1956	1958	1960	1962	1964	1965	1966	1967	1968	1969	1970	1971	1972	1973	1974	1975	1976
271.9	296.6	332.3	363.8	411.7	444.3	481.8	508.7	558.7	605.5	648.9	702.4	770.7	852.5	932.4	1030.3	1149.8
72.0	64.5	78.9	88.1	102.1	118.2	131.3	128.6	141.2	156.4	152.4	178.2	207.6	244.5	249.4	230.2	292.0
91.8	106.5	113.8	132.2	145.1	153.7	174.3	195.3	212.8	224.6	237.1	251.0	270.1	287.9	322.4	361.1	384.5
2.3	0.4	2.4	2.4	5.5	3.9	1.9	1.4	−1.3	−1.2	1.2	−3	−8	0.6	−3.1	13.6	−2.3
438	467.9	527.4	586.5	664.4	720.1	789.3	834.1	911.5	985.3	1039.7	1128.6	1240.4	1385.5	1501	1635.2	1823.9
47.3	52.8	56.9	61.0	66.6	70.8	76.5	83.1	90.9	99.8	109.1	118.9	130.9	142.9	164.8	190.9	209.0
390.7	415.2	470.4	525.5	597.8	649.3	712.7	751.0	820.6	885.6	930.6	1009.7	1109.5	1242.6	1336.2	1444.2	1615
244.6	259.6	296.4	327.2	370.7	399.5	442.6	475.2	524.3	577.6	617.2	658.8	725.1	811.2	890.2	949.0	1059.3
47.0	51.4	51.9	56.5	60.6	65.2	69.6	71.1	75.4	78.9	79.8	86.1	97.7	115.2	115.5	121.6	134.3
13.1	14.5	16.2	17.8	18.6	19.2	19.9	20.4	20.2	20.3	20.3	21.2	21.6	23.1	23.0	22.0	21.5
47.4	42.4	52.3	61.6	74.8	86.0	92.0	89.6	96.5	93.7	81.6	95.1	109.8	123.9	114.5	133.0	160.6
6.6	9.4	10.7	14.1	17.3	19.7	22.6	25.4	27.2	32.2	38.4	42.6	46.2	53.9	68.8	76.6	80.8
358.7	377.3	427.5	477.1	542.1	589.6	646.7	681.7	743.6	802.7	837.5	903.9	1000.4	1127.4	1211.9	1302.2	1456.4
2.9	2.7	3.2	4.3	5.0	5.4	5.2	5.5	6.2	6.1	6.4	7.7	8.7	12.7	15.7	13.3	17.2
47.3	52.8	56.9	61	66.6	70.8	76.5	83.1	90.9	99.8	109.1	118.9	130.9	142.9	164.8	190.9	209
35.7	38.9	46.7	51.9	59.4	63.2	64.7	70	78.8	86.2	92.7	102.1	109.2	119.9	130.1	137.5	151.2
−0.9	1.7	−0.6	0.7	1.2	1.9	6.4	4.8	4.3	2.9	6.9	11.3	8.7	8	10	17.7	24.5
438	467.9	527.4	586.5	664.4	720.1	789.3	834.1	911.5	985.3	1039.7	1128.6	1240.4	1385.5	1501.0	1635.2	1823.9
2141.1	2162.8	2376.7	2578.9	2846.5	3028.5	3227.5	3308.3	3466.1	3571.4	3578	3697.7	3898.4	4123.4	4099	4084.4	4311.7
2.0	−1.0	2.5	6	5.8	6.4	6.6	2.5	4.8	3.0	0.2	3.3	5.4	5.8	−0.6	−0.4	5.6
20.45	21.64	22.19	22.74	23.34	23.78	24.46	25.21	26.3	27.59	29.06	30.52	31.82	33.6	36.62	40.03	42.3
21.64	22.19	22.74	23.34	23.77	24.45	25.21	26.29	27.59	29.05	30.52	31.81	33.6	36.6	40.03	42.29	45.02
98.6	90.1	110.9	124.6	143	158.1	169.1	171.1	183.3	199.8	194.3	211.4	241.6	294.6	304.0	298.4	342.7
97.7	91.9	110.4	125.3	144.2	160.0	175.6	175.9	187.6	202.7	201.2	222.7	250.3	302.6	314.0	316.1	367.2
16.6	23.3	25.7	30.3	16.0	18.1	20.8	25.5	30.2	32.9	38.5	44.5	49.6	60.4	70.1	81.4	92.9
1502.3	1553.7	1664.8	1803.5	2006.9	2131	2244.6	2340.5	2448.2	2524.3	2630	2745.3	2874.3	3072.3	3051.9	3108.5	3243.5
8.4	8.5	7.2	8.3	8.8	8.6	8.3	9.4	8.4	7.8	9.4	10.0	8.9	10.5	10.7	10.6	9.4
168.2	174.1	180.8	186.6	191.9	194.3	196.6	198.8	200.7	202.7	205.1	207.7	209.9	211.9	213.9	216	218.1
11.8	−2.7	11.3	7.6	7.2	9.7	10.5	−1.4	6.2	17.6	−7.3	−20.4	−6.9	4.5	−4.6	−66.9	−45.7
10.0	11.4	16.4	19.1	22.4	23.4	31.3	34.9	38.7	44.1	46.4	51.2	59.2	75.5	85.2	89.3	101.3
38.1	37.4	43.3	46.9	56.7	63.3	68.3	70.4	80.8	85.9	85.0	96.9	110.4	123.5	122.3	133.5	158.9
130.8	141.7	152.9	162.8	178.7	191.6	208.8	217.1	235.7	253.2	272	285.5	308	343.1	384.5	420.7	458.3
102.9	117.4	136.1	154.1	176.4	189.5	204.7	221.2	242.3	266.4	292	320	352.3	385.9	425.5	476.1	532.6
271.9	296.6	332.3	363.8	411.7	444.3	481.8	508.7	558.7	605.5	648.9	702.4	770.7	852.5	932.4	1030.3	1149.8
—	—	140.7	147.8	160.3	167.8	172.0	183.3	197.4	203.9	214.3	228.2	249.1	262.7	274.0	286.8	305.9
—	—	0.5	1.8	4.6	4.7	2.5	6.6	7.7	3.3	5.1	6.5	9.2	5.5	4.3	4.7	6.7
—	—	312.4	362.7	424.7	459.2	480.2	524.8	566.8	587.9	626.4	710.1	802.1	855.3	901.9	1,016.0	1,151.7
—	—	4.9	8.1	8.0	8.1	4.6	9.3	8.0	3.7	6.5	13.4	13.0	6.6	5.4	12.7	13.4
—	—	315.2	371.3	442.4	482.1	505.4	557.9	607.2	615.9	677.0	775.9	885.8	984.9	1,069.7	1,169.9	1,309.7
—	—	5.2	8.9	9.0	9.0	4.8	10.4	8.8	1.4	9.9	14.6	14.2	11.2	8.6	9.4	11.9
3.0	1.8	1.4	1.3	1.0	1.9	3.5	3.0	4.7	6.2	5.6	3.3	3.4	8.7	12.3	6.9	4.9

ECONOMICS

ENHANCED EDITION

PRENTICE HALL SERIES IN ECONOMICS

ECONOMICS

Explore & Apply

ENHANCED EDITION

RONALD M. AYERS
University of Texas at San Antonio

ROBERT A. COLLINGE
University of Texas at San Antonio

PEARSON

Prentice
Hall

Upper Saddle River, New Jersey 07458

Library of Congress Cataloging-in-Publication Data

Ayers, Ronald M.
  Economics: explore & apply enhanced edition / Ronald Ayers, Robert Collinge.--1st ed.
    p. cm.
  ISBN 0-13-146394-2
  1. Economics. 2. Microeconomics. 3. Macroeconomics. I. Collinge, Robert A. II. Title.

HB171.5.A888 2003
330--dc22

2003025051

Executive Acquisitions Editor: Rod Banister
Editor-in-Chief: P. J. Boardman
Managing Editor (Editorial): Gladys Soto
Senior Development Editor: Lena Buonanno
Director of Development: Steve Deitmer
Project Manager: Marie McHale
Editorial Assistant: Joy Golden
Media Project Manager: Victoria Anderson
Marketing Manager: Kathleen McLellan
Marketing Assistant: Melissa Owens
Managing Editor (Production): Cynthia Regan
Production Editor: Michael Reynolds
Production Assistant: Joe DeProspero
Associate Director, Manufacturing: Vinnie Scelta
Production Manager (Manufacturing): Arnold Vila
Design Manager: Maria Lange
Designer: Steven Frim
Interior Design: Karen Quigley
Cover Design: Kathryn Foot
Cover Illustration/Photo: Dennis Galante/CORBIS
Manager, Print Production: Christy Mahon
Print Production Liaison: Ashley Scattergood
Composition: Carlisle Publishers Services
Full-Service Project Management: Carlisle Publishers Services
Printer/Binder: R.R. Donnelley/Willard

Credits and acknowledgments borrowed from other sources and reproduced, with permission, in this textbook appear on appropriate page within text (or on page 795).

Pearson Education LTD.
Pearson Education Singapore, Pte. Ltd
Pearson Education, Canada, Ltd
Pearson Education–Japan

Pearson Education Australia PTY, Limited
Pearson Education North Asia Ltd
Pearson Educación de Mexico, S.A. de C.V.
Pearson Education Malaysia, Pte. Ltd.

10 9 8 7 6 5 4 3 2 1
ISBN 0-13-146394-2

To my former professors
–Ron

To Mary
–Bob

ABOUT THE AUTHORS

RONALD M. AYERS

Ronald Ayers is Associate Professor of Economics and Director of the Teaching and Learning Center at the University of Texas, San Antonio. He teaches principles of microeconomics and macroeconomics, as well as the university's core curriculum course in political economy and various field courses, including labor economics, money and banking, and industrial organization. His classes have ranged from small honors sections to lecture sections of 300.

After receiving Bachelor's and Master's degrees from the University of New Orleans, he subsequently received his Ph.D. in economics from Tulane University. Earlier in his career, Dr. Ayers served as a faculty member at Loyola University (New Orleans), Ohio State University, and Texas A&M University. He has also worked as a consultant for the City of San Antonio and several private consulting firms and attorneys. In recent years he was awarded the President's Distinguished Achievement Award for Core Curriculum Teaching, the College of Business Teaching Award, and the U.T. System Chancellor's Council Teaching Award. He also was named a Senior Fellow, Texas Higher Education Coordinating Board, in 2000. In 2001–2002, Professor Ayers was elected to serve as the Chair of the University's Faculty Senate.

Dr. Ayers has published chapters in *Putting the Invisible Hand to Work: Concepts and Models for Service-Learning in Economics* (University of Michigan Press) and *U.S.-Mexican Economic Relations: Prospects and Problems* (Praeger Publishing Company). In addition, he has published articles in many different journals, including the *National Social Science Journal* and the *Journal of Urban and Regional Information Systems*. Along with Robert Collinge, Professor Ayers has written *Economics by Design: Principles and Issues,* forthcoming in its third edition. When he is not pursuing his interest in how people learn, Dr. Ayers enjoys spending time with his dogs, collecting books, and tinkering.

ROBERT A. COLLINGE

Robert Collinge is Professor of Economics at the University of Texas, San Antonio. Among other courses at the graduate and undergraduate levels, Dr. Collinge has taught micro principles, macro principles, or the combined survey/issues class in each of his 16 years at UTSA. In the last few years, Professor Collinge has twice been awarded his University President's Outstanding Achievement Award, once for overall teaching and once for teaching at the core curriculum level. Most recently, he has received his College's Combined Teaching, Research, and Service Excellence Award. Along with Ronald Ayers, Professor Collinge co-directed his University's Center for Economic Education.

After undergraduate studies at the State University of New York at Buffalo, Bob enrolled at the University of Maryland at College Park, where he went on to receive his B.A., M.A., and Ph.D. degrees. In 1982, he joined the Economics faculty at the University of Louisville. To gain experience outside of academia, Dr. Collinge worked in Washington, D.C., first as a Visiting Economist with the U.S. International Trade Commission, and then as an Economist in the Policy Analysis Department of the American Petroleum Institute.

Professor Collinge's research focuses on the design and analysis of public policies, such as his recent articles in the *Journal of Environmental Economics and Management* and the *Canadian Journal of Economics.* He has contributed to an array of other books and journals, including *The Economic Journal, The Journal of Public Economics,* and *World Development.* Professor Collinge currently serves as a member of the editorial board of *Public Works Management and Policy.* In his free time, Bob enjoys hiking through the woods near his Texas Hill Country home.

BRIEF CONTENTS

CONTENTS

PART 9: MARKET FAILURE AND GOVERNMENT ACTION 607

CHAPTER 24. PUBLIC GOODS, REGULATION, AND INFORMATION 607

A LOOK AHEAD 607

CHAPTER 25. EXTERNALITIES AND COMMON PROPERTY RESOURCES 631

A LOOK AHEAD 631

CHAPTER 26. PUBLIC CHOICE 653

A LOOK AHEAD 653

PREFACE

A BOOK FOR TODAY'S STUDENTS

Taking your first course in economics can be like finding yourself in a foreign country where you do not know the language. You want the freedom to explore various interesting spots, but you cannot read the street signs for direction and you struggle when trying to communicate with the locals. There may be several different, exciting paths you can choose, but you are not sure which is best. To get your bearings in the country and reach your destinations, you need to learn something about the country's language.

Students in a principles of economics course face many of the same challenges as a wandering traveler. They have registered for the course, but they face the hurdle of learning a new language that includes many new terms and concepts. They also face the challenge of learning how to read and interpret graphs. *Economics: Explore & Apply, Enhanced Edition,* was written to help students learn the language of economics. We engage students with familiar real-world examples and applications that bring economics to life. Our goal is to encourage students to apply the concepts they learn in this book to personal, business, and social issues that will face them long after their economics course is over. We teach students how to analyze events in the world around them and draw their own conclusions. To achieve our goal, we implement three key tools:

1. Real-world applications
2. Sound pedagogy
3. Straightforward presentation

REAL-WORLD APPLICATIONS

Principles of economics is often a required course for a variety of majors, since its subject matter relates to so many of life's issues: Should I stay in school, or quit and get a full-time job? Which major should I select? Why does it matter if the Federal Reserve increases or decreases interest rates, or if Microsoft is a monopoly? To help students find the answers to such questions and fulfill the purpose of this course, we emphasize both economic tools and the application of those tools. Many of our applications deal with recent events that underscore the importance of economics, such as: tradeoffs the United States faces in Iraq; violence associated with illegal drugs; economic implications of unethical business practices; and why some European countries have not adopted the euro. Such economic issues make it all the more important for students to understand the market economy and the principles that underlie effective public policy.

Explore & Apply

We continually motivate learning and retention of concepts with examples and brief applications throughout this book. Additionally, each chapter concludes with an in-depth *Explore & Apply* section that drives students to use the economic principles they have just learned. Each *Explore & Apply* looks at a current issue and places the student in the position of analyzing the issue using the economic tools presented in the chapter. Whether in class or over coffee, debating these policy issues can be both interesting and instructive. The result is that students retain the concepts and are ready to apply them to the many additional issues they will encounter beyond the confines of this textbook and the course.

The *Explore & Apply* sections include domestic and international topics, and several interweave technology-related issues. Sample topics include:

- What has motivated China to transition toward a market economy?
- How does Internet technology contribute to economic growth?
- How are the budget deficit and the trade deficit related?
- How do incentives affect healthcare?

Each *Explore & Apply* includes two *Thinking Critically* questions that promote economic reasoning and encourage students to debate a policy issue. A compass icon, located in the chapter-opening learning objectives and various places in the chapter, identifies material and questions related to the *Explore & Apply* sections. Below are excerpts of narrative, a graph, and *Thinking Critically* questions from the Chapter 3 *Explore & Apply*.

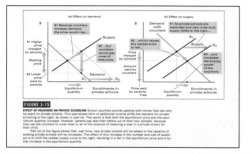

To keep the *Explore & Apply* sections up to date and to strengthen class discussions, we offer two kinds of web support materials at www.prenhall.com/ayers:

1. Updates on each *Explore & Apply* section and supporting exercises.
2. Ten custom-filmed videos that further explore the issues at hand. Current statistical information and interviews with professionals and students highlight the various viewpoints on each policy issue. Tips on how to use these videos appear in the book's Instructor's Manual.

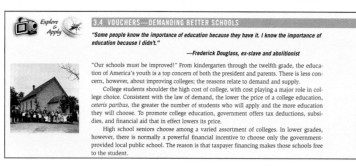

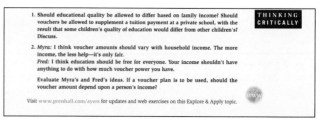

PEDAGOGY

Our pedagogical features support our goal of helping students learn the language of economics and apply what they have learned.

- **Learning Objectives.** Each chapter opens with a list of objectives that establishes the goals and organization of the chapter. We repeat these learning objectives and use them as an organizational tool for the end-of-chapter summary. The linking of the learning objectives and summary provides students with a helpful and coherent way to review the concepts in each chapter. One learning objective per chapter supports the *Explore & Apply* section.

- **Snapshots.** Students retain economic concepts best when they see how these concepts relate to their immediate world. We include three Snapshots in each chapter to reinforce key concepts that have been presented.

- **QuickChecks.** Three or more questions with answers interspersed throughout each chapter allow students to check their knowledge of key concepts before moving on.

- **Margin Definitions.** This running glossary allows students to check their understanding of key terms.

- **Graphs.** Reading and interpreting graphs is a key part of understanding economic concepts. Colors are used consistently to reinforce key concepts. For example, the supply and aggregate supply curves are red, the demand and aggregate demand curves are blue, and shifts in curves are shown with a different shade. Call-out boxes are inserted into the graphs to help students interpret them. Graph captions are clear and self-contained so that students can understand how and why curves are shifting.

- **Extensive Array of End-of-Chapter Pedagogy.** Each chapter ends with a wide array of summary and self-test materials that appeal to a variety of teaching and learning styles:

  Summary and Learning Objectives summarize the key points of the chapter and tie those points back to the learning objectives that opened the chapter.

  Key Terms List gives students an opportunity to review the concepts they have learned in the chapter. A page reference is included next to each term so that students can easily locate the definitions.

  Test Yourself questions in true/false and multiple-choice formats give students self-assessment opportunities and support the *Explore & Apply* section. Solutions appear at the end of the book.

  Questions and Problems are annotated by topic. The annotation appears before each question and problem so that instructors can easily make assignment choices. Solutions to even-numbered items appear in the back of the book. All solutions appear in the Instructor's Manual.

  Working with Graphs and Data problems, new to the *Enhanced Edition*, help students build their skills in drawing, reading, and interpreting graphs and data.

  Web Support Materials encourage students to visit www.prenhall.com/ayers to access more self-test quizzes, Exploring the Web exercises, news articles, and much more.

SNAPSHOT COMPETING WITH COMPARATIVE ADVANTAGE

Many great athletes are multitalented, possessing strength, speed, and muscle coordination that dwarf that of the general population. These qualities are needed for success in a variety of sports, yet few athletes play more than one sport professionally, even though they might be able to do so. Simply look at the sports pages. Venus Williams makes headlines by swinging a tennis racket, while Tiger Woods swings a golf club and Barry Bonds swings a bat. Their choices tell the rest of us about their comparative advantages.

The best teams exploit the comparative advantages of their players. Each player has a job to do and specializes in doing it well. Whatever the sport, owners and fans expect this principle of comparative advantage to be followed and demand coaches who will best exploit the talents of their players. But even the best coaches can err, as when Cleveland Indians' baseball coach Tris Speaker said in 1921, "Babe Ruth made a great mistake when he gave up pitching. Working once a week, he might have lasted a long time and become a great star." ◄

QUICKCHECK

List three cases in which shifts in demand and/or supply would result in a lower price and a greater quantity.

Answer: One case occurs when supply shifts to the right and demand does not change. A second case is when supply and demand both shift to the right, but the shift in supply is larger. A third case is when supply shifts right and demand shifts left, with the shift in supply being larger than the shift in demand. These cases are shown in Figures 3-11 (case 1), 3-13(b), and 3-14, respectively.

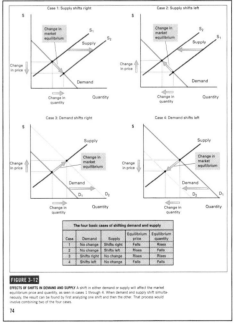

FIGURE 3-12

EFFECTS OF SHIFTS IN DEMAND AND SUPPLY A shift in either demand or supply will affect the market equilibrium price and quantity, as seen in cases 1 through 4. When demand and supply shift simultaneously, the result can be found by first analyzing one shift and then the other. That process would involve combining two of the four cases.

74

STRAIGHTFORWARD PRESENTATION

One of the most frequent complaints about many existing textbooks is that they offer more material than can be covered adequately during the term. *Economics: Explore & Apply, Enhanced Edition,* responds to this concern by covering essential concepts without bogging down the reader in too much detail. The book accomplishes this objective by emphasizing the intuition of economics and focusing on those concepts that are at the heart of macro-economics analysis. The result is a 29-chapter book that can easily be read and taught from with an ample but not excessive reading amount of material.

Enhanced Edition

The *Enhanced Edition* builds on our other book, *Economics: Explore & Apply,* by providing more detail and more in-depth coverage of key economic concepts. There is new material on GDP, expanded multiplier coverage, new coverage of crowding out, additional material on antitrust, and greater detail on exchange rates, just to name a few. Updates include:

- **More-Detailed Graphs**—The *Enhanced Edition* has added more detailed labeling of selected graphs to help students understand the shifts versus movements in curves and make these difficult concepts understandable.
- **Updated Data**—Data has been updated throughout to include 2003, wherever possible.
- **Working with Graphs and Data**—Helps students build their skills in drawing, reading, and interpreting graphs and data.
- **Additional Test Bank**—A new test bank is available, which adds additional questions to the already robust preexisting test banks. The test bank is written by the authors for continuity with the text.
- **29 *Explore & Apply* Sections**—In the *Enhanced Edition*, many of the *Explore & Apply* sections have been updated to continue to address today's current economic issues. An example of this new updating can be found in Chapter 2's *Explore & Apply* that highlights the recent war in Iraq and the cost of keeping the peace.
- **Snapshots**—Three brief applications of the concepts are highlighted in each chapter, which allow students to pause and consider the concepts they have just learned. New Snapshots address recent research and events, such as the impact of Europe's aging population on retirement security.
- **Chapter 3, *Demand and Supply***—This chapter includes a more thorough treatment of market demand and how it is derived, including new graphs to make the concepts clearer. In addition, there is expanded coverage of how surplus and shortage move the market to equilibrium. More intuitive graphs are used in the *Explore & Apply* section that analyzes school vouchers.

MACROECONOMICS ORGANIZATION

Economics: Explore & Apply, Enhanced Edition, is available in three separate volumes. A combined volume includes the topics of macroeconomics and microeconomics. Split volumes are also available for those who teach either macroeconomics or microeconomics.

Please see the Alternative Sequences chart on preface page xxxii. Common to all three volumes is Part 1, "A Journey Through the Economy" (Chapters 1–4), which covers the goals of economics, various economic systems, production possibilities, comparative advantage, demand and supply, market efficiency, and price controls.

The Macroeconomics portion of *Economics: Explore & Apply, Enhanced Edition,* is flexible enough to be used by those who favor a short-run emphasis or a long-run emphasis. For example, we have isolated the income–expenditure model (Keynesian cross) in Chapter 10,

"Aggregate Expenditures," so that instructors who do not cover this model can easily skip the chapter without loss of continuity.

Part 2, "Monitoring the Macroeconomy" (Chapters 5–7), covers GDP measurement, inflation, and unemployment.

In *Part 3,* "Aggregate Demand and Aggregate Supply" (Chapters 8–10), Chapter 8 introduces the two primary schools of macro thought, associating Keynes with short-run analysis and classical with long-run analysis. The chapter develops the model of aggregate demand and aggregate supply as a unifying framework. Chapter 9 builds upon Chapter 8 by exploring in greater detail the issues involved in short-run analysis, including issues. Issues of deficits, debt, and other aspects of fiscal policy. Chapter 10 furthers comprehension of the macro equilibrium and the role of fiscal policy by examining the Keynesian aggregate expenditures model that underlies the aggregate demand curve.

Part 4, "Incentives for Productivity" (Chapters 11–12), covers issues related to implementing fiscal policy and how incentives for growth are strongly influenced by the specifics of government fiscal policy design.

Part 5, "Money in the Macroeconomy" (Chapters 13–14), covers money, the Fed, and the logic behind Fed policy actions. These topics are positioned so as not to disrupt the step-by-step building process found in Chapters 8 through 12.

Updates and additions in Macro include:

- **Chapter 5, "Measuring National Output"**—This chapter discusses in more detail how to compute GDP, including a recognizable equation for computing GDP. In addition, comprehensive definitions for real and nominal GDP, and a more complete circular flow diagram, are presented to help students understand these critical foundations of macroeconomics.

- **Chapter 8, "A Framework for Macroeconomic Analysis"**—This chapter includes early coverage of aggregate demand and aggregate supply and allows instructors the flexibility to decide which models are best suited for their students. The *Enhanced Edition* offers expanded coverage of the differences between Keynesian and classical economic thought and a comprehensive discussion of aggregate demand and its shift factors.

- **Chapter 9, "Fiscal Policy and Short-Run Instability"**—This chapter examines short-run instability within the context of fiscal policy throughout the chapter. The multiplier effect is introduced and explained conceptually and through graphical analysis. The output gap and inflationary/recessionary gaps are also introduced along with the appropriate fiscal policies to address them. This coverage exposes students to short-run adjustment processes, including cost–push inflation and the inflationary spiral. Finally, the limitations of fiscal policy are considered with reference to the crowding-out effect.

- **Chapter 10, "Aggregate Expenditures"**—The Keynesian cross is isolated in one chapter. By focusing on the keys of the income-expenditure model, the chapter allows instructors to streamline their presentation and not overwhelm their students with excessive mathematical detail. This chapter can be covered or skipped without losing continuity. To facilitate student understanding, the chapter revisions include two new circular flow graphs that relate expansionary and contractionary fiscal policy to the circular flow, plus additional coverage of multiplier concepts, including numerical examples.

- **Chapter 11, "Fiscal Policy in Action"**—This chapter has been streamlined to more clearly focus on the macro components of government spending and tax policies. It includes a new example of how seemingly simple tax rates can turn befuddlingly complex in application.

MICROECONOMICS ORGANIZATION

Our microeconomics chapters follow the traditional layout that has for many years served economics students well. We emphasize incentives and choice, the foundations for a vibrant market economy.

Part 6, "Microeconomic Foundations" (Chapters 15–18), covers elasticity, consumer behavior, and how firms make production decisions. Part 7, "Output Markets" (Chapters 19–21), covers the market structures of pure competition, monopoly, oligopoly, and monopolistic competition. Part 8, "Input Markets" (Chapters 22–23), shows that input markets also have their structures, with the labor market of particular significance to earnings. Market economies sometimes fail to produce the goods we value and other times send price signals that misguide our choices. In Part 9, "Market Failure and Government Action" (Chapters 24–26), we show that government actions can help remedy market failures, but those actions often have failures of their own. We include a full chapter on public choice to emphasize the economic significance of incentives within government. Chapter 20, "Monopoly and Antitrust," now has expanded coverage of antitrust and regulation.

THE GLOBAL ECONOMY

Whether it be economic incentives in China, the multinational nature of the work force, or treaties on the global environment, international economic issues are integrated throughout the book. Furthermore, they appear in many of the *Explore & Apply* sections, Snapshots, and comparative tables and figures. Our book concludes by looking at the global marketplace in *Part 10, "The Global Economy."*

In Chapter 27, "Into the International Marketplace," and Chapter 28, "Policy Toward Trade," we examine the balance of payments, exchange rates, free-trade agreements, and arguments for trade restrictions. In Chapter 29, "Economic Development," we study the forces that can lead some countries to develop strong economies and other countries to stagnate.

CURRENCY AND ACCURACY

At all times, we strive for currency of content. Graphs and tables include the most recent data available. Throughout the book, we apply economic analysis to genuinely current issues—the ones that appear in headlines today and promise to continue making headlines in years to come. We will also keep the *Explore & Apply* sections current via the book's web site.

Economics: Explore & Apply, Enhanced Edition, was developed based on our over forty years' combined experience teaching the principles of economics course, as well as the input of approximately 100 professors. We realize the extreme importance of accurate graphs, equations, questions and problems, and solutions. To ensure the highest level of accuracy, we carefully and painstakingly evaluated each chapter and also formed an *Accuracy Review Board* of four economics professors who checked every word, number, equation, and figure in the book. The board members were Paul Comolli, University of Kansas; Barry Kotlove, Edmonds Community College; Matthew Marlin, Duquesne University; and Garvin Smith, Daytona Beach Community College. The supplement package was checked for accuracy by Warren Bilotta, Louisiana State University, Alexandria; Jack Bucco, Austin Community College; Ronald Elkins, Central Washington University; Jeff Holt, Tulsa Community College; and John C. Wassom, Western Kentucky University; and Peter Shaw, Tidewater Community College.

SUPPLEMENTS ADVISOR AND COORDINATOR

We understand how important it is for instructors to have a supplement package that is comprehensive, coordinated with the main text, and easy to use. Professor Mary Lesser of Iona College, who has taught the principles of economics course for 20 years, served as the advisor and coordinator for the extensive print and technology supplement packet that accompanies *Economics: Explore & Apply, Enhanced Edition.* Professor Lesser ensured that each supplement, including the test banks, instructor's manuals, study guides, and PowerPoint presentations met the highest standards of quality. Her script ideas and overall direction on the *Explore & Apply* custom-video series helped the film crew focus on topics that resonate with today's students. She also helped develop many of the media supplements, including the *Explore & Apply* activebook™.

PRINT SUPPLEMENTS

Economics: Explore & Apply, Enhanced Edition, has a comprehensive supplements package that is coordinated with the main text through the numbering system of the headings in each chapter. The major sections of the chapters are numbered (1.1, 1.2, 1.3, and so on), and that numbering system is used consistently in the supplements to make it more convenient and flexible for instructors to develop their course assignments.

Study Guide

The authors have personally prepared the comprehensive study guide that accompanies the text. Tied directly to sections of the text, the study guide enhances and reinforces economic concepts for increased student comprehension. Each chapter of the study guide includes approximately 90 questions. Each chapter features the following elements:

- **Chapter Reviews.** A comprehensive summary of the key concepts of the chapter, including the *Explore & Apply* sections.
- **Study Checks.** These problems are included throughout the Chapter Review for quick practice with the concepts just covered.
- **Self Tests.** 25 true/false/explain, 25 fill-in-the-blanks, and 25 multiple-choice questions give students an opportunity to test their knowledge.
- **Grasping the Graphs.** This section provides students with practice in labeling and analyzing key graphs from the book.
- **Solutions.** Detailed answers to all study guide questions.

Instructor's Manual

Two Instructor's Manuals, Macroeconomics and Microeconomics, written by Rose LaMont of Modesto Junior College and Peter Mavrokordatos of Tarrant County College, provide the following teaching support materials:

- **Exercises** to use in the classroom.
- **Sample Syllabi.**
- **Solutions** to all problems in the book.

Test Banks

Six test banks are available—three for microeconomics and three for macroeconomics. Four of the six test banks were prepared by Scott Hunt of Columbus State Community College, Richard Gosselin of Houston Community College, Andrew Dane of Angelo State University, and Kathy Wilson of Kent State University. The test banks include approximately 10,000 questions, organized by chapter section. Each question is keyed by degree of difficulty as easy, moderate, or difficult. *Easy* questions involve straightforward recall of information in the text. *Moderate* questions require some analysis on the student's part. *Difficult* questions usually entail more complex analysis. To help instructors select questions quickly and efficiently, we have used the skill descriptors of fact, definition, conceptual, and analytical. A question labeled *fact* tests a student's knowledge of factual information presented in the text. A *definition* question asks the student to define an economic term or concept. *Conceptual* questions test a student's understanding of a concept. *Analytical* questions require the student to apply an analytical procedure to answer the question. Two of the six test banks, with multiple choice and true or false questions, were prepared by Professors Ayers and Collinge.

The test banks include questions with tables that provide students with the numbers that they need to use in solving for numerical answers. They also contain questions based on the graphs that appear in the book. The questions ask students to interpret the information presented in the graph. There are also many questions in the test banks that require students to sketch out a graph on their own and interpret curve movements. Test bank questions also support the *Explore & Apply* sections.

Color Transparencies

All figures and tables from the text are reproduced as full-page, four-color acetates.

INTERNET RESOURCES

Prentice Hall's Internet Resources provide students with a variety of interactive graphing and self-assessment tools. It also supplies numerous current news articles and supporting exercises.

Companion Website   http://www.prenhall.com/ayers

The Companion Website connects students to self-test quizzes and to articles and exercises that provide the most current information on economic issues. All Internet articles and exercises include questions for the students with suggested answers provided for the instructor.

For Students and Instructors

- **In the News.** These articles invite students to read articles from newspapers such as the *Wall Street Journal,* and examine the relevance and controversy of economic issues. In the News includes a summary of the article, questions, and additional resources.
- **Internet Exercises.** These invite students to explore the vast resources of the Internet and assess the information in historical and current economic analysis.
- *Explore & Apply* **Updates.** These updates steer students toward the latest web information concerning the topics discussed in the *Explore & Apply* sections. For each *Explore & Apply,* there is an article summary, additional links and references, and questions.
- **Practice Quizzes.** These self-test quizzes allow students to test their understanding of the concepts and receive immediate feedback for correct and incorrect answers. The results can be e-mailed to the students' professor.

OneKey for Instructors and Students

Available by using the access code packaged with every new text, OneKey uses all of the content of the Companion Website listed previously as well as the following additional interactive resources:

- **Active Graphs.** Two levels of interactive graphs help students to understand economic concepts. Forty-two Active Graphs Level One, support key graphs in the text. These JAVA applications invite students to change the value of variables and curves and see the effects in the movement of the graph. Seventeen Active Graphs Level Two, include exercises that ask students to modify graphs based on an economic scenario and questions. Students receive an instant response detailing how they should have changed the graph.

- **Animated Graphing Tutorial with Audio.** Guides the student through a multimedia version of Chapter 1 Appendix: "Working with Graphs and Data."
- **Egraph and Graphing Questions.** This electronic tool allows students to create precise, colorful graphs, using Flash technology. Students can e-mail these graphs to their professor or print and save them. To apply this technology, we have included *Graphing Questions* that require students to analyze information gathered on the web, then create graphs using the Graphing Tool. Complete answers, with graphs, are included.

Research Navigator™

Research Navigator™ is an on-line academic research service that helps students learn and master the skills needed to write effective papers and complete research assignments. Students and faculty can access Research Navigator™ through an access code found in front of *The Prentice Hall Guide to Evaluating Online Resources with Research Navigator*. This guide can be shrinkwrapped, at no additional cost, with our text. Once you register, you will have access to all the resources in Research Navigator™ for six months.

Research Navigator™ includes three databases of credible and reliable source material.

- EBSCO's ContentSelect™ Academic Journal database gives you instant access to thousands of academic journals and periodicals. You can search these on-line journals by keyword, topic, or multiple topics. It also guides students step-by-step through the writing of a research paper.
- The *New York Times* Search-by-Subject™ Archive allows you to search by subject and by keyword.
- Link Library is a collection of links to web sites, organized by academic subject and key terms. The links are monitored and updated each week.

The Econ Tutor Center

Staffed with experienced economics instructors, the Prentice Hall Econ Tutor Center provides students with one-to-one tutoring on concepts and problems in the book. Students can access the Tutor Center via toll-free phone, fax, e-mail, or interactive web. Please contact your Prentice Hall representative for information on how to make this service available to your students.

ON-LINE COURSE OFFERINGS

To accommodate various teaching styles, we offer a complete range of technology-support materials.

WebCT

Developed by educators, WebCT provides faculty with easy-to-use Internet tools to create on-line courses. Prentice Hall provides content to help instructors create a complete on-line course. Please contact your local Prentice Hall sales representative for further information.

Blackboard

Easy to use, Blackboard's simple templates and tools make it easy to create, manage, and use on-line course materials. Prentice Hall provides content so that instructors can create online courses using the Blackboard tools. Please contact your local Prentice Hall sales representative for further information.

TECHNOLOGY SUPPLEMENTS FOR THE INSTRUCTOR

The following technology supplements are designed to make teaching and testing easy.

TestGen-EQ Test-Generating Software

The test banks appear in print and as computer files that may be used with the TestGen-EQ test-generating software. This computerized package allows instructors to customize classroom tests. Instructors may edit, add, or delete questions from the test banks; edit existing graphics and create new graphics; analyze test results; and organize a database of tests and student results. This new software allows for flexibility and ease of use. It provides many options for organizing and displaying tests, along with a search and sort feature. *Economics: Explore & Apply, Enhanced Edition,* is supported by a comprehensive set of test-item files with approximately 10,000 questions. These test-item files are described in detail under the "Print Supplements" section of this preface.

PowerPoint Lecture Presentations

The PowerPoint presentations, by Paul Harris of Camden County College, offer summaries and reinforcement of key text material. Many graphs "build" over a sequencing of slides so that students may see the step-by-step process of economic analysis. Instructors can create full-color, professional-looking presentations and customized handouts for students. The PowerPoint presentations are included in the Instructor's Resource CD-ROM and are downloadable from www.prenhall.com/ayers for students to access using their OneKey access code.

Explore & Apply Videos on VHS Cassette

A series of ten custom-filmed videos support the *Explore & Apply* sections. The videos dig deeper into the issue presented in each chapter and highlight various viewpoints of the policy issue being discussed. A guide is packaged with the videos, which provides summaries, lecture tips, discussion questions, and exercises.

■ ***Explore & Apply* Video Series.** A series of ten custom-filmed videos support the *Explore & Apply* sections. The videos dig deeper into the issue presented in each chapter and highlight various viewpoints of the policy issue being discussed. A guide to using the videos is included and provides summaries, lecture tips, discussion questions, and exercises.

Instructor's Resource CD-ROM

The Instructor's Resource CD-ROM allows instructors to easily access and edit the Instructor's Manual, test banks, and PowerPoint presentations.

SUBSCRIPTIONS: *WALL STREET JOURNAL, FINANCIAL TIMES,* AND *ECONOMIST.COM*

Analyzing current events is an important skill for economic students to develop. To sharpen this skill and further support the book's theme of exploration and application, Prentice Hall offers you and your students three *news subscription* offers:

The Wall Street Journal *Print and Interactive Editions Subscription*

Prentice Hall has formed a strategic alliance with the *Wall Street Journal,* the most respected and trusted daily source for information on business and economics. For a small additional charge, Prentice Hall offers your students a ten-week subscription to the *Wall Street Journal* print edition and the *Wall Street Journal Interactive Edition.* Upon adoption of a special package containing the book and the subscription booklet, professors will receive a free one-year subscription of the print and interactive versions as well as weekly subject-specific *Wall Street Journal* educators' lesson plans.

The Financial Times

We are pleased to announce a special partnership with The *Financial Times.* For a small additional charge, Prentice Hall offers your students a fifteen-week subscription to The *Financial Times.* Upon adoption of a special package containing the book and the subscription booklet. Professors will receive a free one-year subscription. Please contact your Prentice Hall representative for details and ordering information.

Economist.com

Through a special arrangement with *Economist.com,* Prentice Hall offers your students a twelve-week subscription to *Economist.com* for a small additional charge. Upon adoption of a special package containing the book and the subscription booklet, professors will receive a free six-month subscription. Please contact your Prentice Hall representative for further details and ordering information.

ACKNOWLEDGMENTS

We would like to start by expressing our hearty thanks to Rod Banister, Executive Editor, Gladys Soto, Managing Editor, and Lena Buonanno, Senior Developmental Editor, for their ceaseless commitment to quality. Michael Reynolds, Production Editor, skillfully managed all phases of the production process and ensured a quality product. The extensive print and technology supplements that accompany this book are the result of the dedication Marie McHale, Project Manager; Victoria Anderson, Media Project Manager; and Joy Golden, Editorial Assistant. Kathleen McLellan, Executive Marketing Manager, and David Theisen, National Sales Director for Key Markets, provided recommendations through various phases of the book development and created an innovative marketing strategy. Abby Reip and Julie Tesser, our photoresearchers, located the dynamic and effective photographs that appear in each chapter. Along with the rest of the team at Prentice Hall, their hard work and vision were instrumental in achieving the finished products we have been discussing in this preface.

In addition to having the expertise of the Prentice Hall staff, we benefited from the expertise of many professors who teach the principles of economics course. We extend our special thanks and appreciation to Mary Lesser of Iona College for her careful attention to the extensive supplement package.

Special thanks also go to the members of our *Accuracy Review Board,* who helped us identify and correct accuracy issues: Paul Comolli, University of Kansas; Barry Kotlove, Edmonds Community College; Matthew Marlin, Duquesne University; and Garvin Smith, Daytona Beach Community College.

We owe a debt of gratitude to our talented and dedicated supplement authors: Andrew Dane of Angelo State University, Richard Gosselin of Houston Community College, Paul Harris of Camden County College, Scott Hunt of Columbus State Community College, Rose LaMont of Modesto Junior College, Peter Mavrokordatos of Tarrant County College, Leonie Stone of State University of New York, Geneseo, Kathy Wilson of Kent State University, and Fernando Quijano.

We also owe a great deal to the many reviewers and focus-group participants who assisted us in developing this book. The following professors provided us with thoughtful recommendations and constructive criticism:

Cinda Adams, Chattanooga State Technical Community College

Christie Agioutanti, City University of New York, Baruch

Carlos Aguilar, El Paso Community College

Uzo Aguelfo, North Lake College

Ercument G. Aksoy, Los Angeles Valley College

Frank Albritton, Seminole Community College

Newton E. Aldridge, Hinds Community College

Khalid Al-Hmoud, Texas Tech University

Farhad Ameen, SUNY, Westchester Community College

Len Anyanwu, Union County College

Hamid Azari-Rad, State University of New York, New Paltz

Mina N. Baliamoune, University of North Florida

Getachew Begashaw, William Rainey Harper College

Adolfo Benavides, Texas A&M University, Corpus Christi

Victor Brajer, California State University at Fullerton

Fenton L. Broadhead, Brigham Young University, Idaho

Kathleen K. Bromley, Monroe Community College

Jack A. Bucco, Austin Community College

Melvin C. Burton, Jr., J. Sargeant Reynolds Community College

Regina Cassady, Valencia Community College

Chandana Chakraborty, Montclair State University

Marc C. Chopin, Louisiana Tech University

Pam Coates, San Diego Mesa College

John P. Cochran, Metropolitan State College of Denver

Paul Comolli, University of Kansas

Bienvenido S. Cortes, Pittsburg State University

Chandrea Thomas Crowe-Hopkins, College of Lake County

Rosa Lea Danielson, College of DuPage

M. R. Davoudi, North Harris College

Irma T. de Alonso, Florida International University

Amrik Singh Dua, Mount San Antonio College

Rex Edwards, Moorpark College

Michael D. Everett, East Tennessee State University

William George Feipel, Illinois Central College

Clara V. P. Ford, Northern Virginia Community College

Kirk D. Gifford, Ricks College

Lynde O. Gilliam, Metropolitan State College of Denver

Michael G. Goode, Central Piedmont Community College

Richard Gosselin, Houston Community College

John W. Graham, Rutgers University

Julie Granthen, Oakland Community College

Chiara Gratton-Lavoie, California State University at Fullerton

Mehdi Haririan, Bloomsburg University

Paul C. Harris, Jr., Camden County College

Victor Heltzer, Middlesex County College

Michael G. Heslop, Northern Virginia Community College

Rick L. Hirschi, Brigham Young University, Idaho

James H. Holcomb, University of Texas, El Paso

Norman Hollingsworth, Georgia Perimeter College

Jeff Holt, Tulsa Community College

R. Bradley Hoppes, Southwest Missouri State University

Yu Hsing, Southeastern Louisiana University

Safiul Huda, Community College of Rhode Island

Scott Hunt, Columbus State Community College

Paul E. Jorgensen, Linn-Benton Community College

Thomas Kemp, Tarrant County College, Northwest Campus

Jenni Kim, Pasadena City College

Marcelle Anne Kinney, Brevard Community College

Barry Kotlove, Edmonds Community College

Louis H. Kuhn, Edison Community College

Rose LaMont, Modesto Junior College

Phillip Letting, Harrisburg Area Community College

Kenneth E. Long, New River Community College

Kjartan T. Magnusson, Salt Lake Community College

Matthew Marlin, Duquesne University

Pete Mavrokordatos, Tarrant County College

Diana McCoy, Truckee Meadows Community College

Erika Weis McGrath, Golden Gate University

Shah Mehrabi, Montgomery College

Saul Mekies, Kirkwood Community College

Barbara Moore, University of Central Florida

Francis Mummery, Fullerton College

John Nader, Grand Valley State University

Kelly Noonan, Rider University

Alex Obiya, San Diego City College

Charles C. Okeke, College of Southern Nevada

Paul Okello, Tarrant County College

Shawn Osell, Anoka-Ramsey Community College, Augsburg College

Charles Parker, Wayne State College

Elizabeth Patch, Broome Community College

Michael C. Petrowsky, Glendale Community College

Marilyn Pugh, Prince George's Community College

Fernando Quijano, Dickinson State University

Robert Reichenbach, Miami Dade Community College

Charles A. Reichheld, III, Cuyahoga Community College

Teresa Riley, Youngstown State University

James N. Roberts, Tidewater Community College

Fred D. Robertson, Hinds Community College

Larry Lynn Ross, University of Alaska, Anchorage

Sara Saderion, Houston Community College

Ramazans Sari, Texas Tech University

Reza Sepassi, McLennan Community College

Peter Mark Shaw, Tidewater Community College

William L. Sherrill, Tidewater Community College

Ken Slaysman, York College of Pennsylvania

Garvin Smith, Daytona Beach Community College

Noel S. Smith, Palm Beach Community College

David Sollars, Auburn University

Leonie L. Stone, State University of New York, Geneseo

James L. Swofford, University of South Alabama

Lea Templer, College of the Canyons

J. Ross Thomas, Albuquerque Technical and Vocational Institute

Donna Thompson, Brookdale Community College

Anthony Uremovic, Joliet Junior College

Abu Wahid, Tennessee State University

Chester G. T. Waters, Durham Technical Community College

Paul R. Watro, Jefferson Community College

Mark W. Wilkening, Blinn College

We also wish to thank the many students at the University of Texas at San Antonio, who class tested the manuscript in various stages. They provided us with inspiration and were a great source of feedback.

We welcome comments about the book. Please write to us c/o Economics Editor, Prentice Hall Higher Education Division, One Lake Street, Upper Saddle River, NJ 07458.

Ronald M. Ayers

Robert A. Collinge

Save a Tree!

Many of the components of the teaching and learning package are available in electronic format. Disk-based and web-based supplements conserve paper and allow you to select and print only the material you plan to use. For more information, please ask your Prentice Hall sales representative.

ALTERNATIVE SEQUENCES

MACROECONOMICS

LONG-RUN EARLY	SHORT-RUN EARLY
1 The Economic Perspective	1 The Economic Perspective
2 Production and Trade	2 Production and Trade
3 Demand and Supply	3 Demand and Supply
4 The Power of Prices (optional)	4 The Power of Prices (optional)
5 Measuring National Output	5 Measuring National Output
6 Unemployment	6 Unemployment
7 Inflation (Can be covered before Chapter 6)	7 Inflation (Can be covered before Chapter 6)
8 A Framework for Macroeconomic Analysis	8 A Framework for Macroeconomic Analysis
13 Money, Banking, and the Federal Reserve	9 Fiscal Policy and Short-Run Instability
14 Monetary Policy and Price Stability	10 Aggregate Expenditures (Can be covered before Chapter 9)
12 Economic Growth	11 Fiscal Policy in Action
9 Fiscal Policy and Short-Run Instability (optional)	12 Economic Growth
11 Fiscal Policy in Action	13 Money, Banking, and the Federal Reserve
10 Aggregate Expenditures (optional)	14 Monetary Policy and Price Stability
27 Into the International Marketplace	27 Into the International Marketplace
28 Policy Toward Trade	28 Policy Toward Trade
29 Economic Development (optional)	29 Economic Development (optional)

MICROECONOMICS

TRADITIONAL MICRO	POLICY EMPHASIS
1 The Economic Perspective	1 The Economic Perspective
2 Production and Trade	2 Production and Trade
3 Demand and Supply	3 Demand and Supply
4 The Power of Prices	4 The Power of Prices
15 Elasticity: Measuring Responsiveness	15 Elasticity: Measuring Responsiveness
16 Consumer Behavior (optional)	16 Consumer Behavior (optional)
17 The Firm and Production	17 The Firm and Production
18 Costs and Profit-Maximizing Output	18 Costs and Profit-Maximizing Output
19 Pure Competition	19 Pure Competition
20 Monopoly and Antitrust	20 Monopoly and Antitrust
21 Oligopoly and Monopolistic Competition	21 Oligopoly and Monopolistic Competition
22 Markets for Labor and Other Inputs	26 Public Choice
23 Earnings and Income Distribution	24 Public Goods, Regulation, and Information
24 Public Goods, Regulation, and Information	25 Externalities and Common Property Resources
25 Externalities and Common Property Resources	22 Markets for Labor and Other Inputs
26 Public Choice (optional)	23 Earnings and Income Distribution
27 Into the International Marketplace (optional)	27 Into the International Marketplace (optional)
28 Policy Toward Trade	28 Policy Toward Trade

EXPLORING GRAPHS

In order to understand economic concepts, it is important to practice and develop your skills in reading and interpreting graphs. Prentice Hall has developed two levels of interactive graphing tools to help you achieve these goals. Use the code packaged with the book for access to these valuable interactive tools along with other important OneKey resources.

Active Graphs Level One include 42 exercises that require you to consider several key concepts in sequence. Below is a list of Active Graphs Level One, to accompany *Economics: Explore & Apply, Enhanced Edition*. Look for the OneKey logo next to figures in the book, then go to the web site, www.prenhall.com/ayers, to find a corresponding interactive graph.

ACTIVE GRAPH / Level One	FIGURE REFERENCE
Constructing and Working with Graphs	Figures 1A.1, 1A.2
Nonlinear Relationships	Figure 1A.3
The Marginal Principle	Figure 1A.4
Curves, Which Way Do They Shift?	Figure 1A.5
Shifting a Curve	Figure 1A.5
Opportunity Costs	Figure 2.1
Scarcity and the Production Possibilities Curve	Figure 2.4
Comparative Advantage and Specialization	Table 2.2
The Demand Curve and the Law of Demand	Figure 3.1
The Supply Curve and the Law of Supply	Figure 3.4
The Market Demand Curve	Figure 3.7
The Market Supply Curve	Figure 3.8
Market Equilibrium	Figure 3.9
The Demand Curve and Consumer Surplus	Figure 4.2
The Supply Curve and Producer Surplus	Figure 4.4
Market Efficiency	Figure 4.5
The Effect of Imports and Exports on Social Surplus	Figures 4.7, 4.8
Rent Control	Figure 4.9
Agricultural Price Supports	Figure 4.10
Supply and Demand for Labor	Figure 4.11
Real Versus Nominal	Definitions in text
Aggregate Demand, Aggregate Supply, and Inflation	Figures 8.13, 8.14
Shifts of Aggregate Demand and the Classical Aggregate Supply Curve	Figure 9.1
Shifts of Aggregate Demand and the Keynesian Aggregate Supply Curve	Figure 9.9
Introduction to the Phillips Curve	Figure 9.14
The Multiplier	Figure 10.6
Government Spending and Taxation	Definition in text
From Income–Expenditure to Aggregate Demand	Figures 10.11, 10.12
Crowding Out in the Long Run	Definition in text
The Investment Decision	Definition in text
How Banks Create Money	Definition in text
Monetary Policy	Figure 14.2

Active Graphs Level Two, include 35 exercises and problems that allow you to manipulate variables and shift curves based on an economic scenario. Students can assess their understanding of a concept before moving on. Below is the list of Active Graphs, Level 2, to accompany *Economics: Explore & Apply, Enhanced Edition*. Look for the OneKey logo next to figures in the book, then go to the web site, www.prenhall.com/ayers, to find a corresponding interactive graph.

ACTIVE GRAPH / Level Two	FIGURE REFERENCE
Understanding Graphs	Figures 1A.1, 1A.2
Production Possibilities Frontier: Understanding Opportunity Cost	Figure 2.2
Production Possibilities Frontier: Understanding Growth	Figure 2.11
Supply and Demand: Understanding Equilibrium	Figure 3.9
Supply and Demand: Understanding Shifts (I)	Figure 3.11
Supply and Demand: Understanding Shifts (II)	Figure 3.11
Supply and Demand: Understanding Shifts (III)	Figure 3.11
Supply and Demand: Understanding Shifts (IV)	Figure 3.11
Market Efficiency	Figure 4.5
Aggregate Supply and Aggregate Demand: Demand Side Inflation and Deflation	Figure 8.13
Aggregate Supply and Aggregate Demand: Supply Side Inflation and Deflation	Figure 8.14
Short-Run Instability: The Slope of the Aggregate Supply Curve	Figure 9.8
Short-Run Instability: The Inflationary Spiral	Figure 9.13
Aggregate Expenditures	Figure 10.7
Saving and Investment: The Equilibrium Interest Rate	Figure 12.3
The Money Market and Monetary Policy	Figure 14.9
Monetary Policy: The Liquidity Trap	Figure 14.10
Calculating Elasticity	Figure 15.6
Using Elasticity: Analyzing the Effect of an Excise Tax	Figure 15.10
Marginal Product and Average Product	Figure 17.4
Shutting Down or Breaking Even	Figure 18.3
Maximizing Profit at the Price-Taking Firm	Figure 18.8
Pure Competition in the Long Run	Figure 19.4
Long-Run Supply	Figure 19.7
Marginal Revenue for a Single-Price Monopoly	Figure 20.4
Maximizing Profit for a Single-Price Monopoly	Figure 20.8
Regulating a Natural Monopoly	Figure 20.12
The Dominant Firm Model	Figure 21.2
The Kinked Demand Curve Model	Figure 21.5
Monopolistic Competition	Figure 21.6
The Market for Labor	Figure 22.3
Dealing with Congestion	Figure 24.4
Moral Hazard	Figure 24.9
Understanding Externalities	Figure 25.2
Understanding Tariffs and Quotas	Figure 28.5

Explore & Apply Topics by Chapter

The following is a list of the *Explore & Apply* topics used in the text. The video icon identifies those *Explore & Apply* topics supported by Prentice Hall's custom video series produced exclusively for this text. Like the *Explore & Apply* topics, the videos examine today's hot policy issues—the price of homeland security, business ethics, pollution controls—from various points of view.

CHAPTER 1

THE ECONOMIC PERSPECTIVE

A LOOK AHEAD

Choosing the right mix of government and free enterprise involves questions of economics, philosophy, and politics. Economic incentives can lead to the success or downfall of political systems. As discussed in the Explore & Apply section in this chapter, China's leaders recognized the importance of incentives. They shifted the country's policies away from government directive in order to draw upon the incentives found in a dynamic market economy.

Any country's economic system reflects its choices about how to organize economic activity. Scarce resources and unlimited wants force us to make choices, whether they be the grand choices we make as a nation or the personal choices we make in everyday living. Economics examines how to make choices well. This chapter sweeps across the economic landscape to provide the context for our choices.

LEARNING OBJECTIVES

Understanding Chapter 1 will enable you to:
1. **Describe how scarce resources and unlimited wants lead to the study of economics.**
2. **Distinguish between microeconomics and macroeconomics.**
3. **Identify three basic questions that all economies must answer.**
4. **Recognize the strengths of the marketplace and motivations for government involvement.**
5. **Understand what a model is and why models are best kept simple.**
6. **Explain why incentives are important for economic prosperity.**

economics studies the allocation of limited resources in response to unlimited wants.

Economics *studies the allocation of limited resources in response to unlimited wants.*

1.1 SCARCE RESOURCES, UNLIMITED WANTS

scarcity a situation in which there are too few resources to meet all human wants.

Economics is about choice. We are forced to choose because of **scarcity,** which means that society does not have enough resources to produce all the goods and services we want to consume. Both individually and as a society, we seek to choose wisely.

Securing the most value from limited resources is the objective of economic choice. At a personal level, we each have our own economy. We have limited income to spend on the many things we want. For this reason, we might forgo the new Porsche automobile we've long dreamed of in order to pay tuition at Highbrow College. Usually, however, resource scarcity does not force us into all-or-nothing decisions. We might be able to purchase a used Dodge Neon and still afford tuition at Home State University.

MAKING DECISIONS AT THE MARGIN

the margin the cutoff point; decision making at the margin refers to deciding on one more or one less of something.

When something is scarce, we must choose. We commonly make choices at **the margin,** meaning incrementally—in small steps. Decision making at the margin is about the choice of a little more of this and a little less of that. It's about weighing and balancing the benefits and costs of alternatives. We consider the *marginal benefit* of our action and compare it to the *marginal cost.* If we take the action, we must have in mind that its marginal benefit exceeds its marginal cost. Otherwise, we wouldn't do it. It's such a natural part of our behavior that we don't pause to give it a second thought.

Table 1-1 provides examples of choices facing a consumer, a business, and a government. Each choice is considered at the margin and is phrased as a question. In the study of economics, questions will often be posed in this manner in order to emphasize the marginal nature of many decisions.

RESOURCE ALLOCATION AND SCARCITY

It is not a scarcity of money that is at the root of economics. Scarce resources lead to scarce goods, whether or not money is involved. To illustrate that point, consider what would happen if everything were declared to be "free." Supermarkets, department stores, discount stores, and other retailers would quickly be picked bare. People would complain that they did not take

TABLE 1-1   EXAMPLES OF CHOICES AT THE MARGIN

Choices Facing a Consumer:
- Should I eat the last slice of pizza?
- What is the best use of the next hour of my time?
- How should I spend the last dollar in my pocket?

Choices Facing a Business:
- Should revenues be used to hire another worker or to upgrade the office computer system?
- Should one more entree be added to a restaurant's menu? Should one be deleted?
- Should the restaurant stay open an hour later, or close an hour earlier?

Choices Facing Government:
- Should we add another freeway exit ramp?
- Should a new elementary school be built?
- How badly does the city need another water treatment plant?

home everything they wanted or that they arrived too late to obtain anything at all. This is often what happens during humanitarian relief efforts, in which food and other aid is distributed from the back of a truck. The result seen in Somalia and other recipient countries is that the fastest and strongest, rather than the neediest, get the goods. Free distribution is not an economical way to allocate scarce resources and the goods and services they produce.

Resource allocation refers to the uses to which resources are put. How resources are used depends partly upon *technology*, which refers to the techniques of production. When new technologies are created, the results can include new ways of doing things, new product choices, and new uses for resources. For example, the development of the Internet meant that existing television cables could also be used to deliver web sites to home computers.

When society makes choices about what will be produced, it is also choosing its allocation of resources. The choices can literally be a matter of life and death, such as involving a nation's healthcare system. In wealthier nations, it might seem as if scarcity of resources doesn't apply, and that more and better healthcare could be provided for all, apparently without giving up anything else. But since more healthcare requires a greater number of doctors and nurses, where would they come from? Some people who otherwise would have sought careers in engineering, teaching, business, and other fields would have to obtain their degrees in medicine. As a consequence, there would be less *output* of goods and services elsewhere in the economy. The consequences of resource scarcity cannot be avoided.

STUDENTS OF ECONOMICS—ALWAYS EXPLORING, ALWAYS APPLYING *SNAPSHOT*

"Let's explore that mountain pass!" shouts the hiker. "Let's explore the financing options," suggests the car dealer to the customer. "Let's explore the possibility of sending astronauts to Mars," argues the scientist. Like these three, everyone is an explorer. We think through our possibilities in life, and that is exploration.

Exploring can involve web surfing, visiting a bookstore, or mingling with one another. It expands our knowledge and experience, which we can then apply in order to make better choices. For example, our explorations can lead to writing a better term paper, finding a good book, making new friends, or other applications.

Students of economics are most assuredly explorers. As a student, you explore the principles and issues of economics, then apply what you learned from your explorations. You apply economics to choosing a career, a mate, a senator, and what to eat for breakfast. The exploration of economics and its application to life's choices are found throughout this book. The Explore & Apply section that precedes each chapter summary offers the opportunity to dig deeper into an issue. Like Daniel Boone, Ponce de León, and John Glenn, you are now a pioneer on a journey of discovery. ◄

QUICKCHECK

Would $2 million satisfy all of your wants?

Answer: It would be quite difficult to discover someone with $2 million who would decline to accept a third million. Even billionaires would accept another billion, if only to better endow their trust funds. Unless you would actually decline to accept that third million, then $2 million does not satisfy all of your wants. Essentially, your wants are unlimited.

1.2 SURVEYING THE ECONOMIC LANDSCAPE

We have seen that economics applies to a vast expanse of choices. To make progress in the study of economics, it is useful to narrow our field of vision by dividing economics into two broad categories: microeconomics and macroeconomics.

MICROECONOMICS—COMPONENTS OF THE ECONOMY

microeconomics analyzes the individual components of the economy, such as the choices made by people, firms, and industries.

Microeconomics studies the individual parts of the economy. It looks at the choices of individuals in their roles as consumers and as workers. It also includes the choices of businesses—*firms*—which are the companies that produce goods and services as their outputs. Microeconomics also studies the industries within which firms operate, where an *industry* is composed of firms producing similar outputs. For example, the airline industry includes United Airlines, American Airlines, Southwest Airlines, and many other airlines.

markets make possible the voluntary exchange of resources, goods, and services; can take physical, electronic, and other forms.

market prices serve as signals that guide the allocation of resources.

Microeconomics revolves around the interaction of consumers and producers in **markets**. Markets can take physical, electronic, or other forms. The common characteristic of all markets is that they make possible the voluntary exchange of resources, goods, and services. **Market prices** serve as the signals that guide the allocation of resources. Participants in the economy make choices based upon the *incentives* provided by the prices they face, meaning that these prices motivate their actions.

Microeconomic applications affect our lives each day. Suppose you decide to go on vacation. What will be your destination? Will you use the services of a travel agent? At which hotel will you stay? If you decide to fly, which airline will you choose? Is the fare lower if you purchase tickets in advance? Why do many airlines reduce the fare if you stay over a Saturday night? How are ticket prices related to government regulation of the airlines? Should government regulate airplane noise? If so, how? As you can see, the list of microeconomic questions is long. Answering them requires us to know the prices of the various alternatives.

MACROECONOMICS—THE BIG PICTURE

macroeconomics analyzes economic aggregates, such as aggregate employment, output, growth, and inflation.

Macroeconomics looks at the big picture. It concentrates on the analysis of economic *aggregates,* total values that describe the economy as a whole. The most important aggregate is *gross domestic product (GDP),* which measures the market value of a country's aggregate output—the market value of the goods and services that a country produces in one year. Macroeconomic issues are often raised in the news. Employment, economic growth, interest rates, inflation, and the federal budget are examples of macroeconomic issues. These issues reflect the macroeconomic goals that each country sets for itself. Widely accepted goals include a high rate of economic growth, low inflation, and high employment.

Macroeconomics was first considered a separate field of study following the 1936 publication of *The General Theory of Employment, Interest, and Money* by British economist John Maynard Keynes [1883–1946]. Keynes suggested macroeconomic answers to the problems of the Great Depression, answers that seemed lacking in the microeconomic mainstream of economic thought. The writings of Keynes and his followers so influenced the economics profession that for three decades after the publication of *The General Theory,* macroeconomics and *Keynesian* economics were virtually one and the same. Today, Keynesian economics is still prominent, albeit not the only perspective on the macro economy.

Pose three questions illustrating microeconomic issues and another three questions illustrating macroeconomic issues.

Answer: The micro questions you ask should be related to an individual, firm, or industry. There are many possible questions. Examples are: Why is the price of a Lexus greater than that of a Toyota? Why do some firms advertise? What do I want for lunch? Your macro questions should be related to issues of the whole economy. Examples are: What is the cause of inflation? Why is there unemployment? What causes an economy to grow?

1.3 THREE BASIC QUESTIONS: WHAT, HOW, AND FOR WHOM?

Every economy must answer three basic economic questions:

1. **What?** What goods and services will be produced and offered for sale and in what quantities? The latest fashions, CDs from established pop stars, medical services, fast food, and countless other items are produced by our economy. What is the reason that these goods are produced, while other items, such as vinyl records and 8-track tapes, are not?

2. **How?** How will goods and services be produced? There are numerous production techniques available. Some methods of production use simple hand tools and much labor. Other production methods employ machines or computers in combination with labor. For example, a shirt could be sewn by hand with no more than a needle and thread. However, most shirts are sewn with a sewing machine that saves on the use of labor. How are these decisions made, and what motivates the development of new and better ways of doing things?

3. **For whom?** Who will consume the goods and services that are produced? People who live on Poverty Row consume less than those who live on Park Avenue, so income matters in the distribution of goods and services. But what determines income? If a family's income is small, should income be redistributed from others who are wealthier? What problems does redistribution cause?

When it comes to deciding what, how, and for whom, society must choose among three kinds of *economic systems.* Government might make the decisions. If so, the economy is termed **command and control.** Alternatively, government might stay out of the picture and allow economic choices to be made entirely in the marketplace. In that case, the economy is characterized by laissez-faire free markets, also termed laissez-faire capitalism. *Laissez faire* means "let it be." **Free markets** are free from government intervention and characterized by freedom of choice in both production and consumption. Free markets are associated with capitalism, in which resources are privately owned.

In practice, all countries have **mixed economies,** meaning that they choose a combination of markets and government. Different countries choose different combinations, with some leaning toward command and control, and others toward laissez faire. The exact mix is influenced by custom, tradition, religion, political ideology, and other factors. Figure 1-1 illustrates this spectrum of choice.

command and control government decrees that direct economic activity.

free markets the collective decisions of individual buyers and sellers that, taken together, determine what outputs are produced, how those outputs are produced, and who receives the outputs; free markets depend on private property and free choice.

mixed economies the mixture of free-market and command-and-control methods of resource allocation that characterize modern economies.

THE SPECTRUM OF ECONOMIC SYSTEMS Command and control involves government allocation of resources. Laissez faire is characterized by private resource allocation. In reality, all countries have mixed economies, with the mix varying from country to country.

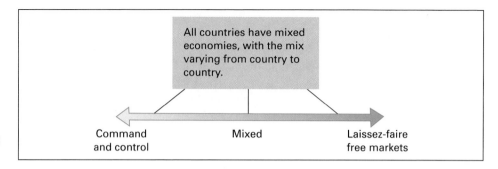

All countries have mixed economies, with the mix varying from country to country.

Command and control   Mixed   Laissez-faire free markets

THE GOALS OF EQUITY AND EFFICIENCY

There are two primary economic objectives to guide countries in choosing how much government to mix with free markets. The first objective is *equity*, which refers to fairness. While we often intuitively sense what is fair, the concept of equity is difficult to pin down. There are commonly accepted principles of equity that apply in certain circumstances, such as in discussions about taxation and government spending. However, equity is ultimately a matter of personal perception. Well-meaning people can reasonably disagree about what is equitable, and their views cannot be proved or disproved.

equity fairness.

The second economic objective is *efficiency*, sometimes called economic efficiency, which means that resources are used in ways that provide the most value—that maximize the size of the economic pie. Efficiency means that no one can be made better off without someone else becoming worse off. Efficiency has both a technological and allocative component, defined as follows:

efficiency means that resources are used in ways that provide the most value; implies that no one can be made better off without someone else becoming worse off.

- **Technological efficiency** implies getting the greatest quantity of output from the resources that are being used. Conversely, for any given output, technological efficiency requires that a least-cost production technique must be chosen.
- **Allocative efficiency** involves choosing the most valuable mix of outputs to produce. For example, the economy might be able to produce the largest number of toothpicks from the resources at its disposal. That choice would be technologically efficient. However, if the economy produces nothing but toothpicks, consumers would not be getting the greatest value from the economy's resources. The economy would be allocatively inefficient, because the wrong mix of goods would have been chosen.

technological efficiency the greatest quantity of output for given inputs; likewise, for any given output, requires the least-cost production technique.

allocative efficiency involves choosing the most valuable mix of outputs to produce.

There is frequently a tradeoff between efficiency and equity, meaning that more equity may result in less efficiency. Likewise, less equity may result in greater efficiency. For example, many people believe that, for the sake of more equity, tax systems should be something like Robin Hood—taxes should take from the rich and give to the poor. However, as taxes paid by the rich rise, their incentives to work and invest can be expected to fall because the rich get to keep less of their earnings. Thus, the more redistributional the tax system, the less productive the economy is likely to be. The economic pie may be divided more equitably, but its size would be diminished.

To see the difficulty in identifying equity and the tradeoff between efficiency and equity, suppose that on the first day of class your instructor reads the following grade policy: "The final grades of all students who have earned an *A* or *B* will be reduced by enough points to bring each of them down to a *C*. The points taken away from them will be distributed among the students who earn a *D* or *F* so that they also receive a *C*." Your instructor supports the equity of this policy by arguing that it recognizes the many differences in learning abilities and opportunities. Perhaps you would agree that the policy is fair. Perhaps you would disagree. In either case, though, the policy is likely to reduce the number of high grades available for redistribution. In an effort to promote equity, this instructor's policy changes students' incentives to work hard for excellence.

COMMAND AND CONTROL—WHO NEEDS MARKETS?

The marketplace seems cluttered with choices. Wouldn't it be better to do away with seemingly unnecessary variety, skip all the advertising, and just have government direct the economy for the good of us all? Throughout history, many countries have embraced economic systems that promised to eliminate the perceived disorder of the marketplace. Often, these efforts have involved government *central planning* that sets production plans for most goods, which are produced by government-owned state enterprises.

Even the most well-meaning central planners cannot know our desires as well as we can know them ourselves. Moreover, nothing ensures that only the most well-meaning central planners will rise to the top. Even if they do, they face difficulties in motivating actual producers to do their bidding. For example, if the government plan assigns farmers production quotas measured by the ton, farmers will seek to maximize the weight of their crops and ignore their quality. The result of command-and-control methods is often inefficiency, in which resources are squandered on the production of the wrong goods and services or wasted through use of the wrong production techniques.

Centrally planned economies must also match production to consumption. If production fails to match their plans, then the government may be forced to ration goods and services. Government *rationing* occurs when consumers are permitted to buy only limited amounts of the goods they want. Rationing has been adopted in the United States, but on a temporary basis and with mixed results. For example, gasoline, tires, sugar, meat, and other essentials were rationed during World War II. When the war emergency was over, rationing was quickly ended by popular demand.

THE INVISIBLE HAND—WHO NEEDS GOVERNMENT?

Is it not something of a mystery that goods and services are regularly offered for sale in quantities that satisfy the wants of consumers? After all, there is no commander-in-chief ordering an army of workers to bring those goods to market. In *The Wealth of Nations,* published in 1776, Scottish philosopher–economist Adam Smith explained this puzzle. Smith described how the **invisible hand** of the marketplace leads the economy to produce an efficient variety of goods and services, with efficient production methods as well. Guided by this invisible hand, producers acting in their own self-interests provide consumers with greater value than even the most well-intentioned of governments.

invisible hand the idea that self-interest and competition promote economic efficiency without any need for action by government.

The reasoning behind the invisible hand is straightforward. To prosper in the marketplace, producers must provide customers with goods and services that they value. Those producers who are best at doing so thrive. Those who pick the wrong goods and services to produce, or who produce them in an inferior manner, lose out. For this reason, an essential ingredient of the invisible hand is *competition,* which pits rival firms against one another in a contest to win the favor of consumers.

Free markets offer people opportunity—the opportunity to get ahead or to fall behind. The market rewards people who use their abilities to satisfy their fellow citizens, so long as that satisfaction is embodied in a good or service that can be sold in the marketplace. As the saying goes, "Build a better mousetrap, and the world will beat a path to your door."

All participants in a market economy, including consumers, businesses, investors, and workers, make choices on the basis of information conveyed by market prices. The use of prices to answer the three basic questions—what, how, and for whom—characterizes *the price system*. **Prices provide information about scarcity.** For example, you could probably not afford to hire your friend's favorite rock star to perform at her birthday party. The scarce talents of superstars generally command a price that only a very large audience can pay. Responding to this market price, superstars would skip the birthday party in favor of the concert. More generally, **it is the price system that allocates resources in a market economy to their highest-valued uses.**

Price changes lead to changes in both consumer and firm behavior. Following the onset of relatively low gasoline prices in the 1980s, consumers moved up—literally—to gas-guzzling sport-utility vehicles and pickup trucks, with some even sporting monstrous V–10 engines. Light-truck divisions at automakers became profit centers, while companies that relied heavily upon the manufacturing of small cars suffered. However, during times when gasoline prices spike upward to significantly higher levels, just the opposite occurs. Those are the times that small car dealers prosper while the owners of pickups and SUVs are left to their regrets at the gas pump.

Guided by market prices, free-market choices lead the economy toward allocative efficiency. The preferences of consumers dictate answers to the "what" question. Competition provides the incentive for firms to choose least-cost production techniques, thus answering the "how" question. The "for whom" question is answered when people offer their labor and other resources in the marketplace—their incomes reflect the value of these resources to others.

MIXING GOVERNMENT WITH THE MARKETPLACE

market failure situation in which the market outcome is inefficient.

For various reasons, markets sometimes fail to achieve efficiency, a situation known as **market failure.** And when it comes to equity, markets seem amoral—sometimes fair and sometimes not. Markets seem fair in rewarding those who work instead of lying on the beach all day, but can seem unfair in the opportunities presented to one person relative to another. So government steps in to correct the inefficiencies and remedy the inequities that would arise in the laissez-faire marketplace.

Some of the most efficient public policies do not abandon markets. Rather, markets can often be steered back on course with public policies that are minimally disruptive to the workings of the invisible hand, while avoiding the inefficiencies of command and control. For example, government took action against Microsoft in order to increase competition in the marketplace, not to replace it with government planning. Likewise, some of the best pollution-control policies are those that change incentives in the marketplace rather than dictate exactly what firms should do. The identification of market failures and the design of efficient policies to correct them is a major topic within microeconomics.

The distribution of income in the free marketplace rewards those who provide the most value to others. To some extent this arrangement seems fair. To some extent, it does not. For example, through no fault of their own, some people are incapable of providing much of value in the marketplace. This situation could be due to physical impairment or the lack of opportunity to acquire knowledge and skills. The result is poverty. Government attempts to promote greater equity by redistributing income and by providing social services. For example, welfare programs and public housing are government actions that are rooted in the concerns about equity.

Sorting out when government intervention is helpful and how it might best be done is probably the most challenging task facing a nation and one that different countries answer in different ways. The result is that all economies combine government action and the marketplace. Some economies, such as that of Cuba, lie toward the command-and-control end of the spectrum. Others place greater reliance upon the marketplace, but still retain a role for

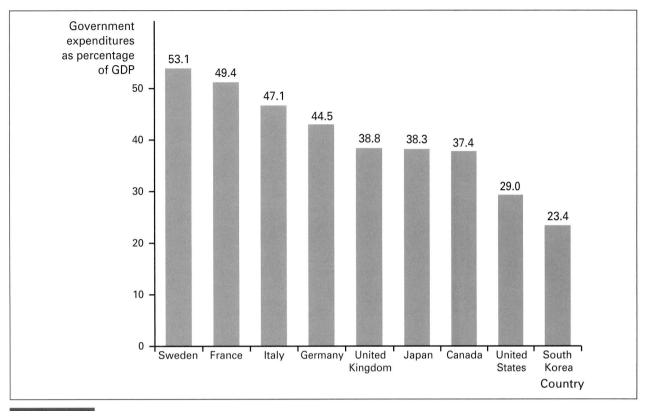

GOVERNMENT EXPENDITURES AS A PERCENTAGE OF GROSS DOMESTIC PRODUCT (GDP), SELECTED COUNTRIES
As evident from the data, countries choose widely varying mixes of government and the widely varying degrees of government involvement in the market economy. For example, while government expenditures account for more than half of Sweden's GDP, they make up less than a quarter of South Korea's GDP.

Source: 2002 Statistical Abstract of the U.S., Table 1328. Data are for 2001.

government. **Helping to identify a proper role for government in a mixed economy is an ongoing theme in economics.**

Figure 1-2 sheds light on the economic significance of government in selected countries. Specifically, the figure shows the fraction of total economic activity (measured by GDP) directly accounted for by government in each country. In effect, the figure shows the cost of government as a percentage of aggregate output. Government's role in the economy is usually greater when the percentage is higher. The data in the figure understate the economic significance of government to the extent that the costs of complying with government regulations are paid for by firms and individuals rather than government.

Unlike in the nineteenth and early twentieth century, the United States can no longer lay claim to having a nearly pure laissez-faire free-market economy. The transition to a larger, activist government has occurred in response to a public perception that government policy provides the only means for correcting inequities and other problems in the marketplace. At the other extreme, few governments still promote central planning because widespread use of command and control in the formerly communist countries was associated with economic stagnation, leaving their citizens with relatively low living standards. China has been quite successful in creating a vibrant market sector that coexists along with state enterprises. Table 1-2 summarizes briefly the key differences between laissez-faire economies, command-and-control economies, and mixed economies.

TABLE 1-2   A BRIEF COMPARISON OF BASIC ECONOMIC SYSTEMS

	LAISSEZ FAIRE	MIXED ECONOMY	COMMAND AND CONTROL
Key Characteristics	Limited role for government implies a small government with few powers. Low taxes. Private property.	Significant role for government. Taxes take a significant portion of national output. Most production of goods and services occurs in the private sector, but there are many regulations and some government production.	Government ownership of property and government directives control the production of goods and services.
Organizing Principle	Invisible hand guides free markets.	Mix of free markets and command and control. Emphasis upon markets relative to government varies from country to country.	Central planning of the economy by government.
Daily Life	Large degree of personal freedom. Most goods and services provided by the private sector, including such essentials as food and education. Market prices and market wages.	Moderate limits on personal freedom because of government regulation and taxation. A few essential goods (education, for example) provided by government, while others (such as food) provided by the private sector. Market prices, with the possibility of some government price controls. Minimum wage laws and a small degree of other government control of wages.	Severe limits on personal freedom due to government control of the economy. Most goods provided by government. Prices set by government rather than the market. Government-set wages.
Countries Where Applied	None, although the United States, Australia, and some other countries value laissez faire in principle.	All countries, including China, Russia, and other countries in transition away from command and control.	None entirely. Cuba and North Korea come the closest.

SNAPSHOT   INTERTWINING ECONOMIC AND POLITICAL PHILOSOPHIES

Bigger or smaller government? An economic stimulus package? Lower taxes? More money for homeland defense? These questions are all answered in the political process. Yet their content is most decidedly economics!

During the eighteenth and nineteenth centuries, economics was called political economy. The term *political economy* makes clear that politics and economics intertwine. Even today, some refer to economics as political economy when they want to emphasize the close ties between economics and public policy. ◀

1.4 ECONOMIC ANALYSIS

The practice of economics involves analysis and problem solving. Sometimes these problems force us to think in terms of value judgments; sometimes they are factual. For example, which of many candidates for liver transplants will receive them? The answer involves a value judgment as to what criteria should be used to allocate scarce transplants. It also involves facts, such as what the possibilities are. Then, we apply logic to solve the problem of how best to meet our objectives with our possibilities.

Care must be taken to avoid faulty reasoning that leads to false conclusions. An example is the *fallacy of composition.* This error in reasoning occurs when it is assumed that what is true at the micro level must also be true at the macro level. In other words, the fallacy of composition involves the observation of a truth about some individual component of the economy accompanied by the assumption that this truth will also apply to the economy at large.

Changes in income can illustrate the fallacy of composition. For example, you would probably consider yourself better off if your income were to double, since that would allow you to purchase twice as much as before. However, to then generalize and think that everyone would be better off if everyone's income doubled would be to commit the fallacy of composition. There would be an important fact missing in that generalization. Specifically, while a change in your personal income would not affect prices, a change in everybody's income would. If prices also doubled, people would be no better off than they had been.

POSITIVE AND NORMATIVE ECONOMICS

Economic pronouncements are in abundant supply from an array of sources. Media commentators, politicians, ordinary citizens, and many economists are often quite eager to share their thoughts. How can we make sense of this mishmash of opinions? Is it truly nothing but opinion?

With some sorting, unsupported opinions can be separated from thoughtful analysis. A good start distinguishes between normative and positive economic statements. **Normative** statements have to do with behavioral norms, which are judgments as to what is good or bad. Examples of normative statements often include "ought" or "should" in them. They imply that something deserves to happen, such as: "The federal government ought to balance its budget."

Positive statements have to do with fact. They may involve current, historical, or even future fact. Positive statements concern what is, was, or will be. The accuracy of positive statements can be checked against facts, although verifying predictions about the future will have to wait until that future arrives. Sometimes it is also hard to judge the accuracy of a statement, although in principle it could be done. For example, "A balanced federal budget will lead to lower interest rates" is a positive statement that would be difficult to verify. Positive economic statements are not necessarily true. However, factual evidence may be introduced to support or refute any positive economic statement. Professional economists generally deal in positive economics, although they might assume some basic normative goals, such as goals of efficiency and equity. Table 1-3 provides examples of positive and normative statements, categorized by whether the subject matter is microeconomics or macroeconomics.

Both positive and normative economics rely upon theory, which is organized thought aimed at answering specific questions. Theories can be tested by logic and, for positive economic theories, by data. Theories are first tested for their internal logic. Does a theory make sense? Sometimes the testing stops there. When feasible, theories are tested by collecting facts to see whether the facts are consistent with the theory. Testing of theories allows us to judge their value, so that the results become more than mere opinion or idle speculation.

For example, consider an economic problem facing Dr. Joan Parker, president of Carbound College. President Parker has commissioned a survey that reveals that the average Carbound

normative having to do with behavioral norms, which are judgments as to what is good or bad.

positive having to do with what is, was, or will be.

TABLE 1-3   CATEGORIZING ECONOMIC STATEMENTS

	MACROECONOMICS	MICROECONOMICS
Positive	The unemployment rate is rising.	People are eating so much chicken that I'll lose my job at the beef-packing plant.
	Inflation is lower today than it was twenty-five years ago.	DVD players are cheaper today than when they were first introduced.
Normative	The unemployment rate is too high.	People should eat more chicken.
	There's no need to worry about inflation.	DVD players are too expensive.

College student spends twenty minutes per day driving around looking for a parking space. Conversations with students lead President Parker to theorize that students will be willing to pay an additional $30 per year in parking fees to cut their search time down to five minutes. Based on past construction costs, the president also theorizes that the required number of parking places could be added for less than this amount. President Parker's theorizing is positive because it is about fact—the benefits and costs of more parking spaces. Before authorizing new parking lot construction, though, the president might be well advised to collect additional data that might more fully indicate if the theory is correct. In the process, President Parker is practicing economics.

ECONOMIC MODELING: THE ROUTE TO HIGHER-LEVEL UNDERSTANDING

models simplified versions of reality that emphasize features central to answering the questions we ask of them.

Economics, like other academic fields such as physics, psychology, and political science, makes extensive use of models. A **model** is a simplification of reality that emphasizes features essential to answering the questions we ask of it. A roadmap is a familiar model. A section of a roadmap is seen in Figure 1-3. In this model the wide red lines that designate interstate highways let us know of major high-speed routes. The circles and yellow splotches show us the locations of towns and larger cities. If our goal is high-speed driving, we want the map kept simple, since we need to read it quickly.

Economic models remove unneeded detail, keeping only features that are essential. Similarly, a roadmap eliminates many features of the terrain, such as trees, houses, and hills. That lack of detail would be inappropriate if the map is for surveying or hiking. For driving, though, including those details would reduce the map's usefulness. A good model need not be totally realistic, even in the features it does include. After all, from a helicopter we would not actually find huge red lines connecting black circles and yellow splotches. The roadmap is merely representative, as a good model should be.

Keep in mind a guiding principle when producing a model. This principle is termed *Occam's razor,* formulated by the fourteenth-century English philosopher William of Occam. Occam argued that reasoning is improved by focusing one's thinking on the most essential elements of an issue. He suggested using a figurative razor to cut away the unnecessary elements from analysis. Occam's razor increases the likelihood that modeling will lead to correct conclusions when the principle is applied correctly.

QUICKCHECK

Categorize the statements below as normative or positive. Explain your reasoning.
   a. The federal government collects more tax revenue than any state government.
   b. After the tornado hit Central City, Uncle Sam moved too slowly in providing aid.

Answers:
   a. Positive. The statement can be checked for its factual accuracy.
   b. Normative. The statement implies that the government should have moved more quickly, without telling us what is meant by too slowly. A positive version of the statement might read as follows: "After the tornado hit Central City, it took two weeks for aid to reach the stricken population. Officials predict a quicker response to future disasters."

FIGURE 1-3

A FAMILIAR MODEL A roadmap is a model. The map is a simplification of reality that retains the features of the landscape that are most important to travelers.

To keep models simple, economists make *assumptions,* meaning that they act as though certain things are true without proving them to in fact be true. One common assumption is termed *ceteris paribus,* which is Latin for holding all else constant. The assumption of *ceteris paribus* allows us to look at one thing at a time. For example, when President Parker was considering whether to add to student parking spaces, the *ceteris paribus* condition in her model might be that student enrollments and driving habits stay unchanged. Effects of changes in student enrollments or driving habits could then be looked at separately.

Economists develop models to explain the choices people make and the consequences of those choices. Economic models may be presented in words, as graphs, or using mathematical equations. If you lack experience in working with graphs you should study the appendix to this chapter, since you will encounter numerous graphical models throughout this book.

MODELS—FROM EINSTEIN'S MIND TO YOURS

SNAPSHOT

The renowned physicist Albert Einstein (1879–1955) was in the business of modeling. The most famous model to come from his mind, summarized in the equation $e = mc^2$, provided key insights that led scientists to the ability to split the atom. It is not only economists and physicists that model, however. Psychologists tell us that all of us walk around with models of life in mind.

Take your model of learning. How do you perceive the learning process? A simple model holds that the job of the instructor is to fill your mind with knowledge. In this model you are a passive recipient of facts, figures, and principles. Students whose internal learning model is similar to this one often fail to prosper academically because some important elements of the learning process have been omitted. Remember, Occam's razor tells us to omit only the nonessential elements from models. As Einstein told us, "Everything should be made as simple as possible, but not simpler."

A more sophisticated learning model allows for the student to interact with the instructor, the material, and other students. Key elements of this model involve setting aside time to reflect on the material, to ask questions, and to work with others. Which model is yours? ◄

Explore & Apply

1.5 FROM MAO TO NOW—MARKET INCENTIVES TAKE HOLD IN CHINA

"Necessity is the mother of invention."

When there are needs, a market economy responds. As a market economy's needs change over time, prices serve as a signal for the invisible hand of the marketplace to meet those needs. For example, when oil seemed scarce, its price went up and new supplies were found. When the price of copper soared, fiber optic cable was developed as an alternative to copper wires.

Some countries have rejected the market economy, only to find that their economic wants and needs were not being met. For much of the twentieth century, the idea of a command-and-control economy had deep, widespread appeal. Many people believed that the unemployment, inflation, depressions, and other problems faced by mixed economies could be avoided through central planning. Charismatic national leaders came into power that century offering to implement command-and-control principles. Lenin in Russia, Mussolini in Italy, Hitler in Germany, Ho Chi Minh in Vietnam, and Mao Tse-Tung in China are the best known.

All these countries have turned away from command and control. Consider China. Chinese civilization is one of the oldest on the planet. Its history is one of extremes, both good and bad. In the mid-to-late twentieth century, that extreme was bad. Faced with grinding poverty and stagnation after the death of Mao, the Chinese leaders decided that a larger role for markets was the only thing that could save their country. They learned from their mistake.

Like the former Soviet Union and other communist countries, the People's Republic of China was guided by the philosophy of the controversial nineteenth–century theorist, Karl Marx. **Marx stated the core philosophy of *communism* as: "From each according to his ability, to each according to his need."** This idea was used to justify a strong central government that would allocate resources according to the communist idea of equity. That idea focused on equal outcomes rather than equal opportunities. Equality would be achieved by government ownership of resources and central planning of the economy.

Marx's idea was not easy to put into practice. What does a person need? A chicken in every pot? Rice and beans? A glass of wine and a loaf of bread? We each have different ideas when it comes to fulfilling our personal needs. People want more, and yet make do with little. How is a government to know what people want? The result is that Marxist governments expounded a philosophy of *egalitarianism,* in which everyone would get identical access to everything from soap to medical care.

Unfortunately for an economy, egalitarianism provides little incentive for people to be productive. If a country's government distributes the same amount of goods and services to everyone, its people are not motivated to work their hardest and do their best. In this system, smart people act stupid. There is no incentive to do otherwise. Indeed, the smarter you act, the more that might be expected of you and the more risks you run. Great efforts were made in China under Chairman Mao to submerge individual identity into a collective mentality that always put the needs of the state before the needs of the individual. Egalitarianism went so far as to see that everyone—men, women, and children—wore the same "uniform," which consisted of denim pants and jacket topped with a small-billed denim military-style cap.

With central planners attempting to direct the "what," "how," and "for whom" of production, poor choices were made and resources were squandered. Everyone had a job, but productivity and purchasing power lagged badly behind the West. China, already the most populous nation on earth, faced a population explosion that promised to lead to mass starvation and unrest unless the economy could be made to perform; thus, the turn to the market. Table 1-4 shows selected key events in the economic transition from command and control to the market, a transition that is still occurring.

| TABLE 1-4 | SELECTED MILESTONES IN CHINA'S TRANSITION TOWARD A MIXED ECONOMY |

YEAR	EVENT
1978	Transition from a planned to a market-oriented economy begins.
1979–1983	Collective farming is replaced by "household responsibility system" of individual farms.
1980	Special economic zones are created to experiment with market reforms.
1986	Foreign investment law is passed.
1988	Enterprise law allows for the existence of privately owned stock companies.
1990	Chinese stock markets are established.
1993	Modern corporate system at state-owned enterprises is introduced.
1994	China allows the exchange value of its currency to be set on world markets, reflecting the common practice of market economies.
1999	China's economy becomes the world's second largest, behind only that of the United States.*
2001	Price controls on key items are lifted as China is admitted as a member of the World Trade Organization.
2003	The deadly SARS virus takes hold in Southern China, causing death and temporarily slowing economic activity.

*As ranked by The International Monetary Fund's purchasing power parity index.

THE ROLE OF GOVERNMENT IN A MARKET ECONOMY

The advantage of a market economy is that the marketplace rewards those producers best able to offer goods and services of value to others. The better a person is at providing things of value to others, the more will be that person's income. Those who fail to provide value, and their employees, will experience unemployment. In this way, each person has an incentive to develop his or her productive potential to the maximum of his or her abilities. The marketplace rewards ability and industriousness with more income. That seems fair, to some extent.

A problem arises when, through no fault of their own, people do not all have the same potential. Furthermore, people may develop their potentials in ways that seem productive at the time, but turn out not to be. For example, elevator operators found their skills obsolete when the ingenuity of manufacturers created automatic push-button elevators. That example reflects the changing opportunities in society, but hardly seems fair to many of the people whose livelihoods are involved. In other cases people find themselves with disabilities that prevent them from reaching their full potential to provide for others. This situation does not mean that they are worth any less as humans, although they tend to earn less income than people without disabilities. Again, that does not seem fair.

Enter government, with its power to tax. Specifically, government redistributes wealth by imposing taxes that take wealth from those who can afford to give and that give to those in need. Taken to an extreme, this redistribution of wealth would eliminate incentives for individuals to behave more productively and lead to stagnation. Therefore, in taxing, government must weigh the tradeoff between equity and incentives for efficiency. In the case of China this has meant the willingness to keep taxes relatively low and tolerate inequality in income and wealth. While the majority of its citizenry remain poor, other Chinese have been allowed to become millionaires, with all the trappings of wealth. This change has generated great controversy in China, with many older citizens seeking a return to the former ways of the country.

In China, Russia, and other transition economies in Eastern Europe and elsewhere, the urge to impose new government regulations as a response to every problem must be tempting. The invisible hand is just that, invisible. For this reason, it is often not well understood, at least until people have a chance to observe it in action. What the mix of markets and government ultimately chosen by China will look like is anyone's guess. What we can say is that China seems to have learned the value of mixing incentives into the recipe for its economy.

THINKING CRITICALLY

1. *Jesse:* **I like the idea of a strong central government. We need freedom and opportunity within limits, where government keeps us from going too far.**

   Lee: **When people harm others or take their property, then government needs to intervene. Otherwise, government should keep out, since it's just one group imposing its version of morality on everybody else.**

   This exchange illustrates that the mixed economy involves much more than the magnitude of taxes and government regulation. What are some other points of contention in how "free" free markets should be?

2. **Some people think that the more democratic a country, the greater reliance it will place upon free markets. Do you think this is true? Explain.**

 Visit **www.prenhall.com/ayers** for updates and web exercises on this Explore & Apply topic.

SUMMARY AND LEARNING OBJECTIVES

1. **Describe how scarce resources and unlimited wants lead to the study of economics.**
   - Economics is the study of how to allocate scarce resources to satisfy unlimited wants. Scarcity forces people to make choices, both individually and collectively.
   - Economic choices are often made at the margin, meaning in increments rather than all or nothing. The choices made by individuals, businesses, and government determine the economy's allocation of resources.

2. **Distinguish between microeconomics and macroeconomics.**
   - Economic issues can be classified as falling within microeconomics or macroeconomics. Microeconomics deals with the individual parts of the economy, such as consumers or firms. Macroeconomics looks at the big picture, including gross domestic product, unemployment, inflation, money, and interest rates.

3. **Identify three basic questions that all economies must answer.**
   - The three basic economic questions are what, how, and for whom. The *what* question refers to the choice of goods and services produced. The *how* question is about the choice of production methods. The *for whom* question relates to who receives the output the economy produces.

   - To answer the three questions, countries choose a mix of laissez faire and command and control. The result is that all countries have mixed economies, with the mix varying from country to country.

4. **Recognize the strengths of the marketplace and motivations for government involvement.**
   - In making decisions about the choice of system, countries can be guided by two economic objectives: equity and efficiency. Equity refers to fairness; efficiency to getting the most value from economic resources. Efficiency is of two types: allocative and technological. The first refers to producing the highest-valued mix outputs; the second to producing any particular output in the least-costly way.
   - In a free-market economy resources are allocated as if, in Adam Smith's famous phrase, by an invisible hand. A laissez-faire or hands-off policy by government means that market prices guide the allocation of resources.
   - When the market fails to achieve efficiency, government tends to take action. Government action is also directed toward equity issues. Such government actions include the government provision of goods and services.

5. **Understand what a model is and why models are best kept simple.**
   - ■ Sound logic is essential to proper economic analysis. Care must be taken to avoid the fallacy of composition, which is the error of assuming that what is true for the part is true for the whole.
   - ■ Economic analysis can involve normative or positive statements. Normative economics involves value judgments about whether something is good or bad. Positive economics concerns facts.
   - ■ Economic analysis is practiced using models, often expressed with graphs. Occam's razor suggests that models ought to be stripped down to their necessary elements. They should be as simple as possible, while still conveying the essence of an issue.

 6. **Explain why incentives are important for economic prosperity.**
   - ■ Egalitarianism was a key feature of the economy in China under Chairman Mao. That economy was also characterized by central planning, which led to the inefficient use of resources. For this reason, China's leaders introduced market incentives. How much government to mix with the private marketplace is a choice that each country must make. Care must be taken that incentives are sufficient to promote productivity.

KEY TERMS

economics, 2
scarcity, 2
the margin, 2
microeconomics, 4
markets, 4
market prices, 4
macroeconomics, 4

command and control, 5
free markets, 5
mixed economies, 5
equity, 6
efficiency, 6
technological efficiency, 6

allocative efficiency, 6
invisible hand, 7
market failure, 8
normative, 11
positive, 11
models, 12

TEST YOURSELF

TRUE OR FALSE

1. The problem of resource scarcity has been solved in recent years through advances in technology.
2. Industry studies are examples of macroeconomic analysis.
3. The tradeoff between efficiency and equity means that increases in efficiency will often be accompanied by less equity.
4. Adam Smith's concept of the invisible hand is that the free marketplace functions better when the hand of government guides it.
5. Occam's razor is a principle that is used in the drawing of roadmaps.

MULTIPLE CHOICE

6. Economics is primarily the study of
   a. stocks and bonds.
   b. allocating limited resources to meet unlimited wants.
   c. methods to eliminate scarcity.
   d. why consumers want what they do.

7. Making decisions at the margin is about
   a. all-or-nothing choices.
   b. choices involving money.
   c. incremental choices.
   d. normative economics.
8. Macroeconomics looks at
   a. the "big picture."
   b. only the government portion of the economy.
   c. only the business portion of the economy.
   d. the behavior of individuals, but not of firms.
9. Which of the following is the best example of microeconomics?
   a. A study of new automobile prices.
   b. Evaluation of the Federal budget.
   c. A statement about what ought to be.
   d. A history of U.S. inflation.

10. The three basic questions an economy must answer are
    a. why produce; how much to produce; who to produce it?
    b. what to produce; how to produce it; who to consume it?
    c. what to produce; why produce; how to produce?
    d. when to produce; how to produce; what to produce?
11. Command-and-control economies are characterized by
    a. reliance upon free markets.
    b. adherence to the principles of capitalism.
    c. economic freedom.
    d. government decision making.
12. Laissez faire is the term for
    a. the philosophy that hard work is bad for a person.
    b. government command-and-control policies.
    c. let it be.
    d. a partnership between government and business.
13. Which of the following is NOT an advantage of market allocation of resources over central government allocation of resources?
    a. Markets distribute income in the most equitable manner possible.
    b. Market prices allocate resources to their highest-valued uses.
    c. People out for their own self-interest in the marketplace have more incentive to provide products of value to others than would government bureaucrats.
    d. Competition among firms causes products to be produced in the most technologically efficient manner.
14. In a capitalist economy, economic activities are coordinated by
    a. tradition.
    b. prices.
    c. government.
    d. business firms.
15. The concept of a mixed economy refers to a mixture of
    a. positive and normative economics.
    b. microeconomics and macroeconomics.
    c. government and free markets.
    d. command with control.
16. Efficiency means
    a. resources are distributed in a fair manner.
    b. all material wants are satisfied.
    c. no one can be made better off, except at someone else's expense.
    d. technology does not change.
17. The idea that the economy should produce its outputs with the least costly combinations of inputs is known as
    a. allocative efficiency.
    b. technological efficiency.
    c. economic efficiency.
    d. equity.
18. The invisible hand of the marketplace refers to the tendency for
    a. government to control the economy behind the scenes.
    b. pollution and other side effects of market activities to harm the economy.
    c. producers to conspire with each other, so as to get as much money as possible out of consumers' pockets.
    d. sellers out for their own self-interests to provide the most valuable assortment of products at the lowest possible prices.
19. Which of the following is the best example of a positive economic statement?
    a. New York should repeal its income tax.
    b. An increase in the minimum wage is likely to increase unemployment.
    c. It is unfair to subsidize farmers.
    d. The price of gasoline is just fine!
 20. In response to the inefficient use of resources in China in the days of Mao Tse-Tung, recent Chinese policy has emphasized
    a. egalitarianism.
    b. central planning.
    c. free Internet access.
    d. market incentives.

QUESTIONS AND PROBLEMS

1. *[scarcity]* Describe how scarcity affects the following decision makers:
    a. the president of the United States.
    b. a business executive.
    c. a city manager.
    d. the mother of a baby.
2. *[the margin]* Think back over all the decisions you have made in the last twenty-four hours. Select a few of the clearest examples of decisions made at the margin.
3. *[resource allocation]* Explain how the economy's resource allocation depends in a small way upon the choices you make. For example, how does your choice of going to college affect the economy's resource allocation?
4. *[microeconomics versus macroeconomics]* Identify each of the following topics and issues according to whether they are more appropriate to the study of microeconomics or macroeconomics.

a. the U.S. unemployment rate.

b. electricity prices.

c. gross domestic product.

d. money.

e. advertising by the tobacco industry.

5. *[three economic questions]* List and briefly explain the three economic questions that every economy must answer.

6. *[economic systems]* What are the three types of economic systems? Which of these best describes the economic systems of Canada, the United States, and Western Europe? Discuss the characteristics of this type of economic system.

7. *[equity and efficiency]* Each of the following situations describes an aspect of the issues of equity or efficiency. Identify each situation, according to whether it relates to equity, technological efficiency, or allocative efficiency. Explain why you chose the answers you did.

   a. Jane, a supervisor at the Built-Rite construction company, is concerned because her company does not offer health insurance to its part-time employees, while full-time employees are covered.

   b. Ted, the owner of Ted's Automotive, a small automobile repair shop, has rearranged the layout of the tools and equipment in the shop in order to service more customers each week.

   c. Juanita, a professor of economics at Home State University, is pondering whether to curve the grades on the last test her students took.

   d. Jason, the president of a medium-sized company producing shoes, has decided to stop producing the model #102 running shoe because of a lack of sales.

   e. Ramiro, the owner–manager of BookMax, a chain of discount book stores, has decided to install a $1,000,000 automated shipping system to more quickly and accurately respond to orders that are placed by customers on its web site.

8. *[tradeoffs]* Explain why there could be a tradeoff between efficiency and equity, using taxation as an example.

9. *[role of prices]* During World War II, sugar, gasoline, meat, and other goods were rationed by the U.S. government. Families were issued ration cards that allowed them to buy a government–determined quantity of rationed goods. Why would the government bypass the free market in time of war? Is government rationing, rather than rationing by price, a good idea? How does government rationing affect the allocation of resources?

10. *[role of prices]* If farmers stopped farming or transportation workers quit shipping the food that farmers grow, we might wake up one morning to discover our cupboards bare. Why don't we lose sleep over that possibility? What causes food and other goods to appear in stores?

11. *[mixed economy]* Explain how choices made between government's spending of taxpayer money, or taxpayers spending that money themselves, affect the allocation of society's resources.

12. *[political economy]* Why is economics sometimes called political economy? Explain.

13. *[fallacy of composition]* Ralph the theater manager knows that he can walk from a first row seat to the rear exit in fifteen seconds. When the fire marshal asked Ralph how long it would take his customers to leave the theater in the event of a fire, Ralph responded that it would take fifteen seconds. What flaw in Ralph's reasoning has caused him to commit the fallacy of composition?

14. *[positive versus normative economics]* Why is the statement "Movies today are too violent" a normative statement? Convert the statement into a positive statement. Is your positive statement true? What sort of evidence could be used to establish the truth or falsity of the statement you wrote?

15. *[economic models]* Generally speaking, what is the purpose of an economic model? What guidance does Occam's razor give in creating models? Why do economists make assumptions in developing models? What does the assumption of *ceteris paribus* mean?

16. *[economic models]* Suppose that a college president is developing a model that the administrator hopes will explain how much students will be willing to pay for additional campus parking. Briefly comment on how each of the following might influence student willingness to pay.

    a. Class schedules.

    b. Available bus service.

    c. Students' incomes.

 Visit **www.prenhall.com/ayers** for Exploring the Web exercises and additional self-test quizzes.

WORKING WITH GRAPHS AND DATA

Economists draw graphs in order to clarify thoughts and show economic relationships in a way that can be more easily understood than with words alone. Graphs that present factual information are often drawn as line graphs, bar charts, and pie charts, all of which are seen in this book.

Other graphs represent economic models and contain lines that are referred to as curves. As you read this book, you should study each graph and read its caption. The horizontal line is commonly called the *X* axis and the vertical line the *Y* axis, with the specific labels of the axes varying from graph to graph, depending on what the graph is modeling. Pay attention to both labels and to what the graph is trying to tell you.

When it comes to graphs of models, you will understand the graph better if you can draw it yourself. If you are able to visualize economic relationships graphically, can put an explanation of the graph into your own words, and can draw the graph, you will greatly increase your understanding of economic concepts.

MODELS: DIRECT VERSUS INVERSE RELATIONSHIPS

Each axis of the graph of a model is labeled with the name of a variable, where a variable refers to the name of anything that can change. For example, the price of a pound of tomatoes is a variable because the price could be any of many different values. The price can change with the passage of time. Likewise, the quantity of tomatoes sold is a variable because the quantity sold can change from one time period to the next.

Within the axes, a relationship between two variables is shown by a curve—a line. Some graphs will have more than one curve in them. Other graphs will only show one curve.

Curves that slope upward to the right show a *direct relationship*, also termed a *positive relationship*, between the variables. Curves that slope downward to the right show an *inverse relationship*, also termed a *negative relationship*.

An example will help. Suppose we are interested in the relationship between the average annual quantity of umbrellas sold and the average annual quantity of rainfall, measured in inches. Hypothetical data for these variables in five communities are given in Figure 1A-1.

The relationship between rainfall and umbrella sales is clearly positive, because increases in rainfall are associated with a greater number of umbrellas sold. In Figure 1A-1, the data on the left are plotted in the graph on the right, with rainfall measured on the horizontal axis (the axis that goes left to right) and umbrella sales on the vertical axis (the axis that goes up and

Hypothetical data on yearly rainfall and umbrella sales			
Data point	Community	Yearly rainfall	Umbrella sales
A	Center City	30 inches	100 units
B	Moose Haven	40 inches	200 units
C	Blountville	50 inches	300 units
D	Houckton	60 inches	400 units
E	Echo Ridge	70 inches	500 units

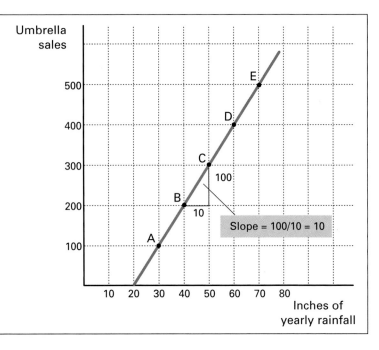

FIGURE 1A-1

A POSITIVE SLOPE A curve that slopes upward to the right illustrates a positive relationship between two variables, also called a direct relationship. The slope of the curve in this figure is positive and constant, equaling 10.

down). A curve is drawn through the plot of data points. The curve slopes upward to the right, again confirming the direct relationship between the two variables.

In contrast, the graph in Figure 1A-2 shows a curve that slopes downward to the right, indicating an inverse relationship between variables. The axes are labeled to show the relationship between the sales of woolen coats, measured on the vertical axis, and the average January temperature, measured on the horizontal axis, in five cities. A greater quantity of coats are sold when temperatures are lower. The data that are plotted in Figure 1A-2 are observable in the table on the left side.

THE SLOPE OF A CURVE

The slope of a curve is measured by the amount of change in the variable on the vertical axis divided by the amount of change in the variable on the horizontal axis. Slope is sometimes referred to as the "rise over the run." In Figure 1A-1, the slope of the curve equals 100 (the rise, or vertical change) divided by 10 (the run, or horizontal change), which equals 10:

Slope = (change in variable on vertical axis)/(change in variable on horizontal axis)
       = rise/run
       = 100/10 = 10

Applying the definition of slope to Figure 1A-2, the slope of the curve in Figure 1A-2 equals -10, a negative value because the vertical change involves a decrease. Downward sloping curves always have a negative value for their slope.

Straight lines are linear and always have a constant slope. This means that if you know the slope between any two points on the line, you know the slope everywhere on the line. Thus, in Figure 1A-1 the slope equals 10 all along the curve and in Figure 1A-2 the slope equals -10 everywhere on that curve.

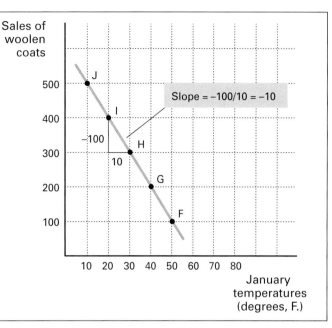

Hypothetical data on sales of woolen coats and average January temperatures			
Data point	City	Coat sales	Average January temperature
F	Tropical city	100 units	50 degrees
G	North town	200 units	40 degrees
H	Snowbound	300 units	30 degrees
I	Cold city	400 units	20 degrees
J	Arctica	500 units	10 degrees

FIGURE 1A-2

A NEGATIVE SLOPE A curve that slopes downward illustrates a negative relationship between two variables, also called an inverse relationship. The slope of the curve shown is negative and constant, equaling −10.

The slope of a nonlinear curve changes from one point to the next on the curve. In Figure 1A-3 graphs (a) and (b) both show curves that have a positive slope. However, the slope becomes decreasingly positive in (a), but increasingly positive in (b). Graphs (c) and (d) show curves with negative slopes. In (c), the slope becomes decreasingly negative, while the slope becomes increasingly negative in (d). Figure 1A-3 illustrates another point about graphs. Notice that these graphs do not have numbers. Graphs of models will often be presented this way when the numbers are less important than the type of relationship between the variables.

Many economic relationships are portrayed as linear. This convention simplifies the analysis, in keeping with the principle of Occam's razor, and allows us to focus our attention on the analysis rather than the shape of the curve. When curves are drawn as nonlinear, the nonlinearity will typically be important to the analysis.

Merely glancing at a curve is often revealing. When the curve slopes upward to the right, you know that it has a positive slope and thus shows a direct relationship between the variables on the axes. Likewise, when the curve slopes downward to the right, it has a negative slope that portrays an inverse relationship between the variables.

The slope of a curve provides information at the margin. The downward sloping curve in Figure 1A-4 shows the incremental spending by the customers of a restaurant in response to additional hours of operation. Note that the slope of the curve equals −25, because incremental customer spending decreases by $25 every additional hour the restaurant remains open. The owners of the restaurant could use this information, in conjunction with data relating to the cost of staying open, to reach a decision about how long to stay open.

SHIFTS AND INTERSECTION POINTS

A change in the relationship between two variables is indicated by a shift in a curve. For example, suppose that umbrellas become a fashion accessory to be carried even when it is

NONLINEAR RELATIONSHIPS The graphs in parts (a) through (d) show nonlinear relationships since the curves in the graphs are not straight lines. The two axes are labeled X and Y, which can represent any two variables. The slopes are:
(a) becoming decreasingly positive as X increases,
(b) becoming increasingly positive as X increases,
(c) becoming decreasingly negative as X increases,
(d) becoming increasingly negative as X increases.

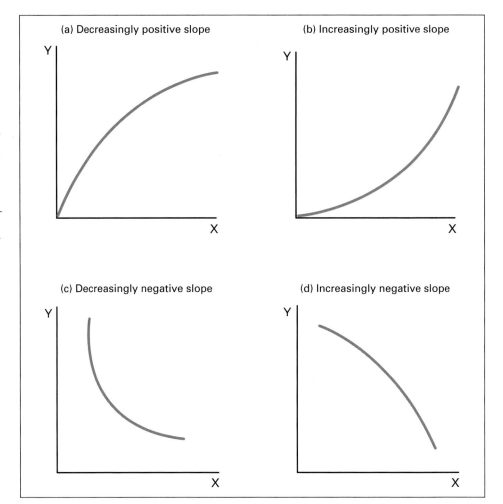

INFORMATION AT THE MARGIN
Incremental spending by customers at this restaurant decreases as it stays open longer. The slope shown equals −25, which means that the additional spending by restaurant customers decreases by $25 with each passing hour.

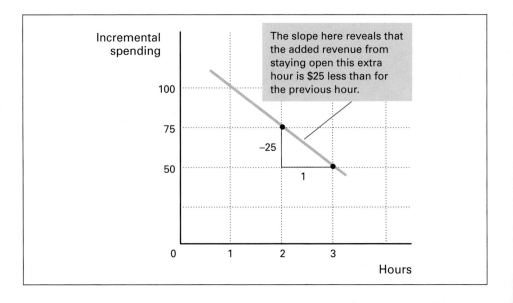

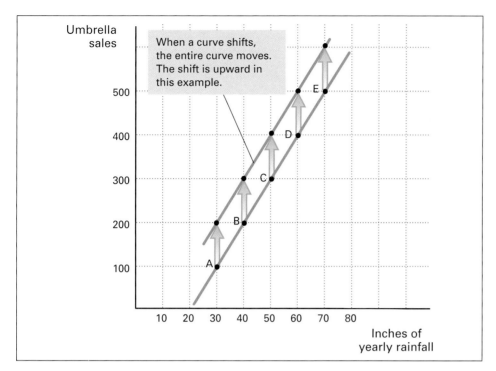

FIGURE 1A-5

A SHIFT IN A CURVE When a curve changes position, we say there has been a shift in the curve. A shift represents a new relationship between the variables. This curve shifts upward because umbrellas have become more popular. The shift indicates that 100 additional umbrellas will be sold for each level of rainfall.

not raining. The curve shown in Figure 1A-5 would shift up. In this example, the sales of umbrellas increase by 100 units in each community. If the popularity of umbrellas fades, the curve would shift back down. The student should also be aware that **there is a difference between a shift in a curve and a movement along a curve.** A change in the amount of rainfall will cause a movement along the curve, as in moving from one point to another in Figure 1A-5. For example, the original curve in Figure 1A-5 shows that umbrella sales would increase from 100 to 200 units if rainfall increased from thirty inches to forty inches a year. That increase in sales is a movement along the curve. The increase in umbrella sales from 100 to 200 units would also occur if rainfall stayed at thirty inches a year, but the curve shifted upward, as shown in Figure 1A-5. This time the increase in sales is associated with a shift in the curve, not a movement along it.

Some graphs show two different relationships between the variables on the axes. Each relationship will be illustrated by its own curve. You have just seen this possibility illustrated by a shift in a curve. However, another case involves two relationships that are independent of each other. An example of this possibility occurs when two curves intersect (cross each other). When two curves intersect, the intersection point will sometimes be of particular interest. **At the intersection point the values of each variable will be identical for both relationships—both curves.** Their values are equal only at that point. For example, Figure 1A-6 shows two curves, one that slopes upward and one that slopes downward. The two curves intersect at a point, labeled *A* in the figure. The figure shows that at the intersection point the *X* value is 2 and is the same on both curves. The *Y* value is 75 and is also the same on both curves.

POINTS OF TANGENCY

While points of intersection are frequently of interest in economics, there is another case in which two variables will take on equal values. This is the case where two curves are

AN INTERSECTION POINT At the intersection point of two curves, their values are identical. Point *A* shows a value of 2 for variable *X* and 75 for variable *Y*. Only at that point does curve 1 equal curve 2.

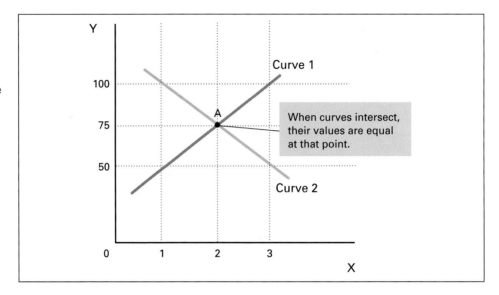

TANGENCY A tangency occurs when two curves touch each other, but do not intersect. Their values at the point of tangency are identical.

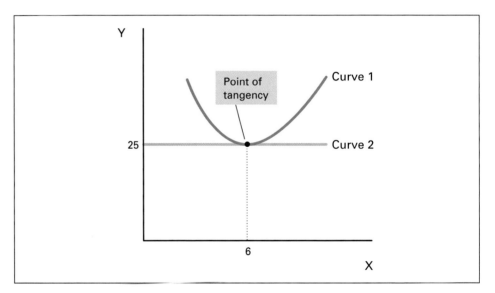

tangent to each other. To be tangent means to touch at a point. Figure 1A-7 shows the idea. The U-shaped curve labeled curve 1 is tangent to the horizontal line labeled curve 2. In this case the tangency point is at the bottom point, called the *minimum point,* of the U-shaped curve. The value of X at the tangency point equals six. The horizontal line has a constant Y value of twenty-five. The U-shaped curve has a value of twenty-five only at the tangency point. To put in another way, the U-shaped cuve has a value of twenty-five only when X equals six.

Points of tangency do not necessarily have to be between a horizontal line and a U-shaped curve. Anytime two curves touch each other, but do not intersect, there is a tangency point.

TIME-SERIES AND CROSS-SECTIONAL DATA

Numerical data are important in economic analysis. Data can be presented in a table or a graph. In general, graphs of data are preferred to tables when the details of the data are less

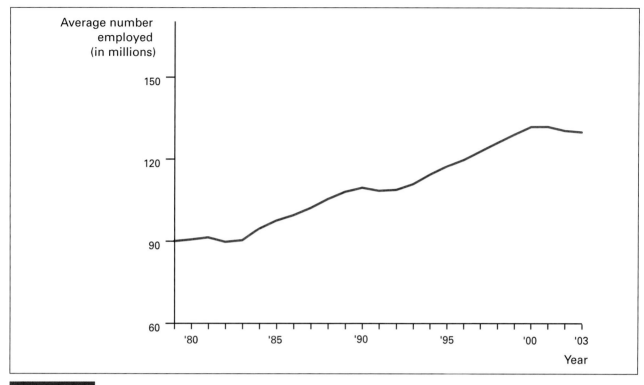

FIGURE 1A-8

TIME-SERIES DATA: NUMBER EMPLOYED The yearly average number of people employed in the United States since 1979 is an example of time-series data. Time-series data show how something changes with time.

Source: Federal Reserve Bank of Dallas on-line data base. These data refer to total nonagriculture employment. Data for 2003 are current through the month of July.

important than the general pattern, since general patterns are more easily ascertained by looking at a graph than at a table.

Time-series data show the values of a variable as time passes. Economists utilize time-series data when changes in the value of a variable over time are the focus of interest. The number of people employed in the United States for each year between 1979 and 2003 is an example of time-series data, as shown by the line chart in Figure 1A-8. Notice that these data could have been presented in a table, but that a table would require more careful study than the graph. The graph easily reveals that the trend in employment was up, since in most years employment increased. Employment moved down, against the trend, in 1982, 1991, 2002, and 2003 because of economic slowdowns in those years.

Cross-sectional data are fixed at a moment in time, but vary in some other way. In other words, cross-sectional data change because of some cause that is unrelated to the passage of time. The April 2003 unemployment rate for the United States, Canada, Japan, France, Germany, Italy, and the United Kingdom is an example of cross-sectional data. These data are shown in Figure 1A-9 (see page 28) as a bar chart. The bar chart shown would be useful to an economist studying differences in country unemployment rates in the year cited.

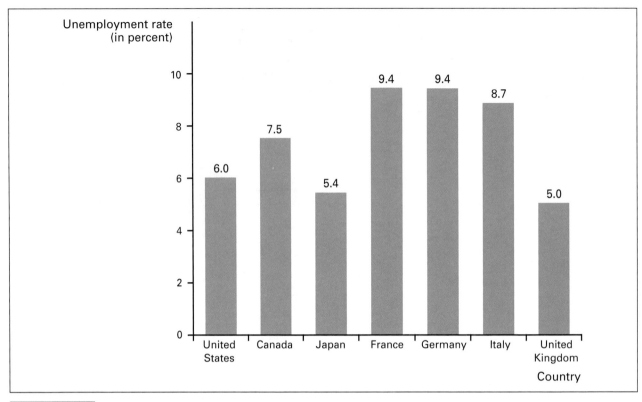

FIGURE 1A-9

CROSS-SECTIONAL DATA: COUNTRY UNEMPLOYMENT RATES The average unemployment rate in each of several countries is an example of cross-sectional data. These data are not time-series data, because they are for a single month and year, April 2003.

Source: OECD, *Main Economic Indicators,* August 2003.

SOURCES OF ECONOMIC DATA

Economic research utilizes data in order to identify problems and issues, and to provide evidence about the causes of economic phenomena. Much of the numerical data economists use is collected by various levels of government. Important nongovernmental sources of data include industry trade associations, the United Nations, the Organization for European Community Development (OECD), the International Monetary Fund (IMF), World Bank, Standard and Poor's, Moody's, and Robert Morris Associates.

A short list of useful sources of data follows:

- *Economic Report of the President.* Annual. Roughly one-third of the book is a compilation of numerous data tables selected from among those issued by government agencies. The text is written by the President's Council of Economic Advisers, and provides a professional assessment of the performance of the economy. Written to be understood by the general public, the Economic Report is probably the best place for both novices and experts to start a general search for data about the U.S. economy.

- *International Financial Statistics.* Monthly. Published by the International Monetary Fund in English and other languages, the book presents several hundred large pages of finely printed economic data on the world at large, and on specific countries throughout the world. The focus is on the financial side of economic activity, such as inflation, interest rates, government budgets, and exchange rates. There is also data on a variety of non-financial features of world economies, such as the composition of exports and imports. To promote easy access, the IMF also provides a CD-ROM version.

- **Federal Reserve Bulletin.** Monthly. The user will find extensive data on money, banking, interest rates, and finance, along with news relating to the financial environment. Also featured are articles that analyze economic developments. Articles are written to be accessible to the general reader.
- **Survey of Current Business.** Quarterly. This publication of the U.S. Department of Commerce offers a rich source of data on business conditions.
- **City and County Data Book.** Annual. What is the population of your hometown? What is the average age of its residents? Average income? This data source provides information about the economies of U.S. cities and counties.
- **Statistical Abstract of the U.S.** Annual. This source contains hundreds of data tables, packed full of facts about the United States.
- **The Internet.** The Internet has marked a huge change in the way data are retrieved. There are numerous sites offering economic data. Some data sets are free; others are not. For example, the *Economic Report of the President* is freely available on-line, as are many other data sets from the federal government.

EXERCISES

1. Consider the relationship between a college student's grade in a course and the amount of time spent studying. Draw a graph with the vertical axis labeled "grade" and the horizontal axis labeled "time spent studying" that shows the general relationship you would expect between these variables. Do you think the relationship would necessarily be linear? What factors other than study time would affect the grades of college students? How would changes in these other factors shift the curve in the graph you have drawn?

2. Gross domestic product data for the imaginary country of Janica are as follows: 1998 GDP = $175 billion; 1999 GDP = $145 billion; 2000 GDP = $164 billion; 2001 GDP = $200 billion; 2002 GDP = $215 billion. Plot the GDP data on a graph in which the vertical axis measures GDP and the horizontal axis years. Connect the data plots to create a line graph.

WORKING WITH GRAPHS AND DATA

1. *[direct versus indirect relationships]* Draw graphs indicating the following relationships. Also describe the mathematical relationships between the variables. Be sure to label all axes.

   a. Susan has discovered that as her income fell last year she bought fewer concert tickets.
   b. David, a cross-country runner, experienced decreasing times running the mile as he increased his time sprinting during practice.
   c. Robert, an avid bodybuilder, recognized that as he increasingly lifted more weight on his presses, it reduced his yardage on his drives on the golf course.
   d. Molly's car got the same gas mileage when she used 87-, 89-, and 93-octane gasoline on separate occasions.
   e. As John ate more popcorn during the movie, he felt that his total satisfaction from the popcorn grew at a decreasing rate.

2. *[time-series and cross-sectional data]* Mike is preparing data for a paper he is writing for his Cultural Diversity course. He has collected the data on per capita or average income (GDP) for the following countries:

Year	Albania	Austria	Bulgaria	Czech Republic	Romania
2002	$4,500	$27,700	$6,600	$15,300	$7,000
2001	$3,700	$26,100	$6,200	$12,900	$6,800
2000	$3,000	$25,000	$5,100	$12,200	$5,900
1999	$1,650	$23,400	$4,300	$11,700	$3,900
1998	$1,490	$22,700	$4,100	$11,300	$4,050
1997	$1,370	$21,400	$4,300	$10,800	$4,500
1996	$1,110	$19,700	$4,630	$11,100	$5,200

a. If Mike decided to present the growth of average income for a single country from 1996 to 2002 from the previous table, what type of graph would be appropriate? Draw the graph.

b. What type of data is Mike dealing with when he draws the graph that indicates the growth of average income of a single country from 1996 to 2002?

c. If Mike wanted to compare average yearly incomes across the five nations for a single year, what type of graph could be used? Draw the graph.

d. What type of data is Mike dealing with when he draws the graph that indicates the average income of all five countries in 1996?

e. How might Mike present the entire table of data representing average incomes across five countries over the period of 1996 to 2002?

f. What type of data would he be presenting in case *e* above?

3. *[direct versus inverse relationships and the slope of a curve]* Cynthia sells ice cream in five locations in Florida. She observed the following variations in her sales of ice cream based on the temperatures where her shops are located:

Data Point	Store Location	Ice Cream Sales	Temperature (°F)
A	Tallahassee	100	80
B	Tampa	120	84
C	Orlando	140	88
D	Fort Myers	160	92
E	Naples	180	96

Jason, Cynthia's brother, sells coffee at the same locations. He recorded the following data:

Data Point	Store Location	Coffee Sales	Temperature (°F)
E	Tallahassee	70	80
F	Tampa	65	84
G	Orlando	60	88
H	Fort Myers	55	92
I	Naples	50	96

a. Draw the relationship between the temperature and ice cream sales at Cynthia's shops.

b. What type of relationship exists between the temperature and ice cream sales?

c. What is the slope along the line you drew between points B and C? Between C and D?

d. Interpret what the slope is telling Cynthia about her ice cream sales.

e. Draw the relationship between the temperature and coffee sales at Jason's shops.

f. What type of relationship exists between the temperature and coffee sales?

g. What is the slope along the line you drew between points F and G? Between G and H?

h. Interpret what the slope is telling Cynthia about her brother's sales of coffee.

CHAPTER 2

PRODUCTION AND TRADE

A LOOK AHEAD

What does the word *model* bring to mind? A fashion model? A model airplane? A model citizen? In this chapter, we will model the essence of economics—scarcity and choice. While models are designed with different purposes in mind, the economic model shares a common trait with other models. That trait is a studied simplicity that highlights the features of greatest significance.

The basic model of economics developed in this chapter extends from our daily routines as individuals to the grand plans of our society—from our choice of occupations to the rise and fall of nations. For example, the twentieth century has been dubbed "America's century" to reflect the strengths of the U.S. economy in providing for its citizens and in defeating its adversaries. In the Explore & Apply section that concludes this chapter, we will discover how economics helps us better understand those victories. As we journey through the twenty-first century, we will encounter new and sometimes fearsome choices, such as those we have already seen in the conflict in Iraq. Economic models can help us to recognize our options so that we will choose well.

LEARNING OBJECTIVES

Understanding Chapter 2 will enable you to:
1. **Analyze tradeoffs facing both individuals and countries.**
2. **Categorize the types of resources an economy possesses.**
3. **Model a country's production possibilities, and how these possibilities respond to technological development.**
4. **Describe how economies can grow faster if they are willing to cut back on current consumption.**
5. **Visualize the flow of goods and services, resources, and money in the economy.**
6. **Explain how people and countries gain from trade by specializing according to comparative advantage.**
7. **Convey how economic strength can lead to victory, sometimes without a fight.**

Explore & Apply

2.1 SCARCITY AND CHOICE

There is no such thing as a free lunch.

Economics exists because resources are scarce relative to our wants. Scarcity means we have to make choices. Take lunchtime for example. Suppose your school cafeteria holds a Student Appreciation Day and offers a free sandwich buffet between noon and 1:00 next Thursday. Would you go? Your decision depends upon opportunity costs.

OPPORTUNITY COSTS

opportunity costs the value of the best alternative opportunity forgone.

Opportunity costs represent the value of forgone alternatives. Specifically, the opportunity cost of an action is the value of the single most highly valued alternative choice that has been forgone. Perhaps you contemplate how good the cafeteria's sandwiches are, relative to other things you could eat. You might also consider how pleasant the surroundings are, relative to other lunch spots. You would also want to check your calendar—your time may be needed for something of higher priority, such as studying for an exam. If you choose to eat the cafeteria's sandwiches, you must give up the value of the best alternative way to spend that time. While no money is taken, the lunch is in reality far from free.

The money you pay for an item could have alternatively been spent on something else. The value of the best alternative use of that money is an opportunity cost, but not usually the only opportunity cost. The value of forgone alternative uses of time or other nonmonetary resources must also be included. To compute your own opportunity cost of going to college, for example, you must compute what you would be doing if you were not in school. Would you be working? Then the cost of a semester is tuition plus the forgone earnings from the job you would have had. Maybe you would have been spending all of your time at the beach. That, too, has an opportunity cost. Only you can know how high it is, because only you can know what value you receive from lying in the sun and listening to the surf.

SNAPSHOT   "THE GRASS IS ALWAYS GREENER ...

... on the other side of the fence," the saying goes. Take marriage, for example. How many married men and women do not catch themselves envying the freedom of their single friends—freedom to meet new people and do what they want, when they want to do it? How many of those single friends do not look back with envy of their own, seeing the warmth and security of sharing one's life with someone special? Oh, those opportunity costs! We cannot have it all! ◄

RESOURCES

Resources are combined to produce outputs of goods and services. *Inputs* is another name for resources, which are usually divided into the categories of land, labor, capital, and entrepreneurship. We refer to the ability of a resource to produce output as that resource's *productivity*.

land natural resources in their natural states.

Land refers to all natural resources in their natural states. These gifts of nature include such things as minerals, water, and soil. Neither motor oil nor gasoline would fall under the category of land. Rather, they are products that use land as an input. The crude oil from which the motor oil and gasoline were derived is land.

labor the human capacity to work.

human capital acquired skills and abilities embodied within a person.

Labor refers to people's capacity to work. It ignores the increased labor productivity from acquired skills and the development of peoples' abilities, which constitute **human capital.** Human capital is a special case of an economy's third resource, capital.

Just before leaving office in 2001, President Clinton designated as parkland millions of acres of land owned by the federal government. Since the government already owned the land, is it true that there were no opportunity costs to the president's decision?

Answer: No. Although the government did not have to spend money to acquire the land, there were still opportunity costs. For one, national parklands are restricted in terms of their uses. Thus, mineral exploration is curtailed. Ranchers are also not allowed to graze their animals in national parks. By converting the land into a park, the federal government gave up the opportunity of selling it. These opportunity costs are difficult to estimate, but are real nonetheless. The opportunity costs account for the public protests that accompanied the president's action.

Capital is anything that is produced in order to increase productivity in the future. Along with human capital, there is also *physical capital,* which includes buildings, machinery, and other equipment. For example, a college education adds to human capital, and the classroom in which that education was obtained is physical capital. The classroom aids in the production of an education, and the education aids in productivity in the workplace.

capital anything that is produced in order to increase productivity in the future; includes human capital and physical capital.

Caution: The definition of capital used in economics differs from that used in finance. Financial capital refers to financial instruments, such as stocks, bonds, and money.

Entrepreneurship is taking personal initiative to combine resources in productive ways. Rather than accepting jobs where orders are handed down from above, entrepreneurs blaze new trails in the world of commerce. If you start your own business, you are an entrepreneur. Entrepreneurs take risks, but have the potential to become the economy's movers and shakers. Countries tap the creative potential of entrepreneurship in order to improve the value they get from other resources. In the process, the entrepreneurs themselves are sometimes handsomely rewarded.

entrepreneurship personal initiative to combine resources in productive ways; involves risk.

The possibilities for combining an economy's resources depend upon technology. **Technology** refers to possible techniques of production. Technological advances both improve the selection of goods and services and the manner in which we can produce them. As technologies change, the relative values of various resources also change. For example, natural harbors declined in significance in response to the technology of air transportation. While the value of land around harbors diminished, air travel increased the importance of other resources, such as the human capital needed to pilot the planes.

technology possible techniques of production.

2.2 PRODUCTION POSSIBILITIES

Land, labor, capital, and entrepreneurship combine in various ways to produce the output of various goods and services. This section examines the output opportunities these combinations allow and the resulting choices that all economies must make.

MODELING SCARCITY AND CHOICE

Recall that a model is a simplification of reality. Following the principle of keeping a model simple, a good model emphasizes only those features pertinent to solving the problem at hand. This section models the essence of economics, which is scarcity and choice. An economy's scarce resources limit its options, so it must make choices about what to produce. We can model these options, and possibilities for choice among them, with a production possibilities frontier.

production possibilities frontier
a model that shows the various combinations of two goods the economy is capable of producing.

The **production possibilities frontier** illustrates scarcity and choice by assuming that only two goods can be produced. This simplification is appropriate, because understanding choice between any two goods allows the understanding of choice between each good and any other. It is termed a *frontier* because it represents the limits of output possibilities, given current resources and technology. Frontiers of knowledge and capability are made to be expanded, and the production possibilities frontier is no exception. Over time, as people and firms accumulate more resources and learn new production techniques, the production possibilities frontier will expand.

Consider the fictional economy of Castaway Island, inhabited exclusively by a castaway named Hank. Hank has the island to himself, and it provides for all his material needs. Still, he must spend time gathering food to eat. His options are to catch fish or harvest coconuts. He values both of these foods in his diet and can spend up to eight hours a day to obtain them. Figure 2-1 illustrates a production possibilities frontier for Hank's economy.

The graph of production possibilities in Figure 2-1 reveals the same information as the table, but does so in a visual way that can be interpreted at a glance. Each row of the table corresponds to a point on the graph. For example, the combination of three fish and sixteen coconuts can be read from the third line of the table or seen as point *C* on the graph.

Relationships among data are more readily apparent in the graph than in the table in Figure 2-1. For example, a basic message of the production possibilities frontier is that the more fish Hank catches, the fewer coconuts he can collect. A glance at the graph reveals this relationship. The inverse relationship between fish and coconuts illustrates the opportunity cost of Hank using his limited resource, time.

The opportunity cost of more fish is the number of coconuts forgone. The table in Figure 2-2 shows these opportunity costs. Since we are showing the opportunity cost of more fish, Figure 2-2 rearranges the rows in Figure 2-1 to start with row F, which corresponds to zero fish.

As Hank increases his catch from zero fish (row F in the table) to a maximum of five fish (row A), we see the number of coconuts he collects drop at an increasing rate. In other words, the opportunity cost of the first fish is only one coconut. The opportunity cost of two fish is giving up three coconuts. Then opportunity costs really jump. The opportunity cost of four fish is 12 coconuts, which is quadruple the opportunity cost of two fish. Five fish

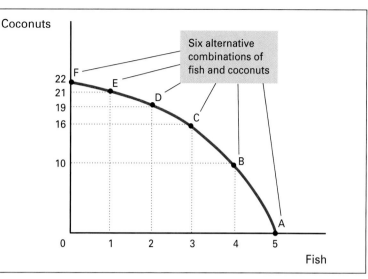

Production possibilities frontier on Castaway Island		
Data point	Fish caught per day	Coconuts collected per day
A	5	0
B	4	10
C	3	16
D	2	19
E	1	21
F	0	22

FIGURE 2-1

THE PRODUCTION POSSIBILITIES FRONTIER ON CASTAWAY ISLAND The production possibilities frontier is a curve that illustrates an economy's options from which to choose. If Hank devotes all of his labor to collecting coconuts, he will have 22 coconuts but no fish, as shown by point *F*. Alternatively, he could catch one fish and still have 21 coconuts, as shown by point *E*. Points *A, B, C,* and *D* on the production possibilities frontier illustrate other possible combinations of the two goods.

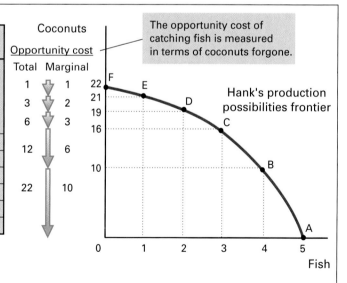

Measuring opportunity cost on Castaway Island			
Data point	Fish caught per day	Opportunity cost (total number of coconuts forgone)	Marginal opportunity cost (change in number of coconuts forgone)
F	0	0	undefined*
E	1	1	1
D	2	3	2
C	3	6	3
B	4	12	6
A	5	22	10

* Marginal opportunity cost is undefined in this cell because *marginal* signifies a change in something. In the first row there has not yet been a change in the number of fish.

FIGURE 2-2

MEASURING OPPORTUNITY COST ON CASTAWAY ISLAND The opportunity cost of fish can be measured at the margin or in total. The marginal opportunity cost is measured one fish at a time. The first fish costs one coconut, the second costs another two coconuts, and so forth. The total opportunity cost is the sum of the marginal opportunity costs, as shown on the left. For example, the total opportunity cost of two fish is three coconuts.

carry an opportunity cost of 22 coconuts, meaning that Hank must give up all coconuts if he wants to catch five fish.

The final column in Figure 2-2 shows *marginal opportunity cost,* which is the additional opportunity cost from catching one more fish. In economics, marginal means incremental— referring to one additional unit of a good or service. For example, you can see that the marginal opportunity cost of the second fish equals 2, computed as the difference between the opportunity cost of two fish and one fish. Similarly, the marginal opportunity cost of the fifth fish equals 10, which is the difference between the opportunity cost of four fish and five fish. The graph in Figure 2-2 duplicates the graph in Figure 2-1, except that Figure 2-2 shows the marginal and total opportunity costs.

law of increasing cost the rise in the marginal opportunity cost of producing a good as more of that good is produced.

The numbers in Figure 2-2 illustrate a principle known as the **law of increasing cost,** which states that as an economy adds to its production of any one good, the marginal opportunity cost of that good will rise. The reason is that resources are often specialized, being more suitable to producing one output than another output. So to increase the output of a good, the most appropriate resources are used first, followed by resources that are increasingly less appropriate for producing that good.

Because marginal opportunity cost increases as output increases, the production possibilities frontier is bowed outward, meaning that its slope becomes increasingly negative. In contrast, if marginal opportunity cost were constant, the production possibilities frontier would be a straight line with a constant downward slope. To understand the law of increasing cost and why the production possibilities frontier is bowed outward in Hank's case, consider the choices he must make.

Each daylight hour, Hank has to choose between fishing and gathering coconuts. The most productive fishing occurs at certain hours of the day when the fish are biting. While all hours are equally well suited to gathering coconuts, Hank knows that the number of coconuts gathered per hour declines as he spends more hours per day gathering, because he gathers the most accessible coconuts first. Knocking a few hours off of coconut gathering allows Hank to fish when the fishing is best and comes at a cost of relatively few coconuts forgone. Adding more hours to his fishing time leads to less and less incremental productivity in fishing and takes away increasingly more productive hours in gathering. The result is the law of increasing cost.

Like Hank, economies are forced to make choices about how to use scarce resources. In producing any good *X,* an economy first uses resources that are best suited to producing *X.* If the economy keeps adding to the production of good *X,* it uses resources that are increasingly less well suited to *X,* but increasingly better suited to some other good, *Y.* The result is that the production of good *Y* drops at an increasingly rapid rate as *X* production increases. The production possibilities frontier bows outward because resources are not equally suited to the production of different goods.

For instance, classrooms are well suited to producing education, but not to producing automobiles. Resources are often specialized to perform limited tasks: fish hooks are great for fishing, cooktops for cooking, coal mines for mining coal, and so on. They can sometimes be used for other purposes, but will not be as productive in these uses. For example, coal mines are fine places to grow mushrooms and have led to commercial production under such brand names as Moonlight Mushrooms. However, until the coal seams are fully mined, the coal output is likely to be of higher value.

Figure 2-3(a) shows a production possibilities frontier without numbers, since the idea of a production possibilities frontier transcends any particular numbers. If you have trouble with a graph without numbers, however, just put in some illustrative numbers as is done in Figure 2-3(b). All points within or along the production possibilities frontier are feasible combinations of two goods. For the economy to reach that frontier, it must use all of its resources. It must also use these resources efficiently in the technological sense of getting

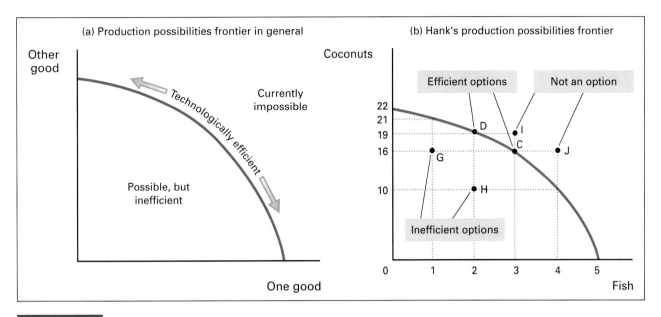

FIGURE 2-3

POSSIBILITIES FOR EFFICIENCY All points on the production possibilities frontier are output combinations that are technologically efficient and feasible, as shown in (a). Points within the production possibilities frontier are also feasible, but are not efficient. Points outside the frontier cannot be reached with current resources and technology.

For example, (b) shows Hank's production possibilities on Castaway Island. On this graph, point *G* represents 16 coconuts and 1 fish. That combination of outputs is possible, but Hank could do better at point *D* by producing 19 coconuts and 2 fish. Likewise, point *C* is more efficient than point *H*. Both *C* and *D* are efficient in a technological sense, meaning that at either point, Hank cannot produce more of one good without giving up some of the other. Hank would like to achieve points *I* or *J*, but does not have the resources and technology to do so.

the most output for given inputs. Otherwise, the economy would be inefficient and at a point inside the frontier. In short, **any point along the production possibilities frontier is a technologically efficient combination of outputs.** Points inside the frontier are inefficient and points outside the frontier are currently unattainable.

Recall from Chapter 1 that, while *technological efficiency* is part of economic efficiency, there is also another part, *allocative efficiency*. Allocative efficiency implies a specific point on the production possibilities frontier that is the most valuable combination of outputs. In general, **there will be only one point on the production possibilities frontier that is allocatively efficient,** and we cannot know what it is by sight. However, the invisible hand of the market economy will tend to lead the economy to that point on the production possibilities frontier that is the allocatively efficient combination of outputs. In Hank's case, his preferences for fish vis à vis coconuts will guide his use of time so that he picks the combination of fish and coconuts that provide him with the most satisfaction.

ECONOMIC GROWTH AND TECHNOLOGICAL CHANGE

Land, labor, capital, and entrepreneurship—these are the resources available to the economy. Production possibilities will depend on how much of each resource the economy has and on the technology that is available to make use of those resources. As resources increase

> ### QUICKCHECK
>
> **Are all points along a production possibilities frontier equally efficient? Is an economy indifferent among them?**
>
> **Answer:** All points on the production possibilities frontier are technologically efficient, meaning that it is impossible to produce more of one good without giving up some of the other. However, while technological efficiency is necessary for overall economic efficiency, so too is allocative efficiency, which identifies the specific point on the production possibilities frontier that is the most valuable combination of outputs. Not all points on the production possibilities frontier are allocatively efficient, meaning there is a point that will be preferred over others since it best reflects wants.

economic growth the ability of the economy to produce more or better output.

or technology improves, production possibilities grow and the economy's entire production possibilities frontier shifts outward, as shown in Figure 2-4(a). **When the production possibilities frontier shifts outward, the economy experiences economic growth.** Economic growth occurs when the economy uses expanded production possibilities to produce an output of greater value. In the event of natural disasters, the exhaustion of natural resources, or anything else that causes an economy's resource base to shrink, the country's production possibilities will also shrink, which would lead to negative economic growth. Figure 2-4(b) illustrates negative economic growth as a shift inward of the production possibilities frontier.

Let's return to the economy of Castaway Island for examples of positive and negative growth. Hank might find some netting that has washed ashore that he can use to catch fish or to collect the coconuts as they fall to the ground. The netting is capital that allows him to catch more fish and to collect more coconuts per hour. This shifts Hank's production possi-

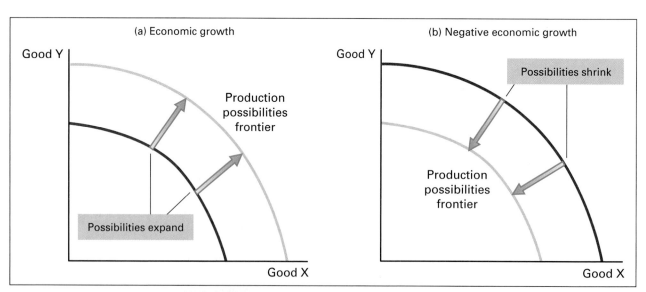

FIGURE 2-4

ECONOMIC GROWTH Economic growth shifts the production possibilities frontier outward, as shown in (a). More resources or improved technology have this effect. Negative economic growth, seen in (b), is associated with a shift inward in the frontier. Negative growth can be caused by the destruction of resources, such as from natural disasters or warfare.

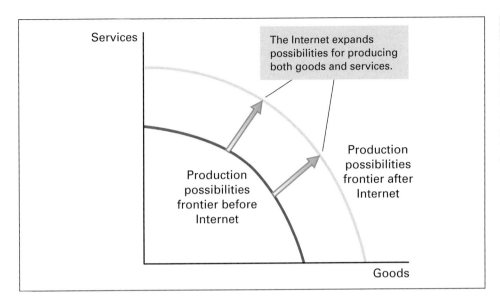

FIGURE 2-5

ECONOMIC GROWTH FROM THE INTERNET The efficiencies brought about by the Internet shift the production possibilities frontier outward. The equipment that allows this flow is capital, and includes such things as fiber optic cables and personal computers.

bilities frontier outward. Alternatively, were Hank to overfish and a coconut blight to strike, fewer fish and coconuts would be available. His production possibilities frontier would shift inward.

Closer to home, the Internet has improved information flows and allowed more efficient choice. The result is that the economy is able to obtain more output from its scarce resources. The Internet is at least partly capital because it was produced in order to make information flow easier, which can increase the production of other goods and services. It includes such components as the computer and modem from which you connect, the lines upon which the data travel, and the routers and switches that direct that data to the right places. Adding this Internet capital to the economy causes the production possibilities frontier to shift outward, as shown in Figure 2-5.

MODELING GROWTH—IMPOVERISHED COUNTRIES FACE A DIFFICULT TRADEOFF

It takes capital to make use of technological change and increase labor productivity. Since capital represents output that is produced now for the purpose of increasing productivity later, the creation of capital comes at the expense of current consumption. This choice can be illustrated with the production possibilities frontier, as shown in Figure 2-6.

For example, at point *A* the economy is devoting nearly all of its resources to producing goods for current consumption. The result is that the amount of capital it possesses decreases over time, because of equipment wearing out, buildings falling into disrepair, and other forms of *depreciation.* With its economy producing too little new capital to offset depreciation of existing capital, the production possibilities frontier shifts inward. Point *B,* in contrast, trades off some current consumption for significantly more production of capital, more than enough to offset depreciation. The result is that the production possibilities frontier shifts out over time.

When an economy is characterized by widespread poverty, the route to economic growth involves particularly tough tradeoffs. For countries to reduce poverty, they must channel resources into amassing capital. Those resources are taken away from the production of goods that meet current needs, such as food and housing. Yet Bangladesh, Somalia, and other countries that can ill afford to sacrifice current consumption are the ones most in need of the economic growth that such a sacrifice would bring.

FIGURE 2-6

CAPITAL'S ROLE IN GROWTH
Sacrificing current consumption in favor of producing more capital hastens economic growth, but may be painful in the present. For example, choosing point *B* provides the capital needed to expand production possibilities over time. In contrast, choosing point *A* allows for more current consumption, but shrinks the production possibilities frontier over time. This is because not enough new capital is produced to offset the depreciation of existing capital.

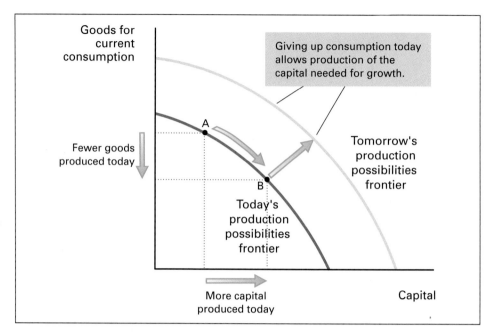

Goods for current consumption

Giving up consumption today allows production of the capital needed for growth.

Fewer goods produced today

A

B

Tomorrow's production possibilities frontier

Today's production possibilities frontier

More capital produced today

Capital

SNAPSHOT

JAPANESE RICE FOR NORTH KOREAN ROCKETS

Was it a test missile or a satellite launch vehicle that North Korea fired in the direction of Japan? Either way, the Japanese were not amused by this unexpected projectile hurtling their way late in the summer of 1998. In response, Japan was quick to cut off its food aid to North Korea. After all, it was the food aid that allowed North Korea the luxury of devoting resources to developing its expertise in rocketry. Food aid from Japan was meant to help the North Koreans survive, not to allow them to reallocate their resources toward financing investment in new, threatening capabilities, now thought to include nuclear weapons. ◀

GENERAL AND SPECIALIZED GROWTH

Technological change can increase productivity across a broad range of industries, as with the better information flows made possible by modern computers and telecommunications. Oftentimes, however, technological change is specific to an industry. For example, an advance in biotechnology might improve cucumber yields but have no effect on the steel industry.

Figure 2-7 illustrates the difference between general growth and specialized growth, where the economy starts from the original production possibilities frontier. In the case of general growth, productivity in both the pretzel and pumpkin industries increases. In the case of specialized growth, productivity increases in only one industry.

The production possibilities frontiers in the graph labeled Specialized Growth in Figure 2-7(b) indicate technological improvement in only the pretzel industry. To see why growth occurred in the pretzel industry but not the pumpkin industry, consider the output of each good separately when none of the other is produced. When no pretzels are produced, the technological change has not affected the production possibility for pumpkins, because the point on the vertical axis is the same as before. However, when no pumpkins are produced, the technological change has allowed an increase in the possible output of pretzels. We know this because the intercept on the horizontal axis has moved to the right. Whatever that maximum quantity of pretzels had been, it is now higher. **Specialized growth thus pivots**

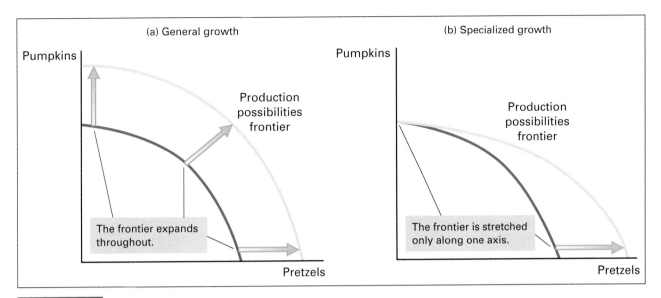

FIGURE 2-7

GENERAL AND SPECIALIZED GROWTH Broad-reaching technological change brings general growth, which shifts the entire production possibilities frontier (ppf) outward as shown in part (a). Specialized technological change brings specialized growth, which causes the production possibilities frontier to expand in the direction of the industry to which the new technology applies. In part (b), that industry is pretzels.

the production possibilities frontier in the direction of more output in the industry affected by the technological change.

In summary:

- The production possibilities frontier shows how much of one good can be produced for any feasible amount of another good.
- If an economy is on its frontier, the opportunity cost of producing more of one good is less of the other good.
- The production possibilities frontier is bowed outward, consistent with the law of increasing cost, which notes the increasing marginal opportunity cost of additional output.
- Every point along the production possibilities frontier is technologically efficient.
- Points inside the frontier imply some unemployed or misallocated resources and are thus inefficient.
- Points outside the frontier are unattainable with current resources and technology.
- Economies grow by acquiring resources or better technology, which shifts the frontier outward.
- If the economy acquires resources that are specialized in the production of a certain good, the production possibilities frontier expands outward in the direction of more of that good.

2.3 THE CIRCULAR FLOW OF ECONOMIC ACTIVITY

Production possibilities frontiers are about *possibilities*. What a market economy will actually choose to produce is decided through the interaction of consumers and businesses. In effect, consumers vote with their money for the assortment of goods and services that is offered. **Money** is a medium of exchange, meaning that it facilitates the exchange of goods and services. Without money, people would be forced to exchange goods directly, a situation

money a medium of exchange that removes the need for barter; also a measure of value and a way to store value over time.

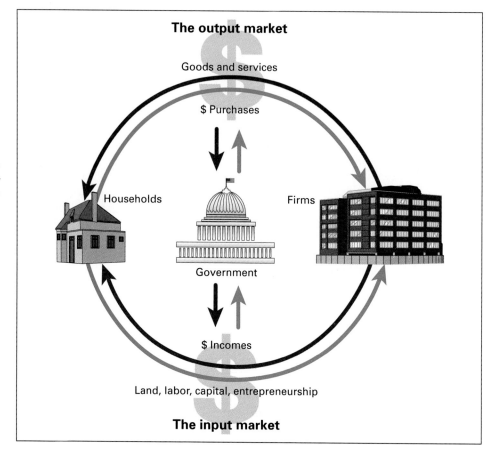

FIGURE 2-8

THE CIRCULAR FLOW OF ECONOMIC ACTIVITY The sale of goods and services by business firms occurs in the output market, while the purchase of resources by firms occurs in the input market. The circular flow model shows that household income depends on the sale of resources, as seen by the arrows that pass through the input market along the bottom of the flow. The arrows through the output market indicate that household spending determines outputs. Taxes, regulations, and other government actions will influence both markets.

The output market

Goods and services

$ Purchases

Households   Firms

Government

$ Incomes

Land, labor, capital, entrepreneurship

The input market

barter the exchange of goods and services directly for one another, without the use of money.

circular flow a model of the economy that depicts how the flow of money facilitates a counterflow of resources, goods, and services in the input and output markets.

output market the market where goods and services are bought and sold.

input market the market where resources are bought and sold.

known as **barter.** Barter would be very difficult in a complicated economy. For example, to buy a mystery novel, you would have to provide something the bookseller would want in return. What do you have? Would you offer a chicken? What if the bookseller is in the mood for Buffalo wings? Money comes to the rescue—it greases the wheels of commerce.

Many things have served as money through the years. In prisoner-of-war camps during World War II, cigarettes served as money. Traditionally, gold, silver, and other scarce metals have been considered money, since they are inherently scarce and relatively easy to transport in the form of coins. Paper is even easier to transport, which is why it is the most common form of money in use today. However, for paper or anything else to be used as money, its quantity must be limited, which is why counterfeiting is illegal. Government must also be careful about printing too much currency if it wishes its currency to retain value as money.

Figure 2-8 illustrates the **circular flow** of economic activity, a model that depicts how markets use the medium of money to determine what goods and services are produced and who gets to buy them. The top part of the diagram illustrates the **output market** in which businesses sell goods and services to consumers. The actual assortment of goods and services is determined by how much households are willing to pay relative to business firms' production costs.

The bottom part of the diagram shows the **input market,** which illustrates that households supply the resources of land, labor, capital, and entrepreneurship. All of these resources are ultimately owned by people, who make up households. The sale of resources to business firms provides the income that households use to buy products. Since people own businesses, business profits also belong to households. For this reason, the circular flow of inputs and outputs is maintained by a counterflow of dollars.

Through taxation, regulation, and production, government influences the mix of goods that is produced and the manner in which resources are used. The circular flow diagram could be expanded to include foreign commerce, banking, or other economic details, but can become complex and difficult to interpret.

2.4 EXPANDING CONSUMPTION POSSIBILITIES THROUGH TRADE

For their own self-interest, economies engage in trade with other economies. This is true for national economies, regional economies, local economies, and even personal economies. For example, we each have our own production possibilities. Yet, if we each had to rely upon our own production possibilities frontier and could not trade, we would be hard-pressed to live as well as Hank the castaway. Instead, we trade with one another. We trade our labor services for income to let us buy what we want. We trade so that we can consume more quantity and variety than we could produce on our own. Cities, states, and countries trade among themselves for the same reasons individuals trade with one another.

People specialize in their jobs according to their interests and opportunities. They then use the income they earn in order to purchase goods and services. Note that this is a two-part decision. First people decide what to produce; then they decide what to consume. The economies of countries engaged in international trade operate the same way.

SPECIALIZATION ACCORDING TO COMPARATIVE ADVANTAGE— THE BASIS FOR TRADE

In order to gain from trade, an economy must *specialize* according to its **comparative advantage. An economy has a comparative advantage in producing a good if it can produce that good at a lower opportunity cost than could other economies.** This means the economy chooses to produce those things it does well relative to other things it could be doing. Contrary to popular belief, trade is not based on **absolute advantage,** which refers to the ability to produce something with fewer resources than could others. **To gain from trade, specialize according to comparative advantage, whether or not you have any absolute advantage.**

The principle of comparative advantage holds even in our imaginary wanderings through space, as illustrated in the Star Trek series that got its start in the 1960s. One of the early mainstays was the pointy-eared science officer named Mr. Spock. With his mental prowess and physical strength, Spock had an absolute advantage in performing a variety of tasks. For example, he might have been a master at quickly cleaning the passageways of the *Starship Enterprise.* However, he did not spend his time mopping the floors because, as Spock would say, "That would be illogical!" It would waste his time.

Logic suggests making the most productive use of our time. We don't have time to do everything, something today's college students know well. College students follow their comparative advantages and specialize when selecting their majors and careers. For example, Michael Jordan selected economics as his major and basketball as his career. With his physical prowess and mental savvy, he could have excelled at other majors or other careers. But he had to make a choice. He chose basketball, where he could dazzle. He tried baseball for a time, but quickly returned to his area of relative strength.

Even if a person cannot do anything well, he or she can still do some things relatively better than other things. It might take Doug longer to mow yards than it would take other people. Yet, if that is what Doug could do best, he would mow yards. Other people would be delighted to hire him because he would charge them less than the opportunity cost of their own time were they to do the mowing themselves. Michael Jordan might hire him. It would be irrelevant whether Michael could mow his own lawn faster. The opportunity cost of his time would be too high.

comparative advantage the ability to produce a good at a lower opportunity cost (other goods forgone) than others could do.

absolute advantage the ability to produce a good with fewer resources than other producers.

These lessons apply to any economy, whether the economy is that of an individual or that of a country. Countries gain from trade whether or not they have an absolute advantage in anything. The country can start off rich or poor and still gain from trade. While a country is constrained to produce along or inside its production possibilities frontier, it can exchange some of its own output for the output of other countries. Goods and services a country sells to other countries are termed **exports.** Exports are traded for **imports,** which are goods and services a country buys from other countries. **Through trade, a country can consume a combination of goods and services that lies outside its production possibilities frontier, meaning that the country's consumption possibilities will exceed its production possibilities.**

exports goods and services a country sells to other countries.

imports goods and services a country buys from other countries.

International trade is more important to small countries than to large countries. This is because the larger the country, the more opportunities there are to specialize internally. For example, the United States produces potatoes in Maine and Idaho for sale throughout the other states. Likewise, Michigan specializes in automobile production, Texas in oil and gas production, and so forth. If the United States were broken into fifty different countries, this trade among states would all be international. As it is, the tremendous diversity of resources found within the United States leads it to have one of the smallest proportions of international trade relative to its output of any country in the world. Figure 2-9 shows the proportion of various countries' exports relative to their outputs. The smaller the country, typically, the higher that ratio is, and the more it gains from trade. These gains occur because smaller countries would be hard pressed to produce the variety of goods and services that are available through trade.

Economists rarely compute the goods in which countries have their comparative advantages. Rather, markets do that quite effectively on their own. If a country has a comparative advantage in producing certain goods, it can produce those goods cheaply, relative to the other goods that it could produce. Those goods in which it has a comparative advantage will be the goods it can offer at the best prices in the international marketplace. Thus, without any economic research, economies engaging in international trade naturally tend to export those goods for which they have a comparative advantage and import the rest.

COMPUTING COMPARATIVE ADVANTAGE

Although people and countries act according to comparative advantage whether or not they sit down to compute it, a hypothetical computation helps to clarify its meaning. Consider a model involving two countries, Japan and England, that can each produce only computer memory chips and oil. Assume that all computer memory chips are interchangeable and that oil is also identical. The productivity of workers is shown in Table 2-1. Note that in this example Japan's workers are more productive at both producing oil and manufacturing computer chips, meaning that Japan has an absolute advantage in both computer chips and oil production. However, because a worker cannot do two things at one time, countries must allocate each worker to producing either one good or the other. To maximize its gains from trade, each country chooses to produce according to its comparative advantage.

The key to computing comparative advantage is to measure opportunity cost. In this case, the choices are simple. To produce computer chips, a country must allocate labor away from oil production and thus forgo some oil. Likewise, to produce oil, a country must forgo computer chips. Thus, the opportunity cost of computer chips is the oil forgone, and the opportunity cost of oil is the computer chips forgone. We can use some simple algebra to compute the opportunity cost of a single barrel of oil or computer chip, so as to allow comparison of opportunity costs between countries. Applying this math to Table 2-1 yields the results shown in Table 2-2. By specializing according to this comparative advantage, countries will gain the most from trade.

In Japan, we see that making a computer chip requires giving up the ability to produce 2/5 or .4 barrels of oil, while in England the computer chip costs 3/5 or .6 barrels of oil. Since Japan has a lower opportunity cost of producing the computer chips, it is said to have a comparative advantage in computer chips. Verify for yourself that England has a comparative advantage in oil.

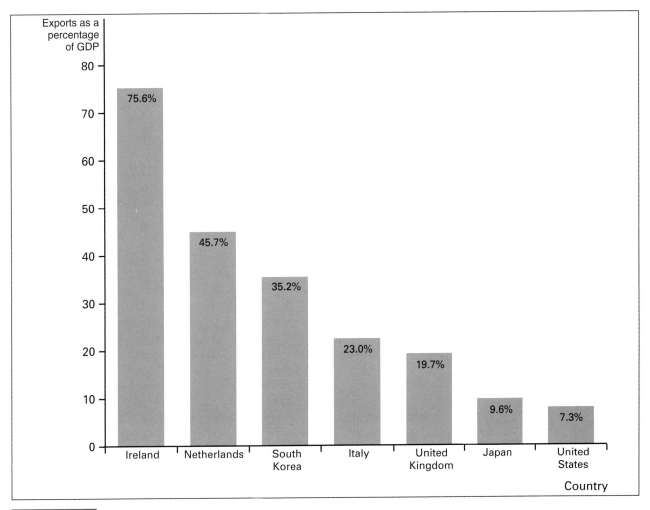

FIGURE 2-9

EXPORTS AS A PERCENTAGE OF GROSS DOMESTIC PRODUCT Countries with larger economies usually export a smaller percentage of their output than do countries with smaller economies. The United States and Japan are two of the world's largest economies and both export a relatively small percentage of their output.

Source: OECD web site. Percentages compiled from 2001 data.

TABLE 2-1 PRODUCTIVITY PER WORKER IN JAPAN AND ENGLAND

COUNTRY	COMPUTER MEMORY CHIPS	BARRELS OF OIL
Japan	10 units per day	4 per day
England	5 units per day	3 per day

TABLE 2-2 COMPUTING OPPORTUNITY COST AND COMPARATIVE ADVANTAGE

PRODUCT LOCATION	OPPORTUNITY COST	OPPORTUNITY COST PER UNIT
Computer chips in Japan	of 10 chips is 4 barrels	2/5 barrel of oil = .4 barrels*
Computer chips in England	of 5 chips is 3 barrels	3/5 barrel of oil = .6 barrels
Oil in Japan	of 4 barrels is 10 chips	5/2 computer chips = 2.5 chips
Oil in England	of 3 barrels is 5 chips	5/3 computer chips = 1.67 chips**

*Lower opportunity cost per unit of computer chips implies comparative advantage in Japan.
**Lower opportunity cost per unit of barrels of oil implies comparative advantage in England.

SNAPSHOT

COMPETING WITH COMPARATIVE ADVANTAGE

Many great athletes are multitalented, possessing strength, speed, and muscle coordination that dwarf that of the general population. These qualities are needed for success in a variety of sports, yet few athletes play more than one sport professionally, even though they might be able to do so. Simply look at the sports pages. Venus Williams makes headlines by swinging a tennis racket, while Tiger Woods swings a golf club and Barry Bonds swings a bat. Their choices tell the rest of us about their comparative advantages.

The best teams exploit the comparative advantages of their players. Each player has a job to do and specializes in doing it well. Whatever the sport, owners and fans expect this principle of comparative advantage to be followed and demand coaches who will best exploit the talents of their players. But even the best coaches can err, as when Cleveland Indians' baseball coach Tris Speaker said in 1921, "Babe Ruth made a great mistake when he gave up pitching. Working once a week, he might have lasted a long time and become a great star." ◄

Explore & Apply

2.5 GUNS OR BUTTER?—GROWTH CAN BRING BOTH

After the cessation of major hostilities in the Iraq war of 2003, the electricity in Iraq was sporadic and the streets dangerous. A common perception was that if the United States truly wanted those things fixed, it could do it. America was seen by Iraqis and by people around the world as a superpower, with abilities beyond the realm of other countries. The United States had developed such a strong and vibrant economy that it could accomplish whatever it set out to do. However, even for a superpower, there are tradeoffs, including tradeoffs that were evident in America's attempt to win the peace in Iraq.

The United States has seen its production possibilities grow rapidly to allow it to produce both more guns (military might) and more butter (consumer goods). However, neither the United States nor any other country is able to escape opportunity costs, as illustrated by the choices facing U.S. forces in Iraq. For example, to the extent that U.S. troops spend their time guarding the electric lines, they are unavailable for other duties, including rooting out those still fighting against them.

The United States' economic success has led it to victory before, emerging triumphant in the major conflicts of the twentieth century. On December 7, 1941, the Empire of Japan attacked Pearl Harbor and drew the United States into World War II. As President Roosevelt reported the next day, that attack also caused "severe damage" to American military capabilities. At the time, Japanese military might extended through much of the Far East, and

Nazi Germany controlled most of Europe. Yet, the United States was able to quickly convert many civilian industries to military production and play a pivotal role in defeating both the Nazis and the Japanese three-and-a-half years later. The world marveled at the ability of the U.S. economy to accomplish this feat. The United States had not sought war, but nonetheless proved able to win.

Nearly five decades later, the United States economy was again able to defeat a foreign adversary that had engaged it in a "cold war." This time, the adversary was the Union of Soviet Socialist Republics, a country armed to the teeth and openly hostile to the United States. Yet, when the United States decided to strengthen its armed forces in the 1980s, the Soviet Union struggled so hard to keep pace that it impoverished its own people and lost its will to exist. The Soviet Union was formally dissolved in 1991 without a shot being fired, breaking up into several different countries, including Russia. That's the best kind of victory, unlike, in the words of Ronald Reagan, "The bloody futility of two World Wars, Korea, Vietnam and the Persian Gulf."

Now, as we seek to surmount the unfolding terrorist threats of the twenty-first century, the lessons of America's twentieth-century success can help guide our way. How has the United States been able to maintain prosperity during peacetime and yet still have the wherewithal to be victorious in wartime? The secret has been the vibrancy of a strong U.S. economy, meaning that the United States has been able to maintain production possibilities that exceed those of its adversaries.

HOW EFFICIENCY LEADS TO GROWTH

"We will bury you."
> —Nikita Khrushchev, Soviet Premier, speaking to the United Nations in 1960

"I pledge allegiance to the flag of the United States of America ...."
> —Sergei Khrushchev, son of Nikita Khrushchev, taking oath of citizenship in 1999

Figure 2-10 depicts the production possibilities frontier for a country with a strong economy, such as the United States in the 1980s, and another production possibilities frontier for an adversary with a weak economy, such as the Soviet Union in the 1980s. The axes of the production possibilities frontier are labeled *guns* and *butter,* where guns represents military output and butter represents output for civilian consumption. In Figure 2-10(a), the Soviet Union is shown to be producing more guns in the 1970s than produced in the United States. However, because of its strong economy, the United States could increase its production of guns to exceed that of the Soviet Union and still have more butter for its civilians. When the Soviets tried to match U.S. spending on guns in the 1980s, their production of butter fell so low that the Soviet people were forced to endure severe hardships. The result is shown in Figure 2-10(b).

To maintain a strong economy, a country must use its existing resources and technology efficiently. As shown in Figure 2-11, moving from an inefficient economy to an efficient economy allows the production of both more guns and more butter. The economy must use the right people and the right capital to produce the right goods in the right way. By producing more in the present, the economy also has more ability to put aside some current consumption of guns and butter in favor of investing in new capital and better technology that will allow production possibilities to grow over time. In other words, the more efficient an economy is in the present, the more ability it will have to expand its production possibilities for the future, as shown by the long arrow in Figure 2-11.

The United States has been able to use its production possibilities with relative efficiency and achieve significant economic growth over time by relying in large measure upon the marketplace to allocate resources. The lure of profit in the market economy has motivated people and companies to look for the most valuable products to produce, keep costs as low as possible, and invest in new capital that expands the country's production possibilities frontier.

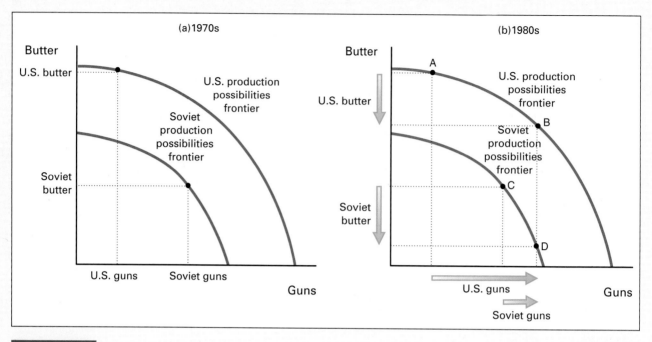

FIGURE 2-10

GUNS AND BUTTER In the 1970s, the Soviets are seen in (a) to devote more resources to their military (guns) than did the United States, even though production possibilities for the Soviets were less. The result was a lower standard of living in the Soviet Union (less butter). In the 1980s as shown in (b), the Soviets decided to match what was by then a higher U.S. output of guns. This reduced still further the already meager Soviet output of butter, resulting in a standard of living that the Soviet people would not accept. In 1991, the Soviet Union dissolved itself in favor of market-oriented economies that chose fewer guns and more butter.

FIGURE 2-11

SHAPING THE FUTURE Today's choices shape future possibilities. Increasing efficiency within the economy, such as moving from point *A* to point *B*, allows the production of both more guns and more butter. In addition, a more efficient economy has more possibilities for growth over time, which would shift the production possibilities frontier outward.

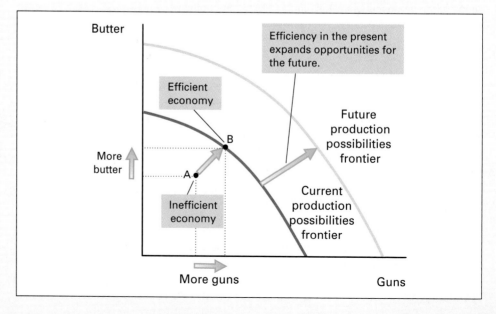

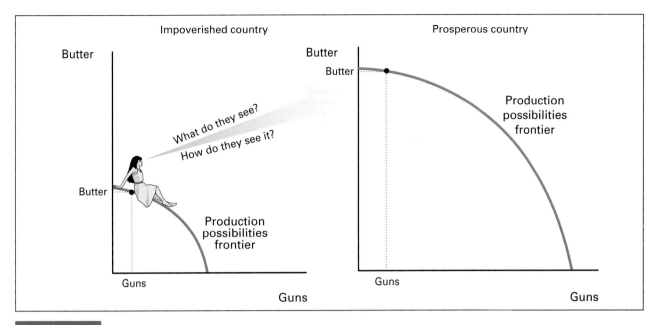

FIGURE 2-12

LOOKING TOWARD PROSPERITY Will impoverished countries choose to emulate prosperous countries and follow their path to success? Such a path would be one of peace and mutual self-interest. Alternatively, the view from below could be one of resentment, providing a spawning ground for ongoing conflict.

These actions constitute the invisible hand of the marketplace that motivates individuals out for their own self-interests to best serve the needs of others.

While there are exceptions in which either markets or government policies have failed to achieve efficiency, it is its reliance upon a market economy that has generally allowed the United States to prosper relative to its adversaries with more centralized economies. In contrast, as former Soviet Premier Mikhail Gorbachev told Columbia University students in March 2002, the Soviets had created an "unreal system" of "pure propaganda." In that system, the ruling politicians "were discussing the problem of toothpaste, the problem of detergent, and they had to create a commission of the Politburo to make sure that women have pantyhose."

The twentieth century has not always brought victory to the United States or other prosperous countries. As the United States learned in Cuba and Vietnam, citizens of impoverished countries can be stubborn adversaries when their patriotic zeal is aroused. Why not peace, with its promise of prosperity?

Whether the world in the twenty-first century sees economic victory or the impoverishment of warfare might hinge in part upon attitudes. Are people of impoverished nations inspired to replicate for themselves the success of the United States and other developed countries? Or is that prosperity seen as out of reach and the source of resentment and ongoing conflict? While economic analysis can help frame the questions, such as in the manner of Figure 2-12, only time will reveal the answers.

1. While it clearly helped the United States in World War II and in the Cold War against communism, does a strong economy do any good in battling terrorism? Explain.

2. Describe ways in which the U.S. government attempts to be efficient in how it spends money militarily. Give an example in which spending might be inefficient and explain why that might happen.

THINKING CRITICALLY

Visit www.prenhall.com/ayers for updates and web exercises on this Explore & Apply topic.

SUMMARY AND LEARNING OBJECTIVES

1. **Analyze tradeoffs facing both individuals and countries.**
   - Opportunity costs, which are the value of forgone alternatives, influence the choices people make.
   - The concept of opportunity cost makes clear that nothing is free. By considering the opportunity cost of an action, both people and countries can make better choices.

2. **Categorize the types of resources an economy possesses.**
   - Resources include land, labor, capital, and entrepreneurship. Land refers to natural resources in their natural states. Labor refers to the human ability to work. Capital is produced to increase future productivity. Physical capital includes buildings, machines, and equipment. Human capital represents acquired skills and abilities. An entrepreneur takes risks by combining the other resources in productive ways.
   - Human capital is different from physical capital because it is embodied within a person.

3. **Model a country's production possibilities, and how these possibilities respond to technological development.**
   - The production possibilities frontier represents all combinations of two goods that would be technologically efficient.
   - The production possibilities frontier typically has a bowed outward shape. Points outside the frontier are not now attainable. Points inside the frontier are inefficient. Inefficiency arises from unemployment and/or misallocated resources. Only points on the frontier are both attainable and efficient.
   - Opportunity costs are illustrated by the production possibilities frontier. Movement from one point to another on the frontier means that more of one good is produced, but less of the other. The amount by which the production of the other good decreases equals the opportunity cost of the increase in the first good.
   - Economic growth expands the frontier by shifting it outward. Such growth can occur if a country adds more capital or other resources, or experiences technological change that enhances its productivity. Specialized growth pivots the frontier outward in the direction of more output in the industry affected by technological change.

4. **Describe how economies can grow faster if they are willing to cut back on current consumption.**
   - Depreciation shifts the frontier inward because it decreases the amount of capital. The effect of depreciation on the frontier can be overcome by producing new capital, with the amount of that production being at least large enough to offset depreciation.
   - Capital production comes with an opportunity cost since it requires the sacrifice of current consumption.

5. **Visualize the flow of goods and services, resources, and money in the economy.**
   - The circular flow graph shows how economic activity depends upon markets. Flows of goods and services go toward the household sector as households make purchases. Goods and services are sold in the output market. Households earn the incomes needed to make those purchases by selling the resources they own to businesses. Resources are bought and sold in the input market. Money is used to make it easier for market exchanges to take place.

6. **Explain how people and countries gain from trade by specializing according to comparative advantage.**
   - Countries specialize according to their comparative advantage, as do people. A comparative advantage in the production of a good requires that a country have a lower opportunity cost of production than other countries. Trade according to comparative advantage allows countries to consume beyond their production possibilities frontiers, thus benefiting the countries that trade.
   - A country has an absolute advantage if it is able to produce something with fewer resources than other countries. It is not necessary to have an absolute advantage in the production of a good to benefit from specialization and trade.
   - A country's comparative advantage can be computed, which entails first computing opportunity costs of each good's production within a country and then comparing the results with the same computation for other countries. The country with the lowest opportunity cost of producing a good has the comparative advantage in that good. If there are just two countries and two goods, a comparative advantage by one country in one good implies a comparative advantage for the other country in the other good.

Convey how economic strength can lead to victory, sometimes without a fight.

- A stronger economy can produce more guns and more butter than a weaker economy. A stronger economy's production possibilities frontier will be outside that of a weaker economy. The difference in eco-nomic prosperity illustrated by the location of the production possibilities frontiers can lead to envy and resentment of wealthy countries by the citizens of relatively poor ones. Alternatively, poorer countries can aspire to peacefully become prosperous themselves.

KEY TERMS

opportunity costs, 32
land, 32
labor, 32
human capital, 32
capital, 33
entrepreneurship, 33
technology, 33

production possibilities frontier, 34
law of increasing cost, 36
economic growth, 38
money, 41
barter, 42
circular flow, 42
output market, 42

input market, 42
comparative advantage, 43
absolute advantage, 43
exports, 44
imports, 44

TEST YOURSELF

TRUE OR FALSE

1. If you decide to buy a Butterfinger candy bar, instead of an equally priced Almond Joy, the opportunity cost of your purchase is the value you would have received from that Almond Joy.
2. The axes of the production possibilities frontier are labeled price and quantity.
3. Economic growth is represented on a production possibilities frontier as a shift outward of that frontier.
4. The circular flow model of economic activity assumes that resources are owned by businesses.
5. With international trade, a country is able to produce outside its production possibilities frontier.

MULTIPLE CHOICE

6. The opportunity cost of a new city police contract is
   a. the amount of money it takes in order to provide the city with the most highly qualified personnel.
   b. the value of the other goods and services that the city and taxpayers will be forced to give up in order to pay for the contract.
   c. the cost to victims of crimes that the new contract would prevent.
   d. the value of the opportunities that city policemen acquire by accepting it.

7. Which of the following items is the best example of an economic resource?
   a. A stock certificate.
   b. A one-hundred dollar bill.
   c. A tractor.
   d. A plate of spaghetti and meatballs.
8. Which of the following is the best example of earning income from human capital?
   a. Melody takes a job as an interpreter for the hearing impaired.
   b. Josie invests her life savings into her own business, "Jeans by Josephine."
   c. Seth toils all day in the hot summer sun as a common laborer, just to earn enough money to keep food on the table.
   d. J.R. kicks up his heels and watches the royalty checks flow in from his oil fields.
9. A production possibilities frontier shows combinations of
   a. inputs that can produce a specific quantity of output.
   b. outputs that people consume.
   c. outputs that can be achieved as technology improves.
   d. outputs that can be achieved in a given time period with all available resources employed using current technology.

10. If a nation's production possibilities indicate that 1,000,000 battle tanks and 6,000,000 houses could be produced, or alternatively, 750,000 tanks and 8,000,000 houses could also be produced, the opportunity cost of each additional house would be
    a. 250,000 tanks.
    b. 8 tanks.
    c. 0.125 tanks.
    d. 2,000,000 houses.

11. As a nation develops economically, its production possibilities frontier
    a. remains stable.
    b. shifts toward the origin.
    c. shifts away from the origin.
    d. becomes steeper, but does not shift.

12. Suppose an economy produces only gizmos and widgets. If there is a technological advance in the production of widgets, the economy's production possibilities frontier will shift
    a. outward along the widget axis, but not along the gizmo axis.
    b. outward along the gizmo axis, but not along the widget axis.
    c. outward along both axes.
    d. inward along both axes.

13. Of the points listed in Self-Test Figure 2-1, the fastest rate of economic growth would occur at
    a. A.
    b. B.
    c. C.
    d. D.

14. All points along the production possibilities frontier are
    a. technologically efficient.
    b. allocatively efficient.
    c. economically efficient.
    d. equitable.

15. In a circular flow diagram, the output market is where
    a. goods and services are exchanged for money.
    b. resources are exchanged for money.
    c. consumer outlays of dollars are exchanged for wages, rent, interest, and profits.
    d. resources are exchanged for goods and services.

16. Money in the economy today
    a. is needed in order for barter to occur.
    b. is primarily commodity money.
    c. facilitates the circular flow of economic activity.
    d. is an economic resource along with land, labor, capital, and entrepreneurship.

17. In order to gain from trade, it is necessary to
    a. specialize according to comparative advantage.
    b. specialize according to absolute advantage.
    c. find a trading partner with an absolute advantage in something.
    d. find a trading partner without an absolute advantage in anything.

18. When a country can produce a good with fewer resources than any other country, the country has
    a. a comparative advantage.
    b. a resource advantage.
    c. an absolute advantage.
    d. an unfair advantage.

19. A country has a comparative advantage in the production of a good if it can produce that good _____ than can other countries.
    a. with fewer raw materials
    b. at a lower opportunity cost
    c. at a higher quality
    d. with fewer labor-hours

20. By having an efficient economy today, a country's future production possibilities frontier will allow the production of
    a. both more guns and more butter.
    b. more guns, but not more butter.
    c. more butter, but not more guns.
    d. neither more guns nor more butter.

SELF-TEST FIGURE 2-1
PRODUCTION POSSIBILITIES FRONTIER

QUESTIONS AND PROBLEMS

1. *[opportunity cost]* Provide plausible opportunity costs for each of the following choices.
    a. Valerie stays home from work to watch an especially interesting episode of the Ricki Lake program.
    b. Frank spends Saturday night watching videos with his friend Erica.
    c. Renee spends Saturday afternoon playing golf with her church singles group.
2. *[entrepreneurship]* Do management skills differ from entrepreneurial skills? Explain.
3. *[resources]* Explain the concept of capital, as it is used in economics. Part of your answer should distinguish between human capital and physical capital.
4. *[production possibilities frontier]* Suppose the country of Baseballia's production possibilities frontier between baseballs and bats is as shown in the table below.

BASEBALLIA'S PRODUCTION POSSIBILITIES FRONTIER

Number of Baseballs Produced per Hour	Number of Baseball Bats Produced per Hour
0	10
5	9
10	7
15	4
20	0

    a. What is the opportunity cost of producing 20 baseballs?
    b. What is the opportunity cost of producing 15 baseballs?
5. *[production possibilities frontier]* What would a straight-line production possibilities frontier between coconuts and fish on Castaway Island say about opportunity costs?
6. *[general growth]* Draw a production possibility graph that shows general growth. Briefly state how the numbers in the production possibilities frontier table in question #4 above would change if the economy of Baseballia experienced general growth.
7. *[production possibilities frontier]* Draw the original production possibilities frontier in Figure 2-7. How does the frontier change when technological change affects only the pumpkin industry?
8. *[money]* What is meant when money is described as a medium of exchange? Is money a part of the circular flow diagram?
9. *[circular flow]* In the circular flow diagram, how do households earn incomes?
10. *[trade]* California and France both produce wine.
    a. Without international trade, U.S. consumers would be unable to consume French wines, but they would still be able to consume California wines.

Would this arrangement be better for the United States as a whole? For any particular groups within the United States?
    b. Do you think France imports U.S. wines? Explain.
11. *[trade]* Succinctly evaluate the validity of the following:
    a. "The United States is losing its competitive edge to other countries with more diligent and skilled workers. The problem is that we are becoming increasingly incapable of producing anything that other countries would want to buy. We are fast on our way to becoming a nation of burger flippers."
    b. "The U.S. standard of living has been the envy of the world. Unfortunately, because we have allowed imports from countries where working conditions are dismal and labor is cheap, our own standard of living is rapidly being pulled down to match the competition."
12. *[absolute advantage]* Briefly explain the difference between the concept of absolute advantage and the concept of comparative advantage. Which principle explains how countries specialize?
13. *[comparative advantage]* Since the principle of comparative advantage applies to people as well as economies, identify at least three areas in which you have a comparative advantage relative to your friends.
14. *[consumption possibilities]* Draw a graph of the production possibilities frontier. Then comment on the validity of the following statements, referring to the graph you have drawn:
    a. A country that trades with other countries will produce at a point outside its production possibilities frontier.
    b. A country that trades with other countries will consume at a point on its production possibilities frontier.
15. *[comparative advantage]* Explain the sport your favorite athlete has chosen to play in terms of that person's comparative advantage. How does an athlete's comparative advantage change with age?
16. *[computing comparative advantage]* Suppose that there are two countries, Tryhard and Trynot. In Tryhard, each hour of labor can produce either 8 units of good *X* or 8 units of good *Y*. In Trynot, each hour of labor can produce either 2 units of good *X* or 4 units of good *Y*. Compute the opportunity cost of: (a) one unit of *X* in Tryhard; (b) one unit of *Y* in Tryhard; (c) one unit of *X* in Trynot; and (d) one unit of *Y* in Trynot. If these countries trade only goods *X* and *Y*, which country will produce *X*? Which will produce *Y*? Explain.

WORKING WITH GRAPHS AND DATA

1. *[opportunity cost and comparative advantage]* Suppose you receive the labor productivity data for airplane and bulldozer production in Mexico and Brazil listed below.

PRODUCTIVITY PER WORKER IN MEXICO AND BRAZIL

Country	Bulldozers	Airplanes
Mexico	3 days per unit	12 days per unit
Brazil	2 days per unit	10 days per unit

 a. What is the opportunity cost to Mexico of producing a bulldozer?

 b. What is the opportunity cost to Mexico of producing an airplane?

 c. What is the opportunity cost to Brazil of producing a bulldozer?

 d. What is the opportunity cost to Brazil of producing an airplane?

 e. Which country has the absolute advantage in the production of bulldozers?

 f. Which country has the absolute advantage in the production of airplanes?

 g. Which country has the comparative advantage in the production of bulldozers?

 h. Which country has the comparative advantage in the production of airplanes?

 i. Which of the following trade offers would be acceptable to both Mexico and Brazil?

  1. 1 airplane = 6 bulldozers

  2. 1 bulldozer = 0.33 airplanes

  3. 1 airplane = 4.5 bulldozers

2. *[production possibilities frontier]* You are presented with data that generates the production possibilities frontier (PPF) in Graph 2-1. As your country's economic advisor you need to:

 a. Explain the reasons why your country is currently producing at point A.

 b. Explain why your country cannot produce at point Z presently.

 c. Explain how the current economy, operating at point A, could reach the production level at point B on the PPF.

  You discover that if the economy produces at point B on the PPF, it is able to produce just enough capital goods to replace all the worn out capital used in the production process during the year. Assume *ceteris paribus* and answer the following questions.

 d. Using the information above, what would next year's PPF appear like if the economy currently produced at point B? Draw a graph of a PPF incorporating this information.

 e. Using the information above, what would next year's PPF appear like if the economy currently produced to the right of point B? Draw a graph of a PPF incorporating this information.

 f. Using the information above, what would next year's PPF appear like if the economy currently produced to the left of point B? Draw a graph of a PPF incorporating this information.

3. *[opportunity cost and comparative advantage]* Assume that the United States and Thailand have an equal amount of resources that could be devoted to the production of television sets and/or rice production. Graphs 2-2 and 2-3 below depict the productivity of each country's respective labor force.

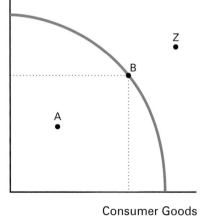

GRAPH 2-1

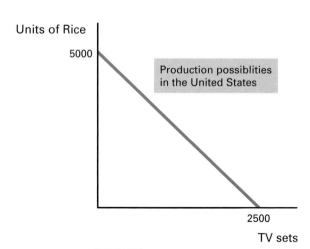

GRAPH 2-2

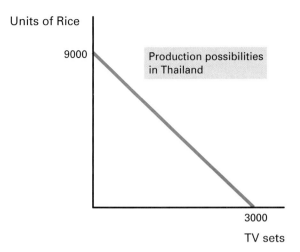

GRAPH 2-3

a. What is the slope of the PPF depicting production in the United States?

b. Interpret what the slope indicates for the United States.

c. What is the opportunity cost of the United States to produce a unit of rice?

d. What is the opportunity cost of the United States to produce a TV set?

e. What is the slope of the PPF depicting production in Thailand?

f. Interpret what the slope indicates for Thailand.

g. What is the opportunity cost of Thailand to produce a unit of rice?

h. What is the opportunity cost of Thailand to produce a TV set?

i. Which nation holds the absolute advantage in rice production?

j. Which nation holds the absolute advantage in TV production?

k. Which nation holds the comparative advantage in rice production?

l. Which nation holds the comparative advantage in TV production?

m. If Thailand specialized in the production of the good it has a comparative advantage in and decided to trade 1,000 units of rice at a rate of 1 unit of rice for 0.4 units of a TV, what combination of rice and TV sets would Thailand consume?

n. If the United States specialized in the production of the good it has a comparative advantage in and decided to trade 1,000 units of rice at a rate of 1 unit of rice for 0.4 units of a TV, what combination of rice and TV sets would the United States consume?

4. *[opportunity cost]* Suppose the fictional economy of Sunshine Island is capable of producing straw hats and walking canes. Its production possibilities frontier (PPF) is represented by the data in the following table:

Data Point	Straw Hats per Hour	Walking Canes per Hour	Opportunity Cost (Total Walking Canes Forgone)	Marginal Opportunity Cost of An Additional Straw Hat (Change in Number of Walking Canes Forgone)
A	0	55		
B	1	50		
C	2	43		
D	3	31		
E	4	17		
F	5	0		

a. Complete the opportunity cost and marginal opportunity cost columns in the table.

b. Draw the production possibilities frontier for Sunshine Island. Label the horizontal axis as "Straw hats per hour" and the vertical axis as "Walking canes per hour." Label the curve with the letters PPF$_1$. Label points A through F on the frontier.

c. On your graph place an X at the point where 3 straw hats and 20 walking canes would be produced. What is the significance of point X?

d. On your graph place a Y at the point where 3 straw hats and 40 walking canes would be produced. What is the significance of point Y?

e. Suppose that the number of walking canes produced in data points A through E increases by 5 at each point, so that Sunshine Island's production possibilities are represented by the new points: (AA) 0 hats and 60 canes; (BB) 1 hat and 55 canes; (CC) 2 hats and 48 canes; (DD) 3 hats and 36 canes; (EE) 4 hats and 22 canes. Point FF will be identical to the original point F. In your graph draw the new production possibilities frontier using these data and label it PPF$_2$.

f. What type of technological change would cause a shift from PPF$_1$ to PPF$_2$?

 Visit www.prenhall.com/ayers for Exploring the Web exercises and additional self-test quizzes.

CHAPTER 3

DEMAND AND SUPPLY

A LOOK AHEAD

"Teach a parrot the terms 'supply and demand' and you've got an economist!" That humor from Thomas Carlyle has been handed down for decades in introductory economics courses. While not literally true (we hope), it does point out how central the concepts of supply and demand are to economic analysis.

How are the prices of music CDs, apartment rents, and the prices of other goods and services determined? Why do people build so many homes where hurricanes are known to strike? What do cows eat? The answers? "Squawk, supply and demand!" This chapter fills in the details of these answers and shows how to answer a host of additional questions about the workings of supply and demand that underlie the market economy. The Explore & Apply section that concludes the chapter discusses how public policy might tap into the forces of supply and demand to improve our schools.

LEARNING OBJECTIVES

Understanding Chapter 3 will enable you to:
1. **Distinguish between the general notions of demand and supply used in ordinary conversation and the precise notions employed in the study of economics.**
2. **Explain what it means to shift demand and supply and why shifts might occur.**
3. **Describe how the marketplace settles on the equilibrium price and quantity.**
4. **Specify how demand and supply shifts cause market equilibriums to change over time.**
5. **Identify the changes to equilibrium that result from simultaneous changes in demand and supply.**
6. **Discuss how vouchers use competition to improve the quality of schooling.**

Explore & Apply

Competition provides consumers with alternatives. The competition by producers to satisfy consumer wants underlies markets, which are characterized by demand and supply. Market economies rely upon competition, and thus upon demand and supply, to answer the three basic economic questions: *What? How?* and *For whom?* The economic definitions of demand and supply are more precise than the fuzzy notion that demand is something a person wants or needs and supply is what is available. Rather, demand and supply are both defined as relationships between price and quantity. We start by looking at demand.

3.1 DEMAND

demand relates the quantity of a good that consumers would purchase at each of various possible prices, over some period of time, *ceteris paribus.*

quantity demanded the quantity that consumers would purchase at a given price.

Demand *relates the quantity of a good that consumers would purchase at each of various possible prices, over some period of time, ceteris paribus.*

Demand is a relationship, not a single quantity. For a given price, demand tells us a specific quantity that consumers would actually purchase if given the opportunity. This quantity is termed the **quantity demanded.** In other words, demand relates quantity demanded to price over the range of possible prices. To emphasize that demand is a relationship and not just a single point, demand is also sometimes called a *demand schedule.* A demand schedule is a table that shows possible prices and their quantities demanded. When the numbers in a demand schedule are plotted in a graph, the line that is plotted is called a *demand curve.* In other words, the terms *demand, demand schedule,* and *demand curve* all refer to the same thing.

Demand must be defined for a set period of time. For example, demand for coffee will be quite different if the period in question is one day, one week, or one year. Moreover, anything else that might influence the quantity demanded must be held constant. This is termed the *ceteris paribus* condition. It means that we only look at one relationship at a time, where **ceteris paribus** is the Latin for holding all else constant.

ceteris paribus holding all else constant.

Suppose we want to know how an increase in water rates will affect the amount of water people use on their lawns. To avoid mixing up the effects of price and rainfall, for example, we might estimate one demand curve for times of normal rainfall and another for times of drought. This approach allows us to focus exclusively on the relationship between price and quantity demanded.

BY WORD, BY TABLE, BY GRAPH

There are various ways to express relationships between variables. One is to provide a schedule, which is a table showing various values of the variables. Another is to show the data with a graph. For example, the data shown in Figure 3-1 make up a demand schedule. The data can be plotted on a graph to form the demand curve labeled Demand, also shown in the figure. The horizontal axis is labeled Quantity to denote the quantity demanded at each possible price. Since price is measured in dollars, the dollar sign provides the label for the vertical axis.

law of demand as price falls, the quantity demanded increases.

Note how the graph pictures an inverse relationship between price and quantity demanded. As price rises, quantity demanded falls. As price falls, quantity demanded rises. This relationship is termed the **law of demand.** It is an empirical law, meaning that no one enforces it, but buyers almost always adhere to it because it makes sense. When the price of an item falls, consumers not only can afford to buy more, but will also substitute the lower-priced good for higher-priced alternatives.

You've heard the saying "a picture is worth a thousand words." That saying usually applies to supply and demand analysis in general and to the law of demand in particular. While a table of data can be useful for applications calling for numerical calculations, a graph is ordinarily better suited for broader messages, such as the inverse relationship between price and quantity demanded. When the specific data are less important than the

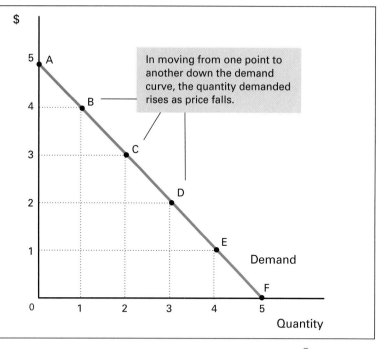

Demand		
Data point	Price ($)	Quantity demanded
A	5	0
B	4	1
C	3	2
D	2	3
E	1	4
F	0	5

In moving from one point to another down the demand curve, the quantity demanded rises as price falls.

FIGURE 3-1

DEMAND Demand slopes downward, showing that price and quantity demanded are inversely related. For example, as the price drops from $4 to $1, the quantity demanded rises from 1 unit to 4 units. This is seen as a movement from point *B* to point *E* along the demand curve.

QUICKCHECK

What is the minimum quantity demanded and the maximum quantity demanded in Figure 3-1?

Answer: At a price of $5, the quantity demanded is zero units, which is the minimum. At a price of $0, the quantity demanded is 5 units, the maximum. These quantities occur where demand intersects the axes.

general nature of the relationship, it is common to draw a graph without attaching any numbers to that graph, as is done in many of the graphs in this chapter and the rest of this book.

If you are uncomfortable with a graph without numbers, recall the simple solution mentioned in Chapter 2: Add some numbers. Even though the numbers would be artificial, the graphical relationship may then become easier to comprehend. For example, we could have labeled Figure 3-1 with different numbers or with no numbers at all. The graph would still impart the notion that price and quantity vary inversely.

SHIFTING DEMAND VERSUS MOVEMENTS ALONG A DEMAND CURVE

Price is not the only influence on how much people buy. Quantities purchased are also dictated by income, tastes, the prices of other goods, and various other factors. By holding all but price constant, the *ceteris paribus* assumption lets us focus on one thing at a time. This approach provides order to what otherwise might seem like a jumble of simultaneous changes.

What happens to demand when other influences on demand change? Changes in other aspects of the world have the potential to shift the entire demand curve, leading to a new relationship between price and quantity. This is shown by a change in the position of the demand curve—a shift. Anything that causes the curve to shift is termed a *shift factor.* **An increase in demand occurs when demand shifts to the right. A decrease in demand occurs when demand shifts to the left.** Figure 3-2 summarizes these shifts. Note that a change in the price of the good neither increases nor decreases demand—demand does not shift. Rather, **a price change would change the quantity demanded, which involves** *moving along the demand curve,* **but would not change the demand curve itself.** A lower price results in a movement down the demand curve, while a higher price causes a movement up the demand curve.

Consider an example of demand shifting that is associated with a fast-growing economy. An upward surge in the economy often causes family incomes to rise. With more income at their disposal, some families will decide to buy new homes. That decision increases the demand for new homes. To the extent that higher income causes consumers to

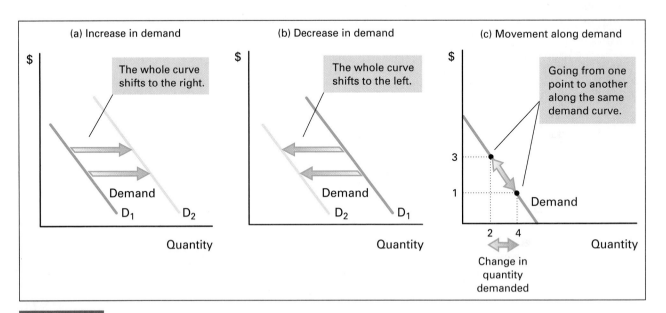

FIGURE 3-2

A SHIFT IN DEMAND VERSUS A MOVEMENT ALONG DEMAND Demand shifts when there is a change in any shift factor. An increase in demand moves the demand curve to the right, as shown in (a). A decrease in demand moves the demand curve to the left, as shown in (b). A change in price does not shift demand. Rather, a price change causes a movement along the demand curve to a new quantity demanded, as shown in (c).

buy more of any good at a particular price, the higher income increases demand, depicted by the rightward-pointing arrows in Figure 3-2(a).

Whether it be a hurricane's pounding surf that washes away expensive beachfront homes, a swollen river that engulfs entire communities along its course, or sliding mud that obliterates whatever stands in its way, the effects of wind and rain cost U.S. citizens billions of dollars annually. Much of this loss is a direct result of expensive structures being built in harm's way. For example, huge amounts of real estate development occur in some of the most at-risk areas, including California hillsides, property fronting the beaches of Florida, and in the flood plains of scenic West Virginia rivers.

Is the large amount of building in risky areas proof of people's shortsighted irrationality? More likely, it is evidence of the law of demand in response to government low-interest loans for rebuilding and other assistance that reduce the cost of disasters to their victims. Specifically, disaster assistance lowers the price of taking the risk to build in disaster-prone locations. The lower price leads people to do more building there. Thus, by the law of demand, the unintended consequence of compensating disaster victims for property losses is that there will be a larger amount of property lost when the next disaster strikes.

To reduce the amount of risk-taking, it is increasingly common for government aid to be contingent upon the recipients rebuilding in safer spots. Even so, disaster aid lowers the expected price of risk-taking for the rest of us. We respond to this lower price by daring to live closer to our country's scenic but dangerous places. ◄

CHANGES IN DEMAND

As listed in Table 3-1, various events are likely to shift demand. **For *normal goods*, an increase in income shifts demand to the right.** However, there are many goods that people buy less of as their incomes rise. These are termed **inferior goods. An increase in income shifts the demand for inferior goods to the left.** Is there anything you would buy less of as your income increases? Perhaps you would eat fewer hot dogs and cans of tuna, and more steak and fresh fish. If so, for you, hot dogs and tuna would be inferior goods, and steak and fresh fish would be normal goods.

Changes in the prices of substitutes and complements also shift demand. A **substitute** is something that takes the place of something else. Different brands of coffee are substitutes. So are coffee and tea. A **complement** is a good that goes with another good, such as ketchup on hot dogs or cream in coffee. The degree to which one good complements or substitutes for another will vary according to each person's tastes and preferences. For example, many coffee drinkers prefer to take their coffee black. For them, coffee and cream are not complements. Likewise, to the extent a consumer is loyal to a particular brand of a product, other brands might not be viewed as acceptable substitutes unless the price difference is dramatic.

What would happen to demand for a good if the price of a substitute changes? To answer questions like this one, it often helps to be specific. For example, consider how much Sparkle Beach laundry detergent shoppers purchase at various possible prices. Those quantities would go up or down depending upon the prices of Tide, Surf, All, and other possible substitutes. If the price of the substitutes rises, *ceteris paribus,* shoppers buy more Sparkle Beach. Their demand for Sparkle Beach shifts out. Likewise, should the substitutes be reduced in price, *ceteris paribus,* shoppers would buy less Sparkle Beach—demand shifts in. Thus, **demand varies directly with a change in the price of a substitute.**

Conversely, **demand varies inversely to a change in the price of a complement.** Since complements are the opposite of substitutes, a change in the price of a complement shifts

normal goods demand for these goods varies directly with income.

inferior goods demand for these goods varies inversely with income.

substitutes something that takes the place of something else, such as one brand of cola for another.

complements goods or services that go well with each other, such as cream with coffee.

TABLE 3-1 CHANGES IN DEMAND

SHIFT FACTORS	DEMAND SHIFTS TO THE LEFT WHEN	DEMAND SHIFTS TO THE RIGHT WHEN	EXAMPLES
Price of substitutes	The price of a substitute decreases.	The price of a substitute increases.	A decrease in the price of butter causes the demand for margarine to decrease. An increase in the price of butter causes the demand for margarine to increase.
Price of complements	The price of a complement increases.	The price of a complement decreases.	An increase in the price of computers decreases the demand for software. A decrease in the price of computers increases the demand for software.
Income, when the good is normal	The good is normal and income decreases.	The good is normal and income increases.	The demand for jewelry decreases when income decreases. The demand for jewelry increases when income increases.
Income, when the good is inferior	The good is inferior and income increases.	The good is inferior and income decreases.	The demand for thrift store clothing decreases when income increases. The demand for thrift store clothing increases when income decreases.
Population	Population decreases.	Population increases.	The demand for shoes decreases when population decreases. The demand for shoes increases when population increases.
Consumer expectations of future prices	Consumers expect the price to decrease in the future.	Consumers expect the price to increase in the future.	Demand for coffee decreases because consumers expect the price of coffee to decrease later. Demand for coffee increases because consumers expect the price of coffee to increase later.
Tastes and preferences	Tastes and preferences turn against the product.	Tastes and preferences turn in favor of the product.	The demand for action movies decreases because consumers prefer less-violent movies. The demand for action movies increases because consumers prefer more-violent movies.

demand in the opposite direction from what would occur if there were a change in the price of a substitute. For example, peanut butter is complementary to jelly. An increase in the price of jelly would decrease consumption of jelly and anything that goes with it. Demand for peanut butter would shift to the left. Likewise, a decrease in the price of jelly would shift demand for peanut butter to the right.

Changes in tastes and preferences will also shift demand. Over time, as some items become more popular, their demand curves shift out. Other items see their popularity fade and their demand curves shift in. Producers often use advertising in an attempt to influence tastes and preferences toward their particular brand of product.

Changes in population, in expectations about future prices, or in many other factors can cause demand to shift. **Demand will increase or decrease to the extent that population increases or decreases. A change in consumer expectations about future prices will shift demand in the present.** For example, if you expect prices to fall in the future, you might put off your purchases now, in effect shifting your current demand curve to the left. You would be treating future purchases as a substitute for current purchases. For some products, other

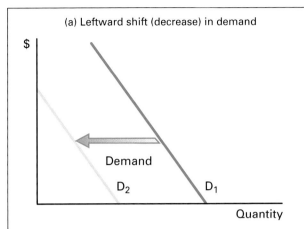

(a) Leftward shift (decrease) in demand

Demand

D₂   D₁

Quantity

Demand shifts left when:
• Price of a substitute decreases.
• Price of a complement increases.
• Good is normal and income decreases.
• Good is inferior and income increases.
• Population decreases.
• Consumers expect price to fall in the future.
• Tastes and preferences turn against the product.

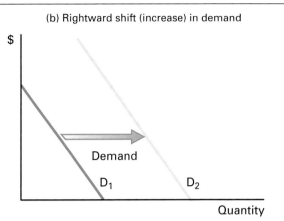

(b) Rightward shift (increase) in demand

Demand

D₁   D₂

Quantity

Demand shifts right when:
• Price of a substitute increases.
• Price of a complement decreases.
• Good is normal and income increases.
• Good is inferior and income decreases.
• Population increases.
• Consumers expect the price to rise in the future.
• Tastes and preferences turn in favor of the product.

FIGURE 3-3

FACTORS THAT SHIFT DEMAND Factors that shift demand to the left are listed in (a), along with a graph showing the leftward shift. Factors that shift demand to the right are shown in (b), along with a graph showing the rightward shift.

factors could be significant, such as conjectures about future technologies that might make products with current technologies obsolete.

Summing up, when consumers buy less of a good at each price, demand shifts to the left. When consumers buy more of a good at each price, demand shifts to the right. Table 3-1 and Figure 3-3 summarize the causes of these shifts. A change in the price of the good causes a change in the quantity demanded, but does not shift demand. Rather, a change in price causes a movement along the demand curve.

NEW COKE? OR OLD COKE IN A NEW BOTTLE?   *SNAPSHOT*

It was either a stroke of marketing genius or just dumb luck. But what it did for demand is one for the record books. The year was 1985 when, losing market share to its arch-rival Pepsi, the Coca-Cola Company tossed aside its secret recipe and ceased making "the real thing." Instead, Coke drinkers were presented with a reformulated New Coke that tasted oh-so-syrupy sweet. It seems that taste tests found consumers favoring the sweeter taste of Pepsi over traditional Coke, but found New Coke beating all. Market research notwithstanding, New Coke was a huge flop.

"Bring back the real thing!" cried Coke customers, and back it came under the name Coca-Cola Classic. Curiously, even though the formula is the same as that of traditional Coke, Coke Classic has proven more popular. Was it the publicity? The near loss of something millions of Coke drinkers took for granted? Was it nostalgia? Whatever the reasons, the demand for Coke shifted to the right and has stayed shifted ever since. In the back of their minds, it's what Coke's owners were hoping to find. ◀

3.2 SUPPLY

supply relates the quantity of a good that will be offered for sale at each of various possible prices, over some period of time, *ceteris paribus.*

quantity supplied the quantity that will be offered for sale at a given price.

Supply *relates the quantity of a good that will be offered for sale at each of various possible prices, over some period of time, ceteris paribus.*

The first thing to note about supply is its symmetry with demand. Supply tells us the quantity that will be offered for sale at various prices. This quantity is termed the **quantity supplied.** Note that supply and quantity supplied are not synonyms. Supply refers to the entire set of data that relates price and quantity and is thus also called a *supply schedule* or *supply curve.* Quantity supplied is the quantity associated with a single point on that schedule. As price changes, quantity supplied changes, but supply does not.

Supply is often referred to as the supply schedule or supply curve in order to emphasize that it is not any single quantity. Like demand, supply must be specified for a set period of time, such as a day, month, or year. The *ceteris paribus* condition makes sure that all else is held constant, so that we can focus clearly on the relationship between price and quantity supplied.

BY WORD, BY TABLE, BY GRAPH

law of supply as price rises, the quantity supplied increases.

Just as with demand, supply can be presented as a table or as a graph. Figure 3-4 shows an example of supply. In contrast to the downward-sloping demand curve, the supply curve nearly always slopes upward to the right. This direct relationship between price and quantity supplied is known as the **law of supply.** As price rises, the quantity offered for sale by producers increases. The reason is that a higher price means higher revenue per unit sold, which will in turn cover the cost of producing some additional units.

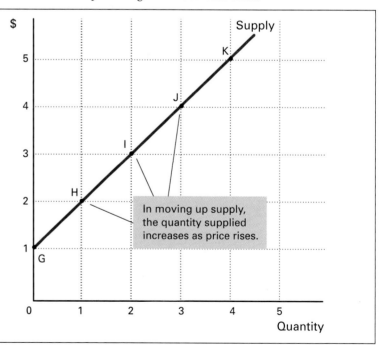

Supply		
Data point	Price ($)	Quantity supplied
G	1	0
H	2	1
I	3	2
J	4	3
K	5	4

In moving up supply, the quantity supplied increases as price rises.

FIGURE 3-4

SUPPLY Supply slopes upward. An increase in price leads to a greater quantity supplied. For example, an increase in price from $3 to $5 would cause the quantity supplied to increase from 2 to 4 units. This result is seen as a movement from point *I* to point *K* along the supply curve. The supply curve itself remains unchanged.

CHANGES IN SUPPLY

An *increase in supply* occurs when the entire supply curve shifts to the right, with more quantity supplied at each particular price. Likewise, a *decrease in supply* occurs when the entire supply curve shifts to the left, showing less quantity supplied at any particular price. A change in price does not shift supply, but rather causes a *movement along the supply curve.* Figure 3-5 illustrates these three possibilities.

Supply's most important shift factors differ from those for demand. Remember, for demand, the most important shift factors are income, prices of substitutes and complements, tastes and preferences, and consumer expectations about future prices. When it comes to supply, changes in expectations as to future prices are still important, but it is the expectations by producers, and not by consumers, that matter. The other important supply shift factors are different from the demand shift factors. In addition to producer expectations as to future prices, important shift factors include: (1) the number of firms; (2) prices of inputs; (3) technological change; (4) restrictions in production; (5) prices of substitutes in production; and (6) prices of jointly produced goods.

Why would expectations of future prices be important to a seller? To answer that question, suppose you own an oil field, and that it costs you $1 per barrel to pump your crude oil from the ground. How much oil would you offer for sale if the price were $15? $20? Why would you think twice about pumping your oil field dry if the selling price were $1.50?

For each possible current price, you would ask yourself how likely it would be for the price to go higher in the future. If you thought prices were on their way up, you would put off your pumping until later. If you expect prices to remain flat or to drop in the future, you would pump more now. If your expectations change, your entire supply schedule for pumping oil in the present would shift. For example, if you become convinced that the world is about to run out of oil, your supply curve in the present would shift far to the left, so that

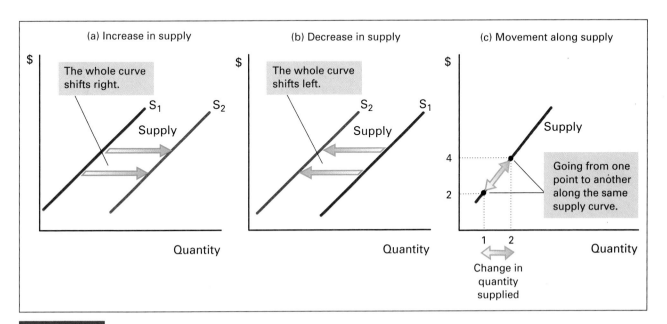

FIGURE 3-5

A SHIFT IN SUPPLY VERSUS A MOVEMENT ALONG SUPPLY Supply shifts when there is a change in any of its shift factors. An increase in supply moves the supply curve to the right, as shown in (a). A decrease in supply moves the supply curve to the left, as shown in (b). A change in price does not shift supply. Rather, a price change causes a movement along the supply curve to a new quantity supplied, as shown in (c).

you would retain plenty of oil to sell at high prices in the future. Thus, **today's supply curve shifts in the opposite direction from changes in expected future prices.**

If the price of labor or other input prices fall, firms see their expenses drop, and are willing to produce more at any given price. Hence, a decline in input prices increases supply, meaning that supply shifts to the right. Were input prices to increase, supply would decrease, meaning that it would shift to the left. In that case, fewer units are offered for sale at any given price. In general, **supply will shift in the opposite direction from changes in input prices.**

Firms adopt technological change in order to produce more output per unit of input. This has the same effect as a decrease in input prices. **Technological change in the production of any good shifts its supply to the right.**

Firms sometimes face restrictions in how they are allowed to do business. **Production restrictions decrease supply.** For example, a contract between a firm and its labor union might restrict the firm's ability to hire, fire, and make work assignments. Such restrictions have the potential to increase per-unit production costs. Likewise, automobile makers must meet exhaust-gas emission standards by installing catalytic converters, which adds to the cost of each car. For any given price, the automakers will offer fewer units for sale because of the increased expense of producing an automobile. This expense shifts the supply curve of automobiles to the left.

Additional shift factors could be important in some applications. For example, the 1990s saw thousands of acres in the South converted from cotton to corn because of the relatively high price of corn. As the price of corn rose, *ceteris paribus,* cotton plantings fell and the cotton supply curve shifted to the left. If the price of corn were to fall, conversely, the cotton supply curve would shift to the right. More generally, **supply varies inversely to the price of a substitute in production.** Be aware that substitutes in production are not the same as the substitutes in consumption that shift demand. After all, would you be willing to trade in your morning corn flakes for a hearty bowl of cotton flakes?

Turning to another agricultural example, some products are produced jointly, such as beef and leather. An increase in the popularity and price of beef would lead to a movement up the supply curve for beef. The greater quantity supplied of beef means that more cattle are raised for slaughter, which has the effect of shifting the supply of leather to the right. In brief, more leather would be offered for sale at each price of leather, in response to people consuming more steak and hamburger. Thus, **supply varies directly with the prices of products that are jointly produced.**

Summing up, when producers offer to sell less of a good at each price, supply decreases. When producers offer to sell more of a good at each price, supply increases. Table 3-2 and Figure 3-6 (see page 68) summarize these shifts. Remember that a change in the price of the good causes a change in the quantity supplied, but does not shift supply. Rather, a change in price causes a movement along the supply curve.

SNAPSHOT   THE LIVESTOCK GOURMET ON A HOT SUMMER DAY

While humans huddle by their air conditioners to escape the sweltering summer sun, life is good for some Iowa pigs and cattle—they enjoy a gourmet feast of tasty wet corn feed. On particularly hot days, farmers in the vicinity of the Cargill corn processing plant in Eddyville, Iowa, can buy this high-quality feed for a very low price. It's not that Cargill pities overheated animals. Rather, it is the availability of electricity that shifts out Cargill's supply of wet feed.

The many air conditioners that run on exceptionally hot days stress the ability of the local electric company to provide power. The ensuing power shortage leads to electricity cutbacks and leaves Cargill with huge piles of perishable wet feed, because there isn't enough electricity to dry and store it. The result is that, although power curtailment is not one of the more common things that shift supply, it's one that leaves some cows very contented. ◀

| TABLE 3-2 | CHANGES IN SUPPLY |

SHIFT FACTORS	SUPPLY SHIFTS TO THE LEFT WHEN	SUPPLY SHIFTS TO THE RIGHT WHEN	EXAMPLES
Number of sellers	The number of sellers decreases.	The number of sellers increases.	The supply of shoes decreases when the number of shoemakers decreases. The supply of shoes increases when the number of shoemakers increases.
The price of labor or other inputs	The price of labor or any other input rises.	The price of labor or any other input falls.	The wages of shoemakers rise, which decreases the supply of shoes. The wages of shoemakers fall, which increases the supply of shoes.
Production restrictions and technology	Government, labor union, or other restrictions on production practices increase cost.	Technological change lowers cost.	The garment workers' labor union negotiates extra holidays for its members, which increases the cost of making clothing, thus decreasing the supply of clothing. Technological improvements in sewing machines lower the cost of making clothing, thus increasing the supply of clothing.
Price of substitutes in production	The price of a substitute in production rises.	The price of a substitute in production falls.	The price of corn rises, causing the supply of wheat to decrease. The price of corn falls, causing the supply of wheat to increase.
Price of jointly produced products	The price of a jointly produced product falls.	The price of a jointly produced product rises.	The price of beef falls, causing the supply of leather to decrease. The price of beef rises, causing the supply of leather to increase.
Producer expectations of future prices	Producers expect prices to rise in the future.	Producers expect prices to decline in the future.	Wheat farmers expect the price of wheat to rise and so withhold wheat from the market, causing the supply of wheat to decrease. Wheat farmers expect the price of wheat to decline, and so rush wheat to the market, causing the supply of wheat to increase.

3.3 EQUILIBRIUM—DEMAND MEETS SUPPLY AND THE MARKET CLEARS

Now that we have taken a close look at demand and supply, let's put them together to see how prices are determined. We will first need to make clear the distinction between demand and supply at the individual level and at the market level.

MARKET DEMAND AND SUPPLY

Demand can be one individual's or the market's as a whole. Likewise, supply can be from one firm or all firms in the market. Most of the time when economists use demand and supply analysis, they have in mind demand and supply for the entire market. When necessary, the terms *market demand* and *market supply* can be used to clarify that demand and supply are for the entire market rather than for a single buyer or seller.

The market is the bringing together of buyers and sellers. While most people think of a market as a physical location, markets usually extend well beyond any single place. Markets can be local, regional, national, or multinational in scale. For example, gold, crude oil, and

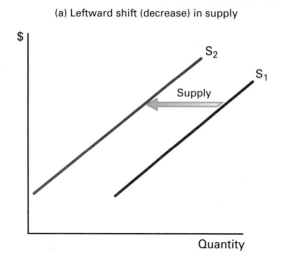

(a) Leftward shift (decrease) in supply

Supply shifts left when:
• The number of sellers decreases.
• The price of labor or other input rises.
• Producers expect the price to rise in the future.
• Government, labor, or other restrictions on production
  practices increase cost.
• Price of a jointly produced product falls.
• The price of a substitute in production rises.

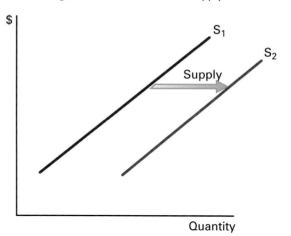

(b) Rightward shift (increase) in supply

Supply shifts right when:
• The number of sellers increases.
• The price of labor or other input falls.
• Producers expect the price to fall in the future.
• Technological change lowers cost.
• Price of a jointly produced product rises.
• The price of a substitute in production falls.

FIGURE 3-6

FACTORS THAT SHIFT SUPPLY Factors that shift supply to the left are listed in (a), along with a graph
showing the leftward shift. Factors that shift supply to the right are shown in (b), along with a graph
showing the rightward shift.

many other commodities are sold in global markets, with only minor variations in price
throughout the world.

Market demand is the sum of all the individuals' demands in that market. Summing
individuals' demands is straightforward if you remember to add quantities, not prices. For
each price, the quantity demanded in the marketplace is the sum of the quantities
demanded by all consumers. On the graph of demand, as we will see in Figure 3-7, **market
demand is the horizontal summation of individuals' demand curves.** An example will
demonstrate this process.

For simplicity, we will consider a market with only two consumers, Jack and Jill. Jack and
Jill are both interested in purchasing—what else?—pails of water. While climbing the hill for
pails of water is great aerobic exercise, there is always some danger of tumbling down. So both
Jill and Jack are willing to buy pails of water. The quantities they demand depend upon price, as
shown by Jill's and Jack's demand curves in Figure 3-7(a) and Figure 3-7(b). These demand
curves combine into a market demand, as shown in Figure 3-7(c). To obtain market demand,
Jill's and Jack's quantities demanded are added at each possible price. As always, it is quantities
that are added, not prices. Since quantity—the number of pails of water—is measured on the
horizontal axis, we say that market demand is the horizontal sum of individual demand curves.

Market supply depicts the total quantity offered for sale in the market at each price. To
obtain market supply, merely add the quantities offered for sale by all sellers at each price.
Graphically, **market supply is the horizontal summation of each seller's supply curve.**
Continuing with the example, Figure 3-8 shows the supplies of two sellers of pails of water—
Wally and Wanda—and how their supplies sum to market supply.

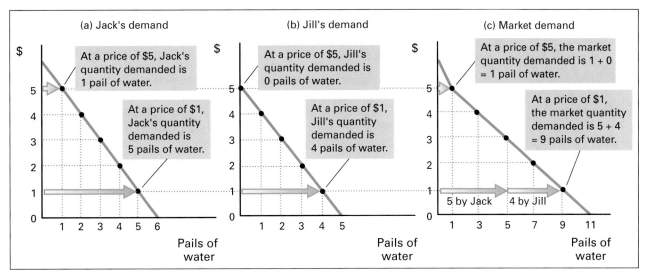

FIGURE 3-7

MARKET DEMAND Market demand is the horizontal summation of each individual's demand curve. In other words, the market quantity demanded at any particular price is the sum of each person's quantity demanded at that price. For example, part (a) shows that, at a price of $1, Jack would be willing to purchase 5 pails of water. Part (b) shows that, at a price of $1, Jill would purchase 4 pails of water. Adding together the quantities demanded by both Jack and Jill at a price of $1, part (c) shows that the market quantity demanded would be 9 pails of water. Likewise, at a price of $5, Jack would be willing to buy 1 pail of water. However, Jill would not buy any at that price. Taken together, the market quantity demanded at the price of $5 would be one pail of water.

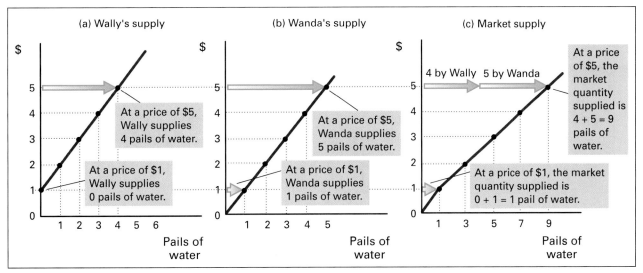

FIGURE 3-8

MARKET SUPPLY Market supply is the horizontal summation of each seller's supply curve. In other words, the market quantity supplied at any particular price is the sum of each person's quantity supplied at that price. For example, part (a) shows that, at a price of $1, Wally would be unwilling to sell any pails of water. Part (b) shows that, at a price of $1, Wanda would offer 1 pail of water for sale. Adding together the quantities supplied by both Wally and Wanda at a price of $1, part (c) shows that the market quantity supplied would be one pail of water. Likewise, at a price of $5, Wally would be willing to sell 4 pails of water and Wanda would offer 5. Taken together, the market quantity supplied at the price of $5 would be 9 pails of water.

ARRIVING AT AN EQUILIBRIUM

When supply and demand meet in the marketplace, a market price is created. While individual sellers are free to price their products however they wish, **there is only one price that *clears the market*, meaning that the quantity supplied equals the quantity demanded.** The market-clearing price and the resulting quantity traded comprise what is known as the **market equilibrium**, meaning that there is no tendency for either price or quantity to change, *ceteris paribus*.

market equilibrium a situation in which there is no tendency for either price or quantity to change.

Market equilibrium is determined by the intersection of supply and demand, as shown in Figure 3-9. A market equilibrium is associated with an *equilibrium price* and an *equilibrium quantity*. In our example, the market equilibrium occurs at a price of $3 and a quantity of five pails.

surplus the excess of quantity supplied over quantity demanded, which occurs when price is above equilibrium.

At any price above the equilibrium price, there would be a **surplus**, representing the excess of quantity supplied over quantity demanded. For example, a price of $4 would be too high, resulting in a surplus of four pails. In that case, Wally and Wanda would compete with each other for sales by lowering their prices. More generally, in any market in which a surplus occurs, some sellers would cut their prices slightly in order to be the ones that make the sales. Other suppliers would then be without customers, and would consequently lower their own prices enough to capture customers from their competitors. This leapfrogging process would continue until the quantity demanded and supplied are equal, which occurs at the equilibrium price.

shortage the excess of quantity demanded over quantity supplied, which occurs when price is below equilibrium.

A price that is below the equilibrium price results in a **shortage**, equal to the amount by which quantity demanded exceeds quantity supplied. For example, a price of $2 would be too low and result in a shortage of four pails. Because there is not enough water to meet demand at that price, Jack and Jill would scramble to be the first to buy. More generally,

Finding market equilibrium				
Price ($)	Quantity demanded	Quantity supplied	Surplus	Shortage
5	1	9	8	–
4	3	7	4	–
3	**5**	**5**	**0**	**0**
2	7	3	–	4
1	9	1	–	8
0	11	0	–	11

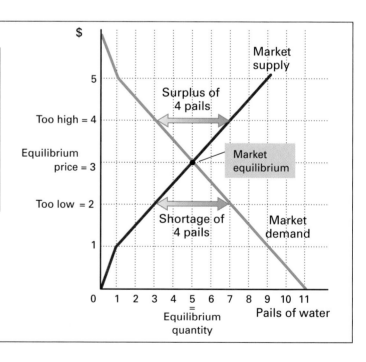

FIGURE 3-9

MARKET EQUILIBRIUM Market equilibrium occurs where demand and supply intersect. In this example, the equilibrium is at a price of $3 and a quantity of five pails. Any price above $3 would lead to a surplus, causing price to fall until the equilibrium is reached. Any price below $3 would lead to a shortage, causing price to rise until the equilibrium is reached.

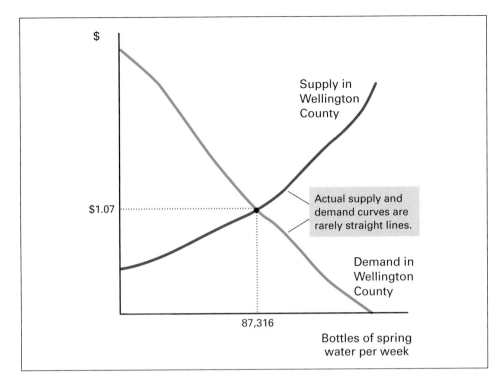

$

Supply in
Wellington
County

$1.07

Actual supply and
demand curves are
rarely straight lines.

Demand in
Wellington
County

87,316

Bottles of spring
water per week

FIGURE 3-10

DOES REALITY FIT THE MODEL?
When supply and demand analysis is applied to the real world, the number of buyers, the number of sellers, and the equilibrium quantity are each likely to be quite a bit larger than in the model we used in the last few figures. Likewise, the large numbers involved in real markets will probably mean that market demand and supply curves are also not straight line segments like the ones shown in those figures. For example, a more realistic market might look like the figure shown here. However, to the extent that the extra details in real markets are unimportant to our analysis, the principle of Occam's razor, discussed in Chapter 1, suggests that we should ignore those details and keep our model as simple as possible.

whenever there is a shortage in any market, buyers compete against each other for the limited quantities of the goods that are offered for sale at that price. For sellers, shortages provide an opportunity both to raise prices and to increase sales, a doubly appealing prospect. Price would thus rise to its equilibrium value, the point at which the shortage disappears. Thus, without any guidance, the invisible hand of the market eliminates either surpluses or shortages and leads to the market-clearing equilibrium.

To some, it may seem that the analysis in Figures 3-8 and 3-9 is overly simplistic. After all, who among us has even seen a pail of water for sale? Remember from Chapter 1, however, that the principle of Ocean's razor suggests that models should be as simple as possible, eliminating all unnecessary details of reality. For example, Figure 3-10 depicts the market for bottles of spring water of Wellington County, an example that might seem more realistic. The equilibrium quantity of 87,316 is quite large relative to our other example. The supply curve slopes generally upward and the demand curve generally downward, but neither curve is smooth or straight. The question we must ask ourselves, though, is whether adding these details of reality would help us better understand the principles of supply, demand, and market equilibrium. If the details just get in the way, Sir William of Occam would tell us to get rid of them.

Suppose either demand or supply were to change. For example, suppose an increase in consumer income or a decrease in the price of a complement shifts demand to the right. One of the most common mistakes students make is to think this shift in demand would also shift supply. It would not, because demand is not a shift factor for supply. Rather, the rightward shift in demand leads to a movement up the supply curve and results in a new, higher equilibrium price and quantity. More generally, **a change in supply would cause a movement along demand. Similarly, a change in demand would cause a movement along supply.**

For practice, you might draw the basic supply and demand diagram, and then sketch a few shifts in either demand or supply. Note the effect on the equilibrium price and quantity. Note also that shifting demand does not cause a shift in supply or vice versa.

QUICKCHECK

In Figure 3-9, how much would be sold if the price is $4? If the price is $2?

Answer: Remember that each sale requires both a buyer and a seller. If the price is $4, then three pails of water would be sold, because three is the quantity demanded. If the price is $2, it would still be three pails of water sold, this time because three is the quantity supplied.

CHANGES IN THE MARKET EQUILIBRIUM

The market equilibrium will change whenever supply or demand shift. Adjustment from one equilibrium to the next can be thought of as a four-step process:

Step #1   For some reason, a shift occurs in either supply or demand.

Step #2   The price that had been in equilibrium now causes either a surplus or shortage.

Step #3   If there is a surplus, price adjusts down; if there is a shortage, price adjusts up.

Step #4   In response to changes in price, consumers adjust their quantities demanded and producers their quantities supplied until the two are equal and the market is again in equilibrium.

Figure 3-11 shows these steps for the cases when supply shifts to either the right or the left. A similar analysis could be done for instances in which demand shifts either to the right or left. In actual application, the four steps commonly occur so gradually or so rapidly that we are not even aware of the process.

Taken one curve at a time, there are only four shifts possible. Supply could increase, in which case the entire curve would shift to the right. Alternatively, supply could decrease, in which case the entire curve would shift to the left. Likewise, demand could increase, in which case the entire curve would shift to the right. Alternatively, demand could decrease, in which case the entire curve would shift to left. These shifts and their effects on equilibrium price and quantity are shown and summarized in Figure 3-12 (see page 74). The four rows of the table, labeled case 1 through case 4, match the four graphs in the figure.

Whether it be in the market for meals, metals, or memory chips, we can expect both demand and supply to shift over time. To understand the effects on price and quantity when there are simultaneous shifts in supply and demand, look at each shift separately. In other words, we would combine two of the four cases listed in Figure 3-12 .

Table 3-3 (see page 75) summarizes the results from simultaneous shifts in supply and demand. Notice that in each of the cases in Table 3-3, the change in either equilibrium price or quantity is listed as uncertain to indicate that the direction in which the equilibrium price or quantity will move cannot be known without additional information. The direction in which either price or quantity changes will be uncertain when the shifts in demand and supply pull the equilibrium in opposite directions.

For example, if supply shifts to the right and demand shifts to the right also, we would look at the combination of cases 1 and 3 in Figure 3-12. This combination tells us that equilibrium quantity will definitely rise, but that equilibrium price might rise, fall, or remain unchanged. Specifically, when we look at them separately, both the demand and supply shifts result in a higher equilibrium quantity. However, case 1 pulls price lower while case 3 pulls price higher. Whether price rises, falls, or stays the same will depend on the relative strengths of those pulls. Figure 3-13 (see page 75) illustrates these possibilities by combining differently proportioned increases in supply and demand. Figure 3-13(a) shows identically proportioned increases in supply and demand, resulting in a constant price; Figure 3-13(b) shows a shift in demand that is weaker than the shift in supply, which causes the equilibrium price to fall; and Figure 3-13(c) shows a shift in demand that is larger than the shift in supply, resulting in a higher price.

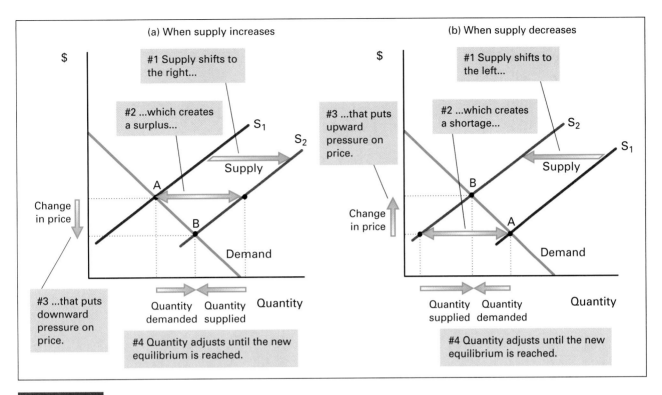

FIGURE 3-11

FOUR STEPS TO A CHANGE IN EQUILIBRIUM The process of changing from one equilibrium to another can be thought of as occurring in four steps. Part (a) shows what happens when supply increases. In this case, the four steps in moving from the starting equilibrium (labeled A) to the new equilibrium (labeled B) are:

#1   Supply shifts to the right.
#2   A surplus occurs at the starting price.
#3   Competition among producers causes the price to fall.
#4   As price falls, the quantity demanded increases and the quantity supplied decreases until the two become equal, after which there is no more tendency for either price or quantity to change.

Part (b) shows the affect of a decrease in supply. In this case, the four steps in moving from the starting equilibrium (labeled A) to the new equilibrium (labeled B) are:

#1   Supply shifts to the left.
#2   A shortage occurs at the starting price.
#3   Competition among producers causes the price to rise.
#4   As price rises, the quantity demanded decreases and the quantity supplied increases until the two become equal, after which there is no more tendency for either price or quantity to change.

   Can you apply this analysis? For example, how would you interpret the observation that the price of digital camcorders has fallen in the last ten years, and people are now buying more? One possibility is case 1, in which demand stays constant while supply shifts to the right. Case 5 is more likely to represent reality, however, with both demand and supply shifting to the right. This result is shown in Figure 3-13(b). Demand shifted as population increased and camcorders became an increasingly popular addition to the gadgets of modern life. However, the increase in supply was even more pronounced, which explains why prices have fallen.

   Continuing with the same example, suppose that video cell phones or other technologies take hold that cause demand for digital camcorders to fall in the future. If supply were to continue to increase, the result would be case 8. While the equilibrium price would definitely drop, the equilibrium quantity might rise, fall, or remain unchanged. Figure 3-14 illustrates the possibility that the equilibrium quantity would rise, which would occur if supply shifts to the right more than demand shifts to the left.

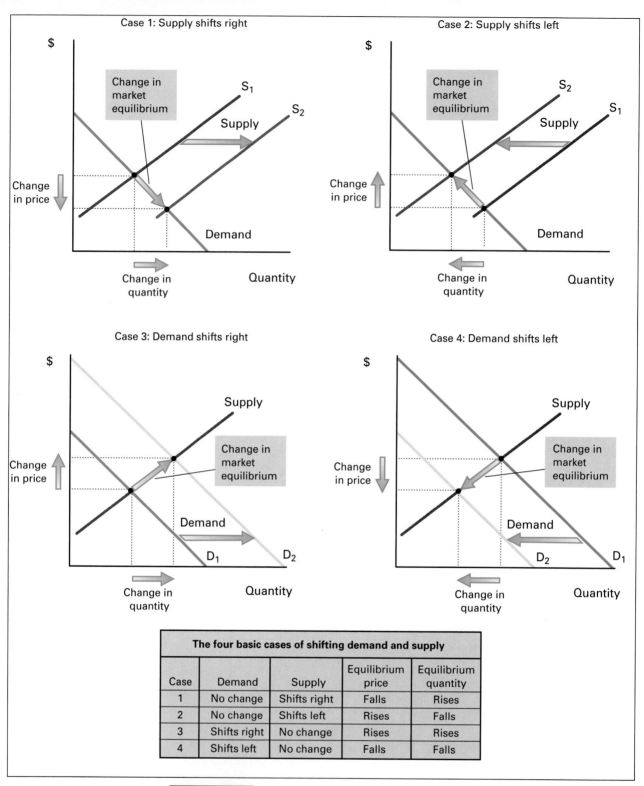

The four basic cases of shifting demand and supply				
Case	Demand	Supply	Equilibrium price	Equilibrium quantity
1	No change	Shifts right	Falls	Rises
2	No change	Shifts left	Rises	Falls
3	Shifts right	No change	Rises	Rises
4	Shifts left	No change	Falls	Falls

FIGURE 3-12

EFFECTS OF SHIFTS IN DEMAND AND SUPPLY A shift in either demand or supply will affect the market equilibrium price and quantity, as seen in cases 1 through 4. When demand and supply shift simultaneously, the result can be found by first analyzing one shift and then the other. That process would involve combining two of the four cases.

TABLE 3-3   CASES 5 THROUGH 8 EACH COMBINE TWO OF THE FOUR CASES IN FIGURE 3-11

CASE	DEMAND	SUPPLY	EQUILIBRIUM PRICE	EQUILIBRIUM QUANTITY
5 (cases 1 and 3)	Shifts right	Shifts right	Direction uncertain	Rises
6 (cases 2 and 4)	Shifts left	Shifts left	Direction uncertain	Falls
7 (cases 2 and 3)	Shifts right	Shifts left	Rises	Direction uncertain
8 (cases 1 and 4)	Shifts left	Shifts right	Falls	Direction uncertain

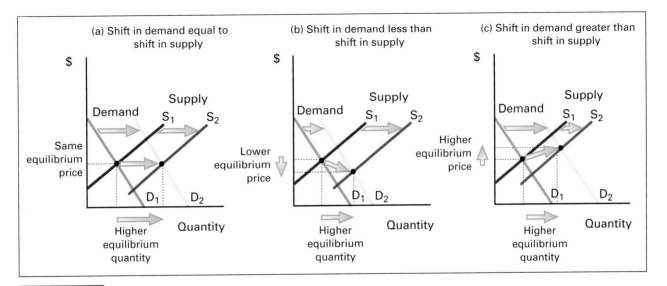

FIGURE 3-13

COMBINING AN INCREASE IN DEMAND WITH AN INCREASE IN SUPPLY When supply and demand both shift to the right, the equilibrium quantity increases. Equilibrium price might go up, down, or not change at all, depending upon the relative magnitudes of the shifts. Equal magnitude shifts are shown in (a), which leaves equilibrium price constant. As shown in (b), an increase in supply that exceeds the increase in demand causes a lower equilibrium price. By the same token, (c) shows that an increase in demand that exceeds the increase in supply causes equilibrium price to rise. These examples represent a combination of cases 1 and 3 from Figure 3-12.

QUICKCHECK

List three cases in which shifts in demand and/or supply would result in a lower price and a greater quantity.

Answer: One case occurs when supply shifts to the right and demand does not change. A second case is when supply and demand both shift to the right, but the shift in supply is larger. A third case is when supply shifts right and demand shifts left, with the shift in supply being larger than the shift in demand. These cases are shown in Figures 3-11 (case 1), 3–13(b), and 3–14, respectively.

FIGURE 3-14

A LARGE INCREASE IN SUPPLY COMBINED WITH A SMALL DECREASE IN DEMAND When demand shifts to the left by a smaller amount than supply shifts to the right, equilibrium price will fall and equilibrium quantity will rise. While both the shift in supply and in demand pull price downward, the two shifts pull quantity in opposite directions. The reason quantity rises in this example is that the shift in supply is larger than the shift in demand.

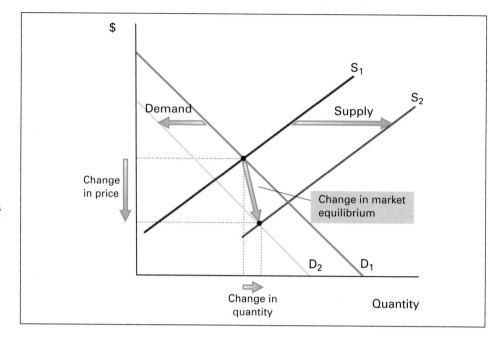

3.4 VOUCHERS—DEMANDING BETTER SCHOOLS

"Some people know the importance of education because they have it. I know the importance of education because I didn't."

—*Frederick Douglass, ex-slave and abolitionist*

"Our schools must be improved!" From kindergarten through the twelfth grade, the education of America's youth is a top concern of both the president and parents. There is less concern, however, about improving colleges; the reasons relate to demand and supply.

College students shoulder the high cost of college, with cost playing a major role in college choice. Consistent with the law of demand, the lower price of a college education, *ceteris paribus,* the greater the number of students who will apply and the more education they will choose. To promote college education, government offers tax deductions, subsidies, and financial aid that in effect lowers its price.

High school seniors choose among a varied assortment of colleges. In lower grades, however, there is normally a powerful financial incentive to choose only the government-provided local public school. The reason is that taxpayer financing makes those schools free to the student.

Free public schooling was established in the nineteenth century to promote equal opportunity—an equal start in life. However, public schools are not all the same, and the gap between the best and the worst is not likely to close on its own. Schools in wealthy neighborhoods often spend more per pupil than schools in poor ones. Some schools are bureaucratic, inefficient, and ineffective, while others have strong academic reputations. Inefficient schools are insulated from competitive pressures to reform because even the best private schools find it hard to compete with "free" tuition. In addition, it would take moving to a new school district to enroll in a different public school.

If there were no free public schools, the invisible hand of the marketplace would cause schools to become efficient at responding to the demands of parents. While parents lack formal teaching credentials they could be guided by reputation or brand name in much the same way that they are guided in buying the family car and refrigerator. Schools that are most efficient at providing value would gain students, while others would lose them. However, because family incomes differ, the market outcome would not achieve equal educational opportunities for all children. The political outcome has been to sacrifice the efficiency of competition for the veneer of equity provided by equal access to free public schools. But is there a way to achieve our goal of equity in a manner that is less costly to the efficiency of free markets? Can we introduce competition to achieve more efficient schools?

Limited competition is provided by *charter schools,* a form of public school. Charter schools are started when a group of parents form or hire a nonprofit organization to set up a new school that meets state specifications. The new school receives a state contract called a charter to operate a school for a limited time, usually five years, after which the charter is renewed if the school meets educational standards. Because charter schools call for parental involvement, they are more accountable to parents than traditional schools. Recently, over 250,000 students were enrolled in about 800 charter schools in thirty-seven states.

INTRODUCTION TO VOUCHERS

Much more competition can be achieved through *vouchers,* which provide money that recipients can spend, although spending is restricted to a certain category of goods. The Food Stamp program provides low-income recipients with vouchers—food stamps—that can only be used on food purchases. Food Stamp recipients buy what they want rather than being forced to eat the offerings of a government-run food kitchen. A similar situation holds true when vouchers are applied to education. *School vouchers* provide parents with money that they must spend on schooling their children. With vouchers, the money is received by the school of each parent's choosing rather than being spent directly by the government-run public school.

School vouchers were first proposed in 1955 by Nobel-prize-winning economist Milton Friedman. Today, voucher programs of one sort or another are underway in Ohio, Florida, Texas, and elsewhere. Still, vouchers are poorly understood and controversial.

Figure 3-15 illustrates the effects of school vouchers in the market for private schooling. Figure 3-15(a) shows that demand shifts to the right as parents have more income to spend on schooling, with that additional income provided in the form of school vouchers. When demand shifts to the right, there is a movement up the supply curve to a higher price (tuition) charged by private schools, along with a larger equilibrium quantity of enrollments. Although the price is higher, the cost to each parent is actually lower because parents can use vouchers to cover most of the tuition. The result is that parents enroll more children in private schools.

The larger market for private schooling would bring in more suppliers as time goes by. Figure 3-15(b) shows the effect over time as new schools are built and staffed. As the number of suppliers increases, supply shifts to the right. In other words, at any given price, there are more openings at private schools than there would otherwise have been. The consequence of this increase in supply is that the market equilibrium moves down the demand curve, possibly leading to the same price that was charged prior to the voucher program. After spending their vouchers, parents quite possibly find that tuition is free, just as it would be in public schools.

One argument that has been used against vouchers is that they would weaken public schools, because vouchers would deprive them of students and the revenues associated with those students. Figure 3-16 illustrates the market for public schools that are provided free of charge by government. While there are significant costs of building, maintaining, and staffing the schools, parents can enroll their children in the public schools without charge. However, if private schools also become costless to parents, as illustrated in Figure 3-16, the demand for the public schools would shift to the left. The reason is that private schools represent a substitute for public schools, and demand shifts to the left when the price of a substitute goes down, as it would in this case.

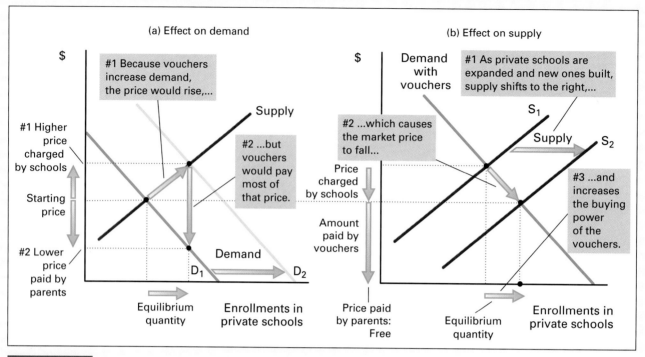

FIGURE 3-15

EFFECT OF VOUCHERS ON PRIVATE SCHOOLING School vouchers provide parents with money that can only be spent on private schools. This specialized form of additional income shifts the demand for private schooling to the right, as shown in part (a). The result is that both the equilibrium price and the equilibrium quantity increase. However, parents pay less than before out of their own pockets, because they use the vouchers to cover most or all of the expense of reserving a seat in a private school for their child.

Part (b) of the figure shows that, over time, new private schools will be added or the capacity of existing private schools will be increased. The effect of this increase in the number and size of suppliers is to shift the market supply curve to the right, resulting in a fall in the equilibrium price and a further increase in the equilibrium quantity.

Because parents are charged a price of zero when they enroll their children in the public school, the market equilibrium is nothing more than the intersection of the demand curve with the horizontal axis. As demand shifts to the left, this equilibrium likewise shifts to the left, as shown in Figure 3-16. There would be fewer children in the public schools, with consequent decreases in tax funding for those schools. The schools that would be hit the hardest are those that parents think are doing the worst job or that face competition from private schools that parents think are doing a very good job.

With vouchers, the location, design, and operation of schools is driven by parental choice. Such radical change has proven difficult to enact into law. Most proposals for school vouchers retain support for public schools, either by restricting vouchers to apply to public schools only, or by providing vouchers just to students who attend "failing" public schools. A *pure voucher system* would permit children to attend any school, whether church sponsored or not. In the summer of 2002, the U.S. Supreme Court upheld a lower court ruling that allows vouchers so long as their purpose is to promote education, not religion. Similarly, financial aid is available to college students even if they attend a college operated by a religious denomination.

Opponents of vouchers fear that the competition for voucher money would cause schools to shortchange educational objectives and promote popular, but not very worthwhile, activities. For example, schools might de-emphasize academic achievement, while

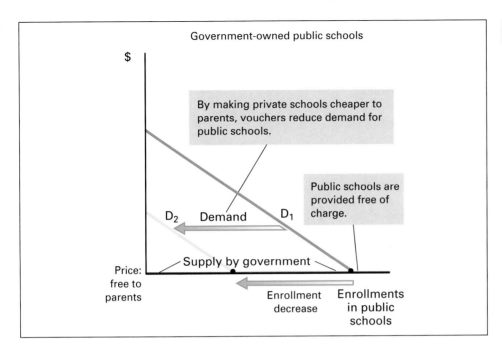

Government-owned public schools

By making private schools cheaper to parents, vouchers reduce demand for public schools.

Public schools are provided free of charge.

D₂ Demand   D₁

Supply by government

Price: free to parents

Enrollment decrease   Enrollments in public schools

FIGURE 3-16

EFFECT OF VOUCHERS ON PUBLIC SCHOOLING Public schools would see a decline in demand as vouchers lower the price paid by parents for the substitution of private schooling for their children. The idea of vouchers is to increase incentives for efficiency in both public and private schools, with the result that the least efficient public schools would be the ones that would shrink the most or shut down.

emphasizing football. Schools could also appeal to parents' religious preferences to gain enrollments and the dollars they bring.

Voucher opponents predict that competition would impede learning in other ways. For example, private schools might seek corporate sponsors who would pay for the right to put advertisements in school learning materials, thus possibly distracting students from learning. Voucher critics want to see schooling remain in the hands of educational professionals whose motives they feel would be more focused on learning and less on money.

Another criticism of vouchers relates to funding. Public schools are funded on the size of their enrollments. By reducing enrollments, vouchers would also drain public schools of money and jobs. Less money would cause the public schools to shrink in size. Just like inefficient companies in other sectors of the free market, inefficient public schools would whither and die. So, too, would inefficient private schools. The process might be hard on both the faculty and students.

Perhaps more time and experience with vouchers will clarify the issues. By promoting competition, vouchers offer the promise of improved schools. Would parents demand well for their children or should that choice be left to educational professionals? You be the judge.

1. **Should educational quality be allowed to differ based on family income? Should vouchers be allowed to supplement a tuition payment at a private school, with the result that some children's quality of education would differ from other children's? Discuss.**

2. *Myra:* **I think voucher amounts should vary with household income. The more income, the less help—it's only fair.**
   Fred: **I think education should be free for everyone. Your income shouldn't have anything to do with how much voucher power you have.**

   Evaluate Myra's and Fred's ideas. If a voucher plan is to be used, should the voucher amount depend upon a person's income?

THINKING CRITICALLY

Visit www.prenhall.com/ayers for updates and web exercises on this Explore & Apply topic.

SUMMARY AND LEARNING OBJECTIVES

1. **Distinguish between the general notions of demand and supply used in ordinary conversation and the precise notions employed in the study of economics.**

   - Supply and demand analysis captures the essential role of competition in the free marketplace. The what, how, and for whom questions you studied in Chapter 1 are answered by demand and supply in a market economy.

   - Demand is more than merely wanting a good or service. Demand is a relationship between price and quantity. By the law of demand, market demand curves slope downward, indicating an inverse relationship between price and quantity demanded. In other words, at each possible price there is a specific quantity demanded.

   - Like demand, supply is also a relationship between price and quantity. Supply shows the quantity supplied for each possible price. Unlike the demand curve, market supply curves slope upward, reflecting the law of supply. Thus, price and quantity supplied are directly related.

2. **Explain what it means to shift demand and supply and why shifts might occur.**

   - Demand will shift with changes in the price of a substitute or complement, a change in income, a change in population, changes in expectations, and changes in tastes or preferences. An increase in demand shifts the demand curve to the right. A decrease in demand shifts the demand curve to the left.

   - Two goods are substitutes for each other when the goods are similar and serve the same purpose. An increase in the price of a substitute for a good will increase the demand for the good. Two goods are complements to each other when they are used together. An increase in the price of a complement for a good will decrease the demand for the good.

   - An increase in income will increase the demand for a normal good, but reduce the demand for an inferior good.

   - There is a distinction between a change in demand and a change in quantity demanded. A change in demand means the demand curve shifts. A price change causes a movement from one point to another on a demand curve and results in a change in quantity demanded.

   - Supply slopes upward, indicating a direct relationship between price and quantity supplied. A price change causes a change in quantity supplied and is seen as a movement along a supply curve. A change in supply means that the whole supply curve shifts. An increase in supply is seen as a shift to the right in the supply curve, while a decrease in supply occurs when the supply curve shifts to the left.

   - Supply will shift with a change in the prices of substitutes in production, changes in the prices of jointly produced products, changes in union work rules or government regulations that change costs, changes in technology, changes in input prices, and changes in seller expectations.

   - A shift in supply causes a movement along the demand curve, while a shift in demand causes a movement along the supply curve.

3. **Describe how the marketplace settles on the equilibrium price and quantity.**

   - The interaction of supply and demand leads to a market equilibrium price and quantity, from which there is no tendency to change. Market equilibrium occurs at the intersection of demand and supply. At this point, quantity demanded equals quantity supplied.

   - A market price that is less than the market equilibrium price will cause a shortage, in which case the price will adjust upward toward the equilibrium price. The shortage will be gone when the price reaches its equilibrium level. A price that is above the market equilibrium price will cause a surplus. The price will adjust downward toward the market equilibrium price until the surplus is eliminated.

4. **Specify how demand and supply shifts cause market equilibriums to change over time.**

   - Demand and supply usually shift with the passage of time. When the demand or supply of a good shifts, then the good's price and quantity adjust to a new market equilibrium. There are four cases involving a shift in either demand or supply, but not both: an increase in demand, a decrease in demand, an increase in supply, and a decrease in supply.

   - An increase in demand by itself causes an increase in the market equilibrium price and quantity. A decrease in demand by itself causes a decrease in the market equilibrium price and quantity. An increase in supply by itself causes a decrease in equilibrium price, but an increase in equilibrium quantity. A decrease in supply alone increases the equilibrium price and decreases the equilibrium quantity.

5. **Identify the changes to equilibrium that result from simultaneous changes in demand and supply.**

   - More complicated cases involve simultaneous shifts in both demand and supply. Either the direction of change in equilibrium price or in equilibrium quantity will be uncertain in each of these cases.

- When demand increases and supply increases, the equilibrium quantity will increase, but the direction of change in the price will be uncertain. When demand increases and supply decreases, the equilibrium quantity will be uncertain, but the equilibrium price will increase.

- When demand decreases and supply increases, the equilibrium quantity will be uncertain, but the equilibrium price will decrease. When demand decreases and supply decreases, the equilibrium quantity will decrease, but the equilibrium price will be uncertain.

 6. Discuss how vouchers use competition to improve the quality of schooling.

- School vouchers increase competition in the market for education. Vouchers are controversial because of the fear that the public schools would be harmed. However, the efficiency of public schools would likely be increased because of their need to compete with private schools for students and money.

KEY TERMS

demand, 58
quantity demanded, 58
ceteris paribus, 58
law of demand, 58
normal goods, 61

inferior goods, 61
substitutes, 61
complements, 61
supply, 64
quantity supplied, 64

law of supply, 64
market equilibrium, 70
surplus, 70
shortage, 70

TEST YOURSELF

TRUE OR FALSE

1. If price rises, demand falls.
2. *Ceteris paribus*, if the price of Coca-Cola rises, the quantity sold of Pepsi will fall.
3. If something happens that leads producers to expect the price to rise in the future, supply will initially shift to the left.
4. If the market clears, there is likely to be a shortage.
5. If demand and supply both shift to the left, the equilibrium quantity will definitely fall but the equilibrium price might either rise, fall, or remain the same.

MULTIPLE CHOICE

6. The law of demand states that consumers
   a. must not buy more than they need.
   b. must not waste what they buy.
   c. must pay for what they buy.
   d. will buy more as the price falls.
7. Demand and supply curves are drawn assuming *ceteris paribus*, which means
   a. consumers and producers care only about money.
   b. that product is the only product in existence.
   c. to ignore all assumptions.
   d. that all other things are held constant.
8. Assume that used cars are an inferior good and that new cars are a normal good. If consumer incomes increase, the demand for
   a. used cars will decrease, and the demand for new cars will increase.

   b. used cars will increase, and the demand for new cars will decrease.
   c. both new and used cars will decrease.
   d. both new and used cars will increase.
9. An increase in the price of football tickets would cause the _____ basketball tickets, a substitute, to _____.
   a. demand for; increase.
   b. supply of; increase.
   c. demand for; decrease.
   d. supply of; decrease.
10. Which of the following would be most likely to shift the demand for widgets?
   a. A change in the price of widgets.
   b. Unionization of the widget industry.
   c. Discovery of a valuable use for by-products generated in the production of widgets.
   d. A news report that widget prices are expected to increase in the future.
11. An upward-sloping supply curve means that
   a. consumers will wish to purchase more at higher prices.
   b. consumers will wish to purchase more at lower prices.
   c. business firms will wish to sell more at higher prices.
   d. business firms that lower their prices will desire to sell more.
12. A decrease in supply is illustrated as
   a. a downward shift in the supply curve.
   b. a shift to the left in the supply curve.

c. an upward movement along the supply curve.

d. a downward movement along the supply curve.

13. Which event is most likely to result in an increase in the price of a Whopper hamburger at Burger King?

  a. French fries go up in price.

  b. New competing hamburger restaurants open.

  c. Beef prices increase.

  d. Scientists declare that hamburgers are a health hazard.

14. In Self-Test Figure 3-1, which of the following would cause a movement from point *A* to point *B*?

  a. An increase in the cost of inputs.

  b. A decrease in the cost of inputs.

  c. An increase in demand.

  d. A decrease in demand.

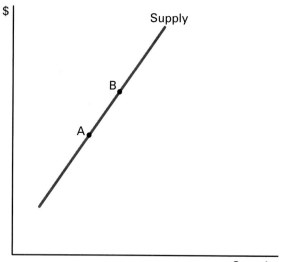

SELF-TEST FIGURE 3-1

15. Suppose a new technique is discovered that is expected to result in cars and houses of the future obtaining all of their energy requirements from roof-mounted solar panels. In the present-day market for oil, it is most likely that

  a. demand would shift to the right.

  b. demand would shift to the left.

  c. supply would shift to the right.

  d. supply would shift to the left.

16. If research reveals that carrot juice cures cancer, it is likely that

  a. the supply of carrot juice will increase, which will increase the quantity demanded.

  b. demand for carrot juice will increase, which will increase the quantity supplied.

  c. neither the demand for carrot juice nor the supply of carrot juice will increase.

  d. both the demand for carrot juice and the supply of carrot juice will increase.

17. Let Jack and Jill be the only two consumers in the market for pails of water. Jack's demand schedule is:

Price	Quantity Demanded
$1	10
$2	5
$3	0

Jill's demand schedule is:

Price	Quantity Demanded
$1	15
$2	10
$3	5
$4	0

Which of the following would be the market demand for pails of water?

a.

Price	Quantity Demanded
$1	12½
$2	7½
$3	2½
$4	0

b.

Price	Quantity Demanded
$1	15
$2	10
$3	5
$4	0

c.

Price	Quantity Demanded
$1	25
$2	15
$3	5
$4	0

d.

Price	Quantity Demanded
$1	15
$3	10
$5	5
$7	0

18. When there is an initial shortage, market prices eventually reach equilibrium because

  a. supply increases.

  b. price decreases.

  c. price increases.

  d. equilibrium output falls.

19. If the demand and supply of a product both decrease (shift to the left), then
    a. both price and quantity must fall.
    b. price rises, but quantity remains constant.
    c. quantity falls, but the change in price cannot be predicted without more information.
    d. price falls, but the change in quantity cannot be predicted without more information.

 20. School voucher plans are likely to do all of the following EXCEPT
    a. increase the amount of control that parents have over schools.
    b. threaten the job security of teachers in the public schools.
    c. violate the constitutional separation between church and state.
    d. increase the amount of educational choices available.

QUESTIONS AND PROBLEMS

1. *[demand]* Do price and quantity demanded show an inverse or a direct relationship between each other? Draw a graph showing a plausible demand curve for milk. Be sure to correctly label the axes of your graph.

2. *[individual and market demand]* Draw a single graph indicating someone's demand curve for hot dogs. Be sure to label the axes of your graph appropriately. Label the demand curve with the words Individual's Demand. On this graph, indicate what market demand would be if there were only two people willing to buy hot dogs, and if each had a demand curve identical to the one you just drew. Label this curve Market Demand.

3. *[demand]* Suppose Clare's demand for tomatoes is represented by the figures in the accompanying table. Draw and label the axes of a graph that shows Clare's demand for tomatoes. Scale the axes appropriate to the figures in the table. Plot the price–quantity pairs from the table in your graph, then connect the points plotted and label the resulting curve with the word Demand. Is the demand curve you plotted a straight line? Why are most of the demand curves in the text drawn as straight lines?

Price per Pound	Quantity Demanded per Week (in pounds)
$1.00	0
75 cents	1/2
50 cents	3/4
25 cents	1
Free	2

4. *[demand]* Why does insurance increase the number of homes that are built in areas prone to hurricane damage? Explain, using a graph of demand.

5. *[substitutes]* List at least five substitutes for your favorite soft drink, in order, starting with the best substitute, second best, and so on. Comment on whether the products on your list are good substitutes. How much would the price of your favorite soft drink have to increase before you would begin to purchase the best substitute?

6. *[complements]* Name at least one other good that would be a complement for each of the following goods: pencil, baseball, personal computer, postage stamp, sugar, and butter. What effect on the demand for each of these goods would there be if the price of a complement for the good were to increase (decrease)?

7. *[inferior goods]* Keeping in mind the economic definition of inferior goods, list several products that would be inferior goods for you personally. Do you think that these would also be inferior goods for most other people?

8. *[normal versus inferior goods]* When Mr. Johnson lost his job, thus cutting his income, his demands for various products changed. The accompanying table lists five normal goods and five inferior goods for Mr. Johnson. However, the goods may not be in the correct column. Bearing in mind the distinction between normal and inferior goods, use your best judgment to rearrange the goods by placing them in the correct column. Will the demand for the normal goods increase or decrease because of Mr. Johnson's income reduction? Will the demand for the inferior goods increase or decrease?

Normal Goods?	Inferior Goods?
Generic paper towels	Antique furniture
Restaurant food	Tickets to pro football games
Tommy Hilfiger clothing	Used cars
Fresh vegetables	Home-brewed coffee
Spam	Ramen noodles

9. *[demand]* As in the chapter, suppose Jack and Jill are the only two consumers in the market for pails of water. However, suppose that their demand curves

change over time from the data in the chapter to the following:

Price	Jack's Quantity Demanded	Jill's Quantity Demanded
$1	10	15
2	5	10
3	0	5
4	0	0

a. Compute market demand.
b. Compute the quantities purchased in total and by Jack and Jill individually if the price per unit is $2.
c. Graph Jack's demand and Jill's demand on separate graphs. Note that, if you connect the data points you are given, you are actually inferring additional data. For example, connecting the data points on Jack's demand implies that Jack would be willing to purchase 2.5 pails of water at a price of $2.50 per pail.

10. *[demand versus quantity demanded]* Is there a difference between a *change in demand* and a *change in quantity demanded*? Explain.

11. *[direct or inverse supply curve]* Does a supply curve show a direct or an inverse relationship between price and quantity supplied? Draw a graph showing a plausible market supply curve for spinach. Be sure to correctly label the axes of your graph.

12. *[shift factors for supply]* In each of the situations that follow, state whether supply would increase or decrease. Sketch each shift by drawing a graph for each case.
a. The price of a substitute in production falls.
b. The price of a jointly produced product falls.
c. Sellers expect prices of their output will increase in the future.
d. The technology of production improves.

13. *[supply versus quantity supplied]* Explain why an increase in *quantity supplied* is NOT the same as an increase in *supply*. Which of these would be associated with a rightward shift in the supply curve? Which would be associated with a movement up the supply curve?

14. *[equilibrium]* Explain what is meant by saying that, at equilibrium, the market clears. Why do markets tend toward equilibrium?

15. *[surplus]* Will a surplus result from a price that is above the equilibrium price or a price below the equilibrium price? Why would a surplus be only temporary?

16. *[shortage]* Will a shortage result from a price that is above the equilibrium price or a price below the equilibrium price? What adjustment will take place so that the shortage eventually disappears?

17. *[surplus, shortage, equilibrium]* Fill in the surplus or shortage in the table below. In each case identify whether the number is a surplus, shortage, or neither. Identify the equilibrium price, and explain why a price above equilibrium would not last.

Price	Quantity Demanded	Quantity Supplied	Surplus or Shortage
$7	12	30	
$6	15	25	
$5	19	19	
$4	23	10	

18. *[adjustment to equilibrium]* Suppose that a market is initially in equilibrium. Now suppose that demand increases. At the initial equilibrium price, will the effect of the increase in demand be to create a surplus or a shortage? What must happen for the market to attain a new equilibrium?

19. *[shifts in demand and supply]* Fill in the missing information in the following table by stating whether equilibrium price and quantity will increase or decrease in each case.

Demand	Supply	Equilibrium Price	Equilibrium Quantity
Shifts to the right	Does not shift		
Shifts to the left	Does not shift		
Does not shift	Shifts to the right		
Does not shift	Shifts to the left		

20. *[shifts in demand and supply]* Using a graph of supply and demand, demonstrate how a leftward shift in demand, accompanied by a rightward shift in supply, can result in the equilibrium quantity rising. On a separate graph, demonstrate how the equilibrium quantity could alternatively have fallen.

WORKING WITH GRAPHS AND DATA

1. *[market demand and market supply]* There are three (3) consumers in the market for coffee: Ableman, Bart, and Connor. The table below indicates the number of pounds of coffee each consumer is willing and able to purchase at various prices. Assume that the entire market demand for this coffee is comprised of these three consumers.

Price	Ableman	Bart	Connor	Market
$5.00	0	0	0	
4.50	0	0	1	
4.00	1	0		3
3.50	4	2	3	
3.00	7	4	4	
2.50	10	6	5	
2.00		8	6	27
1.50	16	10	7	
1.00	19		8	39
0.50	22	14	9	
0.00	25	16	10	

a. Complete the table.
b. Draw a graph showing each consumer's demand curve for coffee. Label the vertical axis "Price" or "$" and the horizontal axis "Quantity."
c. Draw a graph showing the market demand for coffee. Label the vertical axis "Price" or "$" and the horizontal axis "Quantity."

There are also three (3) suppliers of this type of coffee. The table below indicates the manufacturer's ability and willingness to supply coffee to the market.

Price	Xanos	YabbaDabba	Zebra	Market
$5.00	5	10	12	
4.50	4.50	9	10.5	
4.00	4		9	21
3.50	3.50	7		18
3.00	3	6	6	
2.50	2.50	5	4.5	
2.00		4	3	9
1.50	1.50	3	1.5	
1.00	1	2		3
0.50	0.50	1	0	
0.00	0	0	0	

d. Complete the table.
e. Draw a graph showing the supply curves of the individual producers of coffee. Label the vertical axis "$" and the horizontal axis "Quantity."
f. Draw a graph showing the market supply curve. Label the vertical axis "$" and the horizontal axis "Quantity."
g. Draw a graph showing the market demand and supply curves on the same graph and identify the equilibrium price and quantity in the market. Identify the amount each consumer will purchase and manufacturer will produce. Label the vertical axis "$" and the horizontal axis "Quantity."
h. At what price is there a shortage of coffee of 18 pounds?
i. What occurs when the price of coffee is $4.50 a pound?

2. *[market equilibrium]* Begin with the respective market in equilibrium as depicted in Graph 3-1. Read each of the following situations, taking note of the market and the event that takes place. For each situation you are to:
   i) identify the appropriate shift factor that is changing.
   ii) identify whether it impacts demand or supply.
   iii) indicate the proper direction of the shift.
   iv) shift the appropriate curve.
   v) determine the resulting change in the equilibrium Price ($) and Quantity due to the event.

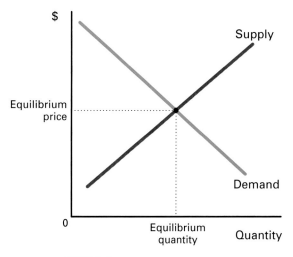

GRAPH 3-1

a. Market: Leather
   Event: The price of beef increases
b. Market: Automobiles
   Event: Consumers expect higher auto loan interest rates in the future
c. Market: Urban Housing
   Event: More people move into the urban area from the rural areas
d. Market: Wood burning stove
   Event: The price of natural gas increases
e. Market: Delivery services
   Event: Wages of delivery workers increase
f. Market: Corn
   Event: Mississippi River floods thousands of acres of farm fields

3. *[demand and supply]* Soft drink manufacturers have observed the impact of temperature on the sales of their products. Some have designed vending machines to adjust the price of their product based on the outside temperature. The table below indicates the data from one particular study of soft drink sales and temperature.

Price	Sales	Temperature (°F)
$0.75	70	80
1.25	75	85
1.25	125	90
1.50	150	95
1.00	100	85
1.75	75	90
1.00	50	80
2.00	100	95
1.50	50	85
1.50	100	90
1.75	125	95
1.25	30	80

The supply curve of soft drinks in this study is depicted by the table below:

Price	Quantity Supplied
$2.00	150
1.75	125
1.50	100
1.25	75
1.00	50
0.75	25
0.50	0

a. Draw the demand and supply curves for soft drinks identified in this study.
b. Identify the equilibrium quantities and the equilibrium prices the vending machines should charge.

4. *[shift factors for demand and supply]* Begin with the respective market in equilibrium as depicted in Graph 3-2. Read each of the following situations, taking note of the market and the events that take place. For each situation you are to:
   i) identify the appropriate shift factors that are changing.
   ii) identify which shift factor impacts demand and which impacts supply.
   iii) indicate the proper direction of the shift for each curve.
   iv) shift the appropriate curve.
   v) determine the possible resulting changes in the equilibrium Price and Quantity due to the events.

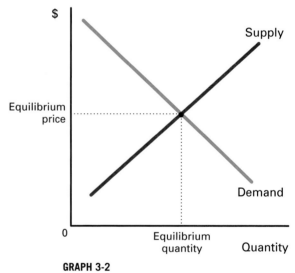

GRAPH 3-2

a. Market: Peanut Butter
   Event: The price of jelly increases *and* a drought reduces the peanut crop.
b. Market: Apartments
   Event: The price of single family homes increases *and* more apartments are converted into condominiums.
c. Market: Automobiles
   Event: Consumers expect higher prices of automobiles in the future *and* new technology lowers automobile production cost.
d. Market: Soccer tickets
   Event: Urban population is decreasing *and* a larger stadium is built.

 Visit www.prenhall.com/ayers for Exploring the Web exercises and additional self-test quizzes.

THE POWER OF PRICES

A LOOK AHEAD

The United States shines like no other country, at least when looked at from outer space. Electric power and lighting are taken for granted as inalienable rights. Yet there was a time not long ago when the lights went dark, first in California and later in New York. Fingers of blame pointed to public policy. As we will see in the Explore & Apply section that concludes this chapter, the culprit in California was a policy that ignored some basic economic lessons concerning supply, demand, and market price.

Prices are powerful! They guide the marketplace to produce the right things in the right way and distribute them to those who place the most value upon them. Sometimes the results of the market price system seem unfair. But tampering with market prices can be perilous in terms of efficiency. As we will see, sometimes the effect is to harm the very people the policies intend to help.

LEARNING OBJECTIVES

Understanding Chapter 4 will enable you to:
1. **Interpret how demand represents marginal benefit and supply represents marginal cost.**
2. **Explain the concept of social surplus and how it is divided between consumers and producers.**
3. **Demonstrate how both exports and imports increase efficiency while simultaneously harming either consumers or producers.**
4. **Identify inefficiencies associated with price ceilings.**
5. **Show why price supports are unnecessary and potentially counterproductive.**
6. Pinpoint the economic flaw in California's deregulation of electricity.

Explore & Apply

price signals help consumers decide how much to buy and help producers decide how much to sell.

The marketplace depends upon **price signals,** meaning that the market price sends a message to consumers and producers. The price signals to consumers how much of a good they will wish to buy, and signals to producers how much of a good they will wish to sell. When the market equilibrium price rises, consumers respond by buying less of a good and producers respond by offering more for sale. Just the opposite is true when price falls. We start Chapter 4 by examining why these price signals are desirable. We then examine various public policies that are intended to either lower or raise prices from their market equilibrium values.

4.1 PRICE SIGNALS FOR EFFICIENT CHOICE

Consumers buy something because they expect that they will be better off by doing so. The same holds true when producers sell something. Therefore, when a consumer buys a good that a producer sells, both parties are better off. The mutual gains from such market exchanges lead the economy to greater efficiency. This section looks at how gains are measured, how much is gained by consumers and producers, and how market prices can maximize these gains, including when trade occurs internationally. Later chapters examine exceptions, such as possible reasons for restricting international trade.

MARGINAL BENEFIT AND CONSUMER SURPLUS

marginal benefit the incremental value of an additional unit of a good.

The demand curve depicts the quantity that would be purchased at each of various prices, *ceteris paribus.* Another way of looking at it is that the demand curve shows the maximum price the consumer would pay for each quantity that might be purchased. This maximum price is the consumer's **marginal benefit**—the incremental value of each additional item consumed. Figure 4-1 illustrates this way of looking at demand.

Consider Dwight, who is shopping for blue jeans. Dwight won't buy blue jeans if the price is over $20. He'll buy one pair if the price is $20, two pair if the price is $15, or three pair if the price is $10. In other words, the first pair is worth $20 to him, the second pair is worth an extra $15, and the third an extra $10. His marginal benefits from blue jeans, therefore, are $20 for the first pair, $15 for the second, and $10 for the third. Table 4-1 shows how demand translates into marginal benefit and total benefit. Dwight's *total benefit* from his blue

FIGURE 4-1

MARGINAL BENEFIT Demand is the marginal benefit to consumers. Marginal benefit declines as quantity demanded rises. The length of the arrows represents the marginal benefit of the quantities 1, 2, and 3, respectively.

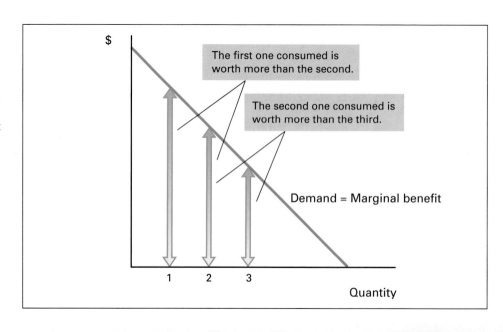

TABLE 4-1   DWIGHT'S DEMAND, MARGINAL BENEFIT, AND TOTAL BENEFIT

| (A) DWIGHT'S DEMAND FOR BLUE JEANS | | (B) DWIGHT'S BENEFITS FROM BUYING BLUE JEANS | | |
PRICE	QUANTITY	QUANTITY	MARGINAL BENEFIT	TOTAL BENEFIT
$20	1	1	$20	$20
$15	2	2	$15	$35
$10	3	3	$10	$45

jean purchases is the sum of his marginal benefit from each pair. So, if he buys three pair, the blue jeans would bring Dwight $45 worth of total benefit, where $45 = $20 + $15 + $10.

Since Dwight must pay for the blue jeans he buys, the remaining value to him of his blue jean purchases equals the total benefit from the blue jeans minus what he pays. This value is termed **consumer surplus,** which is the difference between the total benefit and total cost to the consumer. Graphically, it is the demand curve minus price, as shown in Figure 4-2(a). Therefore, if the price of blue jeans is $10, then Dwight would buy three pair at a cost of $30. Subtracting that $30 from his total benefit of $45 would leave him with a consumer surplus of $15, as shown in Figure 4-2(b).

consumer surplus consumers' total benefit minus cost; graphically, demand minus market price.

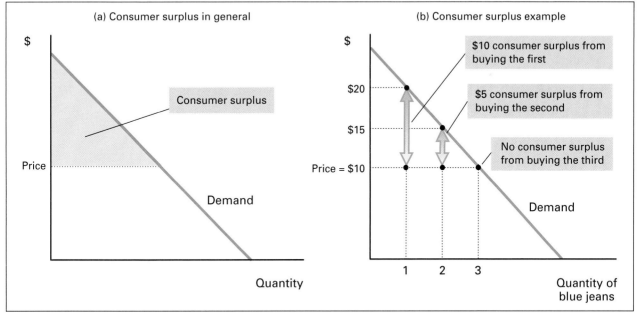

FIGURE 4-2

CONSUMER SURPLUS Consumer surplus is the area under the demand curve and above the market price. It is what consumers gain from their purchases after deducting the cost. The general idea is shown in graph (a).

Graph (b) applies this idea to the example of Dwight. At a price of $10 per pair of jeans, Dwight buys three pair and receives $15 worth of consumer surplus. His consumer surplus equals the sum of the consumer surplus from the first, second, and third pairs, which is $10 + $5 + $0 = $15. If the price were higher, Dwight's consumer surplus would be lower, as shown in Table 4-2.

TABLE 4-2   DWIGHT'S CONSUMER SURPLUS FROM BLUE JEANS

PRICE	QUANTITY BOUGHT	TOTAL BENEFIT	TOTAL PAID	CONSUMER SURPLUS
$20	1	$20	$20	$0
$15	2	$35	$30	$5
$10	3	$45	$30	$15

Table 4-2 computes Dwight's consumer surplus for three different prices of blue jeans. As you can see in that table, **consumer surplus varies inversely with price.** The greater the price, the less is consumer surplus, and the lower the price the greater is consumer surplus.

MARGINAL COST AND PRODUCER SURPLUS

Supply, like demand, can be viewed in two ways. A supply curve shows the quantity that would be offered for sale at each of various prices, *ceteris paribus.* The supply curve also depicts the minimum price that the producers of a good would be willing to accept for each quantity offered. That minimum price is the producer's *marginal cost,* which is the incremental cost of producing each additional item offered for sale. Figure 4-3 illustrates this way of looking at supply.

Consider Buddy, who sells blue jeans. Buddy won't offer any blue jeans for sale if the price is under $5. He is willing to sell one pair if the price is $5, two pair if the price is $7.50, or three pair at a price of $10. Those prices are also his marginal costs when he produces the first three pair of blue jeans. Table 4-3 shows how supply translates into marginal cost and total cost. Buddy's *total cost* of blue jeans sold is the sum of his marginal cost from selling each pair. So, if he sells three pair of blue jeans, he would incur total costs of $22.50, where $22.50 = $5 + $7.50 + $10.

producer surplus producers' revenue minus production cost; graphically, market price minus supply.

The value Buddy receives from the sale of his product equals total revenue minus total cost. This value is termed **producer surplus,** which is the excess of revenue to producers over their costs of production. Graphically, it is the market price minus the supply curve, as shown in Figure 4-4(a) on page 92. If the price of blue jeans is $10 in our example, then Buddy would sell three pair for a total revenue of $30, where total revenue is computed by multiplying price by quantity. Subtracting the total cost of $22.50 from the $30 would leave him with a producer surplus of $7.50, as shown in Figure 4-4(b).

QUICKCHECK

Suppose coffee costs $1 per cup at Handy Stop Shop and $1.05 per cup at Gas'n N Goin' next door. If you buy coffee at Handy Stop Shop, does this mean your consumer surplus from coffee is only five cents?

Answer: No, consumer surplus does not depend upon alternative prices for the same product. Rather, it asks you what is the most you would be willing to pay to avoid doing without the product altogether and then subtracts the price you actually pay. Thus, whatever your consumer surplus from a cup of coffee may be, it is five cents more if you buy your coffee at Handy Stop Shop than at Gas'n N Goin'.

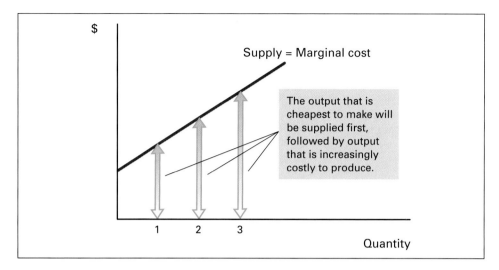

FIGURE 4-3

MARGINAL COST Supply is the marginal cost to producers. Marginal cost increases as quantity produced rises. The length of the arrows represents the marginal cost of the quantities 1, 2, and 3, respectively.

TABLE 4-3   BUDDY'S SUPPLY, MARGINAL COST, AND TOTAL COST

(A) BUDDY'S SUPPLY OF BLUE JEANS		(B) BUDDY'S COSTS OF PRODUCING BLUE JEANS		
PRICE	QUANTITY	QUANTITY	MARGINAL COST	TOTAL COST
$5	1	1	$5	$5
$7.50	2	2	$7.50	$12.50
$10	3	3	$10	$22.50

Table 4-4 computes producer surplus for three different prices of blue jeans. As seen in that table, **producer surplus varies directly with price.**

To clarify the concepts of producer surplus and consumer surplus, consider the on-line auction house, eBay. Perhaps you have personally bought or sold something there. If you bid to buy an item, it's in your interest to bid the very most that you would be willing to pay. That doesn't mean you'll have to pay that amount, because eBay only charges you the lowest bid price that would make you the winner. If you win, your consumer surplus is the difference between your maximum bid and what you actually wind up paying.

Likewise, if you offer an item for sale, you can specify a minimum price, below which you would not be willing to sell. If your item sells, your producer surplus is the difference between the price it sells for and the minimum price that you had specified. The final result of this process is that both the buyer and the seller are likely to be better off.

TABLE 4-4   BUDDY'S PRODUCER SURPLUS FROM BLUE JEANS

PRICE	QUANTITY SOLD	TOTAL COST	TOTAL REVENUE	PRODUCER SURPLUS
$5	1	$5	$5	$0
$7.50	2	$12.50	$15	$2.50
$10	3	$22.50	$30	$7.50

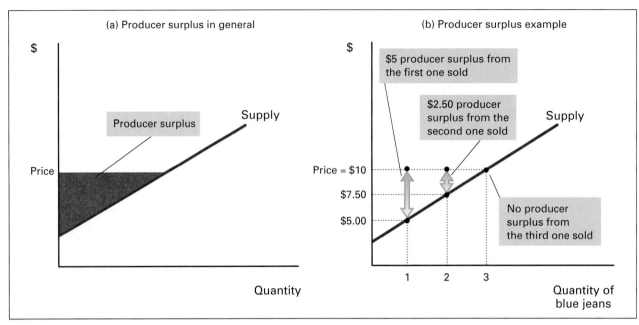

FIGURE 4-4

PRODUCER SURPLUS Producer surplus is the area above the supply curve and under the market price, as shown in (a). It is what producers gain from their sales after deducting their costs.

Graph (b) shows that, at a price of $10 per pair of jeans, Buddy sells three pair and receives $7.50 worth of producer surplus. His producer surplus equals the sum of his producer surplus from the first, second, and third pairs, which is $5 + $2.50 + $0 = $7.50.

QUICKCHECK

What is the difference in meaning between the terms *surplus, consumer surplus,* and *producer surplus*?

Answer: A surplus exists when the market price is above the equilibrium price, as discussed in Chapter 3. The surplus equals the quantity supplied minus the quantity demanded at that price. In contrast, consumer surplus refers to the value that a consumer receives in excess of what was paid for the purchase—it equals demand minus the market price. Producer surplus is the value a seller receives in excess of cost—it equals market price minus supply.

THE EFFICIENCY OF THE MARKETPLACE

social surplus the sum of consumer surplus and producer surplus.

Markets are efficient to the extent that they maximize social surplus, which is the sum of consumer and producer surplus. Social surplus is the difference between how much a good is worth and how much it costs to produce. It is the total value the economy gains by having the good produced and consumed. In the blue jeans example, the social surplus at a price of $10 would be $22.50, which equals $15 in consumer surplus for Dwight plus $7.50 in producer surplus for Buddy.

Any time marginal benefit exceeds marginal cost, social surplus would increase if more of the good were to be produced and sold. That is just what the marketplace does. Producers keep on selling until their marginal cost just equals the market price. Likewise, consumers keep on buying until their marginal benefit equals the market price. This means that marginal benefit equals marginal cost at the market equilibrium price and that social surplus is maxi-

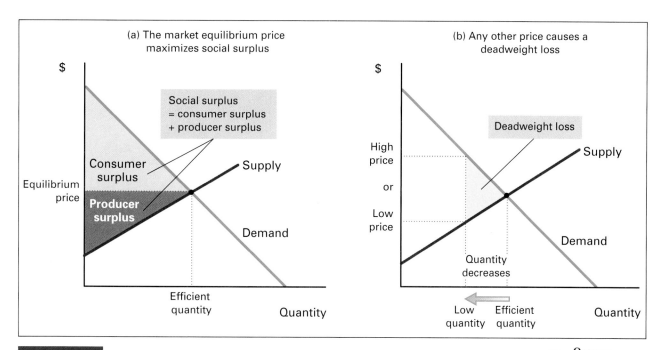

(a) The market equilibrium price maximizes social surplus

(b) Any other price causes a deadweight loss

FIGURE 4-5

EFFICIENCY OF THE EQUILIBRIUM PRICE The market equilibrium price leads to the efficient quantity, as shown in (a). No other quantity would generate a larger total of consumer and producer surplus. Any other price, such as either of the prices shown in (b), would lead to a lower quantity sold. If the price is high, the quantity falls because consumers aren't willing to buy as much. If the price is low, quantity falls because producers aren't willing to sell as much. In either case, there is a triangular area of deadweight loss that shows how much social surplus is forgone relative to the amount at an efficient quantity.

mized. Any more output would add more cost than benefit. Thus, the *rule of efficiency* states that **the efficient output occurs when society's marginal benefit equals marginal cost.**

To the extent that demand equals marginal benefit and supply equals marginal cost, the market outcome is efficient. However, there are exceptions when either demand does not equal marginal benefit or supply does not equal marginal cost. For example, pollution represents a situation in which there are *external costs* that are not reflected in either demand or supply. Likewise, there is no market demand for the *public goods* of clean air and national defense, even though we collectively receive benefits from both. These are examples of **market failure**—instances in which the market outcome fails to achieve efficiency. While market failure is not a topic in macroeconomics, it is a major topic in microeconomics.

Barring instances of market failure, the marketplace achieves an efficient output through price adjustments. At the market equilibrium price, marginal benefit equals marginal cost and social surplus is maximized. Figure 4-5(a) illustrates how the market price—also the equilibrium price—signals an efficient quantity that maximizes social surplus. In this figure the intersection of demand and supply establishes the efficient quantity. Since demand represents marginal benefit and supply represents marginal cost, the rule of efficiency is satisfied. Any other price, such as the high price or low price shown in Figure 4-5(b), would lead to less output and a smaller social surplus.

The triangular area of forgone social surplus caused by inefficient pricing is called a **deadweight loss.** The size of the deadweight loss will decrease when the price is closer to the market price, but increase when the price moves farther away from its equilibrium value. Prices that differ from their equilibrium values will not persist because those prices will adjust toward equilibrium. The deadweight loss will in this way eventually disappear.

market failure instances in which the market outcome fails to achieve efficiency.

deadweight loss reduction in social surplus caused by inefficient price; shown graphically as a triangular area.

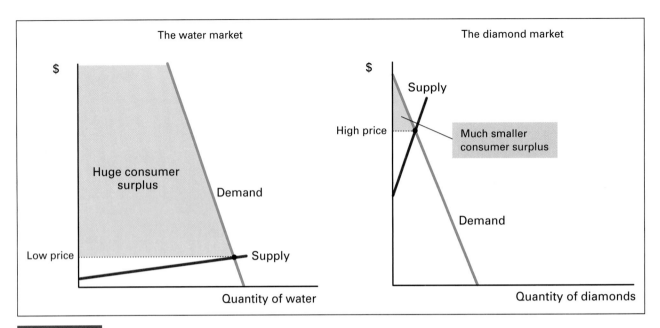

FIGURE 4-6

THE PARADOX OF DIAMONDS AND WATER Price measures the value of consuming one more unit of a good. Consumer surplus measures the total value to consumers from all of their consumption of the good. While the marginal benefit from a glass of water is far less than from a diamond, as revealed by the relatively low price of water, the total benefit from all water as measured by its consumer surplus is immensely larger than it would be for all diamonds.

SNAPSHOT   **THE PARADOX OF DIAMONDS AND WATER**

Some necessities that have a great deal of intrinsic worth are priced lower than luxuries we could easily do without. For example, people pay much more for a diamond than for a glass of water, which seems paradoxical. If we were stranded in Death Valley with neither water nor diamonds, which would seem the better bargain—a diamond for a nickel or a glass of water for a one-hundred-dollar bill?

The paradox disappears when we realize that price merely tells the value of a good at the margin. The last bit of water is not worth much when water is plentiful. It is the scarcity of diamonds that keeps that price high. To understand the total value of a good, though, we must look beyond price to consumer surplus. As shown in Figure 4-6, the consumer surplus from water purchases is vastly greater than the consumer surplus from diamond purchases. It is consumer surplus that truly measures the total value consumers receive from the things they buy. ◄

THE EFFICIENCY OF IMPORTS AND EXPORTS

Questions of efficiency often arise in the context of international trade. If a country chooses not to engage in international trade, the market prices of its goods and services would reflect only the supply and demand within that country. Those prices are called *domestic* prices. Opening an economy to international trade will change market prices in a country by bringing into its markets a world of new consumers and producers. *World prices* of goods and services are determined by the supply and demand from all countries.

Countries that trade buy goods and services from other countries—their *imports.* They also sell goods and services to other countries—their *exports.* Whether a country imports a good or exports a good will depend upon whether the good's world equilibrium market price is below or above what the country's price would otherwise have been—its domestic price.

In other words, **the result of trade is that the price in the domestic market will come to equal the world market price.** If the domestic price rises to meet a higher world price, then the country exports the good. If a lower world price causes the domestic price to drop, then the country imports the good, meaning that it is purchased from producers in other countries. In either case, there are some people within the country who gain and others who lose. However, as we will see, the gains can be expected to exceed the losses.

Figure 4-7 shows the case of a world price of a good that would lead a country to import that good. Domestic consumers will not be willing to pay any more than the world price. Producers will also refuse to sell for less than the world price. Because the domestic quantity supplied is less than the quantity demanded, consumers make up the difference with imports, as shown in Figure 4-7(a).

Adding together consumer surplus and producer surplus, it is apparent by looking at Figure 4-7(b) that the total increases. Specifically, allowing imports increases social surplus by the amount labeled. Although the lower price will cause producer surplus to shrink, the increase in consumer surplus is seen to more than compensate for that loss. Because the gains to consumers more than offset the losses to producers, efficiency calls for allowing imports.

Figure 4-8 is similar to Figure 4-7 except the world price is above the domestic price. In this case, the price difference causes the domestic quantity supplied to be greater than the domestic quantity demanded. This difference between quantity supplied and quantity

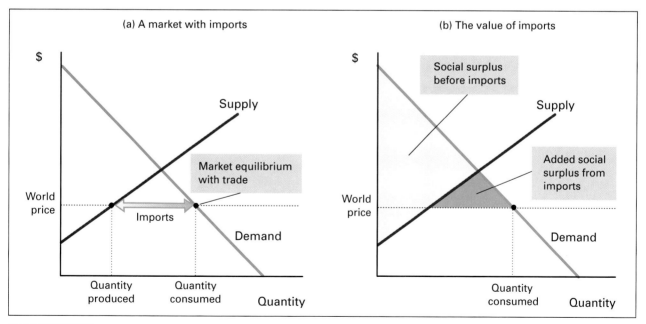

FIGURE 4-7

THE EFFICIENCY OF IMPORTS Imports result from a world price that is below what the country's equilibrium price would have been without trade. The lower world price causes the country's consumption to rise and production to fall, with the difference being the amount imported, as shown in (a).

Trade leads to an efficient quantity consumed because it increases the value of social surplus by the added triangular area shown in (b). However, the gains go disproportionately to consumers. Producer surplus is smaller because of the lower price.

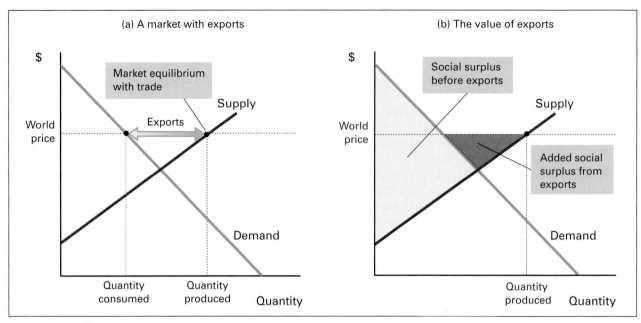

FIGURE 4-8

THE EFFICIENCY OF EXPORTS Exports result from a world price that exceeds what the country's equilibrium price would be without trade. The higher world price causes the country's consumption to fall and production to rise, with the difference being the amount exported, as shown in (a).

Trade leads to an efficient quantity produced because it increases the value of social surplus by the added triangular area shown in (b). However, the gains go disproportionately to producers. Consumer surplus is less because of the higher price.

QUICKCHECK

Since consumers gain from imports, but domestic producers lose, isn't a country just as well off to forgo imports altogether? Similarly, since consumers lose from exports, but domestic producers gain, isn't a country just as well off to do without exports? Explain.

Answer: No, consumers gain more from imports than producers lose. Likewise, producers gain more from exports than consumers lose. Thus, both imports and exports bring net gains to the country.

demanded results in an excess quantity of the product. This excess is exported, as shown in Figure 4-8(a).

Adding together consumer surplus and producer surplus in Figure 4-8(b) shows that the total increases. Specifically, allowing exports increases social surplus by the amount labeled. Although the higher price will cause consumer surplus to shrink, the increase in producer surplus is seen to more than compensate. Because the gains to producers more than offset the losses to consumers, efficiency calls for allowing exports.

In short, consumers come out winners from imports, but producers lose. Producers come out the winners from exports, but consumers lose. In each case, though, the gains exceed the losses. So, whether it be from imports or from exports, the country as a whole comes out the winner.

4.2 PRICE CEILINGS—HOLDING PRICES DOWN

In 1973, the Organization of Petroleum Exporting Countries (OPEC) succeeded in restricting oil supplies to Western countries and achieving a dramatic spike upward in energy prices. In response, Congress enacted temporary gasoline price controls, which capped price increases and cut into the social surplus. This action caused fuel shortages, with drivers losing much time and patience in long lines at the gas pumps. Yet the problem of gasoline shortages and wasteful gas lines has little to do with gasoline and much to do with the economics of a **price ceiling,** which is a law that establishes a maximum price that can be legally charged for a good. As discussed in the following sections, price ceilings arise in various contexts.

price ceiling a maximum price that can legally be charged for a good.

PROMOTING AFFORDABLE HOUSING—ARE RENT CONTROLS THE ANSWER?

With rising populations in competition for scarce land, major cities sometimes choose rent controls as a way to insulate tenants from higher housing costs. **Rent controls** hold the monthly price of rental housing to below its equilibrium level. Price tries to rise, but bumps up against the rent control ceiling. As we will see, the long-term consequences often differ from what proponents have in mind.

rent controls a price ceiling applied to the price of rental housing.

The market for rental housing is like other markets in which demand slopes down and supply slopes up. Demand slopes down because prospective tenants are unwilling to rent as many apartments when prices are high as when they are low. Some people continue living with their parents. Others choose to share rental homes and apartments with roommates. Still others live on their own, but rent smaller and less-desirable quarters than they would have preferred. The supply of rental housing slopes upward as higher rental prices motivate prospective landlords to partition off rental rooms, repair vacant apartments, and in other ways increase the quantity of housing supplied.

Figure 4-9 illustrates a housing market with rent controls in place. **For these rent controls to be meaningful, the ceiling price must be set below the market equilibrium price.** The result is a housing shortage, as shown in Figure 4-9(a), in which less housing is offered for lease, while more housing is demanded.

One effect of rent controls is to transfer wealth from current landlords to current tenants, as shown in Figure 4-9(b). Such **transfer payments,** in which one party's loss is another's gain, are not themselves inefficient since they merely redistribute social surplus. However, when transfer payments are caused by government price controls, there are multiple sources of inefficiency that shrink social surplus. The first inefficiency is the deadweight loss triangle associated with a less-than-efficient overall quantity, such as labeled in Figure 4-9(b).

transfer payments the redistribution of social surplus from one party to another; rent controls create transfer payments from landlords to tenants.

A second source of inefficiency comes from misallocating apartments that are leased. For example, even though Tanisha in Figure 4-9 would get a larger benefit from the apartment than would Candice, the landlord would receive the same payment from either and so might well rent the apartment to Candice. Since any tenant would be constrained to pay the same rent and there are more potential tenants than available apartments, the landlord would find it easy to discriminate, whether on the basis of income, occupation, or anything else the landlord thinks is important. It might be difficult to prove if that discrimination was illegal, such as based on race, color, or creed.

A third inefficiency involves **search costs,** which are the costs of finding an apartment. Since landlords have plenty of prospective tenants for rent-controlled apartments, they do not need to advertise. As a result, some enterprising would-be tenants have taken up such tactics as reading the obituaries or, to get the jump, listening to police radios and checking out emergency rooms. In the absence of rent controls, there would be little or no need for such wasteful behavior.

search costs the costs of finding something; rent controls increase search costs for rental housing.

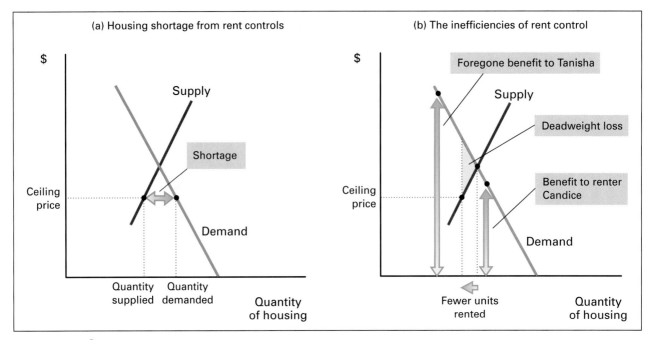

FIGURE 4-9

RENT CONTROLS A rent control law imposes a ceiling price that leads to a shortage of rental housing, as shown in (a). As shown in (b), the inefficiencies of rent controls include a deadweight loss from fewer units rented and an inefficient allocation of apartments among prospective tenants. For example, a landlord might rent an apartment to Candice, since she is willing to pay the ceiling price. However, that might leave Tanisha without an apartment, even though it is worth more to her.

The inefficiencies of rent controls are likely to get worse over time as demand grows with an increasing population while rent-controlled apartments are allowed to deteriorate. For example, New York City and Washington, D.C., have seen rent-controlled housing crumble for decades. A look at some of the aging cities of Europe also reveals deep scars from rent control. Paris has had some rent controls in place for over two hundred years. The rent-controlled apartment houses in Paris have seen little modernization in that time, with few apartment units containing their own plumbing facilities. In the rent-controlled period between 1914 and 1948, almost no new rental housing was constructed in all of France.

While rent controls have problems, there are also problems associated with removing them. The immediate effect of abolishing rent controls is that rents jump to their market equilibrium value. That value could be quite high if rent controls have been in place for a long time and the housing shortage has become severe. Higher rents would eventually shift supply to the right as old apartments are refurbished and new ones are built. However, this process would take time and the only immediate effect would be higher rents.

There are alternatives to rent controls. One alternative is to identify the needy and assign them housing vouchers. **Housing vouchers** are government grants that the recipient can spend only on housing. Thus, even though the price of rental housing may be high, housing vouchers can bring it within reach of impoverished tenants.

housing vouchers government grants that recipients can spend only on housing.

ANTI-GOUGING LAWS

price gouging price increases in response to increased demand related to emergencies.

Rent controls are far from the only time government seeks to keep prices down. For example, local governments have often attempted to protect consumers against **price gouging,**

If rent controls are removed, is there likely to be as much illegal discrimination against apartment applicants?

Answer: No, uncontrolled rents will clear the market, meaning that the shortage of apartments will be eliminated. Landlords will no longer have the luxury of picking from a crowd of applicants all offering the same rent. In competing for tenants, landlords have a financial incentive to avoid discrimination. Those who insist on discriminating on the basis of irrelevant prejudices are by definition accepting less than the most valuable offer. Because the price of discrimination has risen, its quantity will fall.

which is the disparaging term for hiking up prices in response to temporary surges in demand. The idea is to promote equity. The cost is in terms of efficiency, though, because high prices in times of emergency prevent shortages and allocate sought-after goods to those who value them the most.

Profitably high prices also motivate rapid restocking, which means that prices do not stay high for long. For example, when hurricanes move toward the coast, oceanfront homeowners seek out plywood to board up their windows. If stores can raise prices, they have an incentive to send out extra trucks for new supplies. Otherwise, homeowners must scramble to snatch up and hoard supplies before the shelves go bare. If homeowners are lucky, stores might use the occasion to generate goodwill and restock promptly despite the extra costs.

Local governments also often have laws against *ticket scalping*—the practice of buying tickets at the price set by concert promoters and then reselling at whatever the market will bear. Scalping is a form of *arbitrage*, which means buying low and selling high. Arbitrage directs goods to their highest-valued uses, thus efficiently allocating seats at concerts, ball games, and other events. As for equity, however, opinions differ. Good seats get snared quickly by scalpers, many of whom hire stand-ins to buy up blocks of tickets. Those seats are made available to true fans, but the price might be much higher.

SCALPING THE STONES   *SNAPSHOT*

From the honky-tonk women of Memphis to the fear-no-SARS partiers of Toronto, over four decades of touring has taught the Rolling Stones all about how to rock the crowd. And their fans have learned all about the crowds of scalpers that grab up the best seats! Their techniques? One ticket reseller paid $20 each to the brothers of a college fraternity just for standing in the ticket line. That reseller hired over 150 stand-ins for a single Rolling Stones concert. Who could blame Stones' fans for crying that they "can't get no satisfaction"?

Some fans—those willing to spend extra money to avoid the time in line—were glad for the choice and convenience offered by the scalpers, who these days usually put their tickets up for auction at eBay, uBid, or other on-line auction sites. Others cried that it wasn't fair to fans or promoters, who want to generate excitement with below-market ticket prices. Which should it be? During their 2002–2003 World Tour, the Rolling Stones played in stadiums, arenas, and clubs in cities including Boston, Chicago, and Los Angeles. Concert tickets sold out quickly, leaving many fans with two choices: wait for another tour or pay an above-market price. The price of some tickets on eBay reached $3,000. The fans who didn't pay got to know all too well the words of Mick Jagger, "You can't always get what you want." If you have the money, though, "you can get what you need!" ◄

4.3 PRICE FLOORS—PROPPING PRICES UP

price floor (price support)
minimum price guaranteed to producers by the government.

Although consumers are better off when prices are low, producers prefer them high. Both groups often turn to government for help. If politics dictates propping up prices, government can establish a **price floor,** also termed a **price support,** which sets a minimum price that producers are guaranteed to receive. One way to implement a price floor is for government to agree to buy at that floor price. This approach can cause surpluses to pile up at taxpayer expense. Such is the case of agricultural price supports. Note that the term *surplus* in this context refers to a quantity of output, specifically the excess of what is produced over what is consumed, not to the term *social surplus* that is also used in this chapter. We will also look at minimum wage laws, which have no budgetary cost to government but nevertheless do have significant costs to both job applicants and employers.

AGRICULTURAL PRICE SUPPORTS

Although only 2 percent of the United States' labor force currently derives a living from agriculture, the political influence of agriculture has been strong enough to maintain agricultural price supports in the United States since the 1920s. These price supports have been justified on two counts. One is that they sustain the lifestyle of the family farm, an American tradition. However, the reality is that family farming has continued to decline, and a disproportionate amount of price support payments have gone to large farms and corporations. The second justification is that they ensure a plentiful supply of food for American consumers. This line of reasoning does not withstand the logic of economic analysis.

Figure 4-10 shows the effects of an agricultural price support, such as for corn or wheat. By holding price above the equilibrium, there is more farm output produced, but less consumed. The result is a surplus, as shown. Such agricultural surpluses have averaged many billion dollars' worth of foodstuffs annually in the United States. Agricultural price supports have increased in recent years, most notably with President Bush's 2002 signing of a farm bill estimated to cost taxpayers $190 billion over ten years. With the Census Bureau estimating the U.S. population to be about 287 million at the time of signing, the $190 billion cost

FIGURE 4-10

PRICE SUPPORTS Price supports cause a surplus because they prompt consumers to reduce consumption even as producers increase production. Applied to the grain market, the support price shown in this graph generates additional production at a cost that is greater than its value, causing a triangular area of deadweight loss. A second triangular area of deadweight loss results from the reduced consumption brought by the artificially higher price. Additional deadweight loss can be expected when government distributes the surplus grain it has purchased.

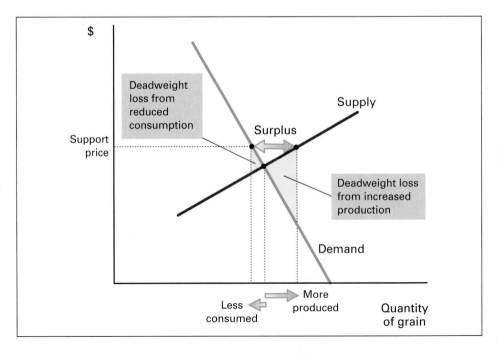

> ### QUICKCHECK
>
> **What determines the amount of the surplus when there is a price support? Will there be a surplus if the support price is set below the equilibrium price?**
>
> **Answer:** Other things equal, the higher the support price, the larger will be the surplus. There will be no surplus when the support price is at or below the equilibrium price.

of the legislation translates to an average of $662 apiece from every man, woman, and child in the United States.

The effect of agricultural price supports is to transfer money from both taxpayers and consumers to those in the agriculture industry. Maintaining a high price redistributes social surplus from consumers to producers. There is a deadweight loss associated with both increased production and decreased consumption, as shown in Figure 4-10. Additional deadweight loss can be expected to occur because government must buy and dispose of the surplus quantity, which is nearly impossible to do in an efficient manner. Government cannot merely sell the surplus to the highest bidder, because it must prevent the surplus commodities it buys from being distributed to people who would otherwise purchase that product in the marketplace. To do otherwise would merely mean more of a surplus that government would be forced to buy, because those who received from government would buy less from farmers.

One option is to give the surplus quantity away in a relatively unpalatable form, such as by turning excess milk into powdered milk. Another option is to export the surplus in a manner that does not compete with other agricultural exports. For example, foreign aid to impoverished countries might work, to the extent that the aid does not supplant other food exported from the donor country. However, recipient countries often fear becoming too dependent upon food aid based on unpredictable agricultural surpluses. The dependency arises when farmers in those countries are driven out of business by the low food prices that years of plentiful food aid brings.

There are other options. To rid itself of surplus butter, for example, Denmark offers it for a reduced price if the buyer agrees to export that butter by baking it into Danish butter cookies. Still another common practice is to store surplus commodities until they are no longer edible and then discard them. It's like the fate of leftover food in a refrigerator!

THE MINIMUM WAGE

The **minimum wage,** which is a requirement that employers pay no less than a specified wage rate, has been a cherished American tradition since the Great Depression of the 1930s. We all remember our first jobs. We each remember how hard we worked to find a job and how we deserved no less than that minimum wage for the work we did. For many, the job served as a springboard toward great success in life. Backing for the minimum wage also arises out of American compassion for the downtrodden. Americans cherish the notion that no one should be exploited. On the face of it, the minimum wage seems like a good protection against such exploitation. On closer examination, however, the case is arguable.

People support the minimum wage with the idea of reducing poverty. The minimum wage has the potential to reduce poverty by increasing the wages paid to low-skilled labor. That is also its problem. The higher wage means that more people are willing to work. These extra workers include many college and college-bound students already on the road to success. The lure of a higher minimum wage would detour some short-sighted students away from that path—in other words, the opportunity cost of following it has become greater for them.

The higher wage for low-skilled labor also means that fewer jobs are offered. Fast-food restaurants, car washes, and other businesses "make do" with fewer people, but train and

minimum wage lowest wage legally allowed to be paid to workers.

TABLE 4-5   SELECTED STUDIES ON THE EFFECTS OF THE MINIMUM WAGE

AUTHOR(S)	YEAR PUBLISHED	FINDINGS IN BRIEF
Peterson	1957	The minimum wage reduces employment.
Mincer	1976	Unemployment caused by the minimum wage is concentrated among minority teens.
Hammermesh	1982	The minimum wage reduces teenage employment.
Behrman, Sickles, and Taubman	1983	The minimum wage helps whites and hurts blacks.
Bonilla	1992	Increase in the minimum wage leads to lower incomes for single parents.
Neumark	2002	Cities with local minimum wage laws experience less poverty, but a greater number of unemployed.

Source: The first four studies and many others are referenced in *50 Years of Research on the Minimum Wage*, Joint Economic Committee, 1995.

work them harder. They also may replace some labor with capital, such as automated dishwashers and car-washing equipment. The result is that along with higher wages comes a surplus of labor—or a shortage of jobs, depending upon how you look at it. The least employable—those with poor language, computational, or social skills—are out of luck. They cannot get that first job they need to start climbing the ladder of success. They cannot join the "jobs club"—it has become too exclusive.

Table 4-5 presents the findings from just a few of the many studies conducted over the last fifty years on the effects of the minimum wage. The overwhelming majority of them conclude that whatever help it provides to some recipients, the minimum wage also causes harm among those it is intended to help.

Figure 4-11 shows how minimum wage laws increase the number of people seeking low-skilled work while decreasing the number of jobs available. For example, Tony would not have worked for the equilibrium wage. With a minimum wage, however, Tony might wind up taking Dave's job, even though Dave would have been willing to work for less. Because higher wages are offset by fewer jobs, there is no guarantee that minimum wage laws actually increase the total amount firms spend to employ low-skilled workers.

As was the case with rent controls, minimum wage requirements make it easier to discriminate. With numerous applicants for each job opening, employers can pick and choose as they wish. It would be quite difficult to prove if they choose to discriminate on an illegal basis.

There are alternatives to the minimum wage. One alternative is for a so-called *living wage* that would increase the minimum wage so high that a person could live on it, or possibly even support a family on it. A living wage would be attractive to numerous prospective job seekers, but would accentuate the problems with the minimum wage, as previously discussed.

Another alternative is to subsidize the earnings of low-income workers. Such a subsidy is already embedded in the U.S. personal income tax—the earned income tax credit. The drawback is that earnings subsidies come at a high budgetary cost, because they reduce government tax collections or involve actual cash payments. Minimum wage laws also have high costs, but these costs are borne by businesses, consumers, and those unable to find a job.

Subsidies to education also serve as an alternative to the minimum wage. Such subsidies include free public schooling or government financial assistance to students attending private schools, subsidized student loans for college students, and subsidized tuition at

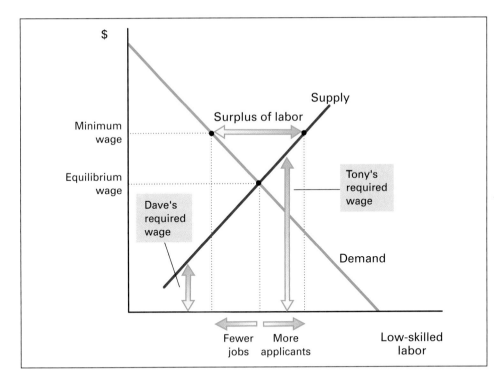

FIGURE 4-11

THE MINIMUM WAGE Minimum wage laws make it tough to find a job, especially for the least-experienced and least-skilled job seekers. The higher wage causes fewer jobs and more applicants. Some of the new applicants (such as Tony) take jobs from others who need the jobs more desperately (such as Dave).

public universities. The more widely available are educational opportunities, the more skills the workforce will acquire. The result is that the supply of low-skilled labor shifts to the left as the opportunity cost of accepting such jobs rises for workers with more human capital that can be applied elsewhere. As shown in Figure 4-12, the leftward shift in supply increases the equilibrium wage for low-skilled labor, which is the purpose of minimum wage laws. The advantage of education subsidies is that they help people develop their skills, leaving the low-skill jobs for those who need them most.

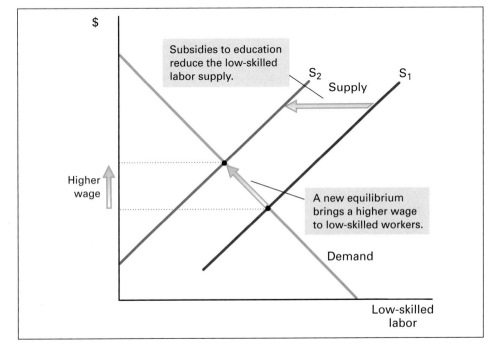

FIGURE 4-12

AN ALTERNATIVE TO THE MINIMUM WAGE Subsidies to education reduce the supply of low-skilled labor, which causes a higher equilibrium wage. Unlike the minimum wage, all workers willing to work at that higher wage will get jobs.

SNAPSHOT   HOMELESS AND WITHOUT A JOB

The homeless often carry a disturbing sign—"Will Work for Food." Although the offers are often a sham, advocates for the homeless are quick to point out that many of the homeless are indeed eager to find steady work. More often than not, however, there are no steady jobs offered to them.

Lack of a home is itself an impediment to finding a job. For example, employers may worry about the employee's personal health and hygiene, and about whether or not the employee is a drifter. For these reasons, potential employers are usually unwilling to pay the minimum wage to the homeless. There are too many other applicants with fewer problems. While employers would be willing to offer jobs at lower wages, such job offers are prohibited.

The homeless are thus caught in the grips of a political vise. Minimum wages are one side of this vise while so-called flophouses that offer cheap nightly lodging are on the other side. Many flophouses have closed down, however, because the residents could not afford rent increases that would be needed to pay the expense of renovation. The law demands such renovation to provide accessibility for the physically challenged. It also requires security from hazards such as fires, lead in pipes and paint, and asbestos. Such government policies are intended to add fairness to what is sold in the marketplace. Together with minimum wages, however, those policies block access to those markets for the very people who need it most, the homeless. ◄

4.4 AROUND THE WORLD—BLACK MARKETS AS A SAFETY VALVE

Price controls are practiced throughout the world. In Taiwan, the Statute for Salt Administration applies price controls to salt. The price of oil is also regulated in order to provide Taiwanese companies with stable prices on what is an important input in manufacturing. Venezuela lifted its price controls in 1996 as a condition for receiving foreign aid. Belarus, a country that once was part of the Soviet Union, made a similar pledge. Price support programs have been common in agriculture. Belgium and other countries of Europe have found that attempts to cut price support programs have been met with vociferous protests from farmers.

black market market in which goods are bought and sold illegally; associated with price controls.

Any time government tries to hold prices above or below market equilibrium, it provides profit opportunities to those willing to take advantage of them. **Black market** activity is said to occur when goods are bought and sold illegally. Under rent controls, for example, it is not uncommon to hear of prospective tenants bribing landlords for an apartment. Sometimes this black market may seem somewhat gray, as when the bribes are merely offers of gifts, or agreements by tenants to "fix up the place." There are also many reports of people being hired "off the books" for less than the minimum wage, especially when the unemployment rate is high.

The black market is nothing more than the free market trying to assert itself when government has attempted to influence that market through taxes or regulation. Regulation could take the form of price controls or the outright ban of market activities. In either case, it is hard to keep willing buyers and sellers from negotiating mutually beneficial illegal deals.

Governments often owe a debt of gratitude to black markets that temper destructive policies. For example, Cubans rely heavily on the black market in their country. If they had to depend upon government rations, they could not obtain enough food to survive. Similarly, the shelves were often bare in the government stores when the countries of Eastern Europe were under communism. These countries relied in large measure on the industriousness of black marketers to keep their economies going.

Recognizing the critical role played by the black market in their economy, the centrally planned former Soviet Union legalized private for-profit agricultural production on approximately 3 percent of its arable land. Despite the small acreage involved, this market-driven component of agriculture produced nearly one-third of all Soviet agricultural output.

4.5 THE PRICE OF POWER

Explore & Apply

With their governor losing a recall election and their state facing an $38 billion budget deficit by October of 2003, California voters may well have wished that their elected officials had known more about the economic consequences of the price ceilings they'd enacted a few years earlier. The fiscal disaster in 2003 was brought about in no small part by a different kind of disaster in 2001. This was no earthquake or tidal wave. Instead, California felt painful shortages of electricity, the lifeblood of modern commerce. Inadequate electric supplies prompted rolling blackouts that cut off electricity to 670,000 households and businesses for two hours at a time. In San Francisco and elsewhere across the state, traffic snarled and motorists screamed as traffic lights died, elevators ground to a halt, and computer screens abruptly turned black. The rolling blackouts were imposed without warning, so as not to alert burglars and robbers that security systems would fail. Even the technological elite of Silicon Valley were not immune, with Cisco Systems and other industry titans complaining of billions of dollars of lost commerce.

EFFECT OF ELECTRICITY DEREGULATION IN CALIFORNIA

Nature was not to blame for California's fiasco. State government was. In order to increase the efficiency with which electricity was generated and distributed at the wholesale level, California lawmakers deregulated the wholesale electricity market. Deregulation scaled back government regulations that applied to previously regulated firms, and the state's wholesale caused the state's wholesale electricity providers to compete for customers.

Competition reduces costs through weeding out inefficiencies. *Ceteris paribus,* greater efficiencies in wholesale electricity production and distribution cause the wholesale electricity supply to shift to the right and the price of electricity in the wholesale market to fall, as shown

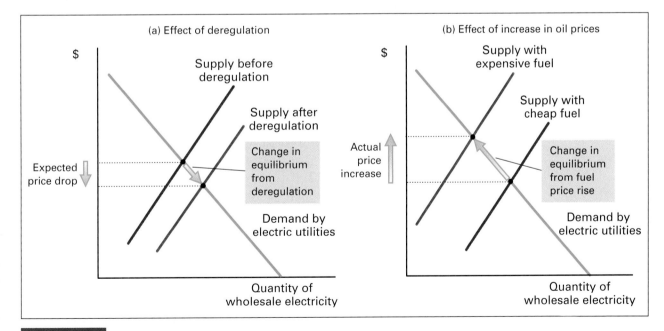

FIGURE 4-13

CALIFORNIA'S WHOLESALE ELECTRICITY MARKET Increased competition after deregulation was expected to shift supply to the right and lower electricity prices, as shown in (a). However, soaring prices of crude oil, coal, and natural gas—inputs into the production of electricity—more than offset the effects of deregulation. The result was that electricity supply in fact shifted to the left, causing the price to increase as shown in (b).

FIGURE 4-14

CALIFORNIA'S RETAIL ELECTRICITY MARKET Higher wholesale electricity prices caused the supply of retail electricity to shift to the left. Ordinarily, that would cause consumers to face a higher price of electricity. However, with retail electricity prices held down by California law, the result was a shortage as the market moved from point *A* to point *B*. The market would achieve the equilibrium shown at point *C* if controls were lifted and price allowed to rise.

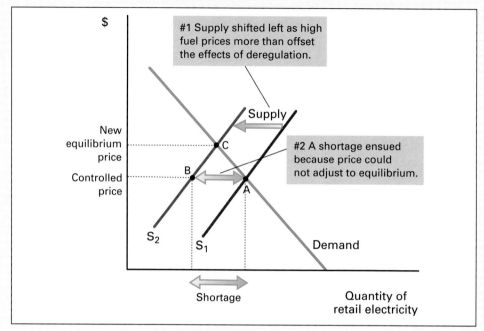

in Figure 4-13(a). Utilities pay less for the electricity they distribute and these savings are passed along to the utilities' residential and business customers. California lawmakers, therefore, felt comfortable promising California voters that their electricity rates would not go up, at least not very much, and might even go down. Making this promise was a big mistake.

In the real world many things can change at once. In particular, world crude oil prices skyrocketed, more than doubling soon after California's deregulation of wholesale electricity took effect. The prices of natural gas, coal, and other substitutes for crude oil likewise increased. Since oil and other fuels are significant inputs into the production of electricity, rising fuel prices shifted the supply of electricity at the wholesale level significantly to the left. That leftward shift more than offset any rightward shift caused by deregulation. As shown in Figure 4-13(b), the decrease in the supply of wholesale electricity caused the wholesale price of electricity to rise sharply.

Left to itself, the marketplace will not allow a shortage for long. The price of electricity at the retail level will rise in response to a shortage. In turn, consumers will consume less electricity, and producers will provide more, until an equilibrium is reached. However, because of the lawmakers' promise that consumer electricity prices would be held in check, the market was not left to itself. Rather, rates were held down to less than the market equilibrium price. The result in the retail electricity market was a shortage, as shown in Figure 4-14.

There was no incentive for the utilities to provide additional electricity because the controlled price they were allowed to charge their customers was less than what they were paying for the electricity they bought on the wholesale market. Losses among the California utilities climbed to $13 billion (as reported by SoCal Edison and Pacific Gas & Electric) and they were teetering on the brink of bankruptcy before the state fashioned a plan to keep the power on. Under the terms of that plan, California borrowed $10 billion to tide the utilities through, with California taxpayers responsible for repaying this added debt. Many additional billions were wasted in securing unneeded long-term electricity supplies that were later sold by California at a loss. All in all, the decision by California lawmakers to hold electricity rates below the market equilibrium price turned out to be a very costly proposition for the very customers they sought to protect.

The restructuring of the electricity industry toward more competition is not just a California event. About half of the states are currently active in this effort, with the transition from regulation to deregulation underway in state after state. The experience of California, one of the first to venture down this path, should remind other states to take care in how they mix regulation and deregulation. Among the states that have deregulated electricity without the problems experienced by California are Texas and Pennsylvania, in which consumers are estimated to have saved $5 billion from successful deregulation. The lesson from California is that, tempting as they may sound politically, the fundamental economics should not be ignored: price ceilings cause shortages.

1. **Californians wound up paying a high "price" because the state held down the price of electricity. Explain.**

2. **California's tough environmental regulations were a factor in preventing the construction of new power plants in California in the 1990s. The result is that California wound up importing more of its power from elsewhere. Explain how that decision might or might not have been efficient. If the tough regulations were inefficient, why would California have imposed them?**

Visit **www.prenhall.com/ayers** for updates and web exercises on this Explore & Apply topic.

SUMMARY AND LEARNING OBJECTIVES

1. **Interpret how demand represents marginal benefit and supply represents marginal cost.**
   - Marginal benefit equals the incremental value associated with the consumption of additional units of a good. The marginal benefit of any unit of a good is measured by how much consumers are willing to pay for it, as shown by their demand curves. The demand curve slopes downward, indicating the marginal benefit of additional consumption decreases.
   - Marginal cost equals the incremental cost associated with producing additional units of a good. The marginal cost is equivalent to the price required to induce a producer to supply a particular quantity. The supply curve slopes upward, depicting the increase in marginal cost that occurs as more units of output are produced.

2. **Explain the concept of social surplus and how it is divided between consumers and producers.**
   - Social surplus is the sum of consumer surplus and producer surplus.
   - Consumer surplus is the difference between the market price and the price that consumers are willing to pay. The total amount of consumer surplus is shown as a triangular area bounded by the market price and the demand curve.
   - Producer surplus is the difference between the market price and the price that producers would be willing to receive in order to sell their goods. Producer surplus is represented by the triangular area bounded by the market price and the supply curve.
   - Because social surplus is the sum of consumer and producer surplus, social surplus is also represented

by a triangular area. This area is bounded by the demand curve and the supply curve.
   - A price that deviates from the equilibrium price will create a deadweight loss, which represents the loss of social surplus.
   - The paradox of diamonds and water is that the price of water, a necessity, is less than the price of diamonds. The paradox is resolved by recognizing that price reveals only marginal benefit. The consumer surplus from water is higher than from diamonds.

3. **Demonstrate how both exports and imports increase efficiency while simultaneously harming either consumers or producers.**
   - Exports occur when a country's domestic price of a good is below the world price of that good.
   - Imports occur when a country's domestic price of a good is above the world price of the good.
   - When a country opens its doors to trade, its domestic prices are replaced by world prices for traded goods.
   - Imports increase a country's social surplus. The bulk of the increase goes to consumers since consumer surplus increases with the consumption of imports, but producer surplus shrinks because of cuts in domestic production.
   - Exports also increase a country's social surplus. The bulk of the increase goes to producers since producer surplus increases with the production of more goods for export. Consumer surplus shrinks because production that is exported cannot be consumed by domestic consumers.

4. **Identify inefficiencies associated with price ceilings.**

- For the sake of equity, government often seeks to change free-market prices. Unfortunately, because price signals are basic to how markets operate, changing these signals sacrifices market efficiency.

- Anti-gouging laws are examples of price ceilings. Price ceilings hold price below the market equilibrium, resulting in shortages. Market quantity will be less than the equilibrium quantity, which is also the efficient quantity. The lower the price ceiling is set by government, the greater the shortage that results.

- Rent controls are an example of a price ceiling. A number of cities around the world have enacted rent control legislation, although a number of these laws have been repealed in the United States recently. When rent controls are present, the incentive to provide new rental housing is reduced.

- Housing vouchers are an alternative to rent controls. Housing vouchers avoid the shortages created by rent controls, but require that government set aside money for the vouchers.

5. **Show why price supports are unnecessary and potentially counterproductive.**

- When a price is kept higher than the market equilibrium price because of a government price floor, also called a price support, the result is a surplus in which production rises and consumption falls. The higher the price floor, the greater the surplus.

- Black markets are a response to price ceilings. Black markets are illegal, but arise anyway when price ceilings are present. Goods are sold in black markets at or above their market equilibrium prices.

- Minimum wage laws are another example of price floors. Minimum wages that are set above the market equilibrium wage decrease the quantity demanded of labor while increasing the quantity supplied of labor. The result is that minimum wage laws create unemployment.

- Educational subsidies provide many of the same benefits as the minimum wage. Educational opportunities reduce the ranks of low-skilled workers by shifting the supply of low-skilled labor to the left. The shift in supply increases the wages of the remaining low-skilled workers. In this way educational subsidies increase the wages of low-skilled workers without creating unemployment.

- When surpluses or shortages are present because of price ceilings and supports, markets are not efficient.

 6. **Pinpoint the economic flaw in California's deregulation of electricity.**

- The flaw involved price ceilings. Rising fuel prices increased the wholesale price of electricity just as California was deregulating the market for wholesale electricity. Rather than being allowed to pass on their price increases, electric utilities serving consumers were forced to hold rates down because of government imposed price controls. The result was shortages of electricity and accompanying power outages.

KEY TERMS

TEST YOURSELF

TRUE OR FALSE

1. Consumer surplus is greater for diamonds than for water.
2. For an economy to be efficient, it must eliminate producer surplus.
3. A price ceiling set below the market equilibrium price results in a shortage.
4. Rent controls provide a good way to fight discrimination in housing.
5. Consumers in the United States have more food on their tables than they would without agricultural price supports.

MULTIPLE CHOICE

6. If Yvette would be willing to pay up to $10 for one gizmo, up to $8 for a second, and up to $6 for a third, and the price of gizmos is $6 apiece, then Yvette's consumer surplus totals
    a. $24.
    b. $18.
    c. $6.
    d. $4.

7. Efficiency requires that
    a. total consumer surplus equal zero.
    b. market prices be fair.
    c. marginal social benefit equal marginal social cost.
    d. people buy low and sell high.

8. The benefits of price ceilings are received by
    a. consumers able to buy the product.
    b. producers able to sell the product.
    c. all consumers.
    d. all producers.

9. If the government places a price ceiling of $1.20 on a good with an equilibrium price of $1.00, then
    a. there will be a shortage of the good.
    b. there will be a surplus of the good.
    c. neither a surplus nor a shortage will occur.
    d. if demand for the good decreases, the government will not let the price go below $1.00.

10. Over time, rent controls that remain in place lead to
    a. increased renovation of old apartments.
    b. a greater ability for tenants to move to the best apartment for their needs.
    c. increasingly severe housing shortages.
    d. rents that are higher than they would be if the controls were to be removed.

11. Housing vouchers offer an alternative to rent controls by
    a. ensuring that landlords keep their word to keep rents low.
    b. giving prospective tenants the ability to pay higher rents.
    c. setting up detailed standards landlords must adhere to in order to qualify for permits to offer rental units.
    d. constructing new, low-rent public housing on government-owned land.

12. Anti-gouging laws that keep prices of essentials low in times of emergency are likely to
    a. be efficient.
    b. lead to surpluses.
    c. lead to shortages.
    d. distribute the available goods fairly.

13. Ticket scalping is most likely to be
    a. neither efficient nor equitable.
    b. equitable, but not efficient unless on-line auctioning is banned.
    c. efficient, but of questionable equity.
    d. both efficient and equitable, but very unfair.

14. Of the following, the best example of a black market is
    a. the sale of secondhand furniture at a used-furniture shop.
    b. a mail-order purchase of a computer.
    c. renting an apartment for more than the rent-controlled price.
    d. discriminating against minority applicants for a job opening.

15. A price floor placed on a good is a _____ that will normally result in a _____.
    a. maximum price; shortage
    b. maximum price; surplus
    c. minimum price; shortage
    d. minimum price; surplus

16. Compared to a free-market equilibrium, agricultural price supports have the effect of
    a. increasing both the quantities supplied and demanded.
    b. decreasing both the quantities supplied and demanded.
    c. increasing the quantity supplied and decreasing the quantity demanded.
    d. decreasing the quantity supplied and increasing the quantity demanded.

17. Which of the following is NOT a way that governments dispose of agricultural surpluses?
    a. Let the surpluses rot in storage.
    b. Sell the surpluses to purchasers in the marketplace, without restrictions on the use or resale of the commodities involved.
    c. Give the surpluses away in an unappealing form to the poor.
    d. Give the surpluses to needy countries that are unable to afford enough food.

18. If the minimum wage is set below the equilibrium market wage, the effect will be
    a. a surplus of labor.
    b. neither a surplus nor a shortage of labor.
    c. unemployment of labor.
    d. higher wages.

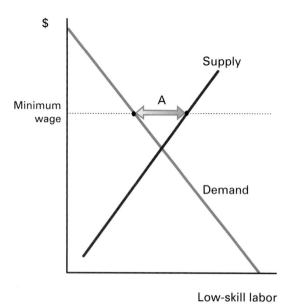

SELF-TEST FIGURE 4-1

19. In Self-Test Figure 4-1, the two-headed arrow labeled *A* represents the
    a. surplus of labor caused by the minimum wage.
    b. shortage of labor caused by the minimum wage.
    c. inefficiency of the minimum wage.
    d. efficiency of the minimum wage.
20. Minimum wage laws would most likely DECREASE
    a. the number of homeless people without jobs.
    b. opportunities for the least employable to gain job experience.
    c. discrimination in the job market.
    d. wages paid for low-skilled labor.
21. The reason California suffered from a shortage of electricity in 2001 is fundamentally because of
    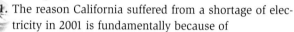
    a. insufficient regulation by the state.
    b. too many people.
    c. antiquated power lines.
    d. price controls on retail electricity.

QUESTIONS AND PROBLEMS

1. *[consumer surplus]* Compute consumer surplus in the market for pails of water, described in Figure 3-9.
2. *[consumer surplus]* Of all the purchases you have made in the last three months, which one has given you the largest amount of consumer surplus? State the amount of consumer surplus by subtracting what you paid for the item from the amount you would have been willing to pay.
3. *[social surplus]* Using a supply and demand graph, illustrate the area of social surplus. Explain how the area of social surplus can be broken down into two parts, the areas of consumer and producer surplus.
4. *[efficient output]* Is the efficient output equal to the equilibrium output? Explain.
5. *[diamonds and water]* Why is water so much cheaper than diamonds, when water is so much more important to human life?
6. *[imports and exports]* When the world price of a good is less than what a country's price would be without trade, will the country import or export the good? Will the country produce any of the good itself? Will it gain from trade? Explain, using a graph as part of your explanation.
7. *[imports and exports]* When the world price of a good is more than what a country's price would be without trade, will the country import or export the good? Will the country produce any of the good itself? Will it gain from trade? Explain, using a graph as part of your explanation.

8. *[price ceiling]* For a ceiling price to have any effect in a competitive market, must it be set above or below the equilibrium price? Explain by drawing two graphs. The first graph should show the ceiling price above the equilibrium price; the second graph should show the ceiling price below the equilibrium price. Each graph should be accompanied by an explanation noting the effects of the price ceiling in that graph.
9. *[efficient quantity; price ceiling]* Using the data provided in the accompanying table, fill in the last column and then provide answers to the following questions.

Price	Quantity Demanded	Quantity Supplied	Surplus (+) or Shortage (−)
$12	7	9	
11	8	8	
10	9	7	
9	10	6	
8	11	5	
7	12	4	

a. What is the efficient quantity?
b. What price results in the efficient quantity?
c. Suppose a price ceiling of $8 is established. Does a surplus or shortage result? What is the amount of the surplus or shortage?
d. Suppose a price ceiling of $7 is established. Describe its effect.

e. Suppose a price ceiling of $11 is established. What is its effect?

f. Suppose a price ceiling of $12 is established. Why does it have no effect?

10. *[efficiency versus equity]* Comment on the efficiency and equity aspects of ticket scalping.

11. *[price ceilings]* Do price ceilings increase or decrease social surplus? Explain.

12. *[rent controls]* Rent controls lower rents for those lucky enough to have apartments. However, there are several problems. List three inefficiencies of rent control.

13. *[price floors]* For a price floor to have any effect in a competitive market, must it be set above or below the equilibrium price? Explain by drawing two graphs. The first graph should show the price support above the equilibrium price; the second graph should show the price support below the equilibrium price. Each graph should be accompanied by an explanation noting the effects of the price support in that graph.

14. *[price floors]* Do price floors increase or decrease consumer surplus? Explain.

15. *[price floor]* Using the data in question #9, what would be the effect of a price floor set at a price of $8? What would be the effect of a price floor set at a price of $11? What would be the effect of a price floor set at a price of $12? Since the goal of a price floor is to increase the income of producers, which price(s) in the data table would logically be chosen as a floor price?

16. *[minimum wage]* Is the minimum wage law an example of a price ceiling or a price floor? Explain.

17. *[minimum wage]* Minimum wage laws are an American tradition. Although the laws seem caring and do raise wages for minimum wage labor, there are many problems. List five problems caused by minimum wage laws and briefly indicate why each occurs. Why are minimum wage laws so popular?

18. *[black markets]* What is a black market? Explain why black markets might arise as a consequence of price controls, but not as a consequence of price supports. What function do black markets perform? Are black markets legal?

WORKING WITH GRAPHS AND DATA

1. *[demand and supply]* Draw demand and supply curves that indicate the following situations:
   a. Consumer surplus is equivalent to producer surplus.
   b. Consumer surplus > producer surplus.
   c. Consumer surplus < producer surplus.
   d. Consumer surplus = 0.
   e. Producer surplus = 0.

2. *[demand and supply]* The tables following depict Monty's demand and value from purchasing sleeves of unique golf balls from a manufacturer and the manufacturer's supply curve of these sleeves of unique golf balls and their cost of production. (A sleeve of golf balls is three balls.)

Quantity Demanded (Sleeves)	Monty's Perceived Value
1	$20
2	16
3	12
4	8
5	4

Quantity Supplied (Sleeves)	Manufacturer's Cost of a Sleeve
1	$2
2	4
3	6
4	8
5	10

a. Draw the demand and supply curves for sleeves of these unique golf balls.

b. Identify the equilibrium price and quantity for Monty.

c. Identify the area of Monty's consumer surplus on the graph.

d. How much consumer surplus does Monty obtain?

e. Identify the producer surplus of the manufacturer on the graph.

f. How much producer surplus does the firm receive?

g. How much social surplus does this market create?

3. *[demand and supply; consumer and producer surplus]*
   The tables below indicate the domestic markets for rice
   in Japan and Thailand, respectively.

JAPANESE DOMESTIC RICE MARKET

Price/lb	Quantity Demanded (Thousands of lbs)	Quantity Supplied (Thousands of lbs)
$5	210	300
4	250	250
3	270	220
2	300	120
1	390	15
0	500	0

THAI DOMESTIC RICE MARKET

Price/lb	Quantity Demanded (Thousands of lbs)	Quantity Supplied (Thousands of lbs)
$5	40	225
4	75	175
3	100	150
2	120	120
1	160	80
0	200	0

a. Draw the demand and supply curves depicting the
   Japanese domestic rice market.
b. What is the domestic equilibrium price and quantity
   of rice in Japan?
c. Identify the areas of consumer and producer surplus
   on the graph in the Japanese domestic rice market.
d. Draw the demand and supply curves depicting the
   Thai domestic rice market.
e. What is the domestic equilibrium price and quantity
   of rice in Thailand?

f. Identify the areas of consumer and producer surplus
   on the graph in the Thai domestic rice market.
g. Suppose that the world price of rice were $3 per
   pound. Indicate the trading pattern that would take
   place between Thailand and Japan at this price.
h. Draw the Japanese domestic market for rice if the
   price were now $3 per pound.
i. Indicate how the trading pattern impacts Japanese
   social surplus.
j. Draw the Thai domestic market for rice if the price
   were now $3 per pound.
k. Indicate how the trading pattern impacts Thai social
   surplus.

4. *[minimum wage]* The table below presents the data
   from a local labor market.

Wage per Hour	Quantity Demanded of Workers	Quantity Supplied of Workers
$10	100	10
12	90	30
14	80	50
16	70	70
18	60	90
20	50	110

a. Draw the demand and supply of labor using the
   table above.
b. Identify the equilibrium wage and number of workers hired.
c. Identify the wages that could be used as an effective
   minimum wage.
d. Choose one of the hourly wages prices that could be
   used as an effective minimum wage and depict it on
   the graph.
e. What effects are caused by the application of an
   effective minimum wage?

Visit **www.prenhall.com/ayers** for Exploring the Web exercises and additional self-test quizzes.

CHAPTER 5

MEASURING NATIONAL OUTPUT

A LOOK AHEAD

If we as a society are to achieve our macroeconomic goals, we need ways of measuring our successes and failures. Government collects and makes available to anyone who is interested a vast amount of statistical information about our economy. This chapter starts with the measurement of the nation's aggregate output. Statistics on aggregate output provide a revealing glimpse of the health of the whole economy.

Accurate statistics can help paint a clear picture of the economy—where it's been, where it's at now, and where it's going. Statistics on the aggregate economy also guide decision makers in government as they allocate funds to education, defense, healthcare, and other government programs. It turns out that the data used by Congress are often contentious, since Congress needs to make policy decisions based on projections of future data. The Explore & Apply section at the end of this chapter discusses how Congress wrestles with this issue.

LEARNING OBJECTIVES

Understanding Chapter 5 will enable you to:
1. **Present three widely accepted goals for the economy.**
2. **Define gross domestic product (GDP), discuss its components, and the ways in which it can be measured.**
3. **Distinguish real GDP from nominal GDP.**
4. **Track the stages of the business cycle.**
5. **Identify the advantages and disadvantages of static and dynamic scoring.**

Explore & Apply

Macroeconomics deals with the economy as a whole. The millions of individual microeconomic decisions of people, businesses, and government in their totality represent the nation's economy. Everyone thus influences the economy at least a little bit, and the performance of the economy likewise affects everyone.

5.1 MACROECONOMIC GOALS

Economic growth, full employment, and low inflation are the three primary goals of macro policy. Economic growth occurs when the economy's total output of goods and services increases. Higher living standards are a by-product of economic growth. In effect, growth enlarges the economic pie, allowing many people bigger slices. Table 5-1 shows a handful of the many ways in which the United States standard of living has improved. Economic growth in the United States has promoted changes in our living standards that range from greater computer ownership to greater life expectancy. Because the wealth of our nation increases as a consequence of economic growth, more of us are able to own our homes, go to college, and access the Internet.

An economy grows because of increases in available resources and improvements in technology. Economists usually believe that the economy can sustain a long-term growth rate of about 2.5 percent per year. Strong economic growth in the late 1990s offered hope that the U.S. economy is capable of growing faster than previously believed possible. Because of that strong growth, some optimists argue that a sustained growth rate of as much as 5 percent is possible. Over the long run, differences in the economy's growth rate can make a large difference in living standards. It would take about 29 years for aggregate output to double at a 2.5 percent growth rate, but only half that time in the more optimistic case of 5 percent annual growth.

Doubling times, such as that for aggregate output, can be estimated using the *rule of seventy-two.* Whatever the percentage growth rate of a variable is, dividing that number into 72 will reveal the approximate doubling time. For example, a 5 percent growth rate means that output doubles about every 14.4 years, because 72/5 equals 14.4.

In reality, economic growth does not occur smoothly. The economy surges and stumbles at periodic intervals. These ups and downs in the growth of output sometimes put the economy above, and other times below, its long-run sustainable growth rate.

High employment is a major goal of public policy. When economic growth falls short, unemployment is usually the result. Concerns over unemployment motivate economists to develop macro models designed to help us better understand its causes and identify policies to achieve full employment. In subsequent chapters you will study some of these models.

Inflation **is a sustained rise in the general price level.** Inflation is usually expressed in terms of the *inflation rate,* the annual percentage increase in the general level of prices. Policymakers in government seek to preserve the value of money by keeping the inflation rate low. In practice, the economy has experienced some inflation every year since 1955. Annual inflation reached a peak of 13.5 percent in 1980 before declining sharply after that. By 2003, the inflation rate had fallen to slightly more than 2 percent. When the inflation rate is low and stable, history shows that public concern over inflation subsides. However, even a seemingly low inflation rate, such as 3 percent, would cause the price level to double in about 24 years. If inflation were to reach 10 percent today, and stay at that rate permanently, it would take a little more than 7 years for the price level to double. Seven more years after that, the price level would have doubled again, and so forth. Such behavior of the price level explains why increases in the inflation rate merit concern, especially for people living on fixed incomes.

In addition to the three primary goals, policymakers may have additional goals for the economy. For example, equity in the distribution of the nation's income may be a concern. Keeping interest rates low in order to make borrowing affordable for consumers and businesses is sometimes brought up as a goal. The foreign exchange value of the dollar is

TABLE 5-1	EFFECTS OF GROWTH: SELECTED CHANGES IN THE U.S. STANDARD OF LIVING

INDICATOR, YEARS COMPARED, AND INDICATOR VALUES

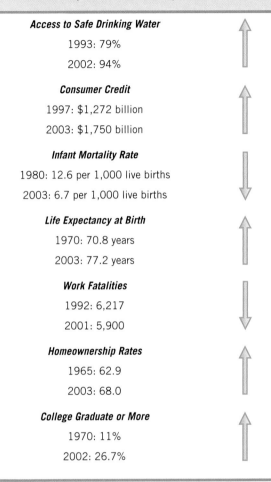

Access to Safe Drinking Water

1993: 79%

2002: 94%

Consumer Credit

1997: $1,272 billion

2003: $1,750 billion

Infant Mortality Rate

1980: 12.6 per 1,000 live births

2003: 6.7 per 1,000 live births

Life Expectancy at Birth

1970: 70.8 years

2003: 77.2 years

Work Fatalities

1992: 6,217

2001: 5,900

Homeownership Rates

1965: 62.9

2003: 68.0

College Graduate or More

1970: 11%

2002: 26.7%

Sources: Various publications of U.S. government agencies, including the *Statistical Abstract of the United States.*

another. Stability in the banking industry, and in financial markets, such as the stock and bond markets, also receives attention from policymakers. The achievement of the three primary goals will often contribute to the achievement of other goals.

5.2 MEASURING NATIONAL OUTPUT

From the earliest days of American history, the government has kept statistical records. As the economy has grown larger and more complex, the importance of keeping track of the economy has increased. Policymakers rely on government data to design policies that will improve economic performance and help achieve the macro goals of economic growth, full employment, and low inflation.

The value of goods and services produced is the single most important measure of the nation's output. According to the circular flow of income, the value of national output must be identical to the value of national income. This equality occurs because every dollar that buyers spend on output represents income to the sellers of that output as depicted in the circular flow model shown in Chapter 2.

The economy's output of goods and services is diverse, running the gamut from A to Z, including the proverbial kitchen sink. One way to measure output is to classify the goods and services produced according to who is purchasing the output. To this end, purchases are classified by dividing the economy into four sectors, each identified with a different type of purchaser. These are the household, business, government, and foreign sectors. Each unit of output eventually finds its way to one of these sectors. The output is valued at *market value*, which is measured by market prices (the prices paid by the purchasers). Apples, oranges, the kitchen sink, and all other goods and services are valued by the common dollar-denominated yardstick of market prices.

gross domestic product (GDP)
the market value of the final goods and services produced in the economy within some time period, usually one quarter or one year.

Output is measured by tallying the market value of *final goods and services*—those that are sold to their final owners. The most widely reported measure of the economy's output is **gross domestic product (GDP),** the market value of the final goods and services produced in the economy within some time period, usually one quarter or one year. Spending on *intermediate goods*—goods used to make other goods—is not included in GDP so as to avoid counting the same output twice. For instance, a new Ford Focus purchased by a consumer includes a new battery and tires as standard equipment. Since the total value of the Focus includes the value of these and other input components, the values of the new Focus and its inputs should not be counted separately. While the value of the Focus is included in GDP, the values of the battery, tires, and other intermediate goods are not included in GDP. On the other hand, replacement batteries and tires are counted because they are purchased by their final users. For this reason, GDP includes expenditures by car owners who replace their old tires and batteries with new ones from Sears, Wal-Mart, AutoZone, and other retailers.

In order to track spending in different parts of the economy, GDP is measured as the sum of spending on output by households, businesses, government, and the rest of the world. Thus, we turn our attention now to consumption spending, investment, government purchases, and the effect of foreign commerce on GDP. This way of looking at GDP is termed the **expenditure approach.**

expenditure approach method of computing GDP that sums consumption, gross investment, government purchases, and net exports.

THE EXPENDITURE APPROACH TO GDP

The expenditure approach to computing GDP is based on the idea that the sum of all the spending that occurs in purchasing the nation's output will equal the value of its production. GDP is thus measured as the sum of spending on output by U.S. households, businesses, government, and the rest of the world. When the expenditure approach is taken, the following equation holds true:

$$GDP = C + I + G + NX$$

where

- C = consumption spending by households
- I = gross investment by the private sector
- G = government consumption and investment spending on goods and services
- NX = net exports

We now turn our attention to how each of these four types of expenditures affects GDP.

CONSUMPTION

consumption spending
purchasing by households; makes up the majority of GDP spending.

Purchasing by households comprises **consumption spending.** Household spending makes up the majority of spending in the U.S. economy, generally close to 70 percent of total spending. This spending may be on services or on consumer durable or nondurable goods. Nondurable goods are consumed quickly, by definition in one year or less. Food is an example. Durable goods have an expected life span of more than one year, such as automobiles. Note that the purchases of new houses by consumers are included in investment spending, as explained below.

INVESTMENT

Investment—spending now in order to increase output or productivity later—is the most variable component of GDP over time. Although there are many forms of investment, such as a college student's investment in the human capital provided by an education, GDP statistics record only three measurable types:

- Purchases by firms of **capital,** such as new factories and machines.
- Consumers' purchases of **new housing,** a form of consumer capital.
- The market value of the **change in business inventories** of unsold goods.

investment spending now in order to increase output or productivity later; includes spending on capital, new housing, and changes in business inventories.

Purchases of capital allow firms the opportunity to increase their future outputs of goods and services. As such, a pickup truck purchased by a firm is counted as an investment. If that same truck had been purchased by you for your personal use, it would have been included in consumption. New homes are included under investment because they provide an ongoing stream of housing services over many years. In that sense the purchase of a new house is an investment.

To see why the change in business inventories is included as an investment, consider an increase in inventories. Inventories increase when firms deliberately produce more than they can immediately sell. Inventories also increase when demand falls short of firms' estimates, as when the economy slows down. Inventory investment is different from investment in capital in that an increase in inventories may be unintended. Nonetheless, accumulations of inventory represent investment because they allow for increased sales in the future. When goods in inventory are sold, inventory investment shows a decrease and other spending an equivalent increase.

Investment may be measured as either gross or net. **Gross investment** is the total amount of investment that takes place. Gross investment by private sector firms, *gross private domestic investment,* is the measure of investment used to compute GDP. It usually amounts to between 15 and 18 percent of GDP. **Net investment** is gross investment minus depreciation. Because plants and machines wear out or become technologically obsolete, net investment will be less than gross investment. A positive value for net investment measures the increase in the economy's productive capacity. A negative value for net investment means that depreciation exceeded the total amount of investment, which implies that the productive capacity of the economy declines. When the focus is on net investment, **net domestic product (NDP)** is a more appropriate measure than GDP. NDP equals GDP minus depreciation.

gross investment the total amount of investment.

net investment gross investment minus depreciation.

net domestic product (NDP) gross domestic product minus depreciation.

ARE DISASTERS GOOD FOR THE ECONOMY?   *SNAPSHOT*

Hurricanes, floods, and earthquakes are good for the economy, right? After all, they force people to spend more, which increases output. Isn't an increase in output a reason to rejoice?

Clearly, something is amiss with this reasoning. What is the key to understanding this faulty logic? Spending on additions to our stock of goods and services increases living standards. However, spending that follows natural disasters merely replaces goods in order to bring living standards back to some semblance of their former levels. ◀

GOVERNMENT PURCHASES

Governments at the federal, state, and local levels accounted for about 19 percent of the total purchasing of goods and services in the U.S. economy in 2003. Although estimates are imprecise, perhaps one-tenth of government purchasing could be classified as investment.

> ## QUICKCHECK
>
> **What would a value of net investment equal to zero say about the economy's ability to produce goods and services?**
>
> **Answer:** Net investment equal to zero implies that the economy's productive capacity did not grow. The investment that occurred merely replaced depreciated capital. For example, if 100 machines wore out during the year, net investment equal to zero means that the 100 machines were replaced, and the total number of working machines remained constant.

Examples of government investment include new highways and other infrastructure, such as government-owned buildings, including schools, offices, and airports. Government also pays for social services provided by teachers, social workers, parole officers, and others. These are civilian goods and services. Defense goods, such as tanks, missiles, and the services of military personnel, are also purchased.

Government *transfer payments,* such as Social Security and unemployment benefits, are received by individuals who do not provide goods and services in return. **Government purchases and investment should be distinguished from government transfer payments. The latter are not included in the computation of GDP.** In Figure 5-1, transfer payments are contrasted to government expenditures that count toward GDP. The figure shows that transfer payments have become increasingly important over time. To the extent that transfer payments are used by the households that receive them to buy goods and services, they are counted as consumption spending. Through this backdoor route, the dollars received as transfers do ultimately contribute to GDP.

NET EXPORTS

Some of the output produced by the economy is purchased by foreigners in the form of exports. Exports should be included when GDP is computed because they represent goods and services produced. However, consideration of the role of foreign commerce on GDP must not stop there. Because a portion of spending by U.S. consumers, businesses, and government is on imports, it is necessary to subtract imports from exports in order to compute GDP. In other words, a part of consumption spending, investment, and govern-

> ## QUICKCHECK
>
> **Are each of the following included in computing U.S. GDP?**
> 1. **New Corvettes built in Bowling Green, Kentucky?**
> 2. **New Honda Accords produced in Marysville, Ohio?**
> 3. **New Accords produced in Japan, but purchased by U.S. residents?**
> 4. **New Ford cars produced in Ford plants in Great Britain and purchased by residents of Britain?**
>
> **Answers:** (1) Yes, although the value of any imported components would be subtracted. (2) Yes, since the nameplate or ownership of the company does not matter. As in (1), the value of imported engines, transmissions, or other components are not part of U.S. GDP. (3) No. Japanese-built Accords purchased by American consumers are an import. Recall that imports are subtracted from exports in the calculation of GDP. (4) No. U.S. GDP measures U.S. production, not production by U.S. firms in other countries.

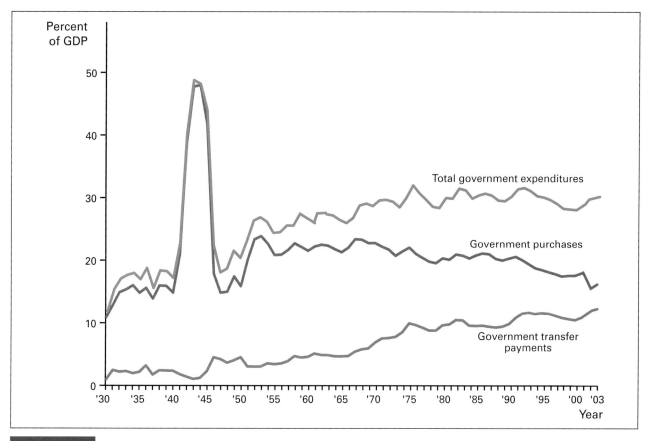

FIGURE 5-1

GOVERNMENT PURCHASES VERSUS GOVERNMENT TRANSFER PAYMENTS Government expenditures take two forms: purchases and transfer payments. When the government purchases goods and services GDP increases. However, transfer payments do not represent payments for production, and are not counted toward GDP. As a percentage of GDP, transfer payments have risen significantly over time, while government purchases are back to what they were at the start of the 1950s. The spike seen in the 1940s was caused by World War II.

Source: Computed from National Income and Products Account data.

ment purchases is on goods not produced in the United States. The value of these imports should not be counted in GDP.

  Exports minus imports defines *net exports.* It is the value of net exports that goes into GDP. A negative value for net exports means that spending on imports is greater than spending on exports; a positive figure means that spending on imports is less than spending on exports. The value of net exports varies from year to year, but has been negative for many years. For example, in 2003, exports equaled $1.03 trillion, about 9.6 percent of GDP. Imports equaled $1.52 trillion, about 14.2 percent of GDP. Net exports were thus equal to −$0.49 trillion, about −4.6 percent of GDP.

net exports exports minus imports.

THE EXPENDITURE APPROACH AND THE CIRCULAR FLOW OF ECONOMIC ACTIVITY

In Chapter 2 you saw a simple model of the circular flow of economic activity. In the simple model, goods and services were purchased in the output market by households and by government. Households earned the money to make purchases by exchanging resources for

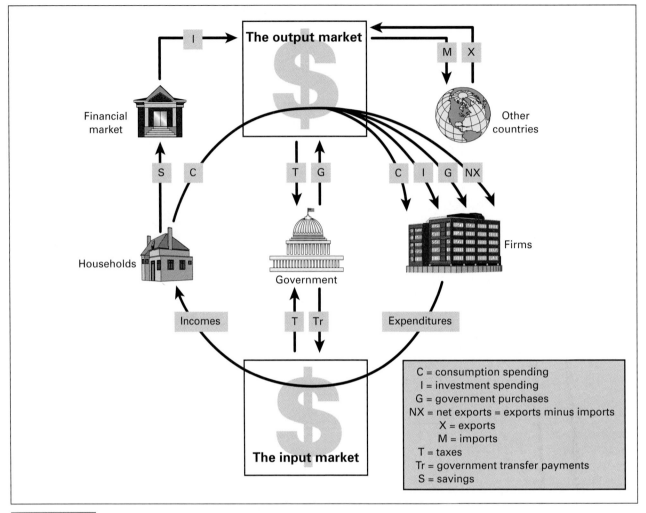

THE CIRCULAR FLOW AND EXPENDITURES Economic activity arises from four sources: households, businesses, government, and other countries. Spending on the country's total output, and hence its GDP, is
represented by the equation: GDP = C + I + G + NX. In the equation C is the symbol for consumption spending by households, I represents investment spending, G is government purchases, and NX is
net exports. Investment spending requires that saving (S) takes place. The financial market exists to
convert savings into investment. This process involves banks using savings deposits to make loans to
investors. The government affects the circular flow through its purchases (G), and also through taxation
(T) and transfer payments (Tr). Taxes flow to government from the output and input markets.
Government purchases allow the government to acquire goods and services, while transfer payments
(Tr) join with expenditures by businesses on inputs to go to households as income.

incomes in the input market. Figure 5-2 expands on the simple circular flow model to show
the categories of expenditures.

Let's start with households. Incomes are received by households, represented by the
arrow in the lower left quadrant pointing toward households. Incomes are either spent on
consumption (C) or saved (S). Consumption spending involves a flow of money to the output market. Saving flows from households to the *financial market,* where *financial intermediaries* such as banks function to turn savings into investment spending (I). Banks take savings deposits and lend those funds to businesses that need to borrow money to finance new
factories, equipment, and other business investments.

Government consumption purchases and investment (G) are represented by the arrow leading from government to the output market. Other countries, shown in the figure as the rest of the world, spend to buy U.S. exports (X); thus, the arrow is pointing from the rest of the world to the output market. U.S. consumers buy imports (M) from the rest of the world, which is indicated by the arrow leading from the output market to the rest of the world.

The spending by consumers, investors, government, and the rest of the world converge in the output market as goods and services are sold. These four kinds of spending are shown in the upper right quadrant of the diagram as C, I, G, and NX, where NX stands for net exports (the value of exports minus the value of imports).

Other flows are significant in the circular flow. The government collects taxes (T) from the sale of output in the form of sales taxes. This is represented by the arrow from the output market to the government. The government also collects income taxes, which are taxes on the earnings of labor inputs. This flow is symbolized by the arrow from the input market toward government. Government also provides transfer payments (Tr), such as Social Security and welfare payments, which are received as income.

The flow of spending from firms that goes through the input market is labeled as expenditures. This spending is done by firms in order to acquire the inputs needed for production to occur. These expenditures are received as incomes, so labeled in the diagram, by households. The single arrow labeled incomes in Figure 5-2 could be split into several parts, since income takes different forms. We now turn our attention to the income approach to measuring GDP, where you will learn about several kinds of income.

THE INCOME APPROACH TO GDP

The **income approach** to measuring GDP is based on the logic of the circular flow model, which shows that the production of goods and services provides income for those involved in that production. For example, workers receive wages, the proprietors (owners) of businesses receive income from operating their businesses, landlords receive rents, corporations earn profits, and savers earn interest income. All of these incomes are created when the economy produces output. Let's take a look at each of the incomes in turn.

income approach method of computing GDP that sums various forms of income.

COMPENSATION OF EMPLOYEES Wages and salaries paid by businesses and government, and received by workers, are included in the compensation of employees. This income category also includes the value of fringe benefits such as paid vacation and health insurance.

PROPRIETOR'S INCOME Businesses owned by individuals alone, or with partners, earn for their owners what is called *proprietor's income.* Examples of proprietor's income include the earnings of individual farmers and small business owners. Doctors and lawyers who own their own practices also receive proprietor's income.

RENTAL INCOME OF PERSONS Individuals who own property that is rented or leased to others receive rental income. Mini-storage units, homes, office space, house trailers, recreational vehicles, and many other kinds of property are rented or leased in exchange for rental income.

CORPORATE PROFITS *Corporations* are businesses that are owned by their shareholders. The profits received by corporations arise from many different kinds of production. Some farms are organized as corporations, as are some medical and legal practices. Of course, the country's largest businesses, such as Wal-Mart and Exxon, are corporations, too. Whatever the size of the corporation, its profits are computed and added to the other incomes that make up GDP.

NET INTEREST People often receive interest payments, such as the interest paid by their banks on their savings accounts. Many people also make interest payments, such as for a mortgage, student loan, or car loan. *Net interest* equals the value of interest payments received minus the value of interest paid. It is net interest that is used to compute GDP using the income approach.

FOUR ADJUSTMENTS TO INCOME Four factors complicate the income approach and must be taken into account in order to compute an accurate value of GDP. These four factors are:

■ *Depreciation: Capital Consumption Allowance.* You know that the expenditure approach to GDP includes gross investment. Recall that the value of gross investment includes depreciation, which is called capital consumption allowance. Depreciation is then added to incomes to arrive at GDP when we take the incomes approach.

■ *Indirect Business Taxes.* Taxes that businesses implicitly treat as costs are called indirect business taxes. The sales and excise taxes that consumers pay are examples. Businesses collect these taxes and pass them on to the government. An indirect business tax that most people are familiar with is the gasoline tax, a tax which is included in the price that motorists pay at the pump. That portion of the price represented by the tax does not go to any of the income categories. Yet the full price paid by the purchasers of gasoline goes into the computation of GDP when we take the expenditure approach. For this reason, indirect business taxes are added to incomes to arrive at GDP.

■ *Net Income of Foreigners.* Just as the expenditure approach considers the role of foreign commerce on GDP, the income approach considers the role of incomes earned by Americans living abroad and foreigners living in the United States. Net income of foreigners is defined as the incomes earned by citizens of other countries living in the United States minus the income of Americans living in other countries. This is a logical statement when you consider that adjustment follows when foreigners living in the United States help produce our goods and services, thus increasing our GDP, while Americans living abroad contribute to the GDP of the country where they reside.

TABLE 5-2 COMPUTING 2003 GDP USING THE INCOME APPROACH

(BILLIONS OF DOLLARS)	
Incomes	
Compensation of employees	6,081.2
Proprietor's income	784.4
Rental income	126.9
Corporate profits	816.5
Net interest	703.3
Equals National Income	8,512.3
Adjustments to National Income	
Capital consumption allowance	1,421.4
Indirect business taxes	835.9
Net income of foreigners	10.2
Statistical discrepancy	−91.4
Equals GDP	$10,688.4

Source: U.S. Department of Commerce, Bureau of Economic Analysis, *The National Income and Product Accounts,* Tables 1.9 and 1.14. The value shown for indirect business taxes includes adjustments for other business items, as shown in Table 5-A2 in the Appendix. All values are for the first quarter of 2003.

- *Statistical Discrepancy.* Since the measurement of large amounts of income is subject to error, the computation of GDP using the income approach requires the inclusion of an adjustment called the statistical discrepancy. In effect, it forces the GDP numbers calculated from the income approach to equal the GDP numbers calculated from the expenditure approach.

Table 5-2 shows the computation of GDP in 2003 using the income approach. Note in the table that the sum of all incomes is called *national income.*

5.3 GROSS DOMESTIC PRODUCT—A CLOSER LOOK

As we have seen, the expenditure approach includes the four kinds of spending that, when added together, sum to GDP:

- Consumption spending
- Gross investment
- Government purchases
- Net exports

Let's show GDP as the sum of these in an equation, and then show their values in 2003, in trillions of dollars:

GDP = Consumption spending + Gross investment + Government purchases + Net exports
$10.7   + $7.51   + $1.61   + $2.05   − $0.49
          (70%)   (15%)   (19%)   (−4.6%)

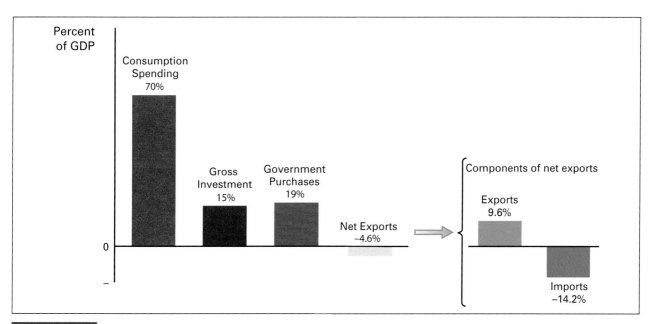

FIGURE 5-3

THE FOUR COMPONENTS OF GDP GDP equals the sum of the four categories of spending. Net exports equals the value of exports minus the value of imports. Net exports have a negative value because the value of imports outweighs the value of exports, as shown. Percentages do not add to 100 because of rounding.

Source: Bureau of Economic Analysis, *National Income and Product Account Tables,* Table 1.1.

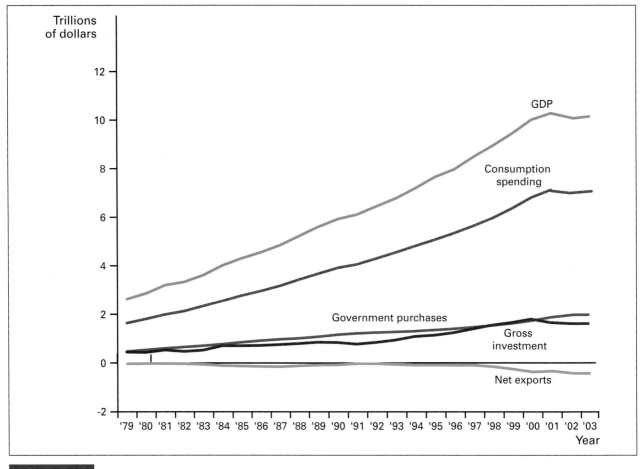

FIGURE 5-4

TRACKING GDP AND ITS COMPONENTS OVER TIME GDP is the sum of the four components shown in the figure: consumption spending, gross investment, government purchases, and net exports.

Source: 2003 Economic Report of the President, Table B-1; and Bureau of Economic Analysis, *National Income and Product Accounts Tables,* Table 1.1. Data are nominal values, meaning they have not been adjusted for price changes.

Note that net exports enters the equation with a minus sign because exports were less than imports. The percentage each item contributes to GDP is shown in parentheses. The percentages shown are rounded, which is why they do not sum to 100 percent. Figure 5-3 illustrates the components of GDP graphically. Figure 5-4 shows their behavior over time.

There are other features of GDP that should be noted. One is that only private sector investment is counted in gross investment, since government investment is counted in government's contribution to GDP. Gross investment includes U.S. investment spending by foreign citizens as well as by U.S. citizens. Thus, if a citizen of France purchases a new condominium in New York City, the transaction enters GDP through investment. However, if this same person purchases U.S.-made business machines and ships them to France, the transaction enters GDP through net exports.

Per capita GDP is GDP per person. The total U.S. GDP in 2003 is seen to be $10.7 trillion ($10,688,408,000,000—a trillion is a million millions or a one followed by twelve zeros). This number is more easily placed into perspective when divided by the U.S. population that year of about 291 million people. Performing that division, we see that per capita GDP for 2003 was

$36,729. This is the amount of output produced that each person would receive if output were divided equally among every person living in the United States, whether adult or child.

GDP AS VALUE ADDED

As an alternative to the expenditure approach, **GDP may also be viewed as the sum of values added in the economy.** Each firm takes inputs of materials and intermediate goods and increases their value through the firm's production process. **Value added** equals the revenue from the sale of output minus the cost of purchased inputs.

value added the difference between revenue and the cost of purchased inputs.

Let's examine the computation of value added by looking at the steps in the production of a single jar of dill pickles. A seed company produces cucumber seeds that are sold to a farmer. Suppose it takes 30 cents worth of seeds to grow the cucumbers in a jar of dill pickles. Assuming the seed company buys no intermediate goods, this initial step generates 30 cents of value added by the seed company. The farmer who purchases the 30 cents worth of seeds subsequently sells the resulting cucumber crop to a pickle maker for $1.00. The farmer has added value equal to 70 cents. The pickle maker sells the pickles it produces to a supermarket for $1.50, and in so doing contributes another 50 cents in value added. When the supermarket sells the pickles to shoppers for $2.25 a jar, which is the market value of a jar of pickles, an additional 75 cents is contributed toward value added.

The $2.25 market value of the jar of pickles represents the value of the production of a final good, since that is the sum of money spent by consumers who will eat the dill pickles in question. The spending of the $2.25 on each jar of pickles is spending on a final good that increases GDP by that amount. This $2.25 worth of GDP can be computed by summing the values added at each step of production:

Increase in GDP from production of a jar of pickles = $0.30 + $0.70 + $0.50 + $0.75 = $2.25

Figure 5-5 illustrates the computation of value added for this example.

CONTRASTING GDP TO GNP

Until 1992, the chief measure of the economy's output was *gross national product (GNP)*. GNP differs from GDP in that the value added to production by resources located outside the United States, but owned by U.S. citizens, is counted in GNP. Unlike GDP, GNP excludes value added within the United States by foreign-owned resources. Typically, U.S. GDP and GNP differ by less than 1 percent, so that either can be used to evaluate the performance of the economy. Table 5-3 shows the relationship between GDP and GNP, using data from

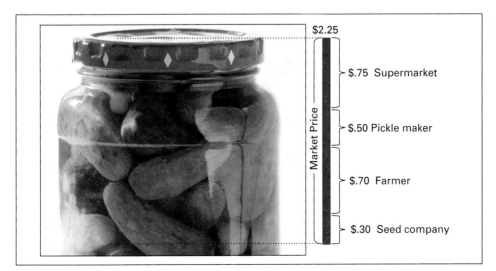

FIGURE 5-5

VALUE ADDED Value added is the firm's revenue minus the cost of the inputs it purchases from other firms. Jars of pickles sell for their market value, $2.25. Since pickles are a final good, GDP increases by $2.25 for each jar of pickles produced. Of the $2.25 in total value added, the seed company contributed 30 cents for supplying the seeds, the farmer 70 cents for growing the cucumbers, the pickle maker 50 cents for making the pickles, and the supermarket 75 cents for selling the pickles.

TABLE 5-3	ADJUSTMENTS TO GDP TO OBTAIN GNP
Gross domestic product in 2003 (billions of dollars)	$10,688.4
Plus: Income received from the rest of the world	281.3
Minus: Income payments to the rest of the world	291.5
Equals: Gross national product in 2003	10,678.2

Source: Bureau of Economic Analysis, *National Income and Product Account Tables,* Table 1.9. Data for 2003 are first quarter data stated on an annual basis.

2003. Other measures of an economy's output and the income created by the production of output are discussed in the Appendix to this chapter.

Let's consider an example where the value of production would be included in U.S. GNP, but not U.S. GDP. Holden cars and light trucks are produced in Australia by Holden, Ltd., whose parent company is U.S. auto giant General Motors. Holden's income in the form of profit represents income earned by U.S.-owned resources. Thus, Holden is an example of a firm located in another country that contributes to U.S. GNP, as recorded in the second line in Table 5-3, *Income received from the rest of the world.*

Just as U.S. firms own factories in other countries, foreign companies also own factories in the United States. Consider American Honda Motor Company, owned by Honda of Japan. A company factory in Marysville, Ohio, produces Honda Accords sold in the United States. Earnings from the production of this factory and other Honda facilities located in the United States are examples of value added that is included in U.S. GDP. This value added must be subtracted from U.S. GDP when U.S. GNP is computed, as recorded in the third line in Table 5-3, *Income payments to the rest of the world.*

INTERPRETING GDP—THE UNDERGROUND ECONOMY, HOUSEHOLD PRODUCTION, AND INTANGIBLES

underground economy market transactions that go unreported to government.

The value of many of the goods and services produced in our economy goes unreported in the GDP statistics. Market transactions that go unreported make up the **underground economy.** Some of these goods and services are illegal. For example, while a drugstore's sales of prescription medications are included in GDP, the crack cocaine sales of a drug dealer are not. The underground economy includes other goods and services that, while not illegal, are not reported to government so that their producers can avoid paying taxes. In sum, the existence of an underground economy means that GDP understates the economy's true output.

Estimates as to the size of the underground economy vary greatly, which is to be expected since the essence of that economy is that it is not reported to the government. For example, one study estimates that illegal activity alone—specifically concerning drugs, immigrant labor, and pornography—accounts for 10 percent of total economic activity in the United States (Schlosser, 2003). That study estimates that 3 million Americans grow marijuana, with 100,000 to 200,000 doing so for a living. The value of that crop, growing mostly in America's heartland, is said to exceed the value of U.S. corn production. Estimates of this sort are controversial, however, in part because they are so difficult to prove. They can only be hinted at by reference to supporting statistics, such as the observation that 724,000 people were arrested for marijuana offenses in the United States in a recent year.

The government's statisticians ignore some output deliberately, because they don't know how to place a value on it. For example, GDP does not include the value of *household production,* which is the production of goods and services for use within the household. So, if you cook your own dinner tonight, the value of that service does not appear in GDP. But if you eat out, the value does. That's because there is a market price for a restaurant meal but not for a home-cooked meal. As a result, if all married couples were to divorce and pay one another for their household services, GDP would skyrocket despite the economy not actually producing any more than it had before.

GDP is often used as a proxy for our well-being. This practice is convenient, but can also be misleading. For example, just looking at GDP, it might be hard to fathom how anyone could be nostalgic for the past. After all, GDP is up, and so is the variety of goods and services we can buy. Yet, there is more to life, including *intangibles* that cannot be measured easily. Unmeasured intangibles of value include simplicity, love, freedom, harmony, neighborliness, and many other qualities. On the downside, intangibles include pollution, loneliness, and traffic congestion.

Then there are the things that are measured, but that do not actually indicate that the people are better off. For example, increases in military spending increase GDP, but do nothing to increase a country's welfare above what it had been in the past if the spending is in response to heightened dangers in the world. Likewise, increased spending on cigarettes adds to GDP in the same way as increased spending on healthcare made necessary by previous smoking. It would be useful to have a single *measure of economic welfare* that could take into account the effects of intangibles on our overall standard of living. Although economists and social scientists have tried to develop such a measure, their efforts have failed to lead to a widely accepted alternative to GDP itself.

SHHH! WANT A ROLEX? HOW ABOUT A "HONEY DO"?

SNAPSHOT

While it is obviously difficult to measure unreported activity, estimates place the underground economy at up to 15 percent of total economic activity in the United States. Other countries see even higher percentages. As a general rule, the more burdensome a country's taxes and regulations, the larger its underground economy.

Most people think that the underground economy consists of prohibited goods and services, such as drugs and prostitution, along with stolen or counterfeit items. Yes, that Rolex watch being hawked on the street corner is probably fake or stolen. But there is much more. A significant portion of the underground economy consists of legal goods that are sold off the record in order to avoid taxes or regulatory requirements.

Examples of this type of underground activity include toxic wastes illegally dumped, workers illegally employed, goods sold without the collection of sales taxes, and services sold without required paperwork. Yes, the underground economy may even include that friendly handyman willing to take on the "honey-do-this, honey-do-that" odd jobs—no license inspected, no credit cards accepted, and no tax collected. ◄

DISTINGUISHING NOMINAL GDP FROM REAL GDP

Increases in the measured value of a nation's output, its GDP, may occur for two reasons:

- Because of an increase in the output of goods and services. The more boats, books, beans, and other goods and services the economy produces, the greater will be the value of a country's gross domestic product.
- As a consequence of price increases in the form of inflation. Inflation artificially "pumps up" the value of gross domestic product. An increase in GDP due solely to price increases does not increase economic welfare since there is no increase in output to make people better off.

In reality, when GDP rises there is usually a mix of both an increase in output and a price increase. Removing the effects of price changes from the value of GDP allows us to identify the changes in output.

Nominal GDP is the value of GDP expressed in current dollar terms. The nominal value may be thought of as "what you see is what you get." By contrast, **real GDP** adjusts the

nominal GDP GDP that is stated without adjusting for inflation.

real GDP the value of GDP after nominal GDP is adjusted for inflation.

Part 2: Monitoring the Macroeconomy

nominal value of GDP for inflation. Real GDP expresses GDP in terms of a constant value of money—dollars with the same purchasing power.

The *GDP price index,* also called the *GDP chained price index,* is an index of prices that measures price changes over time, linking each year with the next. An increase in the value of the GDP price index over time indicates that the general level of prices has increased. The GDP price index is used to compute real GDP, as follows:

$$\text{Real GDP} = \frac{\text{Nominal GDP}}{\text{GDP price index}} \times 100$$

TABLE 5-4 **U.S. NOMINAL AND REAL GROSS DOMESTIC PRODUCT, SELECTED YEARS**

SELECTED YEARS	NOMINAL GDP (IN TRILLIONS)	GDP PRICE INDEX (IN CONSTANT 1996 DOLLARS)	REAL GDP (IN TRILLIONS OF 1996 DOLLARS) [NOMINAL GDP/GDP PRICE INDEX]
1961	$0.546	22.43	$2.434
1971	1.129	30.52	3.699
1981	3.131	62.37	5.020
1987	4.742	77.58	6.112
1988	5.108	80.22	6.368
1989	5.489	83.27	6.592
1990	5.803	86.53	6.706
1991	5.986	89.66	6.676
1992	6.319	91.85	6.880
1993	6.642	94.05	7.062
1994	7.054	96.01	7.347
1995	7.401	98.10	7.543
1996	7.813	100	7.813
1997	8.318	101.95	8.160
1998	8.782	103.20	8.510
1999	9.274	104.69	8.859
2000	9.825	106.89	9.192
2001	10.082	109.42	9.215
2002	10.446	110.66	9.439
2003	10.688	111.90	9.551

Source: Adapted from *2003 Economic Report of the President,* Tables B-1 and B-3, and Bureau of Economic Analysis, *National Income and Product Accounts.* Slight variations from the values in the sources may occur because of rounding. 2003 data is annualized from the first quarter. Final 2003 data are likely to vary from stated.

Table 5-4 shows the values of U.S. nominal GDP and the GDP chained price index for selected years. These data are used to compute the values for real GDP shown in the last column. To see how the computation of real GDP works, let's pick a year, 2003 for example, and compute real GDP. Looking at the table we see that nominal GDP in that year equaled $10.688 trillion. The GDP chained index equaled 111.90. What then is the value of real GDP in 2003? Divide the nominal value by the value of the GDP price index and multiply by 100: ($10.688 ÷ 111.90) × 100. Performing this computation shows the real value of GDP in 2003 to be $9.551 trillion (rounded to the third place following the decimal). You should compute real GDP for additional years, using the values given in the table for nominal GDP and the GDP chained price index, to confirm your ability to perform this calculation. Your computations should be identical to those shown in the last column of Table 5-4.

Let's look more closely at Table 5-4. Observe that the GDP price index column states that the values for this price index are expressed relative to the purchasing power of the dollar in 1996. The arbitrary choice by government statisticians of the year 1996 as a reference point for the chained index has two implications. One is that the real GDP and the nominal GDP have the same value in 1996, as you can see by looking at the table. The second is that picking a particular year as a reference point for the GDP price index allows us to express real GDP in terms of a constant value of money, which in this case is the value of the dollar in 1996. Thus, the column heading for real GDP states that the figures given are expressed in 1996 dollars.

REAL GDP ACROSS COUNTRIES

Most, if not all, nations of the world compute the value of real GDP for their economies. The size of a nation's real GDP is probably the best indicator of the size of a country's economy and the significance of that economy on the world's economic stage. Table 5-5 shows real GDP for eight countries, including the United States. The table also shows real GDP for the continent of Europe as a whole.

TABLE 5-5   REAL GDP ACROSS COUNTRIES (IN BILLIONS OF DOLLARS)

COUNTRY OR CONTINENT	REAL GDP*
United States	$9,196.4
Canada	741.6
France	1,831.5
Germany	2,708.0
Italy	1,234.3
Japan	5725.5
Mexico	375.2
United Kingdom	1,260.8
Europe	11,125.4

*Values for 2002 expressed at 1995 prices and 1995 exchange rates. Because of differences in measurement techniques, the value for real U.S. GDP varies slightly from the value given in Table 5-4. The value of real GDP for Europe includes only countries belonging to the Organization for Economic Cooperation and Development (OECD).

Source: OECD, *Main Economic Indicators,* July 2003, page 243.

The U.S. economy is seen to tower over that of any country in the table. For example, Japan's economy is only about 60 percent as large as that of the United States. Of particular note are the relatively small size of the economies of America's neighbors, Canada and Mexico. While the U.S. economy is the world's largest, when the twenty plus countries of Europe are taken as a whole, the European continent is seen to have a larger real GDP than that of the United States.

5.4 THE BUSINESS CYCLE—THE UPS AND DOWNS IN ECONOMIC ACTIVITY

Cycles in economic activity have been a feature of economies throughout history. In the twentieth century, the Great Depression of the 1930s stands out as an economic collapse of historic proportions in the United States and other countries around the world. Although most downturns in the economy are mild and short-lived, we still worry about the cyclical nature of our economy.

STAGES OF THE BUSINESS CYCLE

business cycle the uneven sequence of trough, expansion, peak, and recession that the economy follows over time.

recession a sustained decrease in real GDP.

The term **business cycle** refers to the expansions and contractions in economic activity that take place over time. Figure 5-6 shows the stages of a business cycle as a smooth curve. The low point in economic activity is called the *trough.* Following the trough is the *expansion* stage. When the expansion is ready to end, the economy reaches its *peak,* and then falls into **recession** in which real GDP decreases. An especially severe recession is termed a *depression.* Subsequently, another trough will mark the point where the process begins repeating itself.

FIGURE 5-6

STAGES OF THE BUSINESS CYCLE
The stages of the business cycle are not smooth in reality. The duration and intensity of stages can differ dramatically over time, although the long-run trend is upward.

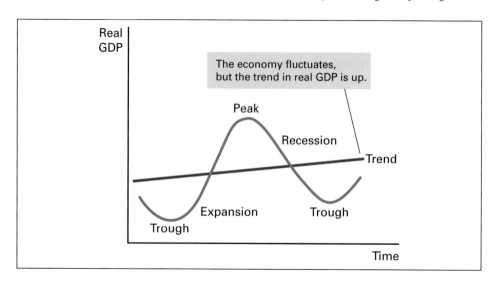

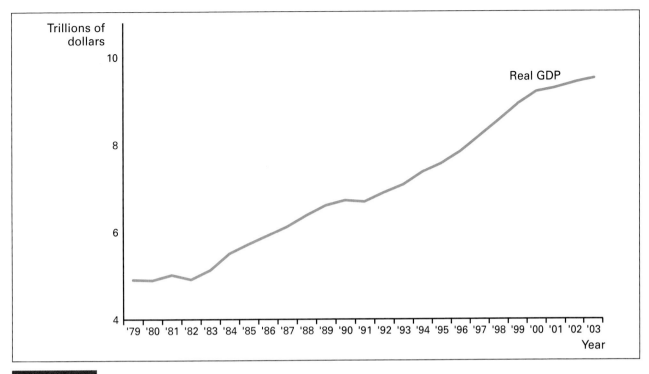

FIGURE 5-7

THE UPWARD TREND OF REAL GDP When real GDP is viewed over many years, the upward trend becomes apparent.

Source: 2003 Economic Report of the President, Table B-2, and Bureau of Economic Analysis, *National Accounts Data.*

The economic fluctuations represented by the business cycle are an example of *short-run* features in the economy. The business cycle occurs around an upward trend in real GDP. Economic trends describe persistent features in the economy. Thus, trends describe the *long-run* features of the economy.

In the real world, the ups and downs in the economy do not occur in such a smooth fashion. Expansions typically last much longer and are much stronger than recessions. Thus, the business cycle occurs within the context of a rising trend in real GDP. Figure 5-7 reveals the upward course of GDP over time. Figure 5-8 shows that, since the Great Depression of the 1930s, recessions in the United States have been infrequent, mild, and short lived. None of the post-war recessions has come close to matching the Great Depression in length or magnitude.

Who decides when the economy leaves one stage of the business cycle and enters the next stage? In the United States, that job is not left to government economists, whose judgment might be swayed by political considerations. Instead, an independent organization, the National Bureau of Economic Research (NBER), is entrusted with the dating of business cycle turning points. To accomplish this task, the NBER considers the depth and duration of the downturn, along with the dispersion of its effects throughout the economy.

Because important indicators of the economy, such as GDP, employment, and industrial production, sometimes move opposite to each other, the job of the NBER is a difficult one. In many instances, the NBER will not announce the onset of a recession until it has observed the indicators for months. There are also often delays in dating the beginning of expansions.

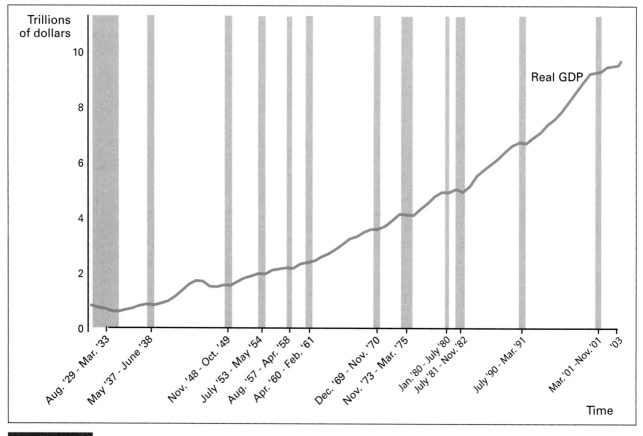

FIGURE 5-8

REAL GDP SINCE 1929 People living during the Great Depression of the 1930s would have found it difficult to agree with the idea that the trend in GDP was upward. In contrast, the ten recessions since the
end of World War II in 1945 have been relatively short and mild, thus reducing public fear that another
Great Depression might occur. Recessions are identified in the graph by the shaded vertical bars.

Source: Bureau of Economic Analysis, *National Accounts Data,* and National Bureau of Economic Research, *Business
Cycle Expansions and Contractions.*

SEASONAL ADJUSTMENTS—HELPING TO ISOLATE CYCLICAL EFFECTS

Many economic variables move either up or down at the same time each year. For example,
construction activity slows down during the winter because of bad weather and picks up
during the warmer months. Retail sales increase during the Christmas season. Agriculture
follows seasonal patterns. Thus, downswings in economic activity do not always indicate
recession, just as upswings do not always signal expansion.

These seasonal effects make it difficult to disentangle actual growth in economic variables from changes in them due to seasonal volatility. That is why most published economic
data are seasonally adjusted, using statistical models. Seasonal adjustments to data help
reveal the underlying trends. For example, when construction activity drops off in January,
the seasonally adjusted data can tell us whether the decline is merely the usual winter slowdown or whether construction is stronger or weaker than usual for that time of year.

Seasonal adjustments can reveal unusual strength or weakness in the economy. For
example, if the seasonal adjustment shows that the January decline in construction activity
is not as sharp as usual, and many other economic measures are also above their seasonal
norms, we have compelling evidence that the economy is expanding.

READING THE INDICATORS—LEADS AND LAGS

There are hundreds of economic indicators capable of illuminating various aspects of the economy. History has shown that some of these indicators, called **leading indicators**, will usually change direction before the economy does. Examples include the index of building permits, housing starts, and manufacturers' new orders for durable goods. These data series and several others are combined to form a composite index of leading indicators, which receives much attention from the media.

leading indicators statistics that are expected to change direction before the economy at large does, thereby indicating where the economy is headed.

Other indicators, the *lagging indicators,* usually change direction only after the economy has already done so. The unemployment rate and expenditures on new plants and equipment are examples. Many indicators change direction about the same time the economy changes direction. These are called *coincident indicators.* Examples include the index of industrial production and the prime interest rate charged by banks.

Investors and businesspeople need predictions about the future in order to plan effectively, which motivates their interest in the leading indicators. Unfortunately, the leading indicators do not always give an accurate prediction of the future direction of the economy, and thus must be used with care.

GLOBAL ECONOMY, YES—GLOBAL RECESSION, WHO COULD KNOW?   *SNAPSHOT*

In 1998, the economies of Asia and the Far East were in turmoil. Indonesia entered a depression. Bad bank loans in Japan caused the lengthy recession there to deepen. The Russian economy teetered on the brink of disaster. In the second half of the year, the U.S. stock market reacted so negatively that investors wondered if the long-feared "bear market" was upon them. President Clinton even called the situation the most dangerous for the world economy in fifty years. Yet, in the following two years, the U.S. economy boomed and the U.S. stock market soared to record heights.

April of 2000 ushered in a different phenomenon. This time it was U.S. stocks that came crashing down from their historic highs, with one major market indicator losing over a quarter of its value in a single week and continuing a generally downward course for over two years. As panic gripped Wall Street, finance ministers from around the world met in Washington to discuss the latest turn of events. Would the tightening financial situation crush developing countries in a financial vise? Would Wall Street's troubles become the world's?

Although investors and finance ministers alike sought definitive answers to those questions, seeking knowledge in the leading indicators and other evidence, there was really only one answer that could have been known for sure. And that was: "Time will tell." For the last sixty years, time has told that economic downturns have been mere blips against the upward trend in GDP. ◄

QUICKCHECK

Does the government declare when the economy enters a recession? Explain.

Answer: No, it is not a government agency that performs this task. Instead, the National Bureau of Economic Research, a private organization that is less likely to be influenced by politics than a government agency, is charged with the task of announcing that a recession has begun, and that a recession has ended.

5.5 USING ECONOMIC DATA TO SET POLICY

"My son ... was a Marine Corps company commander in Iraq, and I actually have less concern about him being in Iraq in that capacity than I do about what the future may hold for him and his new daughter because of this fiscal imbalance."

— David M. Walker, Comptroller General, General Accounting Office

With the 2004 deficit in the federal budget predicted to be $475 billion and the accumulating debt of the United States forcing Congress to add another trillion dollars to what had been a $6.4 trillion debt ceiling, policymakers in Congress are hardpressed to know if the U.S. economy will be able to afford the obligations of its government. For this, the federal government must have answers, even if they are not the ultimate answers. The government must know whether there are macroeconomic problems. If there are problems, it must know how serious those problems are. Otherwise, government cannot know which actions to take, or even whether to take action at all. Thus, it turns to economic statistics.

Of course, just knowing economic data does not mean that government will choose to budget sensibly. The federal budget deficit—a shortfall of federal revenues below expenses—is evidence. Until the surpluses of 1998–2001, the federal government incurred a budget deficit every year between 1960 and 1997. Then the deficits hit again, rising from the $165 billion deficit in 2002 to a $475 billion deficit projected for 2004. No end is in sight, either, as the federal government also borrows additional hundreds of billions of dollars from trust funds that will be needed later to finance Social Security and Medicare benefits to the elderly.

FISCAL IMBALANCE

The amounts involved can be mind-boggling. For example, in July of 2003, the American Enterprise Institute published a study that estimated the federal government's fiscal imbalance to be $44.2 trillion, where *fiscal imbalance* is defined as the amount of *extra* money that the federal government would need today in order to fund its current tax and spending policies indefinitely into the future. As seen in Figure 5-9, future Medicare and Social Security obligations make up the vast majority of the financing needs.

The $44.2 trillion fiscal imbalance is not as grim as it initially seems. Even though the estimated fiscal imbalance is about four times the current GDP, the GDP measure is annual and growing, allowing the government decades to rectify the fiscal imbalance through altered tax or spending policies. Still, to make sensible decisions, Congress needs to project the future. Yet Congressional projections of future GDP and tax revenues are always highly contentious, so much so that they were even prohibited until a couple years ago.

Until the legislation expired in the summer of 2003, Congress adhered to the Budget Enforcement Act of 1990. Under this legislation, Congress would not allow itself to make policy changes that would increase the budget deficit from whatever it would otherwise have been. Under this legislation, policy changes that would add to the budget deficit must be balanced by other changes that would offset that effect.

Avoiding policies that would add to the budget deficit sounds like a reasonable thing to do, but it brings back that basic statistical problem—measuring the effects on government revenues and expenses of alternative public policies. Because such statistics are not immune from politics, the Budget Enforcement Act required that Congress use a simplifying assumption. Specifically, Congress required itself to use what is called *static scoring*, which assumes that there would be no general changes in macroeconomic behavior as a result of government policy changes. The alternative to static scoring is called *dynamic scoring*, a process that would allow for consideration of all behavioral changes over time caused by changes in government policy.

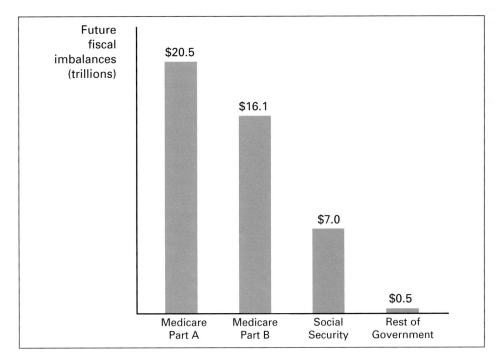

FIGURE 5-9

FUTURE FISCAL IMBALANCES The $44.2 trillion question is how to pay for future Social Security and Medicare obligations. Projections are particularly significant for these programs, because they target retirees, and the population profile is changing. The figure breaks down Medicare obligations into its two components, with Part A being hospitalization coverage and Part B being all other medical coverage. With the exception of paying for Social Security and Medicare, current federal tax policies appear more or less adequate to finance government spending.

Source: Gokhale and Smetters, 2003.

Static scoring led to serious problems. For example, it nearly forced Congress to abandon its goal of promoting freer international trade. Although U.S. negotiators had spent years convincing other countries to lower their tariffs, the United States was almost unable to reciprocate with lower tariffs of its own. Static scoring made it very difficult to pass revisions to the General Agreement on Tariffs and Trade because static scoring looked only at the cost to the Treasury Department of losing tariff revenues on the pre-existing quantity of imports.

Although the entire purpose of reducing trade barriers was to promote trade, static scoring rules assumed that the volume of trade would remain constant. Thus, any tariff cut was automatically scored as a revenue-loser by the same percentage that the tariffs were cut. Budget rules meant that tariffs could not be cut without other policy changes that would add revenues or cut expenditures in other areas to offset the purported revenue loss. It was only through an extraordinary act of juggling other elements of the budget that the congressional budgetary rules were finally satisfied.

Static scoring is stupid, you might say. Washington policymakers know that taxes can change our behavior. Static scoring has been a budgetary mainstay because it provides an obvious baseline estimate, the baseline being the status quo. Analysts may know that behavior will change, but are unlikely to agree on exactly what forms the changes will take or how significant will be their effects. Because of such disagreement, dynamic scoring must inevitably lead to controversy.

Everyone in the budget process knows that static scoring gives wrong answers. Still, as the saying goes, the devil you know is better than the devil you don't know. If the government were to follow a dynamic scoring standard, who could tell what controversies would lie buried beneath the surface?

Consider the possibilities. There was hot debate over President George Bush's recently enacted tax cuts when, on May 16, 2002, the Congressional Joint Committee on Taxation (JCT) issued a report urging Congress to modify its budget rules in order to allow dynamic scoring. The Committee pointed to economic studies suggesting that, while cutting tax rates would reduce the amount of tax revenue per dollar earned, a significant portion of that revenue loss would be offset by revenues gained from an increase in aggregate economic activity. Senate Majority Leader Tom Daschle objected. In a public letter to House Speaker Dennis Hastert on June 25, 2002, Daschle declared, "Having JCT include the macroeconomic effects into its cost estimates would subject the committee's work to huge potential errors and would only serve to undermine its credibility."

The problem of budgetary discipline also arises on the spending side. For example, advocates of social programs often find themselves attracted to the dynamic standard, arguing that cutting back spending on social programs could cause tax revenues to decline over time. The idea is that money spent on social programs helps to develop productive, taxpaying citizens who pay back many times more than they received. Thus, they sometimes argue, cutting social spending would threaten to increase rather than decrease budget deficits.

The issue of static versus dynamic scoring underscores the old adage that politics makes strange bedfellows. Conservatives seeking to cut taxes find themselves allied with liberals seeking to expand government spending on social programs. Both support dynamic scoring. On the other side are conservatives and liberals who fear political manipulation of the budget process. Whatever the immediate outcome of this tug-of-war, the issue will remain with us.

Is it better to adhere to static scoring that we know gives wrong answers or to allow our elected officials the leeway to use their best judgments as to which forecasts to accept? Do we trust them to think well? Is it better to analyze and maybe get it wrong than not to analyze at all?

Since 2002, the answer has been to let Congress use its best judgment without the straitjacket of static scoring. Along with this answer have come soaring budget deficits, growing at a rate that cannot be sustained. Policymakers don't intend to sustain it, either. The different political parties merely offer differing predictions as to whether a growing GDP will get us out of our current fiscal predicament.

THINKING CRITICALLY

1. **Senate Majority Leader Tom Daschle was quoted in this Explore & Apply as declaring, "Having JCT include the macroeconomic effects into its cost estimates would subject the committee's work to huge potential errors and would only serve to undermine its credibility." Using your own words, explain what he meant and why others might disagree.**

2. **These days, the biggest check on government spending might seem to be the $7.38 trillion *debt cap,* which holds down federal debt to a little over two-thirds of GDP. In practice, however, Congress periodically raises the ceiling rather than eliminate the U.S. budget deficits. Why isn't the debt cap more effective at holding down government budget deficits? Should it be enforced more strictly? Why does Congress keep raising it?**

 Visit www.prenhall.com/ayers for updates and web exercises on this Explore & Apply topic.

SUMMARY AND LEARNING OBJECTIVES

1. **Present three widely accepted goals for the economy.**
   - The three goals for the economy are economic growth, full employment, and low inflation.
   - An annual growth rate of 2.5 percent is usually considered sustainable. Evidence from the late 1990s suggests a possible sustainable growth rate of up to 5 percent.

   - The rule of seventy-two can be used to compute doubling times. For example, at a 2.5 percent rate of growth, the economy's output would double in approximately 29 years. A growth rate of 5 percent would cut this doubling time in half.
   - In order to know whether the nation is meeting its macro goals, government collects data that measure the aggregate economy.

2. **Define gross domestic product (GDP), discuss its components, and the ways in which it can be measured.**

   - Gross domestic product (GDP) is the most widely reported measure of the aggregate economy. It measures the value of final goods and services produced by an economy within some time period. Intermediate goods are used to make other goods. To avoid double counting, GDP does not count the production of intermediate goods, since their value is included in the value of final goods.

   - Using the expenditure approach, GDP equals the sum of consumption, investment, government purchases, and net exports. Per capita GDP is GDP per person, computed by dividing GDP by the population. GDP is an imperfect measure of a nation's well-being, because it does not count the value of goods and services produced in the underground economy and at home.

   - The largest component of total spending in the United States is consumption spending, which includes most spending by consumers.

   - Total spending also includes investment, government purchases, and net exports. Investment is the sum of three items: spending on capital by businesses, spending on new housing by consumers, and the change in business inventories.

   - Government spending is the sum of spending on purchases of goods and services by governments at the local, state, and national levels. Government transfer payments are not directly included in the computation of GDP.

   - Net exports equal the value of exports minus the value of imports. Net exports have been negative in the recent past.

   - Using the income approach, GDP equals the sum of compensation of employees, proprietor's income, rental income, corporate profiles, and net interest.

   - Gross national product (GNP) is computed by first adding income received from the rest of the world to GDP, and then subtracting income payments to the rest of the world. GNP and GDP typically differ by a relatively small amount.

   - The value of production that occurs at home is not counted in GDP. Neither is the value of goods and services produced for the underground economy. Thus, GDP is an imperfect measure of a nation's well-being.

3. **Distinguish real GDP from nominal GDP.**

   - A nominal value is expressed without regard to price changes. A real value has been adjusted for price changes. The GDP price index is used to compute real GDP from nominal GDP.

   - Nominal GDP, when divided by the GDP price index and multiplied by 100, equals real GDP. Real GDP provides a more accurate measure of the economy's actual output over time than does nominal GDP. Nominal GDP will rise whenever production increases, but also because of inflation. Real GDP will only rise when production increases.

4. **Track the stages of the business cycle.**

   - The business cycle refers to the expansions and contractions in economic activity that take place over time. In the expansion phase, real GDP rises. Real GDP reaches its maximum at the peak of any business cycle. During the recession phase, economic activity declines. Real GDP reaches its lowest level at the trough of the business cycle.

   - The leading indicators are various data series that are supposed to predict turning points in the business cycle. Since they do not always predict accurately, anyone using them to make decisions must proceed with caution.

5. **Identify the advantages and disadvantages of static and dynamic scoring.**

   - Static scoring and its opposite, dynamic scoring, are alternative methods for gauging the effects of a policy action taken by government. In contrast to dynamic scoring, static scoring assumes that policy changes have no macroeconomic effects. Dynamic scoring is potentially more accurate than static scoring, but also allows for more opportunities to manipulate predicted outcomes to match political preferences.

KEY TERMS

gross domestic product (GDP), 116
expenditure approach, 116
consumption spending, 116
investment, 117
gross investment, 117
net investment, 117

net domestic product (NDP), 117
net exports, 119
income approach, 121
value added, 125
underground economy, 126

nominal GDP, 127
real GDP, 127
business cycle, 130
recession, 130
leading indicators, 133

TEST YOURSELF

TRUE OR FALSE

1. Low unemployment is a widely accepted goal of macro policy.
2. The investment component of GDP includes spending on human capital.
3. Net exports equal about 5 percent of GDP.
4. When there is an increase in nominal GDP, there must also be an increase in real GDP.
5. When real GDP decreases during the business cycle, the lowest point is called the peak.

MULTIPLE CHOICE

6. Applying the rule of seventy-two, it would take _____ years for GDP to double at a steady growth rate of 3 percent in GDP.
   a. 216   c. 24
   b. 72   d. 3

7. A loaf of french bread is used by a bakery to cut into croutons that are sold to Bridgette. The value of the loaf of french bread is not counted in GDP because it is a(n) _____ good. The value of the croutons are counted in GDP because they are a(n) _____ good.
   a. final; intermediate
   b. intermediate; final
   c. consumption; investment
   d. investment; consumption

8. The consumption spending portion of GDP includes
   a. durable goods, nondurable goods, and services.
   b. goods, services, and new houses.
   c. intermediate goods, but not final goods.
   d. about 90 percent of all production that occurs in the economy.

9. Gross investment equals
   a. net investment plus depreciation.
   b. investment adjusted for the effects of inflation.
   c. a negative component of GDP.
   d. the change in business inventories.

10. Which of the following is an example of a transfer payment?
    a. A school district pays the salary of a teacher.
    b. A senior citizen is issued a Social Security check by the government.
    c. A farmer raises a field of corn from seed.
    d. A little boy and girl spend their allowances at Chuck E. Cheese's pizza restaurant.

11. How are transfer payments treated in the measurement of GDP?
    a. Transfer payments are included in the government component of GDP.
    b. Transfer payments are changes in business inventories and are thus included in the investment component of GDP.
    c. Transfer payments are subtracted in the computation of GDP.
    d. GDP does not count transfer payments directly.

12. Net exports are computed as
    a. exports minus depreciation.
    b. exports minus imports.
    c. exports minus GDP.
    d. imports minus exports.

13. Which item in the income approach to measuring GDP is the largest?
    a. compensation of employees.
    b. proprietor's income.
    c. rental income.
    d. corporate profit.

14. U.S. gross national product (GNP)
    a. is another name for gross domestic product (GDP).
    b. excludes net exports, since its purpose is to compute national consumption and investment.
    c. includes production by U.S. firms in other countries and excludes production by foreign firms in the United States.
    d. is no longer computed, having been replaced by GDP.

15. Per capita GDP is
    a. GDP minus net exports.
    b. GDP adjusted for inflation.
    c. GDP per person.
    d. computed by taking the legal output and the illegal output of the economy and adding them together.

16. How is the output of goods in the underground economy treated in the computation of GDP?
    a. They are difficult to measure accurately, but the government estimates their value and adjusts GDP to reflect that value.
    b. They are included in GDP as one of the components of investment.
    c. Government produces goods for the underground economy and, thus, they are included in the government purchases component of GDP.
    d. They are not counted.

17. To compute real GDP when given nominal GDP, we must also know
    a. nothing else, since real and nominal GDP are generally equal.
    b. the value of consumption spending.
    c. the value of gross investment.
    d. the value of the GDP chain-type price index.

18. If the real value of GDP decreases from one year to the next, it is most likely that
    a. inflation is a problem in the economy.
    b. real GNP is up.
    c. consumption spending is down while government purchases are up.
    d. the economy is in a recession.

19. The leading indicators are
    a. a group of New York City investors who predict the stock market.
    b. government economists whose job it is to indicate solutions to problems with the economy.
    c. statistics that are used to predict the future direction of the economy.
    d. almost always wrong, but interesting anyway.

20. The primary difference between static and dynamic scoring is that
    a. static scoring is legal but dynamic scoring is illegal.
    b. static scoring considers real values of variables, but dynamic scoring considers nominal values.
    c. static scoring is favored by Congress, but dynamic scoring is favored by the president.
    d. static scoring assumes that behavior does not change when policies change, but dynamic scoring allows for the possibility of behavioral changes.

QUESTIONS AND PROBLEMS

1. *[macro goals]* List the three primary macroeconomic goals and briefly discuss why the achievement of these goals is desirable.

2. *[macro goals]* The U.S. Constitution refers to the rights of "life, liberty, and the pursuit of happiness." Explain how this constitutional right relates to the three primary macro goals. Does it appear from this phrase that the Constitution goes beyond promoting these goals? Explain.

3. *[macro goals]* After obtaining the most recent edition of the *Economic Report of the President* from your library or the Internet, compare the discussion of macroeconomic goals in this chapter with those discussed in the *Report*. Are all the goals mentioned in the chapter also in the *Report?*

4. *[final versus intermediate goods]* Explain why GDP excludes the value of intermediate goods, while including the value of final goods and services.

5. *[components of GDP]* Explain each of the four components of GDP. Include in your explanation answers to the following: (a) Is investment measured as gross or net? (b) Does the government component include transfer payments? (c) Which component has a negative value?

6. *[expenditure approach]* Suppose you have the following information available to compute the GDP of the country of Traczania: Consumption spending = $150; Gross investment = $55; Net investment = $50; Government purchases = $75; Government transfer payments = $30; Imports = $25; Exports = $20. Compute Traczania's GDP.

7. *[income approach]* List and explain the five different incomes that sum to the value of national income. Briefly discuss the adjustments that are necessary to arrive at the value of GDP.

8. *[GNP versus GDP]* Explain how gross national product (GNP) differs from gross domestic product (GDP). Is the difference between the values of GDP and GNP large or small in percentage terms?

9. *[GDP and household production]* Jane and John spent last Saturday morning cleaning their apartment. Is the value of those services counted in the measurement of GDP?

10. *[GDP and the underground economy]* What is meant by the underground economy? Is the output of the underground economy counted in measuring GDP?

11. *[value added]* Jay Jones runs a small business out of his home, making bird houses from scrap lumber that he finds in dumpsters. Last year Jay sold $8,000 worth of his birdhouses to happy birdwatchers. How much value added did Jim contribute to GDP last year? Is the value added equal to spending by consumers on his birdhouses? Explain.

12. *[per capita GDP]* What is *per capita* GDP? Under what circumstances would *per capita* GDP tell us more about the state of the economy than would GDP?

13. *[real versus nominal GDP]* What is the purpose of computing the real value of GDP? Explain how the GDP price index is used to compute real GDP.

14. *[business cycle]* Illustrate graphically the stages of the curve you draw. Be sure to include appropriate labels on the axes and on the business cycle.

15. *[business cycle]* Go to your library or the Internet and read at least three articles about the current condition of the economy in magazines such as *Business Week,* the *Economist,* or *Fortune,* or in a business newspaper such as the *Financial Times* or the *Wall Street Journal.* What stage of the business cycle is the economy currently in? Which single statistic is the most useful in answering this question? What economic problems are discussed in the articles you have read? Explain.

WORKING WITH GRAPHS AND DATA

1. *[computing GDP]* Given the information below calculate the following:
   a. GDP
   b. NDP
   c. NI
   d. Imports

Compensation to employees	$1,400
Depreciation	350
Government purchases	900
Exports	900
Corporate profits	400
Rental income	100
Consumption expenditures	1,100
Proprietor's income	500
Indirect business taxes	300
Net interest income	150
Gross domestic private investment	500

2. *[GDP]* Solve the following GDP problems.
   a. Suppose that nominal GDP was $6 trillion in 1998. The GDP price index was 102 for 1998, where the GDP price index for 1996 was 100. What was real GDP in 1998?
   b. Real GDP in 2000 was $10 trillion. The GDP price index for 2000 was 107. What was nominal GDP in 2000?
   c. Real GDP in 2002 was $412 trillion and the nominal GDP was $14 trillion. What was the GDP price index in 2002?

3. *[real and nominal GDP; GDP price index]* Given the data in Graph 5-1, interpret the growth of real GDP, nominal GDP, and the GDP price index for each time period (t0–t1;t1–t2; t2–t3; t3–t4).

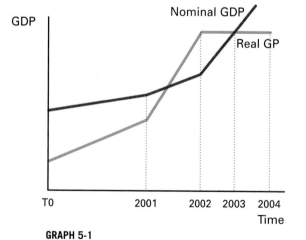

GRAPH 5-1

   a. Time period t0–t1
   b. Time period t1–t2
   c. Time period t2–t3
   d. Time period t3–t4

4. *[business cycle]* Graph 5-2 depicts a fictional nation's real GDP over time.

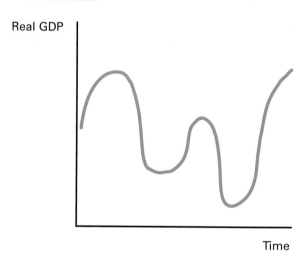

GRAPH 5-2

   a. Identify the number of business cycles in the graph.
   b. Label the parts of each business cycle.
   c. Discuss the trend of real GDP in this economy.

 Visit www.prenhall.com/ayers for Exploring the Web exercises and additional self-test quizzes.

APPENDIX 5

THE NATIONAL INCOME AND PRODUCT ACCOUNTS

The purpose of national income accounting is to summarize the millions of daily economic transactions in a form that economists, government planners, politicians, and others can easily use and understand. The development of the national income and product accounts began in the 1930s in response to the need to evaluate depressed economic conditions, and the growing realization that the government's existing collection of data meant that it already possessed the primary data that could be used to construct the accounts.

The Bureau of Economic Analysis (BEA), an arm of the U.S. Department of Commerce, is responsible for the preparation of the final reports detailing the national income and product statistics. These reports are prepared using data obtained from other government agencies. Individual tax returns, obtained from the Internal Revenue Service, are an important source of data. Survey data are also extensively employed.

Users of BEA data are familiar with the notion of preliminary and revised data. Preliminary data are estimates that are subject to change. Revised data incorporate changes in data made necessary as more complete information becomes available with the passage of time. Data may be revised several times before the BEA is satisfied with its accuracy. The process of revision can occasionally drag on for years.

Most data are available at quarterly or annual intervals, although some data are available monthly. The monthly Commerce Department publication, the *Survey of Current Business,* is the primary source of national income and product data. BEA-developed data can also be found in other government publications, including the annual *Economic Report of the President.*

In calculating GDP it is useful to recognize that every dollar of production creates an equivalent dollar of spending. **Since every dollar of spending generates a dollar of income for someone, the values of production and income are also equal.** Goods and services are produced and sold, with the dollars spent by purchasers being collected by businesses. These dollars go toward the payment of incomes—wages to workers, for example.

The equality of production and income means that GDP can be calculated in two ways, as seen in Table 5A-1. On the left side of the table, GDP is obtained by measuring the total value of production. The **expenditure approach** sums spending on consumption, investment, government purchases, and the value of net exports. On the right side of the table, the **incomes approach** sums various income items plus other charges against GDP. Proprietor's income is received by persons who own unincorporated businesses, such as farmers and physicians. Net interest is interest received by individuals minus individuals' interest payments.

TABLE 5A-1   TWO APPROACHES TO MEASURING GDP

EXPENDITURE APPROACH	INCOMES APPROACH
Personal Consumption Expenditures	**Compensation of Employees**
Durables	Wages and salaries
Nondurables	Supplements
Services	
	+
+	**Proprietor's Income**
Gross Private Domestic Investment	+
Business capital investment	**Rental Income of Persons**
New housing	+
Inventory change	**Corporate Profits**
+	+
Government purchases	**Net Interest**
Federal	+
State and local	**Other Charges Against GDP**
+	Capital consumption
Net Exports	Indirect business taxes
	Other items, net
	Statistical discrepancy
=	=
Gross Domestic Product	**Gross Domestic Product**

Source: Adapted from Federal Reserve Bank of Richmond, "The National Income and Product Accounts," *Macroeconomic Data: A User's Guide,* 1994, 3rd edition.

Because of imperfections in data collection, product and income are not exactly equal. This necessitates the inclusion of the statistical discrepancy as part of the "other charges" on the income side. Other complications associated with the income approach force the inclusion of several additional charges. Capital consumption measures depreciation in the nation's capital stock. Indirect business taxes are federal excise taxes as well as state and local sales taxes included in the value of purchases. These complications make the incomes approach less useful than the more straightforward expenditure approach for most macro analyses.

By making adjustments to GDP, other measures of aggregate economic activity can be calculated as follows:

- *Gross national product (GNP):* GNP = GDP + income received by U.S. firms and workers outside the United States − income received by foreign firms and workers within the United States
- *Net national product (NNP):* NNP = GNP − capital consumption allowances
- *National income (NI):* NI = NNP − indirect business taxes − business transfer payments + statistical discrepancy + subsidies less surplus of government firms

TABLE 5A-2	THE U.S. NATIONAL INCOME AND PRODUCT ACCOUNTS (IN BILLIONS OF DOLLARS)	

Gross Domestic Product	**10,688.4**
Plus: Income received from the rest of the world	281.3
Minus: Income Payments to the rest of the world	291.5
Equals: **Gross National Product**	10,678.2
Minus: Capital consumption allowances and other adjustments	1,421.4
Equals: **Net National Product**	9,256.8
Minus: Indirect business taxes	821.7
Minus: Business transfer payments	44.9
Plus: Statistical discrepancy	91.4
Plus: Subsidies less surplus of government enterprises	30.7
Equals: **National Income**	8,512.3
Minus: Corporate profits and other corporate adjustments	816.5
Minus: Net interest	703.3
Minus: Social Security taxes	764.1
Minus: Wage accruals less disbursements	1.4
Plus: Government transfer payments to persons	1,304.9
Plus: Personal interest income	1,075.8
Plus: Personal dividend income	451.2
Plus: Business transfer payments to persons	35.9
Equals: **Personal Income**	9,094.8
Minus: Personal tax and non-tax payments and other adjustments	1,077.2
Equals: **Disposable Personal Income**	8,017.6

Source: Survey of Current Business, August 2003, Tables 1.9 and 2.1. The values given are annualized from the first quarter of 2003. Values may vary slightly from the sums shown because of rounding.

- *Personal income (PI):* PI = NI − corporate profits − net interest − Social Security taxes − wage accruals less disbursements + government transfer payments to persons + personal interest income + personal dividend income + business transfer payments to persons
- *Disposable personal income (DPI):* DPI = PI − personal tax and non-tax payments

As the adjustments show, national income accounting can be quite complex. Each of the measures defined above is used for a specific purpose, thus justifying the effort. For example, disposable personal income shows how much income people actually have available to spend. Economists use this data to forecast consumer spending. Table 5A-2 shows the values of the five national income statistics previously listed. As you can see, GDP and GNP are nearly identical in value. The other measures of product and income will always be less than GNP or GDP.

EXERCISES

1. If you manage a major chain of retail stores, and are developing your plans as to how much inventory to stock for the Christmas season, which of the national income and output measures would you be most interested in? Why?

2. GNP rather than GDP was the primary focus of national income accounting until the early 1990s. Under what circumstances would GNP be of more interest to economists than GDP? Given the difference between GNP and GDP, why do you think that attention shifted to GDP?

CHAPTER 6

UNEMPLOYMENT

A LOOK AHEAD

Too many unfilled jobs and not enough qualified people—not a bad problem to have! The United States found itself in just that situation as the twentieth century drew to a close, with an unemployment rate that hovered at 4 percent, the lowest since 1969. Unfortunately, the recession that occurred in 2001 caused unemployment to reverse course. After the recession ended, the economy experienced two years of a so-called job-less recovery. Are government policies toward the workplace to blame? Consequences of such policies are examined in this chapter's Explore & Apply section.

This chapter is about the labor force and unemployment. You will learn what it means to be a labor force participant. You will also see how the unemployment rate is calculated. We discuss the causes of unemployment within the framework of the four types of unemployment, as well as the economy's overall path toward full employment. While U.S. unemployment is the primary interest here, you will also see that unemployment is a problem with global dimensions.

LEARNING OBJECTIVES

Understanding Chapter 6 will enable you to:
1. **Identify who is part of the labor force and who is not.**
2. **Explain how the unemployment rate is calculated.**
3. **Elaborate on unemployment in other countries.**
4. **Divide unemployment into different types and explain the implications of each.**
5. **Describe the natural rate of unemployment and its converse, full employment.**
6. **Discuss how the quality of employment can deteriorate when mandates increase labor costs.**

Explore & Apply

Employment and unemployment top the list of macroeconomic concerns. The reason is straightforward—most people's incomes come from their jobs. To understand unemployment, we must measure it in total and by types. Knowing what it is helps us to identify how much of it we can expect.

6.1 MEASURING UNEMPLOYMENT

An economy with unemployment is wasting resources and producing at a point inside its production possibilities frontier. The concept of unemployment applies to any resource that lies idle. In common usage, however, unemployment refers to idle labor.

THE LABOR FORCE AND UNEMPLOYMENT

labor force individuals age 16 and over, excluding those in the military, who are either employed or actively looking for work.

The U.S. *civilian labor force*—the **labor force**—is composed of individuals age 16 and over, excluding those in the military, who are either employed or actively looking for work. The labor force typically expands as the adult population increases. The labor force also expands as job opportunities improve, which causes some of the people not previously in the labor force to look for work.

The labor force can be divided into two parts, consisting of the employed and the unemployed. The employed are those who work for pay, and the unemployed are those who do not work, but are seeking jobs. The **unemployment rate** is the fraction of the labor force who are unemployed, expressed in percentage terms:

unemployment rate the ratio of the number of unemployed persons to the number of persons in the labor force.

$$\text{Unemployment rate} = \frac{\text{Number of unemployed}}{\text{Labor force}} \times 100$$

Table 6-1 shows the U.S. population, civilian labor force, and unemployment data from 1979 through 2003. When we take the ratio of the civilian labor force to the population age 16 and over, the result is the **labor force participation rate** (or just the *participation rate*):

labor force participation rate the ratio of the labor force to the population age 16 and over; expressed as a percentage.

$$\text{Participation rate} = \frac{\text{Labor force}}{\text{Population}} \times 100$$

Over this period there has been a consistent increase in the participation rate. This trend is primarily caused by the increase in the participation of women in the U.S. labor force.

Labor force participation and job creation depend on each other. When the economy is in the midst of a strong expansion, potential workers become aware that job opportunities are available that would be absent in a weaker economy. The result is that some persons who would choose not to join the labor force when job openings are relatively scarce are enticed to enter the labor force by the prospect of a good job. This job seeking is in addition to the normal expansion of the labor force that occurs when young graduates look for their first jobs and people who have temporarily left the labor force reenter it. The latter group includes women who return to the labor force after having left their jobs to raise families, and retirees who wish to supplement their incomes. When the expansion of the labor force brought on by a strong economy is added to the normal increase, the result is that the unemployment rate does not fall as much as it otherwise would. The reason is that the additional job seekers will be counted as unemployed until they find and accept work.

There are many influences on the labor force participation rate.

- **Increased opportunities for women and minorities** have led to an increase in the participation rate over time.
- **Opportunities for workers to take early retirement** have grown. Since retirees are not part of the labor force, the influence of improved retirement opportunities has been to limit the increase in the participation rate.

TABLE 6-1 POPULATION, LABOR FORCE, AND UNEMPLOYMENT

YEAR	POPULATION AGE 16 AND OVER (MILLIONS)	LABOR FORCE (MILLIONS OF CIVILIANS)	LABOR FORCE PARTICIPATION RATE (IN PERCENT)	NUMBER OF UNEMPLOYED (IN MILLIONS)	UNEMPLOYMENT RATE (IN PERCENT)
1979	164.9	105.0	63.7	6.1	5.8
1980	167.7	106.9	63.8	7.6	7.1
1981	170.1	108.7	63.9	8.3	7.6
1982	172.3	110.2	64.0	10.7	9.7
1983	174.2	111.6	64.0	10.7	9.6
1984	176.4	113.5	64.4	8.5	7.5
1985	178.2	115.5	64.8	8.3	7.2
1986	180.6	117.8	65.3	8.2	7.0
1987	182.8	119.9	65.6	7.4	6.2
1988	184.6	121.7	65.9	6.7	5.5
1989	186.4	123.9	66.5	6.5	5.3
1990	188.0	124.8	66.4	6.9	5.5
1991	189.8	125.3	66.0	8.4	6.7
1992	191.6	127.0	66.3	9.4	7.4
1993	193.6	128.0	66.2	8.7	6.8
1994	196.8	131.1	66.6	8.0	6.1
1995	198.6	132.3	66.6	7.4	5.6
1996	200.6	133.9	66.8	7.2	5.4
1997	203.1	136.3	67.1	6.7	4.9
1998	205.2	137.7	67.1	6.2	4.5
1999	207.8	139.4	67.1	5.9	4.2
2000	209.7	140.9	67.2	5.6	4.0
2001	211.9	141.8	66.9	6.7	4.8
2002	214.0	142.5	66.6	8.3	5.8
2003	221.8	146.6	66.1	9.0	6.1

Source: *2003 Economic Report of the President,* Table B-35, and U.S. Department of Labor. Data for 2003 are current through September, and are seasonally adjusted.

- ■ **Better healthcare** has allowed workers who might have been too sick to stay in the labor force in earlier times to continue on.
- ■ **Government aid,** such as generous welfare programs, can cause workers to stay out of the labor force.

POPULATION AND LABOR FORCE
The U.S. adult population in 2003 of 221.8 million people is represented by the pie chart, where each adult fits into one of the slices. Adults who have jobs are counted in the 137.6 million employed. Those who are unemployed are grouped in the slice that contains 9.0 million unemployed persons. These two slices of the pie make up the labor force of 146.6 million people. The rest of the population, are not in the labor force.

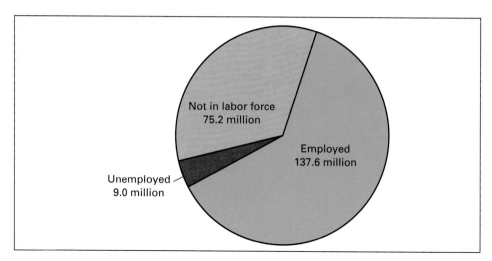

■ **Individual attitudes** toward labor change. When people put great value on their involvement in the labor force, the participation rate will be higher than when work is not so highly valued for its own sake.

Figure 6-1 enlarges on Table 6-1 by showing labor force concepts in a pie chart, where the pie represents the adult population. There are three slices to the pie. Two of the slices represent people in the labor force, the employed and the unemployed. The third slice represents people not in the labor force. Figure 6-2 elaborates on Table 6-1 by breaking down the overall labor force participation rate in the table into the rates for men and women.

SNAPSHOT

DEMOGRAPHY—POPULATION STATISTICS TO LET US GLIMPSE THE FUTURE

Demography is the study of population statistics. Demographers offer us small glimpses of the future. Because birth rates and death rates change slowly, demographers can predict with little error how many people of various ages will comprise the labor force in ten, twenty, or even thirty years. Demographers tell us to expect an aging work force. The large numbers of baby boomers born from 1946 to 1964 were followed by the much smaller number of babies born in the 1970s and 1980s.

As the baby boomers grow older, and with fewer young workers to enter the labor force, the average age of the labor force must rise. An older labor force has important consequences, good and bad, for both the unemployment rate and our lifestyles. Middle-aged workers do not change jobs as often as young workers. As a consequence they are less likely to be unemployed. And while retirees look forward to taking it easy, their rising numbers will place increasing stresses on the nation's ability to provide for us all. With this glimpse of the future in hand, the nation can plan to deal with the problem of an aging labor force and growing population of retirees. ◀

UNEMPLOYMENT RATES IN THE UNITED STATES AND AROUND THE WORLD

As already mentioned, to be counted as unemployed a person must be at least 16 years of age and without work, but actively looking for a job. Separating the employed from the unemployed would seem easy, but there are many details to consider. For example:

■ Are you employed if your job is not full time? Yes, people are counted as employed regardless of how many hours they work, just so long as it's one hour a week or more for pay.

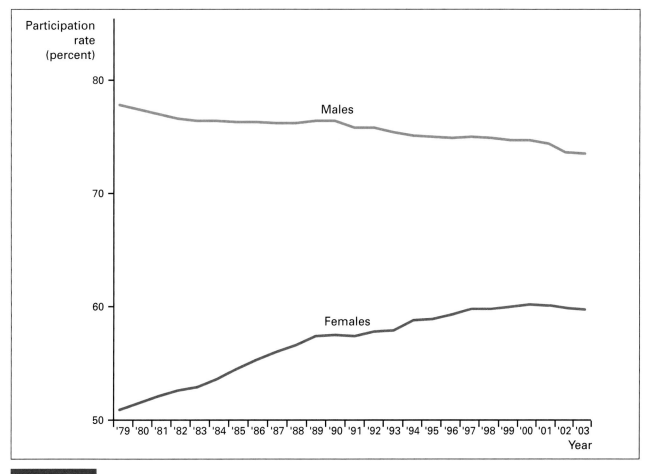

FIGURE 6-2

LABOR FORCE PARTICIPATION RATES FOR MEN AND WOMEN The labor force participation rate of women has increased dramatically over time, from about 50 percent in 1979 to about 60 percent today. For men, the labor force participation rate has dropped slightly over time but has remained in the general vicinity of 75 percent. When men and women are taken together, the overall participation rate is about 66 percent, as seen in Table 6-1.

Source: 2003 Economic Report of the President, Table B-39, and U.S. Department of Labor.

■ Can someone who works without pay be counted as employed? Again, yes, just so long as that person is working in a family business for at least fifteen hours a week.

■ Does going to school count as having a job? No. For students, school may seem to be a full-time job, but it's not considered that way by government statisticians. Neither are students counted among the unemployed, unless they are looking for jobs.

   In the United States the Bureau of Labor Statistics (BLS) estimates the number of employed and unemployed, and hence the unemployment rate. The estimates are based on a monthly survey of households and employers, and a tally of unemployment insurance claims. The last column in Table 6-1 shows yearly average unemployment rates since 1979. Figure 6-3 offers a longer view of unemployment, showing yearly unemployment rates since 1947.

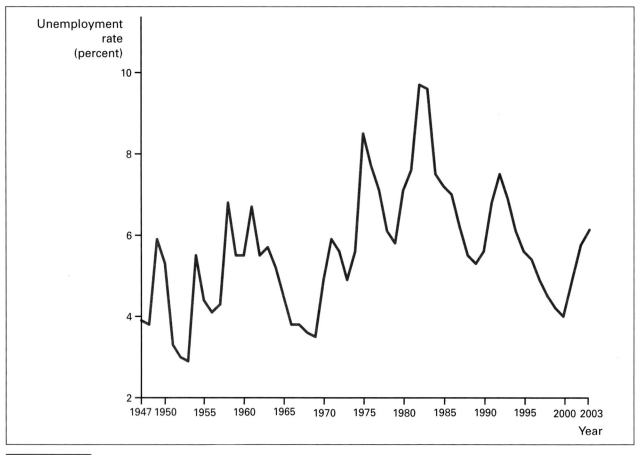

FIGURE 6-3

HISTORY OF THE U.S. UNEMPLOYMENT RATE The U.S. unemployment rate changes frequently. When the economy slows down, the unemployment rate rises. Faster economic growth promotes a lower unemployment rate. The unemployment rate fell significantly during the 1990s, but bounced upward in 2001 as the economy slowed.

Source: 2003 Economic Report of the President, Table B-35, and U.S. Department of Labor.

discouraged workers people who would like to have a job, but have given up looking; not counted as unemployed because they are not included in the labor force.

The unemployment rate, while useful, does not tell us all that we would like to know about the labor market. Some workers who have part-time jobs would like to have full-time jobs. Those workers are *underemployed.* Other workers would like to have a job, but have tried unsuccessfully to find one in the past and have given up looking. Because they have stopped looking, they are not counted in the unemployment statistics. Such would-be workers are called **discouraged workers.** Government estimates put the number of discouraged workers at about 480,000 people toward the end of 2003. **The presence of discouraged workers would cause the reported unemployment rate to understate true unemployment because discouraged workers are not in the labor force.** Concerns over the accuracy and meaning of the unemployment rate have led some economists to coin a saying about it: "The unemployment rate is like a hot dog. It's hard to tell what's in it."

People are unemployed for a variety of reasons, with some reasons of more concern than others. For example, some people are unemployed because they have voluntarily left their jobs. These unemployed persons are of less concern than the unemployed who have been involuntarily laid off. Some other people who are unemployed are actually earning

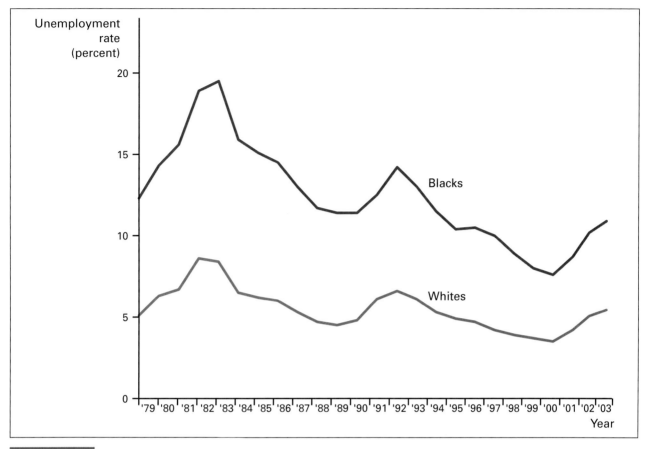

FIGURE 6-4

UNEMPLOYMENT RATES FOR BLACKS AND WHITES Despite recent signs of convergence, unemployment rates for blacks are consistently higher than unemployment rates for whites. However, when the unemployment rate among whites decreases (or increases), typically the black unemployment rate will also decrease (or increase).

Source: 2003 Economic Report of the President, Table B-42, and U.S. Department of Labor.

incomes in the underground economy. **The underground economy causes the reported unemployment rate to overstate true unemployment.**

Unemployment rates can vary among different segments of the population. For example, Figure 6-4 shows that the unemployment rate for blacks has been consistently higher than that for whites, although the gap has narrowed in recent years. Teenage unemployment is a significant contributing factor, with over 31 percent of black teenage males and 28 percent of black teenage females unemployed in 2002, compared to unemployment rates of about 16 percent for white teenage males and 13 percent for white teenage females.

Historically, male unemployment rates have been close to female unemployment rates. However, when only heads of households are considered the unemployment rate for men is much less than for women. Figure 6-5 shows those unemployment rates over time. Unemployment among heads of households is particularly significant because it can affect the well-being of entire families.

The unemployment rate does not tell us the *duration of unemployment*—how long a person has been unemployed. Short spells of unemployment among workers are of less

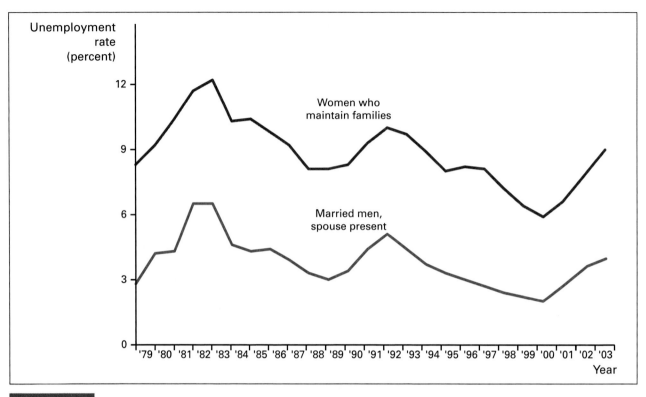

FIGURE 6-5

UNEMPLOYMENT RATES FOR MALE AND FEMALE HEADS OF HOUSEHOLDS The men and women in this graph provide the primary financial support for their families. The men have a significantly lower unemployment rate than the women.

Source: 2003 Economic Report of the President, Table B-42, and U.S. Department of Labor.

concern than long-term unemployment. The median duration of unemployment in 2003 was about 10 weeks. Figure 6-6 shows that unemployment tends to be of relatively short duration.

Having looked at unemployment in the United States, let's turn our attention to other countries. Recent unemployment rates for several major economies are presented in Figure 6-7 on page 154. By examining these data we can make a few generalizations about unemployment around the world. First, there is some tendency for unemployment rates to rise and fall together across countries. This tendency for unemployment rates to move together reflects the modern global economy that has led to increased economic interactions among countries. Note, however, that this tendency is not a hard and fast rule.

Four of the countries in Figure 6-7 experienced relatively high unemployment rates during the 1990s. While *changes* in the level of unemployment tend to move together, the *level* of unemployment itself is a different matter. Relative to their historical norms, Japan, France, Sweden, and Germany all exhibited high unemployment rates during the 1990s. The Japanese economy was bogged down in a stubborn recession during the period. France and Sweden suffered from high labor costs, along with traditions and government regulations that impeded their abilities to compete with other countries in the international marketplace. At the same time, Germany was dealing with the problem of integrating the economically backward East Germany into its economy.

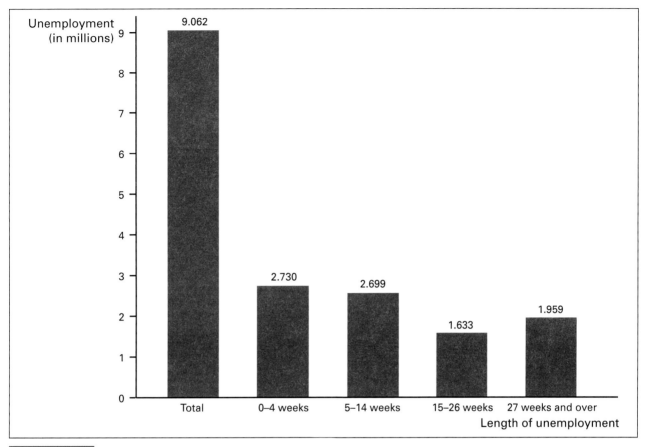

FIGURE 6-6

DURATION OF UNEMPLOYMENT Most unemployed people are unemployed for relatively short periods of time. The long-term unemployed, people who were unemployed for twenty-seven weeks or longer, make up only 22 percent of the total number of unemployed.

Source: U.S. Department of Labor. The data are for July 2003.

QUICKCHECK

Suppose the labor force in the country of Ecommercia equals 150 million people. Six million of these have no job and are looking for work. Another one million people have no job but are not looking for work. What is the unemployment rate? What is the labor force participation rate?

Answer: The unemployment rate equals 4 percent (6 million/150 million) since the one million people not looking for work are not in the labor force. It is impossible to calculate the labor force participation rate without more information. Specifically, to compute the participation rate would require us to know the population age 16 and above as well as the size of the labor force.

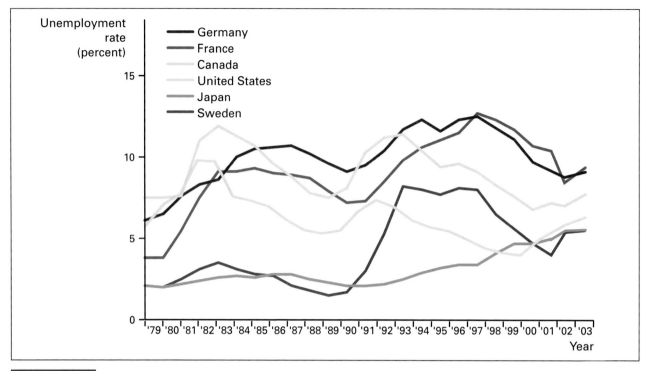

COUNTRY UNEMPLOYMENT RATES Unemployment rates around the world vary. Note that the United States, Sweden, and Japan succeeded in keeping their unemployment rates below 10 percent during the entire twenty-five years covered in the figure. The data are adjusted to U.S. methodologies.

Source: Comparative Civilian Labor Force Statistics, Ten Countries, 1959–2002, Table 2, U.S. Department of Labor, and OECD, and Organization for European Cooperation and Development (OECD), 2003.

6.2 IDENTIFYING TYPES OF UNEMPLOYMENT

Unemployment can be divided into the following four types:

frictional unemployment
unemployment associated with entering the labor market or switching jobs.

seasonal unemployment
unemployment that can be predicted to recur periodically, according to the time of year.

structural unemployment
unemployment caused by a mismatch between a person's human capital and that needed in the workplace.

cyclical unemployment
unemployment from a downturn in the business cycle that affects workers simultaneously in many different industries.

- **Frictional Unemployment**—occurs when someone enters the labor market or switches jobs.
- **Seasonal Unemployment**—recurs periodically, according to the time of year.
- **Structural Unemployment**—caused by a mismatch between a person's human capital and that needed in the workplace. This mismatch can be caused by an evolving structure of the economy as some industries rise and others fall. It can also be caused by minimum wage laws or other structural *rigidities* that inhibit job creation or the movement of workers into new jobs.
- **Cyclical Unemployment**—results from a downturn in the business cycle and affects workers simultaneously in many different industries.

Structural and cyclical unemployment are usually of most concern, because they represent *involuntary unemployment,* meaning that employees have little choice in the matter. In contrast, frictional and seasonal unemployment frequently represent *voluntary unemployment,* which can be planned for and more easily overcome.

SEASONAL AND FRICTIONAL—WAITING FOR THE OLD OR SWITCHING TO THE NEW

Seasonal unemployment affects workers in agriculture, many tourism-related occupations, education, tax accounting, professional sports, and some other industries. There is usually little concern over this unemployment, because it can be planned for—it is part of the job. Workers are not even counted as unemployed if they have labor contracts that restart after the off-season, such as often occurs in teaching and professional sports.

Frictional unemployment occurs when people are between jobs, either because they were fired and have yet to line up new jobs or have quit voluntarily, such as in preparation for moving somewhere else or trying something new. Either way, their stay on the unemployment roles is likely to be brief. Frictional unemployment also includes many young people entering the labor market for the first time and older workers reentering the work force after an absence to raise children.

Changing jobs does not imply frictional unemployment. Most voluntary job switching is done without it; people line up new jobs before leaving their old ones. However, involuntary job changes, such as in response to layoffs and firings, commonly do result in frictional unemployment. In the case of involuntary frictional unemployment, publicly provided unemployment compensation acts as a safety net. It allows the job seeker to hold out longer in search of the best job opportunity.

STRUCTURAL—HUMAN CAPITAL MISMATCHES AND LABOR MARKET RIGIDITIES

Changes in the structure of the economy can give rise to structural unemployment, as demands for some types of goods and services give way to demands for others. This change in structure arises from such factors as technological change, international trade, and changing ways of doing business. For example, computers and telecommunications have opened doors to many types of jobs, but have cost many types of jobs, too.

Former telegraph operators exemplify structural unemployment. Once a valuable skill, the ability to speedily send coded messages over telegraph lines now has no market. Telegraph operators who were displaced by the technology of telephones could not easily find other employment at comparable wages. Their skills were not in demand. Until they retrained or found new jobs (usually at much lower wages), the ex–telegraph operators were structurally unemployed.

Rigidities that inhibit labor movement and the creation of new jobs can also cause structural unemployment. For example, the federal minimum wage law introduces a rigidity by making it difficult for workers with little human capital to find a job. Further rigidities arise from the regional nature of many jobs. For example, there may be pockets of unemployment in inner cities and some regions of the country, while there are plenty of job openings in suburbia or other states. If regional migration were without cost, such locational rigidities would vanish.

Human capital is often specific to a particular firm or kind of job—**specific human capital**—and does not apply readily to other firms or other jobs. As telegraph operators learned the hard way, workers with specific human capital are most prone to structural unemployment. It is a risk that people take voluntarily, since the best-paying jobs usually involve specific human capital. In contrast, **general human capital** involves such skills as language and math. General human capital is easily transferred from job to job. Those who possess it are less likely to be structurally unemployed. For most students, an undergraduate economics education represents general human capital. Economics majors are qualified to hold a variety of jobs in business and government. However, graduate training in economics is more specialized, and thus represents specific human capital. Students who earn a doctoral degree in economics usually build a career as a business or government economist, or as a college teacher of economics.

Structural unemployment is a necessary part of economic evolution. Without structural unemployment, there would be no progress—no industrial revolution, no railroad, no automobile, no computer. Those skilled workers who lose their jobs often find the transition to new jobs difficult, since economic change has depreciated the human capital that supported

specific human capital human capital that is specific to a particular firm or kind of job.

general human capital skills such as language and math that are easily transferred from job to job.

their incomes. They are usually forced to evaluate their alternatives, and either take a job with lower pay or drop out of the labor force to retire or learn new skills.

Examples of structural unemployment are frequently poignant, involving older workers who have advanced high up career ladders that collapse out from under them. Sometimes the reason involves imports. For example, the United States imports much of its steel from the countries of Europe and the Far East. Blast furnaces in America's "rust belt" that were built before World War II could not compete with the newer, more technologically advanced facilities in other countries. In response, America's primary steel producers laid off many highly skilled workers. Those skills and a powerful union had combined to increase steelworkers' earnings to levels far above what they could earn in other occupations. Does a 50-year-old ex-steelworker go back to school and start over, compete with teenagers for a minimum-wage job, or retire early and hope the money holds out? The choices are painful.

Structural unemployment is not only found in blue-collar jobs. Corporations have eliminated many white-collar managerial jobs in corporate downsizings in recent years. Like their blue-collar counterparts, former managers find that job openings are few and competition is fierce. Their choices are often little better than those of the 50-year-old steelworker just mentioned.

The government sometimes offers job-training programs to cushion the blows of structural unemployment. The question arises, though, as to the form of that training. For example, should the government train people to be hair stylists? That would take the jobs of other hair stylists or force them to work at lower wages. Such human capital is also so specific that it would not be pertinent for many of the structurally unemployed. The 50-year-old steelworker would probably not enroll.

SNAPSHOT   A WORLD WITHOUT CHANGE

Change is distressing. It disrupts our lives and makes us scramble to adapt to it. It causes stress in our lives, especially when it causes us to lose our jobs. Just ask the bank tellers who lost their jobs to automatic teller machines. Or the typewriter repair people who just never learned about computer keyboards. Or the many others whose skills became obsolete when technology or tastes changed against the industries or occupations in which they worked. They are the structurally unemployed.

When spending patterns change, so do the available jobs. The only way to avoid such disruption would be to freeze ourselves in time. For example, if change had been forbidden in the early 1960s, then we would still be watching the TV shows, listening to the music, and driving the cars of that era. Life would be pretty much like dwelling in a museum. ◀

CYCLICAL—A SYSTEMIC DISORDER

A troublesome form of unemployment is caused by downturns in the business cycle, *panics* as they were called in the nineteenth century. In these periodic downturns, which we refer to as recessions today, people in numerous sectors of the economy lose their jobs simultaneously. There just does not seem to be enough spending to go around, at least for awhile. Cyclical unemployment is thus a *systemic disorder*—a problem felt throughout the entire economy. The increase in U.S. unemployment in 1991 and 1992, and again in 2001, exemplifies cyclical unemployment since those increases were associated with the mild recessions that occurred at those times. In contrast, the higher unemployment in 2002 and 2003 was associated with the so-called jobless recovery.

Cyclical unemployment is a temporary phenomena because recessions are temporary. As the economy pulls out of a recession, job creation leads the cyclically unemployed to

---

QUICKCHECK

Categorize each of the following cases according to the type of unemployment described: (1) long-term unemployment related to lack of marketable skills; (2) temporary unemployment related to finding a job or switching jobs; (3) unemployment related to a recession; (4) lack of a job because of the time of year.

Answer: (1) structural; (2) frictional; (3) cyclical; and (4) seasonal unemployment.

---

return to their old jobs or find new ones. In this way cyclical unemployment diminishes and eventually disappears.

6.3 UNEMPLOYMENT INSURANCE AND THE NATURAL RATE OF UNEMPLOYMENT

Unemployed workers who qualify are able to collect state-provided *unemployment insurance* payments to help tide them over during a spell of unemployment. Benefits vary from state to state, paid for by taxes on employers. Workers who are laid off for economic reasons qualify for unemployment benefits, but workers who are fired do not. Otherwise, incentives would exist for workers to provoke their own firings in order to undeservedly collect benefits. Unemployment insurance programs were instituted on a widespread basis in the United States during the 1930s in order to alleviate some of the human suffering that accompanies unemployment. These programs partner the state governments with the federal government in providing cash benefits to the unemployed. Figure 6-8 shows how the average weekly unemployment check has grown over time.

By making it easier for the unemployed to stay unemployed, unemployment insurance contributes to a higher unemployment rate. If there were no unemployment insurance, the unemployed would be forced to take work or apply for welfare benefits as soon as their savings ran out, even if they were not happy with the jobs available to them. Unemployment insurance affords workers the time to find better jobs, thus increasing the *duration of unemployment.* Unemployment insurance programs build in some provisions that are designed to discourage idleness on the part of the unemployed. These provisions include a requirement that, to receive benefits, recipients must demonstrate evidence of applying for work each week. There are also limits on how long unemployment insurance can be received. Typically, unemployment insurance benefits are exhausted after one year or less.

In countries around the globe, unemployment rates average significantly closer to zero than to 100 percent. This is no coincidence. People look for ways to work because work puts food on the table. Even in the Great Depression of the 1930s, unemployment in the United States never exceeded 25 percent of the work force, and was as high as 20 percent for only four years, 1932–1935. Given that income is critical to living, however, it does not take many percentage points of unemployment to cause severe human trauma. The Great Depression was proof of the misery that high unemployment can bring.

Over time, the unemployment rate does not tend toward zero, exactly. Rather, the tendency is for unemployment to settle at a few percentage points above zero, due to the inevitable presence of seasonal, frictional, and structural unemployment. The minimum sustainable level of unemployment is termed the **natural rate of unemployment,** and is thought to be around 5 percent of the U.S. work force today.

natural rate of unemployment
the minimum sustainable level of unemployment; associated with zero cyclical unemployment.

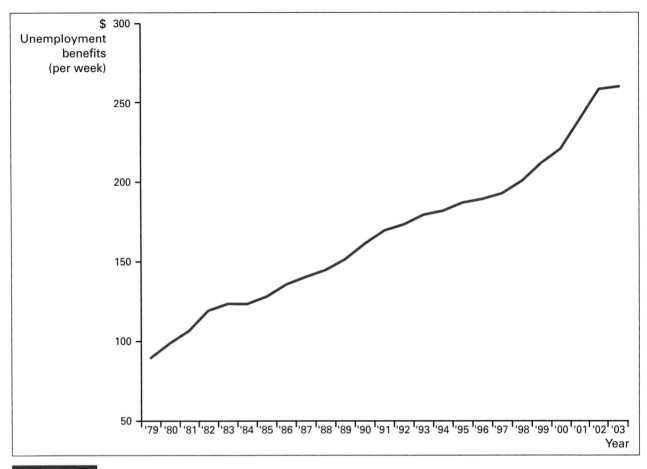

FIGURE 6-8

THE GROWTH IN THE AVERAGE WEEKLY UNEMPLOYMENT BENEFIT Average unemployment benefits have increased over time. The checks received by the unemployed are not intended to replace all of the income they earned when they had jobs.

Source: 2003 Economic Report of the President, Table B-45, Employment and Training Administration, and U.S. Department of Labor.

The economy would tend toward a lower natural rate in the absence of unemployment insurance and other social *safety net* programs, such as Medicaid, food stamps, and additional programs designed to cushion the impact of unemployment or poverty. Without the safety net, the unemployed would be subject to greater misery, and a correspondingly greater incentive to grasp at any job offer, without regard to its long-term consequences for their future prospects. From an employer's perspective, minimum wage laws, liability laws, and many other policies discourage job formation because of the cost of complying with them. Other government policies, such as employment-related tax breaks for businesses, can have the opposite effect. Thus, government policies can and do affect the level of employment. Because of government actions, it is likely that the natural rate of unemployment has risen from a little over 2 percent a century ago to somewhere in the vicinity of 5 percent today.

full employment 100 percent minus the natural rate of unemployment.

The flip side of the natural rate of unemployment is **full employment,** which equals 100 percent minus the natural rate of unemployment. Because the natural rate of unemployment exceeds zero, full employment occurs when the employment rate is less than 100 percent. In short, economies will always have people who are looking for jobs.

What are some reasons that the natural rate of unemployment is higher today than it was a century ago?

Answer: Unlike a century ago, the out-of-work today need not fear starvation or resort to private charity. Unemployment compensation, food stamps, and other programs provide a safety net that removes some of the urgency about finding a job right away. Another reason is structural unemployment caused by minimum wage laws, laws that did not exist a century ago.

FORECASTING JOBS LOST TO IMPORTS—NO MARKET FOR THE NATURAL RATE?

SNAPSHOT

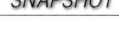

We must have an income, and so we work. If we are out of work, we offer to work for less pay, which tends to drive wages down. As wages fall, prices fall. Our incomes then buy more goods, and more people can work to produce them. The process continues until all but about 5 percent of us have jobs. That is the logic of the natural rate of unemployment.

When it comes to international trade, though, the media has no patience for logic—it wants numbers to drum up interest! How many jobs do we gain from trade? How many do we lose? Reporters eagerly seek out so-called experts who provide numerical forecasts that international trade cuts down on aggregate employment. Other experts then reply with numbers showing just the opposite.

As usual, reality lies somewhere in the middle. Imports cost jobs in import-competing industries. However, the logic of a natural rate of unemployment leaves no room for international trade to have any lasting effect on unemployment in the aggregate. Workers who lose their jobs to imports would find other jobs. That is why, when faced with low-priced imported beef, many South Texas ranches switched from raising cattle to raising wild game for hunters. More generally, that is why, even as the United States imported a then-record $271.3 billion more goods than it exported in 1999, that year's unemployment rate was lower than it had been in thirty years! Unfortunately, logic usually lacks the eye-popping magic of charts with numbers, and therein seems to lie the market. ◄

6.4 EMPLOYING LABOR—HIDDEN CONSEQUENCES OF THE LAW

Explore & Apply

"But what we do know is that if we have a sufficiently flexible labor market..., that jobs will be created."

—*Federal Reserve Chairman Alan Greenspan, July 15, 2003*

When jobs are being created, we don't think much about it. But when job creation stalls, or even reverses course to become jobs lost, then there is an issue. Such was the case in July 2003 when the U.S. Labor Department reported that 486,000 jobs had been lost since January. Since the economy was on the rebound from the mild recession of 2001, people were calling it the jobless recovery. Yet, the leader of the Federal Reserve, perhaps America's most influential economic policymaker, speculated that "jobs will be created" in testimony before Congress that month. He did make that statement conditional, however, upon a "sufficiently flexible labor market." What did he mean?

The flexibility of employers to hire workers, fire workers, and manage them in the meanwhile is important to job creation. Lack of flexibility means higher costs, and because of higher costs, fewer jobs. The chief impediment to labor market flexibility is associated with the requirement that employers comply with labor market regulations. Let's see why.

Employers incur expenses associated with complying with employment laws and regulations. Hiring new employees is no longer as simple as advertising a job, interviewing the applicants, checking the references, and making the best choice. Firms must be careful to avoid lawsuits in this process. The lawsuits could come from the federal government, perhaps while it guards against discrimination. A lawsuit could also come from someone who was not hired. Such a lawsuit might allege an unfair hiring process. While many lawsuits involve an honest difference of opinion, frivolous lawsuits designed to harass defendants have resulted in the common use of the phrase "lawsuit abuse."

Jobs nowadays must be advertised using very careful wording. Prior to the passage of the Equal Pay Act of 1963, Title VII of the Civil Rights Act of 1964, and the Age Discrimination in Employment Act of 1967, if a particularly appealing applicant came along, an employer could tailor the job to suit that applicant's unique abilities. Such actions today would wave the red flag of lawsuit over discriminatory treatment of those who were not hired. Hiring exactly according to a written advertisement avoids this problem, but also lowers the expected payoff to the firm from advertising a new opening. This caution increases the cost of producing the firm's output. These costs are not measured in official statistics.

Information about prospective employees is increasingly hard to come by. The Equal Employment Opportunity Commission (EEOC) issues detailed guidelines about questions that are or are not appropriate to ask of job candidates. The same questions must be asked of each candidate. The employer cannot revise the list once interviewing has started, even if it becomes obvious that some pertinent questions have been overlooked. This very formal process makes it difficult for an employer to get a feel for whether an employee will fit into the organization.

Letters of recommendation are often nearly devoid of meaningful information. The threat of lawsuits bears much of the blame. After all, previous employers or others who know of reasons why someone should not be hired have no incentive to reveal it. Even if their information is true, they might still be sued for slander, defamation of character, or some other charge. There could even be dangers of lawsuits from future employers if letters of recommendation are misleadingly glowing.

Since the certain expense and uncertain outcome of a lawsuit is something few letter writers wish to face, letters of recommendation are often little more than reports on such dry, objective facts as a job applicant's previous position and duration of employment. The upshot is that hiring firms face an increasingly risky process, one less likely to match the best-qualified person to the job. This process increases per-unit production costs above what they might have been. It also affects the decision about whether to hire, since the hassles of hiring can be avoided by working current employees longer hours or more efficiently. The result is fewer employees per unit of output.

Government regulations and mandates have also increased employment costs. For example, the Americans with Disabilities Act mandates that firms accommodate a variety of employee disabilities. Usually, for example, a firm cannot simply fire a worker for showing up to work inebriated, since that might be a symptom of alcoholism. Alcoholism is a covered disability. Health and safety regulations, anti-discrimination laws, family leave requirements, and other government actions are intended to make the workplace better. They also increase per-unit production costs.

Such cost increases even arise from government-mandated protections for employees about to lose their jobs. For example, consider the requirement that firms notify their employees at least sixty days prior to closing a production facility and laying off employees that work there. In those sixty days, firms can expect to see both productivity and quality drop, perhaps precipitously. After all, employees are not usually motivated to do their best if they know that they will be out of work shortly. If they choose to produce at all, firms must be prepared for high absenteeism, low productivity, and even sabotage. In these ways, legislation designed to cushion the blow of unemployment has the unintended side effect of increasing firms' production costs.

DO GOVERNMENT POLICIES HELP EMPLOYEES?

Despite all the government presence in the employment process, life on the job isn't necessarily any easier. This is not surprising. The same incentives that reduce the number of employees

TABLE 6-2 **PERCENTAGE OF EMPLOYED WHO WORK 55 TO 99 HOURS A WEEK, BY OCCUPATION AND SEX**

PERCENTAGES FOR MEN	
Physicians	44
Firefighters	41
Clergy	40
Restaurant and Hotel Managers	32
Vehicle Sales	26
Lawyers	25
Total:	10
PERCENTAGES FOR WOMEN	
Physicians	32
Lawyers	18
College Faculty	16
Marketing Managers	12
Restaurant and Hotel Managers	12
Total:	3

Source: Daniel Hecker, How Hours of Work Affect Occupational Earnings, *Monthly Labor Review*, October 1998.

firms wish to hire also motivate firms to obtain more productivity from the employees they already have. From the employees' perspective, finding new jobs is more difficult. Because all employers face similar incentives to increase productivity, employees have little recourse but to bear down and be more productive. Thus, we see the rise of workweeks that are much longer than the traditional forty hours. Table 6-2 shows the results of a survey of workers that identified those who work long hours, classified in the survey as 55 to 99 hours a week. The occupations shown are selected from those that exhibit the highest percentage of workers who fall into that classification. Men tend to work longer hours than women, an average of 44 hours for men and 41 hours for women. In addition to showing data for specific occupations, the table also shows that 10 percent of men and 3 percent of women work long hours.

Incongruously, we also see more temporary and part-time positions. The reasons for both trends are similar. Part-time and temporary workers are easier to hire and fire and require fewer federally mandated benefits. For example, firms will go to extraordinary lengths to stay below fifty full-time employees. By law, firms that exceed that threshold find themselves subject to an array of costly mandates and regulations. Part-time and temporary workers often provide the flexibility to avoid that threshold.

Taken as a whole, then, the increasing presence of well-intentioned laws pertaining to the workplace is threatening one of the mainstays of middle-class American existence, the forty-hour workweek. Part-time and overtime work is on the rise. Whether or not these changes are for the long-term good, is it any wonder that jobs seem stressful? Employment statistics measure the quantity of employment. We have no federal measure of its quality. The increasingly common reports of violence in the workplace give reason to wonder. According to the BLS, workplace violence accounted for 16 percent of the 5,900 workplace fatalities in 2001 (excluding the 9/11 terrorist attacks). Additionally, there were over 23,000 assaults and violent acts in the workplace that did not end in fatalities.

Few Americans would wish to repeal the laws or regulations that aim to eliminate discrimination and other workplace problems. However, a recognition of the costs of these mandates can help alleviate the unavoidable burdens. A little less stress on the job might contribute to a higher quality of life for all.

THINKING CRITICALLY

1. This Explore & Apply notes that laws and regulations are enacted in order to accomplish some worthy end. However, because these benefits are not elaborated upon, you might get the impression that legislation and litigation have imposed costs in excess of their benefits. Have they? Justify your answer with some specific examples.

2. What characteristics would a high-quality job have for you personally? If you worked at a job that failed to provide your desired characteristics, would you be willing to quit and join the ranks of the unemployed? Why or why not? What sorts of considerations would lie behind your decision?

 Visit www.prenhall.com/ayers for updates and web exercises on this Explore & Apply topic.

SUMMARY AND LEARNING OBJECTIVES

1. **Identify who is part of the labor force and who is not.**
   - The civilian labor force equals the number of persons age 16 and over who have a job or are looking for one. The labor force participation rate is found by dividing the labor force by the population age 16 and over. Currently, the U.S. labor force participation rate is about 66 percent.

2. **Explain how the unemployment rate is calculated.**
   - The unemployment rate equals the number of unemployed persons divided by the civilian labor force, multiplied by 100. The unemployment rate must be interpreted carefully, because of the existence of discouraged workers. Discouraged workers are not counted in the labor force because they have given up looking for work. If they were counted, the reported unemployment rate would rise.
   - The reported unemployment rate is higher than the true unemployment rate because of the underground economy. Note that the underground economy biases the reported unemployment rate in the opposite direction from discouraged workers.

3. **Elaborate on unemployment in other countries.**
   - There is a tendency for changes in unemployment rates across countries to move together. In contrast, the level of unemployment varies significantly across countries.

4. **Divide unemployment into different types and explain the implications of each.**
   - Unemployment of labor comes in four basic types: seasonal, frictional, structural, and cyclical.
   - Seasonal unemployment is related to the time of year. Examples include the department store Santa Claus without a job after Christmas, and the farm worker who becomes unemployed after the crop is harvested.
   - Frictional unemployment is associated with job switching and entry into the labor force. Frictional unemployment cannot be eliminated since, even though most job switches occur without unemployment time, there will always be some new jobs that cannot be lined up prior to departure from the old. Even when there is time between jobs, the frictionally unemployed typically do not stay unemployed for long.
   - Structural unemployment occurs when job skills become obsolete. Without skills that are in demand in the labor market, the structurally unemployed will remain unemployed for an extended time. Job training programs can reduce structural unemployment.
   - Cyclical unemployment is associated with the business cycle. During recessions, workers are laid off and the unemployment rate rises accordingly.

5. **Describe the natural rate of unemployment and its converse, full employment.**
   - The natural rate of unemployment is the minimum unemployment rate the economy can sustain in the

long run. The natural rate changes over time. Currently, it is estimated to be around 5 percent.

- A natural rate of unemployment implies the existence of full employment and the absense of cyclical unemployment.
- Unemployment insurance programs offer financial support to the unemployed. However, they also offer an incentive to remain unemployed. Thus, the existence of unemployment insurance increases the unemployment rate.

 6. Discuss how the quality of employment can deteriorate when mandates increase labor costs.

- Because of various government actions, the expense of hiring and employing labor is higher than it otherwise would be. Employment-related government mandates are intended to create a more equitable workplace. However, the higher costs might cause some firms to cut back on their use of labor. Job stress and uncertainty can be a side effect.

KEY TERMS

labor force, 146
unemployment rate, 146
labor force participation rate, 146
discouraged workers, 150

frictional unemployment, 154
seasonal unemployment, 154
structural unemployment, 154
cyclical unemployment, 154

specific human capital, 155
general human capital, 155
natural rate of unemployment, 157
full employment, 158

TEST YOURSELF

TRUE OR FALSE

1. Persons over the age of 65 are excluded when the labor force is counted.
2. Recently, the U.S. labor force participation rate has been around 67 percent.
3. Persons who work but receive no pay, such as in a family business, are never counted as employed.
4. Frictional unemployment is associated with the business cycle.
5. The natural rate of unemployment is the unemployment rate associated with full employment.

MULTIPLE CHOICE

6. To be counted as employed, someone must work for pay
   a. at least 1 hour a week.
   b. at least 15 hours a week.
   c. at least 35 hours a week.
   d. for at least as many hours as that person wants to work.
7. The civilian labor force does not include
   a. workers under the age of 16.
   b. the unemployed.
   c. part-time workers.
   d. anyone working in a family business without pay.
8. The long-term trend in the labor force participation rate in the United States has been
   a. flat.
   b. up.
   c. down.
   d. cyclical.

9. To be counted as unemployed, an individual must
   a. not have a job.
   b. not have a job and be looking for work.
   c. not have a job, be looking for work, and be willing to accept the first job offer he or she receives.
   d. have held a job in the past, not have a job now, be looking for work, and be willing to accept the first job offer.
10. Discouraged workers
    a. are counted among the employed.
    b. are counted among the unemployed.
    c. would increase the unemployment rate if they were counted among the unemployed.
    d. have no effect on the labor force and unemployment statistics regardless of how or whether they are counted.
11. How does the underground economy affect the measurement of unemployment?
    a. It causes the reported unemployment rate to be higher than the true unemployment rate.
    b. It causes the reported unemployment rate to be lower than the true unemployment rate.
    c. It has no effect on the reported unemployment rate.
    d. It affects the reported unemployment rate in varying, but unpredictable, ways.
12. The duration of unemployment is an important aspect of unemployment because it tells us
    a. the probability that someone will become unemployed.
    b. the average age of the unemployed.
    c. how long people are unemployed.
    d. the lost income that is associated with unemployment.

13. Which type of unemployment is associated with a recession?
    a. Frictional.
    b. Seasonal.
    c. Structural.
    d. Cyclical.

14. Which type of unemployment is associated with technological change?
    a. Frictional.
    b. Seasonal.
    c. Structural.
    d. Cyclical.

15. Which type of unemployment is typically long term?
    a. Frictional.
    b. Seasonal.
    c. Structural.
    d. Cyclical.

16. The current best estimate of the natural rate of unemployment is around
    a. 0 percent.
    b. 1 percent.
    c. 5 percent.
    d. 7 percent.

17. The natural rate of unemployment
    a. remains constant over time.
    b. is higher today than a century ago.
    c. is lower today than a century ago.
    d. changes every day, so that it is sometimes higher than in the 1970s, but sometimes lower than then.

18. Full employment
    a. occurs only when 100 percent of the labor force is employed.
    b. equals 100 minus the natural rate of unemployment.
    c. is achieved when no one is frictionally unemployed.
    d. is a concept that is useful in the abstract, but never actually occurs in reality.

19. Unemployment insurance
    a. has no effect on the unemployment rate.
    b. increases the unemployment rate.
    c. decreases the unemployment rate.
    d. has unpredictable effects on the unemployment rate.

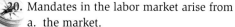

20. Mandates in the labor market arise from
    a. the market.
    b. government.
    c. firms.
    d. workers.

QUESTIONS AND PROBLEMS

1. *[civilian labor force]* How would the labor force be affected if those in the military were included? What effect would including the military in the labor force have on the unemployment rate?

2. *[labor force]* Can you think of a logical reason for excluding persons under the age of 16 from the labor force statistics, but not excluding persons over age 65 or even age 70 from the statistics? Explain.

3. *[labor force participation]* a) Provide several examples of individuals who would choose not to participate in the labor force. b) The labor force participation rate among men between 35 and 44 years of age is nearly 100 percent. What would explain such a high labor force participation rate?

4. *[labor force participation rate]* How is the labor force participation rate calculated? What is your best guess about the labor force participation rate among students in your economics class?

5. *[unemployment rate]* How is the unemployment rate calculated? Are discouraged workers included?

6. *[unemployment rates over time]* Use the data in Table 6-1 to answer the following questions.
    a. What is the highest unemployment rate in the table and what year did it occur?
    b. What is the lowest unemployment rate in the table and what year did it occur?

    c. Is there an easily discernable long-term trend in unemployment rates? Explain.

7. *[differences in unemployment rates]* Would you expect the average unemployment rate among high school graduates to be the same as the average unemployment rate among college graduates? Explain.

8. *[labor force and unemployment rate]* Suppose the country of Worklandia has a population of 100,000 persons age 16 and above. Of these persons 70,000 are working, 3,000 have no job, but are looking for a job, 7,000 of them are discouraged workers, and the rest are either students or retired. What is the labor force participation rate in Worklandia? What is the unemployment rate in that country?

9. *[types of unemployment]* List three instances when you or someone you know has been unemployed. For each, explain the type of unemployment, such as frictional, seasonal, structural, or cyclical.

10. *[structural unemployment]* Explain the role of human capital in the ability of an individual to find and keep a job.

11. *[seasonal unemployment]* Provide at least two examples of workers who are likely to become seasonally unemployed in each of the following cases.
    a. The day after Christmas.
    b. The day after the Super Bowl.
    c. The day after the last day of school.

12. *[influences on unemployment]* How does the "work ethic" of a country affect its labor force participation rate and its unemployment rate? Is it possible for a country to have too strong a work ethic? Explain.

13. *[natural rate of unemployment]* Why do economists reject the notion that the natural rate of unemployment equals zero? Why is the natural rate stated to be in the vicinity of 5 percent instead of an exact number?

14. *[full employment]* The employment rate in percent equals 100 minus the unemployment rate. What employment rate represents full employment in the United States? Explain.

15. *[imports and employment]* Explain why the logic of the natural rate of unemployment leaves no room for international trade to have any lasting effect on aggregate employment.

WORKING WITH GRAPHS AND DATA

1. *[labor force, labor force participation rate, unemployment]* Leveltown researchers have collected the following data pertaining to its labor market. You are to assume that there is one job per person.

Population 16 and over	Labor force	Employed	Unemployed	Labor force participation rate	Unemployment rate
800,000	500,000	450,000			

a. Create a table that starts with the data and columns shown. Fill in the three unmarked entries for the first line in that table. You will be adding to this table in the subsequent sections of this problem.

b. Suppose that Acme Corporation moves to Leveltown and creates 10,000 additional jobs, *ceteris paribus*. Write a general statement on the impact of this event on the unemployment rate.

c. Suppose that 100,000 more people are willing to work today than in the original table you filled out in part a. How would this change the data? (Do not use the information for question b here.) Add a third line to the table showing the effect of this event. Describe its impact on the unemployment rate.

d. Suppose that the previous two events occur simultaneously. That is, Acme corporation creates 10,000 new jobs and 100,000 more people are looking for work. Add a fourth line to the table that reflects these events. Describe their joint impact on the unemployment rate.

e. Suppose you are the mayor of Leveltown and running for re-election. What would you say about the labor market in Leveltown in order to promote your campaign?

f. Suppose that you were the mayor's opponent in the election. What information would you report from this labor market data in order to promote your campaign?

2. *[unemployment rate]* Graphs 6-1 and 6-2 indicate the unemployment rate and the level of employment in the village of Hedgehog. You are to explain to the local government the relationship between these two variables for each time period.

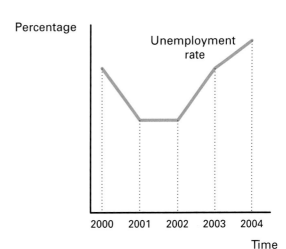

GRAPH 6-1

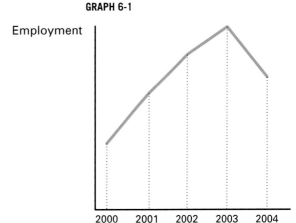

GRAPH 6-2

3. *[labor force participation]* Solve the following unemployment problems.
   a. There are 8,000,000 people in the population who are 16 years of age or older. Eighty percent of these people are willing to work. The economy is currently experiencing a 10 percent unemployment rate.
      i) How many people are in the labor force?
      ii) How many people are unemployed?
      iii) How many people are employed?
   b. Currently the economy has 140,000,000 employed people. Five million are unemployed. The labor force participation rate is 67 percent.
      i) How many people are in the labor force?
      ii) How many people are 16 years of age or older?
      iii) What is the unemployment rate in the economy?
   c. There are 10,000,000 unemployed workers in the economy. The unemployment rate is 8 percent and there are 200,000,000 people 16 years of age or older.
      i) How many people are there in the labor force?
      ii) How many people are employed?
      iii) What is the labor force participation rate?

4. *[unemployment rate]* Graph 6-3 indicates the unemployment rates of two countries, X and Y, over a period of time. Answer the questions that follow by interpreting the graph and the information provided in the question.
   a. Which country had the highest unemployment rate in 2001?
   b. Which country experienced the largest growth in its unemployment rate from 2000 to 2001?
   c. Which country had the greatest amount of unemployment in 2001?

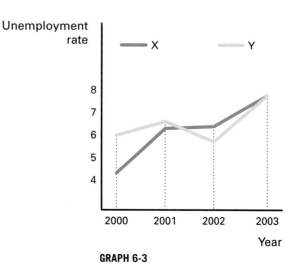

GRAPH 6-3

   d. Which country had the highest unemployment rate in 2003?
   e. Which country experienced the largest growth in its unemployment rate from 2002 to 2003?
   f. Which country had the greatest amount of unemployment in 2003?
   g. Suppose that you learned that country X included its military in its employment data. How might that affect your answers to questions a, b, and c?
   h. Suppose that you learned that country Y included discouraged workers as being unemployed in statistics. How might this impact your answers to questions a, b, and c?

 Visit www.prenhall.com/ayers for Exploring the Web exercises and additional self-test quizzes.

CHAPTER 7

INFLATION

A LOOK AHEAD

Inflation—widespread, persistent price increases—can hurt people. It can change their behavior and keep them awake at night worrying about whether their incomes will keep up with prices. It can lower their standard of living when their incomes fall behind. In America, inflation has been a fact of life, but at least that inflation has been mild. In some other countries, inflation has been severe. In the Explore & Apply section in this chapter you will see how people make adjustments in their lifestyles in response to inflation. You will also see how people might respond to *deflation*—a general decline in prices.

Low inflation is a basic macroeconomic goal. As you read this chapter you will see why we prefer low inflation, the several ways that inflation is measured, and some ways that have been devised by people to defend themselves against the harmful effects of inflation.

LEARNING OBJECTIVES

Understanding Chapter 7 will enable you to:
1. **Describe inflation rates in the United States and other countries.**
2. **Discuss the effects of inflation that cause low inflation to be a macroeconomic goal.**
3. **Compute, interpret, and use a price index to compute a real value.**
4. **Identify problems with price indexes and efforts to improve them.**
5. **Explain how people respond to price changes, and how their responses affect the measurement of prices.**

Explore & Apply

Do you notice price changes when you go shopping? Most people do, especially when prices are rising fast. This chapter will show you how changes in the cost of living are measured and why it is important to keep track of inflation.

7.1 THE GOAL OF LOW INFLATION

You have learned that there are three fundamental goals for our economy: economic growth, high employment, and low inflation. How well have we achieved the last goal? Let's take a look at the behavior of prices over time to answer that question.

MODERN HISTORY OF U.S. INFLATION

price level prices of goods and services in the aggregate.

The **price level** refers to the prices of goods and services, when considered in the aggregate. Even with no training in economics it is easy for you to recognize that the price level today is higher than it was when you were born. For example, by going to the library and taking a peek at twenty-year-old copies of your local newspaper, you would see that back then a basic economy car cost about $4,000, a man's dress shirt $10, a gallon of regular gas 80 cents, and a pound of bananas 20 cents. These items today might average about $13,000, $20, $1.40, and 40 cents, respectively. Many other items commonly purchased are also more expensive. A few items have gotten cheaper. Examples include television sets, cell phones, and other electronics. Overall, however, since most prices are higher, we say that the price level is also higher today than twenty years ago. Most of the time the price level increases from one year to the next.

inflation persistent, widespread increases in the price level.

Inflation is a persistent increase in the price level. Thus, inflation is not the same as a one-time increase in the prices of a few products. Rather, inflation involves widespread price increases, affecting the prices of many goods and services. Inflation can be mild, meaning that price increases are typically small for most goods, or severe, in which case price increases tend to be large. Any amount of inflation robs people of their purchasing power, *ceteris paribus*.

inflation rate the annual percentage increase in the price level.

The **inflation rate** is the annual percentage increase in the price level. We can compare the inflation rate in one year to the inflation rate in other years. In the United States, so long as the inflation rate stays at approximately 3 percent or less, most Americans are satisfied that the goal of low inflation has been accomplished. Once the inflation rate gets much over 3 percent, people tend to become worried.

As the inflation rate rises beyond the 3 percent threshold, people expect the federal government to "fight" inflation. In the United States, the last bout of relatively high inflation occurred in the 1970s. Every president in that decade fought for his political future by taking a stand against inflation. For example, in the mid-1970s President Ford tried to popularize a small lapel button that said WIN. WIN stood for Whip Inflation Now. Most people thought the WIN buttons were silly and ineffective. Partly because of inflation, candidate Jimmy Carter beat President Ford in the 1976 election. Ironically, the inflation rate had fallen every year of the Ford presidency, but promptly rebounded under Carter. When inflation rates reached new highs during the Carter years, Carter himself was turned out of office by Ronald Reagan's 1980 victory. As you can see, presidents may need to pay attention to inflation or pay the consequences. Because inflation was low during the last decade, it has become less of an election issue than it used to be.

Let's check the U.S. inflation rate over the years by looking at Figure 7-1. This figure shows the annual inflation rate in the United States since 1945, the last year of World War II. We can see that the inflation rate fluctuates. The somewhat high inflation in the late 1940s after World War II, and during the second year of the Korean War (1950–1953), subsided throughout the rest of the 1950s and early 1960s. Inflation began to increase as the Vietnam

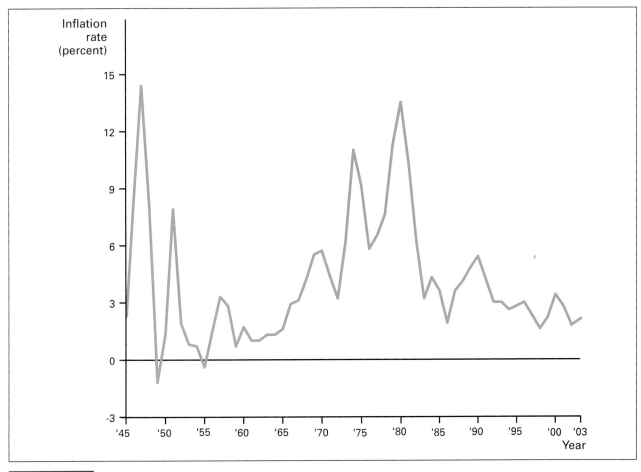

FIGURE 7-1

THE U.S. INFLATION RATE SINCE 1945 The annual inflation rate changes from year to year. The relatively high inflation rates in some years tell us that the goal of low inflation is sometimes elusive.

Source: 2003 Economic Report of the President, Table B-64, and Bureau of Labor Statistics. The inflation rates shown are based on the Consumer Price Index.

QUICKCHECK

What is the price level? How is the inflation rate related to the price level?

Answer: The price level refers to the prices of goods and services in the aggregate. An inflation rate is expressed as an annual percentage increase in the price level.

War heated up in the mid-to-late 1960s, continued to rise during the 1970s, and peaked in the early 1980s. Most of the 1980s were characterized by declining inflation rates. Inflation stayed relatively low in the 1990s. Although there are periodic fears that a new outbreak of high inflation is about to begin, such fears had not been realized by 2003, as the United States continued to experience the relatively low inflation that characterized the 1990s. As the figure shows, however, the inflation rate can rise significantly from one year to the next, so no one knows what the future holds.

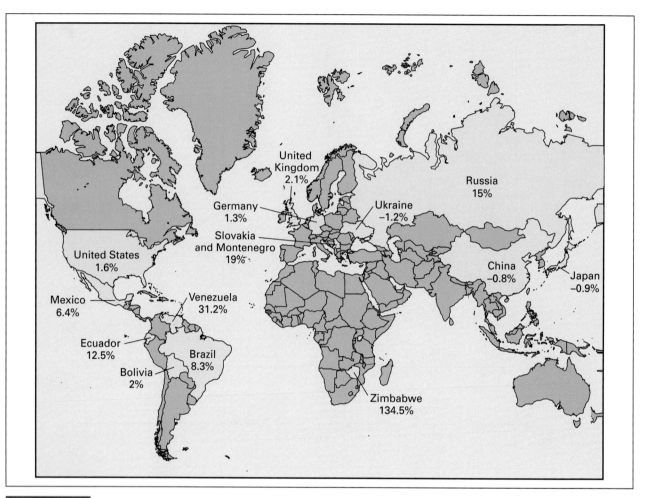

FIGURE 7-2

INFLATION RATES IN SELECTED COUNTRIES Inflation rates vary significantly from country to country.
Developing countries tend to have higher inflation rates than do developed countries.

Source: Central Intelligence Agency, *The World Factbook, 2003.* The inflation rates are for consumer prices.

INFLATION—A WORLDWIDE PHENOMENON

Inflation is not confined just to the United States. The Central Intelligence Agency (CIA) estimates that the median inflation rate in the world in 2002 was 3.3 percent. Throughout recent history, inflation has been most severe in developing nations, ones facing a variety of economic and social problems. The CIA estimates that typical developing countries had inflation rates between 5 percent and 60 percent in 2002, which is markedly higher than the typical 1 percent to 4 percent inflation rate in developed countries. A few countries, such as Japan, have had lower inflation rates than the United States. Figure 7-2 shows recent inflation rates for selected countries. The figure reveals that inflation is a near universal fact of life in the modern world.

Countries with very high inflation rates usually try to bring them down because high inflation is unpopular. Political instability can be the result of letting inflation get out of control. For example, Bolivia had an 11,000 percent (!) inflation rate in 1985, which brought about a change in its government the next year. Figure 7-2 shows that Bolivia has been able to successfully rein in its inflation of the 1980s. Other countries, including Brazil and Venezuela, have also suffered from very high inflation rates in the last decade or two. Similarly, they have brought their inflation rates down to no more than two digits, also documented in Figure 7-2. However, countries with a history of high inflation seem to swerve back and forth between extreme increases in the price level and relative price stability.

Seeking a solution to its high inflation, Ecuador adopted a policy of *dollarization* in 2001. Dollarization replaces a country's currency with the U.S. dollar. By dollarizing its economy, Ecuador expects to be better off because its inflation rate should mirror the relatively low U.S. inflation rate. Dollarization should also provide for a more stable economy and government since the value of the dollar is relatively stable. In the year following dollarization, the inflation rate in Ecuador fell sharply from 96 percent to 12.5 percent.

DEFLATION AND DISINFLATION

When the inflation rate is negative, *deflation* is said to occur. That would happen if the price level declined from one year to the next. Severe, persistent deflation has yet to occur in modern U.S. history, although the economy showed slight deflation in 1949 and 1955, which you can see in Figure 7-1. More recently, prices of raw materials and some other goods, such as personal computers, fell significantly in the late 1990s, but not enough that we could say there was deflation. As for other countries, Figure 7-2 shows that Japan experienced a small negative value for its inflation rate, indicating mild deflation.

Shoppers benefit from persistently falling prices by being able to buy more with their incomes, which means that their purchasing power is increased by deflation. For example, if deflation caused all prices to drop by 10 percent, then other things equal, everyone's income would buy 10 percent more. Borrowers, on the other hand, see declining values of the items they have purchased using debt, while the size of their debts remain constant. The family that borrowed $100,000 to finance the $100,000 purchase price of a new home would find that their home was worth only $90,000 after a 10 percent deflation, but their debt would stay at $100,000.

Deflation is not a macroeconomic goal because deflation tends to be associated with economies in trouble. In the 1930s, the U.S. economy experienced significant deflation during the Great Depression. Sixty years later, a decade characterized by recession and weak growth in Japan has also been associated with deflation in that country. The conclusion drawn by many economists is that deflation must be avoided in order for an economy to prosper.

Disinflation differs from either inflation or deflation. *Disinflation* means that the rate of inflation declines. For instance, if we observed inflation rates of 7 percent followed by 2 percent over two consecutive years, disinflation would have occurred. Disinflation is sometimes confused with deflation, but they are not the same. You can see in Figure 7-1 that disinflation occurs quite frequently. It is identified in the figure with dips in the line showing the inflation rate.

SNAPSHOT   "WATCH FOR FALLING PRICES"—CAN WAL-MART HELP KEEP INFLATION IN CHECK?

It's all about low prices at Wal-Mart. The slogan in the title is designed to keep customers coming back by convincing them that Wal-Mart strives to give them more for their money. You've probably seen the ads that show the old higher prices and the new lower prices of specific items.

How does Wal-Mart bring down those prices, and what effect does the retail giant have on inflation? Wal-Mart is able to cut prices when it finds ways to increase the efficiency with which it operates and thereby cut its operating costs. Efficiency increases help keep inflation in check. ◄

7.2 THE HARM FROM INFLATION

In spite of relatively little inflation in the United States in recent years, the fear of higher inflation persists. This fear causes people to pay attention to inflation data. Toward the middle of each month, the government makes public the inflation rate for the previous month in a news release that is reported by the media. Of course, even without access to inflation data, people can tell a lot about the inflation rate just by visiting their local supermarket or discount store. For many Americans, the ultimate inflation tale is the story told by a cash register tape.

Energy and food prices are subject to wide fluctuations caused by temporary shifts in their supplies. Excluding food and energy prices from the computation of the inflation rate reveals what is termed *core inflation*. The core rate of inflation is of special interest when food and energy inflation rates differ significantly from the overall inflation rate. Otherwise, core inflation and the overall inflation rate will not differ much. Table 7-1 shows the U.S. inflation rate and the core inflation rate. In 2000, for example, the core inflation rate of 2.4 percent is less than the inflation rate of 3.4 percent. That difference occurred because energy prices skyrocketed in percentage terms in 2000.

Even with relatively low inflation, as in recent years, select groups of people can be hurt. There will be some people whose incomes do not keep up with inflation and other people whose incomes keep up with or exceed inflation. The first group will be hurt; the latter group probably will not be.

Most workers expect and receive an annual raise in pay. To them a good pay raise is one that provides an increase in their purchasing power, meaning that it exceeds the inflation rate. In contrast, people who live on a fixed income see no increase in their income. Thus, inflation eats away at their purchasing power. Over time, through no fault of their own, their standard of living declines. **Inflation hurts those on fixed incomes.**

One group that can benefit from inflation is borrowers. Because inflation erodes the purchasing power of money, borrowers repay their debts with dollars that are worth less and less. Of course, on the other side are the lenders who receive those devalued dollars as the debts of the borrowers are paid off. Thus, when lenders and borrowers are compared, it is the lenders who are hurt by inflation.

Perhaps the greatest harm from inflation is the opportunity cost of the time and other resources spent trying to avoid the harm inflicted by inflation. One obvious response by consumers to inflation is to seek out substitute goods whose prices have not risen as much as the prices of similar goods. Shoppers must spend time, energy, gasoline, and other resources trying to dodge the inflation bullet.

Inflation motivates businesses to offer new products. The interest in cheaper substitutes motivated retailers to begin offering generic brands. Generic products, with plain labels like "Green Beans" and "Paper Towels," are cheaper than their brand name equivalents. Inflation might also cause businesses to trim the sizes of their products rather than raise their prices.

TABLE 7-1   THE CORE RATE OF INFLATION

The core rate of inflation excludes food and energy prices from the computation of the inflation rate. These items' prices are particularly volatile. By excluding them, we get a better idea of the price changes in a broad range of other goods and services. All data are percentages.

YEAR	INFLATION RATE (INCLUDES FOOD AND ENERGY PRICES)	CORE INFLATION RATE (EXCLUDES FOOD AND ENERGY PRICES)
1979	11.3	9.8
1980	13.5	12.4
1981	10.3	10.4
1982	6.2	7.4
1983	3.2	4.0
1984	4.3	5.0
1985	3.6	4.3
1986	1.9	4.0
1987	3.6	4.1
1988	4.1	4.4
1989	4.8	4.5
1990	5.4	5.0
1991	4.2	4.9
1992	3.0	3.7
1993	3.0	3.3
1994	2.6	2.8
1995	2.8	3.0
1996	3.0	2.7
1997	2.3	2.4
1998	1.6	2.3
1999	2.2	2.1
2000	3.4	2.4
2001	2.8	2.6
2002	1.6	2.4
2003	2.1	1.5

Source: 2003 Economic Report of the President, Table B-63, and Bureau of Labor Statistics. The inflation rates shown were computed using the Consumer Price Index. Data for 2003 are current through mid-year and are expressed on an annual basis.

ANTICIPATED AND UNANTICIPATED INFLATION

By making the distinction between anticipated inflation and unanticipated inflation, we can more easily discuss the gains and losses produced by inflation. *Anticipated inflation* is expected by the public. *Unanticipated inflation* is inflation that catches the public by surprise.

People can take anticipated inflation into account in wage negotiations, mortgage loans, the tax system, and a variety of other contractual agreements. In theory at least, everyone is thus able to defend against losses imposed by anticipated inflation. For example, if workers anticipate the inflation rate will be 3 percent next year, they can try to negotiate 3 percent wage increases to offset that inflation.

When inflation is unanticipated, the story changes. An increase in inflation that causes the inflation rate to be higher than expected provides borrowers with a windfall. Because borrowers win, lenders lose. To see this possibility, suppose I borrowed $1,000 from you to be repaid in one year. We both anticipate an inflation rate of 2 percent over the year, and agree that an additional 3 percent **interest** to compensate you for the use of your money is fair. Thus, we strike a deal that I will repay you $1,050: the original sum of $1,000 I borrowed, plus $20 (2 percent of $1,000) to make you whole for the loss of purchasing power you suffer because of inflation, plus another $30 (3 percent of $1,000) for giving up the use of your money for the year.

Now suppose inflation proves greater than we anticipated. For example, suppose inflation rises to 5 percent. The $1,050 I repay you provides you with no reward for giving up the use of your money. You lose. I win, because I was able to use your money without having to pay you for its use. In other words, I used your purchasing power, and later returned the same purchasing power to you. If inflation had risen to a rate greater than 5 percent, I would have returned less purchasing power to you than you had before. You would be an even bigger loser, and I would be a bigger winner.

interest payment made by a borrower to compensate a lender for the use of money.

INDEXING TO OFFSET INFLATION'S EFFECTS

A response to the winners and losers problem created by unanticipated inflation is called **indexing**—automatically adjusting the terms of an agreement to account for inflation. *Cost of living adjustment (COLA)* clauses in labor agreements are a form of wage indexing. COLAs call for periodic upward adjustments in the wages of workers to match increases in inflation. Social Security payments feature a COLA. People who receive monthly Social Security checks find those checks get larger each year because of the built-in COLA.

indexing automatically adjusting the terms of an agreement for inflation.

If we indexed our loan agreement in the previous section, we would agree to adjust the amount I repaid you according to the inflation rate. If the inflation rate were to be 5 percent over the year of our loan agreement, I would be required to repay you $1,080, equal to the $1,000 I borrowed, plus the additional 3 percent interest you wanted ($30), plus the 5 percent ($50) to make up for the reduction in purchasing power caused by inflation. In other words, an **interest rate**, the price of borrowed money, that is indexed to inflation rises when inflation rises and falls when inflation falls.

interest rate the price of borrowed money; expressed as a percentage.

A number of high-inflation countries have resorted to indexation to deal with inflation. In the United States, variable-rate home mortgages are a form of indexing. When market interest rates rise because of inflation, home buyers find their monthly payments also rising because the interest rate built into their mortgage agreement rises accordingly. Traditional fixed-rate home mortgages are not indexed. Lenders who make fixed-rate loans take the risk of inflation-induced losses in exchange for a higher interest rate than is initially attached to an otherwise-similar variable-rate mortgage.

Indexing can benefit savers. Millions of Americans have loaned money to the federal government by buying U.S. Savings Bonds, receiving fixed interest payments in return.

The fixed interest payments mean that these bonds are not indexed for inflation. Inflation thus reduces the purchasing power of the interest payments as the years go by. Because of people's fears of inflation, the U.S. Treasury began to offer indexed bonds called *Treasury Inflation-Protected Securities (TIPS)* in 1997. Savers who buy TIPS bonds will find their interest earnings rise as inflation rises and fall as inflation falls. This feature of these bonds makes them attractive to savers who worry about unanticipated inflation. Meanwhile, the old-fashioned savings bond is still available for other less-worried savers.

IS A LITTLE INFLATION GOOD FOR THE ECONOMY?   *SNAPSHOT*

Goal: low inflation. Why not just say, "Goal: zero inflation"? Some say a little inflation is good for the economy. The argument goes like this: Rising prices create expectations of more inflation, and prompt consumers to buy now to beat the coming price increases. Those rising prices also provide businesses with more profits that they can use to expand their production of goods and services. Thus, GDP rises and unemployment is kept low.

Based on this view, inflation is like a mild stimulant to the economy, just as caffeine is to tired, overworked people. However, we should recognize that inflation causes consumer purchasing power to fall so that consumers cannot keep up the extra spending that inflation initially causes. Furthermore, experience from the 1970s showed that a little inflation can easily become a lot of inflation. That experience showed that inflation can become less like caffeine and more like a strong narcotic. Still, today we accept a little inflation and go about our business. ◄

7.3 MEASURING INFLATION

Which prices are going up the fastest? Is our income keeping up with price increases? Price indexes can help inform us about inflation.

A *price index* measures the average level of prices in the economy. There are several price indexes, each created for a specific purpose, with a different set of prices measured.

- The **consumer price index (CPI),** the best-known price index among the public, measures prices of typical purchases made by consumers living in urban areas.
- The **producer price index (PPI)** measures wholesale prices, which are prices paid by firms.
- The **GDP chained price index** and the **GDP implicit price deflator** are the most broadly based price indexes because they include prices across the spectrum of GDP.

Let's look at the CPI first since it is the most-used price index.

THE CONSUMER PRICE INDEX

To understand the CPI, let's start with the concept of the *base period*. **The base period is an arbitrarily selected initial time period against which other time periods are compared.** The CPI is assigned a value of 100 during the base period. For instance, the base period for the CPI is presently 1982 to 1984, and the CPI has been assigned an average value of 100 over that period of time.

Table 7-2 reproduces values of the CPI for selected years. The table shows, for example, that the CPI for 1951 equals 26. That value means that a dollar's worth of consumer purchases in the base period would have cost 26 cents in 1951. The table also shows that the CPI for 2003 equals 183.9. On average, a consumer would have needed $1.84 to pay for the

consumer price index (CPI) measures prices of a market basket of purchases made by consumers living in urban areas.

producer price index (PPI) measures wholesale prices, which are prices paid by firms.

GDP chained price index a price index used to compute real GDP by linking together successive years of data.

GDP implicit price deflator index of prices across the spectrum of GDP; ratio of nominal GDP to real GDP.

TABLE 7-2   **THE CONSUMER PRICE INDEX, SELECTED YEARS**

The CPI typically rises year to year, as is seen here. The average value of the CPI for 1982, 1983, and 1984 equals 100 because the 1982–1984 period is the base period.

YEAR	CONSUMER PRICE INDEX	
1951	26	
1961	29.9	
1971	40.6	
1979	72.6	
1980	82.4	
1981	90.9	
1982	96.5	Averages to 100, the base-period value
1983	99.6	
1984	103.9	
1985	107.6	
1986	109.6	
1987	113.6	
1988	118.3	
1989	124.0	
1990	130.7	
1991	136.2	
1992	140.3	
1993	144.5	
1994	148.2	
1995	152.4	
1996	156.9	
1997	160.5	
1998	163.0	
1999	166.6	
2000	172.2	
2001	177.1	
2002	179.9	
2003	185.2	

Source: 2003 Economic Report of the President, Table B-60, and Bureau of Labor Statistics. Data for 2003 is current through September.

purchases that cost a dollar during the base period. Notice that the CPI for years before the base period exhibits values less than 100 because prices were lower than in the base period.

We can use the CPI data to compute the inflation rate. The inflation rate is calculated by taking the percentage change in the CPI as follows:

$$\text{Inflation rate} = \frac{\text{Change in price index}}{\text{Initial price index}} \times 100$$

For example, from Table 7-2, the CPI equaled 179.9 in 2002 and 177.1 in 2001. The change in the CPI between 2001 and 2002 was 2.8 units, equal to 179.9 minus 177.1. When 2.8 is divided by 177.1 and the result multiplied by 100, the annual rate of inflation is seen to be 1.6 percent:

$$\text{Inflation rate in 2002} = \frac{2.8}{177.1} \times 100 = .016 \times 100 = 1.6 \text{ percent}$$

The inflation rate you just computed is the same as shown in Table 7-1. All the inflation rates in that table are computed in the same way.

What prices are measured by the CPI? If it were possible to count all the consumer prices in the economy, the number of different prices would likely be in the millions. It is unrealistic to expect so many prices to be used in the computation of a price index. The calculation of the CPI is based upon the prices of selected goods and services that consumers typically purchase. **The collection of goods and services used in the calculation of the CPI is called the *market basket*.** The market basket represents a sampling of the items that consumers buy that make up a significant part of their budgets. The market basket is based on extensive surveys of consumer purchases. There are around 200 specific categories of goods and services in the market basket, ranging from apples to women's dresses. Each item in the market basket is assigned a *weight* that reflects its importance in consumers' budgets. For example, personal care items such as shampoo have a smaller weight than gasoline. The BLS computes the CPI for the market basket every month. This effort requires Bureau of Labor Statistics (BLS) employees in eighty-seven urban areas to collect a total of 80,000 different prices.

The 200 or so specific categories of goods in the CPI market basket are divided into eight broad expenditure categories, as shown in Figure 7-3. All goods and services in the market basket belong to one of these categories. The weight on each category, which reflects the relative importance of the categories to consumers, is also shown in the figure. The relative importance is stated as a percentage of total spending by the average consumer. For example, housing expenditures are the largest component of the expenditure categories, amounting to 40.9 percent of expenditures by average consumers. The weights are so important in contributing to the accuracy of the CPI that they are now updated every two years, rather than every ten years, as in the past. Current weights help to ensure that the CPI reflects how people are spending their money.

Weights can be used to identify the sources of inflation. For example, suppose that there is a price increase of 10 percent in housing, with no price changes for the other expenditure categories. The inflation rate as measured by the CPI would equal 4.09 percent, computed as 10 percent multiplied by 0.409 (the weight on housing, after it is converted from a percent to decimal form). The knowledge that the increase in the CPI is concentrated in the price of housing can be used to design policies that target inflation from that source.

Let's see how to compute a price index based on the CPI market basket of items. The formula for the consumer price index is:

$$\text{CPI} = \frac{\text{Cost of market basket at current prices}}{\text{Cost of market basket at base period prices}} \times 100$$

The consumer price index measures the increase in the price of the market basket between the current year and the base period. It uses base period quantities throughout.

FIGURE 7-3

**CPI MARKET BASKET
EXPENDITURE CATEGORIES**

Source: Bureau of Labor Statistics,
*Relative Importance of Components
in the Consumer Price Indexes: U.S.
City Average, December 2002.* The
weights are for 1999–2000, and are
obtained by surveys of consumers.

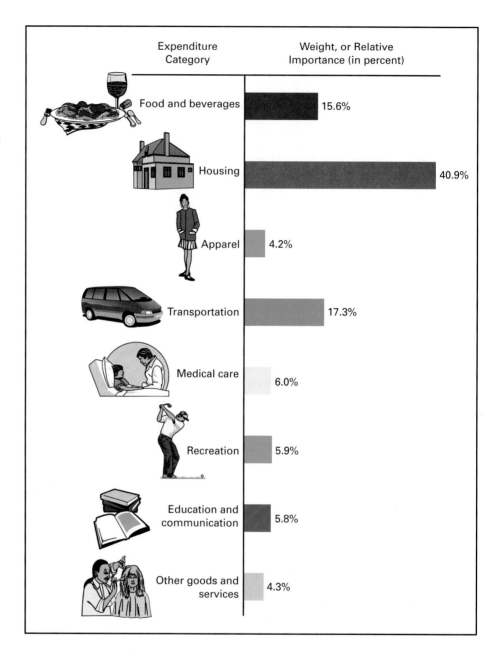

An example in which this price index is calculated for a market basket of three goods can help clarify the procedure. Suppose we wish to calculate the price index for a market basket of apples, oranges, and bananas. In the base period five apples, four oranges, and two bananas are purchased. The prices in the base period were 30 cents each for apples, 20 cents each for oranges, and 10 cents each for bananas. Currently, apples are still 30 cents each, but oranges have also risen to 30 cents each, while bananas have risen to 20 cents each. These prices and quantities are presented in Table 7-3.

Perform the calculation as follows:

$$\text{Price Index example} = \frac{(.30 \times 5) + (.30 \times 4) + (.20 \times 2)}{(.30 \times 5) + (.20 \times 4) + (.10 \times 2)} \times 100 = \frac{3.10}{2.50} \times 100 = 1.24 \times 100 = 124$$

TABLE 7-3	DATA USED IN PRICE INDEX EXAMPLE		
BASE PERIOD QUANTITIES	**BASE PERIOD PRICES**	**CURRENT PRICES**	
Apples: 5	Apples: $.30 each	Apples: $.30 each	
Oranges: 4	Oranges: $.20 each	Oranges: $.30 each	
Bananas: 2	Bananas: $.10 each	Bananas: $.20 each	

QUICKCHECK

What is the significance of the base period for the CPI? How is the base period selected?

Answer: The base period provides a point of reference to which the current price level can be compared. The CPI is set to a value of 100 during the base period. The selection of the base period is arbitrary.

In the base year the market basket cost $2.50. Now that same market basket costs $3.10. The index number of 124 indicates that the market basket costs 24 percent more than in the base year. The computation of this simplified price index gives you an idea of how the CPI is computed. The actual CPI calculation follows this procedure, but is more complicated because of some problems with price indexes that we will discuss a little later in the chapter.

CHANGING INCOMES, CHANGING LIFESTYLES, CHANGING WEIGHTS

SNAPSHOT

The twentieth century has run its course. Looking back we can see that the century was characterized by ever-increasing prosperity for Americans. Oh, there were interruptions on the way up—the Great Depression, then World War II, and a number of relatively mild recessions. However, the overall prosperity allowed for major lifestyle changes: a shorter workweek, a house in the suburbs, and a car in every garage.

Changes in people's lifestyles mean that the things that they spend their money on change. People can only spend so much on necessities like food and clothing before they have enough to meet their needs. The relative importance of necessities in their budgets thus falls. Their weights in the CPI market basket decrease. At the same time, new goods and services are introduced to the marketplace. When these are successful, the market basket weights will change to reflect that success. Thus, the expenditure category weights in Figure 7-3 are a snapshot of spending patterns at a point in time. The weights were different in the past and will be different in the future. ◄

USING THE CPI: NOMINAL VALUES VERSUS REAL VALUES

An increase in GDP due solely to price increases does not increase economic well-being. We can use a price index to adjust economic measures for the effects of inflation. The **nominal value** of a variable is not adjusted for inflation. The **real value** of a variable adjusts for inflation. The real

nominal value a value that is not adjusted for inflation.

real value a value that results from adjusting a nominal value for inflation.

value is expressed in terms of the value of the dollar during a selected base period. The time period chosen as the base period is not very important. What is important is that each year's measuring units be the same—dollars with the same purchasing power.

The distinction between real and nominal values is important not only to the study of macroeconomics, but also to individuals. Consider a worker whose weekly pay increases from $100 to $110. That worker has experienced a 10 percent increase in nominal income. If the price level remains constant, the worker's real income is also 10 percent greater. However, if the price level increases by 10 percent, the $110 of current income will purchase only as much as $100 purchased in the past. That means that the real income has not changed.

The following formula shows how to use a price index to compute a real value:

$$\text{Real value} = \frac{\text{Nominal value}}{\text{Price index}} \times 100$$

For example, suppose Jason earned nominal incomes of $39,000 a year in the base period and $40,500 in the current year, a 3.8 percent increase over the base period. Is Jason better off in the current year than in the base period? If the price index in the current year equals 105, then:

$$\text{Jason's real income} = \left(\frac{\$40,500}{105}\right) \times 100 = \$38,571.43$$

Jason's real income, which measures his purchasing power, has fallen since the base period. In terms of his real income he is not better off.

Figure 7-4 exemplifies the importance of real measures by showing the nominal and real values of the minimum wage since its enactment in 1938. As the figure shows, the purchasing power of the minimum wage has been in a long-term decline since the late 1960s, with periodic slight upticks when it is increased by Congress.

The distinction between a nominal and a real value is important in other instances. An *interest rate* is the price of borrowed money, expressed in percentage terms. If it is not adjusted for inflation, it is called a *nominal interest rate*. A *real interest rate* measures the percentage payment in terms of its purchasing power. To compute a real interest rate it is not necessary to know the value of a price index. Instead, all that is needed is the inflation rate and the nominal interest rate. To obtain the real interest rate, subtract the inflation rate from the nominal interest rate:

$$\text{Real interest rate} = \text{Nominal interest rate} - \text{Inflation rate}$$

Recall our earlier example where I borrow $1,000 from you. We agree that I am to repay you $1,050 in one year. The nominal interest rate is 5 percent (the interest payment of $50 divided by the amount borrowed). With an inflation rate of 2 percent, the real interest rate is only 3 percent. You, the lender in this example, will increase your purchasing power by 3 percent when the loan is repaid. The real interest rate in the United States is contrasted to the nominal interest rate in Figure 7-5 on page 182. The real interest rate and the nominal interest rate typically move in the same direction, but the nominal rate is higher than the real rate.

PRICE INDEXES FOR OTHER PURPOSES

Let's consider the three other price indexes mentioned earlier: the producer price index, the GDP implicit price deflator, and the GDP chained price index. The producer price index (PPI) focuses on the prices received by U.S. producers, as measured by the revenue they receive. The prices are those of the outputs sold by producers to other producers as intermediate goods, and sold by producers directly to consumers. The PPI often foretells increases in the CPI because price increases at the producer level will usually be passed on

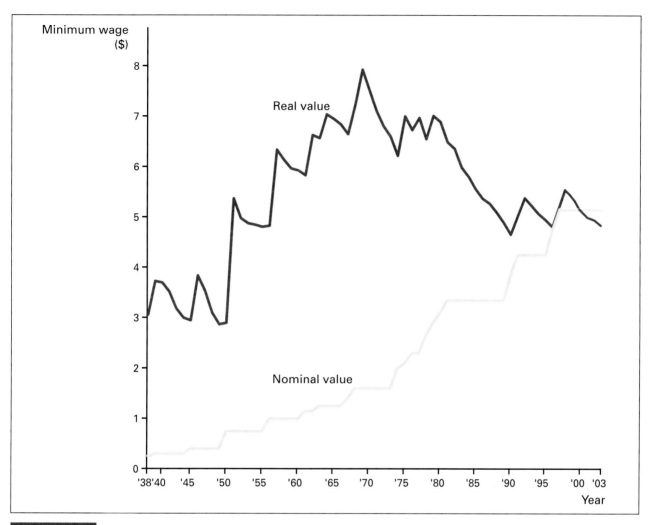

THE REAL AND NOMINAL VALUES OF THE MINIMUM WAGE, 1938–2003 The figure shows the nominal and real values of the minimum wage since its inception in 1938. The real value of the minimum wage is in terms of year 2000 dollars. Expressing the real value in terms of dollars in that year makes the real and nominal values identical in the year 2000, which you can see in the figure. You can also see that the minimum wage had the greatest purchasing power in 1968, when the nominal value of $1.60 would have bought the equivalent of a nominal wage of nearly $8.00 in 2000.

Source: Bureau of Labor Statistics, and author's calculations.

later to consumer prices. Thus, the PPI is watched for hints about the future course of consumer prices.

Prior to 1978, the PPI was called the wholesale price index, a name that reflected the idea that many of the prices in the PPI are wholesale prices, rather than the retail prices used to compute the CPI. The name change occurred in order to emphasize that the prices in the PPI are those received by producers no matter who makes the purchase, whether it be another firm or a consumer.

The GDP chained price index and the GDP implicit price deflator, as you would guess from their names, are for gross domestic product. Both indexes, published by the Department of Commerce, use 1996 as the base period, meaning that the values of the indexes are equal to 100 in that year.

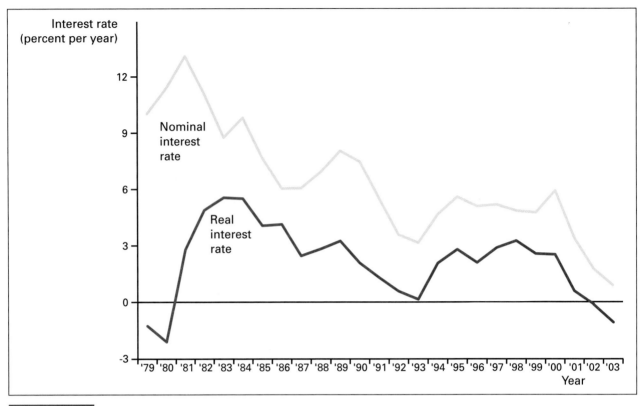

FIGURE 7-5

THE REAL AND NOMINAL INTEREST RATES The real interest rate was negative in 1979 and 1980 because the inflation rate was higher than the nominal interest rate. The rising real interest rates in 1981, 1982, and 1983 resulted from efforts to bring inflation under control. Negative real rates appeared again in 2002 and 2003 as the nominal interest rate fell below the inflation rate.

Source: 2003 Economic Report of the President, Tables B-63 and B-73, and Federal Reserve System. The real interest rate was computed using the six-month T-bill rate as the nominal interest rate.

Let's look at the GDP implicit price deflator first. It is computed as:

$$\text{GDP implicit price deflator} = \frac{\text{Nominal GDP}}{\text{Real GDP}} \times 100$$

Let's apply the formula. In 2003 nominal GDP equaled $10,688.4 billion and real GDP equaled $9,552.0 billion. Substituting in the formula, we have:

$$2003 \text{ GDP implicit price deflator} = \frac{10,688.4}{9,551.0} \times 100 = 111.90$$

This value says that the price level has risen over 9 percent since the 1996 base year. The GDP implicit price deflator is broad-based because it reflects price changes in the entire spectrum of goods and services that go into GDP.

In order to compute the GDP implicit price deflator, we must know the value of real GDP. Real GDP is computed from nominal GDP, using the GDP chained price index:

$$\text{Real GDP} = \frac{\text{Nominal GDP}}{\text{GDP chained price index}} \times 100$$

The computation of real GDP using this price index was shown in Chapter 5. Chained-type methods provide the best way to estimate a price index. We turn now to discussing why a chained-type index is superior, and how the computation of the CPI has been revised in response.

CHAIN METHODS TO IMPROVE PRICE INDEXES

The GDP chained price index is a type of *chain-weight* index, because it links quantities (weights) in two successive years, then moves forward a year and does that link again, and so forth. This continuous linking, two years at a time, forms a chain, and hence the name. For example, the calculation of 2003 GDP involves prices and quantities for 2002 and 2003. Similarly, the calculation of 2004 GDP involves prices and quantities for 2003 and 2004. A chained-type price index provides the most accurate data on changes in the cost of living, since it uses current weights in its computation. This consideration has led to changes in the CPI, including the decision to offer a new chained CPI alongside the traditional CPI.

Prior to 1999 the CPI was calculated using *fixed weights* throughout the market basket. Fixed weight price indexes provide consistently incorrect results because they assume that people do not change their consumption when prices rise. In fact, as prices change, people typically substitute relatively cheaper goods for goods that have become relatively more expensive. The inaccuracy introduced into the CPI by this behavior is termed the *substitution bias*. **The substitution bias causes inflation to be overstated.** This bias is inherent in a fixed-weight price index. Other biases creep into price indexes because it is difficult to account for quality changes that improve products. Similarly, unless a price index immediately takes into account the introduction of new products, it will be biased.

It was recognized long ago that the substitution bias caused the CPI to overstate inflation, and a solution to the problem was sought. Through the years since its inception in 1913, the method of computing the CPI has been improved repeatedly. In January 1999, the CPI was improved again to provide a partial solution to the substitution bias. That change better measures the cost of living when people respond to inflation by cutting their consumption of goods whose prices have risen the most, and increasing their consumption of items whose prices have not. The revision to the CPI has lowered the computed inflation rate slightly, providing a more accurate assessment of price changes.

In an effort to provide even more accurate inflation data, another type of CPI was introduced in August 2002. This CPI is called the C-CPI, with the first C standing for chained. A chained price index uses continuously updated expenditure weights. As discussed earlier in relation to Figure 7-3, the CPI weights are updated every two years. In contrast, the new C-CPI is chained monthly. In effect, the weights for the C-CPI are updated continuously.

The C-CPI supplements, but does not replace, the older CPI. Both price indexes are useful, but the method of computation is different. The current CPI assumes that the share of the consumer's budget spent on an item stays fixed for the two years between updates in the weights. Thus, it retains some of the disadvantage of a fixed weight index. The C-CPI makes no such assumption, and instead assumes that consumers substitute freely among items as prices change. Thus, the C-CPI may be viewed as an effort to overcome fully the problem of substitution bias.

QUICKCHECK

What is the substitution bias that causes the traditional CPI to overstate the impact of inflation on actual consumers?

Answer: Computing inflation using the traditional CPI will tell you the percentage by which the cost of goods in the market basket will have increased. However, consumers will substitute away from goods that have risen the most in price and toward those that have risen the least, thus mitigating the effect of that inflation.

7.4 ADJUSTING TO PRICE CHANGES—NO PRECISION IN THE CPI

The consumer price index (CPI) is used in three ways:

- As an economic indicator. As such, it is used by the government and the public to determine whether the nation is meeting its goal of low inflation.
- To convert nominal economic values into real values. A worker's average real income is superior to nominal income as a measure of economic progress.
- To adjust selected monetary payments upward as prices increase. The annual cost-of-living adjustment in Social Security payments is an example.

Consider how people might react to a soaring CPI.

Hyperinflation is inflation out of control, with prices rising quickly. Take an annual inflation rate of 10,000 percent, for example. A look at the CPI would be unnecessary to conclude that inflation was out of control. A trip to any store would do that. What would a dollar be worth after just one year of such continuous hyperinflation? The answer: less than a penny. To put it another way, it would take over $100 at the end of a year of such hyperinflation to purchase what $1 would have purchased at the beginning of the year.

The most widely documented hyperinflation occurred in post–World War I Germany in the years 1922–1923. Germany had to pay war reparations to the Allies. Unable to raise enough money by taxing or borrowing, the German government turned to the printing press. Before the presses stopped and currency reform occurred, prices had increased by a factor of 1.5 trillion. In comparison, if the United States suffered an inflation of similar magnitude, a $50 sleeping bag would rise in price to $75 trillion.

Imagine a hyperinflated world. It would be difficult to carry enough cash to make a simple purchase since that purchase might cost you millions of dollars. You might want your wages paid daily, or even more often. That's because a dollar received now would have more purchasing power than a dollar received later—even a few hours later. You would also want to budget enough time to spend your money. You might take time off from work during the day to go spend your wages as soon as you receive them. Hyperinflation turns money into a hot potato: Get rid of it quickly before it loses more value.

Hyperinflation has also struck other countries. Imagine yourself peering from your apartment window in Buenos Aries, Argentina, in 1989. You spy an armored car pulling up to La Dora Restaurant down the street, and carting away sacks of money. It is midnight. You recall seeing the same event every night at midnight. Come to think of it, you'd seen bags of money carted away from that same restaurant every day at noon. Have you witnessed an illegal money laundering operation? Actually, these events were real, but represented the restaurant getting its money into an interest-earning bank account as quickly as possible. At a 1989 inflation rate of 100 percent per month, it did not take long for the Argentine currency to lose much of its value.

With prices changing quickly, everyone tries to adjust. One type of adjustment is the behavioral changes that individuals make in order to try to cope with inflation. Individual adjustments can be as simple as searching out cheaper places to shop and substituting chicken for steak. Some people barter—they enter into direct exchanges of goods and services with other people, with no need for money to change hands. Other people exchange their country's currency for foreign currencies that are stable in value. These adjustments can be stressful and costly in terms of a person's time.

Another type of adjustment revolves around the changes in business practices that increase the cost of doing business. For example, businesses must devote resources to constantly keep track of prices, making changes as often as necessary. Other businesses may be forced into costly redesigns of their products in response to higher labor and materials prices. These costs are likely to be passed on in the form of higher consumer prices. Higher prices, followed by higher costs, followed by even higher prices can result in an *inflationary spiral,* with inflation feeding on itself.

With all these examples of individual and business behavioral changes, you can see that hyperinflation would be a giant headache. The time needed to cope with it decreases individual productivity, which reduces the production of goods and services, in turn reducing the standard of living. Some of the adjustments that people make in response to hyperinflation are also made on a smaller scale in response to ordinary levels of inflation.

Hyperinflation is one extreme. At the other extreme is deflation, which would be associated with price declines so widespread as to bring the consumer price index down on an ongoing basis. When deflation occurs, the value of money increases. As in the case of inflation, people's behavior changes. For example, if all prices declined 10 percent over the next year, then by the end of the year 90 cents would buy what it would have taken about a dollar to buy at the beginning of the year. Since people would recognize that their money was becoming more valuable because of deflation, they would tend to save more and spend fewer dollars. With people spending less, businesses would have to cut back on the production of goods and services. Such cutbacks might necessitate laying off workers. In this way the unemployment rate would rise and the economy could fall into a recession.

Deflation would also have effects on borrowing and lending. Borrowers would be discouraged from borrowing because of the high real interest rate that results from deflation. Consider the equation for the real interest rate presented earlier in the chapter:

$$\text{Real interest rate} = \text{Nominal interest rate} - \text{Inflation rate}$$

In our example, the inflation rate equals -10 percent, the minus sign indicating deflation. Even if the nominal interest rate were zero, which is as low as the nominal interest rate can go, then the real interest rate would equal 10 percent:

$$\text{Real interest rate} = 0 - (-10) = +10 = 10 \text{ percent}$$

A real interest rate of 10 percent makes it expensive to pay back borrowed money, thus discouraging borrowers, and causing people to spend even less.

Businesses might respond to deflation by being less open about the true price of their products. For example, maintaining list prices for goods might allow them to be sold at list price to some buyers and at a discount to other buyers. U.S. new-car buyers have become familiar with this practice. Although the automakers have offered buyers incentives of up to $5,000 per vehicle, rather than cut the Manufacturers Suggested Retail Price (MSRP) by that amount, the automakers offer rebates, which in effect cut the price of the car by the amount of the rebate.

Although U.S. prices fell about 10 percent a year from 1930 to 1933, the most recent example of deflation is found in Japan. Japan's economy has been troubled for more than a decade, and rightly or wrongly, many policymakers in the United States blame deflation for those troubles. Low U.S. inflation rates in 2002 and 2003 led some to fear that deflation was about to strike a blow against the economic recovery then underway in America. Thus, it should not be surprising that Federal Reserve Chairman Alan Greenspan testified before Congress on July 15, 2003, that "…we face new challenges in maintaining price stability, specifically to prevent inflation from falling too low."

HOW THE CPI MEASURES THE PRICE LEVEL

Whether caused by inflation or deflation, the changes in behavior we've discussed make it more difficult to measure the price level accurately. Since the CPI is widely used, it should reflect price changes as precisely as possible. Changes in product design present a particular challenge to the accurate measurement of inflation. To understand this point, recall the earlier example in which the prices of apples, bananas, and oranges were used to illustrate the computation of the CPI. Those computations implicitly assumed that the three products remained unchanged. Suppose, however, that improved varieties of all three goods have been introduced in the marketplace since the base period. The improvements offer consumers greater satisfaction, which they are

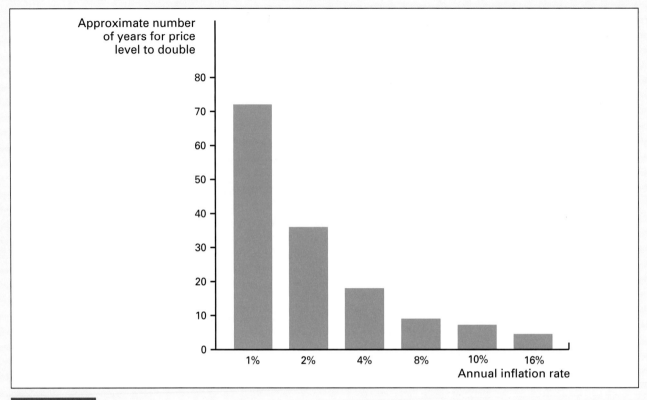

APPLYING THE RULE OF SEVENTY-TWO TO COMPUTE THE EFFECTS OF INFLATION The rule of seventy-two is used to compute the approximate doubling times. In this figure the rule of seventy-two is used to compute how long it would take the price level to double when the inflation rate takes on different values.

willing to pay for. In this context, the value of the CPI does not accurately reflect inflation, but a willingness to pay for improvements in product quality. Thus, unless a price index adjusts for product quality improvements, the price index will overstate the inflation rate.

The CPI adjusts price changes for product improvements through a method called an *hedonic model.* Although hedonic models use statistical methods and are complicated in practice, in concept they are quite simple. In a hedonic model each product is viewed as a bundle of characteristics, where the model is used to estimate the value of each characteristic. Can you identify several characteristics of a college textbook that provide value? In the CPI, the number of pages, the type of cover (soft or hard), and the use of color are a few examples of the characteristics that affect the value of a textbook.

Let's see how the hedonic approach works. Suppose that the previous edition of your math textbook sold for $65, but that the new edition carries a price of $75. If both editions were identical, then the entire price increase would be viewed as inflation and would enter into the computation of the CPI. However, suppose the new edition has more pages and the book has gone from black and white to color. To a significant extent the two books are different products. A hedonic model estimates the value of the improvements in the book, concluding, let's say, that the increased pages have a value of $5, while color has a value of $4. Then $9 of the $10 price increase is accounted for by quality improvements. The remaining $1 of price increase not related to improvements increases the CPI. Although hedonic models help improve the accuracy of the CPI, they are not perfect.

Even if the CPI were perfectly accurate, your personal inflation experience would probably be different. The CPI measures changes in average prices. You may live in an area of the country that is experiencing price increases that outstrip the average. For a variety of reasons your purchasing may not mirror that of the average consumer. If you are chronically ill, you may spend a larger-than-average fraction of your income on medicines. If you are in college, increases in tuition will hit you harder than the average citizen. If you have a long commute between home and work, increases in the price of gasoline make your personal inflation experience different from the CPI.

Even relatively low inflation can add up over time. The rule of seventy-two allows an estimate of how many years it would take prices to double for any inflation rate. The calculation involved in the rule of seventy-two is simple: Take an inflation rate and divide it into seventy-two. The result is the time it takes prices to double. Figure 7-6 shows doubling times for selected annual inflation rates between 1 percent and 16 percent.

Figure 7-6 shows that an increase in the inflation rate can have dramatic long-term effects. For instance, a sustained 2 percent inflation rate would mean that it would take almost half of the average person's lifetime for prices to double. At a 4 percent inflation rate, not much higher than in recent U.S. experience, prices would double about four times over a lifetime. At a 10 percent inflation rate, prices would double a total of ten times for someone living into his or her seventies.

1. **Consumers often substitute cheaper goods for similar goods that have risen in price. From a student perspective, what are some substitutes for a new math textbook? Would these substitutes be acceptable substitutes from a professor's perspective? Explain.**

2. **How easy is it for consumers to identify improvements in personal computers? Since personal computers today are cheaper than they were five years ago, what effect does including them in the CPI market basket have on the inflation rate? Explain.**

Visit **www.prenhall.com/ayers** for updates and web exercises on this Explore & Apply topic.

SUMMARY AND LEARNING OBJECTIVES

1. **Describe inflation rates in the United States and other countries.**

   - Inflation occurs when there is a sustained rise in the general price level, which includes the prices of many goods and services. The inflation rate is stated as an annual percentage increase in the price level. Over time, U.S. inflation rates have fluctuated up and down.

   - Inflation occurs in many countries. The inflation rate in some countries is quite high, but relatively low in other countries. Some countries that have experienced very high inflation rates have looked to a policy of dollarization to bring down inflation. Dollarization was enacted in Equador, which replaced its own currency with the U.S. dollar.

   - Deflation and disinflation sound similar, but are not the same. Deflation means a fall in the price level. Deflation would involve a decrease in the CPI. Disinflation is a fall in the inflation rate. Disinflation is illustrated by an inflation rate of 3 percent one year and 2 percent the next. This situation is not deflation because the CPI increases in both years. Deflation is not a macroeconomic goal since deflation is often associated with a weak economy.

2. **Discuss the effects of inflation that cause low inflation to be a macroeconomic goal.**

   - People on fixed incomes suffer from reduced purchasing power because of inflation. Compared to people who are able to earn larger incomes, those on fixed incomes lose because of inflation. Relative to lenders, borrowers gain from inflation. This effect of inflation occurs because borrowers repay their debts with money that will buy less because of the rise in the price level.

   - The core inflation rate excludes food and energy prices from the computation of the inflation rate. Under some circumstances it can provide a clearer picture of inflation and its harm.

   - Anticipated inflation is expected by people. Unanticipated inflation takes them by surprise. People are able to adjust their financial affairs to adjust for the effects of anticipated inflation.

   - Indexing allows people to take account of future inflation and protect their purchasing power. Social Security payments are an example of an indexed income since Social Security checks are adjusted upward in amount each year to reflect the prevailing inflation rate. Cost-of-living adjustments (COLAs) allow workers to receive automatic upward adjustments in their pay that are tied to the inflation rate.

3. **Compute, interpret, and use a price index to compute a real value.**
   - Several price indexes, including the consumer price index (CPI), the producer price index (PPI), the GDP chained-type index, and the GDP implicit price deflator, measure inflation. The CPI is the best known of these.
   - The base period for a price index is an initial time period, currently 1982 to 1984 for the CPI, to which prices in other time periods are compared. The base period is selected arbitrarily. By convention, the value of a price index equals 100 during the base period.
   - As the price level rises, the value of the CPI increases. The CPI for 2003 equals 183.9, which is interpreted to mean that the price level in 2001 is 84 percent higher than in the base period. Alternatively, it would take $1.84 to purchase what $1.00 purchased in the base period.
   - The CPI is calculated using items that urban consumers typically purchase, the so-called market basket of goods and services. There are about 200 categories of goods and services in the CPI, grouped into eight major expenditure categories. The relative importance of an expenditure category is used as a weight in the computation of the CPI. Currently, the CPI is computed using weights that are updated every two years.
   - The formula used to compute a price index is: Cost of market basket at current prices ÷ Cost of market basket at base period prices, multiplied by 100.
   - Price indexes are used to compute a real value from a nominal value. With knowledge of the nominal value of a variable and the value of a price index it is possible to compute the real value of the variable. Real values are useful to know. For example, the real value of the minimum wage over time shows us that the purchasing power of the minimum wage has varied significantly.
   - The producer price index (PPI) is used to measure inflation in the prices of goods and services sold by U.S. producers. The GDP implicit price deflator measures a broad spectrum of prices. It is computed as: GDP implicit price deflator = Nominal GDP ÷ Real GDP × 100. The GDP chained price index also measures prices across the spectrum of GDP.

4. **Identify problems with price indexes and efforts to improve them.**
   - The CPI is an imperfect measure of inflation. Using the CPI to measure inflation suggests that the effects of inflation are more severe than they really are. The reason has to do with biases in fixed-weight price indexes, including the substitution bias. A chain-weight index, such as the GDP chained price index, is intended to provide a better approximation to true inflation.

5. **Explain how people respond to price changes, and how their responses affect the measurement of prices.**
   - The CPI is used for three purposes: an economic indicator, to find real values, and to adjust monetary payments. In the case of hyperinflation, behavior changes necessary to limit the harm caused by rapidly rising prices will be widespread. Behavioral changes create difficulties in computing and interpreting price indexes. Product design is a particular challenge. The CPI attempts to adjust for quality changes so as to avoid overstating price increases. The method used is called a hedonic model.

TEST YOURSELF

TRUE OR FALSE
1. The goal of low inflation is explicitly stated to be an inflation rate of 0 percent.
2. Compared to other countries in recent history, the United States is among the group of four or five countries with the highest inflation rates.
3. Disinflation is associated with a fall in the price level.
4. Inflation hurts borrowers while benefiting lenders.
5. A chain-weight price index links quantities in one year to the next.

MULTIPLE CHOICE

6. Which of the following best fits the definition of inflation?
   a. A one-time increase in a few prices.
   b. A one-time increase in many prices.
   c. A sustained increase in a few prices.
   d. A sustained increase in many prices.

7. In which decade was U.S. inflation highest?
   a. 1960s.
   b. 1970s.
   c. 1980s.
   d. 1990s.

8. Deflation is associated with
   a. a rising price level.
   b. a falling price level.
   c. an inflation rate that is higher this year than last year.
   d. an inflation rate that is lower this year than last year.

9. The core inflation rate excludes
   a. energy prices.
   b. the price of medical care.
   c. food prices.
   d. both food and energy prices.

10. The distinction between anticipated and unanticipated inflation is important because
    a. unanticipated inflation is always greater than anticipated inflation.
    b. unanticipated inflation is harmful, but anticipated inflation is not.
    c. anticipated inflation is harmful, but unanticipated inflation is not.
    d. both types of inflation are potentially harmful, but people can make arrangements to minimize the damage from anticipated inflation.

11. Treasury Inflation-Protected Securities (TIPS) are an example of
    a. a policy to reduce the inflation rate.
    b. one of the goods in the CPI market basket.
    c. indexing to protect against unanticipated inflation.
    d. a deliberate effort to inflict harm on lenders when inflation rises.

12. When you see a value of the consumer price index (CPI) of less than 100, you know
    a. that there has been a misprint since the CPI cannot be under 100.
    b. nothing in particular since the CPI can be any value at any time.
    c. that there has been price inflation within the last year.
    d. that either you are looking at the CPI for a year prior to the base period, or there has been deflation since the base period.

13. The goods and services included in the computation of the consumer price index (CPI) are referred to as the _____

a. base period.
b. fixed weights.
c. market basket.
d. price level.

14. How is an inflation rate computed?
    a. The inflation rate equals the value of a price index.
    b. The inflation rate equals the change in the value of a price index.
    c. By the following computation: (change in price index/initial value of price index) multiplied by 100.
    d. By the following computation: change in price index multiplied by the initial value of the price index.

15. Using a price index, a real value is computed by
    a. multiplying a nominal value by the price index, and then dividing by 100.
    b. dividing a nominal value by the price index, and then multiplying by 100.
    c. averaging two nominal values.
    d. dividing the current nominal value by the base period nominal value.

16. The best way for workers to determine whether their earnings have kept up with inflation over the last ten years is to
    a. see if the nominal value of earnings is at least the same as ten years ago.
    b. see if the real value of earnings is at least the same as ten years ago.
    c. multiply the earnings figure from a decade ago by the current value of the consumer price index.
    d. multiply the current earnings figure by the value of the consumer price index from a decade ago.

17. When the real value of GDP is computed by the government
    a. the CPI is used.
    b. the PPI is used.
    c. the GDP chained price index is used.
    d. no price index is necessary because the real and nominal values of GDP are always identical.

18. A chained price index is
    a. the least accurate type of price index.
    b. superior to other types, because it links successive years of prices and quantities together.
    c. superior to other types, because it links the CPI and PPI together to cover more prices than either the CPI or PPI cover separately.
    d. superior to the CPI, but definitely inferior in accuracy to an implicit price deflator.

19. The substitution bias causes the CPI to
    a. overstate the effects of inflation.
    b. understate the effects of inflation.
    c. more accurately reflect the effects of inflation.
    d. be nearly useless as a measure of inflation.

20. When a country experiences hyperinflation it is likely that
a. people will hold on to money.
b. hyperinflation was a goal of that country's macro policy.

c. cash will be spent very quickly.
d. the country's standard of living will be improved.

QUESTIONS AND PROBLEMS

1. *[history of U.S. inflation]* Use the information conveyed by Figure 7-1 to characterize the decades of the 1950s, 1960s, 1970s, 1980s, and 1990s as to how well the goal of low inflation was met. Use your general knowledge of history and politics to speculate on why inflation remained under better control in some decades than others.

2. *[world inflation]* Are other countries' inflation rates similar to that of the United States? Explain, referring to the data in Figure 7-2.

3. *[deflation]* Refer to the example in the chapter that computes a price index for apples, bananas, and oranges. Provide price data for that example that illustrates deflation. Compute the price index using the prices you provided. Based upon your computation, state how a price index will behave when there is deflation.

4. *[core inflation]* Suppose that data shows the overall inflation rate equals 5 percent, but core inflation equals 3 percent. What is the cause of the difference in these percentages? Which is more likely to provide the most accurate gauge of inflation? Explain.

5. *[harm from inflation]* The minimum wage is adjusted upward at unpredictable intervals. Congress must pass legislation increasing the minimum wage, legislation the president must sign before the increase takes effect. How is the group of minimum wage workers affected by inflation?

6. *[anticipated versus unanticipated inflation]* Why is unanticipated inflation usually considered more harmful than anticipated inflation?

7. *[indexing]* Is indexing practiced in the United States? Explain.

8. *[CPI base period]* Why does an understanding of the CPI require you to understand the base period concept?

9. *[CPI market basket]* Why does an understanding of the CPI require you to understand the concept of the market basket?

10. *[computing a price index]* Suppose that in the base period consumers purchase eight pounds of grapes, seven pounds of potatoes, and three pounds of bacon. The prices per pound were $1, $.50, and $2, respectively. In the current year, these prices are $2, $1, and $3, respectively. Compute and interpret a price index using these data.

11. *[CPI]* Suppose that the CPI in year 5 equals 123 and in year 6 equals 130. What was the inflation rate in year 6?

12. *[real versus nominal values]* Three years ago Johnson earned $100 a week. Today he earns $125 a week. He would like to know whether his real income is higher today than it was three years ago. If the consumer price index increased from 150 to 175, has Johnson's real income risen, fallen, or remained the same? Explain.

13. *[chain weights]* What is the purpose of computing a chain-weighted price index? Is the CPI an example of a chain-weighted index?

14. *[real chained GDP]* Suppose that a country's nominal GDP equals $1,000. Also suppose its GDP chained price index has a value of 125. What is the value of this country's real GDP?

15. *[substitution bias]* Explain how the substitution bias in the CPI affects the reported inflation rate.

WORKING WITH GRAPHS AND DATA

1. *[CPI]* You are provided with the following consumer data for the years of 2002 and 2003.

GOOD	PRICE 2002	QUANTITY 2002	PRICE 2003	QUANTITY 2003
Orange juice	$3/gallon	25 gallons	$3.05/gallon	26 gallons
Paper towels	$2/package	20 packages	$2.10/package	19 packages
Gasoline	$1.20/gallon	1,000 gallons	$1.40/gallon	1,050 gallons

a. Calculate the CPI for 2003 using 2002 as the base year.

b. What is the inflation rate for 2003?

c. Calculate the growth rate of the price of orange juice from 2002 to 2003.

d. Calculate the growth rate of the price of paper towels from 2002 to 2003.

e. Calculate the growth rate of the price of gasoline from 2002 to 2003.

f. What is the average of the growth of the three prices found in questions c, d, and e?

g. Why does this answer vary from the inflation rate you found in question b?

2. *[real versus nominal values]* Solve the following problems.

a. Nolan Ryan, a famous Major League baseball pitcher, was the first player to earn a million dollars in 1980. The CPI of 1980 was 82.3, base 1983. What salary would Nolan Ryan need to receive in 2003 in order to maintain his purchasing power of 1980, knowing that the CPI in 2003 was 183.3, base 1983?

b. A country's nominal GDP was $3 trillion in the base year of 2000. In 2003 its nominal GDP grew to $4 trillion, while its real GDP was at $3.5 trillion. How much inflation did the country experience over this time period?

c. Suppose that your annual income in 2001, the base year, was $50,000. You received a $3,000 increase in your salary in 2002. Inflation during 2002 was 2 percent. What was your real income in 2002? Were you better off, just as well off, or worse off in 2002 compared to 2001?

d. Suppose that your annual income in 2001, the base year, was $50,000. You received a $3,000 increase in your salary in 2002. Inflation during 2002 was 6 percent. What was your real income in 2002? Were you better off, just as well off, or worse off in 2002 compared to 2001?

3. *[interest rates and inflation]* Graph 7-1 depicts the nominal and real interest rates over a five-year period. You are to interpret the relationship between the real and nominal interest rates as well as what it implies about the inflation rate in each respective time period.

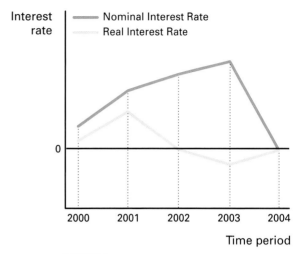

GRAPH 7-1

4. *[real versus nominal values and CPI]* Graph 7-2 shows a country's real and nominal GDP over several years. For each respective time period from one year to the next, indicate the relationship between the nominal and real GDP and the implied relationship to the inflation rate or CPI. Assume that 2000 is the base period.

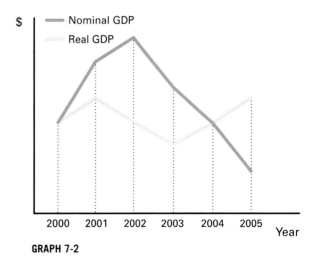

GRAPH 7-2

 Visit www.prenhall.com/ayers for Exploring the Web exercises and additional self-test quizzes.

CHAPTER 8

A FRAMEWORK FOR MACROECONOMIC ANALYSIS

A LOOK AHEAD

The twentieth century ended with a string of prosperous years for the United States economy. Productivity surged and unemployment fell to record lows. Because of its success, the economy faded into the backs of our minds. Then, as the twenty-first century unfolded, productivity sagged and unemployment reared its ugly head. Business profits were slim, bankruptcies were up, and stock prices were down. People with their jobs on the line or their savings decimated by stock-market declines demanded action from the federal government. In response they got tax rebates and interest-rate cuts, but nothing seemed to help.

Then came the terrorist attacks of September 11, 2001 and the start of the war on terrorism. Immediately, fears of future attacks caused the stock market to plunge and 100,000 people were laid off in the airline industry alone, as travelers decided it was safer to stay home. The monthly unemployment rate jumped by ½ percent, the largest one-month leap in twenty-one years. Some urged the government to take action to shore up the economy. Others said it would be best to wait and let the economy take care of itself. This chapter frames these choices and the tradeoffs involved. The Explore & Apply section that concludes this chapter pays particular attention to the macroeconomic consequences of the war against terrorism.

LEARNING OBJECTIVES

Understanding Chapter 8 will enable you to:
1. **Contrast the perspectives of classical economists to those of Keynesians.**
2. **Describe why aggregate demand slopes downward.**
3. **Explain why the price level does not matter in the long run, but does in the short run.**
4. **Interpret and explain the macro equilibrium.**
5. **Relate the difference between demand-side and supply-side inflation in the long run.**
6. **Interpret how the war against terrorism can cause both inflation and lower output, and ways in which these effects might be countered.**

Explore & Apply

"Prior to 1929, kids had too much of everything. Then after the crash, they didn't have enough of anything. So they became too much concerned with economic problems. We began to think too much about sharing the wealth, instead of creating it. Youth should create something, and it should have something to create."

> *—Perry Mason, by Earl Stanley Gardner, The Case of the Drowning Duck, 1942*

The above passage was written as America was preparing to enter World War II. Having endured a lingering depression for over a decade, the state of the U.S. economy was high on people's minds. Then World War II brought forth a massive civilian and military mobilization that brought with it a new resolve and new spending. After the war, the economic crisis was over and America prospered like never before. Unemployment fell from the 14.6 percent in 1940 (before the war) to 3.9 percent in 1946 (after the war had ended). The one and only Great Depression of the twentieth century was over.

In late summer of 2001, Americans were again troubled by a declining economy. Unemployment was under 5 percent, but up from its lows of under 4 percent. Stock prices had been in a jagged slide since March of the previous year. Business profits were squeezed and layoffs announced. Having lived comfortably for decades, U.S. citizens were not used to worrying about the overall economy, but that started to change.

The September 11 terrorist attacks killed thousands of Americans. The Dow-Jones Industrial Average of stock prices reacted by falling nearly 15 percent in a single week, exceeded only by the 15.5 percent drop in 1933 during the depths of the Great Depression. Consumers held tight to their money and business investment was at a standstill. During October 2001, businesses cut their payrolls by 415,000 jobs, the largest one-month decline in over two decades. All at once, it seemed, everybody wanted to know what was to become of the economy. How did it work? What could be done?

8.1 A FIRST LOOK AT AGGREGATE DEMAND AND AGGREGATE SUPPLY

In Chapter 3, you learned about the demand and supply model. In order to conduct macroeconomic analysis, we need a different model–the aggregate demand and aggregate supply model. Figure 8-1 shows the similarity, with part (a) of that figure repeating the example of supply and demand for pails of water that was used in Chapter 3. Part (b) shows the *aggregate supply and aggregate demand model* that we will use in analyzing the macroeconomy. As noted in both cases, market forces push the economy toward an equilibrium in which there's no tendency for further change to occur.

The most fundamental difference between these two models is what they measure on the horizontal and vertical axes. In the micro model of supply and demand, the horizontal axis measures the quantity of a good, in this case pails of water. In the macro model of aggregate supply and aggregate demand, on contrast, the horizontal axis measures real GDP, which includes pails of water, the kitchen sink, and everything else produced in the economy.

On the vertical axes, the measures are also different. The supply and demand model uses the price of the product, measured in dollars. A change in this price, such as a change in the price of pails of water, would make the product either more or less expensive than other products that consumers could purchase. In contrast, the vertical axis of the aggregate supply and aggregate demand model measures the price level, which is an index of all prices. If the price level rises, pails of water and everything else would become uniformly more expensive. Figure 8-1 makes note of these differences.

Equilibrium in any particular micro market will normally be reached much more rapidly than equilibrium in the macroeconomy. The reason is that consumers and producers find it easy to observe the prices in that market. For this reason, it's relatively easy for them to make the adjustments that bring the market into equilibrium. If the market price is higher than the equilibrium value, a surplus would develop that would soon pull the market price lower. If the market price is lower than the equilibrium value, a shortage would develop that would soon bring the market price higher, as summarized in the three steps following:

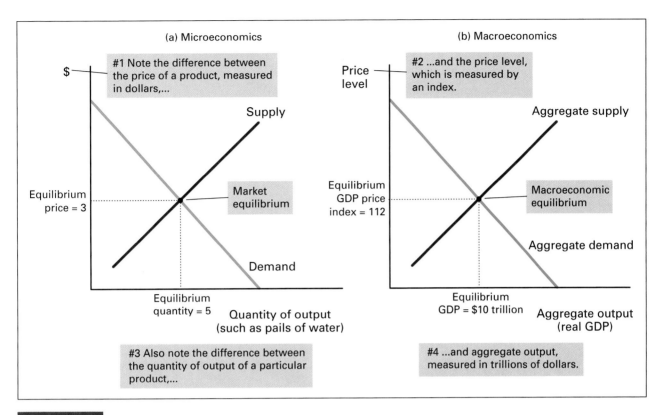

FIGURE 8-1

COMPARING MICRO TO MACRO ANALYSIS The model of supply and demand relates the quantity of a particular product to its price, as shown in part (a). The market equilibrium occurs when the quantity demanded equals the quantity supplied. In this example from Chapter 3, the equilibrium is at a price of $3 and a quantity of five pails of water. Any price above $3 would lead to a surplus, causing price to fall until the equilibrium is reached. Any price below $3 would lead to a shortage, causing price to rise until the equilibrium is reached.

In the macroeconomy, there is a multitude of markets, each of which is separately trying to achieve its equilibrium value, while influencing one another in the process. The macroeconomy is shown in part (b), where the vertical axis measures the price level and the horizontal axis measures real GDP. While the principles of adjusting to equilibrium are generally the same in the micro- and macro-economies, the speed of adjustment can be dramatically slower in the macroeconomy.

Step #1: At the starting price, there is either a surplus or shortage, meaning that the market is not in equilibrium.

Step #2: If there is a surplus, price adjusts down; if there is a shortage, price adjusts up.

Step #3: In response to changes in price, consumers adjust their quantities demanded and producers their quantities supplied until the two are equal and the market is again in equilibrium.

In the macroeconomy, the process of adjusting to equilibrium is very similar, as follows:

Step #1: At the starting price level, the economy is not at equilibrium, meaning that the aggregate quantity demanded is either more or less than the aggregate quantities supplied.

Step #2: If the price level starts above the equilibrium, there would be surplus capacity that would pressure the price level lower. If the price level starts below the equilibrium, there would be shortages and the price level would be pushed up.

Step #3: Changes in the price level would lead to changes in the behavior of consumers and firms until the economy stops at the macro equilibrium.

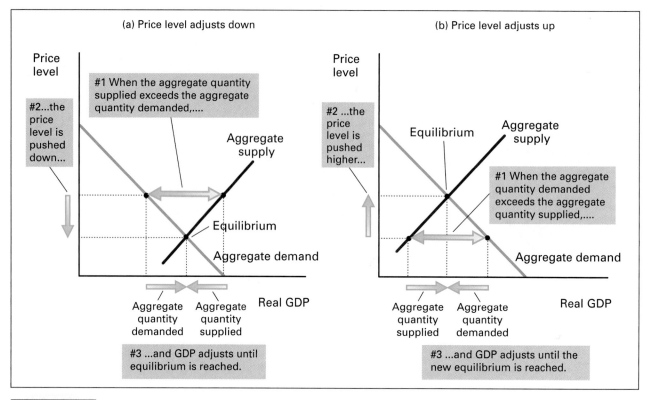

FIGURE 8-2

ADJUSTMENT TO THE MACRO EQUILIBRIUM At its equilibrium value, there is no tendency for the price level to change. However, if the price level starts out either too high or too low (step #1), that means that there are disequilibriums in various markets throughout the economy. As these markets adjust toward equilibrium, the price level is pushed toward its equilibrium value (step #2). In this process, the economy will move along its aggregate demand and aggregate supply curves until the point of equilibrium is reached (step #3). Part (a) shows the adjustment process to a lower price level, and part (b) to a higher price level.

Figure 8-2 shows these three steps in the adjustment process to the macro equilibrium. Unlike when the price of an individual item changes, however, it's often not obvious to individuals or businesses when the price level changes. In the next section, we will see why macroeconomics is controversial. We will also lay the foundation for a more detailed look at the AD/AS model. We'll see that the specifics and significance of the adjustment process have been the source of considerable controversy within the economics profession between classical and Keynesian economists. Later in this chapter we will take a more detailed look at aggregate demand and aggregate supply.

8.2 KEYNESIAN SHORT-RUN AND CLASSICAL LONG-RUN PERSPECTIVES

long run involves underlying economic forces that make themselves felt over time.

short run a period of time during which the economy transitions to the long run.

Answering sweeping macroeconomic questions about employment, output, and inflation requires providing near-term events with a long-term perspective and context. This context is called the **long run,** which involves underlying economic forces that make themselves felt over time. For example, economic growth is a long-run consideration. In contrast, the **short run** represents more immediate and transitory economic developments, such as the increased unemployment in the months following the September 11 attacks. Much of the difference of opinion within the economics profession concerns how much weight to attach to short-run versus long-run outcomes. The issues are especially contentious when the policies that are best for long-run economic health come at the price of short-run problems.

KEYNESIAN AND CLASSICAL SCHOOLS OF THOUGHT

During the Great Depression of the 1930s, the biggest short-run problem was unemployment. It was against this backdrop that, in 1936, John Maynard Keynes authored *The General Theory of Employment, Interest, and Money*. In this path-breaking work, Keynes took issue with the mainstream of economic thinking at the time. Instead of accepting that government should sit back and wait for the economy to pull itself out of recession, he proposed ways in which government could actively manage the economy toward prosperity. Keynesian theory came to define the field of macroeconomics for nearly half a century. Before it, the field of macroeconomics did not even exist.

After the work of Keynes and the economic recovery seemingly brought about by the government spending of World War II, it appeared that government had a duty to shepherd the economy through times of economic distress. In the United States, that duty was embodied in the Employment Act of 1946. When the problem was too little spending and too few people employed, the government could go far toward solving the problem through spending more itself and giving its citizens incentives to do likewise. At the time, there seemed to be no macroeconomic tradeoffs in this course of action. As time progressed, however, efforts by the government to keep unemployment low started to cause the unwanted side effect of inflation in the 1960s and 1970s.

As a result, the emphasis in economics shifted away from short-run cures and toward looking for policies that would facilitate smooth long-run economic growth without significant inflation. From this perspective, government should not adjust its policies in order to promote spending when unemployment rises, but should rather provide the stability that allows the economy to adjust on its own.

Macroeconomic theory can be placed within either of two broad categories, depending on whether the emphasis is on short-run or long-run processes. These schools of thought are:

- **Keynesian,** which suggests that government action is an appropriate response to short-run macroeconomic problems.
- **Classical,** which suggests that a steady policy aimed at the long run best allows the economy to take care of itself.

Since classical economics represented the conventional wisdom prior to the Great Depression and before the publication of Keynes' *General Theory*, let's first consider some key ideas of the classical school of thought:

- *Say's Law.* "Supply creates its own demand." One of the earliest expressions of the classical viewpoint was by the French economist, Jean Baptiste Say (1767–1832). According to Say, the aggregate value of what is produced will provide the income with which to buy it. Periods of unemployment are thus *disequilibriums* that will be corrected when the marketplace figures out the profit-maximizing mix of goods and services to produce.
- *Full employment.* According to the classical view, unemployment is nothing more than a transitory disequilibrium in the marketplace—the time markets take to adjust to their market-clearing equilibriums. Specifically, there is a surplus of workers in the labor market. The market response is for wage rates to fall until the surplus is absorbed and full employment is obtained. In response to lower labor costs, competition forces output prices to fall. These wage and price adjustments are supply and demand in action.

Keynesian a macroeconomic school of thought that emphasizes the short run and the importance of fiscal policy.

classical a macroeconomic school of thought that emphasizes the long run and reliance upon market forces to achieve full employment.

Say's Law supply creates its own demand; the aggregate value of what is produced will provide the income with which to buy it.

QUICKCHECK

What is the essential difference between the Keynesian view and the classical view of the economy?

Answer: Keynesians emphasize the importance of the short run, while classical economists emphasize the importance of the long run.

TABLE 8-1 KEYNES IN HIS OWN WORDS, WITH COMMENTS*	
QUOTE FROM KEYNES	**COMMENT**
If supply creates its own demand, why are we having a worldwide depression?	Shows Keynes' rejection of a cornerstone of the classical school of thought, Say's Law. Refers to the Great Depression of the 1930s.
In the long run we are all dead.	Probably Keynes' most famous statement. Implies that waiting for the economy's tendency to correct itself is not acceptable.
The ... economic problem is not—if we look into the future—the permanent problem of the human race.	Reflects Keynes' belief that proper policy actions could overcome the depression.
The ideas of the economists and the political philosophers, both when they are right and when they are wrong, are more powerful than is commonly understood. Indeed, the world is ruled by little else. Practical men, who believe themselves to be quite exempt from any intellectual influences, are usually the slaves of some defunct economists.	Emphasizes the high importance of economics and economic policymaking to the average person, although that importance is usually not recognized.
I believe myself to be writing a book on economic theory which will largely revolutionize—not I suppose all at once, but in the course of the next ten years—the way the world thinks about economic problems.	Foresaw that the *General Theory* would revolutionize economics.

*Comments are interpretations by the authors.

- *Downwardly flexible wages and prices.* Even if the economy began to experience a recession, both wages and prices would adjust downward to ensure that workers remained employed and the goods and services produced would be sold. Given enough time, the classical economists had no doubt that wage and price flexibility would assert themselves if the economy began to experience difficulties.
- *Minimal government intervention in the economy.* Adam Smith is often credited as the father of classical economics. Smith's *Wealth of Nations* (1776) took the position that the invisible hand of the marketplace would ensure that the economy performs up to its potential, without help from the government.

In order to advance his own position that massive government spending programs were required to pull the economy out of the Great Depression, Keynes first had to undermine the foundations of classical economics. His first target was Say's Law, which led him to question the other classical beliefs. Keynes held out the following ideas:

- *Saving and investment.* When Keynes looked around, he saw people desperate for work. Say's Law, he concluded, is "equivalent to the proposition that there is no obstacle to full employment." Surely Say's Law is wrong, he reasoned. Buy why? Keynes' thoughts turned toward the motives to save and to invest. He saw the act of saving as motivated by the all too human desire to hoard, or to accumulate wealth. For investment to occur, however, people had to be optimistic about the future, since investing involves risk. In other words, while investment cannot occur without savings to finance it, the mere existence of savings does not guarantee that investment will take place. People may be pessimistic about the future and want to hoard. The result would be insuffucient aggregate demand, which causes unemployment unless the price level falls to adjust to the smaller amount of money in circulation. As we see below, Keynes assumed that would not happen in the short run.

- *Sticky wages and prices.* Keynes argued that wage and price cuts were rare. Without them, the price level could not fall. Since Say's law relies on flexible prices, sticky wages would keep the adjustments from happening and prevent the economy from making the transition to a full-employment equilibrium.
- *Unemployment.* Keynes' reasoning led him to conclude that the classical equilibrium of full employment was false. An *unemployment equilibrium* would be the outcome when aggregate demand is not sufficient to keep everyone employed.
- *Government must intervene.* Keynes believed that when the economy experienced downturns, increased government spending was the only way to make up for the lack of spending by households and businesses.

It is clear that Keynes took economics from the long-run perspective of the classical school to a short-run perspective, which was in tune with the massive unemployment people were experiencing during the Great Depression. You can get a better idea of Keynes' thinking by referring to Table 8-1, which presents some of Keynes' ideas in his own words.

Economists today use the concepts from both schools of thought. However, they may emphasize the concepts from one school or the other depending on the severity of the short-run problems in the economy. We will now proceed to develop the models of aggregate demand and aggregate supply. This model can both provide the short-run and long-run context for macroeconomic analysis, as we will see in this and following chapters.

KEYNES—THE MAN AND THE ECONOMIST   *SNAPSHOT*

John Maynard Keynes (1883–1946), the man, still intrigues us nearly sixty years after his death. Likewise, Keynes the economist still influences us. His father was a noted economist and his mother the first female mayor of Cambridge, England, which perhaps explains the many interests that Keynes pursued. He has been described as an intellectual, an academic, a pacifist, a statesman, a mathematician, a successful stock market speculator, a journalist, an art collector, a bibliophile, a patron of the arts, a husband of a famous Russian ballerina, the father of macroeconomics, and the name behind Keynesian economics. Whew! That's a lot, but it barely scratches the surface of all that has been said about Keynes. Blessed with a powerful mind and an engaging personality, Keynes the man was among the towering public figures of his day.

Keynes the economist is best known for the *General Theory of Employment, Interest, and Money* (1936), which offered a way to pull the world out of the depression. The book proposes a policy of more government spending, even if those expenditures exceed tax revenues. That is a controversial idea even today. In 1940 the problem was different, and Keynes responded by writing *How to Pay for the War.* He foresaw that once the Second World War was over, the overriding economic problem would not be depression, but inflation. His policy to prevent inflation? The government should not spend more than the amount of its tax revenues, a policy the opposite of that in the *General Theory.* We see that Keynes was able to adjust his thinking to suit new problems. That was a hallmark of his entire life. Keynes never stood aside and merely observed. His writings were focused on policy recommendations. Were he alive today, he would have much to say, and whatever he said would be heard. ◄

8.3 MODELING THE MACROECONOMY WITH AGGREGATE DEMAND AND AGGREGATE SUPPLY

The economy does not always achieve the three primary goals of low inflation, high employment, and economic growth. Through an understanding of why we sometimes fail to achieve our goals, we can better deal with the problems of high inflation, unemployment, and economic

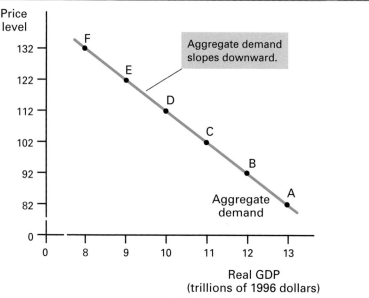
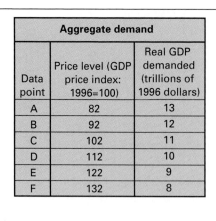

Aggregate demand		
Data point	Price level (GDP price index: 1996=100)	Real GDP demanded (trillions of 1996 dollars)
A	82	13
B	92	12
C	102	11
D	112	10
E	122	9
F	132	8

FIGURE 8-3

AGGREGATE DEMAND An aggregate demand curve shows the relationship between the price level and the quantity of real GDP demanded. The price level and real GDP are inversely related, resulting in the downward slope to aggregate demand. Points *A* through *F* in the table are plotted as points *A* through *F* in the graph.

stagnation. The model of aggregate demand and aggregate supply provides the framework for thinking about the macroeconomy's performance. In this section you will look at:

■ Aggregate demand
■ Long-run aggregate supply
■ Short-run aggregate supply
■ The macroeconomic equilibrium

We turn our attention to aggregate demand first.

AGGREGATE DEMAND

aggregate demand relates how much real GDP consumers, businesses, government, and foreign buyers will purchase at each price level; graphically, aggregate demand slopes downward.

Aggregate demand tells us how much real GDP consumers, businesses, government, and foreign buyers would collectively purchase at each price level. The aggregate demand curve, like the demand curve for a single good, slopes downward. The table and graph in Figure 8-3 shows that the quantity of real GDP varies inversely with changes in the price level. A higher price level results in a smaller quantity of real GDP demanded, while a lower price level leads to an increase in the quantity of real GDP demanded.

The reasons for the downward slope of aggregate demand are different from the reasons for the downward slope in the demand for an individual good. In the microeconomy, a demand curve reveals the quantity of a good or service that would be purchased at each of various possible prices. For example, as the price of Pepsi rises, the quantity demanded falls. This occurs for two reasons. The first is because consumers substitute Coca-Cola and other beverages in place of Pepsi. The second is because the purchasing power of consumers is reduced because of the higher price of Pepsi. Less purchasing power means fewer purchases will be made.

In contrast, the downward slope to aggregate demand occurs because a change in the price level affects aggregate spending in four ways:

1. The **purchasing power effect:** A lower price level allows consumers to receive more goods and services for any given number of dollars they spend. A higher price level means consumers receive fewer goods and services for any number of dollars they spend.

2. The **wealth effect:** A higher price level would reduce the real value of savings and lead consumers to spend less out of their current incomes. Conversely, a lower price level causes consumers to spend more of their current incomes because the lower price level increases the value of their savings.

3. The **interest-rate effect:** A higher price level increases interest rates, which represent the cost of borrowing. In turn, because of the higher cost of borrowing, households and firms will decrease the quantity of real GDP demanded. The interest-rate effect would work in reverse in response to a lower price level.

4. The **international substitution effect:** If the price level in the United States rises, while the price level in other countries stays the same, U.S. consumers will shift their buying of goods toward imports from other countries, and away from U.S.-made goods. Similarly, foreigners will also reduce their purchases of U.S.-made goods and substitute goods from other countries. The international substitution effect would work in reverse if the U.S. price level fell. The international substitution effect is not very significant for the U.S. economy.

Consider how these effects would operate in your life if tomorrow you woke up to find that the price level was half what it was when you feel asleep the night before. If your income stayed the same, you could buy twice as much as before. That is the purchasing power effect. Likewise, your savings would be worth twice as much. That would motivate you to spend more of your income, illustrating the wealth effect in action. Finally, recognize that the lower U.S. price level would leave the prices of imports from other countries unchanged. The lower prices on U.S. goods and the unchanged prices on imports would cause you to purchase more U.S. goods, which is the international substitution effect.

We have just seen that the aggregate demand curve slopes downward. A movement up the curve will occur when the price level rises. A movement down the curve will occur when the price level falls. The purchasing power effect, the wealth effect, the interest-rate effect, and the international substitution effect provide the rationale for the downward slope. We now turn our attention to shifts in aggregate demand, including a discussion of the shift factors.

purchasing power effect the effect of the price level on consumers' ability to buy goods and services.

wealth effect the change in the fraction of current income spent caused by a price-level change affecting the real value of savings.

interest-rate effect A higher price level increases interest rates, causing households and firms to decrease the quantity of real GDP demanded.

international substitution effect a change in the price level changes the quantity demanded of real GDP through its effects on imports and exports. A rise in the price level causes consumers to buy more imports, thus reducing the quantity of real GDP demanded. A lower price level causes consumers to substitute domestic goods for imports, thus increasing the quantity of real GDP demanded.

SHIFTS IN AGGREGATE DEMAND

When the economy's aggregate demand curve shifts to the right, there has been an increase in aggregate demand. When the aggregate demand curve shifts to the left, there has been a decrease in aggregate demand. Part (a) of Figure 8-4 shows an increase in aggregate demand, while part (b) of the figure shows a decrease in aggregate demand.

QUICKCHECK

The lower the price of movies, the more movies you choose to see, according to the law of demand. Would this behavior be different if prices were to fall in the same proportion throughout the economy?

Answer: When the price of movies drops but other prices remain constant, consumers substitute movies for other forms of entertainment. That substitution effect of a price change would not occur if all prices dropped simultaneously. However, if the general price level falls, the purchasing power of your income increases and so you might watch more movies because of the purchasing power effect. You also feel wealthier and so might watch more movies on account of the wealth effect.

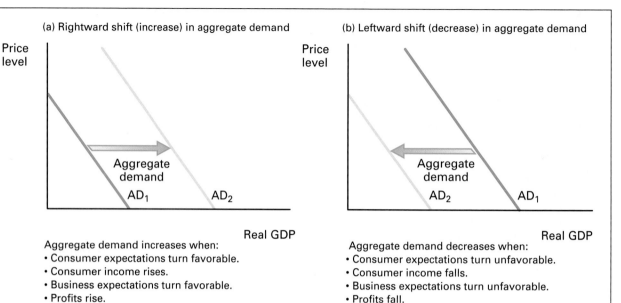

FIGURE 8-4

FACTORS THAT SHIFT AGGREGATE DEMAND Factors that shift aggregate demand to the right are listed in (a), along with a graph showing the rightward shift. Factors that shift aggregate demand to the left are shown in (b), along with a graph showing the leftward shift.

The aggregate demand curve, just like the demand curve for a single product, is drawn under the assumption of *ceteris paribus.* Influences on aggregate demand other than the price level can change. When that happens, the aggregate demand curve will shift. The other influences on aggregate demand, called the *shift factors for aggregate demand,* include influences related to spending by:

■ Consumers
■ Investors
■ Government
■ Foreign buyers

Let's consider the shift factors for each group. Among consumers, changes in expectations about the economy and expectations about their own future prospects can shift aggregate demand. When expectations are positive, aggregate demand will increase. When expectations are negative, aggregate demand will decrease. For example, consumers may cut back on spending if they fear that employers will be laying off workers because of an economic downturn. Spending cutbacks based on fearful expectations such as this one cause a decrease in aggregate demand. In general, when expectations are such that consumers are motivated to spend, aggregate demand increases. When expectations point in the other direction, aggregate demand decreases. A second influence on aggregate demand is consumer incomes. When incomes fall, perhaps because workers have been laid off, aggregate demand will decrease. A rise in incomes will increase aggregate demand.

Businesses spend on buildings, equipment, research, and other investments, and are likewise influenced by their expectations and incomes. Investment occurs in the expectation of a future return in the form of profits from that investment. When the future course of the economy looks rosy, investors expect that the returns on their investments will be high. This causes an increase in investment spending, and thus an increase in aggregate demand. When the future looks bleak, investors cut back on investment spending and aggregate demand shifts to the left. In addition to being influenced by expectations, businesses often finance investments from their profits. When profits fall, business investment is cut back because of insufficient funding. Aggregate demand decreases as a consequence. When profits increase, business investment tends to rise. Aggregate demand then increases.

Additional government spending increases aggregate demand, while cutbacks in government spending decrease aggregate demand. Higher taxes lead to a decrease in aggregate demand since higher taxes leave less income for workers to spend. Lower taxes, however, spur aggregate demand to increase by allowing workers to keep more of what they earn.

Foreign buyers of goods, services, and investments also influence aggregate demand. When their incomes rise, aggregate demand will increase, since an increase in their incomes allows them to spend more. When their incomes fall, the effect on aggregate demand is the reverse. The purchasing power of foreign currencies also affects the ability of foreign buyers to make purchases. An increase in the purchasing power of foreign currencies shifts aggregate demand to the right because of an increase in spending by foreign buyers. A decrease in the purchasing power of foreign currencies shifts aggregate demand to the left because decreased purchasing power means that foreign buyers will be able to spend less.

The shift factors for aggregate demand are summarized below the graphs in Figure 8-4. In reality, aggregate demand is buffeted by changes from these and many other sources. Some changes pull aggregate demand to the right, while at the same time other changes pull aggregate demand to the left. What matters most to the economy is whether the ultimate outcome of all the influences is an increase or a decrease in aggregate demand.

Economic problems relating to unemployment may result from decreases in aggregate demand. For example, from Keynes' perspective, the Great Depression resulted from a lack of aggregate demand. Since the 1930s, a great deal of economic policy has been motivated by the idea that having sufficient aggregate demand is important to economic prosperity. As mentioned earlier in the chapter, increased government spending was a key policy recommendation by Keynes. We see now that this recommendation was equivalent to a policy to increase aggregate demand.

AGGREGATE SUPPLY IN THE LONG RUN AND THE SHORT RUN

The output of goods and services that consumers purchase comes primarily from business firms. In the circular flow model, we see that firms employ labor and other resources in order to produce output. The total quantity of output, called aggregate output, is equivalent to an economy's GDP. In the United States, the decisions of ExxonMobil, General Motors, Microsoft, and millions of other firms lead to the production of output, which contributes to GDP.

How will aggregate output behave when the price level changes? To answer that question, we must look toward **aggregate supply,** the relationship between aggregate output, as measured by real GDP, and the price level. Aggregate supply assumes that the price level is the only influence on the production of aggregate output. In other words, like the supply curve for an individual good, an aggregate supply curve is drawn assuming *ceteris paribus*. As you will see momentarily, when other influences make themselves felt, the aggregate supply curve will shift.

Exactly how the aggregate supply curve appears depends on whether we are looking at production from a long-run or short-run perspective. As discussed in Chapter 6, the economy tends toward a natural rate of unemployment in the long run. From a long-run perspective, then, the price level does not matter—the economy will produce at full employment no matter whether a cup of coffee costs twenty cents or twenty dollars.

aggregate supply the relationship between aggregate output, as measured by real GDP, and the price level.

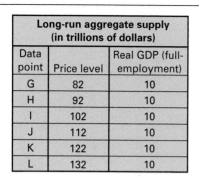
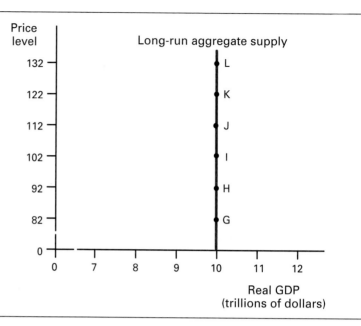

Long-run aggregate supply (in trillions of dollars)		
Data point	Price level	Real GDP (full-employment)
G	82	10
H	92	10
I	102	10
J	112	10
K	122	10
L	132	10

FIGURE 8-5

LONG-RUN AGGREGATE SUPPLY The long-run aggregate supply curve is vertical at the full-employment level of real GDP. The price level is irrelevant to the quantity of real GDP because full employment is determined by resource availability and the economy's ability to utilize resources. Points G through L plot the full-employment level of GDP, which is assumed to be $10 trillion. In the long run, this quantity of real GDP will be produced no matter the price level.

full-employment output (full-employment GDP) the real GDP the economy produces when it fully employs its resources.

Full-employment output, also termed **full-employment GDP,** is the real GDP the economy produces when it fully employs its resources. In other words, the economy has an unemployment rate exactly equal to the natural rate of unemployment. Recall that the natural rate will vary depending on structural features of the economy, such as its age profile and the amount of unemployment compensation available to those out of work. Estimates place the natural rate of unemployment at around five or six percent in the U.S. today. So full-employment output is produced by the remaining 94–95 percent of the work force. **In the long run the desire of people to receive incomes and the desire of firms to earn profits holds unemployment down and real GDP near its full-employment level.**

long-run aggregate supply the idea that, in the long run, the price level does not affect the amount of GDP the economy produces; graphically, long-run aggregate supply is vertical at full-employment GDP.

Long-run aggregate supply shows the relationship between full-employment GDP and the price level. The value of full-employment output will be the same whether the price level is low or high, so the long-run aggregate supply curve is drawn as a vertical line at full-employment output. Suppose that $10 trillion is the economy's full-employment level of GDP. Figure 8-5 shows the long-run aggregate supply curve as a vertical line at $10 trillion.

As evidence that the price level does not matter in the long run, consider that the price level today is quadruple what it was in the 1960s. However, market wages have also adjusted upward. Other than requiring that we earn and spend about four times as much to obtain the same quantity of goods and services, the rise in wages and prices has had little long-run significance for the aggregate economy.

In the short run, an economy's aggregate output can be equal to, greater than, or less than its full-employment output. For example, unemployment of resources causes aggregate output to be less than its full-employment level. An economy can produce more than the full-employment level temporarily. This would happen if workers toiled more than the usual number of hours, perhaps in order to meet a surge in aggregate demand. The **short-run aggregate supply** curve shows the relationship between the price level and aggregate output (real GDP) in the

short-run aggregate supply tells how much output the economy will offer in the short run at each possible price level.

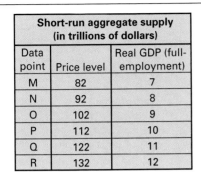

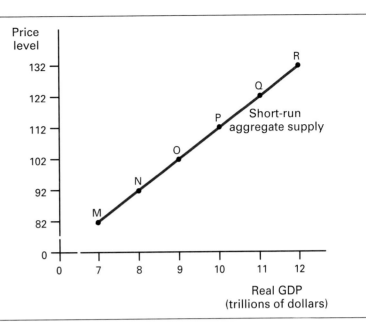

Short-run aggregate supply (in trillions of dollars)		
Data point	Price level	Real GDP (full-employment)
M	82	7
N	92	8
O	102	9
P	112	10
Q	122	11
R	132	12

FIGURE 8-6

SHORT-RUN AGGREGATE SUPPLY In the short-run, aggregate supply will increase as the price level increases. Real GDP can be less than the full-employment level, equal to it, or greater. The value of real GDP depends on the price level in the short run. For example, point M shows that $7 trillion of output, which is less than the full-employment output of $10 trillion, would be produced at a price level of 82. Unemployment would exceed the natural rate and real GDP would fall below the full employment level of $10 trillion. At a price level of 132, in contrast, the economy would produce more than it could sustain in the long run. Point R shows that output would climb to $12 trillion, which exceeds the full employment output of $10 trillion.

short run. This curve will slope upward, since a higher price level, other things equal, will induce firms to produce more goods and services. Similarly, a lower price level will cause aggregate output to fall. A short-run aggregate supply curve is shown in Figure 8-6.

SHIFTS IN AGGREGATE SUPPLY

When the price level changes, there is a movement along an aggregate supply curve. Movements along aggregate supply must be distinguished from shifts. An aggregate supply curve will shift when an influence on aggregate supply changes. As shown in Figure 8-7, an increase in aggregate supply is indicated by a shift to the right, while a decrease in aggregate supply is indicated by a shift to the left. This is true whether we are looking at long-run aggregate supply, shown in parts (a) and (b) of the figure, or short-run aggregate supply, as shown by parts (c) and (d).

The causes of the shifts in aggregate supply vary according to whether it is long-run aggregate supply that shifts or short-run aggregate supply that shifts. Later in this chapter you will see what makes the long-run aggregate supply curve shift. Chapter 9 further examines shifts in short-run aggregate supply.

AGGREGATE DEMAND AND AGGREGATE SUPPLY DETERMINE THE MACRO EQUILIBRIUM

If we bring together aggregate demand, long-run aggregate supply, and short-run aggregate supply, we can show the idea of a **macroeconomic equilibrium,** when aggregate demand equals aggregate supply. At the macro equilibrium, real GDP will be at its full-employment level. The aggregate demand curve and the long-run aggregate supply curve will intersect at the equilibrium

macroeconomic equilibrium where aggregate demand equals aggregate supply.

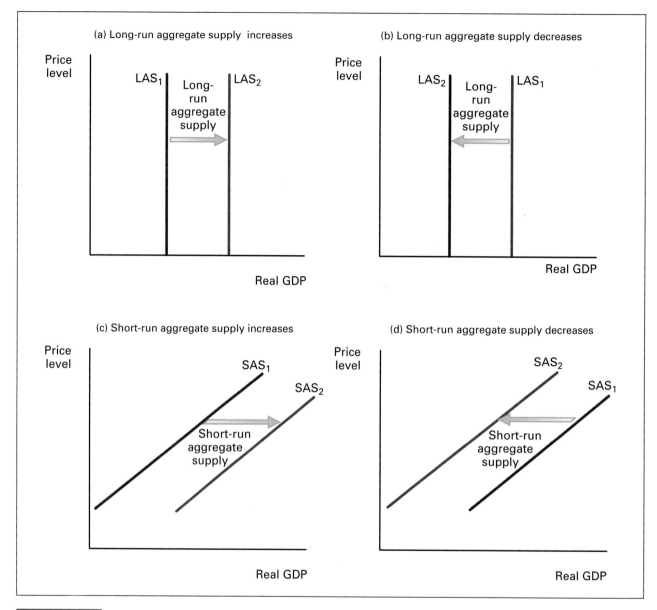

FIGURE 8-7

SHIFTS IN AGGREGATE SUPPLY Part (a) shows that an increase in long-run aggregate supply (LAS) is indicated by a rightward shift in the curve. Part (b) shows that a decrease in long-run aggregate supply is indicated by a leftward shift in the curve. Parts (c) and (d) show shifts in the short-run aggregate supply (SAS) curve. The rightward shift in part (c) illustrates an increase in short-run aggregate supply. The leftward shift in part (d) illustrates a decrease in short-run aggregate supply. The initial position of each curve is indicated by the subscript 1, while the new position is labeled with the subscript 2.

point. Furthermore, the short-run aggregate supply curve will intersect aggregate demand and long-run aggregate supply at this same point. The macro equilibrium is shown in Figure 8-8.

As you will see in subsequent chapters, the macro equilibrium changes when any of the three curves in the figure shift. For now, we ignore the short-run aggregate supply curve, and all the issues associated with the short run, in order to take a long-run perspective on the economy. Three questions will be examined:

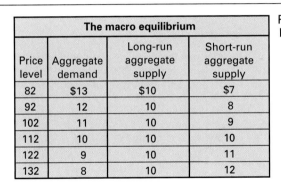

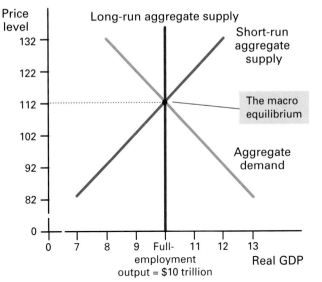

FIGURE 8-8

THE MACRO EQUILIBRIUM In this example, the macro equilibrium is achieved when the price level equals 112. Only at that price level will aggregate demand, long-run aggregate supply, and short-run aggregate supply be equal. Graphically, the macro equilibrium occurs when the three curves intersect.

- What is the long-run macro equilibrium and why is it important?
- What could prevent the long-run macro equilibrium from being achieved?
- What causes a change in full-employment GDP?

In answering these questions we apply the model of aggregate demand and long-run aggregate supply.

8.4 ACHIEVING FULL-EMPLOYMENT EQUILIBRIUM

Figure 8-9 shows a downward-sloping aggregate demand curve, along with a vertical long-run aggregate supply. The intersection of these two curves represents a long-run macroeconomic equilibrium, termed the **full-employment equilibrium** because it occurs at the full-employment output. The figure labels both the full-employment equilibrium and the price level that supports it.

At any price level above the full-employment equilibrium price level, aggregate spending will be insufficient to support full-employment output. Unemployed workers will compete for jobs, which will drive down wages. Competition in the output market will force firms to lower prices in response to these lower wages. The lower price level that results means that spending will buy more output and thus lead to greater employment. The process continues until the economy reaches full employment and the corresponding full-employment GDP, as shown in Figure 8-9.

If the actual price level were below the equilibrium shown in Figure 8-9, the economy would "overheat," with aggregate purchasing power exceeding the economy's ability to produce. Firms would compete for workers, thus driving their wages up. Competitive firms would pass on these higher wages to consumers by raising their prices. The resulting increase in the price level would soak up the excess purchasing power, thus leading the economy back to its long-run equilibrium.

full-employment equilibrium
the long-run macroeconomic equilibrium that occurs at a full-employment output.

THE LONG-RUN MACRO EQUILIBRIUM The long-run macroeconomic equilibrium occurs where aggregate demand intersects long-run aggregate supply. Competition prevents the price level from remaining either too high or too low, resulting in a movement along the aggregate demand curve until full employment is reached.

For example, the high price level at point *A* on aggregate demand is associated with unemployment. As workers compete to get jobs, they drive down wages and production costs. Competition then forces down prices. In contrast, at point *B*, there are not enough workers to produce all the output people want to buy. Competition drives up wages and prices, a condition known as overheating.

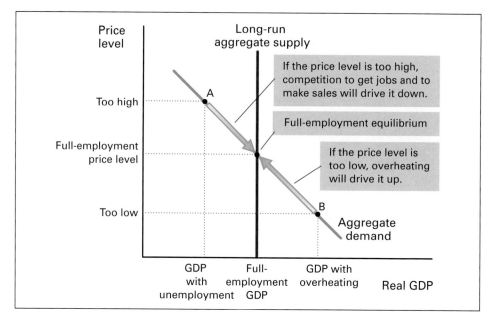

sticky wages wages that are slow to adjust, usually in a downward direction.

sticky prices prices that are slow to adjust, usually in a downward direction.

The debate between classical and Keynesian economists often comes down to the question of nothing more than whether government should wait for a movement along aggregate demand or to take action to *manage aggregate demand,* meaning to shift the aggregate demand curve itself. We proceed by looking at the adjustment process along aggregate demand, and leave possible policy options for aggregate demand management to chapters that follow.

If a market is not at equilibrium, forces of supply and demand will cause the price to change until the equilibrium comes about. That is the classical analysis: Wage and price adjustments will lead to a long-run macro equilibrium that is characterized by both full employment and its associated full-employment output. Keynesians do not dispute this point, but dispute its relevance when the economy faces immediate macroeconomic problems that call for prompt solutions. Of particular note is the existence of downwardly **sticky wages** and **sticky prices,** where downwardly sticky refers to an inflexibility that makes it difficult for wages and prices to fall. If wages are sticky, the downward movement in wages required to reach a long-run equilibrium could take too long. The downward stickiness could be due to labor contracts between a union and its employees. It could also be due to human psychology—when firms cut wages, their workers resent it.

One reason for wage and price stickiness is that some markets might not move to equilibrium easily. Changes in the demand for outputs make it appropriate for some wages and prices to rise or fall relative to other wages and prices. However, there is resistance to change—*rigidities*—within both labor and output markets. Stores have leases and contracts that are not easily adjusted. In some cases, the contracts are with unions that resist wage cuts.

In principle, wage and price stickiness might occur in either direction—whether for price increases or for price decreases. In practice, **wage and price stickiness is most pronounced in a downward direction,** meaning that there is more stickiness when markets resist lower wages and prices. For example, it is natural for workers to resent a wage cut, no matter what the macroeconomic circumstances might be. Firms that cut wages run the risk of lower productivity and lower quality output from their workers. The problem is

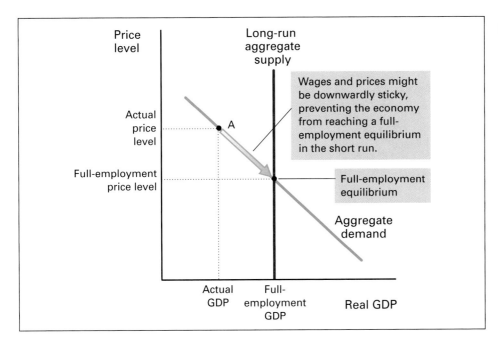

FIGURE 8-10

DOWNWARDLY STICKY WAGES AND PRICES Wages and prices that are downwardly sticky would prevent the economy from moving rapidly to a full-employment equilibrium. For example, the economy might start at point *A*, with a price level that is too high to reach full-employment output. In the long run, that price level will fall, but wage and price stickiness might prevent it from doing so in the short run.

often exacerbated by a lack of information and trust. When employers attempt to downsize or close operations, employees balk, which causes adjustments in employment and output to occur slowly.

Figure 8-10 sums up the significance of downwardly sticky wages and prices. While wages are not listed explicitly in this figure, wages paid by firms will be a big factor in determining their costs and the prices they charge. In other words, higher wages are associated with a higher price level. When the price level is too high to sustain a full-employment equilibrium, it must adjust downward to reach that equilibrium. Sticky wages and prices can get in the way of that adjustment.

For example, if the actual price level is above the full-employment price level, such as at point *A,* wage and price stickiness would prevent it from dropping fast enough that the full-employment equilibrium can be reached quickly. By delaying movement down the aggregate demand curve to a full-employment equilibrium, wage and price stickiness can mean a prolonged period in which both output and employment are below the economy's potential.

DOES ACTUAL GDP LIVE UP TO ITS POTENTIAL?

For most of its history, the U.S. economy has been successful at living up to its potential. In other words, actual GDP has been in the vicinity of *potential GDP*, which is the amount that we can expect the economy to achieve at full employment. This history is shown in Figure 8-11.

Periods of unemployment in which actual GDP falls short of potential GDP represent transition times in a market economy—the time markets take to adjust to their market-clearing equilibriums. These transitions are the recessions shown by the shaded vertical bars in Figure 8-11. During a recession, there is a surplus of workers in the labor market. As they compete for jobs, workers drive down wages until the labor surplus is absorbed. In response to lower labor costs, competition forces output prices to fall, too. These wage and price adjustments reflect supply and demand in action in the many markets that make up the economy as a whole. These adjustments can take time, however, the significance of which forms the crux of the debate between classical and Keynesian economists.

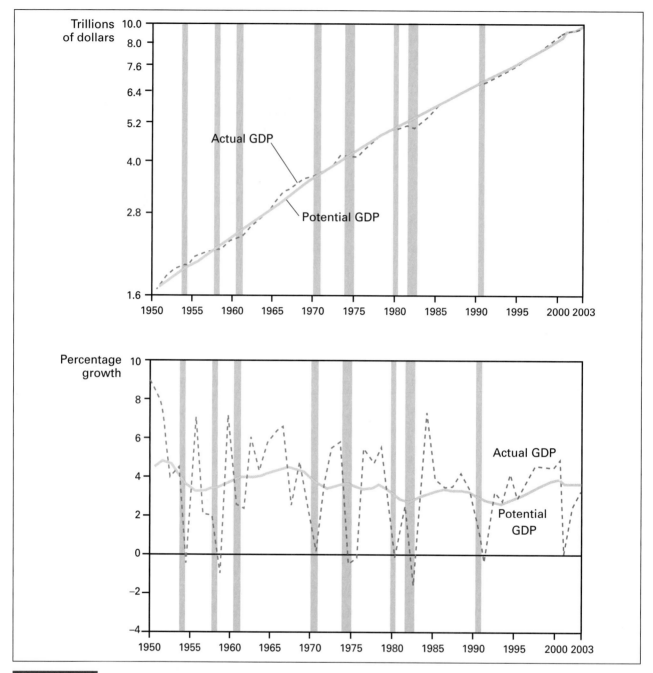

FIGURE 8-11

ACTUAL AND POTENTIAL GDP Over time and with some short-run zigs and zags, actual real GDP in the United States has generally been close to the economy's full-employment potential. The top graph shows actual and potential GDP in trillions of dollars. The bottom graph shows the percentage growth in both. Actual GDP is seen to be more volatile than potential GDP. Recessions are indicated by the shaded vertical bars. During recessions, actual GDP falls short of potential GDP.

Source: Congressional Budget Office, 2001 and 2003, using data from the Department of Commerce, Bureau of Economic Analysis and National Income and Product Accounts.

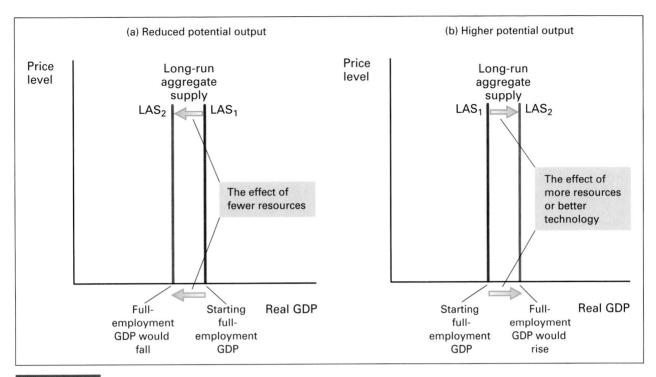

FIGURE 8-12

LONG-RUN AGGREGATE SUPPLY Long-run aggregate supply is graphed as a vertical line at full-employment GDP, which implies that the price level does not affect an economy's potential output in the long run. As shown in (a), a loss of resources reduces full-employment output and shifts aggregate demand to the left. Conversely, as shown in (b), long-run aggregate supply shifts to the right over time as the economy acquires greater resources and better technology that increase the amount of output produced at full employment.

In the long run, potential GDP changes so that long-run aggregate supply shifts. This occurs in response to changes in the amount of resources available to the economy and in the technology available to use these resources. For example, warfare or natural disasters could destroy resources, which would reduce full-employment output and shift aggregate supply to the left, as shown in Figure 8-12(a).

More commonly, economies add resources and improve technology over time. The result is economic growth that increases full-employment output and thus shifts long-run aggregate supply to the right, as shown in Figure 8-12(b).

QUICKCHECK

What would be the effect on long-run aggregate supply of an earthquake that destroys an economy's productive capacity? Why?

Answer: The long-run aggregate supply would shift to the left. This movement shows that, even if the country's work force is fully employed, there would be less output.

SNAPSHOT   A STORY TOLD IN A MILLION WAYS

If products linger on the shopkeeper's shelf, the prices eventually get lowered to clear the inventory. If you can't find a job with the skills you have, you eventually acquire new ones. If no one will pay you what you ask, you eventually lower your salary expectations. However, if the headhunters are beating at your door with salary offers that you just can't pass up, then you demand a higher salary where you are or switch jobs.

These are stories told over and over for millions of people and products all across the land. Put together, it is nothing more than the economy heading toward full-employment output at an equilibrium price level. But the stories of how to get there are told in ways that are unique to the circumstances of the individuals and firms involved. Each and every story is significant—they are the micro behind the macro of economics. ◄

8.5 ROOT CAUSES OF INFLATION

To fight or prevent inflation, policymakers must identify the source. This section shows how the model of aggregate supply and aggregate demand can help by distinguishing between demand-side and supply-side causes of inflation. This distinction also has implications in regard to full-employment output.

DEMAND-SIDE INFLATION AND DEFLATION

demand-side inflation occurs when aggregate demand shifts to the right. The result is a movement up the long-run aggregate supply curve to a higher price level, but no change in full-employment output.

Aggregate demand tends to increase—shift to the right—over time. This shift occurs in response to general growth in purchasing power as consumer spending increases, government spending increases, or, most generally, as more money circulates throughout the economy. The effect of an outward shift in aggregate demand is shown in Figure 8-13(a). *Ceteris paribus,* in the long run, the effect is to keep output the same and increase the price level. This effect is known as **demand-side inflation.**

Alternatively, if aggregate demand were to shift to the left, the effect would be **demand-side deflation** as shown in Figure 8-13(b) on page 214. Demand-side deflation is not common, but can have significant disruptive effects when it happens. Many economists point to the difficulties of adjusting to a lower price level as being a root cause of the Great Depression.

demand-side deflation occurs when aggregate demand shifts to the left. The result is a movement down the long-run aggregate supply curve to a lower price level, but no change in full-employment output.

SUPPLY-SIDE INFLATION AND DEFLATION

supply-side inflation occurs when long-run aggregate supply shifts to the left. The result is a movement up the aggregate demand curve to a higher price level and lower full-employment output.

Changes on the supply side of the economy can also cause either inflation or deflation. If long-run aggregate supply were to shift to the left, we would see **supply-side inflation** in which the same amount of spending is able to buy fewer goods at higher prices. Supply-side inflation is shown in Figure 8-14(a), see page 214. Note that full-employment GDP decreases as long-run aggregate supply shifts to the left.

One possible source of supply-side inflation is a **supply shock,** which is an unexpected event that is major enough to affect the overall economy. Supply shocks, such as caused by wars, natural disasters, or disruptions to oil imports, cause real changes in productive capacity. The terrorist attacks of September 11 caused a supply shock, the economic effects of which are discussed in this chapter's Explore & Apply section. Supply shocks are behind what is called the **real business cycle,** in which GDP rises or falls in response to major events that cannot be foreseen. Although we don't know what the shocks will be, we can be pretty sure that additional shocks will occur.

supply shock an unexpected event that is major enough to affect the overall economy; shifts aggregate supply.

real business cycle when GDP rises or falls in response to major events that cannot be foreseen.

Aggregate supply might alternatively shift to the left in response to a change in the laws governing business practices within a country. Recent years have witnessed a number of laws and lawsuits that have changed the way firms can operate. Most notably, firms have

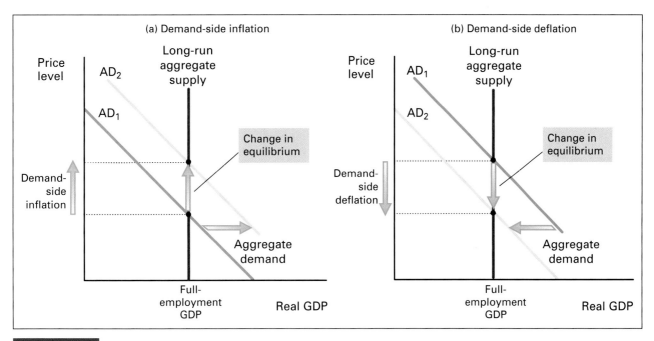

FIGURE 8-13

DEMAND-SIDE INFLATION AND DEFLATION Aggregate demand shifts to the right in response to increased government spending or increased spending by consumers, as shown in (a). The equilibrium price level increases, a result known as demand-side inflation. Spending might increase in response to an increase in the amount of money circulating in the economy.

Aggregate demand shifts to the left when there is less money circulating, such as when the government collects more tax revenue or when consumers are fearful and inclined to hoard cash. The leftward shift in aggregate demand pushes the price level down, resulting in demand-side deflation as shown in (b).

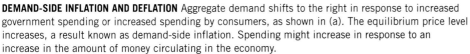

QUICKCHECK

Would the economy be better off if the government were to declare that all incomes shall henceforth be doubled? Use aggregate demand and aggregate supply analysis to support your answer.

Answer: If the economy is working up to its potential, then doubling everyone's income could not increase output, but would rather cause demand-side inflation that increases prices to offset the increased wages. With everyone having more money to spend, aggregate demand would shift to the right. The economy would move to a new long-run equilibrium at the same output and a higher price level.

seen their production costs increase in response to higher indirect employee costs, higher costs of complying with government regulations, and higher legal costs. Ongoing technological improvements that increase productivity can mask these effects.

On the bright side, technological change or an increase in resources increases the output associated with full employment. The result is a rightward shift in long-run aggregate supply. For example, the advent of e-commerce opened up possibilities for on-line shopping that have increased competition. It has also opened up possibilities for on-line payment

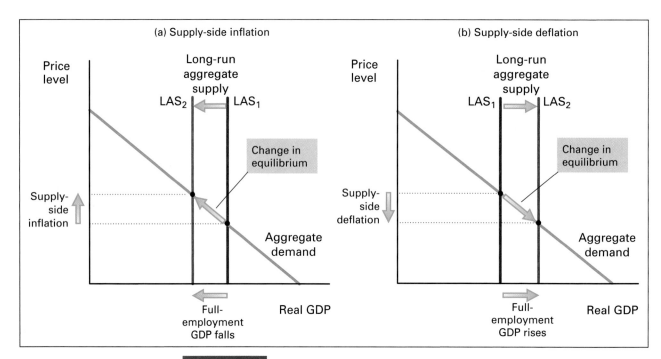

FIGURE 8-14

SUPPLY-SIDE INFLATION AND DEFLATION IN THE LONG RUN A leftward shift in long-run aggregate supply causes supply-side inflation, as shown in (a). Although unemployment remains unchanged, output falls and the price level rises. Explanations for this shift could include the destruction of resources in warfare or government restrictions on business practices.

In contrast, technological change or additional resources would shift aggregate supply to the right, resulting in supply-side deflation. In that case, without changing employment, output would rise and the price level would fall as shown in (b).

supply-side deflation occurs when long-run aggregate supply shifts to the right. The result is a movement down the aggregate demand curve to a lower price level and higher full-employment output.

methods that have reduced the costs of making transactions. As aggregate supply shifts to the right, the economy moves down the aggregate demand curve to a lower equilibrium price level. This process is called **supply-side deflation,** and is associated with an increase in full-employment GDP, as shown in Figure 8-14(b).

SNAPSHOT   THE REAL BUSINESS CYCLE—SOME SHOCKING SURPRISES

Cars, wars, oil cartels, computers, and power outages may not seem to have much in common, but they do. They have all shocked the economy in one way or another. How could ordinary citizens have foreseen the potential of the auto or the disruptions of World War II? We did not know of the oil crisis of the 1970s before it happened, and we did not know that it would disappear in the 1980s. Nor can we know the extent to which technology will alter our lifestyles or when the power grid will shut down.

All of these things and more jolt the economy, either to make it more productive or to knock it back a notch. They represent real changes in aggregate supply to which businesses and individuals must adjust. Policymakers can predict these events no better than the rest of us, and so can do little to avert these disruptions to the smooth path of economic growth. When it comes to the real business cycle, then, it is best to expect the unexpected! ◄

8.6 CLASSICAL VERSUS KEYNESIAN—THE GREAT DEBATE CONTINUES

This chapter started with reference to the Great Depression, which was ended by World War II and the massive government spending associated with it. Keynesian analysis was thought to have been proven correct. As President Richard Nixon phrased it in 1972, "We are all Keynesians, now." However, just as Nixon was proclaiming that Keynes had won, the economics profession was focusing in a more classical direction. It began to emphasize its microeconomic foundations, such as incentives facing individuals and firms that can influence the performance of the overall economy.

Economic analysis influences people's politics and vice versa. For example, political liberals often adopt Keynesian policy prescriptions. The reason is presumably not because most liberals have studied the economy in detail and are convinced of the validity of the Keynesian economic model. More likely, political liberals tend to believe that an activist government can be a powerful force for good in the world. Keynesian economics calls for government to be just such a force. It provides justification for a large government, but leaves open specific categories of spending.

A similar analysis applies to political conservatives, who tend to adhere to a classical perspective on the role of government. Conservatives usually distrust big government, preferring instead a more laissez-faire approach. Classical analysis suggests that much government action does more harm than good to the macroeconomy, which is in keeping with the conservative perspective.

While some controversy in macroeconomics is positive, concerning factual issues of cause and effect, most disagreement among macroeconomists is normative. For example, modern Keynesian models incorporate classical analysis of the long run. What makes these economists and their models Keynesian is that they discount the significance of the long run, preferring instead to emphasize practical issues in the workplace that inhibit adjustments to full employment. Thus, the disagreement between modern Keynesians and classical economists often boils down to the degrees to which they are willing to trade off short- and long-run objectives.

8.7 FIGHTING TERRORISM—WHAT PRICE DOES THE ECONOMY PAY?

Explore & Apply

"The world is not ending."

—New York Mayor Rudy Giuliani after the September 11 terrorist attacks

On September 11, 2001, hijackers turned four passenger airliners into terrorist bombs, demolishing the World Trade Center skyscrapers in New York City and destroying a portion of the Pentagon in Washington, D.C. One of the hijacked planes crashed in rural Pennsylvania. About three thousand people lost their lives from these attacks. Immediately, before any more hijackings could be committed, the U.S. Federal Aviation Authority grounded all planes until security could be tightened. It was only when expensive and time-consuming security measures were in place that planes resumed flying. The country prepared for war, the war against terrorism.

No one could know at the time just what would lie ahead. One thing was certain, however, and that was the addition of tighter security throughout the country. The added security measures meant that it became more expensive to do business. The security industry prospered, as demand and prices went up in that line of business. However, numerous other industries suffered as they faced higher costs of production and slower deliveries of their raw materials.

The added costs for security services cause an increase in the real costs of producing the final goods and services recorded in GDP. The economy's limited resources are thus not

FIGURE 8-15

SUPPLY-SIDE EFFECTS OF TERRORISM The war on terrorism causes firms to spend more on security, which takes resources that could otherwise produce final goods and services. For this reason, the output associated with full employment decreases and shifts long-run aggregate supply to the left. The macroequilibrium adjusts from *A* to *B*, reflecting a higher price level and less output. Either an increase in full employment during wartime or the adoption of improved technologies holds the potential to offset these effects.

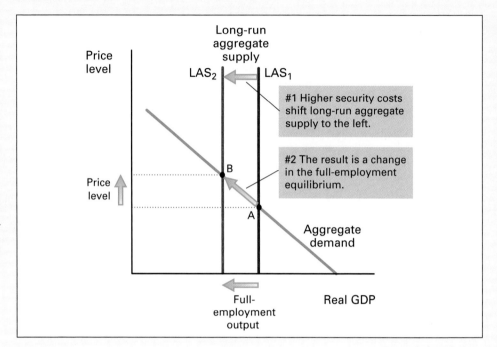

capable of producing as much final output, meaning that full-employment output falls. Note that full employment itself remains the same, but the output associated with it is less. The result is a shift to the left in the long-run aggregate supply curve, as shown in Figure 8-15, which leads to a new full-employment equilibrium at a higher price level and a lower level of output.

This shift can be moderated or even completely offset by advances in technology that increase productivity. For example, advances in monitoring and scanning cameras can reduce the need for security personnel, freeing them up to be productive in other ways. More generally, technology is applied to the workplace in order to increase productivity. To the extent it does so, the effect is to increase full-employment output and shift aggregate supply to the right, which is exactly opposite to the changes shown in Figure 8-15.

Other influences might also shift aggregate supply to the right. Looking back to World War II, we find that patriotism led to far more hours of work from the general population than was the norm either before or after the war. In effect, wartime full employment was higher than peacetime full employment. Taken by itself, the result was an increase in long-run aggregate supply.

HOW TERRORISM AFFECTS DEMAND

The 2001 terrorist attacks also had a significant effect on the demand side of the economy. The shock and uncertainty caused businesses to postpone new investments and consumers to postpone new purchases. For a while, it seemed everyone was hanging tight to their money and not allowing it to circulate as rapidly as it previously had. Airlines, hotels, amusement parks, and cruise ships all begged for customers. Some went bankrupt. Hundreds of thousands of Americans lost their jobs and millions more worried about their job security. The result was a leftward shift in aggregate demand. In other words, for any given price level, less output was demanded, as shown in Figure 8-16.

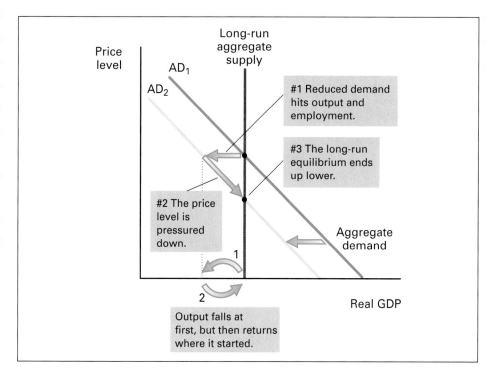

FIGURE 8-16

DEMAND-SIDE EFFECTS OF TERRORISM If the threat of terror makes people more cautious about spending, aggregate demand would shift to the left. The result would be:
#1 Firms throughout the economy would be unable to sell all of their output. Unemployment would rise and output would fall at first.
#2 To sell unsold output, firms would lower prices and the price level would fall.
#3 Output would return to the full-employment output once the price level adjusts to a new equilibrium.

The aggregate demand shift would be avoided if government's extra wartime spending exactly offsets the spending slowdown in the private sector, or as people return to their previous spending habits.

Taken by itself, this leftward shift in aggregate demand would have the effect of pushing prices lower, as shown. Before the price level would have a chance to adjust downward, output would fall and unemployment would rise. Were aggregate demand and aggregate supply both shifting left simultaneously, however, their influences would tend to offset each other in regard to price. Therefore, only output would fall.

There was considerable question following the September 2001 attacks as to how long it would take for consumers to resume their former patterns of spending. The answer was significant in terms of what the government should do. In particular, the government was not only spending additional money to combat the terrorists, but was also taking actions to lower borrowing costs and increase the amount of money circulating in the economy. The idea was to offset any drop in aggregate demand.

While intended to merely offset a drop in aggregate demand, such government actions ran the risk of going too far and actually increasing aggregate demand above what it had been before, particularly once the initial fears subsided and people returned to more normal spending patterns. If aggregate demand were to increase, demand-side inflation would be the result, as shown Figure 8-17(a). Figure 8-17(b) shows how the situation could easily get out of hand, with demand-side inflation adding to supply-side inflation, causing the economy to move from point *A* to point *B*, and on to point *C* in the figure. This situation is stagflation, in which output falls even as prices rise.

In response to the war against terrorism, there are also additional real and important macroeconomic consequences that lie hidden beneath the surface of the aggregate-demand/aggregate-supply model. For example, for the purposes of this model, it does not matter whether GDP is composed of military spending that we wish was unnecessary or spending on consumer goods and services that would be the alternative in peacetime. It matters to our standard of living, but we do not see these things in the aggregate economic analysis.

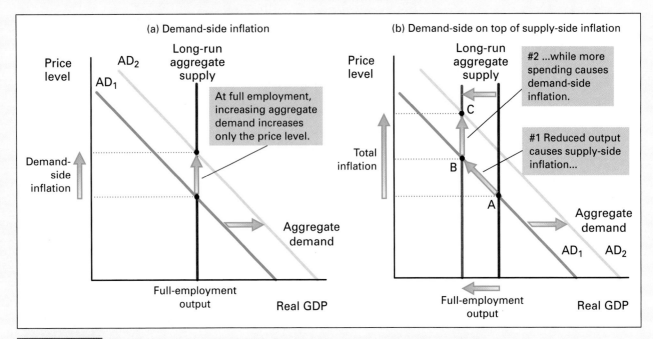

FIGURE 8-17

A DOUBLE DOSE OF INFLATION Graph (a) shows the demand-side inflation that could occur if government spending rises dramatically while the economy is already at full employment. The macro equilibrium would rise as shown. The higher government spending might reflect the costs of fighting a war, or merely the costs of tax and spending programs intended to offset an economic downturn.

The demand-side inflation might follow an initial supply-side inflation from higher costs of security and transportation. In graph (b), the leftward shift in long-run aggregate supply causes supply-side inflation. Because the economy is unable to produce as much output as previously, it moves up the aggregate demand curve from point *A* to point *B*. Then, if government steps in with additional purchases that increase aggregate demand, the economy experiences further inflation as it moves up the long-run aggregate supply curve from point *B* to point *C*. The combined effect is a double dose of inflation.

1. **Identify some additional effects of the war on terrorism that would shift aggregate supply or aggregate demand.**

2. **What could cause wartime full employment to exceed peacetime full employment? Give some examples from the United States' actual wartime experience.**

 Visit **www.prenhall.com/ayers** for updates and web exercises on this Explore & Apply topic.

SUMMARY AND LEARNING OBJECTIVES

1. **Contrast the perspectives of classical economists to those of Keynesians.**
   - Aggregate demand and aggregate supply are used to model the macroeconomy. The model places the price level on the vertical axis and real GDP on the horizontal axis.
   - John Maynard Keynes' *General Theory of Employment, Interest, and Money* (1936) revolutionized economics and launched the new field of macroeconomics.

Keynes distinguished between the long run and the short run, observing that "In the long run we are all dead."

   - The earlier classical economists took a long-run perspective on the economy, a perspective that has been summarized as Say's Law: Supply creates its own demand. According to classical economics, the long-run tendency in the economy is toward full employment. For this reason, government intervention should be limited.

- Keynesian economics dismisses the relevance of Say's Law. Keynes showed that when saving is greater than investment, the economy can find itself stuck in an unemployment equilibrium. In order to combat unemployment, Keynes recommended that government spending make up for the lack of spending by consumers and investors.

2. **Describe why aggregate demand slopes downward.**
   - There are four possible reasons for the downward slope to aggregate demand: the purchasing power effect, the wealth effect, the interest-rate effect, and the international substitution effect.
   - The aggregate demand curve is downward sloping because a lower price level may increase the purchasing power of money and prompt people to spend more, known as the purchasing power effect. The wealth effect states that a lower price level increases the real value of savings, encouraging people to spend more of their current incomes. The international substitution effect occurs when a lower price level causes people to purchase goods made in their country, in place of imported goods.

3. **Explain why the price level does not matter in the long run, but does in the short run.**
   - When the economy's resources are fully utilized, the economy attains its full-employment output, also called full-employment GDP. In the long run the economy tends toward the full-employment output because people desire to earn incomes.
   - Full-employment GDP could occur at any price level. For this reason, the long-run aggregate supply curve is vertical at full-employment output. Since the price level could be any value, the price level does not affect the quantity of real GDP in the long run.
   - The short-run aggregate supply curve is upward sloping rather than vertical. This means that in the short run, an increase in real GDP is associated with a higher price level, while a decrease in real GDP is associated with a lower price level.
   - In the short run the price level and the quantity of real GDP are related, but in the long run they are not.

4. **Interpret and explain the macro equilibrium.**
   - The macroeconomic equilibrium occurs at the intersection of the aggregate demand, long-run aggregate supply, and short-run aggregate supply curves.
   - The macro equilibrium is characterized by full employment because it occurs at a point on the long-run aggregate supply curve. It is sometimes called the full-employment equilibrium.

- When the price level is higher than the full-employment price level, the economy will experience unemployment, and actual GDP will be less than full-employment GDP. The economy's tendency to adjust to full employment requires that the price level fall.
- When the price level is lower than the full-employment price level, the economy will overheat. Aggregate demand will be greater than long-run aggregate supply and actual GDP will exceed the full-employment level. Overheating causes the price level to adjust upward. Along with a higher price level will come a decrease in actual GDP back to its full-employment level.
- Downwardly sticky wages and prices make it difficult for the economy to adjust to the full-employment equilibrium when the price level is too high.
- Over the long run, the economy of the Untied States tended to produce an actual value of GDP that was very close to its potential value.

5. **Relate the difference between demand-side and supply-side inflation in the long run.**
   - Increases in aggregate spending, such as those caused by additional consumer and government spending, shift aggregate demand outward and lead to demand-side inflation. Demand-side deflation would accompany a leftward shift in aggregate demand.
   - Inflation and deflation can also arise from shifts in the long-run aggregate supply curve. An outward shift in long-run aggregate supply leads to supply-side deflation. A leftward shift in long-run aggregate supply leads to supply-side inflation.
   - Changes on the supply side of the economy influence inflation and deflation. An increase in the natural rate of unemployment will occur when legislation and other forces make it more difficult for employers to hire workers and for workers to switch jobs. Supply-side inflation is the outcome.

6. **Interpret how the war against terrorism can cause both inflation and lower output, and ways in which these effects might be countered.**
   - The war on terrorism will cause the macroeconomic equilibrium to change. Aggregate supply will shift to the left because of the need to devote resources to increase the country's security, causing the price level to rise. Aggregate demand will also shift to the left to the extent that uncertainty inhibits consumer spending, causing the price level to fall. Government spending can offset the drop in consumer spending. If aggregate demand rebounds strongly, the economy could see a combination of supply-side and demand-side inflation pushing the price level upward.

KEY TERMS

long run, 196
short run, 196
Keynesian, 197
classical, 197
Say's Law, 197
aggregate demand, 200
purchasing power effect, 201
wealth effect, 201

international substitution effect, 201
aggregate supply, 203
full-employment output (full-
    employment GDP), 204
long-run aggregate supply, 204
short-run aggregate supply, 205
macroeconomic equilibrium, 205
full-employment equilibrium, 207

sticky wages, 208
sticky prices, 208
demand-side inflation, 212
demand-side deflation, 212
supply-side inflation, 212
supply shock, 212
real business cycle, 212
supply-side deflation, 214

TEST YOURSELF

TRUE OR FALSE

1. Both classical and Keynesian economists agree that the economy is most usefully characterized through a long-run perspective.
2. One explanation for the downward slope of aggregate demand is the savings effect, which states that people save more as they earn more.
3. The long-run aggregate supply curve illustrates that full-employment GDP is independent of the price level.
4. Supply-side inflation occurs when there is a decrease in aggregate supply.
5. The aggregate demand and aggregate supply model can explain inflation but not deflation.

MULTIPLE CHOICE

6. Say's Law is
   a. a foundation of Keynesian economics.
   b. saving equals investment.
   c. that prices and wages are sticky.
   d. "Supply creates its own demand."
7. "In the long run we are all dead" is a statement that best expresses
   a. Keynesian economics.
   b. classical economics.
   c. both Keynesian and classical economics.
   d. neither Keynesian nor classical economics.
8. The aggregate demand curve is
   a. upward sloping to the right.
   b. downward sloping to the right.
   c. vertical.
   d. horizontal.
9. An aggregate demand curve
   a. shows the quantity of a good or service that will be purchased at each of various possible prices.
   b. reveals how much real GDP consumers, businesses, and government will purchase at each price level.
   c. portrays how much real GDP the economy will produce at various price levels.

d. shows the relationship between interest rates and spending in the economy.
10. Full-employment GDP
   a. must be equal to actual GDP.
   b. must be less than actual GDP.
   c. must be greater than actual GDP.
   d. could be less than, equal to, or greater than actual GDP.
11. Because of the desire of people to have an income, the long-run tendency of the economy is to
   a. move up and down with the business cycle.
   b. produce the full-employment level of output.
   c. behave in unpredictable ways.
   d. exhibit stable prices.
12. If the economy is producing more than full-employment GDP, it's future path is most likely to be given by arrow _____ in Self-Test Figure 8-1.
   a. A
   b. B
   c. C
   d. D

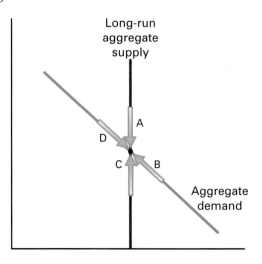

SELF-TEST FIGURE 8-1

13. In Self-Test Figure 8-2, point *A* represents
 a. total unemployment.
 b. an increase in unemployment.
 c. a decrease in aggregate demand.
 d. a smaller output associated with full employment.

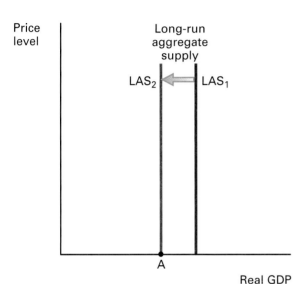

Price
level

Long-run
aggregate
supply

LAS₂ ← LAS₁

A

Real GDP

SELF-TEST FIGURE 8-2

14. Graphically, a long-run macro equilibrium occurs
 a. anywhere along an aggregate demand curve.
 b. anywhere along the long-run aggregate supply curve.
 c. at the intersection of an aggregate demand curve and the long-run aggregate supply curve.
 d. at any value of real GDP so long as the long-run aggregate supply curve and an aggregate demand curve do not intersect.

15. If the economy starts at point *A* in Self-Test Figure 8-3, it is likely to see
 a. the price level increase over time.
 b. the price level decrease over time.
 c. unemployment rise over time.
 d. full-employment output fall over time.

16. Which of the following is most likely to cause the shift in aggregate supply shown in Self-Test Figure 8-2?
 a. An increase in aggregate demand.
 b. A decrease in aggregate demand.
 c. A decrease in consumer spending.
 d. The destruction of resources in warfare.

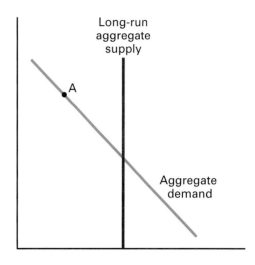

Price
level

Long-run
aggregate
supply

A

Aggregate
demand

Real GDP

SELF-TEST FIGURE 8-3

17. Demand-side inflation occurs when
 a. the long-run aggregate supply curve shifts to the left.
 b. inflation causes the aggregate demand curve to shift to the left.
 c. the aggregate demand curve shifts to the right.
 d. inflation rises above 3 percent per year.

18. Supply-side deflation is a phenomena associated with
 a. more government rules and regulations.
 b. decreased consumer spending.
 c. an aggregate demand curve that shifts to the right.
 d. improved technology.

19. The supply shock of a natural disaster is associated with a _____ shift in long-run aggregate supply and a _____ price level.
 a. leftward; lower
 b. leftward; higher
 c. rightward; lower
 d. rightward; higher

20. The war on terrorism could shift aggregate supply to the left and aggregate demand to the right as a consequence of increased government spending. The result would be
 a. demand-side inflation only.
 b. supply-side deflation only.
 c. a combination of demand-side inflation and supply-side inflation.
 d. a combination of demand-side deflation and supply-side deflation.

QUESTIONS AND PROBLEMS

1. *[classical versus Keynesian]* State the essential difference between the classical and Keynesian schools of thought. If you were a public policymaker and received conflicting advice from a classical and a Keynesian economist, how would you choose? Explain.

2. *[aggregate demand]* Define aggregate demand. Draw a graph of aggregate demand. What are four effects that explain the slope of the aggregate demand curve?

3. *[downward slope to aggregate demand]* List and explain the four causes of the downward slope to the aggregate demand curve.

4. *[full-employment GDP]* Must actual GDP always be equal to full-employment GDP? Explain.

5. *[full-employment GDP]* Explain how it is possible for actual GDP to temporarily exceed full-employment GDP.

6. *[long-run aggregate supply]* Explain why the long-run aggregate supply curve is drawn as a vertical line. At what point on the horizontal axis is the long-run aggregate supply curve located? Why would the long-run aggregate supply curve shift outward?

7. *[long-run aggregate supply]* Why does the price level not make a difference to full-employment output in the long run? Illustrate your answer by drawing a long-run aggregate supply curve and explaining the implications of the vertical nature of the curve.

8. *[short-run aggregate supply]* Does the short-run aggregate supply curve indicate that the price level matters in the short run? Explain.

9. *[macroeconomic equilibrium]* Illustrate graphically the idea of the macroeconomic equilibrium. Does the macroeconomic equilibrium require an equilibrium in both the short-run sense and the long-run sense? Explain.

10. *[long-run macro equilibrium]* Illustrate graphically and explain the long-run macro equilibrium.

11. *[aggregate demand/aggregate supply model]* Draw a graph that shows the long-run aggregate supply curve and an aggregate demand curve. Be sure to label the axes and the point on the horizontal axis that represents full-employment GDP. Illustrate on your graph an economy with unemployment. What is the cause of unemployment? Describe how the economy will adjust toward full employment.

12. *[aggregate demand/aggregate supply model]* Redraw the aggregate demand/aggregate supply graph you created in the preceding question. Illustrate on your graph an economy that is overheating. What is the cause of overheating? How will the economy adjust toward full employment?

13. *[inflation]* On separate graphs, show demand-side and supply-side inflation, labeling the axes, curves, and changes in output and the price level. Explain how the two might occur together.

14. *[deflation]* On separate graphs, show demand-side and supply-side deflation, labeling the axes, curves, and changes in output and the price level. Explain how the two might occur together.

15. *[Classical versus Keynesian]* Which group, political liberals or conservatives, is more likely to take Keynesian positions on the economy? Explain.

WORKING WITH GRAPHS AND DATA

1. *[long-run macro equilibrium]* Use Graph 8-1 to answer the questions that follow.
   a. Label the long-run macroeconomic equilibrium as point *C*.
   b. At point *A* on the aggregate demand curve, what is the value of real GDP? Label it GDP$_A$. What macroeconomic problem is associated with the value of real GDP you identified?
   c. At point *B* on the aggregate demand curve, what is the value of real GDP? Label it GDP$_B$. What macroeconomic problem is associated with the value of real GDP you identified?
   d. Explain how the economy adjusts to the long-run macro equilibrium. What can be said about employment at the long-run equilibrium level of GDP?

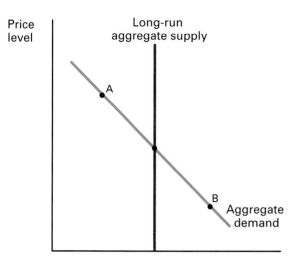

GRAPH 8-1

2. *[the macro equilibrium]* Full employment output in the country of Mordania is $600 Mordanian dollars. Its price level, aggregate demand, and short-run aggregate supply are shown in Table 1.

Price Level	Aggregate Demand	Short-run Aggregate Supply
90	750	450
95	700	500
100	650	550
105	600	600
110	550	650
115	500	700
120	450	750

a. Plot aggregate demand, short-run aggregate supply, and long run aggregate supply on a graph. Be sure to label the axes of your graph.

b. What is the value of the price level at the macro equilibrium? Label it on graph.
c. What is the value of real GDP at the macro equilibrium? Label it on your graph.

3. *[actual and potential GDP]* Graph 8-2 depicts the record of the actual and potential GDP of the United States. Answer the questions that follow.

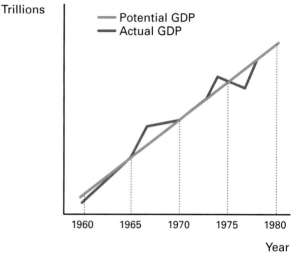

GRAPH 8-2

For each of the following years or periods listed following:
i) Describe the relationship between the actual and potential GDP.
ii) What does the situation imply with respect to aggregate demand and long-run aggregate supply?
iii) What is the macroeconomic problem associated with this situation?

    a. 1965   c. 1970–1973
    b. 1965–1970   d. 1975–1977

4. *[changes in the macro equilibrium]* Display the following situations by shifting the appropriate curve(s) in
Graph 8-3. Also, describe the outcome with respect to
full-employment GDP and macroeconomics problems
that may arise.

a. Increased government spending
b. Technological advances are utilized throughout the
economy
c. Decreased household income
d. Increased government restrictions on business
practices
e. Domestic terrorism

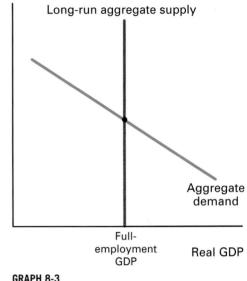

GRAPH 8-3

 Visit www.prenhall.com/ayers for Exploring the Web exercises and additional self-test quizzes.

CHAPTER 9

FISCAL POLICY AND SHORT-RUN INSTABILITY

A LOOK AHEAD

Debt is a four-letter word, one that has gotten many people in trouble. Debt can crimp a person's lifestyle and even lead to personal bankruptcy. Many countries have felt the financial straitjacket of debt. In the United States, for example, the federal government has amassed debt of over $6 trillion and a deficit in the federal budget that increases that debt as the years go by. Irresponsible? Perhaps, perhaps not. As we will see in the Explore & Apply section that concludes this chapter, there is cause for both personal and national debt. There are also questions about the effect on the economy of policies that add more.

Deficit spending might be intended to offset economic downturns and reduce economic instability. As the economy transitions from one long-run equilibrium to another, it is buffeted by the short-run ups and downs of the business cycle. This chapter examines the issues of short-run instability by adding to the model of aggregate supply and aggregate demand introduced in Chapter 8. We will find possible ways for government tax and spending policies to help the economy out of recession. We will also uncover potential problems with these policy actions, including getting them to take effect at the proper time and creating inflation that can undermine the policy's intent.

LEARNING OBJECTIVES

Understanding Chapter 9 will enable you to:
1. **Distinguish between expansionary and contractionary fiscal policy, and identify their relevance to the macro equilibrium.**
2. **Explain how balancing the full-employment budget is consistent with a budget deficit.**
3. **Discuss how fiscal policy to stabilize the economy is subject to lags, and how the lags can be overcome automatically.**
4. **Identify the characteristics and significance of short-run aggregate supply.**
5. **Describe demand-pull and cost-push inflation, and how they can be part of an inflationary spiral.**
6. **Analyze the rationale and limitations of deficit spending.**

Explore & Apply

225

The short-run instabilities of the business cycle often seem more compelling than the long-run tendencies discussed in the previous chapter. Whenever there is an economic downturn, the press and public call upon government to do something about it. People want action!

For example, the economic downturn that started in March of 2001, together with four years of surplus in the federal budget, led President Bush and Congress to authorize refunds of some tax payments in August of that year. Taxpayers received checks for up to $300 per person or $600 per couple. The idea was to energize the economy. To bring the economy out of what then appeared to be a deepening recession, President Bush requested, and Congress enacted, $100 billion worth of tax cuts and new spending. It's hard to know if these or other government policies had the desired effect. The economy did recover, but it took a long time and was influenced along the way by terrorism, warfare, power failures, and other events.

In the short run, the economy is constantly buffeted one way or another by changes in consumer attitudes toward spending, and business attitudes toward investing, with the causes of these changes frequently difficult to pin down. Sometimes consumers are loose with their pocketbooks, buying with seemingly reckless abandon. Other times, perhaps worried by political or international events, consumers can seem downright stingy. Even greater instability holds true for business spending, because businesses always have to concern themselves with the future, and that future sometimes looks rosy and sometimes bleak.

This chapter models short-run instability within the context of aggregate demand and aggregate supply, extending the analysis of the previous chapter. Instabilities are looked at from a fiscal policy perspective, where fiscal policy is the government's combination of taxation and spending policies. Those policies are often adjusted in an attempt to minimize macro instability and keep the economy on an even keel. Analysis of specific policies, such as the 2003 tax cuts and Social Security, are deferred to Chapter 11.

9.1 FISCAL POLICY TO STABILIZE THE BUSINESS CYCLE

unemployment equilibrium a short-run equilibrium GDP that is less than full-employment GDP.

fiscal policy government tax and spending policy designed to shift aggregate demand rightward.

Suppose the economy starts at an **unemployment equilibrium,** characterized by a price level that is too high to achieve full-employment GDP, but that refuses to fall because of sticky prices. If the price level cannot fall to correct the unemployment equilibrium, the only solution is to shift aggregate demand rightward by increasing spending power. The shift can be accomplished by **fiscal policy,** which is government policy toward taxation and spending. It can also be accomplished through *monetary policy,* which has to do with varying the quantity of money that is available to spend. We will examine specific fiscal policy tools in Chapter 11 and the tools and goals of monetary policy in Chapter 14. Here we focus on the general strategies of fiscal policy government can use to manage aggregate demand in order to reduce economic fluctuations.

FISCAL STIMULI AND FISCAL DRAGS

expansionary fiscal policy (fiscal stimulus) increased government spending or reduced taxation intended to stimulate aggregate demand.

When the economy finds itself stuck at an unemployment equilibrium, Keynesians advocate using **expansionary fiscal policy,** also called a **fiscal stimulus,** which is increased government spending or reduced taxation intended to *stimulate* aggregate demand and move the economy toward full employment. The Works Progress Administration and other New Deal public works programs of President Franklin Roosevelt are examples of stimulative fiscal policies. Indeed, World War II seemed to prove the validity of Keynesian economics, since the massive amount of government spending it involved paved the way from the Great Depression of the 1930s to the prosperity of the 1950s. With more government spending, aggregate demand shifts to the right, as shown in Figure 9-1(a). The Keynesian idea is to

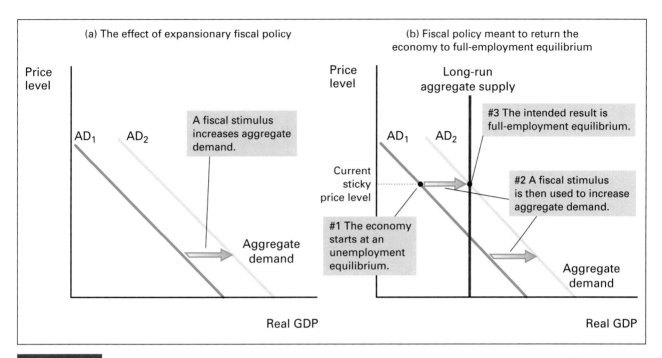

(a) The effect of expansionary fiscal policy

(b) Fiscal policy meant to return the economy to full-employment equilibrium

Price level

AD₁   AD₂

A fiscal stimulus increases aggregate demand.

Aggregate demand

Real GDP

Price level

Long-run aggregate supply

AD₁   AD₂

Current sticky price level

#3 The intended result is full-employment equilibrium.

#2 A fiscal stimulus is then used to increase aggregate demand.

#1 The economy starts at an unemployment equilibrium.

Aggregate demand

Real GDP

FIGURE 9-1

EXPANSIONARY FISCAL POLICY Expansionary fiscal policies shift aggregate demand to the right by adding to government and/or consumer spending, as shown in (a). When the economy starts at an unemployment equilibrium, Keynesians would suggest using expansionary fiscal policy to shift aggregate demand to the right. As shown in (b), the idea is to shift aggregate demand just far enough to reach long-run aggregate supply at full-employment output and achieve a full-employment equilibrium.

shift it just enough to reach full-employment output, as shown in Figure 9-1(b), thus solving unemployment problems without causing inflation.

Alternatively, when the economy *overheats*—or grows so fast that inflation threatens— government can use a **contractionary fiscal policy,** also called a **fiscal drag,** to slow it down. Contractionary fiscal policy might involve higher taxes or less government spending. Figure 9-2(a) and (b) illustrate how contractionary fiscal policy can shift aggregate demand to the left to avoid overheating.

contractionary fiscal policy (fiscal drag) reduced government spending or increased taxation intended to decrease aggregate demand.

THE MULTIPLIER EFFECT

The amount of government spending or tax changes only needs to be a relatively small percentage of the desired shift in aggregate demand. The reason is that fiscal policy actions are enhanced by the **multiplier effect,** in which subsequent rounds of private sector behavior reinforce the initial change in spending. For example, if the government increases its spending, people in the private sector will have increased incomes from that spending and in turn spend more themselves. This process generates an ongoing cycle of greater income and greater intended spending. At each stage in the cycle, however, some income is likely to be saved, thereby slowing down the cycle and eventually bringing it to a halt.

multiplier effect occurs when an initial change in spending leads to additional rounds of spending changes; causes aggregate demand to shift further in the same direction as its initial shift.

The multiplier effect is depicted in Figure 9-3. Part (a) shows the multiplier effect for an expansionary fiscal policy, such as an increase in government spending or a decrease in taxation. In this case, as seen in the figure, the multiplier effect from the initial increase in aggregate demand is for aggregate demand to increase again and again, but by a smaller amount each additional time. Part (b) shows just the opposite, which would occur in

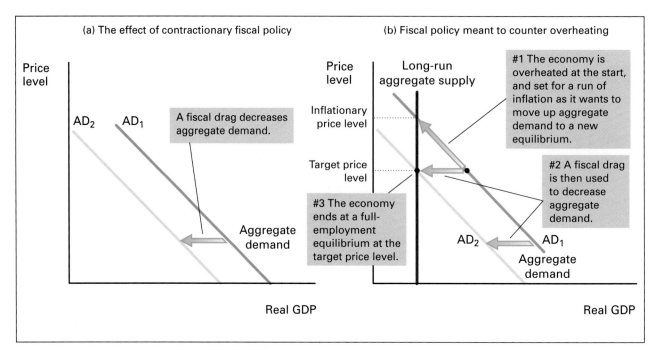

FIGURE 9-2

CONTRACTIONARY FISCAL POLICY Contractionary fiscal policies shift aggregate demand to the left by reducing government or private sector spending, as shown in (a). When the economy starts overheating, such that it is likely to cause inflation as it moves up aggregate demand to a long-run equilibrium, contractionary fiscal policy can be used to shift aggregate demand instead. As shown in (b), the idea is to shift aggregate demand just far enough to the left to reach long-run aggregate supply at the current price level so as to achieve a full-employment equilibrium.

response to a contractionary fiscal policy, such as a decrease in government spending or an increase in taxation. In that case, the initial decrease in aggregate demand is accentuated by further rounds of decreases, albeit smaller decreases each time. Observe that the multiplier effect shifts the aggregate demand curve in its entirety, which could lead to changes in the price level that could partially or fully offset any output changes caused by the multiplier.

If the economy is starting at an unemployment equilibrium, as shown in Figure 9-4(a), the tendency for prices is to be adjusted downward, traveling from long-run equilibrium A to long-run equilibrium D. However, since wage and price stickiness can cause the downward adjustment in the price level to be a slow and painful process, policymakers choose to instead take action to increase aggregate demand. To achieve full-employment output under these circumstances, the policymakers would wish to shift aggregate demand to the right just enough for it to intersect long-run aggregate supply at the current price level, meaning at long-run equilibrium C. The difference between the starting unemployment equilibrium given by point A and the desired full-employment equilibrium at the same price level, given by point C, is called the output gap. In short, the **output gap** equals the full-employment GDP minus the actual GDP.

Expansionary fiscal policy that is designed to close the output gap would need to factor in the multiplier effect. The amount of new spending needed to close the output gap without change to the price level is called the **recessionary gap,** where the recessionary gap is smaller than the output gap by the amount of the multiplier effect. Figure 9-4(b) shows how the output gap can be divided into the recessionary gap (point A to point B) and the multiplier effect from spending to close that gap (point B to point C). Put another way, to the

output gap full-employment GDP minus the actual GDP.

recessionary gap when combined with the multiplier effect, the amount of new spending needed to close the output gap without change to the price level.

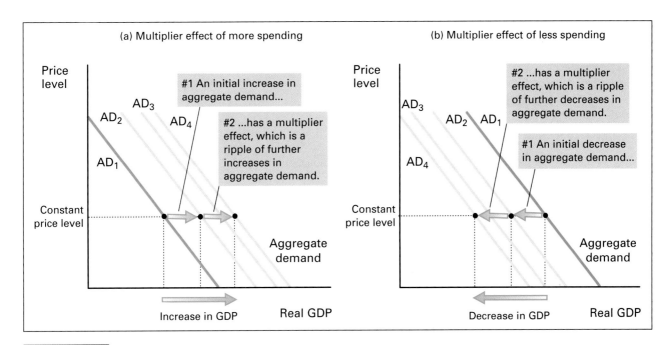

(a) Multiplier effect of more spending

(b) Multiplier effect of less spending

FIGURE 9-3

THE MULTIPLIER EFFECT The impact of expansionary fiscal policy can be much larger than the amount of increased government spending or decreased taxation. The shift in aggregate demand occurs in multiple rounds, with the direct effect of the policy being only the first round. Indirect effects occur as the spending increases some people's incomes, which leads them to spend more, which increases other people's incomes, causing those people to spend more, and so forth. The result is that the after-effects of the policy change continue to shift aggregate demand to the right, as shown in part (a), with the shifts becoming progressively smaller because people don't spend every penny of the income they receive. The same sort of multiplier effect would occur in reverse if the government were to choose a contractionary fiscal policy. Part (b) depicts this result.

extent that fiscal policy causes some initial change in spending, the resulting change in GDP would equal that change in spending plus the multiplier effect, as follows:

Change in GDP = Initial change in spending + Multiplier effect

The recessionary gap is the initial change in spending that, along with the multiplier effect, would just close the output gap.

Figure 9-4(b) illustrates a situation in which the economy is overheating, meaning that it is producing more output than it can sustain on a long-term basis. The market response to overheating is to push the price level up until the economy's output drops to full-employment output, which would be to move from point A to point D in Figure 9-4(b). However, policymakers might prefer to avoid this inflation, and choose instead contractionary fiscal policy that would shift aggregate demand to the left until the full-employment equilibrium is reached without inflation. That goal is seen in Figure 9-4(b) as the movement from point A to point C.

To accomplish this goal, policymakers would need to factor in the multiplier effect of their actions, where this time the multiplier effect would accentuate the leftward shift of the aggregate demand curve. The amount by which spending must be cut in order to achieve full employment without inflation is termed the **inflationary gap,** which is shown as the arrow from point A to point B in Figure 9-4(b). Because of the multiplier effect (point B to point C), the inflationary gap will be smaller than the required reduction in GDP (point A to point C).

inflationary gap when combined with the multiplier effect, the amount by which spending would need to be cut to reduce GDP to full-employment GDP at a constant price level.

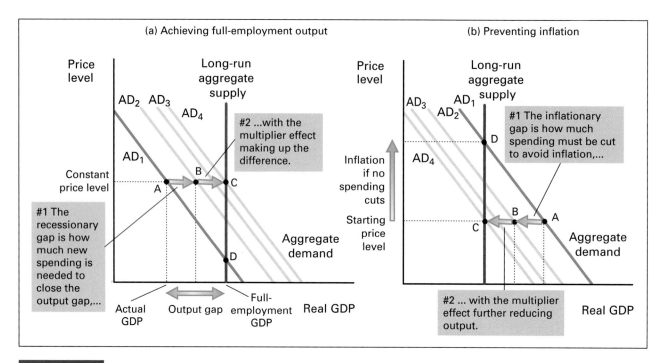

FIGURE 9-4

IDENTIFYING FISCAL POLICY NEEDS If the economy starts at an unemployment equilibrium, such as shown by point A in part (a), downwardly sticky prices might prevent the rapid movement to the full-employment equilibrium given by point D. To avoid the need for the price level to fall, policy-makers might wish to shift the aggregate demand curve to the right until the economy reaches full-employment GDP at point C. The difference between the starting GDP and full-employment GDP is termed the output gap, as labeled in the graph.

Only part of the output gap needs to be closed directly by fiscal policy. The fiscal stimulus aims to close only the recessionary gap, which is the difference between point A and point B in part (a). The rest of the shifting, from point B to point C, would come from the multiplier effect.

In part (b) of the figure, point A represents an economy that is overheating and prone to inflation, which would lead it to the long-run equilibrium labeled D. To avoid that inflation, policymakers could use contractionary fiscal policy to reduce aggregate demand. The aim would be to reach a new long-run equilibrium at the starting price level, shown as a movement from point A to point C. The fiscal drag need not be this entire distance, though, because the multiplier effect will enhance it. Specifically, aggregate demand would need to be reduced by the amount of the inflationary gap, which is the distance from A to B. The multiplier effect would take care of the rest, moving the economy from B to C.

crowding-out effect when borrowing to finance government spending displaces private-sector spending.

There is a considerable amount of controversy within the economics profession as to how effective fiscal policy can be. The point of contention is whether and to what extent there is a crowding-out effect. The **crowding-out effect** occurs if an increase in government spending relative to tax revenue—*government net spending*—displaces an equal amount of private-sector spending. For example, if the government spends $10 in order to stimulate the economy, that $10 must have come from somewhere. There are three options for increasing government net spending. Government could:

- *Print the money.* Adding to the money supply would be inflationary and akin to a tax, as discussed further in later chapters.
- *Raise taxes.* Raising taxes as a contractionary fiscal policy that would counter the expansionary fiscal policy of increasing spending.

■ *Borrow the money.* The crowding-out effect suggests that there must be an offsetting decrease in private-sector consumption or investment to free up the money to loan to the government. The reduction in private-sector spending would have a contractionary effect on the economy, which would tend to offset the expansionary impact of the additional government spending.

By the same token, a contractionary fiscal policy that would reduce government net spending would tend to be offset by the same three effects, albeit operating in the opposite direction. Studies that have tried to prove or disprove the multiplier effect have been inconclusive, perhaps because so many things go on at once in the macroeconomy.

THE MULTIPLIER EFFECT OF FISCAL POLICY— THIS WAY, THAT WAY, OR NO WAY?

SNAPSHOT

The multiplier effect is a popular concept. When a public spending program is proposed, usually someone will point out how that spending will lead to further rounds of spending by those who receive the government money. When a tax cut is proposed, usually someone will point out that consumers will be left with more money to spend, and that increased consumer spending will increase jobs and lead to further spending by those who get the jobs. But can the economy have it both ways, winning with more government spending and at the same time winning with lower taxes?

The catch is that the money for public spending must come from somewhere. If it doesn't come from taxes, then it comes from government borrowing. When the government borrows, it sucks in money that would otherwise have paid for consumer or business spending. Taking that money out of the private sector has an offsetting multiplier effect of its own, reducing jobs, incomes, and spending. That's the crowding-out effect. When government uses fiscal policy to spur the economy, the crowding-out effect has the potential to negate that policy. If so, government might find that its fiscal stimuli do nothing more than redistribute income, changing which outputs the economy produces and which people get to produce them. From the standpoint of the macroeconomy, there could be no effect at all. ◄

BALANCING THE BUDGET

A **balanced budget** occurs when government revenue equals government spending. In other words, tax revenue inflows just equal government expenditure outflows. Economists often suggest that fiscal policy should be set so that the budget roughly balances over the course of the business cycle. The idea is that, when the economy is overheated and contractionary policy is in order, the government would run a **budget surplus** in which tax revenue exceeds government spending. When economic health is poor and expansionary policy is needed, the government would then choose a **budget deficit** in which government spending exceeds tax revenue. The surpluses could help pay for the deficits.

In practice, however, there is a significant tilt toward the expansionary side, even when the economy is doing well. To assess this tilt, we can look at the **full-employment budget,** which is an estimate of what government revenue and spending would be were there full employment. When the full-employment budget is in deficit, as it was from 1992 to 2001, the economy is said to have a **structural deficit.** For this reason, despite being in the vicinity of full employment for much of the past two decades, the U.S. government has run substantial budget deficits in the large majority of those years, as seen in Figure 9-5. The result of the accumulation of past budget deficits and surpluses is, on balance, a U.S. **national debt** approaching $7 trillion in 2004. The debt represents how much money the government owes.

balanced budget occurs when government revenue equals government spending.

budget surplus occurs when government collects more revenue than it spends.

budget deficit occurs when government collects less revenue than it spends.

full-employment budget estimate of government revenue and spending were the economy to be at full employment.

structural deficit occurs when the economy has a budget deficit, even when at full employment.

national debt how much money the government owes.

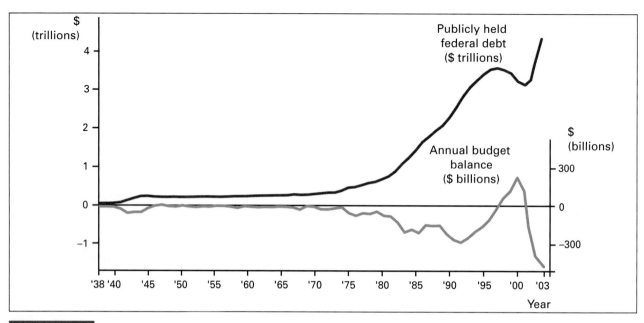

FIGURE 9-5

THE U.S. BUDGET Budget deficits have been the norm in modern U.S. history. These deficits have added to the national debt over time. This figure shows the portion of the debt held by the public. Including debt from one government agency to another, the national debt totaled over $6 trillion in 2002.

Source: 2003 Economic Report of the President, Table B-78, and Congressional Budget Office.

SNAPSHOT   SQUANDERING THE SURPLUS?

For four glorious years—from 1998 through 2001—the United States government experienced the luxury of a budget surplus. The national debt got a chance to decline for the first time in three decades. It was more than nice. The declining national debt instilled hope that the country could actually afford its commitments, such as to Social Security for the looming wave of retiring baby boomers. Then reality struck.

First came the stock market slide and later a mild recession, which caused the government to pay out more in unemployment insurance and other assistance. The September 11 terrorist attacks added the need for massive amounts of government spending on national security. All of this combined to create a mentality in Washington, D.C., of spend and spend some more. By the middle of 2002, the economy was expanding, but so too was government spending. With massive new commitments to agriculture, the military, homeland security, and with a 2003 budget deficit approximating $400 billion, a return to the days of budget surpluses was no longer in sight. ◄

FISCAL POLICY CHOICE: DISCRETIONARY OR AUTOMATIC?

discretionary policy public policy adjusted through explicit changes made by lawmakers.

Both expansionary and contractionary fiscal policy are examples of **discretionary policy**—public policy adjusted at the discretion of lawmakers. Unfortunately, even the best intentioned discretionary public policy is unlikely to follow the Keynesian policy prescription of managing aggregate demand in order to counter short-run instability. The reason has to do with the three *fiscal policy lags*:

recognition lag time before policymakers recognize that a problem exists.

■ The **recognition lag**—It takes time to know that the economy is in a recession. For example, although not an official standard, it usually takes approximately two consecutive quarters of declining GDP before the authoritative National Bureau of Economic Research

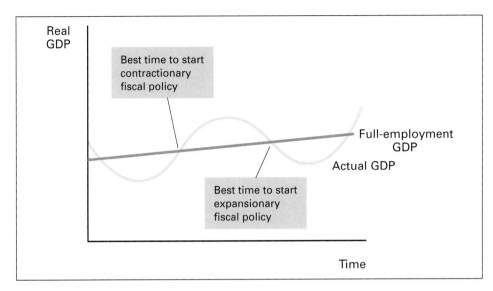

FIGURE 9-6

FISCAL POLICY TIMING The best time for contractionary fiscal policy is when the economy starts to overheat, meaning that it is exceeding full-employment GDP. The best time for expansionary fiscal policy is when the economy has fallen into a recession below the full-employment GDP. Lags make it hard to fine-tune discretionary fiscal policy such that it follows these prescriptions. Automatic stabilizers, in contrast, tend to push down the economy's peaks and push up its troughs without any change in the policies themselves.

(NBER) declares a recession. In late November of 2001, the NBER declared that the economy was in a recession that started in March of that year. It took until mid-2003 for the NBER to declare that the recession had ended in November 2001!

■ The **action lag**—Time between when the problem is recognized and when policies are enacted. Tax and spending bills are not passed overnight. For example, the fiscal stimulus aimed at the 2001 recession was not passed until 2002.

■ The **implementation lag**—Time between when policies are enacted and when they take effect. It's great to build a highway, but most people expect to have it planned out before crews are sent to lay asphalt! Once spending is authorized, the details must be planned and the money spent, which takes time. It also takes time before tax changes can take effect.

action lag time between when the problem is recognized and when policies are enacted.

implementation lag time between when policies are enacted and when they take effect.

Because of fiscal policy lags, the business cycle may have turned by the time the money starts flowing from an expansionary fiscal policy. The spending may be more likely to cause inflation than to reduce unemployment. Policy lags make it very difficult, if not impossible, to *fine-tune* the economy to even out the ups and downs of the business cycle. Fine-tuning would require that contractionary fiscal policy start when the economy pushes above full-employment GDP. Likewise, when the economy sinks to less than full-employment GDP, then finely tuned fiscal policy should be expansionary. Figure 9-6 shows both possibilities.

Instead of discretionary policy, lawmakers can rely on **automatic stabilizers.** Automatic stabilizers are components of existing fiscal policies that stimulate the economy when it is sluggish and act as a drag when it overheats. The U.S. economy has automatic stabilizers embedded within its system of taxation and spending.

automatic stabilizers features embedded within existing fiscal policies that act as a stimulant when the economy is sluggish and act as a drag when it is in danger of inflation.

Consider automatic stabilizers on the tax side. As personal and corporate incomes fall during recession, so too does the amount collected by the federal government in personal and corporate income taxes. The reduced tax burden on individuals and companies helps reduce the severity of that recession. Alternatively, if the economy is booming, income taxes bring in revenue, which is contractionary because it removes some of the excess purchasing power. No policy action is necessary.

On the spending side, payments for welfare, unemployment compensation, and other social programs rise as the economy slows and more people seek these safety-net services. Conversely, this spending falls when the economy heats up, just as Keynesian policy prescribes. Again, the action to stabilize the economy is automatic; no policy adjustments are needed. Taken as a whole, the automatic stabilizers are intended to be expansionary if the economy is below full employment and contractionary when the economy is overheating.

> ## QUICKCHECK
>
> **(a)** Once federal spending is approved, why is there an implementation lag? Use a new highway as an example. **(b)** Must all fiscal policies have a long implementation lag? Explain.
>
> **Answer:** (a) Projects must first be planned. A new highway requires a considerable amount of surveying before the specifics of its route and features are established. Land must then be acquired. There continues to be a sequence of employing different types of labor and other inputs for different phases of the construction. The final product may not be completed for several years. (b) Projects that require little planning will have a shorter implementation lag.

If the economy is at full employment, fiscal policy should be neutral, since there is no need to either stimulate or slow down economic activity.

9.2 THE SHORT-RUN ADJUSTMENT PROCESS

In principle, as seen earlier in Figure 9-1, expansionary fiscal policy can shift aggregate demand rightward until it achieves full-employment output at the current price level. In practice, however, the economy does not behave quite this simply. The most notable complexity is a tendency toward inflation when policymakers try to stimulate aggregate demand. In order to understand this response, we will distinguish between aggregate supply in the short run and aggregate supply in the long run.

SHORT-RUN AGGREGATE SUPPLY

short-run aggregate supply tells how much output the economy will offer in the short run at each possible price level.

Recall that aggregate supply tells how much output the economy has to offer at each possible price level, based on the potential productivity of its resources. In the long run, the price level does not matter to this potential. In the long run, higher wages that are only the result of inflation will have no influence on behavior because workers recognize that the higher wages are merely necessary to pay for higher costs of living. Therefore, in the long run, aggregate supply is unaffected by the price level, causing it to be vertical.

However, **short-run aggregate supply**—the amount of output the economy has to offer in the short run—will depend on the flexibility of wages and prices. If we make the extreme Keynesian assumption that wages and prices cannot fall, then any reduction in aggregate demand below the full-employment equilibrium would reduce GDP, but not the price level. The resulting short-run aggregate supply curve in that case is horizontal up to full-employment GDP, and then becomes vertical as shown in Figure 9-7(a).

Figure 9-7(b) shows a more realistic upward-sloping short-run aggregate supply as it relates to long-run aggregate supply, which is always vertical at full-employment GDP. In the short run, the amount of output produced can even exceed full-employment GDP, as workers offer to work overtime or seek out extra jobs. Conversely, if workers expect more inflation than actually occurs, the output they would produce at the actual price level would be less than full-employment GDP.

Two reasons for the upward slope of aggregate supply are as follows:

structural rigidities impediments within the economy that slow adjustment to a long-run equilibrium.

■ **Structural rigidities**—Impediments within the economy that slow adjustment to a long-run equilibrium. As new spending power is added to the economy, it tends to raise wages and prices where it first hits, before eventually diffusing throughout the economy. Wages and prices in the sectors of the economy most directly affected by the spending will rise before

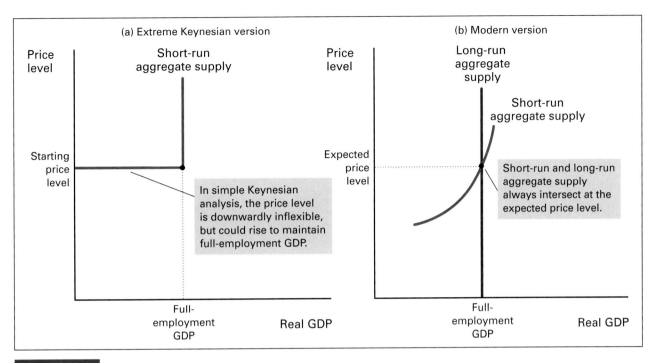

FIGURE 9-7

SHORT-RUN AGGREGATE SUPPLY In extreme Keynesian analysis, the price level cannot fall, which explains the horizontal section of the aggregate supply curve shown in Part (a). If the economy tries to exceed full-employment output, though, the price level would immediately rise, which explains the vertical section of that curve.

Part (b) shows a more realistic short-run aggregate supply curve in which short-run aggregate supply slopes upward, intersecting long-run aggregate supply at the expected price level. Structural rigidities and the production effect explain the upward slope of short-run aggregate supply. According to the production effect, a drop in the price level can lead workers to cut back on hours of work, causing GDP to fall. An increase in the price level would have the opposite effect, possibly leading to output that exceeds full-employment GDP.

the extra spending can circulate more generally throughout the economy. The result is a higher output in those sectors, but also a higher overall price level.

- **The production effect**—When the price level rises and labor supply curves remain unchanged, firms can profit by increasing output and employment. As firms in the aggregate attempt to raise output they run into production bottlenecks that constrain their ability to do so. For this reason, the slope of the short-run aggregate supply curve tends to become steeper as real GDP increases. If the economy is already at full employment, firms will employ workers overtime, thus allowing the economy to exceed full-employment output temporarily.

the production effect when a higher price level causes firms to increase output, employing workers who are willing to work extra hours to the extent that they do not correctly anticipate inflation.

The production effect relies upon workers being fooled by inflation or deflation. After all, if the price level changes, workers should adjust their own labor supply curves accordingly. In the event of inflation, for example, individual wage requirements should rise, thus shifting each worker's labor supply curve upward. However, while it is easy for workers to know past rates of inflation, it is much more difficult to recognize price-level changes in the present. People seeing wages going up are likely to first respond by offering to work more and then adjust their **inflationary expectations** later. Since an increased price level is associated with higher wages, a higher price level brings forth more work effort as workers are fooled by inflation, but only in the short run. For the

inflationary expectations predictions about future inflation that people factor into their current behavior.

FIGURE 9-8

THE SHORT-RUN MACROECONOMIC EQUILIBRIUM
The short-run macroeconomic equilibrium is given by the intersection of aggregate demand and short-run aggregate supply. The price level and GDP at this equilibrium are those the economy is actually at, rather than those toward which it tends in the long run.

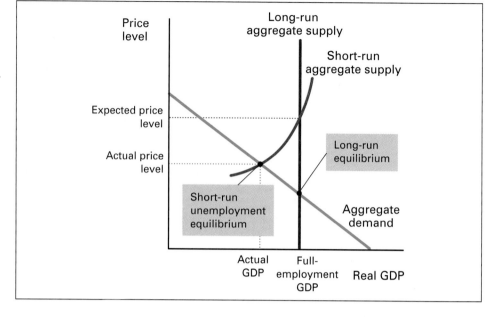

short-run macroeconomic equilibrium where the economy tends in the short run, given by the intersection of aggregate demand and short-run aggregate supply.

economy to be in long-run equilibrium, workers must have accurate wage and price expectations. For this reason, **short-run aggregate supply always intersects long-run aggregate supply at the expected price level.**

The intersection of aggregate demand and short-run aggregate supply constitutes a **short-run macroeconomic equilibrium,** as shown in Figure 9-8. In this case, the macro equilibrium is also an unemployment equilibrium, because it occurs at less than full-employment GDP. The short-run macro equilibrium consists of an equilibrium price level and an equilibrium GDP. These are labeled in the figure as actual price level and actual GDP, since the short run is where the economy actually is at any given point in time. As before, short-run aggregate supply intersects long-run aggregate supply at the expected price level.

The long-run aggregate supply is a reference toward which the economy tends over time. Therefore, whereas the long-run equilibrium occurs where aggregate demand intersects long-run aggregate supply, the short-run equilibrium is where aggregate demand intersects short-run aggregate supply.

SNAPSHOT   "TOMORROW IS ANOTHER DAY!"

"I will never go hungry again!" avowed Scarlett O'Hara in the movie *Gone With the Wind.* She was determined to make a better future. In the meantime, though, she was forced to work with what she had. For Scarlett, it was the red earth of her one-time plantation *Tara.* For the economy, it is the output and price level that actually do occur. Collectively, we must first take stock of where we are before we can make progress toward where we want to be. In other words, it takes a short run to make it through to the long run! ◀

DEMAND–PULL INFLATION

Chapter 8 discussed demand-side and supply-side inflation in the context of changes in either aggregate demand or long-run aggregate supply. That discussion involved the long run. Here we discuss the short-run counterparts. Consider first **demand-pull inflation,** which is caused by an increase in aggregate demand that pulls the economy up the short-run

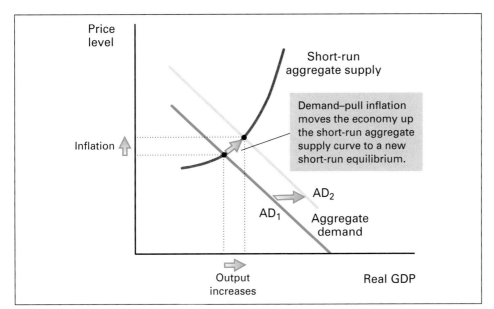

FIGURE 9-9

DEMAND–PULL INFLATION
Stimulative fiscal policy shifts
aggregate demand, moving the
economy up the short-run aggregate supply curve. The result is
an increase in output along with
demand–pull inflation.

FIGURE 9-10

**INFLATION FROM FISCAL
STIMULUS** Expansionary fiscal
policy shifts aggregate demand.
While the intention might be to
move the economy to full-
employment output at a constant price level, the reality is a
movement up the short-run
aggregate supply curve. Some of
the added spending that is
intended to increase output is
instead eaten up by inflation.

aggregate supply curve, such as shown in Figure 9-9. **Demand–pull inflation occurs when
a rightward shift in aggregate demand moves the economy to both a higher output and
a higher price level.**

Demand–pull inflation might be caused by expansionary fiscal policy that is meant
to move the economy toward full employment. For example, suppose the economy starts
at the unemployment equilibrium given by the intersection of aggregate demand and
short-run aggregate supply, labeled point 1 in Figure 9-10. To reach full employment, the
government might select the fiscal policy stimulus of spending an extra $20 billion on
new ballistic-technology military equipment. The idea would be to shift aggregate

demand–pull inflation occurs
when a rightward shift in
aggregate demand moves the
economy up short-run
aggregate supply; associated
with greater employment and
output.

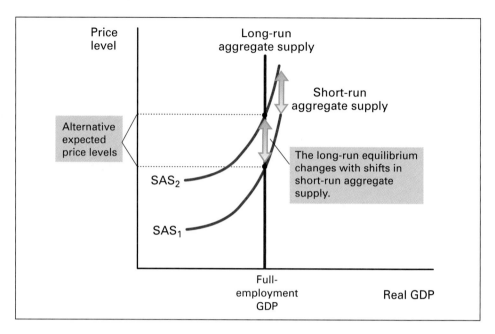

demand far enough to the right to reach full-employment GDP at the current price level, as shown by point 2 in the figure.

Instead of full employment at the current price level, though, the result of the extra spending is likely to be inflation plus a less-than-intended increase in output, given by point 3 in Figure 9-10. The reason is that the added demand for jobs would be concentrated in the defense industry. Workers with the human capital used in the defense industry would be in great demand and would see their salaries increase, a situation that would contribute to inflation. Meanwhile, job seekers without the required skills would remain unemployed. The result is shown as a movement up the short-run aggregate supply curve in the general direction of full-employment output, but also in the direction of a higher price level.

COST–PUSH INFLATION

Inflation could also arise from an upward shift in the short-run aggregate supply curve. Because the short-run aggregate supply curve intersects long-run aggregate supply at the expected price level, a change in the expected price level will shift short-run aggregate supply vertically, as shown in Figure 9-11. For example, if the expected price level increases, short-run aggregate supply shifts vertically upward until its intersection with long-run aggregate supply occurs at the new expected price level. Likewise, if the expected price level decreases, short-run aggregate supply shifts downward, intersecting long-run aggregate supply at the new expected price level.

Such shifts are likely because workers revise their expectations over time. For example, as inflation rose significantly from 2 percent in 1960 to 6 percent in the early 1970s, most people commenced to factor inflation into their labor supply decisions—they developed inflationary expectations, and could be fooled only by actual inflation that turned out differently from what they came to expect. Thus, stimulative fiscal policies that shifted aggregate demand to the right were offset by upward shifts in the short-run aggregate supply curve.

cost–push inflation occurs when an upward shift in short-run aggregate supply causes the economy to move up the aggregate demand curve to a higher price level and less output.

When aggregate supply shifts up, the economy moves up the aggregate demand curve to a point of higher prices and lower output, as shown in Figure 9-12. Inflation that is caused in this way is called **cost–push inflation. Cost–push inflation reduces output and increases the price level.** Recall from Chapter 8 that this combination is known as *stagflation*—the simultaneous occurrence of inflation and economic stagnation.

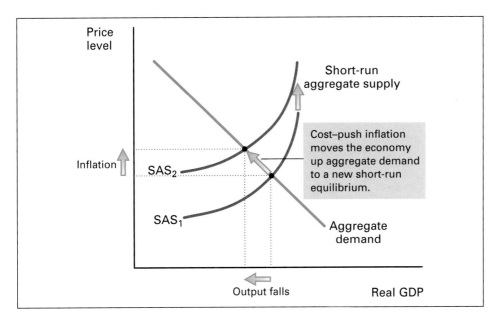

FIGURE 9-12

COST–PUSH INFLATION When an increase in inflationary expectations causes an upward shift in short-run aggregate supply, the result is cost–push inflation, in which output falls and the price level rises.

QUICKCHECK

What is the difference between cost–push inflation and demand–pull inflation?

Answer: Cost–push inflation involves a movement up the aggregate demand curve as prices rise. It is caused by the inflationary expectations of workers and firms that drive up production and output costs. Demand–pull inflation occurs when the aggregate demand curve shifts outward, which causes a movement up the short-run aggregate supply curve.

9.3 SHORT-RUN PATHS TO LONG-RUN STABILITY

Over the course of time, an economy is constantly in the short run. However, the short runs differ from one year to another. If they differ very much, the economy is likely to be in trouble, as we will see below.

THE INFLATIONARY SPIRAL

The shifting short-run aggregate supply becomes a moving target for government policy-makers. If government chases an upwardly shifting aggregate supply by using ever more stimulative policies that shift out aggregate demand, the result would be the reinforcement of inflationary expectations. As inflationary expectations rise, short-run aggregate supply shifts up and output falls, which prompts more fiscal stimuli in an ever-repeating cycle. The result is an ongoing **inflationary spiral** of alternately rising and falling output along with a continually rising price level, as shown in Figure 9-13.

 In the inflationary spiral, demand–pull and cost–push inflation feed upon each other. Cost–push inflation is caused by past experiences with inflation, which were most likely caused by policies that had allowed aggregate demand to increase. To counter cost–push inflation and keep the economy near full employment, policymakers might choose to expand aggregate demand again. That would reinforce inflationary expectations in future periods, causing another round of cost–push inflation. Thus, if government responds to cost–push inflation by stimulating aggregate demand, the result is likely to be an inflationary spiral of demand–pull inflation followed by more cost–push inflation, continuing in a cycle that goes on and on.

inflationary spiral alternately rising and falling output along with a continually rising price level.

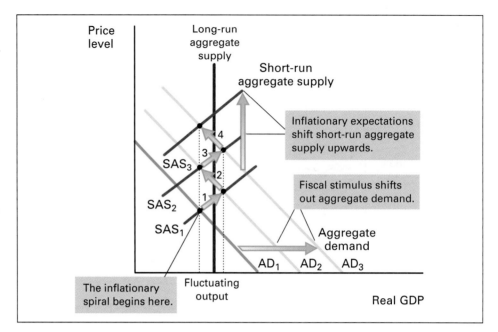

FIGURE 9-13

SPIRALING INFLATION When stimulative policy increases aggregate demand, the result can be an inflationary spiral, which is an ongoing sequence of demand–pull inflation (arrows 1 and 3 pointing upward to the right), followed by cost–push inflation (arrows 2 and 4 pointing upward to the left) as short-run aggregate supply shifts to reflect higher expectations of inflation. Output is seen to fluctuate near the full-employment level.

QUICKCHECK

How can government policy to stimulate the economy cause spiraling inflation? Explain with reference to demand–pull and cost–push inflation.

Answer: Government stimulative policy can shift aggregate demand to the right, leading to demand–pull inflation by moving the economy up the short-run aggregate supply curve to higher output. As workers get hit by this inflation, they demand higher wages, which shifts short-run aggregate supply upward, causing in turn cost–push inflation and its associated reduction in output. Government might respond to the falling output and associated higher unemployment with additional fiscal stimulation, thus taking the economy into a second round of demand–pull inflation. The pattern continues, with output rising from the demand–pull inflation and falling from the cost–push inflation, while the price level rises all the time. That sequence forms the inflationary spiral.

THE PHILLIPS CURVE—A MATTER OF INFLATIONARY EXPECTATIONS

In the 1970s, the United States experienced the inflationary spiral we described in the previous section. Policy during those years was often based on the mistaken belief in the permanent existence of a so-called Phillips curve, named after economist A.W. Phillips, who first identified it. The **Phillips curve** is a graphical representation of data that, from the 1950s in Great Britain and the 1960s in the United States, depicted a distinct curvilinear tradeoff between the goals of low unemployment and low inflation, as seen in Figure 9-14 for the United States. The evidence seemed so convincing that many economists at the time hailed the Phillips curve as a newly revealed fundamental truth.

By the end of the 1960s, the Phillips curve relationship was falling apart, as shown by the later data points in Figure 9-14. Data beyond the decade of the 1960s showed no systematic relationship between unemployment and inflation. The Phillips curve is now viewed as a short-run phenomenon that did not hold up in the long run. However, as the inflationary experiences

Phillips curve a graphical representation of data from the 1960s in the United States that shows a short-run tradeoff between low unemployment and low inflation.

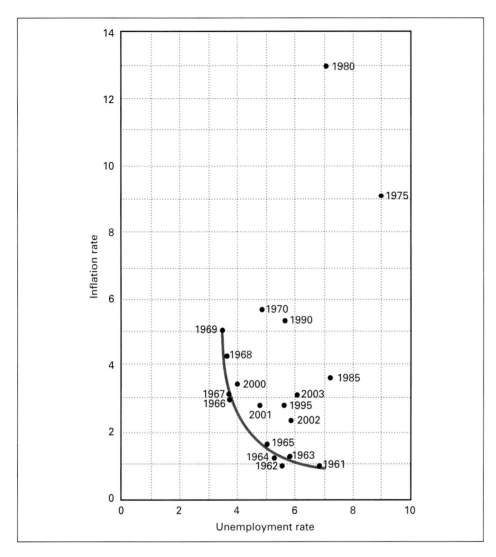

FIGURE 9-14

THE PHILLIPS CURVE The Phillips curve showed a tight, inverse relationship between inflation and unemployment in U.S. data from the 1960s. In later decades, though, the relationship no longer held true.

Source: 2003 Economic Report of the President, Tables B-42 and B-63, and Bureau of Labor Statistics. Data for 2003 are current through September.

of the 1960s and 1970s pass into history, there is a danger of people forgetting the possibility for inflation, which could lead to the Phillips Curve re-emerging as a short-run issue.

There are two ways for people to form their inflationary expectations. One way is through **adaptive expectations,** where we form our expectations about future prices according to our past experiences. So if the price level goes up at a rate of 2 percent per year, we would expect inflation of 2 percent to continue on into the future. If prices rise or fall in a manner inconsistent with the past, adaptive expectations could lead to our being fooled and slow to adjust our wage demands.

For example, a big new government spending program might add to both GDP and inflationary pressures in the short run before people catch on. In the 1960s, government spending in the United States did increase significantly in response to the Vietnam War and social programs. The prolonged period of time in which the public was apparently tricked by unexpectedly high inflation suggests that the public was basing its expectations on what it had previously experienced rather than forming its opinions based on current policy actions. With a U.S. economy characterized by adaptive expectations in the 1960s, increased government spending would cause lower unemployment and higher inflation, exactly what the Philips curve of the time showed.

adaptive expectations when we form our expectations about future prices according to our past experiences.

By the 1970s, people and businesses had learned to factor the effects of inflation into their personal and business plans. Government could no longer inflate its way to lower unemployment. This limitation on government's ability to manage the economy was shown by the combination of high inflation and unemployment—*stagflation*—experienced in that decade. People had learned to predict more accurately the impacts of public policy.

These days, public policy is unlikely to succeed if it depends on assuming that government knows more than consumers and firms in the marketplace. With the instant communications of the modern world, people are more likely to have **rational expectations** in which they correctly predict the implications of government policy action and thus cannot be systematically tricked. With rational expectations, we keep up with the news analyses and base our expectations on the best information available to us. Public policies that have been debated in Congress, commented on by the media, and passed into law are not likely to surprise us.

The rise of rational expectations explains the demise of the Phillips curve relationship of the 1960s. In those years, government actions that caused inflation also caused people to work more because they didn't recognize that inflation. People at the time were tricked by higher wages into working more. They later came to understand that the higher wages were only in nominal terms, not in real terms, because prices were rising to match. From then on, it became standard practice for workers to compare wage increases to their expected cost-of-living increases. The more experience they had with being surprised, the more attention they paid to inflation predictions in the media.

If people have rational expectations, government policy that is intended to stimulate the economy will have no predictable effect. In other words, the best guess is that policy actions will not change the economy much in either direction. The idea of rational expectations provides support to the classical argument that government should step back and let the macroeconomy take care of itself.

rational expectations when people correctly predict the implications of government policy action and thus cannot be systematically tricked.

CLASSICAL OR KEYNESIAN—BOTH SEEK THE SAME STABILITY

Figure 9-15 depicts a sustainable long-run macro equilibrium, in which the expected and actual price levels are equal. The expected price level is given by the intersection of short- and long-run aggregate supply. The actual price level is given by the intersection of short-run

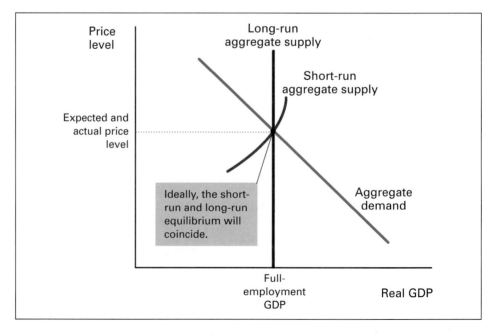

FIGURE 9-15

THE MACRO POLICY IDEAL Macro policy aims to achieve the full-employment output and a stable price level, which occurs when the actual price level equals that which is expected. The actual price level is given by the intersection of short-run aggregate supply and aggregate demand. The expected price level is given by the intersection of short-run aggregate supply and long-run aggregate supply.

TABLE 9-1   SUMMARY OF CLASSICAL AND KEYNESIAN VIEWS

	CLASSICAL	KEYNESIAN
Focus	Long-run issues, especially economic growth.	Short-run issues, especially unemployment.
Prices and Wages	Prices and wages will adjust upward or downward as needed to reach a full-employment equilibrium.	Prices and wages adjust upward without difficulty, but are downwardly sticky and thus unable to lead the economy from an unemployment equilibrium to full employment.
Fiscal Policy	Government should not attempt to manage aggregate demand.	Government should actively adjust taxes and spending in order to manage aggregate demand.
Shortcoming	Remedying unemployment requires patience.	Remedying unemployment can lead to demand–pull inflation and possibly an inflationary spiral.

aggregate supply and aggregate demand. Because these intersections both occur at the same point (a point on long-run aggregate supply), the economy is at full employment. Whether achieved through government policy intended to manage aggregate demand, or through a hands-off policy of giving short-run aggregate supply time to adjust on its own, this long-run macro equilibrium is usually considered to be the ideal outcome of macro policy.

To achieve long-run stability and avoid the inflationary spiral, classical economists advocate maintaining the policy goal of low inflation, no matter the short-run consequences. The United States followed that policy in the early 1980s, after a decade when inflation had risen to the double-digit range. The result was a couple of years of jarring recession during which people adjusted their inflationary expectations downward. Afterward, the economy returned to full employment, but at a much lower rate of inflation.

Table 9-1 summarizes the differences between the classical and Keynesian approaches to achieving economic stability. Bear in mind that both schools of thought have the same goal for the economy, which is to reach full-employment output without inflation. The essential difference is that the Keynesians will set aside long-run goals to combat the short-run hardships of unemployment, while classical economists "keep their eyes on the horizon" to obtain a sustainable long-run equilibrium of stable prices and full employment.

9.4 DEFICITS AND DEBT—DO WE SPEND TOO MUCH?

"I place economy among the first and most important virtues, and public debt as the greatest of dangers."

Explore & Apply

—*Thomas Jefferson*

Why do babies cry? You'd cry, too, if you were born over $23,000 in debt. On average, that is how much debt Uncle Sam has already rung up for each U.S. citizen, babies included. The federal government continues to add to that national debt each year in which it operates with a budget deficit. In 2003, the budget deficit was $400 billion and the gross national debt stood at $6.8 trillion. About half of this debt was owed from one government agency to another, with the other half owed to the public.

The national debt can be thought of as the *stock* or inventory of accumulated past budgetary imbalances, and the deficit as a *flow* that adds to that debt. That debt represents almost 60 percent of the $10.4 trillion value of U.S. GDP. Interest payments alone account for about 14 percent of total federal government spending. The Congressional Budget Office estimates that, between 2004 and 2013, the U.S. will add another $1.4–$3.7 trillion to its debt.

Is it fair? Is our government doing the right thing by spending our next generation's money, without them having any voice in the matter? After all, in the 1773 Boston Tea Party, the colonists of Massachusetts rebelled against unjust English taxes. Their rallying cry of "Taxation without representation is tyranny!" provided one more spark to the fire that formed the United States of America. Is our government engaging in tyranny against future American citizens?

To answer these questions, ask yourself when debt is justified. You may run up debt to pay for a college education. If you expect a payback in the form of a better income down the road, some debt while in college seems justifiable. What if you "own" a home? Few people own their homes outright. Yet most homeowners, even those with hefty mortgages to pay off, do not consider themselves debtors. Government statisticians count homeowners as debtors, though.

Most people are willing to take on debt when that debt allows them to purchase assets of greater value. The homeowner who takes on a mortgage and the lender who offers that mortgage figure that the value of the house is more than enough to cover the balance due on the mortgage. Indeed, most homeowners with mortgages view the difference between the value of their homes and what they still owe as a primary source of their savings.

Government statisticians take a different view. When the government measures how much Americans have saved, it subtracts from that savings figure the amount that is owed on mortgages. The value of the homes is left out because it is difficult to measure. Since there are so many homeowners with mortgages in the United States, America's savings rate then appears artificially low when compared with that of other countries.

Likewise, when the government reports its own debt, it does not offset this debt with the value of the assets it owns. After all, how do you value assets of the government? Those assets include such things as parks, highways, military bases, military equipment, a judicial system, and much more. Taken as a whole, we know the value is quite high. We also know that new babies born as U.S. citizens will obtain benefits from these assets for years to come. From this perspective, expecting future citizens to bear some of the costs does not seem so bad.

Would the next generation accept this deal, to be born with both the privileges and obligations of being a U.S. citizen? While we cannot ask them, we can observe their parents answering that question with their actions. It would be most unusual to find an expectant mother seeking to leave the United States so that her baby would be born elsewhere. In contrast, immigrant couples frequently seek entry into the United States so their babies can be born as U.S. citizens.

Just because most people believe that, on balance, there is a positive value to living in the United States does not tell us that the United States has the right amount of debt. If the accumulation of debt exceeds the accumulation of assets, the value of our country diminishes over time. Conversely, if the United States holds down debt by cutting back on public investments, the country runs the risk of missing out on investment opportunities that would look good in hindsight. U.S. opportunities for economic growth would diminish, meaning that long-run aggregate supply would not shift rightward as rapidly as it could.

THE RELATIONSHIP BETWEEN THE BUDGET DEFICIT AND THE TRADE DEFICIT

As a country, we often accuse ourselves of being on a spending binge, one we will have to pay for later. As evidence, we point to both the federal budget deficit and the U.S. *trade deficit*. The trade deficit is the amount by which the value of goods we import exceeds the value of goods we export. Because we spend more of our dollars on foreign goods than foreigners return in exchange for American goods, foreigners have extra dollars left over to invest in the United States. Those investments represent future obligations of this country to other countries. Yet,

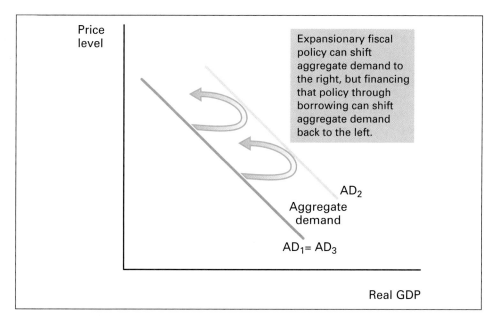

Price level

Expansionary fiscal policy can shift aggregate demand to the right, but financing that policy through borrowing can shift aggregate demand back to the left.

AD$_2$

Aggregate demand

AD$_1$= AD$_3$

Real GDP

FIGURE 9-16

CAN FISCAL STIMULI WORK? The effectiveness of deficit spending that is intended to shift aggregate demand to the right may in practice be offset by an increased trade deficit, together with less consumption and investment spending at home by U.S. residents, which shifts aggregate demand back to where it started.

while it is the collection of our individual actions that leads us to a trade deficit, we don't usually consider ourselves to be personally engaging in irresponsible spending.

The $400 billion budget deficit differs from the amount of the trade deficit, which has been running well over $400 billion in recent years. Still, the two are related, so much so that they have been dubbed the *twin deficits*. By running a budget deficit, the U.S. government leaves more money in the pockets of consumers, some of which they spend on imports. Those U.S. dollars that consumers spend on imports come back to the United States, such as when foreigners buy U.S. exports or invest in the United States.

When the government borrows money to finance the budget deficit, that borrowing tends to draw more investment dollars into the United States in response to the expanded investment opportunities. To obtain dollars to invest in the United States, foreign investors must bid them away from other uses, such as foreign purchases of U.S. products. For this reason, holding all else constant, the higher the federal budget deficit, the higher the trade deficit.

The existence of the twin deficits runs counter to the idea that government fiscal policy can spend the economy out of an unemployment equilibrium. The problem is illustrated in Figure 9-16. If the government attempts to shift aggregate demand to the right through deficit spending, it generates offsetting effects that shift aggregate demand back to the left. Specifically, the higher U.S. trade deficit reflects a reduction in spending on U.S. goods as foreigners substitute purchases of U.S. debt for purchases of U.S. products.

By the same token, the same higher interest rates that cause foreigners to invest in the United States rather than buy U.S. goods will likewise crowd out private sector investment, because the more money investors put into secure government debt, the less there is left over for private sector investments. Together, these effects might offset the government's expansionary fiscal policy and leave the economy back where it started, as seen in Figure 9-16.

About 80 percent of government debt is owed to itself or to private U.S. investors. Nevertheless, as the federal government adds to its debt, so too do U.S. citizens. Attracting additional foreign investment accumulates obligations to repay that debt in the future. Is that dangerous? After all, Bolivia, Argentina, and many other struggling countries have endured economic crises brought about by foreign debt obligations that they were unable to repay.

When it comes to the United States, the dangers of foreign debt are few. Latin American and other debtor countries ran into problems repaying their debts in large part because their debts were denominated in U.S. dollars, which meant they had to acquire those dollars. To the extent that the United States owes financial debt to citizens of other countries, that debt is also denominated in dollars. The critical difference is that those are homemade dollars; the United States controls the presses that print the money it owes.

Some people worry over a sudden exodus of foreign investment, possibly as a means to exert political pressure. Such worries are unfounded. If foreigners for some reason wish to stampede out of the United States, they would have to leave behind all but a small fraction of their assets. By investing in the United States, foreigners allow us political and economic control over things of great value to them. In that way, foreigners acquire a strong interest in having our economy perform well and in maintaining good political relations.

We have seen that a budget deficit and consequent increase in the federal debt can be justifiable. We have also seen that this expansionary fiscal policy tends to increase the trade deficit and international debt, but that the consequences of those increases are not as worrisome as many people think. Just how much debt is the right amount, however, remains an open question.

THINKING CRITICALLY

1. **Keynesian fiscal policy suggests that deficit spending can be justified to pull the economy out of an unemployment equilibrium. Yet federal budget deficits have characterized most years in recent decades, even when the economy has been at or near full employment. What are some likely explanations for this expansionary fiscal policy?**

2. **"Our federal government exploits babies by giving them a huge debt upon birth—a debt they did not ask for, but will be forced to repay. Let's care for our children and grandchildren. It's time for the government to stop running budget deficits and to start repaying our massive public debt!" Evaluate this view, including in your discussion an assessment of the proper role of government debt.**

Visit www.prenhall.com/ayers for updates and web exercises on this Explore & Apply topic.

SUMMARY AND LEARNING OBJECTIVES

1. **Distinguish between expansionary and contractionary fiscal policy, and identify their relevance to the macro equilibrium.**

   ■ An expansionary fiscal policy, also called a fiscal stimulus, occurs when government increases spending or decreases taxation. Expansionary policies are intended to shift the aggregate demand curve to the right in response to a stagnant economy.

   ■ A contractionary fiscal policy, also called a fiscal drag, occurs when government decreases spending or increases taxation. Contractionary policies are intended to shift the aggregate demand curve to the left in response to an overheating economy.

   ■ The impact of fiscal policy on aggregate demand is enhanced by the multiplier effect, in which the initial shift in aggregate demand is amplified by additional rounds of shifting.

   ■ Government borrowing to finance expansionary fiscal policies can cause the crowding-out effect, which is a displacement of private-sector spending that can offset the effects of the expansionary policy. By the same token, the effects of contractionary policy might be reduced or eliminated to the extent that government borrows less and in this way leaves more money to be spent in the private sector.

2. **Explain how balancing the full-employment budget is consistent with a budget deficit.**

   ■ The federal budget records the revenue and spending of the federal government. A balanced budget occurs when the two are equal. A budget surplus is when revenue exceeds spending, and a budget deficit is when spending exceeds revenue. Because the federal budget has mostly been in deficit, the United States has compiled a national debt of over $6 trillion.

   ■ The full-employment budget estimates what federal revenue and spending would be if the economy were at full employment. It's sometimes argued that the government should balance its budget over the course of the business cycle, running surpluses during booms and deficits during recessions. Doing so would help stabilize the economy. It also means that the government could have a budget deficit or a surplus even though the full-employment budget is balanced.

3. Discuss how fiscal policy to stabilize the economy is subject to lags, and how the lags can be overcome automatically.

- Discretionary fiscal policy is the term applied to deliberate changes in fiscal policy that are designed to affect the macroeconomy.

- Discretionary fiscal policy is subject to errors because of the three fiscal policy lags. These lags include the recognition lag, the action lag, and the implementation lag. The recognition lag refers to the length of time before a problem is recognized. The action lag refers to the amount of time it takes to decide on an appropriate policy response and pass the legislation that reflects policy. The implementation lag occurs because policy changes take time to begin to affect the economy.

- Working to counter the problems of an unemployment equilibrium and overheating are the automatic stabilizers that are built into the economy. When the economy slows down, the automatic stabilizers increase government spending. When the economy overheats, government spending tends to decrease. An example of the automatic stabilizers is unemployment benefits.

4. Identify the characteristics and significance of short-run aggregate supply.

- Unlike long-run aggregate supply, which is vertical, short-run aggregate supply slopes upward to the right. This means that in the short run an increase in the price level will result in an increase in real GDP.

- The upward slope to the short-run aggregate supply curve occurs for two reasons. The first is structural rigidities. As new spending takes place, it tends to raise wages and prices in selected sectors of the economy. That spending also increases production and employment.

- The second reason for the upward slope to short-run aggregate supply is the production effect. A rise in the price level can prompt firms to profitably employ labor for more hours. Overtime work can result in an economy that temporarily produces more than the full-employment level of output. The production effect relies upon workers' labor supply curves

remaining constant, which will only occur if workers are unaware of the true level of inflation.

- Short-run aggregate supply always intersects long-run aggregate supply at the expected price level. The reason is that a long-run macro equilibrium requires that workers and firms have accurate price expectations.

5. Describe demand–pull and cost–push inflation, and how they can be part of an inflationary spiral.

- Demand–pull inflation describes an increase in the price level that results from an increase in aggregate demand.

- Cost–push inflation occurs in response to an upward shift in the short-run aggregate supply curve. The short-run aggregate supply curve will shift upward whenever there is an increase in inflationary expectations on the part of workers or firms. The effect of cost–push inflation is to reduce real GDP.

- Demand–pull inflation can lead to cost–push inflation and an inflationary spiral, which refers to a sequence of demand–pull and cost–push inflation that creates an ongoing rise in the price level. Demand–pull inflation increases output and the price level. This increase in the price level sets off an increase in inflationary expectations that leads to cost–push inflation and an accompanying reduction in real GDP. To counter the cut in production, policymakers would see to it that aggregate demand increased, thus causing another round of demand–pull inflation. This process could continue indefinitely.

6. Analyze the rationale and limitations of deficit spending.

- An enduring feature of the modern American economy is the presence of a budget deficit, trade deficit, and huge national debt. These features are related, with ongoing budget deficits adding to the national debt and also attracting foreign investment dollars. Because those foreign investment dollars might otherwise have gone to purchase American goods and services, the budget deficit and trade deficit are often called the twin deficits.

- Although people worry a great deal about the large deficits and national debt, at least some of this borrowing is offset by assets. For example, while future taxpayers inherit debt, they also inherit roads, a system of government, and other assets of value.

- If the government attempts to shift aggregate demand to the right through deficit spending, the trade deficit and other offsetting effects might shift aggregate demand back to the left.

KEY TERMS

unemployment equilibrium, 226
fiscal policy, 226
expansionary fiscal policy (fiscal stimulus), 226
contractionary fiscal policy (fiscal drag), 227
multiplier effect, 227
output gap, 228
recessionary gap, 228
inflationary gap, 229
crowding-out effect, 230
balanced budget, 231

budget surplus, 231
budget deficit, 231
full-employment budget, 231
structural deficit, 231
national debt, 231
discretionary policy, 232
recognition lag, 232
action lag, 233
implementation lag, 233
automatic stabilizers, 233
short-run aggregate supply, 234

structural rigidities, 234
the production effect, 235
inflationary expectations, 235
short-run macroeconomic equilibrium, 236
demand–pull inflation, 237
cost–push inflation, 238
inflationary spiral, 239
Phillips curve, 240
adaptive expectations, 241
rational expectations, 242

TEST YOURSELF

TRUE OR FALSE

1. An unemployment equilibrium will be corrected if wages and prices are able to adjust downward.
2. The implementation lag occurs because it takes time to recognize that a problem exists with the macroeconomy.
3. Aggregate demand will increase in response to a fiscal stimulus.
4. Balancing the budget over the course of the business cycle results in surpluses in some years and deficits in others.
5. When workers expect a higher price level, short-run aggregate supply will shift upward.

MULTIPLE CHOICE

6. The multiplier effect refers to the tendency for there to be
   a. a need to budget extra money for government programs because they always wind up costing more than originally estimated.
   b. the tendency for private-sector borrowing to increase when government borrowing increases.
   c. the tendency for private-sector borrowing to decrease when government borrowing increases.
   d. additional rounds of spending that shift aggregate demand in the same direction that fiscal policy had shifted it in the first place.
7. To the extent that the crowding-out effect occurs, expansionary fiscal policy is likely to be
   a. more effective.
   b. less effective.
   c. characterized by fraud.
   d. associated with a balanced budget.

8. An example of an automatic stabilizer is
   a. the U.S. income tax system.
   b. the Internet.
   c. sticky wages.
   d. the full-employment equilibrium.
9. The federal budget deficit
   a. has not existed since 1997.
   b. is the accumulation of all federal debts.
   c. equals the national debt minus the budget surplus.
   d. is the amount by which government spending exceeds its revenue over the course of a year.
10. Short-run aggregate supply always intersects long-run aggregate supply at
    a. the expected price level.
    b. the actual price level.
    c. the long-run equilibrium price level.
    d. an unemployment equilibrium.
11. If the economy starts at the point indicated in Self-Test Figure 9-1 and aggregate demand does not shift, the long-run equilibrium would occur at point
    a. A.
    b. B.
    c. C.
    d. D.
12. If the economy starts at the point indicated in Self-Test Figure 9-1 and aggregate demand shifts to the right as shown, the new short-run equilibrium will occur at point
    a. A.
    b. B.
    c. C.
    d. D.

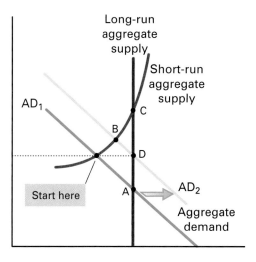

SELF-TEST FIGURE 9-1

13. In Self-Test Figure 9-1, the expected price level is associated with point
    a. *A.*   b. *B.*
    c. *C.*   d. *D.*
14. The short-run aggregate supply curve holds
    a. the price level constant.
    b. real GDP constant.
    c. workers' labor supply curves constant.
    d. nothing constant.
15. Suppose the economy is in an unemployment equilibrium. An increase in aggregate demand caused by a fiscal stimulus
    a. must cause a fall in the price level.
    b. will most likely cause a rise in the price level.
    c. cannot affect the price level.
    d. will affect the price level, but in an unpredictable way.

16. Cost–push inflation occurs when
    a. the long-run aggregate supply curve shifts to the right.
    b. the short-run aggregate supply curve shifts upward.
    c. the short-run aggregate supply curve shifts downward.
    d. a shift in aggregate demand moves the economy up the short-run aggregate supply curve.
17. In an inflationary spiral, output
    a. always rises.
    b. always falls.
    c. alternately rises and falls.
    d. remains constant.
18. In an inflationary spiral, the price level
    a. always rises.
    b. always falls.
    c. alternately rises and falls.
    d. remains constant.
19. When the expected and actual price level are equal, the macroeconomy is
    a. overheated.
    b. in an unemployment equilibrium.
    c. experiencing inflationary expectations.
    d. at the long-run macro equilibrium.
20. The difference between the federal budget deficit and the national debt is that the budget deficit represents the
    a. accumulation of past debts, while the national debt is the amount by which spending exceeds revenues each year.
    b. amount by which spending exceeds revenues each year, while the national debt represents the accumulation of past deficits and surpluses.
    c. amount of money the country owes that it cannot pay back.
    d. amount of money the United States owes foreign countries, while the budget deficit represents the amount of money the United States owes in total.

QUESTIONS AND PROBLEMS

1. *[expansionary fiscal policy]* Show an unemployment equilibrium on a graph and explain how an expansionary fiscal policy can achieve full employment.
2. *[overheated economy]* Explain the appropriate fiscal policy response when the economy overheats.
3. *[fiscal policy lags]* What are the three fiscal policy lags that complicate the task for policymakers of using fiscal policy to manage the economy? Explain each of the lags.
4. *[automatic stabilizers]* Write a brief essay on the contribution that the automatic stabilizers play in creating a stable economy. Provide examples of the automatic stabilizers and use them to illustrate their

significance. Why is there an interest in using fiscal policy to stabilize the economy when the automatic stabilizers are available?
5. *[federal budget]* When the economy is at full employment, should the federal government run a budget deficit, surplus, or neither? Explain.
6. *[full-employment budget]* Is the full-employment budget usually balanced? Explain.
7. *[national debt]* How was the U.S. national debt of over $6 trillion created? Who is owed this debt?
8. *[short-run aggregate supply]* Illustrate graphically the short-run aggregate supply curve. Also include on your

graph the long-run aggregate supply curve. At what point must the short-run aggregate supply curve and long-run aggregate supply curve intersect? Label the correct axis accordingly.

9. *[structural rigidities]* In regard to the short-run aggregate supply curve, what is the significance of structural rigidities? Your explanation should be stated within the context of an example of structural rigidities.

10. *[production effect]* In regard to the short-run aggregate supply curve, what is the significance of the production effect? Your answer should be stated within the context of workers' labor supply curves.

11. *[short-run unemployment equilibrium]* When the actual price level is below the expected price level, explain why there will be a short-run unemployment equilibrium. If fiscal policy shifts aggregate demand to the right, explain what will happen to the actual price level.

12. *[demand–pull and cost–push inflation]* On separate graphs, show demand–pull and cost–push inflation, labeling the axes, curves, and changes in output and the price level.

13. *[inflationary spiral]* Explain how cost–push inflation might prompt policymakers to take actions that subsequently cause demand–pull inflation. Then explain how this demand–pull inflation could lead to another round of cost–push inflation. What is the sequence of demand–pull inflation followed by cost–push inflation called? Illustrate this process graphically using the aggregate demand–aggregate supply model.

14. *[Phillips curve]* According to the Phillips curve, what characterizes the relationship between inflation and unemployment? Draw a Phillips curve, making sure to label the axes. Does evidence accumulated after the 1960s support those conclusions?

15. *[inflationary expectations]* What do you expect the inflation rate to be over the next year?
    a. Did you arrive at an answer to this question by adaptive expectations?
    b. What are rational expectations? Are rational expectations or adaptive expectations more likely to be accurate?

16. *[macro thought]* Summarize the Keynesian and classical views on fiscal policy.

WORKING WITH GRAPHS AND DATA

1. *[fiscal policy]* Answer the following questions based on Graph 9-1.

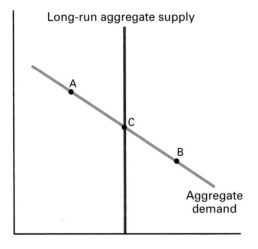

GRAPH 9-1

a. If the economy is operating at point A, what macroeconomic problem is the economy experiencing?
b. If the economy is operating at point A, what type of fiscal policy could be used to theoretically alleviate this problem?
c. Indicate on the graph how this would take place.
d. Explain the outcome of this fiscal policy.
e. If the economy is operating at point B, what macroeconomic problem is the economy experiencing?
f. If the economy is operating at point B, what type of fiscal policy could be used to theoretically alleviate this problem?
g. Indicate on the graph how this would take place.
h. Explain the outcome of this fiscal policy.
i. If the economy is operating at point C, what macroeconomic problem is the economy experiencing?

2. *[inflationary spiral]* Use point A on Graph 9-2 as a starting point to explain how spiraling inflation could take place. Show each step on a graph and explain your reasoning behind the changes made on the graph.

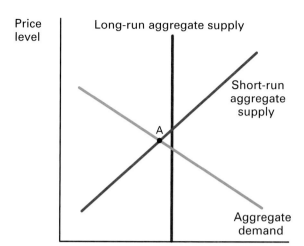

Price level

Long-run aggregate supply

Short-run aggregate supply

A

Aggregate demand

Real GDP

GRAPH 9-2

3. *[expansionary fiscal policy, cost-push inflation, crowding-out effect]* Use Graph 9-3 as a starting point to answer the questions that follow.

Price level

Long-run aggregate supply

Short-run aggregate supply

Aggregate demand

Real GDP

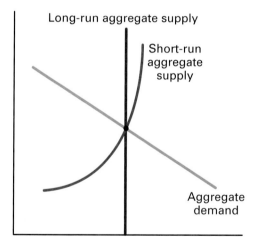

GRAPH 9-3

a. Explain why the slopes of the short-run aggregate supply and the long-run aggregate supply curves differ.
b. What is meant by the macroeconomic "ideal" and where is it found on the graph?

c. Suppose that the short-run aggregate supply curve shifts to the left. Draw it. What is the short-run outcome? How might an economy correct this situation?
d. Explain why your solution may not achieve the macroeconomic ideal.
e. Identify the expected price level in Graph 9-3.
4. *[unemployment, inflation, Phillips curve]* Answer the following questions about unemployment rates, inflation rates, and the Phillips curve.
   a. Use the data from the table below to plot the unemployment rates and inflation rates of this economy.

Year	Unemployment rate	Inflation rate
1980	3.0	5.0
1981	3.2	4.5
1982	3.5	4.0
1983	4.0	3.0
1984	4.5	2.5

   b. How does this relate to the Phillips curve?
   c. What might cause a movement along the curve you drew for the 1980–1984 period?
   d. Use the data from the table below to plot the unemployment rates and inflation rates of this economy.

Year	Unemployment rate	Inflation rate
1985	6.0	2.0
1986	5.5	3.0
1987	5.0	3.5
1988	5.5	3.2
1989	4.5	4.0

   e. How does this relate to the Phillips curve?
   f. What might cause the shift in the curve you drew for 1980–1984 to the curve representing 1985–1989?
   g. Use the data from the table below to plot the unemployment rates and inflation rates of this economy.

Year	Unemployment rate	Inflation rate
1990	6.0	7.0
1991	5.0	6.5
1992	4.0	6.0
1993	4.5	4.0
1994	4.0	3.5

   h. How does this relate to the Phillips curve? Explain.

 Visit www.prenhall.com/ayers for Exploring the Web exercises and additional self-test quizzes.

CHAPTER 10

AGGREGATE EXPENDITURES

A LOOK AHEAD

Spend your money and give people work. It sounds like such a patriotic thing to do: Buy, buy, and buy some more. In doing this, you will help out others, but you might also find yourself on the verge of personal bankruptcy. Is this really the way the economy works? Should you consume for the sake of giving others jobs? Is spending the key to keeping economic depression at bay? This chapter's Explore & Apply examines the Great Depression, noting what we thought we knew then and what we think we know now.

Interpreting the Great Depression is not the only place where economists disagree. As the joke goes, "If you line up all the economists in the world end to end, you still won't reach a conclusion!" The joke is itself quite a stretch, because economists share a great deal of common ground. The model of aggregate supply and aggregate demand represents that meeting of the minds. This chapter highlights the demand side of the economy, using Keynesian analysis that at one time defined the whole field of macroeconomics. The Keynesian income-expenditure model of the economy underlies the aggregate demand curve we have already studied.

LEARNING OBJECTIVES

Understanding Chapter 10 will enable you to:
1. **Summarize the perspective of Keynes and Keynesian economics.**
2. **Illustrate the income–expenditure model.**
3. **Explain the adjustment process to an expenditure equilibrium.**
4. **Describe how new spending can have a ripple effect throughout the economy.**
5. **Distinguish the tax multiplier from the balanced-budget multiplier.**
6. **Graph the relationship of the income–expenditure model to aggregate demand.**
7. **Compare economic analyses of the Great Depression.**

Explore & Apply

Policymakers have always worried about there being too few jobs to keep everyone employed. In the nineteenth century, they worried about workers displaced by the Industrial Revolution. Today, they worry about workers displaced by imports or Internet technologies. For example, if we have what we need and new technology can produce it with fewer people, what are the remaining people to do? Or what if people start making do with fewer goods and services? How can the economy keep everyone employed?

As discussed in Chapter 8, economists are relatively unconcerned with these questions in the long run, as markets have time to adjust—the evidence across time and across countries suggests that there is always something to do, if only a person has the time to find it. As people discover those jobs, they move the economy toward its full-employment output. In this process price levels adjust, which is why the model of aggregate supply and aggregate demand has the price level on the vertical axis. In contrast, in the model presented in the current chapter, the price level is not a variable. Here we dig deeper into the demand side of the economy, using a Keynesian model, called the income-expenditure model, that focuses on the short run, before prices have time to adjust. We will see how the aggregate demand curve is derived from the Keynesian model.

10.1 "IN THE LONG RUN, WE ARE ALL DEAD"

With the famous line above, John Maynard Keynes (1883–1946) spotlighted the need to address immediate problems facing the unemployed. In response to the pressing problems of the Great Depression, Keynes offered a new, short-run perspective that came to be called *Keynesian economics.* Prior to that time, economists emphasized long-run economic tendencies, viewing short-run fluctuations around the long-run trends as transitory problems that would correct themselves. That long-run way of looking at the macroeconomy became known as *classical economics.* Both classical and Keynesian perspectives are still used today.

In keeping with a short-run perspective, Keynes chose to ignore long-run tendencies toward full employment. In a nutshell, he took the view that problems of unemployment could be solved if only people and their government would buy more goods and services. Recall that consumption directly accounts for about 70 percent of GDP. It also motivates business investment spending. The Keynesian model is based around understanding how much spending is likely to occur at different levels of GDP and how the government can influence that spending to make sure that the economy lands at full employment.

10.2 THE INCOME—EXPENDITURE MODEL

One person's spending is another person's income—the two go hand in hand. Likewise, the circular flow model from Chapter 2 tells us that aggregate income and output must be equal.

Aggregate national income = Aggregate national output

Money spent on a cheeseburger, for example, is split into income to the employees and owners of the restaurant, as well as to the suppliers of the cheese, meat, and other inputs that go into the burger. For this reason, gross domestic product can be viewed as a measure of both output and income, as noted on the horizontal axis of Figure 10-1. That figure depicts the **income–expenditure model,** which shows planned and actual expenditures at each possible level of real GDP.

The 45-degree line in Figure 10-1 maps the GDP from the horizontal axis to the vertical axis. The vertical axis is labeled expenditure, because GDP measures output by adding up the value of all final goods and services that are purchased. Those purchases are expenditures that sum to the economy's **aggregate expenditures,** which include consumption, investment, government purchases, and net exports. So, if the economy has produced $5 trillion worth of GDP, we collectively have made $5 trillion worth of aggregate expenditure to buy it.

income–expenditure model shows planned and actual expenditures at each possible real GDP.

aggregate expenditures consumption + investment + government + net exports.

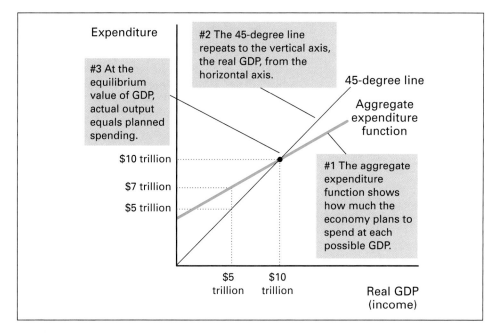

FIGURE 10-1

THE INCOME–EXPENDITURE MODEL The income–expenditure model shows planned and actual expenditures at each possible level of real GDP, where GDP measures both aggregate output and income. The model contains three components:

#1 The aggregate expenditure function shows how the economy's spending plans are based on its GDP. For example, at a GDP of $5 trillion, we would plan to spend $7 trillion.

#2 The 45-degree line notes the amount that the economy actually produces. So at a GDP of $5 trillion, we in fact have only $5 trillion of new output.

#3 The expenditure equilibrium is the one point at which planned expenditures and actual GDP are the same. In this case, the expenditure equilibrium occurs at $10 trillion.

Unfortunately, what we plan to spend and what we earn are not always the same. We might plan to spend $7 trillion when our aggregate income is only $5 trillion. In that case, $5 trillion is not an equilibrium GDP, because our spending plans cannot be sustained. The **aggregate expenditure function** tells what the economy's planned spending will be at each level of real GDP. There will be only one level of GDP where planned spending equals output. That GDP occurs at the **expenditure equilibrium,** which is given by the intersection of the aggregate expenditure function and the 45-degree line in the income–expenditure model shown in Figure 10-1. The expenditure equilibrium is the level of GDP that the economy tends toward in the short run, at a given price level.

aggregate expenditure function shows the economy's planned spending for each possible level of real GDP.

expenditure equilibrium the level of GDP that the economy tends toward in the short run, at a given price level.

COMPONENTS OF AGGREGATE EXPENDITURES

The aggregate expenditure function shows that the economy's planned spending depends upon its income, the latter measured by actual GDP. Aggregate expenditures can be divided into the following two types:

- **Autonomous spending** would occur even if people had no incomes.
- **Induced spending** depends upon income.

autonomous spending spending that would occur even if people had no incomes.

induced spending spending that depends upon income.

Autonomous spending includes both investments and goods and services that will be purchased no matter what the national income might be. For example, if it became necessary, people would draw upon their accumulated wealth to buy such necessities of life as food and shelter. Even college students without any earnings have been known to draw down their parents' bank accounts in order to pay for room and board at school!

Figure 10-2 shows how aggregate expenditures equal the sum of autonomous and induced spending. Autonomous spending by itself is depected by a horizontal line, since it does not vary with income. In contrast, induced spending is entirely dependent upon income. Therefore, the line showing induced spending starts at zero GDP and rises from there. When autonomous spending and induced spending are added together, the result is an aggregate expenditure function that has both a positive vertical intercept and a positive slope. In other words, the aggregate expenditure function starts at autonomous spending and rises from there.

AUTONOMOUS AND INDUCED SPENDING Aggregate expenditures have an autonomous component that does not vary with actual GDP and an induced component that does. The higher the GDP, the more consumers will want to spend. For this reason, induced spending and aggregate expenditures in total both rise as GDP increases. There is only one point at which planned aggregate expenditures equals actual GDP. That equality occurs only at the expenditure equilibrium, which is $10 trillion in this example.

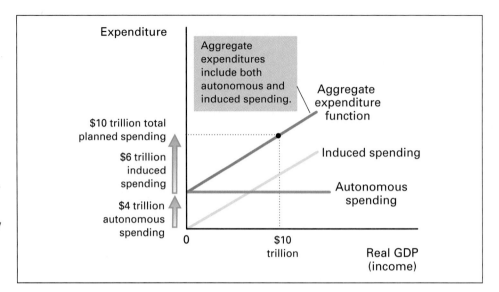

The components of aggregate expenditures are merely the components of GDP, which are:

GDP = Consumption + Investment + Government purchases + (Exports − Imports)

or, for short,

$$GDP = C + I + G + (X − M)$$

Exports minus imports is alternatively termed *net exports,* as presented in Chapter 5.

consumption function shows planned consumption spending for each possible level of real GDP.

Far and away the largest component of GDP is consumption. Plotting consumption spending for each possible level of real GDP gives the **consumption function,** as shown in Figure 10-3. Because of autonomous spending, the consumption function has a positive vertical intercept. From there, it slopes upward because of the **marginal propensity to consume (mpc),** which is the fraction of incremental income that people spend. It is computed as the slope of the consumption function, equaling 3/5 in the example shown in Figure 10-3. A worker with an mpc of 3/5 and who is given a $1/hour raise would spend sixty cents out of that dollar and save the rest.

marginal propensity to consume (mpc) the fraction of additional income that people spend.

THE CONSUMPTION FUNCTION The consumption function shows how much consumers intend to spend at various possible values of GDP, which is the economy's actual income. The slope of the consumption function is the marginal propensity to consume, given by the change in planned spending divided by the change in income.

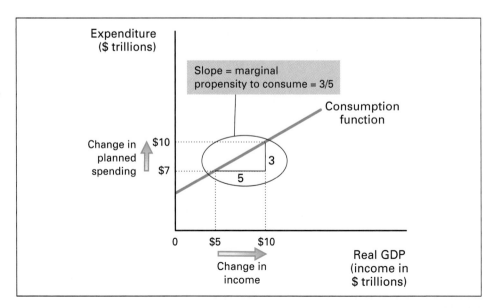

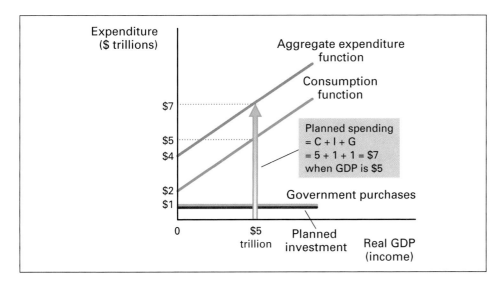

FIGURE 10-4

THE AGGREGATE EXPENDITURE FUNCTION The aggregate expenditure function shows planned spending at each possible quantity of real GDP. It equals the sum of consumption, investment, and government purchases. (Net exports would also be included.) In the example, autonomous expenditures are 2 + 1 + 1 = $4 trillion. If GDP is $5 trillion, planned expenditures would be $7 trillion, including $3 trillion in induced consumption. The slopes of the aggregate expenditure function and consumption functions are equal, both being the marginal propensity to consume.

The fraction of additional income that people save is termed the **marginal propensity to save (mps).** Adding together the marginal propensity to save and the marginal propensity to consume must yield a total of one, since there is nowhere else for income to go:

$$mpc + mps = 1$$

marginal propensity to save (mps) the fraction of additional income that people save.

Investment and government purchases are of roughly comparable size. Figure 10-4 shows these components, where for simplicity planned government purchases and planned investment spending are assumed to be completely autonomous and thus to be constant as GDP changes. For this reason, the slope of the aggregate expenditure function and consumption function are the same, both equaling the marginal propensity to consume.

MODELING THE EXPENDITURE EQUILIBRIUM

Recall that the expenditure equilibrium occurs where the aggregate expenditure function intersects the 45-degree line, as shown in Figure 10-1. At the expenditure equilibrium, the economy's actual GDP equals its planned spending. **When the economy is not at equilibrium, actual GDP and planned spending differ. The difference shows up in business inventories.** In particular, businesses plan to maintain some amount of inventories, but cannot predict exactly how much of their products consumers will buy. For example, toy sellers cannot predict exactly how many Xbox video games and other items consumers will buy at Christmas. The result is that business plans go awry and they find themselves with either too little inventory or too much inventory. Unintended inventory changes show up as the difference between planned and actual investment, as follows:

Expenditure equilibrium: Aggregate expenditures = Actual GDP

where

Aggregate expenditures = Consumption + Planned investment + Government purchases + Net exports

and

Actual GDP = Consumption + Actual investment + Government purchases + Net exports

which implies that the expenditure equilibrium occurs where planned investment = actual investment.

Does the aggregate expenditure function include actual investment or planned investment? What are the other types of spending that make up aggregate expenditures?

Answer: The aggregate expenditure function shows planned spending, including planned investment spending. The aggregate expenditure function sums planned spending on consumption, investment, government spending, and net exports.

Another way to understand the expenditure equilibrium is to consider what would happen if real GDP were either above or below it. If the economy produced less than the equilibrium, planned spending would exceed output. With buyers clamoring for more than the economy in fact produces, businesses would see their inventories decline.

The next step after a decline in inventories is a surge in orders to suppliers, as businesses would want to replace those inventories. In response, manufacturers and other suppliers would increase output. The result is an increase in GDP produced.

The process does not stop there. The workers in the factories would take home more pay, and spend some of it. That extra spending is induced consumption (induced by the extra income). Inventories are then drawn down again, which means that firms will again increase output. This process continues, but not forever. At each round, the increases in output and income get smaller until, eventually, an equilibrium is reached.

Figure 10-5 illustrates the process of moving to the expenditure equilibrium. The economy starts at a GDP that is below equilibrium. The initial inventory drawdown and resulting increase in output is the vertical arrow at point 1. As the amount of GDP produced rises to replace these lost inventories, real GDP increases and adds induced spending that leads to a second inventory drawdown, which is not as large as the first. Additional rounds of inventory drawdowns and output increases lead to the expenditure equilibrium shown as point 2.

Conversely, if production were to exceed the equilibrium, planned spending would not keep pace with production and inventories would build up. In response to the buildup in inventories, firms would cut back output and jobs as Boeing did in 2002 following the drop in air travel after September 11. The output cuts cause income to drop. In turn, induced spending falls and inventory levels would continue to be high. Firms would continue to postpone ordering and GDP would continue to fall until an expenditure equilibrium is reached. At the expenditure equilibrium, there are no further unplanned changes in inventories.

What sorts of situations would occur if the economy is not at an expenditure equilibrium?

Answer: The situations would depend on whether the economy is producing more or less than the expenditure equilibrium GDP. If the economy is producing more, there'll be an inventory buildup and consequent reduction in production. If the economy is producing less than the equilibrium GDP, inventories will be drawn down and firms will order increased output.

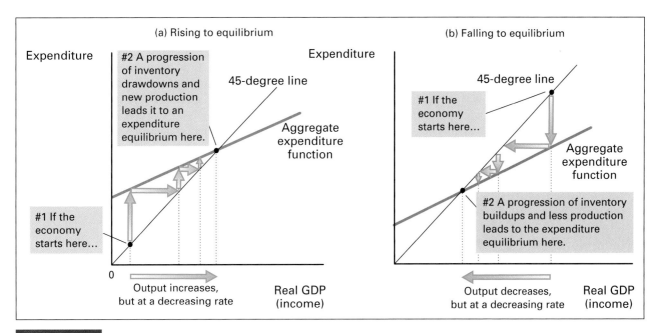

FIGURE 10-5

THE EXPENDITURE EQUILIBRIUM When GDP is below the expenditure equilibrium, there is an unintended drop in business inventories. Output is increased to replace these inventories, as shown in (a). Producing more output adds to income, leading to more consumption. Therefore, inventories drop again, production rises again, and on and on, as depicted by the sequence of arrows in the graph. The process continues until an expenditure equilibrium is reached. At that equilibrium, actual GDP and planned spending are equal and there are no unplanned inventory changes.

Graph (b) shows the process in reverse. In this case, the economy starts by producing more than can be sold, leading to inventory buildups. Then come order cutbacks, layoffs, lower incomes, and lower consumption. That causes more inventory buildup, which leads to more layoffs, and so forth as shown by the sequence of arrows. The process continues until an expenditure equilibrium is reached.

CHRISTMAS STOCKINGS AND JANUARY RESTOCKINGS   *SNAPSHOT*

Jingle jingle jingle! These are not the bells retailers listen for in those merry days before Christmas. They are the chimes of coins landing in the cash register drawer. How many coins? That can only be known at the end of the year. And what a Christmas present it would be to see those shelves bare!

Empty shelves following Christmas would provide a present for the economy, too. The new year would start with new orders to the warehouses and additional orders to the factories. More orders mean more jobs and more income and spending. The effect of retailers underestimating Christmas demand on the macroeconomy would be an increase in GDP toward its true equilibrium value. The only hint of a Grinch would be if the economy is already at full employment. In that case, inflation would surely dampen the exuberance of the new year.

There is a flip side to this happy story. The retailers might have overestimated Christmas shopping enthusiasm. In that case, the shelves would overflow and the after-Christmas orders would not go. The days of January would be grim as employment drops along the path to a lower expenditure equilibrium. ◄

10.3 CHANGING THE EXPENDITURE EQUILIBRIUM

An expenditure equilibrium implies that there are no unplanned inventory buildups or drawdowns that would prompt a change in business plans. Thus, all businesses must correctly forecast the demand for their products. The world is not that precise. Because there will always be some forecasting errors, the economy can only approximately achieve an equilibrium. In addition, that equilibrium will change when the aggregate expenditure function changes, such as in response to people changing their consumption preferences or businesses changing their investment preferences. The reasons could be as simple as attitudes toward world events, with planned expenditures increasing when we are optimistic and decreasing when we are pessimistic. Then there is government, which can change the aggregate expenditure function directly by altering its spending policies, or change it indirectly by altering tax policies that affect consumer spending or business investment.

THE MULTIPLIER EFFECT

multiplier effect sequence of spending that takes the economy from one equilibrium to another.

When there are changes in autonomous spending, the changes are magnified by the **multiplier effect,** which is a sequence of cause and effect, much like the ones shown in Figure 10-5. However, instead of taking us from a disequilibrium to an equilibrium as in that figure, the multiplier effect takes the economy from one equilibrium to another.

The multiplier effect works as follows: Adding autonomous spending causes a higher GDP, which causes more induced spending. That's because money that one person spends autonomously adds to the income of others, which in turn induces them to buy more output. This process generates an ongoing cycle of greater income and greater output. At each stage in this cycle, however, some income is likely to be saved, thus eventually bringing the cycle to a halt.

For example, suppose that Dawn spends her wages to buy boots at Betty's Bargain Basement. Dawn's spending in turn provides Betty with income that she spends at J-Mart, which in turn, well, you get the story! Through this multiplier effect, as shown in Figure 10-6, any given change in autonomous spending adds up to a considerably larger change in equilibrium GDP.

FIGURE 10-6

THE MULTIPLIER EFFECT The multiplier effect is the induced spending caused by a change in autonomous spending. The higher the marginal propensity to consume, the steeper the aggregate expenditure function and the greater the multiplier effect. Through the multiplier effect, a change in autonomous spending results in a much larger change in equilibrium GDP. The example shows this result for an autonomous spending increase.

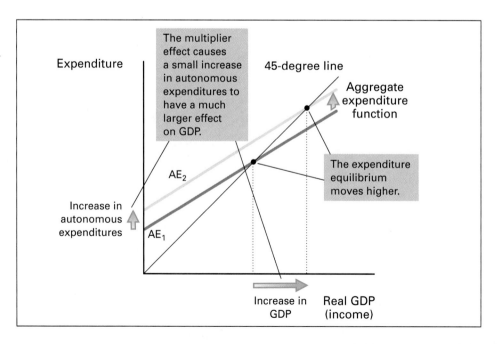

TABLE 10-1	SPENDING DEPENDS UPON THE MARGINAL PROPENSITY TO CONSUME (MPC)

(Assume autonomous spending = $1,000, mpc = 0.6, mps = 0.4)

INCOME	SPENDING	SAVINGS
$0	$1,000	−$1,000
$1,000	$1,600	−$600
$2,000	$2,200	−$200
$3,000	$2,800	$200
$4,000	$3,400	$600
$5,000	$4,000	$1,000

The strength of the multiplier effect depends upon the proportion of income that is devoted to consumption. To the extent that people save their incomes, for example, those savings represent a *leakage* out of the multiplier process. Table 10-1 illustrates how the value of the marginal propensity to consume determines the increase in spending as income rises from zero to $5,000. The table assumes that autonomous spending is $1,000. Although actual values of mpc and mps depend upon consumer confidence, the table will (for simplicity) assume that the mpc is a constant 0.6, meaning people spend sixty cents out of each additional dollar of income. Savings are also shown in the table, because income not spent is saved. Thus, the mpc of 0.6 implies an mps of 0.4. A negative value for savings, which occurs at lower income values in the table, means that there is *dissaving*—spending out of existing savings.

The multiplier effect works through the following formula:

Change in autonomous spending × Expenditure multiplier = Change in equilibrium GDP

In this equation, the **expenditure multiplier** is the multiple by which equilibrium real GDP grows as a result of an increase (an *injection*) of new autonomous spending. The expenditure multiplier is sometimes called the *autonomous expenditure multiplier* for clarity or merely just the *multiplier* for short. If autonomous spending rises, **the expenditure equilibrium will rise by the increase in autonomous spending multiplied by the expenditure multiplier.** The price level is assumed to remain unchanged.

For example, if investors gain confidence in the economy and so increase their autonomous investment spending, equilibrium GDP would rise by more than that amount. Specifically, the equilibrium GDP would equal the increase in autonomous investment multiplied by the multiplier. Conversely, if autonomous spending were to decrease, the expenditure multiplier would reveal how much real GDP would fall.

If people always spend every penny of income they receive, the expenditure multiplier would be infinite and the multiplier formula would lead to an infinite GDP. For example, if Ann were to receive $1,000 in income, she would spend $1,000. That would provide others with $1,000 in income, which they would spend, thus providing others with $1,000 in income, and so forth. In practice, however, leakages and possible price increases eventually bring the multiplier process to a halt. For example, if the mps were to equal 0.2, Ann would only spend $800, and 20 percent of that $800 would be saved by those receiving it, so that the next round of spending would amount to only $640.

expenditure multiplier
the multiple by which equilibrium real GDP grows as a result of an increase (an injection) of new autonomous spending.

| TABLE 10-2 | ROUNDS OF SPENDING FOR THE EXPENDITURE MULTIPLIER (ASSUME THE MPC = 0.8, SO THAT THE MPS = 0.2) |

SPENDING ROUND AND AMOUNT RECEIVED	AMOUNT SPENT (80% OF AMOUNT RECEIVED)	AMOUNT SAVED (20% OF AMOUNT RECEIVED)
#1: $1,000	$800	$200
#2: $800	$640	$160
#3: $640	$512	$128
#4: $512	$409.60	$102.40
#5: $409.60	$327.68	$81.92
… through an infinite number of rounds		
Totals:	$5,000	$1,000

Because 20 percent of the $640 received in income is saved, the next round of spending would amount to $512. The spending behind the multiplier effect is tracked through the first five rounds in Table 10-2. Notice that, because of the leakage from the spending stream caused by saving, the amount spent decreases with each successive round of spending. The process shown would continue through an infinite number of rounds until there is nothing left of the original $1,000 to spend. The expenditure multiplier computes the value of the amount spent through an infinite number of rounds of spending. We see in Table 10-2 that the total equals $5,000.

We can use the formula for the expenditure multiplier to compute the value of total spending shown in the last row of Table 10-2.

The multiplier is computed as the reciprocal of the percentage of new income that isn't spent on consumption. If the only options for using additional income are to spend it or save it, the multiplier formula becomes the reciprocal of the marginal propensity to save:

$$\text{Expenditure multiplier} = \frac{1}{(1 - \text{mpc})}$$

or, equivalently,

$$\text{Expenditure multiplier} = \frac{1}{\text{mps}}$$

Again, **the multiplier is multiplied by a change in autonomous spending to reveal the change in equilibrium GDP.** The change in autonomous spending could be undertaken by the government, businesses, or consumers. For example, if government spending rises by $10 billion, and the marginal propensity to save is 0.2, the expenditure equilibrium will rise by (1/0.2) multiplied by $10 billion, which equals 5 multiplied by $10 billion, or $50 billion.

Note that nothing in the foregoing analysis indicates whether the expenditure equilibrium occurs at full employment. However, **there must be some idle resources for the multiplier effect to occur.** If an injection of new spending occurs when the economy is already at full employment, consumers and others bid up prices by seeking to buy more output than the economy is capable of sustaining. The result is inflation, implying a rising price level that offsets the multiplier effect by making money not go as far in real terms. Thus, rising prices thwart the multiplier effect, even to the extent that extra spending might cause no increase at all in real GDP.

If the expenditure equilibrium occurs below full-employment GDP, there will be unemployment, and thus downward pressure on prices until full-employment GDP is achieved. However, this point is where Keynes draws the line from his classical predecessors. Regarding the expenditure equilibrium, Keynes wrote, "There is no reason for expecting it to be *equal* to full employment." Keynes went so far as to dismiss any possibility for prices to fall, because that process would only occur in the long run. Remember, "In the long run, we are all dead." Accordingly, **Keynesian multiplier analysis assumes a constant price level.**

RECESSION AND INFLATION WITHIN THE INCOME–EXPENDITURE MODEL

If the expenditure equilibrium lies below full-employment GDP, it is called an **unemployment equilibrium.** Along with the unemployment equilibrium comes an **output gap,** in which actual GDP falls below full-employment GDP, as shown in Figure 10-7. At an unemployment equilibrium, there is too little planned spending for the economy to achieve full-employment GDP. The shortfall in spending is called a **recessionary gap,** which is a shortfall in the aggregate expenditure function below that necessary to achieve a full-employment equilibrium.

The recessionary gap is shown in Figure 10-7. Keynes suggested that the government could increase spending by just this amount and the multiplier effect would do the rest. More generally, an increase in autonomous spending in an amount equal to the recessionary gap would shift up the aggregate expenditure function by just enough to lead to a full-employment equilibrium. This result assumes a constant price level. As we saw in Chapter 9, expansionary fiscal policy might raise the price level and have a diminished effect on output, particularly as the economy approaches full-employment GDP.

If the expenditure equilibrium occurs past full-employment GDP, the multiplier analysis does not apply because inflation will not allow it to stay there. This possibility is referred to as an **inflationary gap,** which is the excess of the aggregate expenditure function above that consistent with a full-employment equilibrium. The inflationary gap is shown in Figure 10-8. Because the productive capacity of the economy could not keep up with the economy's appetite to buy, the result would be inflation. Inflation would continue until it eroded the real value of planned aggregate expenditures and shifted the aggregate expenditure function down to intersect the 45-degree line at a full-employment equilibrium.

unemployment equilibrium a short-run equilibrium GDP that is less than full-employment GDP.

output gap the amount by which full-employment GDP exceeds actual GDP.

recessionary gap shortfall in the aggregate expenditure function below that necessary to achieve a full-employment equilibrium; this gap might persist in the short run unless the government takes action.

inflationary gap excess in the aggregate expenditure function above that necessary to achieve a full-employment equilibrium; this gap will be corrected by inflation.

THE RECESSIONARY GAP The recessionary gap is the shortfall in the aggregate expenditure function below that needed for full employment. Note that the recessionary gap is much smaller than the output gap, which is the shortfall in actual GDP below full-employment GDP. The recessionary gap could be closed by shifting the aggregate expenditure function up with additional autonomous spending. The gap is how much extra autonomous spending is needed.

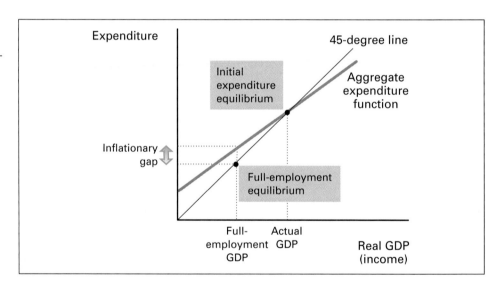

THE INFLATIONARY GAP The inflationary gap is the excess in the aggregate expenditure function above that needed for full employment. In trying to produce more than is possible, the economy overheats and produces inflation. In turn, the inflation shifts down the aggregate expenditure function and closes the gap.

SNAPSHOT   **CONSUMED WITH CONFIDENCE**

Are you a confident consumer? Do you plan to purchase a new house or car in the next year? Various surveys attempt to measure consumer confidence each month, with an eye to predicting how consumers are going to behave in the near future. These surveys underscore an important point: Spenders will become savers when they fear the economy is on the verge of turning down. That's because they fear that hard times might require them to dip into their savings and so they feel more comfortable building up those savings.

When consumers spend less, businesses have to throttle back production. Workers, in turn, might lose their jobs. In this cyclical pattern, a lack of consumer confidence becomes a self-fulfilling prophecy for the economy. That's probably why there always seems to be a government official or economist reassuring us that all is well with the economy. If we believe the economy is sound, we keep spending and our spending helps keep the economy sound. ◄

MAKING POLICY WITH MULTIPLIERS

To prevent an unemployment equilibrium, in which the economy is stuck in recession, Keynesians argue that either autonomous spending or the multiplier itself must be increased. The multiplier will increase to the extent that people decrease their marginal propensity to save. Because savings represent a leakage out of the multiplier process, Keynesians emphasize the value of consumption. If people consume a greater fraction of their income, the multiplier increases and equilibrium occurs at a higher GDP.

For example, if the marginal propensity to save were to equal 1, that would mean that people save every dollar they receive. In that case, the expenditure multiplier would equal $1/1 = 1$, meaning that the effect of an extra dollar of spending is that dollar and no more. If the mps equals 0.2, in contrast, people save only twenty cents per dollar of additional income. In that case, an extra dollar of spending would generate $1 multiplied by $(1/0.2)$, giving a result of $1 multiplied by 5, which equals a $5 increase in equilibrium spending and output. Thus, a decrease in the marginal propensity to save means that equilibrium income will be a greater multiple of autonomous spending.

How can the multiplier be increased or autonomous spending be stimulated? According to Keynes, when business conditions are bad, the private sector is unlikely to make it better! Because he doubted increases in private sector spending, Keynes was a strong advocate of increasing government spending during recessions. Keynesian analysis also suggests that the government can use tax cuts to stimulate the economy.

Figure 10-9 illustrates expansionary fiscal policy within the context of the circular flow of income and output, repeating a figure seen in Chapter 5. As noted by the flow arrows in Figure 10-9, expansionary policy can involve government collecting less tax revenue or spending more on goods and services or transfer payments. When government taxes less, it leaves more money in people's pockets to spend on consumption or to invest in the private sector. Some consumption spending might go to the rest of the world, which represents a leakage out of the circular flow. To the extent that money returns, however, it becomes an injection back into the flow.

Figure 10-9 also shows the crowding-out effect, in which an increase in government borrowing as a result of expansionary fiscal policy diverts money that might have gone into consumption, causing it to go instead into the financial market. When the financial sector converts those savings into loans, private-sector borrowers must compete against the expanded needs of government borrowing. The result is that government borrowing to finance an expansionary fiscal policy tends to displace borrowing by firms in the private sector.

Figure 10-10 shows the effects of a contractionary fiscal policy within the context of the circular flow of income and output. The flow arrows in this figure are just opposite to those in Figure 10-9. Likewise, the effects are also opposite from those in the previous figure. The circular flow models presented here are meant to give a general idea of how government fiscal policy interacts with the rest of the economy.

Keynesians note that people might save some of their higher after-tax income rather than spend it all. In other words, the **tax multiplier**—the expansionary effect of a tax cut or contractionary effect of a tax increase—would be less than the expenditure multiplier by the amount of the initial round of spending. When multiplied by a change in taxation, the tax multiplier gives the change in equilibrium GDP.

tax multiplier the expansionary effect of a tax cut or contractionary effect of a tax increase; $-mpc/(1 - mpc)$; when multiplied by a change in taxation, gives the change in equilibrium GDP.

For example, if the government spends a dollar, taxpayers with an mpc of 70 percent will get that dollar and proceed to spend seventy cents. If the government merely cuts taxes by a dollar, the first effect to be felt on the economy is that taxpayers will spend their mpc of, in this case, seventy cents. So the tax multiplier starts at the marginal propensity to consume and proceeds from there. The result is that, instead of a multiplier of $1/(1-mpc)$, the tax multiplier formula is:

$$\text{Tax multiplier} = \frac{-mpc}{(1 - mpc)}$$

and

Change in taxes owed to government $\times$ Tax multiplier = Change in equilibrium GDP

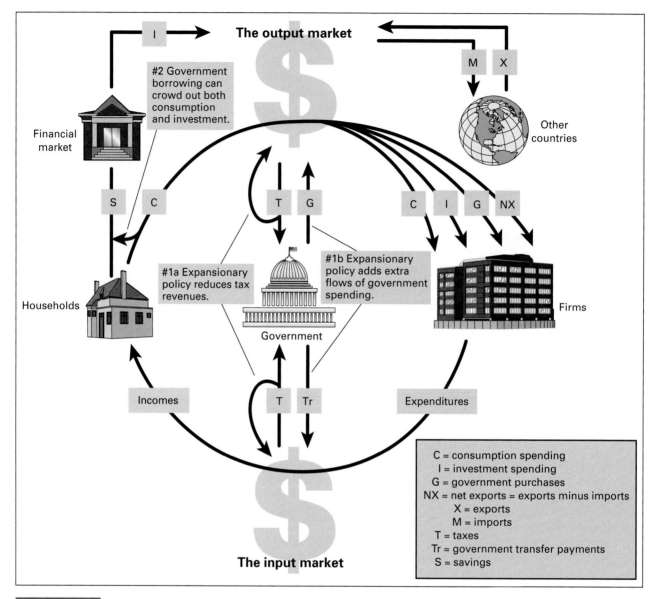

The output market

#2 Government borrowing can crowd out both consumption and investment.

Financial market

#1a Expansionary policy reduces tax revenues.

#1b Expansionary policy adds extra flows of government spending.

Households

Government

Firms

Other countries

Incomes

Expenditures

C = consumption spending
I = investment spending
G = government purchases
NX = net exports = exports minus imports
X = exports
M = imports
T = taxes
Tr = government transfer payments
S = savings

The input market

FIGURE 10-9

EXPANSIONARY POLICY AND CROWDING OUT The circular flow model discussed in Chapter 5 is used here to show the mechanisms by which government can implement fiscal policy to increase equilibrium GDP. The policy options are to either (a) reduce taxes or (b) increase government spending, as labeled by boxes #1a and 1b in the figure. A tax cut in the output market would leave more revenue in the economy that might become consumption and investment spending. Likewise, a tax cut in the input market would leave more income that households would have available to spend.

Alternatively, an increase in government spending would increase GDP directly if government spends the money on goods and services, or indirectly if government spends it on transfer payments. However, to the extent that government must borrow money to finance the tax cut or increase in spending, it will find itself competing with the private sector in the financial market. This situation can lead to a crowding-out effect, as labeled in box #2, that would negate the effectiveness of the fiscal policy.

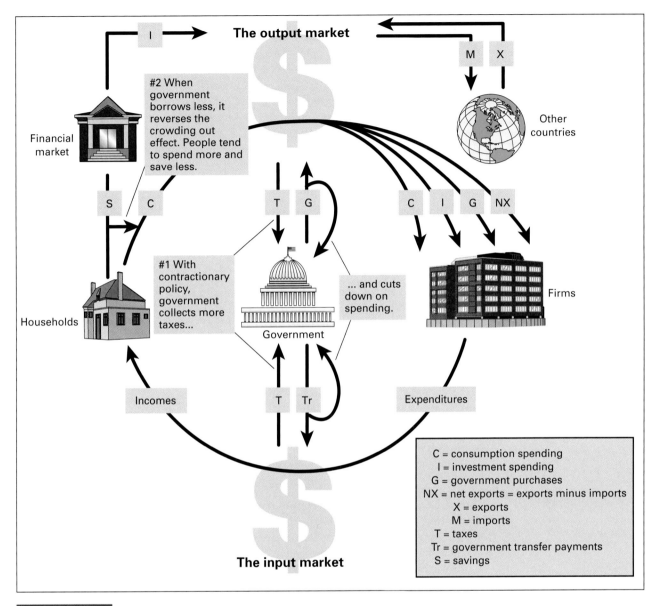

The output market

#2 When government borrows less, it reverses the crowding out effect. People tend to spend more and save less.

Financial market

Other countries

S　C

T　G

C　I　G　NX

#1 With contractionary policy, government collects more taxes...

... and cuts down on spending.

Firms

Households

Government

Incomes

T　Tr

Expenditures

C = consumption spending
I = investment spending
G = government purchases
NX = net exports = exports minus imports
X = exports
M = imports
T = taxes
Tr = government transfer payments
S = savings

The input market

FIGURE 10-10

CONTRACTIONARY POLICY The circular flow model repeats the model in Figure 10-9, except that in this case the government is seeking to slow down the economy. To do so, it can either raise taxes on output or income, or it can reduce spending on goods and services or on transfer payments. The effects are exactly opposite to those shown in Figure 10-9. The effectiveness of contractionary fiscal policy is called into question by the crowding-out effect acting in reverse. Specifically, the money that government does not borrow remains in the economy to finance private-sector purchases. Although not shown in the diagram, more of what is saved would go into private-sector investment.

The tax multiplier is preceded with a negative sign because an increase in taxation reduces after-tax income and thus reduces aggregate expenditures. For example, suppose the mpc equals 0.6. The tax multiplier would be computed as $-0.6/(1-0.6) = -0.6/0.4 = -1.5$. The outcome of a \$5 increase in taxes when the multiplier effect is figured in will be a \$7.50 decrease in equilibrium GDP. Because the tax multiplier is smaller than the expenditure multiplier, **Keynesians view extra government spending as the most effective policy to cure a recession.**

In this model, financing extra government spending with an identical increase in taxation would have an expansionary effect because the expenditure multiplier exceeds the tax multiplier. The **balanced-budget multiplier** combines the expenditure multiplier for an increase in government spending and the tax multiplier because taxes would increase to finance that spending. Adding these multipliers together gives a balanced budget multiplier of one, as follows:

balanced-budget multiplier
the effect on equilibrium GDP per dollar of additional government spending when that spending is paid for by additional taxation; this multiplier equals one.

$$\text{Balanced budget multiplier} = \frac{1}{(1 - \text{mpc})} - \frac{\text{mpc}}{(1 - \text{mpc})} = \frac{(1 - \text{mpc})}{(1 - \text{mpc})} = 1$$

and

Change in balanced-budget government spending $\times$ 1 = Change in equilibrium GDP.

In other words, when financed by a tax increase, an increase in government spending increases equilibrium GDP by exactly the amount of that extra spending, without a further multiplier effect.

For government to put its fiscal policy into effect, it may need to consider even more complexities than those we've addressed so far. For example, not only do savings represent a leakage out of increased spending, but so too do taxes and imports. The complex multiplier that considers these effects would appear as:

Complex multiplier = $1/(\text{mps} + \text{mpt} + \text{mpi})$,

where:

mps is the marginal propensity to save
mpt is the marginal propensity to tax
mpi is the marginal propensity to import

The marginal propensity to tax refers to the proportion of each additional dollar of income that is used to pay taxes. Similarly, the marginal propensity to import is the proportion of each additional dollar of income that is used to purchase imports. Other complications, such as a marginal propensity to invest, could further complicate the formula.

When the complex multiplier is applied to a change in autonomous spending, we have:

Change in equilibrium GDP = Complex multiplier $\times$ Change in autonomous spending

For example, if we suppose that the mps = 0.4, the mpt equals 0.1, and the mpi also equals 0.1, then the complex multiplier equals 1/0.6, which is 1.67. Thus, for a \$5 increase in autonomous spending,

Change in equilibrium GDP = $1.67 \times \$5 = \$8.35$

Table 10-3 summarizes multiplier analysis. It presents the formula for each multiplier along with a numerical example and the assumptions underlying the formula.

In Table 10-3 we see that the effect of introducing taxes and imports results in a value for the complex multiplier that is less than the value of the expenditure multiplier, which leaves out taxes and imports for simplicity. Thus, if there were no taxes and imports to be concerned about, a \$5 increase in autonomous spending would lead to a \$12.50 increase in equilibrium GDP. Both taxes and imports reduce the amount of additional spending that can take place, so that the ultimate increase in equilibrium GDP falls to just \$8.35. In the real world of economic policymaking, placing exact estimates on these values is rarely done, but rather tax and spending programs are adjusted over time in the direction that policymakers intend them to go.

| TABLE 10-3 | THE MULTIPLIERS COMPARED MPC = 0.6, MPS = 0.4, MPT = 0.1, MPI = 0.1 |

MULTIPLIER	FORMULA	MULTIPLIER VALUE	CHANGE IN EQUILIBRIUM GDP FOR A $5 CHANGE IN AUTONOMOUS SPENDING (OR TAXES):
Expenditure Multiplier	$1/(1 - mpc) = 1/mps$	2.5	$12.50
Tax Multiplier	$-mpc/(1 - mpc)$	−1.5	−$7.50
Balanced Budget Multiplier	$(1 - mpc)/(1 - mpc)$	1	$5
Complex Multiplier	$1/(mps + mpt + mpi)$	1.67	$8.35

THE PARADOX OF THRIFT—DOES SAVING MORE SAVE LESS?   *SNAPSHOT*

The baby boomers are aging. Their retirement looms and their lifestyles are threatened. Maybe they should save their money. "A penny saved is a penny earned," Benjamin Franklin told us. However, Keynesians might not agree.

According to Keynesian analysis, when consumers plan to save a higher fraction of their incomes, the result is a flatter aggregate expenditure function and a smaller multiplier. All else equal, the result is a lower equilibrium GDP. The economy winds up saving a higher fraction of a smaller income. Our incomes might drop so much that our total savings might even be lower than before—that's the *paradox of thrift*. In this Keynesian model, the baby boomers should keep on spending.

Economists today are not so quick to discard Ben Franklin's advice, at least not for the long run. In the long run, the paradox of thrift does not exist. Instead, price levels adjust to take the economy to a full-employment GDP no matter what fraction of income we save. But if you worry about escaping a short-run unemployment equilibrium, frugality might be something for the economy to avoid. ◄

10.4 AGGREGATE DEMAND—AN EXPENDITURE EQUILIBRIUM FOR EACH PRICE LEVEL

When the price level changes, the aggregate expenditure function shifts and generates a different expenditure equilibrium. The reason is that a change in the price level changes the real value of consumer wealth. For example, a higher price level represents inflation that erodes wealth and purchasing power. In response, there is less planned spending at each level of GDP, meaning that the aggregate expenditure function shifts down. Autonomous and induced spending are both less, because inflation has diminished the real value of savings. The expenditure equilibrium drops to a lower GDP, as shown in the upper portion of Figure 10-11.

If we were to plot the expenditure equilibrium for each price level, the result would be the aggregate demand curve that we've used in the previous two chapters. To see how, consider again Figure 10-11. The lower portion of this figure illustrates that a higher price level is associated with the lower expenditure equilibrium, the same information as above but now plotted explicitly. This relationship between the price level and the expenditure equilibrium is nothing more nor less than aggregate demand.

> ### QUICKCHECK
>
> **If the price level rises, what happens to the aggregate expenditure function and the aggregate demand curve?**
>
> **Answer:** The aggregate expenditure function shifts down as the real value of wealth falls in response to the higher prices it takes to buy goods and services throughout the economy. However, the aggregate demand curve does not change. Rather, there is a movement up the curve to a point that reflects the new higher price level and lower expenditure–equilibrium GDP.

FIGURE 10-11

FROM THE INCOME–EXPENDITURE MODEL TO AGGREGATE DEMAND

As the price level rises, planned real spending falls, as shown by the downward shift in the aggregate expenditure function in the top graph. The result is that the expenditure equilibrium falls. Aggregate demand, shown in the bottom graph, is nothing more than a plot of the expenditure equilibrium that would occur at each of the various possible price levels. When the price level rises, therefore, the demand-side GDP falls and the aggregate demand curve slopes down.

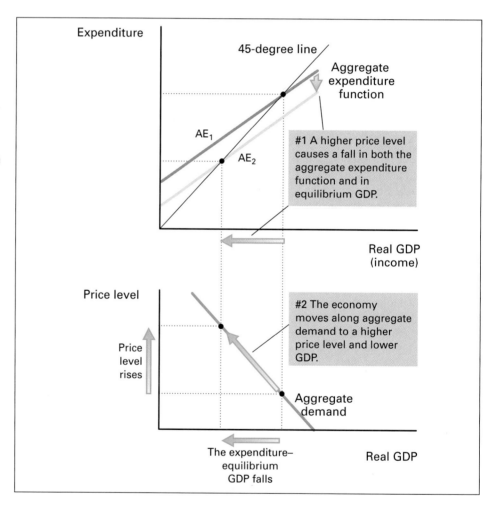

If the price level remains constant and the aggregate expenditure function shifts for any other reason, aggregate demand shifts as well. The reason is that the price level, while not itself changed, would now be associated with a different expenditure equilibrium. This result is shown in Figure 10-12.

Holding the price level unchanged, the top graph in Figure 10-12 shows the aggregate expenditure function shifting down in response to a decrease in autonomous spending. Perhaps the decrease is the result of lower government spending or higher taxation. The decrease in the autonomous expenditure function causes the expenditure equilibrium to

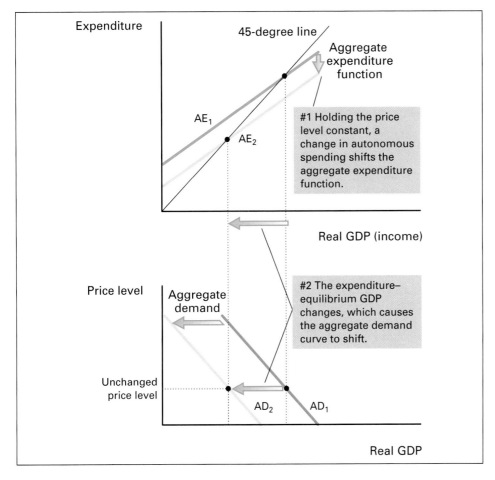

Expenditure

45-degree line

Aggregate expenditure function

AE₁

AE₂

#1 Holding the price level constant, a change in autonomous spending shifts the aggregate expenditure function.

Real GDP (income)

Price level

Aggregate demand

#2 The expenditure–equilibrium GDP changes, which causes the aggregate demand curve to shift.

Unchanged price level

AD₂   AD₁

Real GDP

FIGURE 10-12

SHIFTING BOTH THE AGGREGATE EXPENDITURE FUNCTION AND AGGREGATE DEMAND If the autonomous expenditure function shifts for a reason other than a change in the price level, the aggregate demand curve would also shift. In the example shown in the top graph, the aggregate expenditure function shifts down in response to a decrease in autonomous spending. As a consequence, the expenditure–equilibrium GDP is lower. Also as a consequence, as shown in the lower graph, aggregate demand shifts to the left. The shift in aggregate demand shows the bottom expenditure–equilibrium GDP at the existing price level and at various other possible price levels.

occur at a lower real GDP. Since the price level has not changed, the result is that aggregate demand shifts to the left, as shown in the bottom portion of Figure 10-12. There is now a lower expenditure–equilibrium GDP at the current price level. The equilibrium GDP would be lower at any other price level, as well.

10.5 THE GREAT DEPRESSION—AT THE TIME AND WITH THE BENEFIT OF TIME

Explore & Apply

Nearly every American has been haunted by the images—grainy flickering newsreel pictures and black-and-white stills of bread lines, bank runs, hunger, and desperation from which we cannot turn away. These images of the Great Depression have become part of our subconscious. Many fear that it may happen again. We even capitalize the words to emphasize its place in our heritage. Otherwise, future generations might dismiss it as just a long recession. The United States' survival through the Great Depression gives us hope that Americans can overcome whatever adversity might strike.

Some years are indelibly stamped on our collective memory. One such year is 1929. In August of 1929 the U.S. economic expansion reached its peak. Was the subsequent drop just another bump on the road to permanent prosperity? Most people, if they even noticed the economic downturn at all, thought so.

After all, the "Roaring 20s" witnessed unprecedented prosperity as the average American family seized the opportunity to buy its first automobile, as well as a radio that would tune in

the soap operas, dramas, and comedies offered by the expanding web of network-affiliated stations. Many also dabbled in stocks, shares of ownership in the booming businesses around them. It was a new age of permanent prosperity in which the consumer and investor both shared in the wealth.

There were a few missed beats as the economy marched forward in time to the music of this new age of jazz, flappers, and speakeasies. A couple of brief, mild economic downturns did occur along with a more severe recession at the beginning of the decade. Farmers in particular did not share in the general prosperity. However, the wealthy made out quite well. The Revenue Act of 1926 legislated huge tax cuts, fueling the demand for stocks issued by companies like General Motors (GM), General Electric (GE), and the Radio Corporation of America (RCA).

There were also more intellectual pursuits if one so desired. For example, 1922 saw the publication of Ludwig von Mises's *Socialism: An Economic and Sociological Analysis,* followed the next year by John Maynard Keynes's *Tract on Monetary Reform.* But why bother to read the difficult works of these and other intellectuals when there was so much easy money to be made in the new national pastime—stock picking? This was one gamble where everyone could win, or so it seemed until October 29, 1929, "Black Tuesday." The stock market crashed and did not recover. The party was over and the country would not fully recover for over a decade.

The 1929 crash of the stock market was followed by deepening economic troubles, which most people blamed on the market crash. The economy did not begin to recover until 1933. The recovery, never strong enough to convince the country that its troubles were behind it, was interrupted by a second severe downturn in 1937. Thus, in the course of more than a decade a nation struggled to overcome its economic troubles.

DID KEYNES UNDERSTAND HOW TO FIX THE ECONOMY?

The tools of Keynesian economic analysis can help us understand the problems of recession and its meaner relative, depression. In Figure 10-13, we see a situation in which GDP starts far short of that needed for full employment. In order for the economy to produce full-employment GDP, the aggregate expenditure function must be shifted upward to intersect the 45-degree line at the higher level of GDP. Keynes called for the government to make this shift happen by filling the recessionary gap with extra autonomous spending. If the government would just spend this extra amount, the multiplier effect would take over and bring the economy to full employment.

Unfortunately, this analysis does not answer several important questions. If we grant that the crash of the stock market destroyed enough wealth to push the aggregate expenditure function down from the full-employment level, why did the aggregate expenditure function continue to shift downward until 1933? Once the economy did begin to recover in 1933, why was the recovery so weak? What could have been done to strengthen the recovery? The Keynesian analysis neither tells us why the Great Depression occurred, nor why the economy remained trapped so long.

Even today, economists differ over the cause or causes of the Great Depression. The simplest explanation is that the stock market crash caused the aggregate expenditure function to shift downward as previously described. However, economists are well aware of the dangers of the *fallacy of causation* in which an event is attributed to another event that preceded it. Just because one event occurs before a second one does not mean that the first event caused the second one. Many economists would label the stock market explanation as an example of the fallacy of causation. After all, the economic downturn began in August of 1929, while the market did not crash until October.

What else could have caused the Great Depression? In the 1992 presidential debate that CNN broadcast on *Larry King Live,* candidate Al Gore presented candidate Ross Perot with a framed picture of Senators Smoot and Hawley, authors of the *Smoot–Hawley Tariff Act,* passed in 1930. Gore criticized Perot for favoring raising tariffs on imports into the United

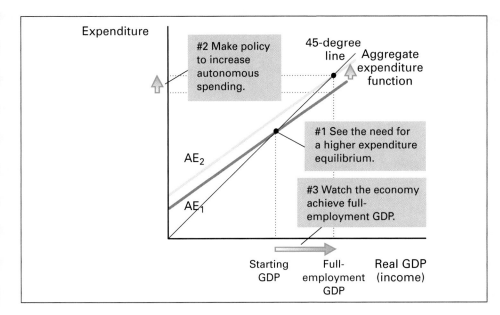

FIGURE 10-13

KEYNES'S CURE FOR DEPRESSION
When the economy is in depression, Keynes suggests the government should take action. First, observe the extent of the problem. Second, solve it by increasing aggregate demand enough to fill the recessionary gap, shown by the arrows pointing upward. Third, await the multiplier effect that will lift the economy to full-employment GDP.

States. Many analysts believe that the Smoot–Hawley tariffs turned what might have been an ordinary recession into an economic disaster. By smothering international trade with high tariffs and precipitating retaliation by other countries, the Smoot–Hawley Act disrupted commerce. Soon the depression had spread to become a worldwide phenomenon.

We know that other suspects lurk in the pages of history. Economist Milton Friedman points his finger at the Federal Reserve, America's central bank. The Federal Reserve failed to rescue the banking system and allowed bank failures to multiply. By the time President Roosevelt declared a so-called bank holiday on his Inauguration Day, March 4, 1933, about a third of the country's money had been swallowed by bank failures. As one survivor of the era, Vince Olsen, put it, "A nickel would go a long way in those days. The problem was that nobody had a nickel." If the Fed had acted decisively to save the nation's banks and its money supply, the Great Depression would not have occurred.

Others point to the nation's unequal distribution of wealth as the culprit, decrying such actions as the Revenue Act of 1926 that cut the federal income tax on a million-dollar income from $600,000 to $200,000. As the rich took a larger fraction of national income and wealth, some argue that the nation began to save too much, resulting in too little aggregate demand. In addition to advocating government spending, for example, Keynes also urged consumers to increase the marginal propensity to consume and in that way get more money circulating in the economy.

With the passing of the Hoover presidency into history on March 4, 1933, President Franklin D. Roosevelt took the oath of office while promising the American people a New Deal. The nation witnessed an energetic, if not always successful, effort to banish the Great Depression through legislation. The first theme of action was to reform the nation's financial and banking system to make banks stronger and safer. However, the government did not repay the money lost when banks failed. A program of deposit insurance was not enacted until June of 1933, and that program was not retroactive.

A second theme of the New Deal, the one for which it is most widely known, is embodied in various pieces of legislation to provide "relief" in the form of money and services for those in distress. The government attempted to set up a social safety net so that business downturns would no longer bring such personal devastation.

A third theme is government influence over market prices. Prime examples are minimum wage laws and agricultural price floors. The purpose of these actions was to put purchasing power into the hands of workers and farmers, a very large group in those days. Support for workers was also embodied in legislation that supported the efforts of labor unions to organize workers.

There was a widespread belief early on that a balanced federal budget would be the soundest fiscal policy. Thus, the Revenue Act of 1932 raised tax rates from a 25 percent maximum rate to 63 percent. Keynes abhorred that policy.

Even years prior to its publication date in 1936, drafts of Keynes's *General Theory of Employment, Interest, and Money* were the talk of the town in Washington. The ideas of this already well-known English economist offered the best hope that the country could find a way out of the Great Depression. Keynes suggested that an economy ought to use government deficit spending to stimulate the economy and close any recessionary gap. A tax cut might achieve the same result, but with less certainty because taxpayers might save the money received from a tax cut rather than spend it. Thus, the Keynesian remedies for unemployment can be summarized as "spend, spend, spend." Only the government has deep enough pockets for that.

Keynes recommended that the deficit spending that governments use to fight off recessions should be balanced by a budget surplus during good economic times. The problem is that the Keynesian medicine of deficit spending has proved to be an addictive drug for governments around the world. Severe, protracted unemployment such as in the Great Depression has not been seen since.

Economists today pay homage to Keynes for his powerful logic and insights into the role of aggregate demand in the macroeconomy. But economists also recognize the importance of money, taxes, aggregate supply, property rights, international trade, and other factors in promoting a healthy economy.

THINKING CRITICALLY

1. **Why would deficit spending prove to be addictive to governments? Would a deficit created by tax cuts be more or less desirable than a deficit created by more government spending? Explain.**

2. **What practical difficulties would a government face in closing a recessionary gap with government spending? Can you identify any alternatives besides a tax cut to close such a gap?**

 Visit www.prenhall.com/ayers for updates and web exercises on this Explore & Apply topic.

SUMMARY AND LEARNING OBJECTIVES

1. **Summarize the perspective of Keynes and Keynesian economics.**
   - Keynesian economics takes a short-run perspective, whereas classical economics emphasizes long-run tendencies and views unemployment as a temporary phenomenon that will be corrected by market forces. In response to the classical contention that unemployment will be corrected by the market, Keynes wrote, "In the long run, we are all dead."

2. **Illustrate the income–expenditure model.**
   - Keynesian economics is portrayed with an income–expenditure model. There are two curves in the income–expenditure graph. The first is a 45-degree line. Since at every point along any 45-degree line the value on one axis equals the value on the other axis, the 45-degree line in the expenditure–equilibrium graph illustrates all points where spending and real GDP are equal. The second curve is the aggregate expenditure function, which shows how much spending is planned at each level of real GDP.
   - An expenditure equilibrium occurs when aggregate planned spending equals real GDP, shown graphically by the intersection of the aggregate expenditure function and the 45-degree line. When real GDP and aggregate planned spending are equal, the economy's output of goods and services are all purchased.

- Planned spending can be autonomous or induced. Autonomous spending is the amount of spending that would occur if people had no incomes. Even if people had no incomes, autonomous spending would be some positive amount because people would spend out of accumulated savings.

- Induced spending is the spending that occurs because people earn incomes. Induced spending is in addition to autonomous spending. The larger one's income, the greater his or her induced spending.

- The aggregate expenditure function sums the four components of aggregate spending: consumption, planned investment, government spending, and net exports (net spending by foreigners).

3. **Explain the adjustment process to an expenditure equilibrium.**

   - An expenditure equilibrium is associated with inventories of goods and services that are neither being drawn down nor built up.

   - Aggregate spending that is less than real GDP causes a recessionary gap. A recessionary gap is associated with unemployment because planned spending is less than production, which results in a buildup of inventories of unsold goods. Producers would cut back production to eliminate an additional buildup of inventories. Production cutbacks typically involve layoffs of workers. Thus, a recessionary gap leads to higher unemployment.

   - An inflationary gap is the opposite of a recessionary gap. An inflationary gap leads to a decrease in inventories. Businesses will increase production in an effort to restore inventories to their desired level.

   - In addition to recognizing the implications of differences between planned and actual investment, Keynesian analysis also points out the significance of various aspects of consumer behavior. The marginal propensity to consume (mpc), which is the fraction of an additional dollar that is spent, plays a key role in the aggregate expenditure function. The maximum value of the mpc is one, indicating that 100 percent of an additional dollar is spent. The minimum value of the mpc is zero, indicating that none is spent. Typically, the value of the mpc for the economy will be somewhere between zero and one.

4. **Describe how new spending can have a ripple effect throughout the economy.**

   - Keynesian economics emphasizes the distinction between saving and spending. Every additional dollar of income must either be spent, or by definition, saved. The fraction of an additional dollar of income that is saved is the marginal propensity to save (mps).

   - The sum of the marginal propensity to consume and the marginal propensity to save must equal 1 [mpc + mps = 1]. The reason is that the fraction of an additional dollar not spent must be saved. For example, if consumers spend ninety cents of each additional dollar of income they receive, they save ten cents by definition. Thus, the mpc = 0.9 and the mps = 0.1.

   - Multiplier effects of spending are an important element of Keynesian economics. Induced spending and autonomous spending both contribute to reaching an expenditure equilibrium. When saving or consuming are consumers' only options, the expenditure multiplier equals 1/mps.

   - The expenditure multiplier assumes there are unemployed resources in the economy. It also assumes a constant price level.

   - Rather than rely upon downward price adjustments, Keynes recommended increased government spending to move the economy to full employment. This spending will spread and, through the multiplier effect, lead to even more spending.

5. **Distinguish the tax multiplier from the balanced-budget multiplier.**

   - The tax multiplier shows the expansionary effect of a tax cut or the contractionary effect of a tax increase on the economy. The tax multiplier will have a value of $-mpc/(1 - mpc)$, which is less than the expenditure multiplier.

   - Combining the expenditure multiplier with the tax multiplier gives a balanced-budget multiplier that equals one. This means that an increase in government spending financed by higher taxes increases equilibrium income by the amount of extra government spending.

   - One objection to Keynesian multiplier analysis is that the tax multiplier ignores how changing taxes changes work and investment incentives. Keynesian multiplier analysis also ignores the crowding-out effect, which occurs when government borrowing reduces funds available for private sector investment.

6. **Graph the relationship of the income–expenditure model to aggregate demand.**

   - The income–expenditure model can be used to derive an aggregate demand curve. A higher price level shifts the aggregate expenditure function downward; a lower price level shifts it upward. The relationship between the price level and the expenditure–equilibrium GDP is plotted in aggregate demand.

■ If the aggregate expenditure function shifts for any reason other than a change in the price level, aggregate demand will shift. The new aggregate demand curve shows the new expenditure equilibrium for the existing price level and for each other possible price level.

 7. Compare economic analyses on the Great Depression.

■ There is disagreement over the cause or causes of the Great Depression. There is also disagreement over the success of Keynesian policy in pulling the country out of that depression. Keynesian analysis models the Great Depression as a severe recessionary gap.

KEY TERMS

income–expenditure model, 254
aggregate expenditures, 254
aggregate expenditure function, 255
expenditure equilibrium, 255
autonomous spending, 255
induced spending, 255

consumption function, 256
marginal propensity to consume (mpc), 257
marginal propensity to save (mps), 257
multiplier effect, 260
expenditure multiplier, 261

unemployment equilibrium, 263
output gap, 263
recessionary gap, 263
inflationary gap, 263
tax multiplier, 265
balanced-budget multiplier, 268

TEST YOURSELF

TRUE OR FALSE

1. John Maynard Keynes offered a long-run perspective on the macroeconomy.
2. If you had no income, you would still engage in autonomous spending.
3. The marginal propensity to consume is normally less than one.
4. An expenditure equilibrium occurs where the aggregate expenditure function intersects the vertical axis.
5. An injection of new autonomous spending will leave equilibrium real GDP unchanged when the marginal propensity to save equals 0.5.

MULTIPLE CHOICE

6. An expenditure equilibrium is
   a. achieved when aggregate demand involves no induced spending.
   b. the level of real GDP the economy tends toward in the short run, at a given price level.
   c. when tax revenue is exactly equal to government spending.
   d. the point where the economy is always at.
7. Suppose actual spending equals planned spending. Then we can say that
   a. the economy is at an expenditure equilibrium.
   b. real GDP is the most it can possibly be.

   c. autonomous spending equals zero.
   d. aggregate demand has shifted to the left.
8. Referring to Self-Test Figure 10-1, point A represents
   a. autonomous spending.
   b. induced spending.
   c. an unemployment equilibrium.
   d. the multiplier effect.

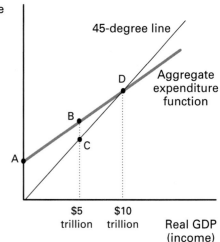

SELF-TEST FIGURE 10-1

9. Referring to Self-Test Figure 10-1, an economy that produces real GDP equal to $5 trillion would have
   a. a recessionary gap equal to $B - C$.
   b. an output gap equal to $B - C$.
   c. an inflationary gap equal to $B - C$.
   d. a drawdown of inventories equal to $B - C$.

10. Referring to Self-Test Figure 10-1, point D represents
    a. full-employment GDP.
    b. an expenditure equilibrium.
    c. induced spending.
    d. the inflationary gap.

11. In the income–expenditure model, the 45-degree line shows
    a. the amount of autonomous spending.
    b. the amount of induced spending.
    c. the expenditure multiplier.
    d. that the economy's income is actually the same as its output.

12. The aggregate expenditure function includes all of the following EXCEPT
    a. consumption.
    b. planned investment.
    c. net exports.
    d. unintended changes in business inventories.

13. The marginal propensity to consume equals
    a. the fraction of total income that people consume.
    b. the fraction of additional income that people consume.
    c. the fraction of savings that people plan to spend within the next year.
    d. one in most cases.

14. The sum of the marginal propensity to consume and the marginal propensity to save equals
    a. the amount of a person's income.
    b. zero.
    c. one.
    d. a value greater than zero, but less than one.

15. The expenditure equilibrium will rise by the increase in _____ _____ multiplied by the expenditure multiplier.
    a. autonomous spending
    b. aggregate demand
    c. induced spending
    d. idle resources

16. To cure a recession, Keynes suggested that the most effective action the government could take would be to
    a. reduce government regulations.
    b. raise wages.
    c. reduce prices.
    d. increase government spending.

17. According to the balanced-budget multiplier, a simultaneous increase of $50 billion in both government spending and taxation would
    a. have no effect.
    b. increase equilibrium output by $50 billion.
    c. decrease equilibrium output by $50 billion.
    d. decrease output by $50 billion multiplied by the crowding-out effect.

18. Crowding out
    a. is what Keynesian economic policies aim to achieve.
    b. occurs if government borrowing increases interest rates.
    c. refers to the effort to move large numbers of people out of poverty with Keynesian policies.
    d. happens every time there is an increase in aggregate demand.

19. The paradox of thrift, if true, suggests that people should
    a. save more.
    b. spend more.
    c. vote more often.
    d. spend the same amount of money, but spend it more wisely.

 20. In Self-Test Figure 10-2, the arrow labeled A represents the
    a. marginal propensity to consume.
    b. amount of inflation that can be expected to close an output gap.
    c. increase in autonomous spending needed to close a recessionary gap.
    d. amount of inflation that can be expected to close an inflationary gap.

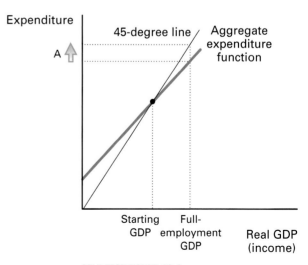

SELF-TEST FIGURE 10-2

QUESTIONS AND PROBLEMS

1. *[Keynesian versus classical perspectives]* "In the long run, we are all dead." Evaluate this quote from a macroeconomic perspective, taking first a classical position and then a Keynesian position.

2. *[income equals output identity]* The circular flow model implies that aggregate national income equals aggregate national output. Review the circular flow model in Chapter 2 and then explain why this implication is present in the model.

3. *[45-degree line]* What role does the 45-degree line play in the model of expenditure equilibrium?

4. *[autonomous and induced spending]* Provide an estimate of your family's autonomous spending. What is your family's approximate actual spending? What is the difference between the actual spending figure and your estimate of autonomous spending called? Why is actual spending different from autonomous spending?

5. *[expenditure equilibrium]* Illustrate graphically an expenditure equilibrium. Be sure to label the axes. Show the amount of autonomous spending, the amount of induced spending, and the point that represents the expenditure equilibrium.

6. *[recessionary gap]* Using the graph you created in the previous question, illustrate and explain the effects of a recessionary gap.

7. *[inflationary gap]* Apply the income–expenditure model to illustrate a situation in which business inventories are being unintentionally depleted. Explain the effects of this inventory depletion within the context of that model.

8. *[mpc and mps]* Explain why the sum of the marginal propensity to consume (mpc) and the marginal propensity to save (mps) must equal one. What value do you estimate your personal mpc to have?

9. *[expenditure multiplier]* What is the formula for the expenditure multiplier? What role does the expenditure multiplier play in the expenditure equilibrium? What assumption does the expenditure multiplier make about the price level?

10. *[expenditure equilibrium]* Suppose the marginal propensity to save is 0.4 and autonomous spending is $1 trillion.
    a. Identify the value of the expenditure equilibrium.
    b. To increase the expenditure equilibrium by $1 trillion, what change in autonomous spending would be needed? Why is this amount less than $1 trillion?

11. *[Keynesian policy]* Why does Keynesian economics view an increase in government spending as a better cure for a recession than a tax cut?

12. *[mps and equilibrium income]* Suppose there is a decrease in the mps. Does Keynesian analysis predict an increase, decrease, or no change in equilibrium income? Explain.

13. *[balanced-budget multiplier]* The balanced-budget multiplier can be shown to equal one. What is the significance of this for the expenditure equilibrium?

14. *[paradox of thrift]* What is the paradox of thrift? Is it relevant to the economy today?

15. *[deriving aggregate demand]* Using two possible price levels, show how aggregate demand can be derived from the income–expenditure diagram. Label the axes and all curves and equilibrium points on both the income–expenditure graph and the aggregate demand graph.

WORKING WITH GRAPHS AND DATA

1. *[income–expenditure model]* Use Graph 10-1 to answer the questions that follow.
   a. What is the equilibrium real GDP of the economy pictured in the following graph?
   b. How much autonomous spending is there in this economy?
   c. How much induced spending is taking place in the economy when it is at its equilibrium?
   d. What portion of income is attributable to induced spending?
   e. What is the marginal propensity to consume (mpc) in this example?
   f. What is the marginal propensity to save (mps) in this example?
   g. What is the expenditure multiplier in this example?

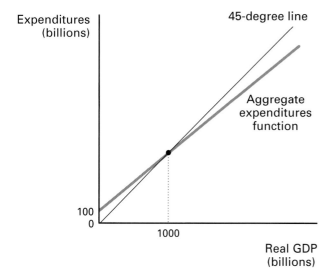

GRAPH 10-1

2. *[income–expenditure model]* Use Graph 10-2 to answer the questions that follow.

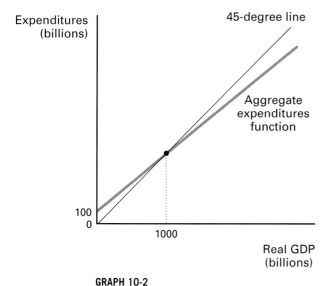

GRAPH 10-2

Suppose that the Federal Government increased government purchases by $50 billion, *ceteris paribus*. Draw a new aggregate expenditures function depicting the new equilibrium GDP of the economy and answer the following questions.

a. What is the equilibrium real GDP of the economy pictured in your new graph?

b. How much autonomous spending is there in this economy?

c. How much induced spending is taking place in the economy when it is at its equilibrium?

d. What portion of income is attributable to induced spending?

e. What is the marginal propensity to consume (mpc) in this example?

f. What is the marginal propensity to save (mps) in this example?

3. *[income–expenditure model]* Use Graph 10-3 to answer the questions that follow.

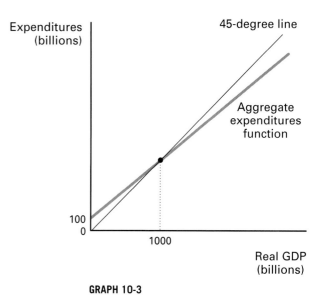

GRAPH 10-3

Suppose that the marginal propensity to consume changes to 0.75, *ceteris paribus*. Draw a new aggregate expenditures function depicting the new equilibrium GDP of the economy and answer the following questions.

a. What is the equilibrium real GDP of the economy pictured in your new graph?

b. How much autonomous spending is there in this economy?

c. How much induced spending is taking place in the economy when it is at its equilibrium?

d. What portion of income is attributable to induced spending?

e. What is the marginal propensity to save (mps) in this example?

f. What is the expenditure multiplier in this example?

4. *[recessionary, inflationary, and output gaps]* Use Graph 10-4 to answer the questions that follow.

   a. Suppose that the economy shown in Graph 10-4 produces at point A, but that full-employment output is a GDP of 250. Identify what type of gaps would exist. (Hint: What is the significance of point Z?)

   b. How large is each gap, respectively?

   c. Now suppose that full-employment output occurs at a GDP of 2000, but the economy only actually produces a GDP of 1000. Identify the types of gaps that would exist under this assumption. (Hint: What is the significance of point X?)

   d. How large is each gap, respectively?

   e. Draw two graphs showing the respective gaps.

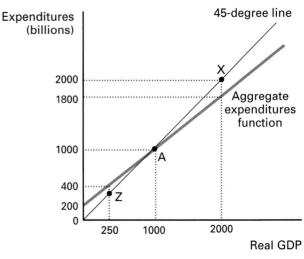

GRAPH 10-4

 Visit www.prenhall.com/ayers for Exploring the Web exercises and additional self-test quizzes.

CHAPTER 11

FISCAL POLICY IN ACTION

A LOOK AHEAD

To take from the rich and to give to the poor was the model of Robin Hood of storybook fame. Some considered him a hero, others thought he was nothing more than a thief. So it is with our system of taxation and income redistribution: We hate to pay but we like to receive. As Winston Churchill put it, "Taxation is the price we pay for living in a free society." However, we do demand a say in what sort of taxes we are expected to pay, as well as the choices our government makes in spending those taxes. Those choices are the subject of this chapter.

One such choice involves how to pay for homeland security. Both government and industry have found themselves facing higher costs to maintain security. The airline industry was particularly hard-hit. Paying for added security in air travel and elsewhere in the economy is the subject of this chapter's Explore & Apply section. We will see that there are repercussions elsewhere in the economy when government picks up the tab for security in air travel or security in any other industry.

LEARNING OBJECTIVES

Understanding Chapter 11 will enable you to:
1. List the major sources of revenue for government in the United States.
2. Explain the principles of tax equity and how they apply to fiscal policy.
3. Interpret why the U.S. income tax is structured as it is, and why critics suggest changing it.
4. Show why workers pay more Social Security tax than they see withdrawn on their pay stubs.
5. Justify the use of consumption taxes, including the value added taxes of Canada and Europe.
6. Discuss issues of market efficiency and tax equity as they relate to security costs.

Explore & Apply

"We acted to come out of that recession. . . . We acted with tax relief."

—President George W. Bush, September 1, 2003

In his 2004 reelection campaign, President Bush has highlighted his fiscal policy as a central achievement of his administration. This fiscal policy has revolved around cutting taxes in order to stimulate spending and economic growth. It involved the nuts and bolts of addressing the specifics of the tax and spending changes. As we will see in this chapter, the specifics of fiscal policy hit home when we pay our taxes in April and when we contemplate how much to work and how much to play. The details involve incentives for efficiency and effects on equity, the two overriding economic goals we discussed in Chapter 1. Effects on efficiency and equity can differ significantly among policy options, even if the tax and spending totals are the same.

11.1 POLICY IN PRACTICE

"In this world nothing can be said to be certain, except death and taxes."

—Benjamin Franklin

Few things are less popular than taxes, since taxes represent money that is taken from us involuntarily by the government. However, we all like to be the recipients of government spending. If we live in the U.S. economy, with its large variety of both taxes and government activities, we are likely to see both.

SPENDING AND TAXATION

Government spending in the United States encompasses a vast array of programs. Some of these programs go toward the purchase of goods and services, such as highways or national defense. Others are regulatory programs, such as those conducted by the Occupational Safety and Health Administration or the Environmental Protection Agency. In addition, a large fraction of government spending goes toward **transfer payments** that redistribute income from one group to another. Transfer payments include unemployment compensation, welfare, and other *safety-net programs* that provide economic security. Transfer payments account for approximately 44 percent of total federal spending. Figure 11-1 shows the growth in transfer payments and other components of federal spending over time.

transfer payments the redistribution of income from one group to another.

Because taxes take roughly 30 percent of gross domestic product (GDP), taxpayers are acutely concerned that they not be taken advantage of—in other words, that all pay their fair share. This is the goal of equity. Because taxes can discourage work effort and investment, a second goal in taxation is efficiency. **To achieve efficiency, taxes that are intended to raise revenues should do so in a manner that affects our behavior the least.** Efficiency in taxation gives citizens the greatest possible incentive to be productive.

The personal income tax is the single largest source, providing 46 percent of all revenues. As U.S. citizens accumulate income over the course of the year, the federal personal income tax claims those earnings at incremental rates that increase from 10 percent to 15 percent, to 25 percent, to 28 percent, to 33 percent, and to 35 percent. This incremental tax rate on incremental income is known as the **marginal tax rate,** which equals 25 percent for most American taxpayers.

marginal tax rate the percentage of incremental income that is taken by the federal income tax.

Marginal tax rate = Change in tax payment ÷ change in income

In other words, the average citizen pays twenty-five cents to the IRS on each additional dollar he or she earns. Marginal tax rates are shown in Table 11-1. Note that the marginal tax

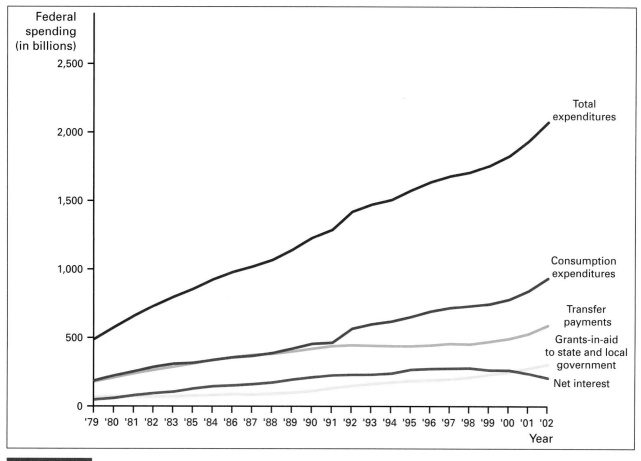

FIGURE 11-1

FEDERAL SPENDING Spending by the federal government has grown rapidly over the last century, especially spending on transfer payments, interest on the national debt, and grants-in-aid from the federal to state and local governments. Slightly more than half of federal purchases are related to national defense.

Source: 2003 Economic Report of the President, Table B-84.

TABLE 11-1 MARGINAL PERSONAL INCOME TAX RATES FOR SINGLES, FOR TAXES DUE APRIL 15, 2004

TAX RATE	TAXABLE INCOME
10%	up to $7,000
15%	$7,001–$28,400
25%	$28,401–$68,800
28%	$68,801–$143,500
33%	$143,501–$311,950
35%	$311,951 or more

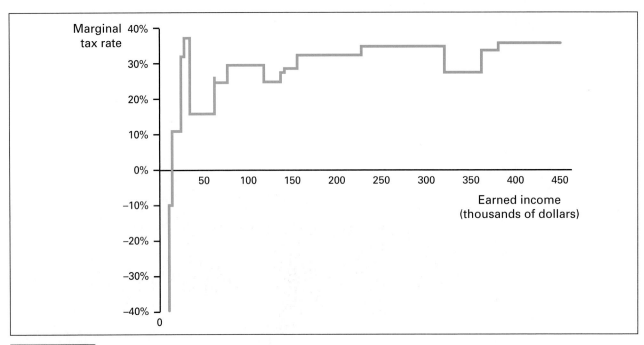

FIGURE 11-2

TAX RATE COMPLEXITIES When people compute actual taxes, complexities arise that distort marginal tax rates away from the schedule shown in Table 11-1. In this example, the tax return is for a single parent of two dependent children, with special circumstances as described in the accompanying text. Circumstances vary by individual, but often result in highly complex tax computations.
Source: Institute for Research on the Economics of Taxation, 2003.

rate differs from the *average tax rate,* which equals a person's total tax liability divided by total income at the end of the year.

$$\text{Average tax rate} = \text{Total taxes owed as a percentage of total income}$$

The amount of income withheld from your paycheck is based on your projected average tax liability.

Applying marginal tax rates in practice can get complicated, because there are exclusions, deductions, phase-ins of some benefits, and phase-outs of other benefits. For example, consider taxpayer Fay, a single mother with two teenage children: Freda and Philo. Fay earns labor income, but she does not save. Because daughter Freda required substantial healthcare, Fay incurred $4,500 of medical bills last year. Suppose that Fay's itemized deductions, excluding medical, are 20 percent of her adjusted gross income (AGI), that her deductible state and local taxes are 5 percent of her AGI, and that she chooses the greater of itemized deductions or the standard deduction. Figure 11-2 shows Fay's marginal tax rate at various income levels.

As you can see, the tax return becomes complex, which is the point of the illustration. Initially Fay's marginal income tax rate was −40 percent due to the phase-in of the Earned Income Tax Credit (EITC), which begins on the first dollar earned and maxes out at about $4,200 for an income of about $10,500. At about that point, the EITC hits its plateau and the child credit becomes refundable (paid by the government even if no taxes are due from the taxpayer), which accounts for a stretch where Fay's effective marginal tax rate is −10 percent. The next stretch, where her marginal tax rate is 11.06 percent, is due to the child credit phasing in at a 10 percent rate while her EITC phases out at a 21.06 percent rate. At

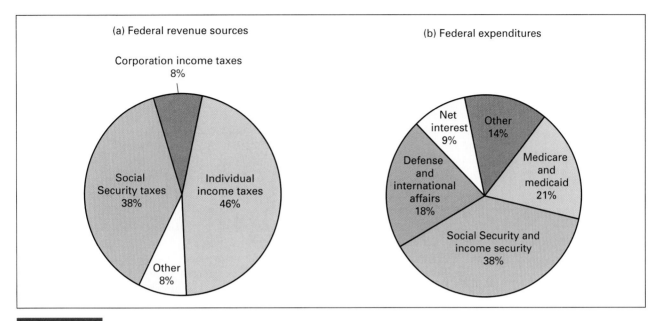

FIGURE 11-3

FEDERAL REVENUE SOURCES AND EXPENDITURES Individual income taxes and Social Security taxes are the most important sources of revenue for the federal government. Together, as shown in part (a), they account for 84 percent of federal tax revenue. On the expenditures side, as shown in part (b), 38% of federal spending goes toward Social Security and income security. At 21% of total federal spending, healthcare is becoming an increasingly prominent component of the federal budget. Another 18% of the budget is taken by spending on national defense and international affairs.

Source: 2003 Economic Report of the President, computed from Table B–80. The data are for 2002.

an income of about $23,500, her effective marginal rate jumps to 31.81 percent because the child credit is fully phased in, the regular income tax kicks in at a 10 percent rate, the EITC is still being phased out, and each extra dollar of income reduces the medical deduction she can claim. These are just a few of the complications of applying the simple marginal tax rates in Table 11-1 to the reality of benefit phase-ins and phase-outs. We might mention that, were she to earn between $155,000 and $365,000 of income, Fay would also need to factor in the alternative minimum tax, which is designed to keep rich people paying a significant portion of their income in taxes.[1]

Figure 11-3 illustrates the relative importance of revenue sources for the U.S. federal government. As seen in Figure 11-3(a), Social Security taxes, inclusive of the hospitalization portion of *Medicare*—health insurance for the elderly—account for 38 percent of federal revenues, second only to the share of the personal income tax. The Social Security tax is a *payroll tax,* in which the government deducts a flat 7.65 percent from the amount of money the employer pays, plus another 7.65 percent from the amount of money the employee receives. Taken together, the Social Security tax collects 15.3 percent of a worker's payroll income, up to a maximum individual income of $84,900 in 2002, after which only the 2.9 percent Medicare hospitalization tax continues to be collected.

Figure 11-3(b) shows how the taxes collected are spent. The largest category of spending is on Social Security and other forms of income security. Other federal spending goes to pay for national defense, pay the interest on the national debt, and provide healthcare.

---

[1]We would like to thank Michael Schuyler of the Institute for Research on the Economics of Taxation for this example.

With the corporation income tax, government takes approximately 30 percent of corporate profits. The corporation income tax brought in revenues of $149 billion in 2002, which equalled about 8 percent of total federal revenues. The corporation income tax has proven to be quite controversial over time because, while it may seem fair to tax corporations as though they are people, the **tax incidence** of the corporation income tax—meaning who ultimately winds up paying the tax—is on real people who directly or indirectly own the corporations and who also pay personal income taxes or other taxes relating to that ownership.

tax incidence identifies those who eventually wind up paying a tax.

Additional taxes are assessed by states and localities. Most states rely heavily on a combination of individual income taxes, sales taxes, revenue from the federal government, and other charges. The two most important sources of revenue at the local level are property taxes and sales taxes. States have to be careful not to tax any one source of revenue much more heavily than do other states, or that revenue source will migrate to the less-taxing state. This problem plagued New York in the 1960s and 1970s, as the poor moved in to receive generous welfare benefits, while many of the wealthy moved away to avoid paying the high income taxes that financed those benefits.

When all the revenues received by all units of government are added together, the result is that **government revenues in the United States are over 30 percent of the value of production.** Another way of looking at this is that the average American must work until "Tax Freedom Day" each year—which will occur in late April of 2004—in order to have enough money to pay the government.

QUICKCHECK

What is the difference between the average tax rate and the marginal tax rate? Why is the marginal tax rate more likely to influence your decision about how much to work?

Answer: The average tax rate divides your total taxes into your total income. The marginal rate is the amount of taxes taken out of the last dollar that you earn, and would directly affect the pay you receive for working one more or one less hour.

EVALUATING EQUITY

Taxes are used to redistribute income from the haves to the have-nots, and in the process remedy some of the inequities that arise in a free-market economy. People's views on equity vary widely, however, which means that issues of equity in taxation—*tax equity*—become a matter of hot debate. Some basic principles can help frame this debate. The two most fundamental principles of tax equity are as follows:

benefit principle states that a fair tax is one that taxes people in proportion to the benefits they receive when government spends those tax revenues.

ability-to-pay principle states that those who can afford to pay more taxes than others should be required to do so.

- The **benefit principle** states that a fair tax is one that taxes people in proportion to the benefits they receive when government spends the tax revenues.
- The **ability-to-pay principle** states that those who can afford to pay more taxes than others should be required to do so.

The gasoline tax would appear to satisfy the benefit principle of tax equity, because gasoline tax revenues are *earmarked* for—restricted to—highway construction and repair. The more someone drives, the more government-funded highways the person drives on, and the more gasoline tax the person pays. In general, *user fees* are designed to meet the benefit principle of tax equity.

The benefit principle cannot be applied to programs whose purpose is to redistribute income. To see why not, consider food stamps (like money but only spendable on food). According to the benefit principle, food stamp recipients should pay for the cost of those food stamps. However, this would have the effect of defeating the fundamental purpose of the food stamp program, which is to help those in need. Food stamps are of no help if you have to pay for them! Thus, to justify redistributional programs, a different principle of tax equity is invoked—the ability-to-pay principle. The idea of the ability-to-pay principle is that the more a person is able to pay, the more that person should pay.

Many people interpret the ability-to-pay principle to mean that taxes designed for redistributing income should be progressive. A **progressive tax** collects a higher percentage of high incomes than of low incomes. In contrast, a **regressive tax** collects a higher percentage of low incomes than of high incomes. A **proportional tax** collects the same percentage of income, no matter what the income is. A *flat tax* that taxes all income at the same tax rate would be proportional. In practice, proposals for a so-called flat tax almost always provide for some exemptions that make the tax progressive overall.

The key here is percentage. A tax that collects $1,000 from a poor person earning $10,000 and $10,000 from a rich person earning $1 million is regressive, because the poor person pays 10 percent of his or her income, whereas the rich person pays only 1 percent.

Sometimes it is hard to determine whether or not a tax is progressive. For instance, consider the Social Security tax, which is defined broadly to include the Medicare tax. The Social Security tax may be considered either proportional, regressive, or progressive, depending on which aspects of the system are under scrutiny. Up to the 2002 limit of $84,900 of payroll income received, the tax is proportional at 15.3 percent. Because the marginal payroll tax rate beyond that point drops to only 2.9 percent (the Medicare component), the average tax rate declines with income and the overall tax is regressive. However, if Social Security benefits are included along with the taxes, the Social Security system as a whole is highly progressive, as will be discussed in more detail later in this chapter.

> **progressive tax** a tax that collects a higher percentage of high incomes than of low incomes.
>
> **regressive tax** a tax that collects a higher percentage of low incomes than of high incomes.
>
> **proportional tax** a tax that collects the same percentage of high incomes as of low incomes.

PROGRESSIVE—WHAT'S IN A WORD?   *SNAPSHOT*

The terms *progressive* and *regressive* are loaded—they make an implicit normative judgment about what is good and bad. After all, who could argue against progress? Would you prefer to regress? That would be moving backward, not forward. Bear in mind, though, that there is nothing magical about the terms.

The ability-to-pay principle of equity says that, to finance government, the rich should pay more than the poor. It does not specify whether the higher taxes should be less than, more than, or exactly in proportion to the higher income. For instance, it would make life simpler if we had one flat-rate income tax, with no exemptions, deductions, exclusions, and so on. Such a tax would be proportional, but would it be fair? That judgment is entirely up to you. ◀

TRADING OFF EFFICIENCY AND EQUITY

Economic efficiency involves getting the most valuable output from the inputs available. It bakes the biggest economic pie. In general, taxes are efficient to the extent that they do not change our behavior, with the most efficient tax being the one we cannot influence or escape.

QUICKCHECK

If your tax bill rises as your income rises, does that mean the tax is progressive?

Answer: Not necessarily. For the tax to be progressive, it must not only collect more revenue from you as your income rises, but it must also take a higher fraction of your total income.

To see how taxes cause inefficiency, consider an increase in the income tax. Some workers, especially those who are not heads of households, would cut back their work efforts. Even those who do not cut back would find that getting ahead in the workplace would bring less reward. For this reason, people are less likely to invest their time and money to acquire more human capital. Corporate income taxes mean that businesses also don't invest as much, either, because the corporation income tax cuts down on the return to that investment.

For an efficient tax, we can turn to the *head tax*. In short, if you have a head, you pay the tax! Since head taxes are efficient and require virtually no paperwork, should all of our other taxes be replaced by head taxes? You probably see the problem. While the economic pie would be large, most of us would consider it to be sliced very unfairly. In other words, head taxes would not be equitable.

in-kind benefits a government-provided good or service, as opposed to cash.

Not only are tax laws written with an eye toward equity, but government spending is often targeted toward promoting equity directly through provision of a social safety net. This safety net targets the needy with both cash transfers and **in-kind benefits,** which are any benefits other than money. Social Security is far and away the largest cash transfer program, redirecting a significant amount of current earnings to current retirees. The largest in-kind program is Medicaid, which provides health insurance for the impoverished.

A tradeoff between efficiency and equity pervades our system of tax and spending programs. Ideally, to provide a broad and generous safety net, the government might guarantee good housing, good food, and good health insurance for everyone. The better the guarantees, however, the more the programs will cost and the less the incentives will be to work and invest. There are three reasons for this inefficient reduction in work incentives, as follows:

■ There is less need to better yourself to the extent that the government guarantees you a comfortable lifestyle. As the saying goes, necessity is the mother of invention.
■ If you choose to forge ahead anyway, your greater ability to take care of yourself causes you to lose eligibility for many welfare-type programs. Over some ranges of income, the loss of benefits from Medicaid, subsidized housing, food stamps, and other welfare programs more than offsets the value of extra income earned.
■ Obtaining the money for safety-net programs requires the government to either tax or borrow, which would need to be repaid from future tax revenue. With taxes comes less incentive to work and invest.

We could eliminate the second problem if we offer eligibility to everyone, regardless of income. However, that policy would accentuate the third problem.

There is no ready answer to the dilemma of choosing between a generous safety net and incentives for economic productivity. This is an area of seemingly endless political debate and compromise. We don't want the income tax burden to be so high that our economy stagnates because we have little to gain personally by being productive. However, our economy can afford to provide some degree of economic security for those in need. Choices of this sort are why policymakers face what has been called *the big tradeoff* between efficiency and equity in the design of government tax and spending programs.

11.2 SOCIAL SECURITY

Social Security is far and away the government's largest program, with the Social Security tax alone accounting for more than a third of Federal revenue, as was shown in Figure 11-2. For this reason, we use Social Security as our focus to examine the issues that arise in fiscal policy.

Social Security collects taxes on all payroll income, and allots the proceeds for *OASDI* and *HI,* which stand for old age, survivors, and disability insurance, and hospitalization

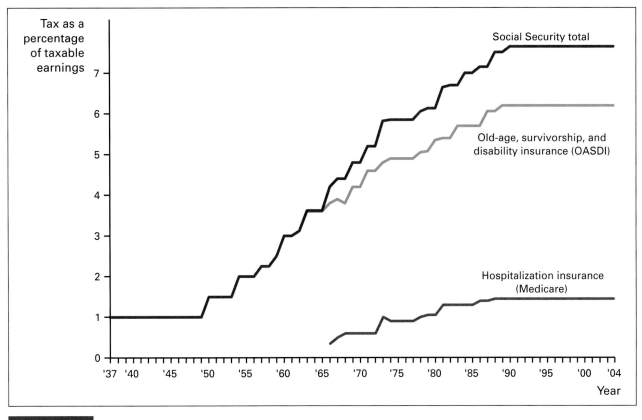

FIGURE 11-4

SOCIAL SECURITY TAX RATES OVER TIME Social Security rates are shown as a percentage of taxable earnings. Rates apply to both employees and employers, so that the total tax rates are double those shown. Hospitalization insurance is more commonly known as Medicare.

Source: U.S. Social Security Administration.

insurance, respectively. The hospitalization portion is more commonly known as Medicare. The combined employer and employee Social Security tax rate is 15.3 percent of the first $84,900 of that income as of 2002, where the threshold has been adjusted upward over time in response to wage inflation. For income over that threshold, the Social Security tax is eliminated except for the 2.9 percent Medicare component. The rates have risen over time, as shown in Figure 11-4.

Turning to Social Security's impact on wages, consider Figure 11-5, which illustrates the economy's supply and demand for labor. The sellers are the people who offer labor; the buyers are firms. The supply of labor is shown as a vertical line because the quantity of labor supplied depends primarily on the natural rate of unemployment rather than on the specifics of tax policy. The portion of the Social Security tax paid by employers reduces their after-tax demand for labor by the same percentage as the tax, since the value of labor to the firm is reduced by the amount of tax that must be paid for that labor. This reduction is shown in the figure by a downward shift in labor demand, a shift that is just sufficient to cover Social Security taxes.

As seen in Figure 11-5, requiring the firm to pay Social Security taxes causes the equilibrium wage to be lower by exactly the amount of the tax. In effect, the tax burden has been *shifted* from employers to employees. The result is that workers effectively pay the full 15.3 percent Social Security tax. Many employees are unaware of the true magnitude of the Social Security tax, because only half of the combined 15.3 percent rate appears on their pay stubs.

FIGURE 11-5

EFFECT OF SOCIAL SECURITY TAX ON WAGES The employer share of the Social Security tax is passed on to workers in the form of lower wages. The market-equilibrium wage rate falls by 7.65 percent as firms' willingness to pay for workers falls by 7.65 percent in response to the employers' 7.65 percent share of the Social Security tax.

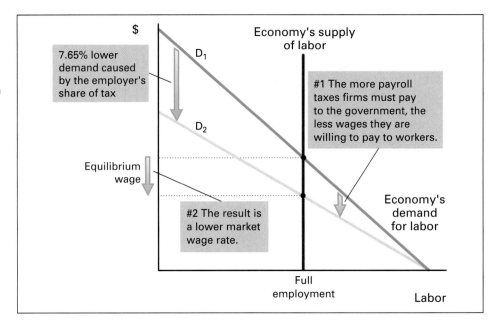

INCOME REDISTRIBUTION—NOT JUST FOR EQUITY

pay-as-you-go referring to Social Security, meaning that current workers pay for current retirees.

Social Security is primarily **pay-as-you-go,** meaning that current workers pay for people who are currently retired. In this way, **Social Security redistributes income from one generation to another.** This redistribution started off in a small way. When Social Security was first established in 1935, the first pension was not planned to begin until 1942. The Social Security program plays an important part in providing for families, children, and older persons in times of stress. But it cannot remain static. Changes in our population, in working habits, and in our standard of living require constant revision. The tax rate was initially set to reach only 5 percent in total, with 2½ percent levied on the pay of workers and another 2½ percent on the employers doing the paying. In contrast, the current combined tax rate is 15.3 percent.

In 1945, the ratio of workers to retirees was about 50 to 1. It is currently about 3 to 1, and predicted to drop to only about 2 to 1 by 2030. Therefore, the burden on workers rises. To keep benefits constant, the Social Security Administration estimates that, by 2034, the tax rate would need to rise to almost 21 percent (18 percent, excluding Medicare). Without a tax increase, benefits would need to fall to three-fourths of their current amount.

Social Security also redistributes income within generations. The ratio of payments to retirees relative to the amount they contributed in their working years is much higher for the low income than for the high income. Payments are also adjusted on the basis of need, which is determined in part by the number of dependents a person has. Thus, even though the Social Security tax took out the same portion of each person's income when he or she was working, the percentage that Social Security gives back is much higher for the poor.

On an after-tax basis, Social Security may even pay the retired low-income worker more than he or she earned when working. A worker at the maximum income subject to Social Security tax, in contrast, is likely to receive only about 30 percent as much as when employed. The upshot is that, when Social Security taxes and payments are combined, the Social Security system is highly progressive. Low-income workers have money redistributed their way from the tax dollars paid by higher-income workers.

The redistribution from higher-income workers to lower-income workers is one reason participation in Social Security is required by law. If it were optional, workers with above-average incomes would quit, leaving no money to redistribute. Workers would also be

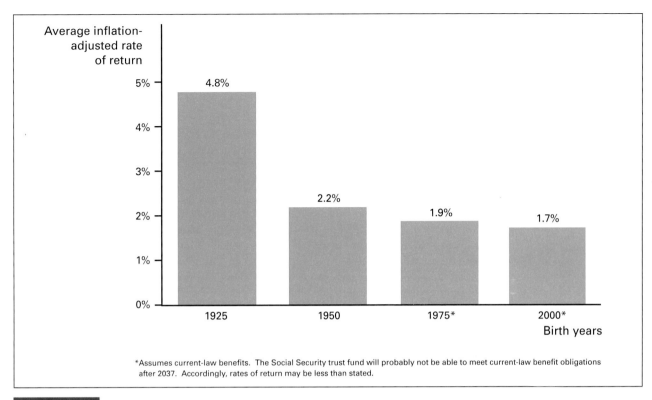

*Assumes current-law benefits. The Social Security trust fund will probably not be able to meet current-law benefit obligations after 2037. Accordingly, rates of return may be less than stated.

FIGURE 11-6

RETURNS FROM SOCIAL SECURITY The rate of return from Social Security has fallen from generation to generation. Those born in 2000 can expect the rate of return on the Social Security contributions they make during their lifetime to be nearly 1.7 percent, according to government estimates.

Source: June 2002, http://www.whitehouse.gov/infocus/social-security/.

deterred from joining voluntarily by intergenerational redistribution, which gives current retirees a much better deal than can be expected by current workers.

If the present structure of Social Security were to be offered by any private business, the owners of that business would be prosecuted for fraud for running an illegal *ponzi scheme,* in which the money from current investors is used to finance paybacks to longer-term investors. Ponzi schemes are very risky; if new investors ever stop coming, the most recent investors lose their money.

Social Security has a significant advantage over the typical ponzi scheme, however. New investors are forced into the system by the government and its power to tax. However, if the government changes its mind down the road, investors who have yet to receive a payback could lose out. Even if Social Security were fully financed, though, the low returns it offers would dissuade potential investors. Figure 11-6 illustrates these returns. Note that the return to those born in early years greatly exceeds the return to those born in later years.

A TRUST FUND OF IOUS

There is a **Social Security trust fund,** which is the depository for Social Security tax revenues. The trust fund is currently building up because tax revenues exceed Social Security payouts. However, the size of that trust fund pales in comparison to the expected future demands against it. Moreover, all savings held in the Social Security trust fund take the form

Social Security trust fund the buildup of Social Security tax revenues above what is paid out in benefits; kept in the form of government bonds.

of special government bonds. Since a bond is merely a promise to pay in the future, savings within the Social Security trust fund are nothing more than government IOUs.

To pay those IOUs, the government must either create extra money or collect extra tax dollars in the future. Either way, future taxpayers pay. If the government creates new money, taxpayers pay the tax of inflation that eats away the value of their earnings. Otherwise, the trust fund bonds would be redeemed out of general tax revenues, which would require higher personal income taxes or other general taxes. Even if the Social Security trust fund were to stack a warehouse full of its special government bonds, it would still be up to future taxpayers to pay them off. Thus, for the economy as a whole, balances in the Social Security trust fund are not in themselves real savings.

Social Security also reduces private savings to the extent that people expect to receive Social Security checks in the future. Workers substitute the government's promises for their own savings. Moreover, because the Social Security tax reduces take-home pay, current workers have less money that could be saved. The reduction in the national saving rate because of Social Security means there is less money for investment, and thus less economic growth, as will be discussed in the next chapter. The result is that, when current workers retire, the economic capacity of the country to support them will be smaller than if Social Security never existed in the first place.

For the Social Security trust fund to represent real savings, it must generate real capital that will increase the country's production possibilities in years to come. This could come about either directly through investment in capital or indirectly through a paydown in other government debt. If tax inflows into Social Security are greater than the payment outflows, the surplus that is used to buy federal bonds could in turn be used by the Treasury to buy back its other bonds and thereby reduce the national debt. A lower national debt would reduce the crowding-out effect and make room for greater private investment that increases the economy's productive capacity. When Social Security reaches a point where it must cash in its government bonds and draw down its trust fund, the federal government could then increase federal debt once more. In the interim, though, the economy would have grown to be better able to support that debt. That is the ideal situation, but one that is politically difficult to implement. Instead, we are faced with a continuing Social Security budget surplus that is more than used up by other government spending. As a result we see an overall federal deficit that is projected to continue.

Rather than use the trust fund to pay down other government debt, the federal government might directly invest the Social Security trust fund in the production of real capital. It could take one of two routes:

- The **government could produce the necessary capital itself.** Government production may be justified to the extent that the needed investment applies to the provision of public goods, such as highway infrastructure needed for smoothly flowing traffic. Beyond this, however, direct government investment would lead the economy in the direction of command and control.
- The **government could invest the money in the marketplace, perhaps establishing or designating mutual funds to buy stock in private companies.**

In either case, the danger is that the investments would move the economy toward inefficient central planning and be allocated to firms based on politics rather than economic merit.

The amounts in question are not inconsequential. For the Social Security trust fund to be **fully funded**—able to pay off all its future obligations without recourse to future taxation—it would need to own well over a year's worth of GDP. In other words, the buildup of savings in the Social Security trust fund would need to greatly expand the country's current productive capacity for that savings to be real in a macroeconomic sense. Having the government take over such a large part of the economy's ownership of capital would not be capitalism as we know it in the United States.

fully funded the idea of having enough revenue in the Social Security trust fund to be able to pay off all obligations to current workers without recourse to taxing future workers.

Most people consider investing in government bonds to be very secure. Yet, the Social Security trust fund's investment in government bonds is a source of insecurity. Explain.

Answer: At a personal, microeconomic level, government bonds are very secure because they are backed by the full faith and credit of the government. They will be repaid. When it comes to the macroeconomy, however, the bonds do not represent real savings because they are just IOUs that must be repaid by future taxpayers. They do not add to the productive capacity of the economy directly.

SUPPLEMENTING SOCIAL SECURITY

Individuals do save for their own retirement. **Individual retirement accounts (IRAs)** promote that saving by allowing a limited amount of tax-free or tax-prepaid contributions, the latter termed _Roth IRA_. The contribution limit in 2003 is $3,000, which is scheduled to rise to $4,000 in 2005. The government has been reluctant to increase that limit very much, because any increase in tax-free savings would deplete current tax revenues. The government has also been content to accumulate bonds in the Social Security trust fund, because the special Social Security bonds that the Social Security Trustees buy from the Federal Treasury mean that any extra money collected by Social Security taxes are transferred into general government revenues that can be spent wherever the government chooses.

If the government wants to promote private saving, its options include:

- Increasing or eliminating the contribution cap on IRAs.
- Eliminating the taxation of income that is saved.
- Requiring that individuals save some fraction of their earnings for their own retirement.

The third option has led to proposals for **Personal Security Accounts,** which would be retirement accounts financed by a payroll tax, but that would be under the individual's own control and ownership. **Personal Security Accounts could only supplement, not replace, Social Security as it now stands,** for three reasons:

- **Social Security depends on current workers to support current retirees.** With Personal Security Accounts, workers are saving to support themselves.
- **Social Security redistributes income from wealthier workers to poorer ones.** With Personal Security Accounts, workers keep their own savings.
- **Personal Security Accounts are riskier, with workers making their own investment choices.** They would still need a Social Security fallback in case their personal investment choices lose their value.

While politically contentious, proposals for Personal Security Accounts have been looked on favorably by American presidents of both political parties. President Bill Clinton even included the idea in his 1999 State of the Union address. Workers who get to keep control of their own savings might be more inclined to accept the double tax of paying for current retirees and also building up savings for their own retirement. Such an approach has the economic advantage of maintaining a free-market allocation of investment. Companies that offer mutual funds and other forms of investment would compete for savings, and the winners would be those companies that offer the best services and investments.

individual retirement accounts (IRAs) tax-free savings accounts earmarked for retirement income.

Personal Security Accounts retirement accounts individuals own, but that they are forced to contribute to by the government.

SNAPSHOT   THE OLD WORLD, GROWING OLDER

If the United States thinks that it faces trouble with Social Security, it should just look across the Atlantic Ocean. A recent study by demographer William Frey of the Brookings Institution projects that the median age in Europe in 2050 will be 52.3 years old, over 14 years higher than the current European median age of 37.7. In contrast, Frey estimates the median age in the United States will rise only slightly, to 35.4 years old. Austrian economist Erich Streissler suggests that, to be realistic about its Social Security needs, Europeans would need to keep working until they are 80. That would be quite a shocker to Europeans who have grown accustomed to retiring at age 55. The Organization for Economic Cooperation and Development estimates that, today, fewer than 40 percent of Europeans between the ages of 55 and 65 continue to work.

The pressures are mounting for change. In France, after two weeks of a heat wave that was responsible for the deaths of over 11,000 elderly people in August, 2003, Prime Minister Jean-Pierre Rafarin proposed that French workers work an extra day each year with all proceeds going to finance care for the aged. With the French workweek limited to thirty-five hours, and with eleven public holidays and five full weeks of vacation per year also mandated by law, the French public appear willing to make that one sacrifice. However, workers in France, Germany, Austria, and elsewhere have made it clear that they are not about to go much further than that. In the words of Karlheinz Nachtnebel of the Austrian Trade Union Federation, following a general strike in that country, "The European social model is at stake and it has to be defended." ◀

11.3 TAX REFORM

The debate over Social Security taxes is a microcosm of the debate over taxes in general. It seems like nearly every year there is a move afoot to reform our taxes. Perhaps this is because taxes are always a compromise. Those who pay want to pay less. Those on the receiving end want to receive more. Within the give and take of the political process, though, the economic goals of efficiency and equity are treated with considerable respect by legislators interested in the country's prosperity.

A tax is efficient only if it does not *distort* relative prices within the economy, since price signals are what allocate resources to their highest-valued uses. By taxing all income equally, distortions are minimized. Efficiency thus calls for a *broadly based tax,* meaning one that it is difficult to escape, where the **tax base** refers to that which is taxed. **It is less disruptive to the workings of the economy to tax as wide a spectrum of income or consumption as possible at a low rate, rather than to single out a few things for especially high rates of taxation.** By spreading taxes broadly, people have few ways to escape them and not as much incentive to try; inefficient changes in behavior are kept to a minimum. Much of the complexity of the current income tax code stems from innumerable provisions that remove income from taxation, thus narrowing the tax base.

tax base that which is taxed.

IMPROVING THE INCOME TAX

The ability-to-pay principle of equity suggests that some income should be taxed more than other income, depending on how needy the person is. Exempting low incomes concentrates the tax base and leads to inefficiencies. Thus, the personal income tax is a compromise between efficiency and equity. Unfortunately, the compromise accomplishes neither goal fully and is also complicated.

There are many alternatives to the particular set of taxes chosen in the United States. For example, some have suggested that the United States should adjust its income tax to become a **consumed-income tax,** in which dollars that are saved would not be counted as income when the tax is applied. The consumed-income tax would remove the bias against saving that is present in a more general income tax, which taxes money when it is earned and also taxes

consumed-income tax an income tax that does not tax income that is saved.

interest on that money when it is saved. The flip side is that, although a consumed-income tax would promote savings, some people view it as a tax deduction for the rich and not for the poor, because the ability to save rises sharply with income.

CONSUMPTION TAXES—FIRST CHOICE AROUND THE WORLD

Most of us are familiar with state or local *sales taxes* that collect a percentage of the prices consumers pay. Sales taxes are one form of **consumption tax,** which takes money as you spend it rather than as you earn it. This tax gives people a greater incentive to save, and may be partly responsible for the higher saving rates in other countries relative to the United States. Most countries of the world, including Canada and the countries of Europe and the Far East, rely much more heavily on consumption taxes as a source of public revenues than does the United States.

consumption tax a tax on spending rather than on income.

The most common form of consumption tax in other countries is the **value added tax (VAT).** A VAT collects the difference between what companies earn in revenues and previously taxed costs, which would mostly be the cost of material inputs. For example, the wheat farmer would pay a tax on the difference between revenues from the sale of the crop and the costs of fertilizer and other materials used to grow it. Taxing value added yields the same tax revenues as a retail sales tax set at the same rate, since the price of a final product is nothing more than the sum of the values added. Some advocate that the United States adopt the VAT as a means of promoting increased national saving. Others point out that it could help resolve trade disputes with Europe, which has complained that its industries must compete with tax-free U.S. exports. Two recent rulings from the World Trade Organization support that claim.

value added tax (VAT) a form of consumption tax that collects the difference between what companies earn in revenues and their previously taxed costs.

Just as with the income tax, value added taxes and sales taxes should be broadly based in order to achieve efficiency. Singling out some goods to tax while leaving others untaxed would distort choices away from the more highly taxed goods, since taxing sales in an industry shifts its supply curve, as shown in Figure 11-7. The tax will add an additional marginal cost of sales, which will shift the supply curve up by the percentage at which the tax rate is set. Tax revenues will equal the quantity of output multiplied by the amount of tax per unit, determined by the market equilibrium with the tax in place. The area of these tax revenues is labeled in the figure.

In Figure 11-7(a), the tax is assessed only on one good and not on substitutes for that good. In Figure 11-7(b), the tax is assessed on the same good and also on substitutes for the good. The difference is that demand will be steeper in (b), because consumers are unable to avoid the tax by buying untaxed substitutes for the good. The result is that the broadly based tax shown in (b) will be less distorting to consumer choice and therefore more efficient. It will also bring in more revenue because there is a greater quantity of output sold.

E-COMMERCE—A TAXING QUESTION

SNAPSHOT

Go to the store and pay sales tax; go on-line and skip it! Such has been the practice throughout the forty-seven states that impose sales taxes. To some it seems fair and reasonable. They say, "Let the Internet stay tax free!" To others, requiring shippers to pay sales tax for items shipped out of state is just too complex.

New taxes are never popular. Consumers enjoy buying tax-free items over the Internet, and do not take kindly to a tax that causes these items to cost more. Nonetheless, tax revenue must come from somewhere. Broadening the tax base by taxing e-commerce would allow lower sales tax rates overall without changing the amount that government collects in total. Maybe consumers just don't think that those tax cuts would happen!

As for complexity, modern database software should be able to handle it with ease. If a significant number of companies were required to charge taxes that varied from locality to locality and from state to state, you can bet that profit-seeking software makers would be eager to help out. So don't be too surprised to see a tax on e-commerce, even though nobody likes a tax. ◄

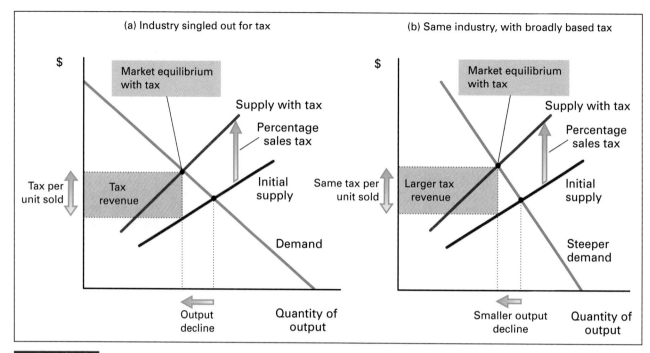

FIGURE 11-7

THE TAX BASE AND TAX REVENUE Taxes should usually be broadly based in order to be efficient. Graph (a) depicts an industry that is singled out for a sales tax. Supply in that industry is reduced, as the new supply curve appears higher by the amount of the sales tax percentage. The resulting equilibrium occurs at a new lower quantity and a higher price, inclusive of the tax. Tax revenue equals the tax per unit sold at the new market equilibrium multiplied by the new equilibrium quantity, as labeled by the shaded rectangle.

Graph (b) shows the exact same thing, with one difference: substitutes for the product are also taxed, which means that demand is steeper because consumers are less able to shift away from the taxed good. Therefore, the quantity purchased does not fall as much and tax revenue is consequently somewhat more. Because the broadly based tax causes less change in behavior, it is more efficient.

11.4 PAYING FOR HOMELAND SECURITY

Airplanes, buildings, oil pipelines, water supplies, nuclear power plants, letters in the mail—the list of potential terrorist targets is seemingly endless. Defending these points of vulnerability can potentially be accomplished in many different ways. Who is to pay for all these security measures?

Three possibilities suggest themselves:

1. **Use general tax revenues,** such as the $37.6 billion of financing budgeted in 2004 for the Department of Homeland Security.
2. **Levy taxes on specific industries** for which the federal government provides security. For example, air travelers are assessed a surcharge to help defray the expenses of federally provided airport security. That approach is in keeping with the benefit principle of taxation, in which the beneficiaries of government spending are the ones who pay the taxes.
3. **Mandate that industries facing security threats be responsible,** with any costs merely absorbed by the companies or passed along to their customers.

To gain perspective on which is the best alternative, consider the example of safeguarding air travel. To guard against the threat of bombs and hijackings, airline passengers are

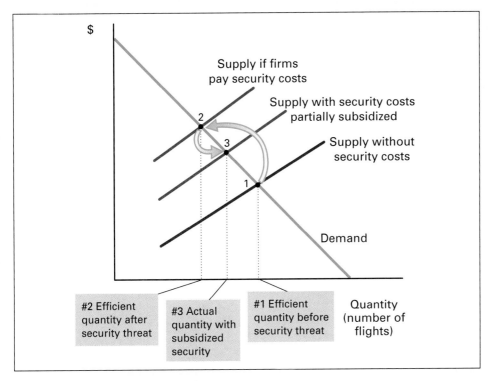

FIGURE 11-8

PAYING FOR SECURITY IN THE AIRLINE INDUSTRY The cost of protecting against security threats shifts the supply curve for the threatened industry to the left. The result is that the price of air travel increases and the number of flights decreases as the market equilibrium changes from point 1 to point 2. For example, the need to provide airport security increases the cost of air travel and shifts supply to the left as aging planes are not replaced and some airlines go out of business. The new equilibrium is associated with fewer flights and higher fares.

Government subsidies can off-set some of these effects, such as shown by the equilibrium point 3. In the case of airlines, govern-ment has provided direct financial assistance to airlines and also provides a great deal of airport security. Only some of those sub-sidies are financed by a surcharge on passenger tickets.

screened by means of federal marshals, surveillance equipment, X-ray machines, wands, and so forth. This screening is expensive and is a genuine cost of providing air transporta-tion. If each airline company has to pay those costs on its own, the costs would be reflected in supply, just as would any other cost of doing business. To the extent that heightened con-cerns over security cause companies to increase spending on security, supply shifts to the left and the quantity of air travel decreases. This result is shown in Figure 11-8 as the move-ment from point 1 to point 2.

USE OF SUBSIDIES AS AN OPTION

Alternatively, the federal government could give airlines *subsidies,* in which government picks up some of the cost of providing security. Figure 11-8 shows that when the government par-tially subsidizes increased security spending, it achieves the output given by point 3, which is greater than if firms are forced to pay all of the costs themselves, but less than if there was no security threat. The reason is that the leftward shift in supply as a result of increased security needs is partially offset by a rightward shift in supply as firms are able to obtain government money to pay for some of that added security. If government were to provide the security itself, or if subsidies to firms in the industry were to cover the entire cost of security, there would be no shift in supply. In that case, price and output would remain unchanged.

Comparing the alternative approaches requires us to specify our goals. The two most fundamental goals in economics are efficiency and equity, both of which might come into play in considering the best policy. Meeting the goal of efficiency requires that each good be produced only up to the point for which its marginal benefit equals its marginal cost. As dis-cussed in Chapter 4, the market accomplishes this mission to the extent that the intersection of demand and supply is also the intersection of marginal benefit and marginal cost. However, **if the costs of necessary security measures are paid for by government subsi-dies, the market supply will no longer represent the complete marginal cost**. Instead, the

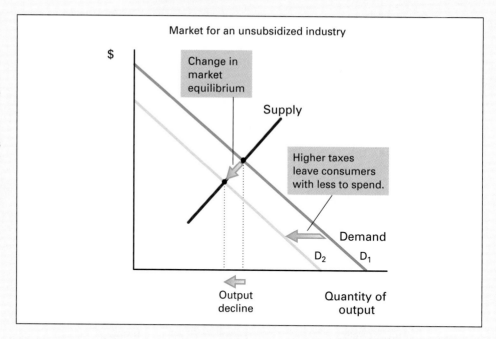

FIGURE 11-9

THE HIDDEN COST OF SUBSIDIES
When the economy is at full employment, subsidizing some industries hurts other industries. When government uses tax dollars to pay the subsidies, it reduces demand for the various unsubsidized goods and services by reducing the after-tax income consumers have available to spend. The result is that output shrinks in the unsubsidized portion of the economy.

output will be greater than the efficient quantity and the price will be lower than the price that achieves efficiency.

When the government gets directly involved in providing security, such as with screening mail for anthrax or checking airline passengers for weapons, the same principles of market pricing apply. With the mail, screening costs are reflected in the postage we pay. With airline security, the government adds a security charge of $2.50 to each passenger's ticket. Both of these practices are consistent with market efficiency.

Government action and taxation cannot replace the marketplace in one element of efficiency, however. In particular, the government lacks competition to ensure that its actions are technologically efficient. For this reason, for example, we have little way of knowing if the anthrax screening procedures used by the United States Postal Service are the most cost-effective. Likewise, there might be alternative combinations of equipment, personnel, and passenger waiting times that could achieve an equal amount of airport security, combinations that the government has little incentive to optimize. These possible inefficiencies represent a cost of government actions, not a definitive reason against taking those actions.

The upshot of this discussion is that when government does take action, efficiency suggests that it should tailor its practices as closely as possible to those of the marketplace. Rather than just using general tax revenues to provide government services, the implementation of user fees tailors price adjustments from industry to industry to match the costs of increased security in the various industries.

Politics does not always ensure that user charges are assessed in the right amount or even assessed at all, in which case, distortions can occur in the pattern of economic activity away from what is efficient. In particular, if the costs to government of providing security are not reimbursed by user fees, the result is a subsidy to the industries government is protecting. This subsidy comes from general tax revenue, which reduces the amount of income taxpayers have to spend throughout the rest of the economy. When incomes are reduced by the taxes that pay for security, the demand for many goods and services will decrease, such as shown in Figure 11-9. For those industries, output is reduced.

The myriad of new security measures to safeguard against terrorism have costs that cannot be avoided. Whether it be taxpayers or customers, someone will pay. Economic analysis can provide guidance to policymakers on how to design taxes in an efficient manner. Whether policymakers follow this advice is of course up to them.

1. **How much security would the airline industry have to provide to ensure that you would travel as much as before the terrorist attacks? What is the maximum user fee for security you would be willing to pay to secure your safety when you travel by airplane?**

2. **How much individual liberty would you be willing to give up to achieve greater security? For example, do you favor profiling that targets individuals with a particular appearance for security measures? If not, would you suggest the same security measures be used on people of all ages and appearance? More generally, explain how the loss of individual liberty represents a cost to society of terrorism.**

Visit www.prenhall.com/ayers for updates and web exercises on this Explore & Apply topic.

SUMMARY AND LEARNING OBJECTIVES

1. **List the major sources of revenue for government in the United States.**

   - Taxes are used by government to pay the costs of providing public goods. Taxes also finance income redistribution through the provision of transfer payments. Safety-net programs that provide economic security transfer tax dollars to those in need. Welfare and unemployment compensation are examples.

   - Two goals for taxes are equity and efficiency. Tax equity is about fairness. The goal of efficiency in taxation is to maintain incentives for people to be productive. To raise revenue efficiently, a tax should be designed to change people's behavior the least.

   - A marginal tax rate is different from an average tax rate. A marginal tax rate states the percent of additional income that is collected in taxes. An average tax rate states the percent of total income that is taken in taxes.

   - Taxes take about 30 percent of GDP. The personal income tax raises the largest share of the federal government's revenue. Federal personal income tax rates start at 10 percent for people with very low taxable incomes and increase to 15 percent, 25 percent, 28 percent, 33 percent, and 35 percent as incomes rise. This series of tax rates provides an example of marginal tax rates, since each of these rates applies to increments of income.

   - The federal government also collects Social Security taxes, including a Medicare hospitalization tax. There is also a corporate income tax that takes about 30 percent of corporate profits.

   - Tax incidence refers to who ultimately pays a tax. In the case of the corporate income tax, the tax ultimately reduces the income of shareholders.

   - State and local governments also collect taxes. States' individual income taxes, sales taxes, and revenues from the federal government make up most of the revenues states receive. Local governments tend to rely on property taxes and sales taxes for their revenues.

2. **Explain the principles of tax equity and how they apply to fiscal policy.**

   - The two fundamental principles of tax equity are the benefit principle and the ability-to-pay principle. The benefit principle provides the justification for earmarked taxes, such as the gasoline tax. It suggests that those who pay a tax should be the same as those who receive benefits from how that tax revenue is spent. The benefit principle cannot apply to redistributional programs, since the point of those programs is to provide assistance from taxpayers to the needy.

   - The ability-to-pay principle states that those with more ability to pay taxes should actually pay more taxes. The federal income tax is modeled according to this principle, weighing concepts of tax equity against concepts of efficiency.

3. **Interpret why the U.S. income tax is structured as it is, and why critics suggest changing it.**

   - A tax may be progressive, regressive, or proportional. A progressive tax collects a larger fraction of income as income increases. The federal income tax is progressive since the marginal tax rate rises as a person's income reaches a threshold level. For example, the income tax starts at 10 percent for low-income individuals and rises to 35 percent for those with relatively high incomes.

- A regressive tax collects a smaller fraction of income as income increases. For example, a tax that collects $1,000 from a person earning $10,000 and $10,000 from a person earning $1,000,000 is regressive since the first person pays 10 percent of his or her income toward the tax, while the second person pays only 1 percent of income toward the tax.

- A proportional tax collects the same fraction of income as income changes. If the person earning $1,000,000 in the previous example paid $100,000 in taxes, the same 10 percent as the low-income person, then the tax would be proportional.

- A flat tax applies a single tax rate to all income. Thus, a flat tax is an example of a proportional tax. While the tax rate is the same for all taxpayers, recognize that people with higher incomes still pay higher taxes. A flat tax, if enacted, would be transparent (meaning easily monitored). In reality, any flat tax likely to be enacted would involve exempting low incomes.

- It can be difficult to tell whether a tax is progressive, regressive, or proportional. Depending on whether Social Security benefits are included with the tax, Social Security can be viewed as representing a progressive, regressive, or proportional tax.

- In pursuing the twin goals of equity and efficiency in the tax system, there are tradeoffs. More equity can mean less efficiency, and vice versa. In the pursuit of equity, government programs provide cash and in-kind benefits.

- An efficient tax does not distort relative prices within a country. Efficiency calls for a broadly based tax that virtually everyone must pay.

4. **Show why workers pay more Social Security tax than they see withdrawn on their pay stubs.**

- The Social Security tax is the second-largest source of federal revenue. Both employees and employers contribute toward Social Security taxes, each paying 7.65 percent of a worker's gross pay to the federal government, for a total of 15.3 percent. The burden of employers' contributions is shifted to workers in the form of lower worker pay. Thus, the ultimate incidence of the Social Security tax is on workers because the market wage rate declines by the amount of the employer's share of the tax.

- The Social Security system is a pay-as-you-go system, with current workers paying for the benefits received by current retirees. It is predicted that the system will run out of money in the relatively near future. Individual retirement accounts promote saving for retirement. Personal Security Accounts, although politically contentious, might supplement Social Security if enacted into law.

5. **Justify the use of consumption taxes, including the value added taxes of Canada and Europe.**

- A consumption tax takes revenue for the government as people spend their money rather than as they receive income. Sales taxes are one form of a consumption tax. Many countries impose a consumption tax called a value added tax (VAT). As its name suggests, the VAT taxes value added, which is the difference between a firm's previously taxed costs and its revenues. A VAT will yield the same tax revenue as a sales tax set at the same percentage.

- Whatever taxes are imposed, a broader tax base, associated with eliminating tax "loopholes," combined with lower tax rates can reduce possibilities for inefficient behavior brought about by efforts to avoid taxes.

6. **Discuss issues of market efficiency and tax equity as they relate to security costs.**

- The terrorist threat imposes additional costs on firms in specific industries, such as the airline and pipeline industries. These costs could be paid for by government subsidies to firms. Subsidies often run counter to market efficiency.

KEY TERMS

TEST YOURSELF

TRUE OR FALSE

1. The tax rate on incremental income is called the marginal tax rate.
2. Broadening the tax base is a very inefficient way to raise revenues.
3. Tax shifting refers to people being able to delay paying taxes until after April 15.
4. A progressive tax is any tax that takes more money from the rich than from the poor.
5. A flat tax collects the same number of dollars from everybody.

MULTIPLE CHOICE

6. An average tax rate is
   a. additional taxes owed as a percentage of additional income.
   b. total taxes owed.
   c. total taxes owed as a percentage of total income.
   d. the percentage of income not collected in taxes.
7. The corporate income tax takes about _____ percent of corporate profits.
   a. 10
   b. 20
   c. 30
   d. 50
8. The two most important sources of revenue for local governments are sales taxes and
   a. personal income taxes.
   b. corporate income taxes.
   c. Social Security taxes.
   d. property taxes.
9. A value added tax is an example of a
   a. property tax.
   b. Social Security tax.
   c. income tax.
   d. consumption tax.
10. The benefit principle and the ability-to-pay principle refer to
    a. whether a tax is progressive or regressive.
    b. principles of tax efficiency.
    c. principles of tax equity.
    d. legal principles that question the constitutionality of Social Security.
11. The gasoline tax
    a. is used to fund various government programs.
    b. is the best example of a progressive tax.
    c. seems to satisfy the ability-to-pay principle.
    d. reflects the benefit principle, since those who pay the tax tend to receive the benefits.

12. If a tax collects 5 percent of the income of those making less than $100,000 and 10 percent of the income of those making $100,000 or more, then the tax is
    a. progressive.
    b. regressive.
    c. proportional.
    d. flat.
13. If a tax collects $1,000 per person, no matter what a person's income might be, then the tax is
    a. a head tax, which is regressive.
    b. progressive.
    c. a user fee.
    d. proportional.
14. Efficiency in taxation
    a. is less important than equity in taxation.
    b. is best exemplified by the progressivity of the income tax.
    c. is increased when a tax is also more equitable.
    d. often involves a tradeoff with equity.
15. An efficient tax
    a. distorts relative prices.
    b. changes peoples' behaviors.
    c. is paid entirely by employers.
    d. may not be equitable.
16. When added together, the employer share and the employee share of the Social Security tax total just over _____ percent of an individual's wages.
    a. 5
    b. 10
    c. 15
    d. 24
17. Personal security accounts would be financed by
    a. employers.
    b. government.
    c. individuals.
    d. small- to medium-sized firms, but not large corporations.
18. Savings in the Social Security system consist of
    a. IOUs.
    b. shares of stock.
    c. mostly hundred-dollar bills.
    d. gold.
19. In most countries, _____ provide the primary source of government revenue.
    a. tariffs
    b. personal income taxes
    c. corporate income taxes
    d. consumption taxes

20. Self-Test Figure 11-1 is most likely to represent which of the following?
   a. A subsidized industry.
   b. An unsubsidized industry, when other industries receive significant subsidies.
   c. An unsubsidized industry, when other industries likewise receive no subsidies.
   d. An industry that subsidizes its customers.

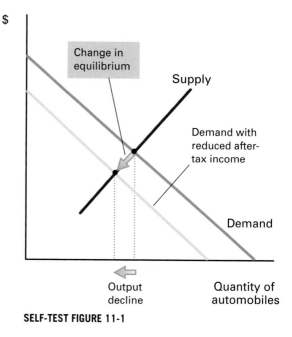

SELF-TEST FIGURE 11-1

QUESTIONS AND PROBLEMS

1. *[transfer payments]* How does the idea of a safety net relate to the concept of transfer payments? Explain, using a specific example.

2. *[marginal tax rate]* If Sam earns $100,000 a year and pays $10,000 in income taxes, can you determine his marginal tax rate? Explain.

3. *[average tax rate]* If Sue earns $100,000 a year and pays $10,000 in income taxes, can you determine her average tax rate? Explain.

4. *[tax revenues]* Without looking at the pie charts in the text, draw a pie chart showing sources of federal revenue. Slice the pie you draw in order to show the relative importance of each source of revenue. After you finish your drawing, compare it to the pie chart in the text and make any corrections needed to your drawing.

5. *[tax base]* What is the tax base? Why is it efficient to lower tax rates while broadening the tax base? Explain.

6. *[tax equity]* Most people want taxes to be fair. Yet there are strong disagreements over what constitutes tax equity. Using an example and the concepts of equity discussed in this chapter, explain why such disagreement can reasonably persist.

7. *[tax equity]* Which principle of tax equity, the benefit principle or the ability-to-pay principle, is in closest agreement with your own personal idea of what is fair? Explain.

8. *[progressive versus regressive]* Suppose that you have been chosen by the president of your college or university to design a tax system that would tax students at your school in order to provide funding for student athletics. You will be allowed to impose a tax on one of the following: tickets to school football games, soft drinks from vending machines on campus, or textbooks sold from your campus book store. Evaluate each alternative within the context of equity, efficiency, and whether the tax you choose would be regressive or progressive.

9. *[flat tax]* On balance, do you think it is a good idea to adopt a flat tax? If such a tax is adopted, how much income should be exempted? Explain your reasoning.

10. *[payroll tax]* Is the term payroll tax another way of referring to the income tax? Explain.

11. *[Social Security tax]* Using a graph and labeling the axes, curves, and all relevant information, demonstrate how employees wind up paying the employer portion of Social Security taxes.

12. *[taxes and incentives]* Why is it difficult to design aid to the poor that provides work incentives? Explain with reference to cost and the level of the safety net.

13. *[tax reform]* Income taxes provide the government with information about your earnings. Information from tax returns has been used to convict bootleggers, narcotics smugglers, and others with large unreported incomes of tax law violations, even when the government could not prove that their income was obtained illegally. Some supporters of tax reform would prefer to abandon the income tax altogether and replace it with a value added tax or other tax that leaves no paperwork trail and keeps individuals' affairs out of the eyes of government. Do you think the information contained in income tax returns should be used by the government in prosecuting crime? Should we fear that the government will go overboard and misuse tax information to infringe on civil liberties? Explain.

14. *[tax reform]* Mention two examples of a consumption tax. Explain how replacing the personal income tax with a consumption tax might or might not be considered to be tax reform.

15. *[consumption tax]* Do governments in the United States impose a consumption tax? If so, what is the most common type? Do governments in other countries impose a consumption tax? If so, what is the most common type?

WORKING WITH GRAPHS AND DATA

1. *[marginal tax rate]* Below is a table indicating the marginal personal income tax rates for a single person in 2004. Use the table to answer the questions that follow.

Tax Bracket	Marginal Tax Rate	Taxable Income
1	10%	Up to $7,000
2	15%	$7,001–28,40
3	25%	$28,401–68,800
4	28%	$68,801–143,500
5	33%	$143,501–311,950
6	35%	$311,951 or more

a. How much tax would a single person in 2004 pay if he or she earned $40,000?

b. What would the above person's average tax rate be in 2004?

c. How much tax would a single person in 2004 pay if he or she earned $80,000?

d. What would the above person's average tax rate be in 2004?

e. How much tax would a single person in 2004 pay if he or she earned $160,000?

f. What would the above person's average tax rate be in 2004?

g. Comment on the average tax rate as income increases.

2. *[Social Security tax]* Consider the impact of Social Security taxes on wages and employment.

a. Draw an economy which has a vertical labor supply curve and a downward-sloping labor demand curve. The economy presently has no Social Security program.

b. Identify the equilibrium wage. Label it W1.

c. Suppose that the government now imposes a 6 percent Social Security tax on employers. How does this impact the graph you drew in part a?

d. What happens to the equilibrium wage? Why? Label it as W_2.

e. What happens to the equilibrium level of employment? Why?

3. *[paying for security]* Stretching for 40 miles along the western border of Vermont, Lake Champlain is both scenic and an obstacle.

a. Draw demand and supply curves depicting the market for ferry rides across Lake Champlain. Label the equilibrium point as point A, the equilibrium price as P_1, and the equilibrium quantity as Q_1.

b. Recent government regulations call for ferry boat operators to increase security screening of passengers, cars, employees, and their boats. What impact do these new regulations have on the market for ferry boat rides? Draw it and label the new equilibrium as point B, the equilibrium price as P_2, and the equilibrium quantity as Q_2.

c. Complaints from ferry boat firms concerning the additional cost of compliance with the new government regulations has led the government to partially subsidize the cost of implementing these new measures. What impact does this have on the equilibrium in the ferry boat ride market? Draw it and label the new equilibrium as point C, the equilibrium price as P_3, and equilibrium quantity as Q_3.

4. *[the tax base]* Graph 11-1 depicts a hypothetical market for automobiles.

   a. Suppose that the automobile industry is singled out for an increase in the sales tax placed on motor vehicles. Draw the impact of this increase in the sales tax on the automobile industry, and identify the tax revenue to the government using the data above.

   b. How would the effects you describe change if the tax were placed on not only automobiles, but also all other outputs as well?

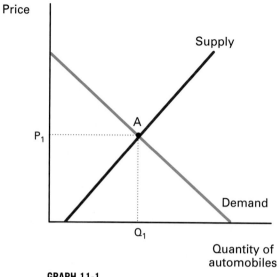

GRAPH 11-1

    Visit www.prenhall.com/ayers for Exploring the Web exercises and additional self-test quizzes.

ECONOMIC GROWTH

A LOOK AHEAD

Packets of electronic data surge from your keystrokes or from your voice. Instantly, you and your co-worker can see the results on your computer screen, hear the results with your headset, or both. It does not matter if your colleague is in New Jersey or New Guinea—the computers and networks of today are found all around the globe. It seems that the possibilities for collaborating on business projects have been expanding at light speed. In reality, today's fiber-optic transmission lines really *do* transfer data packets at the speed of light. Along with new possibilities for interacting and sharing comes new productivity and a *new economy,* the topic of this chapter's Explore & Apply section.

The technology and capital for economic growth do not appear by magic, however. Economies produce them, and produce more and better types if the right incentives are in place. Growth like this offers the only means to maintain or improve living standards in the face of an expanding population. In this chapter, we focus on the incentives for economic growth, and ways to adjust public policies to make those incentives stronger.

LEARNING OBJECTIVES

Understanding Chapter 12 will enable you to:
1. **Identify the sources of economic growth.**
2. **Describe the role of saving and investment in the process of capital formation.**
3. **Analyze how taxation affects both saving and investment activity.**
4. **Provide justification for subsidized higher education.**
5. **Summarize new growth theory and supply-side economics.**
6. **Discuss the key role of labor productivity in economic growth.**

Explore & Apply

economic growth the change in real GDP over time.

In Chapter 11, we saw that government tax and spending policies could change incentives, such as the incentives to work, to save, and to acquire human capital. In turn, these changes affect **economic growth,** which is usually measured by the change in real GDP over time. (Sometimes a real GNP measure is used, instead.)

Economies turn resources into outputs of greater value. The possibilities for doing so expand over time as the economy develops new technologies and acquires new resources. In other words, the economy's possibilities for production increase, which is why Chapter 2 showed economic growth to be an outward shift in the production possibilities frontier. This chapter examines the process more closely to see how the rate of economic growth might be improved. If the growth is in per-capita real GDP, a country can look forward to a better standard of living for its people.

12.1 THE SEEDS OF GROWTH

Economic growth does not just happen. It takes a combination of resources and technology, along with a policy environment to nurture that combination. These are the matters to which we now turn.

SOURCES OF GROWTH—LABOR, TECHNOLOGY, CAPITAL FORMATION, AND ENTREPRENEURSHIP

The U.S. economy has probably been studied more extensively than the economy of any other country. Evidence from the United States reveals quite a bit about what factors are important to growth, as the United States has a history of increasing real GDP. Table 12-1 summarizes U.S. economic growth according to the terms of office of recent presidents.

From 1947 to 1973, the average real GDP growth rate averaged around 4 percent. Real GDP growth diminished in the 1970s to under 3 percent during the Carter administration. GDP growth picked up steam a couple of years into the Reagan administration to give an annual growth rate average over Reagan's eight years of 3.5 percent. It then stumbled again to less than 2 percent in the following four years under George Bush. Growth was picking up in the final months of the first Bush administration to average a bit under 4 percent in the

TABLE 12-1   ANNUALIZED GROWTH RATES BY PRESIDENCY

PRESIDENCY	YEARS	GROWTH RATE
Kennedy–Johnson	1961–1968	4.9
Nixon–Ford	1969–1976	3.0
Carter	1977–1980	2.7
Reagan	1981–1988	3.5
Bush I	1989–1992	1.7
Clinton	1993–1999	3.7
Bush II	2001–2003	3.0

Source: BEA's NIPA Revision, Released March 30, 2000. Clinton and Bush II growth rates were computed by the authors from NIPA annual growth rates.

eight years of the Clinton administration. Shortly before Clinton left office, growth slowed and recession took hold in President George W. Bush's first year in office.

While growth was previously stated in terms of presidential administrations, growth is not directed from the top down. It is also sometimes hard to know what the economy's growth rate is at any given point in time, because it takes time to compile the data used to report GDP. This lag can have political repercussions. For example, following the election of President Bill Clinton in 1992, it was widely speculated that President Bush would have instead been re-elected if only voters had recognized the then-occurring economic recovery just a little sooner.

Most U.S. economic growth is attributable to increases in labor and capital, as well as technological change. Both technological change and additional capital increase **labor productivity,** which is output per hour worked. Although there is still some question as to why U.S. economic growth began turning upward in the mid-1990s, many analysts believe that technological change, embodied in the personal computer and the Internet, played a significant role. In turn, technological change increased labor productivity. Increases in labor productivity mean that more GDP is produced for each hour worked by the labor force. Figure 12-1 shows the percentage change in labor productivity in the United States since 1959.

labor productivity output per hour worked.

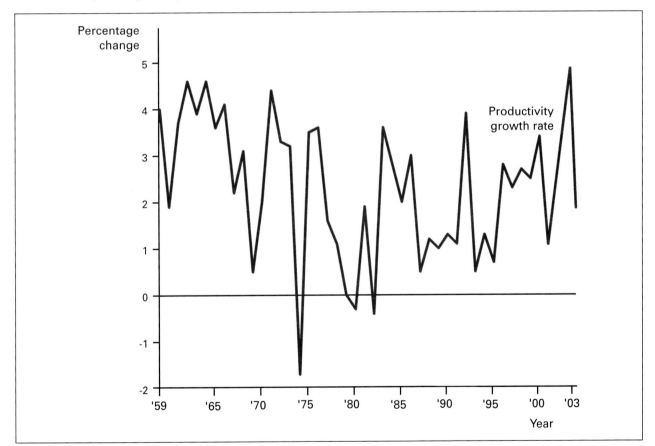

FIGURE 12-1

THE ANNUAL CHANGE IN LABOR PRODUCTIVITY Labor productivity rises and falls as additional capital is made available to workers. Technological change can also contribute to a rise in labor productivity as better equipment on the job makes labor more productive. The business cycle also affects labor productivity, with productivity typically falling in the early part of a recession, and rising as the economy later pulls out of the recession. Government regulations also affect labor productivity.

Source: 2003 Economic Report of the President, Table B-50, and Bureau of Labor Statistics, *Survey of Current Business,* Table D1. The data represent output per hour of all persons in the business sector. Data for 2003 are through February.

The figure makes clear that labor productivity does not necessarily increase each year. Why does the growth rate in productivity decrease in some years, and even become negative at times? One important factor is economic slowdowns. When the economy slows down, or enters a recession, labor productivity tends to fall at first because businesses decrease the production of goods and services in response to reduced aggregate demand. However, they also try to retain their workers in order to avoid the costs of recruiting and training new workers when aggregate demand picks back up. Thus, less production, combined with the same amount of labor, must decrease labor productivity. Later, when a recession nears its end, production is at first increased without a corresponding increase in labor employed. Labor productivity rises at that point in the business cycle.

capital formation the creation of new capital.

Labor productivity is associated with how much capital—both physical capital and human capital—labor has at its disposal. The labor productivity statistics suggest correctly that the United States has been quite successful at accumulating capital. The creation of new capital is termed **capital formation.** Capital formation requires initiative, since producing capital requires that people identify what additional outputs need to be produced or technologies should be employed. In market economies, entrepreneurs make these choices based on their best judgments of what is most profitable, meaning of most value to both consumers and producers. The struggle for profit weeds out entrepreneurs who do not make these choices well. Thus, one of the keys to capital formation is allowing this competitive search for profit. Where central planning is practiced, that key is lost. Thus, in Cuba, North Korea, and other economies in which government exercises too heavy a hand, the quantity and quality of capital formation is impaired. Figure 12-2 shows capital formation in the United States over time.

SNAPSHOT   THE ENTREPRENEURIAL ROAD TO RICHES—TAKING THE RISK AND SHARING THE REWARD

The odds of striking it rich as an entrepreneur may not be great—one in two hundred, they say—but the potential payoff does motivate people to try. If successful, the economy wins the products and the entrepreneurs gain a tidy profit.

Entrepreneurial success stories lie behind the companies we take for granted. Former economics major Sam Walton used the concept of one-stop shopping at everyday low prices to smash Wal-Mart's way to success, and in the process propel the Walton family to first place among America's wealthy. Bill Gates amassed his fortune by positioning Microsoft to provide the industry-standard interface for the personal computer. Talk on the phone? Craig McCaw said "take it with you," and took home $11.5 billion from his sale of McCaw Cellular Communications Corporation. Chat over coffee? Howard Shultze earned his fortune by opening Starbucks Coffee Company as a place to hang out over a steaming brew. FedEx your important papers? That was Fred Smith's idea. It was Domino's that delivered for Tom Monaghan, and Motown that recorded Berry Gordy's profit.

The common theme to the success stories of America's modern entrepreneurs is insight into what the public likes to do and how they could do it better or more conveniently. But it takes more. Without the risks inherent in trying to build companies from the ground up, there would be neither entrepreneurial success nor the economic growth that it engenders. ◄

QUICKCHECK

How can entrepreneurship increase labor productivity?

Answer: Entrepreneurship can add to productivity by organizing resources in better ways.

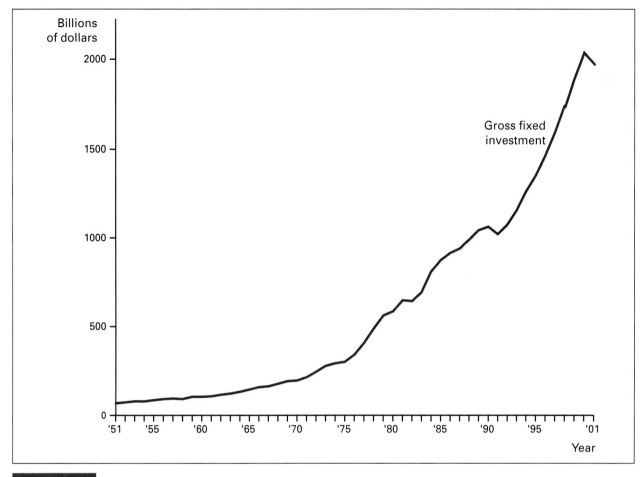

FIGURE 12-2

CAPITAL FORMATION Economic growth is associated with the creation of new capital, termed capital formation. Capital formation, usually rises, but has dipped during recessions.

Source: National Income and Product Accounts, Table 5.16. The data are for gross fixed investment, and include both private and government investment.

NURTURING GROWTH—SAVING AND INVESTMENT

Capital formation requires investment, which can be coordinated centrally through government. For example, government ordinarily finances the construction of highways, because it would be very difficult for private investors to acquire rights of way or to charge for highway usage. Indeed, rebuilding highways, especially bridges on the U.S. interstate highway system, is thought to be one of the major investment needs in the United States today.

More typically, investment is a decentralized process that responds to supply and demand in the marketplace. Investors finance the capital formation that is necessary to take advantage of market opportunities. For example, investors who expect to profit from the sale of gum balls, livestock feeders, big-screen televisions, or any other product must first finance the capital necessary to produce that product. Firms invest when they wish to do any of the following:

- Expand their scale of operations
- Implement better production techniques
- Produce new goods that their old factories are ill-suited to manufacture

To acquire human capital, individuals invest in themselves. This investment includes the time and money it takes to attend college or otherwise acquire new skills.

Private investors have a strong personal incentive to invest wisely. Because their own resources are on the line, private investors can be relied on to investigate closely which products are likely to succeed and which are not. While no one can foresee the future with certainty, investors who judge the best are rewarded in the marketplace with additional funds for further investment.

saving putting aside income for later use.

Saving is when income is put aside for later use. Central to understanding the process of capital formation is the observation that **saving provides the funding for investment.** In general, the more saving, the more investment. Sometimes people invest their savings themselves, such as when they buy houses or stocks. Other times, savers deposit their money into financial intermediaries, such as banks and mutual funds, which then invest that money.

Savers look to investments for good returns without excessive risk. Without aiming to do so, **government reduces private saving and investment.** This reduction happens in two ways. First, **government taxes away income that might be saved.** Second, **government taxes the returns on investments,** thus making them less attractive. In contrast, **government also adds to investment** to the extent that it directly invests the tax revenues it receives. The government investment in highways is an example. So, too, are government investments in schools, the criminal justice system, and elsewhere in the economy. In turn, these investments are used in the private sector. For example, the production of gum balls, restaurant meals, family vacations, and innumerable other goods and services benefit from an efficient transportation system, educated workers, and the system of laws.

Without government, aggregate saving and investment would be equal. This equality would be true because money saved would either be directly invested or would find its way into investment through banks and other financial institutions. With government, the situation is more complicated because tax dollars can be directed toward government investment or government consumption purchases. Thus, the total amount saved plus the total amount taken in taxes must equal the sum of private investment, government investment, and government spending on consumption items. Lumping together private and government investment, and simply calling the sum investment, we have the following equality:

$$\text{Investment} + \text{Government consumption} = \text{Saving} + \text{Taxation}$$

or, equivalently,

$$\text{Investment} = \text{Saving} + \text{Taxation} - \text{Government consumption}$$

Some investment funds also come from abroad and, likewise, some saving becomes investment in other countries.

Investment is a current expense that is made in the expectation of receiving income in the future. When firms borrow to finance new investment, the expected future income must be sufficient to pay off the amount borrowed, plus interest. The amount of interest depends upon the interest rate. **Higher real interest rates raise the cost of investing.** Some investments that would be undertaken at low real interest rates will not be undertaken when those rates are high. This result causes the investment demand curve to slope downward, as shown in Figure 12-3.

The money for investment comes from saving. While people will save some money whether they are paid interest or not, in general the higher the interest rate, the greater the supply of saving. For this reason, the supply of saving curve is shown as upwardly sloping in Figure 12-3. There is only one point of equilibrium, which determines the actual interest rate. The market equilibrium equates the quantity of saving supplied to the quantity of investment demanded, as shown in the figure.

Investment is also affected by other factors, such as business confidence (which encompasses expectations about the future), current economic growth, and opportunities pre-

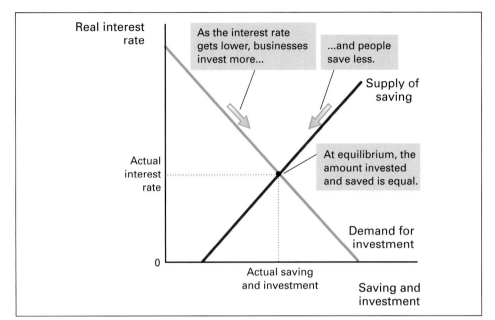

Real interest rate

As the interest rate gets lower, businesses invest more...

...and people save less.

Supply of saving

Actual interest rate

At equilibrium, the amount invested and saved is equal.

Demand for investment

0

Actual saving and investment

Saving and investment

FIGURE 12-3

THE EQUILIBRIUM INTEREST RATE
Interest rates are determined in the marketplace by the intersection of investment demand and saving supply. This rate determines the quantity of actual saving and investment. The equilibrium will change if either demand or supply shifts, such as in response to changes in confidence about the future.

sented by technological change. Increases in any of these variables would shift the investment demand curve to the right. Decreases would shift it to the left.

Government fiscal policy can also shift investment demand. An expansionary fiscal policy can stymie the capital formation needed for economic growth. Specifically, when the government increases spending or cuts taxes in order to stimulate the economy, it often finances the difference with borrowing by selling government bonds to investors. However, **government borrowing is in competition with private sector borrowing, and thus can cause higher interest rates.** The resulting reduction in private investment spending is called the **crowding-out effect** of expansionary fiscal policy. In other words, the crowding-out effect represents money that would have gone to private sector investment, but instead goes to finance government borrowing. However, because so much goes on at once in the macroeconomy, it is difficult to interpret from investment data whether, and to what extent, the crowding-out effect actually occurs.

crowding-out effect when government borrowing attracts money that would otherwise have gone to private sector investment.

12.2 INFLUENCING GROWTH THROUGH PUBLIC POLICY

The world's economies represent a mix of markets and government, with government actions holding the potential to either help or hinder economic growth. Understanding the likely effects of public policies requires an understanding of the incentives facing prospective investors. The key elements are risk and return.

THE INVESTMENT DECISION—RISK AND RETURN

"Success represents the 1 percent of your work that results from the 99 percent that is called failure."

—Soichiro Honda, founder, Honda Motor Company

Private investors do not know with certainty which products will sell and which will not. They accept some risk of failure, in the hopes of getting a return that compensates for that risk. There is always risk ex ante, meaning before the outcome is known. Investors assess

expected return the value of an investment if successful, multiplied by the probability of success; expressed as a percentage.

actual return the value an investment actually had, judged after the fact; expressed as a percentage.

the **expected return**—the value of the investment if successful, multiplied by the probability of success. The **actual return** can be viewed ex post, meaning after the fact. Ex post, an investment might have turned out fabulously, or it might have failed miserably.

As an example of the difference between expected return and actual return, consider movies. Some movies reap unexpected success at the box office and prove extremely profitable for their investors. In contrast, other movies, some with huge budgets and high expectations, are flops at the box office and lose enormous amounts of money for their investors.

The uncertain return on investment has important implications for public policy toward industry. Consider pharmaceuticals. The production cost of many cutting-edge drugs is very low, although their prices are often quite high. The high prices help pay for the many years of research and testing required to bring a successful drug to market. They also help pay for the many more drugs that failed to make it through the research and testing phase. In November 2002, Vice President Ferdinand Massari of Drugmaker Pharmacia put it this way, "For every new drug you see in the store, there are probably 10,000 that were tested and didn't make it!"

If prices for pharmaceutical drugs are held down by government regulation that aims to make drugs more affordable, less investment would occur in the pharmaceutical industry because there would be less expectation of profit. Investors would be less willing to accept the considerable risk of failure in the hope of only a modest profit from success. The result would be a slower pace of growth in that industry, leading to fewer new drugs. **Thus, the tradeoff is whether to make current drugs more affordable or to allow the quest for profit to lead to new and improved pharmaceuticals down the road.**

THE INCENTIVE EFFECTS OF TAXATION

In addition to regulation, taxes can also affect growth. For example, the United States personal income tax discourages saving behavior by taxing interest income earned on savings, but not taxing the alternative of current consumption. Figure 12-4 shows how a tax on saving increases the market interest rate and discourages investment. Savers face a lower return because of the tax, which makes them unwilling to save as much at each real interest rate. For this reason, taxing the return to saving shifts the supply of saving curve to the left,

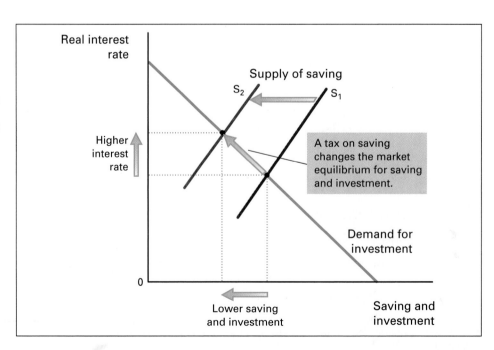

FIGURE 12-4

EFFECT OF THE INCOME TAX The personal income tax requires savers to pay a tax on their interest incomes, which reduces people's willingness to save and shifts the supply of saving curve to the left. The result is a higher equilibrium interest rate and less actual saving and investment.

resulting in a higher equilibrium interest rate and less saving and investment. In this way, taxation of the return on saving discourages both saving and investment.

Because saving is so important to economic growth, there is concern over the low *personal saving rate* in the United States in recent years. Figure 12-5 illustrates the fluctuations in the percentage saved out of disposable personal income since 1929. In 2000 and 2001, the personal saving rate plunged to lows not seen since the Great Depression.

Investment is also discouraged by other taxes, such as the tax on capital gains. **Capital gains** represent the difference between the current market value of an investment and its purchase price. The **capital gains tax** takes a percentage of this difference when the investment is sold. Because investors know about the capital gains tax when making investment decisions, it too diminishes capital formation. The reduction in investment demand means that banks pay lower interest rates on savings. Likewise, individuals who invest directly in stocks or anything else subject to capital gains taxation also see their expected returns reduced. The upshot is that the capital gains tax leads to less saving and investment.

capital gains the difference between the current market value of an investment and its purchase price.

capital gains tax a tax on the capital gains from investments that are sold.

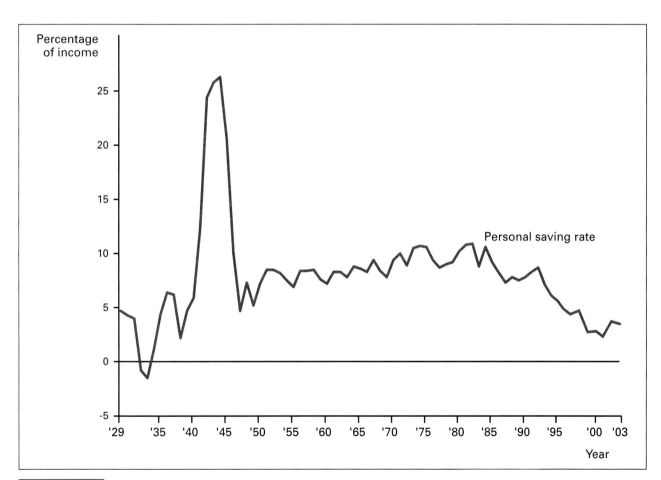

FIGURE 12-5

U.S. PERSONAL SAVING RATE The personal saving rate was low during the Great Depression because incomes were low. The personal saving rate soared during World War II because goods were rationed and people could not spend as much as they wished. In the 1990s, the personal saving rate fell as Americans consumed more and saved less.

Source: National Income and Product Account Tables, Table 2.1. The personal saving rate equals personal saving as a percentage of disposable personal income. Data for 2003 are current through the second quarter.

QUICKCHECK

Explain why the capital gains tax discourages investment.

Answer: Investors place their money at risk in the hope of seeing their investments grow. By taking a cut out of that expected return, the capital gains tax reduces the expected pay-off and thus makes the investment less attractive.

SUBSIDIZING RESEARCH AND DEVELOPMENT

external benefit when some benefits are received by third parties who are not directly involved in the decision.

Even without the inhibiting effects of taxes and regulations, the private sector may not devote an efficient amount of financial capital toward increasing future productivity. This shortfall occurs when there are external benefits from investment in research and development (R&D). An **external benefit** occurs when some benefits are received by third parties who are not directly involved in a decision, such as the decision to research or invest. In effect, these third parties siphon off benefits that would otherwise have gone to the firms undertaking the R&D. The result is a lower expected benefit to investors, which is likely to reduce the amount of resources they devote to R&D.

research aimed at creating new products or otherwise expanding the frontiers of knowledge and technology.

development when technology is embodied into capital.

While often lumped together, there is a significant distinction between research and development. **Research** is aimed at creating new products or otherwise expanding the frontiers of knowledge and technology. **Development** occurs when that technology is embodied into capital or output. For example, research may be aimed at uncovering a superconducting material that allows electricity to flow unimpeded at ordinary temperatures. If the research is successful, many companies could then incorporate the advance in knowledge (research) to design their own products (development), such as transmission lines, electromagnets, or computers.

property rights rights of ownership.

External benefits are most prominent at the research stage, especially when the research involves the creation of knowledge that can be applied to the production of many different products, as in the example just given. It is difficult for any one investor or group of investors to assert ownership—**property rights**—over the range of applications that can arise from basic advances in knowledge. For this reason, given that the odds of achieving a significant knowledge breakthrough are quite small, private investors usually avoid investments in basic research.

To correct this market failure, and perhaps as a counterweight to the Federal tax code's general distortion against investment, the government subsidizes research. Sometimes the government funds research directly, such as cancer research at the National Institutes of Health. Sometimes subsidies are indirect, such as public support of universities that require faculty to conduct research along with their teaching. There is controversy over how generous these subsidies should be, however, since the diffusion of knowledge throughout the economy makes measuring the value of basic research practically impossible.

Much more controversy exists when government subsidizes development. For example, the U.S. Department of Energy funded a variety of alternative energy demonstration projects after the dramatic rise in world oil prices in 1973. However, most of the investments in windmills, solar energy, shale oil, and other forms of alternative energy were never commercially viable. Even gasoline blended with ethanol (alcohol made from corn) survives in the marketplace only because of ongoing government subsidies.

Such investments are examples of development rather than basic research. Development by one firm does give other firms ideas about what will be successful and what will not, and thus involves external benefits. However, this situation holds true for airline services, fast-food locations, new toys, and a host of other goods and services offered in the marketplace. Competitors learn from each others' successes and mistakes. Such minor external benefits pervade any market economy. It would be inefficient to single out some and not others.

UNIVERSITIES—ADVANCING THE FRONTIERS OF KNOWLEDGE   *SNAPSHOT*

New ideas and information can confer significant external benefits, particularly if businesses can apply the knowledge to develop more valuable goods and services. The trouble is that the value of new ideas and information is often not known until they are produced, and then the applications could be in a variety of industries. Firms that engage in basic research might be unable to claim property rights to this growth in the knowledge base, since patent laws more effectively protect development than research. Firms that advance the knowledge base might even see competitors use that knowledge as well as, or better than, they do themselves.

So, where are advances in knowledge to come from? Often it is universities that are the sources. Government and academia both recognize the role of universities in engaging in valuable research that companies fear to undertake on their own. Government subsidies or grants often provide the funds that make it possible. ◄

12.3 PROPERTY RIGHTS AND NEW GROWTH THEORY

The prospect for business profits in the future can lead to research and development in the present. While not new in itself, this idea is a cornerstone of what is called **new growth theory.** New growth theory stresses the association between productivity growth over time and technological advances that are embodied in new capital. Since no one can know beforehand which lines of research will prove fruitful and which will fail, economies that handsomely reward productive ideas will grow the fastest. Productive ideas can include all sorts of things, including how to make wireless local computer networks, how to genetically engineer a disease-preventing potato, how to organize a firm, and any number of other thoughts.

According to new growth theory, the ideas behind new technologies are promoted most effectively by allowing individuals to claim property rights, and the associated monopoly power, over ideas they have. *Monopoly power* is the idea that others can only imitate, but not duplicate, your product. Profits associated with monopoly power provide the incentive to create even better ways of doing things. The idea that private property is the key to growth, however, is far from new.

New growth theory contrasts with mainstream prescriptions for growth in the decades following the Great Depression of the 1930s and World War II. The viewpoint at that time was that government was the centerpiece of economic development. This view of growth was consistent with the high degree of confidence in government that characterized that period in history. For example, the American public works projects and World War II itself were seen as instrumental in moving the economy from the ravages of depression to

new growth theory
emphasizes the importance of new ideas in generating economic growth, and of intellectual property rights in providing the profit incentive to generate those ideas.

decades of peace and prosperity. Aid to Europe under the Marshall plan was also credited with getting that continent back on its feet. Confidence in the ability of government to direct the economy along a pathway of growth rose in the 1930s with the New Deal, and peaked during the period from the 1950s through the early 1970s.

Although new in contrast to the prevailing economic wisdom of that period, new growth theory actually taps into themes that have been central to economic analysis for centuries. For example, private property is central to Adam Smith's idea of the invisible hand of the marketplace, discussed in Chapter 1, which gives entrepreneurs an incentive to invest and grow the economy in their search for profit. Likewise, private property and the unfettered freedom to use it form a central theme of the *Austrian school* of economic thought, which got its start with the writings of Ludwig von Mises (1881–1973) in the early twentieth century. **Austrians emphasize that government rules and regulations that restrict the use of private property impede progress, which in von Mises's words, "is precisely that which the rules and regulations did not foresee."**

12.4 SUPPLY-SIDE POLICY

supply-side economists (supply siders) economists who emphasize incentives for productivity and economic growth, such as lower marginal tax rates and less regulation.

Those economists who particularly emphasize policies aimed at growth are called **supply-side economists,** or **supply siders** for short. Supply siders focus on increasing the value of what the economy can produce in the long run (the supply side), rather than on any desire to change consumers' spending behavior (the demand side). Supply siders figure that the short-run business cycle will sort itself out over time, and will lead to a larger economic pie in the long run if government does not intrude. This long-run, free-market orientation places supply siders squarely within the classical school of economic thought.

The objective of supply-side policy is to ensure that the output associated with full employment is as high as possible. Supply-side policies are designed to increase productivity, such as through increasing capital formation. The intended effect of such policies is to shift long-run aggregate supply to the right, as depicted in Figure 12-6.

FIGURE 12-6

GOAL OF SUPPLY SIDERS Supply-side economists seek to increase productivity, which would cause long-run aggregate supply to shift to the right. This increase would increase long-run per-capita GDP.

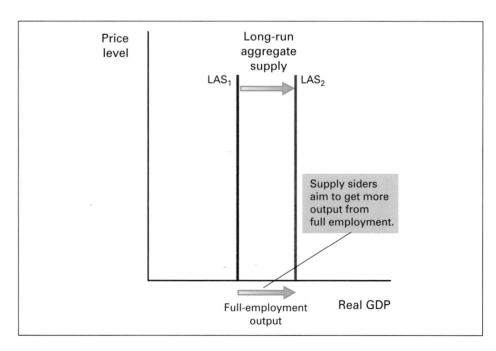

Full-employment output will change in response to changes in *structural features of the economy*, including resources and technology. Structural features also include government policies that change how workers and firms behave. Examples include unemployment compensation, minimum-wage laws, and other public policies that affect the natural rate of unemployment.

Supply siders are concerned with any government policies that might cut productivity or lead to structural unemployment. They look with suspicion at the work disincentives embedded in many safety-net programs, and at regulations that make it more costly for firms to hire and fire employees. They emphasize that regulations should be designed with an eye toward minimizing their impact on productivity.

Supply siders are most known for their focus on tax policies. They recommend keeping marginal tax rates low in order to leave a higher fraction of incremental earnings in the hands of individuals and investors. In this way, there is more incentive to invest and be productive. The result is a higher full-employment output. The reason is partly that there will be more work effort provided at the full-employment equilibrium in response to greater marginal rewards for that effort. Mostly, however, output will be greater because investors will have greater incentives to build up the economy's stock of physical and human capital, and thereby increase the productivity of its labor.

Because the concern of the supply siders is with the long run, they have little use for activist fiscal policies designed for short-run goals. **Supply siders often see an expansionary fiscal policy as an excuse for a greater government presence in the economy, and worry about the increased regulatory and tax burdens that presence may bring.**

Following the election of President Ronald Reagan, the U.S. Congress passed sweeping changes in the tax code. The 1982 tax changes adopted the supply-side agenda of cutting marginal tax rates in order to promote growth. Such growth was intended to provide greater prosperity in the future, as well as a greater tax base over time. Beginning in 1983, after the tax cuts took effect, and lasting through the end of that decade, the economy witnessed real economic growth every year along with an inflation rate that was much lower than in the preceding decade. The average growth rate from 1983 through the end of the Reagan presidency in 1988 was a very respectable 4.1 percent.

Because Congress did not curtail spending in line with its tax cuts, the federal government ran a large budget deficit in the 1980s. The budget deficit exceeded 6 percent of GDP in 1983, although it fell to just under 3 percent by 1989. The Reagan-era budget deficits look like Keynesian fiscal policy run amok, with the fiscal stimulus of a tax cut applied to marginal tax rates at the high end of the income spectrum, rather than to rates paid by those struggling to make a good life for themselves. **Critics thus refer to supply-side policies as** *trickle-down economics.* The term suggests that the policies intend to make the rich richer, so that they might spend a bit more and help the rest of us. **In fact, that is not the process that the supply siders have in mind.** Supply siders aim at productivity, not spending.

The U.S. economy grew in the 1980s after the tax cuts. The rich did indeed get disproportionately richer, at least in terms of the income they reported to the IRS. They also became more productive and paid more taxes. While the tax cuts of the 1980s reduced real federal tax revenues from most groups in the economy, the tax cuts greatly increased tax revenues from the highest income groups. The top 5 percent of income earners increased their share of total income tax payments from 36 percent in 1980 to 43 percent in 1990. Upward mobility also became more commonplace as a result of the lower tax rates. Looking at the lowest fifth of the income distribution in 1980, for example, 86 percent had advanced beyond that by 1988, with 16 percent even making it all the way to the top fifth of the income distribution.

THE LAFFER CURVE Increasing tax rates will increase tax revenues, but only up to a point. After that point, higher tax rates are self-defeating and actually reduce tax revenues. At a tax rate of 100 percent, there would be no personal incentive to earn any income at all.

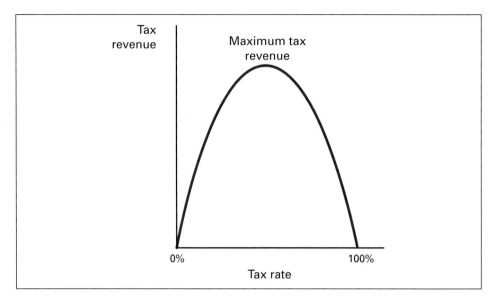

SNAPSHOT   **ON THE BACK OF A NAPKIN**

At a tax rate of zero percent, the government collects no revenue. It can increase revenues by increasing tax rates, but there are limits. After all, a tax rate of 100 percent would also generate no tax revenue—no one would bother to earn money if Uncle Sam took it all. Arthur Laffer, a young UCLA economist, discussed this at lunch one day in the 1970s. He sketched the hump-shaped relationship between tax rates and tax revenues on the back of his napkin. Ever since, as shown in Figure 12-7, that sketch has been called the *Laffer curve.*

Promoted by some of the supply siders, the Laffer curve proved to be a potent idea in the early 1980s. It surely would be nice if government could cut its tax rates and see both the economy and its tax revenues grow. Congress went on to cut tax rates in 1982, and—lo and behold—the economy grew and the rich wound up paying more taxes. They paid more taxes because economic growth meant there were more of them and they had more income.

Unfortunately, although overall federal tax revenues increased by $1.1 trillion in the 1980s, that was not enough to overtake government spending. The Laffer curve became a laughingstock among the I-told-you-so crowd. Yet, no one can dispute its logic. Perhaps, if the right tax is found to cut, the Laffer curve will rise to prominence once more. ◀

Explore & Apply

12.5 THE NEW ECONOMY—IS IT REAL?

"We have entered a new era in which brains count for more than brawn."

—Royal Bank of Canada Newsletter

American prosperity seemed strong and enduring in the 1990s. The vitality of the economic boom indicated that the economy had changed in some fundamental way. The media needed a catch phrase that would describe what was happening and help define the decade for posterity. In this way, America's economy became the "new economy." That expression was soon on just about everyone's lips, symbolized by the wealth created in California's Silicon Valley. The fast-growing, entrepreneurial firms that dot Silicon Valley were a hallmark of the new economy. Today, the question is whether the new economy is still alive, or ever really was.

You may remember the old economy, with its emphasis on boring old industries, its recurring recessions and high unemployment, its inability to eliminate poverty, and its association with government budget deficits and a host of other ills. Contrast that mental picture to the new economy, which emphasizes the application of technology to raise living standards. The new economy is about high technology and its promise to revolutionize everyday life. From the spectacular special effects in the movie *Twister*, improved treatments for AIDS, and on-line auctions at e-Bay, the range of impacts associated with the new economy is wide.

How much about the new economy is ballyhoo? Consider that new economy centerpiece, the Internet. Over half of U.S. households are currently connected, and that number continues to grow. The Internet provides access to information and entertainment, and allows people to communicate instantly with each other. For buyers and sellers, the Internet provides opportunities to meet in cyberspace to transact business. The problems and failures associated with the Internet are often glossed over, however, when these benefits are raised in conversation. Try as we might to prevent them, problems like crippling new yet-to-be-named viruses threaten millions of computers. Hackers are another problem, able to penetrate allegedly secure web connections and steal millions of dollars. In addition, Internet failures include the liquidation of many Internet businesses that never came close to making a profit. For example, buying groceries on-line from home through Webvan was once touted as a threat to traditional supermarkets. No more!

The Internet bubble, exemplified by Webvan and a host of other failed on-line firms, began to deflate near the end of the longest economic expansion in U.S. history. That upswing in the economy began in the early 1990s and ended with the recession that started in March 2001. Some economists began to question whether the new economy was dead, or even whether it ever existed at all. Let's try to answer such questions, using the framework of macroeconomics.

The three macro goals of high growth, high employment, and low inflation all fell into place for the United States during the presidency of Bill Clinton. Economists will study this era for years to come, seeking to establish with certainty all the factors that accounted for the nation's superior economic performance. Alan Greenspan, chairman of the Federal Reserve at the time, has commented that the economy was revitalized by fundamental changes in the 1990s. Behold technology.

HOW TECHNOLOGY IMPACTS GROWTH

The new economy is characterized by the application of technology to increase business productivity. The growth of computers in the workplace increases the productivity of labor. More productive labor means incomes rise in the long run. Furthermore, increased productivity is the closest thing to a "magic bullet" for the economy. Increased productivity can translate into meeting the three macro goals. Strong productivity growth can keep the economy growing, keep workers employed, and act as a brake on inflation.

Before we discuss how productivity growth can strengthen the economy, let's examine the U.S. productivity data in Table 12-2. This table shows that, when cheaper and easier-to-use technology was provided to workers throughout the economy in the 1990s, workers became more efficient. Output per worker increased. Businesses increased production in response.

Table 12-2 tracks economic performance for four separate time periods: 1979 to 1990, 1990 to 1995, 1995 to 2000, and 2000 to 2001. Row (1) shows the acceleration in the growth rate of labor productivity between 1995 and 2000 relative to the earlier years in the table. In the 1995 to 2000 time period, each year American workers produced 2.7 percent more output per hour worked than in the previous year. Compared to the earlier periods, labor productivity roared ahead in the mid-to-late 1990s. The last column shows that labor productivity slowed down from 2000 to 2001, most likely because of the recession in 2001.

TABLE 12-2   SOURCES OF CHANGE IN UNITED STATES LABOR PRODUCTIVITY, 1979–2001

ITEM	1979 TO 1990	1990 TO 1995	1995 TO 2000	2000 TO 2001
(1) Output per hour (Labor productivity)	1.6	1.5	2.7	1.3
(2) Contribution of capital	0.8	0.5	1.1	1.7
• Contribution of information technology capital	0.5	0.4	0.9	0.8
• Contribution of other capital	0.3	0.1	0.2	0.9
(3) Contribution of labor	0.3	0.4	0.3	0.6
(4) Contribution of technological change and other factors	0.5	0.6	1.4	−1.0

Source: Adapted from *Multifactor Productivity Trends,* Bureau of Labor Statistics, USDL 02–128, April 8, 2003. Row (4) shows multifactor productivity, which measures the joint influences of technological change, efficiency improvements, and other influences on economic growth.

Rows (2) through (4) explain the sources of growth in labor productivity: increases in capital, labor, and technological change. Note that information technology capital, such as computers, fax machines, and so forth, contributed significantly to soaring labor productivity in the 1995 to 2000 period. The same is true of technological change, as shown in row (4). The data in this table allow us to separate the hoopla about the new economy from the substance. What we see is that something fundamental did indeed change in the mid-1990s. Technological change, especially as it related to increases in information technology capital like computers, contributed mightily to the burst in labor productivity, which in turn contributed mightily to the nation's increased prosperity. The question raised by the negative value in row (4) for 2000 to 2001 is whether the value has turned positive again as the economy expanded in 2002 and 2003.

The current new economy is not the first time in American economic history that everyone sensed a permanent change for the better because of technology. The Industrial Revolution in the late 1700s was the first. In the United States, that revolution was sparked when Samuel Slater illegally smuggled from England the plans for the textile mill he built in Rhode Island. Throughout history, the economy has been revitalized again and again. The railroad, the automobile, radio, television, and now the computer and the Internet have created new economies in turn.

As in the current new economy, those episodes from history were also filled with hype, speculation, and excess. Life was made better, too, because in spite of the hype, what was new was real. So, the next time you place an order for a music CD at Amazon.com, remember that the new economy is much more. Most fundamentally, it is the building block for economic growth.

Yet doubts linger, for web worms, viruses, and even power failures have the potential to grind the new economy to a halt. For a day or two in the summer of 2003, we were reminded how fragile a thing this new economy can be. That was when, from Cleveland to Manhattan, the new economy blacked out. The culprit? Not enough upkeep of that old economy goliath of steel and wire—those basic and boring power transmission lines. It served as a reminder: For the economy to work, it takes old and new alike!

1. Until the widespread adoption of personal computers and word processing software in the mid-to-late 1980s, office paperwork was usually typed on an electric typewriter. Describe how the productivity of typists was increased when they shifted to the new technology. Also describe how the human capital that typists needed was changed by the new technology.

THINKING CRITICALLY

2. Should government subsidize Internet access for the poor? Explain, making reference to the benefits and to the problems that could be expected.

Visit www.prenhall.com/ayers for updates and web exercises on this Explore & Apply topic.

SUMMARY AND LEARNING OBJECTIVES

1. **Identify the sources of economic growth.**
   - Labor, capital, technological change, and entrepreneurship are important determinants of growth.
   - In the United States, economic growth averaged about 4 percent from 1947 to 1973, but growth fell off after that. From 1992 until the recession that started in 2001, the growth rate in the United States was again in the vicinity of average during the earlier era.
   - Economies grow through accumulating resources. They have the most control over capital, which in turn improves labor productivity. New capital requires capital formation. Entrepreneurs must identify new products or new technologies and produce new capital according to these opportunities.

2. **Describe the role of saving and investment in the process of capital formation.**
   - Funds for investment come from savings. Together, investment demand and the supply of saving determine the amount of investment.
   - Government both increases and decreases investment. Taxes reduce saving that could be used for investment. However, the government invests some of the taxes it collects, making investments in highways, schools, airports, and elsewhere.
   - The following equation describes the fundamental relationship between investment, saving, and government: Investment = saving + taxation − government consumption. The right-hand side of the equation shows that investment is financed by dollars that are saved and paid in taxes. However, some tax dollars pay for government consumption, and this item must be subtracted.
   - Government fiscal policy can result in a crowding-out effect in which government spending replaces private investment.
   - The interaction of investment demand with the supply of saving creates an interest rate equilibrium. The equilibrium real interest rate makes the actual amount of investment equal to the amount of saving. Graphically, this model of investment shows the investment

demand curve to be downward sloping and the supply of saving curve to be upward sloping. The market equilibrium occurs at the intersection of these two curves.

3. **Analyze how taxation affects both saving and investment activity.**
   - Taxing interest income reduces the supply curve of saving, which leads to a higher equilibrium real interest rate and less investment. A second example is the capital gains tax, which imposes a tax on the rise in value of an investment. Some current regulations also discourage investment.

4. **Provide justification for subsidized higher education.**
   - Government promotes technological advancement through subsidies for basic research, such as is conducted at colleges and universities. Otherwise, the existence of external benefits would lead to too little of such research.

5. **Summarize new growth theory and supply-side economics.**
   - New growth theory recognizes the key role played by research and development in economic growth. This school of thought promotes the idea that property rights to ideas must be protected in order for businesses to have the incentive to engage in research and development.
   - Supply siders seek to minimize structural features of the economy that discourage work effort and capital formation. Reducing regulations and marginal tax rates have been two of their emphases. Supply siders believe that their policies will shift the long-run aggregate supply curve to the right.

6. **Discuss the key role of labor productivity in economic growth.**
   - The new economy is seen as more than just a catch phrase. Information technology capital and technological change both contributed to the rise in productivity that occurred after 1995. This rise in labor productivity has been a key ingredient of economic growth.

KEY TERMS

economic growth, 306
labor productivity, 307
capital formation, 308
saving, 310
crowding-out effect, 311
expected return, 312

actual return, 312
capital gains, 313
capital gains tax, 313
external benefit, 314
research, 314

development, 314
property rights, 314
new growth theory, 315
supply-side economists (supply
  siders), 316

TEST YOURSELF

TRUE OR FALSE

1. An economy will grow faster when it chooses to produce more consumer goods and fewer capital goods.
2. Saving is used to finance investment.
3. Higher real interest rates shift the investment demand
   curve to the left.
4. A tax on saving shifts the supply curve of saving to the
   left, thus increasing the real interest rate.
5. Supply-side economics favors more government regulation relating to the health and safety of workers.

MULTIPLE CHOICE

6. Technological change and additional capital
   a. increase labor productivity.
   b. decrease labor productivity.
   c. have no effect on labor productivity.
   d. affect labor productivity in unpredictable ways.
7. U.S. economic growth
   a. has generally been characterized by a 5 percent or
      more growth rate since the 1960s.
   b. varied with each president.
   c. was on a downward trend in the 1990s, but has
      recently reversed its course.
   d. is no longer considered an important economic goal.
8. Capital formation is also referred to as
   a. property rights.
   b. technology.
   c. the real interest rate.
   d. investment.
9. Investment equals
   a. saving − taxation.
   b. saving + taxation.
   c. saving + taxation + government consumption.
   d. saving + taxation − government consumption.
10. In Self-Test Figure 12-1, the movement from point A to
    point B is most likely to be caused by
    a. external benefits from research.
    b. external benefits from development.
    c. supply-side policies.
    d. the personal income tax.

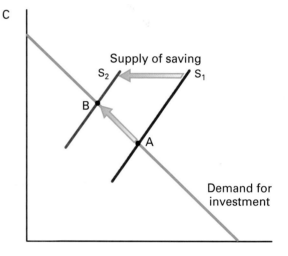

SELF-TEST FIGURE 12-1

11. In Self-Test Figure 12-1, the movement from point A to
    point B is most likely to cause
    a. less capital formation.
    b. more capital formation.
    c. higher capital gains.
    d. more saving.
12. In Self-Test Figure 12-1, axis C should be labeled as
    a. planned investment.
    b. actual investment.
    c. actual saving.
    d. the real interest rate.
13. Higher real interest rates
    a. increase the amount of investment.
    b. decrease the amount of investment.
    c. have no effect on the amount of investment.
    d. have varying and unpredictable effects on invest-
       ment.

14. The crowding-out effect refers to
    a. the crowds of people who attend sports events and rock concerts.
    b. the crowd mentality of investors who rush to buy the latest "hot" stocks.
    c. private sector borrowing that makes it difficult to finance the government.
    d. the reduction in private investment spending when the government borrows.

15. The capital gains tax takes a percentage of
    a. the purchase price of an investment.
    b. the selling price of an investment.
    c. the difference between the purchase price and the selling price of an investment.
    d. the expected return on an investment minus its actual return.

16. External benefits
    a. are most likely during the research phase.
    b. are most likely during the development phase.
    c. are equally likely during the research and development phases.
    d. explain why firms undertake research and development.

17. Research and development are the cornerstones of
    a. supply-side economics.
    b. the Laffer curve.
    c. old growth theory.
    d. new growth theory.

18. Supply siders emphasize
    a. increases in aggregate demand.
    b. higher real interest rates.
    c. a balanced federal budget.
    d. policies that shift the long-run aggregate supply curve to the right.

19. The Laffer curve shows that the effect of increasing taxes too much is
    a. less economic growth.
    b. less tax revenue.
    c. more unemployment.
    d. that only the rich get richer.

20. The new economy is characterized by
    a. the application of technology to increase business productivity.
    b. the need to rebuild bridges and highways to account for today's heavier traffic loads.
    c. widespread goofing off as workers are less accountable for their actions.
    d. the extra pollution it causes.

QUESTIONS AND PROBLEMS

1. *[labor productivity]* What is meant by the term labor productivity? What factors most strongly affect your personal labor productivity (or, if you have no job, the labor productivity of your closest family member with a job)? What actions can a person take to increase his or her labor productivity?

2. *[labor productivity]* Explain why the growth rate in labor productivity usually falls during the early part of a recession, but rebounds when the economy begins to improve.

3. *[capital formation]* Does capital formation affect labor productivity? Explain.

4. *[capital formation]* Provide examples of the kinds of capital formation that might have occurred when each of the following entrepreneurs launched his or her business:
   a. Bill Gates (Microsoft)
   b. Sam Walton (Wal-Mart)
   c. Howard Schultz (Starbucks Coffee)
   d. Berry Gordy (Motown Records)

5. *[government effect on investment]* Explain how government both reduces and increases investment at the same time. In light of your answer, interpret the following equation from the chapter: Investment = saving + taxation − government consumption.

6. *[saving and investment]* Why does the supply of saving slope upward? Why does investment demand slope downward? Identify the equilibrium in this market.

7. *[saving and investment]* Illustrate graphically and explain the significance of the market equilibrium real interest rate.

8. *[saving and investment]* Illustrate graphically the effect of an increase in the demand for investment on the real interest rate. Could an increase in the supply of saving offset the interest rate effect your graph illustrates? Explain.

9. *[government investment]* List three examples of government spending that might be considered investment. Would the private sector have undertaken these projects if government did not? Explain.

10. *[effect of taxation]* Using a supply and demand graph, explain how taxation of interest earnings reduces the amount of saving and investment.

11. *[crowding-out effect]* An expansionary fiscal policy can reduce private investment spending through the crowding-out effect. Explain how the crowding-out effect could occur.

12. *[personal saving rate]* Figure 12-5 shows that the personal saving rate was very high in the United States during

World War II (1942–1945), but is extremely low today. Speculate as to why the war brought about high annual savings rates. Would you expect that the war on terrorism would lead to an upward spurt in the personal saving rate?

13. *[research and development]* What is the difference between research and development? Why is the argument for the government subsidizing research stronger than the argument for subsidies to development?

14. *[theories of growth]* Explain the similarities and dissimilarities between new growth theory and supply-side economics.

15. *[supply-side economics]* Explain why critics of supply-side economics refer to it as "trickle-down economics." Explain why supply siders object to this characterization. Which president is known for promoting a supply-side agenda?

16. *[Laffer curve]* How could the Laffer curve be used by government policymakers? Illustrate your explanation with a graph showing the Laffer curve.

WORKING WITH GRAPHS AND DATA

1. *[equilibrium interest rate]* Observe how the principles of supply and demand analysis are used periodically throughout the study of economics.
   a. Draw a market for investment funds using demand and supply curves. Be sure to appropriately label the curves and axes. Indicate the equilibrium in the market.
   b. Explain how the market arrives back at equilibrium if the interest rate is above the equilibrium interest. Indicate this on the graph.
   c. Explain how the market arrives back at equilibrium if the interest rate is below the equilibrium interest. Indicate this on the graph.

2. *[supply-side economists]* The exercise asks you to apply the principles of aggregate supply and aggregate demand.
   a. Draw a graph depicting a macroeconomic equilibrium according to the perspective of the supply siders.
   b. Suppose that the government imposes new regulations that reduce worker productivity. According to supply-side theory, what will be the impact of these new regulations? Draw the impact on the graph.
   c. Suppose that the government decided to use expansionary fiscal policy. According to supply-side theory, what will be the impact of this expansionary fiscal policy? Draw the impact on the graph.
   d. Suppose that the government decided to reduce the marginal tax rates. According to supply-side theory, what will be the impact of this decrease in tax rates? Draw the impact on the graph.

3. *[Laffer curve]* The Laffer curve is often associated with supply-side economics.
   a. Draw a Laffer curve and label the axes.
   b. Explain the relationship shown by the curve.
   c. Explain how maximum tax revenue is achieved.

4. *[capital formation]* Graph 12-1 depicts the market for saving and investment. To answer the following questions, start in each case by reproducing the graph and noting the equilibrium. Then mark how it changes.

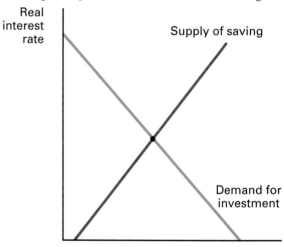

GRAPH 12-1

   a. What is the impact of a decrease in the capital gains tax on this market? Draw it on your graph.
   b. What is the impact of an increase in the marginal income tax rates? Draw it on your graph.
   c. Suppose that the federal government subsidizes saving by providing $0.01 for each additional dollar of income saved. *Ceteris paribus,* or holding all else constant, what impact does this have on the above market? Draw it on your graph.
   d. What is the impact of an increase in the capital gains tax? Draw it on your graph.

 Visit www.prenhall.com/ayers for Exploring the Web exercises and additional self-test quizzes.

CHAPTER **13**

MONEY, BANKING, AND THE FEDERAL RESERVE

A LOOK AHEAD

"Closed by Order of the Federal Deposit Insurance Corporation." Such signs were posted on hundreds of banks in the 1980s. For the individual depositor, bank failure is an unsettling event, but usually just a minor inconvenience. Depositors soon regain access to their money, along with receiving word of the name of the bank that has taken over their accounts.

Most depositors need not worry about permanently losing their savings because of bank failures. The government's deposit insurance, currently in the amount of $100,000 per bank account, has offered peace of mind to depositors since the 1930s. In this chapter's Explore & Apply section, you will learn why bank failures, although rare today, can occur and why they are worrisome to people. While repeated bank failures usually have little impact on individuals, they can ultimately reduce public confidence in the banking system and make bank loans less available.

Commercial banks are the banks we find on Main Street. The Federal Reserve (the Fed) is the U.S. *central bank,* a special kind of bank charged with regulating money and commercial banks. Together, the commercial banks and the Federal Reserve make up the U.S. banking system, which plays an instrumental role in shaping the quantity of money. Money, in turn, is itself at the heart of the macroeconomy. This chapter begins by examining money, its functions, and how it is measured. A discussion of banking and the Fed completes the chapter.

LEARNING OBJECTIVES

Understanding Chapter 13 will enable you to:
1. **Identify the types, functions, and liquidity of various money measures.**
2. **Describe key elements of the banking industry.**
3. **Discuss how banks create money.**
4. **Describe the structure, functions, and policy tools of the Federal Reserve.**
5. **Work through the process of monetary expansion using the deposit multiplier.**
6. **Explain why the banking crisis of the 1980s occurred and whether another banking crisis could happen.**

Explore & Apply

Meeting the macro goals of high employment, low inflation, and economic growth is made easier by the existence of money and banks, including a central bank. In previous chapters money has stayed in the background, but here it comes front and center, along with banks and the Federal Reserve.

13.1 MONEY

money what is commonly used to buy and sell things.

barter exchange of one good for another.

Money is whatever is commonly used in an economy to buy and sell things. To put money into perspective, imagine a world in which it did not exist. To fulfill our wants, we would have to either swap one good for another—**barter**—or produce on our own all the goods and services we consume. Both alternatives are inefficient. Money provides us with higher living standards; that's why money is no fad and never goes out of style. In one form or another, money has been in continuous use from the earliest days of civilization. Among the important qualities of money are *portability* and *divisibility*. Money should be easy to carry around, and divisible to make it convenient to spend and receive change.

THE CHARACTERISTICS OF MONEY

Everyone knows what money is. It's the rectangular pieces of paper with pictures of presidents and the shiny metallic coins that we carry with us when we go shopping, right? Not quite. If it has value, is portable, and doesn't turn to mush, it has probably served as money somewhere. Among Native Americans, wampum (seashells) was used as money. Livestock, produce, tobacco, colonial currency, foreign currency, and furs were money at various times in the early days of America.

Gold was money for thousands of years. Given the long history of monetary gold, it may surprise you that gold is not used as money in the United States today. What, then, performs the role of money? Government-issued currency and coins are money, but they are most assuredly *not* the largest part of the money that we own. The electronic notations of bankers representing checking account money hold that distinction, as we'll see in the next section.

Money performs the following functions:

medium of exchange the purchasing function of money.

store of value the function of money related to holding wealth.

unit of account a use of money that occurs when the value of one item is compared with the value of another in terms of monetary units.

fiat money money not backed by a commodity; money by decree of law.

- **Medium of exchange.** Money is used to make purchases. Money must be acceptable to sellers, who will find it so only if they believe that others will, too.
- **Store of value.** Money is a means of holding wealth, but by no means the only one. Real estate, jewelry crafted of precious stones and metals, and stocks and bonds also serve as stores of value, because they are not perishable. Conversely, food and clothing are not used as money.
- **Unit of account.** The market values of goods and services are expressed as prices, which are stated in terms of money. The monetary unit varies from one nation to another. These monetary values are used for a variety of purposes, including measuring GDP and comparing goods.

Fiat money is money because the law says it is. Paper currency and current U.S. coins are examples. Because the government accepts fiat money, individuals and businesses do as well. Look at your paper money and see this reminder that our money is fiat money: "This note is legal tender for all debts, public and private." Gold and silver coins, once a commonplace form of money in the United States, are examples of *commodity money*. Commodity money is made from precious metals. In contrast, coins today are made from cheaper metals. The silver dimes that once filled change drawers in store cash registers have been replaced by dimes made of cheaper metals. Paper currency in the United States is not backed by gold, silver, or any other precious metal. As fiat money it does not need to be.

Unfortunately, commodity money is subject to **Gresham's law**—bad money drives out good. In other words, people have the incentive to nick, shave, or otherwise reduce the metallic content of coins. A little bit of gold shaved from the edges of enough coins can add up to a nice little nest egg. When the shaved coins are spent, they will be accepted by sellers who do not examine them closely. If they notice later, anyone possessing such an altered coin tries to spend it first and hoard the better, unaltered ones that contain more precious metal. This practice forces recipients of commodity money to examine it carefully, weigh it, and even bite it. People do not wish to examine their money this closely, and thus turn to fiat money instead. Of course, fiat money must be designed so that it is not easily counterfeited.

The governments of virtually all nations today hold a monopoly on the production of fiat money. The profit from the difference between the value of money and the cost of producing it is called *seigniorage*. For example, the U.S. Mint has reported that the cost of making 1,000 pennies, with a face value of $10, was $8.21 in 2000. The difference between the face value and the cost, equal to $1.79, is an example of seigniorage. Seigniorage is much greater for higher denomination coins and paper money.

Gresham's law bad money drives good money out of circulation.

SNAPSHOT

DEBIT OR CREDIT?

That plastic card that you swipe through the reader at your local Home Depot could be a traditional credit card, like those used for more than fifty years, but it is increasingly likely to be a more recent invention, the debit card. What is the difference? The debit card immediately transfers the amount of your purchase out of your checking account and into the store's deposit account. In effect, it saves you the trouble of writing a check, and eliminates the possibility of bouncing a check. You can't use a debit card to make a purchase unless you have the amount of your purchase in your account.

In contrast, a credit card provides you with a loan in the amount of the purchase. When you receive your monthly statement you must repay at least part of the loan. The debit card came much later than the credit card because debit cards would not be practical without high-speed computer networks. Debit cards make it easier for consumers to spend their checking account money. Like credit cards, debit cards are not money. Even if every bank depositor were issued a debit card tomorrow, the amount of money that exists would not change. It would just be easier to spend. ◄

LIQUIDITY: M1, M2, AND M3

When paper money and coins are deposited in banks, money changes form. Deposits into checking accounts create **demand deposits,** also termed *checkable deposits.* More money is held in the form of checkable deposits than in any other form. These deposits are money because

demand deposits checking account deposits at commercial banks.

checks—orders to a bank to make payment—are generally accepted by sellers. Traveler's checks are also generally accepted by sellers of goods and services. In addition, currency may be transformed into any of several "near monies," such as balances in savings accounts.

liquidity how easily and quickly an item can be turned into a spendable form.

Liquidity refers to how easily and quickly something of value can be converted into spendable form. An item is highly liquid if it is spendable without delay. Money is highly liquid, but some types of money are more liquid than others. Three definitions of money, termed the *monetary aggregates,* categorize various types of money according to how liquid they are. The monetary aggregates include M1, M2, and M3. M1 is the most liquid of these and totaled $1.3 trillion in mid-2003. M2 is slightly less liquid and totaled $6.1 trillion that year, while M3, which is much less liquid, totaled $8.9 trillion. The specific components of each category are as follows:

M1 most liquid measure of money; currency plus demand deposits, traveler's checks, and other checkable deposits.

- **M1:** The sum of currency and coins in the hands of the public, demand deposits, other checkable deposits, and traveler's checks. These forms of money are the most easily and immediately spendable. **Currency stored in bank vaults is not counted in the money supply because it is not available to make purchases.**

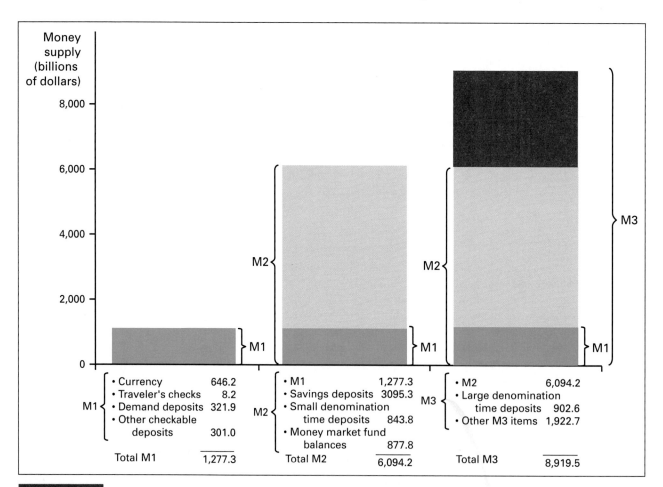

FIGURE 13-1

THE COMPONENTS OF M1, M2, AND M3 The M1 measure of the money supply includes only the most liquid items. Less-liquid items are added to arrive at M2 and M3. The bars rise in height when the additional components of the M2 and M3 money supply are added. Values are in billions of dollars.

Source: Money Stock Measures, August 14, 2003. The data shown are for July 2003. The values in the figure vary slightly from those in the source because of rounding.

- **M2:** M1 plus the balances in savings deposits, "small" time deposits, and balances in money market mutual funds. *Time deposits* are certificates of deposit (CDs), which can be withdrawn without penalty only after some period of time, such as one or five years. The Fed considers CDs small if they are less than $100,000!

- **M3:** M2 plus large time deposits (at least $100,000), and several other near monies. These additional components of M3 are even less likely to be spent than the items in M2.

M2 obtained by adding savings deposits, small time deposits, and money market fund balances to M1.

M3 expands M2 by adding large time deposits and several other near monies.

Figure 13-1 illustrates how the M2 and M3 measures of the quantity of money build on the M1 measure. Figure 13-2 shows that the money supply, whether measured by M1, M2, or M3, grows each year.

Because currency and coins are immediately spendable, they are completely liquid. Demand deposits are only slightly less liquid, because businesses often require check writers to present some form of identification before the check is accepted. Savings account deposits are slightly less liquid than demand deposits, but can be converted into demand deposits or currency with a trip to the bank.

Financial assets, such as stocks and bonds, are not counted in the money supply figures. They are nonetheless relatively liquid because they can be readily sold in the financial marketplace at fair market value, although brokerage fees reduce their liquidity. In contrast, most nonfinancial assets are not very liquid. For example, automobiles, furniture, and personal belongings are difficult to sell quickly at their market value. Similarly, the sale of real estate usually involves large broker's fees.

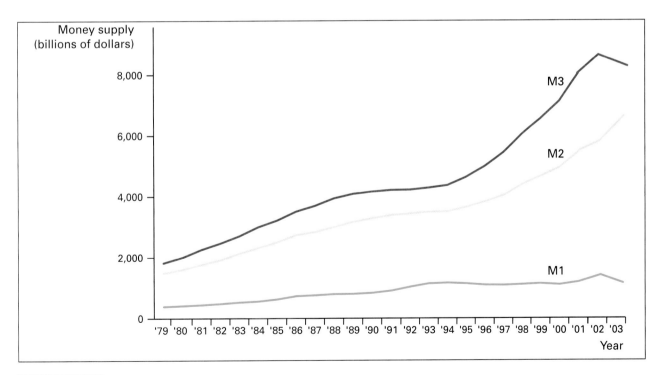

FIGURE 13-2

THE GROWTH OF THE M1, M2, AND M3 MONEY SUPPLY Over many years the money supply grows larger, no matter whether measured as M1, M2, or M3.

Source: 2003 Economic Report of the President, Table B-69, and the Federal Reserve. The 2003 data are through July.

QUICKCHECK

State the effect on the money supply in each of the following instances:
a. Check printing companies print more blank checks.
b. An individual deposits $9,000 in currency into a checking account in the bank.
c. An individual moves $500 from a savings account to a checking account.

Answer: (a) The printing of more blank checks does not change the money supply since it is the balances in demand deposit accounts that are measured by M1. (b) Depositing currency into a checking account leaves the money supply the same. (c) Moving balances from a savings account to a checking account leaves the M2 money supply the same. The M1 money supply increases because this move increases demand deposits.

SNAPSHOT

THE EURO—OUT WITH THE OLD AND IN WITH THE NEW

U.S. residents take it for granted that the same dollar bills are just as spendable in New York as New Orleans. Europeans, on the other hand, have historically had to contend with changes in currency and coins even for short trips that cross borders between countries. That has recently changed.

January 1, 1999, marked an historic moment in monetary history. The three-year transition to a new monetary unit began in eleven of the countries making up the European Monetary Union. The German mark, the French franc, the Italian lire, and the other familiar currencies issued by many European countries began to disappear in 2002, replaced by the euro. More countries may also make the jump to the euro as time passes. The Monetary Union also requires a new European Central Bank to conduct monetary policy, which was once the job of central banks in individual countries.

Why would countries risk confusion by dropping their familiar currencies, not to mention the loss of control over their own money? These changes are all part of a long-term effort to integrate the economies of Europe to make them more competitive with the United States and Japan in the global marketplace. A common currency will also ease the burdens on harried travelers who would rather worry about the price of lodging in the night's ski chalet than about having the right currency to pay that price! ◀

13.2 MONEY AND BANKING IN THE UNITED STATES

As Americans moved westward during the first 100 years of the country's existence, new banks were needed to facilitate commerce whenever towns grew up. For the most part, banking regulation was weak, and so banks were easy to start. The legacy of that frontier history lives on, as the United States today has more banks than any other country. Currently, about 7,900 U.S. commercial banks and 1,450 savings institutions accept deposits and make loans.

THE BANKING SYSTEM

Since the mid-1980s the number of banks in the United States has plummeted because of bank failures and bank mergers. More specifically, the number of banks fell an astonishing 33 percent between 1990 and 2003. During this period the United States has seen the rise of megabanks—large banks that do business in many locations. Megabanks thrive in today's climate of *interstate banking* as legal barriers against branching across state lines have fallen. On-line banking from home or work using the Internet has become common, allowing people to check their account balances, pay bills, or transfer funds among accounts. The fact is that banks are becoming more national, and even international, institutions in terms of their reach.

Banks are regulated by both state and federal governments. Bank regulation is designed to protect against unsound banking practices that could bankrupt both depositors and government insurance funds. Bank regulation is controversial. Since regulations inhibit banks from responding to the demands of their customers, regulations can lead to inefficiencies in the financial system. For example, under the Glass–Steagall Act of 1933, banks were barred from offering insurance and brokerage services. The act was intended to keep banks away from risky investment activities that could endanger the banking system. Over time, the inefficiencies created by Glass–Steagall were recognized and a number of its provisions were relaxed because of changes in the law, regulatory interpretations, and court decisions. Yet the act stayed on the books.

Congress finally killed off the Glass–Steagall Act in 1999 after twelve attempts to do so in the prior twenty-five years. Why was it so difficult to abolish a law that many, including Federal Reserve Chairman Alan Greenspan, felt inhibited the competitiveness and efficiency of the U.S. financial system? For one reason, insurance and brokerage firms were happy that banks could not enter their markets to compete with them. For another, smaller banks were content to stay out of these businesses and were pleased that their larger competitors were forced out, too. The lesson? Good economics and good politics do not always go hand in hand.

To understand how our banking system operates, it is useful to consider a simplified *balance sheet* showing the assets and liabilities of a bank, as seen in Table 13-1. The assets are things that a bank owns, and reveal how banks use funds. In a balance sheet, assets are always listed on the left side. The liabilities are what the bank owes, and reveal how a bank raises funds. Liabilities are listed on the right side.

Take a look at bank assets first. The two most liquid assets, vault cash and deposits held by the Federal Reserve, are normally lumped together to form what are called *cash assets*. Bank deposits at the Fed are cash assets for banks because banks can cash in their deposits at the Fed in the same way that you can go to your bank and withdraw cash from your checking or savings accounts. The sum of vault cash plus deposits with the Fed is called **bank reserves**. Bank reserves are highly liquid and so are available immediately to meet

bank reserves vault cash plus deposits held by the Fed.

TABLE 13-1   A BALANCE SHEET—MAJOR ASSETS AND LIABILITIES OF BANKS

ASSETS	LIABILITIES
Vault cash (part 1 of bank reserves)	Customer deposits
Deposits held by the Federal Reserve (part 2 of bank reserves)	Federal funds
Loans	Discount loans
Securities	
Other	

depositor withdrawals. This liquidity provides banks with a margin of safety should depositor withdrawals unexpectedly increase.

Banks hold some fraction of their deposits on reserve to meet the cash needs of their customers. Individual banks are also required by law to meet the *reserve requirements* imposed by the Fed. The current reserve requirement of approximately 10 percent for demand deposits means that banks must hold at least $10 in reserves for every $100 of customer deposits. Reserves in excess of **required reserves** are called **excess reserves.** Hence, total reserves equal required reserves plus excess reserves.

Bank reserves are a non-income-producing asset. This characteristic motivates banks to minimize the amount of bank reserves held so long as the banks are meeting the reserve requirement and are satisfied with the margin of safety provided by the quantity of reserves held. If bank reserves provide banks with no income, how then do they earn revenues? Loans and securities provide the answer.

The next asset in Table 13-1 is loans, which represent promises by borrowers to repay borrowed funds. Bank loans go to both the household and business sectors. Banks lend to borrowers in order to earn income in the form of interest. Bank loans are extended to borrowers for many purposes, such as to finance a business, a car, home improvements, and college tuition. Interest rates that borrowers pay on a bank loan vary, mainly depending on the purpose of the loan, and the risk to the bank that the loan will not be repaid in full. One interest rate on bank loans that is widely known to the public is the *bank prime lending rate.* This interest rate applies to short-term business loans. When there are changes in interest rates, the prime rate is usually singled out by the news media to represent interest rates in general.

Interest payments on investments purchased by banks also provide banks with income. *Securities,* in the form of **bonds,** are interest-paying investments. The government issues bonds when it borrows money from investors in order to pay the expenses of government that are not covered by tax collections. Large business firms also issue bonds in order to borrow money. Investors that purchase bonds include individuals, banks, and other financial institutions. Many people are familiar with U.S. Savings Bonds, which provide a safe investment vehicle for small savers. Banks do not invest in these bonds. Neither do they invest in bonds issued by business firms. Instead, they mostly purchase federally issued short-term bonds called *T-bills,* which is short for *Treasury bills.* T-bills are an attractive investment because their owners can easily convert them to cash. T-bills come in large denominations of $10,000 each. To the federal government, T-bills and other Treasury bonds are debt because they represent money the government borrows.

Although banks are prohibited by law from investing in risky securities, loans to borrowers do carry a risk of non-repayment. Sometimes loans go sour when borrowers are unable to repay them. It is normal for a small fraction of loans to be uncollectible. The expenses generated by bad loans raises the cost of borrowing and reduces the profits earned by banks. If the amount of bad loans goes beyond norms, banks might not be able to pay off their depositors. That possibility is why the *Federal Deposit Insurance Corporation (FDIC)* insures deposit accounts up to $100,000. This insurance reduces the likelihood of bank runs, in which numerous depositors simultaneously seek to withdraw funds because of fears about the financial soundness of a bank. The tradeoff is that FDIC insurance allows banks to make riskier loans without scaring away their depositors. These depositors know that their funds are secure no matter how many unsound loans a bank may make.

Banks also own other assets, such as their buildings, equipment, and fixtures. These assets are needed in order to do business with the public.

Now take a look at the liabilities in Table 13-1. Bank deposits are liabilities because they are funds owed to depositors. Banks also raise funds by borrowing, both from each other and from the Federal Reserve. Funds borrowed from other banks are called *federal funds.* The interest rate that banks charge on loans to other banks is called the **federal funds rate.** The federal funds rate is determined by the supply and demand in the marketplace for fed-

required reserves bank reserves held to meet the Fed's reserve requirement; expressed as a percentage of deposits.

excess reserves the amount of bank reserves that exceed the amount needed to meet the reserve requirement.

bonds interest-paying investments; also called securities.

federal funds rate interest rate on loans that banks make to other banks.

eral funds. Most of the funds borrowed in the federal funds market are repaid the next day. Although the federal funds rate is not widely known among the general public, as you will soon see, it is probably the most significant interest rate in terms of the Federal Reserve's monetary policy influence on banks.

Borrowings by banks from the Federal Reserve are called *discount loans* because the Federal Reserve is said to "discount" its loans. To discount a loan means that banks are required to pay the interest on loans from the Fed when the loans are made rather than as they are repaid. The rate of interest charged is termed the **discount rate,** which is set by the Fed. Funds borrowed by banks at the so-called "discount window" at the Fed are typically repaid quite rapidly because banks need these funds to meet a temporary shortfall in the reserve requirement.

discount rate interest rate set by the Fed on loans it makes to banks.

For simplicity, the balance sheet in Table 13-1 ignores *net worth*, which is assets minus liabilities. By definition, the value of the sum of the assets must equal the value of the sum of the liabilities plus net worth for any balance sheet.

KEY BANK INTEREST RATES

Table 13-2 shows yearly data for the prime rate, federal funds rate, and the discount rate since 1979. Observe that the prime rate is greater than the federal funds rate and the discount rate every year. This difference illustrates the idea that banks can borrow funds at interest rates lower than the interest rates they charge borrowers. In this way, banks profit from their loans. Observe also that in general the three interest rates move in the same direction over time. Thus, year to year increases or decreases in the cost of borrowing for banks is translated into increases or decreases in the cost of borrowing for their customers.

In addition to banks, there are other *financial intermediaries,* bank-like institutions that accept funds from savers in order to make loans or investments. With minor exceptions, the discussion of banks in this text also applies to credit unions and savings and loans. Insurance companies, mutual funds, pension funds, and finance companies are examples of nonbank financial intermediaries, because, although they are not banks, they invest the funds they raise.

DO BANKS DISCRIMINATE IN MAKING LOANS? *SNAPSHOT*

"Redlining!" Some banks have been accused of this illegal practice, which makes it tough to get a loan if you're in a low- and moderate-income neighborhood. Redlining violates the 1977 Community Reinvestment Act (CRA), which requires banks to service their entire community. The law does not require them to abandon sound banking principles, and banks defend themselves by noting that the profit motive prompts them to reject risky loans no matter the neighborhood.

The Federal Reserve assesses bank compliance with the CRA. It's found that of over 5,800 banks examined since 1990, just 38 have been in "substantial noncompliance" with the law, with another 208 rated as "needs to improve." Bank examinations, such as those called for by the CRA, provide a transparency to bank decision making that can help us know the extent of redlining and other potential problems in the banking system. ◀

TABLE 13-2	KEY INTEREST RATES: THE PRIME RATE, FEDERAL FUNDS RATE, AND DISCOUNT RATE

YEAR	PRIME RATE	FEDERAL FUNDS RATE	DISCOUNT RATE
1979	12.67	11.20	10.29
1980	15.26	13.35	11.77
1981	18.87	16.39	13.42
1982	14.85	12.24	11.01
1983	10.79	9.09	8.50
1984	12.04	10.23	8.80
1985	9.93	8.10	7.69
1986	8.33	6.80	6.32
1987	8.21	6.66	5.66
1988	9.32	7.57	6.20
1989	10.87	9.21	6.93
1990	10.01	8.10	6.98
1991	8.46	5.69	5.45
1992	6.25	3.52	3.25
1993	6.00	3.02	3.00
1994	7.15	4.21	3.60
1995	8.83	5.83	5.21
1996	8.27	5.30	5.02
1997	8.44	5.46	5.00
1998	8.35	5.35	4.92
1999	8.00	4.97	4.62
2000	9.23	6.24	5.73
2001	6.91	3.88	3.40
2002	4.67	1.67	1.17
2003	4.00	0.96	2.00

Source: Federal Reserve. Interest rates for 2003 are those effective August 8, 2003. All others are yearly averages. After January 8, 2003, the discount rate refers to discount window primary credit.

HOW BANKS CREATE MONEY

When a bank makes a loan, the quantity of money in the economy increases. To see how, suppose you hope to borrow the cost of a new PT Cruiser, $18,000, from your bank, Homestate University National Bank. After discussing your loan request with loan officer Softheart, the loan is approved. Soon you'll be behind the wheel of your first new car.

If you receive the loan as currency, the amount of currency in the hands of the public, which includes you, is greater than before the loan. Recall that this currency, while inside the bank's vault, was not included in the money supply. Once you receive the $18,000, the M1, M2, and M3 money supplies increase by that amount.

You might not feel safe with $18,000 cash on your person. For this reason, you probably received the loan in the form of an $18,000 check deposited in your checking account. Again, the M1, M2, and M3 money supplies increase by $18,000. We can illustrate the effect of a loan on a bank's balance sheet by referring to the changes in Homestate University National Bank's balance sheet, seen below. The bank acquires an asset, your IOU promising to repay the loan. Customer deposits increase on the other side of the balance sheet because the bank increases your account by $18,000 when the loan is made.

HOMESTATE UNIVERSITY NATIONAL BANK: BALANCE SHEET CHANGES WHEN A LOAN IS MADE

ASSETS		LIABILITIES	
Loans	+ $18,000	Customer deposits	+ $18,000

When you pay for your new car, the bank's balance sheet will change again. Customer deposits decrease by $18,000 since you no longer have that money in your account. Bank reserves will also fall by $18,000 since the bank will either lose $18,000 in vault cash, or see its deposits at the Fed reduced by that amount. The balance sheet effects are shown below.

HOMESTATE UNIVERSITY NATIONAL BANK: BALANCE SHEET CHANGES WHEN A LOAN IS SPENT

ASSETS		LIABILITIES	
Reserves	− $18,000	Customer deposits	− $18,000

When borrowers repay bank loans, the quantity of money falls. If a loan is repaid with currency, the money supply decreases because there is less currency in the hands of the public. If a loan is repaid by writing a check, the money supply falls due to fewer demand deposits. Say that you repay your $18,000 loan all at once. That wipes out your IOU and increases the bank's reserves, as shown.

HOMESTATE UNIVERSITY NATIONAL BANK: BALANCE SHEET CHANGES WHEN A LOAN IS REPAID

ASSETS		LIABILITIES
Reserves	+ $18,000	
Loans	− $18,000	

13.3 MEET THE FED

In the United States, it is the Federal Reserve that performs the central banking functions at the heart of the monetary system. So, in addition to looking at money and banks, we are now ready to look at the Federal Reserve. The Fed is known to the public for engineering changes in short-term interest rates. However, the Fed does much more. Let's take a look at the Fed and its responsibilities.

STRUCTURE AND FUNCTIONS OF THE FEDERAL RESERVE

Federal Reserve System U.S. central bank; conducts monetary policy, holds bank deposits, and performs several other functions.

In England, it is affectionately known as the "Old Lady of Threadneedle Street," but it is officially called the Bank of England. In Germany, it is the Bundesbank; in Canada, the Bank of Canada; and in Hong Kong, the Hong Kong Monetary Authority. What is it? A central bank, a bank that is an arm of the government charged with seeing to it that the monetary system functions efficiently. In Europe as a whole it is called the European Central Bank. The U.S. central bank is called the Fed, short for **Federal Reserve System.** It was created by the *Federal Reserve Act of 1913* in response to recurring problems of bank failure and the belief that a central bank could contribute to U.S. economic stability. With its creation, Congress sought to provide the banking system with the stabilizing influence of a central bank. To this end, the Fed does the following:

- **Functions as a banker's bank.** The Fed holds reserves for commercial banks.
- **Functions as a lender of last resort.** The Fed lends reserves to sound banks that are temporarily short of reserves. Withdrawals by depositors deplete reserves. If depositors become concerned about a bank's ability to pay, the rush to withdraw funds can create a bank run.
- **Supervises banks.** Banks are held accountable for complying with the federal laws and regulations that apply to banks. The Fed is one of several government agencies that is responsible for overseeing compliance.
- **Conducts monetary policy.** The Fed was established for the purpose of providing an elastic money supply—a quantity of money that responds to the demands of the economy. Monetary policy involves the Fed in changing short-term interest rates and the quantity of money.
- **Issues currency.** Paper money in the United States is mostly made up of Federal Reserve Notes, which you can verify by looking at the front of the currency in your wallet or purse. Currency is printed by the U.S. Treasury, but put into circulation by the Fed.
- **Clears checks.** When you write a check, the check must clear, meaning that your bank must reduce your account by the amount of the check. The Fed operates facilities that process and transport checks to the banks upon which they are written so that the banks can clear them.

Congress also sought to keep the Fed *independent,* meaning free from political pressures that might lead it to take actions that would harm the economy in the long run. Because the Fed does not depend upon Congress for its income, but instead earns income from its investments and from providing banking services, the Fed is one of the more independent central banks around the world. This fact is important because evidence shows that countries with independent central banks suffer less inflation. To further insulate the Fed from the political process, the Fed is divided into three components:

- The *Board of Governors,* which is responsible for the overall direction of the Federal Reserve and its policies.
- The *Federal Open Market Committee (FOMC),* which conducts monetary policy.
- The *Federal Reserve Banks,* which regulate and provide a variety of services for banks.

There are seven members of the Board of Governors. They are appointed to fourteen-year nonrenewable terms by the president, with the advice and consent of the Senate. Terms are staggered so that one term expires every two years, which minimizes political influence over the Fed. One of the seven is named by the president to chair the Board. The chairperson, who serves a four-year renewable term, is the most powerful individual in the Fed and one of the most powerful people in the country. As of 2003, Alan Greenspan held the position.

The FOMC consists of twelve members, the seven members of the Board plus four rotating district bank presidents, as well as the president of the New York District Bank. The president of the New York Fed is always a member of the Committee because New York City is the hub of the United States' financial markets. The FOMC usually meets at intervals of approximately four to six weeks, making adjustments in the conduct of monetary policy in accordance with its assessment of economic conditions.

There are twelve regional Federal Reserve Banks, as shown in Figure 13-3. Together with their branches, these Banks perform the routine functions of the Fed. Chances are that you have benefited from their services today. Federal Reserve Banks issue currency, which bears the location of the issuing bank. Commercial banks within a district make deposits of reserves into their district's Federal Reserve Bank. Federal Reserve Banks also operate the Fed's check-clearing operations, which allow funds to be expeditiously transferred from check writers' accounts to the accounts of the banks that cash the checks. These banks also participate in the supervision of commercial banks in their districts.

INFLUENCING THE MONEY SUPPLY: OPEN MARKET OPERATIONS

The principal method the Fed uses to influence the money supply is called open market operations. **Open market operations** occur when the Fed enters the financial marketplace to buy or sell government securities, such as Treasury bonds or Treasury bills. The Fed does not itself issue government securities; the U.S. Department of the Treasury issues Treasury bonds and bills. The Fed can only obtain them in the open market, hence the name. Open market operations allow currency, in the form of Federal Reserve Notes, to make its way into circulation.

open market operations buying and selling of Treasury bonds and Treasury bills by the Fed; tool of monetary policy.

For example, suppose your Aunt Elvira sells a bond to the Fed for $10,000. The Fed issues a check written on itself, payable to Aunt Elvira. When she deposits the check in her checking account at Investors' National Bank, demand deposits in the banking system increase by the amount of the check. Thus, the money supply increases. If she had cashed the check instead, currency in the hands of the public would have increased. Either way, the money supply rises.

When an individual buys a bond sold by the Fed, the money supply decreases. Suppose the buyer pays for the bond by writing a check. When the buyer's bank pays the Fed, the buyer's checking account is reduced by the amount of the check. Thus, demand deposits decrease, as does the money supply.

The bulk of the Fed's open market operations involve banks directly. An open market sale to a bank by the Fed decreases bank reserves. Fewer reserves mean that the bank is able to do less lending. Thus, open market sales tend to reduce the money supply. A greater volume of open market sales is consistent with a tighter policy.

An open market purchase by the Fed from a bank increases bank reserves, which in turn tends to increase the money supply because banks have more money to loan. However, whether loans are actually made and the money supply actually increased depends on the willingness of banks to make loans and on the desire of the public to borrow. **Thus, the Fed influences, but does not control, the money supply.**

However, by conducting open market operations, **the Fed controls the monetary base.** The **monetary base** is the sum of currency held by the public plus bank reserves. **An open market purchase by the Fed always increases the monetary base by the amount of the purchase; an open market sale always decreases the monetary base by the amount of the sale.**

monetary base sum of currency in circulation plus bank reserves.

Let's look at four kinds of open market operations, and examine their balance sheet effects.

■ Fed buys a $10,000 bond from a member of the public, and the seller deposits the funds received in a commercial bank.

FIGURE 13-3

THE FEDERAL RESERVE SYSTEM The Federal Reserve System is divided into twelve district national banks—those chartered by the federal government—which are automatically members of the Federal Reserve. Banks with state charters may join at their option. Whether or not they are members of the Federal Reserve System, however, all banks have nearly equal access to the Fed's services and are subject to its regulations. Thus, although only about 3,000 banks are formal members, in practical terms all banks fall under Federal Reserve regulation.

Source: http://www.federalreserve.gov/otherfrb.htm.

BANK BALANCE SHEET CHANGES: PUBLIC SELLS BOND

ASSETS		LIABILITIES	
Reserves	+ $10,000	Customer deposits	+ $10,000

■ Fed buys a $10,000 bond from a commercial bank.

BANK BALANCE SHEET CHANGES: BANK SELLS BOND

ASSETS		LIABILITIES	
Bonds	− $10,000		
Reserves	+ $10,000		

■ Fed sells a $10,000 bond to a member of the public. The buyer writes a check to pay for the bond.

BANK BALANCE SHEET CHANGES: PUBLIC PURCHASES BOND

ASSETS		LIABILITIES	
Reserves	− $10,000	Customer deposits	− $10,000

■ Fed sells a $10,000 bond to a commercial bank. The bank pays for the bond by having its account at the Fed reduced by $10,000.

BANK BALANCE SHEET CHANGES: BANK PURCHASES BOND

ASSETS		LIABILITIES	
Reserves	− $10,000		
Bonds	+ $10,000		

In which of the four types of open market operations did the money supply immediately change at the completion of the transaction? To answer that question look for a change in customer deposits. When the Fed buys or sells a bond to the public, the money supply changes immediately. When the transaction involved a bank, there was no immediate change in the money supply. However, when bank reserves increase, banks are able to make more loans. When bank reserves decrease, the opposite is true. This means that **any open market operation has the potential to change the money supply, if not now, then later.**

In which cases did the monetary base increase? Since all four cases saw a change in bank reserves, the monetary base changed in all cases. As previously stated, any open market operation changes the monetary base immediately.

QUICKCHECK

If Aunt Elvira, who sold a $10,000 bond to the Fed, deposited the Fed's check into her savings account, would the money supply increase?

Answer: The M1 money supply would remain unchanged. However, M2 and M3 would rise, because these measures include savings accounts.

THE MONEY MULTIPLIER AND THE MONETARY BASE

The effects of open market operations do not stop with the initial purchase or sale. Secondary effects magnify changes in the money supply or monetary base. For example, an open market purchase from an individual increases the money supply once when the seller receives the proceeds of the sale. If those funds are deposited in a bank, and then loaned to someone, the money supply increases again. This process can continue over and over.

money multiplier the amount by which a new deposit is multiplied to arrive at the actual increase in the money supply; maximum value is given by the deposit multiplier.

The *money multiplier* shows the total effect on the money supply of each dollar of open market operations. To see how the money multiplier works, return to Aunt Elvira's sale of a bond to the Fed. When her checking account increased with the deposit of the Fed's check, we saw that demand deposits in the banking system increased.

If we assume for simplicity that Investors' National Bank was just meeting a 10-percent reserve requirement prior to the $10,000 deposit, then the bank will find itself holding excess reserves of $9,000. Actual reserves have increased by $10,000, but the bank is only required to hold 10 percent of that amount, equal to $1,000, as required reserves. The bank is thus able to make loans up to the amount of excess reserves and still meet the reserve requirement.

As it happens, your best friend wishes to borrow $9,000 to finance the purchase of a used Saturn automobile. After your friend speaks with loan officer Pushover at Investors' National Bank, the loan is approved. That loan increases the money supply by $9,000. The auto dealer deposits your friend's check into the dealer's bank. That bank will then have excess reserves to lend. The amount of required reserves equals $900, so excess reserves equal $8,100, the amount that can be loaned.

This lending–depositing–lending sequence could continue. Someone can borrow $8,100. When the loan is spent and someone else deposits the $8,100 in his or her bank, that bank will have excess reserves, which it is able to lend. At each succeeding step in the process, the sum of money loaned, which is new money, grows smaller because each succeeding bank in the sequence must hold a portion as required reserves. Thus the process is eventually exhausted when the last bank in the sequence has essentially nothing left to lend.

What is the total of new money created when the expansion of the money supply is complete? The answer depends on the money multiplier.

$$\text{Money supply} = \text{Money multiplier} \times \text{Monetary base}$$

The money multiplier can vary according to loan prospects and people's behavior, and is thus hard to calculate with precision. However, an upper bound can be found by calculat

deposit multiplier upper bound on the value of the money multiplier; computed as 1 divided by the reserve requirement.

ing the *deposit multiplier*—**the maximum possible value of the money multiplier.** The deposit multiplier is calculated by assuming that all money is held as demand deposits and that banks do not hold excess reserves. In practice, the true value of the money multiplier will be less than the deposit multiplier.

The deposit multiplier is the reciprocal of the percentage reserve requirement, meaning

$$\text{Deposit multiplier} = \frac{1}{\text{Reserve requirement}}$$

For example, if the reserve requirement equals 10 percent, then 1 divided by 10 percent equals 1/0.1, which gives a deposit multiplier of 10. To use this multiplier, multiply the Fed's original open market purchase of $10,000 by the multiplier, 10. The total of new money in that case is $100,000.

You can follow the process of money creation that follows an open market operation by referring to Figure 13-4. The process starts when Aunt Elvira deposits the $10,000 she received from the Fed in Investors' National Bank. Let's refer to Investors' National Bank as

Bank	Deposits received	Reserves kept	Loans made
Investors' National Bank = 1	$10,000	$1,000	$9,000
2	$9,000	$900	$8,100
3	$8,100	$810	$7,290
4	$7,290	$729	$6,561
5	$6,561	$656	$5,905
6	$5,905	$590	$5,315
7	$5,315	$532	$4,783
8	$4,783	$478	$4,305
9	$4,305	$430	$3,875
10	$3,875	$388	$3,487
Totals: Banks 1 – 10	$65,134	$6,513	$58,621
Totals: Infinite number of banks	$100,000	$10,000	$90,000

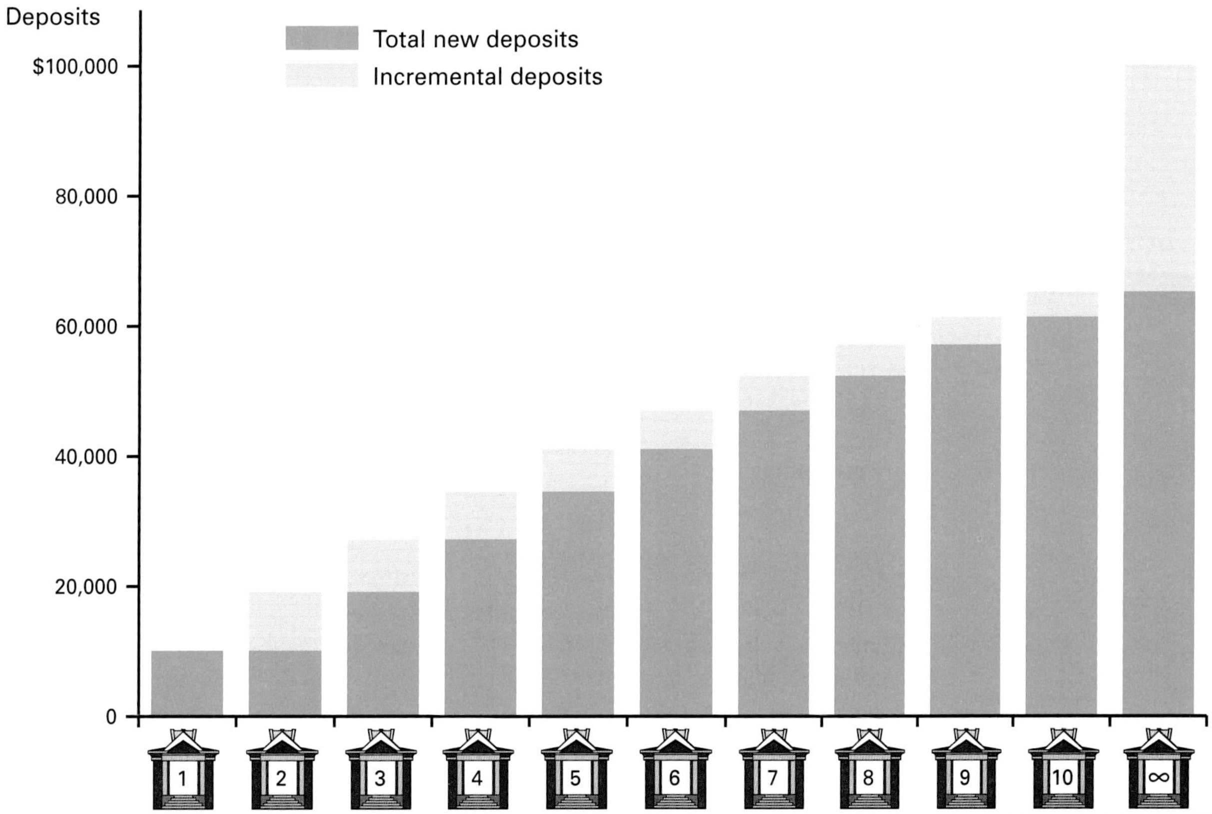

FIGURE 13-4

CREATION OF DEPOSIT MONEY, 10 PERCENT RESERVE REQUIREMENT You can track the expansion in the money supply by following the actions of the banks in the table. The graph presents the same information visually.

Bank 1, and follow the actions of the other banks in the process. Note that each loan expands the money supply.

- **Bank 1.** The bank keeps required reserves of 10 percent of the $10,000 deposit, equal to $1,000. It makes loans totaling $9,000 ($10,000 deposit − $1,000 reserve requirement = $9,000) with the rest.
- **Bank 2.** The $9,000 loan from Bank 1 is spent by the borrower, and is then deposited in Bank 2 by the person receiving the money. Bank 2 keeps $900 in reserves. It loans the $8,100 difference between the $9,000 deposit and the $900 it keeps in reserves.
- **Bank 3.** The borrower of the $8,100 spends the amount of the loan, and the individual receiving that money deposits it in Bank 3. Bank 3 keeps 10 percent in reserves, equal to $810. It loans the balance, $7,290, to a customer.
- **Banks 4 to 10.** Each of these banks keeps 10 percent of the deposit it receives as reserves, and makes loans with the other 90 percent. By the time that Bank 10 has completed its role in the process, $65,134 has been received as deposits by Banks 1 through 10, and $58,621 in loans have been made.
- **All other banks.** The process described continues through an infinite number of banks. Because the amount of deposits received shrinks with the involvement of each additional bank, there will be a limit on the amount of deposit money that is created. The deposit multiplier formula allows you to compute that amount of money, which is $100,000 in this case.

The following three factors affect the money multiplier, and thus the actual expansion of the money supply:

- **The reserve requirement:** Changes in the reserve requirement would change the deposit multiplier, and thus the maximum value of the money multiplier. A lower reserve requirement means that banks are able to lend a greater fraction of deposits; a higher reserve requirement has the opposite effect.
- **The public's desire to hold currency instead of deposits:** If people hold more of their money as currency and less as deposits, banks will have fewer dollars to lend. If Aunt Elvira had taken the original $10,000 from the sale of her bond as currency and buried it in her backyard, the multiple expansion of the money supply would not have taken place, thus reducing the multiplier effect.
- **The bank's desire to hold excess reserves:** Excess reserves may be held in order to meet unexpected depositor withdrawals, or because lending opportunities seem poor. Reserves that are not loaned out do not add to the money supply. **Excess reserves reduce the multiplier effect.**

OTHER TOOLS OF THE FED

In response to unexpected customer withdrawals, banks may wish to borrow from the Fed in order to maintain their required reserves. Recall that loans from the Fed to banks are called discount loans, and the rate of interest charged is called the discount rate. An increase in the discount rate makes it more costly for banks to borrow; a decrease makes it less costly.

Increases in the discount rate tend to decrease the quantity of money by prompting banks to borrow less from the Fed. Conversely, a decrease in the discount rate leads banks to borrow more from the Fed, which tends to increase the amount of money in circulation. Thus, **a change in the discount rate tends to cause the money supply to change in the opposite direction.**

Changes in the discount rate are typically front-page news because they are an easily understood signal of the Fed's policy intentions. The Fed may wish to see the money supply

TABLE 13-3	THE FED'S MONETARY POLICY OPTIONS	
TIGHTER MONETARY POLICY		**LOOSER MONETARY POLICY**
Open market sale of securities		Open market purchase of securities
Increase in discount rate		Decrease in discount rate
Increase in reserve requirement		Decrease in reserve requirement

QUICKCHECK

When the Fed lowers the discount rate, why does it become more likely that the money supply will increase?

Answer: A lower discount rate lowers the cost to banks of borrowing reserves from the Fed. Banks that are short of reserves are more likely to borrow reserves from the Fed and less likely to borrow from other banks. Thus, more funds are available in the banking system to lend to the public.

grow faster to stimulate growth and employment. An increase in the discount rate signals a tighter policy. Perhaps the Fed would like to slow down monetary growth to fight inflation.

The Fed could change the money supply dramatically by altering the reserve requirement. A decrease in required reserves would increase the money multiplier and spur monetary growth. An increase in the reserve requirement would reduce the money multiplier and thus decrease the money supply. Excess reserves, which banks are able to lend to borrowers, would become required reserves, which cannot be used to make loans.

The Fed is reluctant to increase reserve requirements because banks without sufficient excess reserves would be forced to sell securities or call in loans—actions that could prove disruptive to the bank and its customers. Thus, while potent, changes in reserve requirements are rarely used as an instrument of monetary policy. Table 13-3 summarizes the Fed's options in setting monetary policy. A *tight monetary policy* is intended to slow the economy down in order to keep inflation in check. A *loose monetary policy* is intended to have an expansionary effect on the economy. Monetary policy is discussed in detail in the next chapter.

13.4 HIGH-PRICED HOUSING—ARE BANKS AT RISK?

Housing prices in the United States have risen nearly 10 percent per year for the last decade. Is there a so-called *housing bubble,* a situation in which real estate prices have gotten so out of hand that they are poised to collapse? In the words of one influential magazine, "This may well be the single most important question currently hanging over the world economy" (*The Economist,* May 29, 2003).

After surveying housing data throughout the world and over time, that magazine predicted real estate price declines of 15 to 20 percent over the next few years in the United States, and declines of 30 percent or more in other countries. In contrast, Federal Reserve Chairman Alan Greenspan testified to Congress that the mortgage market remained strong. "The notion of a bubble bursting and the whole price level coming down seems to me, as far as a national nationwide phenomenon, is really quite unlikely."

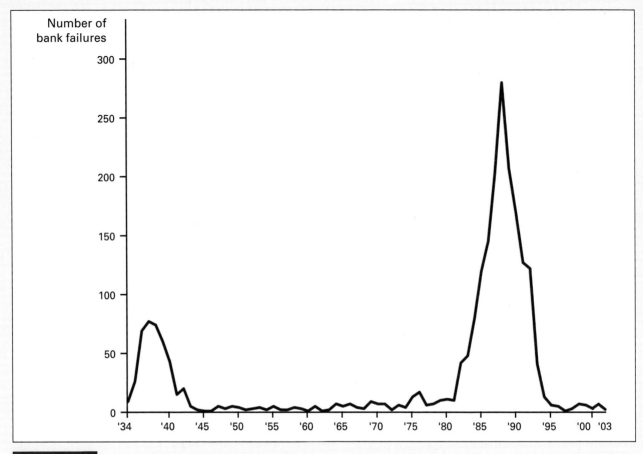

ANNUAL NUMBER OF U.S. BANK FAILURES Bank failures in the United States soared in the 1980s and did not return to normal until the mid-1990s. The number of bank failures in this period far exceeded those during the Great Depression of the 1930s.

Source: Federal Deposit Insurance Corporation.

While no one can know for sure what the future holds, real estate ownership is definitely a large part of personal wealth an a major influence on consumption. For example, the real estate owned by a typical household in America is about six times as much as that household's ownership of shares of stock. There is also no doubt that many years of falling interest rates have made home mortgages easier to afford and so helped fuel the increase in home prices. However, after reaching forty-five year lows in the early summer of 2003, interest rates on home mortgages started to rise and real estate prices showed some signs of weakness.

WHY BANKS FAIL

With mergers and acquisitions sweeping the industry, banks look very healthy today. Yet, as seen in Figure 13-5, it was bank failures that were sweeping the industry little more than a decade ago. The overwhelming majority of those failures revolved around bad real estate loans. It was the dramatic decline in oil prices in the late 1980s that precipitated a fall in real estate prices in Texas and some other parts of the country. In turn, people found themselves owing more on their home mortgages than their homes were worth in the market. It was a financial disaster for many that resulted in a glut of houses for sale and a sharp drop in their selling prices. Banks found themselves with a huge increase in bad loans, loans which homeowners could not or would not repay. Many banks failed.

The nature of economic shocks is that we do not see them coming. There's always the possibility that something unexpected will shock housing prices either up or down. If housing prices drop, there would probably be more bank failures. However, with the benefit of experience, there's reason to expect that the shock to the banking system might not be as severe as in the past. To understand why, we start with a look at U.S. banking regulations, and their origins in the New Deal of the 1930s.

Following upon the heels of bank runs after the stock market crash in late 1929, the 1930s witnessed the closure of many banks. The consequent loss of depositors' money led to New Deal legislation that created the Federal Deposit Insurance Corporation (FDIC) to insure funds deposited in banks, as well as to the passage of the Glass–Steagall law to restrict the investment-related activities of banks. The purpose of the FDIC insurance was to restore public confidence in the banking system; the purpose of Glass–Steagall was to prevent bank failures by keeping banks away from risky investments.

For many years afterward, bankers could pay depositors low interest rates because of the FDIC insurance and because depositors had few alternatives. The financial climate was also favorable, with low inflation and stable interest rates as the norm. In the 1960s, though, the climate started to change. Inflation was no longer quite so low and the public intuitively understood that a 3 percent interest rate on deposits meant that savings accounts were not a very attractive use of money. Bankers had to start competing for deposits with more than a free toaster for every new account.

The second round of legislation that shaped today's banking system occurred with the passage of the *Depository Institutions Deregulation and Monetary Control Act of 1980 (DIDMCA)*. This legislation loosened the regulatory knot that was holding back the banks. Regulation Q, which limited the interest rates banks could pay on deposits, was also rolled back. Now banks were freer to compete for depositors' money. But how could they pay the higher interest rates that they needed in order to compete, and yet still maintain their profitability? The answer is that in the competition for deposits that came to characterize the latter 1970s and the 1980s, banks had to take on a large volume of what proved to be high-risk loans and investments. The alternative was to keep their rates on deposits low and see depositors flee to other banks, savings and loans, money market mutual funds, or even the bond market, all of which offered higher returns. After all, with the FDIC insurance, the only thing depositors cared about was high interest rates.

If it hadn't been for the FDIC insurance, depositors would likely have shopped for banks that invested wisely. They would have had to pay attention to the ratings in *Consumer Reports* magazine, or other publications that would have found it informative to their readership to profile the safety ratings of banks. Such actions by depositors would have been the only way to ensure that their money was safe.

MORAL HAZARD

The problem of *moral hazard* occurs when people change their behavior because of insurance. When the price of risk goes down, people will do riskier things. It is clear that the moral hazard problem led both depositors and bankers to take on more risk than they otherwise would have accepted. For the bankers' part, they could seek out lending opportunities with higher returns but greater risk without experiencing howls of protest from depositors worried about the safety of their deposits. Depositors could sleep soundly as long as their deposits did not exceed the $100,000 FDIC limit.

In practice if not in law, the government even guaranteed deposits above the $100,000 level by adopting a policy of "too big to fail," and by encouraging the merger of insolvent banks—those whose asset values fell below the value of their liabilities—with sound banks.

Both of these government policies were equivalent to insurance. A large bank that was deemed too big to fail because its failure might diminish public confidence in the banking system was allowed by bank regulators to continue to operate. Some other troubled banks were forced to merge with sound banks. In these cases the sound banks acquired only the good loans of the merged bank. The government took over ownership of the bad loans.

The market also found a way to extend deposit insurance to those with deposits of more than $100,000 through deposit brokering. Deposit brokers could guarantee that any amount of deposits was insured by breaking up large deposits into blocks of amounts less than $100,000 and then placing these blocks with different banks. For example, a $1,000,000 deposit could be placed into ten different banks in $100,000 blocks. With this innovation, the FDIC limits became meaningless.

Could another massive wave of bank failures occur? The healthier economy of the 1990s did much to restore bank profitability and cut bank failures. Although the economy turned down in the 2001 recession, the number of bank failures remained steady. There is always some increase in bad loans when the economy turns down, however. To the extent that bank loans are for the most part sound, banks will be able to survive an uptick in the number of loans that are not repaid. Thus, the answer to the question is equivalent to asking about the soundness of bank loans. So long as deposit insurance creates moral hazard issues, that answer will remain unclear.

THINKING CRITICALLY

1. **Based upon what you have learned about the U.S. banking system, reply to the following questions:**
   a. **To prevent bank failures, should there be more or less regulation of banks?**
   b. **Make a case for the position you take. For example, if you believe that more regulation is called for, explain what regulations you would want to see enacted. If you believe in less regulation, explain why.**
   c. **Critique the position you took in part a. For example, if you favored more regulation, for what reasons might that be a bad idea? If you favored less regulation, what are the dangers?**

2. **Should another wave of bank failures occur in the future, what response should the government take? Specifically, should the government try to keep banks going or should it let them fail? What would be the consequences of each policy for the economy?**

Visit **www.prenhall.com/ayers** for updates and web exercises on this Explore & Apply topic.

SUMMARY AND LEARNING OBJECTIVES

1. **Identify the types, functions, and liquidity of various money measures.**
   - Money increases economic efficiency by eliminating the need to barter.
   - Money performs three functions. Money must be a medium of exchange, meaning that it is usable to make purchases. Money also functions as a store of value and a unit of account.
   - Paper currency in the United States is an example of fiat money, which is money because the government says it is money. Commodity money in the form of U.S. silver or gold coins is no longer minted. One shortcoming of commodity money is that it is subject

to Gresham's law—bad money drives good money out of circulation.
   - An item has the characteristic of being liquid when it is easily and quickly spendable. Currency is highly liquid.
   - Various parts of the money supply exhibit varying degrees of liquidity, although in general any component of the money supply can be considered liquid in relative terms. The M1, M2, and M3 money supplies are defined according to decreasing liquidity, respectively.
   - M1 is the most liquid measure of the money supply because it contains only currency and coins in circulation; checking account balances, also known as demand deposits; and the value of traveler's checks.

- M2 adds to M1 savings account balances plus small time deposits and money market mutual funds. M2 is considered a less-liquid measure of the money supply because savings account balances are not spendable without first converting them to currency or demand deposits.

- M3 adds to M2 several additional items that are typically less liquid than the items making up M2. Thus, M3 is considered the least liquid measure of the money supply.

2. **Describe key elements of the banking industry.**

- The U.S. banking system includes 7,900 or so commercial banks that accept deposits and make loans, plus 1,450 savings institutions.

- Bank regulation is designed to provide for a stable banking system.

- A bank's balance sheet shows its assets and liabilities. The assets include vault cash, deposits held by the Federal Reserve, loans, and securities. Vault cash plus deposits held by the Federal Reserve equals bank reserves. Banks must meet the reserve requirement set by the Federal Reserve. Assets show what a bank does with funds that are deposited with it.

- Loans and securities, which are government bonds, provide banks with income.

- The liabilities include customer deposits, federal funds, and discount loans. Federal funds are the amount of reserves that a bank has borrowed from other banks. Discount loans are funds borrowed from the Federal Reserve.

- The Federal Deposit Insurance Corporation (FDIC) insures deposit accounts up to a maximum of $100,000.

- Key interest rates include the prime rate, the federal funds rate, and the discount rate. The prime rate is also called the bank prime lending rate. This interest rate applies to short-term business loans. The Federal funds rate is the interest rate on funds that banks borrow from other banks. The discount rate is set by the Fed and applies to loans that the Fed makes to banks.

3. **Discuss how banks create money.**

- Banks create money when they make loans. When loans are repaid, the money supply decreases.

- A borrower is provided with deposit money through the stroke of the banker's pen when the loan is granted.

4. **Describe the structure, functions, and policy tools of the Federal Reserve.**

- The Federal Reserve controls the monetary base and thereby influences the quantity of money.

- The Federal Reserve is composed of three primary parts: the Board of Governors, the Federal Open Market Committee, and twelve regional Federal Reserve District Banks.

- The tools of monetary policy are open market operations, changes in the discount rate, and changes in the reserve requirement. Most monetary policy is conducted through open market operations.

- Open market operations occur when the Fed buys or sells securities. Fed purchases of securities tend to increase the money supply. Fed sales of securities tend to cause the money supply to decrease.

- The Fed also influences interest rates, which in turn affect other aspects of the economy.

5. **Work through the process of monetary expansion using the deposit multiplier.**

- The monetary base is the sum of currency in circulation plus bank reserves. The money supply equals the money multiplier multiplied by the monetary base.

- An initial deposit of new money into a bank results in an expansion of money through the money multiplier effect. The maximum value of the money multiplier is called the deposit multiplier. The value of the deposit multiplier is computed by taking the reciprocal of the reserve requirement. Thus, when the reserve requirement equals 10 percent, the deposit multiplier equals 1/.10, which is 10.

- With a deposit multiplier of 10, a $10,000 open market purchase by the Fed could conceivably result in an expansion of the money supply by $100,000. This expansion of the money supply would occur as the result of a lending–depositing–lending sequence.

6. **Explain why the banking crisis of the 1980s occurred and whether another banking crisis could happen.**

- The number of bank failures in the United States soared during the 1980s and early 1990s. Banks failed because of bad loans. The role of moral hazard created by the FDIC deposit insurance helps to explain the incentive to make risky loans.

- The strong economic growth of the 1990s helped bring down the number of bank failures as the decade unfolded. However, bank loans that appear to be sound can sour when the economy is in a recession. Moral hazard arising from deposit insurance remains a feature of the banking system, which could lead to additional bank failures.

money, 326
barter, 326
medium of exchange, 326
store of value, 326
unit of account, 326
fiat money, 326
Gresham's law, 327
demand deposits, 327

liquidity, 328
M1, 328
M2, 329
M3, 329
bank reserves, 331
required reserves, 332
excess reserves, 332
bonds, 332

federal funds rate, 332
discount rate, 333
Federal Reserve System, 336
open market operations, 337
monetary base, 337
money multiplier, 340
deposit multiplier, 340

TEST YOURSELF

TRUE OR FALSE

1. In fulfilling its medium of exchange function, money is set aside in savings accounts.
2. M3 includes only currency and checking account balances.
3. Federal funds represent bank reserves that have been borrowed by commercial banks at the discount window at the Fed.
4. The importance of the Federal Open Market Committee (FOMC) is that it conducts monetary policy.
5. An open market purchase of securities by the Fed would tend to increase the money supply.

MULTIPLE CHOICE

6. Barter is most likely to occur when
   a. money takes the form of commodity money.
   b. M1 is the dominant form of money.
   c. Gresham's law requires people to barter.
   d. there is no money.
7. The U.S. one dollar coin is an example of
   a. commodity money.
   b. fiat money.
   c. money that is neither commodity money nor fiat money.
   d. something that looks like money, but is not since it is coined from nearly worthless metals.
8. Which is NOT a function of money?
   a. Standard of measurement.
   b. Unit of account.
   c. Store of value.
   d. Medium of exchange.
9. The liquidity of money refers to its
   a. country of origin.
   b. denomination.
   c. store of value function.
   d. medium of exchange function.

10. Currency held in bank vaults is
    a. part of the M1 money supply.
    b. part of the M2 money supply.
    c. part of the M3 money supply.
    d. not part of the M1, M2, or M3 money supply.
11. The value of stocks is
    a. part of the M1 money supply.
    b. part of the M2 money supply.
    c. part of the M3 money supply.
    d. not part of the M1, M2, or M3 money supply.
12. Which statement about the Glass–Steagall Act is correct?
    a. The act was passed in the 1980s in response to the increase in bank failures of that decade.
    b. The act was repealed in 1999.
    c. Banks deposits were insured by the act, which also created federal deposit insurance.
    d. Bank reserves are required to be held as vault cash or as deposits at the Fed under the terms of the act.
13. A bank's total reserves equal
    a. required reserves.
    b. excess reserves.
    c. required reserves + excess reserves.
    d. required reserves − excess reserves.
14. Suppose a bank makes a loan in the amount of $1,000. Which of the following statements is correct about the immediate effect of the loan?
    a. The loan increases the money supply by $1,000.
    b. The loan leaves the money supply the same as it was before the loan.
    c. The loan changes the money supply by some amount that is impossible to determine from the information given.
    d. The loan decreases the money supply by $1,000.

15. Which of the following is NOT a function or activity of the Federal Reserve System?
    a. Lender of last resort.
    b. Accepts deposits from the public.
    c. Supervises banks.
    d. Clears checks.
16. If the money supply equals $100 and the money multiplier equals 10, then the monetary base must equal
    a. $1,000.
    b. $100.
    c. $10.
    d. an amount that cannot be determined from the information given.
17. If the reserve requirement were 20 percent and the Fed purchased $100 of securities in an open market purchase, then the money supply could potentially expand by a maximum of
    a. $5.
    b. $20.
    c. $100.
    d. $500.

18. Discount rate changes by the Fed
    a. change the interest rate on discount loans by the Fed to commercial banks.
    b. are a tool of monetary policy that is clearly superior to open market operations.
    c. tend to have no effect on the money supply.
    d. cause the reserve requirement to increase.
19. Which of the following is consistent with a looser monetary policy?
    a. Open market sale of securities.
    b. Closer supervision of banks by the Fed.
    c. Decrease in discount rate.
    d. Increase in reserve requirement.
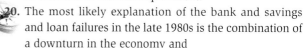
20. The most likely explanation of the bank and savings and loan failures in the late 1980s is the combination of a downturn in the economy and
    a. deposit insurance.
    b. fraud.
    c. too much government oversight of investments by banks.
    d. collusion among a few giant banks aimed at reducing consumer choice.

QUESTIONS AND PROBLEMS

1. *[money]* Suppose it became lawful for anyone to issue money without any government restrictions of any kind. What factors would influence an individual to either accept or reject privately issued money? What institutions might arise in the free market to help a person decide whether to accept or reject a particular private monetary note?
2. *[money]* Although the castaways on *Gilligan's Island* were marooned for several years on an "uncharted desert isle" they apparently had no money and saw fit not to adopt any item to use as money. Speculate on the circumstances under which a group of people stranded without money on an island might see fit to invent money. In your discussion be sure to include answers to the following questions: What form might their money take? Would a smaller or larger group of people be more conducive to the invention of money? Would the length of time they expected to remain on the island be a factor in how useful money would be to them? Would barter be a good alternative to money?
3. *[monetary aggregates]* List the components of M1, M2, and M3. Explain why the additional items in M3 make it a less-liquid measure of the money supply than M1.
4. *[balance sheet]* Create a personal balance sheet for yourself. The value of your assets equals the value of

the things you own. Your liabilities equal what you owe to others. Their value equals the amount of your loans outstanding, including the interest owed on the loans. On your personal balance sheet, what is the ratio of assets that are not liquid to assets that are liquid? Since liquid assets generally offer lower rates of return, why bother to hold them? Explain.
5. *[balance sheet]* Are loans an asset or a liability to a commercial bank? Explain.
6. *[bank reserves]* What are the two places that banks can use to keep their reserves? Speculate on the decision process by which a bank decides how much of its reserves to keep in each place.
7. *[bank liabilities]* List and explain three major liabilities of commercial banks. Are a bank's liabilities best described as its sources of funds or its uses of funds? Explain.
8. *[Fed's functions]* Suppose that you are the president of a commercial bank. List the functions of the Federal Reserve System. Then describe how your bank would interact with the Fed in relation to each function.
9. *[Fed's components]* List and briefly describe the three components of the Federal Reserve System.
10. *[monetary policy]* Explain the following sentence from the text: "The Fed influences, but does not control, the money supply."

11. *[open market operations]* What are open market operations? What form would open market operations take if the Fed wished to see an increase in the money supply?

12. *[money multiplier versus deposit multiplier]* Distinguish between the money multiplier and the deposit multiplier. Why is the value of the money multiplier likely to be less than the value of the deposit multiplier?

13. *[deposit multiplier]* What is the formula for the deposit multiplier? Compute the value of the deposit multiplier when the reserve requirement equals 25 percent.

14. *[federal funds rate versus discount rate]* What is the federal funds rate? What is the discount rate? Are the two rates necessarily equal?

15. *[monetary policy]* What Fed actions are consistent with a looser monetary policy? Which are in accord with a tighter policy?

WORKING WITH GRAPHS AND DATA

1. *[money]* Given the figures below, calculate M1, M2, and M3, respectively.

Coins	$ 400
Saving deposits	2,600
Large denomination time deposits	800
Demand deposits	300
Travelers checks	20
Money market fund balances	1,000
Other checkable deposits	260
Small denomination time deposits	970
Currency	200

2. *[interest rates]* Use the following table to answer the questions that follow.

Year	Prime Rate	Federal Funds Rate	Discount Rate
1991	8.46	5.69	5.45
1992	6.25	3.52	3.25
1993	6.00	3.02	3.00
1994	7.15	4.21	3.60
1995	8.83	5.83	5.21
1996	8.27	5.30	5.02
1997	8.44	5.46	5.00
1998	8.35	5.35	4.92
1999	8.00	4.97	4.62
2000	9.23	6.24	5.73
2001	6.91	3.88	3.4
2002	4.75	1.79	1.25

a. Define the following interest rates:
   1. prime rate
   2. federal funds rate
   3. discount rate

b. Interpret the relationship between the prime rate with the federal funds and discount rates.

c. Interpret the relationship between the federal funds rate and the discount rate.

d. Could the discount rate ever be higher than the federal funds rate? Explain and interpret.

3. *[open 5 economy operations]*
   a. Suppose that the Fed just bought $100,000 of bonds from Bank One. Record the first five iterations of the impact of this purchase of bonds by the Fed in the table below. Assume the banks loan out all excess reserves and no cash is held by any loan recipients. The reserve requirement is equal to 0.2.

Bank	Deposits Received	Reserves Kept	Loans Made
1			
2			
3			
4			
5			

   b. What is the money multiplier in this example?
   c. What is the maximum possible change in the money supply from the Fed's action?

4. *[bank reserves]* Use T-accounts that list the Acme Bank's assets and liabilities for the following transactions. The reserve requirement is 0.10.
   a. Acme Bank sells $50,000 of bonds to the Fed.
   b. Acme Bank lends the maximum legal amount of reserves from the sale of bonds (question a) to Joe so he can purchase a new car.
   c. The Mercedes dealership deposits the proceeds of the sale of the car to Joe back into Acme Bank.
   d. Joe pays $10,000 back to Acme Bank.

 Visit **www.prenhall.com/ayers** for Exploring the Web exercises and additional self-test quizzes.

CHAPTER 14

MONETARY POLICY AND PRICE STABILITY

A LOOK AHEAD

The 1977 amendment to the Federal Reserve Act of 1913 spells out the objective of monetary policy: to "promote effectively the goals of maximum employment, stable prices, and moderate long-term interest rates." The Fed was created to be independent and free to act without interference from the president, Congress, big business, or big labor. The Fed would not be beholden to any branch of government, nor to any special-interest group. The Explore & Apply section in this chapter looks at the issue of central bank independence, and how it promotes a healthy, stable economy.

This chapter revolves around monetary policy and its goals. Monetary policy is established by the Fed, the U.S. central bank that we introduced in the previous chapter. In this chapter we describe the Fed's monetary policy along with the economic theory that guides such policy. Monetary policy affects interest rates, inflation, unemployment, and economic growth, which directly affect the lives of us all. Because of its broad effects, there is often contention over what monetary policy should be. Thus, this chapter also offers a view of the factors that motivate that disagreement.

LEARNING OBJECTIVES

Understanding Chapter 14 will enable you to:
1. **Distinguish between an expansionary and contractionary monetary policy.**
2. **Describe the significance of the money market and the motives for holding money.**
3. **Explain the equation of exchange and its role in the conduct of monetary policy.**
4. **Discuss the monetarist school of thought and its implications for monetary policy.**
5. **Interpret the relationship between monetary policy and interest rates.**
6. **Address the importance of central banks staying independent of political pressures.**

Explore & Apply

The Fed's role in the economy has expanded greatly since its creation in 1913. At that time, the Fed was mainly seen as a "lender of last resort" for troubled banks. As we see in this chapter, the Fed's role today is much more.

14.1 THE AIMS OF MONETARY POLICY

"There have been three great inventions since the beginning of time: fire, the wheel, and central banking."

—Will Rogers

Federal Reserve monetary policy encompasses the three primary macro goals discussed in Chapter 5: high employment, low inflation, and economic growth. *Low inflation* is referred to as *price stability.* In its efforts to keep employment high the Fed must take care not to set off higher inflation. **Many economists argue that price stability should be the Fed's primary goal.** That argument is based on the premise that the economy tends toward full employment, and that monetary policy's greatest impact is on the price level. Nonetheless, the Fed itself makes monetary policy decisions within the context of both employment and inflation because that is what it is legally required to do.

Two realities can help you better understand the conduct of monetary policy:

- **There are conflicts and tradeoffs involved in pursuing a particular monetary policy.** For instance, in bringing down the high inflation of the 1970s the Fed's monetary policy shift toward higher interest rates in the fall of 1979 was widely blamed for creating the two recessions that occurred in the early 1980s. In that particular circumstance, lower inflation came at the cost of a higher unemployment rate.
- **The Fed develops monetary policy surrounded by a whirl of political considerations.** The debates in Congress over appropriate Fed policy can be intense. Unemployment and inflation exact a toll in human suffering.

If you've been unemployed, you know the problem—you don't have enough money to spend! If unemployment in the economy is excessive, as in a recession, the problem is the same: Cyclical unemployment stems from spending that is insufficient to purchase the full-employment level of output at current prices. Thus, to cure the recession, either prices must fall or the quantity of money available to be spent must rise. In general, to maintain full employment, the quantity of money must rise to keep pace with the economy's productive potential. The Fed strongly influences the money supply by conducting open market operations, changing the discount rate, and changing the reserve requirement, as discussed in the previous chapter. The Fed is thus able to utilize these tools of monetary policy to achieve the goals of monetary policy.

If the quantity of money rises too much, then the problem is not one of too little spending power to sustain full-employment output. Rather, the problem is that too much money will be chasing the goods and services that the economy is capable of producing, thus driving up their prices and causing a general inflation. **An overwhelming amount of evidence shows excessive growth in money to be the root cause of inflation.** This evidence is from the United States and from many other countries, and covers episodes of inflation throughout history.

The quantity of money affects aggregate demand, as shown in Figure 14-1. An increase in the money supply is associated with an **expansionary monetary policy,** also called a *looser monetary policy* because the Fed is in effect loosening the purse strings to stimulate the economy with more money. **An increase in the money supply shifts aggregate demand to the right, and thus allows more aggregate output to be purchased at**

expansionary monetary policy monetary policy designed to stimulate the economy; also called a looser monetary policy.

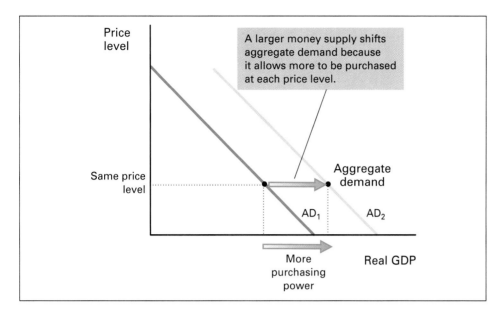

Price level

A larger money supply shifts aggregate demand because it allows more to be purchased at each price level.

Same price level

Aggregate demand

AD₁   AD₂

More purchasing power

Real GDP

FIGURE 14-1

EXPANSIONARY MONETARY POLICY An expansionary monetary policy shifts aggregate demand to the right, which means that more output can be purchased at any given price level. A looser monetary policy is designed to stimulate the economy.

each possible price level. However, to the extent that the increased money supply causes the price level to rise, its effect in terms of increasing real GDP will be reduced or eliminated. That possibility is discussed later in the chapter when we consider the quantity theory of money.

Conversely, a **contractionary monetary policy** would have the effect of drying up liquidity and tightening the economy's purse strings, and is thus alternatively called a *tighter monetary policy*. The effect of a tighter monetary policy would be just the opposite of the expansionary policy shown in Figure 14-1.

There are two monetary policy targets that the Fed can influence as part of monetary policy:

contractionary monetary policy monetary policy intended to slow down the economy; also called a tighter monetary policy.

- *The money supply.* By increasing or decreasing the growth rate of the money supply, the Fed can attempt to stimulate or slow down the economy. Prior to July 2000, the Fed set target ranges for the growth of the M2 money supply. M2 targets are no longer set because the relationship between the size of the M2 money supply and economic performance is not as clear as it was in prior years.
- *Short-term interest rates.* The Fed can also manipulate short-term interest rates, such as the interest rate on short-term government securities, up or down. Lower short-term interest rates stimulate the economy, while higher rates are aimed at slowing it down.

The Fed selects a monetary policy based on whether its focus is on adjustments in the money supply or manipulation of interest rates.

Short-term interest rates provide the current monetary policy focus. To understand this focus, we start by examining the motives for holding money.

14.2 THE MONEY MARKET

Why do people hold on to some of their money rather than invest it? The answer to that question can help us understand the role of money in the economy and how changes in the quantity of money affect the economy. We begin by examining the demand for money.

THE DEMAND FOR MONEY

Why do people typically keep at least some of their wealth as money and not something else? Many other forms of wealth seemingly offer greater returns, or perhaps greater satisfaction. For instance, if you are fascinated by stocks, bonds, and other financial investments, why not invest all your money in those forms of wealth? If your tastes run to hot sports cars, wouldn't you want to hold your wealth in cars in the form of a Ferrari? Whatever your wants, why not just indulge yourself? There are good reasons, as we shall see.

The fact is that people hold some of their wealth as money. The **demand for money** is the quantities of money that people would prefer to hold at various nominal interest rates, *ceteris paribus.* The demand curve for money is illustrated in Figure 14-2. The quantity of money is on the horizontal axis. The nominal market interest rate, on the vertical axis, represents the opportunity cost of holding money. In effect, it is the "price" of holding money because it represents the interest forgone when money is held rather than used to purchase some interest-earning asset, such as a savings bond. Money demand slopes downward because people will hold less money when the market interest rate (the price of money) is high. Likewise, people will hold more money when the market interest rate is low.

For example, if you hold currency, which pays no interest, instead of a U.S. Savings Bond that pays a market interest rate equal to 7 percent, then the 7 percent interest that you forgo is the opportunity cost of holding currency. What would the opportunity cost be if you were holding your money as a demand deposit at a bank that paid you 2 percent interest? In this case the opportunity cost would be the difference between the 7 percent market rate of interest and the 2 percent interest you earned at the bank. Thus, the opportunity cost would be 5 percent.

Let's return to the question of what motivates people to hold money. Why hold money and suffer the loss of the interest income that you could earn by investing in a bond? Three motives make people willing to pay the price of holding money:

■ **Transactions motive:** money is held because of the everyday need to buy goods and services. Thus, there is a *transactions demand for money* because we know we're going to need to fill the car with gas, buy lunch at the cafeteria, grab a soft drink from the vend-

demand for money quantities of money that people would like to hold at various nominal interest rates, *ceteris paribus;* the demand curve for money shows an inverse relationship between the quantity of money demanded and the interest rate, and thus slopes downward.

transactions motive holding money to make purchases.

FIGURE 14-2

THE DEMAND FOR MONEY The demand for money shows an inverse relationship between the market interest rate and peoples' holdings of money.

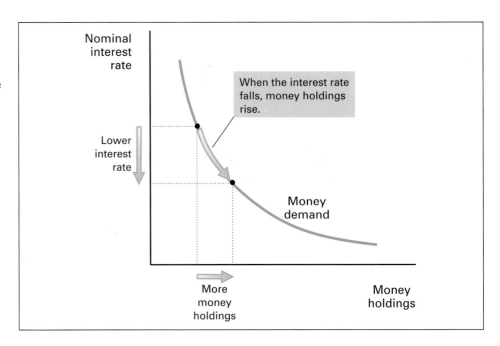

ing machine between classes, and write a check to make a payment on our credit card when we get home.

■ **Precautionary motive:** unforeseen circumstances motivate people to hold more money than called for by their transaction demands. Thus, the *precautionary demand for money* arises from the possibility that people will need extra cash or money in their bank accounts to pay the dentist to fix a broken crown, the auto mechanic for a new radiator, or to buy that new computer at a low sale price that won't last long.

precautionary motive holding money to cover unforeseen needs or wants.

■ **Speculative motive:** people may speculate with some of their money in the sense that they prefer to hold money rather than invest it when stocks, bonds, and other financial investments appear unattractive at their current returns. The *speculative demand for money* increases when people believe that future returns on investments will rise. For example, if people believe that interest rates on bonds will be going up in the near future, the smart thing to do is to wait before investing in bonds.

speculative motive money held because current investment opportunities are unattractive.

CASH—AN ENDANGERED SPECIES? *SNAPSHOT*

With checking accounts and an abundance of credit and debit cards, why carry cash? In certain backwaters of the marketplace, cash still reigns as king. From illegal drug deals, to neighborhood garage sales and campus vending machines, cash is in the catbird seat. For lawbreakers, the opportunity cost of holding cash seems a small price to pay to avoid the paper trail left by checks and bank deposit slips. For the general public, cash is sometimes the most convenient way to buy things. The bottom line? Demand for cash is reduced by financial innovations such as 24-hour ATM machines and sweep accounts that automatically transfer funds from a person's savings account to his or her checking account. Even so, cash is not yet an endangered species. ◄

THE MONEY MARKET EQUILIBRIUM

Like markets for goods and services, the **money market** is characterized by demand and supply. You have just seen that the demand for money is illustrated by a downward-sloping curve. In Figure 14-3 the money market is illustrated by adding a money supply curve to the demand curve for money. The money supply curve is drawn as a vertical line because we are assuming that it is this quantity of money that is supplied to the economy by the Fed. A vertical money supply curve such as this one implies that the money supply is independent of the interest rate. In other words, any interest rate is consistent with the quantity of money shown. The question then is what will the actual market interest rate be?

money market the market where the determination of the interest rate is by the demand and supply of money.

The intersection of demand and supply establishes the money market *equilibrium* in Figure 14-3. The equilibrium interest rate is indicated on the interest rate axis in the graph. This interest rate equates the quantity of money demanded to the money supply. Figure 14-3 is an alternative to viewing the interest rate as determined by saving and investment, which you studied in Chapter 12.

THE SUBSTITUTABILITY OF MONEY AND BONDS

The market interest rate will adjust to the equilibrium interest rate. A market interest rate that is above the equilibrium interest rate will fall until the equilibrium interest rate is reached. Similarly, a market interest rate that is below the equilibrium interest rate will rise. **The key to understanding interest rate changes is to realize that money, bonds, and other investments are substitutes for each other.** When people see relatively high market

FIGURE 14-3

MONEY MARKET EQUILIBRIUM In the money market, the nominal interest rate is the price at which money can be bought (borrowed) or sold (loaned). The equilibrium interest rate occurs at the intersection of the money supply curve and the money demand curve. Market forces will adjust the interest rate until the equilibrium is reached. If the interest rate starts too high, there will be an excess supply of money that causes the rate to fall. If the interest rate starts too low, there will be an excess demand for money that causes the rate to rise.

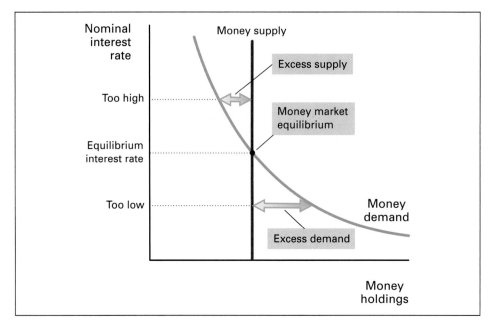

interest rates they will economize on their cash holdings in order to own bonds and other assets that pay those high interest rates. However, when interest rates are relatively low the opportunity cost of holding cash is also low. Therefore, people will hold more cash and fewer bonds.

At any market interest rate other than the equilibrium interest rate in Figure 14-3, the quantity of money demanded will not equal the money supply and the market interest rate will have to adjust to the equilibrium interest rate. To see how this would occur, consider a market interest rate greater than the equilibrium interest rate. This graph shows that the quantity of money demanded is less than the quantity of money supplied when the market interest rate is above its equilibrium value, called an *excess supply of money.* People will react to an excess supply of money by purchasing bonds. In this way people rid themselves of their excess money holdings. When people increase their demand for bonds the interest rate responds by decreasing, since it does not need to be so high to attract buyers to bonds. The decrease in the interest rate will continue until it equals the equilibrium level.

Now consider an interest rate that is below the market equilibrium rate. In this case the quantity of money demanded is greater than the money supply, called an *excess demand for money.* In their efforts to increase their holdings of money, people will sell their bonds. This increase in the supply of bonds must increase the interest rate on bonds because a higher interest rate is needed to make the additional bonds attractive to investors. The market interest rate will increase until it equals the equilibrium interest rate.

Table 14-1 summarizes the adjustment to equilibrium in the money market. The rows of the table are labeled (1) through (3) and show the three possible states of the money market. The columns offer a description of each aspect of the money market for each of the possible states.

The preceding analysis of the money market can help us to understand how monetary policy works. We will return to the money market and how it relates to monetary policy once we look at a theory from economic history that establishes the link between money and prices.

TABLE 14-1	INTEREST RATE ADJUSTMENT AND THE SUBSTITUTION BETWEEN MONEY AND BONDS			
IF THE INTEREST RATE IS	**QUANTITY OF MONEY DEMANDED IS**	**QUANTITY OF INTEREST-PAYING ASSETS DEMANDED IS**	**PUBLIC'S ATTEMPTED RESPONSE**	**INTEREST RATE RESPONSE TO PUBLIC'S ACTION**
(1) at equilibrium	equal to the quantity of money supplied	equal to the quantity supplied of interest-paying assets	No change in the holdings of money or bonds	No change in interest rate
(2) above equilibrium	less than the quantity of money supplied	greater than the quantity supplied of interest-paying assets	Increase holdings of bonds and decrease holdings of money	Interest rate decreases
(3) below equilibrium	greater than the quantity of money supplied	less than the quantity supplied of interest-paying assets	Decrease holdings of bonds and increase holdings of money	Interest rate increases

14.3 GUIDING MONETARY POLICY

The Fed maintains confidentiality when it comes to what economic variables determine monetary policy. For example, transcripts of the Federal Open Market Committee (FOMC) meetings are not released to the public until five years after those meetings take place. Thus, the public remains somewhat in the dark about the details of monetary policy decisions, relying upon the twice-a-year testimony of the chair of the Fed before Congress for clues.

Observers speculate that, in recent years, the Fed has usually followed a **price rule,** by which it conducts monetary policy with the aim of keeping price increases among certain basic commodities, perhaps including gold, within a low target range. The following of a price rule indicates that the Fed's prime concern will often be relative price stability, which means low inflation. We next turn to the equation of exchange, which provides a model to help us understand the cause of inflation and the rationale for monetary policy based on a price rule.

price rule conducting monetary policy in order to keep price increases in basic commodities within a low range.

THE EQUATION OF EXCHANGE—MONEY AND PRICES

The **equation of exchange** was originally proposed in the nineteenth century as a means of explaining the link between money, prices, and output. The equation of exchange reveals that the amount of money people spend must equal the market value of what they purchase, as follows:

equation of exchange $M \times V = P \times Q$; M represents the quantity of money, V is velocity, P is the price level, and Q is aggregate output.

$$M \times V = P \times Q$$

The equation of exchange applies to the aggregate economy. Let's look over the equation one variable at a time.

- *M:* The quantity of money is indicated by M in the equation. Money is used to purchase goods and services.
- *V:* The average number of times money changes hands in a year is called the **velocity of money** (V). The dollar you spend today was spent by someone else earlier, and will be spent again later. The typical dollar will change hands more than once as consumers buy the economy's output of goods and services.

velocity of money the number of times a dollar changes hands in a year.

Total spending is calculated by multiplying the money supply by velocity, as shown in the left side of the equation of exchange. On the right side we have:

- *P:* *P* is a price index, such as the GDP price index, that shows the level of prices in the economy.
- *Q:* The aggregate output of goods and services is represented by *Q*.

When *P* and *Q* are multiplied, the result is the dollar value of aggregate purchases. The total amount of purchasing in an economy is equivalent to the economy's nominal GDP. Thus, **the equation of exchange says that aggregate spending, the left side of the equation, equals nominal GDP, the right side. Because the value of what is bought must equal the value of what is sold, the equation of exchange is always true.** Thus, we may expand the equation of exchange to include the interpretation of each side:

$$M \times V \text{ [total spending]} = P \times Q \text{ [nominal GDP]}$$

The equation of exchange forms the basis for the **quantity theory of money.** The quantity theory assumes:

- The velocity of money (*V* in the equation of exchange) is independent of the quantity of money in the long run. In other words, *V* is assumed not to change when the money supply changes, so that we can treat *V* as a constant value.
- Aggregate output, *Q*, is also independent of the quantity of money in the long run. Aggregate output depends upon the productive capacity of the economy and is assumed to be at its maximum level. This means that *Q* can also be treated as a constant.

These two assumptions leave only *M* and *P*, money and the price level, to vary. Thus, the effect of a change in the quantity of money must be a proportional change in the price level. An increase in the money supply brings a proportionally higher price level. Conversely, a decrease in the money supply lowers the price level proportionally to the decrease in the money supply. Except for determining the price level, the quantity theory suggests that money does not matter, because the economy will always operate at the full-employment level of real GDP. For this reason, the quantity theory cannot explain recessions.

A numerical example can help you grasp the quantity theory. Suppose that an economy's money supply equals $100 and that the velocity of money is constant and equals 2. Each dollar thus changes hands twice each time period, indicating that total spending in the economy is $200 during that time period. This $200 of total spending is also equal to nominal GDP. Suppose now that the money supply rises to $130, and that in accordance with the quantity theory, velocity remains constant at a value of 2. Total spending must then rise to $260. Because the quantity theory assumes that aggregate output (*Q*) is always at its maximum level, aggregate output cannot rise. There is only one way for the right side of the equation of exchange to rise to a value of $260—through an increase in the price level (*P*)!

The link between money and prices can also be clarified by imagining what would happen if, by government decree, we all woke up tomorrow with twice as much money as we have today. One dollar bills would be worth $2 each, five's would be worth $10 each, $100 in a savings account would be transformed into $200, and so forth. Nothing real would have changed, though. Dunkin Donuts would still have the same amount of doughnuts for sale as before, the number of new cars for sale at the dealerships would still be the same, and so on down the line for every good and service. Furthermore, if the economy were at full employment, the ability of the economy to produce more goods and services would be no more than before the increase in the quantity of money. What would you expect to happen next? With everyone having twice as much money to spend as the day before, prices would start to rise immediately in response. In fact, if everyone knew that there was exactly twice as much money, prices would immediately double. Even if people did not know that the total money supply had doubled, prices would still double quickly because of the doubling of

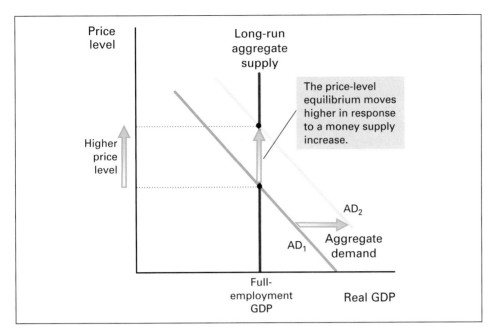

FIGURE 14-4

THE QUANTITY THEORY The quantity theory of money is that, in the long run, an increase in the money supply has no effect except to cause inflation. Aggregate demand shifts out and the economy moves up the long-run aggregate supply curve to a new equilibrium at a higher price level.

demand for goods and services brought about by the doubling of the quantity of money. This exercise in imagination predicts exactly what the quantity theory of money predicts.

The quantity theory can be illustrated with the model of aggregate supply and aggregate demand, as shown in Figure 14-4. An increase in the money supply shifts aggregate demand to the right, because additional money provides greater purchasing power at any given price level. The long-run effect is to move the economy to a new equilibrium at a higher price level. Output remains the same at its full-employment level, as shown in the figure.

TAXATION THROUGH INFLATION—WHAT A MONEY MAKER!   *SNAPSHOT*

The Fed must keep in mind the equation of exchange when conducting its monetary policy. Otherwise, the temptation might be for the Fed to merely buy back as much government debt as possible. The open market purchases of Treasury bonds and Treasury bills that this would require might seem like a painless way to reduce or even eliminate government debt. But painless it is not, as newly printed money used to buy those Treasury securities would cause inflation that eats away at the value of all of our savings. The effect is much like a tax, and indeed is often referred to as the tax of inflation. ◄

QUICKCHECK

If the money supply quadruples, other things being equal, what does the quantity theory predict?

Answer: The quantity theory predicts the price level would quadruple. Prices increase proportionally to the increase in the money supply.

THE MONETARIST PRESCRIPTION

monetarism school of thought that emphasizes the importance of the quantity of money in the economy and a rule for monetary policy; associated with economist Milton Friedman.

Monetarism is a school of economic thought, associated with Nobel prize-winning economist Milton Friedman (1912–   ), that offers a modern version of the quantity theory. Monetarists readily agree with one contention of the original quantity theory: Velocity and aggregate output are independent of the quantity of money in the long run. However, unlike the quantity theory, monetarism acknowledges the existence of a short run.

According to the monetarist view, the quantity of money may indeed affect velocity and aggregate output in the short run. Thus, neither V nor Q in the equation of exchange is viewed as constant by monetarists.

- *Changes in Q.* A reduction in the growth rate of the money supply may cause a reduction in aggregate output, Q. This effect could occur if people cut their purchases of goods and services because there is less money to spend. If that happens, the economy slows down. Hence, monetarism offers an explanation of how too little money can lead to a recession. Table 14-2 summarizes the monetarist view of how changes in the quantity of money affect the economy. The effects of both a looser and a tighter policy are described. A looser policy promotes an increase in nominal GDP through the means of increased spending. A tighter policy slows down the economy, reducing nominal GDP, by making money harder to come by, and thus reducing spending.
- *Changes in V.* The velocity of money can change because of changes in people's need to hold money. For example, the widespread use of debit cards, ATM machines, and other technologies cause people to economize on their money holdings, and thus cause velocity to increase. Figure 14–5 shows the value of velocity over time, confirming that V increased from the mid-1980s to the mid-1990s. If V were constant, the effects of monetary policy would be more predictable. As seen in the figure, velocity is relatively stable from one year to the next, so that the effects of monetary policy are relatively predictable.

To avoid the recession that could result from too little money, or the inflation that could result from too much money, **the monetarist policy recommendation is for the Fed to increase the money supply at a steady rate, equal to or slightly greater than the long-run growth in aggregate output.** If the long-run growth of output tends to be about 2.5 to 3 percent, a steady annual monetary increase of about 3 percent or slightly higher is called for. The idea is to provide sufficient money so that the economy's additional output could be purchased without setting off significant inflation. Figure 14-6 shows the annual growth rates for the M2 money supply over time. The figure shows that money growth has varied significantly from year to year, which runs counter to the monetarist recommendation.

TABLE 14-2   MONEY AS AN INSTRUMENT OF MONETARY POLICY— THE MONETARIST VIEW

EXPANSIONARY (LOOSER) MONETARY POLICY

Increase in the quantity of money → Increased aggregate spending → Increased nominal GDP

CONTRACTIONARY (TIGHTER) MONETARY POLICY

Decrease in the quantity of money → Decreased aggregate spending → Decreased nominal GDP

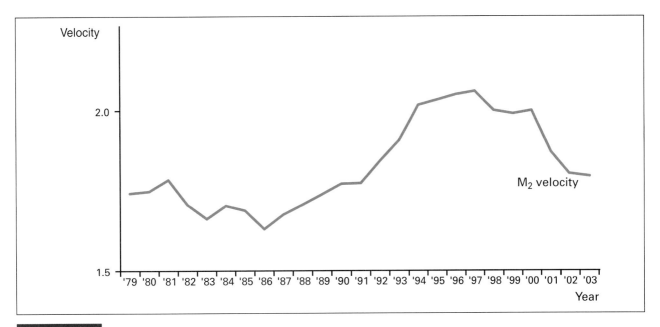

FIGURE 14-5

M$_2$ VELOCITY Changes in velocity complicate monetary policy by making it more difficult for the Fed to achieve its targets. Velocity took an upward turn in the 1980s, as people became more comfortable with financial innovations that allowed them to reduce their money holdings.

Source: Computed by the authors using data from the *2003 Economic Report of the President,* and the National Income and Product Accounts. M$_2$ velocity equals nominal GDP divided by M$_2$.

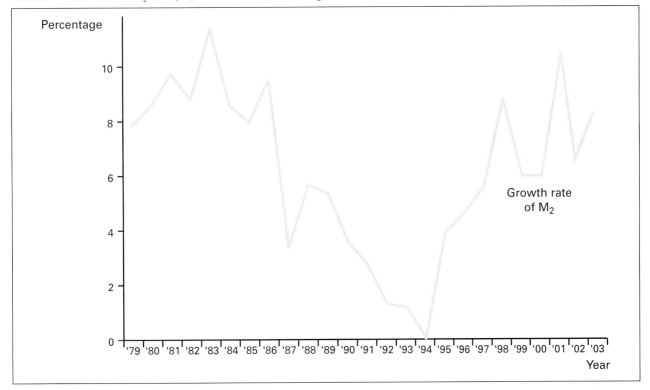

FIGURE 14-6

THE ANNUAL GROWTH RATE OF M$_2$ OVER TIME The M$_2$ money supply has not grown at a steady rate, but has exhibited significant variation over time.

Source: 2003 Economic Report of the President, Table B-69, and the Federal Reserve.

Figure 14-7 illustrates a monetarist version of monetary policy. A macro equilibrium is illustrated by the intersection of the long-run aggregate supply curve and the aggregate demand curve. Economic growth is shown by a rightward shift in long-run aggregate supply. If aggregate demand were to remain unchanged after the increase in long-run aggregate supply, the price level would have to fall in order for consumers to be able to purchase the increased production. In contrast, **monetarists recommend growth in the money supply that just matches the growth in long-run aggregate supply,** thereby avoiding the need for price level adjustments. Thus, the new aggregate demand curve in Figure 14-7 intersects the new long-run aggregate supply at the original price level.

The Fed is sometimes accused by monetarists of being too quick to increase or decrease the growth rate of the money supply. Monetarists claim that an activist policy by the Federal Reserve accentuates economic instability. Monetarists have compared the Fed to a driver who jerks a car's steering wheel first one way, and then the other, before accidentally steering the car off the road and over a cliff. The Fed, of course, denies that monetary policy can accurately be characterized this way. To monitor the Fed, monetarists have established a *Shadow Open Market Committee,* a group of economists that examine monetary policy with a critical eye.

Could the Fed ever adopt monetarism as the guiding principle of monetary policy? That is unlikely for there are some practical problems in implementing monetarism. The basic problem is that the Fed does not control the money supply—it only influences the quantity of money. The Fed controls only the monetary base, as explained in the previous chapter. Growing the monetary base at a slow and steady rate does not mean that the money supply will do likewise. Consumer pessimism or optimism about the economy can greatly affect the money multiplier, which relates the monetary base to the money supply.

FIGURE 14-7

MONETARIST POLICY Monetarists seek to match money-supply growth to growth in the country's productive potential. By doing so, aggregate demand shifts to the right just enough to keep the price level constant.

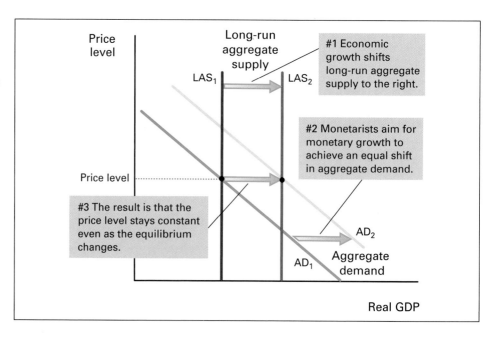

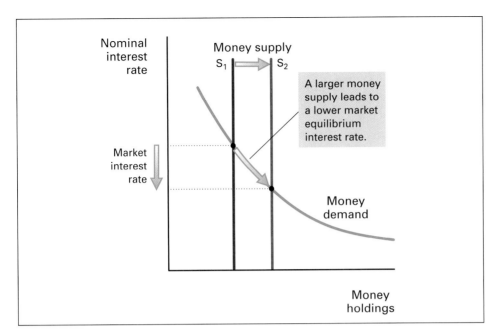

FIGURE 14-8

INTEREST RATES AND THE MONEY SUPPLY An increase in the money supply lowers the interest rate. After the increase in the money supply, the initial interest rate would no longer equate quantity supplied with quantity demanded, so the interest rate falls.

CHANGING THE MONEY SUPPLY

When the Fed conducts open market operations or employs one of the other monetary policy tools to change the money supply, we can trace the outcome in the money market. Refer to Figure 14-8 where an increase in the money supply is shown as a rightward shift in the money supply curve. The result is a lower interest rate.

In Table 14-1, row (2) explained why the increase in the money supply pushes the interest rate down. Once the money supply has been increased, the interest rate associated with the initial equilibrium is too high and the quantity of money demanded is less than the quantity of money supplied. People will buy more bonds in an effort to reduce their money holdings.

QUICKCHECK

Outline the effects of a decrease in the money supply. Why would the Fed pursue a policy that decreases the money supply?

Answer: A decrease in the money supply shifts the supply curve of money to the left and, *ceteris paribus,* causes the interest rate to increase. The interest rate must rise because, at the initial interest rate, the quantity of money demanded is greater than the quantity supplied. In an effort to increase their money holdings, the public sells bonds. In order for those bonds to be sold, the market interest rate will have to increase. A decrease in the money supply describes a contractionary (tighter) monetary policy. The Fed would pursue such a policy to slow down the economy, perhaps to head off an increase in inflation. The decrease in the money supply would shift aggregate demand to the left.

COMPLICATIONS IN CONDUCTING MONETARY POLICY

There are a number of possible difficulties that the Fed could face in designing an effective monetary policy. Five significant possibilities are:

- *Large unpredictable shifts in the demand for money.* Our analysis of monetary policy using the money market showed shifts in the supply of money combined with a stable, unchanging demand curve for money. If there are large unpredictable shifts in the demand for money, then interest rates will fluctuate unpredictably. While it is true that the demand curve for money can shift, we would expect such shifts to mostly occur slowly in response to technological change in financial markets.

- *Interest rate insensitivity among consumers and businesses.* If consumers and businesses ignore interest rate changes in making their spending decisions, then monetary policy would be ineffective. For example, if *expectations* about the future of the economy are pessimistic, it could be that lower interest rates would not increase aggregate demand because spending would not pick up.

- *An unresponsive interest rate caused by a liquidity trap.* A *liquidity trap* occurs when a demand curve for money becomes horizontal at some very low interest rate, as shown in Figure 14-9. Increases in the money supply won't push the interest rate down as when the demand curve for money is downward sloping. A liquidity trap occurs when consumers hold all increases in the money supply rather than buying bonds. The public might hold off from buying bonds if they expect interest rates to increase significantly in the future.

- *Lags in the effects of monetary policy.* Changes in the money supply affect the economy with, as Milton Friedman put it, a "long and variable lag." Today's change in monetary policy may not take effect for months or even years, at which time economic conditions may be quite different from what they were at the moment when the policy was implemented. Therefore, the effects of monetary policy are hard to predict. The long and variable lag in the effects of monetary policy is why monetarists call for a steady increase in the supply of money. Consider the lags in the context of the money market. When new money is put into circulation, it takes time for the public to adjust their holdings of money and bonds. Thus, the interest rate changes that accompany changes in the money supply may not take place immediately. Then, even after the interest rate changes take

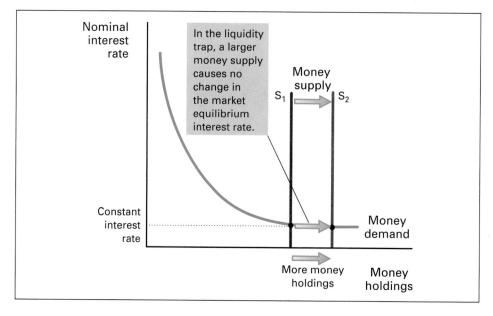

FIGURE 14-9

THE LIQUIDITY TRAP Interest rates might become so low that people ignore them. In that case, increasing the money supply merely increases the amount of cash that people hold.

hold, there can be a lag before the public decides to change its spending. The problem of lags complicates the execution of monetary policy since the Fed's monetary policy actions may not move the economy in the desired direction for many months or even years.

■ *Differential effects of monetary policy.* Certain sectors of the economy, such as housing and the automotive sector, are more interest-rate sensitive than other sectors because purchases of these goods are typically financed with borrowed money. Thus, monetary policy affects these sectors of the economy more than other sectors. For example, a tighter monetary policy that raises interest rates throws more auto and construction workers out of their jobs than workers in other industries. This seems unfair to many people.

In spite of these potential difficulties, the Fed typically conducts monetary policy with a great deal of confidence that monetary policy will be able to achieve its ends.

14.4 THE FEDERAL FUNDS RATE AND MARKET INTEREST RATES

Monetary policy is more than just adjusting the money supply, since monetary policy can also operate through short-term market interest rates. The means by which monetary policy works through interest rates is presented in Table 14-3. This view of the way money affects the economy is Keynesian in its origins. You should compare this table to Table 14-2, which showed how interest rates are not relevant when the quantity of money is the instrument of monetary policy.

Monetary policy goals can be achieved through changes in interest rates. **A key interest rate is the federal funds rate, the interest rate on reserves banks lend to each other.** The federal funds rate, introduced in the last chapter, is the price paid by banks that borrow reserves from other banks. For example, suppose Homestate University National Bank borrows reserves from Coastal Plains National Bank in order to satisfy the reserve requirement that was discussed in the previous chapter. If the federal funds rate is 5 percent, when Homestate repays the reserves it borrowed, it will have to include an interest payment to Coastal Plains that reflects the 5 percent federal funds rate.

The Fed does not directly set the federal funds rate, but can meet its federal funds rate target by changing the quantity of bank reserves through the conduct of open market operations. Open market sales of bonds by the Fed reduce the quantity of bank reserves because banks that buy bonds from the Fed pay for them by transferring the ownership of reserves to the Fed. When banks have less reserves to lend to each other, the result is an increase in the federal funds rate. The higher price of reserves is likely to be passed along to borrowers in the form of higher interest rates on bank loans. Conversely, open market purchases of bonds

TABLE 14-3   INTEREST RATES AS AN INSTRUMENT OF MONETARY POLICY— THE KEYNESIAN VIEW

EXPANSIONARY (LOOSER) MONETARY POLICY

Increase in the quantity of money → Lower interest rates → Increased borrowing → Increased aggregate spending → Increased nominal GDP

CONTRACTIONARY (TIGHTER) MONETARY POLICY

Decrease in the quantity of money → Higher interest rates → Decreased borrowing → Decreased aggregate spending → Decreased nominal GDP

TABLE 14-4   THE INTEREST RATE EFFECTS OF OPEN MARKET OPERATIONS

FEDERAL RESERVE ACTION	BANK RESERVES	FEDERAL FUNDS RATE	SHORT-TERM MARKET INTEREST RATES
Open market sale of securities to banks	Decrease (reserves go to the Fed to pay for securities)	Increases, as reserves leave the banking system	Increase
Open market purchase of securities from banks	Increase (reserves are received from the Fed in payment for securities)	Decreases, as reserves are pumped into the banking system	Decrease

by the Fed tend to reduce the federal funds rate, and can thus lead to lower interest rates on consumer and business loans.

The path by which open market operations affect short-term market interest rates is illustrated in Table 14-4. When the federal funds rate changes because of Fed actions that manipulate the quantity of bank reserves, short-term market interest rates tend to adjust in the same direction. Thus, when the federal funds rate increases, short-term market interest rates tend to go up. When the federal funds rate decreases, short-term market interest rates tend to go down. Consumers shopping for loans find their monthly payments increased or decreased accordingly. The higher monthly payments that go along with higher market interest rates tend to discourage consumer borrowing. The lower monthly payments that accompany lower market interest rates tend to encourage such borrowing.

Monetary policy that targets short-term interest rates can be tight (contractionary) or loose (expansionary), just as with monetary policy that works through the money supply. A tight policy causes real interest rates in the economy to rise, with the goal of keeping inflation in check. If successful, then a tight monetary policy would lead to nominal interest rates that are not much higher than the real rates. For example, if tight monetary policy kept the inflation rate down to zero, real interest rates would equal nominal interest rates. You can see this point clearly by substituting zero for the inflation rate in the equation for the nominal interest rate:

$$\text{Nominal interest rate} = \text{Real interest rate} + \text{Inflation rate}$$

A loose monetary policy causes real short-term interest rates to fall, which leads to more lending by banks to consumers. Such a policy is usually advocated when the economy is weak and inflation is not a problem. Figure 14-10 shows the average yearly federal funds rate since 1979. The nominal federal funds rate is the rate as stated. The real federal funds rate is computed using the equation for a real interest rate.

$$\text{Real interest rate} = \text{Nominal interest rate} - \text{Inflation rate}$$

Because interest rates are an expense to businesses and many households, some politicians and businesspeople argue that the Fed should aim to keep them low. Although the Fed could try to keep real rates low by expanding the money supply, the long-run result would likely be inflation that might cause nominal interest rates to soar as time passes. The reason is that the Fed's open market purchases that are intended to drive down interest rates will, in the long run, increase the money supply and thus inflation. **Monetary policy cannot lower interest rates in the long run, except through lower inflation.** A Fed policy that ignored this principle is often held responsible for the upsurge of U.S. inflation in the 1970s.

The role of the federal funds rate in monetary policy can be appreciated by referring to Figure 14-11. Part of this figure reproduces an actual Federal Reserve press release intended to inform the public about monetary policy. The wording of this press release suggests that

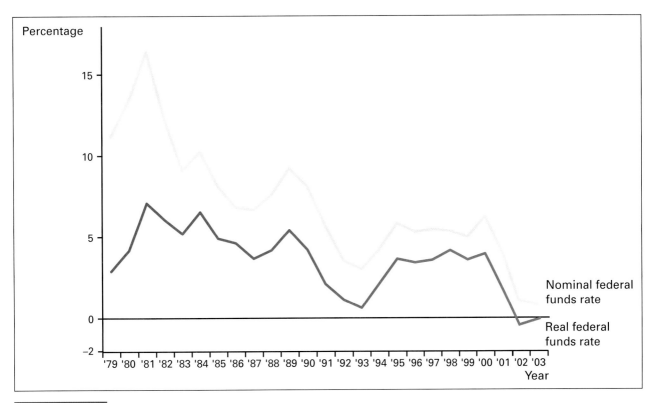

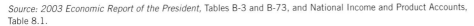

FIGURE 14-10

THE NOMINAL AND REAL FEDERAL FUNDS RATE The real federal funds rate is calculated as the nominal rate minus the change in the GDP implicit price deflator. The real federal funds rate provides a better indicator of the stance of monetary policy than does the nominal rate.

Source: 2003 Economic Report of the President, Tables B-3 and B-73, and National Income and Product Accounts, Table 8.1.

monetary policy was loosened since the Fed's goal was to bring the federal funds rate down to 1 percent. Press releases like this one are provided to the public on a recurring basis by the Fed. The graph shows the drastic drop in the intended federal funds rate throughout 2001. The goal of a lower federal funds rate was motivated by the Fed's effort to shake off the recession that occurred in 2001. The desire to lower the federal funds rate even more in 2002 and 2003 was probably motivated by concerns over deflation.

FED WATCHING—FROM WALL STREET TO MAIN STREET   *SNAPSHOT*

Because the Fed is so powerful, its actions directly affect people's lives. The stock market, mortgage interest rates, returns on investments in bonds—all these and more are subject to the Fed's influence. The consequence is that Fed watching is something of a national sport. Economists, stock market analysts, and policymakers follow the money supply figures closely. The general public is more likely to have a greater interest in how Fed actions affect interest rates. The monthly payment on that new house or car depends not only on how good a deal the consumer is able to find, but also on monetary policy! Hints as to the future direction of monetary policy can be found when the chair of the Fed testifies before Congress each February and July. In between, the Fed issues press releases that explain monetary policy goals. ◄

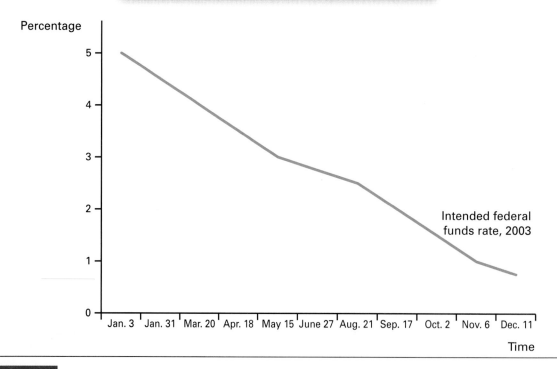

Federal Reserve Release

Press Release

Release Date: August 12, 2003

For immediate release

The Federal Open Market Committee decided to keep its target for the federal funds rate at 1 percent.

The Committee continues to believe that an accommodative stance of monetary policy, coupled with still-robust underlying growth in productivity, is providing important ongoing support to economic activity. The evidence accumulated over the intermeeting period shows that spending is firming, although labor market indicators are mixed. Business pricing power and increases in core consumer prices remain muted.

The Committee perceives that the upside and downside risks to the attainment of sustainable growth for the next few quarters are roughly equal. In contrast, the probability, though minor, of an unwelcome fall in inflation exceeds that of a rise in inflation becoming undesirably low is likely to be the predominant concern for the foreseeable future. In these circumstances, the Committee believes that policy accommodation can be maintained for a considerable period.

Voting for the FOMC monetary policy action were: Alan Greenspan, Chairman; Ben S. Bernanke; Susan S. Bies; J. Alfred Broaddus, Jr.; Roger W. Ferguson, Jr.; Edward M. Gramlich; Jack Guynn; Doanald L. Kohn; Michael H. Moskow; Mark W. Olson; Robert T. Parry; and Jamie B. Stewart, Jr.

Intended federal funds rate, 2003

FIGURE 14-11

MONETARY POLICY THROUGH THE FEDERAL FUNDS RATE The Federal Reserve press release shows the significance of the federal funds rate. The rate was set at 1.75 percent in December 2001 and not changed again until it was adjusted downward to 1.25 percent in November 2002. The press release shows a further drop to 1 percent in August 2003. As seen in the graph, the intended federal funds rate was lowered numerous times in 2001.

Source: Federal Reserve web site. The press release is dated August 12, 2003.

14.5 HOW INDEPENDENT SHOULD A CENTRAL BANK BE?

The same question was asked throughout most of Europe and Japan: "How can we best keep inflation under control now that the inflation rate is low again?" The question became relevant after inflation had been beaten back following a prolonged period of spiraling inflation in the 1970s and 1980s. Country after country answered that question in three words, "central bank independence."

As countries struggled with how to ensure that the goal of low inflation would continue to be met in the 1990s and beyond, the idea of keeping central bankers insulated from political pressures became widely accepted. Politics might call for an expansionary monetary policy that keeps unemployment low, even if that policy leads to an inflationary spiral down the road. Seen in this light, allowing a central bank's policies to be influenced by politics is unacceptable. That is why the European Central Bank (ECB) was created to be independent. That is also why country after country took steps to reform central banking to increase its own central bank independence. Countries that made these reforms are shown in Table 14-5, along with

TABLE 14-5 CENTRAL BANK INDEPENDENCE REFORMS

COUNTRY	YEAR OF IMPLEMENTATION
Australia	None
Austria	1999
Belgium	1993
Canada	None
Denmark	None
Finland	1998
France	1994
Germany	None
Greece	1997
Iceland	2001
Ireland	1998
Japan	1998
Italy	1998
Luxemburg	1999
Netherlands	1998
New Zealand	1990
Norway	None
Portugal	1998
Spain	1994
Sweden	1999
Switzerland	2000
United Kingdom	1998
United States	None

Source: Sven-Olav Daunfeldt and Xavier de Luna, *Central Bank Independence and Price Stability: Evidence from 23 OECD-countries,* June 6, 2003.

the year that the reform took effect. Observe that the United States is not among the reformers, because the Federal Reserve is already among the most independent of central banks. The reasons are many.

The Federal Reserve is unique among government agencies in being subject to relatively few explicit government directives. The Fed has a great deal of independence to conduct monetary policy as it pleases, without interference from Congress, the president, or special-interest groups.

The fear that originally motivated Congress to insulate the Fed from politics is that political pressures could influence the Fed to pursue an expansionary monetary policy at the wrong moment—a policy that would ultimately lead to excessive inflation. Evidence suggests that the inflationary effects of monetary policy do not set in immediately, but appear only after a time lag. Thus, if the Fed were subject to political pressure, decision making could favor short-term popularity at the possible expense of long-term economic goals.

One source of the Fed's independence from political pressure is the structure of the Board of Governors. The president of the United States appoints governors to fourteen-year nonrenewable terms. Governors thus are given the freedom to make policy decisions without the worry of reappointment. Once on the Board, a governor is free to follow the dictates of conscience rather than the decrees of the president or Congress.

Typically, government agencies are funded by Congress. In contrast, the Fed funds itself. By retaining independent control of its own purse strings, the Fed retains independence of action. The Fed's secret of financial independence? The Fed is a banker's bank, and as such earns interest from the discount loans it makes to commercial banks. However, the major source of the Fed's earnings is interest from its holdings of Treasury securities—securities it may have purchased with newly printed Federal Reserve Notes! In recent years the Fed's income has totaled more than a whopping $30 billion each year, much of which it is required to turn over to the U.S. Treasury.

Another source of Federal Reserve independence is found in the financial markets. The Fed's policy actions have the potential to disturb the stock and bond markets, providing substantial gains or inflicting massive losses on the owners of stocks, bonds, and other financial instruments. Financial market participants, called "bond market vigilantes" in the press, stand ready to bail out of investments when they perceive the Fed's actions will threaten the value of those investments. That threat of a sell-off of stocks or bonds influences the Fed to act responsibly in the best long-term interests of the economy.

Even homeowners help keep the Fed independent. Higher expected inflation causes increases in interest rates. The interest rates on adjustable rate home mortgages go up when other interest rates rise. Homeowners with that type of mortgage will see their monthly house payments pushed up by the upward surge in interest rates that accompanies expected inflation. Hence, this segment of the public has a vested interest in seeing that the Fed acts to keep inflation in check.

For the reasons discussed, people have an interest in a stable monetary policy. Thus, the president's appointments to the Board do not go unnoticed. In 1983, for instance, the desire to keep financial markets from losing value influenced Republican President Reagan to reappoint then Board Chairman Paul Volcker even though Volcker had first been appointed to the Board by President Carter, a Democrat. Volcker was perceived by the markets as an experienced policymaker, independent and above politics, and thus a stabilizing influence on the economy. Similarly, President Clinton, a Democrat, was influenced to reappoint Chairman Greenspan, a Republican.

POSSIBLE DRAWBACKS OF THE FED'S ROLE

Critics argue the Fed has too much power, and charge it with decision making that favors its own self-interests and those of special interests, such as bankers. In this view, the Fed is akin to an aristocracy exercising power at the expense of the greater economic welfare. Ostensibly, however, the Fed operates in the public interest. But what is the public interest? Possible goals include stable prices, stable interest rates, a stable foreign exchange value of the dollar, and stable overall economic activity, at a level sufficient to ensure high employment. Unfortunately, these economic variables fluctuate over time, sometimes severely.

Monetarists view the Fed with suspicion. Many monetarists believe that market economies are inherently stable, and that fluctuations in economic activity occur because of unstable monetary policies. If the monetarist view is true, then the Fed must be reined in, since its exercise of monetary policy is harmful. Thus, monetarists seek to limit Federal Reserve power. Others, especially those on Wall Street with a stake in financial stability, look to the Fed to keep the economy humming. While varying views of the Fed are unlikely to be reconciled, it remains true that Fed watching is a national pastime.

1. Since members of the Federal Reserve Board have so much power, should they be elected directly by the public? Explain.

2. How could the Federal Reserve hurt the economy? Provide some examples of Fed actions that could be harmful and of the damage that could be done. How can the Fed help the economy? Provide examples.

Visit www.prenhall.com/ayers for updates and web exercises on this Explore & Apply topic.

SUMMARY AND LEARNING OBJECTIVES

1. **Distinguish between an expansionary and contractionary monetary policy.**
   - Monetary policy has three goals: high employment, low inflation, and economic growth, which are the three macro goals introduced in Chapter 5. Many economists argue that price stability, meaning low inflation, should be the Fed's primary goal.
   - There are sometimes tradeoffs and conflicts in monetary policy. For example, efforts to reduce inflation can slow the economy.
   - Evidence shows that excessive growth in the money supply is the cause of inflation.
   - Monetary policy works through aggregate demand. An expansionary monetary policy shifts aggregate demand to the right, while a contractionary monetary policy shifts aggregate demand to the left.
   - The Fed can influence the two instruments of monetary policy. These instruments are the money supply and short-term interest rates. Prior to July 2000 the Fed set target ranges for the growth of the M2 money supply. M2 targets were abandoned in response to the murkiness of the relationship between M2 and economic performance.

2. **Describe the significance of the money market and the motives for holding money.**
   - The demand for money is made up of the quantities of money that people wish to hold at various interest rates. The interest rate is the price paid for holding money because, when money is held, people forgo the receipt of a certain amount of interest earnings. The demand curve for money is downward sloping, flattening out at a low interest rate.
   - People demand money for three reasons. The first is the transactions motive, which occurs because people must hold a certain amount of money to make purchases. The second is the precautionary motive, which causes people to hold money for a "rainy day." The speculative motive for holding money comes into play when investments offer relatively unattractive returns and people would rather hold cash than stocks, bonds, and other investments.
   - The money market is characterized by the demand for, and supply of, money. A money market equilibrium occurs at the intersection between the demand curve and the supply curve of money. At equilibrium the quantity supplied of money will equal the quantity demanded. A key feature of money market equilibrium is the equilibrium interest rate. The market rate of interest will adjust to equal the equilibrium interest rate.
   - Money, bonds, and other interest-earning investments are substitutes. At relatively high interest rates the public will economize on cash holdings, which pay zero interest, and purchase bonds for the interest they pay. At relatively low interest rates

the public is more willing to hold cash since the opportunity cost of holding cash, the lost interest that could be earned if bonds were held instead, will be low.

3. **Explain the equation of exchange and its role in the conduct of monetary policy.**
   - The equation of exchange is $M \times V = P \times Q$. This equation is an identity, meaning that each side of the equation must always equal the other side. The equation says that total spending ($M \times V$) equals the value of production ($P \times Q$). The equation of exchange forms the basis for the quantity theory of money.
   - The quantity theory of money makes two assumptions about the variables in the equation of exchange. For one, velocity, V, is assumed to be constant. For the other, aggregate output, Q, is assumed to be at its maximum value, which is achieved when there is full employment in the economy. Thus, the quantity theory states that an increase in the money supply, M, on the left side of the equation of exchange will be accompanied by a proportional increase in the price level, P, on the right side of the equation of exchange.
   - The quantity theory of money is illustrated graphically by the model of aggregate demand and aggregate supply. The long-run aggregate supply curve is vertical at full-employment GDP. An increase in aggregate demand occurs when there is an increase in the money supply. The increase in aggregate demand has no effect on output, but increases the price level.

4. **Discuss the monetarist school of thought and its implications for monetary policy.**
   - Monetarists argue that the Fed should target a slow and steady growth path for the money supply, so as to provide enough money for economic growth, but not so much as to cause an unacceptable level of inflation. The monetarist prescription for monetary policy is illustrated by Figure 14-7, which shows that an increase in long-run aggregate supply that is accompanied by a proportional rise in aggregate demand will leave the price level unchanged. According to monetarist doctrine, the way to achieve the desired proportional increase in aggregate demand is to increase the money supply proportionally.
   - Monetary policy actions can increase or decrease the money supply. An increase in the money supply will lower the interest rate, stimulate spending, and thus shift aggregate demand to the right. A decrease in the money supply will increase the interest rate, slow down spending, and thus shift aggregate demand to the left.

5. **Interpret the relationship between monetary policy and interest rates.**
   - Nominal interest rates are expressed without regard to inflation. A real interest rate is computed by subtracting the inflation rate from the nominal interest rate.
   - The federal funds rate is the interest rate on reserves that banks with excess reserves lend to other banks that are in need of reserves. By conducting open market operations, the Fed is able to achieve its target for the federal funds rate.
   - The Fed also influences other interest rates, which in turn affect other aspects of the economy. If the Fed is successful at controlling inflation, real and nominal interest rates will be close together.

6. **Address the importance of central banks staying independent of political pressures.**
   - Central bank independence is thought to insulate central banks from political influences and thus make it more likely that price stability is achieved.
   - Independence arises from a number of sources, including the twelve regional Federal Reserve district banks, the Board of Governors' nonrenewability of terms of appointment, financial market considerations, and the Fed's interest earnings on Treasury securities.

KEY TERMS

TEST YOURSELF

TRUE OR FALSE

1. Federal Reserve policymaking has as its chief aim the reduction of interest rates to 3 percent or less.
2. The precautionary motive for holding money is illustrated by consumers who have cash that they plan to spend soon.
3. The equation of exchange is written as $M \times Q = P \times V$.
4. The quantity theory of money assumes that the quantity of money is a constant.
5. The Fed conducts monetary policy ignoring the federal funds rate.

MULTIPLE CHOICE

6. Conflicts in meeting the goals of Fed policymaking
   a. never occur.
   b. occur, but are ignored by the Fed.
   c. occur, and are considered by the Fed in choosing monetary policy actions.
   d. occur only when the president and Congress disagree about the proper course of monetary policy.
7. The demand for money represents the quantities of money that people want to hold
   a. for transactions purposes only.
   b. at different income levels.
   c. at various interest rates.
   d. at banks.
8. The demand curve for money
   a. does not exist.
   b. is upward sloping.
   c. is vertical.
   d. is downward sloping.
9. The speculative demand for money occurs because
   a. people want to make purchases.
   b. of the need to save for a rainy day.
   c. money that is stolen must be replaced.
   d. sometimes investments are not attractive to people and so they hold money instead.
10. A money market equilibrium occurs
    a. when aggregate demand equals long-run aggregate supply.
    b. the transactions demand for money equals zero.
    c. when the interest rate has adjusted to the level that makes the quantity of money supplied equal to the quantity of money demanded.
    d. when real interest rates and nominal interest rates are equal.
11. The equation of exchange dates to the _____ century.
    a. seventeenth
    b. eighteenth
    c. nineteenth
    d. twentieth

12. The equation of exchange says that the quantity of money multiplied by _____ equals total spending.
    a. the price level
    b. velocity
    c. GDP
    d. the equilibrium interest rate
13. The quantity theory of money assumes that aggregate output is
    a. never at the full-employment level.
    b. always at the full-employment level.
    c. equal to one minus velocity.
    d. unpredictable and unexplainable.
14. The quantity theory of money is best at explaining
    a. how aggregate output is determined.
    b. how the price level is determined.
    c. the significance of interest rates to the economy.
    d. how much money people will save every year.
15. Monetarism recommends that monetary policy
    a. focus on low interest rates.
    b. focus on the stock market, aiming to increase stock prices.
    c. expand the money supply at a steady rate.
    d. be turned over to Congress.
16. Which of the following is most likely to cause the movement indicated by the arrow in Self-Test Figure 14-1?
    a. An increase in aggregate supply.
    b. A decrease in aggregate supply.
    c. An increase in the money supply.
    d. A decrease in the money supply.

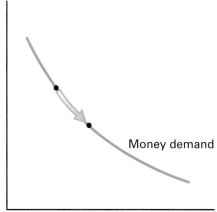

SELF-TEST FIGURE 14-1

17. An increase in the money supply will shift
    a. aggregate supply to the right.
    b. aggregate supply to the left.
    c. aggregate demand to the right.
    d. aggregate demand to the left.
18. A tight monetary policy is associated with
    a. low short-term interest rates.
    b. high short-term interest rates.
    c. alternating increases and decreases in interest rates.
    d. the money supply only, and not interest rates.
19. A monetary policy that aims to keep real interest rates low in the long run by expanding the money supply
    a. is considered the best monetary policy by economists.

b. could lead to higher interest rates because of higher inflation created by the expansion of the money supply.
c. would most likely cause deflation.
d. would violate congressional regulation of the Fed.
20. Operating funds to support the Federal Reserve come mostly from
    a. the budget of the president of the United States.
    b. the Congress.
    c. garage sales, bake sales, and the other charitable fundraisers.
    d. interest earnings.

QUESTIONS AND PROBLEMS

1. *[goals of monetary policy]* List three goals for monetary policy. Explain why there could be conflicts between these goals.
2. *[tradeoffs in monetary policy]* Explain the possible tradeoff if monetary policy is designed to bring down a high inflation rate. In general, why are there tradeoffs in monetary policy?
3. *[monetary policy]* Distinguish between expansionary and contractionary monetary policy. Show graphically their effects on aggregate demand.
4. *[instruments of monetary policy]* What are the two targets of monetary policy? Why would the Fed pick one over the other?
5. *[demand for money]* What are the three motives for holding money? Explain these motives by writing three brief scenarios involving college students acting in ways that illustrate each motive.
6. *[demand for money]* Explain why the "price" of holding money is the interest rate. Will the public wish to hold more or less money as the interest rate decreases?
7. *[demand for money]* Draw a demand curve for money. Be sure to label the axes. Refer to the answer you wrote in question #5 above to explain what could make your personal demand curve for money shift to the right.
8. *[money market equilibrium]* What is meant by an equilibrium in the money market? Illustrate graphically and discuss.
9. *[adjustment to equilibrium]* What causes an excess demand for money? Explain. Is there such a thing as an excess supply of money?

10. *[money and bonds]* Why are money and bonds substitutes? Under what circumstances would someone prefer to be holding bonds rather than money?
11. *[quantity theory of money]* Write the equation of exchange. Define each variable in the equation and then explain why the left side of the equation must equal the right.
12. *[quantity theory of money]* Suppose M = the money supply = $200, V = velocity = 2, and Q = quantity of output = 100 units. What is the price level? According to the quantity theory of money, what happens to the price level if the money supply triples to $600?
13. *[quantity theory of money]* Using the model of aggregate demand and long-run aggregate supply, illustrate the effect of an increase in the money supply predicted by the quantity theory of money.
14. *[monetarism]* What is monetarism? How does it relate to the quantity theory of money? What monetary policy would a monetarist recommend?
15. *[monetarism]* Monetarists refer to a "long and variable lag" in the effects of monetary policy. What does this phrase mean? Why does the long and variable lag lead monetarists to call for the Fed to expand the money supply at a steady rate?
16. *[interest rate instrument]* What is the Keynesian view of how an increase in the quantity of money affects nominal GDP? Explain.
17. *[interest rates]* What is your bank's current nominal interest rate on savings deposits? What is the real interest rate on savings deposits? If the real rate is negative, would people continue to hold dollars in savings accounts? Why?

18. *[federal funds rate]* What is the federal funds rate? Explain its significance to monetary policy.

19. *[interest rates and monetary policy]* Some people urge the Fed to aim at keeping interest rates in the economy very low, both in the short run and the long run. Yet the policies that keep interest low in the long run might sometimes require high interest rates in the short run. Explain, making reference to the distinction between real and nominal interest rates.

WORKING WITH GRAPHS AND DATA

1. *[quantity theory of money]* In the following parts, discuss money and its relationship to the price level.
   a. State the quantity theory of money.
   b. What is assumed about velocity of money in the long run? Why?
   c. What is assumed about aggregate output in the long run? Why?
   d. What do these assumptions (from parts b and c) imply about the relationship between the price level and the money supply?
   e. Using aggregate demand and supply analysis, draw the relationship between the price level and the money supply.

2. *[monetarism]* In the following questions, address the impact of monetary policy on the economy.
   a. Using aggregate demand and supply analysis, explain the monetarist theory with respect to the growth of the money supply when the long-run aggregate supply curve shifts to the right.
   b. Using a graph of aggregate demand and aggregate supply, draw the monetarist theory with respect to the growth of the money supply when the long-run aggregate supply curve shifts to the right.
   c. What impact does this policy have on interest rates? Show, using a graph of money demand and supply.

3. *[money market]* In the following questions, explain the money market and the relationship between money and interest.
   a. Draw a demand curve for money.
   b. Interpret the slope of the money demand curve.
   c. Explain why the money demand curve slopes in this way.
   d. How is an equilibrium interest rate determined?
   e. What is the shape of the money supply curve? Why is it shaped like this?
   f. Graph the money market and label the equilibrium interest rate.

g. Explain the relationship between the interest rate and bonds.

4. *[demand for money]* Show graphically the following complications found in conducting monetary policy using Graph 14-1 as your starting point. For each case, explain whether the money supply curve, the money demand curve, or both, will shift.
   a. The Fed attempts to lower interst rates through open-market operations during a recession. Banks

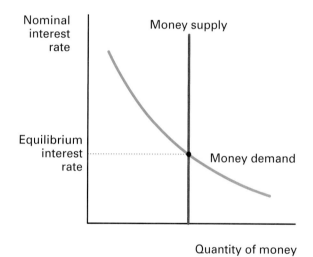

GRAPH 14-1

fear increased defaults on loans, businesses are pessimistic about the near future, and rising unemployment reduces consumer spending.
   b. Business optimism exceeds the Fed's expectations, which defeats the Fed's attempts to stimulate the economy through lower interest rates.
   c. Commercial banks are not as optimistic as the Fed about the Fed's forecast of economic recovery in response to lower interest rates.

 Visit www.prenhall.com/ayers for Exploring the Web exercises and additional self-test quizzes.

CHAPTER 15

ELASTICITY: MEASURING RESPONSIVENESS

A LOOK AHEAD

The "war on drugs" is not intended to enrich drug dealers, but that is what it does. From the mean streets of the inner city to the palatial enclaves of top drug lords around the world, the more government gets tough on drugs, the more lucrative it is for drug dealers to run the risk of selling marijuana, cocaine, heroin, and other illegal drugs. Why the financial prospects of drug dealers are enhanced by government drug policy revolves around the concept of elasticity, as explained in the Explore & Apply section of this chapter.

Elasticity reveals why price changes on some products increase consumer spending, even though similar price changes on other products decrease spending. In this chapter we define the most commonly used elasticities, and show that all elasticities use the same basic formula. You will gain hands-on expertise by using that formula to compute the numerical value of certain elasticities. Such numerical values reveal what merchandise retailers put on sale, what products the government taxes, and even how much study time you should devote to economics!

LEARNING OBJECTIVES

Understanding Chapter 15 will enable you to:
1. **Discuss how elasticity is used to measure the responsiveness of quantity to changes in price.**
2. **Compute the elasticity of demand.**
3. **Describe the conditions under which a price change would increase, decrease, or not change a firm's revenues.**
4. **Discuss the significance of the income elasticity of demand, the cross elasticity of demand, and the elasticity of supply.**
5. **Explain how elasticity determines who ultimately pays a sales tax.**
6. **Discuss how the war on drugs increases crime associated with drug use.**

Explore & Apply

elasticity measures the responsiveness of one thing (Y) to another (X), specifically, the percentage change in Y divided by the percentage change in X.

Social and business issues often revolve around the responsiveness of one thing to another—a concept termed **elasticity** in economics. For example, recall from Chapter 4 that increasing the minimum wage decreases the number of low-skill jobs. But how significant is this effect? Would an increase in the minimum wage increase incomes for the targeted group, or would the job loss be so great that incomes actually fall? The answer lies in elasticity.

15.1 COMPUTING ELASTICITY

Elasticity measures how one variable changes as a result of another variable changing. Although the names of the variables can be anything, the concept remains the same:

$$\text{Elasticity} = \frac{\text{Percentage change in one variable } (Y)}{\text{Percentage change in another variable } (X)}$$

All elasticities arise from this same underlying formula. Different elasticities merely name the variables differently. Therefore, if you know how to compute one elasticity, you can merely substitute variables to compute any other elasticity. For example, if the one variable (Y) changes by 20 percent in response to a 10-percent change in another variable (X), the elasticity equals 2, obtained by dividing 20 percent by 10 percent. This elasticity is called "the elasticity of Y with respect to X."

Elasticity has a broad range of applications. In economics, elasticities are most often used to distinguish the way in which various demand curves differ from one another. There are many other instances in which the concept of elasticity is useful. Farmers might be interested in the elasticity of their crop yields with respect to the amount of fertilizer applied. A high elasticity would mean that a small increase in the amount of fertilizer applied would lead to a significant increase in crop yield. A low elasticity would see yields increasing by a small amount. The elasticity might very well vary from one crop to another. For example, tomatoes might be highly responsive to the application of a particular fertilizer, but corn might not respond at all to that fertilizer. The knowledge of such elasticities can help a farmer to calculate the most cost-effective amounts of fertilizers to apply.

Perhaps you would be interested in the elasticity of your class grade with respect to study time. If that elasticity is high, a small percentage increase in your study time would lead to a large percentage increase in your grade. You would be well rewarded to study more. In contrast, if the elasticity is low, the two variables are not much related.

Computing an elasticity is little more than determining a percentage change. In common usage, a percentage change is defined as the change in something divided by what it started out as. For example, if a person's weight rises from 100 pounds to 150 pounds, we say that his or her weight has risen by 50 percent, that is, by $\frac{50}{100} = \frac{1}{2}$. Curiously, if the person's weight were to drop from 150 pounds to 100 pounds, the percentage change would be -33 percent, that is, $-\frac{50}{150} = -\frac{1}{3}$. In other words, weight rose by half but fell by one-third.

This type of measure will not do for the computation of elasticities. Rather, a measure is needed that is independent of the direction in which the variables are changing. That measure of percentage change is provided by the *midpoint formula*, which computes a percentage change as the change in the variable divided by an amount halfway between the starting and ending amount. Consider the variable Y, which changes from a starting value called Y_0 to another value called Y_1. Symbolically, the midpoint formula to compute the percentage change in Y is:

$$\text{Percentage change in } Y = \frac{\text{Change in } Y}{Y \text{ midpoint}}$$

where

$$\text{Change in } Y = Y_1 - Y_0$$

and

$$Y \text{ midpoint} = \frac{(Y_0 + Y_1)}{2}$$

Likewise, the percentage change in variable X is computed as:

$$\text{Percentage change in } X = \frac{\text{Change in } X}{X \text{ midpoint}}$$

where

$$\text{Change in } X = X_1 - X_0$$

and

$$X \text{ midpoint} = \frac{(X_0 + X_1)}{2}$$

To compute the elasticity of Y with respect to X, divide the percentage change in Y by the percentage change in X:

$$\text{Elasticity of } Y \text{ with respect to } X = \frac{\text{Percentage change in } Y}{\text{Percentage change in } X}$$

Let's apply the midpoint formula to the problem of computing the elasticity of crop yield with respect to the application of fertilizer. Farmer Brown has observed that when he applies 40 pounds of fertilizer per acre, his tomato crop yields 100 bushels, but when he increases the application of fertilizer to 50 pounds, his crop increases to 130 bushels. Table 15-1 shows how to apply the formula and compute the elasticity, which is seen to be 1.17. Pay careful attention to the final computation. Since we have one fraction divided by another, we follow the mathematical procedure that calls for inverting the second fraction (turning it upside down) and then multiplying. The elasticity value is interpreted to mean that for every 1-percent increase in fertilizer Farmer Brown applies, he can expect his tomato crop to increase by 1.17 percent.

QUICKCHECK

Suppose that by increasing her hours of study time per hour of class time from 2 to 3, Andrea can increase her test grade from a 75 to a 95. What is Andrea's elasticity of test grade with respect to study time? Interpret your result.

Answer: Suppose Andrea's study time is called X and her grade is called Y. Using the values provided, the midpoint formula results in: $\dfrac{\left(\dfrac{20}{85}\right)}{\left(\dfrac{1}{2.5}\right)} = \dfrac{20}{85} \times \dfrac{2.5}{1} = \dfrac{50}{85} = 0.588$. This elasticity value is interpreted as indicating that each 1-percent increase in study time results in a 0.588-percent increase in Andrea's numerical grade.

TABLE 15-1	COMPUTING THE ELASTICITY OF CROP YIELD WITH RESPECT TO FERTILIZER APPLIED

(1) Set up the problem:

Y = number of bushels of tomatoes

$\qquad Y_0$ = 100 bushels per acre

$\qquad Y_1$ = 130 bushels per acre

X = amount of fertilizer applied

$\qquad X_0$ = 40 pounds per acre

$\qquad X_1$ = 50 pounds per acre

(2) Compute the percentage change in Y:

$\qquad$ Change in $Y = Y_1 - Y_0 = 130 - 100 = 30$

$\qquad Y \text{ midpoint} = \dfrac{(Y_0 + Y_1)}{2} = \dfrac{(100 + 130)}{2} = \dfrac{230}{2} = 115$

$\qquad$ Percentage change in $Y = \dfrac{30}{115}$

(3) Compute the percentage change in X:

$\qquad$ Change in $X = X_1 - X_0 = 50 - 40 = 10$

$\qquad X \text{ midpoint} = \dfrac{(X_0 + X_1)}{2} = \dfrac{(40 + 50)}{2} = \dfrac{90}{2} = 45$

$\qquad$ Percentage change in $X = \dfrac{10}{45}$

(4) Compute the elasticity:

$\qquad \dfrac{\text{Percentage change in } Y}{\text{Percentage change in } X} = \dfrac{\left(\dfrac{30}{115}\right)}{\left(\dfrac{10}{45}\right)} = \dfrac{30}{115} \times \dfrac{45}{10} = \dfrac{1,350}{1,150} = 1.17$

15.2 THE ELASTICITY OF DEMAND

elasticity of demand
measures the responsiveness of quantity demanded to changes in price; computed as the percentage change in quantity demanded divided by the percentage change in price; expressed as an absolute value.

The **elasticity of demand** measures the responsiveness of quantity demanded to changes in price. For this reason it is sometimes called the *price elasticity of demand*. Some price changes are pretty much ignored by consumers, while others elicit a sharp response. For example, would you hurry on down to your favorite supermarket if the familiar round blue box of table salt were half price? Would your response be different if it were Old Navy selling t-shirts for 50 percent off?

Businesses will answer those questions about your behavior. For example, supermarkets expect little customer response from large cuts in the price of salt, and so do not prominently display salt in their advertising. In contrast, Old Navy and other clothing stores expect to see large increases in sales when they significantly cut the price of certain kinds of clothing. That is why they go to the expense of promoting and advertising sale prices on clothing items—they expect their customers to be very responsive to the lower prices on the sale items and hope that the same customers will purchase many other items while they're at it!

THE FORMULA FOR THE ELASTICITY OF DEMAND

The formula for the elasticity of demand is given by the percentage change in quantity demanded (Q), divided by the percentage change in price (P). Since price and quantity demanded are inversely related, the computation of the elasticity of demand will always result in a negative value. **For convenience, the elasticity of demand is stated as an absolute value, meaning that the minus sign is dropped.** Otherwise the elasticity of demand would always be a negative value, because price and quantity demanded always change in opposite directions.

The elasticity of demand using the midpoint formula is:

$$\text{Elasticity of demand} = \left| \frac{\text{Percentage change in quantity demanded}}{\text{Percentage change in price}} \right|$$

Note the vertical bars around the formula, indicating absolute value. Using Q to stand for quantity demanded, we have

$$\text{Percentage change in } Q = \frac{\text{Change in } Q}{Q \text{ midpoint}}$$

where

$$\text{Change in } Q = Q_1 - Q_0$$

and

$$Q \text{ midpoint} = \frac{(Q_0 + Q_1)}{2}$$

Similarly, using P to stand for price,

$$\text{Percentage change in } P = \frac{\text{Change in } P}{P \text{ midpoint}}$$

where

$$\text{Change in } P = P_1 - P_0$$

and

$$P \text{ midpoint} = \frac{(P_0 + P_1)}{2}$$

Note that **the elasticity of demand is not the same as the slope of demand.** The slope of the demand curve divides the change in price by the change in quantity, without reference to percentages.

Consider Jerry's elasticity of demand for Old Navy t-shirts. At the regular price of $10, he used to furnish his wardrobe with 12 shirts a year. Now that he has discovered that Old Navy lowers the price of the shirts to $8 each when they are on sale, he waits until there is a sale and buys 18 t-shirts a year. Figure 15-1 shows this demand curve. Jerry's elasticity of demand in the price range between $10 and $8 equals 1.8. You should study Table 15-2 to see how this answer was obtained. Note that sometimes students have difficulty in deciding which figures to use as the initial values. The surprising answer is that it doesn't matter! Try it yourself and see. Substitute $8 for P_0 and 18 for Q_0, along with $10 for P_1 and 12 for Q_1. The formula will give exactly the same answer.

FIGURE 15-1

FIGURE 15-1

JERRY'S DEMAND FOR T-SHIRTS
Jerry's demand for t-shirts will
have an elasticity of 1.8 in the
range between $8 and $10.
Note that this value differs from
the slope of −1/3.

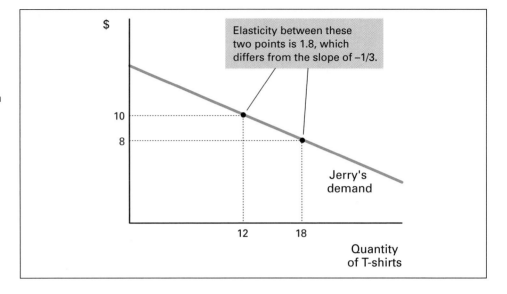

TABLE 15-2 **COMPUTING JERRY'S ELASTICITY OF DEMAND FOR T-SHIRTS**

(1) Set up the problem.

Call the regular price of t-shirts P_0 and the sale price P_1. The quantity purchased by Jerry at the regular price is 12 t-shirts; the quantity purchased at the sale price is 18 t-shirts. The values of the variables are thus:

$$P_0 = \$10 \qquad Q_0 = 12$$
$$P_1 = \$\,8 \qquad Q_1 = 18$$

(2) Compute the percentage change in Q:

$$\text{Change in } Q = Q_1 - Q_0 = 18 - 12 = 6$$

$$Q \text{ midpoint} = \frac{(Q_0 + Q_1)}{2} = \frac{(12 + 18)}{2} = \frac{30}{2} = 15$$

$$\text{Percentage change in } Q = \frac{\text{Change in } Q}{Q \text{ midpoint}} = \frac{6}{15}$$

(3) Compute the percentage change in P:

$$\text{Change in } P = P_1 - P_0 = 8 - 10 = -2$$

$$P \text{ midpoint} = \frac{(P_0 + P_1)}{2} = \frac{(10 + 8)}{2} = \frac{18}{2} = 9$$

$$\text{Percentage change in } P = \frac{\text{Change in } P}{P \text{ midpoint}} = \frac{-2}{9}$$

(4) Substitute into the formula for the elasticity of demand:

$$\left| \frac{\text{Percentage change in } Q}{\text{Percentage change in } P} \right| = \frac{(\frac{6}{15})}{(\frac{2}{9})} = \frac{6}{15} \times \frac{9}{2} = \frac{54}{30} = 1.8$$

QUICKCHECK

Calculate the elasticity of demand for ballpoint ink pens when $P_0 = \$5$, $Q_0 = 15$, $P_1 = \$7$, and $Q_1 = 10$.

Answer: The elasticity of demand equals 1.2 in this range of prices, found by substituting the values given into the elasticity formula.

CLASSIFYING THE ELASTICITY OF DEMAND

The elasticity of demand is classified as inelastic, unit elastic, or elastic, according to its numerical value.

- **Inelastic demand:** Elasticity of demand lies between 0 and 1; in this range, the quantity demanded is relatively unresponsive to price. For example, a 2-percent change in price that leads to a 1-percent change in quantity demanded results in an elasticity of demand equal to 0.5.

- **Unit elastic demand:** Elasticity of demand is equal to 1; in this range, the quantity demanded changes proportionally to changes in price. For example, a 2-percent change in price that leads to a 2-percent change in quantity demanded results in an elasticity equal to 1.

- **Elastic demand:** Elasticity of demand is greater than 1; in this range, the quantity demanded is relatively responsive to changes in price. For example, a 2-percent change in price that leads to a 3-percent change in quantity demanded results in an elasticity equal to 1.5.

inelastic demand demand has an elasticity that is less than 1.

unit elastic demand demand has an elasticity that equals 1.

elastic demand demand has an elasticity that is greater than 1.

The range of numerical values associated with each class of elasticity is portrayed in Figure 15-2.

Other things being equal, the more substitutes there are for a product or the greater the fraction of a person's budget it takes to buy the product, the greater will be its elasticity of demand. Thus, demand for Domino's Pizza is quite elastic, because there are many close substitutes, including other brands of pizza and other types of fast food. Demand for drinking water is quite inelastic, because it takes a tiny fraction of a person's budget and there are no close substitutes for drinking water. However, for any brand of bottled drinking water, the demand will be highly elastic, since other brands and tap water are good substitutes. Table 15-3 shows estimates of the price elasticity of demand for selected products, including several familiar brand names. Notice that items that some people will find to be *necessities*—items that are difficult to do without—tend to have more inelastic demand than *luxuries* that we can easily forgo. For example, public transit is a necessity for the poor who cannot afford their own cars and has less elastic demand than the luxuries of restaurant meals and fresh tomatoes.

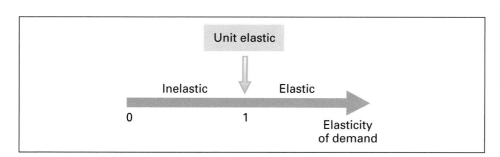

FIGURE 15-2

PRICE ELASTICITY OF DEMAND
This value can range from zero to infinity (in absolute value).

TABLE 15-3　ESTIMATES OF DEMAND ELASTICITIES

PRODUCT	ELASTICITY OF DEMAND
Beef	0.35
Fish	0.39
Public transit	0.40
Peak use business electricity	0.47
Physician services	0.60
Poultry	0.64
Pork	0.69
Fruit	0.71
Peak use residential electricity	1.5
Restaurant meals	2.3
Kellogg's Fruit Loops	2.3
Cheerios	3.6
Coke	3.8
Mountain Dew	4.4
Fresh tomatoes	4.6

Source: Compiled from numerous elasticity studies conducted in various years.

QUICKCHECK

At current market prices, are the market demands for table salt and Old Navy t-shirts more likely to be elastic or inelastic?

Answer: The demand for table salt is likely inelastic since it takes a small part of the budget and there is no good substitute. Old Navy t-shirts probably have an elastic demand because of the many good substitutes for them and because they take a larger part of the budget.

RELATING DEMAND ELASTICITY TO REVENUE

Consumer spending translates into revenue for sellers. The revenue sellers receive equals the quantity sold multiplied by the price, and is called **total revenue.** In other words,

total revenue price × quantity.

$$\text{Total revenue} = \text{Price} \times \text{Quantity}$$

Total revenue, which is the same as total spending by consumers, can be shown graphically as the rectangular area created when a price and corresponding quantity demanded are multiplied by each other. Figure 15-3 illustrates total revenue graphically.

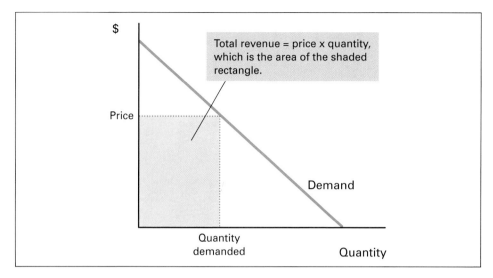

Total revenue = price x quantity, which is the area of the shaded rectangle.

FIGURE 15-3

TOTAL REVENUE Price multiplied by quantity demanded equals total revenue, as shown by the area of the shaded rectangle. The total revenue is received by sellers. Since it represents spending by consumers, total revenue equals total spending.

TABLE 15-4 **THE EFFECT OF A CHANGE IN PRICE ON TOTAL REVENUE**

CHANGE IN PRICE	EFFECT ON TOTAL REVENUE
Higher Price	If demand is inelastic, total revenue rises.
	If demand is unit elastic, total revenue remains constant.
	If demand is elastic, total revenue falls.
Lower Price	If demand is inelastic, total revenue falls.
	If demand is unit elastic, total revenue remains constant.
	If demand is elastic, total revenue rises.

Many people assume that when the price increases, the sellers of a product earn more revenue. However, this assumption is often not true, because quantity demanded falls any time price rises. An increase in price will bring in more revenue only if demand is inelastic, meaning that the fall in quantity demanded is less significant than the rise in price. In contrast, were demand to be elastic, the quantity demanded would be quite responsive to price. Any increase in price would cause a proportionally greater fall in the quantity sold and thus would lower total revenue. Table 15-4 summarizes the price change effects on total revenue.

For example, if demand is elastic, the quantity demanded is very responsive to price changes. The effect of lower prices is to increase purchases so much that total revenue rises. This result has occurred in many industries, ranging from air travel to computing. When computing power was very expensive twenty years ago, the revenues of the computer industry were a mere fraction of current revenues now that computing power is cheap. This example illustrates another point: **The longer the time period that quantity demanded adjusts, the greater the elasticity of demand.** Time lets people adjust, to substitute toward goods that become relatively less expensive and away from those that become relatively more expensive. For example, there is little change in the quantity of mail from a higher postage rate—the bills must still be paid. Longer term, however, people change their behavior. For

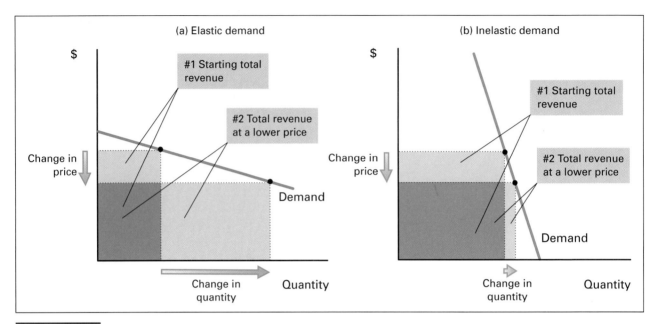

FIGURE 15-4

ELASTICITY AND TOTAL REVENUE Total revenue is the rectangle formed by multiplying price by quantity sold. In the elastic range of demand, as shown in (a), price and total revenue vary inversely. Decreasing price would cause total revenue to rise. The revenue loss from the lower price per unit is more than offset by the revenue gain from the larger quantity sold.

In the inelastic range of demand, as shown in (b), price and total revenue vary directly. Decreasing price would cause total revenue to fall. The additional revenue from increasing the quantity sold does not make up for the revenue loss from the lower price per unit.

example, they might set up on-line billing so that they can pay their bills over the Internet and avoid the postage altogether.

Figure 15-4 illustrates the idea that price changes can sometimes lead to increased total revenue and at other times lead to decreased revenue. Part (a) shows elastic demand, meaning that the total revenue rectangle becomes larger when price is lowered. Part (b) depicts a demand that is inelastic in the price range shown. In such cases, a decrease in price decreases the total revenue rectangle, as seen in the figure.

The elasticity of demand will vary along most demand curves. Along a downward-sloping, straight-line demand curve, demand is unit elastic at the midpoint, elastic above the midpoint, and inelastic below the midpoint. The variation in elasticity is shown in Figure 15-5. To remember, observe that the lower the point on a straight-line demand curve, the less its elasticity. The reason is that, when we move down the demand curve, the percentage change in price becomes larger relative to the corresponding percentage change in quantity demanded.

Table 15-5 provides a demand schedule that includes total revenue. Observe that total revenue increases when price decreases as we move from data point *A* to *B* to *C*. Moving from points *D* to *E* to *F*, total revenue decreases. Let's take the data on price and quantity demanded in Table 15-5 and compute the elasticity of demand in Table 15-6 on page 388. Our purpose is to confirm the relationships between elasticity and total revenue, as well as to show that demand becomes less elastic as we move down a straight-line demand curve.

Table 15-6 computes elasticity between each pair of price–quantity data points in Table 15-5. The computations take the prices and quantities demanded in Table 15-5 and substitute the indicated pairs of data into the midpoint formula. For example, in computing

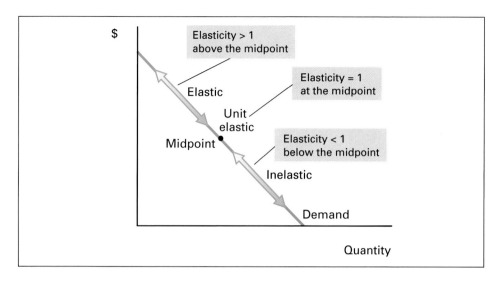

FIGURE 15-5

ELASTICITY ALONG A LINEAR DEMAND CURVE The midpoint of a straight-line demand curve separates the elastic from the inelastic portion. In moving down the linear demand curve, the elasticity of demand declines from elastic to unit elastic to inelastic. The reason stems from elasticity being based upon percentage changes rather than merely upon slope, which remains constant.

TABLE 15-5 **DEMAND AND TOTAL REVENUE**

DATA POINT	PRICE ($)	QUANTITY DEMANDED	TOTAL REVENUE ($) = PRICE × QUANTITY DEMANDED
A	5	0	0
B	4	1	4
C	3	2	6
D	2	3	6
E	1	4	4
F	0	5	0

the elasticity between points *A* and *B,* we observe in Table 15-5 that the absolute value of the change in quantity demanded equals 1, the midpoint between the quantities demanded equals 0.5 (computed as $\frac{(0 + 1)}{2} = 0.5$, the absolute value of the change in price also equals 1, while the midpoint between the two prices equals 4.5 (computed as $\frac{(5 + 4)}{2} = \frac{9}{2} = 4.5$). Substituting into the midpoint formula, we have

$$\text{Elasticity of demand} = \frac{1}{0.5} \div \frac{1}{4.5} = \frac{1}{0.5} \times \frac{4.5}{1} = 2 \times 4.5 = 9$$

You should verify the remaining computations in the table in order to confirm your ability to compute the elasticity of demand using pairs of prices and quantities.

Figure 15-6(a) plots the relationships between demand, total revenue, and elasticity, using the data from Tables 15-5 and 15-6. Figure 15-6(b) shows the more general relationships between these variables. Both figures show that in the elastic range of demand, total revenue increases as price decreases. Total revenue reaches its maximum when the elasticity of demand is unit elastic, which occurs at the midpoint of demand. In the inelastic range of demand, total revenue decreases as price falls.

| TABLE 15-6 | COMPUTING THE ELASTICITY OF DEMAND |

(a) BETWEEN POINTS:	(b) CHANGE IN QUANTITY ÷ QUANTITY AT MIDPOINT	(c) CHANGE IN PRICE ÷ PRICE AT MIDPOINT	(d) ELASTICITY OF DEMAND = (b) ÷ (c)
A and B	$\dfrac{1}{0.5}$	$\dfrac{1}{4.5}$	9
B and C	$\dfrac{1}{1.5}$	$\dfrac{1}{3.5}$	7/3 = 2.33
C and D	$\dfrac{1}{2.5}$	$\dfrac{1}{2.5}$	1
D and E	$\dfrac{1}{3.5}$	$\dfrac{1}{1.5}$	3/7 = 0.43
E and F	$\dfrac{1}{4.5}$	$\dfrac{1}{0.5}$	1/9 = 0.11

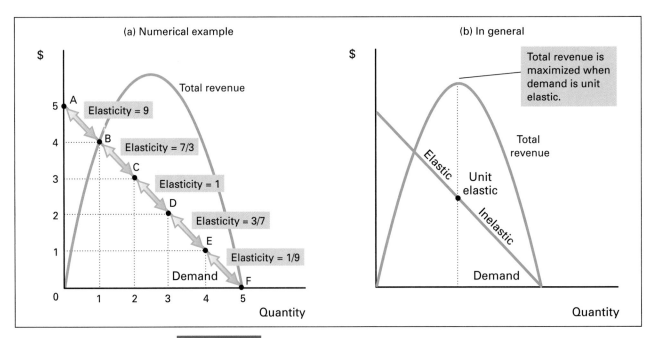

| FIGURE 15-6 |

DEMAND, TOTAL REVENUE, AND ELASTICITY The data from Table 15-5 show the typical relationship between demand, elasticity, and total revenue, as plotted in (a). When quantities are large, the relationships between demand, total revenue, and elasticity will appear as shown in (b). Total revenue is maximized at the midpoint of demand, which is where the elasticity of demand equals one.

QUICKCHECK

Wally's Water Works sells water. Wally has set the price of water at $5 per pail, but wonders if he should charge less. If Wally faces an elasticity of demand for water equal to 0.3, why would he regret lowering his price? What if the elasticity equals 3?

Answer: An elasticity of demand equal to 0.3 means that demand is inelastic. If Wally lowers his price, the increase in sales will not be enough to make up for the loss of revenue per unit. In other words, keeping the price at $5 per pail means that he sells fewer pails but makes more total revenue than if the price is lower. In contrast, an elasticity of demand equal to 3 would mean that Wally faces an elastic demand for his water. In that case, a price reduction would lead to such a large percentage increase in sales that Wally's revenues would rise.

One implication of this analysis is that each firm always seeks to stay out of the inelastic portion of its demand. When demand is inelastic, firms would find their revenues increasing if they reduce output and increase their price. They will do so until they are out of the inelastic range. The result is this general rule: **Each firm seeks to produce in the elastic range of its demand.** Exactly where in that range firms will produce is unclear because the cost of production must be taken into account when deciding on the specific quantity to produce.

FREE SHIPPING!   *SNAPSHOT*

In the summer of 2002, Amazon.com took a chance. For orders over $49, customers would not be charged for shipping. Jeff Bezos, the founder and CEO of the company, wanted to make sure his customers knew about the change in policy, so he sent previous customers an e-mail with the news, adding: "The hope is we'll generate enough new business to offset the cost."

Jeff Bezos did not use the word *elasticity* in his e-mail—most of his customers would not know what it meant. But the concept of elasticity is well known to Jeff Bezos and the rest of the business world. Lower prices can bring in more revenue if demand is elastic. But is it? Not knowing for sure, Jeff Bezos said the free shipping would be a test, lasting from three to six months. After that time, if the policy proved successful, it would continue. Was it? Just check the current shipping fees at Amazon.com to find out. ◀

THE EXTREMES OF DEMAND ELASTICITY

There are three cases in which elasticity is constant throughout the demand curve, as shown in Figure 15-7. Graph (a) depicts a demand that is **perfectly inelastic,** meaning that the elasticity of demand is zero. In other words, the quantity demanded will not depend on price. The corresponding demand curve is drawn as a vertical line. While demand for some goods is highly inelastic, there aren't any goods that do not show at least some responsiveness to price. For example, demand for insulin or certain pharmaceutical drugs is highly inelastic. However, to the extent that patients must actually pay more when the price increases for these necessities, they will skimp on their dosages and thus buy less.

perfectly inelastic elasticity of zero; demand would be drawn as a vertical line.

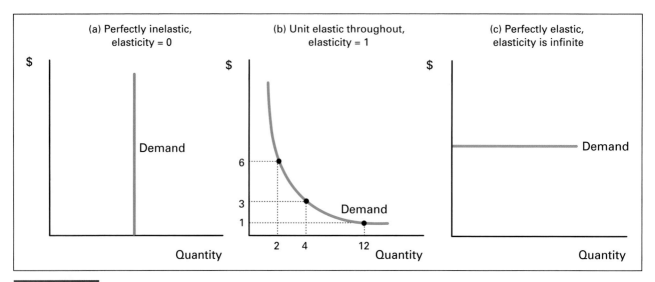

EXTREMES OF DEMAND ELASTICITY The extremes of demand elasticity are:
(a) perfectly inelastic, with demand being vertical;
(b) unit elastic throughout, with demand being a rectangular hyperbola; and
(c) perfectly elastic, with demand being horizontal.

In (b), in which demand is unit elastic everywhere, total spending remains constant no matter what price is charged. For example, if the price is $6, the quantity demanded is 2, and total revenue is 6 × 2 = 12. If the price is $3 and quantity demanded is 4, total revenue is again $12. If price is $1 and quantity demanded is 12, total revenue is still $12.

unit elastic throughout
elasticity of 1; demand would be a rectangular hyperbola that never touches either axis.

Figure 15-7(b) depicts a demand that is **unit elastic throughout.** This shape is referred to as a rectangular hyperbola, because any total revenue rectangle drawn under that demand curve will have the same area. A demand with this shape slopes downward at a decreasing rate, never touching either axis. Whatever price may be, total revenue remains the same. In this example, whether the price is $1, $3, or $6, the total revenue is $12, which is the area of either the 1 × 12, 3 × 4, or 6 × 2 rectangle. This demand would occur if a consumer decides to spend a certain pre-set budget on a product, no matter what the product's price might be.

perfectly elastic elasticity of infinity; demand would be drawn as a horizontal line.

Figure 15-7(c) depicts a demand curve that is **perfectly elastic** throughout, meaning that it has an elasticity of infinity and is drawn as a horizontal line. In other words, the slightest increase in price over some threshold price leads to a complete loss of sales. At any price at or below this threshold, unlimited quantities could be sold. This demand is a close approximation to demand facing the firm in the competitive marketplace, in which there is a very large number of other firms. The firm's demand curve in the competitive marketplace is perfectly elastic at the market price.

For example, if you are a Nebraska wheat farmer, you would sell none of your grain if you price it at even one penny more than the market price set by the interaction of buyers and sellers in the commodity exchanges of Chicago. At or below that market price, however, you could sell all you could produce, no matter how large your farm. Of course, you would have no reason to sell below the market price.

BUDGETING, VEGAS STYLE *SNAPSHOT*

It is quite common for the ordinary tourist vacationing in Las Vegas to set aside a certain amount of money to spend on the slot machines and gaming tables. The tourists keep playing, up and down, until that budget is used up. Of course, some will break the rule and spend over their budgets, but those are usually the ones that lose their money too quickly. Casino owners don't mind that behavior at all.

Indeed, Vegas casino owners count on the "Vegas-style" budgeting for a hefty share of their profits. By choosing a unit elastic demand, the tourists in effect resolve to give their entire budget to the casino owners. It's a peculiar plan. The vacationers do not quit while they're ahead. No, they keep playing until they're in the hole to exactly the tune of their preset budget. Most of them have lots of fun losing their money this way, and the casino owners have lots of fun watching them do it! ◄

15.3 INCOME AND CROSS ELASTICITIES OF DEMAND: THE SIGN MATTERS

Two additional demand elasticities are also referred to frequently, the income elasticity of demand and the cross elasticity of demand. The **income elasticity of demand** measures how demand responds to income. It is computed by dividing the percentage change in quantity demanded by the percentage change in income. If the income elasticity of demand is positive, an increase in income increases demand. **A positive income elasticity of demand indicates the good is normal.** Conversely, **a negative income elasticity of demand indicates the good is inferior** because demand decreases when income rises. Thus, we would expect the income elasticity of demand to be positive for cell phones and negative for canned luncheon meat. That is because when a person has more income it is easier to afford a cell phone, and replace that canned meat with fresh.

Normal goods can be distinguished from inferior goods by the direction of the shift in demand that arises from a change in income. The relationships are laid out in Table 15-7. The table shows that a good is normal when its demand shifts in the same direction as the change in income. When demand shifts in the opposite direction as income, the good is inferior. Can you think of some examples of normal goods for you personally? What are some personal examples of inferior goods?

income elasticity of demand measures how demand responds to income; computed as the percentage change in quantity demanded divided by the percentage change in income.

TABLE 15-7 INCOME ELASTICITY OF DEMAND: NORMAL AND INFERIOR GOODS

CHANGE IN INCOME	CHANGE IN DEMAND	INCOME ELASTICITY	TYPE OF GOOD	EXAMPLE
Increase	Increases	Positive	Normal	Consumer incomes increase, causing the demand for leisure travel to increase.
Increase	Decreases	Negative	Inferior	Consumer incomes increase, causing the demand for store-brand paper towels to decrease.
Decrease	Increases	Negative	Inferior	Consumer incomes decrease, causing the demand for public transit to increase.
Decrease	Decreases	Positive	Normal	Consumer incomes decrease, causing the demand for digital cameras to decrease.

TABLE 15-8 CROSS ELASTICITY OF DEMAND: SUBSTITUTES AND COMPLEMENTS

CHANGE IN THE PRICE OF ANOTHER GOOD	CHANGE IN DEMAND FOR THE FIRST GOOD	CROSS ELASTICITY BETWEEN THE GOODS	RELATIONSHIP BETWEEN THE GOODS	EXAMPLE
Increase	Increases	Positive	Substitutes	The price of fresh broccoli increases, causing the demand for frozen broccoli to increase.
Increase	Decreases	Negative	Complements	The price of coffee increases, causing the demand for donuts to decrease.
Decrease	Increases	Negative	Complements	The price of DVD players decreases, causing an increase in the demand for DVDs.
Decrease	Decreases	Positive	Substitutes	The price of shrimp decreases, causing a decrease in the demand for other seafood.

cross elasticity of demand measures how the demand for one good responds to changes in the price of another good; computed as the percentage change in the quantity demanded of one good divided by the percentage change in the price of another.

Finally, the **cross elasticity of demand** measures how the demand for one good responds to changes in the price of another good. Its formula is given by the percentage change in the quantity demanded of one good divided by the percentage change in the price of another. If this value is positive, the demand for the first good changes in the same direction as the price of the other good. **A positive cross elasticity of demand indicates the goods are substitutes,** such as Coke for Pepsi. Thus, if the price of Pepsi increases, so does the demand for Coke.

If the cross elasticity of demand is negative, the quantity demanded of the good falls as the price of the other good rises, and vice versa. **A negative cross elasticity of demand indicates that the goods are complements,** goods that go together, such as popcorn and movies. If movie tickets become more expensive, fewer people go to the movie theater and less popcorn is sold. Table 15-8 summarizes the relationships that apply to the cross elasticity of demand.

QUICKCHECK

Suppose that a decrease in income increases the demand for potatoes and that a decrease in the price of ground beef increases the demand for potatoes. Using this information, what conclusions can be reached about potatoes?

Answer: Potatoes are an inferior good that complement ground beef.

15.4 THE ELASTICITY OF SUPPLY

elasticity of supply measures the responsiveness of quantity supplied to price; computed as the percentage change in quantity supplied divided by the percentage change in price.

The **elasticity of supply** measures the responsiveness of quantity supplied to price. Its formula is given by the percentage change in quantity supplied divided by the percentage change in price. The formula used to compute the elasticity of demand can be used to compute the elasticity of supply, except that the variable Q will be quantity supplied rather than quantity demanded. Since price and quantity supplied are directly related to each other, the

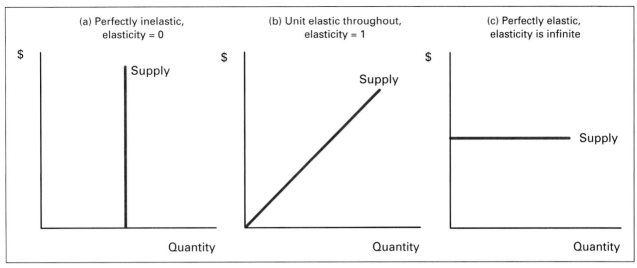

FIGURE 15-8

THE EXTREMES OF SUPPLY ELASTICITY The extremes of supply elasticity are: (a) perfectly inelastic, with supply being vertical; (b) unit elastic throughout, with supply being any straight line starting from the origin; and (c) perfectly elastic, with supply being horizontal.

elasticity of supply will always be positive, thus eliminating the need to take the absolute value, as is done with the elasticity of demand. The elasticity of supply can fall within the following three ranges:

1. **Inelastic supply:** Elasticity of supply lies between 0 and 1; in this range, the quantity supplied is relatively unresponsive to price.
2. **Unit elastic supply:** Elasticity of supply = 1; in this range, the quantity supplied changes proportionally to changes in price.
3. **Elastic supply:** Elasticity of supply is greater than 1; in this range, the quantity supplied is relatively responsive to changes in price.

inelastic supply supply has an elasticity that is less than 1.

unit elastic supply supply has an elasticity that equals 1.

elastic supply supply has an elasticity that is greater than 1.

Compare the classification of elasticity of supply with that of elasticity of demand. Note that, with the exception of substituting supply for demand, they are identical.

As with demand, supply can be *perfectly inelastic, unit elastic throughout,* or *perfectly elastic.* A perfectly inelastic supply curve is vertical, as shown in Figure 15-8(a). Part (b) of that figure shows unit elastic supply, which is any straight line from the origin. This shape is implied by unit elastic's definition, in which the percentage change in price must always equal the percentage change in quantity. A perfectly elastic supply curve is horizontal, as seen in Figure 15-8(c).

15.5 TAX SHIFTING AND THE ELASTICITIES OF DEMAND AND SUPPLY

When a product is taxed, how much of that tax will the buyers pay and how much will the sellers pay? Some people mistakenly think that, even if the tax is levied on sellers, all of the tax will just be passed on to buyers in the form of higher prices. In reality, the answer to the question of who ultimately shoulders the **tax burden**—how much the tax costs after taking into account price changes—depends on the demand and supply elasticities of the product taxed.

tax burden how much the tax costs after taking into account price changes.

If the addition of the tax causes the tax-inclusive price of the product to change by less than the amount of the tax, then both consumers and producers are sharing in the burden of that tax, meaning that they are both worse off. The greater the elasticity of supply relative to the elasticity of demand, the more the tax burden is borne by consumers and the less by producers.

tax shifting when the effects of a tax are transferred from one party to another.

When the effects of a tax are transferred from one party to another, **tax shifting** is said to occur. *Forward tax shifting* occurs when the seller is taxed but is able to pass along all or part of the tax to buyers in the form of a higher price. Conversely, if the buyer pays a sales tax and the seller feels compelled to charge a lower price in order to make that sale, the result is *backward tax shifting,* in which the buyer has effectively shifted some of the tax backward onto the seller.

Figure 15-9 illustrates the effect of a per-unit tax in which sellers must pay a fixed amount per unit of sales. Because the seller must pay the tax for each unit sold, **the effect of the tax is to shift the supply curve upward by the amount of the tax.** Figure 15-9(a) shows a perfectly inelastic demand curve and an upward-sloping supply curve. As seen in the figure, the price of the product rises as the market equilibrium changes. The after-tax price in this case is greater by exactly the amount of the tax. The maximum amount of forward tax shifting occurs when demand is perfectly inelastic because the entire amount of the tax is passed on to buyers. Notice that in spite of the tax, the perfectly inelastic demand results in no change in the quantity of the product bought and sold.

Figure 15-9(b) illustrates the effect of the tax when it is supply that is perfectly inelastic. Supply shifts vertically by the amount of the tax, just as in part (a). However, the shift in supply does not affect the market equilibrium—the equilibrium price and quantity remain unchanged as seen in the figure. In this case, no tax shifting can occur.

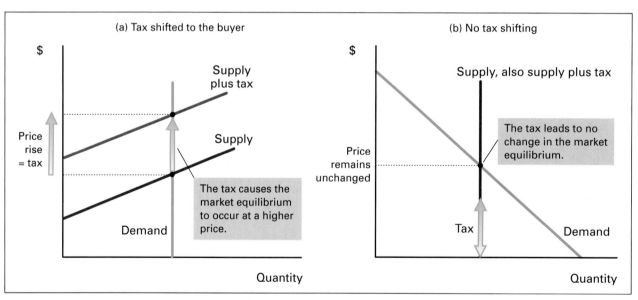

   FIGURE 15-9

THE EXTREMES OF TAX SHIFTING Requiring firms to pay a tax on the output they sell would shift supply up by the per-unit amount of that tax. The more elastic is supply relative to demand, the higher will be the after-tax price and the greater the amount of tax burden borne by consumers. Part (a) shows the extreme of a perfectly inelastic demand, in which case consumers shoulder the entire burden of the tax. Part (b) shows the extreme of a perfectly inelastic supply, in which case producers bear the entire tax burden.

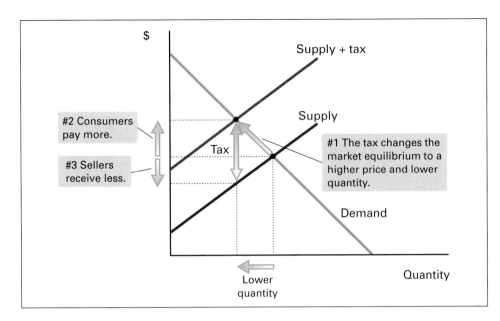

$ Supply + tax

Supply

#2 Consumers pay more.

Tax

#3 Sellers receive less.

#1 The tax changes the market equilibrium to a higher price and lower quantity.

Demand

Quantity

Lower quantity

FIGURE 15-10

PARTIAL TAX SHIFTING The burden of a sales tax is split between buyers and sellers when the tax causes the price to rise by less than the amount of the tax. The exact split is determined by the relative elasticities of supply and demand.

OneKey

Usually, reality lies somewhere in between these extremes, with the **tax burden** shared between producers and consumers, such as shown in Figure 15-10. In that figure, note that the tax-inclusive price is higher than the pre-tax price, but that the increase is less than the tax. In other words, even though consumers pay more, it is not enough to cover the tax. Therefore, producers and consumers end up sharing the tax burden, with the exact amounts depending upon relative elasticities. Specifically, **consumers pay more of the tax if demand is relatively less elastic than supply,** which is consistent with the extreme case shown in Figure 15-9(a). **Producers pay more of the tax if demand is relatively more elastic than supply,** which is consistent with the extreme case shown in Figure 15-9(b).

SIN TAXES—IS IT MORALITY WE'RE AFTER?   *SNAPSHOT*

Cigarettes and alcohol are taxed at much higher rates than virtually any other good. The reason is partly because these "goods" are seen as bad. Just as important, it is because the elasticity of demand is low relative to that of other goods.

If the elasticity were high, people could more easily switch to other goods with lower tax rates. That would cut into tax revenues, which is exactly what happened after Congress passed five luxury taxes in 1990. Higher tax rates on yachts and other luxuries actually brought in less revenue, because so many people refused to buy these items at the higher prices the tax implied. Four of the five luxury taxes were repealed for this reason—demand was too elastic. Because elasticity is higher at higher prices, the amount of extra revenue the government could collect by raising alcohol and tobacco taxes is also limited. Proposals to finance healthcare through taxes on alcohol and tobacco overlook this fact of economic life.

Cigarettes and alcoholic beverages are not the only goods with low elasticities of demand. Milk has a low elasticity of demand, and yet milk is not taxed at all in most places. It seems that the so-called sin aspect of smoking and drinking means that the public, even smokers and drinkers, are less willing to fight higher taxes on those items. Moreover, smoking and drinking can have some harmful effects on others. In contrast, what could be more wholesome than milk?

A caution is in order about taxing sin. If goods are singled out for high taxes because they are bad, it is important to figure out just how bad, and let the punishment fit the crime. ◀

Explore & Apply

15.6 CRIME AND THE MARKET FOR DRUGS

The United States has the highest proportion of its citizens behind bars of any developed country. Sixty percent of those prisoners are convicted on drug-related charges. It sometimes appears that recreational drugs are ripping apart our social fabric. Yet, the more we fight the problem, the worse it seems.

Many images come to mind in association with so-called recreational drugs, including the violence of the drug cartels that produce and sell cocaine, corruption among public officials, and the pathos of addicted babies. Also woven in are the counterculture of the 1960s and the creativity of such classic writers and poets as Edgar Allen Poe and Samuel Coleridge.

We need to do some sorting. We leave aside questions of whether drug use is moral and of where to draw the line on drug laws. Instead, let's employ economic analysis to solve the dilemma of why toughening up our enforcement of drug laws seems to make drug-related problems worse. Then we will examine the implications of disengaging from the drug war.

Government enforcement of drug laws increases the risk involved in getting illegal drugs to market. The supply curve shifts to the left as costs increase and as risk-averse suppliers leave the industry. Remaining suppliers will be those who shrug off the risk, perhaps because they enjoy it or have become accustomed to the lifestyle. For the most part, however, competition will select those suppliers who are best at circumventing the law. Usually that involves the insurance of hooking up with a powerful criminal organization.

From street gangs on up to the reputed drug Mafia, organized crime flourishes under tough drug law enforcement. These organizations offer both connections and firepower to the dealers. In addition, because the drug dealer cannot turn to the police for protection, that dealer becomes easy prey for organized criminals. Here is one source of crime associated with drugs— turf battles in which criminal organizations seek to dominate the sales of drugs in an area.

On the demand side, tough enforcement of the drug laws makes it much more expensive to support a drug habit. Drug users are often addicted to the drugs they use and would go to great lengths to avoid doing without. In other words, the demand for drugs is inelastic because the quantity purchased does not drop proportionally to increases in price. This means that, the tougher we enforce our drug laws, the more money drug users need. Moreover, the tougher we punish a convicted drug offender for the drug use itself, the less the user cares about adding other crimes to the list. Thus, while many addicts can support their habits with legally earned income, others think little of resorting to robberies, burglaries, and other crimes.

Tough enforcement of our drug laws also has the perverse effect of increasing the popularity of the more highly refined drugs, since these drugs are harder to intercept. For instance, "cracking" cocaine to form crack requires only a small amount of cocaine, a drug with very little bulk. Such drugs also tend to be the most addictive. Even marijuana that is grown in the United States today is likely to be much more potent than what members of the counterculture used in the 1960s.

There are numerous possible drug control policies between the current war on drugs and a laissez-faire hands-off strategy. At the extreme, if all drugs were legalized, that would seem to suggest including prescription pharmaceuticals. Should drugstores allow the customer to point and buy "three of those green ones, one of those big red capsules, and twelve of the yellow ones with dots?" This section models some economic implications of moving away from the current war on drugs without specifying the details of how far that movement goes. For example, in 2002, England moved in this direction by decriminalizing marijuana possession and making it subject to no more than a ticket (akin to a parking ticket).

Figure 15-11 depicts the market for recreational drugs, where the model is deliberately nonspecific as to exactly what sort of drugs these are. The addictive nature of drugs leads to an inelastic demand curve. The market price and quantity of drugs in the free market is determined by the intersection of supply and demand. The drug war shifts that supply by

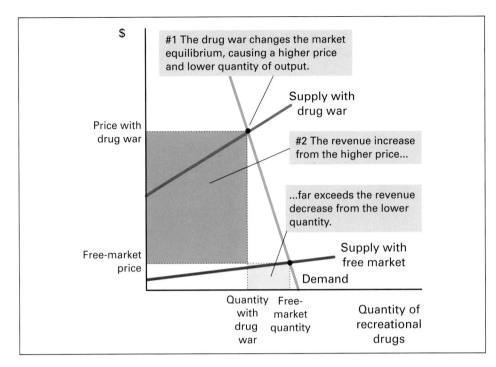

FIGURE 15-11

EFFECTS OF THE DRUG WAR
Tougher enforcement of drug laws make it riskier and more costly to supply recreational drugs, which decreases supply. The drug war causes the market equilibrium price to be higher and quantity to be lower. Because demand is inelastic, the drug war also increases total revenue in the industry. With more money at stake and no recourse to the law, there is an incentive for violence as suppliers compete for control. The higher prices also lead to more property crime among impoverished addicts seeking money to buy drugs.

increasing the riskiness and cost of supplying drugs. The result is a higher equilibrium price and lower equilibrium quantity.

Relative to the outcome under the drug war, the free market would appear to offer both good news and bad news. The good news is that the quantity of spending, given by price multiplied by quantity, would be lower without the drug war. This means less crime to raise money to buy drugs. Since drugs would be sold by legitimate businesses in the free market, the violent territorial crime of the drug rings would also largely disappear. The bad news is that drug use would rise, *ceteris paribus,* because demand always shows an inverse relationship between price and quantity.

Keep in mind that the demand curve keeps constant everything but price. However, moving away from the drug war entails more than just a drop in price. For example, the entire demand curve would shift outward to the extent that users no longer fear being arrested, which would lead to greater usage. Alternatively, the demand curve might shift inward to the extent that drug usage constitutes less of an anti-authority rebellion and is seen more as a matter of responsible personal behavior. Nonlegalistic public policy, such as the current DARE programs that attempt to lead students away from drugs, could contribute to this inward shift.

Moving away from the drug war also eliminates the underhanded marketing efforts of drug pushers and their suppliers. Without tough drug laws, there would be no "pushing" because there would be no money in it. There would be no financial incentive to lure school-children to drug use. Without their wads of cash and the power it buys, pushers would lose their ill-bought status as anti-establishment role models. Free from the pressure of pushers, and without drugs exemplifying rebellion against authority, fewer kids would turn to drugs—demand would shift to the left.

IS LEGALIZATION THE ANSWER?

Some people suggest the legalization of many drugs, but only if we impose high sales taxes to discourage purchases and pay for drug-related problems. However, while taxes can be reasonable, a prohibitively high tax would reopen the doors to criminal pushers and modern-day bootleggers.

Moving away from the drug war toward legalization does raise many questions. Some people are concerned about whether quality would diminish in the workplace, especially when that quality involves personal safety. For example, with drug use legal, what would prevent aircraft maintenance and flight crews from being so "stoned" that it would be unsafe to fly in their planes?

The answer is that, without government prohibitions, the free market would provide its own incentives for a clear-headed work force. The incredibly high cost of a plane crash in terms of replacing the equipment and settling lawsuits would give airlines strong incentives to screen their personnel for drugs, alcohol, or other judgment-impairing problems. In general, companies that employ workers with impaired judgment would lose out in the competitive marketplace to those firms that are more effective at screening out problem workers.

Legal or illegal, drugs do cause problems for both users and innocent victims. For example, driving-under-the-influence laws have reduced but not eliminated the problems of drunk driving. Would a similar approach provide pedestrians and other drivers adequate protection from drivers hallucinating under the influence of LSD? Questions of law aside, recreational drugs are the source of serious problems. For example, seeing cocaine babies and other heart-wrenching consequences of addiction can so enrage people that they want to wipe out drug use at any cost. Does that justify intensifying the drug war? Or is peace the way to victory?

THINKING CRITICALLY

1. *Terri:* **Drug users are wasting away their lives and not being productive members of society.**
Paul: **That's their choice. People should be free to do as they please.**

Should a person have the right to be unproductive? Which lifestyles are unproductive?

2. **Explain why the debate on drug laws is often heated and why well-meaning people disagree.**

 Visit **www.prenhall.com/ayers** for updates and web exercises on this Explore & Apply topic.

SUMMARY AND LEARNING OBJECTIVES

1. **Discuss how elasticity is used to measure the responsiveness of quantity to changes in price.**
   - Elasticity equals the percentage change in Y divided by the percentage change in X, where X and Y are any two variables.
   - The elasticity of demand measures the responsiveness of quantity demanded to changes in price. Likewise, the elasticity of supply measures the responsiveness of quantity supplied to changes in price.

2. **Compute the elasticity of demand.**
   - The formula for the elasticity of demand requires that the percentage change in quantity demanded be divided by the percentage change in price: |Percentage

change in quantity demanded ÷ Percentage change in price|. Because price and quantity change inversely to each other, the computation of the elasticity of demand results in a negative value. The convention is to take the absolute value, indicated by the vertical bars, and express an elasticity of demand as a positive value.
   - To compute the elasticity of demand, use the midpoint formula, which requires the following computations:

$$\text{Percentage change in } Q = \frac{\text{Change in } Q}{Q \text{ midpoint}}$$

$$\text{Change in } Q = Q_1 - Q_0$$

$$Q \text{ midpoint} = \frac{(Q_0 + Q_1)}{2}$$

$$\text{Percentage change in } P = \frac{\text{Change in } P}{P \text{ midpoint}}$$

$$\text{Change in } P = P_1 - P_0$$

$$P \text{ midpoint} = \frac{(P_0 + P_1)}{2}$$

where P_0 is an initial value for price, P_1 is another value for price, Q_0 is the value for quantity demanded when price has the value P_0, and Q_1 is the value for quantity demanded when price has the value P_1. The percentage changes computed using these formulas are then substituted into the elasticity formula: |Percentage change in quantity demanded ÷ Percentage change in price|.

3. **Describe the conditions under which a price change would increase, decrease, or not change a firm's revenues.**
   - The elasticity of demand is particularly important for its insight into the revenue effects of price changes. Inelastic demand, an elasticity less than one, leads to a change in total revenue in the same direction as the price change. Elastic demand, an elasticity greater than one, leads to a revenue change in the opposite direction from the price change. Unit elastic demand, an elasticity equal to one, leads to no change in total revenue.
   - Along a straight-line demand curve, the elasticity changes from one point to the next. The upper half of the demand curve is the elastic range; the lower half, the inelastic range; and the midpoint is unit elastic.
   - A vertical demand curve is perfectly inelastic, while a horizontal demand curve is perfectly elastic. The elasticity of demand is infinite when demand is perfectly elastic. When demand is perfectly inelastic, its elasticity equals zero. When the demand curve is a rectangular hyperbola, then demand is unit elastic throughout.

4. **Discuss the significance of the income elasticity of demand, the cross elasticity of demand, and the elasticity of supply.**
   - The income elasticity of demand measures the change in demand that results from a change in income.

Inferior goods have a negative income elasticity. Normal goods have a positive income elasticity.
   - The cross elasticity of demand measures the change in the quantity of one good in response to a change in the price of another good. Two goods are complements when their cross elasticity is a negative value. Two goods are substitutes when their cross elasticity is a positive value.
   - The elasticity of supply is similar in concept to the elasticity of demand except that quantity supplied replaces quantity demanded in defining and computing the elasticity of supply. A vertical supply curve is perfectly inelastic. A horizontal supply curve is perfectly elastic. An upward-sloping supply curve that starts at the origin is unit elastic.

5. **Explain how elasticity determines who ultimately pays a sales tax.**
   - The effect of a tax on a good is to shift up the supply curve of the good by the amount of the tax. When demand is perfectly inelastic, the tax is paid for by consumers because the price rises by the full amount of the tax. As demand becomes more elastic, less of the tax is passed on to consumers and more of the tax is paid by the sellers.
   - When supply is perfectly inelastic, the tax is fully paid by producers because price does not change at all. As supply becomes more elastic, more of the tax is passed on to consumers.

 6. **Discuss how the war on drugs increases crime associated with drug use.**
   - The inelastic demand for illegal drugs means that efforts to reduce supply will result in markedly higher prices and greater total spending.
   - The illegality of the industry and the large amount of money at stake cause both violent crime and property crime. This crime occurs when suppliers stake out their turfs through violence that scares away potential competitors, and when low-income addicts turn to crime to finance their drug habits.

KEY TERMS

TRUE OR FALSE

1. If demand is elastic and price rises, total spending by consumers also rises.
2. If demand is perfectly elastic throughout, the demand curve will be a horizontal line.
3. If price must be lowered from $9 to $8 in order to increase quantity demanded from 7 to 8 units, then the total revenue increases from $63 at 7 units to $64 at 8 units.
4. If you can sell 7 units of output for $9 each, and 8 units for $8 each, the price elasticity of demand for your output is 1.
5. Using the midpoint formula, if the price of a good rises from $3 to $4 and the quantity demanded falls from 2 units to 1 unit, then the elasticity of demand equals 3.5.

MULTIPLE CHOICE

6. The formula for all elasticities is the
   a. change in one variable divided by the change in another variable.
   b. change in one variable minus the change in another variable.
   c. percentage change in one variable divided by the percentage change in another variable.
   d. percentage change in one variable minus the percentage change in another variable.
7. Which of the following price elasticities of demand illustrates elastic demand?
   a. 0.6.
   b. 0.85.
   c. 1.0.
   d. 1.2.
8. The responsiveness of quantity demanded to changes in price
   a. increases over time.
   b. decreases over time.
   c. is not affected by the passage of time.
   d. first decreases, but then increases over time.
9. If the elasticity of demand equals 17, an increase in price would cause total revenue to
   a. increase.
   b. decrease.
   c. remain the same.
   d. increase sharply at first, but then decrease over time until, after seventeen months, revenues return to what they had initially been.

10. Moving down a downward-sloping straight-line demand curve, elasticity
    a. goes from elastic to unit elastic to inelastic.
    b. goes from elastic to inelastic to unit elastic.
    c. goes from inelastic to unit elastic to elastic.
    d. remains constant at unit elastic throughout.
11. Suppose that at a price of $4, the quantity demanded is 4. At a price of $6, the quantity demanded is 1. The elasticity of demand between these points is
    a. 2/3.
    b. 1.
    c. 3/2.
    d. 3.
12. If consumers buy 9 gizmos at a price of $9 and 10 gizmos at a price of $8, then the total revenue for 10 gizmos differs from the total revenue for 9 gizmos by
    a. $9.
    b. $8.
    c. $1.
    d. − $1.
13. If consumers buy 9 gizmos at a price of $9 and 10 gizmos at a price of $8, then demand is
    a. elastic.
    b. unit elastic.
    c. inelastic.
    d. proto-elastic.
14. The total revenue curve corresponding to a downward-sloping straight-line demand curve will appear as a
    a. hump (rising from zero to a maximum, then falling back to zero).
    b. straight line with a positive slope.
    c. downward-sloping straight line, starting at the vertical intercept of demand.
    d. downward-sloping curved line that approaches zero in infinity.
15. An income elasticity of demand that is positive indicates that a good is
    a. normal.
    b. inferior.
    c. a substitute.
    d. a complement.
16. A cross elasticity of demand that is negative indicates that
    a. two goods are substitutes.
    b. two goods are complements.
    c. one good is a substitute and the other is a complement.
    d. both goods are normal.

17. A supply curve that is unit elastic throughout will appear as a
    a. rectangular hyperbola.
    b. horizontal line.
    c. vertical line.
    d. straight line with a positive slope, starting at the origin.

18. An elastic supply is
    a. highly responsive to price.
    b. somewhat unresponsive to price.
    c. impossible.
    d. a limited supply.

19. If demand is more elastic than supply and sellers are responsible for paying a per-unit sales tax, consumers can expect that price will
    a. stay the same.
    b. increase, but producers wind up paying most of the sales tax.
    c. increase, so that consumers wind up paying most of the sales tax.
    d. increase, so that consumers wind up paying all of the sales tax.

20. If the drug war were to be halted entirely, total revenue in the recreational drug industry would equal areas _____ in Self-Test Figure 15-1.
    a. *A + B*
    b. *C + D*
    c. *B + D*
    d. *A + B + C + D*

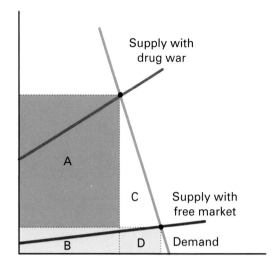

SELF-TEST FIGURE 15-1

QUESTIONS AND PROBLEMS

1. *[elasticity]* Suppose that Thrift Mart's annual Founder's Day sale, where all prices in the store are 50 percent off, results in its sales doubling compared to a typical day when the regular prices prevail. Using this evidence, state Thrift Mart's elasticity of demand.

2. *[elasticity]* As stated in the chapter, students might be interested in their own elasticity of grades with respect to study time. Estimate the response of your grades in the classes you are taking this semester if you increased your study time in each class by 25 percent. State these estimates as elasticities. Are your estimates high or low? Would it be worth your while to study more in each class? Explain.

3. *[midpoint formula]* State the midpoint formula for the elasticity of demand. What purpose does taking an average of the prices and quantities serve in this formula?

4. *[computing elasticity of demand]* Suppose that Hardware Depot lowers the price of its Grass Guzzler lawnmower from $200 to $175 and observes that sales increase from 25 to 30 lawnmowers per week. Compute the elasticity of demand for Grass Guzzler lawnmowers using these data.

5. *[computing elasticity of demand]* Carets Unlimited recently increased the price of unmounted one caret diamonds from $800 to $1,000. Monthly sales of these diamonds has remained steady at 22 diamonds, exactly the same as before the price increase. What is the elasticity of demand for the diamonds?

6. *[classifying elasticity]* Suppose the price of a good changes by 10 percent. Provide examples of percentage changes in quantity demanded for elastic, inelastic, and unit elastic demand. Draw a graph to go with each case.

7. *[extremes of elasticity]* Draw a graph for the case of perfectly elastic demand and another for perfectly inelastic demand. Note the numerical value of elasticity in each case.

8. *[elasticity and revenue]* Durango Dan, owner of Durango Danceland, must decide if he should offer half-price dance lessons on Wednesday nights, when business is slow. After counting up his receipts for a few weeks with Wednesday promotions in place, he concludes that revenues rise when his prices fall. Is demand at Durango Danceland elastic on Wednesday nights? Explain.

9. *[elasticity and revenue]* Suppose that The Artist's Brush, a small art supplies shop, has experimented with prices of $10, $9, and $8 for a standard 16 by 20 inch artist's canvas. The result of this experiment has shown that the sales of this canvas equal $200 per week regardless of the price. What can be concluded about the elasticity of demand for this canvas? Sketch a demand curve that reflects the facts stated here.

10. *[income elasticity]* List three examples of an inferior good that are not mentioned in the chapter. Justify your choice of examples.

11. *[cross elasticity]* Would coffee and tea have a positive or a negative cross elasticity? What sign would the cross elasticity between coffee and cream have? How could this information be useful to a business?

12. *[elasticity of supply]* Suppose the supply of movies is elastic. What can you say about the response of quantity supplied to a 10-percent increase in the price of movie tickets?

13. *[classifying supply elasticity]* What are the three classifications for the elasticity of supply? Are these similar to the classifications for the elasticity of demand? Explain.

14. *[tax shifting]* Suppose the government places a 50 cents a pound tax on hot dogs, collected from hot dog makers. Will consumers have to pay more for a pound of hot dogs if the hot dog market is characterized by perfectly elastic demand? Explain.

15. *[tax shifting]* State a general rule for the amount of tax shifting that will occur when a tax is imposed on a good. Be sure that the rule you state relates the amount of tax shifting to the elasticities of demand and supply.

WORKING WITH GRAPHS AND DATA

1. *[extremes of elasticity of demand]* Use the following tables to answer the questions relating to extreme elasticities of demand.

Perfectly Inelastic Demand			Perfectly Elastic Demand		
Price ($)	Quantity Demanded	Elasticity of Demand	Price ($)	Quantity Demanded	Elasticity of Demand
6				0	
5				1	
4				2	
3	3		3	3	
2				4	
1				5	
0				6	

a. Fill in the quantity demanded column of perfectly inelastic demand.

b. What is the elasticity of demand at any price for this good? Show your work.

c. Draw this demand curve and label it D on Graph 15-1(a).

d. Fill in the price column of perfectly elastic demand.

e. What is the elasticity of demand at any price for this good? Show your work.

f. Draw this demand curve and label it D on Graph 15-1(b).

(a)　　　　　　　　　　　　　　　　(b)

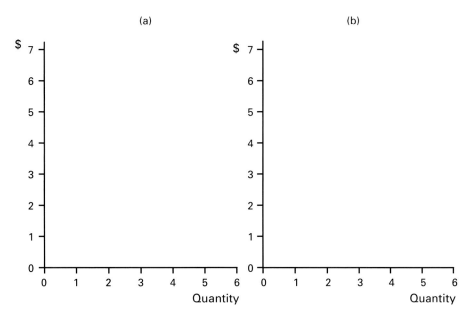

GRAPH 15-1

2. *[elasticity and total revenue]* Use the following table of the demand schedule for a good to answer the following questions about its elasticity of demand.

Price ($)	Quantity Demanded	Total Revenue	Elasticity (classification)	Elasticity (computed value)
5	0			
4	20			
3	40			
2	60			
1	80			
0	100			

a. Fill in the total revenue column. How did you compute total revenue?

b. Fill in the elasticity (classification) column where elasticity is classified as elastic, unit elastic, and inelastic. How do you know?

c. Compute the elasticity of demand between each pair of prices starting at $5 and $4 and going down the demand schedule. Do the classifications of elasticity at different prices agree with your computed values of elasticity?

d. Draw the demand curve using the demand schedule and label it D.

e. Identify the elastic, unit elastic, and inelastic portions of D.

f. Compute the slope of D between two different pairs of prices such as $5 and $4 and $2 and $1. Is it the same as the computed value you got for elasticity between those prices?

3. *[tax shifting]* Use Graph 15-2 to answer the following questions below.

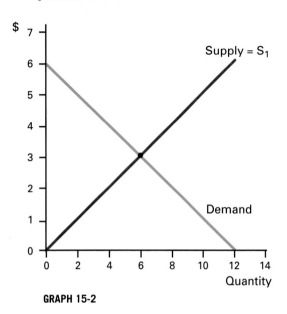

GRAPH 15-2

a. Identify the equilibrium price and quantity in this market.

b. Suppose that the government imposes a $2 tax on each unit of this good. Show the effect on the supply curve and label the new supply curve that includes the tax S_2.

c. Identify the new equilibrium price and quantity.

d. Identify and label the amount of the tax burden that is borne by sellers as sellers receive less. Identify and label the amount of the tax burden that is borne by consumers as consumers pay more.

e. What is the elasticity of demand between the initial equilibrium price and the equilibrium price after the tax is imposed?

4. *[elasticity of supply]* Use Graphs 15-3(a), (b), and (c) to answer the following questions about elasticity of supply.

a. Which graph is unit elastic? Show that it is unit elastic by computing the elasticity of supply.

b. Which graph is perfectly elastic? Show that it is perfectly elastic by computing the elasticity of supply.

c. Which graph is perfectly inelastic? Show that it is perfectly inelastic by computing the elasticity of supply.

d. Assume that the government imposes a tax. For which market would the tax have no effect on equilibrium price? Explain.

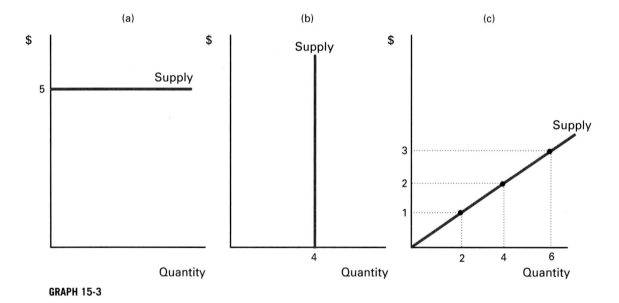

GRAPH 15-3

 Visit www.prenhall.com/ayers for Exploring the Web exercises and additional self-test quizzes

CHAPTER **16**

CONSUMER BEHAVIOR

A LOOK AHEAD

Presidential candidates, pop stars, and even popcorn-king Orville Redenbacher have something in common. They and many others have tried to influence your choices in their favor. Whether the purpose is to get your vote or your money, there will be those who seek to nudge your choices one way or another. What is it that makes us choose as we do? As you read the end-of-chapter Explore & Apply section, you will see that people make bad choices, but that good choices are also possible.

In this chapter we look at consumer behavior, with the goal of explaining the principles behind the law of demand. The concept of utility, which means satisfaction, is central to the chapter. Analyzing consumer behavior with utility will allow you to understand why people make the choices they do, good and bad.

LEARNING OBJECTIVES

Understanding Chapter 16 will enable you to:
1. **Discuss how the income and substitution effects lead to a downward-sloping demand curve.**
2. **Explain why marginal utility diminishes.**
3. **Practice the step-by-step utility-maximization process.**
4. **Apply the rule of utility maximization.**
5. **Relate utility maximization to the demand curve.**
6. Summarize the influences on consumers' choices.

Explore & Apply

American consumers have literally millions of goods to choose from. Why do consumers decide as they do? Answering that question is the goal of this chapter.

16.1 THE LAW OF DEMAND REVISITED

substitution effect a lower price of a good causes a person to buy more of that good instead of alternative goods.

Recall from Chapter 3 that demand slopes downward according to the *law of demand.* In other words, individuals buy more of something when its price falls and less when its price rises. The law of demand is caused in part by the **substitution effect** of a price change, which occurs when a lower price on a good causes a person to buy more of that good instead of alternative goods. Likewise, the substitution effect from increasing the price of a good would drive consumers to buy more of the substitute goods instead of the good with the increased price. An example of the substitution effect is the purchase of a GE television instead of a comparable RCA model because the GE model is on clearance. The result of the substitution effect is a downward-sloping demand curve.

income effect the change in the quantity demanded caused by a price change's effect on real income, which measures a consumer's purchasing power.

For a normal good, the **income effect** of a price change will also cause demand to slope down. The income effect occurs when the price change affects consumer purchasing power, termed *real income,* and thus leads to a change in quantity demanded. A higher price reduces real income while a lower price increases real income. For example, if your income is $50 a week and gasoline sells for $1 a gallon, you could buy as much as 50 gallons a week. If the price of gasoline were $2 a gallon, you could only buy 25 gallons. This reduction in your ability to purchase gasoline when its price increases is an example of the income effect. In most cases the income effect of a price change will be smaller than the substitution effect because few price changes are very significant in terms of a person's overall purchasing power.

SNAPSHOT

FROM A MAC TO A KING

The Big Mac attacks come fast and furious when McDonald's puts its signature feature on sale. Customers gobble down those two all-beef patties, special sauce and all! But when the Big Mac returns to its regular price, sales taper off. What happens to all those burger-hungry customers? Do they all go on a diet together?

A higher price for Big Macs would cause some customers to switch to other menu items at McDonald's. Others turn elsewhere, perhaps to have it their way with flame-broiled Whoppers at Burger King. It is not the income effect that drives these choices, either—when it comes to how many other goods people can afford, changes in the price of Big Macs makes no discernible difference. However, the substitution effect is strong, with lots of people willing to choose ever-so-tasty alternatives. By turning to the likes of the Whopper when the price of the Big Mac goes up, people reduce the quantity of Big Macs demanded. In substituting a Whopper for a Big Mac, the hungry burger hoppers maintain the law of demand. ◄

16.2 UTILITY AND CONSUMER SATISFACTION

utility satisfaction received from consumption of a good.

Consumers buy in order to obtain **utility,** which is the satisfaction received from the consumption of a good. The utility that people gain from their purchases is subjective, varying from person to person. For example, you might know someone who would gain a great deal of utility from an Elvis CD, but none from a CD featuring Mozart. For you, the utility gains may be the opposite. **Utility is not measurable since satisfaction is not measurable.** What we know is that someone who purchases Elvis's music instead of Mozart's, when they are the same price, obtains more utility from Elvis—that much is revealed by the actual choice.

It would be easy to mistakenly conclude that utility is only provided by the "useful" items we purchase. In fact, **utility does not imply that a good is useful.** For example, aspirin is quite useful when we have a headache. Likewise, a bottle of ammonia is useful when we are cleaning. However, if your house were on fire, would you try to save those items? Probably not. Instead, you would save your pets, family pictures, and other items with sentimental value. Many consumer purchases are not particularly useful, but are valued for their beauty or other qualities.

TOTAL AND MARGINAL UTILITY

Although utility is not measurable, it can be modeled as though it were, using the **util** as its unit of measurement. Thus, that bottle of cold Yoo-hoo chocolate drink you gulp down on a hot day might provide you with 22 utils, your purchase of a new pair of shoes might provide you with 500 utils, and so forth.

util unit of measurement of utility; used for illustration only.

We can distinguish between increments to utility and the sum of those increments. For example, suppose you eat two slices of pizza and gain 160 utils from doing so. If the first slice contributed 90 of those utils, then the second slice provided an increment of 70 utils. **Total utility** equals the sum of the utils a person receives from consuming a specific quantity of a good. In this example, your total utility equals 160 utils. **Marginal utility** equals the increments to utility from changes in consumption. Your marginal utility of the second slice of pizza equals 70 utils. Figure 16-1 illustrates the difference between total and marginal utility.

total utility the satisfaction a person receives from consuming a specific quantity of a good.

marginal utility the increments to total utility from changes in consumption.

When you know the amounts of total utility for various amounts of consumption, you can calculate marginal utility by:

$$\text{Marginal utility} = \frac{\text{Change in total utility}}{\text{Change in number of units consumed}}$$

Consider the data in Figure 16-2. The table in the figure shows Vince's total utility and marginal utility associated with his purchases of chewing gum each week. We assume that Vince's preference for chewing gum, measured by his marginal utility, does not change during the week. The table also shows the computation of marginal utility in the last column.

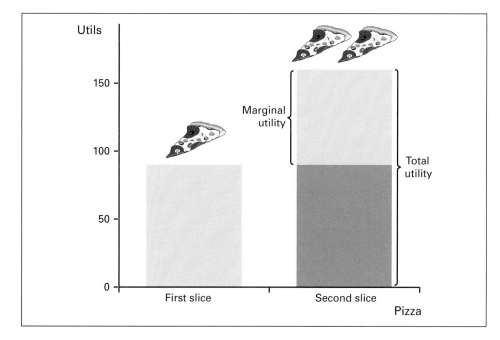

FIGURE 16-1

TOTAL AND MARGINAL UTILITY OF PIZZA One slice of pizza provides a consumer with 90 utils of satisfaction, which is the marginal utility and, since there are no other slices consumed, also the total utility. Two slices of pizza provide 160 utils of satisfaction, the total utility of both slices. The marginal utility of the second slice equals the increase in utility, 70 utils (160 − 90 = 70).

Vince's total and marginal utility			
Number of packs of chewing gum consumed weekly	Total utility	Marginal utility	Computation of marginal utility (change in total utility/change in number of packs consumed)
0	0	undefined	
1	12	12	(12–0)/1
2	22	10	(22–12)/1
3	28	6	(28–22)/1
4	30	2	(30–28)/1
5	30	0	(30–30)/1
6	27	–3	(27–30)/1

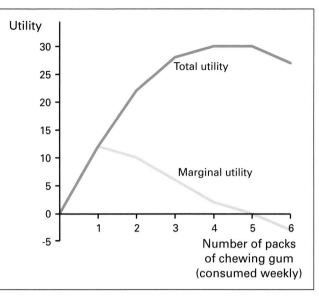

FIGURE 16-2

VINCE'S TOTAL AND MARGINAL UTILITY Vince's total and marginal utility are plotted based upon the data in the table. The total utility curve begins at zero utils when no packs of gum are consumed. Total utility increases when additional packs of gum are consumed, until the fifth pack of gum. That pack has a marginal utility of zero utils. Total utility thus stops rising at that point. The sixth pack of gum provides disutility and so has a negative value for marginal utility. The total utility curve falls when marginal utility is a negative value.

The graph in Figure 16-2 plots the data in the table. Note that the marginal utility curve has a negative slope. Also note that the marginal utility curve crosses the horizontal axis to become negative.

Observe that Vince's total utility increases through the fourth pack of gum. These increases in total utility are reflected in the third column as positive values for marginal utility. The fifth pack provides the same amount of total utility as the fourth, 30 utils. Thus, the fifth pack does not add to Vince's total utility and a value of 0 for the marginal utility is seen in the table. The total utility for six packs of gum is less than the total utility for five packs. This decrease in total utility means that marginal utility is a negative value. Since total utility decreases from 30 utils to 27 utils, marginal utility equals − 3. When marginal utility is negative, as in this case, we say that a good provides **disutility.**

disutility a negative value for marginal utility; associated with consuming too much of a good.

You should verify by reviewing the numbers in Figure 16-2 that total utility can be computed by summing the marginal utilities. For example, the total utility for three packs of gum, which equals 28, can be found by adding the marginal utilities of the first three packs: 12 + 10 + 6 = 28. Note that when the data are graphed:

■ The total utility curve rises so long as marginal utility is a positive number.
■ When marginal utility equals zero, the total utility curve peaks because total utility is at its maximum value.
■ The total utility curve turns downward when marginal utility becomes negative.

law of diminishing marginal utility as consumption of a good increases, marginal utility will eventually decrease.

DIMINISHING MARGINAL UTILITY

Vince's marginal utilities are an example of the **law of diminishing marginal utility,** which decrees that the first unit of a good is the most satisfying, after which additional units pro-

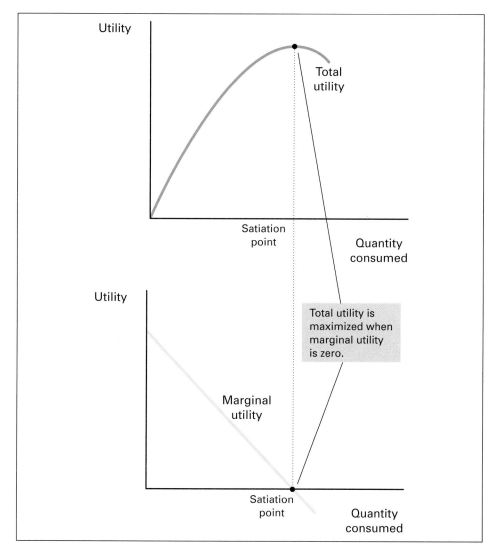

FIGURE 16-3

TOTAL UTILITY AND MARGINAL UTILITY The decreasingly positive slope of total utility leads to diminishing marginal utility, which lies behind the downward slope of the demand curve. Marginal utility is zero at the satiation point.

vide progressively less and less additional utility. There is a **satiation point,** beyond which additional consumption actually reduces total utility. Beyond the satiation point, a good has disutility.

Figure 16-3 illustrates the general relationship between total utility and marginal utility. The top portion of Figure 16-3 shows that total utility rises, reaches a peak, and then falls. The lower portion of Figure 16-3 shows that marginal utility decreases, reaches a value of zero, and then turns negative. The relationship between total utility and marginal utility is such that the following are always true:

- When total utility is increasing, marginal utility will be positive.
- When total utility is at its maximum, the consumer has reached the satiation point and marginal utility will equal zero.
- When total utility is decreasing, marginal utility will be negative.

The law of diminishing marginal utility applies when consumption occurs over a relatively short time period. This means that the second serving of turkey that you eat this Thanksgiving will provide you with less marginal utility than the first serving. In contrast, there is no reason to expect that turkey you eat next year will have less marginal utility than

satiation point quantity for which an additional unit consumed provides zero marginal utility; associated with maximum total utility.

> ## QUICKCHECK
>
> Describe total utility at the satiation point. What does marginal utility equal at that point?
>
> **Answer:** At the satiation point, total utility is at a maximum and marginal utility is zero.

a comparable portion eaten this year. Next year you might not even remember the turkey you ate this year. Consumption in the distant past tends to have no effect on the utility gained from consuming the same good today.

The law of diminishing marginal utility suggests that eventually marginal utility becomes zero, as at the satiation point, and then a negative value. That is what happens to Vince if he consumes five and then six packs of gum within a week. Would you buy so much of a good that your next purchase provides you with zero marginal utility? No, because you spend money in order to gain satisfaction. You would be wasting your money if the purchase gave you no increment of satisfaction. For the same reason you would avoid purchasing so much of the good that the marginal utility of the next unit is a negative value. You would refuse to accept a good that has a negative marginal utility value, even if it was offered free of charge. For example, when Marsha is invited to a friend's pizza party, she is full by the time she eats her fourth slice. Because she has reached her satiation point at four slices, that is all she eats. For her, a fifth slice of pizza in effect becomes a "bad" rather than a good because it has negative marginal utility. "Too much of a good thing," as the saying goes.

Is it possible for marginal utility to increase? To answer this question, consider your favorite snack food. Whether it is potato chips, pizza, a candy bar, or cheese, is the second bite less satisfying than the first? For most people the first bite stimulates the appetite enough to make the second bite, and possibly a few subsequent ones, more satisfying. Thus, marginal utility might increase at first. Nonetheless, marginal utility will eventually diminish as you start to get tired of snacking. The law of diminishing marginal utility is generally applicable.

SNAPSHOT   ENOUGH IS ENOUGH!

A baby's smile, the purring of a cat, the wag of a puppy's tail, or a rainbow in the sky after a storm are always welcome, or so it might seem. And our contentment has cost us not a thin dime. "The best things in life are free," the old saying goes. Yet who wants to watch rainbows ALL day? We go on to other things, not because we like them better in total, but because we like them better at the margin. Enough is enough—when the marginal utility of rainbow watching decreases until it reaches zero, we then turn our attention to something that offers positive marginal utility. ◀

16.3 MAXIMIZING UTILITY SUBJECT TO A BUDGET CONSTRAINT

As much as people would like it to be so, they cannot have it all. Our income, no matter how large it is, limits what we are able to buy. The *budget constraint,* a consumer's income, curbs the amount of total utility that can be obtained. Consumers must choose, while striving to spend their incomes so as to obtain the greatest total satisfaction from their purchases. **Consumers maximize utility subject to their budget constraint. Utility maximization is achieved when the consumer's choices provide the greatest amount of total utility for a specific amount of income.**

SPENDING AT THE MARGIN

Let's show with a numerical example how a consumer maximizes utility. For simplicity we will suppose that Denise has just two choices to make. She must decide how many times she goes to the movies and how many bottles of Pure 'n' Clear spring water to buy. The price of a movie ticket with a student ID is only $3 at the Hollywood Discount Theater that Denise prefers. The price of her favorite water is $1 per bottle. Denise's income is $15 per week. How many movies will Denise see and how many bottles of water will she drink each week when her goal is to maximize the utility she obtains from her spending? To answer this question we need to know her marginal utilities for various quantities of movies and bottles of water. These marginal utilities are presented in Table 16-1 in columns (2) and (5).

In the table, the marginal utilities for both goods have been divided by the respective prices of the goods in columns (3) and (6). When a marginal utility is divided by the price, the result is called the **marginal utility per dollar.** The marginal utility per dollar will be quite useful in helping Denise solve the problem of selecting the amounts of each good that maximize her utility. Observe in the table that the marginal utility per dollar spent upon each good diminishes, which occurs because the marginal utility of each good diminishes.

Denise will purchase a movie ticket when seeing a movie provides her with more marginal utility per dollar than purchasing a bottle of water, but will buy water when that provides more marginal utility per dollar. So long as she always takes the action that provides her with the greatest amount of marginal utility per dollar she will maximize the total utility she obtains with her income. Let's look at Denise's choices step-by-step. Her first choice is whether to purchase the first movie ticket or buy the first bottle of water. Can you correctly predict what she will do based on the figures in Table 16-1? She will purchase the movie ticket because it provides 10 utils per dollar, while a bottle of water offers only 8 utils per dollar. After the purchase of a movie ticket for $3 she will have $12 of income left to spend. What will she do next? Look at the table and see if you can correctly predict her second choice.

marginal utility per dollar
marginal utility divided by price.

TABLE 16-1 **DENISE'S PREFERENCES FOR MOVIES AND BOTTLED WATER**
[Price of movie ticket = $3; Price of water = $1 per bottle; Income = $15 per week]

(1) NUMBER OF MOVIE TICKETS BOUGHT	(2) MARGINAL UTILITY OF MOVIES (IN UTILS)	(3) MARGINAL UTILITY PER DOLLAR FOR MOVIES (MARGINAL UTILITY / PRICE)	(4) NUMBER OF BOTTLES OF WATER BOUGHT	(5) MARGINAL UTILITY OF BOTTLED WATER (IN UTILS)	(6) MARGINAL UTILITY PER DOLLAR FOR BOTTLED WATER (MARGINAL UTILITY / PRICE)
1	30	10	1	8	8
2	27	9	2	7	7
3	24	8	3✓✓	6	6
4✓	18	6	4	5	5
5	8	2.67	5	4	4
6	1	0.33	6	3	3

✓ Utility-maximizing quantity of movie tickets purchased.

✓✓ Utility-maximizing number of bottles of water purchased.

Note: It is assumed in the table that the utilities of each good are independent of the quantity of the other good consumed. This assumption simplifies the analysis because, when two goods are related, the marginal utility of one can change as the amount of the other good consumed changes.

Denise's second choice will be to purchase a second movie ticket because that purchase will provide her with 9 utils per dollar versus 8 utils per dollar from the purchase of the first bottle of water. After spending the $3 to buy the movie ticket she will have $9 of income left to spend. Now what will she do?

Her third choice is between a third movie ticket or the first bottle of water. Each provides exactly the same amount of marginal utility per dollar, 8 utils. When choices provide the same amount of marginal utility per dollar, we say that the consumer is *indifferent* between them. Since Denise is indifferent, she will buy another movie ticket, her third, and buy her first bottle of water. After spending $4 on these purchases, she will have $5 of income left. Her fourth choice will be to buy a second bottle of water, since that provides 7 utils per dollar, which is more than the 6 utils per dollar from the purchase of a fourth movie ticket. Note that the amount of income left after she buys the second bottle of water is only $4.

A fourth movie ticket and a third bottle of water provide Denise an equal amount of marginal utility per dollar, making her indifferent again. Thus, she will purchase another movie ticket for $3 and a bottle of water for $1. This spending exhausts her income and she has maximized utility.

How much total utility will Denise obtain for her $15 in income? We can calculate her total utility as the sum of the marginal utilities from her purchases of each product. Referring to the marginal utilities in Table 16-1, you can see that the marginal utilities for the first four movie tickets are: 30 + 27 + 24 + 18 = 99. The marginal utilities for the first three bottles of water are: 8 + 7 + 6 = 21. When the 99 utils from movies and the 21 utils from water are added together we see that Denise obtains 120 utils of satisfaction. No other combination of movies and water can match that number of utils when her income is $15.

rule of utility maximization
To maximize utility, a consumer adjusts spending until the marginal utility from the last dollar spent on each good is the same.

The process of maximizing utility leads to the **rule of utility maximization:**

> ### Rule of utility maximization
> To maximize utility, a consumer adjusts spending until the marginal utility from the last dollar spent on each good is the same.

When the rule of utility maximization is followed, we say the consumer is in *equilibrium*. For example, Denise's equilibrium involved spending all of her $15 income so that the marginal utility per dollar of movies and water was equal at 6 utils per dollar. The step-by-step utility maximization process led to the outcome suggested by the rule of utility maximization.

Fortunately consumers do not need to measure their utility to follow this rule. As noted earlier, there is no way to accurately measure utility, or to convincingly compare utility across different consumers. For example, who can really say whether their satisfaction is more than, less than, or identical to the satisfaction of someone else? While none of us can measure utility, we all judge it when we decide how to spend. Whether we prefer to emphasize Saturday night "hot spots," mountain biking trips, or social causes, we each allocate our budgets in the ways that maximize our perceptions of our own utility.

To do that, we attempt to divide our spending so that the last dollar spent on each good provides the same marginal utility, whatever the good may be. The marginal utility of a dollar we spend on a good equals the marginal utility of the good itself divided by the price we pay for it. For this to be equal for all goods means that:

$$\frac{\text{Marginal utility of } X}{\text{Price of } X} = \frac{\text{Marginal utility of } Y}{\text{Price of } Y}, \text{ for all goods } X \text{ and } Y$$

To understand why this equality characterizes consumer equilibrium, consider a consumer who receives greater marginal utility from dollars spent on *X* than from dollars spent on *Y*. If *X* and *Y* are ice cream and cookies, respectively, the consumer would cut

QUICKCHECK

Using the example from Table 16-1, show that Denise equates the marginal utility of the last dollar spent on movies to that spent on water.

Answer: Denise's utility-maximizing equilibrium occurred at four movies and three bottles of water, with the following data:

Marginal utility of movies: 18 utils
Price of movie ticket: $3
Marginal utility of water: 6 utils
Price of water: $1

$\frac{18}{3} = \frac{6}{1}$, satisfying the formula above. Additionally, the purchase of four movie tickets plus three bottles of water involves spending the whole of her $15 income. Thus, we know that Denise maximized utility by equating the value she received from the last dollar she spent on movies to the value she received from the last dollar she spent on water.

down on purchases of cookies, and use the extra income to buy ice cream. Even though the budget would be the same, total utility would be greater. We would each be quick to seize such opportunities. By doing so, however, we reallocate our spending until the opportunities to increase total utility are no longer there. Increases in the consumption of ice cream will decrease its marginal utility. At the same time, decreases in the consumption of cookies will increase the marginal utility from consuming cookies. This means that the marginal utility per dollar will ultimately be the same for ice cream and cookies.

UTILITY MAXIMIZATION AND DEMAND

When consumers maximize utility, their individual demand curves for a good are downward sloping. In other words, the quantity demanded of a good will change in the opposite direction to a change in its price. To illustrate that demand is downward sloping, we can derive Denise's demand curve for movies. Suppose that the price of a movie ticket decreases from $3 to $2. When the price decreases to $2, the result will be an increase in the marginal utility per dollar of movies. The marginal utility per dollar for prices of $3 and $2 are presented in Table 16-2. The third column is repeated from Table 16-1 to facilitate the comparison of the marginal utility per dollar for each price. Observing the third and fourth columns in the table reveals that the lower price increases the marginal utility per dollar furnished by the purchase of any quantity of movie tickets. This increase in the marginal utility per dollar will cause Denise to purchase more movie tickets.

Denise's utility-maximizing purchases in Table 16-1 were four movies and three bottles of water. What amounts of each good will she purchase after the price of a movie ticket decreases to $2? Assume as we did in Table 16-1 that her income equals $15 and that the price of water equals $1. Applying the same reasoning process as in Table 16-1, you will find that Denise will now purchase five movie tickets and five bottles of water.

Denise's demand curve for movies is shown in Figure 16-4. Because price and quantity demanded vary inversely, Denise's choices are consistent with the law of demand. In particular, her effort to maximize utility caused her to buy four movie tickets at a price of

TABLE 16-2   A LOWER PRICE FOR MOVIE TICKETS INCREASES MARGINAL UTILITY PER DOLLAR

NUMBER OF MOVIE TICKETS BOUGHT	MARGINAL UTILITY OF MOVIES	MARGINAL UTILITY PER DOLLAR, PRICE = $3 $\left(\dfrac{\text{MARGINAL UTILITY}}{\text{PRICE}}\right)$	MARGINAL UTILITY PER DOLLAR, PRICE = $2 $\left(\dfrac{\text{MARGINAL UTILITY}}{\text{PRICE}}\right)$
1	30	10	15
2	27	9	13.5
3	24	8	12
4	18	6	9
5	8	2.67	4
6	1	0.33	0.5

FIGURE 16-4

THE DEMAND FOR MOVIES When the price of a movie ticket falls, Denise buys more in order to maximize utility. Denise's utility-maximizing process was examined in Tables 16-1 and 16-2. In behaving this way, Denise exemplifies the law of demand, which is that price and quantity demanded vary inversely.

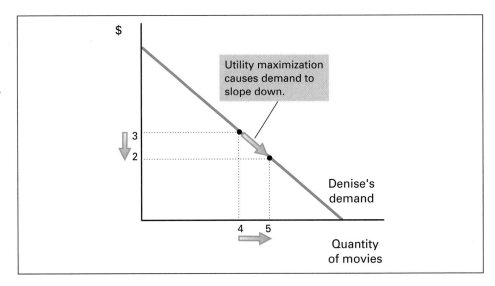

$3, but five tickets at a price of $2. These prices and quantities are shown as points on the demand curve.

Notice that the decrease in the price of movies not only leads to an increase in Denise's quantity demanded of movies, but also to an increase in the number of bottles of water Denise purchases. What accounts for the increase in demand for water? Remember the substitution and income effects discussed at the beginning of this chapter? The lower price of movies causes Denise to substitute more movies because of their lower price. The lower price of movies also increases Denise's purchasing power, which allows her to buy more bottles of water.

HILFIGER AND COMPANY   *SNAPSHOT*

You've seen the names of Tommy Hilfiger, Bill Blass, and Perry Ellis on luggage, clothing, and many other consumer goods. They are just a few of the designers whose names on products ensure a premium price. When status is sold as part of a purchase, the effect is to increase the marginal utility of the purchase. With a greater amount of utility, the demand increases.

Such an increase in demand can convert a $10 t-shirt into a $60 t-shirt when it's a Tommy Hilfiger. That's why the designer's name or trademark is so prominently displayed on designer goods. When consumers buy status, they show it off. Whether it's their impeccable taste or their ability to throw around their money, designer goods send others a message about the buyer. ◄

16.4 MAXIMIZING UTILITY—DO WE WANT WHAT WE CHOOSE?

Explore & Apply

Consumers account for some 70 percent of total spending in the U.S. economy. Predicting consumers' choices is difficult since they are determined by numerous considerations. Consider first the choice of how to spend your time and the effects of that decision on your purchases.

Time has utility. People try to allocate time to give them the greatest amount of satisfaction, taking into account time's opportunity cost. The income and other rewards from time spent at work provides satisfaction. Time spent with families and friends provides another form of satisfaction. Time spent on hobbies and interests also offers satisfaction. We consider the amounts of satisfaction we receive from each of these and more as we decide how to spend our time.

Consumers today have more leisure time than previous generations. While time spent doing nothing has utility, there are many goods that are *complements* to leisure time. Examples include sports and entertainment. The utility from an hour of leisure time can sometimes be increased by filling that time with an interesting activity. Of course, there will still be occasions when we want to be idle, just for the utility produced by resting.

Some goods are time intensive. Consider chess sets. Chess games can go on for hours. A good game of chess requires the players to be skilled at the game. You might not purchase a chess set because developing the necessary skills and finding the time to play would cut into the utility provided by the alternatives. Many other products require us to spend time with them in order to obtain the satisfaction they provide. Television, computers, and video games are just three examples. The more time you have available to use these products, the greater the amount of satisfaction they provide.

Information also has utility. Subscribers to *Consumer Reports* and other magazines receive valuable product information, but at the price of the subscription. Other information has a price too, although not always in terms of money. For example, information costs could include listening to annoying "sales pitches." A consumer must decide how much information to purchase. Product information, like other goods, is characterized by diminishing marginal utility. The rule of utility maximization you studied in this chapter may include information as another good. Thus, the last dollar spent on information should have a marginal utility per dollar equal to the marginal utility per dollar of the last dollar spent on the consumer's other purchases.

Impulse buyers make purchases on the spur of the moment without consulting information sources. Impulse buying may appear to be irrational since impulse purchases may provide less utility than well-planned purchases. However, impulse buying does not necessarily mean that people are ignoring utility. A consumer's time has utility. Impulse buying conserves on time devoted to collecting product information. When the utility of time is taken into account, impulse buying can be viewed as a way to maximize utility.

Some people visit a public library, an appropriate web site, or watch the news to get information. The federal government often publicizes consumer information in these venues. The government's anti-smoking campaign is an example of such consumer information. The government aims to cut the use of tobacco by pointing out that the enjoyment offered by smoking is offset by harm to a person's health. In utility terms the harmful effects of smoking provide disutility.

Other information that influences consumer choices comes from friends and family. People may comment "That cake is delicious. Where did you get it?" because they, too, want to be able to purchase a tasty cake. Word of mouth is especially important when moviegoers select which film to see. The same is true of many other purchases. Some of the choices we make using information supplied by friends end up disappointing us. "How could they recommend that awful movie?" is more a complaint than a question. Thus, people sometimes question the utility of information that comes from friends.

Advertising is intended to affect consumers' choices, generally with the goal of getting us to buy something now. Advertisers will sometimes provide us with useful information in order to loosen our purse strings. The information in the Yellow Pages that relates to opening and closing times, locations, and telephone numbers of businesses is an example of informational advertising. Print advertising for personal computers usually includes numerous technical specifications that promote sales. Other times, advertising seeks to work its effects by influencing our emotions rather than providing us with information. A good bit of TV advertising is of this sort. If a commercial can touch your heart and create good feelings toward a product, you are more likely to buy it. This type of advertising recognizes that utility is subjective. If consumers find that their marginal utilities for a product are increased after viewing a good TV commercial, then that increase in consumers' marginal utilities will translate into an increase in demand for the product advertised.

You don't need to spend a dollar in order to gain utility. A dollar saved can provide more satisfaction than a dollar spent, at least for some people. What is your attitude toward saving and how did you come to hold that attitude? Some people spend every dime they earn and then some more through borrowing. A dollar only has utility for those people when that dollar is spent. For other people, saving has significant utility. Attitudes toward saving and spending may be partially inborn, but are more likely to be the result of the influences of parents, family, and friends. Such attitudes are likely to be formed in childhood. They can be difficult to change.

Consider the compulsive spender. These people have great difficulty in sticking to a budget, even when financial problems hang over them like a dark cloud. When prudence would dictate paying off their bills, they spend. When they ought to be saving, they spend. When they are sleeping, they are dreaming of spending! Ultimately, the motivations of compulsive spenders fall within the realm of psychology. All an economist can say is that if a dollar is spent it must have provided the individual with more utility than if it had been saved.

Giving away your wealth can provide you with utility. That explains why Americans contribute many millions of dollars to charity every year. *Altruism,* a concern for others, is consistent with utility maximization. We may obtain satisfaction from charitable contributions because they make us feel good. Altruism may also be motivated by religious or philosophical beliefs. For example, we might believe that by helping others in this life, we will gain our just rewards in another.

ADDICTIVE BEHAVIOR

Some people make choices that appear to be bad choices to others. The choice to smoke is an example. Overeating is another. Alcohol and drug problems that amount to addictive behavior are a third. Many would like to make different choices, but don't seem to be able to do so.

Figure 16-5 illustrates the binging, then regretting behavior that characterizes people's binges on food, alcohol, shopping, and gambling. The particular binging behavior illustrated is a shopping binge, in which unneeded items are purchased. At the time of the binge, the marginal utility can seem to increase for each successive purchase. Later the reality of the situation sets in, illustrated by the downward-sloping and eventually negative marginal utility curve.

Two aspects of utility analysis can help us better understand addictive and other unhealthy behaviors. One aspect of addiction problems is that we are unable to rationally control the things that give us utility. People who aim to keep their weight down for health reasons cannot help it that chocolate cake provides them with significantly more utility than lettuce. In an effort to provide a massive dose of disutility to problem drinkers, doctors will sometimes prescribe Antabuse, a drug that makes them very sick if they drink. **The other aspect is the time horizon relating to utility. Some things provide immediate gratification, but also produce long-term problems.** Thus, the utility comes now, but the disutility later. The farther into the future the disutility, the more we are inclined to brush it aside. Some addictions might be cured if only the time horizons of the addicted were longer, so that they took into account future problems caused by their addictions.

To conclude, we have seen that good people often make "good" choices, but sometimes make "bad" choices because those choices furnish utility. However, good people are also free to choose. Good choices can replace bad ones. Our families and society can help us to make those good choices. It's all in the utility!

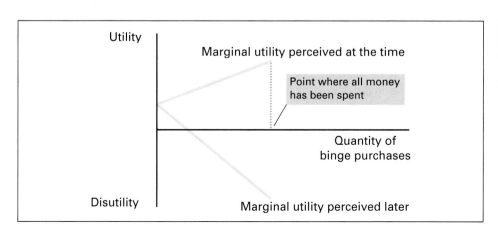

FIGURE 16-5

UTILITY IN HINDSIGHT This person would continue shopping, but regret it later.

THINKING CRITICALLY

1. Most people would agree that addicts commonly make bad choices, at least in regard to things to which they are addicted. What can the government do to help addicts make better choices? In your answer be sure to include how an understanding of utility could help in the design of government policies intended to break addiction.

2. Explain how a person's choice of spouse can be viewed as an exercise in utility maximization.

Visit **www.prenhall.com/ayers** for updates and web exercises on this Explore & Apply topic.

SUMMARY AND LEARNING OBJECTIVES

1. **Discuss how the income and substitution effects lead to a downward-sloping demand curve.**
   - Every price change has a substitution and an income effect. The substitution effect pushes consumers toward cheaper substitutes, while the income effect refers to the change in purchasing power (real income) brought about by a price change.
   - When a price increases, the substitution effect of the increases leads consumers to purchase substitute goods that have not risen in price. Thus, the quantity demanded of the good whose price increases will fall. The income effect of the price increase will cut consumers' purchasing power, thus leading to a reduction in the purchases of all normal goods, including the good whose price increased. The income effect reinforces the substitution effect.

2. **Explain why marginal utility diminishes.**
   - Utility is the satisfaction that someone receives from consuming a good. Utility is subjective and not measurable. The usefulness of a good is unrelated to its utility.
   - In order to illustrate consumer choices, it is sometimes helpful to assume that utility can be measured in units called utils.
   - The total utility a consumer obtains is the sum of the utility from all units of a good. As one more unit of a good is consumed, the increment of utility is called marginal utility. Thus, if someone obtains 80 utils from consuming the first 2 breakfast waffles, and 100 utils when 3 waffles are eaten, then the marginal utility from the third waffle equals 20 utils.
   - Marginal utility diminishes. This statement means that at some point the increment of utility from the next unit consumed will be less than the increment of utility from the previous unit. For example, diminishing marginal utility would imply that a fourth breakfast waffle would furnish less than 20 additional utils.

3. **Practice the step-by-step utility-maximization process.**
   - Consumers arrange their spending to attain the greatest amount of total utility. The process of spending their incomes in this way is called utility maximization. Utility maximization results in a consumer equilibrium, which is a combination of goods that maximizes utility.
   - The marginal utility per dollar equals marginal utility divided by price, which is helpful in discerning a utility-maximizing combination of goods.
   - We say that consumers are indifferent between their choices when those choices provide the same amount of utility. Thus, if a third waffle and a second glass of orange juice each furnish an additional 20 utils, then a consumer would be indifferent between them.

4. **Apply the rule of utility maximization.**
   - The rule of utility maximization states that consumers should arrange their spending so the marginal utility of the last dollar spent on each good is equal. The rule can be stated as an equation. For two goods, A and B, the equation is:

$$\frac{\text{Marginal utility of } A}{\text{Price of } A} = \frac{\text{Marginal utility of } B}{\text{Price of } B}$$

   The equation applies to the last dollar spent on A and on B.

5. **Relate utility maximization to the demand curve.**
   - When a consumer maximizes utility, the consumer's demand curve will be downward sloping. The demand curve can be obtained by assuming that a price changes, and then calculating the consumer equilibrium before and after the price change.

6. **Summarize the influences on consumers' choices.**
   - Consumer choices are subject to varying influences. These include the effects of time, information, family, advertising, and addictive tendencies. Some choices, such as smoking, may provide the consumer with delayed disutility, but the consumer may make that choice anyway.

KEY TERMS

substitution effect, 406
income effect, 406
utility, 406
util, 407

total utility, 407
marginal utility, 407
disutility, 408
law of diminishing marginal utility, 408

satiation point, 409
marginal utility per dollar, 411
rule of utility maximization, 412

TEST YOURSELF

TRUE OR FALSE

1. The substitution effect of a price change occurs because a price change affects consumer purchasing power.
2. Marginal utility equals total utility divided by the amount of a good consumed.
3. Total utility can be obtained by summing marginal utilities.
4. The slope of a total utility curve becomes negative after marginal utility becomes negative.
5. Consumers maximize marginal utility.

MULTIPLE CHOICE

6. When the price of a normal good decreases,
   a. the income and substitution effects both prompt the consumer to purchase more of the good.
   b. the income and substitution effects both prompt the consumer to purchase less of the good.
   c. the income effect prompts the consumer to purchase less of the good, but the substitution effect prompts the consumer to purchase more.
   d. the income effect prompts the consumer to purchase more of the good, but the substitution effect prompts the consumer to purchase less.
7. Which of the following best describes the concept of utility?
   a. Utility is measurable.
   b. The utility of a good must rise the more useful it is.
   c. Utility is subjective.
   d. The utility provided by any particular good will be the same for most consumers.
8. The util is
   a. unrelated to the concept of utility.
   b. measurable with highly sensitive electronic equipment.
   c. used by economists to illustrate diminishing marginal utility.
   d. a special kind of money used in economic experiments.
9. In Self-Test Figure 16-1, point *A* is most closely associated with
   a. maximum marginal utility.
   b. zero total utility.
   c. negative total utility.
   d. satiation.

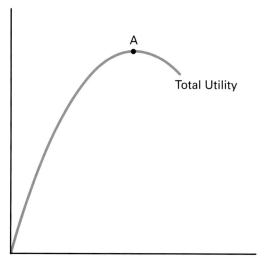

SELF-TEST FIGURE 16-1

10. When the marginal utility from increased consumption is positive, then total utility will
    a. rise.
    b. fall.
    c. remain unchanged.
    d. be unpredictable.
11. Marginal utility will be negative when the total utility curve is
    a. rising.
    b. falling.
    c. at its maximum.
    d. in the negative range.
12. When Jeff drinks a second glass of lemonade, his total utility rises from 20 utils to 25 utils. Jeff's marginal utility of the second lemonade is
    a. 20 utils.
    b. 25 utils.
    c. 5 utils.
    d. not measurable with the information given.

13. Consider the data below on Suzanne's consumption of muffins. Suzanne maximizes her total utility from consuming muffins by eating _____ muffins.

SUZANNE'S UTILITY FROM EATING MUFFINS

Number of Muffins Eaten	Marginal Utility of Muffins (in utils)
1	10
2	5
3	2
4	0
5	−2
6	−8

    a. 1
    b. 2
    c. 4
    d. 6

14. Using the data in question 13 on Suzanne's utility from eating muffins, how many utils of total utility would Suzanne have if she ate five muffins?
    a. − 2
    b. 1
    c. 3
    d. 15

15. Consumer equilibrium requires the consumer to
    a. maximize total utility.
    b. maximize marginal utility.
    c. purchase amounts of each good so that their marginal utilities are equal.
    d. ignore the price of a good in deciding how much to consume and consider only the utility of a purchase.

16. The marginal utility per dollar of a good equals the good's marginal utility
    a. multiplied by $1.
    b. divided by $1.
    c. divided by the price of the good.
    d. multiplied by the price of the good.

17. When Lucy purchases goods A and B in the amounts that maximize utility, then
    a. the marginal utility of A will equal the marginal utility of B.
    b. the total utility from A will equal the total utility from B.
    c. the marginal utility per dollar of A will equal the marginal utility per dollar of B.
    d. A and B must be consumed in equal amounts.

18. The model of utility maximization is
    a. not capable of explaining consumer demand.
    b. good at explaining the demands of some consumers, but not others.
    c. consistent with consumers' demand curves having negative slopes.
    d. applicable to food and clothing purchases, but not the purchases of other items.

19. Suppose that goods X and Y are free (price of X equals $0 and price of Y equals $0). Both goods provide the consumer with utility, and the marginal utility of each good diminishes. A utility maximizing consumer would consume
    a. no X and no Y.
    b. the same amount of X and Y.
    c. X and Y to the point where their marginal utilities are each zero at the satiation points.
    d. amounts of X and Y that cannot be determined.

20. Bad choices, such as shopping, drinking, or gambling to excess,
    a. show that the utility maximization model is not applicable to the behavior of addicts.
    b. cannot be replaced by good choices in the future.
    c. show that the perceptions of the utility provided by consumption can be incorrect.
    d. show that utility only matters after a good is consumed, not before.

QUESTIONS AND PROBLEMS

1. *[substitution and income effects]* Using your purchase of soft drinks as an example, explain how the substitution and income effects of a price increase in your favorite soft drink will affect the quantity demanded of your favorite soft drink, other soft drinks, and also other goods.

2. *[marginal utility]* Calculate the missing values in the following table.

Number of Ice Cream Cones Consumed	Total Utility	Marginal Utility
1	6	6
2		5
3	15	4
4		3
5	20	

3. *[total and marginal utility]* When marginal utility diminishes, does total utility also diminish? Explain.

4. *[total and marginal utility]* When marginal utility is maximized, is total utility also maximized? Will consumers maximize total utility, marginal utility, or both? Explain.

5. *[zero marginal utility]* When Jeff's mom offers him a second scoop of her homemade mashed potatoes at the family dinner table, and Jeff's marginal utility of that second scoop equals zero, how will he respond to his mom? Explain.

6. *[negative value of marginal utility]* Will a consumer purchase another unit of a good when that unit provides the consumer with negative value for marginal utility? Explain.

7. *[marginal utility]* Suppose a new product were invented that offered consumers increasing marginal utility. Also suppose that all other products were characterized by diminishing marginal utility. How much of your income would you spend on this good if your objective were to maximize total utility?

8. *[consumer choice and utility]* Jamie's favorite food is pizza. Jamie eats pizza several times a week, but Jamie also eats chicken, fish, hamburgers, and vegetables. Explain why Jamie does not eat pizza only.

9. *[marginal utility per dollar]* What is marginal utility per dollar? Of what significance is it in the utility-maximization process?

10. *[utility maximization]* Celina must decide how much to spend on books, ice cream, and workouts at the gym. The price of books at her favorite thrift store is $1 each, ice cream costs her $3 a half-gallon at Pik-It-Quik, and she has struck a deal with Arnold's Gym to work out for $10 a session. She has $12 to spend each week. Her marginal utilities for these purchases are presented in the table below. How many books, cartons of ice cream, and workouts will Celina purchase?

11. *[utility maximization]* Refer to Table 16-1 to answer the following:
    a. Verify that while $15 in income could purchase a combination of three movies and six bottles of water, this combination provides less total utility than the four movies and three bottles of water that Denise purchases.
    b. Determine how many movies Denise will see and how many bottles of water Denise would buy if her income were $10.

12. *[rule of utility maximization]* Write an equation that states the rule of utility maximization for three goods, *A*, *B*, and *C*. Restate the rule in words.

13. *[rule of utility maximization]* Suppose a consumer who buys goods *A* and *B* is initially at consumer equilibrium, after which there is an increase in the price of good *B*.
    a. Does the marginal utility of good *A* change? Explain.
    b. Does the marginal utility per dollar of good *A* change? Explain.
    c. Does the marginal utility of good *B* change? Explain.
    d. Does the marginal utility per dollar of good *B* change? Explain.
    e. Before the price increase, was the marginal utility per dollar for the last dollar spent on good *A* equal to the marginal utility per dollar for the last dollar spent on good *B*? Immediately after the price increase, will the marginal utility per dollar for the last dollar spent on good *A* be equal to the marginal utility per dollar for the last dollar spent on good *B*? Explain.
    f. Will the consumer still purchase the combination of *A* and *B* that was purchased at the initial consumer equilibrium? Explain using the income and substitution effects.

14. *[utility and demand]* Is total utility higher when the price of a good is lower? Explain.

15. *[utility and demand]* Explain how the process of utility maximization leads to the law of demand.

# Books	Marginal Utility of Books	# Cartons of Ice Cream	Marginal Utility of Ice Cream	# Workouts at Arnold's Gym	Marginal Utility of Workouts
1	12	1	24	1	30
2	11	2	21	2	25
3	10	3	18	3	20
4	9	4	15	4	15
5	8	5	12	5	10
6	7	6	9	6	5

APPENDIX 16

INDIFFERENCE CURVES, BUDGET CONSTRAINTS, AND UTILITY MAXIMIZATION

Consumer choice can be examined without the artificiality of utils. All that is required is that consumers be able to tell which of two choices they prefer or whether they are indifferent between those choices.

INDIFFERENCE CURVES

Sometimes people are indifferent to the choices before them. In ordinary conversation, this means that we do not care which choice we select. Thus, when faced with choices to which you are indifferent, you might declare, "Might as well flip a coin." **In economic terms, when people are indifferent to the choices before them, they obtain the same amount of utility from each of those choices.** An **indifference curve** shows the combinations of two goods that provide an individual with equal amounts of utility. When we draw an indifference curve, we do not need to state the amount of utility. Instead, our thoughts focus on the idea that the combinations shown are equally desirable to the consumer. For example, suppose Ray often eats a combination plate of chicken wings and jumbo shrimp for supper. He is equally satisfied with the four combinations of chicken and shrimp shown by the table and graph in Figure 16A-1.

The curve in the figure is an indifference curve because it shows the combinations of two goods that provide the same, constant amount of utility. **An indifference curve slopes downward.** The downward slope occurs because, in order for utility to remain constant, the consumption of one of the goods must be cut back when more of the other good is consumed. For example, Ray receives a certain amount of utility when he eats one jumbo shrimp along with eight chicken wings, as indicated by combination A. If a second shrimp were put on his plate and the eight chicken wings were still there, his utility would be higher because he would have more to eat. Because combination B provides Ray with the same utility as combination A, the table tells us that a second shrimp is, to Ray, worth giving up the consumption of three chicken wings. A third shrimp is worth giving up only two chicken wings, and a fourth shrimp is worth giving up only one chicken wing. The number of wings that Ray is willing to give up for an extra shrimp is personal to him. The

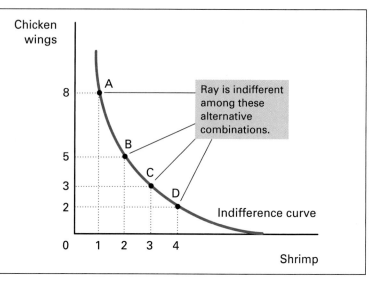

Four meals that leave Ray equally satisfied		
Combination	Jumbo shrimp	Chicken wings
A	1	8
B	2	5
C	3	3
D	4	2

FIGURE 16A-1

RAY'S INDIFFERENCE CURVE Ray's indifference curve between shrimp and chicken wings reveals combinations of the two products that would leave him equally satisfied.

number you would be willing to give up might be different, and thus your indifference curve might look different than Ray's.

Observe that the indifference curve in Figure 16A-1 is curved rather than a straight line. A straight-line indifference curve would violate the law of diminishing marginal utility discussed in this chapter. An indifference curve is drawn as a curved line because that shape is consistent with diminishing marginal utility.

To see why a straight-line indifference curve violates the law of diminishing marginal utility, recall that a straight line has a constant slope. With a constant slope, a consumer would be willing to cut the consumption of one good by the same amount per unit increase in the consumption of another good. For example, if Ray were willing to cut back his consumption of chicken wings by two wings for every extra shrimp consumed, then his indifference curve would be a straight line. Suppose Ray obtains an equal amount of utility by consuming the following combinations: A) one shrimp and eight wings, B) two shrimp and six wings, C) three shrimp and four wings, and D) four shrimp and two wings. You should verify that these combinations plot as a straight line by drawing the indifference curve suggested by these numbers.

Diminishing marginal utility implies that, as more shrimp are consumed, the marginal utility of an additional shrimp falls. Thus, the value to Ray of an additional shrimp will be less than the value of the previous shrimp because an additional shrimp provides less incremental satisfaction. This means that the next shrimp should be worth fewer chicken wings than the previous shrimp. In this case, however, one shrimp is always worth two chicken wings. When Ray has lots of chicken wings and few shrimp, a shrimp is worth two wings; when Ray has few wings and lots of shrimp, a shrimp is still worth two wings. That just isn't plausible. Common sense would dictate that when Ray has more wings, another wing should be of less value to him. Thus, a straight-line indifference curve is illogical and indifference curves are not drawn this way.

THE MARGINAL RATE OF SUBSTITUTION

Rather than discuss the curvature of indifference curves in terms of slope, economists prefer to focus on the idea that we can substitute more of one good in place of less of the other

TABLE 16A-1	THE MARGINAL RATE OF SUBSTITUTION DIMINISHES

(A) BETWEEN POINTS:	(B) CHANGE IN CONSUMPTION OF JUMBO SHRIMP	(C) CHANGE IN CONSUMPTION OF CHICKEN WINGS	(D) MARGINAL RATE OF SUBSTITUTION = I(C) ÷ (B)I
A and B	(2-1) = 1	(5-8) = − 3	3
B and C	(3-2) = 1	(3-5) = − 2	2
C and D	(4-3) = 1	(2-3) = − 1	1

good while maintaining a constant level of satisfaction. The **marginal rate of substitution** is the quantity of one good that must be given up as the consumption of the other good increases by one unit and *total utility remains constant*. Holding utility constant, the marginal rate of substitution can be expressed as:

$$\text{Marginal rate of substitution} = \left| \frac{\text{Change in the consumption of one good}}{\text{Change in the consumption of another good}} \right|$$

This expression applies to changes along an indifference curve because total utility must remain constant when the marginal rate of substitution is computed. The marginal rate of substitution for the choices in Figure 16A-1 are shown in Table 16A-1. Notice that the convention is to express the marginal rate of substitution as a positive number. Also note that the numbers in the table illustrate the *principle of the diminishing marginal rate of substitution.*

Since the same values that were used to plot the indifference curve in Figure 16A-1 are also used to calculate the marginal rate of substitution, it is clear that the marginal rate of substitution tells us something about the indifference curve. By referring to the formula for the marginal rate of substitution, we see that **the marginal rate of substitution is an approximation for the absolute value of the slope of an indifference curve.** The diminishing values of 3, 2, and 1 for the marginal rate of substitution in Table 16A-1 indicate that the indifference curve is steepest at its topmost part and gets progressively less steep as we move down the curve. Curves that graph in this fashion are called *convex to the origin* by mathematicians. Thus, indifference curves are typically convex to the origin. Indifference curves that are convex to the origin will always exhibit a diminishing marginal rate of substitution.

INDIFFERENCE MAPS

A consumer has more than one indifference curve between any two goods, reflecting varying levels of satisfaction. For example, if we were to replace the numbers in the column for chicken wings with larger values, Ray would achieve a higher level of satisfaction. The indifference curve incorporating the new numbers would lie farther from the origin than the indifference curve previously shown. Alternatively, if we were to replace the numbers in the chicken wings column with smaller numbers than the current values, Ray would have less satisfaction. The indifference curve in that case would be closer to the origin than the indifference curve in Figure 16A-1. An **indifference map** shows a set of indifference curves. Figure 16A-2 is an example of an indifference map.

Let's review the indifference curve model of consumer preferences:

■ An indifference curve shows combinations of two goods that are equally preferred by the consumer.

■ Indifference curves slope downward and are convex to the origin, not straight lines.

FIGURE 16A-2

AN INDIFFERENCE MAP An indifference map shows a set of indifference curves. If a person increases consumption of both goods, that person moves to a higher indifference curve associated with more utility. Such an increase in utility is shown by the arrow labeled *more is better*.

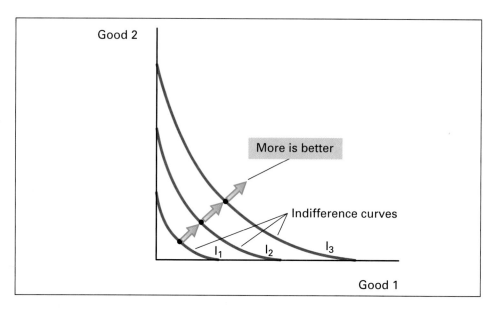

QUICKCHECK

Draw the indifference curve shown in Figure 16A-1. Then draw an indifference curve with double the number of chicken wings in the first curve. Draw a third indifference curve with half the number of chicken wings as illustrated by the original curve.

Answer: The indifference curve with more wings should be farther from the origin than the original indifference curve. The indifference curve with fewer wings should be drawn closer to the origin.

- An indifference curve can be characterized by the marginal rate of substitution, an approximation to the absolute value of its slope. That slope will vary along an indifference curve.
- A consumer's indifference map will have many indifference curves, each indicating a different level of utility. Higher utility levels are shown by indifference curves farther from the origin. In short, more is better.

BUDGET CONSTRAINTS

Consumer choice is limited by the amount of money people can spend and the prices of the goods they buy. The **budget constraint** is a curve that shows a consumer's consumption possibilities for two goods. The budget constraint, also called the budget line, is always a straight line. When there are two goods to choose from, the budget constraint is given by the formula:

Income = (Price of first good × Quantity of first good)
+ (Price of second good × Quantity of second good)

In this formula a consumer knows the prices and income. The quantities of the two goods are the choice variables. The consumer computes various combinations of the two goods that all use up the income.

Ray's $10 Budget Constraint	
Quantity of shrimp: price of shrimp = $1 each	Quantity of chicken wings: price of chicken wings = $.25 each
10	0
9	4
8	8
7	12
6	16
5	20
4	24
3	28
2	32
1	36
0	40

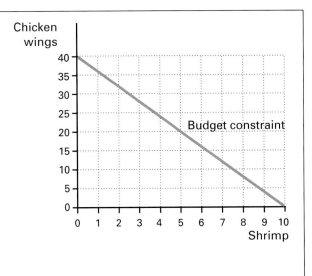

FIGURE 16A-3

THE BUDGET CONSTRAINT The budget constraint will be a downward-sloping straight line, with the slope equal to−(price of one good/price of another good). Ray's $10 budget constraint is drawn based on the data in the table. The slope of Ray's budget constraint is−(price of shrimp/price of wings) =−1/.25 =−4.

Let's illustrate the budget constraint with numbers. Suppose that jumbo shrimp cost $1 each, chicken wings cost 25 cents each, and Ray's income equals $10. Putting these values in the equation for the budget constraint, we have: $10 = ($1 × quantity of shrimp) + ($0.25 × quantity of chicken wings). In Figure 16A-3 we substitute in the equation for various values of the quantity of shrimp and then compute how many chicken wings could be purchased with the income left from the $10. Each row in the table within Figure 16A-3 shows a feasible purchase. For example, if Ray purchases ten shrimp, he can't purchase any chicken wings. But if he buys nine shrimp, he can also buy four chicken wings. Each row in the table shows us how much of both goods Ray can have.

Figure 16A-3 illustrates the budget line for the data in this table. Points outside the budget line require more income than is currently available and thus cannot be purchased now. Points inside the budget line are combinations that cost less than the income available. For example, three shrimp and twenty wings represent a point inside the budget constraint. Combinations inside the budget line are able to be purchased with money left over, but they would provide less utility to the consumer than points on the budget line.

When the consumer's income changes, there will be a new budget constraint that shows the new combinations of goods that the consumer is able to purchase. Figure 16A-4 shows the shift in Ray's budget constraint when he has only $5 in income. The budget line shifts toward the origin, indicating he cannot purchase as much as when his income was $10.

Figure 16A-4 also shows the effect of a price change. In this case, the price of shrimp has doubled, which means that Ray can buy at most only half as much as was possible before. The effect shows up on the graph as an inward pivot. If the price of shrimp dropped, the budget constraint would have pivoted outward.

The slope of the budget constraint in absolute value terms equals the ratio of the prices of the two goods. Thus, a change in a price will alter the slope of the budget line. You should confirm this statement by working through the QuickCheck that follows.

FIGURE 16A-4

SHIFTING THE BUDGET CONSTRAINT The budget constraint will shift in a parallel manner if income changes or will pivot if one of the prices changes. In the examples shown, a decrease in income shifts the budget constraint inward. Alternatively, if the shrimp price doubles, the budget constraint pivots inward until it intersects the shrimp axis at half the number of shrimp that could previously have been purchased.

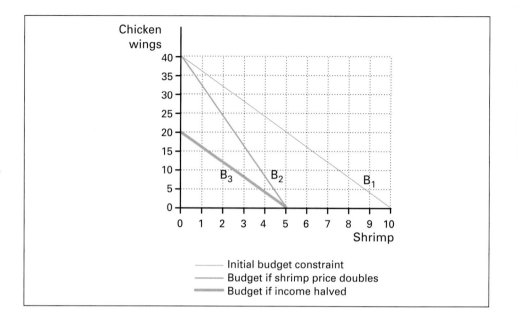

QUICKCHECK

(a) Draw a budget line when Ray's income increases to $20 with the prices of chicken wings and shrimp remaining at 25 cents and $1, respectively. (b) Draw another budget line when his income is $10, but the price of shrimp rises to $2 each, while the price of chicken wings remains at 25 cents.

Answer: (a) An increase in income shifts the budget line farther away from the origin. The budget line for $20 of income will have an intercept at 20 shrimp and another at 80 chicken wings. (b) A price change will alter the slope of the budget line. The budget line for an income of $10, but with shrimp at $2 each, will have an intercept on the shrimp axis of 5 shrimp. The intercept on the chicken wing axis remains at 40 chicken wings.

UTILITY MAXIMIZATION—REACHING THE HIGHEST INDIFFERENCE CURVE

The consumer's objective is to maximize utility, subject to a budget constraint. **Graphically, utility maximization is achieved when the consumer reaches the highest indifference curve attainable along the budget constraint.** The highest indifference curve will be tangent to the budget line, as shown in Figure 16A-5 at point U^*, which is the point of *consumer equilibrium.*

When two curves are tangent to each other, their slopes are equal at the tangency point. Recall that the absolute value of the slope of an indifference curve is the marginal rate of substitution and the slope of the budget line, also in absolute value terms, equals the ratio of the prices of the two goods. What a consumer is *willing to do* is indicated by the marginal rate of substitution. The ratio of prices tells us what the consumer *must do* since the consumer cannot consume beyond the budget line. Thus, at the tangency point in Figure 16A-5, what the consumer is willing to do (the marginal rate of substitution) equals what the consumer must do (the ratio of prices).

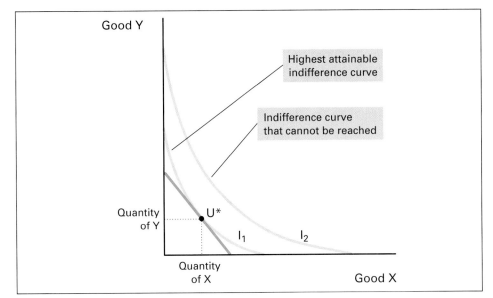

FIGURE 16A-5

MAXIMIZING UTILITY A consumer maximizes utility, U^*, subject to a budget constraint, by choosing a combination of good X and good Y for which the budget constraint is tangent to an indifference curve. Although the consumer would prefer to reach a higher indifference curve, the budget constraint does not allow it.

FROM INDIFFERENCE CURVES TO DEMAND

When there is a change in the price of one of the goods, the utility-maximizing equilibrium point will change. This effect occurs because the slope of the budget line changes with a price change. A lower price will allow the consumer to attain a higher indifference curve; a higher price will push the consumer to a lower indifference curve.

Figure 16A-6 on the next page illustrates the effect of a price change on the consumer's equilibrium point. The quantities chosen are labeled as Q_1 and Q_2. In the lower graph the quantities from the upper graph are plotted and labeled by extending the dotted lines down from the upper graph. The prices that lead to these quantities are called P_1 and P_2, respectively, and are labeled on the vertical axis. When the two price-quantity points are connected by the straight line shown in the figure, the result is a demand curve.

EXERCISES

1. Explain why utility is constant along an indifference curve.
2. Draw a graph with the vertical axis labeled good A and the horizontal axis labeled good B. Then draw a budget constraint and two indifference curves in your graph. The first indifference curve should be tangent to the budget constraint, while the second indifference curve should intersect the budget constraint twice. Explain why the consumer's utility-maximizing equilibrium occurs at the tangency point and not at a point of intersection.
3. Plot a budget line when a consumer has $18 to spend and the price of good A is 50 cents, while the price of good B is $1.
4. Is utility constant along a demand curve? Is every point along a demand curve associated with a consumer equilibrium? Explain.

UTILITY MAXIMIZATION AND DEMAND. When the price of a good falls from P_1 to P_2, the budget constraint rotates from B_1 outward to B_2. The result is that the consumer can move from indifference curve I_1 and utility level $U_1{*}$ to a higher indifference curve, B_2, and a higher utility level, $U_2{*}$. To do so, the consumer will choose to buy the quantity Q_2 rather than Q_1. The demand curve shows this change in quantity demanded resulting from the price change.

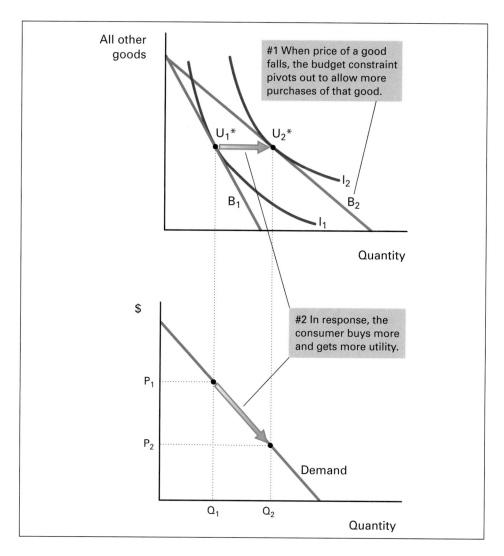

WORKING WITH GRAPHS AND DATA

1. *[total and marginal utility]* Use the following table to answer the questions about total and marginal utility.

Quantity	Utility	Marginal Utility	Calculation of Marginal Utility (change in total utility / change in quantity)
0	0		
1	20		
2	35		
3	45		
4	50		
5	50		
6	45		

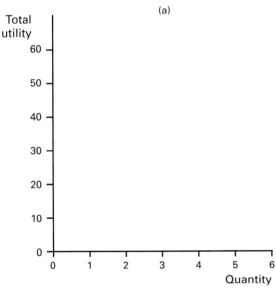

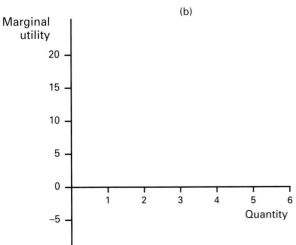

GRAPH 16-1

a. Fill in the marginal utility column and show the computations.
b. Draw the total utility curve and label it TU on Graph 16-1(a).
c. Draw the marginal utility curve and label it MU on Graph 16-1(b).
d. Show the satiation point and label it SP on Graphs 16-1(a) and (b). What is true of total and marginal utility at the satiation point?

2. *[utility maximization]* Use the following table to answer the questions about this utility maximizing consumer.

Quantity of Good X Bought	Marginal Utility of Good X (MUx)	MUx/Px Px = $4	Quantity of Good Y Bought	Marginal Utility of Good Y (MUy)	MUy/Py Py = $2
1	100		1	80	40
2	80		2	60	30
3	60		3	40	20
4	40		4	20	10
5	20		5	10	5

a. Fill in the MUx/Px column when the price of good X is $4.
b. How many units of goods X and Y will this utility maximizing consumer buy if the consumer's income is $14?
c. How much total utility will this consumer enjoy at this level of consumption of X and Y?
d. Based on the conditions for utility maximization, is this consumer maximizing utility? Explain.

3. *[utility maximization and demand]* Use the following table to answer the questions about this utility maximizing consumer to answer the following questions.

Quantity of Good X Bought	Marginal Utility of Good X (MUx)	MUx/Px Px = $2	Quantity of Good Y Bought	MUy/Py Py = $2
1	100		1	40
2	80		2	30
3	60		3	20
4	40		4	10
5	20		5	5

a. Fill in the MUx/Px column when the price of good X is $2.
b. How many units of goods X and Y will this utility maximizing consumer buy if the consumer's

income is $14 when the price of X is $2 and the price of Y is $2?

c. Based on the conditions for utility maximization, is this consumer maximizing utility? Explain.

d. From the previous question, the consumer will buy two units of X and three units of Y when the price of good Y is $4. Draw the segment of the demand curve for good X that would be between the prices of $4 and $2 and label it D on Graph 16-2. Are the consumer's choices consistent with the law of demand?

e. Label the quantity of X purchased as X_2 and the quantity of Y purchased as Y_2.

f. On Graph 16-3(b) identify the two prices and their corresponding quantities of good X and draw the portion of the demand curve that they show.

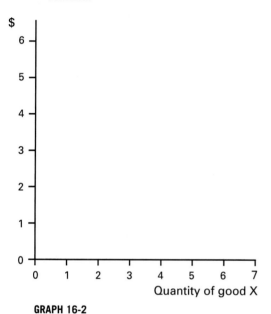

GRAPH 16-2

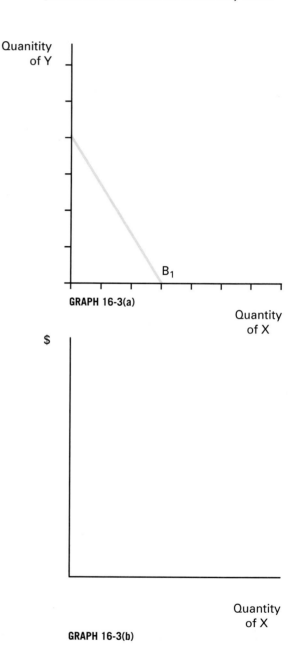

GRAPH 16-3(a)

GRAPH 16-3(b)

4. *[indifference curves]* Use Graphs 16-3(a) and (b) to answer the following questions.

a. Given budget constraint B_1, draw an indifference curve that maximizes this consumer's utility and label the curve I_1. Identify the point, labeled as U_1, that maximizes this consumer's utility.

b. Label the quantity of X purchased as X_1 and the quantity of Y purchased as Y_1.

c. Let the price of X fall. Draw the new budget line and label it B_2.

d. Given B_2, draw an indifference curve that maximizes this consumer's utility and label it I_2. Identify the point, labeled as U_2, that maximizes this consumer's utility.

 Visit www.prenhall.com/ayers for Exploring the Web exercises and additional self-test quizzes.

CHAPTER 17

THE FIRM AND PRODUCTION

A LOOK AHEAD

Bill Gates, Steve Jobs, Sam Walton, John D. Rockefeller, Henry Ford: the names are familiar. So are the companies: Microsoft, Apple, Wal-Mart, Exxon, and Ford. Our familiarity with them illustrates the fundamental role of business in the economy and in our lives. Whether familiar or not, all businesses face ethical issues. The economic perspective on business ethics is discussed in the Explore & Apply section at the end of the chapter.

We begin by examining the legal forms a business can take and the choice among methods of financing. We then show two different ways to measure profit. After pointing out some difficulties that a business can encounter when it grows large, we take an in-depth look at production, the building block of business success.

LEARNING OBJECTIVES

Understanding Chapter 17 will enable you to:
1. **Identify the three legal forms of business and the advantages and disadvantages of each.**
2. **Explain the methods of financing a business.**
3. **Distinguish between accounting profit and economic profit.**
4. **Identify difficulties in maximizing profit that are created by the principal–agent problem.**
5. **Relate the key concepts of production, including the law of diminishing returns.**
6. Recognize and reflect on issues relating to business ethics.

Explore & Apply

firm a business that employs inputs to produce output.

Firms take inputs of resources and produce outputs of goods and services to be sold in the marketplace. The desire for profit, to be discussed in this chapter, motivates firms to produce.

17.1 BUSINESS BASICS

Certain elements of business economics are common to all firms. Choosing a legal form, obtaining financing, computing profit or loss, making the best use of personnel, and producing a good or service are universal experiences for firms. We start with choosing a legal form.

LEGAL FORM—PROPRIETORSHIP, PARTNERSHIP, AND CORPORATION

A firm can choose to operate in one of the following three legal forms: sole proprietorship, partnership, or corporation. Which should it be?

Consider the personal implications if you open a small business, such as a medical, legal, or accounting practice. If you start informally, you'll become a *sole proprietorship*—a business with a single owner. You may want to visit City Hall and file a d.b.a. (doing business as), which lets the public know that you are the operator of a business recognizable by the name you select for your firm. Or you might just print business cards and go to work. You can hire employees if you wish, but remember that you'll be legally liable for injuries caused to or by the employees acting in the course of their duties. You'll also be personally liable for all debts and taxes of the business. If your firm doesn't earn enough income from sales, you will have to tap into your personal resources to pay off your creditors and the tax collector. You'll report the business's profits or losses on your personal tax return.

If you can find one or more people with whom to start your business, you can form a *partnership*. Partnerships are similar to proprietorships. Each partner can hire employees. Each partner is also liable for business debts that the business is unable to pay.

To avoid the disadvantages of proprietorships and partnerships, many firms are formed

corporation a type of firm that is a legal entity separate from the people who own, manage, and otherwise direct its affairs.

as corporations. A **corporation** is a firm that is a legal entity, a thing separate from the people who own, manage, and otherwise direct its affairs. Corporations tend to be big business. While they account for only about 21 percent of businesses in the United States, they earn over 91 percent of the revenues. Figure 17-1 shows the distribution of U.S. firms and the revenues they earn according to their legal form.

stock shares of ownership in a corporation.

Unlike other forms of business, corporations can issue shares of **stock**, which are shares of ownership in the corporation. In addition to being able to issue stock, two major advantages of the corporate form of business are *limited liability* and *perpetual existence*. Limited liability means that the owners are not personally liable for the debts of the business. If you choose to incorporate and the business fails, then creditors cannot lay claim to your personal assets. For example, when United Airlines declared bankruptcy in December 2002, none of its creditors could seize the houses or cars of its stockholders. Perpetual existence means the corporation can outlive its owners, providing that it avoids dissolution through bankruptcy.

The major disadvantage to the corporate form of business is the need to pay a corporation income tax, which takes up to 39 percent of profits. There are also reporting and procedural requirements that other forms of business do not face. These disadvantages explain why few small businesses choose to incorporate. Table 17-1 summarizes the key advantages and disadvantages of the legal forms of business.

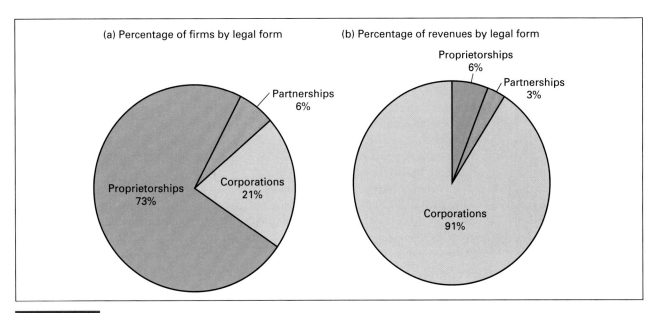

FIGURE 17-1

PERCENTAGE OF FIRMS AND PERCENTAGE OF REVENUES BY LEGAL FORM Although corporations are far out-numbered by proprietorships, corporations receive the lion's share of revenues earned by U.S. firms.

Source: 1997 Economic Census, U.S. Census Bureau. Percentages may not add to 100 because of rounding, as well as the existence of firms whose legal form was unable to be classified, or was in litigation.

TABLE 17-1   COMPARING THE LEGAL FORMS OF BUSINESS

TYPE OF BUSINESS	ADVANTAGES	DISADVANTAGES
Sole Proprietorship	Easy to start; controlled by owner	Owner personally liable for business debts
Partnership	Access to partner's funds	Partners personally liable for all partnership debts
Corporation	Access to funds through issuance of shares of stock; limited liability; perpetual existence	Corporate income tax; corporate reporting and procedural requirements

SNAPSHOT   FRANCHISING—TEAMING SMALL BUSINESSES WITH GIANT CORPORATIONS

You see them everywhere. The names include McDonald's, Best Western, Pizza Hut, Radio Shack, and many others. They are *franchises,* arrangements that let a person or group start a business that uses the name and standards of a parent corporation. The advantage to becoming a franchisee, the holder of a franchise, is the chance to achieve success by putting a well-known name on your business, taking advantage of brand-name advertising, and selling a product mix with a proven track record. Franchise holders also receive training in how to operate their businesses. In return, franchisees pay fees and a percentage of their income or profit to the parent corporation.

Franchising thus pairs the advantages of the corporation with those of the sole proprietor or partnership in the hope of forming a winning team. This teamwork is sometimes contentious, however, as evidenced by the complaints of Subway franchisees, who claimed the parent corporation was franchising so much that franchisees wound up taking each other's customers and profits. ◄

HOW TO FINANCE A BUSINESS

In order to operate, firms must have *financial capital,* the money needed to start or grow a business. Firms can choose one or more of the following four options:

- Use personal funds
- Use retained earnings
- Borrow
- Issue shares of stock

In the case of many small businesses, such as flea market sellers, Amway dealers, and the like, startup financial capital comes from the owners' personal savings. New small businesses often are unable to obtain funds from other sources.

Retained earnings are a firm's savings. Just as the name suggests, retained earnings are monies kept from a business's earnings for the purpose of financing its operations. A business that has never had any earnings, such as a new business, will have no retained earnings. Retained earnings are also called *internal funds.* **Internal funds make up the majority of funds used to finance the operations of U.S. firms.**

Corporations and other firms with established track records and valuable assets are likely to be able to borrow financial capital from banks or other lenders. Only corporations are able to borrow funds by issuing bonds, where a **bond** is a promise to repay borrowed funds at some future date. Businesses that borrow funds must not only repay them, but also pay interest to the lenders, where *interest* is a periodic payment as a percentage of the face value of a bond or loan. While small startups cannot easily borrow from banks, or issue bonds, the owners of these businesses will often borrow funds from friends and relatives. Most firms use a combination of retained earnings and borrowed funds to finance their expansion.

Only corporations have the option of issuing shares of stock. The corporation receives revenue from the initial sale of its stock, but not later when the stock "trades" from one owner to another. Stock exchanges, such as the New York Stock Exchange, the so-called "Big Board," are *secondary markets,* meaning that already existing shares of stock are traded there.

A corporation's market value is given by:

Market value of corporation = Number of shares of stock × Market price per share

The market price of a share of stock is determined by demand and supply in the *stock market,* in which shares of stock are bought and sold, often on a stock exchange. Other things

bond a legally binding promise to repay borrowed funds with interest at a specified future date.

equal, the greater the number of shares of stock, the lower the price per share. It is ultimately buyers and sellers of stock who determine its price and the ultimate value of a corporation. The market value changes as often as the market price of its stock changes.

Only newly issued stock provides funds to a corporation. When new shares are issued, they are sold through so-called public offerings. Despite their name, public offerings are ordinarily not open to the general public. Instead, shares from public offerings are typically purchased by large investment firms that specialize in the purchase and later resale of new shares of stock.

When firms look to sources outside themselves for financing, they are said to be seeking *external funds*. Stocks, bonds, and loans provide external funds. Historically, loans have provided about 60 percent of external funds for U.S. businesses, with bonds providing about 30 percent and stocks about 2 percent. (Other sources of external funds, such as the government, provided the remainder.) External funds are not, however, the primary source of funds for firms. All the external sources of funds—including stocks, bonds, and loans—provide only about 25 percent of the funds that firms use. Thus, as stated earlier, retained earnings provide most financing for firms.

U.S. firms, especially corporations, are not restricted to this country in their search for external funds. Financial markets today are global in scope as financial capital flows relatively freely across international borders. Large pools of savings have developed in other industrial countries—money that can flow to any firm anywhere that offers the greatest expected rewards. Banks also take advantage of opportunities to raise financial capital overseas. The flow of money is a two-way street. Just as U.S. firms and banks can look overseas for financial capital, so too can firms in other countries look outside their borders for funds.

FIVE FOR A DIME *SNAPSHOT*

Little square hamburgers with five holes, onions, and soft buns are the unlikely hero of a classic American success story. The first White Castle opened in Wichita, Kansas, in 1921 with the help of a $700 loan. Selling for a nickel each, the little White Castle hamburger sandwich was popular enough to prompt partners Walter Anderson and "Billy" Ingram to open a second restaurant in 1924. Thus began a steady expansion, creating America's first restaurant chain in the process.

White Castle pioneered fast food. The first fast-food newspaper coupons, in 1932, offered five White Castles for 10 cents! Over the next 70 years, many other innovations followed. One of the most recent was the popular frozen White Castles sold in supermarkets. Today, White Castle has a cult following around the world, often in places far from the chain's few hundred restaurants, which are mostly found in the American Midwest. The firm has never gone public, remaining in the hands of the Ingram family all these years later. The company long ago repaid its $700 loan and today steadfastly avoids the perils of debt. ◀

17.2 THE GOAL OF MAXIMUM PROFIT

profit (economic profit) total revenue minus total cost; unlike accounting profit, economic profit defines cost to include implicit opportunity costs.

Profit, also called **economic profit,** is the difference between total revenue and total cost:

$$\text{Profit} = \text{Total revenue} - \text{Total cost}$$

Total revenue is the sum of income received by a firm. For a firm selling a single product at a single price, total revenue equals the quantity sold multiplied by its price:

$$\text{Total revenue} = \text{Price} \times \text{Quantity}$$

total revenue price × quantity.

total cost the sum of the firm's expenses.

Total cost, which must be subtracted from total revenue to compute profit, is the sum of the firm's expenses.

To say that a firm maximizes profit means that it earns the greatest amount of total profit that it is capable of earning. **The economic analysis of firms usually assumes the goal of profit maximization.** This assumption enhances our understanding of why a firm chooses its specific quantity of output to produce. As we study the behavior of firms in future chapters, we will assume that they maximize profit. We now turn our attention to clarifying economic profit, which will require us to consider total costs in greater depth.

DISTINGUISHING AMONG NORMAL PROFIT, ECONOMIC PROFIT, AND ACCOUNTING PROFIT

"Normal profit is that rate of minimum profit which a firm must earn in order to survive in the market."

—*Alfred Marshall, British economist (1842–1924)*

Firms employ accountants to measure profit for reporting to the government and shareholders. However, the accounting measures do not explain the behavior of firms. For example, firms sometimes pull out of a particular business or operation even when it is profitable according to accounting data. If a firm spends a million dollars to earn one dollar in profit, as reported by its accountants, the owners of that firm would consider themselves to have lost money. They could do better by putting their money in the bank or into other investments.

explicit costs costs accountants aim to measure.

To explain the behaviors of firms, we must distinguish between two components of total cost. All of the costs accountants aim to measure are termed **explicit costs,** no matter what the accountants call them. Explicit costs are all internal to the firm, in the sense that they depend upon decisions that the firm makes. Examples of explicit costs include the cost of labor, raw materials, shipping, insurance, rent, and utilities.

Consider Ali's King-of-Ribs restaurant. The napkins, eating utensils, food, salaries of cooks and servers, and the cost of the ingredients in the dinners served are all explicit costs. However, there are other costs that accountants do not measure. These are **implicit opportunity costs,** or **implicit costs** for short, that are associated with nonpurchased inputs. These costs are the value that the firm's capital and entrepreneur's time would have in their best alternative uses.

implicit opportunity costs (implicit costs) the value that the firm's capital and the entrepreneur's time would have in their best alternative uses.

Implicit costs vary with forces external to the firm, in the sense that the firm has no control over them. Examples include interest rates from alternative investments and the opportunity cost of the entrepreneur's time. Accountants do not try to measure these costs, because they vary in unforeseeable ways over time and among entrepreneurs. A firm that is profitable when John Doe is in charge would probably be unprofitable with Bill Gates at the helm because Bill Gates' time is worth too much elsewhere. Accountants cannot know just what his opportunities are, nor their value. Because the value of alternatives cannot be known, accountants ignore implicit opportunity costs when calculating profit:

$$\textit{Accounting profit} = \text{Total revenue} - \text{Explicit costs}$$

To explain the behavior of firms, however, economists include implicit costs in their calculation of profit.

$$\text{Economic profit} = \text{Accounting profit} - \text{Implicit opportunity costs}$$

Normal profit represents the portion of accounting profit that just covers implicit opportunity costs. **From an economic perspective, normal profit is a cost. It is the accounting profit needed to keep the firm in business.** For this reason, normal profit is the same as a firm's implicit costs. A firm must earn at least a normal profit for its resources to continue to be employed in their current use. If a normal profit is not present or expected in the future, the owners of the firm would make plans to eventually go out of business and *liquidate*—sell off—the firm's assets. Substituting for implicit cost in the equation for economic profit, we have:

$$\text{Economic profit} = \text{Accounting profit} - \text{Normal profit}$$

Figure 17-2 illustrates the relationship between economic profit, accounting profit, and normal profit.

Successful companies are well aware of their implicit costs and the notion of normal profit, even if they cannot know its exact amount. The owners invest their time and money expecting to do at least as well with them as they could elsewhere. For example, Ali had other investment opportunities for the funds he invested in his restaurant. If the best alternative use of his money would have paid a return of $1,000 per month, that is the implicit cost of Ali's investment. Let's take a more detailed look at the King-of-Ribs restaurant's revenue and costs.

Suppose that Ali's restaurant sells an average of 5,000 of its honey-glazed baby back rib dinners each month. Customers pay $10 for each dinner, which is the only item sold at the restaurant. Ali thus earns an average of $50,000 ($10 × 5,000 = $50,000) per month in total revenue. The restaurant incurs two explicit costs, the expenses for food and supplies, and for hired labor. Ali's implicit costs are the opportunity cost of his entrepreneurship (he could try his hand at a different business), the opportunity cost of his own labor hours, and the return on alternative investments. The implicit opportunity costs represent real costs of using Ali's resources of entrepreneurship, labor, and capital in the King-of-Ribs restaurant instead of elsewhere.

Table 17-2 shows the computation of profit for the King-of-Ribs restaurant. In Ali's case, accounting profit equals $10,000, but economic profit equals only $4,000. **Because implicit**

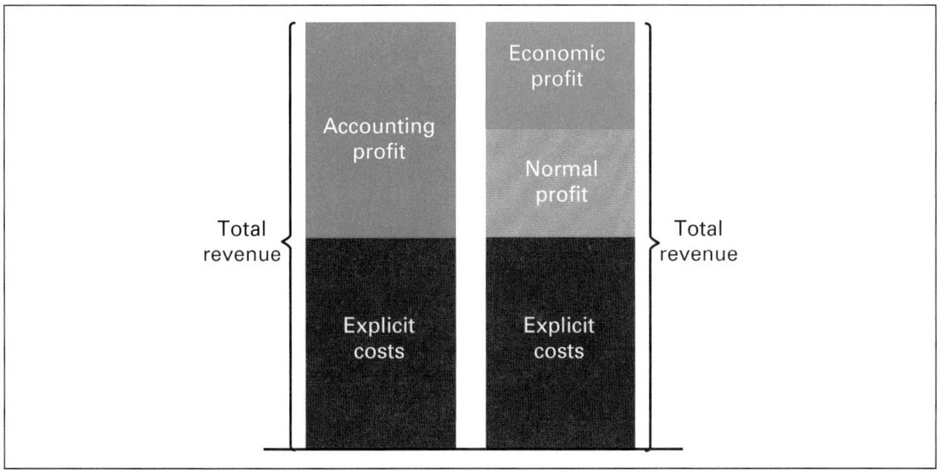

normal profit the portion of accounting profit that equals implicit opportunity costs.

FIGURE 17-2

ACCOUNTING PROFIT VERSUS ECONOMIC PROFIT Accounting profit will be greater than economic profit by the amount of normal profit, which is the portion of accounting profit necessary to keep the firm in business. Normal profit consists of implicit costs that are beyond the scope of the firm, including the opportunity cost of the owners' time and the rate of return on alternative investments. If normal profit is not achieved or expected, profit-maximizing owners will plan to go out of business.

TABLE 17-2	MONTHLY ECONOMIC PROFIT AT ALI'S KING-OF-RIBS RESTAURANT	
Total revenue		$50,000
Minus explicit costs:		
Raw food and supplies	−$27,000	
Hired labor	−$13,000	
Accounting profit		$10,000
Minus implicit costs:		
Value of Ali's entrepreneurship in alternative business venture	−$3,000	
Value of Ali's labor at a different job	−$2,000	
Value of alternative investments that Ali could have made	−$1,000	
Economic profit		$ 4,000

costs are subtracted from accounting profit to obtain economic profit, economic profit will always be less than accounting profit.

Let's suppose that food and labor costs—excluding Ali's own labor, for which he is not explicitly paid—at Ali's King-of-Ribs restaurant increase by exactly $4,000. Assuming all other data stay the same, then economic profit at Ali's drops to zero. Will Ali close his restaurant? No, because while he has no economic profit, total revenue does cover his implicit costs. Thus, the King-of-Ribs restaurant earns a normal profit. That normal profit is sufficient to keep all the resources of the restaurant in their current use.

There are three possible outcomes when economic profit is computed:

excess profit economic profit; the accounting profit in excess of normal profit.

- The firm can earn a positive profit, also called **excess profit,** meaning that total revenue exceeds total cost. For the King-of-Ribs restaurant, the profit is $4,000.

loss occurs when economic profit is negative.

- The firm can earn a negative profit, meaning that total revenue is less than total cost. A negative profit is called a **loss.** When a firm incurs a loss, it may be able to continue in business for awhile. However, if it continues to incur losses, its resources will eventually be put to different uses and the firm will be out of business.

breakeven occurs when economic profit is zero.

- The firm can earn zero profit, meaning that total revenue equals total cost. Zero profit is also called **breakeven,** meaning that the firm earns just enough revenue to provide it with a normal profit, but no more. While a firm would prefer to earn a positive profit, breakeven alone is enough to keep it in business.

THE PRINCIPAL–AGENT PROBLEM—AN ISSUE OF INCENTIVES

"If you want something done right, do it yourself."

—Old saying

While the owners of a firm may seek to maximize profit, not all of the firm's employees are likely to share that goal. Managers and staff often have their own personal agendas. This

How could a firm that earns an accounting profit have an economic loss at the same time?

Answer: The implicit opportunity costs of the owner's time and capital are not considered in computing accounting profit. When these costs are deducted from total revenue, it could be that economic profit is negative, meaning that the firm incurs a loss even though the accounting profits remain positive. For example, if a firm's total revenue equals $10,000, explicit costs equal $9,000, and implicit costs equal $2,000, then the firm earns $1,000 of accounting profit. Subtracting the implicit costs leaves the firm with an economic loss of $1,000.

brings about a **principal–agent problem,** which refers to the difficulties of making employees, who are called agents, act in accordance with the will of the owners, who are called principals. As readers of the comic strip *Dilbert* know all too well, managers may use the firm's resources in ways that contribute little to the revenue of the business. Also, employees are often guilty of *shirking,* which is usually known on the job as "goofing off." The bigger the company, the more distance there is between the owners and the employees and the more pronounced the principal–agent problem is likely to be.

principal–agent problem the difficulty of making agents, such as employees, act in the interests of principals, such as owners.

One way of facing up to the principal–agent problem is to provide employees with economic incentives to maximize the firm's profits. These incentives are sometimes highly personal, as in the case of sales commissions. More often, they depend on the performance of the company as a whole and also of the division of the company in which the employee works. These incentives can take a variety of forms, including:

- *Stock-option plans* in which employees are provided the option to buy stock at a fixed price, irrespective of what the market price of the stock might become. Employees thus have the collective incentive to increase the profitability of the company so that its stock price will go up.
- *Incentive pay* systems that let employees share in the profitability of the firm. An example of incentive pay is the traditional holiday bonus, the value of which depends upon how well the company has done.

When employees are rewarded based upon the company's performance, they have more incentive to work diligently. Perhaps even more importantly, they also have an incentive to keep an eye on one another to ensure that everyone is working hard. Shirking would not be cool!

Sometimes designing a proper system of incentives is problematic and can itself pit the interests of agents against principals. For example, the executives of many companies have been accused by shareholders of devising stock option plans that are too generous to themselves. Also, if your businesses faced the task of devising a scheme of incentive pay as a reward for exemplary performance, how would you measure such performance? If sales doubled in the previous year, would your managers deserve bonuses? Not if your competitors' sales tripled! Only with carefully selected benchmarks is it possible to interpret performance. For example, Enron, Adelphia Communications, Worldcom, and a number of other companies have been accused of misleading their investors into driving up the value of company stock, with the result that insiders could cash out lucrative stock options.

SNAPSHOT   GIVING AWAY OTHER PEOPLE'S MONEY

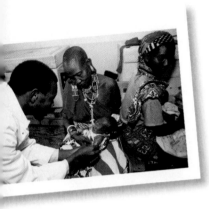

Whether it be to fund public broadcasting or the local cultural museum, firms are often sought out for charitable contributions. Firms, in turn, look for good publicity in making such donations. Should they be charitable when it detracts from profits?

Remember that management is the agent of the owners and is employed to follow the wishes of owners. The owners usually prefer to make their own charitable decisions based on their personal preferences and financial circumstances. Witness Bill and Melinda Gates's decision to set up their own family-controlled foundation for charitable giving, a foundation that started with a net worth of about $24 billion. One of the foundation's objectives has been to vaccinate children in the world's poorest countries, a cause toward which it has already contributed about $850 million. Through this charity, Bill Gates gave away his own money, not the money of shareholders in Microsoft Corporation. Corporate officers must think twice before giving away that which is not theirs to give! For this reason, firms encourage employees to give to the United Way campaign or to make other individual charitable donations out of the employees' own money. ◄

17.3 PRODUCING THE PRODUCT

In order to earn a profit, a firm must have something to sell. It must produce a good or service using labor, capital, and perhaps other inputs. The relationship between the amounts of inputs and the quantities of output a firm produces is called its **production function.**

THE LONG RUN AND THE SHORT RUN

production function the relationship between the amounts of inputs and the quantities of output a firm produces.

Production decisions are made by firms in either a long-run or a short-run context. The **long run** is a time period sufficiently long that all inputs are *variable,* meaning that their quantities can be changed. For this reason, the long run is sometimes called the *planning horizon.* Actual production occurs in the **short run,** a time period where at least one input is fixed. The quantity of a *fixed* input cannot be changed.

long run period of time sufficiently long that all inputs are variable.

While firms employ numerous inputs, our model of the firm simplifies matters by assuming only two inputs. Specifically, assume that labor is a variable input and that capital is a fixed input in the short run. It may be helpful to think of a unit of labor as an hour of work, and a unit of capital as an hour's use of machinery.

short run period of time in which at least one input is fixed.

Modeling production with only two inputs highlights the distinction between variable and fixed inputs. The implications pertaining to labor apply in the real world to any variable input, including variable capital inputs such as pencils and lightbulbs. Likewise, the analysis of capital applies to any fixed input, including long-term employment contracts.

Short-run decision making by the firm focuses only on the variable input. For instance, in your favorite supermarket, another cashier can quickly be put to work when long lines build up, assuming an idle cash register is available. The number of cashiers to put on duty is an example of a short-run decision about a variable input.

While the number of cash registers is fixed in the short run, the long run offers a supermarket enough time to add checkout lanes or even build a larger store. Hence, in the long run, both labor and capital are variable for a supermarket, factory, or any other firm.

PRODUCT—TOTAL, MARGINAL, AND AVERAGE

total product the firm's total quantity of output.

In the short run, when capital is fixed, the amount of output depends on the amount of labor. The output produced is said to be the *product* of labor, since nothing is produced without workers. **Total product** refers to the total quantity of output produced. We will thus use the terms *total product* and *total output* interchangeably. The additional total product from additional units of labor is termed the *marginal product of labor,* or **marginal product** for short:

marginal product additional output produced by the addition of one more unit of labor; change in output ÷ change in labor.

$$\text{Marginal product} = \frac{\text{Change in total product}}{\text{Change in labor}}$$

In contrast, **average product** is the quantity of output per worker:

$$\text{Average product} = \frac{\text{Total product}}{\text{Total labor}}$$

For example, consider a firm that increases its employment of labor from 100 units of labor to 101 units of labor, and experiences an increase in total product from 50,000 units to 51,000 units. The marginal product of the 101st unit of labor is 1,000 units of output. Average product for 100 units of labor is $\frac{50,000}{100}$, which equals 500 units, and for 101 units of labor is $\frac{51,000}{101}$, which equals approximately 505 units of output.

Notice that average product increased in the preceding example. **Average product will increase when marginal product is greater than the initial average product, decrease when marginal product is less than average product, and remain constant when marginal product is equal to average product.**

The relationship between averages and marginals is more general than just average and marginal product. For instance, consider Joyce, who has an average grade of 82 in her economics course after having taken the first two tests. When she takes the next test—the marginal test—her average grade will increase if her grade is greater than 82, or decrease if it is less than 82. Her average remains the same if she gets exactly 82 on that third test. So, in general, a marginal above average pulls the average up; a marginal below average pulls the average down; and a marginal equal to average will not change the average. That rule applies no matter what the marginals and averages are in reference to.

Marginal product is subject to the **law of diminishing returns,** which states that, **when additional units of labor or any other variable input are added to a fixed input, the marginal product of the variable input must eventually decrease.**

Once a firm reaches the point of diminishing returns, each successive unit of labor will add less and less to total product. This is shown in the shape of total product, as seen in Figure 17-3, where diminishing returns set in at the point so labeled.

average product total quantity of output ÷ total quantity of labor.

law of diminishing returns states that when additional units of labor or any other variable input are added in the short run, the marginal product of the variable input must eventually decrease.

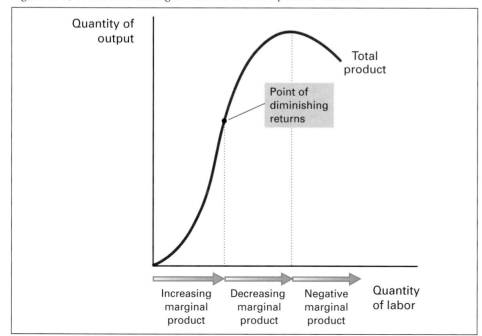

FIGURE 17-3

THE TOTAL PRODUCT OF LABOR CURVE The total product of labor is a short-run relationship between the quantity of output produced and the amount of labor employed. Marginal product is the slope of total product. The law of diminishing returns causes marginal product to decrease at some point, as shown. Marginal product can even become negative, which occurs when total product turns downward so that the slope of total product is negative. In the long run, the firm could vary its capital, which would change total product.

Marginal product equals the slope of total product. To understand why, recall the definition of marginal product, which is the change in total product divided by the change in labor. Also recall that the slope of a curve is found by "rise over run." The "rise" is the change in the variable on the vertical axis—the change in total product in Figure 17-3. The "run" is the change in the variable on the horizontal axis—the change in labor. "Rise over run," the slope of total product, is thus equivalent to marginal product. In the figure, the slope of total product is positive, but decreases (becomes less steep) after the point of diminishing returns. When the slope of total product is decreasing, marginal product must be decreasing as well.

The law of diminishing returns assumes that all labor is of equal quality, which signifies that diminishing returns occur for reasons other than those relating to differences in labor quality. For example, although the 101st unit of labor in the earlier example had a marginal product equal to 1,000 units of output, the 102nd unit of labor will exhibit a marginal product of less than 1,000 units if the firm is past the point of diminishing returns.

The explanation for the law of diminishing returns is found in the commonsense proposition that adding more and more labor to a fixed amount of capital reduces the amount of capital each unit of labor has to work with. Eventually, the effect of less capital per worker reveals itself in the form of diminishing returns. **Because there is a fixed input, the law of diminishing returns applies only in the short run.**

The principle of diminishing returns applies to all types of businesses. For example, Figure 17-4 illustrates marginal and average product for Ali's King-of-Ribs Restaurant.

Ali has a relatively small building. At first, marginal product rises because his employees can specialize. In Ali's case, the major specializations would be the tasks of taking orders, cooking, and cleaning up. After the third worker, the need for specialization is less

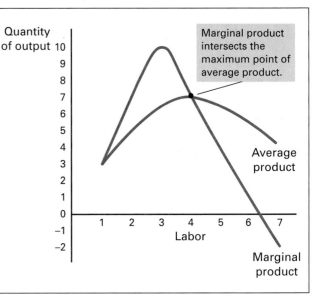

Total, marginal, and average products of labor			
Units of labor	Total product (Quantity of meals per hour)	Marginal product (Change in total product ÷ change in labor)	Average product (Total product ÷ total labor)
0	0	undefined	undefined
1	3	3	3
2	10	7	5
3	20	10	6.7
4	27	7	6.75
5	31	4	6.2
6	32	1	5.3
7	30	−2	4.3

FIGURE 17-4

THE MARGINAL AND AVERAGE PRODUCTS OF LABOR The table shows the calculation of marginal product, which is shown in the graph. For example, when labor increases from 3 to 4 units, total product increases from 20 to 27. This 7-unit increase in total product is the value of marginal product between 3 and 4 units of labor. Note that marginal product becomes a negative value when 7 units of labor are employed. The table also shows the calculation of average product, which is plotted in the graph. For example, average product at 2 units of labor equals 5 because total product ÷ labor equals 10 ÷ 2 = 5. When marginal product is greater than average product, average product will increase. When marginal product is less than average product, average product will decrease.

> ## QUICKCHECK
>
> ### Explain how a student faces the law of diminishing returns.
>
> **Answer:** A student combines ability—an input that is fixed in the short run—with the variable input of time. The output is knowledge as measured by an examination grade. When studying, a point is reached at which each succeeding minute of study time adds less and less to the student's knowledge. Sometimes students press their studying beyond diminishing returns and into negative returns, which start when an additional minute of continuous studying begins to result in mental confusion. Such a student will lament: "I studied too much for the exam."

clear-cut, which puts Ali's restaurant into the region of diminishing returns. For example, the next three workers might "float," relieving the cashier of tending the drive-through window, helping with cleanup, or doing whatever other tasks seem most important at the time. These workers increase Ali's total production, as shown in the total product column, but the marginal product column shows that the increments to output decline.

There is a danger from hiring too many employees. "Too many cooks spoil the ribs," Ali always says, as he imagines excess employees with little to do, chatting and getting in each other's way instead of attending to customers. Suppose Ali mistakenly continues to increase employment to seven workers while keeping his capital constant. In that event, he will reach *negative returns,* in which marginal product is negative. Because output is higher with fewer employees, firms seek to avoid negative returns.

In Figure 17-4, observe that **marginal product intersects average product at the maximum point on average product but in the declining portion of marginal product.** This is because average product is pulled up when marginal product lies above it, and pulled down when marginal product lies below it. **Diminishing returns are associated with the downward-sloping part of marginal product;** negative returns are illustrated by the portion of marginal product that lies below the horizontal axis.

17.4 BUSINESS—ETHICAL IN PRINCIPLE, NOT ALWAYS IN PRACTICE

"He intends only his own gain, and he is in this, as in many other cases, led by an invisible hand to promote an end which was no part of his intention. . . . By pursuing his own interest he frequently promotes that of the society more effectually than when he really intends to promote it."

—Adam Smith, The Wealth of Nations, 1776

The invisible hand Adam Smith describes above is a fundamental concept in economics, which explains how self-interest can be in the public interest. Yet Adam Smith was no advocate of unbridled greed, and had even authored an earlier work, entitled *The Theory of Moral Sentiments* (1759), about morality and virtue. In his renowned *The Wealth of Nations* (1776), Adam Smith made it clear that competition is the key to reining in business self-interest and making sure that the public gets the most for its money. Without competition, Smith thought that firms would join together in a "conspiracy against the public interest." Perhaps he could also have warned us of conspiracies against stockholders' interests by business management and Wall Street insiders.

News of insider trading, misreported profits, bogus stock "buy" recommendations from stockbrokers who were busy selling the stocks they were recommending, excessive salaries, overabundant stock options, and much more has highlighted issues of *business ethics,* the fairness and honesty of business. Unfortunately, the invisible hand is often not present to keep unfairness and dishonesty in check.

In a particularly glaring case, the misrepresentation of Enron Corporation's finances by its auditors camouflaged its deteriorating financial condition, as well as its impending bankruptcy. The indictment and conviction of the auditors, the accounting firm of Arthur Anderson, for obstruction of justice followed within months. The fact that Enron executives were paid $680 million in the year prior to the firm's bankruptcy raised additional ethical and legal issues.

If we cannot rely upon people and businesses to voluntarily act ethically, then at least we can, by the threat of punishment, discourage certain actions by making them illegal. This was the idea behind the legislation to create a new corporate fraud chapter in the federal criminal code, legislation that was unanimously passed by the Senate in July 2002. That legislation, plus additional proposed legislation to stiffen criminal penalties for white-collar crimes, occurred in response to the Enron and other corporate scandals. To put teeth in the new legislation, proposals were made to increase funding for the Securities and Exchange Commission (SEC), the government's watchdog over the stock market.

In spite of regulation of the stock market by the SEC, investors sometimes take it on the chin, even from their brokers. For example, a number of stock brokers increased their profits on "playing the spread" between the bid and ask prices by colluding to keep this spread artificially high. In effect, they were rigging the rules in their favor. When confronted with a class action lawsuit over these practices, these dealers agreed in 1997 to stop colluding and to pay over $1 billion into a settlement fund that would cover the costs of the lawsuit and finance payments to investors who had been harmed.

Laws also protect consumers. Consumer protection laws limit the fraudulent misrepresentation of products by sellers. Consumer safety laws are designed to make sure that the products that we buy do not threaten our safety. Truth-in-lending laws punish lenders who act dishonestly in their dealings with borrowers. Lemon laws are designed to force manufacturers to produce a product that performs the functions it was designed to perform. The antitrust laws govern the behavior of businesses toward their competitors, seeking to ensure that even the little fish can swim with the big sharks of the business world and still survive.

Laws are not always necessary. For example, a few years ago, the owners of some vehicles produced by Ford began to see the paint on their vehicles peeling, which occurred after their warranties had expired. Ford had no legal obligation to assist the owners, who were forced to spend hundreds of dollars each to have their vehicles repainted. Nonetheless, on a case-by-case basis, Ford paid the costs. On the face of it, Ford cut its profit by the amount of the expenses it incurred on behalf of the car owners. However, by having a defect fixed at its own expense, Ford may have been ensuring itself a greater future profit.

A good *reputation* can be critical for the long-term profitability of a firm. Johnson & Johnson, the maker of Tylenol, ensured its good reputation by its actions when someone poisoned bottles of Tylenol that had been sitting on store shelves in 1982 and 1986, resulting in several deaths. The company, at a huge cost, immediately recalled all bottles of Tylenol. The company was praised for its quick action, and Tylenol is as popular today as ever. In contrast, Ford's reputation suffered badly when, in 2001, Ford Explorers were discovered to be equipped with blow-out-prone tires that caused deadly accidents. Although Ford responded to the problem by offering to replace the tires, public opinion had turned against Ford, and the maker of the tires, Bridgestone-Firestone. Ford's chief executive officer, who took the lead in Ford's response to the problem, was subsequently fired.

ACTING ETHICALLY

It is easy to act ethically when doing so contributes to greater profitability, but what about the issues of business ethics that crop up day-to-day? For example, since monitoring within the firm is imperfect, it is often up to employees to be ethical enough to not take credit for other people's work. Other ethical challenges encompass laws and regulations that can sometimes be eluded. Examples include the illicit dumping of toxic wastes, industrial espionage (in which firms steal ideas from one another), and sexual harrassment in the workplace.

How well firms face up to these challenges is a matter of ethics, which are often a part of company policies. Even Enron, in a July 1, 2000, memo to all employees from Ken Lay, Enron's top executive, stated, ". . . We are responsible for conducting the business affairs of the Company in accordance with all applicable laws and in a moral and honest manner." Enron also published a sixty-four-page "Code of Ethics" booklet that was distributed to all employees. Detailed codes of ethics are found in many large businesses, as well as in professional societies, such as the American Accounting Association. Business schools also require their students to study ethics. With business ethics front and center in the business world, the ethical lapses that surface prove all the more disturbing.

Despite all the ethical challenges within business, **the basic nature of business is highly ethical. Rather than being a** *zero-sum game* **in which the winner wins only what the loser loses, business is a** *positive-sum game* **that can bring benefits to all involved.** The reward of profit goes to the owners of firms that are best at responding to consumer wishes. The reward of a high standard of living goes to us all.

1. **In your opinion, what is the greatest ethical problem faced by business people today? What advice could you offer to businesspeople that might promote ethical behavior on their part?**

2. **Should ethics in the business world be a matter of law or of individual conscience? Would your answer be the same if the question pertained to personal ethics? Explain.**

Visit www.prenhall.com/ayers for updates and web exercises on this Explore & Apply topic.

SUMMARY AND LEARNING OBJECTIVES

1. **Identify the three legal forms of business and the advantages and disadvantages of each.**
   - A firm will exist in one of the following legal forms: sole proprietorship, partnership, or corporation. The corporation offers the advantages of limited liability and perpetual existence.
   - Sole proprietorships are easy to start, but saddle their owners with unlimited liability. Partnerships provide access to a partner's funds, but like the proprietorship suffer from the disadvantage of unlimited liability. The corporation has disadvantages, too, in the form of the corporate income tax, and various reporting and procedural requirements not faced by proprietorships and partnerships.

2. **Explain the methods of financing a business.**
   - Financial capital includes personal funds, retained earnings, borrowed funds, and funds raised by issuing stock. Retained earnings, a firm's internal funds, are saved from profits earned by a business. External funds are obtained from investors who buy the firm's new shares of stock, or by borrowing. Borrowing

includes funds borrowed from banks and funds raised by issuing bonds.
   - Existing shares of stock in corporations are bought and sold on stock exchanges. The stock exchanges are secondary markets, meaning that only existing shares of stock are traded there. New issues of stock are sold through public offerings.

3. **Distinguish between accounting profit and economic profit.**
   - Economists assume the goal of the firm is to maximize profit. Total economic profit equals total revenue minus total cost, where total cost includes both explicit and implicit opportunity costs.
   - Accounting profit subtracts only explicit costs from total revenue. Because accounting profit ignores implicit cost, accounting profit will always be greater than economic profit.
   - A firm that maximizes profit may in fact be able to earn an economic profit. Economic profit means that total revenue is greater than total cost. If total revenue is less than total cost, the firm incurs a loss.

- A firm that earns a normal profit but no economic profit receives just enough revenue to cover its implicit opportunity costs. A normal profit ensures that the resources of the firm will stay in their present use. Firms that break even earn zero economic profit, but their revenue is sufficient to provide a normal profit.

- A firm that incurs a loss will eventually go out of business if the losses continue. The reason is that revenue is not enough to cover the amount of implicit costs. In other words, a firm with a loss is not earning a normal profit.

4. **Identify difficulties in maximizing profit that are created by the principal–agent problem.**

- The principal–agent problem exists because employees' goals are not necessarily the same as those of the owners of the firm. Employees and managers may take actions that benefit them at the expense of the firm's profit. Various incentive methods, including bonuses, are used to try to solve the principal–agent problem. Sometimes these incentive methods cause incentive problems of their own.

5. **Relate the key concepts of production, including the law of diminishing returns.**

- A firm's production function relates the amount of inputs used to the amount of output produced. To simplify the study of production, it is assumed that only two inputs, capital and labor, are used in production.

- Production occurs in a short-run and a long-run context. In the short run, at least one input is fixed in quantity. Generally, the fixed input is assumed to be capital. However, in the long run the quantity of capital can vary. Thus, in the long run all inputs are assumed to be variable.

- Total product is the firm's total production. A total product curve shows the amount of output for each amount of the variable input.

- Marginal product is the change in output resulting from a change in input. The marginal product of labor equals the change in total product divided by the change in the quantity of labor.

- Average product is output per unit of input. The average product of labor equals total product divided by the quantity of labor. An average product curve will always be intersected at its maximum point by the marginal product curve.

- The law of diminishing returns states that the marginal product of labor will eventually decrease as more labor is used.

 6. **Recognize and reflect on issues relating to business ethics.**

- Ethical dilemmas occur in the day-to-day operations of a business. Ethical lapses have proven common, as exemplified by the scandals associated with Enron and stock brokers. Many businesses attempt to promote ethical behavior through ethics codes. Professional associations and business schools also promote ethics. The nature of business is ethical since it benefits both consumers and business owners.

KEY TERMS

firm, 434
corporation, 434
stock, 434
bond, 436
profit (economic profit), 438
total revenue, 438
total cost, 438
explicit costs, 438

implicit opportunity costs (implicit costs), 438
normal profit, 439
excess profit, 440
loss, 440
breakeven, 440
principal–agent problem, 441
production function, 442

long run, 442
short run, 442
total product, 442
marginal product, 442
average product, 443
law of diminishing returns, 443

TEST YOURSELF

TRUE OR FALSE

1. Partnerships obtain financing by issuing shares of stock.
2. External funds are a larger source of funds than internal funds for U.S. firms.
3. The value that a firm's capital would have in alternative uses is called an explicit cost.
4. Economists usually assume the goal of a firm is to maximize profits.
5. In the short run, all inputs are variable.

MULTIPLE CHOICE

6. Which of the following is NOT a legal form of business?
   a. Sole proprietorship.
   b. Partnership.
   c. Corporation.
   d. Limited liability.
7. Which of the following types of firms offers its owners protection from personal liability for business debts?
   a. Sole proprietorship.
   b. Partnership.
   c. Corporation.
   d. Limited liability.
8. Startup financing for most small businesses comes from
   a. bank loans.
   b. sale of stock.
   c. issuance of bonds.
   d. personal savings and the savings of family and friends.
9. The stock exchanges are an example of a
   a. primary market.
   b. secondary market.
   c. sole proprietorship.
   d. mutual fund.
10. Explicit costs are
    a. wages and profits.
    b. costs brought on by negative returns in production.
    c. costs that accountants can measure.
    d. costs associated with wasted resources.
11. Suppose a firm earns a return on investment of 5 percent. If investments elsewhere are available paying 8 percent, the firm is
    a. profitable in both an accounting and economic sense.
    b. unprofitable in both an accounting and economic sense.
    c. earning economic profits but not accounting profits.
    d. earning accounting profits but not economic profits.
12. Economic profit equals _____, where normal profit is considered as _____.
    a. total revenue minus total cost; a cost
    b. marginal revenue minus marginal cost; a cost
    c. total revenue minus total cost; revenue
    d. marginal revenue minus marginal cost; revenue
13. When Desico, a producer of drill bits for the oil industry, is said to earn a normal profit, then the firm
    a. earns an economic profit.
    b. incurs an economic loss.
    c. earns just enough to cover its opportunity costs.
    d. will exit the industry.
14. The principal–agent problem occurs when
    a. there is industrial espionage.
    b. a business owner chooses to have no employees but herself.

c. the interests of owners and employees are different.
d. government regulates the stock market.

15. The short run is the
    a. time period in which all inputs are variable.
    b. time period in which all inputs are fixed.
    c. time period in which at least one, but not all, inputs are fixed.
    d. planning horizon.
16. In the long run,
    a. all inputs are fixed.
    b. all inputs are variable.
    c. at least one input is fixed.
    d. one input is variable, while the others are fixed.
17. A firm's total product appears as follows:

Labor	Output
1	2
2	12
3	18
4	20
5	20

Diminishing returns set in with the _____ unit of labor.
    a. second
    b. third
    c. fourth
    d. fifth

18. In Self-Test Figure 17-1, marginal product is positive but decreasing in region
    a. *A*.
    b. *B*.
    c. *C*.
    d. *D*.

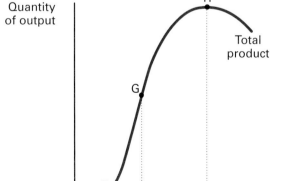

SELF-TEST FIGURE 17-1

19. In Self-Test Figure 17-1, the point of diminishing returns is
    a. *E.*
    b. *F.*
    c. *G.*
    d. *H.*

20. A zero-sum game is one in which
    a. all participants are winners.
    b. all participants are losers.
    c. there are winners and losers and what the losers lose, the winners win.
    d. everyone will refuse to participate since the expected gain is zero.

QUESTIONS AND PROBLEMS

1. *[legal form]* In light of the advantages that corporations possess, why do you think the proprietorship and partnership forms still exist? In your answer, consider the costs and benefits of each form, including the means of financing.

2. *[methods of finance]* List the four methods that a business can use to finance itself. State the advantages and disadvantages of each.

3. *[legal form and finance]* Suppose you wish to start a small lawn care business. Develop a short business plan that states the legal form your business will take and why. Estimate the equipment you will need to start the business and the amount of money each item of equipment will cost. Finally, state in your plan what sources of finance you will pursue to get your business going.

4. *[methods of finance]* What is the difference between internal and external financing? Which type of financing is most commonly used by businesses?

5. *[stock market]* What is a share of stock? Do all corporations issue shares of stock? Do partnerships issue stock? Do sole proprietorships issue stock? Explain.

6. *[stock market]* What is a secondary market? Why is it important to recognize that stock exchanges are secondary markets?

7. *[bond market]* Do all corporations issue bonds? When bonds are issued, what obligations does the issuer take on?

8. *[profit]* State the general definition of profit. What assumption do economists commonly make regarding the firm's behavior toward profit?

9. *[economic profit]* How are implicit costs treated in the calculation of economic profit?

10. *[economic versus accounting profit]* Write two equations where the first equation states accounting profit and the second states economic profit. Why do economists define profit differently from accountants?

11. *[economic profit equation]* Consider the following equation: Economic profit = Total revenue − Total explicit cost − Total implicit opportunity cost = 0. This equation describes a firm that earns no economic profit. Is this firm earning a normal profit? Explain.

12. *[implicit opportunity costs]* Provide examples of plausible opportunity costs in each of the following instances:
    a. $10,000 cash invested in a firm by its owner.
    b. An extra 15 hours of work per week performed for no monetary payment by a business owner.
    c. A business owner's personal automobile used for business purposes.

13. *[normal profit]* When a business earns a normal profit, what is the likelihood that the business will go out of business? Explain.

14. *[principal–agent problem]* What is the principal–agent problem? What does this problem imply about profit maximization?

15. *[inputs]* When economists model production, they assume the firm uses only two inputs. Why do they make this assumption and what are the two inputs?

16. *[long run versus short run]* What is the difference between the long run and the short run? In which of these is there a fixed input? What is the fixed input? Which of these is identified with the planning horizon?

17. *[marginal product]* Is marginal product calculated for the fixed input or the variable input? Why?

18. *[marginal product]* State the definition of marginal product. How does this definition differ from the definition of average product? To which of these does the law of diminishing returns refer?

19. *[diminishing returns]* Suppose you are presented with the three sequences of total product numbers as follows:
    a. 20, 15, 5, 12, 15
    b. 20, 15, 12, 5, 1
    c. 1, 5, 12, 15, 17
    Which illustrates diminishing returns? Why?

20. *[average and marginal product curves]* Graph a typical average product curve and marginal product curve. Be

sure to label the axes of your graph. In the context of marginal product, why does an average product curve rise? In the context of marginal product, why does an average product curve eventually fall? Your graph should show the marginal product and average product curves intersecting at one point. Where is that point?

WORKING WITH GRAPHS AND DATA

1. *[accounting profit versus economic profit]* Use the accounts listed below to answer the questions about the profit of a business.

Total revenue $100,000
Hired labor $25,000
Materials purchased $25,000
Interest that the owner could have
    earned on an alternative investment.............$5,000
Income the owner could have earned by
    renting the firm's building to another
    entrepreneur $4,000
Utility payments $5,000
Income the owner could have earned
    in an alternative business venture $30,000
Cost of shipping the firm's output to buyers $1,000

a. Identify the explicit costs incurred by this business. Why are they explicit costs?

b. Identify the implicit costs incurred by this business. Why are they implicit costs?

c. Assume that this firm has $100,000 in total revenues. How much accounting profit does the firm make? Show your work.

d. How much economic profit (loss) does this firm make? Show your work.

e. If these financial results continue in the long run, will this firm stay in this business?

2. *[total and marginal product]* Use the table of the firm's short-run production function to answer the following questions.

Labor	Total Product	Marginal Product
0	0	
1	4	
2	10	
3	15	
4	19	
5	19	
6	18	

a. Fill in the marginal product column.

b. Draw the total product curve on Graph 17-1(a) and label it TP.

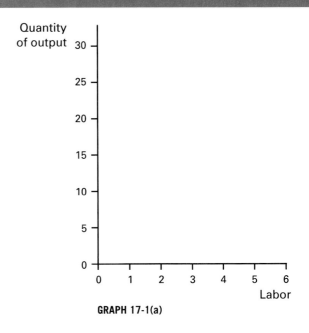

GRAPH 17-1(a)

c. Draw the marginal product curve on Graph 17-1(b) and label it MP.

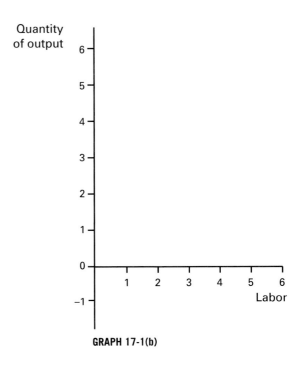

GRAPH 17-1(b)

d. On the "Labor" axis of both graphs identify the range of increasing marginal product and label it "Increasing MP", decreasing marginal product and label it "Decreasing MP", and negative MP and label it "Negative MP."

3. *[marginal and average product]* Use the table of a firm's short-run production function to answer the following questions.

Labor	Total Product	Marginal Product	Average Product
0	0		
1	8		
2	20		
3	30		
4	36		
5	40		
6	42		

a. Fill in the marginal and average product columns.
b. Draw a graph of the marginal product curve labeled MP and the average product curve labeled AP on Graph 17-2.

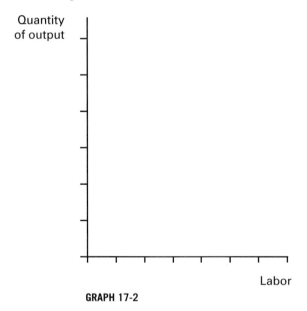

Quantity of output

Labor

GRAPH 17-2

c. Identify the point of diminishing returns as point E. Why does diminishing returns occur?
d. What happens to average product when marginal product is greater than average product?
e. What happens to average product when marginal product is greater than average product?
f. When is average product at a maximum? What is true of average and marginal product at this point?

4. *[accounting profit versus economic profit]* Use the accounts listed below to answer the following questions about the profit of a retail business.

Total revenue $80,000
Hired labor $30,000
Inventory purchased for resale $20,000
Interest that the owner could have earned
  on an alternative investment.......................$2,000
Income the owner could have earned
  by renting the firm's building to
  another entrepreneur.................................$4,000
Income the owner could have earned
  in a different job..$25,000

a. Identify the explicit costs incurred by this business. Why are they explicit costs?
b. Identify the implicit costs incurred by this business. Why are they implicit costs?
c. Assume that this firm has $80,000 in total revenues. How much accounting profit does the firm make? Show your work.
d. How much economic profit (loss) does this firm make? Show your work.
e. If these financial results continue in the long run, will this firm stay in this business?

Visit www.prenhall.com/ayers for Exploring the Web exercises and additional self-test quizzes.

CHAPTER 18

COSTS AND PROFIT-MAXIMIZING OUTPUT

A LOOK AHEAD

Imagine your work and your lifestyle are so intertwined that you cannot separate them no matter how hard you try. You are on the job twenty-four hours a day, seven days a week, working at your own business. Surely this business would pay you well for your dedication. But no, in spite of your best efforts and numerous hardships, you are quite likely to incur losses. Should you quit? This is the dilemma faced by numerous farmers and their families, a dilemma that you will examine in the Explore & Apply section that concludes this chapter.

This chapter is about much more than farming, although farming exemplifies most aspects of running a business. To maximize profit, both farmers and any other business manager must think in terms of costs and revenues. We open the chapter with a detailed look at short-run costs, proceed to the principles of profit maximization, and also discuss the adjustments that a firm faces in the long run in order to maintain profitability.

LEARNING OBJECTIVES

Understanding Chapter 18 will enable you to:
1. **Describe the firm's short-run costs.**
2. **Explain the rule of profit maximization.**
3. **Discuss profit maximization within the context of profit, loss, and shut down.**
4. **Distinguish between economies and diseconomies of scale.**
5. **Describe the factors that motivate U.S. farm policy.**

Explore & Apply

Firms must know their costs of production in order to produce the profit-maximizing quantity of output. As we study cost and profit maximization, the costs you will see will be the economic costs you studied in the previous chapter. As you learned, economic costs include both explicit costs and implicit opportunity costs.

18.1 SHORT-RUN COSTS

To maximize profit, each firm must select its quantity of output. That decision involves considering both costs and revenues. To understand how much output a firm will produce, we first look at short-run costs.

FIXED, VARIABLE, AND SUNK COSTS

fixed cost a cost that does not vary with changes in output.

Fixed inputs are those resources used by a firm that remain constant in amount in the short run. In contrast, the amount of *variable inputs* can change. Firms that produce output incur both fixed and variable costs in the short run, with a **fixed cost** being the expense associated with the use of the firm's fixed inputs. Examples of fixed costs include property taxes, property insurance, rental and lease payments, and executive salaries. These fixed costs exist because the firm uses inputs of real estate, other real property (possibly including office equipment and factory machinery), and executive labor, all of which cannot be increased or decreased in quantity in the short run.

Total fixed cost, the sum of all fixed expenses, remains constant in the short run regardless of the quantity of production. For example, a firm that pays annual expenses of $10,000 in property taxes, $5,000 in property insurance, $15,000 in rent and lease payments, and $175,000 in executive salaries will incur a total fixed cost of $205,000 (= $10,000 + $5,000 + $15,000 + $175,000). Neither increases nor decreases in the firm's quantity of output will change the $205,000 since this expense is unrelated to the firm's quantity of production.

variable cost a cost that varies in the same direction as output.

Variable cost increases as the quantity of output rises and declines as output falls, because a firm's use of variable inputs varies directly with production. Raw materials costs, the wages of hourly labor, and shipping expenses are examples of variable costs. For example, when Dell computes the variable cost of producing a desktop computer, suppose the processor and other components amount to $500, the labor to assemble the computer an additional $100, and the cost of shipping the computer to a buyer another $75. The variable cost of the computer is then the sum of these costs, which equals $675. The more computers Dell sells, the greater the total variable cost. The total variable cost of 100 computers would equal $67,500 (= $675 × 100), but the total variable cost of 1,000 computers would increase to $675,000 (= $675 × 1,000).

Total cost includes *total fixed cost* and *total variable cost*, as follows:

$$\text{Total cost} = \text{Total fixed cost} + \text{Total variable cost}$$

Total cost, like total variable cost, will vary directly with output in the short run. To simplify, we will assume from this point onward that labor is the only variable input and capital the only fixed input. Thus, variable costs are exclusively related to the use of labor (workers) and fixed costs are exclusively related to the use of capital (machines). The principles we will arrive at apply in the more complicated "real world" in which there are many variable and fixed inputs.

sunk cost an irrecoverable cost; irrelevant to decision making.

Some costs that a firm incurs are called **sunk costs,** meaning that they are irreversible—they cannot be recovered. Suppose Mel's Farm Fresh Produce pays an architect $25,000 to design a new produce warehouse, but is unable to obtain the financing to go ahead with construction. The $25,000 is a sunk cost. **Sunk costs are irrelevant to decision making.** Mel will ignore the sunk cost as he makes decisions relating to his firm's existing warehouse, since there is nothing he can do about that cost. Consider another example, a student's decision to drop a college course that doesn't fit well with her schedule. If she drops the course during the first two weeks of the semester, her tuition is refunded. Tuition is not a sunk cost in this case because tuition is recoverable, and so she takes the refund into consideration in making her decision. Once the two-week window of opportunity ends, tuition becomes a sunk cost, and therefore is irrelevant to her decision. She makes her decision then on the basis of her schedule, ignoring the sunk tuition cost.

HOW TO SINK A BUSINESS   *SNAPSHOT*

Some people mistakenly believe that the market value of capital is equal to the cost of producing it. In truth, the value depends upon the capital's ability to generate future profits. No one learned that lesson any harder way than Motorola and other investors in the Iridium satellite network, which spent over $5 billion to place sixty-six satellites into orbit.

   The idea was grand—to have a global cellular phone network accessible from any place at any time. Unfortunately for Iridium, by the time the satellite network was ready to go live, the competitive landscape had changed. The cell phones necessary to link to these satellites weighed too much and cost too much for a mass market to develop. Iridium Corporation went bankrupt and its assets were sold.

   The winning bidder, a company that named itself Iridium Satellite LLC, bought the whole satellite network for a mere $25 million. The bid was accepted because the original $5 billion investment was irrelevant—it was a *sunk cost.* Although the satellites kept spinning in orbit, their costs were sunk, never to be recovered. ◀

RELATING TOTAL PRODUCT TO TOTAL COST

In the short run, with capital fixed in quantity and labor variable, the firm must ask itself how much output to produce and thus how much labor to employ. The answer will depend in part on costs, with costs in turn depending on both the quantity of labor and the *wage rate,* which is the price per unit of that labor.

   To make the decision as to how much labor to employ, the first step is to construct a *labor requirements curve,* which shows the amount of labor needed to produce any given quantity of output. The labor requirements curve is nothing more than the total product curve you studied in the previous chapter with the axes interchanged, as shown in Figure 18-1, minus the portion for which marginal product would be negative. Otherwise, the relationship between labor and output in these two graphs is identical.

   A firm's total variable cost of output will equal the labor requirement for that output multiplied by the wage rate:

$$\text{Total variable cost} = \text{Wage rate} \times \text{Labor}$$

This equation shows that total variable cost equals the cost of labor employed because we assume that labor is the only variable input. Likewise, with capital as the only fixed input, we have:

$$\text{Total fixed cost} = \text{Per unit cost of capital} \times \text{Amount of capital employed}$$

   As seen in Figure 18-2, the shape of total variable cost is identical to that of the labor requirements curve in the prior figure. The only difference is that the vertical axis is now denominated in dollars, rather than units of labor.

   Figure 18-2 also shows total cost and total fixed cost. Total fixed cost is constant at all outputs. Thus, the total fixed cost curve is flat, with a slope equal to zero. When total fixed cost and total variable cost are added to obtain total cost, the total cost curve appears with the same shape as the total variable cost curve. This means that the slopes

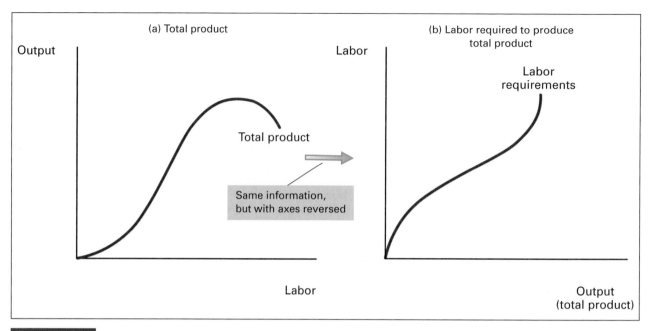

FIGURE 18-1

LABOR REQUIREMENTS CURVE Total labor requirements for each level of output are revealed by looking at the total product curve from a different perspective. The same information is contained in both the total product curve shown in (a) and the labor requirements curve shown in (b). The declining portion of total product is not relevant to labor requirements, because the firm will not hire workers who reduce total output.

FIGURE 18-2

TOTAL COST AND ITS COMPONENTS Total variable cost equals the wage rate × labor requirements, and so has the same shape as the labor requirements curve. So does total cost, which is the sum of total variable cost and total fixed cost. Since fixed costs do not change with output, total fixed cost appears as a flat line. Marginal cost is the slope of the total cost curve or, equivalently, the slope of the total variable cost curve. Marginal cost is minimized where this slope is least, as shown.

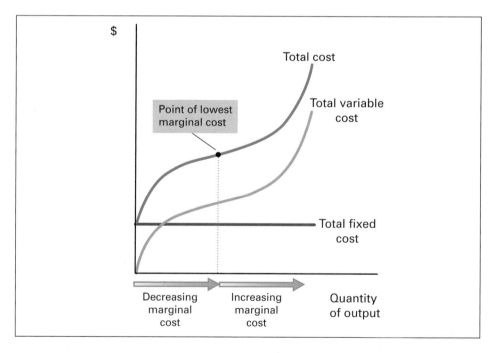

of both total cost and total variable cost are identical. The total variable cost curve starts at the origin, while the total cost curve starts at the point where the total fixed cost curve intersects the vertical axis.

MARGINAL COST AND AVERAGE COST

Marginal cost is the added cost of an additional unit of output, computed by taking the change in total cost and dividing it by the change in the quantity of output. Marginal cost is also called *incremental cost* because it measures the additions to total cost of one-unit increments in output. To take a simple example, if a bakery's total cost of producing 100 cinnamon rolls is $100 and the total cost of producing 101 cinnamon rolls is $101, then the marginal cost of the additional roll is $1. To continue the example, suppose that pushing the production of cinnamon rolls from 101 rolls to 201 rolls pushes total cost up from $101 to $251. In this case output has increased by 100 units. Since total cost has increased by $150, each additional unit of output costs $1.50 (= $150 ÷ 100). Thus, the marginal cost equals $1.50 in the range of output between 101 and 201 rolls.

> **marginal cost** the change in total cost that occurs when there is a one-unit change in output.

Marginal cost is also equal to the slope of the total cost curve, as shown in Figure 18-2. This interpretation of marginal cost requires you to recall that a slope is the "rise over the run." In other words, the slope of a curve is the change in the variable on the vertical axis divided by the change in the variable on the horizontal axis. Since a graph of total cost measures total cost on the vertical axis and the quantity of output on the horizontal axis, the change in total cost divided by the change in quantity is the slope of the total cost curve. It is also the definition of marginal cost, which you can confirm by taking another look at the definition of marginal cost in the first sentence in this section.

Each of the following is a different way to express marginal cost:

■ Change in total cost ÷ Change in quantity of output
■ Change in total variable cost ÷ Change in quantity of output
■ Slope of total cost
■ Slope of total variable cost

The change in total cost is identical to the change in total variable cost because the only other component of total cost is total fixed cost, and that does not vary with output. For the same reason, the slope of total cost and the slope of total variable cost are equal.

In addition to presenting costs in total or at the margin, costs are often stated per unit, meaning on average. Specifically, **average cost** equals total cost divided by the quantity of output:

> **average cost** per-unit cost; total cost divided by the quantity of output; also called average total cost.

$$\text{Average cost} = \frac{\text{Total cost}}{\text{Quantity of output}}$$

Average cost is also called *average total cost* because it is the total of both the fixed and variable components of average costs:

$$\text{Average cost} = \text{Average fixed cost} + \text{Average variable cost}$$

where

$$\text{Average fixed cost} = \frac{\text{Total fixed cost}}{\text{Quantity of output}}$$

and

> **average variable cost** variable cost per unit; total variable cost divided by the quantity of output.

$$\textbf{Average variable cost} = \frac{\text{Total variable cost}}{\text{Quantity of output}}$$

FIGURE 18-3

MARGINAL AND AVERAGE COSTS
Typical shapes of marginal cost, average cost, and average variable cost are as shown. Average fixed cost is the difference between average cost and average variable cost at each quantity. Marginal cost intersects the minimum points of both the average variable cost and average cost curves.

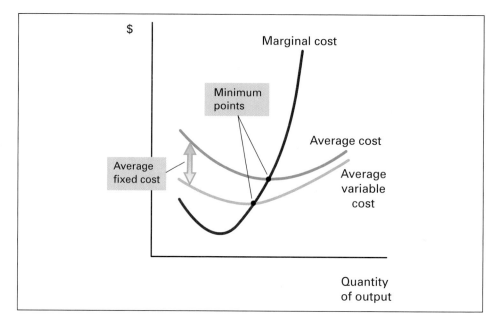

Figure 18-3 shows typical marginal cost, average cost, and average variable cost curves. Marginal cost first falls, and then rises, as labeled in Figure 18-3. **Marginal cost intersects both average cost and average variable cost at their respective minimum points.** The difference between the average variable cost and the average cost curves is average fixed cost.

Average cost, like average variable cost, decreases before reaching a minimum and then increases. Notice that average variable cost begins to increase before average cost. Average cost includes the effect of average fixed cost, which is constantly declining as output increases. Ultimately, the downward pull of average fixed cost is offset enough by the upward pull of average variable cost so that average cost begins to increase.

COMPUTING COSTS

Observe the cost calculations performed by Wendy Webster, owner of WW Wholesale Flour, and presented in the table in Figure 18-4. The first column of the table shows various quantities of output, stopping at seven tons of flour. In the second column, Wendy has calculated her firm's total fixed cost and found that it equals $200. The third column shows her computation of total variable cost. When output equals zero, total variable cost also equals zero. As output increases, so does total variable cost. In the fourth column total fixed cost and total variable cost have been added to obtain total cost. Notice that when output equals zero, total cost equals $200, which is the amount of total fixed cost. Total cost and total fixed cost are always the same when quantity equals zero because total variable cost equals zero at that quantity. Like total variable cost, total cost increases as output increases. Part (a) of Figure 18-4 is a graph that shows the three total cost concepts in the form of a bar chart. Observe that the total fixed cost in each bar is the same height, indicating that total fixed cost does not change.

Column (e) in the table in Figure 18-4 shows the computation of marginal cost. Note that marginal cost initially decreases as output increases. Marginal cost reaches a minimum of $25 before starting to increase. The last three columns in the Figure 18-4 table show the three kinds of average cost. The first is average fixed cost, which will decrease as quantity increases. The decrease in average fixed cost occurs because the constant amount of total

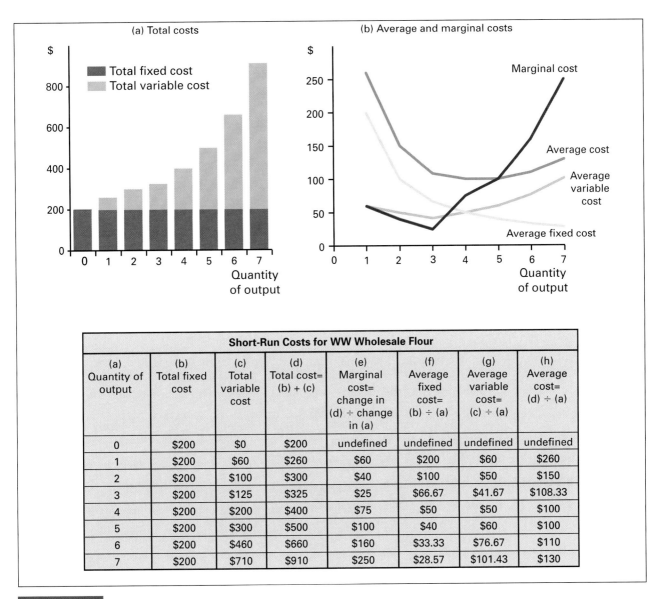

Short-Run Costs for WW Wholesale Flour							
(a) Quantity of output	(b) Total fixed cost	(c) Total variable cost	(d) Total cost= (b) + (c)	(e) Marginal cost= change in (d) ÷ change in (a)	(f) Average fixed cost= (b) ÷ (a)	(g) Average variable cost= (c) ÷ (a)	(h) Average cost= (d) ÷ (a)
0	$200	$0	$200	undefined	undefined	undefined	undefined
1	$200	$60	$260	$60	$200	$60	$260
2	$200	$100	$300	$40	$100	$50	$150
3	$200	$125	$325	$25	$66.67	$41.67	$108.33
4	$200	$200	$400	$75	$50	$50	$100
5	$200	$300	$500	$100	$40	$60	$100
6	$200	$460	$660	$160	$33.33	$76.67	$110
7	$200	$710	$910	$250	$28.57	$101.43	$130

FIGURE 18-4

SHORT-RUN COSTS FOR WW WHOLESALE FLOUR The table shows the components of cost for this sample firm. Part (a) shows how total cost is divided into total fixed cost and total variable cost. Note that, at a quantity of 0, total fixed cost is the only component of total cost. Part (b) shows how the data from the table translates into marginal and average cost curves.

fixed cost is divided by larger quantities of output. In contrast, average variable cost first decreases, reaches a minimum, then increases. Average cost also initially decreases before it reaches a minimum, and then increases. Part (b) of Figure 18-4 is a graph that shows the marginal and average cost data in the table plotted as cost curves.

PRODUCTIVITY AND COST

When labor productivity rises, costs fall. When productivity falls, costs rise. This common sense applies to marginal cost and average variable cost in relation to marginal product and average product, respectively. For example, the smaller the marginal product of an additional worker, the greater the marginal cost of additional output. By the same token, the lower the average product of the employees, the greater the average cost of the output that is produced. Thus, as can be seen in Figures 18-3 and 18-4, the general appearance of the marginal and average cost curves is opposite to the corresponding marginal and average product curves shown in the previous chapter. The result is that marginal cost is shaped like the letter *J*, while average cost is shaped more like the letter *U*. Average cost is at a minimum where it is intersected by marginal cost.

The wage rate for the marginal unit of labor divided by the output of that labor reveals the marginal cost per unit of output. Thus, the lower is marginal productivity, the higher is marginal cost. For example, if an extra hour of work costs $10 and yields five additional widgets, then each extra widget costs $2. This $2 is the marginal cost, as follows:

$$\text{Marginal cost} = \frac{\text{Change in total cost}}{\text{Change in quantity of output}} = \frac{\$10}{5} = \$2$$

Since the change in total cost for the extra hour of work is simply the wage rate, and the change in quantity is the worker's marginal product, marginal cost can be expressed as follows:

$$\text{Marginal cost} = \frac{\text{Wage rate}}{\text{Marginal product}}$$

In our example, if marginal product were to rise to ten widgets per hour, marginal cost would fall to $10/10 = $1. Alternatively, if marginal product were to fall to four widgets per hour, marginal cost would rise to $10/4 = $2.50. More generally, **marginal cost varies inversely with marginal product.**

Similar reasoning shows that **average variable cost varies inversely with average product.** Specifically:

$$\text{Average variable cost} = \frac{\text{Wage rate}}{\text{Average product}}$$

For example, if the wage rate equals $10 per hour and the average product is one widget per hour, then the average variable cost of producing a widget would be $10. However, if productivity were to rise to five widgets per hour, the average variable cost of producing a widget would be $2. Likewise, if workers on average produced ten widgets per hour, the average variable cost would be $1 per widget.

A change in the wage rate would also affect both marginal cost and average variable cost. For example, increasing the wage rate would increase the numerator in each of the previous two offset equations, which would have the effect of increasing both marginal cost and average variable cost. Average cost would likewise increase, since average cost adds together average variable cost and average fixed cost. The result would be a shift upward in both the marginal cost curve and the average cost curve, such as shown in Figure 18-5. Correspondingly, a decrease in wage rates would decrease costs and shift down both the marginal cost curve and the average cost curve.

QUICKCHECK

Explain why marginal cost must eventually rise.

Answer: As the productivity of an additional worker falls, the marginal cost per unit of that worker's output must rise, because marginal cost = wage rate ÷ marginal product.

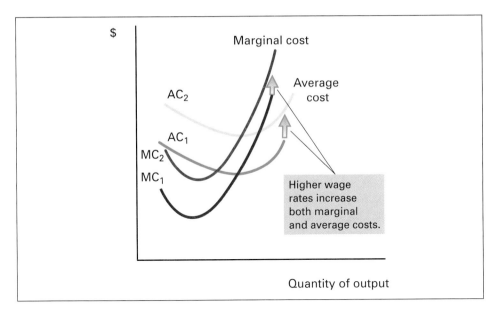

FIGURE 18-5

EFFECT OF HIGHER WAGE RATES
The average and marginal cost curves shift upward when input prices rise. Were input prices to fall, both curves would shift downward.

18.2 MAXIMUM PROFIT IN THE SHORT RUN

Firms produce to earn profit, which is equal to total revenue minus total cost. What quantity of production will maximize profit? The answer lies in comparing costs and revenues.

PROFIT MAXIMIZATION—MAKING DECISIONS AT THE MARGIN

Many firms have no choice but to sell their output for the going market price. For example, if you were to plant a field of soybeans, you would know that the marketplace determines the price. You could charge more than the market price, but you would not sell any soybeans. You could charge less than the market price, but there would be no reason to forgo the extra revenue. In other words, the price you receive would be at the mercy of the marketplace and you would be called a **price taker.**

For price takers, every additional unit of output adds an amount of revenue equal to the market price of the output. This additional income is termed **marginal revenue.**

$$\text{Marginal revenue} = \frac{\text{Change in total revenue}}{\text{Change in quantity of output}}$$

and for price-taking firms:

$$\text{Marginal revenue} = \text{Market price}$$

Suppose WW Wholesale Flour is a price taker. In this case, the market price of a ton of flour is the firm's marginal revenue. Any time another ton of flour is sold that provides marginal revenue greater than its marginal cost, the firm's profit will rise. When the marginal cost of another ton of flour is greater than the marginal revenue, profit will fall. We can illustrate these ideas by referring to Figure 18-6, which adds revenue and profit data to the table in Figure 18-4.

price taker a firm that must sell its output at the market price.

marginal revenue the change in total revenue that occurs when there is a one-unit change in output.

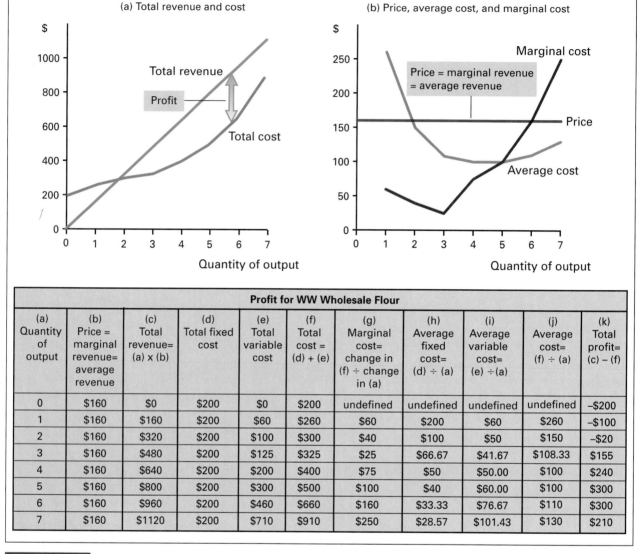

FIGURE 18-6

PROFIT FOR WW WHOLESALE FLOUR Profit is the difference between total revenue and total cost, as seen in column (k). It is also the difference between total revenue and total cost in part (a). The profit-maximizing quantity is given by the intersection of price and marginal cost in part (b).

The table "Profit for WW Wholesale Flour":

(a) Quantity of output	(b) Price = marginal revenue = average revenue	(c) Total revenue= (a) x (b)	(d) Total fixed cost	(e) Total variable cost	(f) Total cost = (d) + (e)	(g) Marginal cost= change in (f) ÷ change in (a)	(h) Average fixed cost= (d) ÷ (a)	(i) Average variable cost= (e) ÷ (a)	(j) Average cost= (f) ÷ (a)	(k) Total profit= (c) − (f)
0	$160	$0	$200	$0	$200	undefined	undefined	undefined	undefined	−$200
1	$160	$160	$200	$60	$260	$60	$200	$60	$260	−$100
2	$160	$320	$200	$100	$300	$40	$100	$50	$150	−$20
3	$160	$480	$200	$125	$325	$25	$66.67	$41.67	$108.33	$155
4	$160	$640	$200	$200	$400	$75	$50	$50.00	$100	$240
5	$160	$800	$200	$300	$500	$100	$40	$60.00	$100	$300
6	$160	$960	$200	$460	$660	$160	$33.33	$76.67	$110	$300
7	$160	$1120	$200	$710	$910	$250	$28.57	$101.43	$130	$210

Referring to Figure 18-6, when the market price of flour is $160 per ton, selling the fifth ton of flour increases profit by $60 because the additional revenue equals the price of $160, while the additional cost is the marginal cost of $100. By a similar calculation, selling the seventh ton subtracts $90 from profit. The firm can do no better than to produce 6 tons, exactly. By producing 6 tons, economic profit at WW Wholesale Flour will be $300, the difference between the total revenue of $960 and the total cost of $660.

Figure 18-6(a) illustrates profit maximization by plotting the total revenue and total cost curves. In that graph profit is shown as the difference between the total revenue and total cost curves. At a quantity of 6 tons of flour, we can see that profit is maximized because no other quantity could increase the vertical distance between the curves. In our example, 5 tons and 6 tons generate the same profit, since the marginal cost of adding the sixth ton just equals its marginal revenue. Figure 18-6(b) illustrates profit maximization with the average and marginal cost curves. The market price, which is equal to marginal revenue for a price taker, intersects marginal cost at 6 tons of flour.

The reasoning we have followed allows the firm to identify the profit-maximizing quantity of flour to produce by following the **rule of profit maximization:**

> ### Rule of profit maximization
> Produce to the point at which marginal revenue equals marginal cost.

rule of profit maximization produce to the point where marginal revenue equals marginal cost.

If the market price of flour changes, WW's output could change. Suppose the price of flour rises to $250. By referring to the marginal cost data for WW Wholesale Flour, we can apply the rule of profit maximization to discover that this increase in market price would cause the firm to expand production to seven tons. Total revenue would equal $250 × 7 = $1,750. By subtracting the total cost of $910 from total revenue, we arrive at the total profit of $840.

The rule of profit maximization is followed any time firms adjust their outputs. Most generally, it means that the firm should take an action whenever that action adds more to revenue than to cost. Specifically, **if an increase in output comes with higher marginal revenue than marginal cost, the firm should produce more. If marginal cost exceeds marginal revenue, the firm should produce less. The only time it should be satisfied is when the two are equal.** If no equality is possible, the rule is to keep producing more as long as marginal cost does not exceed marginal revenue.

The rule of profit maximization reveals the most preferred output at any firm, whether a price taker or not and along whatever dimension output might take. For example, it determines what items are on the menu at Ali's King-of-Ribs Restaurant. Remember Ali from the last chapter? Ali will do anything he can think of for which marginal revenue exceeds marginal cost, and cease doing anything for which marginal cost exceeds marginal revenue. If Ali thinks that offering diners barbecued chicken will add more to total revenue than it adds to total cost, he will offer it. He will adjust the thermostat until his expected marginal cost equals marginal revenue in terms of the temperature of his restaurant. Ali will even provide heated, moist after-dinner napkins if he thinks that the marginal revenue from doing so would exceed the marginal cost. When he is finished, Ali will find that, to a close approximation, marginal revenue will equal marginal cost along all dimensions of his output.

As noted at the start of this section, marginal revenue to a price-taking firm equals the market price. Because price and marginal revenue are equal for a price taker, we can restate the rule of profit maximization accordingly:

> ### Rule of profit maximization for a price taker
> Produce to the point where price equals marginal cost.

The general case of profit maximization by a price taker is illustrated in Figure 18-7. Marginal revenue is shown in the figure by the horizontal line that also portrays the market price. Equating the market price to marginal cost leads to a profit-maximizing quantity, as indicated in the figure. If average cost at this quantity is less than average revenue, given by the market price, the firm will be earning a profit. If average cost at the profit-maximizing output exceeds price, the firm will incur a loss. Because Figure 18-7 shows that price exceeds average cost at the profit-maximizing output, this firm is earning a profit. In the next section we will compare the profitable firm to a firm incurring a loss.

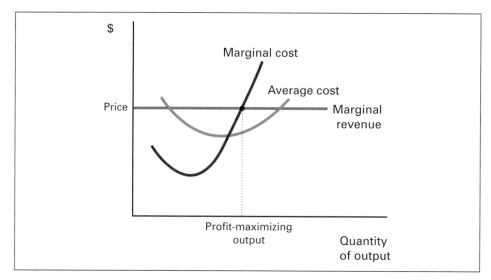

FIGURE 18-7

PROFIT MAXIMIZATION The profit-maximizing output occurs when marginal cost equals marginal revenue. For a price-taking firm, marginal revenue is identical to the market price. This firm is profitable, because price exceeds average cost at the profit-maximizing output.

QUICKCHECK

Would a firm change its output if its marginal revenue exceeds marginal cost? Explain.

Answer: The firm would produce additional output until it gets to the quantity for which marginal revenue equals marginal cost. Until it reaches that quantity, additional output would add more to revenue than to cost and would thus increase profit.

SNAPSHOT   **BURGLARY IS THEIR BUSINESS**

"Crime doesn't pay!" Law enforcement officials everywhere seek to drill that message into the heads of potential criminals. Yes, criminals do think about such things. For example, like businesses in search of profit, thieves plan to keep on stealing only so long as their expected marginal revenue exceeds their expected marginal cost. If punishment becomes more certain or more severe, the expected marginal cost of burglary rises and fewer burglaries are likely to occur.

The difference between legitimate business and thievery is quite simply that businesses do not rob you (some popular complaints notwithstanding). Businesses can only get your money if you offer it voluntarily in exchange for something of value to you. Thieves ignore that nicety. ◄

PROFIT, LOSS, AND SHUT DOWN

When a firm sells all of its output at a single price, that price is the firm's revenue per unit of that output, otherwise known as *average revenue.*

$$\text{Average revenue} = \frac{\text{Total revenue}}{\text{Quantity of output}} = \text{Price}$$

Multiplying average revenue by the quantity of output equals total revenue. By the same token, multiplying average cost by the quantity of output would yield total cost. Thus, a firm's total profit can be expressed as:

$$\text{Profit} = \text{Quantity of output} \times (\text{Average revenue} - \text{Average cost})$$

or, equivalently,

$$\text{Profit} = \text{Quantity} \times (\text{Price} - \text{Average cost})$$

Figure 18-8(a) illustrates a profitable firm. It produces the profit-maximizing output, given by the intersection of marginal cost and marginal revenue (price). The vertical difference between price and average cost at the quantity of output the firm produces is the *average profit* per unit of output. When average profit is multiplied by the quantity produced, the result equals total profit, as shown by the area of the shaded rectangle. This computation applies the length times width formula for the area of a rectangle.

WW Wholesale Flour, presented in Figure 18-6, is similar to the firm in Figure 18-8(a). With the market price of $160 and an average cost of $110, WW Wholesale Flour earns an average profit of $50, which when multiplied by the profit-maximizing quantity of 6, equals the total profit of $300.

Figure 18-8(b) shows a market price that just equals the firm's minimum point on average cost, which would imply that total revenue and total cost would be equal at that point. Such a situation is called *breakeven* and results in zero economic profits. Because total revenue is enough to pay implicit costs, the firm earns a *normal profit*.

If the price were to fall below the breakeven level, the firm would incur losses. **A firm will experience a loss when the price falls below the minimum value of average cost. When a firm operates at a loss, it will seek to minimize the loss.** The *rule of loss minimization* is the same as the rule of profit maximization:

> ### Rule of loss minimization
> Produce to the point where marginal revenue equals marginal cost.

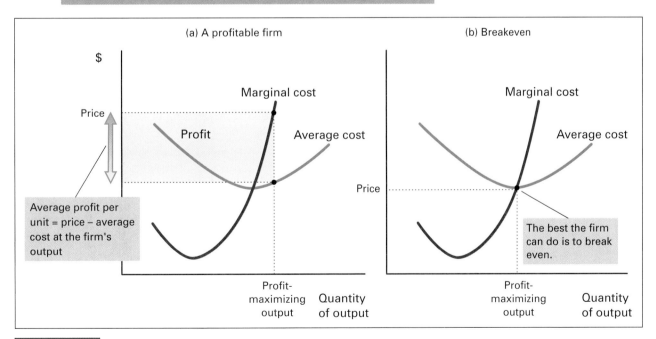

(a) A profitable firm   (b) Breakeven

Average profit per unit = price – average cost at the firm's output

The best the firm can do is to break even.

FIGURE 18-8

PROFIT This firm maximizes profit by choosing the quantity of output for which marginal cost equals price, which is also its marginal revenue. At that chosen quantity, the firm subtracts its average cost from price to obtain its average profit per unit. Total profit is computed by multiplying the per-unit profit by quantity, and is shown by the shaded rectangle labeled "Profit" in (a). In (b), the best the firm can do is breakeven, at which price just equals the minimum point on average cost and economic profit is zero.

> ### QUICKCHECK
>
> **What market price would result in WW Wholesale Flour breaking even? What quantity would the firm produce at that market price?**
>
> *Answer:* The breakeven price equals $100. A firm will break even when the price equals the minimum value of average cost. For WW Wholesale Flour the minimum value of average cost is $100. A market price of $100 would mean that marginal revenue also equals $100. Following the rule of profit maximization, setting the marginal revenue equal to marginal cost means selecting an output of 5 tons of flour. Total revenue and total cost both equal $500 at that output. At a $100 market price this is the best the firm can do.

FIGURE 18-9

A FIRM WITH A LOSS This firm minimizes its loss by producing to where marginal cost equals marginal revenue (price). If price dropped below the minimum point on average variable cost, it would follow the shutdown rule and cease production, losing its total fixed cost.

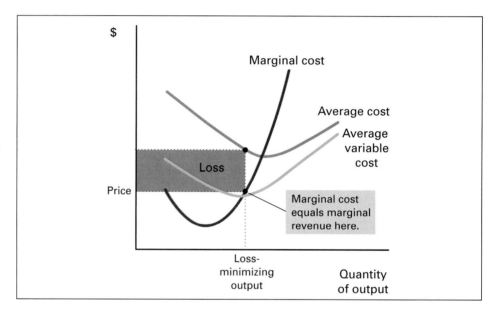

Figure 18-9 depicts the same firm as in Figure 18-8. The only difference is that the firm is now facing a loss because of a drop in the market price below the price shown in Figure 18-8(b). While the firm still produces the quantity for which marginal cost equals marginal revenue, that quantity is now smaller than it was when the market price was higher. The firm has minimized its loss, the area of the shaded rectangle in Figure 18-9. This area is computed similarly to the area of the shaded rectangle in Figure 18-8 except that the market price is shown as less than average cost in Figure 18-9.

$$\text{Loss} = \text{Quantity} \times (\text{Price} - \text{Average cost})$$

Suppose that the market price of flour fell to $75. WW Wholesale Flour will operate at a loss because this price is less than average cost. What output will the firm produce in order to minimize the loss? Marginal cost will equal the marginal revenue of $75 at 4 tons of flour. The loss will equal $100, the difference between the total revenue of $300 and the total cost of $400. **When there is a loss, the computation of profit results in a negative value.**

A profit-maximizing firm will never lose more than the amount of its total fixed cost. Whether the firm is profitable or operates at a loss, it will determine its quantity of output by equating marginal revenue to marginal cost. However, **when price drops so low that revenues are insufficient to pay variable costs, the firm can avoid those costs by ceasing production altogether.** If the firm ceases producing output but retains the capital that would allow it to resume production later, the firm is said to be **shut down.** Since fixed costs must be paid even if the firm produces nothing, **shutdown results in a loss that is equal to the firm's fixed cost.** The *shutdown rule* is as follows:

> ### Shutdown rule
> Shut down if total revenue is less than total variable cost.

By dividing both total revenue and total variable cost by the quantity of output, the shutdown rule can equivalently be stated in terms of average revenue and average variable cost. For a firm that charges a single price, this shutdown rule thus becomes:

> ### Shutdown rule in terms of price
> Shut down if price is less than average variable cost.

When price falls that low, shutting down minimizes the loss, which is limited to fixed cost, which still must be paid.

Price could fall so low that WW Wholesale Flour might shut down. We can identify the *shutdown price* for the firm by checking for the minimum value of average variable cost in Figure 18-6. The table shows that $41.67 is the minimum of average variable cost. Thus, any price below $41.67 will cause WW Wholesale Flour to shut down in order to minimize the loss. For example, let's suppose that the price of flour drops to $25. Were the firm to blindly apply the rule of profit maximization in this case, checking the data in Figure 18-6 reveals the price of $25 equals marginal cost at 3 tons of flour and that total cost is $325 at that output level. Because the total revenue from selling 3 tons of flour at $25 per ton is only $75, the loss would equal $250. By shutting down, the loss can be cut to only $200, the amount of total fixed cost.

The shutdown rule identifies the only exception to the rule of equating marginal cost to marginal revenue. **Shutdown occurs in the short run.** If a firm foresees continuing losses over the long run, it will **exit** the industry, meaning that it will go out of business or change its line of business. This action is the opposite to the **entry** of new firms, which would occur if the industry appears profitable. **Entry and exit occur in the long run.**

Table 18-1 summarizes the revenue and cost conditions that lead a profit-maximizing firm to make the output decisions it does. The revenue and cost comparisons in the table are

shut down when a firm produces no output in order to minimize its loss, which equals total fixed cost; occurs in the short run.

exit when a firm goes out of business or changes its line of business; occurs in the long run.

entry when a firm first opens for business; occurs in the long run.

TABLE 18-1 FOUR OUTCOMES OF SHORT-RUN PROFIT MAXIMIZATION

COMPARISON OF REVENUE AND COST	SET MARGINAL REVENUE = MARGINAL COST AND PRODUCE?	OUTCOME
Price > Average cost or Total revenue > Total cost	Yes	Profit, maximized
Price < Average cost, and Price > Average variable cost or Total revenue < Total cost, and Total revenue > Total variable cost	Yes	Loss, minimized
Price = Average cost or Total revenue = Total cost	Yes	Breakeven (normal profit)
Price < Average variable cost or Total revenue < Total variable cost	No, shutdown	Loss, minimized (equal to total fixed cost)

QUICKCHECK

Suppose a price-taking firm produces 10 units of output. The market price of its output equals $100 per unit. At 10 units of output, average cost equals $105 and average variable cost equals $101. How much profit (or loss) does this firm make? Is the firm maximizing profit (or minimizing loss)?

Answer: Total revenue equals price (average revenue) multiplied by quantity, which is $1,000 in this case. Total cost equals average cost multiplied by quantity, which is $1,050. The firm loses $50. This firm is NOT minimizing its loss, because price is less than average variable cost. By shutting down, the firm would lose the amount of total fixed cost, which is $40. Total fixed cost is computed by first taking the difference between average cost and average variable cost in order to obtain average fixed cost. This computation shows average fixed cost equals $4 ($105 − $101 = $4). When average fixed cost is multiplied by quantity, total fixed cost is obtained ($4 × 10 = $40). This firm should shut down to minimize its loss.

first stated in terms of price and the relevant average cost. By multiplying both the price and the cost by the quantity of output, each comparison is restated in terms of total revenue and the relevant total cost.

18.3 LONG-RUN CHOICES

The long run is the period of time it takes for all inputs to become variable. Since no production can occur without at least some inputs fixed in the short run, such as equipment and a place to use it in, the long run is also termed the *planning horizon*. The firm will choose from different technologies, requiring different proportions of various sorts of capital and labor.

ECONOMIES AND DISECONOMIES OF SCALE

long-run average cost per-unit cost when all inputs are variable.

The production characteristics of a firm in the short run are determined by decisions made in the long run, before the *scale*—size—of the firm is selected. Changing the firm's scale can change its **long-run average cost**—cost per unit of output when all inputs are variable. When the long-run average cost drops as the firm proportionally expands its use of all its inputs, then it experiences **economies of scale,** also called *increasing returns to scale.* For example, doubling the size of a firm might allow it to more than double the amount of output. When the long-run average cost increases as the firm proportionally expands the use of all its inputs, it experiences **diseconomies of scale,** also called *decreasing returns to scale.* This situation might occur if the organization grows beyond a size that can easily be managed.

economies of scale when increasing all inputs causes a more-than-proportional increase in output; associated with declining long-run average cost; also called increasing returns to scale.

diseconomies of scale when increasing all inputs leads to a less-than-proportional increase in output; associated with increasing long-run average cost; also called decreasing returns to scale.

Competitive pressures motivate firms to achieve economies of scale and avoid diseconomies of scale. When all economies of scale have been achieved and diseconomies averted, the firm is said to experience **constant returns to scale.** There is usually a range of possible firm sizes that exhibit constant returns to scale. Within this range, a proportional change in all inputs leads to the same proportional change in output. For example, if this region of constant returns to scale is sufficiently large, doubling the amount of inputs will double the amount of output. Table 18-2 summarizes the response of output according to the type of returns to scale, assuming that all inputs in production double.

constant returns to scale when increasing all inputs increases output by the same proportion; associated with constant long-run average cost.

TABLE 18-2 RETURNS TO SCALE AND RESPONSE OF OUTPUT

TYPE OF RETURNS TO SCALE	WHEN ALL INPUTS DOUBLE, OUTPUT:
Economies of scale (increasing returns to scale)	More than doubles
Diseconomies of scale (decreasing returns to scale)	Less than doubles
Constant returns to scale	Doubles

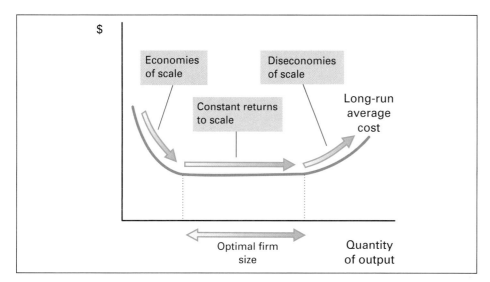

FIGURE 18-10

LONG-RUN AVERAGE COST The region of constant returns to scale reveals which size firms in an industry will have the lowest costs. Firms operating outside this region may find themselves at a cost disadvantage to competitors.

Price takers seek to reach constant returns to scale, because such firms have the lowest possible per-unit costs, which gives them a competitive advantage over other firms that have not achieved constant returns to scale. The relationship between the scale of production and possible economies, diseconomies, or constant returns to scale is illustrated in Figure 18-10. Economies of scale are associated with decreasing long-run average cost, diseconomies of scale with increasing long-run average cost, and constant returns to scale with constant long-run average cost.

IDENTIFYING ECONOMIES OF SCALE

Businesses can often identify any possible economies of scale by asking some commonsense questions as the firm grows in size. Economies of scale would be associated with affirmative answers to any of these questions:

- Would a larger factory allow a more productive layout of machines?
- Can larger-scale machines be found that produce the output more cheaply than current machines?
- Can jobs be broken down into a narrower range of tasks so that greater specialization of labor can be achieved?
- Will suppliers give discounts for the larger orders that will be placed in the future?

Technological change can shift the long-run average cost curve downward by leading to cost-saving innovations in production techniques. In choosing whether to adopt new technologies, the same principle applies as in any business decision. The goal is to maximize profit. If a firm expects the marginal revenue from an action to exceed the marginal cost of that action, the rule says, "Do it!" If not, don't.

SNAPSHOT

BATTLING OVER COSTS—THE $2 BILLION STRIKE AT GENERAL MOTORS

If being big was all that was needed to attain economies of scale, General Motors should have been the lowest-cost producer in the U.S. automobile industry in the 1990s. GM was the biggest auto producer, but its costs were reportedly the highest of the big three automakers. Did GM reach the region of diseconomies of scale, being just too big to manage, or was it merely sluggish about capturing cost savings?

GM management spent much of the decade working to implement the efficiencies that should come with GM's size. One management initiative was *outsourcing*, the practice of buying parts from other companies when it is cheaper to do so. Because outsourcing reduces the number of union jobs in GM plants, GM workers went on strike in 1998 to protest it. That strike cost GM about $2.2 billion before it was settled. The settlement was a victory for GM, allowing it a free hand to eliminate hundreds of jobs and speed up production. GM's decision to hold its ground was motivated by the huge amounts of cost savings it envisioned. Today, the company is among the lowest-cost of the major automakers. ◀

Explore & Apply

18.4 ADJUSTING TO TECHNOLOGY—FEWER FARMERS, MORE FOOD

The country, indeed much of the world, is fed by crops grown on American farms. You might think that farmers would be handsomely rewarded for keeping the rest of us from starvation, and some are. They are the survivors, though. The financial hardships of farming the land have caused the farm population to dwindle from 30 percent of the U.S. population in 1920 to less than 2 percent today.

The problem facing farmers is one of abundance and changing technology. Technology has increased the productivity of farm labor and capital, making much of both obsolete in the process. For example, it was once the faithful mule that pulled the tillers that prepared soil for planting. Today, there are tractors and many different kinds of specialized mechanical planting and harvesting equipment. The intervening time has served as the long run in economic terms, moving us through a series of short runs characterized by different ways of farming. The technological change over this time has also included the development of new crop varieties, fertilizers, and techniques of production.

In farming, all firms must sell at the same market price, despite some of them having cost advantages over others. For example, some farms spread across wide, flat expanses, while others are nestled in river valleys. The result of differences in the physical characteristics of farms is that technological change increases the profit of some farmers while harming others—farmers who cannot adapt to these changes but nevertheless experience the consequent declines in farm output prices. Farmers who are unable to sell their crops at the market price without suffering economic losses will be forced to leave their farms in the long run.

For example, farmers in the choppy hills of Tennessee are at a disadvantage to their counterparts in the Kansas plains when it comes to employing the modern technology of huge combines and other types of farm equipment. Yet, if they grow the same crop, they must sell it for the same price. As technological change takes hold and supply increases, that crop's price drops. Farmers must adopt the changes or exit the industry.

The average number of acres per farm has been increasing, while the number of farms has been shrinking, as seen in Figure 18-11.

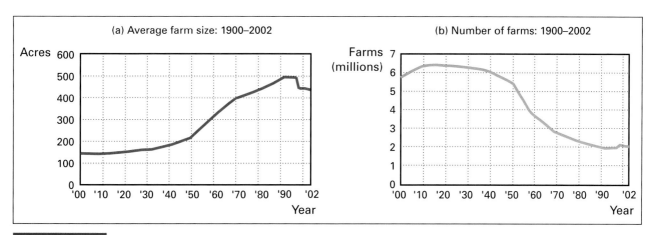

FIGURE 18-11

TRENDS IN FARMING Over time, farm sizes have been increasing and the number of farms shrinking.
Source: Trends in Agriculture, USDA, June 7, 2002, and USDA web site.

Table 18-3 provides additional data that can help you understand the farm problem. We see in the table the ups and downs in farm income. These fluctuations make it difficult for small farms to keep going. Also note the surge in prices paid by farmers for seed, equipment, fertilizer, and so forth, relative to the prices they receive when they sell their crops. The numbers tell us that farmers are caught in a price squeeze. We also see in the table shrinking employment opportunities in farming for most of the last century.

Even though farms disappear, farmland is usually not abandoned. Rather, it becomes part of someone else's farm. When one farmer loses money working a particular piece of acreage, why should another farmer be able to take it over and earn a profit?

An important reason is economies of scale in farming, such as those associated with the use of large-scale equipment, which causes the average cost of farm output to decrease as farms grow larger. For example, farmers waste less time maneuvering their combines when their fields are large. This means that a bushel of corn, wheat, or other commodity can be produced at a lower cost per unit on large farms. Economies of scale are identified with the downward-sloping part of the U-shaped long-run average cost curve. Economies of scale do have limits, though. Since bringing in the crop and equipment uses time and fuel, fields that extend too far can lead to diseconomies of scale, in which average costs rise.

AGRICULTURAL PRICE SUPPORTS

Government programs to help farmers have attempted to drive up prices through supply restrictions and price supports, which were discussed in Chapter 4. The price supports are maintained through *deficiency payments* that compensate farmers for the difference between the support price and any lower market price. The result has been that some farmers have become wealthy while others cannot scrape out a living.

To use agricultural price supports to keep every farmer in business would require a price of output that would provide even the highest-cost producer with at least a normal profit. Consider the three graphs in Figure 18-12. Farmer A is the low-cost producer, farmer B the medium-cost producer, and farmer C the high-cost producer. Don't forget that each cost curve includes an allowance for the farmer's implicit opportunity cost (normal profit).

Farmer C may be the high-cost producer because he or she has higher explicit costs arising from poorer quality of land or poor management skills. Farmer C might also have excellent opportunities for earning income off the farm. In that case, farmer C's higher costs

TABLE 18-3 FARM INCOME, EMPLOYMENT, AND PRICES

YEAR	NET FARM INCOME (BILLIONS OF DOLLARS)	FARM EMPLOYMENT (THOUSANDS)	PRICES RECEIVED BY FARMERS	PRICES PAID BY FARMERS
1979	$27.4	3,765	94	66
1980	16.1	3,699	98	75
1981	26.9	3,582	100	82
1982	23.8	3,466	94	86
1983	14.2	3,349	98	86
1984	26.0	3,233	101	89
1985	28.6	3,116	91	86
1986	30.9	2,912	87	85
1987	37.4	2,897	89	87
1988	38.0	2,954	99	91
1989	45.3	2,863	104	96
1990	44.6	2,891	104	99
1991	38.5	2,877	100	100
1992	47.8	2,810	98	101
1993	44.7	2,800	101	104
1994	48.9	2,767	100	106
1995	36.9	2,836	102	109
1996	54.8	2,842	112	115
1997	50.5	2,867	107	118
1998	45.6	2,827	102	115
1999	46.2	2,977	95	115
2000	48.0	2,952	96	120
2001	45.7	2,923	102	124
2002	36.2	N/A	98	124

Source: 2003 Economic Report of the President, Tables B-97, B-100, and B-101. The values for price in the table are index numbers, with 1990–1992 equal to 100.

result from higher implicit opportunity costs. To keep farmer C farming, the government would have to manipulate prices so that all of farmer C's costs are covered by price. In the process, farmers A and B would grow wealthy on excess profits.

There are several objections to crop prices that keep all farmers farming. For one thing, consumers have to pay the higher prices. Since food is a necessity, high food prices hit the

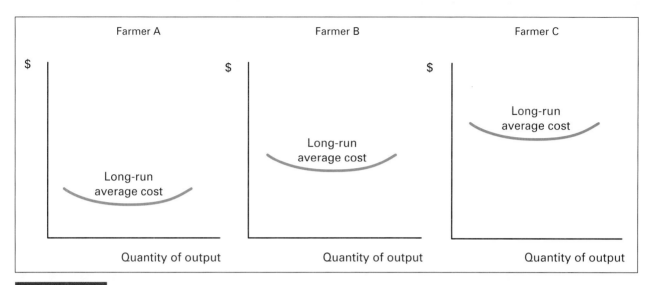

FIGURE 18-12

LOW-, MEDIUM-, AND HIGH-COST FARMS All three farmers face the same price, but the high-cost farmers struggle while the low-cost farmers prosper.

poor the hardest. Another problem concerns where to draw the line at government efforts to help people whose incomes are not enough to keep them in their present line of work. For example, teachers sometimes find it difficult to support a family on their earnings. Should the government eliminate free public schooling and charge students tuition like private schools do so that teachers can be paid more? In general, the incomes of any group cannot be raised without imposing costs on others.

Over six decades of price supports failed to stop the exodus from the farm. For this, we should be grateful. If 30 percent of Americans were still to live on farms, as was true in 1920, many goods and services that we enjoy consuming would simply not be available. People would be growing food instead of, for example, assembling cars, building houses, and making movies.

In farm policy, Washington has tough choices to make. Farming has changed, but how much aid should the government provide to farmers in trying to ease the pain experienced by those who are adversely affected by that change? That question can only be answered by consideration of both economics and politics.

1. **Identify some technological advances that have changed the face of farming. Were these good for farmers? Why did they adopt them? Explain.**

2. **Do you view the government's long-term efforts to help farmers as more of a failure or more of a success? What policies toward farming would be best? Should these policies be applied to other occupations also? Explain.**

Visit www.prenhall.com/ayers for updates and web exercises on this Explore & Apply topic.

SUMMARY AND LEARNING OBJECTIVES

1. **Describe the firm's short-run costs.**
   - In the short run there are both fixed and variable inputs. Thus, short-run costs include fixed and variable costs. Sunk costs are irrecoverable, and thus irrelevant

   to decision making. Total cost is the sum of total fixed cost and total variable cost. Total fixed cost does not change as the quantity of output changes. Total variable cost increases as output increases, as does total cost.

- Marginal cost is the change in total cost divided by the change in the quantity of output. Since only variable costs change, marginal cost also equals the change in total variable cost divided by the change in the quantity of output. Marginal cost measures the increment to total cost when there is a one-unit change in the quantity of output. Marginal cost is especially important in profit maximization.

- Three types of average cost are found by dividing the appropriate total cost by the quantity of output. Average fixed cost equals total fixed cost divided by the quantity of output. Average variable cost equals total variable cost divided by the quantity of output. Average total cost equals total cost divided by the quantity of output.

- Marginal revenue equals the change in total revenue divided by the change in the quantity of output. For a price taker, marginal revenue equals price. Marginal revenue is also the incremental revenue from the production and sale of one more unit of output.

2. **Explain the rule of profit maximization.**
   - The rule of profit maximization is to produce output up to the point where marginal revenue equals marginal cost. For a price taker, the rule can be restated as produce to the point where price equals marginal cost.
   - If price is so low that a firm cannot cover its average cost, it will incur a loss. The rule of profit maximization in this case is to minimize the loss. If the firm produces at all, it will produce the amount for which marginal revenue equals marginal cost.

3. **Discuss profit maximization within the context of profit, loss, and shut down.**
   - Producing according to the rule of profit maximization leads to three possible outcomes: (1) the firm earns an economic profit; (2) the firm breaks even; and (3) the firm incurs an economic loss. When the firm earns a profit, price is greater than average cost. Breakeven occurs when price equals average cost. Loss involves a price that is less than average cost.

- Graphically, profit is represented by the area of a rectangle. The area of the profit rectangle is found by the following: Profit = Quantity × (Price − Average cost). Loss is also represented graphically by the area of a rectangle. Since price will be less than average cost, the computation of loss results in a negative value.

- A firm will not produce (quantity will be set equal to zero) when the firm follows the shutdown rule. This rule says to shut down when price is less than average variable cost. An alternative statement of the rule says to shut down when total revenue is less than total variable cost. Shutting down keeps the loss from exceeding the firm's total fixed cost. Shut down should be distinguished from exit. In shutting down, the firm retains the use of its capital inputs in hopes of putting them to use again in the future.

4. **Distinguish between economies and diseconomies of scale.**
   - Economies of scale occur when output changes by more than the proportion in which all inputs are changed. Diseconomies of scale occur when output changes by less than the proportion by which all inputs are changed. Constant returns to scale occur when output changes by the same proportion by which inputs are changed.
   - Long-run average cost decreases when economies of scale are present, remains constant when there are constant returns to scale, and increases when diseconomies of scale are present. Technological change shifts the long-run average cost curve downward.

5. **Describe the factors that motivate U.S. farm policy.**
   - Technological change and economies of scale have changed farming by reducing the number of farmers. Government policy has aimed to increase the income of farmers who have had difficulty in adjusting to changed conditions. Nonetheless, the exodus from the family farm has continued.

KEY TERMS

TEST YOURSELF

TRUE OR FALSE

1. Total fixed cost equals zero when output equals zero.
2. Marginal cost measures the change in cost that results from a change in output.
3. Average variable cost equals the wage rate divided by average product.
4. To maximize profit in the short run, a firm must always minimize average costs.
5. Diseconomies of scale result in higher per-unit costs.

MULTIPLE CHOICE

6. The labor requirements curve involves reversing the axes of the
   a. total cost curve.
   b. total product curve.
   c. marginal cost curve.
   d. average variable cost curve.
7. When the slope of the total cost curve is graphed, the resulting curve is that of
   a. total variable cost.
   b. marginal cost.
   c. average variable cost.
   d. average cost.
8. Marginal revenue equals the _____ divided by the ____.
   a. change in total cost; change in output
   b. change in total revenue; change in output
   c. change in total revenue; price
   d. price; output
9. In Self-Test Table 18-1, the marginal cost of the fifth bag of peanuts equals
   a. $90.
   b. $30.
   c. $18.
   d. $13.

10. In Self-Test Table 18-1, the average cost of the second bag of peanuts equals
    a. $32.
    b. $16.
    c. $3.50.
    d. $2.
11. In Self-Test Table 18-1, total fixed cost equals
    a. $25.
    b. $10.
    c. $5.
    d. $2.
12. In Self-Test Table 18-1, if Odetta sells peanuts at the market price of $15 per unit, her profit-maximizing quantity of output is
    a. 1 bag of peanuts.
    b. 2 bags of peanuts.
    c. 3 bags of peanuts.
    d. 4 bags of peanuts.
13. A price-taking firm with a loss will
    a. always shut down.
    b. produce to where the price equals marginal cost, unless the price is below average variable cost.
    c. produce to where price equals average cost.
    d. raise its price until it reaches profitability.
14. To maximize profit, the price-taking firm shown in Self-Test Figure 18-1 will produce the quantity associated with point
    a. *A*.
    b. *B*.
    c. *C*.
    d. *D*.

SELF-TEST TABLE 18-1	ODETTA'S WHOLESALE PEANUTS (20-POUND BAGS)

Output (Quantity per Day)	Total Cost
0	$25
1	30
2	32
3	40
4	60
5	90

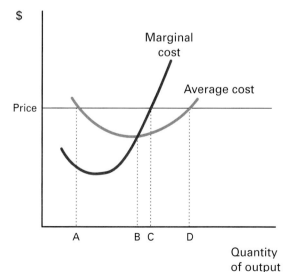

SELF-TEST FIGURE 18-1

15. If it attempts to maximize profit, the firm shown in Self-Test Figure 18-1 will
    a. be profitable.
    b. show losses.
    c. have zero profit.
    d. need more information before determining if a profit potential exists.

16. A firm will shut down if total revenue is less than
    a. total costs.
    b. total variable costs.
    c. total fixed costs.
    d. total explicit costs.

17. What kind of firm is a price taker?
    a. A firm that sets and controls the market price.
    b. A firm with no choice but to sell its output for the going market price.
    c. A firm owned by a religious organization.
    d. All sole proprietorships and partnerships, but never corporations.

18. To maximize profit, a firm will attempt to produce at the point where
    a. average cost is at a minimum.
    b. marginal cost is at a minimum.
    c. total revenue is at a maximum.
    d. marginal cost equals marginal revenue.

19. In Self-Test Figure 18-2, economies of scale occur
    a. in region *A*.
    b. in region *B*.
    c. in region *C*.
    d. at quantity *D*.

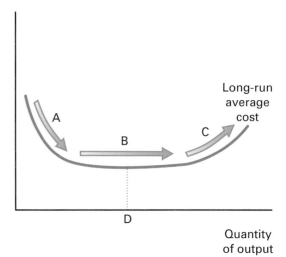

SELF-TEST FIGURE 18-2

 20. Which economic concept provides the most likely explanation for the decline in the number of farms in the United States?
    a. Limited liability.
    b. Perpetual existence.
    c. Diminishing returns.
    d. Economies of scale.

QUESTIONS AND PROBLEMS

1. *[fixed versus variable cost]* Categorize each of the following expenses incurred by Alonzo's Big Time Chocolate Factory as either a fixed cost or a variable cost:
    a. The monthly payment Alonzo makes to the local telephone company.
    b. Payments to his insurance company for automobile insurance on the company car.
    c. Payments to the local utility for electricity to operate the candy-mixing machines.
    d. Alonzo's salary as chief executive officer of the company.
    e. Payroll expenses.

2. *[sunk cost]* "Don't cry over spilt milk." Explain how this saying relates to the concept of sunk costs.

3. *[marginal cost]* RM Motors has the following schedule for total cost:

Quantity	Total Cost
0	$100
1	150
2	175
3	205
4	245
5	290

    a. What is the marginal cost of a fourth vehicle? Of a fifth vehicle?
    b. How will the marginal cost behave? Why?

4. *[total product and labor requirements]* Sketch a total product curve, identifying the region of increasing returns, diminishing returns, and negative returns (review diminishing returns in the previous chapter, if necessary). Be sure to label the axes. Then draw a graph with the axes reversed from that of total product. Sketch a labor requirements curve. What does the curve show? What two cost curves have a shape similar to that of the labor requirements curve?

5. *[computing costs]* Using the data below on output and total variable cost, compute total cost, average fixed cost, average variable cost, average cost, and marginal cost for each output. Total fixed cost is $100.

Output	Total Variable Cost
0	$0
1	50
2	90
3	140
4	200
5	300
6	500

6. *[cost curves]* Draw two graphs. In the first graph, sketch a typical total fixed cost curve, a total variable cost curve, and a total cost curve. In the second graph, sketch a marginal cost curve, an average variable cost curve, and an average total cost curve. Be sure to label the axes on both graphs. Answer the following questions using your graphs.
   a. Which cost curve has a slope equal to zero?
   b. Which cost curve starts at the origin and then slopes upward?
   c. The slopes of which two cost curves are equal to marginal cost?
   d. Which cost curve starts at total fixed cost and then slopes upward?
   e. Which cost curve has a J shape?
   f. Which two cost curves have a U shape?
   g. Which cost curve intersects average total cost? At what point does that intersection take place?
   h. Which cost curve intersects average variable cost? At what point does that intersection take place?

7. *[price taker]* Explain why it would make no sense for a price taker to set a selling price that differs from the market price.

8. *[profit maximization]* A price-taking firm, Moo-town Wholesale Milk and Butterfat, is currently producing 1,000 gallons of milk and butterfat per day. The market price of this output equals $1.50 per unit. Its total fixed cost equals $200 per day, while its total variable cost is $150 per day.

a. Is this firm earning a profit? Show the calculations that led to your answer.
   b. If it is earning a profit, is it maximizing its profit? Explain.

9. *[profit maximization]* What is the rule of profit maximization? How can this rule be restated when the firm is a price taker?

10. *[profit maximization]* Sketch a graph that shows a firm's marginal revenue, marginal cost, and average cost curves. Indicate the profit-maximizing quantity on the graph and label it Q^*. Then explain why the quantity you indicated maximizes profit. Include as part of your explanation why producing $Q^* + 1$ units of output would provide the firm with less profit than producing Q^*. Also, explain why producing $Q^* - 1$ units of output would also provide less profit than Q^*.

11. *[profit maximization]* Suppose a price-taking firm has a total fixed cost equal to $1 and marginal cost as indicated in the following table. Since total variable cost can be calculated by adding the given marginal cost values, fill in the missing values for total variable cost. Then fill in the missing values for total cost. Compute the values for total revenue assuming a market price of $4.25. What output will maximize profit? How much will the profit be? Will output increase when price goes up to $4.50? To $5.25? Explain.

Quantity of Output per Day	Total Revenue	Marginal Cost	Total Variable Cost	Total Cost
0	$0	—	$0	$1
1		$1		
2		0.50		
3		1	2.50	
4		2		
5		3		
6		4		
7		5		
8		6		

12. *[breakeven]* Draw a graph showing a price-taking firm maximizing profit, but breaking even. Your graph should contain market price, marginal revenue, marginal cost, and average cost curves. Indicate the quantity of output the firm would produce. Be sure to label the axes.

13. *[economic loss]* Explain how a firm that maximizes profit might incur an economic loss. Will the firm maximize the loss? Explain.

14. *[profit graph]* Draw the axes for a graph with the vertical axis labeled $ and the horizontal axis labeled Quantity. Sketch an average cost curve and an

accompanying marginal cost curve. Select a price such that the firm earns an economic profit. Show the profit-maximizing quantity by drawing a dotted line from the intersection of marginal revenue and marginal cost to the horizontal axis. Show profit as the area of a rectangle.

15. *[loss graph]* Draw a graph similar to the one in the preceding problem except adjust the price so that the firm incurs a loss. Illustrate the loss as the area of a rectangle.

16. *[shut down]* The owners of Happy Spud Potato Farms have recently seen their firm incur losses because of a downturn in the market price of potatoes. They are trying to decide whether to shut down and take jobs in a factory in a nearby town until the price of potatoes goes up in the future. Here is the information they have accumulated to help them make their decision:
   - Monthly quantity of potatoes sold: 10,000 bushels
   - Price of potatoes: $3 a bushel
   - Happy Spud's marginal cost of growing potatoes: $3 a bushel
   - Total fixed cost (mortgage on farm and other fixed expenses): $6,000
   - Total variable cost of producing 10,000 bushels of potatoes (potato slips, labor, and so on): $29,900

   Will the loss at Happy Spud be minimized by shutting down or by continuing to operate? Explain.

17. *[shutdown graph]* Draw a graph that illustrates the shutdown rule. Label each curve in your graph and explain how the graph illustrates shutdown.

18. *[production, cost, economies of scale]* Within the context of production, explain the difference between the long run and the short run. Repeat your explanation, this time within the context of cost. When does the law of diminishing returns apply, in the short run or the long run? When are economies of scale found, in the short run or the long run?

19. *[economies and diseconomies of scale]* "The fact that so many businesses are big is proof that economies of scale are significant." Comment.

20. *[economies and diseconomies of scale]* Why might a firm want to grow larger if larger means economies of scale are available? Why might a firm want to downsize if it found that it was experiencing diseconomies of scale?

21. *[economies and diseconomies of scale]* Draw a long-run average cost curve. Label the axes and the portions of your cost curve that represent economics of scale, constant returns to scale, and diseconomies of scale.

22. *[shift in long-run average cost]* Price scanning by bar code is common in supermarkets today. Not too many years ago, however, the price of every item purchased was entered by hand. Explain in practical terms how scanners lower costs. Must every supermarket install scanners in order to compete? Is this a long-run or a short-run issue? Explain.

WORKING WITH GRAPHS AND DATA

1. *[total product and total cost]* Use the following table of total product and labor to determine costs for this firm. Assume that labor is the only variable input.

Output (total product)	Units of Labor	Total Variable Cost ($)	Total Cost ($)
0	0		
10	1		
22	2		
33	3		
42	4		
50	5		
54	6		

   a. Draw the labor requirements curve and label it "Labor requirements." Label the vertical and horizontal axes appropriately as "Labor" and "Quantity of output."

b. Fill in the total variable cost column assuming that this firm pays a wage of $10 per unit of labor.

c. Fill in the total cost column assuming that total fixed costs are $10.

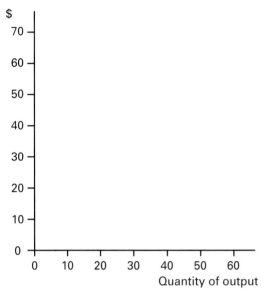

GRAPH 18-1

d. On Graph 18-1 draw the total variable cost curve and label it TVC and the total cost curve and label it TC. Show total fixed costs as TFC.

2. *[computing costs]* Use the following table of output and total cost to determine other costs listed for this firm.

Quantity of Output	Total Cost ($)	Total Variable Cost ($)	Marginal Cost ($)	Average Variable Cost ($)	Average Cost ($)
0	6		undefined	undefined	undefined
1	11				
2	14				
3	18				
4	24				
5	31				
6	39				

a. How much is total fixed cost?

b. Fill in the table.

c. On Graph 18-2 draw the average cost curve and label it AC, the average variable cost curve and label it AVC, and the marginal cost curve and labeled MC.

d. Show how you would find average fixed cost on this graph. Label it as AFC.

e. Where does the MC curve intersect the AVC and AC curves? Label these as E and F, respectively.

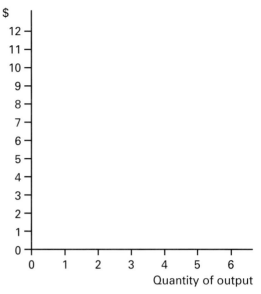

GRAPH 18-2

3. *[profit maximization]* Use Graph 18-3 of a profit-maximizing, price-taking firm to answer the following questions.

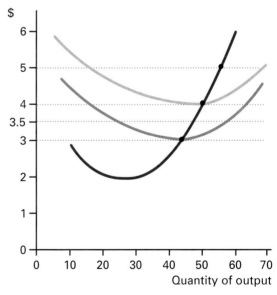

GRAPH 18-3

a. Label the marginal cost curve as MC, the average cost curve as AC, and the average variable cost curve as AVC.

b. If the price is $5 would this firm be making an economic profit? Show the point where profit maximization would occur as point A.

c. At what price would this firm be breaking even, that is, making zero economic profits? Show the point where profit maximization would occur as point B.

d. Identify the price below which the firm would shut down in the short run. Explain.

e. Identify a price at which the firm would definitely continue to operate in the short run but at which it would shut down in the long run. Explain.

4. *[profit maximization]* Use Graph 18-4 that shows a profit-maximizing, price-taking firm to answer the following questions.

   a. Assume that the price that this firm faces is $5. What is the profit-maximizing quantity? Show how you found it.

   b. What is the average cost of producing the profit-maximizing quantity? Show how you found it.

   c. How much is average profit per unit at the profit-maximizing output? Show this on the graph and label it "Average profit."

   d. How much is total profit? Show your work.

   e. Label the area of total profit on Graph 18-4 as "Profit."

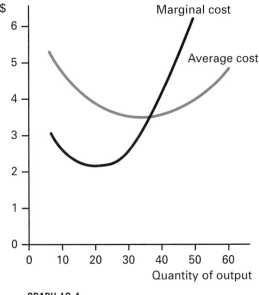

GRAPH 18-4

Visit **www.prenhall.com/ayers** for Exploring the Web exercises and additional self-test quizzes.

CHAPTER 19

PURE COMPETITION

A LOOK AHEAD

On the face of it, the study of racial discrimination and the study of competition in the product market would seem to have little in common. In reality, the type of market into which firms sell their products can make a great deal of difference to the amount of prejudice they express in their choices, as seen in this chapter's Explore & Apply section.

In this chapter we introduce the four market models. We then focus on a market in which many price-taking firms produce identical goods, a market called pure competition. You will see how a purely competitive firm decides how much output to produce, and the implications of this choice. The market price plays a key role in explaining why new firms enter a market, or why existing firms might exit it. The model of pure competition examined in this chapter offers a benchmark of economic efficiency against which all markets can be measured.

LEARNING OBJECTIVES

Understanding Chapter 19 will enable you to:
1. **Name four market types and describe the characteristics of pure competition.**
2. **Illustrate how market demand and supply determine the competitive firm's demand curve.**
3. **Identify the competitive firm's short-run supply curve.**
4. **Describe the long-run equilibrium in pure competition.**
5. **Explain how efficiency is achieved in a purely competitive market.**
6. **Specify the difference between a constant-cost, increasing-cost, and decreasing-cost industry.**
7. **Show how competition can reduce discrimination in society.**

Explore & Apply

In the two previous chapters you learned about business firms. In this chapter we will consider how a firm's actions are influenced by the type of market in which it operates.

19.1 TYPES OF MARKETS

It is clear that there are different types of markets. These different markets are commonly called *industries.* Think about how the municipal water, grocery, and shampoo industries differ. When we buy water we typically face just one seller. When we shop for groceries, there might be several supermarkets in our neighborhood to pick from. Once inside the supermarket, there may be dozens of shampoos from which to choose. Thus, each of these markets is different from the others in terms of the number of sellers.

Markets also differ according to whether the product is homogeneous or differentiated. **Homogeneous products** are identical no matter which firm produces them, and are often called *commodities.* For example, the #2 grade yellow corn produced by farmers is homogeneous. Additional examples include cattle, gold, coal, copper, steel, aluminum, and lumber.

In contrast, **differentiated products** will vary from one producer to the next. One grocery store differs from another, for example, just as the products within also differ from brand to brand. Computers are another example of a differentiated product, varying by brand name and features. These differences lead to four basic **market structures,** which are models of the way markets work. They are:

- **Monopoly**—a market with only one seller of a good without close substitutes. For example, a municipal sewage treatment service or water supply is a monopoly. A monopoly firm maintains a significant amount of control over the price of its product, as will be discussed further in the next chapter.
- **Oligopoly**—a market with more than one seller, where at least one of those sellers can significantly influence price. Oligopoly is usually characterized by just a few significant sellers of a product that can be either homogeneous or differentiated. Passenger airlines and crude oil are both provided in oligopoly markets.
- **Monopolistic competition**—a market with numerous firms selling a differentiated product and with only a slight ability to control price. Retailers such as dry cleaners, music stores, and restaurants are examples. Both oligopoly and monopolistic competition are discussed after the chapter on monopoly.
- **Pure competition**—a market in which there are many buyers and sellers of a homogeneous product. Farmers are an example. The model of pure competition underlies the supply and demand analysis in Chapters 3 and 4.

Figure 19-1(a) shows a grid of market structures according to the number of firms and differentiation of the product among them. Figure 19-1(b) shows the four market structures arranged according to the amount of **market power**—influence over price by the individual firm. Purely competitive firms have no market power. Monopolistically competitive firms have slight market power. Oligopolistic firms may exhibit a significant degree of market power, while monopoly firms usually have more market power than any other type of firm. Market power arises from *barriers to entry,* which are obstacles to joining an industry, and which include anything that makes producing and selling output more difficult for a new firm than for an existing firm. The next chapter looks more closely at these topics. In pure competition, market power does not exist.

Now that we have a brief overview of the four types of market structure, let's focus on pure competition, which is characterized by the following:

---

homogeneous products products that are identical, no matter which firms in the industry produce the commodities.

differentiated products products that vary from one producer to another within the same industry.

market structures models of the way markets work.

monopoly a market with only one seller of a good without close substitutes.

oligopoly a market with more than one seller, where at least one seller can significantly influence price.

monopolistic competition a market with many firms, each with slight market power.

pure competition a market in which there are numerous firms, all of which are price takers. The product is homogeneous and there are no barriers to entry.

market power when individual firms have at least a bit of control over the prices of their outputs; arises from barriers to entry.

(a) Market structure by product and number of firms		
	Homogeneous product	Differentiated product
One firm	Monopoly (example: city drinking water)	Not applicable
Few firms	Oligopoly (example: gasoline refineries)	Oligopoly (example: automakers)
Many firms	Pure competition (example: farmers)	Monopolistic competition (example: restaurants)

(b) Market structure arranged according to market power

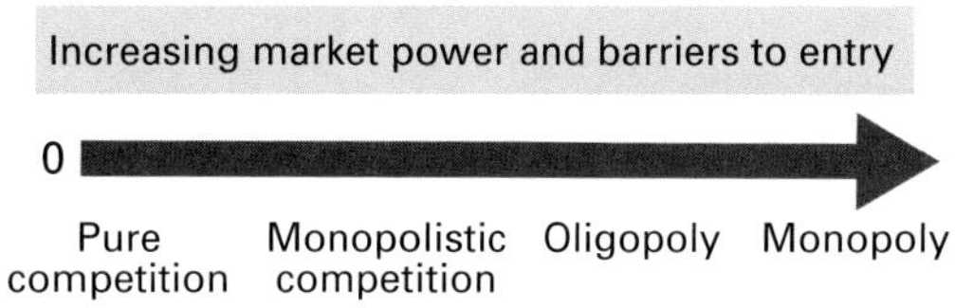

Increasing market power and barriers to entry

0 ⟶

Pure competition   Monopolistic competition   Oligopoly   Monopoly

FIGURE 19-1

MARKET STRUCTURES Market structures differ depending upon how many firms are in the industry and whether their products are homogeneous or differentiated, as shown in (a). Market structure is associated with market power and its associated barriers to entry. As shown in (b), firms in pure competition have no market power. They have some market power in monopolistic competition, more in oligopoly, and the most in monopoly.

- **Numerous buyers and sellers.** As a result, **each firm and consumer is a price taker,** with firms selling their output at the market price and consumers paying that same market price.
- **A homogeneous product.** The market prices of these items are widely available in newspapers and other media reports. Because products are identical, individual firms reap no benefits from advertising: **firms do not advertise in pure competition.**
- **Costless entry and exit of firms.** In the long run, it is easy for firms to start up, called entering an industry, or leave an industry, which is called exit. Firms might leave an industry by going out of business or by shifting the use of their resources to another industry. For example, farmer Brown might plant barley instead of corn.

QUICKCHECK

If you owned a gold coin of known weight and purity, but without collector value, how would you learn what price to ask for if you were selling it?

Answer: You would be a price taker who would sell at the going market price for gold. This price changes often as supply and demand shift. The price at any given moment is determined by supply and demand in the commodity exchanges, such as the Chicago Mercantile Exchange, and can be accessed through various on-line quote services.

SNAPSHOT   ANTIQUARIAN BOOKS IN A DOT-COM WORLD

The Internet has brought buyers and sellers together like never before. Consider the purchase of hard-to-find old books. Well, maybe not so hard to find . . . not any more! Where once the local shopkeeper would do the searching and set the price, now book collectors themselves search the World Wide Web. Booksellers have a huge new market. They also have huge new competition. It is this competition, and not individual sellers, that sets the prices today.

Yes, there are many Mark Twain first editions, and you can find their prices with ease. Those priced too high will not sell. Those priced too low will be sold quickly. The result is that there will tend to be a single market price for any book. Booksellers in the modern world have little ability to control price in what has become a single global market. For as technology changes, so too does market structure! ◀

19.2 THE FIRM'S DEMAND AND SUPPLY CURVES

THE FIRM'S DEMAND

The central implication of pure competition is that firms are price takers. Each firm must decide how much to produce based upon the market price, over which it has no control. Market price is set by the intersection of supply and demand in the marketplace.

Figure 19-2 shows how the equilibrium market price becomes the firm's demand curve. **Although market demand slopes downward to the right, as shown in part (a), the demand facing each firm is horizontal (perfectly elastic) at the market price,** as shown in part (b).

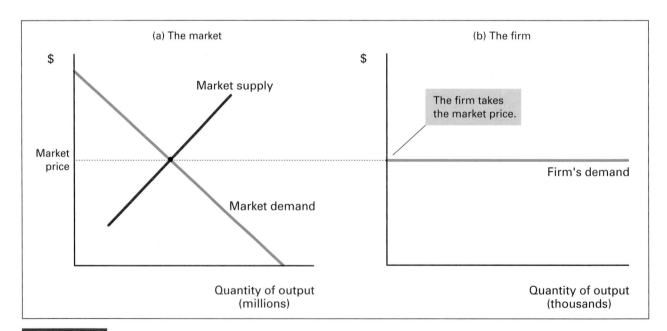

FIGURE 19-2

DEMAND IN PURE COMPETITION The firm in pure competition faces a demand that is horizontal at the market price, because each firm is a price taker, as shown in part (a). The intersection of market demand and market supply sets market price, as shown in part (b). Anything that changes that market equilibrium would lead to a change in price and a corresponding shift up or down in the firm's demand.

The horizontal demand means that the firm is able to sell as much as it wishes at the market price. It has no reason to sell for less than the market price because its horizontal demand curve means that it can sell as much as it wishes at that price. Also, it cannot sell anything if it charges more than the market price. Thus, **a price taker always sells at the market price.**

The individual firm chooses the quantity of output it produces based upon its demand and its supply. To maximize profit, recall that the firm produces at the point where marginal revenue equals marginal cost. Recall also that market price equals the price-taking firm's marginal revenue. Here you have seen that the market price equals the firm's demand curve, too. That makes the firm's demand curve its marginal revenue curve. In the next section we show you that the firm's marginal cost curve is also its short-run supply curve. Thus, the rule of profit maximization, which is to produce at the point where marginal revenue equals marginal cost, is equivalent to producing at the point where the firm's demand and supply curves intersect.

FROM BLUE AGAVE TO BLUE INVESTORS—BETTING ON PRICES　　*SNAPSHOT*

Trying to figure out where market prices are headed has consumed countless hours of effort. For Mexican growers of the blue agave crop, it is about predicting market prices several years down the road when the crop matures enough to be harvested and distilled into tequila. For investors in the stock market, it is about whether prices of the stocks they own will rise or fall.

Yet who can anticipate the ways of purely competitive markets? While many warned of a stock market decline after its phenomenal rise in the 1990s, few could fathom the depths to which prices would tumble. Likewise, the recent surge in popularity of tequila and margaritas was not foreseen by blue agave growers in the mid-1990s. Therefore, as market prices for stocks plunged in 2002, owners of stocks saw their finances crumble. The blue agave growers, in contrast, were greeted with unexpected prosperity as the value of their crops soared higher in response to an unexpected surge in demand. As you can see, life as a price taker is a gamble and the market spins the wheel. ◀

SHORT-RUN SUPPLY

At any price above the shutdown price, the profit-maximizing price-taking firm equates marginal revenue and marginal cost. Because the price-taking firm's marginal revenue equals the market price, the firm produces the quantity associated with its marginal cost curve at that price. For this reason, **the *firm's short-run supply curve* is that part of its marginal cost curve that lies above average variable cost.** This supply curve shows the quantity that the firm will offer for sale at each of various possible prices.

Let us revisit WW Wholesale Flour, a purely competitive price-taking firm that you were introduced to in the previous chapter. The supply curve for WW Wholesale Flour is seen in Figure 19-3(a). At a market price of $160, the marginal revenue curve, which is also the firm's demand curve, intersects the firm's supply curve at six tons of output. If the market price rises, WW sells more. In the graph, a price of $250 indicates the firm's demand curve intersects its supply curve at seven tons of output. That quantity makes marginal revenue (equal to price and to the firm's demand) equal to marginal cost (the firm's supply curve). Also shown in the graph is a typical average variable cost curve, which reaches its minimum where intersected by marginal cost. If the market price falls below the minimum point of its average variable cost curve, WW Wholesale Flour will shut down and offer no flour for sale. This shutdown price is shown in Figure 19-3.

Market supply sums the quantities offered by each firm at each price. For example, if there were 999 price takers in addition to WW in the wholesale flour market, each producing

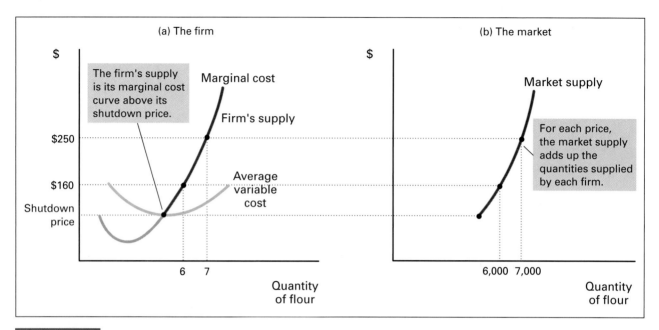

(a) The firm

$

The firm's supply is its marginal cost curve above its shutdown price.

Marginal cost

Firm's supply

$250

Average variable cost

$160

Shutdown price

6   7

Quantity of flour

(b) The market

$

Market supply

For each price, the market supply adds up the quantities supplied by each firm.

6,000 7,000

Quantity of flour

FIGURE 19-3

SUPPLY IN PURE COMPETITION The firm's supply is part of the market supply. The firm's supply is that portion of its marginal cost curve that exceeds average variable cost. Market supply adds together the quantities supplied by all firms at each of the various possible prices. For example, if all firms were identical to the firm shown in (a) and if the market had 1,000 firms, the result would be the market supply shown in (b).

six tons of flour, the total quantity supplied to the market would equal 6,000 tons (6 tons multiplied by 1,000 firms). Similarly, at a price of $250, the quantity supplied to the market would equal 7,000 tons if the firms were all identical to one another. The market supply curve is shown in Figure 19-3(b).

19.3 THE LONG RUN—ENTRY, EXIT, AND EFFICIENCY

The previous section has focused upon the short run, the time period in which all production takes place. Equally important is the long run, which leads from one short-run equilibrium to another.

ENTRY AND EXIT

In the short run, the market price could be sufficiently high that the firm earns profits, or it could be so low that the firm loses money. However, the **long-run equilibrium market price results in the expectation of zero profit for a firm that is considering entry into the industry.** Recall that zero profit, as economists use the term, means that the firm is earning a normal profit measured in accounting terms (normal profit is the accounting profit necessary to keep the firm in business).

Figure 19-4 illustrates long-run equilibrium. The market supply curve in (a) will shift until the market price is just sufficient to cover average cost, shown in (b). When price equals average cost, firms will earn a normal profit and no more shifting will occur. This outcome is indicated graphically in the figure by the firm's demand curve being tangent to its average cost curve at the minimum point of average cost.

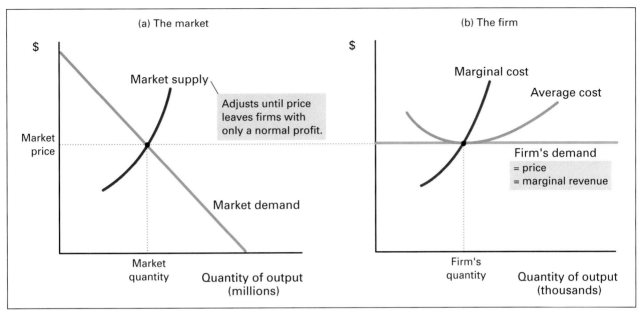

FIGURE 19-4

LONG-RUN EQUILIBRIUM IN PURE COMPETITION The long-run equilibrium in pure competition occurs when the last firm to enter the market earns zero profits, as shown by the firm's average cost curve just tangent to its demand. There would be no reason for a new firm to enter and no reason for an existing firm to exit.

The free entry and exit that characterize pure competition explains why long-run equilibrium occurs. Figure 19-5 illustrates how entry and exit affect market supply. The story behind entry and the achievement of long-run equilibrium is quite simple. The expectation of short-run profit attracts new entrants. Their output shifts the market supply to the right. Entry would continue to occur, increasing market supply and driving market price down, until the expected profit falls to zero.

Likewise, the anticipation of long-run losses would prompt the exit of firms. Exit shifts the market supply curve to the left. The decrease in market supply would continue until the price rises to the level of zero expected profit for firms contemplating entry or exit. Even so, some existing firms will remain profitable in the long run, such as farms with exceptionally fertile and tillable soil.

QUICKCHECK

When will entry occur? What effect will entry have on market supply and price? Once entry is started, when will it stop?

Answer: Entry occurs only when new firms, the entrants, expect to earn a profit. By entering, market supply increases, shown graphically as a shift to the right. The increase in supply causes the market price to drop. Once the market price drops to the point where it equals an entrant's average cost of production, entry will stop.

FIGURE 19-5

ENTRY AND EXIT The lure of profit attracts new entrants (indicated by S_2), which lowers the price until entry stops. Alternatively, losses cause firms to exit the industry (indicated by S_3), which raises the price until exit stops. This process stops when price achieves its long-run equilibrium, as shown in Figure 19-4. Long-run equilibrium is characterized by an absence of entry and exit.

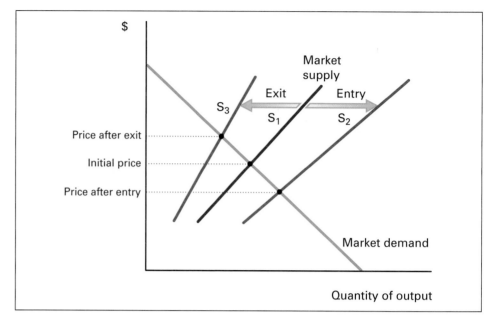

SNAPSHOT   **OLD MCDONALD FARMS AGAIN!**

Old McDonald had a farm, but losses drove him out of business. Exit was painful and distressing. Still, it was also easy, given the well-developed markets for land and farm equipment. Now he wants to give it a second try. Fortunately for McDonald, entry is also easy. Entry merely takes land, equipment, and skill. Although the inputs are expensive, this is not much of a barrier to entry in today's world. Farmers have access to loans or other financial aid, including funds for education. They are also able to lease land and equipment. So, with the easy entry and exit of pure competition, Old McDonald might once more start ahollerin' "Ee-yi-ee-yi-oh!" ◄

THE EFFICIENCY OF PURE COMPETITION

Chapter 4 examined the efficiency of the marketplace. Recall, **the competitive market equilibrium produces an allocatively efficient amount of output. Competition also forces firms to keep costs in check, thus inducing technological efficiency as well.** For these reasons, the model of pure competition is often used as the standard of efficiency by which other market structures are judged.

Figure 19-6(a) shows the efficiency of the purely competitive market output. Recall that social surplus from the production of any one good equals the difference between the total value consumers place on all units of that good and the extra cost of producing all those units. Supply represents the marginal cost of production and demand represents the marginal benefit. At the market equilibrium, these two are equal, an outcome that maximizes social surplus and is thus allocatively efficient. In other words, pure competition produces goods up to the point where the value of the last unit of a good is just equal to what that last unit is worth.

Figure 19-6(b) shows the effect of moving away from the competitive output. Were producers forced to produce more than this competitive output, the value of those extra units would be less than they cost to make, thereby reducing social surplus. This is shown by the triangular area associated with too much output. Likewise, were producers forced to pro-

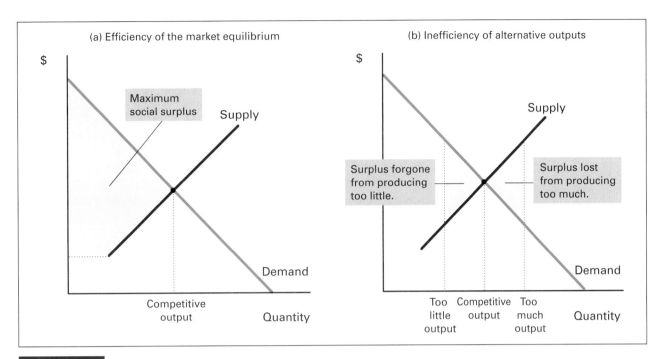

FIGURE 19-6

EFFICIENCY OF PURE COMPETITION In pure competition, the market equilibrium quantity is efficient. In other words, the market outcome maximizes social surplus as shown in (a). Any movement away from that equilibrium would reduce social surplus, as shown in (b). Producing less would forgo some output for which the marginal benefit given by demand exceeds marginal cost given by supply. Likewise, producing more would mean that the extra output added more to cost than to benefit.

duce fewer units, the cost savings would be less than the loss of value from those units. This is shown by the triangular area associated with too little output. Hence, for any particular good, the competitive market price induces consumers and firms to maximize surplus value from that good, which is efficient.

19.4 LONG-RUN SUPPLY

When there is entry of new firms into a purely competitive industry, it is possible that industry costs will be changed. In the following sections, we explain how entry affects costs.

LONG-RUN CHARACTERISTICS OF INDUSTRIES

The expansion or contraction of industries over time sometimes affects the costs of production in that industry. In response to entry, input prices might remain unchanged, rise, or fall, which gives rise to the following three industry types:

- **Constant-cost industry**—An increase in the industry's output does not affect input prices.
- **Increasing-cost industry**—An increase in the industry's output causes input prices to rise.
- **Decreasing-cost industry**—An increase in the industry's output causes input prices to fall.

constant-cost industry when an increase in the industry's output does not affect input prices.

increasing-cost industry when an increase in the industry's output causes input prices to rise.

decreasing-cost industry when an increase in the industry's output causes input prices to fall.

Constant-cost industries are the most common. These industries use few highly special-ized resources. For example, a doubling of the U.S. grain sorghum crop is unlikely to cause any noticeable effect upon land prices, fertilizer prices, equipment rental prices, labor prices, or any of the other costs of production. The reason is that sorghum is a relatively small portion of agriculture as a whole, meaning that sorghum growers could attract land and workers from other industries in the agricultural sector without being required to pay higher prices for those inputs.

Increasing-cost industries are characterized by the use of scarce resources for which an increase in output increases the price of those resources. For example, when telecommuni-cations relied upon signals traveling over copper wire, the increase in demand for telecom-munication networks drove up the price of copper, as copper miners had to resort to extracting copper from less-rich ore. The result was that all telecommunication network providers saw their production costs increase, meaning that telecommunications once seemed to be an increasing-cost industry. Interestingly, technological change in this indus-try took away this source of increasing costs as technology now allows the use of coaxial cable, fiber optics, and wireless networks instead of copper. In addition, there have also been some advancements in mining technology that made it easier to extract copper from low-grade ore.

There are a number of examples of decreasing-cost industries in which increases in industry output result in lower prices. Oftentimes, it is small industries that see decreasing costs as they get large. For example, as the electronics industry expanded in the area of California that became known as Silicon Valley, the movement of skilled labor to the area, the development of specialty suppliers, and increased transportation facilities contributed to lower production costs. Similarly, the rise of the automobile in the early 1900s generated a huge infrastructure of suppliers that drove down costs as the industry expanded.

PERFECT COMPETITION AND LONG-RUN SUPPLY

The three types of industries discussed in the previous section are best analyzed with the model of perfect competition, which is a variant on the model of pure competition. Specifically, the model of **perfect competition** adds to the assumptions of pure competition the further assumption that all firms are identical, with identical access to resources and tech-nology, with all information fully and freely available. The uncomplicated nature of perfect competition makes it very useful for illustrative purposes, such as for long-run industry costs.

perfect competition special case of pure competition in which all firms are identical, with identical access to resources and information.

In a constant-cost industry, the entry of new firms would have no effect on the produc-tion costs of other firms in the industry. Thus, under perfect competition's assumption that all firms are identical, expansion of the industry would lead to the same equilibrium output price. Any higher price would be profitable and would thus attract new entrants that would bring the price down. Any lower price would be unprofitable and would thus lead to exit that would bring the price up.

In an increasing-cost industry, the entry of new firms would not only increase industry output, but would also shift up the cost curves of each firm in that industry. Thus, expan-sion of the industry would lead to a higher equilibrium price of the industry's output. Conversely, in a decreasing-cost industry, the entry of new firms would lower production costs for all firms and thus lead to a lower equilibrium price of output.

long-run supply tells how much will be produced at each of various possible short-run market-equilibrium prices.

These effects are seen by looking at **long-run supply,** which tells how much will be produced at each of various possible short-run market-equilibrium prices. Figure 19-7 shows the effect of an increase in demand for the product of a perfectly competitive industry, the model that assumes all firms have identical cost curves. The increased demand generates profits that attract new entrants into the industry. Newly entering firms shift supply to the right. How far it shifts depends upon which of the three types of industries it is, as shown in the figure. The long-run supply curve connects the initial market equilibrium and the new

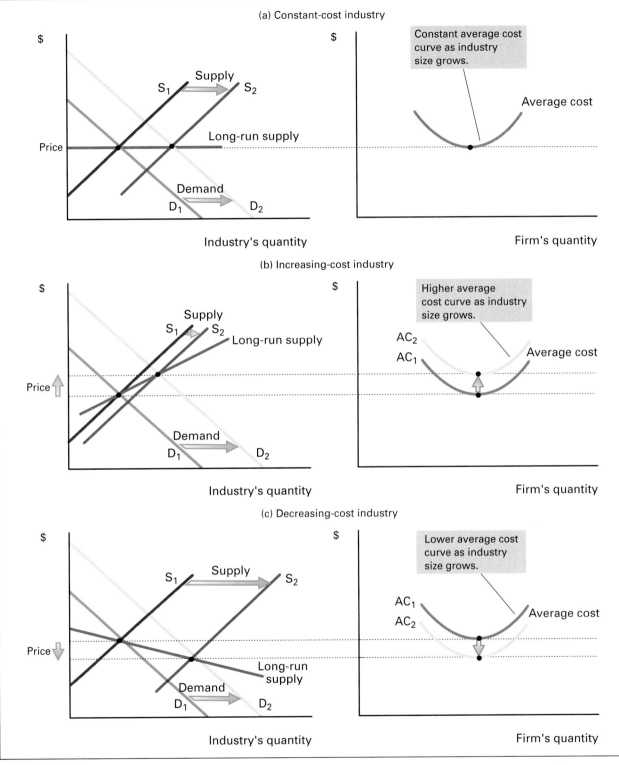

(a) Constant-cost industry

Constant average cost curve as industry size grows.

(b) Increasing-cost industry

Higher average cost curve as industry size grows.

(c) Decreasing-cost industry

Lower average cost curve as industry size grows.

FIGURE 19-7

LONG-RUN SUPPLY Long-run supply is determined by changes in short-run equilibriums over time. How far short-run supply shifts over time in response to a change in demand will depend upon whether an industry is (a) constant cost, (b) increasing cost, or (c) decreasing cost. In a constant-cost industry, increasing industry output does not affect the individual firm's average costs. However, in an increasing-cost industry, the firm's average costs rise as industry output increases. Conversely, in a decreasing-cost industry, the firm's average costs fall as industry output increases.

market equilibrium. Long-run supply is seen to be flat (horizontal, with a slope of zero) for a constant-cost industry, to slope upward for an increasing-cost industry, and to slope downward for a decreasing-cost industry, as shown in Figure 19-7(a), (b), and (c), respectively.

19.5 DISCRIMINATION—NOT LIKELY IN PURE COMPETITION

"The man who exercises discrimination pays a price for doing so."

—Milton Friedman

The remark above was written in the early 1960s, at a time when tension over race in America was at its zenith, and discrimination was often legally required. Why should it be necessary to point out that there is a cost to discrimination? Very few consumers care about the racial and other personal characteristics of the sellers of the products they buy. A good price and high quality are paramount. Because price and quality are more significant to buyers than who makes a good, the marketplace, theoretically at least, should offer opportunities to everyone. How well the promise of opportunity is actually realized in an industry, however, tends to depend at least partly upon its market structure.

Discrimination occurs in the private marketplace, but seldom in markets characterized by pure competition. For example, it was the racially segregated lunch counters at the monopolistically competitive Woolworth five and dime stores that attracted the attention of civil rights organizations of the South in the early 1960s. Likewise, large oligopolistic corporations are often accused of having glass ceilings that prevent the rise of qualified women and minorities. However, in agriculture, mining, and other industries characterized by pure competition, accusations of discrimination are rarely heard. Why is this so? The economic principles you have studied in this chapter offer an answer.

HOW DISCRIMINATION LOWERS PROFIT

Two features of the purely competitive model work to prevent discrimination. One feature is the homogeneous product, which means that the firm has no opportunity to vary the product in discriminatory ways. For example, whites-only restaurants, country clubs, and other facilities are examples of product differentiation, which provide customers with a slightly different environment in which to take advantage of the firm's services. Depending upon biases among prospective customers, such product differentiation might allow the discriminating firm to increase profits. The firm would be tailoring its product to a market niche, the niche of people with similar biases.

Firms in market structures that allow product differentiation might choose to discriminate because, by turning away some customers, they might attract other customers who do not wish to associate with the customers who are turned away. For example, looked at in this way, the decision of Woolworth's half a century ago to not serve blacks at its lunch counters in the Deep South was necessary in order to keep its white customers. Discrimination against blacks increased the profit of Woolworth's relative to a color-blind store policy, since whites had more purchasing power than blacks.

There might be an additional element to this story, though. The denial of service to African Americans by Woolworth's was not necessarily voluntary. Racial segregation was a deeply ingrained custom in the South, and legally mandated in many southern states. Maybe that was because it was recognized that the profit motive in the free marketplace mostly worked against the perpetuation of discrimination.

In a purely competitive market, in contrast, the product must remain homogeneous. There is no opportunity to tailor the output to biases, whether they be mandated by law or merely by customer preferences. There is no such thing as whites-only coal or women-only wheat. No one asks about the race or ethnicity of the roustabout on the offshore drilling platform. Customers do not care which workers produced the lead for the number 2 pencils they use. For this reason, and unlike other market structures, pure competition prevents discrimination in terms of the product itself.

Pure competition also gives firms a strong profit incentive to avoid discrimination. Profit can be viewed as a source of funds to "pay" for discrimination. Pure competition makes profits hard to come by. A firm that is considering entering or exiting the purely competitive market can expect a normal profit, meaning zero economic profit. Using normal profit to pay for discrimination is a luxury such firms can ill afford. In short, to the extent that discrimination occurs on the basis of anything other than a person's abilities, the firm finds itself facing higher production costs.

For example, discriminating against qualified low-wage minority or female workers by denying them employment would force the firm to hire others, perhaps higher-wage white and/or male labor. The practice of not hiring minority or female workers thus shifts the cost of production upward for discriminating firms. **In pure competition, a firm that inflicts higher input costs on itself can find itself going from profit to loss.** Such self-inflicted losses push the discriminating firms toward ultimately going out of business.

Figure 19-8 illustrates a firm that starts out profitable, but that sees its average cost curve shift upward because it discriminates instead of merely hiring the most qualified people. The market price of its output is not sufficient to pay the extra costs this decision imposes. The firm will have to choose whether to change its hiring practices or, in the long run, face the prospect of going out of business.

Society does not rely upon the economic incentives discussed here to rein in discrimination. Instead, civil rights laws have made much discrimination illegal. These laws have undoubtedly reduced blatant instances of discrimination. However, discrimination has taken new, more subtle forms, but ones not immune to the economic incentives of competition and profit.

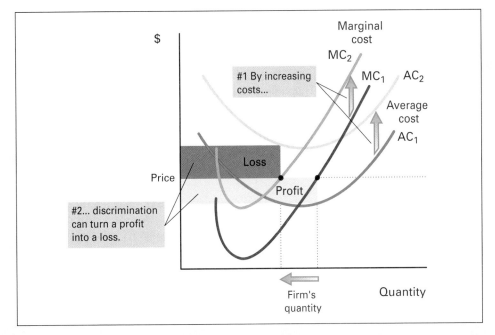

FIGURE 19-8

HIGHER COSTS FROM DISCRIMINATION Discrimination increases marginal and average costs and can mean the difference between profit and loss. The discriminating company with the high costs loses out in competition to the nondiscriminator with the low costs.

THINKING CRITICALLY

1. Suppose that all civil rights laws were declared unconstitutional by the U.S. Supreme Court. Would you expect that discrimination would go back to the levels of fifty years ago? Justify your answer using economics.

2. Why are Chinese, Mexican, and Thai restaurants commonly staffed by people of Chinese, Mexican, and Thai backgrounds, respectively? Are these staffing patterns discriminatory? Does economics help account for these hiring patterns? Explain.

WWW   Visit www.prenhall.com/ayers for updates and web exercises on this Explore & Apply topic.

SUMMARY AND LEARNING OBJECTIVES

1. **Name four market types and describe the characteristics of pure competition.**
   - Market structures refers to types of markets. The four types of markets are: pure competition, monopolistic competition, oligopoly, and monopoly. In pure competition there is a single market price, determined by demand and supply. Firms in purely competitive industries are price takers, selling their output at the market price.
   - Monopoly firms exert a significant amount of influence on the price of their output. Oligopoly firms also influence their prices. Monopolistically competitive firms have only slight influence on their prices. Firms in these three industries are not price takers, since influence over price is inconsistent with price taking.
   - The characteristics of a purely competitive market are: (1) numerous buyers and sellers; (2) a homogeneous product; and (3) free entry and exit. Homogeneous goods are identical across firms in the industry. Free entry means there are no impediments to any firm that wants to produce in the industry. Free exit means there are no impediments to leaving the industry, such as in going out of business, or producing a different output.

2. **Illustrate how market demand and supply determine the competitive firm's demand curve.**
   - Price-taking firms are found in pure competition. Price taking is exemplified by firms in the commodities industries. An individual price-taking firm has no control over its price, which is determined by demand and supply in the market.
   - Market demand is downward sloping. Market demand together with market supply determine the market price of the purely competitive industry's output. Unlike market demand, the purely competitive firm's demand curve is perfectly elastic (horizontal) at the market price.

3. **Identify the competitive firm's short-run supply curve.**
   - The purely competitive firm's supply curve is the segment of its marginal cost curve that lies above its average variable cost curve. When price is below average variable cost, the firm supplies zero output because it will shut down. When price is above average variable cost, the firm maximizes profit by supplying the quantity of output indicated by the intersection of price with marginal cost.

4. **Describe the long-run equilibrium in pure competition.**
   - The long run in a purely competitive market is characterized by zero profit for the firm considering entering or exiting. This outcome is indicated graphically when the firm's demand curve is tangent to the average cost curve. Because entry and exit are free of barriers in pure competition, in the long run, firms will enter or exit until there is no expectation of either a profit or loss.

5. **Explain how efficiency is achieved in a purely competitive market.**
   - Pure competition leads to an efficient quantity of output, meaning that social surplus is maximized. The value of the last unit of output produced equals its marginal cost. Social surplus is reduced when output deviates from the market quantity in pure competition.

6. **Specify the difference between a constant-cost, increasing-cost, and decreasing-cost industry.**
   - In the long run, industries that are perfectly competitive may be characterized as constant cost, increasing cost, or decreasing cost. A firm in a constant-cost industry experiences no shift in its average cost when the industry expands. A firm in an increasing-cost industry employs specialized inputs that increase in price as the industry expands. Because of the price increase, the

industry experiences an upward shift in average cost. A firm in a decreasing-cost industry sees a downward shift in average cost as the industry grows.

- Perfect competition is a variation on pure competition, which assumes identical firms, with identical access to resources, information, and technology. In perfect competition, the long-run supply curve is horizontal for a constant-cost industry, upward sloping for an increasing-cost industry, and downward sloping for a decreasing-cost industry.

 Show how competition can reduce discrimination in society.

- Discrimination on the basis of anything other than productivity increases firms' costs. Since the purely competitive firm cannot differentiate its product, discrimination cannot increase revenue. The result is that the discriminating firm is less likely to be able to achieve a normal profit. Without normal profit, the discriminating firm will exit the industry in the long run.

KEY TERMS

homogeneous products, 482
differentiated products, 482
market structures, 482
monopoly, 482
oligopoly, 482

monopolistic competition, 482
pure competition, 482
market power, 482
constant-cost industry, 489
increasing-cost industry, 489

decreasing-cost industry, 489
perfect competition, 490
long-run supply, 490

TEST YOURSELF

TRUE OR FALSE

1. Both purely competitive and monopolistically competitive markets are characterized by firms that are called price takers.
2. The short-run supply curve for a purely competitive firm is the portion of its marginal cost curve that lies above its average variable cost.
3. Long-run equilibrium in pure competition is characterized by only a normal profit for potential new entrants.
4. Economic efficiency is achieved in purely competitive markets.
5. A long-run supply curve will always slope upward.

MULTIPLE CHOICE

6. Price takers are found in
   a. pure competition.
   b. monopolistic competition.
   c. oligopoly.
   d. all of the above.
7. Market power refers to the ability of a firm to influence its _____. Market power is _____ for price-taking firms.
   a. output; significant
   b. cost; slight
   c. owners; slight
   d. price; zero
8. In pure competition the firm's demand curve will be
   a. upward sloping.
   b. downward sloping.
   c. hump shaped.
   d. horizontal.

9. For a price-taking firm, demand is
   a. equal to price.
   b. less than price.
   c. greater than price.
   d. unrelated to price.
10. A price-taking firm's short-run supply curve is associated with its
   a. total revenue curve.
   b. average cost curve.
   c. marginal revenue curve.
   d. marginal cost curve.
11. Profit maximization calls for the purely competitive firm to produce at the point where its demand curve intersects its
   a. total revenue curve.
   b. average cost curve.
   c. marginal revenue curve.
   d. marginal cost curve.
12. If a potential entrant into pure competition envisions profit, then the model of pure competition says that entry
   a. will definitely occur.
   b. will definitely NOT occur.
   c. might occur, depending upon opportunity costs elsewhere in the economy.
   d. might occur, depending upon how steep the barriers are to entry in that particular purely competitive market.

13. Which statement best describes the long-run equilibrium in a purely competitive market?
    a. The firm's demand curve is downward sloping.
    b. The market will shrink as firms exit.
    c. The number of firms will be stable because there is no incentive for entry or exit.
    d. In the long run, the market will slowly become a monopoly.

14. Graphically, the long run in pure competition is illustrated with price
    a. equal to average cost because profit equals zero.
    b. greater than marginal revenue.
    c. less than marginal revenue.
    d. intersecting marginal cost at a quantity of zero.

15. If Self-Test Figure 19-1 represents a typical firm in the purely competitive widget industry, the market price of widgets will
    a. increase over time.
    b. decrease over time.
    c. remain constant over time.
    d. increase at first, but return later to the original price.

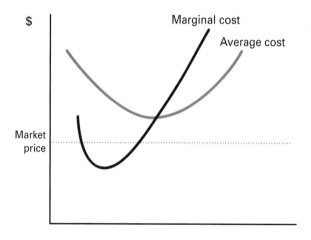

SELF-TEST FIGURE 19-1

16. Exit shifts
    a. supply to the left.
    b. supply to the right.
    c. average cost upward.
    d. average cost downward.

17. Pure competition is
    a. inefficient, because too much output is produced.
    b. inefficient, because too little output is produced.
    c. inefficient, because firms waste resources by competing with one another.
    d. efficient.

18. A decreasing-cost industry is an industry for which
    a. an expansion in the industry will shift firms' cost curves downward.
    b. economic efficiency cannot be achieved.
    c. the industry long-run supply curve is upward sloping.
    d. firms' short-run supply curves are downward sloping.

19. A horizontal long-run supply curve is
    a. impossible.
    b. identified with a constant-cost industry.
    c. identified with an increasing-cost industry.
    d. identified with a decreasing-cost industry.

20. Competitive markets may lessen discrimination because
    a. such markets attract a disproportionate share of minority and women entrepreneurs.
    b. laws against discrimination are more easily enforced because there are fewer firms to police in competitive markets.
    c. entry is quite difficult, so that entrepreneurs who are inclined to practice discrimination can be kept from entering a competitive market.
    d. firms do not have enough profit to pay for it.

QUESTIONS AND PROBLEMS

1. *[market structure]* List the four forms of market structure and briefly describe their characteristics. For each type of market provide an example of an industry or firm that reflects the characteristics of that market.

2. *[market power]* What is market power? In which market structure is market power by firms absent? When market power by firms is absent, what are the firms called?

3. *[homogeneous product and price taking]* Define the term *homogeneous product*. Explain why price taking occurs when products are homogeneous.

4. *[price taker]* What price will a price taker charge for the product it sells? Illustrate that price graphically by drawing two graphs. The first graph will show market demand, supply, and price. The second graph, drawn to the right of the first one, will show the price-taking firm.

5. *[price taker]* In which of the following instances, if any, would the seller likely be a price taker? Explain.
   a. For sale: 1992 Ford Escort.
   b. For sale: 100 shares of General Motors common stock.
   c. For sale: Panasonic 19-inch color television.
   d. For sale: apartment full of furniture.
   e. For sale: silo full of corn.

6. *[market versus firm demand]* If a firm has a horizontal demand curve for its output, will the industry demand curve also be horizontal? Explain.

7. *[graph of firm's short-run supply curve]* Draw a firm's marginal cost and average variable cost curves. Label the axes appropriately. Indicate on your graph the short-run supply curve. State the rule of profit maximization and interpret the rule as it relates to the supply curve in your graph.

8. *[firm's short-run supply curve]* Suppose the minimum average variable cost of producing an ounce of gold at Shiny Yellow Gold Mine is $200 an ounce. That minimum value occurs at a quantity of five tons of gold per month. Further suppose that the marginal cost of producing each ounce of gold is:

Quantity of Gold (tons per month)	Marginal Cost per Ounce of Gold
0	--
1	$50
2	25
3	75
4	125
5	200
6	275
7	350
8	435
9	525
10	750

Fill in the following table with the supply data for Shiny Yellow Gold Mine.

When the Price per Ounce of Gold Is:	Shiny Yellow Gold Mine Will Produce:
$100	
150	
200	
250	
300	
350	
400	
450	
500	
550	
600	

Does your computation of supply show that higher prices are associated with a greater quantity supplied? Is this result consistent with the usual depiction of supply? Explain.

9. *[market supply curve]* Suppose a purely competitive industry is composed of 1,000 identical firms each producing according to the table below. Fill in the missing market supply numbers in the last column of the table.

Price	Single Firm's Quantity Supplied	Market Supply
$1	10	
2	12	
3	14	
4	16	
5	18	

10. *[long run in pure competition]* Is the following statement true or false? Entry in a purely competitive market is free of barriers to entry, which leads to a potential entrant in pure competition earning a long-run economic profit. Explain your answer.

11. *[long run in pure competition]* How does the short-run market supply curve shift when there is entry or exit in a purely competitive market? When will entry occur? What effect does entry have on economic profit? When will exit occur? What effect will exit have on the profitability of the market?

12. *[long-run equilibrium in pure competition]* Explain graphically and in words the proposition that, at equilibrium in pure competition, a firm contemplating entry can expect to earn zero economic profit.

13. *[efficiency of pure competition]* Explain how purely competitive markets achieve economic efficiency. Draw a graph to illustrate your answer.

14. *[constant-cost industry]* Draw a long-run supply curve for a constant-cost industry. As a constant-cost industry expands, why don't the average cost curves of firms in the industry shift upward?

15. *[increasing-cost industry]* Draw a long-run supply curve for an increasing-cost industry. What causes the average cost curves of firms in an increasing-cost industry to shift upward?

16. *[decreasing-cost industry]* Draw a long-run supply curve for a decreasing-cost industry. What causes the average cost curves of firms in a decreasing-cost industry to shift downward?

WORKING WITH GRAPHS AND DATA

1. *[entry and exit]* Refer to Graph 19-1(a) which shows market supply and demand, and Graph 19-1(b), which shows the average cost and marginal cost curves of a firm in the industry.

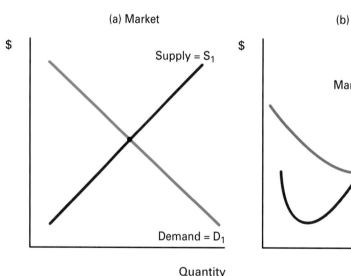

(a) Market

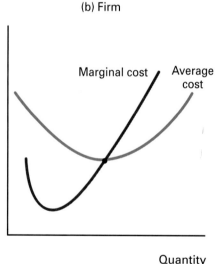

(b) Firm

GRAPH 19-1

a. Identify the equilibrium price in the market and label it P_1. Use P_1 to show the demand curve for the firm in part (b) and label it D_1.

b. Assume that the firms in this market are identical. At price P_1 what would happen in the long run? Explain.

c. Show what would happen in the long run to the supply curve in the market and label the new supply curve S_2.

d. Identify the new equilibrium price in the market and label it P_2. Use P_2 to show the new demand curve for the firm in part (b) and label it D_2.

e. Why would there be no further adjustments to price in this market?

2. *[efficiency of pure competition]* Graph 19-2(a) and (b) contain market supply and demand curves for pure competition.

(a)   (b)

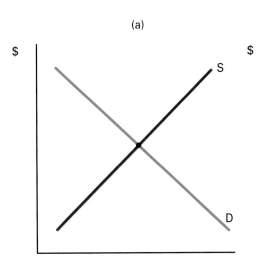

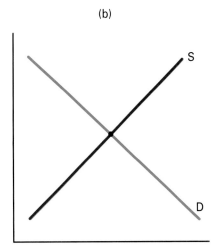

Quantity of output   Quantity of output

GRAPH 19-2

a. Assume that this purely competitive market shown in Graph 19-2(a) is in equilibrium. Show the social surplus that would be produced in this market and label it "Social surplus."

b. This social surplus demonstrates that this market is allocatively efficient. What does this mean?

c. Use Graph 19(b) to show what happens to the social surplus when output increases beyond the equilibrium output. Label the resulting loss in surplus "Lost surplus 1."

d. Use Graph 19(b) to show what happens to the social surplus when output decreases below the equilibrium output. Label the resulting loss in surplus "Lost surplus 2."

e. What can you conclude happens to allocative efficiency when output in a purely competitive market either increases or decreases from its equilibrium quantity?

3. *[firm's short-run supply]* Use the following table of a purely competitive firm's marginal cost curve to answer the following questions.

Quantity:	0	1	2	3	4	5	6	7
Marginal Cost:	—	10	5	10	15	20	25	30
Quantity Supplied:								
Price:	—	0	5	10	16	20	28	30

a. Assume that the minimum value of the firm's average variable cost is $10. Given the quantity-marginal cost information, identify the quantity that this firm will supply at the prices in the lower portion of the table.

b. Draw a graph of the supply curve on Graph 19-3(a) and label it S_1.

c. Suppose that this firm was part of a market with 100 identical firms. Fill in the values for the market quantity for each price in the table below.

Market Quantity:							
Price:	0	5	10	16	20	28	30

d. Draw a graph of the market supply curve into Graph 19-3(b) and label it S_2.

e. Are these supply curves consistent with the law of supply? Explain.

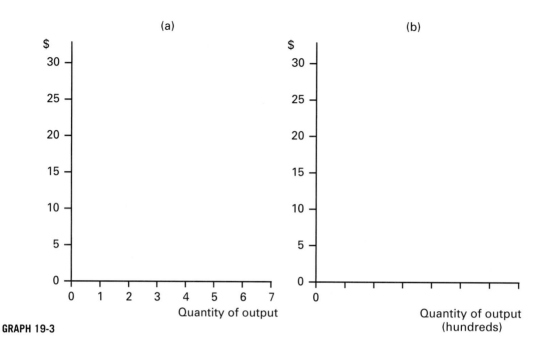

GRAPH 19-3

3. *[discrimination]* Use the average cost (AC$_1$) and marginal cost (MC$_1$) curves in Graph 19-4 for this purely competitive firm to answer the following questions.

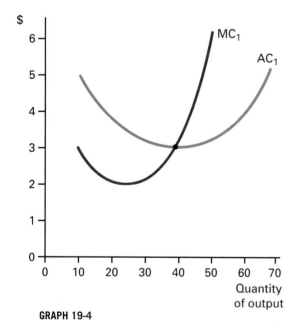

GRAPH 19-4

a. Suppose the market price facing this firm is $3. Draw the demand curve for the firm and label it D$_1$. Show the profit-maximizing quantity as Q$_1$.

b. What are total economic profits for this firm at a price of $3? Why?

c. Suppose that the owner of this firm decides to discriminate by only hiring white males whose wages are higher than those of women and non-white workers. Show what happens if the firm incurs wages that raise the AC and MC curves by $1 per unit. Label the new curves AC$_2$ and MC$_2$. Show the profit-maximizing quantity as Q$_2$.

d. What will be the effect on profit? Explain. Show the change in profit or loss and label it either "Loss" or "Gain."

e. Will this firm stay in business in the long run if it continues to discriminate? Explain.

 Visit **www.prenhall.com/ayers** for Exploring the Web exercises and additional self-test quizzes.

CHAPTER 20

MONOPOLY AND ANTITRUST

A LOOK AHEAD

Most of us can look forward to a visitor every day of the week except Sunday. This visitor sometimes comes bearing gifts, other times bills. The visitor, the U.S. Postal Service letter carrier, is a representative of the country's oldest monopoly. The Postal Service is unique in having its monopoly status mentioned in the U.S. Constitution. This chapter's Explore & Apply section sheds light on technological changes and market shifts that could impact the monopoly status of the Postal Service.

Why should we be concerned with monopolies at all? The model of an unregulated profit-maximizing monopoly shows that a monopoly cuts output and raises price relative to what price and output would be in pure competition. Monopoly creates inefficiency—inefficiency that can persist in the long run. On the face of it, regulation by government seems like a way to avoid the problems created by monopoly. However, regulation is imperfect. For that reason several industries, including trucking and the airlines, have been deregulated and competition has been encouraged. More deregulation is coming, which has created expectations among consumers that the resulting competition will take money out of the pockets of monopoly firms and put it into theirs!

LEARNING OBJECTIVES

Understanding Chapter 20 will enable you to:
1. **Describe how barriers to entry create market power.**
2. **Discuss the profit-maximizing process for a monopolist.**
3. **Explain the inefficiencies of monopoly.**
4. **Name and briefly discuss major U.S. antitrust laws and potentially punishable practices.**
5. **Identify government policies toward monopoly.**
6. **Assess the merits of protecting the U.S. Postal Service from competition.**

Explore & Apply

The previous chapter introduced the four market structures, arranged according to *market power*, which is the ability to set prices. This chapter examines the market structure of monopoly, in which one firm supplies the entire market. As the only seller in a market, a monopoly firm holds more market power than any other kind of firm.

20.1 SOURCES OF MONOPOLY

monopoly when a single firm sells an output for which there are no close substitutes.

A *monopoly* is characterized by a single firm selling an output for which there are no close substitutes. Goods substitute for one another when they fill the same need. For example, if there is only one seller of a good, is the seller a monopolist? Not if another good serves the same purpose. In that case, consumers who are dissatisfied with the price or quality of one good can stop buying it and obtain equivalent satisfaction by purchasing the other.

Whether there are close substitutes for a good or service is often not obvious. Consider your local cable television provider. Usually only one cable company provides service in an area. However, if satellite dishes, network television, theaters, and other recreation are good substitutes, then local cable companies are not truly monopolies.

BARRIERS TO ENTRY

barriers to entry when investors or entrepreneurs find obstacles to joining a profitable industry.

Monopoly is caused by very high **barriers to entry,** which exist when investors or entrepreneurs find obstacles to joining a profitable industry. Barriers to entry include anything that makes producing and selling output more difficult for a new firm than for an existing firm. Monopoly represents the ultimate barrier to entry—one so high that only one firm makes up the entire industry. There are three factors that can create a monopoly:

monopoly by law (legal monopoly) when legal barriers restrict the supply of a good to one firm, and when there are no close substitutes for that good.

- **Monopoly by law** (also called **legal monopoly**) when one firm is protected by law from competition, and there are no close substitutes for the good. First-class mail is an example, where the U.S. Postal Statutes make it illegal for equivalent services to be offered by any other provider. Patents, such as for Cipro, AZT, and other pharmaceutical drugs, could also form the basis for a monopoly by law. Typically, however, the barriers to entry that are formed by patents, trademarks, copyrights, and similar legal protections fall short of those needed for monopoly. The reason is that there are nearly always substitutes for the product.

monopoly by possession when a single firm owns a resource needed in the production of a good for which there are no close substitutes.

- **Monopoly by possession**—when one firm is the only owner of a resource needed to produce a good, and there are no close substitutes for the resource or for the good. Diamonds are an example, with De Beers Consolidated Mines, Ltd., producing a good that is like no other. De Beers has been accumulating diamond mines since 1888 and is easily the largest diamond mining company in the world. Its twenty mines in South Africa, Botswana, Namibia, and Tanzania produce about 40 percent of the world's gem-quality diamonds. It has additional production agreements with the owners of another 40 percent of the world's diamond supply. That 80 percent control of output in the diamond market makes De Beers about as close as reality gets to monopoly by possession.

natural monopoly when one firm can supply the entire market at a lower per-unit cost than could two or more separate firms.

- **Natural monopoly**—when it is cheaper for one firm to produce the entire industry's output than it would be for two or more firms to produce the same output. Again, there must be no close substitutes for the good. Natural monopoly might be called monopoly by technology, because technological advances can sometimes introduce competition. Natural monopoly will be discussed further in the next section.

Barriers to entry bring about market power. This market power reveals itself in the slope of the demand curve facing the firm. If the demand curve slopes down only slightly, it is probably because there are many close substitutes for the firm's product, which leaves the

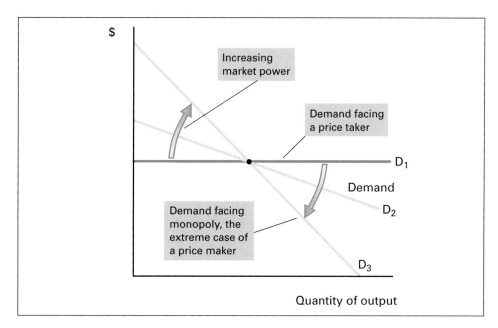

$

Increasing
market power

Demand facing
a price taker

Demand facing
monopoly, the
extreme case of
a price maker

D₁

Demand

D₂

D₃

Quantity of output

FIGURE 20-1

THE EFFECT OF INCREASING MARKET POWER Market power increases as demand steepens. If the firm's demand is horizontal (D_1), the firm is a price taker and has no market power. When demand slopes down (D_2), the firm has market power. Demand curve D_3 would face a monopolist. Monopoly is the extreme case in which demand facing the firm slopes down as steeply as market demand—the two are one and the same.

firm with only a little ability to control price. Holding units of measurement constant, **the steeper the demand curve, the more market power the firm has and the greater its ability to determine price.**

Figure 20-1 shows three possible demand curves facing the firm. If the firm's demand is horizontal (D_1), it is a price taker with no market power. The firm would have market power if its demand curve slopes down (D_2). **Monopoly represents the most market power, in which case the firm's demand is identical to market demand.** The monopolist's demand would slope down relatively steeply (D_3).

No firm's market power is absolute, because no firm can raise prices without reducing the quantity demanded. Even a monopoly will find that if it raises the price enough, it will reach the point where the demand curve intersects the price axis. At that point, the quantity demanded equals zero. The firm would never want to raise the price nearly that high. Rather, it seeks the price that will sell its profit-maximizing quantity. For this reason, a firm with market power is called a **price maker,** in contrast to the price taker found in pure competition.

price maker a firm that faces a downward-sloping demand curve.

IS THE AMERICAN MEDICAL ASSOCIATION HAZARDOUS TO YOUR HEALTH?   *SNAPSHOT*

The American Medical Association (AMA) is not a government agency. Nevertheless, this professional association has much to say about the availability of healthcare. Not only does it have power over the standards for licensing physicians, but it also has considerable input into setting standards for medical schools. For better or for worse, these standards form barriers to entry.

Some critics of the current U.S. healthcare system accuse the AMA of setting unnecessarily high standards, which serve to heighten market power within the medical profession. Critics contend that physicians are motivated by more income. The AMA responds that there is merely a coincidence of self-interest and public interest, and that it is the public interest that guides their actions. They point out that medicine is a life or death proposition, and that the public is best served by allowing only the best physicians to do the serving. ◄

NATURAL MONOPOLY

Natural monopoly occurs when one firm can supply the entire market at a lower per-unit cost than could two or more separate firms. This means that natural monopoly will occur any time that the minimum point on long-run average cost occurs near or to the right of market demand, as illustrated in Figure 20-2(a) and (b), respectively. **Natural monopoly occurs when there are substantial economies of scale.** A potential entrant will think twice about challenging a natural monopolist. To realize economies of scale, the entrant would need to start large, so large that the entrant and the established firm could not both survive. Few investors would be willing to finance such a challenge.

For example, imagine three or four water suppliers each burying water mains along a street and competing for the business of the nearby residents. A single firm could eliminate this wasteful duplication of effort and in the process lower the average costs of providing service. Water companies and local gas and electric companies are examples of *public utili-*

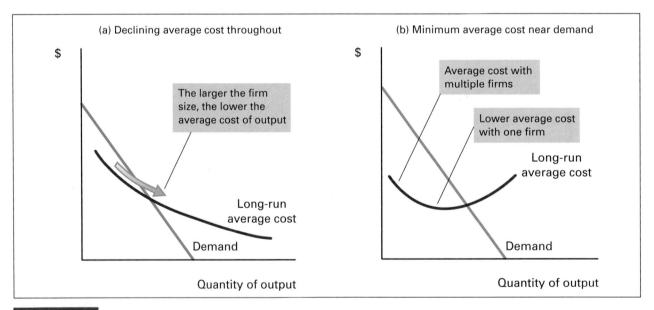

FIGURE 20-2

NATURAL MONOPOLY Natural monopoly occurs whenever one firm can supply the entire market at a lower average cost than could any combination of firms. Graph (a) illustrates a natural monopoly in which long-run average cost declines throughout the relevant range of output. Graph (b) shows a natural monopoly in which long-run average cost reaches its minimum point before intersecting the demand curve, but near enough to demand that one firm could still profitably underprice any combination of two or more firms.

ties, which have distribution lines of pipes, wires, and cables that have traditionally made them natural monopolies.

In recent years, advances in technology have eliminated or scaled back what were once thought to be natural monopolies. For example, local telephone service was a common example of a natural monopoly until near the end of the twentieth century. Today, however, advances in technology for billing and call switching allow customers in many cities to choose among alternative providers of local phone service over the telephone lines. A city's telephone lines have remained owned by one provider, typically, but that isn't a natural monopoly, either. Telephone customers these days have a choice of competing transmission methods, including cable and wireless. More and more people are choosing to rely on their cellular phones or Internet connections for basic telephone service. The result is that telephone service has left the realm of natural monopoly altogether.

Electric service has been another common example of natural monopoly. In this industry, technology has scaled back the natural monopoly portion of the business to only the transmission lines, themselves. As customers in many states already know, it is possible to choose electric power from competing companies, which then feed the electricity into the same power grid for transmission to the customer. Local power lines remain a natural monopoly, since technology has not yet come up with any viable alternatives. That's not to say there have not been attempts. Many dream of solar-powered homes, for example. So far, though, solar collectors on rooftops have proven either too expensive or not feasible. Likewise, septic tanks are usually not a practical substitute for city sewage disposal services, another natural monopoly.

20.2 THE PROFIT-MAXIMIZING MONOPOLY

In competition, firms are price takers and have only to find the intersection between the market price and their marginal cost curves in order to maximize profit. In the long run, competitive firms will have no expectation of profit by entering or exiting an industry. In contrast, monopoly firms must set the price and could potentially earn large and lasting profit. This section examines both the process of profit maximization and the results for the firm and for society.

FINDING THE PROFIT MAXIMUM

Recall from the elasticity chapter that total revenue is maximized when the elasticity of demand equals one, which occurs at the midpoint of a straight-line demand curve. Since the market demand is the demand facing the monopoly firm, it, too, would maximize its revenue when elasticity equals one. Even if production costs were zero, the monopoly would not produce any more than the revenue-maximizing output, since to do so would lower its total revenue, and thus its profit. With a positive marginal cost of production, the monopoly firm will produce less than the revenue-maximizing output. This means that **the monopoly firm always chooses to produce in the elastic range of demand.**

The rule of profit maximization for a monopoly is the same as for all other firms: produce at the point where marginal revenue equals marginal cost. Marginal revenue is the slope of total revenue, as shown in Figure 20-3. Marginal revenue equals zero when total revenue is at a maximum, since the slope of total revenue equals zero at its maximum. Maximum total revenue occurs at the same quantity associated with the midpoint of a straight-line demand curve. The midpoint is also the point of unit elasticity, as shown in the figure and discussed previously in the elasticity chapter. Observe that, for this and any straight-line demand curve, marginal revenue slopes down twice as fast as demand, intersecting the horizontal axis under the midpoint of demand.

MONOPOLY REVENUE Marginal revenue is the slope of total revenue. When total revenue is maximized, marginal revenue equals zero. This outcome occurs at the point where the elasticity of demand is one. The monopolist will avoid producing so much output that marginal revenue is negative.

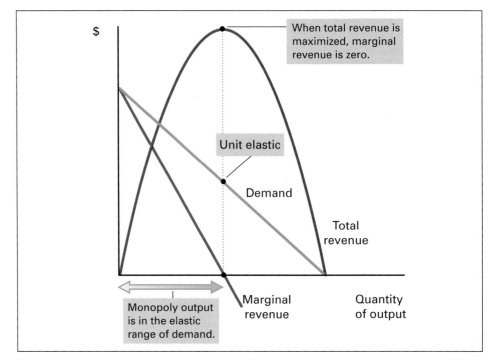

MARGINAL REVENUE LESS THAN PRICE To increase sales of its output, the monopolist must lower the price of that output. The lower price applies to not only the last unit of output that the monopolist sells, but also to all the other units of output. So while the last unit of output adds its price to total revenue, it also subtracts a little bit from the price of all of the other units of output the monopolist had already been selling. This logic explains why the monopolist's marginal revenue is less than its price.

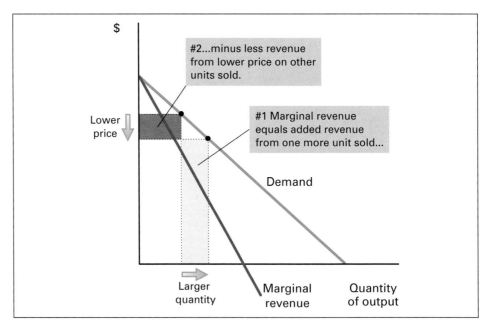

For monopoly, and other firms with downward-sloping demand curves that charge a single price, marginal revenue is less than that price. The reason is that, if such a firm wants to sell more units, it will have to offer potential buyers a lower price. The lower price would then apply to every unit of output that it offers for sale, as shown in Figure 20-4. The result is that the marginal revenue from an extra unit of output would equal the price of that unit minus the price reduction on every other unit sold. For this reason, **a downward-sloping demand curve is associated with a marginal revenue curve that slopes down even more steeply.**

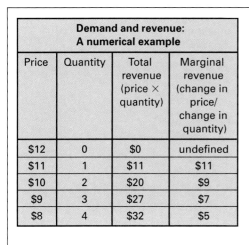

Demand and revenue: A numerical example			
Price	Quantity	Total revenue (price × quantity)	Marginal revenue (change in price/ change in quantity)
$12	0	$0	undefined
$11	1	$11	$11
$10	2	$20	$9
$9	3	$27	$7
$8	4	$32	$5

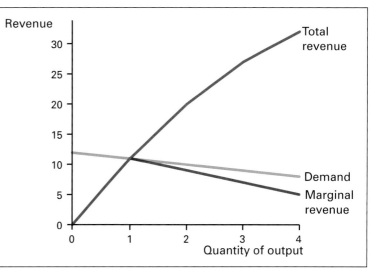

FIGURE 20-5

DEMAND AND REVENUE—A NUMERICAL EXAMPLE The data in the table are plotted to show demand, total revenue, and marginal revenue for a monopoly. Note that the data confirm that marginal revenue has a steeper slope than demand.

Let's now turn to a numerical example. Consider the monopoly shown in Figure 20-5. The firm must reduce its price in order to sell more output. Total revenue, equal to price multiplied by quantity, is shown in the third column. Marginal revenue, the change in total revenue divided by the change in quantity, is computed in the last column. As before, marginal revenue decreases more rapidly than price as quantity increases.

To see why marginal revenue decreases more rapidly than price, consider the price reduction from $10 to $9. This price cut allows the firm to sell three units of output, but also causes the revenue from the sale of the first two units, which would have been $20 at the $10 price, to drop to $18. This drop of $2 means that total revenue will rise by less than the $9 price of the third unit. Specifically, total revenue rises from $20 to $27, an increase of $7, which equals the price of $9 minus the decrease of $2 on the first two units.

To find its profit-maximizing price and quantity, the monopoly firm will calculate its marginal revenue at various quantities. It will then compare marginal revenue to marginal cost at each quantity. At some point the two must be equal, because marginal revenue declines as more output is produced and sold, while marginal cost rises because of the law of diminishing returns. Once the profit-maximizing quantity is determined, the firm will charge the highest price possible that allows it to sell that amount of output. This price is given by the point on the demand curve that corresponds to the output that the firm has chosen. This two-step process—first determine output, then price—is shown in Figure 20-6. Note that the price is higher than either marginal cost or marginal revenue at that output.

Under monopoly, the quantity that will be supplied at any particular price depends on demand. Other things equal, the more elastic is demand, the lower will be the price the monopoly charges. Figure 20-7 illustrates this result, where there are two alternative demand curves. Associated with each is a marginal revenue curve that leads to the same profit-maximizing quantity. The more elastic demand leads to a lower profit-maximizing price at this quantity. The result is different prices associated with the same quantity, depending on demand. **Since there is no unique relationship between price and quantity supplied, the monopolist has no supply curve.**

FIGURE 20-6

MONOPOLY OUTPUT AND PRICE
The unregulated monopoly firm
selects output and price in two
steps. First, the monopolist produces until marginal cost equals
marginal revenue. Second, the
monopolist charges the highest
price that will sell that output.

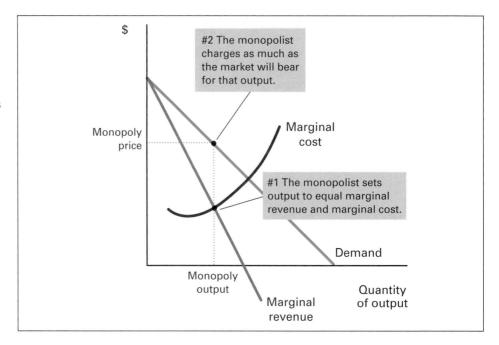

FIGURE 20-7

EFFECT OF DEMAND ELASTICITY
To maximize profit, the monopolist equates marginal cost and
marginal revenue. The resulting
price depends on the elasticity
of demand. The greater the
demand elasticity at the monopoly quantity, the lower will be
the monopoly price. The result
is that a monoploy has no supply curve.

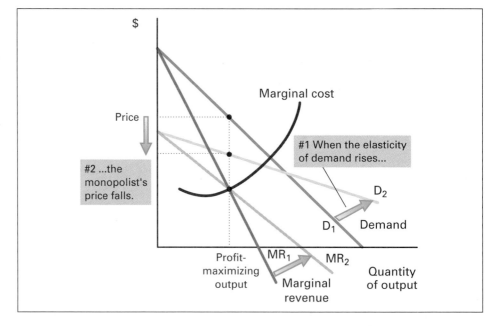

PROFIT, BREAKEVEN, OR LOSS

Figure 20-8 shows graphically a profit-maximizing monopoly. The profit-maximizing quantity in the figure occurs at the point where marginal revenue equals marginal cost. The
profit-maximizing price is set at the corresponding point on the demand curve. The profit is
shown as a rectangle, created when the average profit per unit sold is multiplied by the number of units sold. The average profit per unit is the difference between price and average cost
at the profit-maximizing quantity.

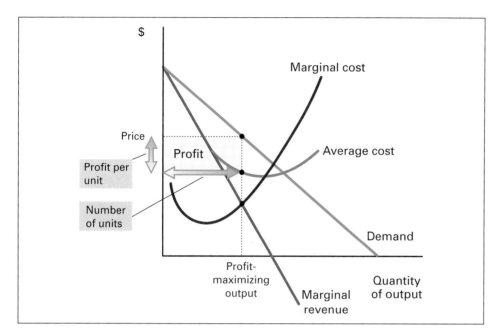

FIGURE 20-8

MONOPOLY PROFIT Total profit equals profit per unit (price - average cost) multiplied by the quantity produced. Profit is shown as the shaded area.

Monopolies can sometimes be quite profitable, since there are no other competitors to undercut their prices. However, merely because a firm is a monopoly does not mean it has a profit. A monopoly firm might find that the best it can do is to breakeven or even to lose money, as shown in Figure 20-9. One reason might be that the monopoly's product is no longer as necessary as it once was. For example, telegraph lines fell into disrepair as telegraph services were displaced by the telephone and, later, the Internet.

Consider an example that allows us to apply the steps that a monopoly firm will take in maximizing profit. Suppose that inventor Archibald Swift has perfected a device that will allow anyone to learn a subject simply by attaching a headband and turning on a machine before going to bed. The device fills the user's mind with knowledge while he or she sleeps. Archibald has formed a corporation, BrainPrinting, Inc., to produce and market the product. BrainPrinting is an unregulated monopoly firm. There are no close substitutes for its product, and government regulators do not control its price or output.

At what price should BrainPrinters be sold? No matter what price Archibald chooses as a starting point, if he wants to increase his sales, he will have to offer potential buyers a lower price. The lower price would then apply to every unit of output that he offers for sale. This means that the marginal revenue from selling an extra BrainPrinter would equal the price of that BrainPrinter, minus the price reduction on every other BrainPrinter sold. Archibald reasons that marginal revenue is thus less than price.

To estimate demand, Archibald test-markets BrainPrinters by offering a one-night trial to a sample of college students, at prices ranging from $12 to zero (free). In the test, the demand schedule for the trial BrainPrinters shows that a price of $12 leads to zero sales, $11 to one sale, $10 to two sales, $9 to three sales, $8 to four sales, and so forth. Notice that the first five prices and corresponding quantities match those in Figure 20-5. Multiplying each price by the corresponding quantity, the total revenue figures are $0, $11, $20, $27, $32, and so on. Since marginal revenue is the change in total revenue resulting from an additional sale, the respective marginal revenue figures are $11, $9, $7, $5, and so forth. This confirms that, as quantity rises, marginal revenue drops faster than price for the price-making firm.

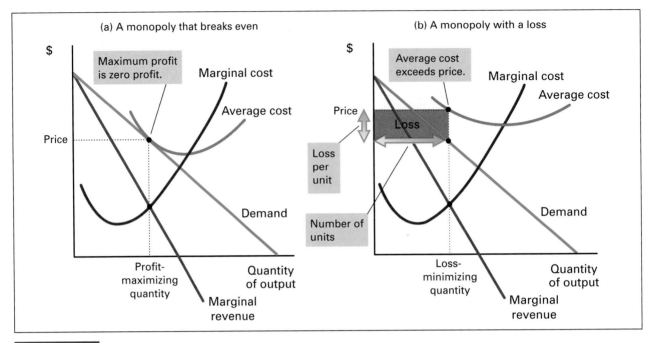

FIGURE 20-9

MONOPOLY BREAKEVEN AND LOSS A profit-maximizing monopolist might find that the best it can do is to break even. As shown in (a), such a firm finds that producing to the point where marginal cost equals marginal revenue allows it to charge a price that merely covers its costs. This result is shown on the graph as average cost just tangent to demand.

If average cost at that point is more than demand, as shown in (b), the firm loses money and would exit the industry in the long run. The loss would equal the loss per unit (average cost - price) multiplied by the quantity produced. Loss is shown as the shaded area.

To find the profit-maximizing price and quantity of BrainPrinters, Archibald will calculate the total and marginal revenues at various prices. He will then produce the quantity for which marginal revenue equals marginal cost.

Table 20-1 demonstrates profit maximization by the BrainPrinting, Inc., monopoly. The first two columns show price and quantity—the firm's demand. Total revenue, in the third column, equals price multiplied by quantity. Marginal revenue, computed in the fourth column, equals the change in total revenue divided by the change in quantity. The fifth column shows total cost. Marginal cost is computed in the next column as the change in total cost divided by the change in quantity. In the second-to-last column average cost is presented, where average cost equals total cost divided by quantity. The eighth column shows total profit, computed as total revenue minus total cost.

The final column reveals that maximum profit equals $24.50, which occurs at either four or five units of output (the latter indicated by ✓ in the table) and a price of either $7 or $8. The reason that two separate combinations show up is that marginal cost and marginal revenue are identical for unit 5, meaning that the firm is indifferent about increasing output from four to five units. More generally, firms keep producing so long as marginal revenue exceeds marginal cost and stop before the reverse holds. Therefore, the firm would not produce the sixth unit, since marginal cost exceeds marginal revenue.

TABLE 20-1 REVENUE AND COSTS FOR BRAINPRINTING, INC., A MONOPOLY FIRM

(1) PRICE	(2) QUANTITY	(3) TOTAL REVENUE	(4) MARGINAL REVENUE	(5) TOTAL COST	(6) MARGINAL COST	(7) AVERAGE COST*	(8) PROFIT
$12	0	$0	Undefined	$3	Undefined	Undefined	$−3
11	1	11	$11	4	$1	$4.00	+7
10	2	20	9	4.5	0.5	2.25	+15.5
9	3	27	7	5.5	1	1.83	+21.5
8	4	32	5	7.5	2	1.88	+24.5
7	5✓	35	3	10.5	3	2.10	+24.5
6	6	36	1	15.5	5	2.58	+20.5
5	7	35	−1	24	8.5	3.43	+11
4	8	32	−3	36	12	4.50	−4
3	9	27	−5	52	16	5.78	−25
2	10	20	−7	70	18	7.00	−50
1	11	11	−9	92	22	8.36	−81
0	12	0	−11	120	28	10.00	−120

*Rounded to the nearest penny.

QUICKCHECK

Suppose a profit-maximizing monopoly firm is incurring a loss. In what way would a graph showing this concept differ from one showing a profit-maximizing monopolist with a profit?

Answer: The difference would be that the average cost curve for the firm with the loss would lie everywhere above the demand curve, causing average cost to be above price at the profit-maximizing (loss-minimizing) output. In both cases, the output will correspond to the intersection of marginal revenue and marginal cost. Also, rather than a rectangle showing profit, there will be a rectangle showing loss. The two situations are depicted in Figures 20-8 and 20-9(b), respectively.

EFFICIENCY AND PRICE DISCRIMINATION

Allocative efficiency requires that each good be produced up to the point at which its marginal cost of production just equals the marginal benefit from its consumption. Yet firms produce to the point where marginal cost equals marginal revenue. It is only because the market price is identical to marginal revenue for price-taking firms that pure competition is efficient.

FIGURE 20-10

THE INEFFICIENCY OF MONOPOLY
Allocative efficiency requires an output for which marginal cost equals marginal benefit (given by demand). However, the unregulated monopoly would choose to produce the output for which marginal cost equals marginal revenue. Since marginal revenue is less than demand, the monopoly produces too little output. The value of the output forgone is the difference between the marginal benefits and marginal costs over that range of output, which is the yellow-shaded area between the demand curve and marginal cost curve. This forgone social surplus is referred to as the triangle of deadweight loss.

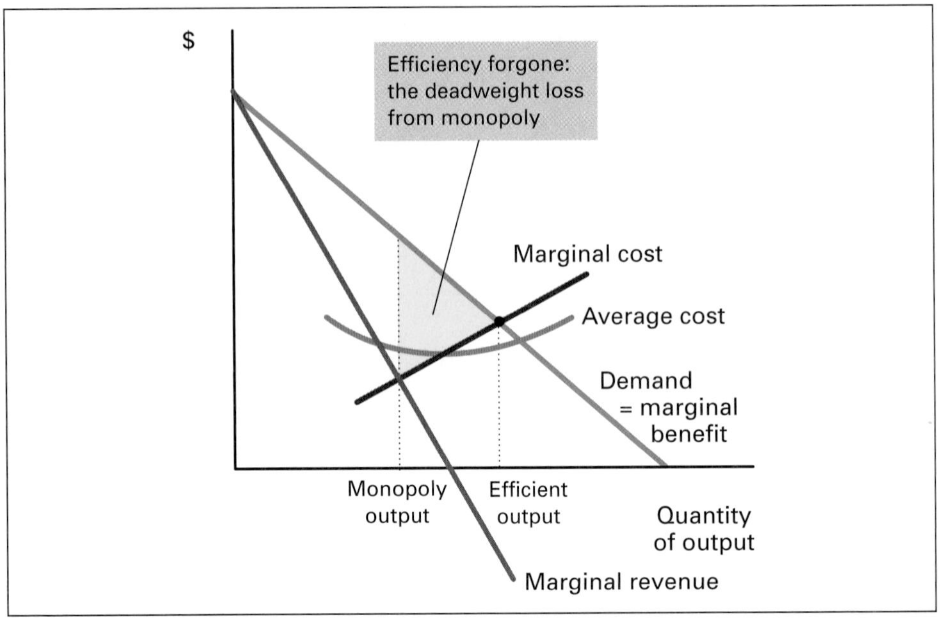

deadweight loss value of efficiency that is not achieved.

limit pricing charging the highest price customers will pay, subject to the limit that the price not be so high that potential competitors enter the industry.

price discrimination charging different prices for different units of output, where the differences do not depend on differences in production costs.

perfect price discrimination price discrimination that perfectly matches the demand curve.

In contrast, at any given point in time, monopoly is allocatively inefficient because the quantity that equates marginal cost and marginal revenue falls short of the quantity that equates marginal cost and demand. The result is that the profit-maximizing quantity is less than the efficient quantity. Figure 20-10 shows these differing quantities and the inefficiency caused by the monopolist's choice. The shaded triangular area is the inefficiency, called **deadweight loss,** which shows the benefits that consumers would have received from the additional output minus the cost the firm would have incurred to produce it. In short, deadweight loss is the value of efficiency that is not achieved.

While the monopolist does not face competition directly, it does face the threat of *potential competition* from new producers or new products. If a monopolist prices its product too high, new substitutes may be developed that draw away the monopolist's customers. Alternatively, a new firm may take the risk of challenging the monopolist's turf. To avoid these possibilities, a monopolist might practice **limit pricing,** which is charging the highest price customers will pay, subject to the limit that the price not be so high that it attracts potential competitors. **The limit price will be lower than the short-run profit-maximizing price.** Although short-run profit is reduced, limit pricing allows the monopolist to earn more profit in the long run by keeping competitors away. It also moves the quantity of output produced in the direction of the efficient amount.

Although an unregulated monopoly will not normally produce an efficient quantity at each point in time, it does have the potential to generate profits that it could invest in research and development to enhance its monopoly status. Competitive firms have neither the incentive nor financial ability to pursue research and development. In addition, the lure of monopoly profit is a powerful motivating force for investment. For these reasons, the overall efficiency of monopoly is a matter of debate. While producing too little and charging too much in the short run, monopoly profits might bring about new and better products in the long run.

The short-run inefficiency of monopoly could be eliminated in theory. The monopolist would need to perfectly match prices to the demand curve, which is a form of price discrimination. **Price discrimination** occurs when a firm charges different prices for different units of output and the differences are not based on the cost of providing the product. Matching prices exactly to the demand curve is the extreme of **perfect price discrimination,** in which the firm charges a different price to each customer equal to the maximum amount

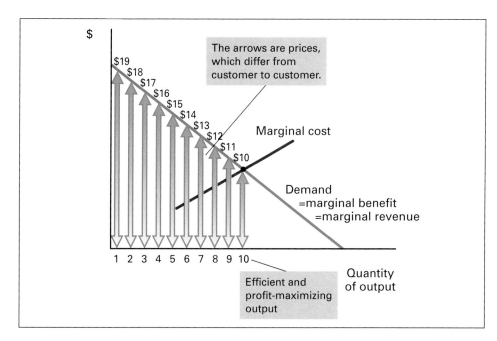

FIGURE 20-11

PERFECT PRICE DISCRIMINATION
Whatever the item is worth to the customer relative to doing without, that is what the customer pays if the monopoly practices perfect price discrimination. The demand curve is also the marginal revenue curve because the firm lowers the price for each succeeding purchaser, not for all purchasers. Consumers would receive no consumer surplus in this case. Perfect price discrimination would lead the profit-maximizing firm to produce an efficient quantity of output. Less-than-perfect price discrimination leads to a less-than-efficient output.

the customer would be willing to pay for the good to avoid doing without it entirely. In other words, the monopolist would capture all consumer surplus by charging the set of prices given by the demand curve.

Figure 20-11 shows an example of perfect price discrimination. In this case, the firm would charge $19 for the first unit of output, $18 for the second, and so forth until the tenth and final unit, which is priced at $10. Each unit of output would retain its separate price. If perfect price discrimination were possible, demand and marginal revenue would be one and the same. By choosing the quantity for which marginal cost and marginal revenue are equal, the monopolist would also be equating marginal cost and marginal benefit. The result would be an efficient output of ten units, as shown in Figure 20-11.

Perfect price discrimination would require that the monopolist not only know each customer's demand curve, but also be able to prevent customers that are charged low prices from reselling the product to other customers charged higher prices. The difficulty of meeting these assumptions means that perfect price discrimination is not observed in practice. Monopolists would like to achieve this goal and the outcome would be efficient. However, consumers would not be happy.

A less extreme example of price discrimination is **multi-part pricing,** in which the price depends on the quantity consumed. For example, the monopolist might set the price very high for the first units consumed, since those are the hardest for customers to do without. Price for additional units could be lower. If used in this manner, multi-part pricing causes marginal revenue to fall somewhere between the extremes of the monopolist with a single price and one able to practice perfect price discrimination. As a result, multi-part pricing can lead to greater efficiency.

Multi-part pricing is often used by municipal electricity or water companies. For example, the utility might charge a low per-unit price to cover marginal cost, but supplement its revenues by also charging each customer a separate monthly service fee to cover the fixed cost of its network of pipes or cables. Similar reasoning explains why it often costs quite a bit to get new telephone service, even though the local phone company need do little more than "flip a switch." The extra money is helping cover the fixed costs of the telephone system.

multi-part pricing a form of price discrimination in which the price depends on the quantity consumed.

20.3 ANTITRUST AND REGULATION

There are various ways in which public policy can address the inefficiencies of monopoly and protect consumers from unfairly high prices. The remedies include breaking up the monopoly, regulating the monopoly, and government ownership. This section discusses these policies and their drawbacks.

ANTITRUST POLICY: AN OVERVIEW

Toward the late nineteenth century, large businesses, called *trusts,* began to dominate and even monopolize various industries. By 1890, public outrage over various alleged abuses of the marketplace by the trusts led to calls for action. Congress responded by passing the *Sherman Act* by the overwhelming vote of 52 to 1 in the Senate and 242 to 0 in the House. This act is the foundation of **antitrust law**—public policies designed to limit the abuse of market power by monopolies—and is enforced by the Justice Department. The focus of the act is on the conduct of a business, although specific illegal actions are not spelled out. In general, it prohibits contracts, combinations, and conspiracies in restraint of trade. It also forbids attempts to monopolize markets, but does not make monopoly itself illegal.

antitrust law public policies designed to limit the abuse of market power by monopolies.

Because of the failure of Congress to write specific provisions into the Sherman Act, it initially proved ineffective at curbing the power of the trusts. Thus, additional legislation was drafted, aimed at spelling out particular anti-competitive behaviors and making them illegal. The *Federal Trade Commission Act* and the *Clayton Act* were signed into law in 1914, thus completing the job of laying the foundation for today's antitrust enforcement. The Clayton Act supplements the Sherman Act by listing specific illegal actions, such as acquiring stock in a competing firm when that action would lessen competition. The Federal Trade Commission (FTC) was created to oversee markets, with the goal of eliminating unfair trade practices. Other antitrust legislation has augmented these laws by preventing firms from taking anti-competitive actions that would give them excessive market power.

Table 20-2 summarizes the key features of the antitrust laws. Note that both the government and competing firms can file antitrust complaints. A violator of the antitrust laws can be forced to pay up to three times the damages it inflicts on other firms. It can also be fined, broken into competing parts, and its employees imprisoned. Sometimes accused firms will sign a consent decree, in which they agree to change their behavior without admitting guilt.

The antitrust laws neither make monopoly illegal nor apply only to monopoly. Rather, they are intended to curb abuses of market power, of which monopolists have the most. They limit the manner in which firms can compete to what is efficient for society and fair to consumers and potential competitors. In considering what constitutes a violation of the law, the Federal Trade Commission will consider the practices listed in Table 20-3. These practices, including the price discrimination we discussed in the previous section, are not

TABLE 20-2   KEY FEATURES OF THE MAJOR ANTITRUST LAWS

LEGISLATION	SUMMARY OF FEATURES
Sherman Act of 1890	Bans monopolization and price-fixing agreements. Establishes criminal and civil penalties.
Clayton Antitrust Act of 1914	Bans certain actions that reduce competition.
Federal Trade Commission Act of 1914	Created the Federal Trade Commission, a government agency that investigates allegations of unfair trade practices.

TABLE 20-3 POTENTIALLY PUNISHABLE PRACTICES: A GLOSSARY OF ANTITRUST TERMS

Exclusive dealing	A firm prohibits its distributors from selling competitors' products.
Exclusive territories	A firm assigns a geographic area to a distributor and prohibits other distributors from operating in that territory.
Predatory pricing	A firm prices a product below the marginal cost of producing it to drive rivals out of business.
Price discrimination	A firm charges different customers different prices for the same product.
Refusals to deal	A firm prohibits rivals from purchasing/using scarce resources (called essential facilities) that are needed to stay in business.
Resale price maintenance	A manufacturer sets a minimum retail price for its product.
Tie-in sales	A firm conditions the purchase of one product upon the purchase of another.

Source: "Does Big Business Need Taming? The Role of Economics in Antitrust Law," *The Regional Economist,* Federal Reserve Bank of Saint Louis, July 1998.

intrinsically illegal. Rather, the behavior becomes illegal when competition is lessened in a significant way, without having overriding business justifications. This judgment is made in court and is known as *the rule of reason.*

COMBATTING MARKET POWER WITH THE ANTITRUST LAWS

While the *Sherman Act* (1890) was the first antitrust law to be passed in the United States, the vagueness of its wording helped to sow the seeds for the passage of the *Clayton Act* (1914) twenty-four years later. Enforcement of the Sherman Act continues to this day. (Note that the Sherman Act and other antitrust legislation is subject to amendment by Congress. The text of legislation presented here incorporates such amendments.) The most important sections of the act include Section 1, which establishes a general definition of illegal behavior.

> Every contract, combination in the form of trust or otherwise, or conspiracy, in restraint of trade or commerce among the several states, or with foreign nations, is declared to be illegal.

Punishment for violating Section 1 ranges up to a $10 million fine and 3 years' imprisonment. Notice that monopolies are not mentioned in Section 1. Section 2 mentions monopolizing behavior.

> Every person who shall monopolize, or attempt to monopolize, or combine or conspire with any other person or persons, to monopolize any part of the trade or commerce among the several States, or with foreign nations . . .

Punishment for violating Section 2 is the same as that for violating Section 1. Nowhere in the second section is monopoly itself declared to be illegal. Rather, it is the actions associated with efforts to "monopolize" that are a crime. While this may seem a fine distinction, in practice the Sherman Act downplays market power to focus on the "restraint of trade" and the monopolization of trade. Exactly what this means was left to the courts, but the implication is that there are illegal monopolies and legal monopolies. The illegal monopolies were to be judged so on the basis of their actions.

The Clayton Act is best understood as a response to the lack of specifics in the Sherman Act. Among its thirty-seven sections, Section 13 states:

> It shall be unlawful for any person engaged in commerce . . . to discriminate in price between different purchasers of commodities of like grade and quality, . . .

> where the effect of such discrimination may be substantially to lessen competition or tend to create a monopoly in any line of commerce, or to injure, destroy, or prevent competition . . .

This passage is about *illegal price discrimination.* The key to understanding when price discrimination is illegal is to note that the law is broken when "the effect of such discrimination may be substantially to lessen competition or tend to create a monopoly. . .". Because of these words, price discrimination that does not lessen competition is acceptable in law.

Section 14 forbids *exclusive dealing,* which refers to prohibiting customers from using the products of your rivals:

> It shall be unlawful for any person engaged in commerce, in the course of such commerce, to lease or make a sale or contract for sale of goods, . . . or fix a price charged therefor, or discount from, or rebate upon, such price, on the condition, agreement, or understanding that the lessee or purchaser thereof shall not use or deal in the goods . . . of a competitor or competitors of the lessor or seller, where the effect . . . may be to substantially lessen competition or tend to create a monopoly in any line of commerce.

Congress established the *Federal Trade Commission (FTC)* to enforce the Clayton Act's prohibition against these and other "unfair trade practices." Over the years, its role has expanded to include consumer protection as well as antitrust. In its role in antitrust enforcement, the FTC is empowered to halt suspected anticompetitive practices temporarily.

The antitrust laws do not apply to labor unions. It would be natural to suppose that labor unions, just like businesses, would be subject to the provisions of antitrust law. After all, labor unions exist to raise the pay and benefits of their membership, which is more easily accomplished when a labor union monopolizes a labor market by making itself the only seller of labor services to the businesses where its members are employed. It is the fact that labor unions do attempt to monopolize the labor market that led to explicit exemptions for them in the Clayton Act. Without this explicit exemption, the effect might well be to outlaw labor unions.

With the 1914 passage of the Clayton Act and the Federal Trade Commission Act, antitrust activity on the legislative front remained quiet for many years. During those years, the courts were interpreting and clarifying antitrust law. It was not until 1936 that the *Robinson-Patman Act* was passed. This act makes *predatory pricing* illegal, where lowering prices to meet competition is allowed, but lowering prices to eliminate competition is not:

> It shall be unlawful . . . to sell goods . . . at prices lower than . . . elsewhere in the United States for the purpose of destroying competition, or eliminating a competitor . . . or, to sell . . . goods at unreasonably low prices for the purpose of destroying competition or eliminating a competitor.

Congress was still not through refining the antitrust laws, however. In 1950, Congress passed the *Cellar-Kefauver Antimerger Act.* This law was intended to close a loophole in the Clayton Act by prohibiting one firm from purchasing the assets of another if the effect was to reduce competition. In 1980, antitrust policy was extended to small businesses through the provisions of the *Hart-Scott-Rodino Antitrust Improvement Act.*

When laws are written, courts can interpret them in various ways. Such has been the case with the antitrust laws. Thus, to fully appreciate the scope of these laws, we must not only examine their wording, but also examine the case law that relates to them.

ANTITRUST LAW AND THE COURTS

There have been many antitrust cases since the passage of the Sherman Act. Every decade since the passage of the Sherman Act has seen its share of antitrust cases. Since 1994, for example, the Justice Department has filed antitrust cases against businesses small and large.

These businesses include Microsoft, Prudential Insurance, the American Bar Association, Ticketmaster, General Electric, Sara Lee, and The Walt Disney Company. Only a handful have been either precedent setting, or have affected the general public in a notable way. In short, most antitrust cases are not front page news. That said, we can identify a few cases that every student of antitrust should be aware of:

- **American Tobacco (1911):** The company was found to be an illegal monopoly and broken into several separate competing companies.
- **Standard Oil (1911):** Found to be in violation of the Sherman Act, the company was broken up into separate oil refining and pipeline companies. This case marked the court's first use of the "rule of reason" in reaching its decision.
- **U.S. Steel (1920):** In spite of the fact that the firm was formed in hopes of monopolizing the market, it was cleared of charges that it was an illegal monopoly. Although a big company, being big is not enough to create a violation of law: ". . . the law does not make mere size an offense."
- **Paramount Pictures (1948):** The U.S. Supreme Court ruled that the major Hollywood film studios had an illegal monopoly because of their ownership of nationwide chains of movie theaters. Ownership of theaters was anticompetitive in the sense that independent film producers had no access to theaters where their movies could be shown. The ruling led the studios to divest themselves of their theaters, thus ending the golden era of Hollywood.
- **Dupont (The cellophane case) (1956):** Although Dupont produced 75 percent of the nation's output of cellophane, the court found that the relevant market was the entire market for packaging materials. Dupont produced only 20 percent of the output when the market was defined in this way, so Dupont was found to be not guilty of violating Section 2 of the Sherman Act.
- **Von's Grocery (1956):** The government challenged the legality of a merger between two Los Angeles area grocery chains, claiming the merger would substantially lessen competition. The U.S. Supreme Court ordered Von's to divest itself of the assets acquired in the merger.
- **IBM (1982):** Big Blue was charged by the Justice Department with being an illegal monopoly, but the case was dropped.
- **Microsoft I (1994):** The company was charged with anticompetitive practices; a settlement was reached instead of a court verdict, in which Microsoft signed a consent decree.
- **Microsoft II (1998):** This time Microsoft was found to be an illegal monopoly. The court's remedy was to order the company to be broken into two separate parts, an order that was subsequently reversed after Microsoft reached a negotiated settlement with the Justice Department in 2002.
- **The compact disc case (2003):** The Compact Disc Minimum Advertised Price Antitrust Litigation led to eight companies involved in the music industry to settle a lawsuit charging them with fixing the retail price of recorded music. Without admitting guilt, the companies agreed to reimburse consumers to the tune of $142 million in cash and merchandise.

Many more cases could be cited when exploring antitrust case law. However, the cases we have examined lead to several observations. The first is that **firms that violate the antitrust laws are sometimes broken into separate pieces.** That happened to AT&T in 1982, and it would have happened to Microsoft in the 1998 case, if the decision had not been reversed. Breakup is considered to be the ultimate punishment.

The second observation is that **the courts pay close attention to the question of the scope of the market.** This idea is perhaps clearest in the cellophane case, but it has played a role in many other cases, including the 1998 Microsoft case. How the market is viewed has a crucial bearing on antitrust outcomes. For example, in a merger involving two pencil manufacturers, the question would be whether the market should be viewed as the pencil market, or the overall market for writing instruments, which includes both pens and pencils. A monopoly in pencil production would not be a true monopoly if consumers can write with pens. In the market for shoes, is there one market, or are there separate markets for men's shoes, women's shoes, and children's shoes? In addition to the product dimension, the market can also be viewed as having a geographic dimension. In the Von's case, it was quite clear that the relevant market was the Los Angeles area, since that is where both merger partners were doing business. In other cases, the market may be wider, and can include the whole country.

The third idea, exemplified by the Von's case, is that **mergers are a focus of attention in antitrust law and enforcement.** We turn our attention to mergers in order to shed more light on their significance.

WHEN MERGERS ARE DISALLOWED

Antitrust policy allows the Justice Department to block mergers. As you have learned already, there are three types of mergers: horizontal, vertical, and conglomerate. The conglomerate merger is usually of little interest from an antitrust perspective since it has limited potential to increase market concentration. The horizontal and vertical merger types almost always have antitrust implications and are the most likely to be blocked. The basic reason for blocking mergers has to do with firms increasing prices after a merger. If the government deems that higher prices are unlikely to result from a merger, the merger stands a better chance for government approval.

Consider first the vertical merger, which involves a combination of firms that are in a buyer-seller relationship with each other. The concern with this type of merger is the possibility of *vertical foreclosure,* where firms that compete with the merged firm lose a supplier or a distributor. Although the Paramount Pictures case did not involve a merger, it illustrates the issue of vertical foreclosure. Only four cities in the United States had an independent theater, a theater not owned by a major Hollywood film studio. Thus, there was little chance for independent film producers who would not play ball with the studios to have their films shown. In the language of antitrust, these film producers were alleged to be *foreclosed* from the marketplace. Following the court's decision against them, the film studios were stripped of the revenues from their theaters and battered by competition from the then new medium of television. For these reasons, they spent much of the next two decades in a fight for financial survival.

Horizontal mergers are likely to draw the close scrutiny of the Antitrust Division of the Justice Department, the arm of the government that decides whether a merger will be allowed. Horizontal mergers involve combining firms that produce similar products. An example is the merger between Compaq and Hewlett-Packard, both computer makers.

Mergers, of whatever type, are allowed when, in the opinion of the government, two conditions are met:

- The market is not concentrated after the merger.
- Entry of new competitors into the market is possible.

When the market is not concentrated, market power is absent. Prices are not likely to rise because of the merger. Even if a market is concentrated, when entry of new competitors is possible, the possibility of new competition is often enough to hold down prices.

Regarding post-merger concentration, the government considers evidence related to the market share of the combined firm following a merger. The method used by the government to measure concentration in merger cases is called the **Herfindahl-Hirschman index (HHI),** which is the sum of the squared market shares of all firms in the market:

$$\text{HHI} = \sum (S_i)^2 = S_1{}^2 + S_2{}^2 + S_3{}^2 + \ldots + S_n{}^2$$

Herfindahl-Hirschman index (HHI) an index of market concentration used by the U.S. Justice Department in the merger approval process; computed by squaring and summing the market shares of all firms in a market; ranges in value from 0 (pure competition) to 10,000 (pure monopoly).

TABLE 20-4 HOW TO COMPUTE THE HERFINDAHL-HIRSCHMAN INDEX

STEPS	DATA AND COMPUTATIONS
1. Obtain market share data for all firms in the industry. In this example there are five firms, A through E, with market shares as shown in the second column.	Firm A = 30% market share Firm B = 30% Firm C = 20% Firm D = 10% Firm E = 10% Total = 100%
2. Square each firm's market share by multiplying it by itself.	Firm A = 30^2 = 900 Firm B = 30^2 = 900 Firm C = 20^2 = 400 Firm D = 10^2 = 100 Firm E = 10^2 = 100
3. Add the values obtained in step 2.	900 + 900 + 400 + 100 + 100 = 2,400

In the formula for the Herfindahl-Hirschman index, the subscripts indicate the number of firms. The formula shows that there are n firms in the market, where n is replaced by the actual number of firms when the formula is applied.

Table 20-4 shows the three steps in computing the HHI. The example supposes there are five firms in an industry, with market shares as given in the table in step 1. After squaring the market shares in step 2, the results are added together in step 3 to obtain the value for the HHI. These steps will apply to any market, no matter the number of firms. When there are more firms, there will be more numbers to square and add together, but the method stays the same.

In order to interpret the value for the HHI, we must recognize the extremes it can take. First, consider that the HHI could be as small as zero. If there are an infinite number of firms of equal size in the market, every value added together in step 3 will be infinitely small. Thus, a value of HHI approaching zero would be obtained if there are many small firms of equal size in the market. In other words, HHI = 0 for pure competition. At the other extreme, the maximum value for HHI is 10,000. This value applies when there is a pure monopoly in the market. A monopoly's market share equals 100. When 100 is squared, the result is 10,000. Thus, HHI = 10,000 indicates a monopoly.

The value of HHI in our example is 2,400. This market is neither purely competitive nor is it a monopoly. How should the value of 2,400 be interpreted? The Justice Department views industries with HHI values above 1,000 as somewhat concentrated, and above 1,800 as highly concentrated. Table 20-5 shows that not only is the level of the HHI of importance to

TABLE 20-5 DEPARTMENT OF JUSTICE HORIZONTAL MERGER GUIDELINES

Change in HHI:	0–50	51–100	>100
HHI over 1,800	Safe	Unsafe	Unsafe
HHI from 1,000 to 1,800	Safe	Safe	Unsafe
HHI from 0 to 1,000	Safe	Safe	Safe

Source: U.S. Department of Justice, *Horizontal Merger Guidelines,* 1992, as revised in 1997.

> ## QUICKCHECK
>
> **Suppose a market is made up of ten firms of equal size. What is the value of the H index? Would a merger between any two of the firms be likely to receive government approval?**
>
> **Answer:** Each firm has a 10 percent market share. Each of these market shares takes on a value of 100 when it is squared. Adding these up, the result is 1,000. If any two firms merge, there will be nine firms left in the industry. The market share of the combined firm would equal 20 percent. Squaring that value, we get 400. The remaining eight firms would still have market shares of 10 percent each. When those values are squared and added, we obtain a value of 800. Adding the 400 to the 800, the H index equals 1,200. The computation is:
>
> $$400 + 100 + 100 + 100 + 100 + 100 + 100 + 100 + 100 = 1,200$$
>
> An H index of 1,200 is of concern to the government and this merger would be looked at carefully for its effects.

the government in making its merger rulings, but so is the magnitude of the change in the HHI after a merger. A change in the HHI of less than fifty points following a merger will in general leave that merger unchallenged by the government, no matter the value of the HHI. An increase of 50 to 100 points in the HHI will likely trigger a government challenge to the merger if the merger puts the HHI over 1,800. An increase of more than 100 points in the HHI will cause the government to challenge a merger when the HHI ends up over 1,000 after the merger. These are guidelines only. Specific cases may vary from them.

SNAPSHOT   FINDING MONOPOLY—MICROSOFT YES, DUPONT NO

Imagine America's wealthiest man and his company pitted against government attorneys. The setting was the courtroom of Judge Thomas Penfield Jackson. The verdict? Microsoft Corporation was found to have a monopoly with its Windows personal-computer operating system. Few computer users could realistically avoid using that operating system. Moreover, Microsoft had abused its monopoly power to thwart potential rivals to its other products, thereby violating the antitrust laws. For example, Microsoft's Internet Explorer was so tied in to Windows that rival Netscape, with its Netscape Navigator and Communicator, could not profitably compete. There was just no good substitute for the Windows operating system, which Microsoft was using as leverage to muscle out competitors to its other software products. So ruled Judge Jackson in 2000. His remedy? Break Microsoft into two companies. That remedy was later overturned by a federal appeals court. Under the new ruling, Microsoft was allowed to remain a single company, but it had to curb its monopoly ways.

The government does not always win its antitrust cases. For example, it lost its 1956 case against DuPont, producer of nearly all cellophane, a clear packaging material. In this case, the court reasoned that cellophane was one of many packaging materials produced by a number of firms. The availability of plastic wrap, wax paper, and other substitutes meant that cellophane had a relatively low market share in the market for packaging materials. Since the court reasoned that the market was for packaging materials, not just cellophane, Dupont was found by the Supreme Court to have no monopoly. ◄

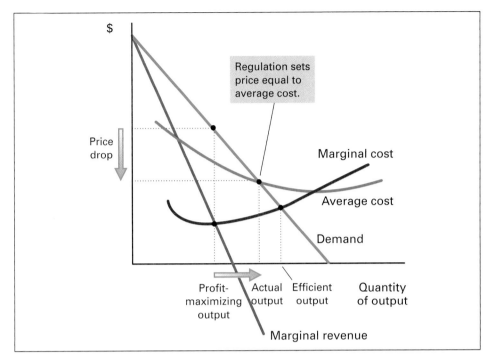

FIGURE 20-12

AVERAGE-COST PRICING In the case of public utilities, regulators commonly attempt to limit monopoly pricing to no more than average cost. The resulting quantity produced more closely approximates the efficient quantity and ensures the firm a normal profit. On the downside, regulators may tend to overestimate the monopolist's costs because they do not know all of the ways that the monopoly could economize and because the regulated monopoly has no incentive to reveal these cost-saving possibilities.

RATE-OF-RETURN REGULATION

If a monopoly is a natural monopoly, the government will typically either own it or regulate it with **rate-of-return regulation** that restricts the monopolist from charging more than average cost. For this reason, rate-of-return regulation is also known as **average-cost pricing.** While it is marginal cost that is used to determine efficiency, average cost is often a close approximation and does at least guarantee that the firm will neither earn excessive profit nor go out of business. For example, the firm in Figure 20-12 will produce less than the efficient quantity, but not nearly as much less than if its price were unrestricted.

rate-of-return regulation (average-cost pricing) restricts the monopoly from earning more than a normal profit; shown by the intersection of the average-cost curve and demand.

The regulation of industry by the federal government, undertaken to ensure "fair prices," has a long history. The Interstate Commerce Commission (ICC), eliminated in the 1970s, was created by Congress in 1887 to regulate the railroads, the primary means of transporting many kinds of goods at the time. In the 1920s and 1930s, as trucking took a larger share of the transportation market, it seemed natural to extend regulation to that industry as well. Airline regulation was also established as regularly scheduled passenger service took hold in the 1930s. Note that regulation was instituted even though these industries were not characterized by monopoly.

A problem with rate-of-return regulation is that the regulated monopolist has little incentive to control costs or to provide innovative services. Thus, over time, regulation can impede change in production techniques and in the development of new products. For this reason, rate-of-return regulation can cause technological inefficiencies even as it corrects allocative inefficiencies. Regulation can also have the effect of stifling new competition, favoring existing firms at the expense of potential competitors. For example, during the more than thirty-year period that the airlines were regulated, startups of new airlines were few.

ALTERNATIVES TO REGULATION

To avoid the inefficiencies of regulation, economists recommend discarding the market process as little as possible. For example, it might be possible to award a **franchise monopoly**—a right to be the exclusive provider of a service—to the firm that offers to provide the

franchise monopoly a right to be the exclusive provider of a service.

> ## QUICKCHECK
>
> **Rate-of-return regulation is intended to restrict a monopolist's price to equal its average production costs. Is this price efficient? If so, why? If not, why not and why use rate-of-return regulation?**
>
> **Answer:** Efficiency requires that the monopolist produce to the point where marginal cost equals demand, not where average cost equals demand as under rate-of-return regulation. Thus, unless marginal cost equals average cost at that point, it would appear that such regulation is not efficient. Still, regulators choose this solution because it is likely to be more efficient than unregulated monopoly and will lead the firm to only a normal profit, meaning zero profit as economists define the term. With zero profit, the firm avoids needing government subsidies to stay in business.

service at the lowest price. In theory, that process should achieve technological efficiency as firms compete for the monopoly franchise. It would also lead to average-cost pricing without regulators needing to know anything about what average costs actually are.

Instead of awarding a monopoly franchise to the lowest bidder in terms of price, franchises can instead be auctioned by local governments as a way of generating revenue. The result would be pricing above average cost, with the profit going to the locality. For example, some cities restrict taxicab service to one or a few companies willing to bid the highest for service rights. By restricting the number of rights granted, cities can generate monopoly profits for the industry that will be passed along to the city in the form of high bids for those rights.

deregulation the scaling back of government regulation of industry.

The concern that regulation breeds inefficiencies over time and sets up barriers to entry has led to the **deregulation** of some industries, in which the government allows market forces to determine price and output. For example, the efficiency of air transportation was significantly increased by deregulation in the late 1970s, in which airlines lost their regulated monopoly status on many routes. The result was less luxurious service, but also the creation of hub-and-spoke route systems that eliminated many nonstop routes in favor of routing travelers through airline hubs, in Chicago, Atlanta, Dallas, and other cities. Travelers may not appreciate the need to make connections, but do appreciate the lower fares these technological efficiencies bring. Only the bus lines were the losers, as the convenience and low fares of the airlines stole their customers. As a consequence, the Trailways bus line exited the market, leaving only Greyhound to provide coast-to-coast service to the mostly low-income clientele that patronizes long-distance travel by bus today.

Deregulation of electricity has also become reality in some states, as technology has advanced to the point where the natural monopoly inherent in power transmission lines can be separated from the production of that power. Deregulation allows power providers the freedom to compete to feed electricity into the power grid, thereby keeping electricity prices as low as possible. As we saw in Chapter 4, however, the deregulation measures must not be halfway. California's deregulation of electricity at the wholesale level coupled with price caps at the retail level led to bankrupt utilities, power outages, and in time much higher costs than if retail prices were left uncapped.

As an alternative to regulation, the federal government has also engaged in government ownership of industry. The giant electric utility, the Tennessee Valley Authority (TVA), is a familiar example to those living in the southeastern states of the United States. The U.S. Postal Service, discussed in more detail shortly, is familiar to even more people. Government ownership is beset with severe enough problems of incentives and finances that it is seen as a policy of last resort, at least in the United States. For example, the controversial government-controlled Amtrak passenger rail service was started because private railroads were exiting the passenger business. However, Amtrak has been unable to stem the losses, losing over $1 billion in 2001 and again in 2002. For 2003, losses were expected to increase to over $2 billion.

Many countries with a history of widespread government ownership have reduced that ownership over the last two decades. These countries, such as Great Britain, Russia, and Brazil, have turned to **privatization,** in which government turns over some of its production to privately owned companies. This can involve an outright sale of government facilities or merely the *contracting out* of public services. For example, in 2001, the U.S. Postal Service contracted out the intercity transportation of priority and first-class mail to FedEx. The economic rationale for privatization is to take advantage of the efficiency of the marketplace, where companies succeed by providing the goods and services that give customers the most value for their money.

privatization the sale of government industries, or government paying private firms to provide public services.

In some instances, privatization may not be feasible because the industry is unprofitable. That does not necessarily mean that the industry should not exist, although it does suggest careful scrutiny is in order. For example, many cities have transportation authorities that provide bus and subway services. These systems are characterized by very high fixed costs, but extremely low marginal costs for additional riders, as shown in Figure 20-13. These characteristics make the transit systems natural monopolies. In the example shown, the consumer surplus—the value to consumers in excess of the price they pay—from the efficient quantity of these transit services is more than enough to cover the loss from providing that quantity at the efficient price.

In this example, there is no price that would avoid a loss, since the average cost curve is everywhere above demand. In some other examples, there might be a price that would cause a private company to at least breakeven, which could be achieved through rate-of-return regulation. However, if that quantity is far removed from the efficient quantity, it might be in the public interest to *subsidize*—help pay for—production of additional output. Direct government ownership is not the only way to accomplish this task, but is often the one that is chosen.

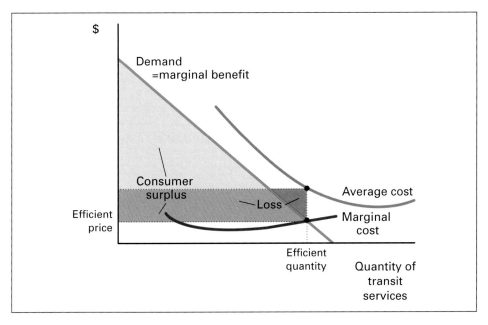

FIGURE 20-13

SUBSIDIZED MONOPOLY
Monopolies may be unable to escape losses, but still be in the public interest if the consumer surplus shown by the triangle is more than enough to cover losses, shown by the shaded rectangle. To obtain the efficient output requires subsidization, either to a private sector monopolist or through government ownership.

SNAPSHOT   THE STATE LOTTERY—ONE MONOPOLY LAWMAKERS LIKE!

Gambling, once the purview of organized crime, is now promoted wholeheartedly by numerous state governments. While the path from the criminal underworld to state-advertised lotteries might seem odd, it is really not surprising. Both outlaws and lawmakers are drawn into the gambling business by the same age-old attraction—the allure of big money. Legislating a government monopoly provides a highly effective barrier to entry. It keeps pay-outs low and profits high.

Is government aiming for efficiency, the idea behind the regulation of other monopolies? Of course not. It's the allure of big profit to keep down the need for tax revenue. Taxpayers don't complain and, if the alternative is no gambling at all, even the gamblers are for it. It's the others in the gamblers' households that wonder just where the money goes. ◀

20.4 THE UNITED STATES POSTAL SERVICE—A MONOPOLY IN THE PUBLIC INTEREST?

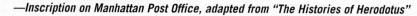

"Neither snow, nor rain, nor heat, nor gloom of night stays these couriers from the swift completion of their appointed rounds."

—*Inscription on Manhattan Post Office, adapted from "The Histories of Herodotus"*

No Madison Avenue advertising agency could think up a better slogan for the Post Office than the motto adapted from the centuries-old Greek scripts of Herodotus. . . . The mail must go through. That principle has inspired the Post Office ever since it was established on September 26, 1789. What is probably the oldest monopoly in America is rich in tradition. For instance, the first Postmaster General was Benjamin Franklin, who was given the title by the Continental Congress in 1775, even before the creation of the Post Office itself.

For more than two centuries the Post Office has grown along with the country. The Postal Reorganization Act of July 1, 1971, established the U.S. Postal Service from what had formerly been the Department of the Post Office. The Postal Service is overseen by a Board of Governors appointed by the president and approved by the Senate. It is intended to be self-supporting. In 2001, the Postal Service had 776,000 career employees and earned $65.9 billion in total revenue. If it were a private-sector company, that revenue would have placed it as the twelfth largest on the *Fortune 500* list of the largest U.S. companies. Unfortunately, that revenue was not enough to offset expenses of $67.6 billion, of which 78 percent were wages and benefits associated with some of the most sought-after blue-collar jobs in the government. The result is that the Postal Office lost $1.68 billion.

To try to make up for that loss, the Postal Service hired FedEx to handle its overnight deliveries and increased the basic rate for mailing a letter from 34 cents to 37 cents. In addition to rate increases to enhance revenues, the Postal Service periodically brings up the possibility of eliminating Saturday delivery as a way to cut down costs. Less controversial plans to keep costs down include developing and installing new automated equipment. Additional challenges include:

■ the growing popularity of e-mail, which has kept postal volume flat even as the number of new postal addresses grows by about 1.7 million each year.

■ the costs of protecting employees and customers from the threat of anthrax or other dangerous substances, including the costs of irradiating mail.

The Senate has debated whether first-class mail delivery should remain exclusively in the hands of the U.S. Postal Service. New Zealand (since 1998) and Sweden (since

1994) have abolished their postal monopolies, with Germany scheduled to follow suit. Even though the trend is toward greater competition in postal services, entrusting delivery of the mail to a governmental postal monopoly is still the norm in countries around the globe.

The U.S. Postal Service is such a monopoly, guaranteed by the postal monopoly statutes and, according to some interpretations, even by the U.S. Constitution. Rivals such as UPS and FedEx are allowed to deliver packages and urgent correspondence, but not other mail. Thus, the law is a barrier to entry that prohibits the rise of competition in postal services. The postal monopoly includes at least two elements of law that act as barriers:

- control over household mailboxes, and
- exclusive rights to delivering first-class mail, which includes personal correspondence, post cards, and many business transactions.

These restrictions explain why private companies do not deliver to household mailboxes, nor do they deliver your bills, or your letters from friends and family.

Even if the postal monopoly laws did not provide a measure of protection to the Postal Service through barriers to entry, it would still have a leg up on its competitors. Specifically, the Postal Service pays no federal income taxes, no state income taxes, and no property taxes. It can also violate certain government regulations with impunity. For example, delivery drivers know that on the busy urban streets with few parking places, traffic cops will walk right past the double-parked Postal Service truck to issue tickets to the similarily double-parked truck of the UPS or other private-delivery service. The reason is the Post Office is exempt from paying traffic fines.

PONDERING PRIVATIZATION

Privatization of the Postal Service would be one option that might increase efficiency in mail delivery. Firms could then compete on an equal footing against one another to capture their share of the first-class mail business, just as they do for parcel delivery. Firms that pay their workers an excessive amount or hire on the basis of politics, cronyism, or anything other than productivity would lose out. Firms that offer poor quality delivery, high prices, and poor hours would also lose. The winners would be those firms that figure out what customers think is worth paying for. Competition would force firms to seek to understand and follow the wishes of postal customers, and provide those services at a low cost.

Privatization of first-class mail delivery would have many hurdles to overcome. One of the first effects of privatization might be confusion, as a jumble of companies competed against each other for customers. Companies would find themselves on overlapping routes, and realize that combining operations would be more efficient by eliminating that overlap. If the postal services are a natural monopoly, only the one most efficient company would survive. However, we see more than one survivor in the package delivery business, so perhaps two or more companies might be able to profitably coexist. Which companies would they be?

Another hurdle is that the Postal Service is committed to *universal access,* in which mail service is offered at equal rates to everyone, despite some addresses being more expensive to serve than others. In this way, local urban delivery of first-class mail subsidizes delivery of first-class mail across greater distances and to rural areas. A more competitive marketplace would price on the basis of cost and eliminate this *cross subsidization,* in which the revenue from some services helps to pay for other services. Competitors would lower prices of the more profitable services and raise the prices of the others.

Dozens of government-provided goods and services have been turned over to the private sector in one place or another. Private-sector provision of services such as garbage collection, tree trimming along city streets, housekeeping and custodial services, forest management, police protection, education, social services, family planning, and many more provide ample evidence of the widespread acceptance of privatization. Yet, there is often resistance to privatization.

Privatization of the U.S. Postal Service that increases the efficiency of delivery might involve layoffs, which the postal workers' unions would oppose. Competition might lead to nonunion workers being hired, which would also be opposed by the unions. For these reasons and because of the public's high regard for letter carriers, Congress would find itself embroiled in controversy if it were to pass legislation to privatize postal services. With unrestricted privatization, prices of each type of service would tend toward the marginal cost of that service. Prices would be more efficient, but whether they would seem fair might depend on the personal impact of the price changes.

THINKING CRITICALLY

1. **Do you believe that universal access is a core mandate of the Postal Service? Should the rural population pay the full cost of providing service to those people who live in remote areas?**

2. **If the Post Office is privatized, how should the government select a new owner? What conditions, if any, do you think should be placed on ownership? Would you prefer to see a privately owned, regulated Postal Service? If so, why? If not, why not?**

 Visit **www.prenhall.com/ayers** for updates and web exercises on this Explore & Apply topic.

SUMMARY AND LEARNING OBJECTIVES

1. **Describe how barriers to entry create market power.**
   - Barriers to entry reduce competition. When there are no barriers to entry, as in the case of pure competition, the firm's demand curve is perfectly elastic (horizontal). Barriers to entry steepen the firm's demand curve and are the root cause of monopoly.

2. **Discuss the profit-maximizing process for a monopolist.**
   - Monopoly occurs when there is a single seller of an output that has no close substitutes.
   - Monopoly firms are price makers—they have some control over their price. As a consequence their demand curves are downward sloping. The monopoly demand curve equals the market demand curve.
   - Monopoly firms include natural monopolies, such as the public utilities. Natural monopoly is created by economies of scale in which the long-run average cost curve is downwardly sloping throughout or nearly throughout the range of demand. One firm is able to supply the entire market at a lower per-unit cost than could two or more firms because of the economies of scale.
   - A monopoly firm maximizes profit at the point where marginal revenue equals marginal cost. The marginal

revenue curve for a monopoly firm will slope downward more steeply than demand. When demand is linear, the marginal revenue curve will be a straight line that is twice as steep as demand.
   - The profit-maximizing monopoly will first select its output where marginal revenue equals marginal cost. As a price maker, it will then identify the point on its demand curve associated with the amount of output produced. The appropriate point on the demand curve indicates the price the monopolist will set.
   - Graphically, total economic profit earned by a monopoly firm is shown by the area of a rectangle. Total profit equals output multiplied by per-unit profit.
   - There is no supply curve in monopoly because there is no one-to-one relationship between price and the quantity produced. Instead, it is possible for the same quantity of output to be sold by a monopoly at different prices in response to a shift in demand.

3. **Explain the inefficiencies of monopoly.**
   - The short-run profit-maximizing output for a monopoly firm will be inefficiently small, while the price will be inefficiently high. The unregulated monopolist produces at the point where marginal revenue equals marginal cost, while the efficient output occurs where demand and marginal cost intersect.

■ The threat of potential competition leads to limit pricing to discourage potential competitors. Limit pricing occurs when a monopoly holds its selling price below the profit-maximizing price.

4. **Name and briefly discuss major U.S. antitrust laws and potentially punishable practices.**

■ Major U.S. antitrust laws include the Sherman Act (1890), Clayton Act (1914), and Federal Trade Commission Act (1914). These laws aim to curb anticompetitive actions by firms.

■ Potentially punishable practices include exclusive dealing, exclusive territories, predatory pricing, price discrimination, refusals to deal, resale price maintenance, and tie-in sales. These practices are not always illegal, but can be illegal when they reduce competition.

■ The antitrust laws are interpreted by the courts and by the U.S. Department of Justice. Various cases have clarified the application of these laws. The Justice Department uses the Herfindahl-Hirschman index (HHI) to determine whether a merger will have significant anticompetitive effects. The HHI squares the market shares of all firms in the market and then adds them together. Its value ranges from 0 to 10,000 with higher values indicating greater market concentration. A value of 1,800 and above represents high concentration to the Justice Department.

5. **Identify government policies toward monopoly.**

■ Monopolies are commonly either owned or regulated by government. Rate-of-return regulation by government aims to bring down the monopoly price. Graphically, price is set by the regulators at the intersection of demand and long-run average cost.

■ An unprofitable monopoly industry might be subsidized by government. In this case, the government pays the monopolist the amount of its operating losses. Public transit companies are a possible example. Two-part pricing is sometimes an alternative to subsidies. The price paid by each consumer will consist of a flat monthly fee plus charges for the amount used. Water companies are a possible example.

 Assess the merits of protecting the U.S. Postal Service from competition.

■ The delivery of mail is characterized by legal monopoly. In the case of first-class mail, the U.S. Postal Service is guaranteed a monopoly by the U.S. Constitution and other law. Private-sector competition in some aspects of mail delivery is allowed. Other competition faced by the Postal Service comes from technological change such as e-mail. Cross-subsidization in Postal Services means that the revenue from some services helps to pay for other services. An alternative to the current Postal Service would privatize the delivery of mail.

KEY TERMS

monopoly, 502
barriers to entry, 502
monopoly by law (legal monopoly), 502
monopoly by possession, 502
natural monopoly, 502
price maker, 503

deadweight loss, 512
limit pricing, 512
price discrimination, 512
perfect price discrimination, 512
multi-part pricing, 513
antitrust law, 514

Herfindahl-Hirschman index (HHI), 518
rate-of-return regulation (average-cost pricing), 521
franchise monopoly, 521
deregulation, 522
privatization, 523

TEST YOURSELF

TRUE OR FALSE

1. One of the best examples of natural monopoly is a taxicab company.
2. A firm facing a demand curve that slopes downward to the right has market power.

3. Fair-rate-of-return regulation of monopoly is designed to provide a monopolist with a normal profit.
4. The price charged by an unregulated monopolist will equal the monopolist's marginal cost.
5. The supply curve for a monopoly firm is upward sloping.

MULTIPLE CHOICE

6. Barriers to entry
   a. increase the number of firms in an industry.
   b. decrease the number of firms in an industry.
   c. have no effect on the number of firms in an industry.
   d. have unpredictable effects on the number of firms in an industry.

7. Market power is indicated by a(n)
   a. horizontal demand curve.
   b. shortage of barriers to entry.
   c. ability to pick your selling price.
   d. *J* shape to the marginal cost curve.

8. Which statement is true about monopoly?
   a. A monopoly is a price taker.
   b. A monopoly will have many good substitutes for its output.
   c. The monopoly demand curve is also the market demand curve.
   d. An unregulated monopoly is always profitable.

9. A natural monopoly occurs when
   a. government grants a patent to a firm.
   b. government prohibits the entry of new competitor firms.
   c. one firm can produce at lower average cost than can any combination of two or more firms.
   d. the product that is monopolized pertains to natural resources.

10. The best example of a natural monopoly is
    a. a local electric utility.
    b. the U.S. Postal Service.
    c. an airline.
    d. a public school.

11. A natural monopoly is characterized by
    a. perfectly elastic demand.
    b. an upward-sloping long-run average-cost curve throughout.
    c. a flat long-run average-cost curve.
    d. a demand curve that intersects long-run average cost near or to the left of the minimum point of the long-run average-cost curve.

12. *Ceteris paribus,* a steeper demand curve indicates
    a. the firm is a price taker.
    b. less market power.
    c. more market power.
    d. the firm is not a monopolist.

13. A marginal revenue curve for a monopoly firm will
    a. be shaped like the letter *J.*
    b. lie below the demand curve.
    c. lie above the demand curve.
    d. be identical to the demand curve.

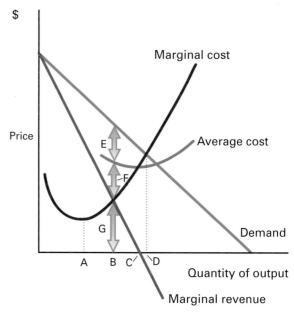

SELF-TEST FIGURE 20-1

14. To maximize profit, the firm shown in Self-Test Figure 20-1 will produce the output associated with quantity
    a. *A.*
    b. *B.*
    c. *C.*
    d. *D.*

15. If it produces at point *B,* the firm in Self-Test Figure 20-1 will achieve a profit per unit equal to the length of arrow(s)
    a. *E.*
    b. *F.*
    c. *G.*
    d. *E + F.*

16. In Self-Test Figure 20-1, the efficient output occurs at quantity
    a. *A.*
    b. *B.*
    c. *C.*
    d. *D.*

17. If a monopolist is able to practice perfect price discrimination, the result will be
    a. inefficient, but consumers will be better off.
    b. inefficient and consumers will be worse off.
    c. efficient and consumers will be better off.
    d. efficient, but consumers will be worse off.

18. Referring to Self-Test Figure 20-2, rate-of-return regulation leads to the price given by
    a. *A.*
    b. *B.*
    c. *C.*
    d. *D.*

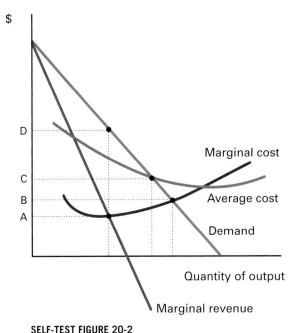

SELF-TEST FIGURE 20-2

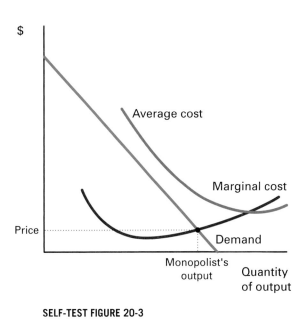

SELF-TEST FIGURE 20-3

19. If the monopoly shown in Self-Test Figure 20-3 charges the price shown, the result is
    a. profit and allocative efficiency.
    b. loss and allocative efficiency.
    c. profit and allocative inefficiency.
    d. loss and allocative inefficiency.

 20. Which of the following best describes a service that is offered at an equal price to everyone, despite some people being more expensive to serve than others?
    a. Antitrust.
    b. Universal access.
    c. Barriers to entry.
    d. Privatization.

QUESTIONS AND PROBLEMS

1. *[barriers to entry]* Provide some examples of barriers to entry. When barriers to entry in an industry are high, is market power more or less? Explain.

2. *[market power]* When a firm has no market power, how does its demand curve appear? As market power increases, how does the appearance of a firm's demand curve change?

3. *[definition of monopoly]* What roles do substitutes play in the definition of monopoly? If there is only one seller in the market, but the firm's product has many good substitutes, is the firm a monopoly? Explain.

4. *[natural monopoly]* How is natural monopoly related to economies of scale? Give an example of a firm that is a natural monopolist.

5. *[price maker]* What is meant when a monopoly firm is described as a price maker? How is a price maker different from a price taker? Is a monopoly ever a price taker?

6. *[monopoly demand]* How is the demand curve of a monopoly firm related to the market demand curve? How will a monopoly demand curve appear graphically?

7. *[monopoly marginal revenue]* Why is marginal revenue less than price for a monopoly? Illustrate by drawing a graph with a monopoly demand curve and the corresponding marginal revenue curve. Be sure to label the axes and the curves.

8. *[monopoly and profit]* Does the mere fact of monopoly guarantee that a firm will earn economic profit? Explain.

9. *[monopoly profit maximization]* State the rule of profit maximization for a monopoly firm. Illustrate graphically a monopoly firm that is maximizing profit.

10. *[monopoly profit maximization]* Change the graph you drew in the previous problem to show the monopoly firm incurring a loss. What rule will the

monopolist apply in order to select the quantity that minimizes the loss?

11. *[monopoly price and profit maximization]* Comment on the following statement: A purely competitive firm will maximize profit at the point where price equals marginal cost, but a monopolist that behaves this way will earn less than the maximum profit.

12. *[monopoly supply]* Does a monopoly firm have a supply curve? Explain.

13. *[monopoly and efficiency]* Is unregulated monopoly economically efficient? Does the monopolist produce more or less than the efficient output?

14. *[monopoly and efficiency]* Draw a graph that shows the output produced by a monopoly and compare it to the efficient output. At the efficient output, to what is price equal?

15. *[limit pricing]* Why would a monopoly firm practice limit pricing? What effect does limit pricing have on a monopolist's profit?

16. *[rate-of-return regulation]* What is the goal of rate-of-return regulation? What price will be set by regulators?

17. *[consumer surplus and subsidies]* Discuss how consumer surplus can justify government subsidies of natural monopolies that incur losses. Support your discussion with a graph, making sure to identify the efficient price and quantity, the area of consumer surplus, and the area of loss.

WORKING WITH GRAPHS AND DATA

1. *[profit maximization]* Use Graph 20-1 of a monopolist to answer the following questions.

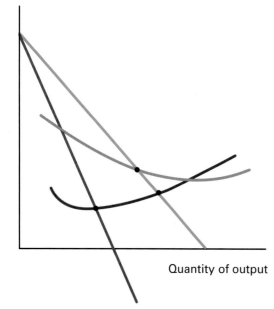

GRAPH 20-1

a. Label the curves in Graph 20-1. Label the demand curve as D, the marginal revenue curve as MR, the average cost curve as AC, and the marginal cost curve as MC.

b. What kind of a monopolist is this firm? What is the source of its monopoly power?

c. Identify the profit-maximizing output and label it Q_1 and the profit-maximizing price and label it P_1. Explain how you determined Q_1 and P_1.

d. Identify the average cost of producing the profit-maximizing output and label it C.

e. How much profit does the firm make? Label the area on the graph that shows profit as "Profit."

2. *[profit maximization]* Use the following table of the demand and total cost of a monopolist to answer the following questions. Note that if the maximum profit occurs at two different output levels, the larger quantity is used as the profit-maximizing quantity.

Price ($)	Quantity	Total Revenue	Total Cost	Marginal Revenue	Marginal Cost	Average Cost	Profit
10	0		$2				
9	1		4				
8	2		5				
7	3		7				
6	4		10				
5	5		14				
4	6		19				

a. Fill in the table.

b. Determine and identify the profit-maximizing output and price.

c. What is true of marginal cost and marginal revenue at the profit-maximizing quantity?

d. Show how you would compute the total profit amount using profit per unit at the profit-maximizing quantity and price.

3. *[inefficiency of monopoly]* Use Graph 20-2 of a monopolist to answer the following questions.

a. Identify the profit-maximizing price and label it P_m and profit-maximizing quantity for this monopolist and label it Q_m.

b. Why is P_m an inefficient price?

c. Identify the efficient price and label it P_e and the efficient quantity and label it Q_e.

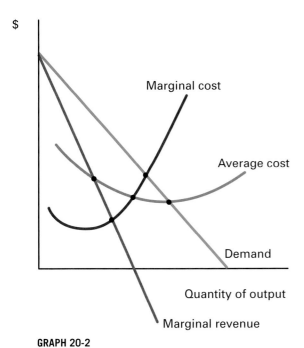

GRAPH 20-2

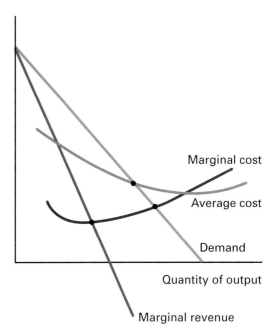

GRAPH 20-3

d. Why is P_e an efficient price?

e. On the graph show the deadweight loss, that is, the value of efficiency that was not achieved as a result of the monopoly, and label it "Loss." Explain.

4. *[regulation]* Use Graph 20-3 of a monopolist to answer the following questions.

a. Identify the profit-maximizing price labeled P_1 and quantity labeled Q_1.

b. Suppose the government decided to impose rate-of-return regulation, which restricts the price that a

monopolist can charge to one that guarantees a normal profit. Identify this price and label it P_2 and the associated output Q_2. Why does this price only guarantee a normal profit?

c. Does the monopolist that is subject to rate-of-return regulation have an incentive to control costs? Explain.

d. Identify the efficient output Q_3 and price P_3. Assume that the government required this private monopolist to charge the efficient price. What problem would exist? Why?

 Visit www.prenhall.com/ayers for Exploring the Web exercises and additional self-test quizzes.

21

OLIGOPOLY AND MONOPOLISTIC COMPETITION

A LOOK AHEAD

What brings mass-market convenience to small-market towns and is the choice of millions of consumers in search of low prices, yet arouses resentment and anger over the market power it wields in small-town America? What is the name of this mighty firm? It's Wal-Mart, the evolution of which is part of "the perennial gale of creative destruction," discussed in this chapter's Explore & Apply section. It is a process that changes the way we live.

This chapter is about businesses large and small. From the cars we drive to the food we eat, we face a wide array of choices. Oligopoly characterizes much of American business. Because the behavior of oligopoly firms is so diverse, economists model oligopoly markets in a variety of ways.

Oligopolists have quite a bit of market power, but not so much as to give any one of them a monopoly of its industry. Firms without much market power often compete by providing consumers with a different product or service than the similar products offered by competitors. Firms in these industries are monopolistically competitive, producing products ranging from physical fitness equipment to family-room furniture.

LEARNING OBJECTIVES

Understanding Chapter 21 will enable you to:
1. **Explain the meaning and significance of mutual interdependence.**
2. **Identify the models associated with oligopoly.**
3. **Describe the characteristics of monopolistic competition.**
4. **Define product differentiation and state its implications.**
5. **Relate how and why firms charge some consumers more than others for the same products.**
6. **Explain why oligopoly brings economic change.**

Explore & Apply

In the last two chapters, we looked at market extremes. We started at the extreme of pure competition, in which firms produce a homogeneous product and cannot price discriminate. We then leapt to the extreme of monopoly, in which there is only one firm in the entire industry. Those models allow us to understand many of the essential characteristics of markets. This chapter adds to that understanding by examining the models of oligopoly and monopolistic competition, which depict markets between pure competition and monopoly.

21.1 OLIGOPOLY—DOMINATION BY A FEW LARGE FIRMS

oligopoly market with multiple firms, at least one of which produces a significant portion of industry output.

mutually interdependent when actions by one firm influence actions taken by other firms in the market.

Oligopoly is characterized by multiple firms, one or more of which will produce a significant portion of industry output. Many oligopoly markets consist of just a few firms. Oligopoly firms are the only firms that are **mutually interdependent,** with the actions taken by one firm influencing actions taken by other firms in the market. Thus, strategy and counterstrategy is the norm in oligopolistic markets.

Mutual interdependence frequently revolves around pricing decisions. For example, the price at which the local cable company offers broadband Internet access will depend in large part upon the price of the substitute DSL broadband access from the local telephone company. Mutual interdependence can also involve product design. For instance, the exploding popularity of sport utility vehicles (SUVs) led small-car maker Saturn to add its first SUV, a 2003 model called the Saturn VUE, to its product lineup. By offering an SUV, Saturn can better compete with its rivals.

differentiated products goods and services that differ among producers.

Oligopoly products may be differentiated or homogeneous. Automobile manufacturing is an oligopoly industry that produces **differentiated products**—products that are similar, but nevertheless differ from one producer to the next. Each vehicle differs from competing models. Styling, colors offered, horsepower, and interior design are just a few of the ways that cars are differentiated. The output of oligopolies is not always differentiated, however. Steel, aluminum, and copper are homogeneous commodities produced by oligopolistic firms.

SNAPSHOT

THEME PARKS—THE THEME IS TO COMPETE

Where once stood miles of orange groves whose bountiful crops helped satisfy the world's thirst for juice, today stand theme parks that satisfy the thirst for fun and adventure. The place is Orlando, Florida, home to Sea World, Universal Studios, and Disney's Magic Kingdom, Animal Kingdom, Epcot Center, and MGM Studios. To attract additional dollars from their visitors, both Disney and Universal offer their own hotels, restaurants, and shops. The strategy is to tie other profit-making activities to the operation of the theme parks. And if one park adds features, its competitors have to add features just to keep up. Such is the nature of designing differentiated products in the head-to-head competition among oligopolists. ◀

MEASURING MARKET POWER—THE FOUR-FIRM CONCENTRATION RATIO

Market power is the ability of a firm to control the price it charges for its output. Purely competitive firms have no market power because they must sell their outputs for the market price. Monopoly firms have the most market power because they have no competitors. In many markets, there is neither pure competition nor monopoly. For this reason we need a method to assess how much market power firms possess. One widely used measure of market power is the **four-firm concentration ratio.** To compute a four-firm concentration ratio:

four-firm concentration ratio fraction of total market sales by the four largest firms.

$$\text{Four-firm concentration ratio} = \frac{\text{Sales by four largest firms in an industry}}{\text{Sales by all firms in an industry}} \times 100$$

In effect, a four-firm concentration ratio equals the percentage of sales accounted for by the four largest firms in a market. A four-firm concentration ratio cannot be greater than 100 since 100 percent of industry sales accounts for all the sales in a market. Since a monopoly market consists of only one firm, the four-firm concentration ratio must equal 100 in that case. An oligopoly with just two, three, or four firms will also have a four-firm concentration ratio equal to 100. At the lower end of the scale, a concentration ratio will approach a value of zero when the industry consists of many small firms. For example, when there are 100 firms of equal size in a market, the four-firm concentration ratio would equal 4.

Table 21-1 shows the four-firm concentration ratios computed by the U.S. Department of Commerce for a selection of industries. Larger numbers in the table show greater market power, but the data must be interpreted with caution. The concentration ratios do not include sales by foreign firms. In addition, the four-firm concentration ratio does not take into account differences in size among the four largest firms. For example, one firm may be much larger than the other three, allowing the largest firm to dominate the market. This case is fundamentally different from the case where the four largest firms are of equal size.

TABLE 21-1 FOUR-FIRM CONCENTRATION RATIOS FOR SELECTED U.S. MANUFACTURING INDUSTRIES

INDUSTRY	CONCENTRATION RATIO (PERCENT)
Cigarettes	98.9
Aircraft	84.8
Tires	72.4
Soap and detergents	65.6
Gloves and mittens	63.8
Cookies and crackers	59.9
Dog and cat food	58.4
Luggage	51.9
Soft drinks	47.2
Boats	41.4
Mattresses	38.6

Source: *Concentration Ratios in Manufacturing*, Table 2. The measure of concentration is the share of value of shipments.

MERGERS AND SPINOFFS

merger when two firms combine into a single firm.

A **merger** occurs when one firm combines with another to form a single firm. One of the best-known examples is the 1998 merger of Chrysler and Daimler-Benz that formed the single firm we know as DaimlerChrysler. In contrast, in a *spinoff,* a firm splits off a portion of its operations into a new company or sells that unit to another firm. The spinoff of Jif peanut butter from Procter and Gamble to jelly maker J. M. Smucker in 2001 offers an example.

There are three types of mergers:

horizontal merger merger of competing firms.

vertical merger merger between a firm and its supplier, or between the firm and a buyer of its output.

conglomerate merger merger between firms in unrelated businesses.

- **Horizontal merger** occurs when a firm merges with a competitor.
- **Vertical merger** occurs when a firm acquires another firm that supplies it with an input, or acquires another firm that buys the product of the acquiring firm.
- **Conglomerate merger** occurs when firms in unrelated businesses merge.

Let's look at some examples of the three kinds of mergers. When a supermarket chain buys another supermarket chain, or a bank buys another bank, a horizontal merger has taken place. The $81 billion acquisition of Mobil Oil by Exxon in 1999 was a horizontal merger. Economies of scale can arise from horizontal mergers. To achieve economies, for example, Exxon expanded many of its gas stations into TigerMarts, while eliminating many of the former Mobil stations altogether. The merger that created DaimlerChrysler, mentioned earlier, is another example of a horizontal merger. The management of both companies expected the merger to promote economies of scale by combining engineering, styling, and other functional units of the two companies.

The objective of a vertical merger that sees a firm acquiring one of its suppliers is to secure reliable delivery of the input. When the vertical merger instead involves a firm acquiring another firm that sells its product, the objective is to ensure a ready market for the firm's output. An example of a vertical merger occurred in 2000 when Internet service provider America Online (AOL) acquired Netscape, supplier of the browser software through which AOL's service is provided. By acquiring Netscape, AOL hoped to utilize Netscape's resources to make its Internet services superior to those of its competitors.

Sometimes mergers have both horizontal and vertical elements. For example, in 2000, AOL also purchased Time Warner, parent company of *Time* magazine and Warner Brothers Pictures. Since Time Warner possessed an extensive cable network, this purchase provided AOL with direct access to put AOL services into the homes of Time Warner customers. In that sense, the merger was vertical. However, Time Warner also provided content. Since AOL also produced its own content, that aspect of the merger was horizontal. This merger offers another lesson on mergers, namely that merged companies do not always prosper. The merged AOL Time Warner failed to live up to the high expectations that management had articulated prior to the merger. The AOL-Netscape merger had the same result.

Mergers have antitrust implications. The Justice Department examines merger proposals, especially those involving horizontal mergers, for their potential effects on competition in the marketplace. One question the Justice Department asks is whether prices will rise because of a merger, with the Justice Department challenging mergers that it thinks would significantly weaken competition and raise prices. For example, the proposed sale of Office Depot to its competitor Staples was abandoned when it appeared that the Justice Department would not approve it.

MERGING INTO BANKRUPTCY   *SNAPSHOT*

Over $30 billion in debt, mostly from acquisitions—that and some multi-billion dollar accounting misstatements is what did in WorldCom. Once known for its long-distance service through its acquired MCI subsidiary, today it is just one more example of a company that expanded itself into the bankruptcy courts. The trend started with Enron, whose numerous partnerships made it a complex company to understand and a financial mess when it became the largest bankruptcy ever in the United States.

After a series of corporate debacles, starting with Enron's in late 2001, investors became leery of companies with too much corporate wheeling and dealing—the plummeting stock prices of such companies showed that uncertainty. The razzle-dazzle of mergers and acquisitions gave way to a realization that, sometimes, they just fundamentally don't make sense. ◄

21.2 OLIGOPOLY MODELS

Oligopoly is the only market structure for which there are a variety of models. As we will now see, the appropriate model depends upon the specific circumstances of the industry. For example, **contestable markets** occur when new rivals can enter or exit the market quickly and cheaply. Contestability can characterize either oligopoly or monopoly. The "quick in and quick out" characteristic of contestable markets limits the ability of the firm or firms already in the market to raise prices. If prices become too high in a contestable market, entry of new firms will occur because such entry is easy. Congressional deregulation of the airline industry in the 1970s brought contestable markets to life in the airports of our major cities, as large carriers could now enter or exit a city's market with relative ease. In contrast, automobile manufacturing is costly and difficult to enter and thus does not meet the criteria of a contestable market.

The **price leadership** model is based on observable oligopoly behavior. In some oligopolistic industries, when one firm changes its selling price, the remaining firms in the industry copy that change. The firm initiating the price change is called the price leader; the copycats are termed followers. At one time or another the cigarette, automobile, and steel industries have exhibited the pattern of price leadership. In effect, the followers in a price-leadership oligopoly have voluntarily placed themselves in the role of price takers. They count on the price leader to set a price that will allow them to stay in business. In the remainder of this section, we examine in greater detail some essential models of oligopoly.

contestable markets oligopoly or monopoly market with quick entry and exit; limits market power of firms already in the market.

price leadership when one firm changes its price and others in the industry follow suit.

OIL FROM OPEC—WHICH MARKET MODEL?

In analyzing oligopoly markets, we must go beyond the models of pure competition and monopoly. For example, OPEC (the Organization of Petroleum Exporting Countries) has played a major role in causing the price of petroleum and its products to fluctuate wildly over the past decades, enough to prompt President Carter in the late 1970s and President Bush in 2001 to declare that the United States was facing an "energy crisis." OPEC is neither a price taker nor the only supplier of the world's oil, so neither the purely competitive model nor the monopoly model apply exclusively. However, used in conjunction with one another, the monopoly and pure competition models can actually reveal what motivates OPEC decisions.

OPEC is made up of eleven developing countries that produce crude oil: Algeria, Indonesia, Iran, Iraq, Kuwait, Libya, Nigeria, Qatar, Saudi Arabia, the United Arab Emirates, and Venezuela. OPEC is an example of a **cartel,** a form of oligopoly in which firms in an industry collude (or in this case countries). *Collusion* means that firms jointly plan price and output. The objective of a cartel is to behave like a monopoly, increasing price to the profit-maximizing monopoly price. To achieve the higher price, the cartel reduces its output and assigns output quotas to its members. While cartels are illegal within the United States, they have at times existed internationally for such items as coffee, tin, and diamonds, in addition to crude petroleum.

cartel occurs when firms collude to eliminate competition among themselves and obtain greater profit.

Cartels are difficult to keep together for three reasons:

- While firms have a collective incentive to keep output low and price high, they have an individual incentive to take advantage of the high price and produce extra output. In other words, each cartel member has the incentive to cheat by selling more than its production quota under the cartel agreement. For example, cheating by OPEC members got so out of hand that, by December 2002, it accounted for over 13 percent of total OPEC output. In a meeting that month, OPEC resolved to stop the cheating. It vowed to increase its official output by over a billion barrels per day, while at the same time reducing its actual output by nearly 2 billion barrels per day. Easier said than done!

- If barriers to entry are not absolute, high cartel profits could induce competition from new entrants or existing firms that are not members of the cartel. For example, high oil prices in the 1970s spurred exploration, which in turn led to major oil finds in Alaska, Mexico, and the North Sea. Because OPEC did not control these new oil fields, the added oil supplies negatively affected OPEC's ability to set price.

- Over time, higher prices can lead to the development of substitutes for the cartel's product. Higher oil prices prompted the development of energy-efficient homes and automobiles, such as the so-called econo-box cars that were produced in the 1970s when oil prices were high, as well as the more recent Toyota Prius and Honda Insight hybrid gas and electric vehicles that are for sale today. Conversely, once oil prices fell in the mid-1980s and 1990s, suburbs sprawled and new-car buyers made gas-guzzling sport-utility vehicles popular.

Figure 21-1 shows nominal and real oil prices since 1970. The real price adjusts the nominal price for inflation and the effects of changes in the value of currencies.

While OPEC tries to behave like a monopolist, it faces competition from many small price-taking oil producers who are not OPEC members. These include the United States, Russia, Norway, Great Britain, and many other countries. To understand this aspect of OPEC's behavior, we turn to the model of a **dominant firm with a competitive fringe,** an oligopoly model that combines the competitive and monopoly models. In this model, the dominant firm, typically the largest in the industry, has a cost advantage over the many smaller firms in the competitive fringe. The dominant firm has no control over other producers, and thus allows them to produce as much as they want at the market price. However, the production decisions of the dominant firm forces that market price to below what it would be if the competitive fringe firms were the only suppliers. This lower price allows the dominant firm a significant share of the market.

dominant firm with a competitive fringe when one large firm sets the price to maximize its profit, and the many smaller competitors that are also in the same market sell at that price.

Figure 21-2 illustrates the model of a dominant firm with a competitive fringe. In part (a) of the figure we show the supply curve of the competitive fringe and the market demand. This market would be purely competitive if the dominant firm did not exist. In application to the world oil market, the competitive fringe consists of all oil producers that are not members of OPEC. OPEC behaves like the dominant firm. Its demand curve is called a *residual demand,* because at any given price, the dominant firm could sell the residual difference between the market quantity demanded and the quantity supplied by the competitive firms.

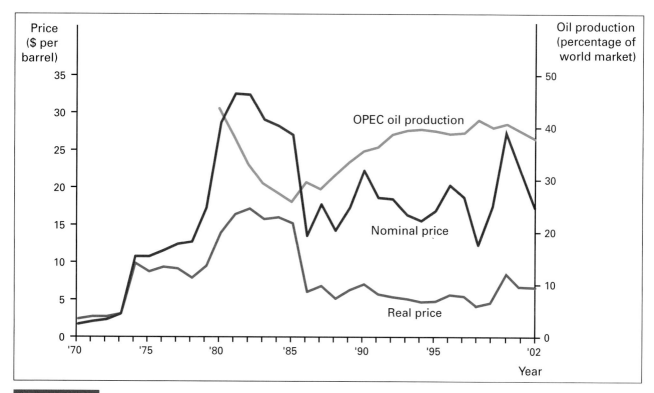

FIGURE 21-1

THE NOMINAL AND REAL PRICE OF OIL SINCE 1970 The real price of oil today is much lower than the nominal price because much of the rise in the nominal price over time has been due to inflation. OPEC's market power became apparent during late 1973 when it allegedly withheld supplies from the world crude oil market. The nominal price of oil tripled by 1974. Since then, OPEC's market power has fluctuated, depending upon demand and supplies of oil from other non-OPEC producing countries. OPEC's share of world crude oil production since 1980 is also shown. OPEC's share dipped during the 1980s before rising. Today, that share is only slightly lower than it was in 1980. Other things equal, a rising share for OPEC increases its market power.

Source: OPEC Annual Statistical Bulletin, 2002, Tables 14 and 73. OPEC's percentage of crude oil production before 1980 is not available.

For example, suppose the price of crude oil is $15 a barrel, and market demand leads to six million barrels per day demanded at that price. If the competitive fringe offers for sale a quantity of one million barrels of crude oil per day, then the dominant firm's quantity demanded would equal the difference of five million barrels. In other words, if the price were $15, OPEC would see its quantity demanded as five million barrels per day, the shortage in the market at that price. The price of $15 and quantity demanded of five million barrels would be one point on the OPEC demand curve. OPEC would compute its residual demand for all other prices in order to arrive at the other points on its demand curve.

The residual quantity demanded is zero if price equals the equilibrium price under pure competition, where market demand and the competitive supply intersect in Figure 21-2(a). Below that price, the residual quantity demanded is positive, shown as "Dominant firm's Demand" in Figure 21-2(b). The process can be thought of as occurring in three steps: (1). The dominant firm computes its residual demand, as just described. (2). The dominant firm maximizes its own profit by producing the output for which its marginal cost equals its marginal revenue. The dominant firm then charges the highest price on its demand curve that would allow it to produce that quantity. (3). The dominant firm's price becomes the market price that faces the price-taking firms in the competitive fringe. The total quantity produced

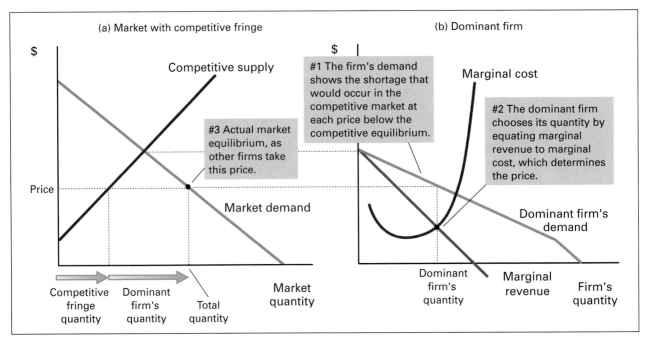

FIGURE 21-2

THE DOMINANT FIRM WITH A COMPETITIVE FRINGE The dominant firm with a competitive fringe chooses its output and price in three steps:

#1 It computes its residual demand, the difference in part (a) between the quantity demanded and the quantity supplied by the competitive firms at each possible price. The residual demand is labeled "Dominant firm's demand" in part (b).

#2 It chooses the quantity that equates its marginal cost to its marginal revenue, labeled "Dominant firm's quantity" in part (b). It charges the price on its demand curve.

#3 The price from step #2 becomes the market price. Firms in the competitive fringe are price takers at that price. The total quantity of output equals the quantity supplied by the competitive fringe plus the quantity supplied by the dominant firm.

in this market is the sum of the quantities produced by the competitive fringe and by the dominant firm, as shown by the addition of the two arrows in (a).

In application to the world market for crude oil, the OPEC cartel is the dominant firm and all other crude oil producers form the competitive fringe.

GAME THEORY

game theory analysis of economic strategies in order to predict how firms will behave; uses a decision tree or a payoff matrix to illustrate the outcomes associated with the choices available.

The mathematics of **game theory** can help us understand the decisions made by oligopolists. Game theory analyzes the behavior of parties whose interests conflict. The tool of analysis is the decision tree or a payoff matrix, which we will explain in a moment.

In game theory the outcome of one player's decision will also depend on a decision made by another. For example, a firm cannot predict the effect of a price cut on its profits unless it considers what competitors will do. If competitors leave their prices unchanged, the effects on the price-cutting firm will be very different than if competitors cut their prices to match or outdo the price cut of the first price cutter. As in poker, chess, and other games, many additional strategies also provide insights into oligopoly behavior. Some strategies are quite complex and involve the use of advanced mathematics.

prisoner's dilemma an oligopoly game that shows the difficulty of enforcing collusion.

A classic game is the **prisoner's dilemma,** which shows the difficulty of enforcing collusion. Two persons, Al and Happy, are suspected by police of being partners in crime. They are arrested and interrogated in separate rooms, where each prisoner is told the following:

*If your partner confesses, while you keep your mouth shut, we'll throw the book at you. Your part-
ner will get off with one year in jail, but you'll do twenty years of hard time. However, if you confess
while your partner keeps quiet, you will get one year of jail time, while your partner gets twenty. If
you both confess, you'll both get five years. If you both clam up, we've still got the evidence to send
you away for three years in the slammer.*

Figure 21-3 summarizes the situation in terms of a *decision tree* and a *payoff matrix* that
show the gains or losses from making a decision when mutual interdependence is present.
These tools of analysis reveal that whatever Al does, Happy is better off confessing.
Whatever Happy does, Al is better off confessing. Guilt or innocence makes no difference.
Confessing is the *dominant strategy* for both Al and Happy, shown by the check marks in the
figure. Collusion between Al and Happy, in the form of an oath by both to keep quiet, results
in a lighter sentence than the five years they both receive by confessing. However, the police
have separated them for the very purpose of preventing collusion. The police have in effect
stacked the deck, preventing the pursuit by Al and Happy of their joint interests.

To see how the prisoner's dilemma applies to oligopoly, consider an oligopoly with
only two firms, X-co and Y-co, in which each firm must choose between a high price and a
low price for its product. The payoff matrix might look like the one shown in Figure 21-4.

The dilemma facing each firm is that it knows that the best collective solution for the
two of them is for both to charge a high price. That solution would bring $20 million in prof-
its to their industry. However, if X-co charges a high price, Y-co's best strategy is to charge a

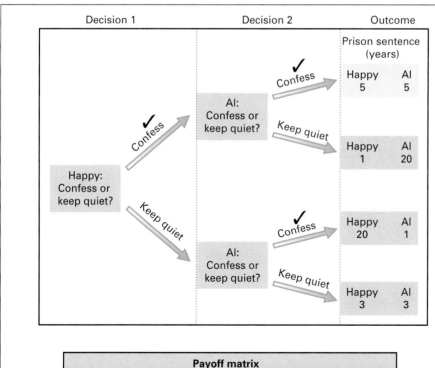

FIGURE 21-3

PRISONER'S DILEMMA In the
prisoner's dilemma, the dominant strategy for each individual
is to confess. In this example,
no matter what Happy does, Al
is better off confessing.
Likewise, Happy is better off
confessing no matter what Al
does. The outcome of these
decisions is a prison sentence of
5 years apiece, as shown in the
yellow boxes. Note that Al and
Happy's collective interest is
better served by collusion, in
which they both keep quiet and
are sentenced to 3 years each.

Payoff matrix		
	Al confesses	Al keeps quiet
Happy confesses	Al gets 5 years Happy gets 5 years	Al gets 20 years Happy gets 1 year
Happy keeps quiet	Al gets 1 year Happy gets 20 years	Al gets 3 years Happy gets 3 years

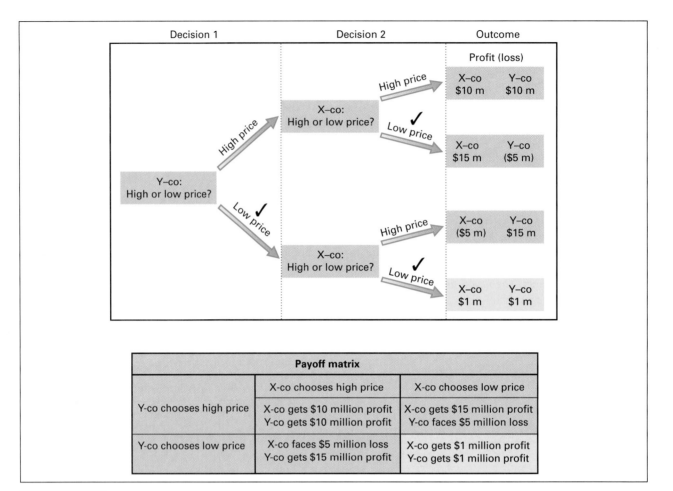

| Decision 1 | Decision 2 | Outcome |

Profit (loss)

High price → X–co $10 m | Y–co $10 m

Low price ✓ → X–co $15 m | Y–co ($5 m)

High price → X–co ($5 m) | Y–co $15 m

Low price ✓ → X–co $1 m | Y–co $1 m

Y–co: High or low price? → High price → X–co: High or low price?

Low price ✓ → X–co: High or low price?

Payoff matrix		
	X-co chooses high price	X-co chooses low price
Y-co chooses high price	X-co gets $10 million profit Y-co gets $10 million profit	X-co gets $15 million profit Y-co faces $5 million loss
Y-co chooses low price	X-co faces $5 million loss Y-co gets $15 million profit	X-co gets $1 million profit Y-co gets $1 million profit

FIGURE 21-4

PRISONER'S DILEMMA IN TWO-FIRM OLIGOPOLY These firms face the dilemma of whether to price high or low. Their collective interest calls for a high price. In the absence of collusion, however, their dominant strategies cause the price to be low.

low price and earn a larger profit by pulling customers away from X-co. Y-co's profit would be $15 million and X-co would lose $5 million. Alternatively, if X-co were to charge a low price, Y-co's best strategy is to also charge a low price so as to avoid losing customers to X-co. Y-co would only earn $1 million in profit, but that would be better than a $5 million loss. Thus, charging a low price is the dominant strategy for Y-co.

Charging a low price is also the dominant strategy for X-co, by the same reasoning. Thus, as shown by the check marked path in Figure 21-4, the firms are led to each charge a low price and share equally in a $2 million profit rather than in a $20 million profit. So, even though each firm knows that their collective best interest involves charging high prices, they are led to each charge low prices!

Because the firms in this example know that they are better off with high prices, they have an incentive to agree to each keep prices high. Such a bargain would involve collusion and lead to a cartel. The antitrust laws in the United States are intended to prevent collusion and thus keep prices low.

Even if firms do form a cartel to keep prices high, the prisoner's dilemma game still comes into play. Each cartel member knows that by cooperating among themselves and raising price while cutting quantity, the member firms making up the cartel can achieve the greatest profit. But reasoned self-interest says that it pays to cheat on the arrangement by increasing sales through secret price cuts. If a member cheats while other members do not, the cheater is better off. If a member does not cheat while other members do, the honest member suffers. No matter what the other members do, a particular member of the cartel is better off by cheating. Cheating is a major reason that OPEC's power has dwindled over time.

At any given point in time, it is always in each firm's interest to charge a low price, even if that means cheating on a cartel agreement. This drives the industry price down. Yet firms know that their long-term interests are served by a high industry price. So, over time, the game playing gets more complicated. For example, when cheating by OPEC members caused the world oil price to drop from $18.68 per barrel in 1997 to $12.28 in 1998, it became obvious to all OPEC members that their collective interest was to stop cheating. The members therefore recommitted themselves to restricting production, with the result that the world oil price rose to $27.60 in 2000 reached an average $31 a barrel in 2003.

Likewise, fare wars routinely break out in the airline industry because it is in each carrier's self-interest to undercut the price of its rivals and take away the rivals' customers. Yet the airlines know that the result is that the rivals do likewise and industry profits plummet. Although airlines are prohibited by U.S. law from colluding on airfares, they have various ways of signaling each other for their collective good. For example, airlines often raise prices, wait a few days to see if rivals match the fare increases, and then lower them again if they do not. In effect, such airlines are signaling their willingness to call off mutually destructive fare wars. Such signaling is not illegal and is widely practiced.

STRATEGY ASSUMPTIONS—THE MODEL OF KINKED DEMAND

Prices in oligopoly sometimes seem sticky, meaning resistant to change. The **kinked demand curve** model offers an explanation. In this model, any firm that raises its price loses a significant fraction of its customers to other firms that are assumed to keep their prices constant. However, if a firm lowers its price, it does not gain customers from other firms because the other firms in the industry would feel the competitive need to lower their prices, too. The result is that the firm would face a relatively flat demand curve for price increases, losing many customers to competitors that keep their prices constant. However, were the firm to lower its price, it would face a steeper demand curve because its competitors would retain their own customers by matching the price drops. The result is a kink in demand at the current price, as shown in Figure 21-5.

kinked demand curve demand curve that is steeper below the current price than above it; predicts that firms will not change price.

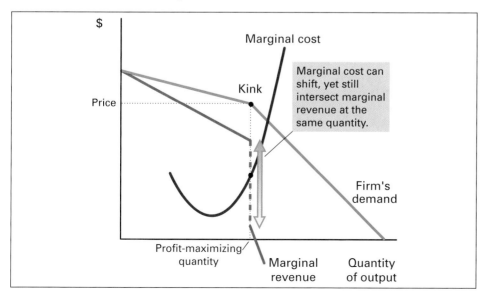

FIGURE 21-5

THE KINKED DEMAND CURVE The kinked demand curve model assumes that firms match price decreases by their competitors, but do not match price increases. As a consequence, marginal revenue is discontinuous (vertical) at the quantity associated with the kink. Marginal cost can rise or fall within the vertical range without affecting either output or price.

The mathematics of marginal revenue cause the marginal revenue curve to be discontinuous directly below that kink, as shown in Figure 21-5. Following the rule of profit maximization, namely to produce to the point where marginal revenue equals marginal cost, firms would ordinarily produce the quantity of output associated with the kink in demand, as shown in Figure 21-5. Even if marginal cost changes, it is likely to still intersect marginal revenue in the discontinuous portion and thus change neither the output nor price. For example, in Figure 21-5, marginal cost could rise or fall within the range shown by the double-headed arrow without changing either price or quantity produced. For this reason, the kinked demand curve leads to so-called sticky prices, namely prices that tend to remain unchanged over time.

The kinked demand curve model represents a particular kind of behavioral game. As with other models, the kinked demand curve model only applies when firms behave according to the assumptions of the model. One reason that there are so many models within oligopoly is that firms do not all play the same game or use the same strategies.

21.3 MONOPOLISTIC COMPETITION—ALL AROUND US

Imagine the diary of a college student: "Walked to Buck's Books and Comics to buy some sci-fi. Dropped in to Piece-A-Da-Pie for lunch. After class, had to drive to CompuWiz to buy more DataSave disks. Gassed up at Gas'n N Go'n, and picked up some Spam. Too long of a wait at the Hair Team. Wound up missing the free buffet at Dancin' Place. Now I'm trying to study for Professor Dobson's course, but I'm too tired."

monopolistic competition a market structure with many firms selling differentiated products and relatively easy entry of new firms.

This college student has had an active day. Much of it was spent dealing with firms operating in markets characterized by **monopolistic competition,** a market structure with many firms, product differentiation, and relatively easy entry of new firms. Many retailers operate in monopolistically competitive markets. In addition, many of the products they sell are also produced by firms in monopolistic competition.

PRICE AND OUTPUT

Monopolistically competitive firms face demand curves that slope downward slightly, because although they are the only providers of their version of the product, other firms offer close substitutes. The result is that firms have only a limited ability to affect prices. For example, Pizza Hut does not just compete with Domino's and other pizza parlors. In addition, it competes with Burger King, Long John Silver's, Taco Bell, and all the other choices for lunch and dinner. Yet nobody else has quite the same products. For this reason, the model of price and output determination under monopolistic competition is akin to that of pure monopoly, but with two exceptions. Specifically, each firm faces a demand curve that is:

- Highly elastic, which gives it a relatively flat appearance.
- Influenced by the firm's own actions and the actions of competitors.

For example, the firm has the incentive to advertise and vary its product as a way of increasing its demand at the expense of its competitors.

Figure 21-6 illustrates price and quantity determination by the monopolistically competitive firm. Like all profit-maximizing firms, the firm we see here produces where marginal cost equals marginal revenue, indicated by the label "Profit-maximizing quantity" in the figure. The firm chooses the price on its demand curve that corresponds to the profit-maximizing quantity. Because demand is highly elastic, marginal revenue slopes down only slightly, too. One consequence is that, like monopoly, the firm does not produce the efficient output (given by the intersection of marginal cost and demand). Unlike monopoly, however, the monopolistically

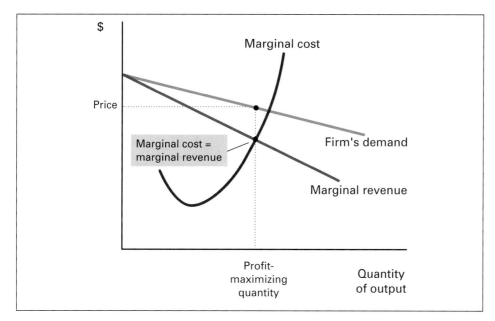

FIGURE 21-6

FIRM'S OUTPUT AND PRICE IN MONOPOLISTIC COMPETITION
Output and price determination under monopolistic competition are the same as under monopoly, except that demand is much more elastic. As a result, the profit-maximizing output occurs close to the efficient output, given by the intersection of marginal cost and the firm's demand.

competitive firm chooses a quantity that is very nearly efficient in the short run. What's more, competition among firms also leads them to develop valuable variations on the product over time. They are constantly looking to "build a better mousetrap."

ENTRY AND EXIT

Monopolistic competition is exciting, because easy entry and exit make it possible for entrepreneurs to test out their good ideas. The same holds true for product variation and advertising. If your version of an industry product is particularly appealing to the public, for example, you can open up shop and possibly grow rich. You would envision a large profit, such as shown in Figure 21-7(a).

The downside is that your vision of the market could be clouded. You might find that your demand is lower or your costs are higher than you anticipated. If so, you would find yourself with losses, such as depicted in Figure 21-7(b). Facing losses, monopolistically competitive firms look for ways to change their advertising or vary their product in order to get to profitability. These changes can potentially affect both the firm's demand and its costs of production.

If the monopolistically competitive firm cannot cover its variable costs of production, it will shut down, just like firms in any other market structure. If the firm cannot find a way to eventual profitability, it will exit the industry in the long run. **Firms will continue to exit or enter until a long-run equilibrium is reached in which additional entrants would expect zero profits.** The zero-profit firm in monopolistic competition is shown in Figure 21-7, part (c).

The ease of entry and exit in monopolistic competition is seen in the restaurant industry. New restaurants constantly open and existing ones close. A few restaurants catch on and even grow into national chains. Others go out of business. Many more allow their owners to just scrape by with zero economic profit, such as the firm shown in part (c) of Figure 21-7.

Note that none of the firms depicted in parts (a), (b), and (c) in Figure 21-7 minimize their average costs of production. Nor do they produce the efficient quantity. These deviations from pure competition are the price we pay for the diversity of choices that monopolistically competitive firms offer us.

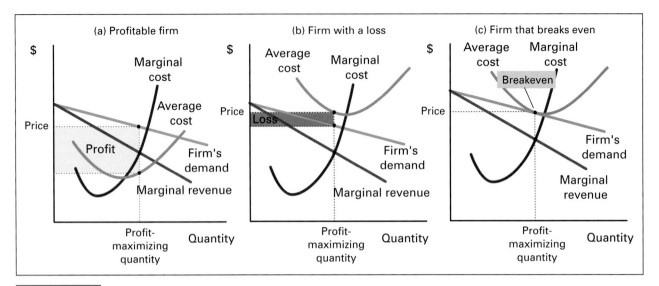

FIGURE 21-7

PROFIT, LOSS, AND BREAKEVEN IN MONOPOLISTIC COMPETITION. As shown in graph (a), profit is the difference between average revenue (which is price) and average cost, multiplied by output. As always, a profit-maximizing output equates marginal revenue and marginal cost.

Loss occurs when average cost exceeds average revenue, as shown in (b). The loss equals the quantity of output multiplied by the difference between average cost and average revenue, which is the area of the shaded rectangle.

Part (c) shows a monopolistically competitive firm with zero economic profit. Note that the average-cost curve is just tangent to demand at the profit-maximizing quantity of output. A firm will neither enter nor exit if it expects zero profit.

QUICKCHECK

There was once a fast-food restaurant named **The Rapid Rabbit.** The owners believed that they had found a lucrative market niche as the only restaurant in town to offer rabbit meat. However, demand was weak and the Rapid Rabbit Restaurant eventually went out of business. Illustrate graphically how weak demand can lead to losses. Explain possible reasons why demand would be weak in this example.

Answer: Your graph should appear similar to Figure 21-7(b). Possible reasons for weak demand include such things as: a poor location, a questionable name, insufficient advertising, and consumers who simply do not want the product.

21.4 WAYS TO COMPETE

It's a big market out there, or so it might seem to a firm in monopolistic competition or oligopoly. A firm in either type of market will always be on the lookout for ways to grab a bigger market share. The firm will also seek ways of getting additional revenue from its customers. This section looks at some of the ways it achieves these goals.

ADVERTISING AND PRODUCT DIFFERENTIATION

The firm's demand is always defined under the condition of *ceteris paribus,* meaning that everything except the firm's price is held constant. In oligopoly markets, each firm's demand will shift when its competitors change their prices and products. Likewise, the demand facing a firm in monopolistic competition will be affected by the availability of the many substitute products from other firms in the industry. Unlike the firm in pure competition, however, the oligopolistic or monopolistically competitive firm is not a helpless victim of market circumstances. Rather, in these market structures, the firm can actively seek to change its own demand curve through the use of product differentiation and advertising.

The key to riches in monopolistic competition is successful product differentiation in such things as style, taste, shape, size, color, texture, quality, location, packaging, advertising, and service. For example, the powerful lure of the trademarked golden arches is one of the features differentiating McDonald's from its competitors. Likewise the thirty-one flavors help differentiate Baskin-Robbins from other sellers of ice cream.

The differentiated nature of products in monopolistic competition and many oligopolies makes it likely that firms will advertise. Some ads focus on facts, such as Yellow Page ads with addresses, phone numbers, and hours of operation. However, much advertising is designed to work on consumers' imaginations and stick in their memories. Advertising slogans permeate our language. Successful advertising, slogans, and sales promotions increase the demand for a firm's version of the industry's output. In addition, advertising that creates customer loyalty for existing firms and their well-known brands forms a barrier to the entry of new firms. Figure 21-8 shows how successful advertising can shift demand and marginal revenue higher when consumers are influenced favorably.

When advertising or otherwise differentiating its product, the profit-maximizing firm is still guided by the same principle that guides its choice of quantity of output: marginal cost equals marginal revenue. **If the marginal revenue generated by advertising exceeds the marginal cost of that advertising, advertising raises profits. Otherwise it does not. Similarly, the profit-maximizing firm will adjust its hours of operation, selection of merchandise, and every other aspect of product differentiation with this same principle in mind.** For example, if a store's marginal revenue from staying open an extra hour in the evening exceeds the marginal cost of staying open the extra hour, the store will choose to stay open that extra hour.

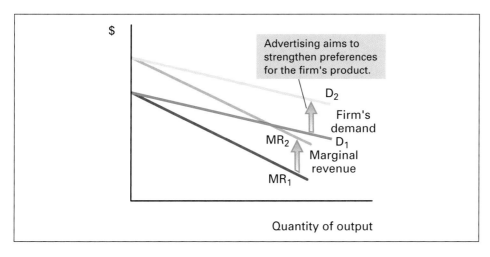

FIGURE 21-8

ADVERTISING TO SHIFT DEMAND
The aim of advertising is to shift demand to the right. An effective ad campaign can bring the firm to profitability or increase the profit it already has. Both oligopolists and monopolistically competitive firms do a significant amount of advertising of their differentiated products.

QUICKCHECK

Under what circumstances would a firm decrease the effectiveness of its advertising or vary its product in such a way that consumers like it less? Provide an example.

Answer: These actions might be either deliberate or unintentional. Firms would deliberately decrease the effectiveness of advertising or make a less-desirable product if the money they save in doing so exceeds the revenue they lose from consumers buying less product. An example would be when a firm reduces the size of its ad in the Yellow Pages, knowing that a smaller ad will save money, but mean fewer customers. Alternatively, firms might launch an advertising campaign or a product variation that is unsuccessful. An example would be a restaurant that plays its background music too loud.

PRICE DISCRIMINATION UNDER MONOPOLISTIC COMPETITION AND OLIGOPOLY

You and your roommate are both flying home on the same airline and to the same city, but your roommate paid $200 more than you did . . . is there something wrong with your ticket? More likely, you bought your ticket further in advance and are the beneficiary of *price discrimination,* which is the selling of a good or service at different prices when such differences are not caused by differences in production costs. Price discrimination under monopoly was discussed in the previous chapter. Examples under monopolistic competition and oligopoly include discounts for senior citizens and students. Coupons that give those who redeem them lower prices also represent price discrimination.

Price discrimination is feasible when different prices can be charged to different market segments. Segments with the highest elasticities of demand usually see the lowest prices, because those consumers are the most price sensitive. For example, it costs no less to screen a movie in a theater filled with children than to show it to adults. Yet adult ticket prices are usually twice those of children's, because adults are less deterred by higher prices—demand for adult tickets is less elastic than demand for children's tickets.

A firm cannot practice price discrimination if buyers who are offered goods at a low price can resell those goods to other buyers at a higher price, a practice called *arbitrage.* For example, pricing adult movie tickets higher than children's would accomplish nothing if adults could see a movie with a child's ticket. The only tickets that a theater could sell would be the child's tickets, purchased by children and then profitably resold to adults at a price less than the regular adult price.

QUICKCHECK

Differences between in-state and out-of-state tuition at public colleges and universities are usually substantial. Is this price discrimination? How can it be justified?

Answer: It is no more costly to serve a student from one location than from another. Therefore, the custom of charging higher tuition to out-of-state students fits the definition of price discrimination. It is justified by the logic that those whose tax dollars have built the schools deserve a lower price. Thus, this price discrimination is intended to satisfy the goal of equity.

There are various ways to implement price discrimination. For example, when airlines require Saturday night stays and advance purchases for flyers to get the lowest rates, much of the reason has to do with price discriminating between the leisure traveler with a relatively elastic demand and the business traveler whose demand is relatively inelastic. Airlines know that business travelers often must make plans at the last minute and rarely want to spend the weekend away from home. Therefore, requiring advance purchases and Saturday night stays is a good way of identifying that traveler. Merely asking at the counter if a person is a business traveler would not work, not when the penalty for a correct answer is to pay more—typically a lot more!

A QUARTER FOR A COKE WHEN YOU'RE COLD   *SNAPSHOT*

On a hot summer day, an ice-cold Coke might sound oh-so-good. But on a cold winter day? The Coca-Cola Company pondered that situation in the fall of 1999 and came up with a solution: Coke machines that set their price in response to the weather and expected demand. Instead of having delivery van drivers twiddling their thumbs while listening to the winter winds, wouldn't it be better to cut the price at Coke vending machines until sales in cold weather rival those when the summer sun sears? And what about those blazing hot days when the delivery people cannot keep the vending machines from running out? Shouldn't price rise to avoid a shortage and give the Cokes to those who value them the most?

With this logic in mind, the Coca-Cola Company made plans to develop smart vending machines that would charge more when demand is high and less when it is low. The strategy of price discrimination seemed efficient and would have involved both price increases some times and decreases other times. But the idea of being charged more when you are the most thirsty just didn't sit well with the Coke-drinking public. In fact, the press coverage was so intensely negative that Coca-Cola was forced to publicly renounce this latest form of price discrimination. ◀

21.5 WAL-MART—CREATIVE DESTRUCTION

Explore & Apply

You can't fight progress, they say, although often that is exactly what we'd like to do. We see the world around us change and we just aren't sure that we like what we see. The old ways that we know give way to new ways that we don't know. What is behind this change, and is it for the best?

Often, change is caused by the decisions made by big businesses located far away from us. For example, consider the way that Wal-Mart, the largest corporation in America, established a dominant oligopoly presence in outlying areas, and in the process changed the character of America's small towns.

Before looking at the effect of Wal-Mart on America's heartland, consider the data in Table 21-2. This table shows the four-firm concentration ratios for several categories of retailing. Depending on how broadly retail trade is defined, retailing is either very competitive or very concentrated. Retail trade itself is highly competitive with countless stores of all types competing for the consumer's dollar. When we look at discount stores, however, we see that the four largest firms have an 87 percent market share. Of those four firms, Wal-Mart is by far the largest. Furthermore, Wal-Mart competes with the other kinds of retailers shown in the table: electronics stores, nurseries, drug stores, and clothing stores. The data in the table are for the United States as a whole, since concentration ratios for local areas are not computed by the Census Bureau. If we were able to obtain market share figures for local areas, we would see Wal-Mart's dominance of some markets even more clearly. We do not need to

TABLE 21-2   FOUR-FIRM CONCENTRATION RATIOS FOR RETAILING

KIND OF BUSINESS	FOUR-FIRM CONCENTRATION RATIO	COMMENT
Discount department stores	87.9	Highly concentrated, indicating probable oligopoly
Radio, television, and other electronics stores	62.3	Relatively high concentration ratio, indicating possible oligopoly
Pharmacies and drug stores	46.6	Moderate concentration
Clothing stores	25.5	Fairly competitive
Nursery and garden centers	12.4	Competitive
All retail firms	7.9	Low concentration ratio indicates retailing is highly competitive

Source: *Concentration of Firms,* Table 6, Census Bureau. The data, the latest available, were compiled from the 1997 Economic Census.

rely upon numbers, however, to understand the effects of Wal-Mart in the marketplace. We can see them for ourselves.

Drive through the heart of many small towns. The hardware stores, drug stores, and groceries of the past are now vacant store fronts. To understand why, keep driving until you see the Wal-Mart at the edge of town. The homogeneous Wal-Mart "big box," each one virtually identical to any other anywhere in America, has superseded the differentiation offered by traditional local retailers.

How did this happen? It was the collective choices of consumers in the free market. Wal-Mart offers reliable one-stop shopping, eliminating the need to crank up the car to make several trips to scattered stores. Just as the "milkman" of yesteryear gave way to supermarkets with their convenience and low prices, many small-town merchants have found themselves unable to compete with Wal-Mart. In spite of the benefits Wal-Mart offers shoppers, many communities have witnessed organized protests when Wal-Mart announces that it is coming to town. Growing bigger is, however, integral to the Wal-Mart philosophy of business. To see how big Wal-Mart is relative to other retailers, refer to Table 21-3, which lists the top ten retailers in the United States including their annual sales. All other retailers are dwarfed by Wal-Mart.

THE OLIGOPOLIST'S MARKET POWER

The Wal-Mart strategy for growth was simple and effective—find many small markets that it could dominate because there was no other large retailer in town, and then use that base to grow into the more competitive urban areas. In short, Wal-Mart became the dominant oligopolist of the small town, even as it was one of many monopolistic competitors in the big city.

Wal-Mart quashes both local flavor, and the personal ties between businesses and their customers that existed in the days when a merchant knew most customers by their first names. It offers different benefits in exchange: convenience, variety, and low prices. How are those low prices achieved? Wal-Mart's business plan emphasizes efficiency in production and distribution. Wal-Mart works with its suppliers to try to reduce their cost of production. Wal-Mart also strategically locates distribution facilities to keep down the cost of restocking its stores.

TABLE 21-3   TOP TEN U.S. RETAILERS

FIRM	SALES (IN BILLIONS)
1. Wal-Mart	$246.5
2. Home Depot	58.2
3. Kroger	51.8
4. Target Corp.	42.7
5. Sears, Roebuck, and Co.	41.4
6. Costco Wholesale Corp.	38.0
7. Albertson's Inc.	35.6
8. Safeway	32.4
9. J. C. Penney	32.3
10. K-Mart	30.8

Source: Stores.org. The data are for 2002.

Wal-Mart has not achieved monopoly status in most small towns, since some competing stores manage to stay in business by offering product differentiation, taking less profit, and becoming more efficient. Likewise, Wal-Mart faces competition from on-line or catalog shopping, but not without shipping fees and the hassles of returning or exchanging items.

The transformation brought about by Wal-Mart in rural America is but a recent example of oligopoly as an agent of change. As observed by Joseph Schumpeter in his 1942 book entitled *Capitalism, Socialism, and Democracy*, new technology provides the impetus for economic growth and higher living standards. "The perennial gale of creative destruction," as Schumpeter termed it, has supplanted one way of doing things with another for as long as mankind has lived. For example, the state-of-the-art personal calculating power of the slide rule was first replaced by the pocket calculator and then by computer spreadsheets. This progression took a mere twenty years or so. Numerous firms ceased to exist because of an inability to adapt to this technological change. Slide rule makers had no expertise in the electronics required to manufacture calculators. The destruction of existing firms and industries occurred concurrently with the emergence of new industries and firms that possessed or acquired electronics expertise.

Schumpeter hypothesized that a prerequisite to innovation is the market power conferred upon firms by oligopolistic market structures. Monopoly and pure competition are not well suited to initiate innovation, in his view. He perceived monopoly firms as possessing the wherewithal, but not the motivation, to conduct research, because monopolists lack the competitive pressures felt by firms in oligopoly markets. Schumpeter also thought that firms in pure competition and monopolistic competition lack the pool of economic profits required to finance research and development.

Viewed in light of Schumpeter's thoughts, Wal-Mart is at the forefront of "the perennial gale of creative destruction" that is taking place in small towns today. While not quite the same as earthquakes, tornadoes, floods, and hurricanes, Wal-Mart has had a dramatic impact on our lives. Schumpeter would say to keep an eye out for more, because oligopoly and a changing way of life go hand in hand.

THINKING CRITICALLY

1. **Using an example other than Wal-Mart, explain how geography can cause a firm to be an oligopolist in one market and a monopolistic competitor in another.**

2. **Schumpeter suggested that oligopoly promotes innovation more than do other market structures. Explain both his reasoning and alternative reasoning that might explain why much innovation comes from individuals and smaller businesses.**

Visit **www.prenhall.com/ayers** for updates and web exercises on this Explore & Apply topic.

SUMMARY AND LEARNING OBJECTIVES

1. **Explain the meaning and significance of mutual interdependence.**
   - An oligopoly market has high barriers to entry and more than one firm. Firms in oligopoly are usually few in number and mutually interdependent, meaning that each firm is aware that the decisions made by its competitors affect its sales and profit. Oligopolies sometimes produce a differentiated product (automobiles), but at other times a homogeneous product (aluminum).
   - Market power is the ability of a firm to control its price. The four-firm concentration ratio provides a measure of market power. The four-firm concentration ratio is computed by taking the sales of the four largest firms in an industry, dividing by the total industry sales, and then multiplying the result by 100. The value of this computation will lie between zero and 100, and is interpreted as the percentage of industry sales made by the four largest firms.
   - Mergers are one means by which market power increases. Mergers are of three types: horizontal, vertical, and conglomerate. The horizontal merger combines two like firms, while the conglomerate merger combines two firms in unrelated businesses. The vertical merger combines a firm with either its supplier or a buyer of its product.

2. **Identify the models associated with oligopoly.**
   - Oligopoly models include contestable markets and price leadership. The contestable markets model describes a market where free entry holds down prices. Price leadership describes a market where one of the firms in the market sends informal price signals to its competitors. That firm is called the price leader because the other firms follow its price changes.

   - A cartel is formed when oligopoly firms band together to collude to limit competition. The OPEC oil cartel is an example. The motivation to form a cartel is to increase the profits of the cartel members. Cartel members have an incentive to cheat on the cartel agreement in order to increase their profit. For that reason and others, cartels tend to break apart. Cartels are illegal in the United States.
   - The dominant firm with a competitive fringe is a model of oligopoly that assumes a market made up of one firm that has a dominant market share plus a large number of smaller firms (the competitive fringe). In this model the dominant firm sets the price that maximizes its profit. The fringe firms can sell all they wish at that price. For example, OPEC can be viewed as the dominant firm and other oil-producing countries as the competitive fringe.
   - Game theory can identify pricing and other strategies for interdependent firms. In the prisoner's dilemma, in the absense of collusion, it is always rational for a prisoner to confess to a crime.
   - The kinked demand curve model of oligopoly assumes firms match price cuts but not price increases. The result is that marginal revenue is discontinuous. This model explains sticky prices, which occur when prices resist change.

3. **Describe the characteristics of monopolistic competition.**
   - Monopolistic competition is a model characterized by many firms producing an output that is slightly differentiated. Because good substitutes are available, the monopolistically competitive firm has slight control over its price. Its demand curve is highly, but not perfectly, elastic.

■ The monopolistically competitive firm will set marginal revenue equal to marginal cost in order to maximize profit.

4. **Define product differentiation and state its implications.**

■ Product differentiation is sometimes present in oligopoly markets, but always present in monopolistic competition. Product differentiation occurs when firms attempt to distinguish their product or service from that of competitors. Product differentiation is intended to increase demand.

■ Advertising is a means of achieving product differentiation. Successful advertising by a firm increases its share of the market.

5. **Relate how and why firms charge some consumers more than others for the same products.**

■ Some firms may be able to practice price discrimination. They charge different customers different prices for the same product when there are no cost differences to justify the price differences. Price discrimination is motivated by the desire for greater profit. It requires that the firm be able to segment the market into categories, such as children and adult customers.

 Explain why oligopoly brings economic change.

■ Wal-Mart used its oligopoly position in America's small towns to provide it with the financial base to enter big city markets, where it faced many more competitors. While achieving its dominant position in small towns, Wal-Mart caused many small businesses to fail because they could not match the low prices and convenience offered by Wal-Mart. Schumpeter calls this type of process "the perennial gale of creative destruction."

KEY TERMS

oligopoly, 534
mutually interdependent, 534
differentiated products, 534
four-firm concentration ratio, 535
merger, 536
horizontal merger, 536
vertical merger, 536

conglomerate merger, 536
contestable markets, 537
price leadership, 537
cartel, 538
dominant firm with a competitive
   fringe, 538

game theory, 540
prisoner's dilemma, 540
kinked demand curve, 543
monopolistic competition, 544

TEST YOURSELF

TRUE OR FALSE

1. If one computer manufacturer merges with another computer manufacturer, the merger is termed a vertical merger.
2. Cartels are illegal in the United States.
3. Cartels are found in monopolistically competitive markets.
4. Entry is difficult in monopolistically competitive markets.
5. Price discrimination occurs when a firm charges different customers different prices because there is a difference in the cost of serving those customers.

MULTIPLE CHOICE

6. Which of the following is the best example of a vertical merger?
   a. A computer manufacturer merges with a computer store.
   b. Two book publishers merge.
   c. A jewelry store merges with a furniture store.
   d. A cosmetics manufacturer merges with a pizza restaurant.

7. Biff's Bigger Burgers buys Bill's Better Burgers. This buyout is an example of which type of merger?
   a. Conglomerate.
   b. Horizontal.
   c. Vertical.
   d. A mix of all three types of mergers.

8. Contestable markets are characterized by
   a. numerous firms, each holding a very small fraction of the market.
   b. high brand-name recognition that prevents new firms from competing.
   c. a need for expensive advertising before potential new firms attempt to enter the market.
   d. potential new rivals that can enter or exit the market quickly and cheaply.

9. Price leadership describes a model of
   a. cartel.
   b. monopoly.
   c. oligopoly.
   d. monopolistic competition.

10. Cartels are difficult to maintain over time for each of the following reasons, EXCEPT that
    a. individual members cheat by charging less than the cartel price.
    b. consumers substitute other goods for the product of the cartel.
    c. new competitors that are not cartel members may enter the market.
    d. legal barriers prohibit any member of the cartel from dropping out.

11. In the game theory model of oligopoly, prices
    a. are set with little concern for whether profits are maximized.
    b. are set strategically, as though firms are all playing a game.
    c. fall when costs rise, and rise when costs fall.
    d. remain stable in response to moderate changes in costs.

12. Which of the following is NOT a model of oligopoly?
    a. Monopolistic competition.
    b. Cartel.
    c. Dominant firm with a competitive fringe.
    d. Game theory.

13. In which market structure do firms ALWAYS produce differentiated products?
    a. Pure competition.
    b. Monopoly.
    c. Monopolistic competition.
    d. Oligopoly.

14. Fast-food restaurants are an example of
    a. pure competition.
    b. monopolistic competition.
    c. oligopoly.
    d. monopoly.

15. Unlike firms in _____, firms in _____ are likely to advertise their products.
    a. pure competition; monopolistic competition
    b. monopoly; pure competition
    c. oligopoly; pure competition
    d. monopolistic competition; pure competition

16. Monopolistically competitive firms
    a. produce homogeneous products.
    b. are also called price leaders.
    c. maximize profit by setting marginal revenue equal to marginal cost.
    d. are few in number.

17. In Self-Test Figure 21-1, the profit-maximizing output would be
    a. A.
    b. B.
    c. C.
    d. D.

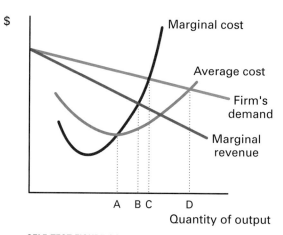

SELF-TEST FIGURE 21-1

18. In Self-Test Figure 21-1, the efficient output would be
    a. A.
    b. B.
    c. C.
    d. D.

19. When a firm practices price discrimination it will charge a higher price in the market segment with
    a. unit elastic demand.
    b. the least elastic demand.
    c. the most elastic demand.
    d. the largest number of buyers.

20. Schumpeter's "perennial gale of creative destruction" is most associated with
    a. innovation.
    b. government action.
    c. hurricanes and other natural disasters.
    d. wars.

QUESTIONS AND PROBLEMS

1. *[mutual interdependence]* Why are oligopoly firms described as mutually interdependent? Explain, making reference to the number of firms.

2. *[differentiated oligopoly]* Today, have you purchased a product produced by an oligopoly? This week? Identify your three most recent purchasing experiences with oligopoly. In each case, identify whether the output of the firm was differentiated or homogeneous.

3. *[four-firm concentration ratio]* Suppose an industry is made up of ten firms, with each firm's sales identical to the other firms. What is the value of the four-firm concentration ratio for the industry? Interpret your result.

4. *[four-firm concentration ratio]* An industry is composed of seven firms, A through G. Use the sales data given for Firms A through G below to compute the four-firm concentration ratio for the industry.

   Firm A: sales = $1,000
   Firm B: sales = $700
   Firm C: sales = $200
   Firm D: sales = $2,000
   Firm E: sales = $400
   Firm F: sales = $500
   Firm G: sales = $200

5. *[mergers]* List and define the three kinds of mergers. Provide an example of each that is different from the example in the text.

6. *[contestable markets]* What characteristic must be present for a market to be contestable? What effect, if any, does contestability have upon the market price?

7. *[cartels]* What is a cartel? What motivates firms to form a cartel? Why is it illegal to form a cartel in the United States? How can OPEC remain a cartel in light of the illegality referred to?

8. *[cartels]* Suppose that in City A there are five new-car dealerships, but in City B there are twenty-five such dealerships.
   a. How likely is it that a cartel of dealerships would be formed in City A?
   b. Is it more or less likely that a cartel of dealerships would be formed in City B than in City A?
   c. If secret, illegal dealership cartels are formed in both cities, which cartel would be most likely to break up?
   d. If secret, illegal dealership cartels are formed in both cities, what evidence might give away the existence of the cartels?

9. *[cartels]* Discuss why cartels are unlikely to be found in pure competition or monopolistic competition. Why do the members of a cartel have trouble keeping the cartel together?

10. *[residual demand]* What is residual demand? Which model is characterized by residual demand? Explain, providing a numerical example.

11. *[dominant firm with a competitive fringe]* Answer the following questions.
    a. What makes a firm the dominant firm?
    b. How is the price set in the dominant firm model?
    c. Are the competitive fringe firms price takers?

12. *[game theory]* The payoff matrix shown below illustrates the choices of prisoner A and prisoner B, who have been arrested for jointly robbing a bank. Will A confess or keep quiet? Will B confess or keep quiet? Explain the decisions made by A and B.

PAYOFF MATRIX

	A confesses	A keeps quiet
B confesses	A get 7 years	A gets 18 years
	B gets 7 years	B gets 2 years
B keeps quiet	A gets 2 years	A gets 4 years
	B gets 18 years	B gets 4 years

13. *[game theory]* Price wars occur when firms engage in repeated price cutting. Many times price will go below the costs to the firm. Create a payoff matrix similar to the prisoner's dilemma, but that shows the pricing decisions of two firms. Use the payoff matrix to explain why price wars occur.

14. *[product differentiation]* Product differentiation is found in oligopoly and monopolistic competition. What purpose does product differentiation serve from a firm's perspective? From society's perspective?

15. *[product differentiation and advertising]* Suppose a fruit grower has developed a new type of grape that tastes somewhat like a peach. The grape is yellow in color. How would you advertise this differentiated grape to consumers?

16. *[demand curve in monopolistic competition]* Is the firm's demand curve in monopolistic competition perfectly elastic as in pure competition? Explain.

17. *[profit maximization in monopolistic competition]* Explain, using a graph, the process of short-run profit maximization in monopolistic competition.

18. *[long-run equilibrium in monopolistic competition]* The long-run equilibrium in monopolistic competition involves zero economic profit. Draw a graph that shows a monopolistically competitive firm with zero profit.

19. *[price discrimination]* Discuss the market conditions required for price discrimination to occur. Generally speaking, is price discrimination illegal? Provide at least one example of price discrimination not mentioned in the text.

WORKING WITH GRAPHS AND DATA

1. *[oligopoly models]* The following table shows the weekly demand and supply schedules for blank CDs that are produced in a market with a dominant firm and a competitive fringe. The table also shows a portion of the dominant firm's marginal cost schedule.

MARKET WITH COMPETITIVE FRINGE   **DOMINANT FIRM**

Price Per CD	Quantity Supplied	Quantity Demanded	Dominant Firm's Quantity Demanded	Total Revenue ($)	Marginal Revenue ($)	Marginal Cost ($)
$10	6	0	____	____	____	—
9	5	2	____	____	____	—
8	4	4	____	____	____	—
7	3	6	____	____	____	3
6	2	8	____	____	____	5
5	1	10	____	____	____	8

a. Fill in the blanks for the quantity demanded and marginal revenue columns for the dominant firm in the table.

b. On Graph 21-1(a) draw and label the market demand curve as D and the market supply curve as S for the market with competitive fringe.

c. On Graph 21-1(b), draw and label the dominant firm's demand curve as D_2, marginal revenue curve as MR, and marginal cost curve as MC.

d. On Graph 21-1(b), identify the price that the dominant firm would charge and the quantity it would produce. Why would it choose this price and quantity?

e. On Graph 21-1(a), show the price charged and total quantity produced in that market. Show the quantity supplied by the competitive fringe firms and the quantity supplied by the dominant firm.

2. *[kinked demand curve]* Use Graphs 21-2(a) and 21-2(b) to answer the questions that follow.

a. Would the oligopolist shown in Graph 21-2(a) be likely to raise its price? Why or why not? Does it face elastic or inelastic demand for its product when it raises its price? How do you know?

b. Would the oligopolist shown in Graph 21-2(a) be likely to lower its price? Why or why not? Does it face elastic or inelastic demand for its product when it lowers its price? How do you know?

c. What kind of expected behavior on the part of competitors accounts for the kink in the demand curve of the firm in Graph 21-2(a)?

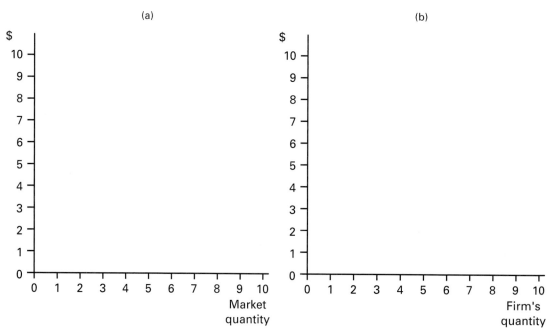

(a)   (b)

Market quantity   Firm's quantity

GRAPH 21-1

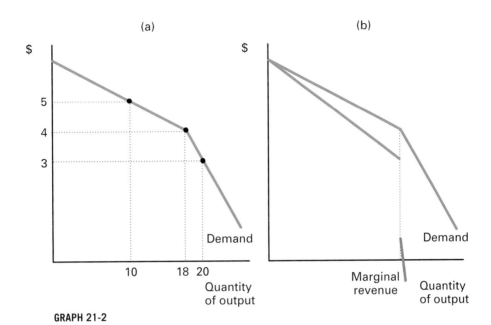

GRAPH 21-2

d. "Since the firm in Graph 21-2(b) maximizes profits, it will change price whenever the marginal cost curve shifts up or down." Evaluate this statement using Graph 21-2(b).

3. *[monopolistic competition]* The following table shows the demand, marginal cost, and average cost schedules for a monopolistically competitive firm.

Price	Quantity	Marginal Revenue	Marginal Cost	Average Cost	Total Revenue
$10	0		—	—	
9	1		$3	$4.00	
8	2		2	3.00	
7	3		5	3.67	
6	4		6	4.25	
5	5		8	5.00	
4	6		11	6.00	

a. Fill in the blank spaces for total revenue and marginal revenue in the table.

b. Draw and label this monopolistically competitive firm's demand curve D, marginal revenue curve MR, average cost curve and marginal cost curve. Label the vertical axis "$" and the horizontal axis "Quantity."

c. Identify the profit-maximizing price on the vertical axis and the profit-maximizing quantity on the horizontal axis.

d. What will happen in the long run if this firm is typical of the firms in this industry? Explain.

4. *[game theory]* Use the following payoff matrix for two competing oligopolists who are looking at the consequences of changing the price that they charge.

	Payoff Matrix	
	Firm B Raises Price	Firm B Lowers Price
Firm A Lowers Price	A gets a $14 million profit.	A gets an $8 million profit.
	B gets a $1 million profit.	B gets an $8 million profit.
Firm A Raises Price	A gets a $12 million profit.	A gets a $1 million profit.
	B gets a $12 million profit.	B gets a $14 million profit.

a. What is the dominant strategy for Firm A assuming that Firm A and Firm B act independently? Explain.

b. What is the dominant strategy for Firm B assuming that Firm B and Firm A act independently? Explain.

c. Could these firms benefit by colluding? Explain.

d. Assuming that the firms do collude, is there any incentive for either of them to cheat?

 Visit www.prenhall.com/ayers for Exploring the Web exercises and additional self-test quizzes.

CHAPTER 22

MARKETS FOR LABOR AND OTHER INPUTS

A LOOK AHEAD

How would you react if your employer forced you to speak a foreign language at work? The French company Alcatel does by requiring its employees to speak in English. Would you be willing to work for a foreign employer, if you could work from home? Computer programmers in India work from home for U.S. companies. New possibilities are presenting themselves to us every day as the internationalization of the workplace proceeds, as explained in the Explore & Apply section that concludes this chapter.

The market for labor affects us all. For most of us, it is our job—our participation in the labor market—that provides our income. But employers do not pay us just because we are human beings. They pay us to produce the goods and services that they can sell. In this chapter we examine the decision-making process that firms will use and how types of labor markets can influence that process. While labor is the case in point, the analysis also applies to capital and other inputs. Whatever the inputs they employ, firms do well to follow the profit-maximizing rule explained in the chapter.

LEARNING OBJECTIVES

Understanding Chapter 22 will enable you to:
1. **State why the demand for labor is a derived demand.**
2. **Use labor demand and supply curves to show how an equilibrium market wage rate is determined.**
3. **Discuss the characteristics of a purely competitive labor market and the wage-taking firm.**
4. **Ascertain the profit-maximizing employment of labor for a wage-taking firm.**
5. **Describe labor markets in which market power over the wage rate is present.**
6. **Relate the similarities between the employment of labor and the employment of other inputs.**
7. **Explain why the employment of labor has become increasingly global in scope.**

Explore & Apply

In the preceding chapters we examined firms from the perspective of the output market. We now turn our attention to the behavior of firms in input markets. The *labor market* involves the exchange of labor services. **Unlike the product market, in which firms are sellers and individuals are buyers, in the labor market firms purchase labor services and individuals supply their labor services to firms.** The market price of labor services is the *wage rate*—the amount an employee is paid per hour. The quantity of labor services is usually measured by the number of hours of labor services exchanged in the marketplace.

22.1 THE MARKET DEMAND FOR LABOR—A DERIVED DEMAND

A market demand curve for labor shows the quantity of labor that employers wish to employ at various wage rates. The lower the wage rate, other things equal, the greater the quantity of labor demanded. For example, if the wage rate drops from $9 to $7, the number of labor hours demanded might increase from 3,000 to 4,000 per day, as shown in Figure 22-1. **Labor demand slopes downward, meaning that higher wage rates decrease the quantity of labor demanded, whereas lower wage rates increase the quantity of labor demanded.**

Economists often study the labor demands in three distinct labor market segments:

- **By occupation:** Occupational labor demands are distinct for dissimilar occupations because labor is associated with human capital that is specific to the occupation—*specific human capital.* That makes it difficult to transfer skills from one occupation to another.
- **By geography:** The demand for labor varies geographically because of differences in the economies of towns and regions. For instance, the demand curve for labor in your hometown would likely differ from the demand curves in most other towns. If business in your town is expanding, the demand for labor there will be strong, unlike in sleepy neighboring villages.
- **By industry:** An industry demand curve for labor shows the quantity of labor employed by all firms in an industry at various wage rates. Various industries may compete for the same pool of workers. For example, many industries employ secretaries, computer programmers, and so forth. In some cases, the demand for a particular type of labor is focused on a particular industry. For instance, the demand for chemical engineers arises mostly from firms in the chemical industry.

FIGURE 22-1

MARKET DEMAND FOR LABOR The market demand curve for labor shows the relationship between the wage rate and the quantity of labor employers would hire. Like the market demand curve for goods and services, a market labor demand curve slopes downward. The price of labor is the wage rate, which is indicated on the vertical axis. This example shows the increase in the quantity demanded from 3,000 to 4,000 units of labor as the wage rate decreases from $9 to $7.

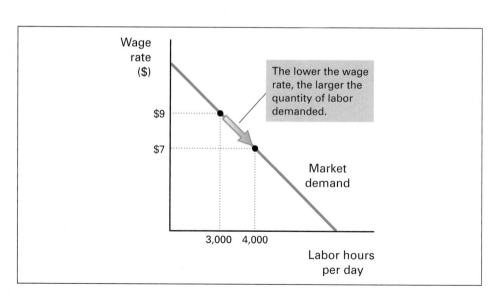

Labor demand is a **derived demand,** which means the demand for labor exists only because there is a demand for the firms' outputs. *Ceteris paribus*, an increase in the demand for a good will increase the demand for labor in the industry that produces that good. To see this idea, suppose that the relationship between labor and the production of soft drinks is such that it takes 1 hour of labor in combination with other inputs to produce 50 cases of soft drinks. *Ceteris paribus*, for every increase in production of 50 cases, the industry will increase its employment of labor by 1 hour. This relationship means that an increase in the demand for soft drinks, which causes an increase in production, will also cause an increase in labor demand. For example, an increase in demand that causes production to increase by 500 cases will increase the demand for labor by 10 hours.

derived demand the demand for labor; exists only because there is a demand for the firm's outputs.

QUICKCHECK

Why is the demand for soft drinks not a derived demand? Is labor demand the only derived demand?

Answer: Soft drinks and other goods are demanded for the value that they provide consumers. The derived demand is for labor to produce those soft drinks. The soft-drink maker also has a derived demand for bottling machines and anything else that makes soft-drink production possible. So, in general, firms have derived demands for all of the inputs they employ.

THE MYSTERY OF THE DISAPPEARING DOT-COM JOBS

SNAPSHOT

Like all good mysteries it happened with little warning. One day prospects for employment in the dot-com world of Internet businesses looked good. The next day job seekers in that industry saw their hopes for employment dashed. What "killed" labor demand at one dot-com firm after another in 2001, with over 100,000 positions eliminated in that year alone?

This is one mystery that is easy to solve. The projections of strong revenue growth in Internet-related businesses proved wildly optimistic. Expected on-line purchases from so-called e-tailers failed to materialize. Many dot-coms were losing money. In response to all the bad news, these firms quickly slashed their hiring of new workers, and laid off current ones.

The lesson is that labor demand can change quickly along with the fortunes of business. The response? Some eager job seekers tried to land one of the relatively few job openings that remained among the dot-coms. Others offered their services to employers in on-line industries that were still hiring. Most found jobs in one industry or another, but few in an industry as glamorous as the dot-coms. Those who were hoping to get back into the dot-com world saw their hopes dashed repeatedly, as Hewlett-Packard, AOL, IBM, and others continued cutting thousands of jobs through 2003. ◄

22.2 THE EQUILIBRIUM WAGE RATE

The last section looked at the market demand for labor. This section brings in supply and market structure. Here you will also know how a firm arrives at its labor demand.

THE MARKET SUPPLY OF LABOR

Workers supply their services to the labor market in exchange for the wages and salaries that they can earn. The market supply curve of labor shows the quantity of labor supplied at various wage rates, such as 4,000 hours supplied at $7 or 5,000 hours supplied at $9, as shown

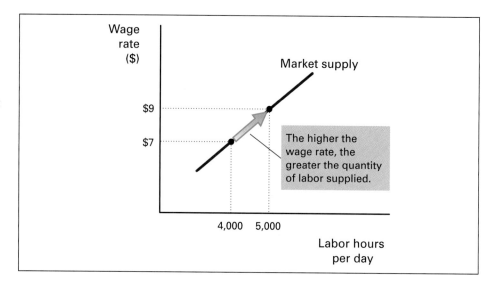

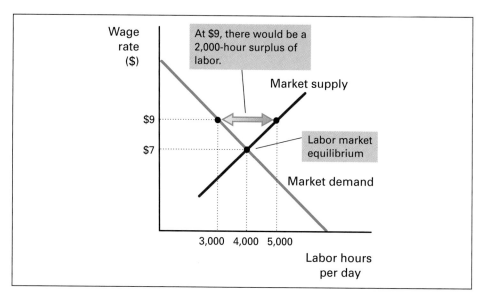

in Figure 22-2. The positive slope of the market supply of labor tells us that higher wage rates attract a greater quantity of labor supplied. Just as labor demand can vary by occupation, area, and industry, so too can labor supply.

The market demand for labor, together with the market supply, determine the market wage rate, as shown in Figure 22-3. The market wage rate in the graph is also called the *equilibrium wage rate,* since this wage rate results in the quantity demanded of labor being equal to the quantity supplied of labor, 4,000 hours in this case. A market wage rate higher than the equilibrium wage rate causes a surplus of labor, such as the surplus of 2,000 labor hours shown in Figure 22-3. Likewise, a market wage rate below the equilibrium wage rate causes a shortage of labor.

The equilibrium wage rate will change when there is a change in labor demand or supply. The market wage rate will increase when there is an increase in labor demand or a decrease in labor supply. A lower market wage rate is brought about by a decrease in labor demand or an increase in labor supply.

JOB ENTREPRENEURSHIP—FINDING WHAT'S HOT   *SNAPSHOT*

What are the "hot" jobs of the future—jobs with plentiful openings and high pay—and how do you get one? The *Occupational Outlook Handbook* projects future labor demand and supply for numerous occupations. Recent projections show that most hot jobs, such as those in medicine or computers, require advanced education or training. Unfortunately, projections of labor demand and supply in specific fields can easily become as dated as yesterday's newspaper.

When "everybody" agrees on what is hot, it may be best to bet on something else. By the time you acquire the needed skills, so have a host of others. Labor supply increases, and lucrative job opportunities become relatively scarce. Instead, the secret to success may lie in being one of the first to identify hot job prospects of the future. There is a risk in taking this initiative: You might be wrong. However, if you follow that lonesome road, you may rightfully dub yourself a "job entrepreneur." ◄

A PURELY COMPETITIVE LABOR MARKET

A **purely competitive labor market** exists when the demand for labor and the supply of labor establish an equilibrium wage rate and quantity of labor. Characteristics similar to those that apply to pure competition in the output market also apply to pure competition in the labor market, including the following:

- There are many buyers and sellers of labor services in the market.
- The services of labor are homogeneous.
- The labor market is free of barriers to entry and exit.

purely competitive labor market labor market with many employers hiring homogeneous labor; employers are wage takers; the equilibrium wage rate is given by the intersection of market supply and demand.

The third characteristic means that workers are free to change jobs or move to labor markets that pay higher wages, if they wish to do so. Employers are also free to enter or exit labor markets. In practical terms, employers can freely relocate.

In a purely competitive labor market, employers are *wage takers*, which means that each will be able to hire as much or as little labor as it wishes at the going market wage rate. **Since one employer by itself cannot influence the market wage rate, employers that are wage takers have no market power over wages.** Figure 22-4 shows a purely competitive labor market. Part (a) shows the market labor demand and supply curves. The intersection of these curves establishes the equilibrium wage rate, labeled "Market wage," and the equilibrium market quantity of labor hired. Since the labor market clears, there is neither a shortage nor surplus of labor.

For a wage-taking firm, the wage rate is the supply curve of labor to the firm. In other words, the firm can purchase as many units of labor as it wishes at the market wage rate. As shown in Figure 22-4(b), the firm's supply curve of labor is horizontal (perfectly elastic) at the market wage rate. The firm will choose to hire the quantity of labor at the point for which the wage rate equals the firm's demand for labor. We now look more closely at the firm's decision about how much labor to hire.

A FIRM'S EMPLOYMENT OF LABOR

We can deepen our understanding of labor markets by looking further at labor demand, this time with the individual employer as the center of attention. We start by asking why labor is valuable to an employer.

marginal revenue product of labor change in the firm's total revenue resulting from the employment of an additional unit of labor.

The value to the firm of any given worker's labor is the revenue resulting from the sale of that worker's marginal product (the output a worker adds to the firm's total product). This added revenue is termed the **marginal revenue product of labor,** defined as the

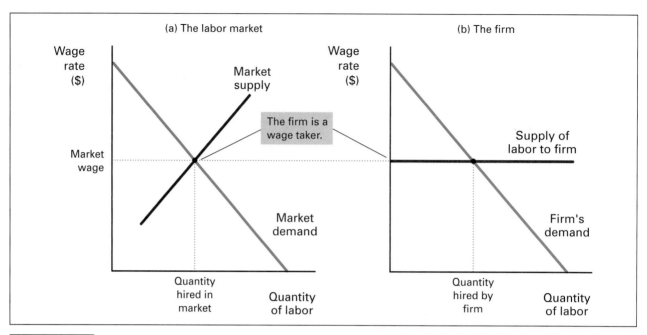

FIGURE 22-4

A PURELY COMPETITIVE LABOR MARKET The interaction of labor demand and labor supply sets the market wage, as shown in part (a). The horizontal supply curve of labor to an employer indicates the employer is a wage taker in a purely competitive labor market. The firm's demand for labor will determine the quantity of labor it hires at that wage as indicated by "Supply of labor to firm" in part (b).

change in the firm's total revenue arising from the employment of an additional unit of labor. Marginal revenue product can be computed in two ways:

$$\text{Marginal revenue product} = \frac{\text{Change in total revenue}}{\text{Change in labor}}$$

or

$$\text{Marginal revenue product} = \text{Marginal revenue} \times \text{Marginal product}$$

Let's compute the marginal revenue product for Jefferson Coal Mining, a producer of coal that is a price taker in the output market. A price taker operates in a purely competitive output market and has no choice but to sell its output at the market price. Data for Jefferson Coal Mining is shown in the table in Figure 22-5. The first two columns show the relationship between the quantity of labor employed and output. Column (c) shows the firm's marginal product of labor, computed as the additional output from a one-unit change in labor. Column (d) contains the market price of the output. Recall that the market price equals marginal revenue for a purely competitive firm, as indicated in that column. Total revenue, shown in column (e), is obtained by multiplying the price by the quantity of output. Finally, column (f) shows marginal revenue product.

The marginal revenue product is the change in total revenue as the firm adds one more unit of labor. Multiplying marginal revenue by marginal product also results in marginal revenue product. Whichever way it is computed, **marginal revenue product measures the value of an additional unit of labor to the firm.** The graph in Figure 22-5 shows the marginal revenue product curve for Jefferson Coal Mining. This marginal revenue product curve is typical in that it slopes downward as more labor is employed.

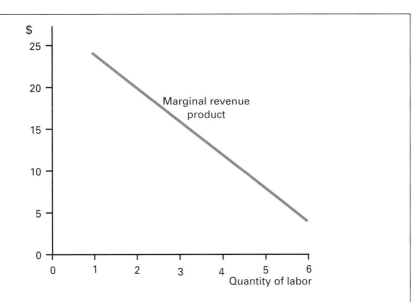

FIGURE 22-5

MARGINAL REVENUE PRODUCT FOR JEFFERSON COAL MINING, A PRICE TAKER Marginal revenue product is downward sloping for a price-taking firm. It is the decrease in the marginal product of labor that causes this downward slope. The marginal revenue product curve in the graph plots the data from column (f) in the table.

Marginal revenue product for Jefferson Coal Mining, a price taker					
(a) Quantity of labor	(b) Output	(c) Marginal product	(d) Output price = marginal revenue	(e) Total revenue = price × quantity	(f) Marginal revenue product = change in total revenue ÷ change in labor = marginal product × marginal revenue
0	0	Undefined	$2	$0	Undefined
1	12	12	2	24	$24
2	22	10	2	44	20
3	30	8	2	60	16
4	36	6	2	72	12
5	40	4	2	80	8
6	42	2	2	84	4

If the firm is not a price taker in the output market, then it is a *price maker*. Price making occurs in monopoly, oligopoly, and monopolistically competitive markets. The computation of marginal revenue product for a price maker is slightly more complicated than when the firm is a price taker. Unlike for a price taker, price and marginal revenue are not equal for a price maker. For a price maker, marginal revenue is less than price.

Consider a price-making firm, The Cutter's Edge, a hair salon and beauty shop. This firm faces a downward-sloping demand curve for its no-frills haircut as shown in the output and price columns of the table in Figure 22-6. Marginal revenue decreases as output increases for a price maker. The result is that the marginal revenue product curves for price-making firms slope downward more steeply than for their purely competitive counterparts, as can be seen by comparing the marginal revenue product columns in Figure 22-5 and Figure 22-6. The graph in Figure 22-6 shows the marginal revenue product curve for The Cutter's Edge. Note that marginal revenue product is negative for the fourth through sixth units of labor.

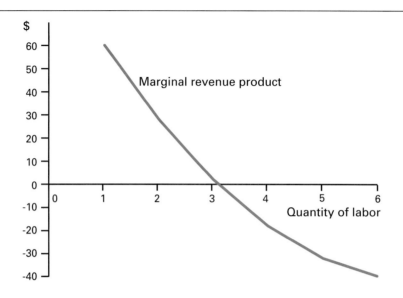

Marginal revenue product for The Cutter's Edge, a price maker						
(a) Quantity of labor	(b) Output	(c) Marginal product	(d) Output price	(e) Total revenue = price × quantity	(f) Marginal revenue	(g) Marginal revenue product = change in total revenue ÷ change in labor = marginal product × marginal revenue
0	0	Undefined	$6	$0	Undefined	Undefined
1	12	12	5	60	5	$60
2	22	10	4	88	2.80	28
3	30	8	3	90	0.25	2
4	36	6	2	72	−3	−18
5	40	4	1	40	−8	−32
6	42	2	0	0	−20	−40

FIGURE 22-6

MARGINAL REVENUE PRODUCT FOR THE CUTTER'S EDGE, A PRICE MAKER Marginal revenue product slopes downward for a price maker. There are two reasons for the downward slope when the firm is a price maker. First, as in the case of the price taker, the marginal product of labor decreases as the quantity of labor is increased, as shown in column (c). Second, for a price maker, price must be decreased in order to sell the additional output that is produced when more labor is employed, as shown in column (d). The decrease in price, which results in less marginal revenue, also contributes to the decrease in marginal revenue product. The marginal revenue product curve in the graph plots the data from column (g) in the table.

To understand how much labor the firm will employ, we must introduce one more concept. The **marginal cost of labor** equals the addition to total cost when there is a one-unit increase in the quantity of labor:

marginal cost of labor
additional cost of employing
an additional unit of labor.

$$\text{Marginal cost of labor} = \frac{\text{Change in total cost}}{\text{Change in quantity of labor}}$$

The market wage rate equals the marginal cost of labor for a wage taker, where a *wage-taking* firm purchases each unit of labor services at the market wage rate. For example, if the market wage rate is $16 per unit of labor, adding any additional unit of labor will always increase the firm's total cost by $16. Thus, the marginal cost of labor is $16 in this instance. When the market wage rate changes because of shifts in the market demand and supply of labor, the marginal cost of labor to the firm will change to match the new market wage rate.

A firm will employ the quantity of labor that maximizes its profit. This quantity of labor can be determined by comparing the marginal revenue product of each unit of labor to its marginal cost. Profit maximization requires a firm to hire additional units of labor so long as labor's marginal revenue product equals or exceeds its marginal cost. Thus, the firm follows the following hiring rule:

> ### *Hiring Rule*
> *Hire up to and including but not beyond the point for which marginal revenue product equals the marginal cost of labor.*

In other words, a firm continues adding labor as long as the revenue it receives from the output produced by one more unit of labor is at least sufficient to cover the added cost resulting from employing that unit of labor. The firm aims to employ labor at the point where the marginal revenue product is equal to the marginal cost of labor.

If there is no quantity of labor that exactly satisfies the equality stated in the hiring rule, the firm will stop hiring when the next hire's marginal revenue product would be less than the marginal cost of labor. After all, firms do not want to pay someone more than the market value of that person's output. For example, Jefferson Coal Mining would employ three units of labor at the $16 market wage rate. Since the marginal revenue product is only $12 when the quantity of labor equals four, the fourth unit of labor will not be employed at any wage rate above $12.

The decision to employ labor at Jefferson Coal Mining is illustrated in Figure 22-7. The market wage of $16 is illustrated in the figure and labeled as the firm's marginal cost of labor curve. Because the firm is a wage taker in the labor market, the marginal cost of labor curve is horizontal (perfectly elastic). Holding all other inputs constant, **the marginal revenue product curve is also the firm's demand curve for labor because it shows how much labor the firm will employ at various wage rates.** Observe that the firm's labor demand curve is downward sloping.

The firm's labor demand curve may shift. For example, *ceteris paribus,* a price-taking firm will increase its demand for labor if the market price of the firm's output increases or if the marginal product of the firm's labor increases. Labor demand would decrease if the price of output fell or if the marginal product of labor decreased.

Let's now assume that The Cutter's Edge faces the same market wage rate of $16 faced by Jefferson Coal Mining so that we can compare the hiring decisions of the two firms. The Cutter's Edge will employ just two units of labor when the market wage rate is $16. The value of the third unit of labor to that firm is its marginal revenue product for three units of labor, equal to $2. Since this value is less than the wage rate of $16, the third unit of labor will not be employed.

HIRING RULE APPLIED BY A WAGE TAKER The marginal revenue product curve is a firm's labor demand curve. The quantity of labor employed by a profit-maximizing firm is the amount for which the marginal revenue product equals the marginal cost of labor. Jefferson Coal Mining will employ three units of labor when the market wage equals $16.

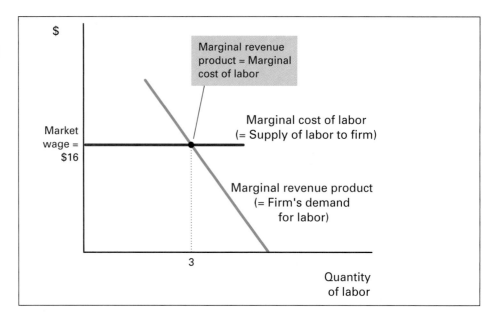

EMPLOYMENT OF LABOR AND THE OUTPUT MARKET Both firms are wage takers, as indicated by the horizontal supply curve of labor. The greater the ability of the firm to set price in its output market, the steeper will be its marginal revenue product curve. The Cutter's Edge, a price maker, hires two units of labor and Jefferson Coal Mining, a price taker, three units of labor when the market wage equals $16. A price taker will employ more labor than a price maker, other things equal.

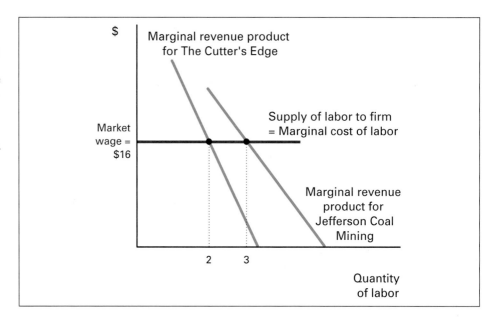

Figure 22-8 illustrates the marginal revenue product curves for The Cutter's Edge and Jefferson Coal Mining and shows each firm's profit-maximizing employment for a market wage rate of $16. Observe that the marginal revenue product curve is steeper for The Cutter's Edge because that firm is a price maker in the output market.

22.3 MARKET POWER OVER THE WAGE RATE

Just as there are four types of output markets, there are also four types of labor markets. The type of market in which a firm sells its output does not determine the type of market in which it buys its labor inputs. For example, oligopoly and monopoly firms in the output market may purchase labor services in a purely competitive labor market. While an output

QUICKCHECK

Other things equal, what would happen to the marginal revenue product data for Jefferson Coal Mining in Figure 22-5 if the price of the firm's output were to double from $2 to $4?

Answer: The marginal revenue product would double. To confirm this, multiply each of the marginal product numbers in the table by $4 and compare the results to the numbers in the table.

monopoly has no competitors in the sale of its product, it may have many rivals as it competes to hire labor.

The model of pure competition in the labor market assumes that both employers and employees are wage takers, meaning that they have no market power over the wage rate. However, market power is often present in the labor market and can drive wage rates either up or down from the competitive level. To the extent that workers gain control of the labor market, the wage rate will increase to more than the competitive level. The wage rate will decrease to less than the competitive level to the extent that employers dominate. These effects are captured in the following labor market models:

- **Monopsony**—only one buyer of labor services, an employer.
- **Monopoly**—only one seller of labor services, a labor union.
- **Bilateral monopoly**—only one employer and only one seller of labor services; a combination of a monopsony employer and a monopoly labor union.

The following sections describe these models.

MONOPSONY—ONE EMPLOYER OF LABOR SERVICES

In the labor market, a firm can have market power over the wage rate. Small numbers of employers result in *monopsony power,* which is the ability to affect wages. **Monopsony employers are able to pay workers less than the competitive wage rate.** The extreme case of monopsony is *pure monopsony*—one buyer of labor's services. A geographically isolated mill town exemplifies monopsony. The mill provides a reason for the town to exist because most of its citizens work there. As the major employer, the mill can offer less than the competitive wage rate to prospective workers. Highly specialized types of labor, such as astronauts or fighter pilots, may also face monopsony in their country's labor market.

Consider a pure monopsony firm—the only employer of labor in a labor market. The table in Figure 22-9 shows data for such a firm. **As the only employer of labor in a particular labor market, the monopsonist faces the market supply curve of labor,** which is shown in the first two columns in the table. The market supply curve of labor is upward sloping. This means the firm must pay a higher wage in order to employ more labor. Thus, in Figure 22-9 the wage rate increases along with the quantity of labor. The firm's total cost of labor for each quantity of labor, shown in the (c) column, is obtained by multiplying the wage rate by the quantity of labor.

Column (d) of the table shows the marginal cost of labor. The marginal cost of labor curve is upward sloping rather than the horizontal line in the case of pure competition in the labor market. Note that, **unlike in the purely competitive labor market, the marginal cost of labor exceeds the wage rate in monopsony.** The reason is that employing additional

monopsony one buyer of labor services in a labor market.

monopoly one seller of labor services in a labor market; for example, a labor union.

bilateral monopoly labor market with a monopsony buyer (employer) and monopoly seller (union) of labor services.

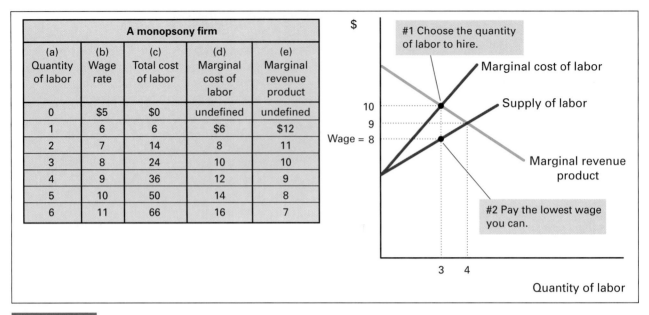

\$				
A monopsony firm				
(a) Quantity of labor	(b) Wage rate	(c) Total cost of labor	(d) Marginal cost of labor	(e) Marginal revenue product
0	\$5	\$0	undefined	undefined
1	6	6	\$6	\$12
2	7	14	8	11
3	8	24	10	10
4	9	36	12	9
5	10	50	14	8
6	11	66	16	7

FIGURE 22-9

A MONOPSONY FIRM A monopsony firm faces an upward-sloping supply curve of labor. It chooses to employ three units of labor, based on the intersection of the marginal cost of labor and marginal revenue product (step 1). It pays a wage of \$8, the minimum needed to attract three workers (step 2). This process contrasts with the four workers paid a wage of \$9 that would arise if the monopsony market behaved in the manner of pure competition.

workers increases the wage rate paid to all workers, not just to the additional workers. The final column of the table shows marginal revenue product data for this firm.

The monopsonist will follow the profit-maximizing rule, which says to employ labor to the point where the marginal revenue product equals the marginal cost of labor. How many units of labor will the monopsonist employ? The answer is three units of labor. Up to that point the marginal revenue product of labor is greater than the marginal cost of labor. Beyond that point, the marginal revenue product is less than the marginal cost. At three units of labor, the marginal revenue product and marginal cost are equal at \$10. However, the monopsonist need not pay a wage rate of \$10. Instead, the supply of labor given by columns (a) and (b) show that the firm can attract three units of labor by paying a wage rate of only \$8. Thus, \$8 is the wage the monopsonist will pay.

Figure 22-9 shows the market supply curve of labor, the marginal cost of labor, the demand for labor (marginal revenue product), and the profit-maximizing employment and wage rate. The monopsonist makes its hiring decision in the following two steps, as shown in Figure 22-9:

- It employs the amount of labor for which the marginal cost of labor equals marginal revenue product.
- It pays the lowest possible wage rate for that labor. The wage rate is given by the supply curve of labor at the quantity of labor chosen in step 1.

Note in Figure 22-9 that if this monopsonized labor market could be transformed into a purely competitive one, the employment of labor would increase to the point where the supply and demand curves for labor intersect. Supply and demand show the competitive wage rate to be \$9 and the competitive level of employment to be four units of labor. This demonstrates that **monopsony labor markets are characterized by less employment and a lower wage rate than in purely competitive labor markets.**

MONOPOLY—A SOLE SUPPLIER OF LABOR SERVICES

Monopolies in the output market possess market power because they can raise prices above the level indicated by the intersection of supply and demand. Monopolies are able to command a higher price for their output by reducing the supply of output. *Labor unions,* which we will discuss more fully in the next chapter, are like monopolies in that unions try to eliminate competition for jobs among workers in order to raise the price of their members' labor services. Just as a monopoly in the output market is the sole seller of a good or service, a labor union could be the sole provider of labor to an employer. If a union is successful in monopolizing the supply of labor's services, it can drive wages higher than would occur in pure competition. Because labor demand curves slope downward, the employment of union labor will be reduced below the competitive level.

Figure 22-10 illustrates the effects when a union monopolizes what would otherwise have been a purely competitive labor market. If the union behaves as a profit-maximizing monopoly, it will restrict the quantity of labor supplied to the point where marginal revenue equals marginal cost, as shown in Figure 22-10. The figure shows that union members will be paid more for their work, but that there will be fewer people working. While unions often have other objectives in addition to profit maximization, Figure 22-10 illustrates the tradeoff between higher wages and fewer job opportunities in unionized industries.

In order to cut the supply of labor to an employer, the union must be able to restrict the size of its membership. One way to restrict membership is to place excessive and hard-to-meet skill or experience requirements on those seeking to join the union. Many workers who might be employed in a competitive labor market will not be able to surmount such an artificial barrier to entry in the union labor market.

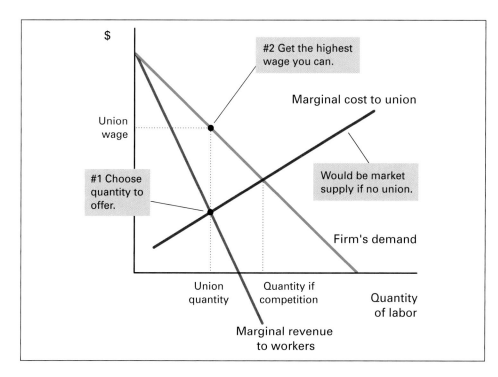

FIGURE 22-10

UNION MONOPOLY IN THE LABOR MARKET When a union monopolizes a labor market, it chooses how much labor to provide (step #1) and gets the highest wage possible for that labor (step #2). There is less labor hired than if the labor market were purely competitive, but the wage rate is higher than the wage rate that would prevail if the labor market were purely competitive.

QUICKCHECK

List the four labor market models. In which model(s) are employers wage takers? *Ceteris paribus,* **in which model will the wage rate be lowest? Does this mean that employment is then highest in this model?**

Answer: The four models are pure competition, monopsony, monopoly, and bilateral monopoly. Employers are wage takers only in the purely competitive model. *Ceteris paribus,* the wage rate will be lowest in the model of monopsony, as employers cut back on labor to drive down the wage rate. For this reason, employment will be less than if the market were competitive.

BILATERAL MONOPOLY—NEGOTIATIONS AND BARGAINING POWER

Bilateral monopoly occurs when a monopsony buyer of labor's services must obtain those services from a monopoly seller, such as a labor union. Professional sports leagues are often a bilateral monopoly. The National Football League, Major League Baseball, and the National Basketball Association are each organized so that the owners' association presents a united front when negotiating with the players' union. Both sides need each other, but disagreements arise over wages and working conditions. **Under a bilateral monopoly, the wage rate depends on bargaining power—whether the employer or representative of the employees bargains more effectively.** The wage bargain that is struck could result in a wage at the competitive level, below it, or above it.

SNAPSHOT   ## "THERE WAS NO JOY IN MUDVILLE . . .

. . . for mighty Casey had struck out," wrote *San Francisco Examiner* sports reporter Ernest Thayer in 1888. When the newspaper published "Casey at the Bat," little could it know the greater sorrow to hit baseball fans just over a century later. On August 13, 1994, baseball's mighty Caseys all struck out at once! Major League Baseball quit for the year, abandoning the late-season pennant race, post-season cheering, and World Series heroics. Instead, there was a players' strike for higher wages and, in response, a lockout by the owners.

This odd situation, one that was very nearly repeated in August 2002, was a natural outgrowth of bilateral monopoly. There was big money to be made by players in driving wages up. To make that happen, their union needed to exhibit bargaining power. Keeping players at home demonstrated just such power. But owners wanted to keep wages down. Their determination to terminate the 1994 season rather than give in to the demands of the players' union demonstrated bargaining power on the owners' part. The result of all this huffing and puffing was a baseball season that brought in far less than the usual amount of revenue. The following spring saw the eventual signing of a new contract and a late start to the season. The result of this bargaining process under bilateral monopoly is that the players, owners, and fans all struck out. ◄

22.4 THE EMPLOYMENT OF OTHER INPUTS

Economists categorize resource inputs into four types: land, labor, capital, and entrepreneurship. So far, we have seen how employers decide how much labor to employ. But labor needs capital, such as tools, machines, and their own skills. Labor may also need natural resources from the land in the form of raw materials. The marginal revenue product can be calculated for any input, as can its marginal cost. **The rule for the profit-maximizing**

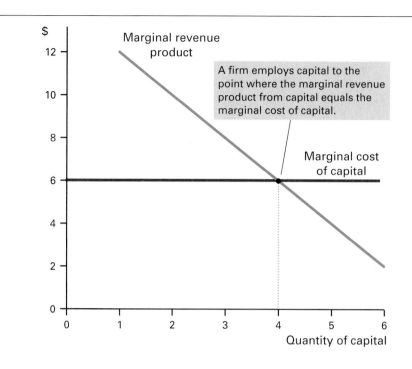

FIGURE 22-11

THE MARGINAL REVENUE PRODUCT OF CAPITAL The marginal revenue product of capital is computed in the same way as marginal revenue product of labor. The difference is that, in this case, the quantity of capital varies and the other inputs are held constant. The marginal revenue product curve in the graph is plotted from the data in column (f) of the table.

The marginal revenue product of capital					
(a) Units of capital	(b) Output (per week)	(c) Marginal product of capital	(d) Output price = marginal revenue	(e) Total revenue = price × quantity of output	(f) Marginal revenue product of capital = change in total revenue ÷ change in capital = marginal product of capital × marginal revenue
0	0	Undefined	$2	$0	Undefined
1	6	6	2	12	$12
2	11	5	2	22	10
3	15	4	2	30	8
4	18	3	2	36	6
5	20	2	2	40	4
6	21	1	2	42	2

amount of labor applies to other inputs: **Employ an input up to the point where its marginal revenue product equals its marginal cost.**

Figure 22-11 illustrates the profit-maximizing employment of capital. The table in this figure shows the quantity of output produced by various amounts of capital. We assume that labor remains constant and that the firm is able to expand the amount of capital that its workers use to produce the firm's output. The marginal revenue product of capital, shown in column (f), is computed in the same way as the marginal revenue product of labor was computed.

The firm will employ capital up to the point where its marginal revenue product equals the marginal cost of capital. Thus, if there is a constant marginal cost of capital of, say, $6 per unit of capital, then the firm in this example will employ four units of capital. If the marginal cost of capital were $8, then only three units of capital would be employed, and so forth.

Computing the cost of capital is not always easy or simple, but is often not as difficult as it might at first appear. In the simplest case, the firm will lease capital at a fixed price per unit. However, even if it owns the capital it uses, the firm pays a price in terms of revenues forgone from not leasing that capital to another firm. For this reason, the marginal cost of capital is usually called the *rental price of capital.* The purchase price of capital is irrelevant to its rental price.

Whatever the purchase price, a firm will employ additional capital so long as the marginal revenue product of capital exceeds the rental price of capital. When the two are equal, the firm stops expanding its employment of capital. If the capital is *lumpy,* meaning that it cannot be varied in minute amounts, the firm will not see an exact equality between marginal revenue product and rental price, but will definitely plan to add no capital that it thinks will have a marginal revenue product of less than the rental price.

22.5 INTERNATIONALIZING THE WORK FORCE

Where were your shoes made? Your pen? Any other item you own? It is easy to know because by law the country where something is made must be indicated somewhere on the product if the product has been imported into the United States. A portion of U.S. imports are made by foreign firms employing foreign workers, but some of these imports are made by foreign workers in factories owned by U.S.-based *multinational firms.* For example, many U.S. clothing makers operate factories in other countries because of cheaper foreign labor and less regulation than they would face in the United States.

Not all U.S. multinational firms export their overseas production to the United States. For example, both Ford Motor Company and General Motors are multinational firms that operate automobile assembly plants and other manufacturing facilities in many countries around the globe. Most of the goods produced in those plants stay in the countries where they are made.

The home base of their employers is of no consequence to the workers who produce the cars. Since multinationals must abide by the labor laws where they operate, and typically follow local employment practices and customs, it doesn't matter to the workers where their employers live.

While the United States is known as the home base for many multinationals, numerous multinationals are also based elsewhere. German car maker BMW, Mexican food producer Bimbo, and Japanese electronics giant Sony are but a few examples. Whatever its home base, a multinational will have facilities and employ workers in multiple countries. For this reason, multinational firms face an international work force, made up of workers who are protected by different labor laws, speak different languages, have different work ethics, and possess varying educations. Sometimes the firm will require that its work force learn a common language to use in internal communications. Sometimes that language is not even native to the country the company calls its home. In the case of the French telecommunications giant Alcatel, for example, employees were told to learn English because that language dominates the telecommunications world.

WORKPLACE DIVERSITY

Workplace diversity is the norm in many countries. Employers are comfortable hiring the foreign born. To some extent this is because the foreign born help plug skill gaps in the work force.

| TABLE 22-1 | U.S. EMPLOYMENT-BASED IMMIGRATION |

YEAR	NUMBER OF IMMIGRANTS
1990	58,192
1991	59,525
1992	116,198
1993	147,012
1994	123,291
1995	85,336
1996	117,499
1997	90,607
1998	77,517
1999	56,817
2000	107,024
2001	179,195
2002	174,968

Source: 2002 Yearbook of Immigration Statistics, Table 4. These immigrants are classified into the following subcategories: priority workers, professionals with advanced degrees or aliens with exceptional abilities, skilled workers, professionals, other workers, special immigrants, and employment creation.

Whether it be a statistics professor from China, a computer systems analyst from India, or a soccer-style NFL field goal kicker from Europe, foreign-born workers are allowed to work in the United States when an employer can demonstrate that no American-born worker is available to fill the job. Table 22-1 shows the number of immigrants admitted to the United States for employment reasons. For the years shown, the total number is well over a million immigrants, about 10 percent of all immigrants allowed into the country. These immigrants were allowed in because their employers certified that American workers to fill those jobs could not be found.

There can be a downside to employing these workers, such as for U.S. citizens who lose out on the field goal kicking and other jobs taken by the foreign workers. For the foreign workers, language barriers intrude, as does the paperwork required by the Immigration and Naturalization Service required to legally employ them. This situation sometimes leads to workplace and social stresses that were never envisioned.

Some employers claim they hire the foreign born because they will do the jobs that American workers will not do. These jobs include low-prestige jobs like janitorial work, physically demanding jobs like picking crops, and other low-paying jobs. This claim is controversial. Some of these jobs are filled by workers who are in the United States working illegally. Their employers are violating the law and subject to criminal penalties if caught, and also subject to seeing their workers deported. The result is that these workers often receive less than the minimum wage, because if they complained they could be forced to leave the country.

Some countries, such as Japan, make it virtually impossible for foreigners to work. However, the internationalization of the work force that characterizes the United States today also applies in many other countries. In England, for instance, workers from the countries that were part of the old British empire are commonly employed because the laws make it easy for that to happen.

Self-employed entrepreneurs who are foreign born add another dimension to the internationalizing of the work force. Take one 22-year-old American, Ally Svenson, for example. When she and her husband moved to London, England, where he had accepted employment with a multinational firm, she found herself wanting a latte of the kind she had enjoyed back in Seattle. Much to her dismay, there was not a latte to be found anywhere in England, a country best known for its tea drinkers. Her response? She founded the Seattle Coffee Company, a chain of coffee shops that she and her partners subsequently sold to Starbucks for $100 million. Her entrepreneurial impulse helped popularize coffee in England. Thousands of foreign-born entrepreneurs have similarly changed the preferences of U.S. consumers, whether it be for foreign cuisine, kung fu lessons, or other previously exotic products.

The Internet and new communications technologies that are arising around the Internet are internationalizing the work force in another way. Many employers are exploiting the potential of the World Wide Web to internationalize their operations. Thus, jobs that in the past would have required American firms to fill them with American workers can now be filled with foreign workers who *stay in their home country*. For example, work on computer applications coordinated from the United States can be accomplished with programers who live in India or most anyplace else in the world. By communicating over the Internet, work can progress simultaneously in each location. Computer software development is currently the most prominent of the jobs that can be done in this way, but employers are finding other applications. Workers in Ireland, for example, now provide many of the back-office services required by U.S. banks.

The Internet is fundamentally changing the way that labor is employed. For this reason, a worker faces competition for jobs not only from fellow citizens, but from labor in other countries. By the same token, a worker in the United States might draw a paycheck from a foreign firm. But change in the labor market is nothing new. Throughout world history, the employment of labor and other inputs has adjusted to change. The U.S. economy, and America's workers, have proven resilient enough to accommodate these changes, with more workers finding employment in the last decade than at any other time in U.S. history.

1. **What problems relating to cultural differences might be created for American workers when foreign firms locate in the United States? Do these problems seem serious enough to justify a policy that would limit the ability of foreign firms to open for business in the United States?**

2. **Write a short paper reflecting upon whether U.S. employers ought to give preference to job applicants born in the United States. Take a position on this issue and justify that position.**

Visit **www.prenhall.com/ayers** for updates and web exercises on this Explore & Apply topic.

SUMMARY AND LEARNING OBJECTIVES

1. **State why the demand for labor is a derived demand.**

   ■ A labor demand curve is downward sloping, meaning that the quantity of labor demanded varies inversely to the wage rate. A labor demand curve can shift. It typically will shift with the state of the economy, shifting to the right with economic growth and to the left with economic slowdowns.

   ■ Labor demand curves exist for various occupations. Different occupations require different skills and have different employment opportunities. These characteristics lead to different labor demands.

   ■ Labor demand curves also exist for various industries. An industry labor demand curve will reflect the occupational mix in the industry.

- A geographic area, such as a city, county, state, region, or country, will have its own labor demand curve.
- Labor demand is called a derived demand. This term means that the demand for labor is related to the demand for goods and services. Other things equal, the greater the demand for goods and services, the greater the demand for labor.

2. **Use labor demand and supply curves to show how an equilibrium market wage rate is determined.**
   - The employment of labor occurs in labor markets that are characterized by demand and supply. Market labor supply curves slope upward, indicating that a greater quantity of labor supplied is associated with higher wage rates. When labor demand and supply are combined, the market wage rate is determined.

3. **Discuss the characteristics of a purely competitive labor market and the wage-taking firm.**
   - Pure competition in the labor market occurs when there are numerous employers hiring a particular type of labor. Employers in pure competition are wage takers. The market wage rate is determined by demand and supply. The supply curve of labor to the firm is perfectly elastic at the market wage rate. A wage-taking firm has zero market power over the wage rate.
   - *Ceteris paribus,* the firm's marginal revenue product for labor is also its demand curve for labor. Marginal revenue product equals the change in total revenue divided by the change in labor. Equivalently, marginal revenue product equals marginal revenue multiplied by marginal product. For a price-taking firm, marginal revenue product equals price multiplied by marginal product.

4. **Ascertain the profit-maximizing employment of labor for a wage-taking firm.**
   - A profit-maximizing employer will hire labor up to the point where the marginal revenue product of labor equals the marginal cost of labor. For a wage taker, the marginal cost of labor is nothing more than the market wage rate.
   - The amount of labor the firm employs will change when the marginal product of labor changes and when the price of its output changes. For instance, an increase in the price of the firm's output or in its mar-

ginal product of labor will shift the firm's demand curve for labor to the right.

5. **Describe labor markets in which market power over the wage rate is present.**
   - Models of the labor market that examine market power over the wage rate include monopsony, monopoly, and bilateral monopoly.
   - Monopsony involves a single employer of labor services. The supply curve of labor to a monopsonist is upward sloping. Employment and the wage rate will be lower in a monopsony labor market than in a purely competitive one. An isolated mill town provides an example of monopsony.
   - Monopoly in the labor market exists when there is a single seller of labor services. A labor union could be an example of monopoly in the labor market. The wage rate will be higher in a labor market monopolized by a single union seller of labor services than in a purely competitive labor market. However, the employment of labor in a unionized labor market will be less than if the labor market were purely competitive.
   - Bilateral monopoly in the labor market involves a single provider of labor services offering those services to a single purchaser of labor services. Wage and employment outcomes cannot be predicted in the case of bilateral monopoly because they depend upon whether the employer or employee has more bargaining power.

6. **Relate the similarities between the employment of labor and the employment of other inputs.**
   - The principles that apply to the market for labor also apply to other inputs such as capital or natural resources. For example, the hiring rule for capital says to employ capital at the point where the marginal revenue product of capital equals the marginal cost of capital.

 7. **Explain why the employment of labor has become increasingly global in scope.**
   - The employment of labor in the United States is affected by competition from workers abroad and by technological change. Foreign labor, both inside and outside the United States, is employed to produce goods and services for companies inside the United States. The Internet is making it possible to spread work around to take advantage of available labor in other countries.

KEY TERMS

derived demand, 561
purely competitive labor market, 563
marginal revenue product of labor, 563

marginal cost of labor, 567
monopsony, 569

monopoly, 569
bilateral monopoly, 569

TEST YOURSELF

TRUE OR FALSE

1. Firms hire up to but not beyond the point where marginal revenue product equals the marginal cost of labor.
2. A labor market might be specific to a particular geographic area or a particular occupation or industry.
3. Monopsony firms pay higher wages than competitive firms, other things equal.
4. An area that has only one major employer provides an example of monopoly in the labor market.
5. To maximize profit, the firm employs additional capital if the marginal revenue product of capital exceeds the rental price of capital.

MULTIPLE CHOICE

6. A market labor demand curve is
   a. downward sloping like the demand curves for goods and services.
   b. upward sloping.
   c. horizontal.
   d. vertical.
7. Which defines the marginal revenue product of labor?
   a. Change in total revenue ÷ change in output.
   b. Change in total revenue ÷ change in labor.
   c. Change in marginal revenue ÷ change in the wage rate.
   d. Change in output ÷ change in input.
8. A marginal revenue product curve shows
   a. a firm's labor supply.
   b. a firm's labor demand.
   c. the market labor supply.
   d. the marginal cost of labor.
9. The marginal cost of labor equals
   a. change in total cost ÷ change in output.
   b. change in total cost ÷ change in labor.
   c. change in total cost ÷ change in the wage rate.
   d. change in output ÷ change in labor.
10. The marginal cost of labor for a wage-taking firm _____ as it hires more labor.
    a. increases
    b. decreases
    c. remains constant
    d. first increases, then decreases
11. A wage-taking firm is currently employing four workers. The marginal revenue product of a fifth worker is $9 an hour and the market wage is $8 an hour. This firm will
    a. employ the fifth worker.
    b. not employ the fifth worker.
    c. be unable to decide whether to employ a fifth worker with the information given.
    d. fire the fourth worker.
12. Under which circumstance will a firm choose to increase its employment of labor?
    a. The marginal revenue product of the next unit of labor is less than the marginal cost of labor.
    b. The marginal revenue product of the next unit of labor is greater than the marginal cost of labor.
    c. The marginal revenue product of the next unit of labor is less than the wage rate.
    d. Fringe benefits paid to the next unit of labor are less than the wage rate.
13. In a purely competitive labor market, the market wage is determined by
    a. the demand for labor.
    b. the supply of labor.
    c. both the demand and supply of labor.
    d. neither the demand nor supply of labor.
14. The market shown in Self-Test Figure 22-1 is
    a. competitive.
    b. a monopsony.
    c. a monopoly.
    d. a bilateral monopoly.
15. In Self-Test Figure 22-1, the wage rate will be given by
    a. A.
    b. B.
    c. C.
    d. somewhere in between A and C, depending upon bargaining power.

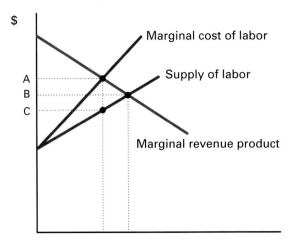

SELF-TEST FIGURE 22-1

16. A monopsony firm
    a. has many competitors in the employment of labor.
    b. is the sole seller of labor services.
    c. is the sole employer of labor services.
    d. faces a horizontal supply curve of labor.
17. The market shown in Self-Test Figure 22-2 is
    a. competitive.
    b. a monopsony.
    c. a monopoly.
    d. a bilateral monopoly.
18. In Self-Test Figure 22-2, the wage rate will be given by
    a. *A*.
    b. *B*.
    c. *C*.
    d. somewhere in between *A* and *C,* depending upon bargaining strengths.
19. Major league baseball exemplifies a labor market that is
    a. competitive.
    b. a monopsony.
    c. a monopoly.
    d. a bilateral monopoly.
20. The percentage of immigrants admitted into the United States for employment reasons in the last decade was equal to approximately _____ percent.
    a. 10
    b. 30
    c. 70
    d. 90

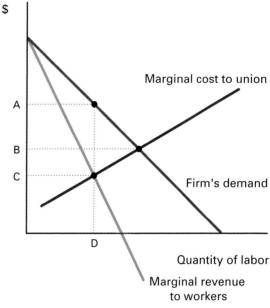

SELF-TEST FIGURE 22-2

QUESTIONS AND PROBLEMS

1. *[derived demand]* Explain how the demand for a firm's product creates a demand for labor at the firm. Other things equal, how will an increase in demand for the product affect the demand for labor?

2. *[derived demand]* In practice, when there is an economic slowdown many employers do not permanently fire unneeded workers. Instead, employers often "lay off" workers, meaning that the employer may call them back to work in the future. How is this practice related to the idea that the demand for labor is a derived demand?

3. *[demand for labor]* When the wage rate rises, does the demand for labor decrease? Explain.

4. *[demand for labor]* Explain briefly the meaning of each of the following: occupational demand for labor; geographic demand for labor; industry demand for labor.

5. *[marginal revenue product]* Explain in your own words the meaning of marginal revenue product. How does this concept relate to derived demand?

6. *[marginal revenue product]* Turn to the table in Figure 22-5. Copy the data in the first three columns onto a sheet of paper. Change the data in the price column to read $5. Compute the total revenue column and the marginal revenue product column using the price of $5. Referring to your computations, what is the highest wage rate that would allow four units of labor to be employed? What is the highest wage rate consistent with the employment of five units of labor?

7. *[changes in labor demand]* Discuss the two causes of shifts in labor demand. For each cause, first explain the circumstances in which labor demand would increase, and then the circumstances in which it would decrease.

8. *[marginal cost of labor]* Define the marginal cost of labor and explain how it affects a firm's employment of labor.

9. *[purely competitive labor market]* Explain graphically why a single employer in a competitive labor market is a wage taker. Is the market wage also equal to the marginal cost of labor? Explain.

10. *[employment of labor]* State the rule for the profit-maximizing employment of labor by filling in the blanks: _____ _____ product = _____ _____ of labor. Restate this rule by writing a sentence or two that explains the rule.

11. *[monopsony]* Using your personal knowledge of labor markets in your hometown, list a few of the largest employers. Are any of these employers likely to possess monopsony power? Explain.

12. *[monopsony]* Using a graph, explain how a monopsony is able to reduce wages and employment below their competitive levels.

13. *[monopoly in the labor market]* How is monopoly in the labor market created? What is the effect when this monopoly power is exercised?

14. *[bilateral monopoly]* Provide an example of a bilateral monopoly in the labor market. Will the wage be the same as, above, or below the competitive wage in the case of bilateral monopoly? Explain.

15. *[bargaining]* Explain how it could be in the interest of baseball players or management to end their season early if they don't get their ways. Could this be in their mutual interest?

WORKING WITH GRAPHS AND DATA

1. *[marginal revenue product]* Consider the labor input and total output of Sunny Farms, which grows and sells raspberries and is a price taker in the output market.

Units of Labor	Baskets of Raspberries	Marginal Product	Output Price = Marginal Revenue	Marginal Revenue Product
0	0	—	—	—
1	20		$3	
2	38		3	
3	54		3	
4	68		3	
5	80		3	
6	90		3	

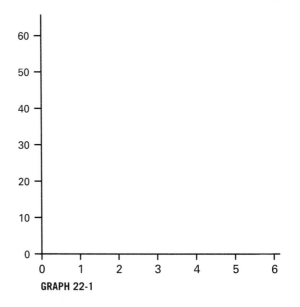

GRAPH 22-1

a. Fill in the marginal product and marginal revenue product columns in the table.

b. On Graph 22-1, draw Sunny Farm's marginal revenue product curve. Label the vertical axis "$" and the horizontal axis "Quantity of labor."

c. Suppose that Sunny Farms is a wage taker. On the graph identify the number of units of labor that Sunny Farms employ if the wage is $42. Why would the firm not hire an additional unit of labor at this wage?

d. Is the marginal revenue product curve the same thing as the demand curve for labor? Explain.

2. *[monopsony]* Consider the supply schedule given for a monopsonist in the following table.

Quantity of Labor	Wage Rate	Total Cost of Labor	Marginal Cost of Labor	Marginal Revenue Product
0	$6			—
1	8			$35
2	10			30
3	12			25
4	14			20
5	16			15
6	18			10

a. Fill in the total and marginal cost of labor columns in the table.
b. On Graph 22-2, draw the supply curve of labor and label it S, the marginal cost of labor curve and label it MC, and the marginal revenue product curve and label it MRP.
c. On Graph 22-2, identify the quantity of labor that this monopsonist would hire and the wage it would pay. Identify the marginal revenue product of the last unit of labor employed by this monopsonist.

d. On Graph 22-2, identify the wage and quantity of labor that would be employed if this monopsonized labor market could be transformed into a purely competitive one.
3. *[union monopoly]* Use Graph 22-3 to answer the following questions about a union.
a. Assume that a union organizes all of the workers in this market and behaves as a profit-maximizing monopolist. Identify the union wage and the union quantity of labor employed on the graph. Label the union wage as W_1 and the union quantity of labor employed as L_1.
b. Identify the wage and quantity of labor employed that would prevail in this market if the union ceased to exist. Label the level of employment as L_2 and the wage as W_2.
c. Why did the wage and quantity of labor change as it did when the union ceased to exist?
d. What does your answer to the question in part c suggest that a union must do to maintain the union wage, assuming that it wishes to continue?

GRAPH 22-2

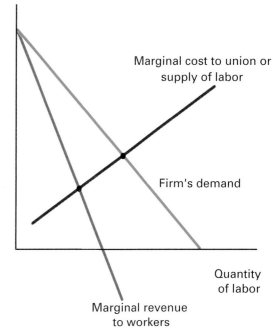

GRAPH 22-3

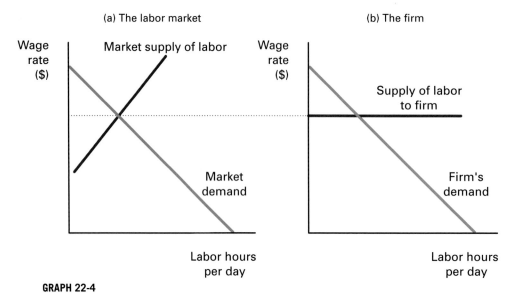

(a) The labor market

Wage rate ($)

Market supply of labor

Market demand

Labor hours per day

(b) The firm

Wage rate ($)

Supply of labor to firm

Firm's demand

Labor hours per day

GRAPH 22-4

4. *[purely competitive labor market]* Use Graph 22-4 on the purely competitive labor market to answer the questions that follow.
   a. Identify the equilibrium market wage as W_1 and the equilibrium quantity of labor as L_1 in Graph 22-4(a).
   b. Identify the equilibrium quantity of labor employed, labeled Q_1, by the firm in Graph 22-4(b).
   c. Is the firm in Graph 22-4(b) a wage taker? How can you tell?
   d. Assume that this market becomes a very desirable labor market for workers to enter. On Graph 22-4(a) sketch what would happen to the market supply of labor curve (label it "Market supply$_2$") and the resulting effect on the equilibrium market wage, labeled W_2 and quantity of labor labeled L_2.
   e. From your answer to part d, sketch what would happen to the firm's supply of labor curve, labeled "Supply of labor to firm 2," and employment, labeled Q_2, on Graph 22-4(b).

 Visit **www.prenhall.com/ayers** for Exploring the Web exercises and additional self-test quizzes.

CHAPTER 23

EARNINGS AND INCOME DISTRIBUTION

A LOOK AHEAD

It takes money to live. Most money comes to us from income earned in the labor market. Typically, peoples' incomes are less when they are young, but rise before leveling out and possibly falling with advancing age, a pattern that describes the life cycle of earnings. As you read about the life cycle of earnings in this chapter's Explore & Apply section, you will see that the lack of education holds down the earnings of high-school dropouts, and that more education increases earnings. College students sacrifice present earnings for greater future earnings.

People receive incomes in the form of wages from labor, rent, interest, and profit. In this chapter you will find answers to the question of why wages differ from person to person. You will also read about poverty, analyze wage differentials between groups such as men and women, and whites and African-Americans, and see how the famous reap earnings from economic rent, savers from interest, and entrepreneurs from profit.

LEARNING OBJECTIVES

Understanding Chapter 23 will enable you to:
1. **Relate the importance of wages and salaries.**
2. **Analyze why higher wages can lead an individual to prefer either more or fewer work hours.**
3. **List and explain the many causes of earnings differentials among workers.**
4. **Assess the extent and significance of poverty and earnings differentials in the U.S. economy.**
5. **Discuss significant differences between the types of income—wages, rent, interest, and profit.**
6. **Discuss the life cycle of earnings through the use of the age/earnings profile.**

Explore & Apply

In the preceding chapter we examined the markets for labor and other inputs. Here we look more closely at the incomes that people receive from the labor market and other sources.

23.1 MEASURING INCOMES

What are the sources of your family's income? Wages from a job, interest from a bank account, and perhaps profit from a business put money into the pockets of many American families. Figure 23-1 shows the relative importance in the United States of the primary sources of national income. In that pie chart we see that wages and salaries provide 71 percent of U.S. national income. Businesses provide another 19 percent in the form of corporate profits plus the income from proprietorships. Interest earnings provide another 8 percent, while rents received by landlords provide 2 percent.

Figure 23-1 does not accurately reflect the meaning of wages as economists use the term. This shortcoming of the data arises because some fraction of proprietor's income is in reality wages, while another part of proprietor's income is profit. Likewise, some wage income is a return to labor; other such income is a return to human capital. Even profit in the figure is based on the accounting definition rather than the economic definition. Despite these data shortcomings, Figure 23-1 clearly shows the importance of wages and salaries as a source of income.

Wages are the incomes that workers earn from their jobs. The size of their incomes depends on two variables: the quantity of labor they supply and the amount they are paid. The quantity of labor supplied is usually measured in hours. The price of labor is the *wage rate*—the amount an individual is paid per hour. When the wage rate is multiplied by hours worked, the result is *earnings,* the income from labor. For example, in October 2003, average hourly earnings of production workers were $15.46, which when multiplied by their average weekly hours of 33.8 resulted in average weekly earnings of $522.55.

Most hourly wage workers who work more than 40 hours a week receive time-and-a-half pay for all hours over 40. Hours in excess of 40 are called *overtime* hours. Overtime wage rates are 50 percent greater than the *straight-time* rate that a worker receives for the first 40 hours worked. The Department of Labor enforces these rules, which arise from the *Fair Labor Standards Act,* enacted by Congress in 1938.

FIGURE 23-1

U.S. NATIONAL INCOME The pie chart shows sources of income in the United States. Wages are by far the largest source of income.

Source: Bureau of Economic Analysis, *National Income and Product Account Tables.* Data are for the first quarter of 2003.

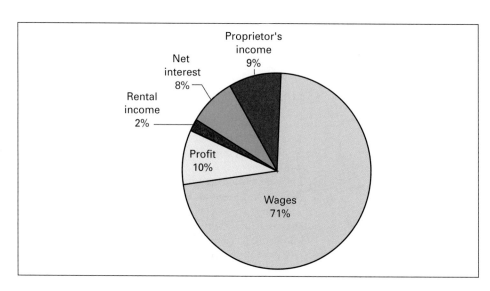

Workers who are paid a *salary* receive a fixed amount of income, no matter how many hours they work. Employers expect salaried employees to work a minimum number of hours per week, typically corresponding to the regular operating hours of the business. If such employees work additional hours, they are not paid for those hours. Labor Department rules govern what types of jobs pay salaries versus hourly wages.

An employer's *total labor costs* are the sum of wages and salaries plus fringe benefits. Some benefits are voluntarily offered by employers; others are required by government. Benefits received by workers include paid vacations, sick leave, and employer contributions to Social Security. *Workers' compensation* coverage (which provides workers who are injured on the job with a stipend while they recuperate from their injuries), paid time off for lunch, and health benefits round out the list of typical benefits. For the typical U.S. employers, benefits account for about 28 percent of labor costs. These labor costs for employers are incomes for the workers who receive them.

23.2 INDIVIDUAL LABOR SUPPLY

Labor force participation reflects the decisions of individuals to offer their services in the labor market. To be counted as a member of the labor force, a person must either have paid employment or be actively looking for it. Examples of nonparticipants include full-time students and retirees.

Individual preferences play a key role in explaining labor force participation, and hence earnings. These preferences are reflected in the individual's labor supply curve. Figure 23-2 illustrates an individual's labor supply curve. Below the **reservation wage,** individuals "reserve" their labor—they choose not to work at all. Note that, unlike supply curves for other things, the individual's supply curve of labor services has a *backward-bending* portion. This shape can be understood by considering the substitution effect and the income effect of increasing wage rates.

As wage rates rise at first, the **substitution effect** of the change in wage rates causes individuals to work more—they substitute away from leisure, because the opportunity cost of leisure becomes higher as wage rates rise. The result is that people offer more hours in response to higher wages, causing the supply curve to slope upward. In place of leisure, workers consume goods and services with their increased earnings.

reservation wage the lowest wage offer an individual will accept.

substitution effect when the wage rate increases, individuals recognize that the opportunity cost of leisure has risen, choose to substitute labor for leisure, and thus offer to work more hours.

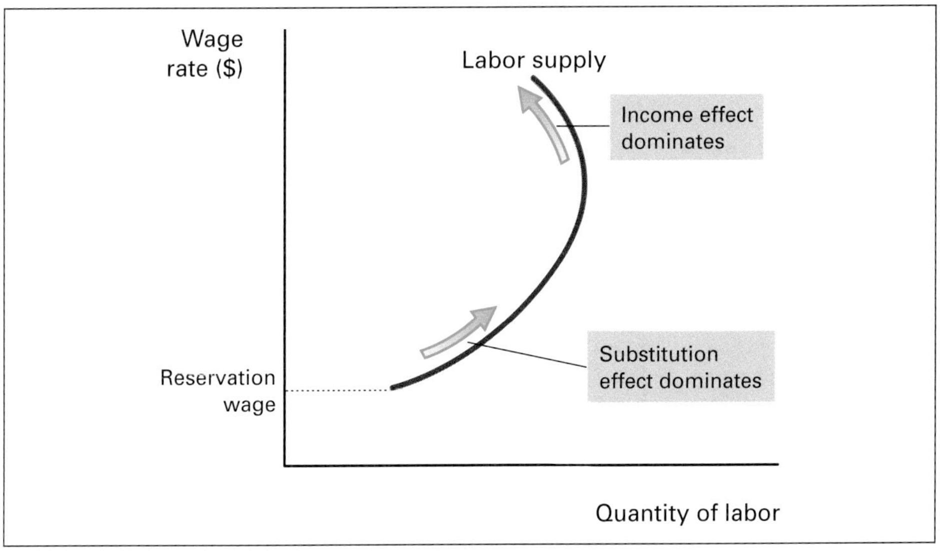

FIGURE 23-2

AN INDIVIDUAL'S BACKWARD-BENDING SUPPLY OF LABOR The backward-bending supply curve of an individual's labor services is explained by the tug of war between the income and substitution effects of a wage change. The income effect is such that, as the wage rate rises, it causes higher income and a desire to take more vacation time to enjoy it. The substitution effect is the response to increase one's labor because it becomes relatively more expensive to take that time off.

income effect when the wage rate rises, individuals offer to work fewer hours because their higher incomes increase their demands for normal goods, including leisure.

As wage rates rise, eventually the **income effect** of the wage change tugs the worker in the opposite direction from the substitution effect. Higher wages bring higher incomes, which prompt workers to demand more of all normal goods. *Leisure*—time away from work—is a normal good. To "buy" more leisure, workers pay the opportunity cost of giving up the income that could have been earned by working. The result is that, as wage rates rise, the income effect prompts workers to offer fewer hours of work.

The supply curve bends backward when the income effect outweighs the substitution effect. This accounts for the huge decline in yearly hours of work for the average American worker over the last 100 years. The standard eight-hour workday and annual paid vacations have permitted workers to enjoy more leisure time as real incomes have risen. Self-employed workers, such as physicians and accountants with private practices, can increase their vacation time to enjoy their substantial income. As seen in Figure 23-2, the substitution effect tends to be stronger at lower wage rates, and the income effect tends to be stronger at higher wage rates. The result is a supply curve that first slopes upward and then bends backward.

Individuals' labor supply curves will vary depending on whether they are *primary workers*, the main source of income in households, or *secondary workers*, whose incomes are not as critical to their households' well-being. The labor supply curves of primary workers are nearly vertical, meaning that they will choose to work about the same number of hours, no matter the wages they are able to receive. The quantity of labor supplied by a primary worker is typically in the range of 35 to 45 hours per week. In contrast, secondary workers have a much more pronounced upward slope and backward bend to their supply curves. Secondary workers are more likely to hold part-time jobs than primary workers.

As an example of an individual's labor supply decisions, consider Elena, a full-time college student. Earning good grades is her priority. The $7 an hour paid by the Burger Barn is below her reservation wage. She could earn $8 an hour by modeling hair styles for Hair Trends, but that amount is not enough to induce her to work, either.

If an employer were willing to pay Elena $10 an hour, she would go to work part-time, but not for a penny less—$10 is her reservation wage. Elena would work more hours if she were offered an even higher wage rate. If she were offered $20 an hour, every hour of leisure time would cost her $20 in lost earnings. She would then be willing to work 25 hours a week.

Because of her commitment to school, Elena would not work more than 25 hours. That is the point where her labor supply curve bends back. For example, if she could earn $30 per hour, she would reduce her hours of work below 25 hours because at $30 an hour her income effect would outweigh her substitution effect.

Elena's reservation wage could change. If she needed money for books, she might lower her reservation wage and apply for a job at the Burger Barn. When she graduates, her reservation wage is likely to go up because the value of her labor is greater. If she doesn't receive a job offer that meets her higher reservation wage, she might eventually lower it. Reservation wages can change when people can't find a job.

Labor supply curves may shift. Many persons receive *nonlabor income* from investments, pension funds, government transfer payments, interest on bank deposits, gifts from relatives, and other sources. The amount of nonlabor income received can affect labor market choices. Generally, **a greater amount of nonlabor income will reduce the labor a worker supplies, while a smaller amount would increase the quantity of labor supplied.** If Elena did not receive income from home, it is likely that her labor supply curve would shift to the right and her reservation wage would decline. Figure 23-3 illustrates the effect of a decrease in nonlabor income.

The *market labor supply* sums the quantity of labor supplied at various wage rates for all the individuals in a labor market. Market supply curves of labor are upward sloping in the range of income that is usually relevant to employers.

An *industry labor supply* sums the quantity of labor supplied to a particular industry at various wage rates. Because higher wage rates in one industry attract workers from other industries, any particular industry supply curve of labor is nearly always upward sloping. It

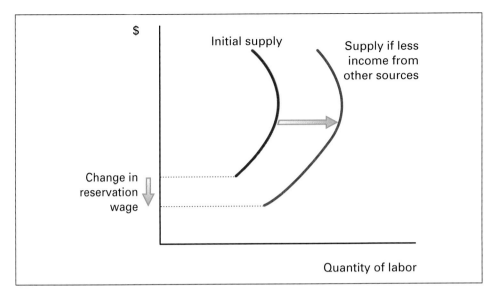

FIGURE 23-3

EFFECT OF A DECREASE IN NONLABOR INCOME A decrease in nonlabor income shifts the labor supply curve to the right and decreases the reservation wage. With less income from other sources, people increase the amount of labor supplied at any wage rate.

QUICKCHECK

Compare the outcome of an increase in the wage rate if Judy's labor supply curve is: (a) upward-sloping; (b) backward-bending; and (c) vertical.

Answer: If Judy's labor supply curve slopes upward, an increase in the wage rate will increase her quantity of labor supplied. If the wage rate intersects the backward-bending portion of her labor supply curve, an increase in the wage rate will decrease her quantity of labor supplied. With a vertical labor supply curve, Judy's quantity of labor supplied would not change.

is also usually quite elastic, meaning that a small increase in the wage rate would result in a large increase in the quantity of labor supplied. For example, as wages rise in the trucking industry, some truckers might work less because of the income effect. However, it is likely that the reduction in work time by individual truckers will be more than offset by an inflow of would-be truckers from other occupations.

TOO RICH TO WORK? OR TOO POOR TO RETIRE?

SNAPSHOT

In the easy money days of the late 1990s, many workers saw their accumulated wealth double and double again. They asked themselves, "Why work?" and commenced with planning for early retirement. Then, in the face of an estimated $7.8 trillion worth of stock market declines in the early 2000s, some of these same people were forced to ask themselves the opposite question. Could they afford to retire?

The riches they had amassed had vanished just as quickly as they had appeared. Lavish spending patterns based on that transitory wealth led many to take on debt. Whether it be to credit card companies or home mortgage lenders, that debt must be repaid. To do so takes an income, and an income once more means work. After being teased with thoughts of early retirement, the cold reality for many people is that they cannot reach that life of leisure even as soon as they originally planned. It all goes to show that labor supply is not just about how many hours of work to offer at any given wage. It's also about whether to work at all! ◄

23.3 SOURCES OF EARNINGS DIFFERENTIALS

Wage differentials among workers sometime seem intuitive. We expect a heart surgeon to earn more than a janitor. Many wage differentials are not so easy to understand, however. Why should physicians earn more than teachers? Why should star athletes earn more than physicians? Individual earnings differ because of a combination of factors, which we will examine next.

OCCUPATIONAL CHOICE AND COMPENSATING WAGE DIFFERENTIALS

Numerous occupations exist. Over 700 basic occupations are cataloged on the Internet database *Occupational Information Network,* also known as *O*NET,* which was created by the U.S. Department of Labor. Occupational choice plays a significant role in earnings power. Generally, the highest-paying occupations are those that require the greatest skills, and the lowest paying are the occupations of the unskilled.

compensating wage differentials additional pay offered by employers to offset undesirable job characteristics.

Different jobs have their own advantages and disadvantages. Most people would rather work at safe jobs in climate-controlled comfort than at dangerous jobs outside in the extremes of weather. Higher pay in the latter jobs can equalize their attractiveness relative to the former jobs. Such increases in pay are termed **compensating wage differentials.**

Sanitation workers, coal miners, and many others have unpleasant or dangerous jobs. To induce workers to take those jobs, employers must pay a compensating differential. Note that even with compensating differentials included, the pay in such jobs may still be relatively low, because skill requirements in many of these jobs are low.

People choose jobs on the basis of numerous job characteristics. Pay, the *pecuniary* attribute, is the most important for some. For others, job security, status, the likelihood of advancement, safe working conditions, interest in the work, or the flexibility of employers in matters of dress or hours is most important. Job features unrelated to pay are called the *nonpecuniary* attributes. Positive nonpecuniary features can offset low pay.

LABOR UNIONS

Workers join labor unions to improve their pay and work environments. At the peak of union membership in 1953, 36 percent of U.S. workers belonged to a union. In 2002 that figure stood at 16.1 million members, about 13 percent of wage and salary workers.

The decline in overall union membership masks the concentration of membership in several key industries. Indeed, government employee unionism has reached record levels, with about 7 million government workers, equal to about 37.5 percent of such workers, belonging to unions. Table 23-1 shows the percentage of workers belonging to a union. In part (A) we see that over one-third of government workers belong to unions, but less than 2 percent of workers in agriculture do. In part (B) we see that union members are concentrated in the blue-collar occupations.

Possibly the most important factor behind the low percentage of union workers in the economy is more global competition in industries where unions have historically been strong. Fewer U.S. workers in these industries mean fewer union members. Examples include the steel and auto industries. Also contributing to the decline in unionism has been the increasing importance of white-collar jobs, in which the appeal of unions is relatively weak. Nonetheless, a recent nationwide survey of workers showed one-third of those surveyed who were not union members would like to be.

In order to reverse the long-term decline in membership, unions reach out for new members. Union efforts to "organize" an employer—have the right to represent its workers—culminate in a secret ballot representation election, under the supervision of the federal

TABLE 23-1 PERCENTAGE OF WORKERS BELONGING TO A UNION

(A) BY MAJOR INDUSTRY

INDUSTRY	PERCENT
Private wage and salary workers	8.5
Agriculture	2.3
Mining	8.5
Construction	17.2
Manufacturing	14.3
Transportation and public utilities	23.0
Wholesale and retail trade	4.5
Finance, insurance, and real estate	1.9
Services	5.7
Government workers	37.5

(B) BY OCCUPATION

OCCUPATION	PERCENT
Managerial and professional speciality	13.0
Technical, sales, and administrative support	8.9
Service occupations	12.6
Precision production, craft, and repair	20.7
Operators, fabricators, and laborers	19.1
Farming, forestry, and fishing	4.3

Source: Union Membership, USDL, Bureau of Labor Statistics, Table 3. The data are from 2002.

government's National Labor Relations Board (NLRB). When more than half of a firm's employees vote in favor of a union, the NLRB certifies the union as the bargaining agent for the workers. Once certified, a union engages in **collective bargaining,** negotiations with employers aimed at improving working conditions, pay, and benefits. Legally, employers must bargain with a union, but are not obligated to reach agreement.

collective bargaining
negotiations between an employer and a labor union.

When firms balk at union demands, which side will prevail? **Union** *bargaining power* **refers to the ability of a union to win an agreement with greater wages and benefits for its members. The primary weapon providing bargaining power to unions is the** *strike,* **or work stoppage.** The ability to shut down an employer is a powerful weapon, although strikers have the incentive to settle a strike because they are not paid wages while on strike. Generally, a strike will be preceded by negotiations. Thus, a strike indicates the failure of negotiations. However, there are *wildcat strikes,* work stoppages that occur spontaneously because of workers' grievances against their employers. When an employer faces a strike, its most powerful source of bargaining power is the right to hire permanent replacements for

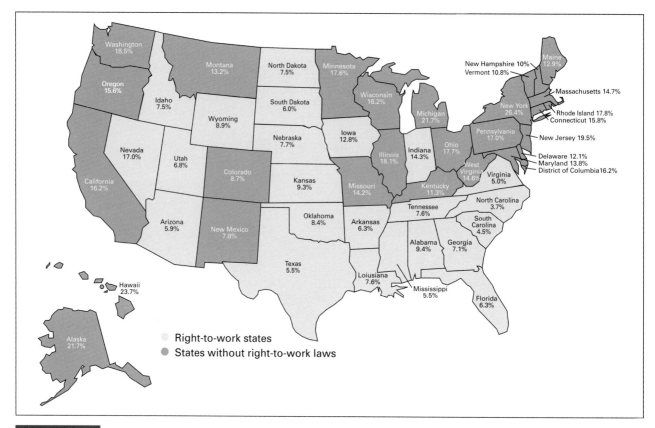

FIGURE 23-4

UNION MEMBERSHIP BY STATE The map shows the percent of employed workers in each state that belong to a labor union. There is wide variation in union membership from state to state. The highest percentage of union members is found in New York, while the lowest is in North Carolina. In general, right-to-work states have a lower percent of union members than do other states.

Source: Union Membership, USDL, Bureau of Labor Statistics, Table 5. The percentages are from 2002. The right-to-work information is also from the USDL, and includes laws and constitutional amendments in effect as of January 1, 2002. Indiana's right-to-work statute applies only to school employees.

striking workers. However, firms often do not exercise that right for fear of violence toward their property or replacement employees.

Union bargaining power is reduced in the twenty-three states with some form of a *right-to-work law,* which permits a unionized firm's workers the option of not joining the union. In these states, union and nonunion workers may work side-by-side on the job. Hence, workers in right-to-work states are less likely to present a united front when labor disputes arise, a situation that decreases union bargaining power. Figure 23-4 shows the percent of employed workers in each state that belong to a union. Union membership is the highest in New York, and the lowest in North Carolina.

Another union weapon is the *boycott,* a campaign to persuade union members and the public to refrain from purchasing the output of a firm with which the union has a disagreement. Boycotts often go hand-in-hand with strikes.

Given the weapons unions have, it should not be surprising that union wages are high. Median weekly earnings for union members in 2002 were $740, approximately 26 percent higher than the $587 for those not represented by unions.

Higher pay means fewer jobs offered by unionized employers, which increases the supply of labor to similar jobs at nonunion employers, and drives down nonunion wages. Furthermore, the kinds of jobs held by union members differ from the kinds held by other workers. Some of the higher pay in union jobs is likely to be compensating differentials, which would be paid even in the absence of unions. The consensus of research on union wages is that, after taking account of all other factors affecting wages, **unions raise wages for their members. However, estimates of the increase vary too widely to know its magnitude with certainty.**

HUMAN CAPITAL AND SIGNALING

Human capital is another important determinant of earnings differentials. Human capital is the knowledge, skills, and other productivity-enhancing attributes embodied within individual workers. Attending college is a prime example of how to increase one's human capital. Sources of human capital include formal schooling, on-the-job training, and classroom-skills training.

It is costly to build a stock of human capital. There are out-of-pocket, explicit costs, as well as the opportunity costs of forgone earnings. For many college students, opportunity costs far exceed the explicit costs. Is a college degree worth the investment? College graduates are less likely to be unemployed than high-school graduates, and earn higher incomes over their adult lives. The $958 median weekly salary in late 2003 for college graduates exceeded the median of $563 for high-school graduates by about 70 percent. The statistics must be interpreted with caution, however, since those going to college may differ in other respects from those who do not. For example, college students might be smarter and more motivated than workers who do not go to college, in which case they would earn more than other people, even without college.

Several studies indicate that the returns to the investment in a college diploma probably increased over the last twenty years, which helps explain why an increasing fraction of high-school graduates attend college. As discussed in Chapter 2, international trade has limited the return to labor in the United States, although it has increased the return to capital, including human capital. There are various other influences, too, such as:

1. The decline in the power of unions to raise wages above competitive levels for their mostly high-school-educated membership.
2. The flow of relatively unskilled immigrants into the United States, many of whom compete for jobs against high-school graduates.
3. The increased desire of employers to hire college graduates for jobs that have not historically required advanced education.
4. The high-tech economy, which places a premium on education.

The **signaling** hypothesis provides an additional explanation for the greater earnings of college graduates. In this view, education provides information to employers about the characteristics of job applicants. Employers believe that more education signals that one is easily trained and reliable.

signaling the view that education provides information to employers about the characteristics of job applicants.

DISCRIMINATION AND EARNINGS

Wage discrimination occurs when a worker who is as productive as other workers doing the same job is paid less because of race, gender, color, religion, or national origin. This discrimination is illegal in the United States. It is difficult to ascertain what part of wage differences between workers occurs as a result of wage discrimination and what part occurs because of productivity differences. Productivity differences among workers often result from differences in human capital, which may reflect differing amounts and quality of schooling. Good schooling requires access to quality schools, which is lacking in many inner-city neighborhoods. It also requires an investment of time and money, which is hard to come by for poor youths whose earnings may be needed within their families.

To the extent that a group experiences systematic discrimination prior to entering the labor market, the outcome is less human capital and lower earnings. For example, blacks may earn less than whites because of such *pre-market discrimination,* in which access to good schooling is denied, and racial stereotyping of black youths occurs. This situation can also harm blacks with higher-than-average human capital to the extent that employers lack essential information about individual job applicants and resort to *statistical discrimination,* which is to judge applicants by the average characteristics of their racial or ethnic group.

Evidence indicates that wage discrimination by employers typically accounts for only a part of wage differentials among racial and gender groups. An individual's age, ability, health, education, marital status, occupation, and number of years of work experience affect his or her productivity and hence earnings. A good part of the lower earnings of minorities and women can be attributed to differences in these attributes.

LUCK AND OTHER INFLUENCES

Wage differentials exist even among individuals who are identical in all measurable attributes that may affect earnings, including race and gender. Such wage differences reflect the effect of difficult-to-measure factors on earnings. Being in the right place at the right time and other forms of luck can play a significant role in wage differences.

Other possible factors creating wage differences include disparities in looks, height, social skills, ambition, selection of a marriage partner, and other tangible and intangible attributes. For example, experiments have shown that good-looking people have an advantage in the labor market. When two people with identical credentials have been sent to the same job interview, the good-looking applicant is usually offered the job while the average-looking one is not. Thus, the greater demand by employers for physical attractiveness will translate into higher earnings for persons possessing such traits.

Wages tend to be related to the cost of living. In localities where the cost of living is high, wages also tend to be high. For example, the cost of living is much higher in New York City than in Mississippi, and so wages tend to be higher in New York City than in Mississippi. Wages also tend to be higher in urban areas than in surrounding rural areas, possibly reflecting a lower cost of living in rural areas. Because of differences in the cost of living, the purchasing power of a particular wage can vary enormously. A wage that barely allows a person to subsist in New York City might allow a comfortable existence in Mississippi. Thus, higher wages do not always mean that the recipients of those wages are better off.

23.4 INCOME INEQUALITY

Income inequality refers to differences in earnings. Here we examine the amount of income inequality. We start with the problem of poverty.

POVERTY

Low wages or lack of a job can create poverty. Poverty is associated with deprivation, which motivates government transfer programs to aid the poor. Some of these transfers are "cash," such as the well-known welfare check. About two-thirds of government transfers to the poor provide *in-kind benefits,* meaning that valuable services are provided instead of money. In-kind benefits include healthcare, food stamps, subsidized housing, and subsidized school lunches. These programs seek to preserve a minimum standard of living for the poor and are commonly referred to as the *social safety net.*

Most households in poverty are very close to the government-set **poverty line.** This income threshold varies by household size and composition, but generally are intended to approximate three times the cost of a nutritionally adequate diet. From 1959 to 1973, the number of persons falling below the poverty line decreased from 22 percent to 11 percent of the population, then stayed within the range of 11 to 15 percent over the following years. The poverty rate in 2002 was 12.1 percent. Poverty rates vary by family status, age, and race. For example, about 26.5 percent of families with a female household head and no husband present fell below the poverty line in 2002. With the safety net provided by Social Security, poverty among the elderly has fallen to 10.4 percent of people over 65, down from 35 percent in 1959. Poverty rates are about three times higher among blacks than whites. Poverty also varies among the states. Louisiana and New Mexico often are among the states with the highest poverty rates each year, while New Hampshire and Minnesota are usually among the states with the lowest rates.

> **poverty line** a government-set income threshold that varies by household size and composition, set to approximately equal three times the cost of a nutritionally adequate diet.

"CUT MY SALARY. PLEASE!"   *SNAPSHOT*

Incentives are changed by the existence of government transfer programs. It is not always easy to predict how people will respond to such incentives. For example, some years ago a professor asked his university's administrators to lower his annual salary by a few hundred dollars. His request was not frivolous. Its purpose was to make his children eligible for subsidized school lunches. The savings from subsidized lunches would have more than made up for his salary reduction. The moral is, those whose earnings are low may have an incentive to reduce their work effort in order to further lower their incomes and qualify for government assistance. ◀

EARNINGS OF WOMEN AND MINORITIES—A WAGE GAP REMAINS

Earnings differentials exist between groups of people. Here we look at earning differences between males and females, and whites and blacks. Even though a substantial fraction of earnings differences are explained by factors other than labor market discrimination, these differences have important social implications. Let's look at women first.

The typical full-time female worker in the United States earns about 76 cents for every dollar earned by the typical male. This figure is up from 59 cents in 1978. The closing of the earnings gap is explained by women workers developing specialized job skills, thereby allowing women to move into professional and managerial jobs. According to the Bureau of Labor Statistics, 18 million American women worked in professional and managerial occupations in 2003, and that number has been steadily increasing.

Although less so now than in earlier decades, women's earnings and rank are negatively affected by *discontinuous labor force participation,* which occurs when a person leaves and later reenters the labor force. Many women leave their jobs after childbirth and do not return to work for several years in order to care for their children. This in-and-out pattern of labor force participation causes women's human capital to depreciate and reduces their years of labor-market experience relative to men. The result is lower earnings. As increasing numbers of women have stayed in the labor force throughout their lives, their earnings as a group have risen relative to those of men and are expected to rise even more in the future.

Explanations for the remaining earnings gap focus on women's occupational choices. Many occupations are dominated by females. Table 23-2 compares the percentage of males in a select group of traditionally male occupations with the percentage of females in another group containing several traditionally female occupations. Many of these female-dominated occupations pay less than the male-dominated ones that involve comparable education and responsibility.

TABLE 23-2 SELECTED MALE-DOMINATED AND FEMALE-DOMINATED OCCUPATIONS

MALE-DOMINATED OCCUPATIONS (PERCENTAGE OF WORKERS WHO ARE MALES)		FEMALE-DOMINATED OCCUPATIONS (PERCENTAGE OF WORKERS WHO ARE FEMALES)	
Automobile mechanics	98.5	Secretaries	98.4
Carpenters	98.3	Dental hygienists	97.8
Firefighters	97.3	Prekindergarten and kindergarten teachers	97.8
Airplane pilots and navigators	96.5	Child care workers	97.0
Truck drivers	94.7	Receptionists	97.0
Engineers	89.6	Cleaners and servants	96.1
Surveyors	84.6	Bookkeepers and accounting clerks	92.9

Source: 2002 Statistical Abstract of the U.S., Table No. 588.

occupational segregation the concentration of women workers in a limited number of occupations.

Occupational segregation, the concentration of women workers in certain jobs, such as nursing and teaching, is often cited as evidence that women are discriminated against in hiring. The reasoning is that women are forced into these jobs because other jobs are not open to them. However, many economists deem this view simplistic, whether or not some aptitudes correlate with gender. Interruptions in women's careers because of childbearing, child rearing, and the need to change jobs because of a husband's job transfer may motivate women to select occupations in which interruptions in labor force participation will be least harmful to their careers. The skills required in these traditionally female occupations are easily transferred from one employer to another and become obsolete only very slowly.

There are other possible explanations for occupational segregation. Gender-based differences in interests may be one factor. In addition, there might be discrimination against women by the educational system, such as school guidance that channels women away from subjects that lead to employment in traditionally male jobs. Employer discrimination in hiring women for some higher-paying jobs is also sometimes pointed to. These explanations are not mutually exclusive, meaning that some combination of them could apply.

The wage gap based upon gender is a worldwide phenomena, not confined just to the United States. According to the latest data from the Organization for Economic Cooperation and Development (OECD), women workers in the United Kingdom earn 76 percent of what men earn; in France, 87 percent; Spain, 71 percent; Japan, 61 percent; and in Sweden, 83 percent.

Table 23-3 compares the earnings of men and women in the United States. The earnings data are provided by race and they include only full-time, year-round workers. Time-series data are provided in order to show the progress that women and blacks have made in closing the wage gap with white males.

Turning to black–white differences, the data show a significant earnings gap between black and white males, with the median black male earning about 78 percent of the amount earned by the median white male in 2001. While narrowing over time, this gap continues to be a source of concern. In contrast, black women earned 88 percent of the earnings of white women in 2001. Black women show a greater attachment to the labor force than do white women, which increases the earnings of black women relative to white women. On average, black women stay in the job market longer than white women because the proportion of households headed by women is greater among black households than among white households.

| TABLE 23-3 | MEDIAN EARNINGS OF YEAR-ROUND, FULL-TIME WORKERS BY RACE AND GENDER |

YEAR	EARNINGS OF WHITE MALES	EARNINGS OF BLACK MALES	EARNINGS OF BLACK MALES AS PERCENT OF WHITE MALE EARNINGS	EARNINGS OF WHITE FEMALES	EARNINGS OF WHITE FEMALES AS PERCENT OF WHITE MALE EARNINGS	EARNINGS OF BLACK FEMALES	EARNINGS OF BLACK FEMALES AS PERCENT OF WHITE MALE EARNINGS
1984	$40,252	$27,471	68%	$25,253	63%	$22,758	56%
1987	40,686	29,091	71	26,658	65	23,810	58
1990	39,505	28,211	71	27,368	69	24,354	62
1993	38,401	28,429	74	27,721	72	24,507	64
1996	39,025	30,482	78	28,485	73	24,702	63
1999	41,778	32,182	77	29,766	71	26,706	64
2001	40,790	31,921	78	30,849	76	27,297	67

Source: 2003 Economic Report of the President, Table B-33. Data are adjusted for inflation and expressed in 2001 dollars.

QUICKCHECK

What effects do discontinuous labor force participation and occupational segregation have on women's earnings?

Answer: Both reduce the earnings of women. Discontinuous participation, which is dropping out of the labor force temporarily, allows women's human capital to depreciate. Occupational segregation concentrates women in certain careers, often those that pay relatively poorly.

THE GLASS CEILING—A LOOK FROM ABOVE   *SNAPSHOT*

The successes enjoyed by Oprah Winfrey, Meg Whitman, and Carly Fiorina suggest the glass ceiling—that symbolic barrier that has kept women from rising to the top—was shattered as the new millennium arrived. Oprah, the social activist, actress, producer, and talk-show queen, had her status among the super successful confirmed in 2003 when *Forbes* magazine declared her a billionaire. Fomer Economics major Meg Whitman rose to command the on-line auction powerhouse eBay. Ms. Fiorina proved that a woman could rise to the top in the high-profile, high-tech world of computers, leading Hewlett-Packard through its successful acquisition of Compaq. Do these and other success stories featuring women reveal that the glass ceiling has been shattered?

Maintaining perspective, Oprah's single billion put her at number 427 on the list of the world's richest people, a list dominated by men. As America's highest-paid female executive, Ms. Fiorina ranked only 116th on a recent *Forbes* list of the best-paid executives. In addition, according to a 2002 survey, just about 1 percent of all Chief Executive Officers were women. Although these numbers do not look encouraging, it is true that more women these days are qualified to rise to the top. Those qualifications include a combination of business degrees and years of experience in the business world. There has also been rigorous enforcement of equal opportunity laws in recent years.

There is a maxim on Wall Street that stockholders care about only one thing—the price of their stock. If hiring a female CEO increases the value of the company, then stockholders would be eager to embrace whichever new Meg Whitman or Carly Fiorina came their way. If there is a glass ceiling that keeps the cream from rising to the top, it would also hold down corporate profit. The stockholders would be eager to be rid of the culprits. Therefore, the market offers hope that the boardroom curmudgeons who might contrive to keep women out would themselves be the ones to go. ◄

23.5 OTHER INCOMES

Up to this point we have focused on earnings in the labor market since that source of income is by far the most important economically. Now, we look at the three other sources of income: rent, interest, and profit.

RENT—WHEN INPUTS ARE IN FIXED SUPPLY

economic rent earnings in excess of opportunity cost when an input is unique.

Economic rent describes earnings in excess of opportunity costs for a unique input—one that is in fixed supply. For example, raw land is always unique because each parcel has a unique location. Numerous inputs can be unique. For example, there is only one Tiger Woods with his unique set of golfing skills and persona.

There is no data to report on economic rent in isolation. For example, the rental income to landlords that was identified in Figure 23-1 includes economic rent, but also includes a return for what is built on the land. Furthermore, economic rent applies to much more than just land.

Movie stars, top corporate executives, and well-known people in law, academia, and other professions can attribute their high incomes in large part to economic rents. When such people have talents and abilities that are exceptionally scarce and valued in the marketplace, they often find themselves earning much more than they could from their next best alternative. The combination of fixed supply and high demand for the talents of superstars results in sky-high earnings. Yet their opportunity cost, their best earnings opportunity outside their current employment, is usually not nearly so spectacular.

Wage determination and economic rent for a superstar with unique talents are illustrated in Figure 23-5. The fixed supply of superstar-quality talents results in a vertical supply curve of labor with that talent. A higher wage will not induce a greater quantity supplied, as would be the case if the supply curve were upward sloping, but not vertical. The position of the demand curve for the superstar's talents determines earnings. When demand is large relative to supply, high earnings are the outcome. The portion of earnings representing economic rent is indicated by the blue shaded area in the figure.

This model applies to a spectrum of workers. Success in many fields requires exceptional skills. The most successful heart surgeons, stockbrokers, economists, attorneys, and business executives, among others, earn economic rents.

Not everyone, even those with unique talents, is able to earn significant economic rents. Your favorite local singers possess talent that is in fixed supply, because nobody else sings just like they do. Nonetheless, without sufficiently large public demand for that talent, they will never get rich by singing. Similarly, many minor league athletes are close to major league quality in their talents, but the public is willing to pay high ticket prices only for major leaguers. Hence, a minor leaguer with 95 percent of the talent of a major leaguer may earn only 1 percent or less of the earnings of the major leaguer. These examples have led to what is sometimes called a superstar economy, with a winner-take-all reward system.

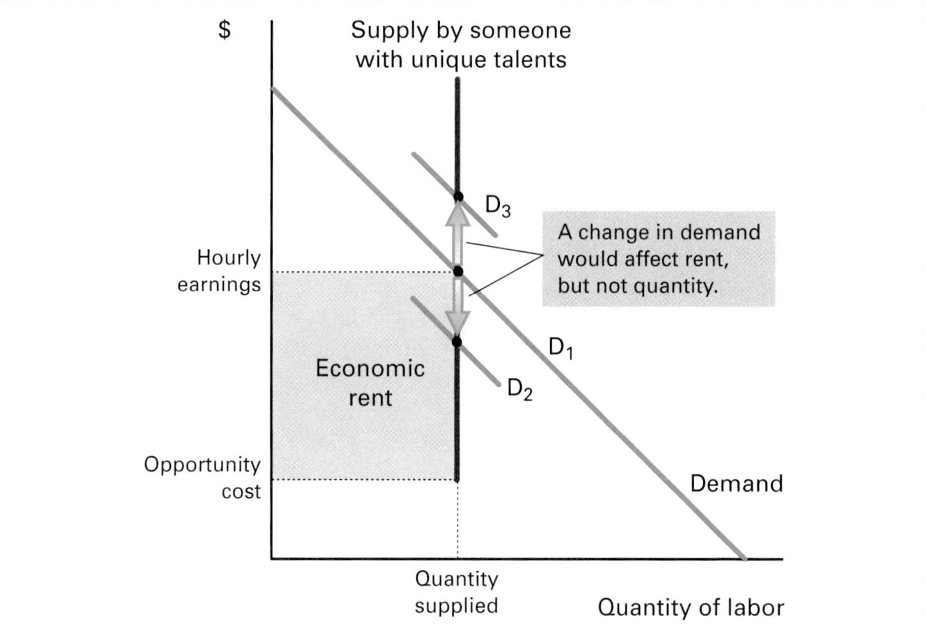
$
Supply by someone with unique talents
D3
A change in demand would affect rent, but not quantity.
Hourly earnings
D1
Economic rent
D2
Opportunity cost
Demand
Quantity supplied
Quantity of labor

FIGURE 23-5

ECONOMIC RENT Economic rent is determined by demand. When demand is large relative to the fixed supply, earnings can be far above opportunity costs.

QUICKCHECK

Does everyone with a unique talent that is in fixed supply earn economic rent?

Answer: No, because there must be a market demand for that talent. For example, the winners of spelling bees, pig-calling contests, and county fair cook-offs exhibit unique, interesting talents, but are rarely able to earn income from those talents.

INTEREST—KEEPING WEALTH PRODUCTIVE

Interest is the price paid for the use of money. In the United States in 2003, interest income represented 8 percent of the total income received. The payment of interest is made by borrowers, while lenders receive interest payments. Often, a *financial intermediary,* such as a bank, credit union, or savings and loan, attracts deposits from savers and lends these savings to borrowers. The government also pays interest to the owners of government *bonds,* which are IOUs of the government. Interest is usually expressed in terms of a percentage, the **interest rate.** A bank that offers savers a 3 percent interest rate will pay $3 in interest per year for each $100 saved.

interest payment made by a borrower to compensate a lender for the use of money.

interest rate price of borrowed money, expressed as a percentage.

Interest rates have sometimes been a source of controversy, with some countries and religions over the centuries questioning whether charging money for the use of money should be allowed. However, while those with substantial wealth certainly gain by being able to "live on interest," the economy gains as well. The reason is twofold:

- The payment of interest to lenders promotes savings that are used to pay for investments in physical and human capital that improve standards of living.
- The requirement that borrowers pay interest makes sure that the money available for investment is used where it will be most productive. Investments should be productive enough to at least be able to cover interest payments.

PROFIT—MOTIVATING THE ENTREPRENEUR

Profit motivates entrepreneurs, who perform the following functions:

■ Combining resources—organizing land, labor, and capital into productive uses;
■ Innovation—implementing new production methods and creating new products; and
■ Taking risks—entrepreneurs face the risk of failure.

These entrepreneurial functions separate the entrepreneur from the hired manager, whose job is to carry out the vision of the entrepreneur.

Entrepreneurs face the possibility of losses as well as profits. Losses can result from a variety of causes, including faulty decision making, bad luck, or stiff competition from other firms. For this reason, some people perceive entrepreneurship as risky business. Even though nearly all workers will receive their paychecks, and nearly all bondholders and bank depositors will receive their interest income, the hard-working entrepreneur runs the risk of reaping no reward. Thus, entrepreneurship is not for everyone. In some countries the lack of entrepreneurs hurts the ability of the country to develop economically.

Economic profit can also be more than just a reward for the successful practice of entrepreneurial skills. Barriers to entry create monopoly and other market structures in which economic profits arise from lack of competition. Perhaps the most surprising aspect of profit is that profit accounts for such a small fraction of national income. Recall from the beginning of this chapter that accounting profit and proprietorship income make up just 18 percent of total national income. From this slice of income comes a significant part of the funds used to push the economy along to greater prosperity, as profits are in effect recycled into additional productive investments.

Explore & Apply

23.6 EDUCATION AND EARNINGS

Why does a student stay in school? For the six-year-old, the answer is simple: "My mother makes me," or "I like school." For older students, the answers to the question are more complex. Make no mistake, the answers are important. After all, schooling provides the foundation for the skilled labor force a modern economy requires. Schooling also offers strong medicine in the fight against poverty.

Clearly, some students do not stay in school as long as they should. We read of the problem of high-school dropouts, whose economic futures look bleak. We also read of the need for more skilled labor, such as more air conditioner repairers, automobile mechanics, computer technicians and programmers, and the like. But to succeed in a skilled occupation often requires at least a high-school education. The result is that most doors of opportunity are closed to dropouts.

At the same time, many of the kinds of jobs that used to be available to dropouts in America have become scarce. Unskilled factory jobs have migrated overseas. Gas-pump jockeys and elevator operators have been replaced by self-service. The power of labor unions to win higher wages for workers is weak because their membership as a fraction of the work force has diminished significantly since the 1950s.

Would more students stay in school if they knew the "economic facts of life" relating to the role of schooling in increasing their earnings and job opportunities? How much schooling is enough? A high-school diploma? A bachelor's degree? A master's? A doctoral degree? Some of the answers can be had by taking a look at Figure 23-6, which shows median earnings by educational attainment.

Considering the model of the life cycle of earnings can help us understand better the decision to pursue additional education. The costs of schooling include both direct costs and opportunity costs. Consider first the opportunity costs. The six-year-old in modern-

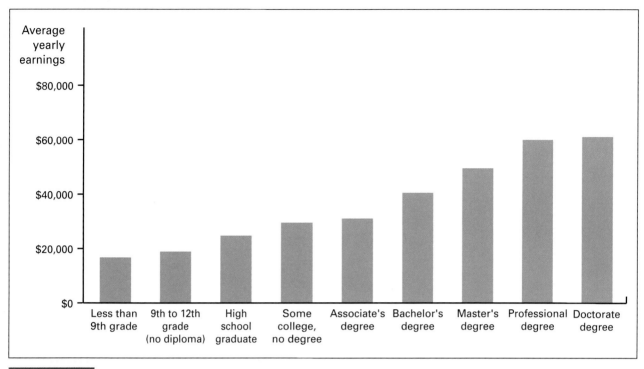

FIGURE 23-6

EARNINGS AND EDUCATION Earnings rise with more education. The earnings shown are annual median earnings for workers age 25 and older.

Source: U.S. Census Bureau, Income 2001. The data are for 2001.

day America can spend the day in school with minimum opportunity cost, at least in terms of money. Young children in America are not expected to work. Indeed, there are laws against child labor. Even if they wanted to work, or their parents wanted them to, there are few job opportunities for six-year-old children. Recognize, however, that bans on child labor were not common until the twentieth century. In the eighteenth and nine-teenth centuries, America's economic foundation was agriculture, and children had to earn their keep by working in the fields. Education was a luxury that many families could not afford, which is still true today in some less-developed countries. Even when child labor is outlawed, it is often commonplace. The opportunity cost of the lost income from sending children to school is often too great to bear, and so the children work.

From kindergarten through twelfth grade, the costs of public schooling are absorbed by the taxpayer—the student need not worry about tuition, books, or fees. Once a student enters college, even a public college, the student or the student's parents must pay out of their own pocket. The cost of tuition and fees in a public university varies from state to state, but averages about $5,000 a year. That cost is far higher at most private universities. When a college student decides to live away from home rather than commute to classes at a local community college or university, the direct cost of schooling rises accordingly. The cost of providing their children with a college education is a significant economic burden

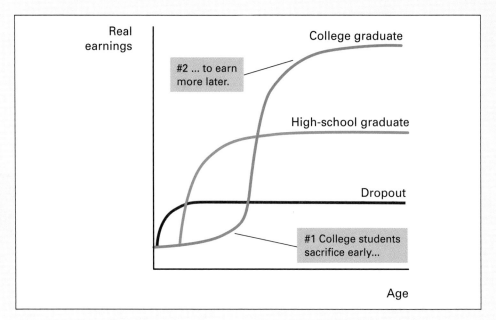

FIGURE 23-7

THREE AGE/EARNINGS PROFILES
Additional schooling postpones earnings, but usually increases them in the long run. This is seen by comparing earnings profiles over time for the high-school dropout, high-school graduate, and college graduate. Dropouts can earn incomes at a young age, but their lack of skills limits their earnings. High-school graduates delay their earnings, but the decision to stay in school pays off because of higher earnings later. When college students graduate, their incomes rise above the income received by high-school graduates.

on working families. Many college students hold part-time jobs in order to ease that burden. Financial aid of various sorts is also available to reduce the burden of college expenses.

THE LIFE CYCLE OF EARNINGS

The *life cycle of earnings* refers to the pattern of an individual's real earnings over time, from entry into the labor force until retirement. Figure 23-7 illustrates a typical life cycle of earnings with a curve called an *age/earnings profile*. This graph shows an individual who enters the labor force after graduating from college at age 21 and who works continuously until retirement at age 66. Note that the age/earnings profile rises steeply in the early years of work as the individual acquires the human capital associated with increasing experience and responsibility. The rise in earnings reflects the individual's increasing productivity.

The age/earnings profile eventually stops rising. Although not shown in the figure, it may even turn down slightly in later years. Perhaps this individual has suffered health problems that have slowed down the advance in earnings, without forcing the individual to retire. In any case, the downturn in earnings is associated with a decline in productivity. When the individual retires, such as at age 66, earnings from labor stop.

Now consider Figure 23-7 again, this time looking at the curve that illustrates the life cycle of earnings for a high-school graduate. This earnings profile starts at age 18 rather than age 21, as in the earnings profile of the college graduate. This earnings profile starts lower than the earnings profile of the college graduate and stays lower. Typically, the gap between the two age/earnings profiles would increase over time because the earnings profile of the high-school graduate will level off while the earnings profile of the college graduate is still rising. This leveling out of the curve reflects reduced opportunities on the job for the high-school graduate to acquire human capital.

A third age/earnings profile is also illustrated in Figure 23-7. This illustration shows the lifetime earnings of a high-school dropout who starts working at age 16. The age/earnings profile starts at the minimum wage and, after rising in response to initial training on the job, remains flat throughout the remainder of an individual's lifetime. The flat earnings profile assumes that the dropout is not able to acquire any human capital on the job, which would increase productivity and thus put a positive slope on the age/earnings profile. It also assumes

TABLE 23-4	EARNINGS BY AGE GROUP
AGE GROUP	**MEDIAN WEEKLY EARNINGS**
16 to 19 years	$305
20 to 24 years	399
25 to 34 years	590
35 to 44 years	669
45 to 54 years	707
55 to 64 years	673
65 years and over	502

Source: *Highlights of Women's Earnings, 2002,* Report 972, September 2003. Bureau of Labor Statistics. The data cover both sexes for the year 2002.

that the minimum wage keeps up with inflation. If the minimum wage rises more slowly than inflation, the age/earnings profile would slope downward. Alternatively, if the minimum wage increased more rapidly than inflation, the age/earnings profile would slope upward. You can put some real-world numbers on the age/earnings profiles by looking at the behavior of earnings in Table 23-4. Older workers earn more than younger workers until earnings begin to reverse among the 55 and up groups. The table mixes together workers of all educational levels.

The study of life cycles of earnings for different types of workers can provide revealing insights into the workings of the labor market. For example, the age/earnings profiles of white workers will have a steeper slope than the age/earnings profiles of minority workers when minority workers are discriminated against on the job. Another example relates to women workers. The discontinuous labor force participation of women will be revealed by a break in the earnings profile. Some kinds of jobs, such as school teaching, allow workers who return to work to resume their earnings at the same level as when they left the labor force. Other jobs, those where human capital depreciates rapidly because of rapid advances in knowledge in the field, punish discontinuous labor force participation by offering lower wages to workers who return after being out of the labor force.

The higher, steeper earnings profile for college graduates indicates that a college education has value. Despite the high costs of obtaining that college education, labor economists have consistently found that a bachelor's degree is a good investment. Even so, there will always be dropouts from high school or college. The reasons are many. The most basic is that while the search for goods and services can explain many facets of people's behavior, there are always nonpecuniary influences. In other words, money is not the only source of satisfaction for human beings. Some students will drop out for love—whether it be for love of another person or love of some particular interest. After all, Bill Gates dropped out of college to follow a dream that created Microsoft. And his earnings profile, while not typical, doesn't look so bad!

1. Draw an age/earnings profile for a female school teacher with three children, and who dropped out of the labor force for one year each time she had a child. Draw a second age/earnings profile for an independently wealthy male worker who drops out of the labor force for five years to pursue his hobby of breeding and raising golden retrievers. Assume that, both before and after dropping out of the labor force, he worked as an Internet software developer for a leading computer software firm.

THINKING CRITICALLY

2. Suppose your little brother, sister, or other close friend or relative has declared that he or she is going to drop out of high school as soon as he or she turns age 16. Write a letter to this person that uses personal, emotional, and economic arguments to persuade him or her to stay in school and go on to college.

 Visit www.prenhall.com/ayers for updates and web exercises on this Explore & Apply topic.

SUMMARY AND LEARNING OBJECTIVES

1. Relate the importance of wages and salaries.

- Wages and salaries represent over 70 percent of U.S. national income. Corporate profit, interest, proprietor's income, and rental income make up the rest of national income.

- The price of labor is the wage rate. Earnings from labor are equal to the wage rate multiplied by hours worked. The Fair Labor Standards Act requires employers who hire labor on an hourly basis to pay overtime wage rates for hours of work in excess of 40 each week. Some workers are salaried, meaning they receive a certain amount of pay no matter how many hours they work.

- Wages and salaries are augmented by fringe benefits to arrive at total labor costs. Fringe benefits account for about 28 percent of labor costs.

- A person's reservation wage is the lowest acceptable wage. When the market wage rate offered by an employer to someone is less than the individual's reservation wage, a person will choose not to work. Only a wage offer above the reservation wage will be accepted.

2. Analyze why higher wages can lead an individual to prefer either more or fewer work hours.

- The backward-bending individual labor supply curve shows that once the wage rate reaches a high enough level, workers may begin cutting back their quantity of labor supplied.

- The behavior of an individual's labor supply is determined by the strength of the income and substitution effects. The substitution effect of a wage increase promotes an increase in the quantity of labor supplied because a higher wage increases the opportunity cost of refraining from working. The income effect of a wage increase promotes a reduction in a person's quantity of labor supplied because a higher wage increases the demand for leisure. A personal labor supply curve bends back when the income effect is stronger than the substitution effect.

- Market labor supply curves are upward sloping, implying that higher wages lead to an increase in the quantity of labor supplied. This assertion is true even if individual labor supply curves bend backward.

3. List and explain the many causes of earnings differentials among workers.

- Important factors determining earnings are the choice of occupation, compensating wage differentials, unions, and differences in the amount of human capital. Luck, the cost of living, discrimination, and even a person's looks can affect earnings.

- Wage discrimination against blacks creates a wage differential between blacks and whites. Such discrimination is illegal. However, blacks may earn less than whites because of pre-market discrimination, in which the access of blacks to human capital is reduced. Individual blacks may also be subject to statistical discrimination, in which an employer judges each member of a group according to the group average.

4. Assess the extent and significance of poverty and earnings differentials in the U.S. economy.

- The government sets a minimum income called the poverty line, based on family size. The poverty rate is the percentage of people or families that receive less income than specified by the poverty line. The overall U.S. poverty rate has stayed within 11 to 15 percent in the last 20 years.

- The poverty problem is one example of problems associated with wage differentials. The wage gap between men and women and between whites and blacks is another. One reason for lower earnings for women is occupational segregation.

5. Discuss significant differences between the types of income—wages, rent, interest, and profit.

- Earnings in excess of opportunity cost are called economic rent. Income in the form of economic rent is received when an input is in fixed supply and the demand for the input is strong enough. Superstars in entertainment and other fields receive economic rents.

■ Interest is the price paid for the use of money. An interest rate is an expression of interest in percentage terms. Interest helps to ensure that borrowed money is put to good use.

■ Profit is the reward for the successful application of entrepreneurship.

 Discuss the life cycle of earnings through the use of the age/earnings profile.

■ The life cycle of earnings looks at the behavior of an individual's earnings over that person's lifetime. The age/earnings profile is a graph that illustrates the life cycle of earnings. The age/earnings profiles of high-school dropouts, high-school graduates, and college graduates will appear very different from one another. The college graduate sacrifices earnings early in life in return for a steeper age/earnings profile during his or her working years.

KEY TERMS

reservation wage, 585
substitution effect, 585
income effect, 586
compensating wage differentials, 588

collective bargaining, 589
signaling, 591
poverty line, 593
occupational segregation, 594

economic rent, 596
interest, 597
interest rate, 597

TEST YOURSELF

TRUE OR FALSE

1. Market labor supply curves are typically backward bending.
2. Evidence is clear that labor union membership has no effect on a person's earnings.
3. Statistical discrimination involves a careful effort to judge each person's characteristics before hiring that person.
4. The poverty line is defined as the earnings provided by full-time, year-round work while earning the minimum wage.
5. The returns to a high-school dropout typically start early but rise relatively little over time.

MULTIPLE CHOICE

6. An individual's labor supply curve will start at the point called the
   a. backward-bending part.
   b. reservation wage.
   c. amount of nonlabor income.
   d. income effect.
7. In the labor supply curve shown in Self-Test Figure 23-1, which of the following points occurs where the income effect dominates the substitution effect?
   a. *A.*
   b. *B.*
   c. *C.*
   d. Either *A, B,* or *C,* depending upon where labor demand intersects the curve.

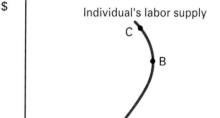

SELF-TEST FIGURE 23-1

8. The job most likely to offer a significant compensating wage differential is
   a. baker.
   b. accountant.
   c. computer repair person.
   d. police officer.
9. Labor unions in the United States represent about ____ percent of workers.
   a. 44
   b. 33
   c. 22
   d. 11

10. A right-to-work law
    a. has no effect on union bargaining power.
    b. increases union bargaining power.
    c. decreases union bargaining power.
    d. has unpredictable effects on union bargaining power.
11. From a signaling viewpoint, earning a college degree will
    a. have no effect on earnings.
    b. decrease earnings.
    c. increase earnings because college increases human capital.
    d. increase earnings because a college degree is associated with personal characteristics employers value.
12. For blacks to have lower earnings than whites,
    a. employers must practice wage discrimination.
    b. statistical discrimination cannot be practiced by employers.
    c. pre-market discrimination could be the cause.
    d. blacks must be more productive than whites.
13. The percentage of American families falling below the poverty line in the last two decades has ranged between
    a. 4 to 8 percent of the population
    b. 11 to 15 percent of the population
    c. 18 to 22 percent of the population
    d. 25 to 30 percent of the population
14. Women earn about what percentage of mens' earnings?
    a. 53 percent
    b. 61 percent
    c. 74 percent
    d. 89 percent
15. Discontinuous labor force participation is associated with
    a. teenage workers.
    b. women workers.
    c. men workers.
    d. black workers.
16. Occupational segregation is often cited as an explanation for
    a. how people choose their life's work.
    b. the concentration of women workers in certain jobs.
    c. jobs that used to be performed in the United States that are now performed abroad.
    d. child labor.
17. A characteristic of the model illustrating economic rent is a supply curve that
    a. slopes upward.
    b. slopes downward.
    c. is horizontal.
    d. is vertical.
18. A large portion of actress Julia Roberts' earnings from starring in movies is
    a. wages.
    b. rent.
    c. interest.
    d. profit.
19. Profit is primarily associated with which input?
    a. Land
    b. Labor
    c. Capital
    d. Entrepreneurship
20. After graduation, the age/earnings profile for a college graduate will
    a. be lower than that of a high-school graduate.
    b. be the same as that of a high-school graduate.
    c. be higher than that of a high-school graduate.
    d. turn downward.

QUESTIONS AND PROBLEMS

1. *[incomes]* Use common sense to speculate on why wages and salaries make up such a large fraction of total income, while profit makes up such a relatively small portion. As a matter of fact, the fraction representing wages and salaries remains relatively stable in the long run. Why do you think this is so? Speculate as to what the world would be like if the percentages were flipped, with wages making up 9 percent of the total and profit accounting for 72 percent.

2. *[total labor costs]* Why are total labor costs more than just wages? Explain by using examples of other labor costs besides wages.

3. *[wages]* Why do some employers offer fringe benefits that exceed those required by government? Why do other employers choose not to offer such fringe benefits? Evaluate and state the advantage to an employer who offers the following fringe benefits:
   a. Free day care.
   b. Flextime—within limits, employees pick their own starting and quitting times.
   c. Employee lunchroom with lunches provided to employees at cost.
   d. Two weeks paid vacation.

4. *[reservation wage]* What is your reservation wage today? What will it be when you graduate from college? What could cause your reservation wage to change over the course of your life?

5. *[backward-bending labor supply curve]* Draw a graph that shows a backward-bending labor supply curve. Does this model apply to your behavior? If so, at what income would your personal labor supply curve start to bend backward?

6. *[income and substitution effects]* Discuss the income and substitution effects within the context of the backward-bending labor supply curve. Must a person's labor supply curve bend backward? Explain.

7. *[earnings differentials]* Some employees automatically pay workers according to seniority—how long they have worked for the employer. Others pay according to a person's productivity—merit. Evaluate the following statements.
   a. "Basing pay raises on seniority rewards mediocrity."
   b. "Merit pay plans allow bosses to reward their favorites and punish those they dislike."

8. *[compensating differentials]* Discuss the notion of compensating differentials for the following occupations:
   a. Nurses.
   b. Forest rangers.
   c. Movie and TV actors.
   d. The occupation that you would like to pursue.

9. *[union wages]* What is the most powerful weapon that unions wield in order to win higher wages for their members? Are unions actually successful at winning higher wages? What is the tradeoff for unions?

10. *[unions]* Americans hold strong opinions about unions, with some favoring unions and others opposed to them. Write a short essay that focuses on your personal views toward unions. Justify your views with information from the chapter and from other sources about the role and effectiveness of unions.

11. *[returns to college]* State and briefly discuss the causes that economists have identified as contributing to the increased return to a college education.

12. *[signaling]* Discuss the merits of the signaling hypothesis. Provide at least three positive characteristics that an employer might reasonably believe a college graduate would possess.

13. *[wage gap]* What factors other than discrimination might explain why women earn less than men? If there were no discrimination against women, would women earn the same as men? Why or why not?

14. *[discrimination]* Is it fair to allow firms to pay more productive workers higher wages, even though productivity differences might be caused by forces beyond a person's control? Explain.

15. *[economic rent]* Do economists use the term "rent" in the same way as the general public? Explain.

16. *[economic rent]* Using a supply and demand graph, illustrate the concept of economic rent. Be sure that your graph shows the opportunity cost, hourly earnings, and area of economic rent. Are all of the earnings in your graph economic rent or just a portion? Explain.

17. *[economic rent]* Is it fair for some people to earn huge economic rents? Should those rents be taxed away? Would taxing rents cause superstars to withhold their talents from the marketplace? Explain.

WORKING WITH GRAPHS AND DATA

1. *[individual labor supply]* Use Graph 23-1 to answer the following questions about the individual's supply of labor curve.
   a. Identify as point *A* on the labor supply curve the reservation wage on the individual's labor supply curve.
   b. Identify as point *B* on the labor supply curve a wage at which the substitution effect dominates the income effect.
   c. Identify as point *C* on the labor supply curve a wage at which the substitution and income effects exactly offset one another.
   d. Identify as point *D* on the labor supply curve a wage at which the income effect dominates the substitution effect.

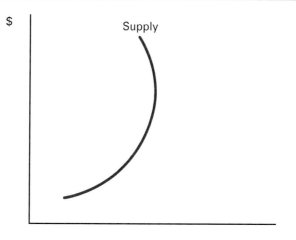

GRAPH 23-1

2. *[labor supply]* Use the following table showing the wage and quantity of labor supplied by Sheila.

Wage rate (dollars per hour)	1: Quantity of labor supplied (hours per week)	2: Quantity of labor supplied (hours per week)	3: Quantity of labor supplied (hours per week)
8	0		
9	10		
10	25		
11	30		
12	32		
13	30		
14	28		

a. Sketch the labor supply curve that relates the wage to the quantity of labor supplied (1) and label the curve S_1. Label the vertical axis "Wage $" and the horizontal axis as "Quantity of labor."

b. Label as point A Sheila's reservation wage.

c. Suppose that Sheila lowers her reservation wage to $8, but is only willing to work for five hours at this wage. Fill in the quantity of labor supplied (2) column. On your graph show the new reservation wage as point B and the effect on the initial labor supply curve of this change in the reservation wage as a dashed line.

d. Assume that Sheila has a sudden increase in non-labor income as a result of an inheritance and reduces her willingness to work by ten hours per week at any wage. Fill in the quantity of labor supplied (3) column. Sketch the new labor supply curve using these numbers and label it S_2. On your graph label the reservation wage as point C.

3. *[economic rent]* Suppose that Vanessa has a unique musical talent. She can work forty hours per week. The supply of labor is vertical at forty hours for her.

a. Suppose that when Vanessa starts out, she can make $20 per hour as a musician. On the graph draw a demand curve and label it D_1 that would allow her to earn $20 per hour for forty hours of work per week.

b. Assume that Vanessa earns $20 per hour for a forty-hour week in her next best employment option as a manager of a retail store. How much economic rent does she make if she decides to be a musician?

Show the amount of economic rent as "economic rent" on the graph.

c. Assume now that Vanessa becomes well-known and popular with the public. She finds that she now earns $50 per hour for a forty-hour week. Draw a demand curve labeled D_2 that would allow Vanessa to earn $50 per hour for a forty-hour week.

d. How much economic rent does Vanessa earn? Show the amount of economic rent as "economic rent" on the graph.

4. *[age/earnings profile]* This question will use Graph 23-2, which shows age/earnings profiles.

a. In Graph 23-2, label the age/earnings profile for the high-school graduate and the college graduate.

b. How does the age/earnings profile of college graduates demonstrate that a college education has value as compared to that of the high-school graduate?

c. What explains the upward-sloping portion of the age/earnings profile for each group in Graph 23-2? What explains the difference in the slopes and height of the two curves?

d. Assume that the age/earnings profile labeled college graduates is for white college graduates. Draw an age/earnings profile for minority workers who are college graduates assuming that they start at the same level of real earnings as whites but that they are discriminated against on the job. Label it "minority workers." How does it compare to the age/earnings profile for white workers?

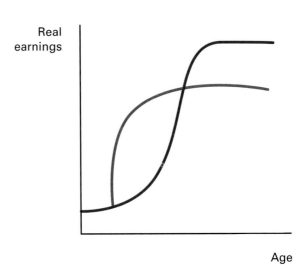

GRAPH 23-2

Visit **www.prenhall.com/ayers** for Exploring the Web exercises and additional self-test quizzes.

CHAPTER **24**

PUBLIC GOODS, REGULATION, AND INFORMATION

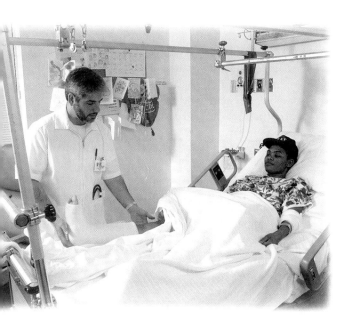

A LOOK AHEAD

The healthcare industry is huge and growing. It also stands at the center of a debate over how much government should do in a market economy. Like food, shelter, clothing, and water, healthcare is crucial to a good standard of living. It is also subject to imperfect information and can be very expensive, with inefficient pricing incentives under health insurance distorting market choices. Government efforts to widen healthcare coverage while reining in costs may solve some problems but can make others worse. The market failures of healthcare and government's role in influencing healthcare outcomes are examined in this chapter's Explore & Apply section.

   Healthcare is hardly unique in being a target for government action. The United States contains over 80,000 separate governments, ranging from education, sewer, and water districts through municipal, county, and state governments, on up to the federal government. Government regulations apply to nearly all elements of the economy. Why is there so much government involvement in what is basically a market economy? Using the perspective of economic efficiency, this chapter examines the rationales.

LEARNING OBJECTIVES

Understanding Chapter 24 will enable you to:
1. **Distinguish among private goods, public goods, externalities, and common property resources.**
2. **Explain why the private marketplace fails to offer public goods in efficient quantities.**
3. **Identify an optimal amount of highway congestion and policies to achieve that amount.**
4. **Describe why government enacts regulations and what principles can guide it toward efficiency.**
5. **Explain the concept of asymmetric information and how it influences market outcomes.**
6. **Apply the analysis of marginal costs and marginal benefits to explain criminal behavior.**
7. **Identify major issues in healthcare and alternative ways of addressing them.**

Explore & Apply

"Technology tells us what can be done. Economics tells us what should be done. Politics tells us what will be done."

This old saying sums up the dilemma facing economists. They are caught in the middle, neither producing goods nor controlling public policy. Rather, economic analysis reveals how the intertwining actions of government and markets can offer citizens the best value. Economics seeks to identify when public policy is needed to meet economic goals, and the types of government actions that are appropriate. Sometimes the action is for the government to produce directly, while at other times government uses regulation to influence production in the private sector.

24.1 IDENTIFYING MARKET FAILURES

The invisible hand of the marketplace leads profit-seeking producers to offer consumers an efficient variety of goods and services. Competition ensures that these goods and services are produced at least cost and in efficient quantities. Efficiency is the market's great success and the reason that market economies have been able to improve living standards over time. However, there are also instances of **market failure,** in which markets do not bring about economic efficiency.

market failure when markets fail to achieve efficiency, as in the case of public goods, externalities, and common property resources.

SOURCES OF MARKET FAILURE

There are two sources of market failure. The first is a lack of competition, which you learned about in the chapter on monopoly. The second source is a good that is not purely private. **Private goods** are *excludable* and *rival,* meaning that people can be excluded from consuming the good and any one person's consumption diminishes the amount that is available for everyone else. For example, your bottle of Arizona Iced Tea would be a private good, because each swig that you offer your friend leaves that much less for you. Most goods are private goods.

private goods goods consumed by one person only—excludable and rival; most goods and services are private.

At the opposite extreme from private goods lie **public goods,** which are *nonexcludable* and *nonrival,* meaning that people cannot be kept from consuming the good, nor does their consumption reduce the amount available for others. The nonrival nature of a public good means that the marginal cost of providing service to additional consumers is zero. The nonexcludable nature of the public good means that, although different people value it differently, we have no choice but to each consume the same amount. National defense provides the best example of a public good. Whether a country's citizens are pacifists, hawks, rich, or poor, and no matter their race, gender, or ethnicity, all consume the same amount of national defense.

public goods goods that are nonexcludable and nonrival, meaning that a person's consumption of the good does not reduce its quantity for others.

Pure public goods are completely nonexcludable and nonrival. To some extent, almost all public goods are impure. An *impure public good* is not consumed with complete equality. Even national defense, the purest of the public goods, is likely to protect people who live in some cities better than the residents of others. But impurities are much more pronounced for many other public goods. Libraries can exclude prospective borrowers. Police patrols provide greater security in some neighborhoods than in others. A fire station provides less protection per house as more houses are built.

An Internet site represents an impure public good. To some degree it is nonrival and nonexcludable. Additional viewers normally add no costs—in other words, the marginal cost is zero. However, it is possible to exclude users who do not register. The fixed cost of providing content and hosting services can be covered by registration fees, or alternatively by advertising. In a similar manner, a national park might charge an entrance fee to cover maintanence, even though the park itself is a public good to the extent that many can use it simultaneously.

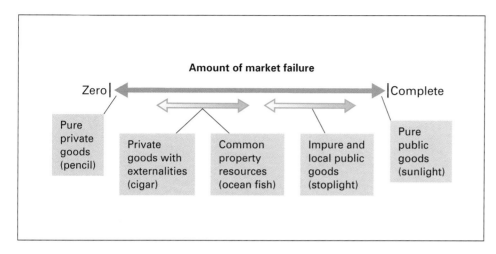

Amount of market failure

Zero | ←——————————————————————→ | Complete

Pure private goods (pencil)

Private goods with externalities (cigar)

Common property resources (ocean fish)

Impure and local public goods (stoplight)

Pure public goods (sunlight)

FIGURE 24-1

THE SPECTRUM OF MARKET FAILURE Market failure depends on the degree of rivalry and excludability. Private goods are completely rival and excludable, while public goods are completely nonrival and nonexcludable. Externalities and common property resources generally fall closer to the private goods end of the spectrum, while local public goods are closer to the pure public goods end of the spectrum. Examples of each good are noted in parentheses.

Impurities in public goods often involve **congestion,** which occurs when the addition of one more user reduces the availability of the good for all other users. **Congestion violates the assumption of nonrivalry needed for a pure public good.** For example, although Internet surfers rarely slow each other down, a particular site can become congested. National parks also become congested. Roughly two out of every five miles of urban Interstate highways are subject to significant congestion nearly every day. Fees can serve to reduce congestion, as we will discover later in this chapter.

Public goods can extend over a wide or limited area. A city's air quality is an example of a **local public good.** Local public goods provide an economic justification for local and regional governments. For instance, it is better to have local streets and highways under the control of municipal and state governments, respectively, rather than to have Congress decide which potholes get repaired and where street lights are to be installed. The same would hold true for the many other public goods that are primarily local or regional in nature.

In between pure public and pure private goods are common property resources and private goods with externalities. Sometimes the ownership of something is common property, meaning that it is shared. Shared ownership occurs most frequently with natural resources, thus leading to the term **common property resource.** For example, an oilfield could straddle two separate properties, with each property owner having the right to pump as much oil as the owner desires. A common property resource generates contention over who gets to use it.

Other times, the production or consumption of private goods leads to costs or benefits to third parties—people or businesses who were not party to the transaction. Such spillover effects onto third parties are termed **externalities.** Externalities can be either negative or positive. Pollution is an example of a negative externality. Negative externalities impose **external costs** on others. For example, to the extent that air pollution causes health problems or decreases people's enjoyment of outdoor activities, the pollution has imposed external costs on its victims. Conversely, positive externalities confer **external benefits.** For example, when a neighbor kills all the mosquitoes on her property and it results in fewer in your own backyard, you receive the external benefits of greater enjoyment of your backyard and savings on pest control. Figure 24-1 summarizes the range of goods and resources from the extreme of pure private goods to the other extreme of pure public goods. We will put aside a detailed examination of externalities and common property resource issues until the next chapter, focusing in this chapter on public goods, regulation, and information.

congestion when adding an additional consumer of a public good detracts from its value to other consumers.

local public good a public good that affects a particular region, such as a city.

common property resource a jointly owned resource, such as groundwater; people have little incentive to conserve common property resources, but rather seek to capture them for their own private use.

externality side effect of production or consumption that affects third parties who have no say in the matter.

external costs when an externality takes the form of costs, such as from pollution.

external benefits when an externality takes the form of benefits, such as from a neighbor maintaining an attractive yard.

THE PRODUCTION OF PUBLIC GOODS

Private goods are consumed and paid for by the individual. Public goods, on the other hand, are consumed simultaneously by everyone regardless of who pays. We share national

FIGURE 24-2

THE VALUE OF A PUBLIC GOOD
The value of a public good is the sum of its value to each person, because everyone consumes the same amount.

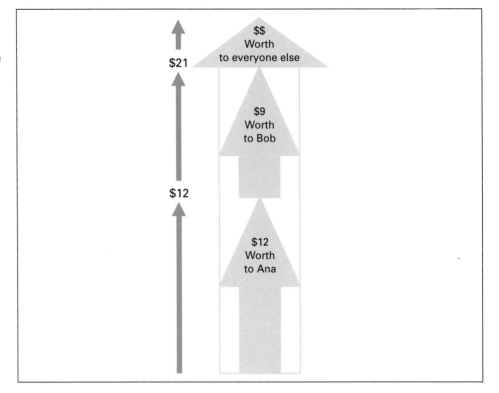

defense, fresh air, and even access to radio signals. Adding more consumers does not diminish the enjoyment we each get from these goods. This arrangement has repercussions on demand that prevent the marketplace from offering an efficient quantity.

Unlike a private good, each unit of a public good is simultaneously consumed by everyone. **The value of a public good is thus the sum of its values to all consumers.** Figure 24-2 illustrates this idea, where the public good is worth $12 to Ana, $9 to Bob, and so forth. It would be efficient to provide this good only if total benefits exceed total costs.

In most applications, the quantity of a public good can vary, which means we must compare the increment to costs with the increment to benefits from producing more of it. In other words, we must consider not only total benefits and costs, but also marginal benefits and marginal costs.

The efficient quantity of a public good is achieved when marginal cost equals marginal benefit, as shown in Figure 24-3. That quantity maximizes social surplus, which is the difference between total benefit and total cost. Maximum social surplus is shown as the shaded area in Figure 24-3.

For private goods, you receive something in exchange for your money. With public goods, the amount you consume seems unaffected by how much you spend. Whether you offer to pay a year's wages or nothing at all makes no discernible difference. You can still consume just as much of the public good as everyone else. The result is a **free-rider problem,** in which everyone has the incentive to let others pay the costs of providing the public good.

free-rider problem the incentive to avoid paying for a public good, because no one person's payment will have any appreciable effect on the quantity of the public good.

The laws of supply and demand apply as much to public goods as to private goods. The lower the price of a public good, the less producers are willing to sell and the more consumers are willing to buy. Unfortunately, because public goods are nonexcludable, they are free to use. You don't need to pay a thing. While we value public goods collectively, we do not volunteer to pay for them individually. Therefore, public goods will not be produced unless the government gets involved.

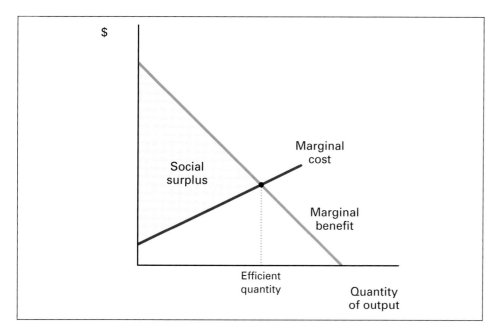

FIGURE 24-3

THE EFFICIENT QUANTITY OF A PUBLIC GOOD Just as for a private good, the efficient quantity of a public good occurs when the marginal benefit of another unit just equals its marginal cost. The shaded area is the social surplus from this quantity.

The solution to the free-rider problem involves taxation. Government compels everyone to contribute, since everyone shares in consuming public goods. How much money people are forced to contribute is then at the discretion of government rather than the consumer directly. Thus, nearly everyone would prefer either more or less government spending on any particular public good.

Sometimes, private entrepreneurs find ways to tie public goods to private goods that individuals or firms are willing to buy. For example, radio and television stations bundle their broadcasts with commercials. Because broadcasts are accessible to all, they are public goods and thus cannot be sold directly. However, commercials are private goods from the standpoint of advertisers. The more valuable the public good aspect of programming, the more stations can charge advertisers for air time. In this and many other cases, there is at least some private provision of public goods. Unfortunately, there is nothing that compels private markets to produce the most efficient quantity or variety of these goods.

The private marketplace also sometimes offers private alternatives to public goods. For example, if all police forces were to be eliminated, there would be a dramatic increase in the sales of firearms, alarm systems, and security guard services. Even so, public safety is likely to be maintained more efficiently through the provision of community-wide police services, a public good.

QUICKCHECK

Much of the content on the Internet is free to use, and yet it costs content providers money to construct and maintain their sites. Explain.

Answer: The free Internet content is offered as a public good in conjunction with advertisements, which hope to induce the web surfer to buy the advertised private goods. Other times, free sites are samples of higher quality restricted sites that the web surfer can access only by paying a fee. The public good is provided because it is tied to private goods.

SNAPSHOT   "WHAT'S A LITTLE SNOW?"

Every year or two, a blizzard will paralyze Washington, D.C., yet work goes on in Buffalo, New York. As one of the snowiest spots in the United States, the people of Buffalo are used to the white stuff. "So what's another foot or two?" they ask as they slog to their jobs, listening to the news reports of prolonged federal government shutdowns and other snow emergencies elsewhere.

True, Buffalonians are battle-hardened veterans of many a' winter campaign. But there is more to the story. What's missing is the part about the efficient choice of a local public good—snow removal. Officials in Buffalo know it's going to snow hard, nearly every year. It is thus efficient for them to spend heavily on snow plows and other capital equipment. With snowfalls much less frequent in other parts of the country, officials there find it more efficient to devote that money to other needs. The result is that when the infrequent blizzard does strike, the Buffalonians drive to work while the Washingtonians wait for a warm, sunny day. ◄

24.2 POLICY OPTIONS

In cases of pure public goods, government has little recourse but to produce the goods itself or provide government payment to private companies who in turn would produce the goods. However, as we move along the spectrum of market failure away from pure public goods, it becomes possible for government to use regulations or price incentives to guide the marketplace toward efficiency.

For example, highways are impure public goods that the government usually constructs by way of contracts with private companies. Once those highways are built, their use is regulated with drivers' licenses and speed limits. In addition, the government might charge for the use of particular highways through the assessment of *user fees,* known more familiarly in this application as tolls. In short, for impure public goods, the government's policy alternatives are of three general sorts:

■ **Government can price the good.** For example, tolls can discourage driving when roads are congested.
■ **Government can produce the good.** For example, most highways are built by government contractors and subcontractors.
■ **Government can regulate the good.** For example, certain highway lanes are reserved for busses or other high-occupancy vehicles—HOV lanes—so as to encourage carpooling or the use of mass transit.

PRICE INCENTIVES—THE CASE OF CONGESTION PRICING

Continuing with the example of highways, we now examine price incentives. Highways are subject to congestion, which you will recall is a frequent trait of impure public goods. Congestion is a special case of externality in which adding another user reduces the benefits received by other users. In the case of highways, additional drivers slow each other down.

Figure 24-4(a) illustrates how an existing highway becomes congested during peak hours. For example, a road that flows smoothly during most hours of the day might become a slow moving sea of vehicles during rush-hour traffic jams. In Figure 24-4(a), the marginal cost of highway usage is assumed to be zero until the point at which congestion sets in. That assumption is largely true for passenger cars, as almost all wear and tear on highways comes from weather and heavy trucks. After the point of congestion, however, adding more vehicles of any sort slows everybody down, which is costly in terms of time, fuel consumption, pollution, vehicle depreciation, and general annoyance.

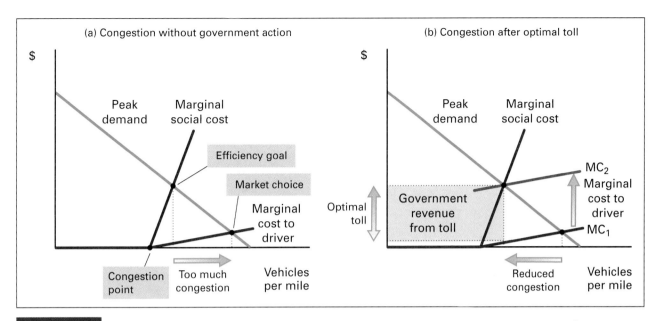

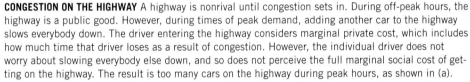

FIGURE 24-4

CONGESTION ON THE HIGHWAY A highway is nonrival until congestion sets in. During off-peak hours, the highway is a public good. However, during times of peak demand, adding another car to the highway slows everybody down. The driver entering the highway considers marginal private cost, which includes how much time that driver loses as a result of congestion. However, the individual driver does not worry about slowing everybody else down, and so does not perceive the full marginal social cost of getting on the highway. The result is too many cars on the highway during peak hours, as shown in (a).

Government can reduce highway usage to an efficient amount by assessing a toll on each driver during times of peak demand, as shown in (b). The optimal toll would increase marginal cost until it intersects demand at the efficient quantity, where the efficient quantity is given by the intersection of demand and marginal social cost. Revenue from the toll is the area of the shaded rectangle, which is obtained by multiplying the number of vehicles subject to the toll by the amount of the toll per vehicle.

The individual driver is motivated to avoid these congested roads only to the extent that it affects that driver personally—marginal private cost. However, there are additional costs to society—marginal social cost—because that driver's presence on the highway makes the problems of congestion worse for everybody else. The result is too much congestion as drivers make their decisions without reference to their own impact on the traffic jam. For this reason, a worker might wait a few minutes to avoid the peak of the evening rush hour, but could care less if his or her entry into the stream of traffic delays others.

Figure 24-4(b) shows how a toll could be used to achieve the efficient amount of congestion by raising the marginal cost perceived by the entering driver. Imposing a toll is becoming increasingly feasible for cities as surveillance technology advances, a reality to which drivers from Houston, Paris, London, Singapore, and numerous other cities can attest. For example, Singapore installed its electronic toll system in 1998, and now adjusts its toll to reflect the time of day and congestion.

Despite scathing protests from irate motorists, London assesses a toll of £5 (about $8) for driving into the downtown area. That toll is assessed remotely, by satellite. Curiously, a poll in early 2003 found that the sixth most popular reason for leaving England was to avoid congestion, with the seventh most popular reason being to avoid the toll that is designed to reduce that congestion.

It is often reasonable for drivers to prefer the inefficient highway congestion to the toll. The reason is that, although achieving efficiency means that society has more to go around, the drivers themselves could be worse off because the toll would collect a large amount of money from them. The total toll revenue is shown as the shaded area in Figure 24-4(b). Even if the money collected from drivers is used for good social purposes, the individual toll-payers no longer have it to spend for their own private purposes. In other words, along with the benefit of less congestion comes an income transfer away from the drivers paying the tolls.

GOVERNMENT PRODUCTION—THE ROLE OF COST-BENEFIT ANALYSIS

cost-benefit analysis the process of estimating the costs and benefits of alternative policy choices.

The previous section discussed how government can use price incentives to make efficient use of an existing highway that is sometimes congested. What if the highway is usually congested—should a new one be built? For the answer to that question and a myriad more, government turns to cost-benefit analysis. Government uses **cost-benefit analysis** to estimate and compare the costs and benefits of alternative policy choices.

Cost-benefit analysis is often complex. For example, to analyze costs and benefits of public actions requires that dollar values be assigned to both monetary and nonmonetary costs and benefits. Consider the seemingly simple matter of speed limits. We can save lives by reducing the speed limit on expressways to ten miles per hour. However, since we value our time as well as our safety, we prefer to go faster. But how much faster? Choosing the best speed limit requires the comparison of *intangibles,* which have no market price. Even so, researchers can often infer the value we implicitly place on intangibles, including the intangibles of safety and time.

For example, consider the value of a *statistical life,* which is the expectation of a life saved or lost as a result of a government action, when no one knows exactly whose life it will be. Raising speed limits costs statistical lives. Likewise, adding police officers saves statistical lives. We do not set speed limits at zero, nor do we spend all of our money on traffic patrols. So implicitly, we place a value on life in a statistical sort of way. Getting a handle on how much a statistical life is worth to us might involve looking at pay differentials between risky and nonrisky jobs, such as how much more pay construction workers receive to work on high-rise buildings where their lives are more at risk.

Another intangible is that, unlike private firms, the government cannot observe the prices at which its products sell in the marketplace because the market for its products does not exist. For example, what is the value of saving a wetland? No one offers to purchase public goods of this sort. Some of the best techniques to reveal the benefits of intangibles involve observing other market prices that relate to the good in question. For example, the cost of noise pollution from airplanes can be estimated by observing market prices for homes under takeoff and landing flight paths, and comparing those to market prices of similar homes in quieter locations.

There are many other techniques that policymakers use, depending on the specific types of intangibles that need measuring. Attaching dollar values provides a common measuring rod by which to measure things that are otherwise seemingly incomparable. Because the economy has scarce resources, such choices must be made.

QUICKCHECK

How can we estimate in dollars the damages from airplane noise?

Answer: Damages from airplane noise can be estimated by comparing the market value of land that is subject to plane noise to the market value of comparable land that is not. The difference in these market prices provides an estimate of the cost of noise.

REGULATION AND THE SPECIFICITY PRINCIPLE— AVOIDING UNINTENDED CONSEQUENCES

Regulation occurs whenever government acts to influence the specifications of goods and services or the manner in which they are produced. Speed limits, smoking bans, seat belt requirements, product standards, and workplace safety laws are a few of the many regulations that affect our daily lives. The extent to which various facets of our economy should or should not be regulated is one of the most controversial topics around.

> *A Few of the Many Things Regulated*
>
> **Regulations apply to:**
> *Labeling requirements for food*
> *Electricity consumption of air conditioners*
> *Width of doorways in the workplace*
> *Emission controls in cars*
> *Use of hard hats at construction sites*
> *Safety of children's toys*
> *Rest requirements for truckers and pilots*
> *Dimensions of wood sold as a 2 × 4*
> *Qualifications of professional wrestlers*

regulation occurs whenever the government acts to influence the specifications of goods and services or the manner in which they are produced.

In determining the type and amount of regulations to apply, policymakers should be aware of the regulations' *administrative and compliance costs.* To achieve efficiency, regulations should only be imposed to the extent that their benefits outweigh their costs, including costs of administration of compliance. **The marginal benefit of additional regulation should equal its marginal cost.** While it is often hard to quantify these benefits and costs, there is often a suspicion that regulation has gone overboard. For example, the paperwork and consulting fees spent on compliance with the myriad of government regulations is a daunting hurdle for new and growing businesses.

To ensure efficiency in regulation, it helps to "hit the nail on the head," a concept that is more formally known as the specificity principle. The **specificity principle** says to target the problem in as precise and narrow a manner as possible. Using the specificity principle, the best solution to a market failure is often not to abandon markets altogether by resorting to government command and control, but rather to correct only the problem within the market that is keeping it from being a success. By following the specificity principle, undesirable side effects of policy actions are kept to a minimum.

specificity principle the idea that policies should be targeted as narrowly and directly at a problem as possible.

APPLYING THE SPECIFICITY PRINCIPLE— RESOLVING URBAN WATER SHORTAGES

The specificity principle can be used to resolve urban water crises, those situations that periodically occur in cities around the country and around the world in which it might seem like a city's reservoirs are inadequate to meet demand. The reasons might be drought, the unexpected contamination of a reservoir, or earthquake damage to water distribution systems. In most cases, the reaction of urban water authorities is to make rules and regulations that govern how water can be used. The authorities might take it on themselves to declare what are essential uses and what are nonessential uses of water. They might set times for watering yards. They might require low-flow plumbing fixtures. They might assess surcharges for excessive water use. However, **the specific problem is not the specifics of water usage, but rather the lack of a market-clearing price.** Fix that underlying problem and the other problems fix themselves.

The complication is that municipal water distribution is a natural monopoly, and thus a legitimate candidate for regulation. In most major American cities, local government either controls the water supply or regulates the price charged by a protected monopoly franchise. Traditionally, as discussed in the chapter on monopoly, regulation takes the form of average-cost pricing, in which the authorities set the price so as to allow the firm only a normal profit. Unlike other cases of regulated monopoly, though, the quantity of water available at any given time is not easily adjustable. The government cannot make it rain. Unfortunately, aiming price to achieve a revenue objective does not allow it to also target the objective of allocative efficiency. That would require that price be set by the intersection of marginal cost and demand—*marginal-cost pricing*—which might be quite a bit higher in some regions.

Figure 24-5 illustrates the regulatory dilemma in the municipal water market, which is that one price cannot hit two targets. For simplicity, marginal cost is shown as vertical in the figure, as though there is zero marginal cost of using current sources up to the sustainable quantity, and no short-run possibilities of supplementing water supplies. Average cost would then be composed of only average fixed cost, and might be quite low as noted in the figure. In times of peak demand, such as in the dry days of a hot summer, there could be a wide gap between the average-cost price and the marginal-cost price. The result is the possible crisis of a water shortage, in which water reserves are drawn down in a manner that cannot be sustained. For example, it has been reported that the fast-growing city of Atlanta might already be using the maximum sustainable capacity of its reservoirs.

Alternatively, local governments frequently price discriminate, with some customers paying a much higher price than is paid by others. For example, authorities might raise the rates to punish large-volume users, and use the extra revenues to lower rates for everybody else. Unfortunately, the result still does not clear the market and is inefficient in that some customers value the last unit consumed more than other customers do.

There are often political reasons that run counter to the specificity principle. Most commonly, local government authorities might aim to keep prices low for the poor to avoid being accused of imposing what might be called a "water tax." If those authorities were to specify the public interest more fundamentally, though, it would be that their actions should not cause additional impoverishment. Therefore, there are really two goals: (1) to avoid a

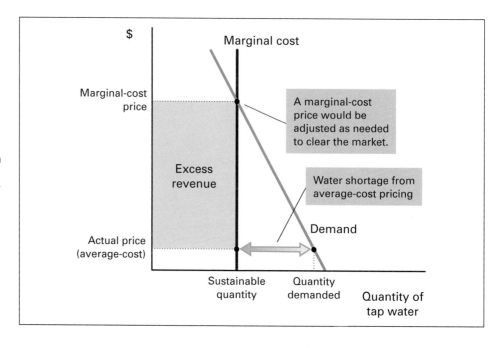

FIGURE 24-5

APPLYING THE SPECIFICITY PRINCIPLE TO AVOID WATER SHORTAGES A marginal-cost price clears the market, which avoids persistent water shortages. However, many cities choose to set the price of tap water on the basis of average cost in order to avoid revenue in excess of that needed to cover costs. A single price cannot satisfy both objectives.

QUICKCHECK

If there is a water shortage, why shouldn't the government just figure out who most needs the available water and allocate it to those people?

Answer: People are the best judges of their own water-use possibilities. Market price matches the product—water—to those for whom it is most valuable, meaning that those who buy it are willing to pay the most for it.

water shortage; and (2) to avoid hurting the poor. Price can only meet one of them. Since there are two goals, the specificity principle would suggest two separate policies, such as:

- A single market-clearing price that adjusts as needed to prevent shortages.
- Financial aid on the basis of income needs.

This second policy would not concern itself with water usage, except in the unlikely event that essential water needs would cost so much that they would affect the amount of income needed to escape poverty.

HEAR YE! MESSAGE YE!—AIRWAVES AT AUCTION   *SNAPSHOT*

The big news? It's about how you get to hear the news, or read the news, or message the news. The news is that government regulation of communication bandwidths now lets the market decide the details of which bandwidths are used for Internet access, cellular phones, paging, instant messaging, personal communication devices, or other modes of service. The Federal Communications Commission used to assign airwave frequencies to potential broadcasters, with all details spelled out. Now, in conformance with the specificity principle, the FCC tries to avoid regulating when the market does not fail. The result is that bandwidth rights are now sold at auction to the highest bidder in the free market. Let the invisible hand rule!

As the airwaves grow increasingly congested with cellular and wireless applications, the FCC has found further market-based avenues toward the public interest. To ensure that the available frequencies are used to their fullest and most valuable extent, the FCC no longer requires each bandwidth owner to obtain a government license for its use. Instead, the FCC now allows bandwidth owners to lease that bandwidth to others. Such efficient exchanges are ho-hum, everyday events in the marketplace. But ensuring that public policy does not tread on market efficiency? That's news! ◄

24.3 IMPERFECT INFORMATION

Everyone makes mistakes and, we hope, learns from those mistakes. We cannot know that we don't like the new flavor of yogurt until we try it. We cannot know if the shoe truly fits until we wear it. We do things that, with better information, we would have done differently. This is the problem of imperfect information, a problem that can lead to market failure. **Imperfect information** occurs when we do not fully understand the choices available to us, or the consequences of those choices.

In the laissez-faire marketplace, there will always be the unscrupulous willing to take advantage of the naive. There will be those who fall victim to scams and frauds because information is not fully shared. While government might step in and seek to help, it must recognize its own imperfections—it is neither all knowing, nor are its actions costless. While recognizing that it cannot solve all of the information problems in the marketplace, government nevertheless can and does look for ways to help.

imperfect information occurs when we do not fully understand the choices available to us, or the consequences of those choices.

For example, investors in Enron Corporation learned firsthand about the implications of imperfect information. At the start of 2001, Enron Corporation had a market value that placed it within the top ten of all U.S. corporations. Yet by the end of that year, Enron was bankrupt, with a debt load of $35 billion. Losing about 6,100 of the 7,500 employees it had in its heyday, Enron was forced to sell its gleaming 1.3 million square foot office tower in the heart of Houston and instead make do in 2004 with rented quarters of one million square feet less. The investors who had bid the price of Enron stock so high had been deceived by complicated and shady accounting practices that they did not understand. The market had made a mistake.

As a result of the Enron debacle, investors and analysts pored over the accounting statements of other companies very, very carefully. Investors had an incentive to do so because their own savings were on the line. This scrutiny caused investors to reallocate their money away from companies with suspect accounting practices, a process that increased both information flow and the efficiency of the market. The government also had a role to play. In 2002, the Securities and Exchange Commission took action to reevaluate the information that public companies were required by law to report to shareholders and when they were required to report it, and Congress enacted new laws governing corporate accountability.

ASYMMETRIC INFORMATION

asymmetric information when one person has access to more information than another on a subject of mutual interest.

When one person has access to more information than another on a subject of mutual interest, that person is said to possess **asymmetric information.** Asymmetric information is responsible for several puzzling facets of modern life. For example, the value of an automobile drops by a couple thousand dollars as soon as it is first sold. The reason is that prospective buyers of a used car are aware that the seller knows more about the car—the shoppers are aware of what they don't know. They figure that they are not told all of the reasons why the car is being sold and expect the car to have problems that will only become apparent over time.

Asymmetric information may be important to the value of the college degree you seek. If you are studying at one of the top ten universities in the country, for example, you are likely to find that your degree will be worth a great deal more in the job market than degrees held by people who have acquired an equal amount of knowledge at lesser-known schools. This is the problem of *credentialism,* in which people's skills and abilities are judged by the reputation of their degrees or other credentials. Employers use credentials as a way to ensure that their employees are intelligent and well trained. Since grading standards vary from school to school, and since the job interview process cannot hope to uncover all of an applicant's skills and abilities, employers pay more for degrees from schools they have heard of and trust. It often seems inequitable, but it can be efficient.

Asymmetric information provides at least part of the explanation for another phenomenon—*cronyism.* Cronyism occurs when employers hire friends, relatives, fellow church members, and so forth. That may be a profitable business practice if these employees are more reliable than strangers. While it seems unfair to applicants outside the group of cronies, cronyism probably does serve to reduce job turnover and minimize false credentials. Fair or not, cronyism offers a way to circumvent asymmetric information.

PROTECTING LIFE AND LIMB—GOVERNMENT'S ROLE IN WORKPLACE SAFETY

The search for profit motivates firms to implement numerous safety measures, even when no regulation forces them to do so. The rationale is that unsafe working conditions lead to various costs, such as those associated with interruptions in production. A dangerous firm must also offer higher wages and better benefits to attract workers. It would be forced to pay higher insurance premiums to cover healthcare expenses and liability. If these costs exceed the cost of the safety measures, a profit-maximizing firm will undertake the safety measures.

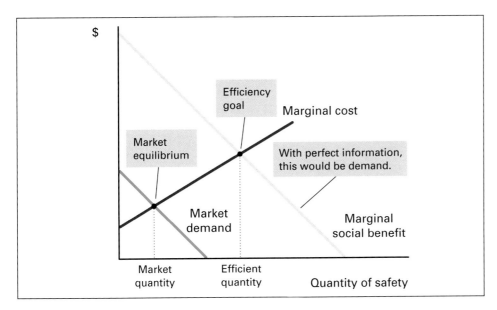

FIGURE 24-6

WORKPLACE SAFETY The efficient quantity of safety at the workplace occurs where marginal cost equals marginal benefit. The quantity chosen in the free market would be less than the efficient quantity if workers underestimate the value of safety measures.

Figure 24-6 shows, in principle, how to choose an efficient amount of safety. The idea is to keep adding safety measures so long as the marginal benefit exceeds the marginal cost. While the search for profit motivates the firm to implement safety measures, not all of the benefits from safety improvements might affect profit. If the safety measures don't, firms will not choose to be safe enough. This situation might occur if workers have insufficient information about the value of safety improvements. For example, the workers might not realize how risky a job actually is and thus be unwilling to sacrifice much pay or other benefits in order to receive extra safety. As a result of their workers' imperfect information, the firm perceives less than the true marginal benefits from safety and implements too few safety measures.

If firms do not undertake an efficient number of safety measures, there is a role for government regulators. Specifically, government regulators might estimate the efficient amount of safety and force firms to achieve that amount. However, it is difficult to estimate these marginal costs and benefits of extra safety, especially since different workers have different preferences when it comes to how much risk they are willing to accept in exchange for extra income.

It is impractical for government safety regulations to be tailored to the wants of different groups of workers. The result is that both firms and workers often complain about rigid work rules and safety measures. Some argue that the government should cut back its regulation of workplace safety. In that case, the government could still make information on workplace safety available to workers so that they could choose more efficiently. On the other hand, backers of government safety regulation point out that there are economies of scale in evaluating information about safety. From that perspective, it seems sensible to let experts in government evaluate the information and make more-informed choices than most workers could do themselves.

PUBLIC SAFETY—CRIME AND PUNISHMENT

Imperfect information is at the heart of criminal activity and the fight against it. Criminals constantly seek to hide their activities, while authorities seek to uncover them. In the United States, there are about 100,000 reported crimes per day (the exact number of actual crimes is unknown because many crimes go unreported).

Technology can provide information that assists in uncovering crime, but can also help the criminals themselves. For example, some parents use so-called nanny cams to

FIGURE 24-7

ECONOMICS OF CRIME Criminals compare their expected marginal benefits to expected marginal costs in deciding how much crime to commit, ignoring the costs to the victims of crime. Increasing the costs and/or lowering the benefits facing the criminal would reduce the amount of crime.

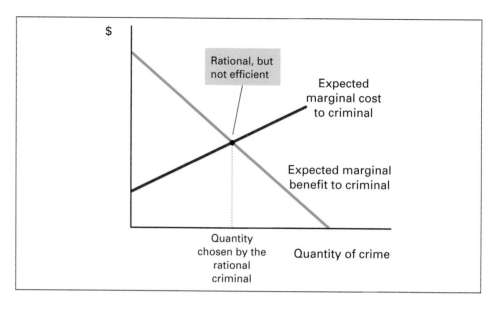

monitor activities in the house while they are away. These nanny cams often include wireless connections to the telephone or the Internet. Parents can dial up the proper connection and see for themselves what the camera sees. Unfortunately, high-tech criminals often can do the same thing, using the same signals that are meant to safeguard the house and its occupants. In this manner, criminals can find out when the parents are gone or when someone is home alone.

The costs of crime and crime prevention take many forms. People lose life and property. They pay higher taxes to support the police and criminal justice system. They also pay for deadbolts, alarm systems, guard dogs, and much more. Some flee to the suburbs or small towns. Others hide behind the walls of security-gated subdivisions in the hopes of escaping crime. Hidden costs include psychic costs associated with the fear of becoming a victim, and the loss of freedom when that fear limits activities.

What makes an individual turn to a life of crime? From an economic perspective, a criminal would consider the relative monetary and nonmonetary returns and weigh them against expected costs. These considerations are illustrated in Figure 24-7. **Because there is uncertainty attached to the outcome of criminal activity, the economic model of crime posits that criminals make decisions based on the** *expected marginal benefits* **and** *expected marginal costs* **of criminal activity.** On the cost side, the prospective criminal considers the uncertain expected punishment, where the

Expected punishment = Punishment for the crime ×
Probability of being caught and convicted

QUICKCHECK

If a thief steals a dollar, does economic analysis say that the punishment should be $1 plus costs of apprehension and prosecution, and no more?

Answer: No, in addition to considering the amount of damage caused by that one criminal incident, it is also important to consider that the thief faces only a small chance of being caught and convicted. For this reason, the punishment might be more severe than the crime.

The uncertainties of catching and convicting criminals mean that, for the punishments to serve as effective deterrents, they often seem harsh relative to the actual crime that the person committed.

Often they are nearly invisible. Other times, they are intentionally obvious. Sometimes they're even phony, just there to make us think twice about breaking the law. Increasingly, they are banned, made illegal by an exasperated public. They are the watchful cameras of the highways, carefully positioned to take our pictures as we speed, run red lights, or merely drive along a toll road. We might get those pictures in the mail, along with a bill for the toll or traffic fine we owe. The totals can be staggering. By 2003, for example, Washington, D.C.'s traffic cameras had caused D.C. drivers to fork over more than $50 million in fines.

Traffic cameras merely enforce the law, so why would anyone be upset? Perhaps it's the impersonality of it all. Perhaps we don't want to be watched so much. Perhaps it is that the penalties for our traffic violations were set with the idea that we usually don't get caught. In contrast, the modern technology of the traffic cam is coming to mean that we usually cannot escape. ◄

24.4 HEALTH INSURANCE—IS THERE A BETTER WAY?

The United States spends about $1.6 trillion per year on healthcare. About $200 billion of that cost goes to the administrative overhead involved with private health insurance. Even so, around 43 million Americans remain uninsured. These are people who find themselves without the healthcare benefits provided by full-time employment, but with too much wealth to qualify for government assistance from Medicaid.

In the August 2003 issue of the *Journal of the American Medical Association,* a "Physicians Working Group" of 8,880 doctors petitioned that the United States do away with its current system of medical coverage in favor of a national health insurance plan, such as those used in Canada or England. These doctors are hoping to persuade the rest of the profession, the large majority of which did not sign the petition (about 860,000 doctors practice in the United States). As we discuss below, while the problems are easy to see, the solutions are not so obvious.

Good health is an essential ingredient in the quality of our lives. Yet proper treatment is expensive and it takes specialized skills to know what to do. Healthcare accounts for roughly 14 percent of U.S. spending, compared to about 10 percent in Canada and 7 percent in Japan. A big part of healthcare's high cost lies in what we buy. Over time, healthcare has come to include increasingly sophisticated techniques. Because of healthcare's high and often unpredictable expenses, we typically resort to insurance. Sometimes that insurance is privately provided. Sometimes it is provided by the government through Medicaid for the poor or Medicare for the elderly. Figure 24-8 shows the sources and uses of medical spending in the United States.

For both physicians and patients, health insurance alters incentives. For example, a patient might pay *co-insurance*—a percentage of costs over some deductible amount. Or a patient might pay 20 percent of yearly healthcare expenses after paying a $300 deductible out-of-pocket.

Healthcare is provided by the insurance company in exchange for annual premiums, usually paid for by a person's employer. Because the per-unit price of healthcare is reduced to the patient, patients seek more of it, just as the law of demand would suggest. However, this lower price to patients does not mean the price paid to the health service providers has

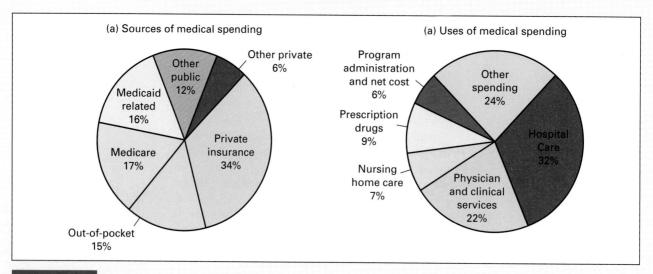

(a) Sources of medical spending

Other private 6%

Other public 12%

Medicaid related 16%

Medicare 17%

Private insurance 34%

Out-of-pocket 15%

(a) Uses of medical spending

Program administration and net cost 6%

Prescription drugs 9%

Nursing home care 7%

Other spending 24%

Hospital Care 32%

Physician and clinical services 22%

FIGURE 24-8

SOURCES AND USES OF MEDICAL SPENDING IN THE UNITED STATES Chart (a) shows the sources of medical spending in the United States for the year 2000. Chart (b) shows the uses of that spending.

Source: Centers for Medicare & Medicaid Services, Office of the Actuary, National Health Statistics Group.

fallen. The result is the problem of *moral hazard* in which the insurance has led to the overconsumption of healthcare services. Figure 24-9 illustrates how moral hazard leads patients to consume too much medical care.

Examples provided by the fifty-year-old National Health Service in Great Britain offer clear evidence of moral hazard. Healthcare in Great Britain is free at the point of service. For that reason, a large proportion of those who make appointments with their family doctors have no good medical reason to do so, resulting in less care for those who really need it. So-called free medical care also delays treatment, sometimes for years if the ailment is placed in a non-urgent category.

FIGURE 24-9

MORAL HAZARD AND PRICE SURPRISES Moral hazard results when insurance lowers the price of healthcare for the recipient, thus causing an increase in the quantity of services demanded beyond what is efficient. Additional inefficiency results when insurance does not cover a charge and the patient is faced with a price surprise—a charge that exceeds what insurers would have paid.

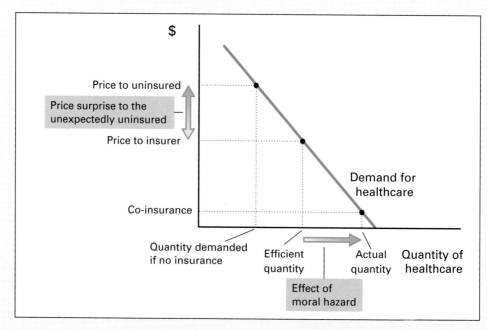

Figure 24-9 also shows another problem in the healthcare market, this one having to do with information. Typically, healthcare providers bill the insurance company for more than contractually agreed-upon rates. This is not usually a problem, as the insurer merely adjusts the charges downward to what is allowable. However, it becomes a problem if for some reason the patient is not covered by insurance. In that case, the patient is surprised with the full charge, labeled in the graph as the price to the uninsured. If this price was known beforehand, patients would have shopped for lower rates or reduced their quantities demanded. The higher price to the uninsured is a way for hospitals, physicians, and other healthcare providers to supplement the low rates paid under government and private insurance plans, rates that cover variable costs but not always fixed costs. The problem revolves around the fairness of this practice to the patient and the efficiency of patient choices in the absence of complete information.

The price of buying insurance is also high for individuals. To understand why, consider the incentives facing insurance companies. These companies are in business to provide a positive return to their investors, not to give away services that cost more than the value of the premiums they receive. Consequently, they try to distinguish between ex ante (before the fact) and ex post (after the fact) conditions. The laws of probability allow insurers to cover conditions ex ante.

For example, suppose you have the same chance as everybody else of coming down with some medical condition. By covering many people, most of whom will have no cause to file claims, the insurer can profitably offer you coverage at a fraction of treatment costs. Ex post is another story altogether. If you already have a condition, the insurance company could make money only if they charged you at least the full cost of treatment. That would be no insurance at all! In other words, once you come down with a condition, you lose your option of initiating insurance coverage at an affordable rate.

Even if you do not have any particular medical problems, you still cannot get an individual policy at a price approaching that of a group insurance plan. For example, if you attempt to purchase insurance with coverage identical to that offered by employers, you would be charged a great deal more. The reason revolves around asymmetric information. Even if you do not have any particular condition yet, you probably know much better than the insurance company which conditions you would be most susceptible to. Asymmetric information leads to the problem of *adverse selection*—those who seek out insurance coverage are the most likely to need it.

Because of adverse selection, the expected cost to the insurance company of writing an individual policy is much higher than the expected cost per person under a group policy. Insurance companies that survive in the marketplace must know this, and thus charge individuals a higher price to reflect the higher costs. The lowest rates go to groups that cannot easily be joined just for the insurance, which explains why most people receive health insurance coverage through their employers.

UNIVERSAL HEALTHCARE

Healthcare expenses can vary dramatically and unpredictably from person to person. This uncertainty motivates us to want insurance. We want others to be covered, too, including the sick and injured who cannot help themselves. This is a motivation for *universal coverage*—equal access to healthcare for everyone—which requires government action to achieve.

Universal coverage would overcome the problem of adverse selection because we would all be in the same group. By forcing everyone to participate, universal coverage would also avoid the free-rider problem, which occurs when people figure that some safety-net level of coverage will be available to them whether they contribute insurance premiums or not. However, universal coverage raises a new set of issues. For example, if everyone is to be covered, what should that coverage consist of? Should we eliminate all choice? Who should pay? What about malpractice? Indeed, by expanding the use of the healthcare system and bureaucracy within that system, universal coverage would probably make the problem of moral hazard worse.

In 1993, President Clinton submitted to Congress a sweeping 1,342 page proposal that called for all Americans to be provided with national health insurance, giving citizens complete freedom to choose their own doctors. However, all doctors would have been forced to charge the same "community standard" price, a form of price control. That prospect frightened many people, and led to the proposal's resounding defeat.

There was good reason for concern. Under community standard pricing, doctors with the best reputations would be flooded with potential patients. The competitive response would have these superior doctors turn many patients away and keep others waiting. There would be long waits prior to scheduled appointments, and then long waits in the office before patients would be seen. The patients wind up paying extra, but the payments are in time, not money. Likewise, doctors with good reputations cannot be expected to spend time on tricky cases when they could process the easy ones much faster for more money. The result would be inefficiency. The best doctors would take the easy cases, leaving the tough ones for the less highly skilled. Even though price controls under universal coverage would not work well, the issue of costly care demands attention. Unfortunately, the solutions remain elusive.

THINKING CRITICALLY

1. **Suppose the government were to enact universal coverage with $2,500 deductibles. What problems would that policy solve? What problems would it cause?**

2. **One of the most significant costs of modern medicine involves malpractice insurance. Should the government limit the amounts that juries are allowed to award victims of medical malpractice, so as to reduce malpractice insurance premiums and thereby lower healthcare costs? Explain.**

 Visit **www.prenhall.com/ayers** for updates and web exercises on this Explore & Apply topic.

SUMMARY AND LEARNING OBJECTIVES

1. **Distinguish among private goods, public goods, externalities, and common property resources.**
    - Market failure occurs when markets fail to achieve efficiency.
    - A good is said to be excludable when someone can be prevented from consuming the good. A good is said to be rival when one person's consumption of the good subtracts from the consumption of another person.
    - Pure private goods are excludable and rival. The goods we buy from retail sellers are almost always private goods.
    - A pure public good, such as national defense, is nonexcludable and nonrival. Pure public goods are consumed equally by everyone. National defense is the best example.
    - Public goods are usually impure, combining to some degree the qualities of a pure public good and a private good. Impure public goods are thus somewhat excludable and rival. Congestion occurs when one user of an impure public good reduces the consumption of another.

    - Between the extremes of pure private goods and pure public goods lie common property resources and private goods with externalities. Common property resources involve shared ownership of natural resources.
    - Private goods sometimes generate externalities. Externalities can be either positive, conferring benefits on third parties, or negative, which impose costs on third parties.

2. **Explain why the private marketplace fails to offer public goods in efficient quantities.**
    - The value of a public good is the sum of the values placed on the good by all the individuals who consume it.
    - The efficient quantity of a public good occurs at the point where marginal benefit equals marginal cost. Social surplus, the area under marginal benefit and above marginal cost, is maximized at this point.
    - The free-rider problem occurs when people seek to consume a public good without having to pay for it. Taxation forces those who would otherwise be free-

riders to pay part of the cost of providing a public good. Were the private sector to provide public goods, free-riding could not be eliminated because private-sector firms have no power to tax.

3. **Identify an optimal amount of highway congestion and policies to achieve that amount.**
    - Highway congestion provides an example of why highways are an impure public good. When another vehicle enters a congested highway, the already slow flow of traffic is further impeded. Each additional vehicle slows down traffic even more. The marginal cost of more vehicles rises accordingly.
    - The efficient number of cars on a congested highway will be less than the actual number.
    - Government policy alternatives that would promote efficiency are of three kinds. First, the government could impose a toll for the use of a highway. Second, the government can produce more highways. Third, use of the highway can be regulated, such as through HOV lanes on a freeway.
    - Cost-benefit analysis is used to make decisions about how much of a public good to produce. Intangibles are things that have no market price. They make cost-benefit analysis complex, since it is difficult to put a value on an intangible. Nonetheless, to be accurate, a cost-benefit analysis must estimate the dollar values of intangibles.

4. **Describe why government enacts regulations and what principles can guide it toward efficiency.**
    - Government regulation specifies product characteristics or production methods. Examples include automobile seatbelt requirements and workplace safety laws.
    - Regulation by the government contributes to greater efficiency only if the benefits outweigh the costs associated with regulation. Costs include both administrative and compliance costs. Regulation is controversial, with concerns over the costs of overregulation at the forefront of the controversy.
    - To enhance economic efficiency, additional regulation should only be carried to the point where the marginal cost and marginal benefit are equal. However, government actions may cause undesirable side effects if not targeted precisely. Precise targeting is an application of the specificity principle.
    - Water shortages exemplify what can happen when the specificity principle is not used. Municipal water markets are characterized by monopoly providers of tap water. Price can be used to avoid shortages if set

on the basis of marginal cost. However, price is often targeted for a different objective, such as to limit revenue. One policy instrument cannot meet both goals simultaneously.

5. **Explain the concept of asymmetric information and how it influences market outcomes.**
    - Imperfect information is a problem for people because better information makes for better decisions. Imperfect information can be the basis for government action, but the private marketplace can also help.
    - Asymmetric information describes a situation where one party to a transaction has information that the other does not have. Used-car buyers and sellers negotiate a sale on the basis of asymmetric information, with the seller having more information than the buyer. Credentialism is one outcome of asymmetric information. Cronyism is another.
    - Lack of information can cause the workplace to be unsafe. Specifically, if workers have imperfect information about job-related risks to their health, they will demand less safety of their employers than they would if they had perfect information. Government health and safety regulations can force employers toward the social optimum, the point where marginal social benefit equals marginal cost.

6. **Apply the analysis of marginal costs and marginal benefits to explain criminal behavior.**
    - Potential criminals make decisions based on the expected marginal benefits and the expected marginal costs of an action. The cost that a criminal would consider is the expected punishment, which is the punishment multiplied by the probability of being caught and convicted.
    - The rational quantity of criminal acts is the quantity associated with the point where the expected marginal benefit equals the expected marginal cost.

 Identify major issues in healthcare and alternative ways of addressing them.
    - Insurance creates the problem of moral hazard. Moral hazard lowers the price of healthcare for patients and thus causes the quantity demanded of healthcare to exceed the efficient quantity. Asymmetric information creates the problem of adverse selection for insurance companies, in which those most in need of insurance are the most likely to seek it. Universal coverage would overcome the adverse selection problem, but not the problem of moral hazard.

KEY TERMS

market failure, 608

private goods, 608

public goods, 608

congestion, 609

local public good, 609

common property resource, 609

externality, 609

external costs, 609

external benefits, 609

free-rider problem, 610

cost-benefit analysis, 614

regulation, 615

specificity principle, 617

imperfect information, 617

asymmetric information, 618

TEST YOURSELF

TRUE OR FALSE

1. Excludable and rival describe pure public goods.
2. Private goods are never pure because of the existence of externalities.
3. An efficient quantity can be identified for a private good, but not for a public good.
4. The free-rider problem is addressed through taxation.
5. Government should establish regulations whenever there is imperfect information.

MULTIPLE CHOICE

6. The distinction between impure and pure public goods is that impure public goods
   a. are rival but not excludable.
   b. are excludable but not rival.
   c. are sometimes either excludable or rival.
   d. must be paid for through taxation, while pure public goods cost nothing.

7. The value of a public good
   a. is indicated by its demand curve.
   b. cannot be known, even in principle.
   c. is the sum of its values to all consumers.
   d. equals the sum of all taxes paid that are spent on the good.

8. The efficient quantity of a good is identified by
   a. public opinion polls.
   b. its market-equilibrium price.
   c. the point where the good's marginal benefit equals its marginal cost.
   d. the government's Office of Equity and Efficiency (OEE).

9. The free-rider problem is associated with
   a. downtown bus terminals.
   b. pure private goods.
   c. the poverty problem.
   d. public goods.

10. In Self-Test Figure 24-1, congestion sets in at quantity
    a. *A.*
    b. *B.*
    c. *C.*
    d. *D.*

11. In Self-Test Figure 24-1, what tax would achieve an efficient result?
    a. *E − F*
    b. *F − C*
    c. *E − C*
    d. *G − D*

12. What technique does the government use to decide how much of a public good to provide?
    a. Specificity analysis
    b. Cost-benefit analysis
    c. Public opinion polls and surveys
    d. None, since politics settle the matter

13. Intangibles
    a. are easily measured.
    b. is another name for the free-rider problem.
    c. are irrelevant to decision making.
    d. are included in cost-benefit analysis.

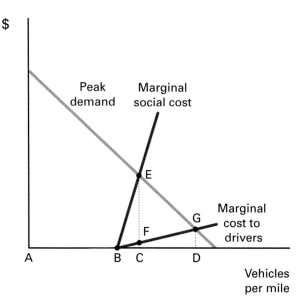

SELF-TEST FIGURE 24-1

14. In assessing costs and benefits, the value of a statistical life is
    a. ignored.
    b. assumed to be zero.
    c. infinite.
    d. based on people's willingness to accept risk.
15. In determining the efficient type and amount of regulation to apply, policymakers should follow the rule that
    a. total benefit = total cost.
    b. marginal benefit = marginal cost.
    c. average cost = average benefit.
    d. marginal revenue = marginal cost.
16. In the municipal water market shown in Self-Test Figure 24-2, the two-headed arrow represents the water
    a. shortage when price is based on average cost.
    b. shortage when price is based on marginal cost.
    c. surplus when price is based on average cost.
    d. surplus when price is based on marginal cost.

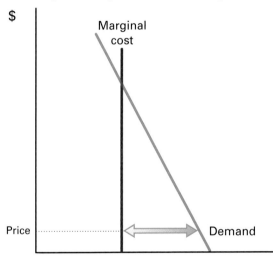

SELF-TEST FIGURE 24-2

17. If policymakers have the objectives of both efficiency and a low burden on the poor, the specificity principle suggests that they should set the price of tap water to equal
    a. zero, because water is a public good.

    b. average cost, because average-cost pricing is both efficient and fair.
    c. average cost and use other policies to address the issue of poverty.
    d. marginal cost and use other policies to address the issue of poverty.
18. Of the following, the most likely explanation for cronyism is
    a. asymmetric information.
    b. the free-rider problem.
    c. common-property resources.
    d. the specificity principle.
19. The expected punishment for committing a crime equals
    a. the punishment for the crime.
    b. the probability of being caught and convicted.
    c. the punishment for the crime plus the probability of being caught and convicted.
    d. the punishment for the crime multiplied by the probability of being caught and convicted.
20. Referring to Self-Test Figure 24-3, moral hazard is most likely to lead to the change shown by arrow
    a. *A*.
    b. *B*.
    c. *C*.
    d. *D*.

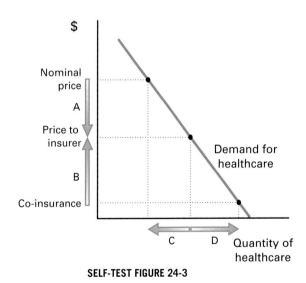

SELF-TEST FIGURE 24-3

QUESTIONS AND PROBLEMS

1. *[public goods]* Define and give several examples of public goods. Categorize each of your examples as a pure public good or an impure public good.
2. *[pure public goods]* Describe the nature of a pure public good and contrast it to an impure public good. Are most public goods pure or impure?

3. *[public goods]* List at least five public goods that are valuable to you personally. Are these public goods provided by the government or the private sector? For the public goods provided by the government, could these public goods also be provided by the private sector? Explain.

4. *[value of a public good]* Suppose that there is a public good consumed by Marsha, Marshall, and Maybell. Marsha values her consumption of this good at $3. Marshall values his consumption of the good at $7. Maybell values her consumption of the good at $1. Assume this public good is a pure public good as you answer the following questions.
   a. Will Maybell consume the good? Why or why not?
   b. Will Marshall consume more, less, or the same amount of this good as Marsha?
   c. What is the value of this public good, assuming that Marsha, Marshall, and Maybell are its only consumers?

5. *[excludability]* Describe what is meant when a good is said to be excludable. Why is the term "rival" also applied to excludable goods?

6. *[market failure]* Is market failure most often associated with purely private goods or with public goods? Explain.

7. *[graphing the efficient quantity of a public good]* Illustrate the efficient quantity of a public good with a graph. Be sure to label the axes, the curves drawn, and the efficient quantity. Write a short paragraph explaining the reasoning behind the efficient quantity.

8. *[free-rider problem]* Explain how the free-rider problem causes private markets to provide too little of a public good.

9. *[highway congestion]* Construct a graph that models the problem of highway congestion. After drawing the axes and labeling them, draw the downward-sloping demand curve for highway use. Then identify the congestion point on the horizontal axis. Add the average cost and marginal cost curves to your graph. Finish the graph by showing the efficient quantity and the actual quantity of vehicles per mile of highway.

   Use this graph to discuss the most congested highway or street that you know. Your discussion should include the following points:
   a. Approximately how many hours per weekday is the highway congested?
   b. Is the highway equally congested on weekends?

c. Provide an estimate of the congestion point for this highway.
   d. Estimate the cost to a driver of the average amount of congestion on the highway.
   e. Do you think that some drivers try to stay off the highway at times of peak congestion? What alternatives are available to them that would make that possible?
   f. Would it be feasible to reduce congestion on this highway by use of a toll? How large do you think the toll would need to be if it were feasible?
   g. What other alternatives might be implemented to reduce congestion on this highway?

10. *[cost-benefit analysis]* The presence of intangibles makes it much more difficult to estimate costs and benefits for public-sector projects than for private-sector projects. Give an example of an intangible that might need to be measured in a public-sector cost-benefit analysis, and suggest how the estimation might be performed.

11. *[regulation]* It is difficult to get a handle on the costs to firms of identifying and complying with regulations. For this reason, such costs are often ignored. Explain why the costs are difficult to compute and what problems arise when they are ignored.

12. *[specificity principle]* Apply the specificity principle to the problem of homelessness by writing five debatable arguments that embody the specificity principle and that could be raised during a discussion about the homeless at a city council meeting.

13. *[specificity principle]* "Water is a necessity and thus should be provided by government to everyone at very low prices." Comment on the assertion that water is a necessity. Does it follow that necessities should be provided cheaply by government? Explain.

14. *[workplace safety]* Should all available safety devices be provided to employees by their employer? Explain your answer in terms of the efficient quantity of safety.

15. *[crime]* Does the economic approach to crime assume that criminals are rational? Explain.

WORKING WITH GRAPHS AND DATA

1. *[congestion pricing]* Graph 24-1 shows the model of congestion of a highway, with no action by the government.
   a. Label the congestion point as point *A*. Why is the marginal cost of using the road equal to zero up to point *A*?
   b. Label the marginal cost to the driver as point *C* and the actual number of vehicles per mile as point *B* during peak demand.

c. Identify the efficient number of vehicles per mile as point *F*. Why is the marginal social cost of the last vehicle to enter the highway higher than the marginal cost to the driver of that vehicle?
   d. Identify the optimal toll as point *E* and draw a curve showing the marginal cost to the driver with the optimal toll.

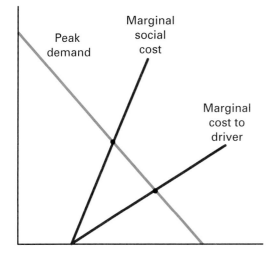

GRAPH 24-1

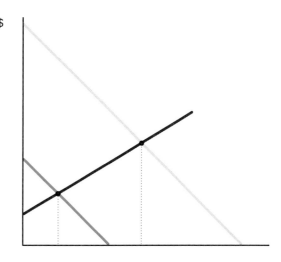

GRAPH 24-2

2. *[efficient quantity of a public good]* Suppose that the marginal cost and marginal benefit of a public good are as shown in the following table.

Quantity of the Public Good	Marginal Benefit	Marginal Cost
0	—	—
1	$11	$2
2	9	3
3	7	4
4	5	5
5	0	6

a. What is the efficient quantity of the public good? Why is this the efficient quantity?

b. Draw the marginal cost and marginal benefit curves. Label them "Marginal benefit" and "Marginal cost." Label the horizontal axis "Quantity" and the vertical axis "$."

c. Show the efficient quantity on the graph. Label the efficient point on the marginal cost and marginal benefit curves as point *E.*

d. Show the social surplus on the graph and label it "Social surplus."

3. *[protecting life and limb in the workplace]* Use Graph 24-2 to answer the questions that follow.

a. Assume that the workers underestimate the value to themselves of safety in this market. Label the market demand curve for safety as D_1 and the marginal cost curve of safety as MC.

b. Identify the market equilibrium point as *A* and the equilibrium quantity of safety as Q_1.

c. Identify the marginal social benefit curve that would result from the provision of perfect safety information. This would be the demand for safety under conditions of perfect knowledge. Label this curve D_2.

d. Show the efficient quantity of safety as Q_2 and label the point on the graph where it is determined as *B.* What economic problem exists that causes there to be a difference between Q_1 and Q_2? What is this problem called if the firms in this market do have perfect information but choose only those that affect the firms' profits and do not implement the others while workers underestimate safety measures that are not implemented?

4. *[healthcare]* Draw a possible demand for healthcare in Graph 24-3.

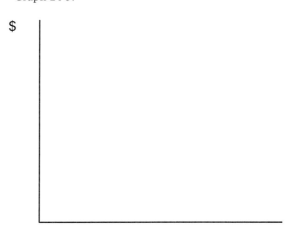

GRAPH 24-3

a. Identify the point on demand corresponding to the price paid by the insurer. Identify the price to the insurer as P_1 and the quantity of healthcare consumed as Q_1.

b. Identify the point on demand that is associated with the co-insurance payment by an insured person. Identify the co-insurance amount paid as P_2 and the actual quantity of healthcare consumed as Q_2. What economic problem is associated with the difference between Q_1 and Q_2?

c. Identify the point on demand that corresponds to the price paid by an unexpectedly uninsured per-

son. Identify the price paid as P_3 and the quantity demanded of healthcare consumed by the uninsured person as Q_3. What is the difference between P_2 and P_3 called?

d. Suppose that an uninsured person wishes to buy private health insurance. What is the price that the person would be likely to pay for insurance for the treatment of a medical condition for which he/she had previously been treated assuming that an insurance company would sell that person a policy? Why?

 Visit **www.prenhall.com/ayers** for Exploring the Web exercises and additional self-test quizzes.

CHAPTER 25

EXTERNALITIES AND COMMON PROPERTY RESOURCES

A LOOK AHEAD

Picture yourself driving down the highway, enjoying the view of rolling green fields of corn or a striking city skyline. These are positive externalities that add to your driving pleasure. And then there are those external costs, you realize, as a car in the other lane cuts you off in order to avoid the mangled tire tread lying in the roadway. To offset your adrenaline surge, you roll down the window for some fresh air. Instead you find yourself engulfed in foul-smelling fumes from other vehicles. You have just experienced a few of the many externalities in life, ones that cause markets to be less than efficient.

If your journey takes you to public land, such as a forest or beach, do you have enough incentive to conserve it for others? Do they have enough incentive to conserve it for you? The common property nature of the resource suggests not, as we shall see.

Government can step into the picture to make us all more concerned with our effects upon one another. But what should government aim for, and what are the best ways to achieve those aims? This chapter focuses on the market failures of pollution and common property resources in identifying the problems and appropriate policies. The Explore & Apply section at the end of the chapter examines what governments can do when externalities extend across countries' borders.

LEARNING OBJECTIVES

Understanding Chapter 25 will enable you to:
1. **Identify examples of externalities and common property resources.**
2. **Analyze the effects of externalities on efficiency.**
3. **Explain why common property resources are likely to be overused.**
4. **Discuss the policy instruments that government can use to promote a better environment.**
5. **Identify the efficient amount of pollution and the policies to achieve it.**
6. **Discuss the issue of transborder pollution and the difficulties in finding solutions.**

Explore & Apply

In the previous chapter we saw how market failure could lead to inefficiencies. This chapter looks more closely at two of those sources of inefficiency. We then examine alternative policy actions that are intended to help.

externalities side effects of production or consumption that affect third parties who have no say in the matter.

common property resource a jointly owned resource, such as groundwater.

Recall that **externalities** occur when the production or consumption of private goods leads to costs or benefits to third parties, meaning people or businesses who are not party to the transaction. Recall that market failure also occurs when the ownership of property is shared, meaning that it is *common property*. Shared ownership occurs most frequently in connection with natural resources such as air and water, thus leading to the term **common property resource.** As shown in the sections that follow, the analyses of externalities and common property resources have much in common.

EXTERNALITIES—WHEN SHOULD THERE BE ACTION?

external costs or benefits value lost to (or gained by) third parties who are not represented by market supply and demand.

Externalities can be either negative or positive. Pollution is an example of a negative externality. Negative externalities impose **external costs** on others. For example, to the extent that air pollution causes health problems or decreases people's enjoyment of outdoor activities, the pollution has imposed external costs on its victims. Conversely, positive externalities confer **external benefits,** such as when a neighbor kills all the mosquitos on her property, which leaves fewer to fly into your own backyard. A few of the many examples of externalities are listed in Table 25-1.

private costs or benefits costs or benefits that are borne by the decision maker, such as a buyer or seller.

social costs or benefits the sum of all costs or all benefits to all members of society; includes both private and external costs and benefits.

Externalities in the form of external benefits or external costs are all around us, although frequently they are of minor significance. Externalities occur when the **private costs or benefits** of an action—those borne by the ones taking the action—differ from social costs or benefits. **Social costs or benefits** are defined to equal all costs or benefits within the economy, including both private and external costs and benefits, as follows:

$$\text{Social cost} = \text{Private cost} + \text{External cost}$$

and

$$\text{Social benefit} = \text{Private benefit} + \text{External benefit}$$

By the same token, consider the costs and benefits associated with each additional unit of output, as follows:

$$\text{Marginal social cost} = \text{Marginal private cost} + \text{Marginal external cost}$$

and

$$\text{Marginal social benefit} = \text{Marginal private benefit} + \text{Marginal external benefit}$$

marginal external costs or benefits externalities that cause market outcomes to be inefficient.

It is externalities that occur at the margin—**marginal external costs** and **marginal external benefits**—that are of most interest in economics, because these externalities at the margin cause market outcomes to differ from what is efficient.

Significant external benefits are not as widespread as significant external costs, but do exist. For example, constructing a beautiful new house in a shabby neighborhood will increase the value of other homes in that neighborhood. Likewise, people who successfully pull themselves out of poverty or other difficult situations serve as valuable role models for others seeking to escape similar situations.

In the case of an external benefit as shown in Figure 25-1, market demand does not include all social benefits. External benefits might arise from education, perhaps because an

TABLE 25-1   EXTERNALITIES ALL AROUND US

SAMPLE ACTIVITIES WITH EXTERNAL BENEFITS	SAMPLE ACTIVITIES WITH EXTERNAL COSTS
Answering questions in class	Allowing your cell phone to ring in class
Looking your best	Being distracted by your cell phone while driving
Having your car washed	Driving a vehicle that emits exhaust gas
Getting immunized against disease	Using river water to remove industrial waste
Inspiring others with your ideas and actions	Burning coal to generate electricity

educated person makes better choices in the voting booth. While of value to others, there is no payment to the individual to motivate him or her to choose the socially efficient amount. For that reason, **when marginal external benefits are present, the free market produces too little—output falls short of the quantity that would be efficient.**

The most obvious external cost is from environmental pollution. For example, fumes from the tailpipe of a diesel bus do not bother either the passengers or the bus company. Rather, the cost is external—the fumes bother the drivers behind. Would you wish to follow a gravel truck that drops sand and pebbles that threaten to damage your vehicle? The cost of chipped paint on your PT Cruiser is of no concern to The Pits Gravel Company unless, perhaps, it fears a lawsuit or government reprisal.

Because external costs or benefits are not felt by the person or firm causing the externality, the free-market price signal fails to generate efficient outputs. For example, Figure 25-2 shows the supply and demand for a product that has an external cost. The supply curve represents marginal private cost, but fails to reflect full marginal social cost. Thus, **when marginal external costs are present, the free market produces too much—output exceeds the quantity that would be efficient.**

Marginal external cost is shown to be rising with output, meaning that the difference between supply and marginal social cost rises with increasing output. This is a typical

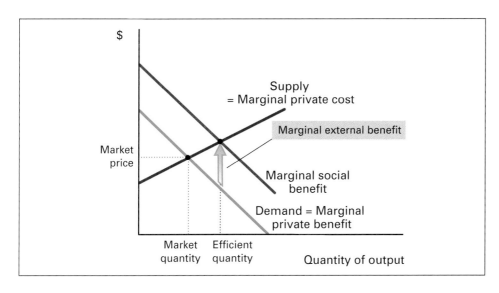

$

Supply
= Marginal private cost

Marginal external benefit

Market
price

Marginal social
benefit

Demand = Marginal
private benefit

Market   Efficient
quantity   quantity

Quantity of output

FIGURE 25-1

EXTERNAL BENEFITS—TOO LITTLE PRODUCED The intersection of market demand and supply determine market quantity. Even if we cannot measure what it is exactly, we can still infer that the existence of any marginal external benefits at this quantity would mean that the market produces less than would be efficient, as shown.

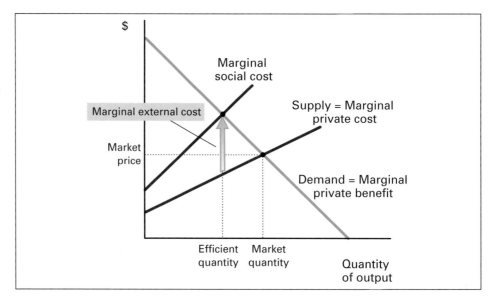

FIGURE 25-2

EXTERNAL COSTS—TOO MUCH PRODUCED When external costs are present, supply lies below marginal social cost and the free market produces more than would be efficient.

result, because the usual external cost comes from pollution and results in a degradation in environmental quality. Environmental quality is a public good, with a demand curve that is downwardly sloping, as discussed in the previous chapter. Pollution reduces the quantity of environmental quality, as shown in Figure 25-3(a). The external cost of smoke from a factory, for example, is the reduction in environmental quality as that smoke disperses. The

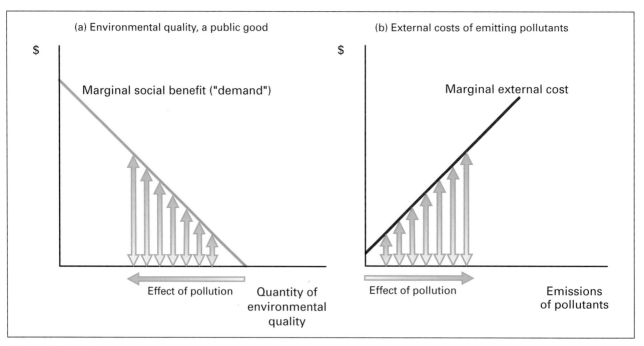

FIGURE 25-3

THE LINK BETWEEN ENVIRONMENTAL QUALITY AND EXTERNAL COSTS Environmental quality is a public good. Pollution reduces the amount of environmental quality, as shown in (a). The marginal external cost curve shown in (b) is a mirror image of the lower part of the "demand" for public goods. It shows the marginal cost of forgoing environmental quality. The curve starts above zero, because there is some environmental degradation that occurs naturally, such as when lightning starts a forest fire.

marginal external costs of pollution are nothing more than the marginal benefits of environmental quality forgone, as shown in Figure 25-3(b). Observe that the marginal external cost curve intersects the vertical axis above zero. The reason is that there are some natural sources of pollution, such as from forest fires started by lightning.

The presence of external costs does not imply that the externality-generating activity should cease. It is efficient to have some pollution, for example. In the course of a day's living, we are each responsible for pollution, such as from the tailpipe of the vehicles that take us where we want to go. Additional pollution is generated in producing the products we buy.

Are manufacturers evil people, who pollute so that we will be miserable? Actually, pollution results from firms using air or water to remove the wastes that are generated by their production of goods and services. The principle of mass balance, a physical law, implies that some waste will always occur when inputs are transformed into outputs. This waste must go somewhere, and water and air provide handy waste removal services.

Lacking government action, polluters pollute too much. The reason is that there is no market for many environmental services. "No market" means just that. The discharge of pollutants into the air, or into lakes, rivers, streams, aquifers, or the ocean can be carried out free of charge because the air and water are publicly owned. There are no sellers of air and flowing water in the marketplace to collect the revenue for their use. The outcome when there is no market is a price of zero.

However, there is a market for some environmental waste-removal services. For instance, firms economize on the solid wastes they generate when they must pay the trash collector to have these wastes disposed of. That's because someone owns the landfill where trash is dumped. In contrast, in the case of liquid and gaseous waste, firms have no incentive to cut back on the production of these pollutants if they can use the publicly owned environment—air and water—to remove these wastes for free.

WHEN MARKETS ARE MISSING

If environmental services provided by common-property water and air were priced, as they would be if sold in a market, firms would economize and pollute less. They would compute how valuable pollution is to them in terms of the extra output it allows. They would also look for alternate ways to produce their output with less pollution. The upshot is that firms would pollute only when the value of their pollution exceeds its environmental costs. That would be efficient.

Occasionally, firms compete on the basis of how environmentally friendly—how "green"—their products are. For example, consumers may pay extra for recycled paper or nontoxic antifreeze. However, consumers rarely seek information on how much pollution is generated in the production of the products they buy, and are rarely willing to pay much of a premium for green products.

Typically, then, competition forces firms to be environmentally neglectful unless there are public policy incentives to be otherwise. Were a firm to go to the expense of cutting back its pollution, that firm would be at a disadvantage in competing against other firms in its industry. Only the heaviest polluters would survive. This is why pollution externalities represent a market failure, one calling for government action to change the rules of the game. The Clean Air Act was one such action. This Act, amended in 1970, has caused the emission of major air pollutants to fall dramatically, as shown in Figure 25-4.

While reliance on public policy is commonplace, it is not the only means to resolve externalities. An alternative would rely on legal safeguards against damage to the property of others. If pollution damages your property, sue for damages! Polluters will seek to avoid damages if they have to pay.

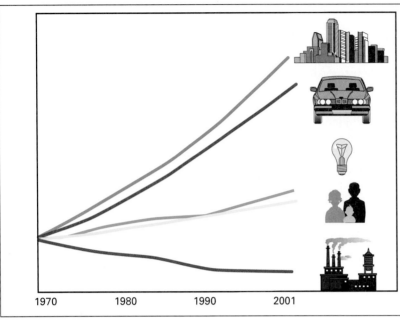

U.S. gross domestic product increased 161%

Vehicle miles traveled increased 149%

Energy consumption increased 42%

U.S. population increased 39%

Aggregate emissions decreased 25% (six principal pollutants)

1970   1980   1990   2001

FIGURE 25-4

COMPARISON OF GROWTH AREAS AND EMISSION TRENDS Between 1970 and 2001, gross domestic product increased 158 percent, energy consumption increased 45 percent, vehicle miles traveled increased 143 percent, and U.S. population increased 36 percent. At the same time, total emissions of the six principal air pollutants decreased 29 percent.

Source: Environmental Protection Agency, *Six Principle Pollutants.*

Coase theorem theory that holds parties to an externality would voluntarily negotiate an efficient outcome without government involvement when property rights are clearly defined.

This idea leads to the **Coase theorem,** named after Nobel Laureate Sir Ronald Coase, which holds that parties to an externality would voluntarily negotiate an efficient outcome without government involvement. Government need merely clearly define and enforce property rights. For example, if the value of changing the amount of an externality exceeds its cost, a mutually beneficial agreement would be struck to accomplish this change. That would be efficient. If the value of change is less than the cost, an agreement would not be reached. That would also be efficient.

Few people believe the Coase theorem offers a general solution to externality problems. For example, imagine your neighbor playing his classic Iron Butterfly album at top volume at 2 A.M. Are you likely to ask how much money that experience is worth to him, and compare the amount with your own willingness to pay to avoid hearing it? Would you offer to pay him enough to get him to turn the volume down? You're a reasonable person, aren't you? "Not at 2 o'clock in the morning!" you say?

Anyway, if you pay once, you'll wind up paying again, even if your neighbor decides that he no longer likes listening. He likes the money. That exemplifies the problem of *strategic behavior,* which interferes with the practical application of the Coase theorem. That problem becomes significantly worse when the effects of the externality are widespread. In addition, identifying specific culprits and bringing together victims becomes quite difficult when many parties are involved. **Transaction costs,** the expense of coordinating market exchanges, would be high. Thus, the Coase theorem applies only in the absence of transaction costs and strategic behavior. In practice, this means we either resort to public policy to remedy the externality or ignore the problem and let the market fail.

transaction costs the expense of coordinating market exchanges.

KEEPING UP WITH THE JONESES   *SNAPSHOT*

Would you be happier with a $50,000 annual income with other people getting half as much, or with a $100,000 annual income with others getting twice as much? In a 2003 study, London School of Economics Professor Richard Layard found that most people would take the first option. It's as though, when others get better off, you get worse off. Dr. Layard termed this phenomenon, "happiness pollution."

Although there is no obvious policy prescription to cure happiness pollution, the idea did suggest to Professor Layard that perhaps we are all working too hard. He suggested raising tax rates so that we have less incentive to work for material gains and more incentive to simply enjoy living. So what if that slows the wheels of progress! Dr. Layard found little evidence to suggest that our hurried lives of today are giving us any greater pleasure than our ancestors could find in the different days of yesteryear. ◀

COMMON PROPERTY RESOURCES—NO INCENTIVES FOR CONSERVATION

Common property resources are owned jointly, including groundwater, public lands, wild animals, and fish in the oceans, lakes, and rivers. Unless government sets up policies to prevent it, anyone can hunt, fish, pump water, and in other ways capture the common property to make it that person's private property.

Common property resources lead to too much production in the present with insufficient regard for the future. The problem is that, when many people own the same resource, no one has any personal incentive to conserve it. Owners have rights to take or use the resource, but have no way of ensuring its preservation. A common property resource generates a race among its owners to exploit the resource as quickly as possible, before others can get to it. Owners ignore the opportunity cost in terms of future value forgone from using something up today.

For example, imagine sharing a very large joint checking account with all other students at your college. How much money would be left in the account by the end of the day? Most likely, each student would figure that others would quickly raid the account. The bank would see a stampede of students, each seeking to be the first to transfer the entire balance to a private account. Common property resources face much the same problem.

A classic article entitled "Tragedy of the Commons" illustrates this problem with reference to the old English commons.* The common pastureland accessible to all quickly turned into a desolate expanse of dirt and mud, while private land nearby was lush and

---

*Garrett Hardin, "Tragedy of the Commons," *Science,* 1968.

QUICKCHECK

Why is common property overused? How can government correct this market failure?

Answer: When ownership is shared, no single owner can profit from saving the resource for future use. Therefore, each owner has the incentive to think only of the present and ignore conservation values. Government can solve this problem through an appropriate user fee or usage restrictions. Assigning property rights to one single owner would also solve the problem.

---

green. Grasses on the commons disappeared because shepherds allowed their sheep to overgraze. Shepherds had no reason to graze their flocks lightly, because the grass they saved would in all likelihood get eaten by someone else's flock. In contrast, on private land nearby, owners sought to conserve some grass to provide for future growth. The sheep were herded to fresh pastures before the grass was munched so short as to become endangered.

The common property resource problem is not a thing of the past. For example, over-fishing along the coast of Maine and in many other ocean fisheries has caused catches to decline dramatically. Another concern is depletion of the ozone layer in the earth's upper atmosphere, as manufacturers in countries around the globe have little incentive to design ozone-friendly products. Likewise, farmers who irrigate their land and cities and towns that tap into groundwater and river water resources have little incentive to practice conservation that would help each other out.

Not only do common property owners have no stake in preserving the resource for future use, but they also do not care if they get in the way of one another's efforts. For example, in fishing or shrimping grounds along the Gulf coast, each additional boat is likely to reduce the amount caught by other boats. Unless all the boats are owned jointly, though, this effect is ignored by the fishermen and shrimpers. Likewise, overfishing today means fewer fish will be available in the future.

Government can solve common property resource problems by selling the common property to a single owner. Most often, however, complete transfers would be impractical or politically unacceptable. For example, few would advocate selling rivers, lakes, and oceans to any single owner. The alternative is for the government to act as the owners' agent and apportion use of the common property so that overuse is avoided. This is the rationale behind fishing and hunting permits, regulation of mesh size on fishing nets, mandated water-saving toilets, and various other restrictions and **user fees**—charges for use of a publicly owned resource.

user fees charges for use of a publicly owned good, service, or resource.

25.2 POLICY TOOLS

Some policy approaches to conservation are more promising than others. This section highlights some prominent policy options for the control of externalities and allocation of common property resources. Although several applications will be mentioned, the focus will be upon pollution and water policy. This focus is warranted because pollution is the most prominent externality, and allocation of common-property water promises to become increasingly significant as the population grows.

MORAL SUASION

"Turn down that thermostat—Don't waste energy!" "Be water tight!" "Don't be a Litter Bug!" "Only YOU can prevent forest fires!"

From U.S. presidents to Smokey the Bear, we are exhorted to do the right thing. These appeals to our social conscience—called **moral suasion**—are the easiest and most high-profile form of public policy available to fight problems associated with externalities and common property resources. Moral suasion makes it clear to the public that the government is taking action. Unfortunately, moral suasion is rarely adequate to the task and often has undesirable side effects.

moral suasion exhortations to do the right thing, as defined by public policymakers.

A fundamental drawback to moral suasion is that it has no way of achieving any particular target, efficient or otherwise. Also, moral suasion imposes all costs of cutbacks on the "moral." A third and perhaps most troubling problem is that moral suasion can lead to a self-righteous intrusion on personal privacy. Even Nathaniel Hawthorne was troubled by moral suasion, as evidenced by his classic novel *The Scarlet Letter* in which the humiliation of public exposure was used as the deterrent against adultery. These days, moral suasion is most likely to take the form of ad campaigns aimed at the public.

STANDARDS AND TECHNOLOGY MANDATES

Technology mandates occur when government instructs producers as to the exact technology to install as a remedy for some public problem. Low-flow showerheads and low-flush toilets are examples of technology mandates designed to avoid wasting water. Catalytic converters on automobiles are mandated to reduce air pollution. Technology mandates are usually chosen because they are easy to observe and enforce, and seem like a very straightforward solution to the problem.

technology mandates government rules that instruct producers as to the exact technology to use in a product or its production.

Sometimes the mandates are indirect, as with smoke-filtering scrubbers on powerplant smokestacks, and other specific pollution control strategies. Here, the Environmental Protection Agency (EPA) specifies emission *standards* that must be met and suggests technologies that will meet these standards. Producers are free to use other technologies, but would be subject to serious penalties if their approaches fail. In contrast, if the EPA's suggested technologies fail, the producers avoid liability. There is thus much risk and little incentive to experiment with potentially better ways of pollution control.

Technology mandates are often much more expensive and annoying than other policy options. For instance, it is a waste of money and an annoyance to require high-tech, low-flush toilets in regions where water is plentiful. If external costs can be added directly to the prices of products, the higher prices would induce conservation in ways that regulators might be unable to mandate. A price of municipal water that fully reflected its opportunity costs would cause customers to seek out an efficient array of plumbing fixtures, without the need for government mandates. By the same token, there would be no need to mandate irrigation techniques in agriculture if farmers always pay the opportunity cost of the water they use. Using prices avoids the inefficiencies caused by the broad brush of technology mandates.

Economic studies on pollution control estimate that market-based alternatives to technology mandates and standards can achieve the same amounts of emission cutbacks at roughly one-third the cost. For example, the EPA's *bubble plan* allows a firm to increase its emissions from some sources if it offsets those increases by decreasing its emissions from other sources within its plant. One Ohio utility plant responded by periodically hosing down its piles of coal to prevent wind-blown coal dust, rather than install expensive smokestack technology. The firm's particulate emissions dropped, while the cost of pollution control dropped even more. The EPA's *offsets plan* extends this flexible concept across firms to capture even more cost savings.

Government planners cannot be expected to foresee all of the options for pollution control. For example, what planner could have mandated that workers reduce pollution and congestion by abandoning their daily auto commute? Could planners in the 1970s have imagined the option of replacing commuters' automobiles with telecommunications? Yet, the recently available technologies of networked home computers and the Internet have led many people to do just that by working at home. Allowing the market to choose this and other less costly strategies of pollution control means that we can have a cleaner environment at a lower cost.

POLLUTION TAXES—ENVIRONMENTAL USER FEES

As an alternative to technology mandates, pollution taxes can reduce pollution without creating the problems associated with technology mandates. Economists often advocate this action, which is referred to as *internalizing* the cost of an externality directly into prices. How would such a tax work? If an activity generates damages, the value of those damages would be estimated, and a tax would be imposed equal to the amount of the marginal external cost at the efficient level of output. In this way, the tax causes perpetrators of the external cost to pay the full marginal social cost of their activities. This means that externalities become part of the decisions of those who cause them, and efficient choices will be made in the marketplace. For example, if smoking a pack of cigarettes causes an average of $1 in health damages to others, then a tax of $1 per pack would represent those damages.

Figure 25-5 illustrates that a corrective tax on cigarettes shifts the supply curve up by the amount of that tax, since sellers now have to collect that extra payment and pass it along to the government. The price would rise and the quantity fall, as the market equilibrium changes. Note that the price rise of 80 cents in this example is less than the tax of $1. Most of the tax is passed on to consumers, because demand is inelastic relative to supply, as discussed in the elasticity chapter. The rest is absorbed by producers in what is now a smaller industry.

Using fees to remedy externalities often encounters difficulties. For example, external damages may depend upon time and place. Smoking at home does not impose the same externality as smoking in a restroom that many people must use. It is not possible to allow

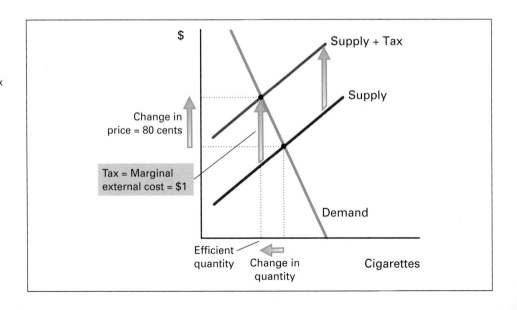

FIGURE 25-5

THE EFFICIENT TAX A tax can internalize an external cost. Efficiency requires that the tax rate be set equal to marginal external cost at the efficient quantity of output.

for this difference in imposing cigarette taxes. In other applications, such as taxes on water pollution from industrial waste, fees could vary depending on such factors as the season and time of day.

Measurement of pollution is another hurdle in the way of applying pollution taxes. For example, it may be difficult to constantly monitor the emission of pollutants, especially for autos and other mobile sources. For stationary sources like factories, one can imagine a system of periodic checks and penalties that would punish cheating. Of greater concern, however, is political support for taxing pollution and providing effective penalties to ensure compliance.

Politicians often seek new revenue sources. In contrast to most taxes, those designed to remedy externalities actually promote economic efficiency. Yet, pollution taxes have proven to have little political support. On the one hand, some well-meaning environmentalists will not accept that the environment is an economic resource. They claim that pollution taxes are merely passed along to consumers, and that pollution is not reduced. This line of reasoning ignores the law of demand. It also ignores the role of competition. Competition forces firms to substitute cheaper inputs for the newly taxed use of environmental services.

On the other hand, producers usually oppose pollution taxes. The reason is that those taxes result in significant transfers of revenues from polluters to the government, revenues that pay for the firms' ongoing emissions of pollutants. This revenue transfer is in addition to money spent directly on pollution control. Thus, pollution taxes lack powerful constituencies.

To overcome political barriers to pollution taxes, policymakers sometimes resort to paying for pollution abatement instead. For example, municipal wastewater treatment plants receive significant federal **subsidies,** which are payments from the federal government meant to encourage actions with external benefits or that reduce external costs. Unfortunately, subsidies for reducing pollution have two undesirable side effects, which are:

subsidies payments to promote actions with external benefits or that reduce external costs.

- Subsidies drain government revenues.
- Subsidies reward polluters and, for this reason, can lead to too many polluting firms.

SMOKING WHILE EATING AND PHONING WHILE DRIVING   *SNAPSHOT*

Anti-smoking laws have cropped up all around the country. Bans on talking on the phone while driving a car are likewise becoming increasingly prevalent. Since both activities are taxed, could not those taxes be set to internalize any externalities so that no heavy-handed prohibitions are needed?

The problem with this proposal is that externalities vary by time and place. A flat tax on cigarettes does not adjust for whether the smoking occurs in a crowded restaurant or in the privacy of one's home. Likewise, talking on a cell phone is not dangerous to other motorists when the talker is not driving on the highway. Since taxes cannot know where the smoking or talking will occur, an alternative is to just ban the activity in situations where the potential for externality is highest.

Bans are not without their costs, however. Smokers value their after-dinner cigarettes just as car callers value the time they save. Therefore, policymakers must weigh the costs and benefits of alternative policies. Sometimes, in fact, the most efficient policy is no policy at all. For example, with no bans on smoking in restaurants some restaurants will differentiate themselves by being smoke-free, some by allowing smoking everywhere, and probably most by having separate sections for smokers and nonsmokers. In the case of smoking while you eat, therefore, the market has a solution. In the case of phoning while you drive, with everyone sharing the same public highways, no market solution is apparent. ◄

MARKETABLE PERMITS—WHOSE PROPERTY?

marketable permits property rights to a specified amount of an activity, such as groundwater pumping or air pollution, where those property rights can be bought and sold; can efficiently achieve quantity targets set by the government.

Marketable permits offer the same economic advantages as taxes, but in a way that has much more political appeal. In application to pollution, **marketable permits** represent property rights to a certain amount of pollutant emissions. The government sets the overall quantity, and then divides up that quantity into a limited number of permits for the various polluters. While these permits could be auctioned, politics causes them more typically to be given away to preexisting polluters without charge.

Because the overall quantity of pollution is controlled directly, environmentalists are usually willing to acknowledge that marketable permits limit total pollution. Polluters prefer this approach to taxes because permits usually require no payment to the government. However, polluters do sometimes worry that the government might take away those rights or impose supplemental charges in the future.

Marketable permits are valuable property rights. The term *marketable* means that those rights can be bought and sold. This feature has appeal not only to producers, but also to economists. If pollution rights are traded, buyers would be firms with high costs of pollution abatement. Likewise, sellers would be firms with low costs of cutting back emissions. This means that emission reductions are undertaken by firms able to do so at least cost.

Trading in emission rights has mushroomed in recent years, so much so that it has formed an industry of its own. Markets for some pollutants are formal and well developed. For example, power plants and other emitters can buy and sell rights for sulfur dioxide emissions on the Chicago Board of Trade. Other pollutants have *thin markets,* where trades are few. When markets are thin, environmental consultants facilitate trading by keeping track of firms willing to sell their permits.

Marketable permits also provide a promising alternative in the allocation of common property resources. Here, a central authority determines how much of the resource can be used now, and still leave enough for the future. For example, the authority might estimate how much water can be pumped from a river without irreparable harm to the river's ecosystem. Pumping rights are then distributed among river users, perhaps in proportion to the users' historical levels of pumping. These rights are then good for each period into the indefinite future. Fluctuations in the river's ability to support pumping might cause the same percentage variations in the quantity allowed per permit.

By allowing permits to be marketable, those valuing water most highly would be the ones that would buy or retain the permits. This outcome is just what economic efficiency prescribes. The main issues are distributional. For example, how are the permits to be initially distributed? Should we compensate feed store owners who lose their livelihoods when local farmers and ranchers sell their water rights to big cities? Political questions of this sort have been the largest obstacles to more widespread use of permits.

APPLYING POLICY DIRECTLY TO POLLUTION

Efficient pollution control can be achieved through either taxes or marketable permits, as discussed in the previous two sections. Since most pollution comes from production rather than from consumption, it is usually best to apply a tax or permit approach directly to pollution rather than to outputs. Sometimes this is difficult or impossible to do. For example, it would take an army of government agents to follow around potential smokers to collect a smoke emissions tax when they light up. In that case, it is far easier to monitor and tax cigarette sales.

When pollution control policy is applied to output, however, pollution is reduced only to the extent that output falls. In contrast, when pollution is taxed directly, polluters also have the incentive to reduce the amount of pollution per unit of that output. It is often feasible to tax pollution directly in cases of stationary-source polluters, such as fac-

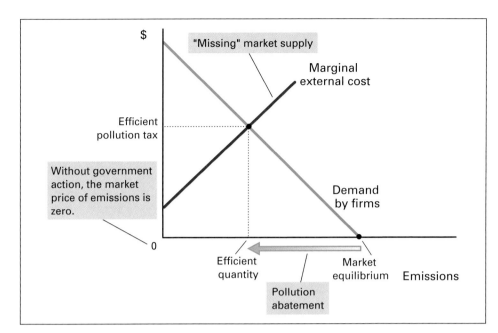

FIGURE 25-6

THE MISSING MARKET FOR POLLUTION To correct problems of pollution externalities in production, the government must first estimate marginal external cost, which is the "missing" market supply curve. The efficient quantity of pollution can be achieved by marketable permits summing to that quantity or through a tax equal to what would be the market-clearing price of a unit of emissions. The result of either policy would be a reduction in pollution to the efficient quantity.

tories. Such taxes require that the government be able to monitor the quantity of pollution that is emitted.

Firms do not pollute for their own sake. Rather, they use the environment to remove waste products, with pollution being the result. For this reason, firms have a demand for the right to emit pollution into the environment. In other words, firms are willing to pay because using the environment to remove wastes is a valuable service to them, just like the services of labor. Firms value this service because consumers value the output that the firms produce. Thus, the benefit of pollution is really the extra value that consumers receive because producers pollute. These benefits are captured in the demand for emission rights, shown in Figure 25-6, the curve that represents firms' willingness to pay for incremental rights to pollute.

Since environmental services are not priced, there is no one in the free market to charge firms for environmental services, because no one owns the environment. For this reason, in the absence of government action, firms are free to pollute as much as they want. In Figure 25-6, the amount that firms pollute in the absence of government action is given by the intersection of demand with the horizontal axis, which is the quantity demanded at a price of zero. In effect, there is a missing market. If a market were to exist, the market supply curve should correspond to marginal external cost, and the market equilibrium would be an efficient quantity. The equilibrium price would equal the efficient tax shown in the figure.

To substitute for the missing efficient market price, the government could charge firms a fee per unit of emissions, where that fee is shown in Figure 25-6 as the efficient pollution tax. **To remedy an externality with a tax, the tax rate must be set equal to marginal external cost at the efficient level of pollution.** Polluters would be forced to pay that price for their emissions in the same manner that they must pay for their other inputs. In this case, it is in effect the government selling them the input of environmental services.

Alternatively, regulators could issue an efficient quantity of marketable permits, which would have the effect of limiting emissions to no more than that amount. The value of the marginal unit of emissions would be the same as the efficient tax, so that competition for emission rights in the marketplace would set a price on those rights just as though there had been an emissions tax.

While the tax solution brings in revenue to the government for every unit of emissions, a marketable permit system will typically bring little or no revenue to the government. The

> ### *QUICKCHECK*
>
> **Why are marketable permits more efficient than technology mandates?**
>
> **Answer:** Technology mandates are inflexible, which can lead to some firms spending much more than others for the same amount of pollution reduction. Marketable permits can achieve overall pollution reduction much more cheaply because the firms that can cut back emissions at least cost will be the ones to do so. In addition, unlike technology mandates, marketable permits make it profitable to improve pollution control technology over time.

reason is that emission permits are usually given free of charge to firms in a region, with those firms then free to sell the emission rights as they see fit. The reason for this manner of distribution is mainly political, since firms in a polluting industry lobby hard to avoid massive payments to the government for polluting activities for which they have historically not been charged. Since either the tax or permit approach allows regulators to create a market that allocates emission rights efficiently, marketable permits have become the policy instrument of choice.

25.3 CARING FOR THE GLOBAL ENVIRONMENT

Policies to control pollution or preserve common property resources require a government to administer them. Yet, oftentimes, these market failures go beyond the confines of any single country. In these situations, the best solutions often involve international cooperation. For example, the world's oceans are common property resources, which leads to the overharvesting of whales and other marine life. They can be exploited without restriction, absent international agreements to the contrary.

Another common property resource, one that countries of the world all share, is the earth's atmosphere. This atmosphere filters out many harmful rays of the sun, protecting us from skin cancer and providing the environment to which humans and other species have adapted over the centuries. The burning of carbon-based fuels, the use of certain aerosol propellants, and other actions of a modern industrial society have the potential to harm this shared resource.

Unfortunately, because of the complexity of the world's environment, it is hard to know just exactly what role mankind has in affecting it. For example, scientists have been unable to prove with certainty that the burning of fossil fuels causes global warming, given historical evidence that the earth has experienced numerous periods of general warming and cooling over the centuries. Even so, just because it is nearly impossible to prove does not mean that it is not occurring, which is why the issue of global warming remains contentious.

It sounds like a good idea for countries of the world to somehow get together and protect the common property resources that we all share. Indeed, countries have gotten together to agree upon such matters as *the law of the sea,* including allowing countries to claim up to 200 miles from shorelines as the countries' own territories. The problem is that agreements are often difficult to reach. For example, President Bush reiterated in 2002 that the United States would not abide by the multilateral *Kyoto Accords* on global warming. This is an agreement signed by representatives of many of the world's countries, requiring them to take actions that would protect the world's environment. The United States would have faced much of the cost of this agreement, including changes in lifestyles and ways of production. While that was fine with the large majority of countries in the world, the United States thought otherwise.

Economists identify pollution as a market failure, because firms and consumers ignore the external costs of their actions. In addition, it is important to recognize that many countries' governments have been responsible for the world's pollution. The environmental legacy of the Soviet Union and its European allies provides a tragic illustration. Environmental devastation there ranged from the ecological death of rivers and lakes to radioactive contamination spread over hundreds of square miles by the 1986 explosion at the Chernobyl nuclear power plant. Secretive, bureaucratic governments cannot be expected to be responsive to their citizens' environmental concerns.

KILLER BEES, FIRE ANTS, HUNGRY RABBITS, AND WALKING FISH   *SNAPSHOT*

Never underestimate the ability of humans to inflict environmental disaster. Take the case of Australia's rabbits, which do significant damage to crops on the island continent. Rabbits are not native to the country, but were introduced when an immigrant youngster's pregnant pet rabbit escaped into the wilds where no natural predators existed. Then there are the fire ants and "killer bees" spreading throughout the United States, threatening people, pets, crops, and the relatively gentle native ants and bees. The ants arrived on boats from South America and found a hospitable climate free of predators. The immigrant bees are the result of a scientific experiment in breeding that went awry when thousands of the pesky critters escaped into the wilds of Brazil and then decided to move north.

Most recently, it is the voracious appetites of the Chinese snakehead "walking" fish that has residents of several states worried. Set free in a Crofton, Maryland, pond when they outgrew their owner's aquarium, these fish found the American environment to be to their liking, free from the predators they had learned to fear in China. Growing up to three feet long and able to travel out of water for three days, these fearsome "Frankenfish" quickly became the predators of frogs, birds, small mammals, and other fish. The situation has prompted the poisoning of ponds and a massive fishhunt to keep them from spreading further. On the bright side, the ugly snakehead fish are reportedly quite tasty! ◄

25.4 BORDERLANDS OF THE SOUTHWEST—WHOSE POLLUTION? WHOSE SOLUTION?

Explore & Apply

Wide open spaces, broad vistas, a freshening breeze—our vision of America's Southwest is one of expansiveness and freedom. It is a place to do and be as we please. The Southwest is part of our psyche; it's a state of mind. It's also a real place with real problems. As ever more people live in the Southwest, unlimited personal freedom comes into conflict with preservation of the environment that attracts them there. The environment of the Southwest is ill-suited to accommodate unrestricted pollution.

As in other parts of the country, citizens of the Southwest must abide by U.S. environmental laws, which means driving cars or operating factories with emission controls in place. The special problem of the Southwest, though, is that those controls apply to only a fraction of the sources of pollution. Much of the air and water pollution has its source in Mexico, an industrializing country with a rapidly growing population and less stringent control over pollutants.

Exemplifying the problem of border air pollution, the city of El Paso, Texas, is in noncompliance with guidelines set by the U.S. Environmental Protection Agency (EPA). However, the EPA allows this noncompliance to continue without penalty. There is a reason.

If you were to fly into El Paso and look out the airplane window as you approach the city, you may have a good idea as to why the EPA makes exceptions for El Paso. On the south side of the Rio Grande you are likely to see a polluted haze that greatly restricts visibility. The haze on the north side is much lighter. El Paso is on the north side and its twin, Ciudad Juárez, is on the south side. Ciudad Juárez has nearly triple the population and

generates proportionally much more pollution than does El Paso. Unfortunately for El Paso, pollution knows no borders.

Transborder pollution is a problem of growing magnitude around the world. The problems are worsening for two reasons. On the one hand, economic growth in the less-developed countries does not emphasize pollution control. Of greater concern to those countries are such tangibles as food, clothing, and shelter. On the other hand, the increased wealth of the developed countries has allowed them the luxury to focus beyond immediate necessities toward the quality and long-term sustainability of lifestyles. Environmental quality is important to both of those lifestyle goals.

Transborder pollution problems come in many forms. Some are global in nature, such as concerns that emissions of chlorofluorocarbons are depleting the earth's ozone layer. The pollution problem of most concern in America's Southwest is more local in nature. Here we have two countries, each of which feels the effects of the other's pollution. What trouble does this cause?

The problem of localized transborder pollution centers on incentives. There is much more incentive to control pollution that affects your own residents than there is incentive to control pollution absorbed elsewhere. For instance, cities along rivers routinely locate sewage treatment plants downstream and city dumps downwind from the city itself. When cities are all governed by one state or country, there are limits to how much pollution exporting is allowed. For example, while sewage from U.S. cities may be discharged down river, at least U.S. law requires that it be treated. Given an absence of a world government, is there some other incentive for neighboring countries to be sensitive to each other's concerns?

POLLUTION CONTROL POLICIES

It would be very difficult for the United States to apply any particular pollution control strategy to firms in Mexico. Options that work well within a jurisdiction don't work as well across jurisdictions. For example, one option long advocated by economists is for the government to impose a tax on emissions of pollutants, such that the external costs of pollution are internalized into the production process. The idea is to make firms pay for environmental services. In other words, firms would be forced to pay for the waste-removal services of the air above or the river next door in the same way they pay for other types of services. In that case, you can rest assured firms would find ways to economize on smoke emissions and discharges into waterways.

A *second-best*, less-desirable alternative would be to tax the output of the firm. This approach would not give firms any incentive to reduce the amount of pollution per unit of output, but it would at least drive up the price of that output. Higher prices would mean fewer sales and thus less pollution. Could we apply either of these tax ideas to transborder pollution?

The answer is the United States probably could not effectively impose pollution taxes on Mexican polluters. The United States could not tax pollution emissions effectively, because it lacks the authority to monitor pollution in Mexico and lacks the authority to impose taxes even if it could monitor that pollution. In principle, the United States could levy a pollution tax on output crossing the border. However, that tax could not effectively differentiate where in Mexico that output was produced. Furthermore, that tax would be politically unpalatable and violate international treaties. Other policy instruments, such as pollution permits or mandated pollution control technologies, would also be infeasible for the same reasons taxes would not work. Where does that leave us?

The best solution may be voluntary cooperation between the United States and Mexico based on mutual self-interest. While both the United States and Mexico gain from trade between the two countries, the gains to Mexico are proportionally larger because it is the smaller country. This cooperative spirit is attested to by the 1994 implementation of the

North American Free Trade Agreement (NAFTA), which incorporated Mexico into a revised and expanded free-trade agreement between the United States and Canada.

NAFTA broke new ground in international trade by writing environmental safeguards directly into the treaty and side accords. For example, NAFTA signatories are obligated to maintain effective enforcement of their own environmental laws, even when the affected pollutants spill over the border. While NAFTA does not itself solve the problems of border pollution, it does provide a framework for cooperation.

What kind of cooperation can the United States legitimately expect from Mexico? Should Mexico maintain environmental standards equal to those in the United States? If so, beware of environmental imperialism. The United States cannot expect the world to follow its standards, at least not without granting the rest of the world's citizens voting rights in U.S. elections. Moreover, uniform environmental standards would not make sense across all countries. After all, maintaining those standards is expensive, and incomes in some countries are much lower than incomes in the United States.

Mexico's per-capita income is less than $6,000 per year. Specifically, in 2001, per-capita income in Mexico was only $5,540, compared to $34,870 per-capita income in the United States. Relative to the average U.S. citizen, the average citizen in Mexico thus consumes less in the way of high-quality food, clothing, shelter, medical care, and so forth. For Mexico to upgrade its control of pollution to match that in the United States would require further reductions in outputs of those goods.

One of the best ways for the United States to see greater control of pollution in Mexico is to see greater per-capita income in Mexico. The reason is that environmental quality is a normal good, meaning that people want more as their incomes rise. The growth in income has been occurring in recent years and will be spurred along as NAFTA continues to be phased in. We are already seeing an increased interest in environmental improvement in Mexico. Over time, we can expect this interest to translate into concrete policy action.

In the meantime, there remain pollution problems along the U.S.-Mexican border. For example, sources of air pollution in the El Paso–Juárez air shed include the burning of tires to fuel brick kilns, dusty unpaved streets, and open-air spray painting of automobiles. The citizens of El Paso want action to clean this up sooner rather than later. So too do citizens of Juárez. Is effective action possible?

Along the border, local governments have an incentive to cooperate in order to address the common pollution problem jointly. That is exactly what El Paso and Juárez have done. Specifically, those governments have formed a single international air quality management district for their region. This district is empowered with the authority to set air quality goals and employ market mechanisms to meet those goals.

Unfortunately, much pollution is left over from the past, especially when it comes to toxins on the land and in the water. Therefore, controlling the flow of new pollutants is not enough; there is the stock of old pollutants to clean up. Who will pay for that cleanup? Part of the answer may be found in the *North American Development Bank*, financed by the governments of Mexico and the United States to fund border cleanup projects. In other words the hands of government and the pockets of taxpayers are likely to be major parts of any final resolution to the transborder pollution problems of the American Southwest.

1. **The production of many of the goods the United States imports from Mexico causes pollution within Mexico. Is this extra pollution fair to the Mexican people?**

2. **When firms in Mexico cause pollution that crosses the border, U.S. residents along the border are damaged. That pollution is an external cost, since the U.S. residents have no way to extract payment for damages from the Mexican polluters. What policies should the United States pursue to reduce this pollution?**

THINKING CRITICALLY

Visit **www.prenhall.com/ayers** for updates and web exercises on this Explore & Apply topic.

SUMMARY AND LEARNING OBJECTIVES

1. **Identify examples of externalities and common property resources.**

   - When market failure occurs, the level of market production is inefficient. Examples of market failure include externalities and common property resources. Externalities involve third parties who are not directly involved in either the production or consumption of a good or service.

   - Externalities can be either positive, conferring benefits upon third parties, or negative, which impose costs upon third parties. Pollution is an example of a significant negative externality. Many externalities do not warrant government action, such as most of those that involve personal attire.

   - Common property resources are defined by shared ownership. Lakes, rivers, and streams are usually common property resources.

2. **Analyze the effects of externalities on efficiency.**

   - Production creates both social costs and social benefits. If there are no externalities, then social costs are equal to private costs. Likewise, social benefits are equal to private benefits in the absence of externalities. However, when there are externalities arising from production or consumption, then social costs will also include the external costs and social benefits will include the external benefits. The following equations characterize social costs and benefits when externalities are present: Social cost = Private cost + External cost; and Social benefit = Private benefit + External benefit.

   - To analyze market efficiency, you must consider marginal social cost, which is represented by the following equation: Marginal social cost = Marginal private cost + Marginal external cost; and Marginal social benefit = Marginal private benefit + Marginal external benefit. These equations are analogous to the equations for social cost and social benefit, except for the addition of the word *marginal* in each term.

   - Demand represents marginal private benefit. When there are external benefits, marginal social benefits exceed demand because marginal social benefits include both private and external components. Graphically, the marginal social benefit curve lies above the demand curve.

   - Market output occurs at the quantity below the intersection of demand and supply. This quantity of output is less than the efficient quantity when external benefits are present. Thus, the market underproduces goods that confer external benefits.

   - The supply curve of a good is equivalent to the marginal private cost of producing the good. The marginal social cost curve will lie above the supply curve whenever there are external costs present.

   - When external costs are present, the efficient quantity of a good is less than the market quantity of the good.

   - The Coase theorem states than an efficient outcome can be negotiated between the parties involved when externalities exist. Private negotiations between the perpetrators of an externality and those harmed by it occur in lieu of government regulation. Based on the Coase theorem, the role of government is limited to the enforcement of property rights. Two features of reality limit the applicability of the Coase theorem. These features are transactions costs and strategic behavior. Transactions costs make negotiations impractical, while strategic behavior involves the repetition of actions for financial gain.

3. **Explain why common property resources are likely to be overused.**

   - Because common property resources are jointly owned, the incentive to conserve them is lacking. People will try to get their share of the resource before others, thus depleting the resource. Overfishing is an example of the misuse of a common property resource.

   - Users of a common property resource ignore that their use of the resource decreases the amount that others can use in the future.

4. **Discuss the policy instruments that government can use to promote a better environment.**

   - Government can choose among various regulatory policy approaches, each of which has different characteristics and implications. Among these policy options are moral suasion, technology mandates, pollution taxes, and marketable permits.

   - Moral suasion attempts to persuade people to voluntarily change their behavior.

   - Technology mandates require the installation of a specified technology.

   - Pollution taxes are a form of environmental user fees. A pollution tax is said to internalize an externality, meaning that the perpetrator of the externality pays for the external cost in the form of the tax. The tax shifts the supply curve upward by the amount of the tax, and thus reduces the amount of the taxed activity.

   - Marketable permits allow firms to pollute, but only up to the permitted amount. Firms have the incentive to reduce their pollution below the allowed amount because they can sell unneeded permits to other polluters.

5. **Identify the efficient amount of pollution and the policies to achieve it.**
   - When pollution can be monitored, taxes or marketable permits can be by far the most efficient policies to control pollution or allocate common property. Since most pollution comes from production and not consumption, taxes or permits can be applied directly to pollution rather than the outputs that are associated with that pollution.
   - Producers demand the use of the environment for waste disposal, but no one but the government has the authority to sell most environmental services. Since the market supply curve is missing, the government must estimate the marginal external cost, which is the missing market supply, and determine the efficient quantity of pollution.

 Discuss the issue of transborder pollution and the difficulties in finding solutions.
   - Transborder pollution crosses national borders. Countries must and do work together to solve such problems. The NAFTA agreement specifically addresses the problem of transborder pollution, offering a framework for cooperation between the United States and Mexico for reducing pollution.

KEY TERMS

externalities, 632
common property resource, 632
external costs or benefits, 632
private costs or benefits, 632
social costs or benefits, 632

marginal external costs or benefits, 632
Coase theorem, 636
transaction costs, 636
user fees, 638

moral suasion, 639
technology mandates, 639
subsidies, 641
marketable permits, 642

TEST YOURSELF

TRUE OR FALSE

1. External costs are associated with positive externalities.
2. Social benefits are the sum of private benefits and external costs.
3. Environmental quality is a public good that is reduced by pollution.
4. The Coase theorem states that carefully crafted government mandates are necessary in order to deal with problems of externalities.
5. Technology mandates are the most cost-effective way to control pollution when pollution is easy to monitor.

MULTIPLE CHOICE

6. The costs associated with a person's actions that the person actually bears are called
   a. social costs.
   b. external costs.
   c. private costs.
   d. private costs + external costs.
7. Spillover costs to third parties are also called
   a. private costs.
   b. marginal costs.
   c. external costs.
   d. internal costs.
8. People who serve as role models to inspire others
   a. impose social costs.
   b. confer private benefits only.
   c. confer external benefits.
   d. are not the cause of any externalities.
9. In Self-Test Figure 25-1, the marginal social cost curve slopes up more steeply than supply because
   a. the demand for environmental quality slopes down.
   b. marginal private cost slopes down.
   c. there are external benefits from larger outputs.
   d. a system of marketable permits is in place.

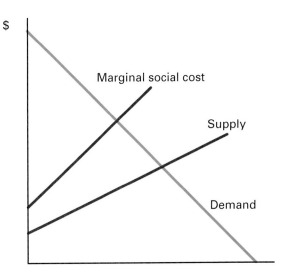

SELF-TEST FIGURE 25-1

10. In Self-Test Figure 25-1, supply represents
    a. marginal private benefit.
    b. marginal social benefit.
    c. marginal external benefit.
    d. marginal private cost.

11. Does the free market ever produce too much?
    a. No.
    b. Yes, when there are external benefits present.
    c. Yes, when there are external costs present.
    d. Yes, when social costs equal private costs.

12. Which of the following is the best example of a common property resource?
    a. A gum ball machine in a barbershop.
    b. The fish in the sea.
    c. A towel for sale at Neiman Marcus.
    d. The movies you rented last week at Blockbuster.

13. The basic reason that overfishing occurs is that
    a. there are no laws against it.
    b. there are laws against it, but they need to be strengthened.
    c. no one person owns the fish before they are caught.
    d. the "fin rights" movement is too disorganized to protect the rights of fish.

14. Common property resource users ignore
    a. taxes, and so use more of the resource than they otherwise would.
    b. taxes, and so use less of the resource than they otherwise would.
    c. the value of conserving the resource for the future.
    d. all of the social costs.

15. Moral suasion is
    a. another name for a pollution tax.
    b. the cost of purchasing a marketable permit.
    c. the process of implementing technology mandates.
    d. an effort to change harmful behavior through appeals to conscience.

16. A pollution tax shifts the
    a. supply curve upward.
    b. supply curve downward.
    c. demand curve to the right.
    d. demand curve to the left.

17. A pollution tax that leads to the efficient quantity must be set equal to
    a. double the market price of the output.
    b. the marginal external cost at the efficient quantity of output.
    c. one-half of the market price of the output.
    d. the cost of a government mandate that would lead to the efficient quantity.

18. Making existing pollution permits marketable among firms would
    a. increase the total amount of pollution.
    b. decrease the total amount of pollution.
    c. reduce pollution-control costs, but have no effect on the total amount of pollution.
    d. increase pollution-control costs, but have no effect on the total amount of pollution.

19. The efficient quantity of pollution caused by the production of output
    a. must be zero.
    b. is determined by the intersection of market supply and demand.
    c. occurs where the demand for the right to pollute equals the marginal external cost.
    d. is the quantity for which firms would be willing to pay government the most money.

20. The North American Free Trade Agreement (NAFTA)
    a. ignores problems of transborder pollution.
    b. outlaws transborder pollution.
    c. neither ignores nor outlaws transborder pollution, but calls for cooperation to control such pollution.
    d. creates a special police force to find and fine polluters.

QUESTIONS AND PROBLEMS

1. *[externalities]* Explain why externalities can be either positive or negative. Which type of externality is associated with a cost? Which is associated with a benefit?

2. *[external benefits]* Discuss any actions that you, a friend, or someone in your family might have taken in the last month that conferred external benefits on a third party. Also discuss any situations within the last month where you or a family member or friend received an external benefit.

3. *[external benefits]* When there are external benefits to an action, does the market produce too much or too little? What policies should the government follow in this case?

4. *[external costs]* Have your neighbors ever imposed an external cost on you or your family? Describe the nature of the external cost. How was the situation resolved?

5. *[external costs]* When there are external costs to an action, does the market produce too much or too little? Should government policy encourage more production or less? Explain.

6. *[pollution and efficient quantity]* "The only acceptable level of pollution is zero pollution." Evaluate this statement using economic principles.

7. *[efficiency and external costs]* Using a graph, illustrate the market equilibrium quantity of a good. Assume that production causes an external cost. Modify your graph to show the marginal social cost and the efficient quantity.

8. *[efficient quantity]* State the equation that must be satisfied for the quantity to be efficient when there are external costs present.

9. *[external costs; Coase theorem]* Stinkigunco, Inc., has a factory located upstream from a small community that uses the river water for drinking. The plant's emissions of pollutants into the water forces the downstream community to treat the water in order for it to be drinkable. Describe the Coasian solution to this problem of externality and comment on its practicality.

10. *[Coase theorem]* Nineteenth-century farmers sometimes had their crops destroyed when steam locomotives traveling the tracks threw off sparks that set fire to their fields. Write a brief essay discussing the merits of the Coasian solution versus government regulation in this instance. Does the Coasian solution make allowances for any government role? (*Note:* At the time, there was no government regulation that dealt with this problem.)

11. *[policy tools]* Explain why, when pollution or common property resource use can be monitored and measured, taxes or marketable permits are preferable to technology mandates and moral suasion.

12. *[moral suasion]* Suppose your hometown holds a contest offering an award for the best essay on how to cut down on the amount of trash thrown out at City Park. Write a brief essay arguing that moral suasion is the best policy. In your essay, include a slogan designed to achieve the desired purpose.

13. *[pollution taxes]* Every time you drive your car it emits some amount of air pollution. Does this mean that a pollution tax should be placed on the sale of new vehicles? Explain.

14. *[pollution taxes]* Illustrate graphically how a pollution tax can lead to an efficient quantity.

15. *[marketable permits]* Using a specific example, explain how to create an efficient marketable permit system to control a measurable pollutant. What problem would arise if the government were to distribute permits free of charge each year based upon how much pollution each firm was responsible for the previous year?

16. *[the market to pollute]* In Figure 25-6, notice that a tax on pollution is one way to reduce the amount of pollution to the efficient quantity. Use the graph in this figure to explain how a system of marketable permits could achieve the same result. Be sure to state what quantity of permits would have to be issued and what price they would command in the permits market.

WORKING WITH GRAPHS AND DATA

1. *[externalities]* The following table identifies the marginal private costs and marginal external costs of production of a good. The marginal external costs are costs associated with pollution.

Quantity	Marginal Private Cost	Marginal External Cost	Marginal Social Cost
0	0	0	
1	$5	$2	
2	10	4	
3	15	6	
4	20	8	
5	25	10	
6	30	12	

a. Fill in the marginal social cost column.

b. Assume that the government does not intervene in this market. Which of these columns represents the market supply schedule? Explain.

c. Draw a graph of the marginal private cost curve and label it MPC. Add the marginal social cost curve and label it MSC. Label the vertical axis "$" and the horizontal axis "Quantity."

d. Sketch in a demand curve (marginal social benefit curve) that intersects both the marginal social cost and marginal private cost curves and label it Demand = MSB.

e. Identify the market quantity as Q_1 and the efficient quantity as Q_2.

2. *[externalities]* Use Graph 25-1, that shows the supply and demand curves for a good, to answer the questions that follow.

a. Label the equilibrium point for this market as *A* and identify the equilibrium price as P_1 and the equilibrium quantity as Q_1.

b. Assume that there are external benefits that result from the production of this good. Sketch a marginal social benefit curve and label it "Marginal social benefit." How is it different from the marginal private benefit curve?

c. Identify the point at which the efficient price and quantity are determined as *E*, identify the efficient quantity as Q_2, and identify the price associated with it as P_2.

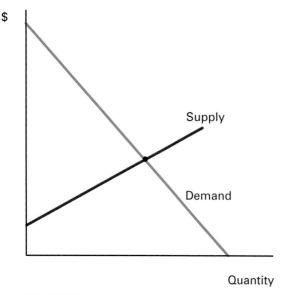

GRAPH 25-1

d. Why would there be a difference between the equilibrium quantity (Q_1) and the efficient quantity (Q_2)?

3. *[pollution taxes]* Use Graph 25-2 to answer the following questions.

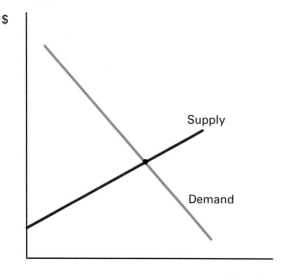

GRAPH 25-2

a. Identify the equilibrium market price as P_1 and quantity as Q_1.

b. Assume that the government imposes a pollution tax on this good. Would the tax affect the supply curve or the demand curve? Sketch the affected

curve after the imposition of the tax and label it either "Supply + Tax" or "Demand + Tax."

c. Identify the new equilibrium price as P_2 and quantity as Q_2.

d. Identify the size of the tax on the graph. Label it "Tax."

e. Assume that this tax is intended to correct externalities associated with the production and/or consumption of this good and result in the efficient quantity being produced. How must the tax be related to marginal external cost?

4. *[tax on pollution]* Graph 25-3 shows the missing market for pollution. Use this graph to answer the following questions.

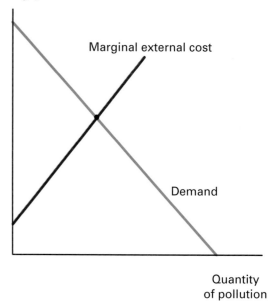

GRAPH 25-3

a. Show the equilibrium market quantity as Q_1 and price as P_1 without government action.

b. Assume that the government is able to identify the marginal external cost and devises a tax based on marginal social cost of the quantity of pollution. Identify the point at which the efficient quantity of pollution and the efficient tax are determined on the graph and label that point *E*.

c. Identify the efficient tax as T and the efficient quantity as Q_2.

d. Assume that the government decides to issue marketable permits that only allow firms to pollute the efficient quantity of pollution. Would the price of these permits be different from the efficient tax? Why or why not?

Visit **www.prenhall.com/ayers** for Exploring the Web exercises and additional self-test quizzes.

CHAPTER

26

PUBLIC CHOICE

A LOOK AHEAD

Big government—we say we don't want it, but we choose to have it. From Franklin D. Roosevelt to John F. Kennedy to Ronald Reagan to Bill Clinton, U.S. presidents have claimed to seek a smaller government. Yet they have not succeeded. Could it be that we really don't want them to? Or does government of the people, by the people, and for the people not reflect the wishes of the people? These questions are addressed in this chapter's Explore & Apply section.

Markets fail when the invisible hand does not guide them well, such as in response to externalities or public goods. In contrast, government has no invisible hand to guide it at all. The result is that the processes of government are often inefficient, with a general tilt toward overspending, as we will see. This chapter examines incentives facing voters on election day, incentives facing our elected representatives in Congress, and incentives facing public servants in government's many administrative agencies.

LEARNING OBJECTIVES

Understanding Chapter 26 will enable you to:
1. **Explain why democracy is imperfect, but still likely to be the best political system.**
2. **Point out why it is reasonable to accept some inefficiencies within government.**
3. **Identify the median voter and explain why that voter holds the key to political outcomes.**
4. **Discuss why legislators engage in vote trading that leads to excessive government spending.**
5. **Describe rent seeking and how it can lead to inefficiency in the political process.**
6. **Explain how both self-interest and the public interest motivate excessive spending within administrative agencies.**
7. **Resolve the apparent contradiction between the public's desire for a smaller government and the data showing increasing government spending over time.**

Explore & Apply

government failure the inefficiency of government processes.

public choice the study of economic incentives within government, including those that face voters, politicians, and the administrators of government programs.

The prior two chapters have examined market failure, which can lead to government action to correct inefficiencies. In addition to market failure, however, there is also **government failure,** which involves inefficiencies within government itself. These inefficiencies are not unexpected, since if government could do everything efficiently, there would be no reason to have markets at all. The field of **public choice** looks at economic incentives within government, including those that face voters, politicians, and the administrators of government programs.

26.1 CHOOSING A POLITICAL SYSTEM

There is no realistic way to get rid of government failure, at least not entirely. But it can help to imagine what such a government might be like, which is where we start.

THE IDEA OF A BENEVOLENT DICTATOR

Economists define a *benevolent dictatorship* as a form of government in which well-meaning and well-informed officials make all of the best choices. Obviously, there is no such thing in practice anywhere in the world. Nor will there ever be, since people make up government, and people have their own views and incentives. A benevolent dictatorship is an abstract form of government that implements the people's wishes without costly political processes and without worrying about providing public servants with incentives.

Dictatorships do not look so benevolent when found in the real world. Although a dictatorship might at first seem like an efficient form of government because it avoids wasting money on political campaigns and political rivalries, there are other inefficiencies that are far more significant. Dictatorships have little incentive to follow the wishes of the public or to avoid waste in government actions. For example, few would argue that the former Taliban religious dictatorship in Afghanistan acted in the best interests of its country. Rather than economic improvement, there was repression, violence, and severe poverty. More generally, prosperous countries of the world are not characterized by dictatorships.

The moral here is that a dictatorship cannot be expected to act in a benevolent manner. This provides justification for a more complicated form of government, one that provides incentives for the government to respond to the wishes of the people.

DEMOCRACY—A MESSY PROCESS TOWARD EFFICIENCY

"Democracy is the worst form of government . . . except for all the others."

—Winston Churchill

Democracy is an answer to the inefficiencies of dictatorship. It provides for a representative government that responds to the wishes of the public. The processes of democracy are costly and messy, however, leading to tremendous expenditures of time and money for political campaigns, as well as to seemingly endless political bickering. Despite these costs, democracies lead the world in standards of living. But all democracies are not created equal in terms of how well they function. One of the challenges in economics is to understand and offer guidance on how to improve incentives within the democratic process.

Economic incentives appear in every aspect of government. Voters face economic incentives in determining whether and how to vote. Legislators face economic incentives in determining which policies to enact and which taxes to levy. Public servants also face economic incentives in determining the level and type of service to provide.

The political process does not provide definitively efficient answers. For example, there is the problem of **cycling,** in which the order of political choices determines the outcome.

cycling when the order of political choices determines the outcome.

| TABLE 26-1 | PREFERENCES OF SUBCOMMITTEE MEMBERS |

OPTION	RANKING BY AGNES	RANKING BY BIFF	RANKING BY CHRISTINA
Increased defense spending	1	3	2
Tax rebates to the poor	2	1	3
Across-the-board tax cut	3	2	1

Let's take the example of a congressional subcommittee with three members voting on which of three alternative ways of stimulating the economy they will recommend to Congress. The alternatives are to increase spending on national security, to send tax rebate checks to the poor, or to cut tax rates across the board.

Table 26-1 uses this example to show how cycling can occur. The first representative, Agnes, prefers increasing spending to cutting taxes, but prefers a tax rebate to the poor over an across-the-board tax cut. The second representative, Biff, prefers cutting taxes to new spending, but would rather that the tax cut be directed to the poor rather than across the board. The third representative, Christina, prefers an across-the-board tax cut and strongly opposes sending out rebate checks. Christina views increased defense spending as preferable to sending out rebate checks, but not as desirable as an across-the-board tax cut. Table 26-1 summarizes the preferences of Agnes, Biff, and Christina.

Table 26-2 shows that the recommendation of the subcommittee will depend on the order in which members consider the alternatives. For example, the subcommittee might first vote on whether to increase defense spending or offer tax rebates to the poor. Two of the subcommittee members would vote for increased defense. However, comparing increased defense with an across-the-board tax cut, two of the three members would vote for an across-the-board tax cut. The subcommittee would therefore recommend an across-the-board tax cut. However, if they were to compare an across-the-board tax cut against tax rebates to the poor, the subcommittee would prefer tax rebates to the poor. This process

| TABLE 26-2 | THE SUBCOMMITTEE'S RECOMMENDATION |

The recommendation will depend on the order in which the subcommittee considers the choices.

CHOICES	AGNES'S VOTE	BIFF'S VOTE	CHRISTINA'S VOTE	THE SUBCOMMITTEE'S CHOICE BETWEEN THE TWO ALTERNATIVES
Tax rebates to the poor or Increased defense spending	for defense	for rebates	for defense	increased defense spending
Increased defense spending or Across-the-board tax cut	for defense	for tax cut	for tax cut	across-the-board tax cut
Across-the-board tax cut or Tax rebates to the poor	for rebates	for rebates	for tax cut	tax rebates to the poor

could go on infinitely, which is why it is called cycling. Whoever sets the *agenda* of which alternatives will be considered first also winds up in effect choosing the alternatives that they will recommend to Congress.

The possibility for cycling illustrates how important it can be to set the agenda. Cycling also illustrates a certain irrationality within the collective choice process. It serves to emphasize that, while democracy is likely to be the best public choice process available, it can sometimes lead to inefficient or even random outcomes.

FEDERALISM—EXPERIMENTING WITH MULTIPLE WAYS

Democracy in the United States is characterized by *federalism*, meaning that there are multiple layers of government. This arrangement has an economic basis: It allows those citizens to vote who are most directly affected by the consequences of the choice. For example, residents of a school district pick members of the board controlling schools within that district. Urban residents vote on the size of their city's police budget, since they are the ones who will be protected by the resulting police force. **Fiscal federalism** examines the design of a federal system of government from an economic standpoint. It suggests that decisions should be made by the level of government most directly affected by those decisions.

fiscal federalism the study of the design of a federal system of government from an economic standpoint.

Many issues are national in scope and thus appropriate to consider at the federal level, meaning at the level of government that presides over all of the other governments. Certainly national defense is one such issue. Another is income redistribution. If income redistribution is left to state-owned localities, little of it can occur. The reason is that only the federal government can effectively take from the rich and give to the poor. If such income redistribution is tried by states and cities on their own, the rich wind up moving out and the poor wind up moving in. The result, as New York City discovered in the 1970s, is that there are too few rich people to tax to pay for aid to the burgeoning population of poor people. In New York City's case, many of the rich moved to Connecticut or New Jersey, both well within commuting distance.

Even when the federal government does not directly control policies at the state and local levels, it often influences these policies through financial incentives. For example, the federal government will withhold transportation aid that goes to highway construction and repair if states do not enforce speed limits and other safety measures that comply with federal guidelines.

Having multiple layers of government has the added benefit of allowing policies to be tried out on a small scale before they are enacted on a large scale. Four of the last five American presidents—George W. Bush, Bill Clinton, Ronald Reagan, and Jimmy Carter—often referred back to their experiences at the state level for guidance on what would work at the national level. Apparently voters recognize the value of this experience, or they would not have voted these former governors into the office of the presidency.

There is sometimes a conflict between the federal governments and states over which government should be the final authority. For example, Oregon legalized medically assisted suicide for terminally ill elderly patients who are capable of making such a choice. The federal government recognizes no such right and promised to prosecute doctors who assist in such suicides. In a similar vein, some localities have legalized the medical use of marijuana. However, under federal law, no medical use of marijuana is allowed. As these examples suggest, the issue of allowing states leeway to try different ways of doing things is fraught with contention.

CHOOSING A PRESIDENT, FLORIDA STYLE   *SNAPSHOT*

It was deep into the night of the presidential election of 2000. The world watched with humor and amazement as bleary-eyed poll workers stared intently at machine-readable ballots, trying to determine voter intent. The world got to learn the meaning of *chad,* those little pieces intended to be punched out of computer-readable cards. The problem was that sometimes the chad was not fully punched—resulting in a dimpled chad. Alas that we would need to learn about such things!

The true lesson is one of federalism, in which different states and even different localities conduct elections in different manners. In hindsight, some states and localities obviously used better methods than others. It was a learning process. But why even have the election determined on a state-by-state basis? Wouldn't it be enough to tally the popular votes across the country and just see who wins the majority?

The answers again revolve around federalism. Tallying votes according to each state and then having the states elect the president through an electoral college makes sure that candidates do not ignore portions of the country altogether. It certainly does influence where time and money will be spent on the campaign trail. ◀

26.2 CHOICES BY THE VOTERS

Because we delegate decisions collectively, none of us gets exactly what we want. Moreover, each candidate for public office represents a **bundled good,** meaning that the voter cannot pick and choose which items on a candidate's agenda to support and which to oppose—one vote buys all. The result is a compromise that is not fully satisfying to anyone. In the case of public goods, such as national defense, the quantity that is chosen by public officials must then be consumed by everyone, no matter their personal preferences. However, the culprit is not the public officials, but the nature of the public good itself—public goods are consumed jointly. Where possible, people prefer to make choices for themselves.

bundled good in the context of voting, occurs when voters must take the whole package, including elements they don't want; candidates represent bundled goods.

A second source of concern over government action has to do with the **principal–agent problem.** Over 19 million workers in this country are employed by government as public servants. Public servants range from teachers to Marines to, until recently, an official tea taster. No matter the job, they are all *agents* of the public (the *principal*). However, because the public is so large, no individual has direct control. For example, we do not advise informing the traffic officer preparing to give you a ticket that he or she is your servant and should follow your orders. This generalized accountability provides a great deal of leeway on the part of the agents to do as they please.

principal–agent problem the difficulty of making agents, such as public servants, act in the interests of principals, such as voters.

QUICKCHECK

When the size of government grows, public dissatisfaction with government can also be expected to grow. Why?

Answer: When choices are made collectively, almost no one gets exactly what he or she wants. Therefore, one explanation for dissatisfaction with bigger government is that growth in the size of the government budget comes at the expense of individuals' abilities to make their own decisions. In addition, the larger the size of the government budget, the larger the size and visibility of inefficiencies within the public sector, such as those caused by the principal–agent problem.

THE MEDIAN VOTER MODEL

A funny thing happens on the road to public office. In U.S. presidential campaigns, for example, Democratic and Republican candidates for president often sound much farther apart on the issues in the primaries than they do when it comes time for the general election. For an explanation of this and other aspects of election outcomes, we can turn to the median voter model.

The **median voter model** says that candidates will seek the support of the decisive swing voter that can tilt the balance from one candidate to the other. This median voter will be quite different in the general election than the median voter in either the Democratic or Republican primaries. The median voter model thus predicts that successful politicians will seek to always follow that median to wherever it moves.

The median voter model is applicable when voters—those who actually vote—can be lined up along a spectrum from left to right. Maybe the spectrum is political, ranging from the left wing to the right wing. Perhaps the spectrum is budgetary, ranging from a lower budget to a higher budget. In any case, the *median voter* is the one for whom 50 percent of the other voters prefer further to the right on the spectrum and 50 percent prefer further to the left. In an election in which all voters pick between two candidates, the candidate chosen by the median voter will win by garnering a minimum of just over 50 percent of the vote. Note that voters are considered to be those people who do indeed vote.

Figure 26-1 illustrates the importance of the median voter in two-candidate elections. In this figure, nine voters and four candidates are lined up along the political or budgetary spectrum. Each voter is numbered. Candidates are labeled by the names Ann, Buck, Carlos, and Darlene. Which candidate would defeat any opponent in a two-person race? The median voter holds the answer.

Voter 5 is the median voter and would vote for Buck against any opponent. If the opponent was to the left of Buck, Buck would also be preferred by voters 6 through 9 and thereby win with a majority of the vote. Likewise, if the opponent was to the right of Buck, voters 1 through 4 would side with the median voter to grant Buck the majority.

Suppose we divide voters into Democrats and Republicans and then hold primary elections to determine each party's candidate. For simplicity, we'll assign voters 1 through 5 and candidates Ann and Buck to the Democrats. Voters 6 through 9 and candidates Carlos and Darlene go to the Republicans. In the Democratic primary, voter 3 now becomes the median

median voter model predicts that, in two-candidate races, the winner will be chosen by the median voter—50 percent of the other voters prefer further to the right and 50 percent prefer further to the left.

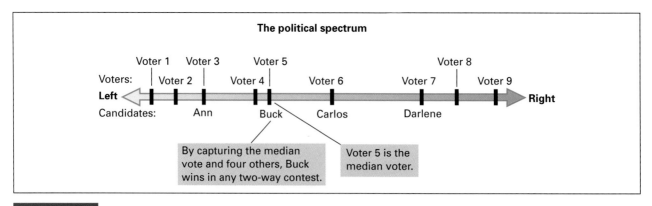

FIGURE 26-1

THE MEDIAN VOTER MODEL The median voter model helps explain the outcome of the political process. Voter 5 is the median voter, because there are an equal number of voters on either side. This voter's preference for candidate Buck would cause Buck to win if running against any single one of the other candidates.

voter and would vote for Ann. In the Republican primary, voters 7 and 8 tie for median voter honors. Their votes would go to Darlene. That means the general election would come down to a race between Ann and Darlene.

Voter 5 has not been forgotten. Between the primaries and the general election, the candidates turn their attentions toward the overall median voter, voter 5. They start sounding more and more alike. The candidate best able to shift to the positions of voter 5 is thus most likely to win the election.

RATIONAL IGNORANCE

Democracy is first and foremost of the people. Yet in most elections below the level of presidential elections, considerably less than half of registered voters bother to vote. Even when registered voters do vote, they often have little idea of what they are voting on. There are many choices on the typical ballot, so many in fact that voters do not have time enough to research all of the candidates and propositions seen on the ballot. Even people who want to be involved find themselves with insufficient time to prepare as well as they would like for the voting process. The result is **rational ignorance** on the part of the voters, meaning that they make a rational choice to remain uninformed on many public issues.

rational ignorance when voters make the rational choice to remain uninformed on many public issues.

Most voting choices are for people rather than specific policy actions. A voter will vote for a candidate based on that candidate's reputation and positions on certain issues. The voter relies on the candidate to address other issues in a similar way. Therefore, voters delegate authority to politicians, who in turn delegate to the administrative bureaucracy. The amount of detail involved in governing the country is too overwhelming to do otherwise. If voters were asked to vote on every issue directly, the amount of rational ignorance would be much greater than it is under the system of voting for candidates.

Political parties are, in part, a response to the rational ignorance of voters. Instead of having to figure it all out for themselves, voters can select political parties according to their philosophical preferences. In this way, voters rely on the political parties to do much of the detailed research into the issues and into the candidates that are running for office. "Voting the party line" can be a reasonable way to address the problem of rational ignorance. If voters pay too little attention, though, political parties and the politicians they produce might too closely align themselves with special interests that do pay attention.

26.3 CANDIDATES AND COALITIONS

To achieve the results constituents expect, the holder of a political office will often find it necessary to compromise and bargain with other elected representatives. In addition, voters' rational ignorance means that politicians and bureaucrats can often safely follow their own personal agendas, even when those agendas conflict with what the public would want them to do. In politics, appearance matters, too.

STAYING IN OFFICE

Most elected officials want to remain in office. Incumbent politicians routinely get reelected, even though *term limitations*—laws that restrict the number of sequential times a politician can hold one public office—are quite popular. Achieving reelection can be accomplished through **logrolling**—vote trading—in order to obtain projects of direct benefit to constituents. Logrolling unfortunately results in massive spending packages that contain numerous local spending projects of questionable merit. These projects (often called *pork*) and

logrolling when politicians trade votes in order to obtain projects of direct benefit to constituents in their districts.

other accomplishments are then reported back to constituents through a newsletter. Left out is any focus on cost, however, even though the pork does not come cheaply.

Remember, to obtain projects for their districts, legislators must vote for all of the other costly items in the legislation, including those of no benefit to their constituents. When voters focus on visible benefits from projects and ignore the less-obvious costs, they are said to suffer from **fiscal illusion,** which tends to bring about excessive spending.

Even if the costs of logrolling are considered, they are still likely to be of little concern to the electorate. After all, the costs are in terms of other districts' wasteful projects that are included in an appropriations bill. However, if a majority of other legislators are signing onto the bill, you don't want your district left out. In other words, if you are going to be paying for other districts' pork, you want pork of your own. Thus, constituents rarely hold pork-barrel politics against their own legislators, even though they may disapprove of the practice in general.

There is good reason to disapprove. *Pork-barrel politics* leads to excessive government spending, as the cost of the myriad of relatively small projects gets lost in the general budget. For example, the constituents in most districts would be delighted to accept federally funded projects, such as for highways or drainage. It does not matter whether the project's benefits exceed its costs, because the costs are spread across the country, while the benefits are concentrated in that district. They are grateful to their elected representatives. For voters in other districts, the project is too small to focus on and has no bearing on the reelection of their own representatives. The result is too much government spending.

One check on logrolling is the line-item veto powers of many state governors. The **line-item veto** allows a governor to veto parts of appropriations bills, rather than having to accept or reject the bills in their entireties. If the governor were to be a Democrat, for instance, he or she could veto all of the Republicans' pet projects, except projects of Republicans who support the governor's agenda. In turn, because Republicans would know their projects would not survive, they would not go along with voting for the Democrats' pet projects. The result would be much less pork. The governors of forty-three states have some form of line-item veto authority. Although Congress voted in 1996 to grant the president line-item veto power, the Supreme Court subsequently ruled this application of line-item veto authority to be unconstitutional. The Justices reasoned that it violated the separation of powers between the president and Congress.

Not all vote trading is inefficient. For example, a worthy project might serve only a portion of the country. Consider levees along a river that benefit the residents of only a few states. Without vote trading, the project would not be passed by Congress, since a majority of states would perceive no benefits. Such projects could still be undertaken, however, if the affected states join forces and proceed on their own. Payment for the project would then come from the residents of those states instead of from general tax revenues.

---

fiscal illusion when voters focus on visible benefits from projects and ignore the less-obvious costs.

line-item veto power that allows a governor to veto parts of appropriations bills, rather than having to accept or reject the bills in their entireties.

QUICKCHECK

Would line-item veto authority for the president stop logrolling in the federal government?

Answer: Logrolling would probably be reduced but not eliminated. For example, friends of the president would not have their pet projects vetoed. However, the president's friends would have a more difficult time lining up support for those projects in Congress, especially if the president routinely vetoes the pet projects of other legislators.

A TAX BY ANY OTHER NAME   *SNAPSHOT*

Sometimes government spending can be financed without a tax, or at least without anything labeled as a tax. A favorite in the political recipe book is to use *unfunded mandates*, which means that the government requires businesses to implement government programs, but to do so at their own expense. For example, if the government thinks that workers should have better healthcare, it has only to mandate that businesses provide better healthcare coverage to their employees. If the government wants to assist the handicapped in getting about, it has only to mandate handicapped parking places, curb cuts, wheelchair ramps, wide doors, and anything else it thinks would help.

In effect, requirements that businesses spend their own money to accomplish public objectives is equivalent to the government assessing a tax of whatever these requirements cost and then undertaking the actions itself. However, there is some question as to whether unfunded mandates lead to proper government decision making. When the government does not have to pay the costs itself, it is much easier to say yes to projects than if those projects must be financed explicitly out of tax revenue. With unfunded mandates, the tax is effectively hidden in the higher costs to firms and higher prices to their customers. ◄

INTEREST GROUPS—THEY PAY ATTENTION

The United States prides itself on its majority rule. Yet legislation is often influenced by small, well-organized minorities, aligned according to special interests. *Special-interest groups* are characterized by a tightly focused agenda and **lobbyists**—agents who promote that agenda within the political system.

lobbyists agents who promote a special-interest agenda within the political system.

The agendas of the special interests often conflict with the interests of most voters. Special interests are frequently able to get their way, however, by paying close attention to the details of legislators' votes. Legislators who vote against special interests know they lose their votes and campaign contributions. However, legislators who favor the special interests and vote against the wishes of the majority often face no adverse consequences. The reason is that the general public interest is often more diffuse, with few voters keying their votes around specific issues. In short, **when the benefits of an action are spread broadly and the costs are concentrated, special interests are frequently successful at preventing the action from occurring.**

For example, few consumers would vote against a legislator for supporting agricultural price supports, even though such supports raise the prices of a broad assortment of foods and beverages. However, if a legislator votes against the price supports, that legislator incurs the ire of those people in agriculture whose livelihoods are at stake. While the number of voters who gain from agricultural price supports is much smaller than the number who lose, the power of the gainers is magnified because they key their votes around this one special-interest issue.

Lobbying by special-interest groups is efficient when it provides information that prevents legislative errors. When legislation targets the actions of a particular industry, for example, that industry's lobbyists are in the best position to provide relevant information on the industry's business practices. For example, congressional staffers attempting to craft sensible pipeline regulations might obtain information on oil and gas pipeline operations from the American Petroleum Institute, which lobbies for the oil industry. Other interested lobbyists would also submit information. Congressional staffers use this information to design policies that are cost-effective, an advantage to both the oil industry and the economy.

Unfortunately, special-interest lobbying is frequently inefficient, because it involves wasteful rent seeking. **Rent seeking** occurs when lobbyists or others expend resources in an effort to come out a winner, such as in the political process. Since economic efficiency looks

rent seeking occurs when lobbyists or others expend resources in an effort to come out a winner in the political process.

at the size of the economic pie, not how it is sliced, the time and money lobbyists spend trying to get the pie sliced to their liking is inefficient.

Some observers contend that an emerging trend in Congress reduces the problems of special-interest lobbying and the rent seeking that comes with it. This trend is toward replacing federal programs with block grants to states. **Block grants** represent sums of money designated to go toward a range of state-administered programs within certain categories of spending. For example, Congress designates a single block grant to finance many of the welfare programs administered in a state. By leaving the details up to the states, block grants mean that Congress need merely decide on the number of dollars to include in the grant, something that voters will monitor relatively closely. Lobbyists must then compete with each other, state by state, over the allocation of that money.

block grant a sum of money transferred from the federal government to states that is designated for a particular type of spending, but where the exact programs are not specified.

SNAPSHOT   YOU MIGHT BE A WINNER!

There is a big difference between competition in the marketplace and competition for favors from government. In the marketplace, the winner is the one that builds the better mousetrap and thereby increases the well-being of all concerned. Lobbying for political favors is not productive in this way. It is more akin to fighting over a prize. The time and money wasted in fighting over who gets the prize is a form of rent seeking and serves little constructive purpose from the point of view of society at large. The value of government policies is often counteracted by the money that interest groups spend in trying to come out among the winners.

Most of us engage in rent seeking, too. You have done so yourself if you have ever returned a sweepstakes entry, such as in the Publishers Clearing House or American Family Publishers multimillion dollar sweepstakes. At the time, you probably wondered if it was worth the time and postage to apply, because you knew that millions of other people would be sending in their entries. That illustrates the problem of rent seeking—the value of the prize is offset by the cost of seeking it, which in this case is the millions of dollars worth of time and postage spent by all the entrants. ◀

26.4 THE GOVERNMENT BUREAUCRACY

Administrative agencies face the task of translating general and often vague legislation into detailed programs that are actually implemented. Employees of the many agencies of government are commonly referred to as government *bureaucrats*. The term is not to their liking, however, since it evokes images of the stodginess, red tape, and delays associated with bureaucracy. Are the employees of the government agencies unresponsive to the citizens they are supposed to serve?

INCENTIVES WITHIN AGENCIES

The employees of government agencies have personal agendas that sometimes conflict with the intent of voters and their elected representatives. Most significantly, **for both public-spirited and self-serving reasons, bureaucrats almost always desire budgets for their agencies that exceed what the average citizen and elected official would prefer.**

To understand this phenomenon, consider who enters any particular government agency. For example, who makes a career in the armed forces? Most likely, it's people of a military persuasion, who are convinced that the armed forces are more important than most people realize. Likewise, those who join the Environmental Protection Agency have keener interests and greater expertise in environmental matters than do most of the rest of

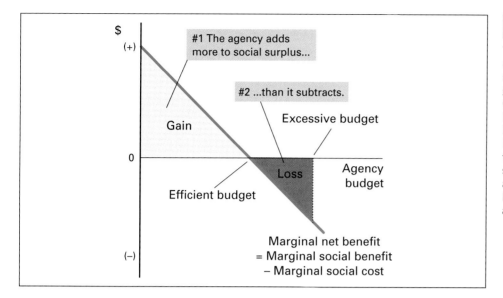

FIGURE 26-2

THE AGENCY BUDGET The efficient budget maximizes social surplus, and occurs where marginal net benefit equals zero. Government agencies have the incentive to seek a budget higher than would be efficient. If the actual budget exceeds that which is efficient, however, some of the gain from the agency's existence is offset by a loss from overspending. Gains and losses are shown.

us. They naturally tend to think that environmental protection deserves a higher priority than it gets.

More broadly, who enters government at all? For the most part, it's people who think government is relatively more important than most citizens realize. Thus, employees of government in general and of agencies in particular truly believe that their missions are more deserving than the political process acknowledges. For these public-spirited motives, they seek to expand the size of their agencies beyond what is efficient.

There are also self-serving reasons why government employees want larger budgets for their agencies. From the top of the agency to the bottom, a larger budget is seen as good job protection. It opens up promotion opportunities and reduces the threat of layoffs. As a manager, the more budget under you, the more power and prestige you enjoy, and the better your qualifications look should you wish to switch jobs later. Indeed, it is usually considered disloyal for any agency personnel to advocate cutting the agency's budget.

Figure 26-2 shows the marginal net benefit of increasing an agency's budget, where *marginal net benefit* equals marginal social benefit minus marginal social cost. At first, if the agency directs its spending toward its most essential missions, the value of agency spending far exceeds its budgetary cost. As its budget size is increased, however, the agency must fund programs of increasingly less merit. When the value of extra spending is less than the cost of that spending, the agency has spent too much.

To achieve economic efficiency, the agency budget should equal the amount for which marginal net benefit is zero, as shown in Figure 26-2. The total net benefit generated by this spending is given by the triangular area labeled "Gain." If the agency spends beyond the efficient amount, total net benefit would decrease. For example, if the actual spending were given by the excessive budget labeled in the figure, the area labeled "Loss" would need to be subtracted from this gain. So long as the gain from having the agency exceeds the loss from an excessive budget, however, it is efficient for the agency to exist.

TURF-BUILDING—STRATEGIES FOR A BIGGER BUDGET

It is one thing for bureaucrats to want an inefficiently large budget—to expand their turf. Getting that budget is another matter. Unfortunately, the struggle over the size of agency budgets is rather one-sided, because the agency is best positioned to know what its spending options are. If an agency is aware of ways to save money, for example, it has little incentive to reveal them. Such *asymmetric information,* in which one party to a transaction knows more than the other, puts legislators at a disadvantage in overseeing agencies.

There are various strategies government agencies use to obtain the budgets they want. For example, agency spending is commonly guided by the philosophy of "use it or lose it." Agencies want to avoid getting caught with extra cash at the end of the fiscal year when the budget expires. Extra cash might indicate to the legislators or public that the agency could accomplish its mission with a smaller budget next time. The response to use-it-or-lose-it incentives is a spending spree near the end of each fiscal year. If you are an agency employee with a pet project, it's a great time to get it funded.

When agencies submit their budgets for review, they are often told to provide a bare-bones alternative budget, perhaps representing a 20 percent reduction from the budget they claim to need. The idea is to give the legislative oversight committee an idea of what services would be sacrificed if the budget were to be reduced. If you are in charge of a government agency and are told to do this, could you manipulate the process to obtain a large budget? Remember, you know more about possibilities for reducing costs in your agency than do the legislators. Would you economize on travel, or on the number of times the trash is collected?

Washington Monument strategy when a government agency offers a bare-bones budget that cuts its most popular functions; intended to increase the chances that a more generous budget will be approved.

To preserve your budget, you would be better off suggesting cuts in something that the public would not in fact want you to cut. The strategy of selecting widely supported projects for potential cuts has been used so often, it's acquired its own name—the **Washington Monument strategy.** Using this strategy, the agency bluffs by offering a bare-bones budget that cuts its most popular functions. For instance, the National Park Service might propose to save money by restricting access to the Washington Monument to between 9 A.M. and 5 P.M. on weekdays, with no access at all on weekends. Evenings and weekends are cut because they are the times of peak tourist demand.

The Washington Monument strategy is used at all levels of government, but not always successfully. In the 1990s, for example, a school district in San Antonio, Texas, claimed that it would be forced to eliminate all school crossing guards unless voters approved a tax increase. Surely the school board did not believe that children's lives deserved the lowest priority. This example of the Washington Monument strategy backfired, though, as voters rejected the tax increase. To safeguard the children's lives, a private individual donated the money needed to pay for crossing guards. In following years, the school district quietly returned to providing the money needed to fund this essential service.

QUICKCHECK

Why is it easy to get projects funded within government agencies at the end of the fiscal year?

Answer: The answer revolves around the concept of asymmetric information. In this case, the agency figures that it knows more than the oversight committee about its spending requirements. It figures that the oversight committee will use actual spending as an indicator of how much budget is required for the following fiscal year. Since agencies usually want as large a budget as is possible, they may not wish to reveal that they can get by with any less than their current budget. So, to avoid future budget cuts, any money that agencies have put aside for unexpected contingencies needs to be spent before the end of the fiscal year, causing projects proposed at that time to have a greater chance of getting funded than if they had been proposed at other times.

26.5 ADDRESSING GOVERNMENT FAILURES

Is there anything citizens can do to counter all the incentives within government to spend too much? The options are limited. For example, limiting the number of years legislators can serve might keep representatives more in touch with the voters. However, such term limits deprive the government of experienced legislators, and also run the danger of focusing legislators' attentions on personal profit opportunities once they leave office.

There is no easy way to provide the proper incentives for efficiency within government. That should come as little surprise. After all, if the government were efficient, there would be little reason to adopt competitive free markets. We turn to government when markets fail. We must merely keep in mind that market failure does not imply government success.

26.6 THE MIXED ECONOMY—ADDING MORE GOVERNMENT

Explore & Apply

"That government is best which governs least."

—Thomas Jefferson

Recall from Chapter 1 that a mixed economy must determine how much to rely on the marketplace and how much to rely on government. It is up to the political process to establish the specifics of this mix. The size of government and its proper role have been debated in the United States from the days of its founding. President Ronald Reagan, for example, was well-known for trying to slow the growth of government. In 1996, even President Clinton proclaimed, "The era of big government is over." On the flip side, Treasury Secretary Alexander Hamilton, pictured on the $10 bill, favored change that would strengthen the power of the federal government. He offered strong arguments favoring the creation of a Bank of the United States, an early version of what we now refer to as a government central bank. More recently, in leading the fight against terrorism, President George W. Bush pushed through significant increases in government spending and powers.

U.S. history shows that the balance of power shifted back and forth between those favoring a bigger government and others who disagreed. Figure 26-3 shows the growth in federal government spending as a percentage of GDP since 1929. This growth is attributable to the growth in transfer payments, as shown in the figure. *Transfer payments,* such as for

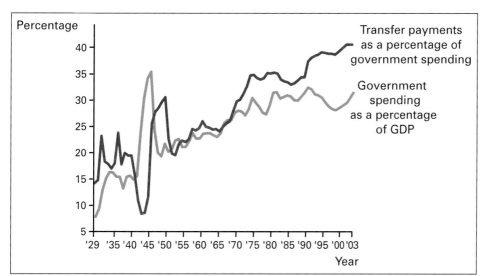

FIGURE 26-3

GROWTH OF AMERICAN GOVERNMENT SINCE 1929
Government spending as a fraction of GDP is today more than three times its value in 1929. Transfer payments as a fraction of government spending rose to historic highs in the 1990s.

Source: Bureau of Economic Analysis, *National Income and Product Account Tables.*

income redistribution and Social Security, refer to government spending that isn't for goods, services, or investments.

What led the country down the path to bigger government? The U.S. Constitution says that government is obligated to "promote the general welfare." The welfare of the country covers a lot. Earliest efforts by the government to promote a growing economy focused on filling the transportation needs of a young nation. From building roads and canals at first, and then later railroads, government provided the resources needed to build a transportation system that would tie the states together and promote commerce. But government was always limited in what it could do because it had no way to raise the money to fund the cost of a "big government," even if there had been agreement that government ought to be bigger.

Following the expansion of government power and influence that necessarily accompanied the Civil War and the Reconstruction era, the federal government continued to take on more responsibilities. To regulate commerce, the Interstate Commerce Commission was created in 1887. The first antitrust law, the Sherman Act, designed to halt the growth of monopoly power, was enacted in 1890. Then came a major event that allowed an unprecedented expansion in the size of the federal government. The federal income tax was enacted into law in 1913, which led to a dramatic increase in federal revenues. All these new laws, agencies, and obligations of government were controversial because they expanded government power and influence. Yet by 1929, the eve of the Great Depression, government's share of aggregate spending was still only a small fraction of its current share.

President Franklin D. Roosevelt promised the nation a New Deal to overcome the misery of the Great Depression. The Supreme Court soon declared a number of these policies unconstitutional, thus acting as a brake on the expansion of government. Not even the popular FDR could bring the American people along in support of his plan to "pack" the Court with new justices who would support all his proposals.

WHY THE ROLE OF GOVERNMENT GREW

After World War II ended in 1945, an explosion of American prosperity enriched consumers as never before. U.S. prosperity ultimately spread to the war-shattered countries of Western Europe and Japan, as the United States served as the engine of growth and these countries got pulled along for the ride. While the government had not been particularly successful in ending the depression in the 1930s, the government proved in the 1940s that it could successfully wage war. Americans were united in their support of their government's war effort and it was natural that these good feelings toward government would continue following the war.

The expansion of government reached its pinnacle with President Lyndon Johnson's Great Society, which added about 500 social programs between 1965 and 1968. Some programs, such as Medicare, have become familiar standbys. Others, such as Model Cities, have long since been forgotten. These programs aimed to meet nearly all of the social issues of the time, and more. They included programs to solve the problems of hunger, homelessness, discrimination, and excess immigration. Great Society programs provided higher minimum wages, vocational training, agricultural subsidies, truth in labeling, clean highways, and on and on.

The big-government expansion of the 1960s seemed too much for many citizens by the end of the 1970s. In 1980, Americans elected Ronald Reagan as their thirty-sixth president. Reagan promised to "get the government off the backs of the American people." As president, Reagan spoke of the need for less government regulation, saying, "Millions of individuals making their own decisions in the marketplace will always allocate resources better than any centralized government planning process." The American people adopted his view that government should be smaller. As Reagan put it, "Government's view of the economy could be summed up in a few short phrases: If it moves, tax it. If it keeps moving, regulate it. And if it stops moving, subsidize it." More pointedly, Reagan stated "There is a threat posed to human freedom by the enormous power of the modern state. History teaches the

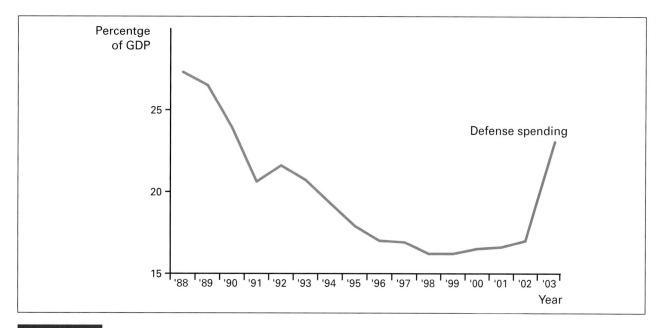

FIGURE 26-4

SPENDING ON NATIONAL DEFENSE After a defense buildup in the 1980s, the economy reaped a "peace dividend" in which it reduced spending on defense. That trend toward lower defense spending appears to have now ended.

Source: Department of Defense, *National Defense Budget Estimates, FY 2003,* Table 7-7.

dangers of government that overreaches—political control taking precedence over free economic growth—secret police, mindless bureaucracy, all combining to stifle individual excellence and personal freedom."

Reagan did oversee a buildup in military spending, but one that was directed at convincing the Soviet Union that it could not afford to maintain its adversarial stance. With the demise of the Soviet Union, the United States in the 1990s was able to reap a so-called peace dividend of lower defense spending needs. As shown in Figure 26-4, military spending was cut dramatically during the administrations of George H. W. Bush and Bill Clinton in the 1990s. In light of terrorist threats and a perception that cuts in the 1990s were too deep, the military spending trend has turned once more to the upside under President George W. Bush, as has spending on farm subsidies and other programs.

Traditional civil service government employment has fallen under President Bush. However, a study released by the Brookings Institution in September 2003 reports that the "true size" of government employment increased by more than one million jobs from 1999 to 2002. This increase was largely in response to the increased use of government contracts and grants.

Government has expanded its presence in other ways that are more difficult to measure. For example, Congress passed what is generally known as the Patriot Act following the terrorist attacks of September 11, 2001. This act greatly increased the surveillance and detention powers of government. More recently, though, pressure has grown in Congress to restrict some of those powers. For example, the U.S. House of Representatives passed legislation in 2003 that would restrict some of government's search powers that had been expanded in that act.

Through considering such legislation, government refines its role in the mixed economy. It is continuously evaluating the marginal costs and marginal benefits of its actions. While public choice analysis reveals that incentives are sometimes flawed in this process, we can be grateful that such a process does exist.

**THINKING
CRITICALLY**

1. In the 2000 campaign for the presidency, neither candidate Al Gore nor candidate George W. Bush proposed to significantly change the size of government. Discuss plausible economic events that would have to occur in the future to prompt a president to again declare that "the era of big government is over."

2. Why do the citizens of some countries seem to prefer big government, while the citizens of other countries prefer a smaller government? What factors might prompt the citizens of countries with big governments to change their preferences in the direction of smaller government?

   Visit www.prenhall.com/ayers for updates and web exercises on this Explore & Apply topic.

SUMMARY AND LEARNING OBJECTIVES

1. **Explain why democracy is imperfect, but still likely to be the best political system.**

   - A benevolent dictatorship is a form of government in which well-meaning and well-informed officials make the best choices. Real-world dictatorships are not of this type, since dictators have little incentive to follow the wishes of the public.

   - Democracy provides for representative government, responding to the wishes of the public, but is still subject to inefficiencies.

   - One problem that can sometimes arise is called cycling, which means that outcomes are determined by the order in which choices are considered. In this case, whoever sets the agenda also determines the outcome. Cycling indicates an irrationality within the collective choice process.

   - Federalism, multiple layers of government, characterizes democracy in the United States. Fiscal federalism looks at the design of a federal system of government from an economic standpoint. From this perspective, decisions should be made by the level of government most directly affected by any decision. Issues that are national in scope are appropriate for consideration by the federal government. National defense is an example.

   - The federal government influences decisions by states and localities through financial incentives, even when it does not make those decisions itself.

2. **Point out why it is reasonable to accept some inefficiencies within government.**

   - Government failure refers to inefficiencies in government itself. The principal–agent problem, rational ignorance, logrolling, and fiscal illusion all contribute to government failure. Pork-barrel politics leads to excessive government spending.

   - Rational ignorance on the part of the public allows politicians to follow their own agendas on many issues. It is rational for the public to remain unaware of much of what their elected servants do because of the public's lack of time to stay fully informed.

3. **Identify the median voter and explain why that voter holds the key to political outcomes.**

   - The median voter model explains why candidates often take similar positions in general elections. The candidate best able to attract the vote of the median voter is most likely to win the election.

   - The median voter is in the middle position regarding issues. Half of the remaining voters will be on one side of the median voter and the other half will be on the other side. Politicians will pitch their appeals to the median voter since that voter will tilt an election result to the candidate receiving the vote cast by the median voter.

4. **Discuss why legislators engage in vote trading that leads to excessive government spending.**

   - Logrolling involves politicians in vote trading. A legislator agrees to support another legislator's bill in exchange for that legislator's support for his or her bill. In this way projects are approved that benefit the voters back home and help the legislator get reelected. Much of the spending that results from logrolling is wasteful and is often referred to as pork. Politicians who bring home the pork often find themselves being repeatedly reelected.

   - Fiscal illusion occurs when voters remember the benefits of government spending but forget about the less-obvious costs. When voters suffer from fiscal illusion, legislators are likely to respond by spending too much relative to taxation.

- The line-item veto, available to forty-three state governors, allows a governor to veto parts of appropriation bills. The line-item veto is thus a weapon against logrolling and pork-barrel spending. A line-item veto for the president was approved by Congress in 1996, but subsequently ruled unconstitutional by the Supreme Court.

5. **Describe rent seeking and how it can lead to inefficiency in the political process.**
   - Special-interest groups and their lobbyists influence government spending. Lobbyists are commonly able to prevent an action that they oppose when the benefits of the action are spread broadly and the costs are concentrated.
   - Lobbying can be efficient when it provides legislators with information that promotes informed actions. Lobbying often involves wasteful rent seeking, in which the special-interest groups' aims are to increase the size of their slice of the economic pie, even if the pie itself is made smaller.

6. **Explain how both self-interest and the public interest motivate excessive spending within administrative agencies.**
   - Government agencies have the incentive to expand their budget beyond the efficient amount. Graphically, a budget that is efficient is identified by the point where the marginal net benefit of the agency is zero. A budget that is too big pushes the value of the marginal net benefit of additional budget allocations into negative values.

- Government agencies employ various strategies to obtain funds. While an agency might be aware of ways to save money, there is no incentive to reveal that information to anyone else. This case is an example of the problem of asymmetric information, in which one party has information that another party lacks, but would find useful.
- Another method to maintain agency budgets is a response to "use it or lose it" rules. If an agency fails to spend all of its budget in one year, then its budget for the next year will possibly be cut by the amount unspent. Hence, agencies facing the end of the year with unspent monies in their budgets tend to find things to purchase with these funds, regardless of whether this spending is efficient.
- Another method to keep an agency's budget up is the Washington Monument strategy. When an agency is threatened by budget cuts, it responds by proposing to eliminate or reduce its most popular programs rather than try to cut the fat out of its spending. Often, protests by the public are enough to restore the threatened agency's funding.

 Resolve the apparent contradiction between the public's desire for a smaller government and the data showing increasing government spending over time.
   - Controversy over the size and role of government has existed throughout U.S. history. Various events, including wars and the Great Depression, led to an increased role for the federal government. Although defense spending declined during the 1990s, that trend has reversed course under President George W. Bush.

KEY TERMS

government failure, 654
public choice, 654
cycling, 654
fiscal federalism, 656
bundled good, 657

principal–agent problem, 657
median voter model, 658
rational ignorance, 659
logrolling, 659
fiscal illusion, 660

line-item veto, 660
lobbyists, 661
rent seeking, 661
block grant, 662
Washington Monument strategy, 664

TEST YOURSELF

TRUE OR FALSE

1. The field of public choice is concerned with economic incentives within government.
2. The median voter model predicts that in general elections politicians will ignore the positions of the median voter.

3. Fiscal illusion refers to the tendency of voters to ignore the benefits of government projects due to their concern over the costs.
4. The president of the United States, like the governors of most states, have line-item veto authority.
5. A government budget that is efficient exhibits a marginal net benefit of zero.

MULTIPLE CHOICE

6. Public choice economics suggests that
   a. markets always fail from the public's viewpoint.
   b. opportunities to correct market failure should be evaluated in light of possibilities for government failure.
   c. the public's choices are equitable, while government choices are efficient.
   d. incentives within government are usually more efficient than those in the marketplace.

7. If members of a congressional committee have preferences that would lead to cycling, then the most powerful person on that committee would be the one
   a. with the most endurance.
   b. with the longest tenure on the committee.
   c. who controls the committee's agenda.
   d. who is the last to vote.

8. Looking at the design of a federal system of government from an economic standpoint is called
   a. fiscal federalism.
   b. rational ignorance.
   c. a benevolent dictatorship.
   d. the median voter model.

9. In Self-Test Figure 26-1, the median voter is
   a. Voter 3.
   b. Voter 4.
   c. Voter 5.
   d. Voter 7.

The political spectrum

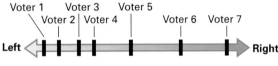

SELF-TEST FIGURE 26-1

10. Under the assumptions of the median voter model, the candidate who receives the vote cast by the median voter will
    a. win the election, with a majority of votes.
    b. lose the election.
    c. receive campaign funds from the government.
    d. receive less than half the votes, but win the election anyway.

11. Rational ignorance occurs when _____ do not have time to fully research candidates.
    a. political parties
    b. bureaucrats
    c. the public
    d. lobbyists

12. Term limits are laws that seek to control government spending by
    a. restricting how much time lobbyists are allowed to spend with a legislator.
    b. outlawing vote trading.
    c. giving each government agency a specific amount of time to spend various items in its budget before losing that budgetary allocation.
    d. limiting the number of times an elected official can serve in a particular position.

13. The line-item veto provides a check on
    a. the median voter.
    b. fiscal illusion.
    c. a benevolent dictator.
    d. logrolling.

14. Pork-barrel politics
    a. increases government spending.
    b. decreases government spending.
    c. has no effect on overall government spending, but impacts specific parts of the budget.
    d. leaves overall government spending and each part of the budget unchanged.

15. Rent-seeking behavior involves
    a. real estate transactions.
    b. illegal government corruption.
    c. measuring the benefits from public housing.
    d. seeking favors from the government.

16. Block grants from the federal government to the states
    a. increase the influence of Washington lobbyists.
    b. decrease the influence of Washington lobbyists.
    c. have no effect on the influence of Washington lobbyists.
    d. grant legislators in the House and Senate the right to travel at the expense of lobbyists in blocks of up to fifteen members of Congress.

17. A government agency has spent too much when the marginal net benefit of its spending is
    a. zero.
    b. any positive value.
    c. a positive value between zero and one.
    d. a negative value.

18. The Washington Monument strategy is
    a. used by budget cutters to reduce government spending.
    b. used by tax cutters to make the case for reduced taxation.
    c. employed by government agencies threatened with budget cuts.
    d. used by government architects to obtain funding for memorials and monuments.

19. Unfunded mandates
    a. provide a means to implement public policy without more government spending.
    b. are illegal, having been declared unconstitutional by the Supreme Court.
    c. are favored by the median voter and voters to the right of the median voter, but not by voters to the left of the median voter.
    d. appear as an item on the federal budget.

20. Of the following, the American president most known for expanding government is
    a. Thomas Jefferson.
    b. Lyndon Johnson.
    c. Ronald Reagan.
    d. Bill Clinton.

QUESTIONS AND PROBLEMS

1. *[government failure]* Explain how the typical taxpayer is made worse off by government failure. In your explanation, provide examples of government failure you have observed. Is government failure likely to be a greater problem when government is big or when it is small? Defend your answer by applying logical reasoning as well as opinion in your answer.

2. *[benevolent dictatorship]* Describe the idea of a benevolent dictatorship. In what respect would a benevolent dictatorship be more efficient than democracy? Why are there no benevolent dictatorships in reality?

3. *[fiscal federalism]* Describe the concept of fiscal federalism and how it provides a rationale for the many layers of government found in the United States.

4. *[principal–agent problem]* State briefly how the principal–agent problem contributes to government failure. Include in your answer whether government failure leads to overspending or underspending, and why.

5. *[bundled good]* Since every elected official can be viewed as a bundled good, why not change the government to allow the public to vote on every issue instead of electing a representative to make choices for them?

6. *[bundled good; government failure]* It is increasingly popular among the states to allow the public to place various propositions on the ballot. When more than 50 percent of votes cast are in favor of a proposition, it is approved and becomes law unless it is held up in the courts. For example, proposals relating to tax cuts, gay rights, and other contentious issues have been on the ballot in various states in recent years. Does the increasing popularity of this method relate to elected officials being bundled goods? Does this popularity also suggest that the public is responding to government failure? Explain.

7. *[voting]* We allow people to buy and sell most of what they own, so should we also allow voters to buy and sell their votes? Alternatively, since most potential voters do not vote, should we eliminate voting and replace it with surveys that measure public opinions? Explain.

8. *[median voter model]* Illustrate graphically a voting scenario in which eleven people will vote in an election that has two candidates. One of the candidates favors tax cuts, while the other candidate favors the status quo. Opinion polls show that five voters generally favor tax cuts, although the intensity of their preferences for tax cuts varies among them. Opinion polls also show that five other voters generally favor the status quo, although the intensity of their preferences also varies. One of the voters is undecided about the wisdom of tax cuts. Answer the following questions after you have drawn your graph.
    a. Where on your graph is the median voter located? Explain.
    b. Is the undecided voter the median voter? Explain.
    c. Why would it be worthwhile for the candidates to aim their campaign advertising and promotions at the undecided voter? Explain.

9. *[rational ignorance]* How does "voting the party line" relate to the problem of rational ignorance? Does it cure the problem? Explain.

10. *[rational ignorance]* How does rational ignorance on the part of voters give elected officials freedoms they would not have if the public became more knowledgeable about government?

11. *[logrolling]* Explain how logrolling can lead to excessive government spending. Would eliminating logrolling cause too little spending?

12. *[pork-barrel politics]* Are you aware of a pork-barrel project in your area? If not, do the research that will allow you to identify such a project. Are local officials and the public proud or ashamed of the elected official who delivered the pork?

13. *[incentives within government]* Illustrate graphically the model that identifies the efficient budget for a government agency. Suppose the actual budget is larger than the efficient budget. Identify such a budget on your graph and shade in the loss of net benefits for the budget you select. Write a brief explanation of why the

larger budget is more likely to be allocated to the agency than the efficient budget. In your explanation be sure to state the names of specific strategies that could lead to this outcome.

14. *[incentives within government]* If you are in charge of rebuilding roads, why might your personal self-interest suggest that you not devote your budget to fixing the worst portions of the roads first? If you leave obvious examples of roads in need of repair, what strategy are you following? Is there a danger to this strategy? Explain.

15. *[term limits]* Many governments have term limits to prevent so-called empire building by holders of public office. For example, the president of the United States can serve only two four-year terms. Is this a good idea? Should the idea be extended to other levels of government? What problems are likely to arise?

WORKING WITH GRAPHS AND DATA

1. *[cycling]* Use the table of preferences of members of a committee of the Senate to answer the following questions.

Policy	Ranking by Mary	Ranking by John	Ranking by Lena
X	2	3	1
Y	1	2	3
Z	3	1	2

Suppose that the three committee members have the following three policies, X, Y, and Z, upon which they will vote. The table shows the committee members' preferences, ranked with 1 being the highest and 3 being the lowest. The policies will be voted on in pairs; that is, a choice will be made between policies X and Y, Y and Z, or X and Z. The chairperson of the committee will choose which two policies to vote on based on his/her ranking of the policy choices. The one to receive a majority vote is sent to the full committee. Only one of the policies will be implemented by a majority vote. Each committee member will vote based on how high he/she ranks the policy choices being voted on.

a. If Mary is the subcommittee chairperson, which pair of policies will be voted on? Which policy will be chosen by majority vote? Explain.

b. If John is the subcommittee chairperson which pair of policies will be voted on? Which policy will be chosen by majority vote? Explain.

c. If Lena is the subcommittee chairperson which pair of policies will be voted on? Which policy will be chosen by majority vote? Explain.

d. Rather than only having one vote, two votes are done where the winner of the first vote is paired against the remaining alternative in the second vote. (For example, in the first vote X would be paired against Y and in the second vote the winner of the X vs. Y vote would be paired against Z.) This means all three possibilities must be voted on. Provide an example of a voting cycle that could occur under this system by showing how the outcome depends on the order in which alternatives are presented.

2. *[median voter model]* Use Graphs and Data Figure 26-1 that illustrates the median voter model to answer the following questions.

Median voter model

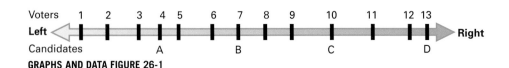

GRAPHS AND DATA FIGURE 26-1

a. Which candidate would win any race when running against any one of the other candidates according to the median voter model?

b. In any race between two of the candidates, how many votes would the winner receive?

c. Assume that candidates A and B and voters 1 through 7 are Democrats and that candidates C and D and voters 8 through 13 are Republicans. If the Democrats hold a primary in which Republicans cannot vote, which candidate will win? Explain.

d. Assume that candidates A and B and voters 1 through 7 are Democrats and that candidates C and D and voters 8 through 13 are Republicans. If the Republicans hold a primary in which Democrats cannot vote, which candidate will win? Explain.

3. *[incentives within agencies]* Use the following table to answer the following questions about a government agency.

Agency Budget (Billions of $)	Marginal Social Benefit (Billions of $)	Marginal Social Cost (Billions of $)	Marginal Net Benefit (Billions of $)
100	500	100	
200	400	133	
300	300	167	
400	200	200	
500	100	233	

a. Fill in the marginal net benefit column.
b. What is the size of the efficient budget? Explain.
c. Using Graph 26-1, draw the marginal net benefit curve.

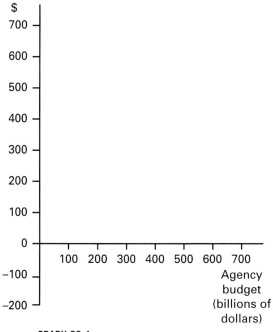

GRAPH 26-1

d. On the graph, show the efficient budget and label it *E*.
e. On the graph, label the area that shows the net social gain from funding the agency "Gain""and the area on the graph that shows the net loss from funding the agency "Loss."

4. *[incentives within agencies]* Use Graph 26-2 to answer the following questions.

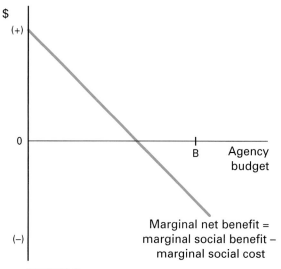

GRAPH 26-2

a. Identify the efficient budget and label it *E*.
b. Identify the gain to society of having the agency funded at the efficient level and label it "Gain."
c. Identify the loss to society of increasing the budget from the efficient level to budget B and label it "Loss."
d. Assume that the agency gets budget B. Is it still efficient for society to have the agency? Explain.

CHAPTER 27

INTO THE INTERNATIONAL MARKETPLACE

A LOOK AHEAD

Euro spells m-o-n-e-y to the French, the Germans, the Italians, and the citizens of nine other countries in Europe. The hopes of millions of people in the countries that make up the euro zone hang on the euro. Discarding their francs, marks, and lira was not an easy decision, but the belief that a common currency could promote prosperity by making it easier to trade is what motivated the adoption of the euro. Will more countries join the euro zone? Is the idea of a common currency a good one? This chapter's Explore & Apply section looks at these questions through the lens of economic analysis. Particular attention is paid to why Great Britain, Denmark, and Sweden have rejected the euro.

Countries currently trade with one another more than ever before in history. Specialization and comparative advantage cause countries to benefit from trade. Yet, no field of economics is more controversial and less understood by the public than international trade. This fact comes as no surprise, since international trade involves all of the elements of the economy within a country's borders—its *domestic* economy. In addition, international trade must also take into account foreign currencies and conflicting interests among countries. Some background information and supply and demand analysis can shed light on this area that at first seems so murky.

LEARNING OBJECTIVES

Understanding Chapter 27 will enable you to:
1. **Identify the balance of payments accounts and their significance.**
2. **Analyze how international trade costs jobs in some industries and creates jobs in others.**
3. **Interpret exchange rates and explain how forces of supply and demand determine their values.**
4. **Describe why an appreciating dollar helps U.S. consumers, but hurts U.S. producers.**
5. **Discuss why the adoption of the euro is controversial in some countries.**

Explore & Apply

The European Community is breaking down the economic barriers among its member countries. The Chinese have embraced international trade as a key to their economic growth. The United States, Canada, and Mexico are ever more closely intertwined economically because of the North American Free Trade Agreement (NAFTA). The Brazilians have granted foreign investors huge stakes in that country's railroad and telecommunications infrastructure. Chrysler Corporation, once the third largest of the big three U.S. automakers, has combined operations with Daimler-Benz, the huge German automaker, to become DaimlerChrysler. The message is clear. Countries around the world are going global. To see how global, we need only check the balance of payments accounts.

27.1 MEASURING INTERNATIONAL TRANSACTIONS

balance of payments accounts measure of a country's economic interactions with other countries.

Countries trade with one another in order to increase their standards of living. Each country records the details of trade in its **balance of payments accounts.** The balance of payments accounts of the United States measure the economic interactions of the United States with other countries. These interactions include the sale of American-made goods and services to other countries, and the purchase of foreign-made goods and services by Americans.

The balance of payments accounts contain subaccounts that categorize the major types of international economic interactions. The two primary subaccounts are:

- the current account
- the capital and financial account

THE CURRENT ACCOUNT

exports goods and services a country sells to other countries.

imports goods and services a country buys from other countries.

current account account that records the monetary value of imports and exports of goods and services, adjusted for international incomes and transfers.

balance of trade the monetary value of exported goods minus the monetary value of imported goods.

trade deficit a negative balance on the merchandise trade account, given when the dollar value of imported goods exceeds the dollar value of exported goods.

A country **exports** goods and services when it sells them to another country. A country **imports** goods and services when it purchases them from another country. The **current account** records the monetary values of

1. **exports of goods and services,** along with income received from abroad.
2. **imports of goods and services,** along with income payments made abroad.
3. **net transfers,** including gifts and foreign aid.

The balance on the current account is the dollar value of exports minus the dollar value of imports, adjusted for international incomes and net transfers. Figure 27-1 shows some leading imports and exports of the United States. Figure 27-2 shows the percentage of total U.S. output accounted for by exports and imports.

The current account divides trade into categories of merchandise and services. The **balance of trade** refers to the merchandise portion only, meaning that it is the value of exported merchandise—tangible goods—minus the value of imported merchandise. The balance of trade is currently in deficit—the **trade deficit**—which means that the value of imported merchandise exceeds the value of exported merchandise. In 2003, U.S. merchandise exports equaled $725 billion, while merchandise imports equaled $1.274 trillion. Thus, when the value of those imports is subtracted from the value of those exports, the trade deficit stood at $549 billion that year. This amount represented nearly 5 percent of the country's gross domestic product (GDP).

When it comes to services—intangible items—the United States exports more than it imports. The result is that the services component of the current account is in *surplus*. Services encompass a diverse array of activities, including the U.S. schooling of foreign citizens, the leasing of rights to broadcast U.S. television shows and movies, and even haircuts for foreign tourists. A wide range of financial and consulting services is also included. Thus,

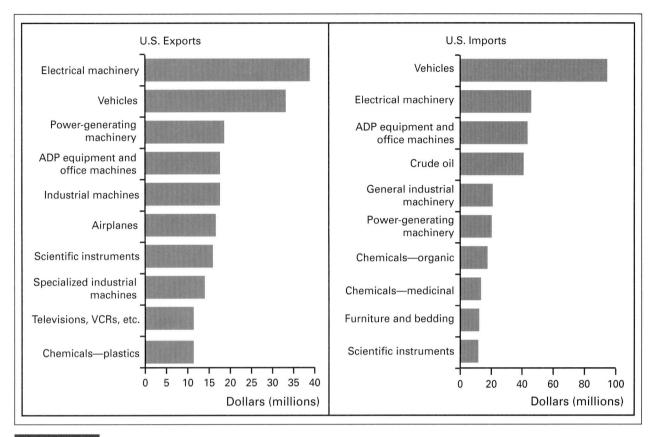

FIGURE 27-1

LEADING U.S. MERCHANDISE EXPORTS AND IMPORTS [MILLIONS OF DOLLARS] Many products, when broadly defined, are both imported and exported. An example is vehicles. However, the exported goods that fall into this category may exhibit different characteristics than those that are imported. Also, note that some goods, crude oil and furniture for example, are among the leading imports, but are not exported in quantities large enough to be included among the leading exports.

Source: U.S. Department of Commerce, *U.S. International Trade in Goods and Services,* July 2003, Exhibit 15. Data values are totals for 2002 exports and imports of goods by principal SITC commodities.

if only services were included, the United States would show a surplus in its current account. **Largely because the trade deficit exceeds the services surplus, the current account as a whole is in deficit.**

THE CAPITAL AND FINANCIAL ACCOUNT

The *capital and financial account,* usually referred to as just the **capital account,** records at flows of investment into and out of the country. Investments counted in the capital account are primarily of two types:

■ **Direct investments:** Examples include foreign investments involving the purchase of tangible income-producing property in the United States such as office buildings, golf courses, and manufacturing plants. Likewise, U.S. investments in similar foreign properties are included in the capital account.

capital account records the monetary value of capital inflows from other countries (foreign investment in the United States), and outflows to other countries (U.S. investment abroad).

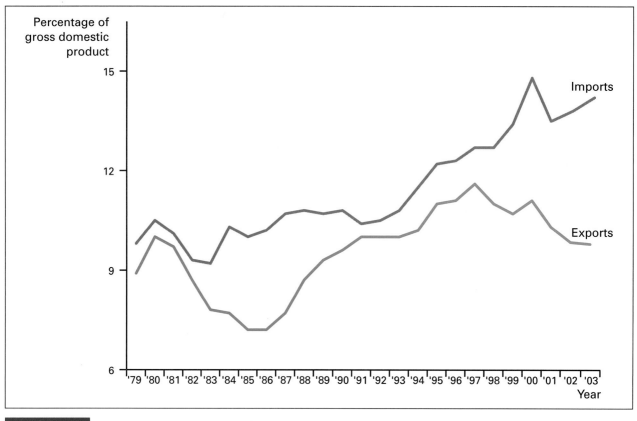

FIGURE 27-2

U.S. EXPORTS AND IMPORTS AS A PERCENTAGE OF GROSS DOMESTIC PRODUCT Whether for imports or exports, the data show an increasingly prominent role for international trade in the U.S. economy.

Source: Calculated from data in the *National Income and Product Accounts Tables*, Table 1.1.

- **Financial investments:** Financial investments are primarily purchases of stocks and bonds. Examples include foreign purchases of stocks issued by American firms and of U.S. government Treasury bonds. The capital account also includes purchases of foreign stocks and bonds by Americans.

   The balance on the U.S. capital account is the dollar value of capital inflows minus the dollar value of capital outflows, with adjustments for government transactions. *Capital inflows* represent dollars that foreigners spend on investments in the United States. *Capital outflows* represent dollars that United States citizens and firms spend on investments abroad. Thus, when looking at the direction of cross-border dollar movements, capital inflows are similar to exports, and capital outflows are similar to imports.

BALANCING PAYMENTS

The balance of payments accounts taken as a whole must have a balance that equals zero. The reason is that, when goods and investments are exchanged among willing buyers and sellers, each buyer and seller must always receive something of equal market value in exchange. For example, consider an export. The recorded worth of both the product sold and dollars received is exactly the same. However, under principles of double-entry bookkeeping, these entries go into different accounts. The result is that, while individual subaccounts

Suppose a country records merchandise exports of $150 billion, merchandise imports of $200 billion, exports of services in the amount of $100 billion, and imports of services of $60 billion. Does this country have a trade deficit? Considering only these transactions, does the current account show a deficit or surplus?

Answer: The trade deficit is $50 billion (computed as: $150 billion minus $200 billion). The services component shows a surplus, in the amount of $40 billion (computed as $100 billion minus $60 billion). The current account deficit would be $10 billion, which is smaller than the trade deficit of $50 billion because of the surplus in services.

can have surpluses and deficits, the overall market value of what is lost and what is gained must be in balance.

Even though the market value of what enters and leaves a country is said to be equal when transactions are voluntary, countries still gain from trade. How can this be? The answer lies in the nature of any kind of trade. Sellers value the goods or investments they sell at less than market value, or they would not care to sell them. Likewise, buyers value the goods and investments they buy at more than market value, or they would not care to buy them. Thus, whenever international transactions occur, both parties gain. These gains are not measured in the balance of payments accounts, because they would be impossible for government statisticians to know.

Even with what is supposed to be measured, the statistical data are imprecise. To force the accounts into balance, it is necessary to include an entry termed *statistical discrepancy.* The statistical discrepancy is often quite large, because data collection is subject to large errors, such as caused by poor recordkeeping, tax evasion, and illegal imports and exports.

Figure 27-3 shows the size of the current account and capital account items in 2002. There is a $482 billion deficit in the current account. When it comes to the capital account, in recent years capital inflows of foreign investments in the United States have exceeded outflows of U.S. investment in other countries, putting the capital account in surplus. The surplus equaled $529 billion in 2002, meaning that $529 billion more investment dollars flowed into the United States than went in the other direction. When the statistical discrepancy is brought in to the balance of payments at the bottom of the table, you can see that the result equals the balance on the current account with the sign reversed. This outcome confirms that the balance of payments accounts as a whole must have a balance of zero, a balance that is forced by the statistical discrepancy (a slight variation from zero may occur because of rounding). Figure 27-3 also shows in a graph the balance on the current account and capital account since 1982. Figure 27-4 summarizes the balance of payments accounts by presenting them in the form of a flowchart.

27.2 THE IMPACT OF INTERNATIONAL COMMERCE

Although international trade increases the aggregate value of a country's consumption, that does not mean that all share in those gains. The reason a country opens its doors to international trade, like the purpose of market trade within countries, is to get more value from the country's resources. However, while the economic pie grows because of trade, some of the slices get smaller. In other words, while there is more to go around, some people will wind up with less.

Current Account	
Exports of goods	$681
Imports of goods	−$1,165
(Balance of trade = −$484)	
Exports of services	$292
Imports of services	−$227
(Balance of services = $65)	
Net income adjustment	−$4
Adjustment for net transfers	−$59
Balance on current account	**−$482**
Capital and financial account	
Net capital account transactions	$1
Foreign investment in the U.S.	$707
U.S. investment in other countries	−$179
Balance on capital and financial account	**$529**
Statistical discrepancy	−$46

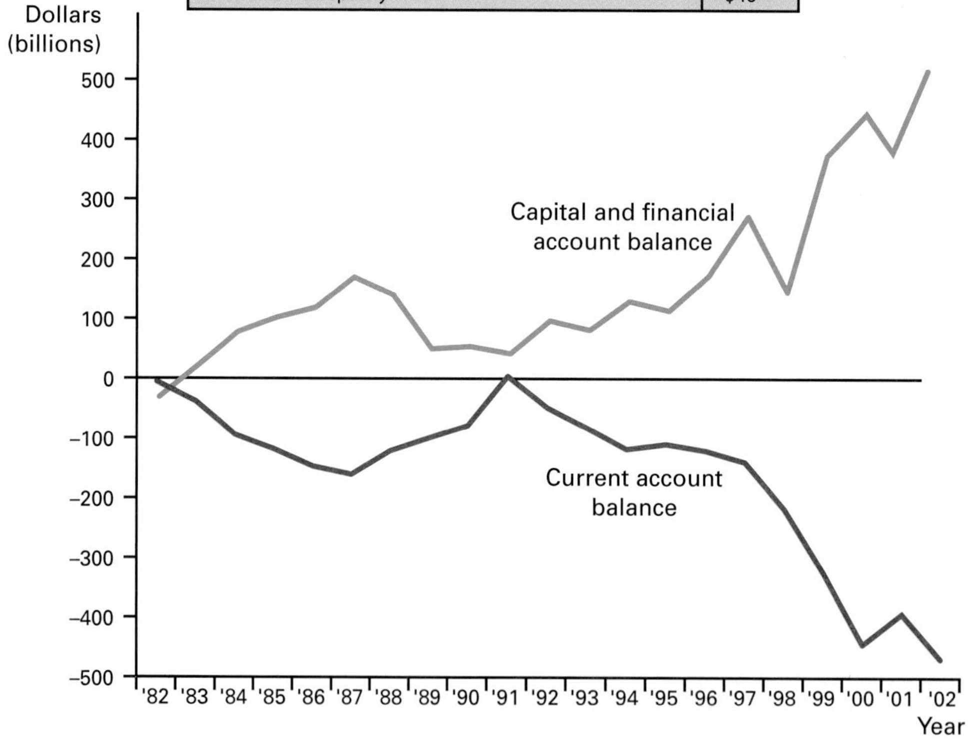

FIGURE 27-3

THE U.S. BALANCE OF PAYMENTS The table in this figure shows the balance of payments items and their 2002 values in billions of dollars. The graph shows the balance on the current account and capital account over time.

Source: Survey of Current Business, August 2003, Table F.2.

BEHIND THE NUMBERS—JOB OPPORTUNITIES LOST AND GAINED

Opportunities in specific industries and types of occupations can change markedly because of international trade. While the manufacturing of goods is still an important part

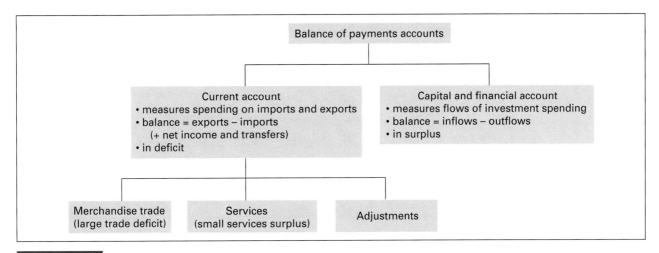

THE BALANCE OF PAYMENTS ACCOUNTS The U.S. balance of payments accounts record the dollar values of economic interactions between the United States and other countries. The two main subaccounts are the *current account,* which measures goods and services, and the *capital and financial account* (usually just called the *capital account*), which measures investment. The current account is in deficit while the capital account is in surplus. Although not pictured, the poor quality of data used to compute the current account and capital account causes there to be another account called *statistical discrepancy* to reconcile the two.

The *balance of trade* refers to the value of exported merchandise minus the value of imported merchandise, which is a portion of the current account. This value is currently quite negative and is called the trade deficit. The services portion of the current account shows a surplus, which reduces the current account deficit to less than the trade deficit.

of the U.S. economy, many U.S. manufacturing industries have shrunk in relative importance as imported goods have replaced those made in the United States. For example, a generation ago, consumer electronic goods such as the TVs and radios that were purchased by U.S. consumers were made by American manufacturers in American factories. Today, that is not the case. Even RCA, which stood for Radio Corporation of America, is now owned by the French. While jobs making televisions are hard to find in the United States because of imports, the global economy has created a bounty of jobs in travel services, entertainment industries, and many other industries that produce goods and services popular with foreigners.

The United States has an abundance of both physical and human capital relative to most, but not all, other countries. This means that the United States is likely to specialize in goods that are *capital intensive.* In other words, for the United States to gain from international trade, it exports goods that use a high proportion of capital in their production, such as airplanes, financial services, and movies. Even U.S. farm exports are capital intensive relative to farm products in other countries because U.S. farmers use so much farm equipment relative to labor in growing and harvesting their crops. In return, the United States imports goods that use a high proportion of labor and land, such as textiles and crude oil.

However, there are exceptions. For example, Japan is in some respects more capital intensive than the United States, which explains why Japan exports so many electronic goods to this country. Over all, though, international trade causes the United States to specialize somewhat in capital-intensive goods. Exports thus increase the demand for different kinds of capital in the United States and increase the prices paid for capital. The prices paid for capital represent income to the owners of capital, including human capital.

By increasing the return to human capital in the United States, international trade opens up attractive employment opportunities for those who have acquired skills and abilities. The return to a college education, a significant source of human capital, is higher than

| TABLE 27-1 | EXAMPLES OF U.S. JOBS GAINED FROM EXPORTS AND LOST TO IMPORTS |

EXAMPLES OF U.S. JOBS GAINED	EXAMPLES OF U.S. JOBS LOST
Aircraft workers	Textile workers
Software designers	Shoemakers
Stockbrokers	Electronics assembly line workers
TV and movie castmembers	Steelworkers
Travel agents	Autoworkers

it would be without international trade. Conversely, job opportunities for low-skilled labor in the United States are harmed by international trade, as imports of labor-intensive goods lead to lower wages and fewer job openings in those industries. Table 27-1 shows examples of jobs lost and gained by U.S. workers as a result of trade. The United States can gain jobs when it can export more of a particular good because of trade, or in response to technological changes that are promoted by trade. Workers who lose jobs because of trade are eligible for help from the Federal Trade Adjustment Assistance Program and other government programs.

SNAPSHOT

YOU CAN'T COMPETE WITH SUNSHINE

The trade deficit is huge, at nearly 5 percent of U.S. GDP. In 1992, presidential candidate Ross Perot even claimed to hear "a giant sucking sound" of jobs being pulled to low-wage countries. For centuries, people have needlessly worried about the jobs that are lost, as though there are only a limited number to go around. Some still do worry, but both long-standing economic theory and the last two decades worth of hard factual evidence from the United States tell us to leave those worries behind.

In recent decades, the United States has run a string of trade deficits, several setting new records. At the same time, it has seen some of the lowest unemployment in its history. The reason is simply that people produce in order to earn the income that allows them to consume. They find their comparative advantages. It does not matter if some things are imported cheaply. As French economist Frédéric Bastiat observed a century and a half ago, French candlemakers lost jobs in competition with sunlight, an import that is completely free. But that did not mean France would have been better off boarding up all its windows. Likewise today: We don't make sunlight and few of us even make candles; we make other things. ◄

EFFECTS OF CAPITAL FLOWS AND IMMIGRATION

International investment can substitute for trade. For evidence, look no further than the highways you travel each day. America's best-selling Japanese cars, the Honda Accord and Toyota Camry, are both made in the United States. The parent Japanese companies built manufacturing plants in Ohio and Kentucky instead of relying on importing cars from Japan.

Immigration can also substitute for trade by affecting trade patterns and the distribution of income within a country. Both capital investment and labor can move among countries, although there are usually some barriers to this migration. In the case of labor, governments commonly limit the number of immigrants overall and from particular countries. Those who want to immigrate must have sufficient money to at least pay for transportation

> ### QUICKCHECK
>
> **How can the international movement of capital substitute for international trade? Use autos as an example.**
>
> *Answer:* Capital flows can lead to production of a good within a country instead of its import from abroad. For example, the Camrys and Accords driven in the United States would be imports were it not for Toyota's and Honda's investment in manufacturing facilities in the United States.

to their new home. Immigrants commonly face difficulties of language and culture, and perhaps discrimination.

The barriers to capital movements arise from diverse sources. Investors often lack information about the risks involved in setting up shop in another country. Many of these risks are referred to as *political risks* because they involve instabilities associated with governments. For example, investors in a foreign land might worry that its government would confiscate their property without paying them for it.

These kinds of political risks are in addition to general business risks associated with investing, and help slow down the flow of capital from one country to another. A further barrier to capital movements occurs when a government limits or refuses to allow foreign investment in the country.

If a country has abundant capital relative to labor, it tends to have lower prices than other countries on capital-intensive goods. That country then tends to export goods that are produced with a relatively high proportion of capital and import goods that are relatively labor intensive. Likewise, labor-abundant countries tend to export goods that require a lot of labor to produce and import goods that require a lot of capital. Immigration provides countries that have relatively less labor an opportunity to increase their amounts of labor. The increase in labor would allow the country the chance to produce within its borders some products that it would previously have imported.

27.3 EXCHANGE RATES

A world traveler quickly discovers that there are dollars, pesos, yen, the baht, and many more currencies. Even countries that use the same name for their currencies usually do not actually share a common currency. For example, although Canada and the United States both use dollars, Canadian dollars are not the same money as American dollars. However, Ecuador is an exception to the rule. Its currency is the dollar—the same U.S. dollar that Americans use. Other countries may share a currency, as is the case with the euro, the common currency for Germany, France, and many other European nations.

Our world traveler probably will need another country's currency when crossing an international border. How can that new currency be acquired? Different monies can be exchanged for one another in *currency markets,* also known as **foreign exchange markets.** Travelers are familiar with the obvious manifestations of currency markets. Hotels, banks, and airports frequently offer a currency exchange for the convenience of foreign tourists and businesspeople. Even taxi drivers are sometimes willing to offer these services.

foreign exchange markets markets in which currencies are bought and sold.

The amount of one country's currency that trades for a unit of another country's currency is called an **exchange rate.** In short, an exchange rate is the price of one currency in terms of another. With exchange rate information, cross-border travelers are equipped to compute how much foreign currency they will be able to obtain for their money. Travelers crossing the border between the United States and Canada in late 2003 who looked up the exchange rate for these currencies found that one U.S. dollar exchanged for about

exchange rate price of one currency in terms of another.

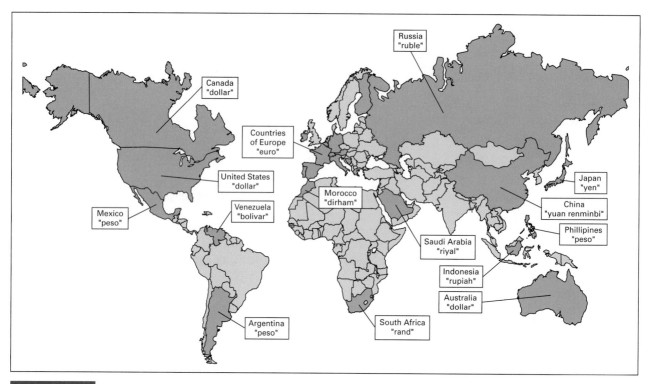

FIGURE 27-5

CURRENCIES OF THE WORLD There is a diversity of currencies in use in the world's many countries. Some countries share a common currency, such as the euro or U.S. dollar, but most countries have their own separate currencies. Thus, the U.S. dollar differs from the Canadian dollar and the Mexican peso differs from the Phillipines peso.

1.34 Canadian dollars. An American with $10 U.S. in hand would be able to acquire $13.40 Canadian. While exchange rates are of direct interest to travelers, they affect all of us, as we will see in the following sections. Figure 27-5 shows the currency of various countries.

MARKET EQUILIBRIUM EXCHANGE RATES— HOW MANY YEN CAN A DOLLAR BUY?

Figure 27-6 illustrates how a currency market operates. The specific example in the figure is for Japanese yen in exchange for U.S. dollars. In this market Americans seek to buy yen (demand) and the Japanese are sellers of yen (supply).

The horseshoe-shaped arrow indicates that, with minor exceptions, U.S. dollars spent on yen never physically make it to Japan. Likewise, virtually none of the yen purchased by Americans ever makes it to the United States. Rather, currencies are exchanged electronically through banks in major financial centers, such as New York, Tokyo, and London.

Although global in nature, the basic operation of this market is easily understood using supply and demand analysis, as depicted in the center of Figure 27-6. Those on the demand side for yen include U.S. buyers of imported goods and services from Japan. They also include U.S. investors interested in such things as Japanese property, stocks, and bonds. Those supplying yen have the same sort of interests, except now the roles are reversed. They may be wanting U.S. goods or services, or U.S. investments. The exchange of currencies thus represents the exchange of goods, services, and investments—both buyers and sellers have a use for each other's currencies.

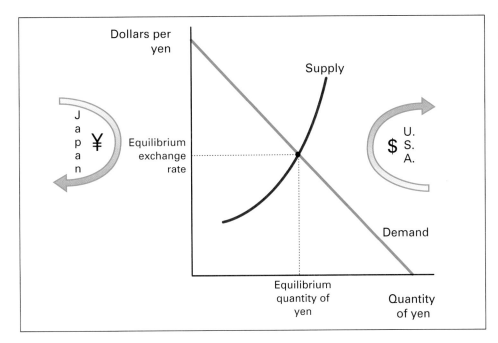

FIGURE 27-6

THE FOREIGN EXCHANGE MARKET—BUYING YEN WITH DOLLARS The equilibrium exchange rate makes sure that all dollars spent on yen are bought by others spending yen for dollars. In essence, the dollars bounce back to be spent in the United States, and the yen bounce back to be spent in Japan.

As usual with supply and demand analysis, the horizontal axis represents the quantity of a good, and the vertical axis represents its price. Quantity here is the total amount of one currency, and price is its value per unit in terms of the other currency. That price is the exchange rate. In our example, we look at the quantity of yen and see its price in terms of dollars per yen. The market equilibrium exchange rate is associated with the intersection of demand and supply, as shown in Figure 27-6. In late 2003, that exchange rate was roughly $.009 per yen, meaning that each Japanese yen cost a little less than one U.S. penny.

At the market equilibrium exchange rate, the total quantity of yen offered for sale is just equal to the total quantity of yen purchased. Moreover, the total number of dollars being spent to obtain yen is just equal to the total number of dollars being received by those selling yen. In other words, all dollars that U.S. residents spend on Japanese imports are received by Japanese sellers of yen. The sellers of yen enter the currency market because they want dollars for some reason.

Exchange rates can greatly affect the prices we see at our local stores. For example, imported products will seem cheaper if the dollar *strengthens,* meaning that it appreciates against many currencies. A stronger dollar buys more of other currencies, although just how much purchasing power is needed to make the dollar strong or how little to make it weak is a normative issue—a matter of subjective opinion. U.S. consumers and U.S. tourists abroad both like a strong dollar. Consider a ceramic vase that costs thirty pesos in Mexico. If the exchange rate is three pesos per dollar, the vase costs the U.S. tourist $10. However, if the exchange rate is six pesos per dollar, the vase costs only $5.

Moreover, not only does a stronger dollar mean that the price of imports is lower to U.S. consumers, it also means that U.S. firms must keep their own prices lower to the extent that their products and imports are good substitutes among consumers. For example, U.S. airlines that fly to Europe must keep their fares competitive with those of Virgin Atlantic, KLM, and other airlines based in Europe even when those airlines' fares decrease in response to a stronger dollar.

Although U.S. consumers benefit from a stronger dollar, U.S. producers of products that compete with imports and foreign tourists in the United States prefer to see the dollar weaken. A weaker dollar means that U.S. goods and services are cheaper to foreigners, and foreign goods and services are more expensive to U.S. citizens. For example, the exchange rate between the dollar and the yen in June of 2002 was about 120 yen per dollar. However, it was over twice that (250 yen per dollar) in 1982, two decades earlier. The Japanese tourist in 2002 thus had more than double the spending power in the United States of that same tourist in 1982. Conversely, it seemed to the U.S. tourist visiting Japan in 2002 that everything was twice as expensive as it had been on a previous trip twenty years earlier.

purchasing power parity
theory that prices would be the same around the world for easily tradeable items.

Some have argued that exchange rates will adjust until there is **purchasing power parity,** meaning that prices would be the same around the world for easily tradeable items. If there were purchasing power parity, a dollar should buy you the same amount of rice in New York as it does in New Delhi. In reality, there are often too many costly details of trade for purchasing power parity to be a good guide. The most significant of these details are transportation and storage costs that increase the price of traded goods. Other details involve public policies and even the cost of real estate where the item is sold. For example, the high price of real estate in New York City raises the price of rice in New York City relative to its price not only in New Delhi, but also relative to its price in New Paltz, which is just upstate.

SNAPSHOT

BUYING THE BIG MAC

Cashiers ring up Big Mac sales all around the world in all sorts of different currencies. When the Big Mac price is converted to a common denominator of dollars, as seen in Table 27-2, its price varies wildly from place to place. For example, in contrast to the $2.71 it cost in the United States, the Big Mac fetched less than half of that price in Russia. How can this be? There are world prices of oil, grain, ball bearings, and all sorts of other things. Is there no world price of a Big Mac?

The answer is that there is no world price for many items, including perishables such as Big Macs. No one flies from Russia to sell you a burger. If they did cart one along in their luggage, we suggest you not eat it . . . no matter the price! ◄

CURRENCY APPRECIATION AND DEPRECIATION

As we have just seen, exchange rates do not remain constant. Currency **appreciation** occurs when a currency gets stronger. **Depreciation** occurs when the currency becomes weaker. Figure 27-7(a) illustrates currency appreciation and depreciation.

appreciation when a currency buys more of other currencies; makes imports cheaper and exports more expensive.

depreciation when a currency buys less of other currencies; makes imports more expensive and exports cheaper.

In Figure 27-7 the demand curve for yen shifts to the right, such as occurred in the 1990s relative to the position of the demand curve in the 1980s. The supply curve of yen is assumed to remain constant. The price of yen in terms of dollars thus rises as shown by the

TABLE 27-2   THE PRICE OF A BIG MAC

COUNTRY	IN LOCAL CURRENCY	IN U.S. DOLLARS
Australia	$3.00 (Australian dollars)	$1.80
Canada	$3.20 (Canadian dollars)	$2.17
China	9.90 Yuan	$1.20
Japan	262 Yen	$2.18
Mexico	23 Pesos	$2.14
Russia	41 Rouble	$1.31
South Africa	13.95 Rand	$1.74
Switzerland	6.3 Swiss francs	$4.52

Source: The Economist, 2003.

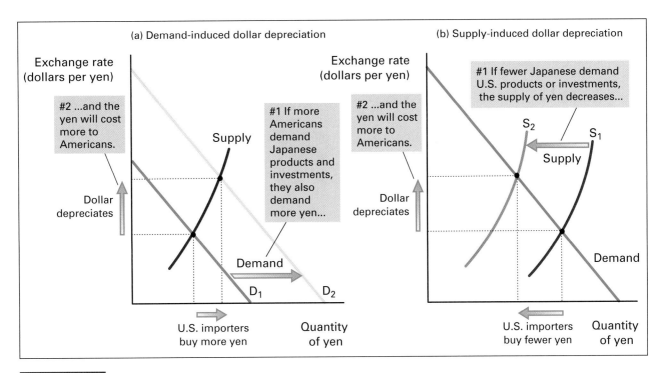

FIGURE 27-7

DEPRECIATION OF THE DOLLAR AGAINST THE YEN The dollar depreciates (and the yen appreciates) as U.S. consumers desire more Japanese products and investments, as shown in part (a), because an increased demand for Japanese products and investments shifts the demand curve for yen to the right. The figure assumes the supply curve of yen does not shift.

Alternatively, the dollar depreciates (and the yen appreciates) if the Japanese decide to buy fewer U.S. goods, services, or investments, as shown in part (b), because that would reduce their desire to supply yen in exchange for U.S. dollars.

upward-pointing arrow on the vertical axis. Since Americans must pay more for yen, we conclude that the dollar has weakened. Since the Japanese receive more per yen, we conclude that the yen has gotten stronger. This scenario illustrates appreciation of the yen and depreciation of the dollar. The dollar depreciation between 1982 and 2003 saw its value drop from 250 yen per dollar to under 110 yen per dollar. Instead of getting two and a half yen for a penny, as in 1982, by 2003 a penny would buy only a little over one yen.

The depreciation of the dollar over time can be traced to an increase in U.S. demand for yen, which drove the dollar price of those yen higher. A dominant force behind the strong yen since the early 1980s has been the demand by American importers for yen to buy the Japanese electronics and automobiles that they sold to U.S. consumers.

The dollar would also depreciate if the supply of yen were to shift to the left, with the result shown in Figure 27-7(b). For example, a private lawsuit making its way through U.S. courts in 2003 sought to seize $161 trillion worth of foreign assets in the United States as compensation for international terrorism. If investors from outside the United States fear that U.S. courts might confiscate their assets as punishment for the actions of their governments, those investors would have a powerful incentive to invest elsewhere. In that case, the supply of all currencies in exchange for the dollar would decrease and the dollar would depreciate, similar to the action shown in Figure 27-7(b) for the yen market.

Figure 27-8 looks at the cases in which the dollar would appreciate against the yen. Remember that, as for any two currencies, when the dollar appreciates against the yen, the yen must depreciate against the dollar. Figure 27-8(a) shows the effect of the demand for yen

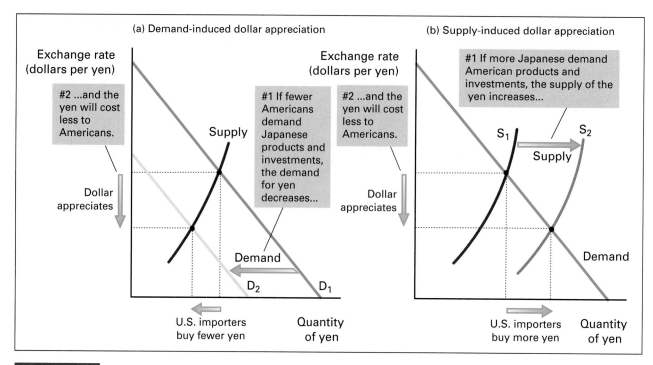

FIGURE 27-8

APPRECIATION OF THE DOLLAR AGAINST THE YEN Appreciation of the dollar (and depreciation of the yen) makes Japanese products cheaper to U.S. consumers, and investments in Japan cheaper to U.S. investors. Dollar appreciation can occur if Americans have less desire to buy Japanese goods, services, and investments, U.S. demand for yen in that case would decrease and the dollar appreciates, as shown by the adjustment in the market equilibrium exchange rate in part (a). Japanese consumers become more receptive to U.S. goods and services, or if Japanese investors see better opportunities in the United States. In either case, the supply of yen in exchange for dollars would increase, as shown in part (a).

shifting to the left, such as might occur if a recession hits the U.S. economy and reduces the ability of Americans to make purchases anywhere, Japan included. The dollar would appreciate and the yen would depreciate in that case.

Figure 27-8(b) shows the effect of an increase in the supply of yen in exchange for dollars. Such an increase would occur if Japanese consumers become more receptive to buying U.S. products or if Japanese investors decide that U.S. investments are more attractive than they had previously been. For example, Japanese exporters might decide that it is a good idea to build more factories in the United States, such as Toyota's decision to start producing its Tundra pickup truck in Texas by 2006. More generally, a supply shift of this sort could be caused by changes in Japanese attitudes toward buying U.S. products, taking U.S. vacations, or investing in the United States.

Table 27-3 summarizes the causes of dollar appreciation and depreciation. It is worth noting that shifts in demand and supply can occur because of changes in the quantities of currencies in circulation. For example, if there is inflation in the United States, U.S. demand for foreign goods, services, and investments would increase because U.S. consumers and investors would have more dollars to spend. As a result, the dollar would tend to depreciate against other currencies. For this reason, monetary policy is one of the primary means by which a country can influence the exchange value of its currency.

Governments sometimes try to influence the market exchange rates. The huge volume of global currency transactions overwhelms the efforts of any individual country. Countries have

TABLE 27-3	**DEPRECIATION AND APPRECIATION OF THE U.S. DOLLAR**

The U.S. dollar depreciates when:

- U.S. demand for foreign goods and services increases.
- U.S. demand for investment in foreign countries increases.
- Foreign demand for U.S. goods and services decreases.
- Foreign demand for U.S. investments decreases.

The U.S. dollar appreciates when:

- U.S. demand for foreign goods and services decreases.
- U.S. demand for investment in foreign countries decreases.
- Foreign demand for U.S. goods and services increases.
- Foreign demand for U.S. investments increases.

been slightly more effective when they work in synchrony. The most important of these joint efforts is conducted through a group of eight countries, called *the G8,* whose members are the United States, Great Britain, France, Germany, Japan, Italy, Canada, and Russia. While these countries slightly affect exchange rates through their buying and selling of currencies in the marketplace, their most effective tools involve monetary and fiscal macroeconomic policies that can change the demand for products and investments that underlie supply and demand in the foreign exchange markets. Even so, the currency markets are so huge that governments can hope for little more than to tweak them slightly in one direction or another. For example, **the value of currencies exchanged worldwide in a single week exceeds the value of an entire year's worth of U.S. output.**

This was not always the case. In the period after World War II, governments from around the world adhered to the *Bretton Woods agreement.* The Bretton Woods agreement was a treaty signed in 1944 at Bretton Woods, New Hampshire, by most of the world's major trading countries. This agreement *pegged* the dollar to gold ($35/ounce) and all other currencies to the dollar. Governments agreed to take whatever actions would be necessary to maintain these rates.

As world commerce grew over the next thirty years, however, the size of currency transactions overwhelmed the ability of governments to follow through on that agreement. The system of fixed exchange rates was modified in stages and was ultimately abandoned as unworkable during a run on the dollar in 1972. This run consisted of dollar selling that overwhelmed governments' abilities to maintain the agreement, thereby precipitating a financial crisis. American tourists abroad felt this crisis personally, as many tourists were stranded, unable to find anyone willing to risk accepting their rapidly depreciating currency. Since that time, the system has been one of **floating exchange rates,** meaning that exchange rates have been allowed to adjust to whatever level the market dictates. However, **because governments still take actions intended to affect market exchange rates, the system is referred to as a** *managed float* **or** *dirty float.*

Although the large majority of world currencies float, countries sometimes reject the float and instead peg their currencies to the U.S. dollar. These countries actively participate in the foreign-exchange markets and take other actions so as to maintain a market price for their currencies that is equal to, or very nearly equal to, an exchange rate peg. A **pegged exchange rate,** also called a **fixed exchange rate,** is any exchange rate that the government commits itself to maintaining. However, a government would typically find it very difficult to maintain that pegged exchange rate if the peg is very far from the freely floating market equilibrium exchange rate.

The most prominent exchange rate pegs are found in Asia, with Malaysia, Hong Kong, and China each pegging their currencies to the U.S. dollar. To maintain their pegs, governments

floating exchange rates exchange rates that adjust according to the forces of supply and demand; called managed float or dirty float if the government attempts to influence these forces.

pegged exchange rate (also called a **fixed exchange rate**) any exchange rate that the government commits itself to maintaining.

must be willing to endure some politically difficult policies. For example, Hong Kong maintains its twenty-year-old currency peg with a mechanism called a *currency board,* which requires it to hold a reserve of U.S. dollars that is sufficient to purchase all of Hong Kong's own currency (the Hong Kong dollar) if that currency were to be redeemed for U.S. dollars at the pegged rate.

When investor doubts about the Hong Kong economy prompted large-scale selling of Hong Kong dollars at times over the last several years, the currency board showed itself willing to pay the pegged rate of one U.S. dollar for every 7.8 Hong Kong dollars, no matter the economic stresses it would face. The currency boards' purchases means that there were fewer Hong Kong dollars circulating within its economy. One consequence to Hong Kong was deflation, such as a 65 percent decline in commercial real estate prices from the mid-1990s through the early-2000s. In turn, the deflation increased the local purchasing power of Hong Kong dollars and brought a stop to the selling of those dollars for U.S. dollars.

Currency boards have been less effective in other countries that have not demonstrated a political willingness to stand behind them. For example, in 1991, Argentina established a currency board to maintain a fixed exchange rate of one Argentina peso per U.S. dollar. However, faced with large-scale government borrowing, social unrest, and massive "capital flight" to other countries, Argentina ultimately abandoned its exchange rate peg and currency board in 2001. Today, it costs almost three Argentina pesos to buy one U.S. dollar, and that price changes constantly as it responds to supply and demand in currency markets.

From 1995 to the time of this writing, China has pegged its currency to the value of the U.S. dollar. From that time to the present, it has taken approximately 8.3 Chinese yuan to purchase one U.S. dollar. This peg has come under considerable pressure, though, in response to both the difficulties China faces in maintaining it and the criticism it has sparked from other countries. By the summer of 2003, the United States, Japan, and the European Union had each asked that China abandon its peg. China said no. If you check the latest exchange rates, you can find out if China still maintains that peg. If the exchange rate remains at about 8.3 to the U.S. dollar, you will know that China has not abandoned the peg.

The pressures for dollar depreciation against the yuan come from the huge U.S. appetite for imported goods and services. While the dollar depreciated by over 25 percent against the euro from the start of 2002 to the summer of 2003, it showed much less movement against currencies of the Far East. For example, during that same period of time, the dollar depreciated by only 10 percent against the Japanese yen. Against the pegged Chinese yuan, the dollar did not change at all. The result is that there was no signal in the exchange markets for U.S. consumers to slow down the pace of their imports from China, resulting in not only a large U.S. current account deficit, but also a large current account surplus in the countries of the Far East. In no small part, this debt takes the form of U.S. government bonds held by the Chinese government. In essence, the Chinese save now what Americans will owe later!

SNAPSHOT

DOUBLING THE WRONG MONEY WON'T MAKE YOU RICH

Interest rates among countries often vary quite dramatically. Yet, it's not a good idea to merely invest your money in countries with the highest interest rates. The value of those high interest rates can be eaten up by the cost of a depreciating currency. Indeed, the highest interest rates are in countries with the highest inflation rates, meaning that the country's currency loses its purchasing power over time. That loss of purchasing power is not just for goods and services, either. It applies equally strongly in the foreign exchange markets.

When you go to convert the foreign currency back to your own, reality hits! You'd find that the lavish interest gains you'd made are eaten away by the higher price you must pay for your own currency. That reality is called *interest rate parity,* meaning that expected returns on investments will be equal across countries, after accounting for expected inflation, risk, and exchange rate adjustments. The foreign exchange markets make it so. ◄

QUICKCHECK

Suppose you are planning a trip from your home in the United States to France.

a. Would your meals and hotel cost you more if the U.S. dollar depreciated or appreciated against the euro just as you embarked on your trip?

b. If the reason for your trip was to find customers in France for a product you make in the United States, which event, depreciation or appreciation of the dollar, would benefit your business?

Answer:

a. Recall that when a currency depreciates it loses value. If the dollar depreciated against the euro, then it would take more dollars to buy the same number of euros. For this reason, as a tourist you would be better off financially if the dollar appreciated. It would take fewer dollars to buy the same number of euros. Thus, U.S. travelers going abroad prefer an appreciating dollar.

b. As a producer of a product, the reasoning is different. An appreciating dollar means that the euro depreciates. As the euro loses value, it means that a citizen of France must spend more euros to get the same number of dollars. As a consequence, U.S. products sold in France carry higher price tags. U.S. producers prefer a depreciating dollar because it makes U.S. goods cheaper when they are sold in other countries.

COMPARATIVE ADVANTAGE AND EXCHANGE RATES— THE MARKET RESPONSE TO CURRENCY PRICE SIGNALS

Companies that import or export products do so in response to market prices, prices that depend centrally upon exchange rates. **Relatively higher prices at home than abroad lead to imports, while relatively lower prices at home than abroad cause exports. The result of the prices in the free market is that countries export goods in which they have comparative advantages, opportunity costs that are lower than for other goods they could produce. They import goods for which other countries have a comparative advantage.** To see the effects of market prices on what will be imported and exported, we consider a hypothetical market for flash memory chips and crude oil, as shown in Table 27-4.

We make the simplifying assumption that there are only two countries, Japan and England. Prices in Japan are given in its currency, the yen (¥), and prices in England in its currency, pounds (£). The relative prices of memory chips and oil in Japan imply that a barrel of oil costs the equivalent of 2.5 memory chips. That is, in Japan 5,000 yen could buy

TABLE 27-4   **RELATIVE PRICES WITHIN COUNTRIES IN THE ABSENCE OF TRADE**

COUNTRY	PRICE OF A MEMORY CHIP	PRICE OF A BARREL OF OIL	OPPORTUNITY COST OF A BARREL OF OIL	OPPORTUNITY COST OF A MEMORY CHIP
Japan	¥2,000	¥5,000	2.5 memory chips (= ¥5,000/¥2,000)	2/5 of a barrel of oil (= ¥2,000/¥5,000)
England	£3	£5	1.67 memory chips (= £5/£3)	3/5 of a barrel of oil (= £3/£5)

TABLE 27-5	OPPORTUNITY COSTS OF MEMORY CHIPS AND OIL BEFORE AND AFTER TRADE			
COUNTRY	**OPPORTUNITY COST OF A BARREL OF OIL BEFORE TRADE**	**OPPORTUNITY COST OF A BARREL OF OIL AFTER TRADE**	**OPPORTUNITY COST OF A MEMORY CHIP BEFORE TRADE**	**OPPORTUNITY COST OF A MEMORY CHIP AFTER TRADE**
Japan	2.5 memory chips	2 memory chips	2/5 of a barrel of oil	½ of a barrel of oil
England	1.67 memory chips	2 memory chips	3/5 of a barrel of oil	½ of a barrel of oil

either one barrel of oil or 2.5 memory chips. By purchasing a barrel of oil, the buyer gives up 2.5 memory chips. In England, a barrel of oil effectively costs 1.67 memory chips because £5 could buy either one barrel of oil or 1.67 memory chips. By similar reasoning, a memory chip costs two-fifths of a barrel of oil in Japan and three-fifths of a barrel of oil in England. The opportunity costs of memory chips and barrels of oil in each country are shown in the last two columns of Table 27-4.

The data in Table 27-4 show that Japan has a comparative advantage in the production of memory chips because the opportunity cost of memory chips is lower in Japan than in England. Recall that comparative advantage occurs whenever the country can produce a good at a lower opportunity cost than could other countries. Looking at England, we see its comparative advantage is in the production of oil because the opportunity cost of oil is lower in England than in Japan. This means that Japan will export to England some of the memory chips it produces, while importing some of its oil from England.

Were the two countries to trade, the terms at which the countries could exchange oil for memory chips would settle somewhere between the two countries' opportunity costs of oil measured in terms of memory chips. For example, the exchange rate between the two goods might be two memory chips per barrel of oil. Equivalently, then, a memory chip would trade for one-half a barrel of oil. Currency exchange rates would adjust to make it happen.

The equilibrium exchange rate causes each country to export the good for which it has a comparative advantage and import the other good. In this way, both countries are better off by specializing and trading, meaning that their consumption possibilities would grow beyond their production possibilities. By trading, Japan obtains a barrel of oil in trade for 2 memory chips, which is less than the 2.5 memory chips a barrel of oil would cost in Japan. Trade allows England to obtain memory chips at the cost of one-half a barrel of oil rather than the cost of three-fifths of a barrel of oil that would prevail without trade.

Table 27-5 summarizes this example. Note that trade causes each country's opportunity costs to converge. A comparison of the before-trade and after-trade opportunity costs in Japan shows that Japan imports oil and exports memory chips. Likewise, a comparison of the before-trade and after-trade opportunity costs in England shows that England exports oil and imports memory chips.

Explore & Apply

27.4 THE EURO—YOU CAN KEEP THE CHANGE

"the euro. Our money."

—slogan of the Euro 2002 Information Campaign

Most Europeans eagerly awaited the conversion from separate national currencies to euro notes and coins. The evidence was 150 million coin kits quickly sold before the changeover, as well as the long lines at ATM machines offering euro cash on January 1, 2002, the day

the euro became spendable. On that day, a common currency would make daily life easier. People would no longer face the costs and annoyances of having to convert one currency to another when traveling or doing business outside one's own country. The common perception was that this day also marked the beginning of a new era of prosperity for the twelve countries of Europe that were initially joining the "euro zone": Austria, Belgium, Finland, France, Germany, Greece, Ireland, Italy, Luxemburg, the Netherlands, Portugal, and Spain.

The conversion from the twelve separate currencies to the euro did not happen overnight. First came many steps toward European economic integration within the *European Union (EU)* (see Figure 27-9). These steps took place over decades. Slowly, the march to European economic unity led to the creation of the euro zone, as any EU country was invited to replace its currency with the euro. However, not every country was sold on the idea of a common currency. Great Britain and Denmark opted out of the euro. Norway, Switzerland, Lichtenstein, and Iceland had no interest, either. If they had, they would have applied for membership in the European Union. Sweden had trouble making up its mind: Its citizens voted against joining the euro zone but then, at the urging of the country's leaders to join, held another vote on the issue on September 14, 2003. The voice of the people spoke again, with the same message: Sweden should stay out of the euro zone!

In contrast to the hesitation of Great Britain, Denmark, and Sweden is the willingness of some other countries to tie their economic fate more closely to the economic stability and prosperity that the euro zone represents to them. The ten formerly communist countries of Eastern Europe, which have relatively low per capita incomes, were by 2003 seeking to replace their currencies with the euro. Predictions are that within a decade there could be as many as fifty countries in the euro zone, or tied to it with exchange rates fixed

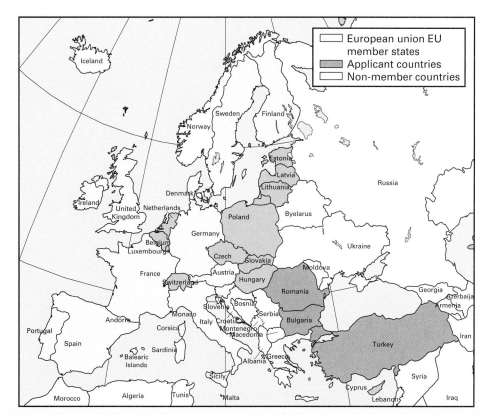

FIGURE 27-9

THE EUROPEAN UNION (EU)
Fifteen countries in Europe are members of the European Union, an international organization of European countries created by the Maastricht Treaty. Most EU countries have adopted the euro as their currency. Great Britain, Denmark, and Sweden are exceptions. The EU traces its roots back to 1950 to the old European Economic Community. The EU's goals include: free trade among members; a common currency, the euro; and free movement of people and capital within the EU. Copyright is owned by the European Commission but reproduction is authorized. © European Communities, 1995–2003.

to the euro (there are already quite a few former colonies of European countries that are tied to the euro through their economic ties to Europe). Why do many want in, while others want to stay out?

The basic questions raised by the creation of the euro is: When is it advantageous for a country to give up its own currency in favor of a common currency? This raises the issue of an *optimal currency area*. Until the creation of the euro, it was almost unheard of for one nation to officially share a currency with another nation. Of course, within a country, diverse regions may have the same currency. In the United States, the dollar is the common currency from "Maine to California." This is true even though the economies of these two states differ greatly from each other, and from the remaining forty-eight states. When we think of Maine, we think primarily of timber, fishing, and other extractive industries. When we think of California, what comes to mind is a giant, diversified economy that, if it were on its own, would be the world's fifth largest. Why should these two states, separated by thousands of miles, and having different resources, climates, populations, and so forth, have the same currency?

In Europe, the countries differ from each other as much as, or more than, the states of the United States differ. That each country has its own language and social customs is obvious. Economically, these countries differ as well. Table 27-6 shows some of these economic differences and provides clues as to why Great Britain, Denmark, and Sweden have rejected the euro. The most striking difference between these countries and the euro zone is the unemployment rate. The euro zone clearly has more unemployment than the three holdouts. In many other respects the table shows the three to be quite similar to the euro zone. Great Britain's stock market did not fall as much as the stock markets in the euro zone. In Denmark and Sweden, stock prices were up significantly. In these countries the leading indicator was also up, and by a higher margin than in the euro zone. The last row in the table shows that government debt (liabilities) is relatively larger in the euro zone. Any of these differences pro-

TABLE 27-6   **THE EURO ZONE COMPARED TO GREAT BRITAIN, DENMARK, AND SWEDEN [ANNUAL DATA FOR JULY 2002 TO JULY 2003, UNLESS OTHERWISE INDICATED]**

	EURO ZONE	GREAT BRITAIN	DENMARK	SWEDEN
Percent Change in Consumer Prices	2.0	3.1	1.9	1.7
Percent Change in GDP (2002 QII to 2003 QII)	0.8	1.8	−0.5	1.5
Percent Change in Composite Leading Indicator	**1.3**	**−1.5**	**3.0**	**6.4**
Unemployment Rate (July 2003)	**8.9%**	**4.9%**	**5.3%**	**5.4%**
Short-term Interest Rate (July 2003)	2.14	3.45	2.14	2.71
Long-term Interest Rate (July 2003)	4.05	4.40	4.17	4.51
Balance on Current Account (June 2003)	$2.92 b.	$3.91 b.	$2.2 b.	$0.00
Percent Change in Stock Prices	**−10.5**	**−3.5**	**11.8**	**12.6**
Percent Change in Broad Money	7.9	7.1	21.4	5.1
Percent Change in Hourly Earnings	3.1	2.9	6.4	3.3
2003 Gross Government Liabilities (percent of nominal GDP)	**75.8**	**51.1**	**50.0**	**59.2**

vide countries with motivation to stay out of the euro zone, but it is probably the lower unemployment rate that has been the deciding factor.

The question behind the study of optimal currency areas is whether the economies that share a common currency might be better off with their own currency. In the case of the United States, the question is whether each state would be better off with its own currency.

ADVANTAGES AND DISADVANTAGES OF ADOPTING THE EURO

Sovereignty over monetary policy—that is both the primary disadvantage and the primary advantage of adopting the euro. While a country can no longer control its own monetary policies, it also no longer has to do so. By abandoning the go-it-alone route, countries choose to be part of a more united Europe. Those countries give up their national currencies and the ability to issue their own money in the quantities they might see fit to create. In short, they have given up an important part of their sovereignty—*monetary sovereignty,* while retaining their national traditions and customs that contribute to their national identity.

Loss of monetary sovereignty is one disadvantage to joining the euro zone. That seems to be a strong motivating factor that keeps Great Britain from joining. In history, the British pound was the world's preeminent currency. Its full name is no longer used in everyday conversation: the pound sterling. The official name still includes the word "sterling," reflecting the old English coin, the sterling, which was made of sterling silver. From 1158 to 1919, Great Britain was continuously on either a gold standard or a silver standard. The British take pride in this history. Today, like other countries' currencies, Great Britain's pound is no longer linked to any precious metal. In addition, it has not been the world's most important currency for decades, ever since the U.S. dollar clearly assumed that role following World War II.

Noneconomic considerations are also important. The rejection of the euro by Great Britain seems at least partially rooted in British pride in the glorious history of the pound sterling, and a certain desire to distance itself from the rest of Europe, with its history of dictators and wars. From this perspective, the English Channel, the body of water separating Great Britain from the European continent, is more than just an inconvenience. In addition to the impetus from purely economic analyses, the British speak from their hearts in saying no the euro.

The future success of the euro, including how attractive the euro will be to Great Britain, Denmark, and Sweden in the future, will depend critically upon the policy actions of one of the world's newest central banks, the European Central Bank (ECB). Just a few years old, the ECB, like its U.S. counterpart, the Federal Reserve, conducts monetary policy for all the countries in the euro zone. When policy makers at a central bank adjust interest rates in order to influence the overall economy, they are conducting monetary policy. The primary goal of monetary policy at both the ECB and the Fed is to achieve price stability. Each country in the euro zone retains its own national central bank (NCB). This structure is somewhat similar to that of the Federal Reserve, where there are twelve regional Federal Reserve Banks.

An NCB has no power to formulate a monetary policy for its country. Prior to the creation of the ECB and the euro, these banks did have that power. Thus, we see another disadvantage to joining the euro zone: **Countries in the euro zone no longer are able to have their own monetary policy.** Individual country monetary policies have been replaced by a "one size fits all" monetary policy. **In practical terms, this means that instead of an interest rate that differs from one country to the next, the euro zone will have a single interest rate.** Prior to the introduction of the euro, interest rates would vary according to the inflation rate, the growth rate in GDP, and other economic conditions in a particular country.

The lack of monetary policy tailored to a country's needs could be a problem. For example, suppose a country in the euro zone is experiencing an unacceptably high level of unemployment, while the other countries in the euro zone are okay with their unemployment rates. Prior to its adoption of the euro, the county's central bankers probably would have invoked a monetary policy designed to stimulate the economy. A decrease in the interest rate is intended to stimulate the economy with monetary policy. There are good reasons to believe that the needed decrease in the interest rate would not be forthcoming when the country is in the euro zone. The ECB is responsible for providing price stability to all countries in the euro zone. It is not its mission to adjust the interest rate to reduce unemployment in a single country. As a member of the British Parliament, Austin Mitchell, put it: Monetary union through the euro is a "disaster waiting to happen on the scale of 1914. Instead of using weapons of mass destruction, we're shouldering the arms of job destruction."

Before joining the euro zone, member countries controlled the foreign exchange value of their currencies. Each currency had an individual exchange rate between it and each of the currencies of other countries. These exchange rates were influenced by the tax and spending policies of the country's government, the monetary policies of its central bank, and the market forces on the demand and supply of its currency. **The euro has replaced each euro zone country's currency with not only a common currency, but also a common exchange rate.** The individual exchange rates between the franc and the mark, the franc and the lira, the franc and the U.S. dollar, and so forth have disappeared.

In the same way that a single interest rate can present a problem for a country in the euro zone, having a single exchange rate can also be troublesome. If the country's economy is sufficiently different from the economies in the other countries, not having its own exchange rate can create problems of unemployment or inflation. For example, suppose that consumers worldwide became more interested in buying French wine. That would cause an appreciation in the euro because of a rightward shift in the demand curve for euros. The appreciation in the euro will make all exports from the euro zone more expensive, other things equal. That could make it more difficult to export, and workers in exporting industries could find themselves unemployed.

Now you see why some countries have said no to the euro. But why have others said yes? First, a common currency promotes trade and travel among neighboring nations. The countries of Europe were already each other's major trading partners, and the introduction of the euro will make that easier. Second, in order to join the euro zone, countries must show that their governments are able to practice fiscal discipline. For example, a condition for joining the euro zone that comes out of the 1997 Growth and Stability Pact is that governments' budgets be close to balanced. A budget deficit, where the government spends more than it receives in taxes, will subject a country to sanctions if it is persistent. Some countries welcome the discipline and the commitment to price stability that exist with membership in the euro zone.

The euro is the creation of a group of countries that have their own reasons for wanting the new currency. Politics, as well as economics, played a role in its creation. The question that the French, the Germans, and others in Europe will find an answer to as the euro experiment unfolds is whether a nation needs its own currency to manage its own economy. While the euro may help bind these countries together in friendship and peaceful trade, these benefits may come at a price. Only the future will tell if some countries that have adopted the euro become seriously disgruntled with it. If that happens, then Great Britain, Denmark, and Sweden will be able to hurl the taunt that everyone on the receiving end hates, "See, I told you so!"

THINKING CRITICALLY

1. **Suppose the framers of the United States Constitution had decided that each state should retain the right to have its own currency, and that the federal government should not become involved in the issuing of currency. Thus, there would be no**

U.S. dollars as we know them today. Discuss the impact of this decision on the country, both in history and today. Do you think the country's standard of living would be higher or lower than it is now if the Constitution prohibited federal money? Also, would it be possible for people living along the borders between states to use more than one currency to purchase goods and services? Explain.

2. Suppose that sometime down the road, France declares the euro to be a failed experiment and announces its intention to return to the franc. Discuss the steps that France would have to take to return to the franc. How long do you suppose it would take the French to abandon the euro? What would become of the euro currency and coins in circulation in France? What would motivate France to pull out of the euro zone?

Visit www.prenhall.com/ayers for updates and web exercises on this Explore & Apply topic.

SUMMARY AND LEARNING OBJECTIVES

1. **Identify the balance of payments accounts and their significance.**
   - The current account records the value of imports and exports of goods and services, with adjustments for international incomes and transfers. Since U.S. imports exceed U.S. exports, the current account is in deficit.
   - The current account includes trade in services and merchandise. The balance on merchandise trade is currently quite negative, and is called the trade deficit. Trade in services shows a surplus, but that surplus is smaller than the trade deficit.
   - The capital account measures international investment flows, which currently are characterized by more foreign investment in the United States than U.S. investment abroad, indicating a surplus. Capital inflows involve investment in the United States by foreigners. Capital outflows occur when there is investment in other countries by U.S. firms and citizens. Investments are of two types: direct investments and financial investments.
   - The balance of payments' balance must equal zero by definition. Because of errors in measurement in the current account and capital account, the balance is forced to zero by including an item called the statistical discrepancy. When the statistical discrepancy is included with the capital account, the result equals the balance on the current account with the sign reversed.

2. **Analyze how international trade costs jobs in some industries and creates jobs in others.**
   - While trade may eliminate specific jobs, in the aggregate a country's total employment will be unaffected.

   - Countries that have abundant capital tend to specialize in the production of capital-intensive goods and export capital-intensive goods to other countries. Likewise, countries that have abundant labor tend to specialize in and export labor-intensive goods.
   - The United States is relatively capital abundant, both in terms of physical and human capital. International trade increases the demand for capital, thus increasing its price. The returns to the human capital possessed by U.S. workers are increased by trade, along with the job opportunities in industries that make use of that human capital. Jobs for low-skilled labor decrease because of trade.

3. **Interpret exchange rates and explain how forces of supply and demand determine their values.**
   - The price of a country's currency in terms of another country's currency is an exchange rate. Exchange rates are determined by the demand and supply of currencies.
   - Exchange rates vary over time. A currency appreciates (gets stronger) when its value in the foreign exchange market rises. A currency depreciates (weakens) when its value falls in the foreign exchange market.

4. **Describe why an appreciating dollar helps U.S. consumers, but hurts U.S. producers.**
   - As a country's currency appreciates, it is able to buy more of other countries' currencies. Currency appreciation results in lower prices for the country's imports, but higher prices for its exports. As a country's currency depreciates, its exports become cheaper, but the price of its imports rises. This effect occurs because currency depreciation increases the price of other currencies.

Discuss why the adoption of the euro is controversial in some countries.

■ Currently, twelve European countries have replaced their individual currencies with the new euro. A number of other countries would like to join the "euro zone." However, a number of others have resisted adopting the euro. The most notable of these are Great Britain, Denmark, and Sweden. Countries that adopt the euro give up monetary sovereignty. A common cur-

rency implies a common interest rate and a common exchange rate. A degree of flexibility held by individual countries to deal with their own economic problems is lost when they join the euro zone. Balancing these costs to joining, promoters of the euro point out the possible benefits: easier trade flows among countries in the euro zone, and greater price stability because of the commitment of the European Central Bank (ECB) to that goal.

KEY TERMS

balance of payments accounts, 676
exports, 676
imports, 676
current account, 676
balance of trade, 676

trade deficit, 676
capital account, 677
foreign exchange markets, 683
exchange rate, 683
purchasing power parity, 686

appreciation, 686
depreciation, 686
floating exchange rates, 689
pegged exchange rate (fixed exchange rate), 689

TEST YOURSELF

TRUE OR FALSE

1. The United States has a deficit in its balance of payments accounts.
2. The balance on the current account equals the dollar value of exported goods minus the dollar value of imported goods.
3. By increasing the return to human capital in the United States, international trade opens up attractive employment opportunities for those who have acquired skills and abilities.
4. If foreign investors decide that investment opportunities in the United States are better than they used to be and so increase their investments in the United States, the dollar is likely to appreciate.
5. An appreciation in the dollar means that consumers pay less for imports.

MULTIPLE CHOICE

6. The balance of payments accounts refer to
   a. the value of exports minus the value of imports.
   b. the values of all international transactions between a particular country and other countries.
   c. a statement of all international transactions among all nations.

   d. a record of spending and taxes collected by the federal government.
7. In the balance of payments accounts, the current account includes
   a. capital flows and merchandise trade.
   b. trade in goods and services.
   c. immigration and trade.
   d. capital flows and services.
8. Which statement best describes a trade deficit?
   a. The dollar value of exported goods is less than the dollar value of imported goods.
   b. Both the dollar value of imports and the dollar value of exports decrease.
   c. The foreign exchange value of a country's currency has increased.
   d. A country invests too much overseas.
9. Which of the following represents a direct investment?
   a. U.S.-grown timber is shipped to Japan.
   b. A shipload of new Korean automobiles is exported to the United States.
   c. A U.S. firm builds a factory in Ireland.
   d. A U.S. citizen gets a haircut abroad.

10. New international investments are measured by the
    a. current account.
    b. capital account.
    c. statistical discrepancy.
    d. trade deficit.

11. The dollars paid by U.S. importers to buy foreign products
    a. circulate abroad until foreigners buy U.S. products.
    b. circulate abroad and do not return.
    c. circulate abroad until Americans buy foreign investments.
    d. usually do not physically leave the country.

12. If the United States were to eliminate international trade, it would be likely to have
    a. an unpredictable impact on the return to human capital.
    b. no change in the return to human capital.
    c. a lower return to human capital.
    d. a greater return to human capital.

13. The euro will strengthen against the dollar when
    a. the demand for euros increases.
    b. the supply of euros increases.
    c. the demand for dollars increases.
    d. the dollar also strengthens against the euro.

14. Suppose that an American import firm purchases some English ironstone dinnerware from an exporter in London. The dinnerware costs £5,000. At the exchange rate of $3 = £1, the dollar price of the dinnerware is
    a. $15,000.
    b. $10,000.
    c. $2,500.
    d. $1,666.67.

15. Currently, currency exchange rates are determined primarily
    a. in the marketplace by demand and supply.
    b. by a computer model developed by the United Nations.
    c. by international gold flows.
    d. in accordance with international agreements negotiated by countries.

16. In Self-Test Figure 27-1, the vertical arrow shows that the dollar
    a. has appreciated.
    b. exhibits purchasing power parity.
    c. exhibits interest-rate parity.
    d. has depreciated.

17. If German-made goods have the same price in Germany this year as last year, but the euro depreciated against the dollar during the year, then the dollar price of German goods sold in the United States would _____ and Americans would buy _____ from Germany.

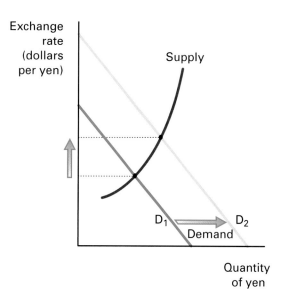

SELF-TEST FIGURE 27-1

    a. increase; less
    b. increase; more
    c. decrease; less
    d. decrease; more

18. Depreciation in a country's currency will cause
    a. the country's exports to drop.
    b. an increase in the number of tourists visiting that country.
    c. windfall gains to speculators holding large quantities of that country's currency.
    d. widespread fear of contracting the disease, and hence a reluctance to accept payment in that currency.

19. Suppose two countries, France and Portugal, produce wine and cloth. If Portugal has a comparative advantage in the production of cloth, then
    a. Portugal must depreciate its currency.
    b. the opportunity cost of cloth is higher in France than in Portugal.
    c. wine will be exported from Portugal to France.
    d. these countries will choose not to trade with each other.

20. When a nation joins the euro zone, which effect will NOT occur?
    a. The same interest rate as other countries in the euro zone.
    b. Use of a common currency, the euro.
    c. Loss of the nation's own monetary policy.
    d. Increase in the nation's monetary sovereignty.

QUESTIONS AND PROBLEMS

1. *[balance of payments accounts]* Discuss the role of the current account in balance of payments accounting. In recent years, has the balance on the current account been positive or negative? Explain.

2. *[balance of payments accounts]* Discuss the role of the capital account in balance of payments accounting. Is the balance on the capital account positive or negative? Explain.

3. *[balance of payments accounts]* Critique the following statement: "There is usually a deficit in the U.S. balance of payments."

4. *[balance of payments accounts]* "The United States runs a trade deficit." Specifically, what does this statement mean? Briefly distinguish the trade deficit from the current account deficit.

5. *[trade and jobs]* Suppose the United States decides to prohibit all imports and exports. Would this approach reduce unemployment in the United States? Explain.

6. *[exchange rates]* Suppose Middle-Eastern investors decide to sell their U.S. investments. What would be the effect on the exchange rate between the dollar and Middle-Eastern currencies? In what way would that harm Middle-Eastern investors who do not sell their U.S. investments?

7. *[exchange rates]* Paperback novels sold in North America typically have two prices marked on their covers, one in U.S. dollars and another in Canadian dollars. Fifty years ago, there would probably only have been one price. Why?

8. *[currency depreciation]* In terms of demand and supply, what causes a currency to depreciate? How does the depreciation of a currency affect its imports and exports?

9. *[exchange rates]* Suppose the U.S. federal government adopts the policy of "What's good for General Motors is good for the country." To this end, the government decides to prohibit the import of all motor vehicles from other countries. Assuming other countries do not change their own trade policies, what would be the impact on the value of the dollar relative to other currencies? What would be the effect on the quantity of other items imported? What would be the effect on jobs in U.S. industries that did not participate in the making of autos?

10. *[exchange rates]* In 1998 the new Volkswagen Beetle and Mercedes-Benz M-class sport utility vehicles were unveiled. Explain, using the concepts in this chapter, why Mercedes-Benz chose to produce its new sport utility vehicle in Alabama rather than in Germany. Why would Volkswagen have decided at about the same time to make the new Beetle in Mexico rather than the United States?

11. *[exchange rates]* Find a recent issue of the *Wall Street Journal* newspaper or other financial publication or web site and check on the exchange rates between several currencies of your choice and the U.S. dollar. Has the dollar strengthened or weakened within the last year relative to these currencies?

12. *[comparative advantage]* Suppose there are only two countries, A and B. Country A is endowed with abundant resources of all types and a highly intelligent and motivated labor force. Country B has few natural resources and its workers cannot seem to do anything well. Both countries are self-sufficient, each subsisting on goods X and Y. The price of both X and Y in country A is $1. In country B, the price of X is £1 and the price of Y is £2. Neither country trades with the other, but both are about to start.

    a. If trade were to occur, what would be its pattern; that is, which country would specialize in which product(s)? Why?

    b. As Trade Minister for country A, would you recommend trading with country B? Why, or why not? What if you were Trade Minister for country B?

13. *[comparative advantage]* Using the example of memory chips and oil production in Japan and England discussed in the chapter, provide a few examples of the characteristics that might explain the comparative advantages held by each country. In other words, what characteristics of Japan would explain why Japan would export memory chips, and what characteristics of England would explain why England would export oil?

14. *[comparative advantage]* Suppose that, without international trade, one Alphanian alpha (the currency of Alphania) would buy either one bottle of wine or one yard of cloth. In the country of Betalia, one Betalian beta would buy either one bottle of wine or two yards of cloth. Which country has a comparative advantage in wine production and which in the production of cloth? Why?

15. *[exchange rates]* In the previous question, what exchange rate between the alpha and the beta would allow both Alphania and Betalia to gain from trade? With trade, what would happen to the price of:

    a. cloth in Alphania?

    b. cloth in Betalia?

    c. wine in Alphania?

    d. wine in Betalia?

WORKING WITH GRAPHS AND DATA

1. *[balance of payments]* The following are international accounts that make up the balance of payments for a country. Use them to compute the following balances in the balance of payments data.

Account	Amount billions $
Imports of Goods	1,000
Exports of Services	400
Capital Inflows	500
Adjustment for Net Transfers	−40
Exports of Goods	800
Capital Outflows	480
Net Income Adjustments	20
Imports of Services	200
Statistical Discrepency	0

   a. The balance of trade.
   b. The balance of services.
   c. The balance on the current account.
   d. The balance on the capital and financial account.
   e. The balance of payments.

2. *[exchange rates]* Use Graph 27-1 of the U.S. foreign exchange market for euros to answer the following questions.

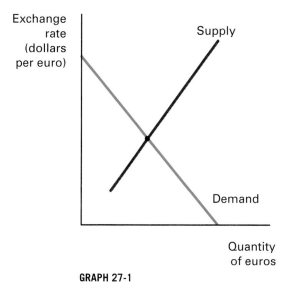

GRAPH 27-1

   a. Identify the equilibrium exchange rate as E_1 and the equilibrium quantity of euros as Q_1.
   b. As a result of the lack of support by France and Germany for the U.S. policies toward Iraq in 2003,

many U.S. consumers threatened to decrease imports of French and German products. Holding other factors constant, show what would have happened to the demand for euros if U.S. consumers had made good on these threats. Label the new demand curve as D_2.
   c. Label the new exchange rate between the dollar and the euro as E_2 and the new equilibrium quantity of euros as Q_2.
   d. Did the dollar appreciate or depreciate? Explain.
   e. What effect would this change in the exchange rate have had on the cost to an American on a vacation to Paris? Why?

3. *[exchange rates]* Use Graph 27-2 of the U.S. foreign exchange market for euros to answer the following questions.

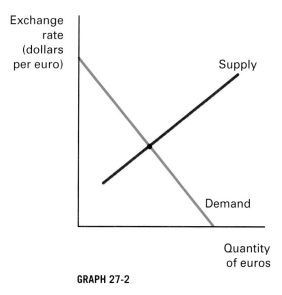

GRAPH 27-2

   a. Identify the equilibrium exchange rate as E_1 and the equilibrium quantity of euros as Q_1.
   b. Draw a supply curve that shows what would happen to the supply of euros if Europeans decided to decrease investment in the United States.
   c. Label the new exchange rate as E_2 and the new quantity of euros as Q_2.
   d. Did the dollar appreciate or depreciate? Explain.
   e. What effect would this change in the exchange rate have on the cost of a bottle of French wine in the United States?

4. *[comparative advantage and exchange rates]* Use the table below to answer the following questions.

Country	Price of One Ton of Wheat	Price of One Ton of Steel	Opportunity Cost of One Ton of Wheat	Opportunity Cost of One Ton of Steel
United States	$100	$200		
Great Britain	£200	£600		

a. Fill in the table.
b. Which good will the United States export if the two countries engage in trade? Explain.
c. Which good will Great Britain export if the two countries engage in trade? Explain.
d. Would the countries engage in trade if the terms at which the two goods were traded were 1 unit of wheat for 2.5 units of steel? Explain.

 Visit www.prenhall.com/ayers for Exploring the Web exercises and additional self-test quizzes.

C H A P T E R **28**

POLICY TOWARD TRADE

A LOOK AHEAD

We walk in them. We talk on them. We drive them. We wave them in the air and shoot them in the sky on Independence Day. What are they? Imports! It's not that we couldn't make all of our own shoes, phones, cars, flags, and fireworks. It is just not in our comparative advantage to do so. Instead, the price signals of the marketplace lead us to specialize and trade. But what about oil? Do we import so much of it that we are held hostage to oil politics? Are the costs of those imports merely the prices the importers pay, or do those imports add security costs, too? As we will see in this chapter's Explore & Apply section, economic analysis can shed light on such questions.

We begin with a discussion of the gains from trade and the policy instruments available in the trade-warfare arsenal. We will see that countries can "beggar thy neighbor" with protectionist policies, but risk losing their own prosperity in the process. To keep protectionist policies at bay and to promote freer trade, countries have joined together in regional trade agreements, reached a major multilateral trade accord termed the GATT, and established the World Trade Organization to enforce the GATT. We'll discover that there is still plenty of controversy over cases in which trade restrictions might be justified.

LEARNING OBJECTIVES

Understanding Chapter 28 will enable you to:
1. **Use the concept of a world price to explain imports, exports, and the gains from trade.**
2. **Discuss the GATT and other trade agreements among countries.**
3. **Distinguish among the various barriers to trade that countries might impose.**
4. **Assess the arguments for and against protectionist policies.**
5. Examine whether an oil import fee can promote energy security.

Explore & Apply

In Chapter 2, we discussed the efficiency of trade. It does not matter if that trade is among individuals, states, or countries—trade can increase our consumption to more than what we can produce ourselves. Yet, over the years, trade has frequently been restricted, and only sometimes for good reason. We start by examining who wins and loses from trade. We then turn to trade agreements . . . and to trade disagreements.

28.1 ASSESSING GAINS FROM TRADE

International trade occurs in response to differences between the price of a good in the country's own market—its domestic market—and the price that the good sells for in the rest of the world—the *world price*. When a country opens its doors to international trade, the price in the domestic market will come to equal that in the world market. If this adjustment means that the domestic price rises to meet the higher world price, then the country exports the good. If the world price causes the domestic price to drop, then the country imports the good, meaning that it is purchased from producers in other countries. In either case, there are some people within the country who gain and others who lose. However, as we will see in this section, the gains can be expected to exceed the losses.

GAINS FROM IMPORTS

We have previously seen how people and countries gain by specializing according to comparative advantage and then trading with others. Here, we look at that general concept as it applies to markets for imports and exports. We proceed by imagining a country that embraces **free trade**—with no policies designed to influence imports or exports—after previously allowing no foreign commerce at all.

free trade international commerce unhindered by policy obstacles.

Before free trade, the country's prices would have been based solely on its own domestic supply and demand curves. However, goods and services that are widely traded among countries have a *world price,* which is the price that the good trades for in the global marketplace. The world price of a good is determined by supply and demand for the good from all trading countries. **Free trade implies that a country's producers must accept world market prices, which would entail a higher price for some goods and a lower price for others.**

Figure 28-1 shows the case of a good's world price that would lead a country to import that good. The supply and demand for the good within the country, labeled "Domestic supply" and "Domestic demand" in the figure, intersect at the price that prevails when the country chooses not to trade, labeled "Price if no trade." However, the world price is less than this domestic price. Domestic consumers will not be willing to pay any more than the world price once free trade is allowed. Producers will also refuse to sell for less than the world price. Thus, it is the intersection of the world price with supply and demand that determines the domestic quantity supplied and demanded, respectively. Because the domestic quantity supplied is less than the quantity demanded, consumers make up the difference with imports, as shown in Figure 28-1.

Imports allow domestic consumers to pay a lower price for goods. They benefit from a lower price per unit for goods that they buy. **They also gain by consuming more of the good,** supplementing the lower quantity supplied by domestic producers with imports from other countries. The gains to consumers are measured by the increase in consumer surplus, defined as the difference between demand and price as discussed in Chapter 4.

Figure 28-2 repeats Figure 28-1, but with the areas of consumer and producer surplus labeled. Without imports, consumers would have received as consumer surplus the area labeled *A* in Figure 28-2, since that is the difference between demand and the price if there was no international trade. With the lower world price, however, consumer surplus

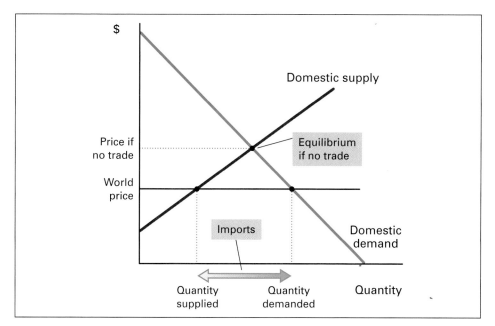

FIGURE 28-1

IMPORTS—EFFECTS ON PRICE AND QUANTITY Imports result from a world price that is below the country's price prior to trade. The lower price causes the country's consumption to rise and production to fall, with the difference being the amount imported.

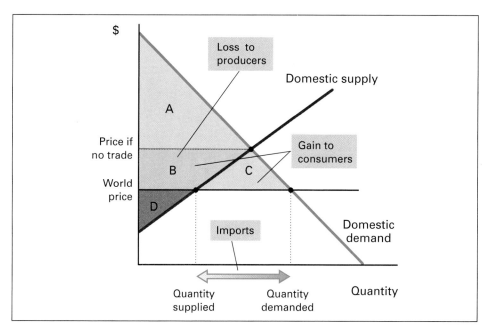

FIGURE 28-2

GAINS AND LOSSES FROM IMPORTS Imports benefit consumers more than they harm producers. Consumer surplus rises from area A to areas $A + B + C$, while producer surplus drops from areas $B + D$ down to area D. Since the gains to consumers exceed the loss to producers, the country on balance is better off.

increases to the areas $A + B + C$, since that is the difference between demand and the new, lower price.

The price drop from imports causes producers to lose, however. In general, producer surplus is defined as the difference between price and supply. In Figure 28-2, producer surplus had been areas $B + D$, which is the difference between the market price without international trade and supply. After the lower price that results from international trade, however, producer surplus drops to only area D. Note that consumers gained areas $B + C$ while producers lost only area B. The implication is that **the gains to consumers from imports more than offset the losses to producers, which reveals that the country as a whole is better off allowing imports.** This result is seen in Table 28-1.

TABLE 28-1 EFFECTS OF REMOVING TRADE BARRIERS IN CERTAIN U.S. INDUSTRIES (MILLIONS OF DOLLARS)

INDUSTRY	TARIFF OR EQUIVALENT	CONSUMER GAIN	PRODUCER LOSS
Ball bearings	11.0%	$64	$13
Benzenoid chemicals	9.0	309	127
Canned tuna	12.5	73	31
Ceramic articles	11.0	102	18
Ceramic tiles	19.0	139	45
Costume jewelry	9.0	103	46
Frozen orange juice concentrate	30.0	281	101
Glassware	11.0	266	162
Luggage	16.5	211	16
Polyethylene resins	12.0	176	95
Rubber footwear	20.0	208	55
Softwood lumber	6.5	459	264
Women's footwear, except athletic	10.0	376	70
Women's handbags	13.5	148	16
Dairy products	50.0	1,184	835
Peanuts	50.0	54	32
Sugar	66.0	1,357	776
Maritime transport	85.0	1,832	1,275
Apparel	48.0	21,158	9,901
Textiles	23.4	3,274	1,749
Machine tools	46.6	542	157

Source: Cletus C. Coughlin, "The Controversy Over Free Trade: The Gap Between Economists and the General Public," *Federal Reserve Bank of St. Louis Review* Jan/Feb 2002, Table 1. Estimates are for 1990.

GAINS FROM EXPORTS

Figure 28-3 is similar to Figure 28-1 except the world price is above the domestic price. In this case, the price difference causes the domestic quantity supplied to be greater than the domestic quantity demanded. This difference between quantity supplied and the quantity demanded results in an excess quantity of the product. This excess is exported, as shown in the figure.

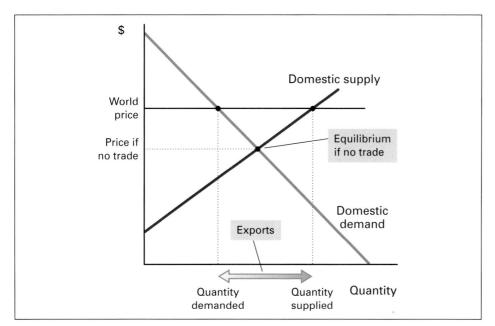

FIGURE 28-3

EXPORTS—EFFECTS ON PRICE AND QUANTITY Exports result from a world price that is above the country's price prior to trade. The higher price causes the country's consumption to fall and production to rise, with the difference being the amount exported.

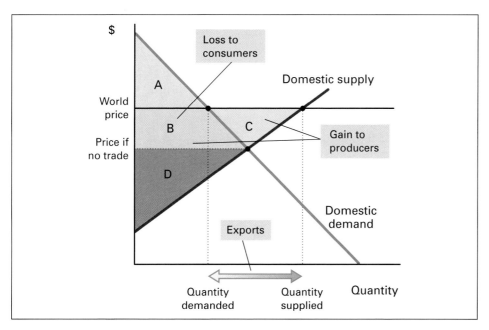

FIGURE 28-4

GAINS AND LOSSES FROM EXPORTS Producers gain more from exports than consumers lose. The country's consumers see their consumer surplus drop from areas $A + B$ to only area A. However, producer surplus rises from area D to areas $B + C + D$. Since the gain to producers exceeds the loss to consumers, the country is better off.

In the case of exports, producers win and consumers lose. Producers win because they sell more at a higher price. Their gain is measured by the increase in producer surplus. Figure 28-4 repeats Figure 28-3, but with consumer and producer surplus labeled. Producer surplus increases from area D, which is what producer surplus would be without international trade, to areas $B + C + D$, which is producer surplus with the higher price that prevails in the world market.

Consumers lose because they must pay the higher world price, and thus consume less. Their consumer surplus drops from areas $A + B$ to only area A in Figure 28-4. Because producer surplus increases by areas $B + C$ while consumer surplus only shrinks by area B,

> ### QUICKCHECK
>
> Since consumers gain from imports, but domestic producers lose, isn't a country just as well off to forgo imports altogether? Similarly, since consumers lose from exports, but domestic producers gain, isn't a country just as well off to do without exports? Explain.
>
> **Answer:** No, consumers gain more from imports than producers lose. Likewise, producers gain more from exports than consumers lose. Thus, both imports and exports bring net gains to the country.

producers gain more than consumers lose. So, on balance, **the country as a whole gains by allowing exports.** In short, both imports and exports lead to more gains than losses.

28.2 TRADE AGREEMENTS

open economy an economy with no restrictions on economic interactions with other countries.

Countries must choose how wide to open their doors to international trade. An **open economy** is one that erects no barriers to international trade and investment. In contrast, a *closed economy* shuts itself off from foreign investment and trade.

MULTINATIONAL EFFORTS TOWARD FREE TRADE— THE GATT AND THE WORLD TRADE ORGANIZATION

Controversy has been the hallmark of efforts toward free trade. Australians witnessed intense anti-trade sentiments firsthand during the 2000 Olympic Games. Australia, like the United States and some other countries, was the site of violent demonstrations in which protesters rebuked the industrialized nations for purported economic exploitation of less-developed countries. Those protesters neglected to point out the reasons that less-developed countries chose open economies, namely that there are benefits from trade in which both countries gain. Trade policies can reduce or enhance an economy's openness.

General Agreement on Tariffs and Trade (GATT) an agreement signed by most of the major trading countries of the world, which limits the use of protectionist policies; enforced by the World Trade Organization.

Countries design their trade policies with an eye toward their own self-interests. Since governments are by nature political, trade strategies usually contain a mix of political and economic objectives. However, most countries recognize that their interests are usually best served by freeing up trade with other countries. This lesson was learned the hard way during the Great Depression of the 1930s. In a misguided fight against the high unemployment of those days, the United States and other countries engaged in *trade wars,* situations in which countries punish each other and themselves through retaliatory trade restrictions.

Most countries have signed the **General Agreement on Tariffs and Trade (GATT)** that aims to avoid trade wars and promote free trade. The GATT was initially signed in 1947 by the twenty-three major trading countries of the world at that time. Over the intervening years, the agreement has been updated and membership has grown to 110 countries. Since 1995, the GATT has been administered by the **World Trade Organization (WTO),** an arm of the GATT created to settle trade disputes among GATT members and monitor compliance with provisions of the GATT.

World Trade Organization (WTO) international organization formed to administer the General Agreement on Tariffs and Trade.

tariff tax on imports.

Smoot-Hawley Act legislation passed by the U.S. Congress in 1930, the Act raised tariffs so high that imports nearly ceased.

The initial impetus for the GATT agreement was the prohibitively high **tariffs**—taxes on imports—imposed by the United States and some other countries in the decade prior to World War II. Most significantly, the **Smoot-Hawley Act** was passed by the U.S. Congress in 1930 as a means to fight the unemployment of the Great Depression. The Act raised import tariffs to an average rate of 52 percent on more than 20,000 products, a level that was so prohibitively high that imports nearly ceased.

Supporters of the Smoot-Hawley Act were surprised by the ultimate outcome. They had expected that high tariffs would protect jobs. But with imports cut back, U.S. exports and foreign investment flows into the country slowed to a trickle because foreigners could not finance their purchase without selling their goods and services to Americans. Rather than lower U.S. unemployment, the Smoot-Hawley Act was followed by even higher unemployment! Such *beggar-thy-neighbor* protectionist policies didn't work for the United States or anybody else. The high tariffs promoted political animosity and isolationism among countries and led to economic tensions that contributed to World War II.

The GATT required significant tariff reductions. It has been strengthened over the years through rounds of trade negotiations that have achieved further reductions in tariffs. The negotiations have also placed restrictions on **quotas,** which limit the quantity of imported products a country allows, and on other **nontariff barriers,** which is a catch-all category for the variety of other actions a country can take to restrict trade. Most recently, the *Uruguay round* of negotiations took eight years of often contentious bargaining before being ratified by the United States and other countries in late 1994. It established the World Trade Organization and dealt with various thorny issues, such as:

- **Tariffs:** Tariffs have been cut by an average of about 40 percent worldwide on thousands of products and eliminated altogether on others, such as beer, toys, and paper. After a phase-in period, the percentage of products that can be imported *duty-free* into industrialized countries will more than double to 44 percent of all imported goods.

- **Agricultural subsidies:** *Subsidies* represent financial assistance to domestic producers. This assistance can lead to inefficient patterns of trade. After particularly heated debate, countries agreed to reduce trade-distorting subsidies to agriculture. Agricultural subsidies have been estimated to cost consumers $160 billion per year.

- **Services:** For the first time, global trade rules will be interpreted to cover services. To reach agreement, many of the details were left vague, especially in regard to banking and other financial services.

- **Intellectual property rights:** New rules were enacted to better protect patents and copyrights, including rights to copy computer software. For example, Malaysia announced in August 2002 that it would begin to crack down on pirated software.

The good intentions of these agreements are not always carried out in reality. For example, the United States and other countries have found it difficult in terms of their own internal politics to make a serious dent in agricultural subsidies. When members violate the GATT agreement, affected countries can turn to the World Trade Organization for recourse. For example, in the late summer of 2002, the World Trade Organization ruled that the United States corporate income tax unfairly subsidized exports. The WTO authorized countries of the European Union to impose up to $4 billion worth of retaliatory tariffs on goods imported from the United States. In response, the United States is considering revising some of its corporate income tax provisions, and might in this way be able to avert many of these penalties.

REGIONAL TRADING BLOCS

The European Union is an example of a regional **trading bloc,** which is an agreement that lowers trade barriers among member countries. The European Union is considered a trading bloc because it has lower trade barriers among its member countries than to the rest of the world. By signing the **North American Free Trade Agreement,** commonly known as **NAFTA,** the United States, Canada, and Mexico also formed a trading bloc. This bloc is envisioned to someday expand southward to include countries of Central and South America, some of which are currently in their own trading bloc called the *Mercosur.*

quota quantity limit on imports.

nontariff barriers any of a variety of actions other than tariffs that make importing more expensive or difficult.

trading bloc agreement among a group of countries that provides for lower trade barriers among its members than with the rest of the world.

North American Free Trade Agreement (NAFTA) trading bloc that includes the United States, Canada, and Mexico.

SNAPSHOT   THE TRADE GAME—NO IMPORTED PICKUP TRUCKS FROM EUROPE

Have you bought a pickup truck imported into the United States from Europe recently? It's not likely, in part because of a decades-old 25-percent tariff that the United States imposed in response to a threatened trade war long since forgotten. The pickup tariff was merely a shot across the bow, so to speak, because Europeans had never had a pickup-truck presence in the United States. The tariff was enacted by the United States as part of strategic maneuvering—a trade game—in which both the United States and Europe were each seeking to both restrict and free up trade in ways that would be of most benefit to their own political constituencies. ◄

trade creation effect trade that would otherwise not take place; adds to efficiency; caused by lower trade barriers among members of a trading bloc.

trade diversion effect trade among members of a trading bloc that would more efficiently be conducted with other countries outside of the bloc.

To the extent that regional trading blocs reduce tariffs and other trade restrictions, the trading blocs promote trade among their members. This trade can come from two sources. First is the **trade creation effect,** which involves an increase in world trade. The trade creation effect is efficient, since it allows countries to specialize according to comparative advantage.

The second is the **trade diversion effect,** which represents trade that would have occurred with countries outside the trading bloc, but that is diverted to countries within a trading bloc solely in response to lower tariff rates within the bloc. An example of trade diversion would be if NAFTA is what induced IBM to assemble its laptop computers in Mexico instead of Taiwan. **Trade diversion is inefficient, since it causes trade to respond to price signals from the government—relative tariff rates—rather than to comparative advantage.**

Economists generally support regional trading blocs as a step toward free trade. However, even supporters of regional agreements have reservations about trade-diversion effects. There are also concerns that regional trading blocs may turn inward and erect higher barriers to the rest of the world. Not only would contentious trading blocs jeopardize gains from trade, but they could also be a threat to world peace.

> ### QUICKCHECK
>
> **Distinguish the trade diversion effect from the trade creation effect of a regional trading bloc. Why is the trade diversion effect inefficient?**
>
> **Answer:** Both the trade diversion effect and the trade creation effect are associated with the formation of regional trading blocs. Member countries of a trading bloc have lowered barriers to trade among themselves, but have not lowered barriers for trade with countries outside the bloc. Lower trade barriers lead to increased trade, which is efficient and is termed the trade creation effect. Unfortunately, there is also the trade diversion effect, which distorts the pattern of existing trade from what it would otherwise have been. Specifically, the trade diversion effect increases trade within the bloc at the expense of trade that would otherwise have occurred between member countries and other countries outside the bloc.

28.3 TRADE POLICY OPTIONS

Counter to the spirit of the GATT and regional trading blocs, all major countries have some restrictions on trade. For better or worse, countries often seek to protect individual industries or sectors of their economies from foreign competition. Policies that accomplish this goal are termed *protectionist,* even though these policies usually harm rather than protect the economy as a whole. Protectionist policies come in two basic forms: tariffs and nontariff barriers. Nontariff barriers can be either quotas—quantity restrictions on imports—or any of a variety of other actions that make importing more difficult. Consider the tariff.

TARIFFS

A tariff is a tax on an imported product. Demand for an imported product tells the quantities of the product consumers would purchase from foreign sources at each possible price. This demand is sometimes called *residual demand,* since it represents demand that is left over after consumers have bought from domestic suppliers. Because buyers have the ability to substitute domestically made products for foreign-made products, the quantity demanded of imports is typically quite responsive to price, leading to a flatter demand curve than for the market as a whole. Likewise, because suppliers of foreign-made goods can sell their products in many countries, the supply of imports is also relatively flat.

Tariffs increase the cost of selling imported products. This increase in turn increases the prices of those products in the domestic market and, by the law of demand discussed in Chapter 3, reduces the quantity that will be sold. That is how a tariff restricts imports. Figure 28-5 illustrates how a tariff raises the price and decreases the quantity of imports, relative to what would have occurred in the free market. Note that the increase in price is less than the amount of the tariff, indicating that importers are often not able to merely pass along the entire tariff to consumers.

By raising barriers to the entry of foreign products, **tariffs can be viewed as a form of price support for domestic producers.** The higher price of imports causes the demand curve to shift to the right for domestic products that are close substitutes. For example, an import tariff on Toshiba laptop computers increases demand for Dell, Compaq, and IBM laptop computers, which in turn causes a new, higher equilibrium price and quantity for those products. The higher price and quantity sold by domestic producers are why an import tariff is said to protect those producers from foreign competition.

Tariffs are said to be *transparent,* meaning that their effects on prices are clear for all to see. The United States has an extensive array of tariffs, most of which are currently below 6 percent and falling. Most other major trading countries also have similar tariffs. With some

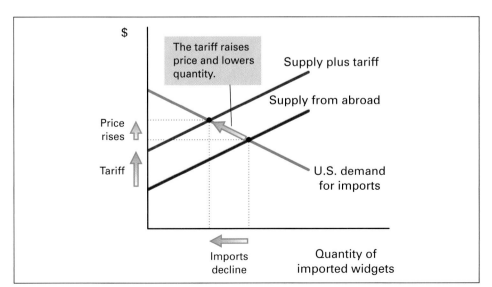

$

The tariff raises price and lowers quantity.

Supply plus tariff

Supply from abroad

Price rises

Tariff

U.S. demand for imports

Imports decline

Quantity of imported widgets

FIGURE 28-5

EFFECTS OF A TARIFF Import tariffs raise prices paid by consumers and thus cause them to buy fewer imports. A tariff on a good imported into the United States helps American producers who can sell at the higher price, but that help comes at the expense of consumers who must pay the higher price.

TABLE 28-2 EFFECTIVE U.S. TARIFF RATES BY SECTOR, 1992–2000 (IN PERCENT)

SECTOR	1992	1993	1994	1995	1996	1997	1998	1999	2000
Food and live animals	1.99	2.07	1.81	1.42	1.41	1.19	1.34	1.36	1.18
Beverages and tobacco	3.33	3.66	2.71	1.76	1.90	2.04	1.10	1.21	0.95
Crude materials, inedible, except fuels	0.36	0.36	0.32	0.24	0.21	0.20	0.20	0.16	0.16
Mineral fuels, lubricants and related materials	0.47	0.48	0.50	0.42	0.35	0.32	0.42	0.35	0.20
Animal and vegetable oils, fats and waxes	1.05	1.19	0.91	0.64	0.53	0.70	0.84	0.76	1.05
Chemicals and related products, n.e.s.	3.64	3.95	3.81	2.23	1.93	1.73	1.56	1.24	1.03
Manufactured goods classified chiefly by material	3.47	3.31	3.16	2.71	2.56	2.42	2.14	1.91	1.76
Machinery and transport equipment	2.00	2.02	1.86	1.53	1.35	1.14	0.94	0.85	0.73
Miscellaneous manufactured articles	8.41	7.81	7.70	6.86	6.45	6.18	5.88	5.54	5.49
Commodities and transactions not classified elsewhere in the SITC	0.02	0.03	0.03	0.05	0.07	0.06	0.10	0.09	0.03
All sectors	3.15	3.07	2.91	2.43	2.20	2.07	1.95	1.76	1.59

Source: United States International Trade Commission, *The Economic Effects of Significant U.S. Import Restraints,* June 2002, page 146.

exceptions, tariff rates are kept low by the GATT. The decrease in U.S. tariff rates in recent years is seen in Table 28-2.

QUOTAS

Import quotas are an alternative to import tariffs and can accomplish the same goals as a tariff. Unlike an import tariff, an import quota restricts the quantity of imports directly and thus cuts off supply from abroad at the quota quantity, as shown by the vertical segment of supply in Figure 28-6. The figure illustrates how the truncated supply from abroad under a quota leads to an increase in prices at home.

GATT limits the extent to which countries can impose import quotas, but does allow quotas for agricultural products and to avoid disruption to countries' domestic economies. While not as widespread as tariffs, most countries have some import quotas.

For example, the United States used to restrict the import of sugar through a set of country-by-country quotas, but have converted them to tariffs with an equivalent effect—*tariff-rate quotas.* These tariff-rate quotas increase the cost of sugar in the United States relative to what it is in the rest of the world. Consumers feel the effects when they buy sugar and sweetened products. Indeed, a primary reason for the use of corn sweetener in U.S. soft drinks has been the high price of sugar in the United States.

voluntary export restraints an alternative to import quotas in which exporting countries agree to voluntarily limit their exports to the target country; leads to higher price received by exporting countries.

As an alternative to tariffs and import quotas, the United States and some other countries have chosen to negotiate **voluntary export restraints,** in which individual exporting countries agree to limit the quantities they export. For example, the *multi-fiber agreement,* currently scheduled for elimination by 2005, sets country-by-country quotas on clothing

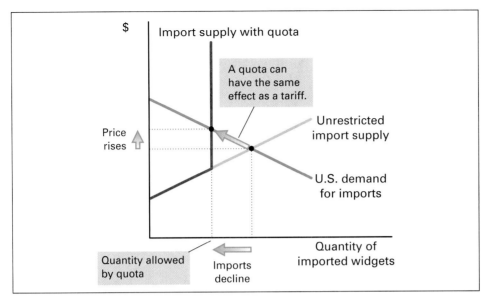

FIGURE 28-6

EFFECTS OF A QUOTA Like an import tariff, a quota also reduces the quantity of imports and increases price in the domestic market. The quota truncates supply from abroad at the maximum allowable import quantity, thus causing import supply to become vertical at that point.

QUICKCHECK

Why are exporting countries better off to agree to a voluntary export restraint than to have the importing country restrict imports with an import quota?

Answer: If the importing country imposes an import quota, exporting countries compete to fill that quota, which drives the prices they receive lower. In contrast, by accepting a voluntary export restraint, the countries are not in competition with one another and can thus receive higher prices for their exports.

---

exports to the United States and some other countries. The alternative would be for the United States or other importing countries to impose import quotas.

The United States offers to forgo quotas in favor of voluntary export restraints in order to maintain good relations with the governments of the other countries involved. Exporting countries know that if they do not agree to the voluntary export restraints, they may face either quotas or some other retaliatory action. Exporting countries can also charge higher prices per unit under a voluntary export restraint than they could if they face import quotas. Exporting countries charge more because they are not competing against one another—they each have their preassigned export restraints and are not allowed to fill those of other exporting countries.

AN ASSORTMENT OF NONTARIFF BARRIERS TO TRADE

Quotas and voluntary export restraints are examples of nontariff barriers to trade, which include all ways other than tariffs that countries make importing difficult. Most nontariff barriers do not restrict imports explicitly; their effects are less obvious than quotas. For example, paperwork and red tape delays can inhibit trade. Under the administration of President Salinas in the early 1990s, for example, Mexico established a clever system to fight corruption and in the process reduce hidden nontariff barriers. The policy required that any application for a license to import a product into Mexico be automatically approved, if not acted on within ninety days. Prior to that time, unless illegal bribes were paid, applications were often delayed until after the market opportunity to sell the product was gone.

Sometimes, nontariff barriers are incidental to accomplishing other objectives. For example, the United States inspects the manufacturing processes of some products made domestically. It cannot do that for most imports, and so resorts to sampling. For this reason, entire shipments of such products as canned foods from China have been discarded because sampling revealed some to be contaminated, labeled improperly, or otherwise not up to U.S. standards. While sampling does increase the cost of importing and is thus a nontariff barrier, its primary purpose is presumably to protect public safety.

At other times, the effects of nontariff barriers on trade seem intentional, but are hard to prove. For example, Japan made it difficult to sell Louisville Slugger baseball bats in its country for many years, because the bats did not meet Japan's guidelines for use in baseball games. Since the Louisville Slugger was the best-selling bat in the world market, U.S. trade negotiators asserted that the Japanese regulators had set their standards for bats in order to restrict competition from U.S. imports.

Still other times, motives conflict. Europe does not allow the import or sale of beef from cattle fed the bovine growth hormones. While illegal in Europe, use of bovine growth hormones was allowed in the United States. Since the U.S. government would not certify its beef exports as hormone-free, the United States was for a time barred from exporting beef to Europe. That ban was lifted after the U.S. restricted imports of some minor European products and threatened to go much further if the Europeans did not back down. Since buyers in either the United States or Europe could always contract with cattle ranchers for whatever sort of animals they desire, U.S. negotiators argued that no government certification would be necessary.

SNAPSHOT

MADE IN MEXICO, BRICK BY BRICK

Americans need not be told which state is responsible for producing the goods they buy. By law, however, they do have a right to know the country of origin for imports. This information must be labeled on each imported item. The law applies to all products, including bricks from Mexico. No big deal, perhaps, except when you realize that brick kilns in Mexico are rarely high-tech. The cost of imprinting *Mexico* into each brick bound for El Norté is a significant fraction of the entire cost of producing that brick. If that labeling requirement forms a nontariff barrier that reduces Mexican brick exports, U.S. brickmakers don't complain! ◄

28.4 THE FREE TRADE DEBATE

If the arguments for and against free trade were to be counted, the free trade side would come up very short. However, the number of objections is not important. It is their validity that matters. **The objections to free trade commonly have limited applicability or are based on questionable logic.** For example, the previous chapter took issue with worries over cheap foreign labor threatening domestic jobs. This section takes a brief look at some additional significant arguments and counterarguments.

NATIONAL DEFENSE—VALID BUT OVERUSED

If imports or exports seriously threaten national defense, it makes sense to restrict them. There is no argument there. However, translating national defense interests into policy requires judgments and debate. For example, the United States restricts the export of certain computers and technology. However, if the United States is an unreliable supplier to other countries, will new technologies evolve elsewhere in places where the government allows producers to reap the profits from exports? Also, how much consideration should be given to civilian uses for products that could also be used in war?

The judgments are often difficult and the source of debate. In 1998, for example, President Clinton's decision to allow China to launch U.S. companies' satellites sparked a heated debate in Congress about the role of satellite and satellite launch technology in the production of intercontinental missiles, which the United States naturally does not want the Chinese aiming its way.

TRADE SANCTIONS—DO THEY WORK?

The United States sometimes uses *trade sanctions,* which restrict trade with countries such as Cuba that have policies it opposes. Note that Cuba's Fidel Castro has had remarkable staying power, even as the trade sanctions contributed to the poverty of the Cuban economy. Trade sanctions allowed Castro to rally Cuba's citizens and point the blame outside its borders. Trade sanctions against Iraq are sometimes pointed to as one reason that Saddam Hussein became so entrenched in power that it took a war to dislodge him in 2003.

Despite their lack of effectiveness, trade sanctions are often popular with the public. For example, when a Chinese fighter jet slammed into a U.S. spy plane in April 2001, and the Chinese government refused to let the crew return home, Americans overwhelmingly backed imposing sanctions. Perhaps in response, diplomacy prevailed and the Americans were allowed to return home.

Another question is whether economic sanctions punish the wrong people, including those in the country that imposes them. For example, the United States would be an unreliable source of goods and services if buyers must fear that their governments might do something that would irritate the United States and cause it to impose trade sanctions. Given the multinational nature of business today, buyers may decide to locate new businesses in countries that are more reliable. Thus, U.S. threats of trade sanctions can backfire and cause U.S. companies to be at a competitive disadvantage relative to similar companies located elsewhere in the world.

ENVIRONMENTAL, HEALTH, AND SAFETY STANDARDS— A LEVEL PLAYING FIELD WITHOUT A GAME

Some U.S. industries cannot produce products as cheaply as similar products from abroad, perhaps because foreign producers face weak government regulation of production. For example, they might not need to do as much to protect the environment and the health and safety of their workers. Should the United States attempt to estimate the extra costs of complying with U.S. standards and then add that cost to imports by imposing an appropriate set of tariffs? Some critics of current trade policy suggest that this approach is the only way to achieve a *level playing field.*

For the United States to impose its own standards on other countries, when effects are localized, would benefit neither the United States nor those countries. Such action could easily be interpreted by those countries' citizens as an act of U.S. arrogance or imperialism. For example, environmental costs of production in poor countries are often less than in the United States because of weaker laws or law enforcement. Higher levels of pollution are likely to be efficient for these countries, because environmental quality is a *normal good*—as incomes rise, people demand more. Poor countries value spending extra income on food and shelter more highly than on extra environmental quality. Thus, poor countries have a higher opportunity cost of environmental quality and might efficiently specialize in industries with a higher pollution content. In contrast, by valuing environmental quality highly, U.S. citizens might prefer that heavy polluters go elsewhere.

DUMPING—RARELY STRATEGIC

dumping selling a good to another country for less than its cost of production.

Dumping is defined as the selling of a good for less than its cost of production. Dumping occurs for many reasons. For example, a company might have overestimated demand for its product and find itself stuck with too much—a clearance sale, so to speak. Alternatively, a company may be selling output at a price that covers wages, materials, and other operating expenses of production, but does not cover the cost of its capital and other costs that it must pay whether it produces or not. Even though the company loses money, it would lose more by not selling. Perhaps it is even able to offset these losses by selling at a higher price in another market where it faces less competition.

Dumping for the above reasons occurs within a country, as well as in international trade. However, dumping is illegal across countries according to the GATT. The United States presumes dumping whenever a foreign company charges less in the United States than it does at home, irrespective of its costs. **The GATT and U.S. law permit anti-dumping tariffs when dumping harms a domestic industry.** However, the world cried foul when, in 2002, the United States slapped anti-dumping tariffs of up to 30 percent on imported steel. Japan immediately retaliated by placing a 100-percent tariff on the token $5 million worth of steel it imports from the United States. Both Europe and Japan took their cases to the World Trade Organization, which ruled in 2003 that the United States had acted improperly in imposing those tariffs. The WTO authorized the European Union to collect up to $2 billion in penalties from the United States if it were to not remove the import fees. The United States appealed the ruling, but lost that appeal.

strategic dumping dumping with the intention of driving the competition out of business.

Consumers gain from the low prices that result from dumping. The only strong economic argument in favor of restricting dumping occurs in the special case of strategic dumping. **Strategic dumping** is dumping that aims to drive the competition out of business so that the firms doing the dumping can monopolize output and drive prices up in the future. However, the prospects for successful strategic dumping are highly questionable in most industries. After all, in a world marketplace, there are numerous potential competitors. Even companies that have been driven out of a particular line of business can often reenter it in the future, should an increase in price make it profitable to do so.

INFANT INDUSTRIES—WHERE ARE INVESTORS?

infant industries startup industries that might be unable to survive the rigors of competition in their formative years.

Developing countries often try to nurture new industries they hope will one day become a source of export earnings. These **infant industries** are thought to need protection in the rough world marketplace. The infant industry argument claims that the government must first identify promising industries and then erect import barriers to protect them. When the infants grow strong enough to fend for themselves, the government should remove the barriers.

The infant industry argument is unconvincing if markets function efficiently. In the free marketplace, *venture capitalists* and other private investors will often support firms through many years of losses. They will do so if they expect that the firms will eventually become profitable and reward their patience. If private investors do not foresee profits down the road, they will withhold their funds, and the businesses will fail.

Unfortunately, there is much less assurance that the government will pick industries that are likely to survive on their own. **Governments often use political considerations to select so-called infant industries.** Even if governments do attempt careful economic analysis, such analyses are unlikely to match those of investors with their own money at risk. The result is that governments around the world have protected industries that never grew strong enough to withstand foreign competition. By requiring government subsidies to stay afloat, and by charging prices above those in the rest of the world, such industries have proven to be expensive for governments and consumers alike.

QUICKCHECK

There are more arguments against free trade than there are in favor of it. Even so, economists are for the most part staunchly pro free trade. Why?

Answer: The arguments against free trade constitute exceptions to the rule that free trade promotes prosperity through increased efficiency. Oftentimes, even the purported exceptions to that rule turn out to be invalid.

FREE TRADE—A WIN-WIN SOLUTION   *SNAPSHOT*

Is limiting free trade just another protectionist barrier, or are the Europeans more aware of the dangers than are Americans? Perhaps the topic would be the sale of beef from livestock fed growth hormones, a practice allowed in the United States but banned in Europe as previously discussed. Perhaps the topic is antitrust. The U.S. Justice Department gave the green light to a merger between General Electric Corporation and Honeywell Corporation, two titans of industrial might. The Europeans put the kibosh on the merger, though, by ruling that the combination was too mighty and could not be allowed to do business in Europe. Maybe good arguments; the result was trade that was less free.

In this international marketplace with so many countries with so many ideas as to what is okay to do and what is not, it is a wonder that free trade can survive at all. Yet it does, to the tune of over $1 trillion in imports and exports done every month by the countries of the world. The protectionists might win a battle here and there, as well they should. But the gains in living standards brought about by free trade are what give us all victory. ◄

28.5 ENERGY SECURITY AND ALTERNATIVE FUELS—AN ISSUE OF OIL IMPORTS

Explore & Apply

"A business scenario can be put together that could have us back on the moon within 10 to 15 years."

—*Dr. "Jack" Schmitt, Apollo 17 astronaut and last man on the moon*

The business strategy Dr. Schmitt had in mind revolved around that most precious of possessions, energy. As he described it in a speech he gave to the Australian Institute of Physics Biennial Congress, in the summer of 2002, his particular plan involved gathering helium-3 from the moon to use in energy-creating fusion reactions here on earth. The cost? Dr. Schmitt estimated it at 200 billion Australian dollars (110 billion U.S. dollars).

While traveling to the moon to gather fuel might seem an outlandish idea, it is but one of many possibilities for developing *alternative fuels,* so-called because they provide an alternative to the traditional fossil fuels of coal, natural gas and crude oil. There are many possibilities along these lines. For example, in his 2003 State of the Union address, President Bush suggested that the United States should focus on developing hydrogen powered vehicles, where the hydrogen in this case would be the alternative fuel.

These alternative fuels have one thing in common—they all cost more than the oil and other fossil fuels that they would replace. For that reason, without government assistance, the marketplace has not financed the development and production of such alternative fuels as ethanol, wind power, and solar power. Those fuels could not compete with cheaper oil. But is oil really cheaper?

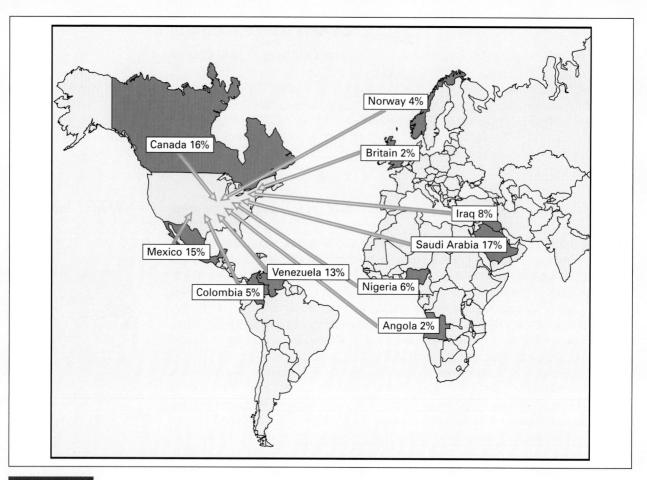

FIGURE 28-7

THE SOURCES OF OIL IMPORTED TO THE UNITED STATES The United States imports oil from many places, with about half coming from the Americas.

Source: Gibson Consulting.

The price of oil in the world market has fluctuated from under $20 per barrel to over $30 per barrel in the last few years. However, the cost of importing that oil into the United States might be significantly higher. There are costs that the importers do not currently pay that perhaps the country as a whole does pay. These are the costs having to do with energy security. Factoring in these costs, estimates of the true cost of imported oil run to as high as $103 per barrel, equivalent to a pump price for gasoline of over $5 per gallon (National Defense Council Foundation, 2003).

HOW AN OIL IMPORT FEE AFFECTS OIL PRODUCTION

The U.S. economy consumes tremendous amounts of petroleum, about 777 million gallons per day as of January, 2002. If placed in one-gallon gas cans, they could encircle the globe six times over. That is 18.5 million barrels of oil per year, with a total price tag of over $50 billion. The U.S. imports 55 to 60 percent of the oil it uses, with imports exceeding 50 percent of the total for the first time in 1994.

Much of that oil comes from countries of this hemisphere, as seen in Figure 28-7. However, because the oil market is global, a disruption in oil exports from the Middle East would bring Europeans and other countries into competition for oil that would otherwise go to the United States. By the same token, the U.S. presence in the world oil market increases petroleum prices and the wealth of oil exporters. This situation means that **the United States is vulnerable to political instability in the Middle East and in other oil-exporting countries.** The United States has spent a large amount of money and put many lives at risk in its efforts to bring peace to the Middle East. It's impossible to know how much of this effort has been motivated by the U.S. interest in secure energy sources. Such *external costs* of oil imports are not reflected in the price paid by importers. To "internalize" them, the United States could levy an *oil import fee,* a common name for an import tariff when applied to oil.

An oil import fee would raise the price of imported oil and encourage the development of alternative fuels. U.S. producers would produce more, and consumers consume less, as shown in Figure 28-8. For ease of analysis, the United States is shown in the figure as a price taker in the world oil market.

If the United States raises the price of imported oil, U.S. oil companies will produce more domestic oil, which increases the price of domestic oil relative to oil available on the world market. The higher price would attract resources from elsewhere in the economy to increase production from existing U.S. oilfields, as well as to increase the search for new supplies. Likewise, some existing industries that consume large amounts of oil would shrink or leave the country. For example, a higher oil price in the United States relative to other countries would probably cause petrochemical production to be moved abroad.

Since oil is a nonrenewable resource, opponents of oil import fees argue that such a fee would "drain America first." Down the road, as U.S. wells are pumped dry more quickly, the United States might be forced to rely even more heavily on foreign supplies. In that view, oil import fees might help in the present, but would make matters worse over time. The economy would grow faster and stronger with cheaper energy and be better positioned to weather energy disruptions if they ever do materialize.

Also, higher oil prices could prompt the substitution of coal and nuclear power, both of which can harm the environment. Oil production itself can cause significant environmental damage. For example, the General Accounting Office estimated in July 2002 that oil companies pumping oil from Alaska's North Slope oil fields will face about $6 billion worth of

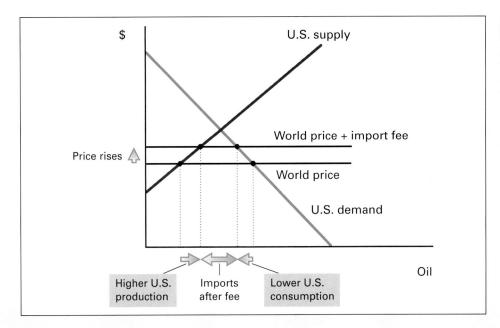

FIGURE 28-8

AN OIL IMPORT FEE An oil import fee would reduce oil imports and increase the U.S. price of oil. Part of the reduction in oil imports would be offset by less oil consumption due to the higher price. The rest would be offset by U.S. oil producers increasing output, also in response to the higher price. The increased U.S. production would deplete U.S. oil reserves more quickly, although the higher price might also prompt additional oil discoveries or development of alternative fuels.

environmental cleanup costs when their wells run dry. Since the opening of the Trans-Alaska pipeline in 1977, oil companies have pumped more than 13 billion barrels of oil and provided about 20 percent of the oil produced in the United States. The prospect of additional environmental damages to the Alaska National Wildlife Refuge caused the U.S. Congress to reject President Bush's proposal to allow oil exploration in that area.

The subject of oil import fees is obviously contentious, with the topic discussed off and on for decades. While the United States does not have an oil import fee, it does have another policy that gives it a measure of protection from the uncertainties of oil politics. Specifically, the United States maintains a *Strategic Petroleum Reserve* in the form of a huge quantity of oil that the U.S. government has been stashing away each year, and that President Bush ordered to be filled to capacity in 2002. That reserve was tapped only once when, in the face of oil prices that had doubled to more than $30 per barrel in 2000, President Clinton ordered a limited sale of oil from the reserve. Whether for this reason or other reasons, the price did drop back after President Clinton's action.

THINKING CRITICALLY

1. **Would the U.S. military have less to do in the Middle East if the United States did not import so much oil? Should this cost differential be covered by an oil import fee? Explain.**

2. **Does the Strategic Petroleum Reserve accomplish the objectives of an oil import fee? Explain.**

 Visit **www.prenhall.com/ayers** for updates and web exercises on this Explore & Apply topic.

SUMMARY AND LEARNING OBJECTIVES

1. **Use the concept of a world price to explain imports, exports, and the gains from trade.**
   - Goods and services that are broadly traded in the world marketplace have a world price, which is determined by the world supply and demand. Free trade means a country will accept the world price, whether it is higher or lower than the country's price before trade.
   - When the world price is below a country's price prior to trade, the country will import the good.
   - Imports increase consumer surplus, but reduce producer surplus. The overall effect is to make the country better off than before trade.
   - A country will export a good whose world price is above the country's price prior to trade.
   - Exports reduce consumer surplus, but increase producer surplus. The increase in producer surplus is more than the loss of consumer surplus, so the country is better off than before trade.

2. **Discuss the GATT and other trade agreements among countries.**
   - The General Agreement on Tariffs and Trade (GATT) is a multilateral agreement, meaning that many

nations have signed it. The 110 GATT signatories include the United States, Canada, Mexico, and countries of Europe. The GATT agreement is administered by the World Trade Organization, which was created to settle trade disputes among countries.
   - Many issues are addressed in the GATT agreement and its updates, such as those made in the Uruguay round of negotiations in 1994. The GATT seeks to cut tariffs, encourage duty-free imports, reduce agricultural subsidies, apply trade rules to services such as banking as well as goods, and protect property rights through the enforcement of rules relating to copyrights and patents.
   - Regional trading blocs are an increasingly common feature of the global economy. An example is the North American Free Trade Agreement that includes the United States, Canada, and Mexico.
   - Regional trading blocs promote trade among their own members. The trade creation effect is efficient, occurring because member countries can more easily specialize according to the principle of comparative advantage. The trade diversion effect occurs when trade that would have occurred with countries outside the trading bloc if the trading bloc did not exist is

instead diverted to countries within the trading bloc. Trade diversion is inefficient because it is a response to differences in tariffs rather than to comparative advantage.

3. **Distinguish among the various barriers to trade that countries might impose.**

- Tariffs are taxes on imported products. A tariff shifts the supply curve of a product upward by the amount of the tariff. However, the price of the product will usually rise by less than the amount of the tariff because importers are not able to pass on the entire amount of the tariff. Nonetheless, a tariff will decrease the quantity imported of the product it is placed on.

- Tariffs are a type of price support for domestic producers. Since tariffs increase the price of imported goods, domestic producers experience an increase in the demand for substitutes for the imports, which leads to higher prices in the domestic market.

- To be transparent means the effects are readily clear to all. Tariffs are an example of a transparent protectionist policy.

- The United States and most countries have lengthy lists of products that are subject to tariffs. For the most part these tariffs are kept low by the GATT. In the United States, most tariffs are below 6 percent.

- Quotas impose a numerical limit on imports. A quota cuts off the supply of an imported product once a predetermined number of units of the product have been brought into the country.

- A country's desire to reduce imports can be achieved by imposing either a tariff or a quota since both tariffs and quotas decrease imports. However, tariffs are more transparent than quotas since consumers usually know little about the existence of quotas or their effect on the price of an import. Quotas on agricultural products are allowed by the GATT, but in general quotas are not as widespread as tariffs.

- A voluntary export restraint is a quota agreement negotiated between countries. A country would prefer that its exports be subject to a voluntary export restraint rather than a quota. The reason is that a quota induces exporting countries to lower their prices as they compete with each other to fill the quota. In contrast, with a voluntary export restraint in place each exporting country is allowed to sell only so much and no more to the other country. This means that each exporting country need not lower its price below that of other exporting countries to sell its product.

- Various other nontariff barriers to trade can be imposed by a country to reduce imports. For example, complicated import rules and regulations in a particular country make it difficult for other countries to sell their goods in that country.

4. **Assess the arguments for and against protectionist policies.**

- Protectionist trade policies seek to protect a country's industry from foreign competition. Because most countries recognize the benefits that come from more international trade, they have jointly agreed to limit their use of protectionist policies by becoming signatories to the General Agreement on Tariffs and Trade (GATT).

- There are a number of possible exceptions to the principle of free trade, although application of these exceptions is often subject to debate. These exceptions include the national defense argument. It may be wise for a country to restrict exports of goods that could be used by another country for hostile purposes. Another arguable justification for not trading arises when a trading partner acts in ways that a country disapproves of, and trade sanctions are imposed. A third questionable justification is that a level playing field should be achieved before trade is allowed. For example, a level playing field would require other countries to adopt U.S. environmental policies.

- Sometimes exporting countries are accused of dumping, which is selling a good for less than the cost of production. The GATT makes dumping illegal and allows a country to impose anti-dumping tariffs in response.

- The infant industry argument for protectionism argues that a country's new industries need to be protected from foreign competition until they are able to compete effectively against the same industries already existing in other countries. This argument is weak if markets function efficiently, since investors will fund new industries that they expect will eventually be profitable.

 5. **Examine whether an oil import fee can promote energy security.**

- An oil import fee might be used to adjust the price of imported oil upward so as to include costs associated with maintaining energy security. The effect would be to encourage use of alternative energy sources, some of which are likely to be environmentally harmful. The Strategic Petroleum Reserve is intended to accomplish some of the same objectives as would an oil import fee.

KEY TERMS

free trade, 704
open economy, 708
General Agreement on Tariffs and
    Trade (GATT), 708
World Trade Organization (WTO), 708
tariff, 708

Smoot-Hawley Act, 708
quota, 709
nontariff barriers, 709
trading bloc, 709
North American Free Trade
    Agreement (NAFTA), 709

trade creation effect, 710
trade diversion effect, 710
voluntary export restraints, 712
dumping, 716
strategic dumping, 716
infant industries, 716

TEST YOURSELF

TRUE OR FALSE

1. The GATT was created in 1995 in order to lower tariffs.
2. A tariff raises the price of an import but leaves the quantity imported the same.
3. Quotas are transparent, but tariffs are not.
4. A country with protectionist policies seeks to encourage imports.
5. Dumping is legal but controversial, with the GATT refusing to take a stand on whether dumping should be outlawed.

MULTIPLE CHOICE

6. The arrow shown in Self-Test Figure 28-1 represents
   a. imports.
   b. exports.
   c. consumer surplus.
   d. producer surplus.

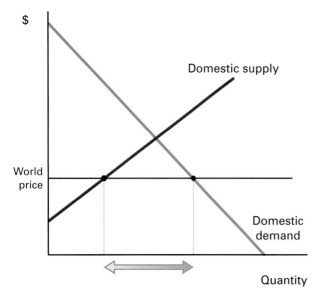

SELF-TEST FIGURE 28-1

7. When a country imports a good, it will
   a. gain more in consumer surplus than it loses in producer surplus.
   b. gain more in producer surplus than it loses in consumer surplus.
   c. find that its gain of consumer surplus is exactly offset by its loss of producer surplus.
   d. find that its gain of producer surplus is exactly offset by its loss of consumer surplus.
8. When the world price of a good is greater than a country's price before trade, free trade will result in that country
   a. importing the good and experiencing an increase in consumer surplus.
   b. importing the good and experiencing a decrease in consumer surplus.
   c. exporting the good and experiencing an increase in consumer surplus.
   d. exporting the good and experiencing a decrease in consumer surplus.
9. The GATT was created in response to
   a. the Great Depression of the 1930s.
   b. the Cold War of the 1950s and 1960s.
   c. Reaganomics, the economic policies of President Reagan in the 1980s.
   d. President Clinton's desire to forge closer relationships with China in the 1990s.
10. The World Trade Organization
    a. is a trading bloc that consists of the United States and the countries of Japan and China.
    b. has many member countries, but not the United States.
    c. competes with the GATT for members, with about half the world's countries belonging to the GATT and the other half belonging to the World Trade Organization.
    d. is a component of the GATT that administers the GATT agreement.

11. An import tariff shifts the _____ curve of imports upward and _____ the price of the good paid by the consumer.
    a. supply; increases
    b. supply; decreases
    c. demand; decreases
    d. demand; increases
12. The effects of a quota will be to _____ the quantity of imports and _____ the price consumers pay for them.
    a. increase; increase
    b. increase; decrease
    c. decrease; increase
    d. decrease; decrease
13. Which is an example of a voluntary export restraint?
    a. A tariff.
    b. A quota.
    c. The multi-fiber agreement.
    d. The GATT.
14. Nontariff barriers to trade
    a. are illegal under GATT.
    b. are allowed by GATT, but are not currently used by any country.
    c. have the effect of reducing a country's imports.
    d. are a good way to increase a country's exports.
15. Trade sanctions
    a. are generally acknowledged to be one of a country's most effective policy weapons.
    b. have been effective in accomplishing America's goals in regard to Cuba.
    c. were strongly supported by the American public as a means of getting China to release some downed U.S. flyers.
    d. are an integrated part of free trade, and explain the strength of the U.S. economy today.
16. Which of the following is NOT offered as a reason to restrict trade?
    a. Infant industries.
    b. Dumping.
    c. Level playing field.
    d. Comparative advantage.
17. Strategic dumping is intended to
    a. result in a cleaner environment.

b. pollute the environment.
c. lead countries to seek a mutually beneficial agreement relating to the environment.
d. drive competitors out of business.
18. The trade diversion effect is
    a. efficient.
    b. inefficient.
    c. equitable, with no effect on efficiency.
    d. inequitable, with no effect on efficiency.
19. The trade creation effect is
    a. efficient.
    b. inefficient.
    c. equitable, with no effect on efficiency.
    d. inequitable, with no effect on efficiency.
20. In Self-Test Figure 28-2, the effect of the oil import fee shown would be to
    a. decrease price by *A*.
    b. decrease the quantity produced in the United States by *B*.
    c. decrease the quantity produced in the United States by *C*.
    d. decrease the quantity consumed in the United States by *D*.

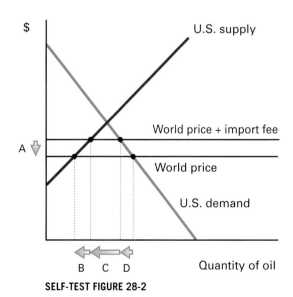

SELF-TEST FIGURE 28-2

QUESTIONS AND PROBLEMS

1. *[imports and exports]* When the world price of a good is below the domestic price, will a country import or export the good? Will the country produce any of the good domestically? Explain, using a graph as part of your explanation.

2. *[imports and exports]* When the world price of a good is above the domestic price, will a country import or export the good? Will the country produce any of the good domestically? Explain, using a graph as part of your explanation.

3. *[the GATT]* What is the relationship between the World Trade Organization and the GATT?

4. *[NAFTA]* In your opinion, should the membership of NAFTA be expanded to include countries in Central America and South America? Why would other countries want to join NAFTA? What benefits might the United States receive if these countries joined? Why might there be opposition to expanding NAFTA?

5. *[tariffs]* Construct a supply and demand graph that illustrates the effects on price and quantity when a tariff is imposed on an imported good.

6. *[tariffs]* As stated in the chapter, most tariffs in the United States are 6 percent or less. Survey your family and friends to see what percentage they think tariff rates in the United States are at. Compute the average of the answers you obtain and compare it to the true figure. Did your family and friends overestimate or underestimate the actual average tariff in the United States? How far off were they? What factors could account for the inaccuracy in their answers?

7. *[tariffs]* Explain why a tariff can be viewed as a price support for domestic producers.

8. *[tariffs versus quotas]* Do consumers prefer tariffs or quotas, given that one or the other will be imposed on a particular import? Explain.

9. *[tariffs and quotas]* Use a supply and demand graph that illustrates the effects on price and quantity when a tariff is imposed on an imported good. Explain how the effects shown on your graph could alternatively be achieved through the imposition of a quota instead of the tariff.

10. *[voluntary export restraints]* From the perspective of producers in an exporting country, why is a voluntary export restraint preferable to a quota on imports of their product?

11. *[nontariff barriers]* List three examples other than quotas of nontariff barriers to trade discussed in the chapter. Then suppose that the United States wished to create a nontariff barrier to the imports of foreign-made televisions. Provide an example of a nontariff barrier not brought up in the text that could apply to television imports.

12. *[protectionism]* Select one of the arguments for protectionism presented in the text and write a short essay critical of the argument you select.

13. *[protectionism]* Suppose you are a member of Congress who wishes to protect tomato farmers, who have a lot of political clout in your area. Which of the arguments for protectionism would you apply to make your case to others in Congress? State your argument briefly and in writing, making sure to explicitly relate it to tomatoes.

14. *[national defense argument]* Name three products that might be able to persuasively use the national defense argument for protectionism. Name three other products where you could make a case, but not one you would support.

15. *[level playing field]* Do you think that nations should be put on a level playing field before being allowed to trade? Explain and defend your position.

WORKING WITH GRAPHS AND DATA

1. *[gains from trade]* Use Graph 28-1, which shows the U.S. domestic supply of a good and demand for that good, along with its price in the world market.

   a. Show the domestic equilibrium price that would exist in the United States if there were no international trade in this good.

   b. Assume that trade began. Label the quantity supplied by U.S. producers and the quantity demanded by U.S. consumers as a result of trade.

   c. Would the United States import or export this good? Explain why. Label the amount imported as "Imports" or the amount exported as "Exports."

   d. Show the gain or loss of producer surplus as a result of trade and label it "Loss to producers" if producers lose or "Gain to producers" if producers gain.

   e. Show the gain or loss of consumer surplus as a result of trade and label it "Loss to consumers" if consumers lose or Gain to Consumers if consumers gain.

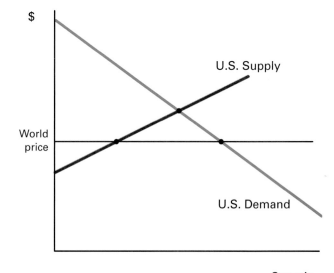

GRAPH 28-1

2. *[gains from trade]* Use Graph 28-2, which shows the U.S. domestic supply curve, the U.S. demand curve, and the world market price of a good that is traded internationally.

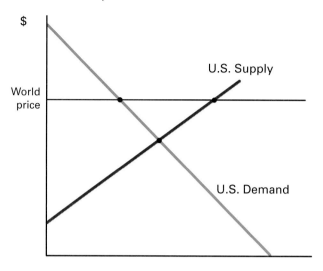

GRAPH 28-2

a. Show the domestic equilibrium price, P_2, that would exist in the United States if there were no international trade in this good.
b. Assume that trade began. Label the quantity supplied by U.S. producers as Q_S and the quantity demanded by U.S. consumers as a result of trade as Q_D.
c. Would the United States import or export this good? Explain why. Label the amount imported as "Imports" or the amount exported as "Exports."
d. Show the gain or loss of producer surplus with trade and label it "Loss to producers" if producers lose or "Gain to producers" if producers gain.
e. Show the gain or loss of consumer surplus with trade and label it "Loss to consumers" if consumers lose or "Gain to consumers" if consumers gain.

3. *[quotas]* Use the following table showing the U.S. import demand schedule and unrestricted import supply schedule.

Price $	Quantity of Imports Demanded	Unrestricted Quantity of Imports Supplied	Import Supply with a Quota
5	10	50	
4	20	40	
3	30	30	
2	40	20	
1	50	10	

a. What is the equilibrium price and quantity of imports?
b. Assume that the government imposes an import quota of twenty units of this good. Fill in the "Import supply with a quota" column.
c. What would be the new price of imports? Explain.
d. Graph 28-3 shows the import demand curve, the unrestricted import supply curve, and the import supply with quota curve. Place the appropriate label on each line in Graph 28-3. Also, label the axes of the graph.
e. On Graph 28-3, show the equilibrium price and quantity of imports when supply is unrestricted and label the equilibrium E_1. Show the equilibrium price and quantity when they are restricted by the quota and label the equilibrium with the restriction E_2.
f. Show on Graph 28-3 how much imports decrease as a result of the imposition of the quota and label it "Imports decrease." Explain the change.

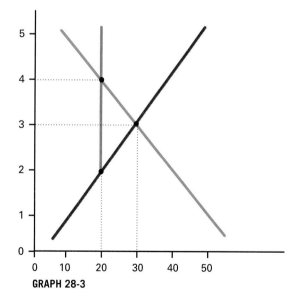

GRAPH 28-3

4. *[tariffs]* Use Graph 28-4, which shows the supply curve of imports of a good into the United States and the demand for imports by U.S. consumers. Answer the following questions concerning this market.

a. What is the equilibrium price and quantity? Label the equilibrium price and quantity as P_1 and Q_1 on the graph.
b. Suppose that the U.S. government imposes a $2 per unit tariff on this good. Draw the new supply curve for imports and label it "Import supply with tariff."

c. What is the new equilibrium price and quantity with the tariff? Label this new equilibrium price and quantity as P₂ and Q₂ on the graph.
d. By how much did imports change? Show the change in imports and label it "Imports decrease."
e. Who benefits and who loses from the tariff? Explain.

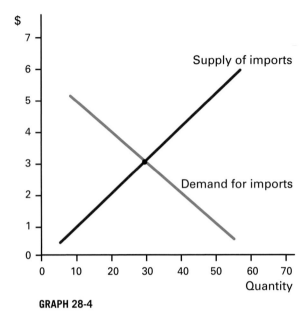

GRAPH 28-4

 Visit **www.prenhall.com/ayers** for Exploring the Web exercises and additional self-test quizzes.

CHAPTER 29

ECONOMIC DEVELOPMENT

A LOOK AHEAD

The watershed events of history are often closely tied to economic forces. In 1989, the world witnessed a Wall come down in Berlin, shattering the symbol of a globe divided into two armed, hostile camps. Tearing down the Berlin Wall epitomized the failure of the centrally planned communist countries to keep up with either the freedom or the living standards in Western economies. The world witnessed communism being replaced with capitalism throughout the former Soviet empire. Yet only now, over a decade later, are the people of the former Soviet Union starting to experience the benefits of a market economy. The Explore & Apply section that concludes the chapter examines the economic forces that have caused this delay.

This chapter examines the transition of economies from poverty to wealth. We start by characterizing the countries of the developing world, noting the need to use development indicators to formulate a goal-oriented development agenda. We then turn to population growth, examining issues both old and new. We emphasize the importance of property rights as a foundation for development. To deal with these and other issues of development, countries can turn to the International Monetary Fund and World Bank for advice and financial help. Created by the wealthy nations to help the poorer ones, these institutions are evidence that in the global neighborhood, neighbors are committed to helping neighbors.

LEARNING OBJECTIVES

Understanding Chapter 29 will enable you to:
1. **Discuss the problems that are a priority for developing countries.**
2. **Describe the goals on the United Nations' development agenda.**
3. **Point out the incentives for population growth.**
4. **Explain the connection between economic development and property rights.**
5. **Identify the roles of the International Monetary Fund and the World Bank in economic development.**
6. **Describe how insecure property rights have hindered economic development in Russia.**

Explore & Apply

727

In earlier chapters, you learned about key economic concepts such as scarcity and comparative advantage. You also saw how institutions such as the Federal Reserve impact the supply of money in an economy. Although our focus so far has been on developed countries, such as the United States, about 40 percent of the 207 countries in the world are less-developed countries where people struggle for basic necessities such as food and water. Economics helps us understand why some countries are rich while others are poor. It also helps us identify and implement solutions for poverty.

developed countries countries such as the United States, Japan, Germany, and the United Kingdom that rely on the free-market system.

less-developed countries (LDCs) nations that lag behind the wealthier countries; also known as developing countries.

transitional economies countries such as Russia, Hungary, and Poland that are moving away from central planning to the free-market system.

29.1 DEVELOPING ECONOMIES AND POVERTY

There are approximately 6.2 billion people in the world living in 207 countries. The International Monetary Fund (IMF) classifies these countries into three groups: developed, less developed, and transitional. **Developed countries** include the United States, Canada, Japan, Germany, France, Italy, and the United Kingdom. The economies in these countries rely on the free-market system. On average, a person working in the United States earns about $37,000 a year. **Less-developed countries (LDCs),** also known as developing countries, include countries in Central and South America, many countries in Asia, and the countries of Africa. A person working in one of these areas may earn as little as $170 a year. **Transitional economies** refer to those countries that are moving away from the central planning of communism and toward the free market. Russia, Hungary, and the Czech Republic are examples of transitional economies. The map in Figure 29-1 highlights the developing countries and transitional

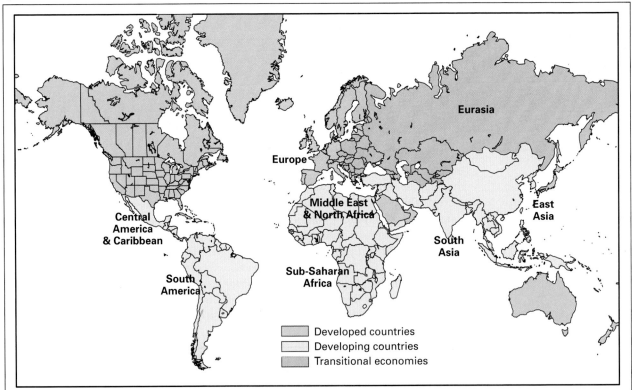

FIGURE 29-1

WORLD MAP Countries are grouped into three categories: developed countries (shown in blue), less-developed countries (shown in light green), and transitional economies (shown in purple). The U.S. Agency for International Development assists developing and transitional economies.

Source: Map available at http://www.usaid.gov/pubs/cbj2003/map.html.

economies served by the U.S. Agency for International Development (USAID), the primary government agency that assists LDCs. As you can see, these countries spread across the globe.

Economic development is a field within economics that studies why some countries remain mired deep in poverty, while other countries prosper. The data that describes a country's economic development are called *indicators*. A country is better off when its development indicators improve over time. The indicators examined in economic development studies vary. **Per capita income is probably the indicator referred to most frequently, but often a set of indicators is needed to assess the level of development in a country.** As we look at the developing countries in this chapter, you will see data on a wide variety of commonly used indicators.

economic development a field of economics that studies the poverty of nations.

PROBLEMS OF THE DEVELOPING ECONOMIES

The LDCs vary in their climate, natural resources, land area, population, and other characteristics. For this reason, there are significant differences in the problems they face. While the LDCs differ, they do share several problems:

- **Poverty.** Per capita income is low.
- **Deficiencies in infrastructure.** *Infrastructure* includes roads, bridges, dams, schools, airports, hospitals, water treatment facilities, sanitation facilities, and other capital that promotes prosperity and well-being.
- **Low life expectancy.** Disease and lack of medical care contribute to health problems and high death rates.
- **High population growth.** Overpopulation creates a lack of opportunity and strains scarce food and water. The result is sometimes malnutrition and even starvation.

The extreme poverty of the LDCs has enormous consequences for the people living in those countries, including the prospect of an early death. Annual life expectancies and per capita gross national income for selected developing countries are both quite low. For comparison, the life expectancy and per capita income in the United States, along with those less-developed countries, are both shown in Figure 29-2. Table 29-1 also shows the striking differences between development indicators in the poorest LDCs and the United States.

TABLE 29-1   LOW-INCOME COUNTRIES COMPARED TO THE UNITED STATES

DEVELOPMENT INDICATOR	LOW-INCOME COUNTRIES	UNITED STATES
Under-five mortality rate (per 1,000)	121.0	8.0
Infant mortality rate	80.5	7.1
Access to improved water source (% of population)	75.7	100.0
Access to improved sanitation (% of rural population)	31.0	100.0
Fixed line and mobile telephones (per 1,000 people)	35.7	1,117.9
Personal computers (per 1,000 people)	6.1	625
Gross national income per capita	$430	$35,060
Life expectancy at birth (years)	58.8	78.0

Source: World Bank, *World Development Indicators* database, by country, 2002 and 2003.

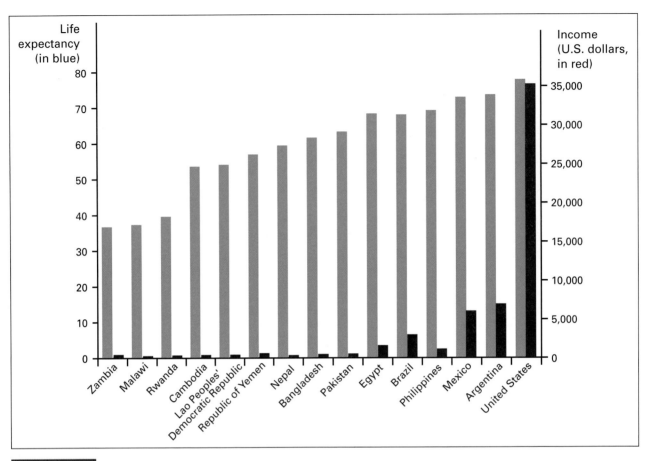

LIFE EXPECTANCY AND ANNUAL PER CAPITA GROSS NATIONAL INCOME There is a clear difference between the development indicators of life expectancy and annual per capita gross national income of developing countries such as Zambia and that of developed countries such as the United States. Economists can use these indicators to identify countries that need assistance.

Source: 2002 World Development Indicators database, World Bank. Gross national income was previously called gross national product in World Bank publications.

STAGES OF DEVELOPMENT—FROM THE COUNTRYSIDE TO THE BIG CITY

To the impoverished worker who toils in the countryside without electricity, indoor plumbing, and safe drinking water, the hope of a better life often involves migrating to a big city. That would be the capital city of Nairobi to the more than 30 million people living in Kenya, the African country about twice the size of Nevada shown in Figure 29-3. Let's briefly consider life in Kenya in order to make several important points about development.

According to the U.S. Central Intelligence Agency (CIA), 75 percent of the population of Kenya can read and write, but 50 percent are unemployed. The chief occupation is farming, which provides a means to survive for 75 to 80 percent of the people. To put that number in perspective, about 2 percent of Americans earn a living from agriculture. Because of Kenya's bountiful wildlife, tourism is a major industry. Small-scale manufacturing is also important. A significant portion of Kenya's manufactured goods are exported to other countries.

Although the country's birth rate is high, so is its death rate, due to the prevalence of HIV/AIDS. The population is growing at better than 1 percent a year. Kenya's per capita GDP of

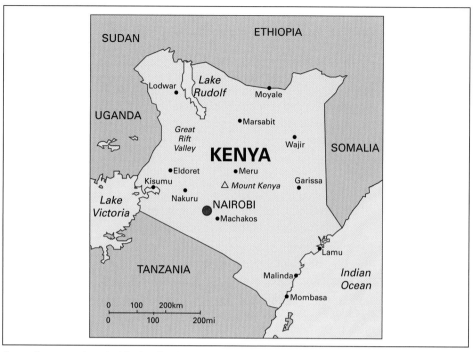

Source: From www.cia.gov/publications/factbook.

FIGURE 29-3

KENYA Kenya is a developing country on the east coast of Africa. While its population is mostly literate, about half of its people are unemployed.

$1,500 is high for a country in Africa. You might be surprised that English is one of the country's two official languages, and that the Protestant and Roman Catholic faiths are professed by the majority of the population. Nairobi is a rapidly growing city of over 2,000,000 people, offering current movies, fine dining, and access to the Internet and other modern technologies.

Like other LDCs, Kenya mixes agriculture and urbanization. To understand this trait of LDCs, consider **Rostow's stages of economic development** model. In 1960, American economic historian Walter W. Rostow suggested that countries pass through five stages in their development.

- ■ **Stage 1: Traditional society.** The first stage in Rostow's model, traditional society, describes a country where subsistence agriculture dominates economic activity.
- ■ **Stage 2: Preconditions for takeoff.** In the second stage, agricultural production rises so as to permit people to trade excess production. Transportation is needed to take crops to distant markets, so that investment in transportation is a key in moving from stage 1 to stage 2.
- ■ **Stage 3: Takeoff.** In the third stage, many farmers leave agriculture to take jobs in industry. Thus, the country begins the process of urbanization, but remains focused on agriculture and just a few manufacturing industries. Again, more investment is needed, this time to create a manufacturing sector.
- ■ **Stage 4: Drive to maturity.** In the fourth stage, there is economic diversification, with many different goods and services produced.
- ■ **Stage 5: High mass consumption.** In the final stage, the production of consumer goods and services dominates economic activity.

Clearly, stage 5 describes the United States and other high-income countries, but where lies Kenya? The answer is not clear. Kenya, like many LDCs, combines stages. It exhibits

Rostow's stages of economic development a model that says that countries begin as traditional societies, pass through the preconditions for takeoff, the takeoff, the drive to maturity, and conclude their development with the stage of high mass consumption.

some qualities associated with traditional society, but has been able to increase its exports, which is consistent with stage 2. The growth of Nairobi suggests the third stage. What are we to make of this?

While Rostow's model can help us view economic development as occurring in a sequence of steps, development does not necessarily occur in the way specified by the model. Furthermore, the model does not identify the causes of movements from one stage to the next. The model is criticized by economists for these reasons, but it is still useful for emphasizing the role of investment in development. Let's turn now to efforts to move nations out of the earlier stages.

A DEVELOPMENT AGENDA

The stated mission of the *United Nations (UN)* is to promote world peace and prosperity through international cooperation. Consider the eight economic development goals set by the United Nations:

Goal 1. Eradicate extreme poverty and hunger. Estimates are that more than a billion people live on less than a dollar a day. Hunger is a problem for 826 million people.

Goal 2. Achieve universal primary education. One-third of children in the LDCs have less than five years of schooling.

Goal 3. Promote gender equality and empower women. Rates of school attendance and participation in the labor force are lower for women than men in LDCs.

Goal 4. Reduce child mortality. A global effort to vaccinate children was launched in early 2000, with the goal of eliminating polio, diphtheria, and other childhood diseases. Millions of children have been vaccinated since that effort began.

Goal 5. Improve maternal health.

Goal 6. Combat HIV/AIDS, malaria, and other diseases.

Goal 7. Ensure environmental sustainability.

Goal 8. Develop a global partnership for development.

The UN plans to achieve these goals by 2015. Those plans still hold, although in late 2003 U.N. Secretary-General Kofi Annan reported that progress on meeting the goals "has been uneven at best". The goals are associated with *targets,* specific results that when achieved will mean each goal has been met. Table 29-2 restates the goals and shows a target for each goal.

TABLE 29-2   **UNITED NATIONS GOALS AND SELECTED TARGETS FOR ECONOMIC DEVELOPMENT**

GOAL	SELECTED TARGET
1. Eradicate extreme poverty and hunger.	Halve the proportion of people whose income is less than a dollar a day.
2. Achieve universal primary education.	Ensure that boys and girls have access to primary schooling.
3. Promote gender equality and empower women.	Eliminate gender disparity in all levels of education.
4. Reduce child mortality.	Reduce by two-thirds the under-five child mortality rate.
5. Improve maternal health.	Reduce by three-quarters the maternal mortality rate.
6. Combat HIV/AIDS, malaria, and other diseases.	Halt the spread of HIV/AIDS.
7. Ensure environmental sustainability.	Reverse the loss of environmental resources.
8. Develop a global partnership for development.	Deal with the debt problems of LDCs.

Source: United Nations.

Regarding the effort to combat HIV/AIDS, the sixth goal, the developing world is home to 95 percent of all HIV/AIDS sufferers. The World Health Organization (WHO) predicts that 70 million people will die in the next twenty years unless drastic action or a major breakthrough occurs in the treatment of HIV/AIDS. One estimate concludes that AIDS has killed more people than all wars and natural disasters throughout history and that 40 million children have already lost one or both parents to AIDS.

One reason that AIDS claims so many lives in the LDCs revolves around missing infrastructure. Without transportation facilities, life-prolonging medicines cannot reach those who need them. Without medical personnel, the sick cannot be properly cared for. Without education, AIDS is more likely to spread. In the LDCs, investments in infrastructure such as roads, hospitals, and schools will complement treatment with drugs in the fight against AIDS.

To track development progress, the UN refers to its world indicators, seen in Table 29-3. Grouping them, the indicators measure just two characteristics. One is infrastructure. The sanitation, water, computer, and telephone statistics shed light on access to capital, which makes people more productive. Note that the rural population has less access than the urban population. The second characteristic is health. The indicators that relate to infants and children's health reveal the effects of poverty.

TABLE 29-3   UNITED NATIONS DEVELOPMENT INDICATORS FOR THE WORLD

INDICATOR	VALUE
1. Sanitation, percentage of population with access to improved sanitation, rural	40%
2. Sanitation, percentage of population with access to improved sanitation, total	61%
3. Sanitation, percentage of population with access to improved sanitation, urban	85%
4. Water, percentage of population with access to improved drinking water sources, rural	71%
5. Water, percentage of population with access to improved drinking water sources, total	82%
6. Water, percentage of population with access to improved drinking water sources, urban	95%
7. Children one-year-old immunized against measles, percent	72%
8. Children under five mortality rate per 1,000 live births	82
9. Infant mortality rate (zero to one year) per 1,000 live births	57
10. Internet users	550 million
11. Internet users per 100 population	9.8
12. Personal computers	575 million
13. Personal computers per 100 population	9.9
14. Telephone main lines in use and cellular subscribers	2 billion
15. Telephone lines and cellular subscribers per 100 population	36.8

Source: United Nations *Millennium Indicators,* U.N. website, 2003. The data are for the latest available year, ranging from 2000 to 2002.

> ### QUICKCHECK
>
> One of the UN goals is to reduce child mortality. The text mentions that the plan to reduce child mortality includes vaccinations against childhood diseases. Will progress in meeting any of the other goals also contribute to lower child mortality? Explain briefly.
>
> **Answer:** Yes. For example, child mortality should also be reduced if hunger and poverty are reduced, since everyone's health partly depends on their diet. Meeting other goals could also reduce child mortality. Children should be healthier if maternal health is improved, and diseases such as AIDS and malaria are diminished.

SNAPSHOT   IT TAKES A HIGHWAY—ONE YOU CAN DRIVE AT NIGHT

Once crops are harvested, they must be transported to the cities before they spoil. Likewise, once goods are produced, they must be brought to buyers. It takes a highway to move the goods. Once the highway is built, other infrastructure is needed—gasoline stations, secondary roads, eating places, repair shops, rest areas, and government inspection stations to weigh and examine cargoes.

Even when all these have been built, the trucks may sit silently as nightfall comes. Trucks carry valuable cargo, which attracts hijackers who prefer the darkness as cover for their lawbreaking. For this reason you might find inspection stations in Africa crowded with trucks. The drivers must stop for inspection, but face long delays. Afterwards, they park overnight rather than venture into bandit-infested territory. Transportation first takes a highway, but then more. In this case, countries in a hurry to raise their living standards have been slowed down because of dangers that lurk in the night. ◄

29.2 POPULATION GROWTH

The world has seen its population grow rapidly, from just under 3 billion in 1960 to over 6 billion today. A longer perspective, as seen in Figure 29-4, shows that population has exploded over the last three-and-a-half centuries, and is projected to keep increasing. Part of the reason for this growth is that advances in medicine and hygiene have lowered death rates, thereby increasing longevity. Birth rates have also been high, however, especially among the segments of the population least able to afford raising children.

THE DISMAL SCIENCE

"the dismal science" a name given to economics because of Thomas Robert Malthus's nineteenth-century predictions of mass starvation.

Economics was once called **"the dismal science."** The term dates to the early nineteenth century. At that time, Thomas Robert Malthus popularized the notion that economics could only hope to delay the day when the world's population finds itself at the brink of starvation.

According to this Malthusian view, starvation is the only force that can keep population in check. While economics can temporarily improve the world, the inevitability of population growth and the limits of the earth's capacity to produce must at some point reduce us all to no more than a subsistence existence. A dismal thought indeed!

Yet, the world has come a long way since the early 1800s, and both population and living standards have increased dramatically. For the most part, people of the world are much

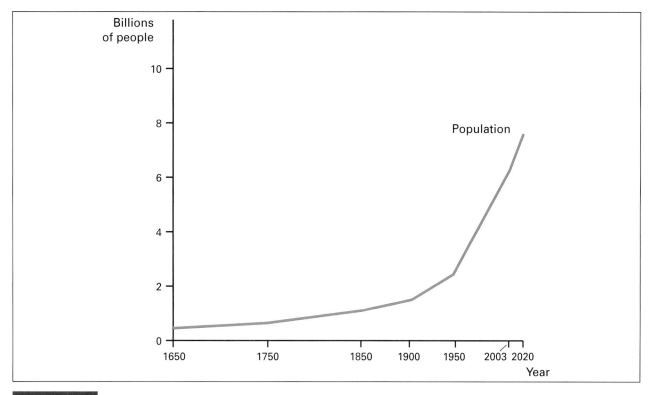

FIGURE 29-4

WORLD POPULATION GROWTH The world population has exploded over the centuries, which leads to concerns about when and how population growth will stop. A look at the data fails to reveal any obvious end in sight.

Source: Census Bureau, *Historical Estimates of World Population* and *Total Midyear Population for the World, 1950–2050.* The data through 1950 are estimates, while the data after 2003 are projections.

further removed from starvation now than then. Since the earth has not expanded, something else must have happened. That something is technology. Technological change has enabled the world to get much more output from its resources than ever imagined by Malthus.

There is still room for concern. If the world continues to experience the same population growth rate that it has over the course of the twentieth century, it must ultimately fill every nook and cranny with people. There would be no room to produce enough food to feed them. Since population grows geometrically, it doubles according to *the rule of seventy-two,* which states that doubling time equals seventy-two divided by the rate of growth. For example, at a growth rate of 1.5 percent, a country's population would double every forty-eight years.

Economic incentives can put a brake on population growth. Specifically, **as countries become wealthier, the opportunity cost of people's time rises.** Because children take time to nurture, people choose to have fewer of them. This is especially true in countries that provide reliable retirement benefits for the elderly. Otherwise, the cost of raising children is offset by the expectation that those children will provide for their parents' retirement. Figure 29-5 shows the fertility rate, meaning the number of children born per woman, in selected developing countries and in the United States. The fertility rate reflects both economic incentives and traditions such as attitudes toward family size.

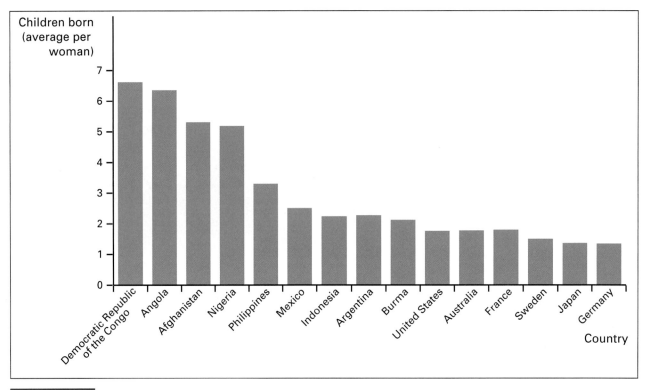

FIGURE 29-5

AVERAGE NUMBER OF CHILDREN BORN PER WOMAN, SELECTED COUNTRIES Generally, developing countries have higher fertility rates than do the developed nations.

Source: 2003 CIA World Factbook.

PROBLEMS WITH THE PRICE SIGNAL

Unless we face the full costs and benefits of our actions, we cannot be expected to make efficient choices. One group that frequently does not bear all the costs of its decisions is parents. For example, ignoring possible external benefits, such as to the Social Security system, efficiency would suggest that parents should pay all costs of rearing children, including costs of food, shelter, and education. However, equity suggests that children should have comparable opportunities. A child born into poverty does not choose to be there, any more than does a child born in more comfortable circumstances. To promote equity, it makes sense for taxpayers to subsidize the infant formula, schooling, school lunches, and other elements necessary to bring up the less-fortunate child. The tradeoff is that those subsidies increase the number of children born into poverty.

To the extent that the costs of rearing children are paid by others, parents face a marginal cost of rearing children that does not reflect the full cost of those children to society. The effect is that those children are subsidized, as shown in Figure 29-6. Figure 29-6(a) shows that this government subsidy can influence parents to choose to have more children than they would were the marginal costs not subsidized. The lower the costs they face, the more rational it is for parents to choose a larger family size or to ignore the precautions that would keep family size down. The result is that government subsidies tend to increase population growth rates.

In some cases, such as that shown in Figure 29-6(b), couples may choose to have children they don't want—so-called *unwanted children*—in order to receive extra government

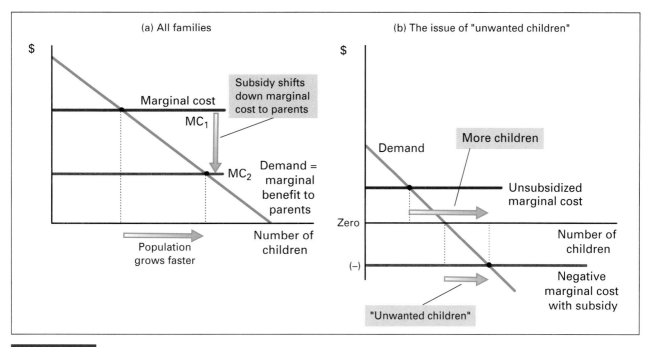

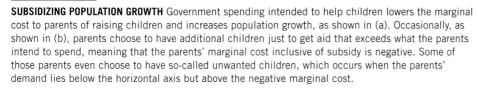

FIGURE 29-6

SUBSIDIZING POPULATION GROWTH Government spending intended to help children lowers the marginal cost to parents of raising children and increases population growth, as shown in (a). Occasionally, as shown in (b), parents choose to have additional children just to get aid that exceeds what the parents intend to spend, meaning that the parents' marginal cost inclusive of subsidy is negative. Some of those parents even choose to have so-called unwanted children, which occurs when the parents' demand lies below the horizontal axis but above the negative marginal cost.

aid or tax write-offs. These are children that the parents would prefer not to have, except for the extra income they cause. In other words, the parents' demand curves would be negative for these children. Public assistance intended to help children may in this way lead to more children who need help.

We know the world cannot sustain an ever-increasing population, nor wish to endure the other stresses of a crowded planet. For these reasons, government policy might seek to influence population growth rates by changing the incentives facing prospective families. Alternatively, countries can turn to command-and-control methods. For example and most notably, for more than two decades China has prohibited a family from having more than one child. Given a cultural preference for baby boys, and modern medical technology, the result has been a demographic nightmare. For example, in 2003, about 109 boys were born in China for every 100 baby girls. Historically, countries where young men could not find mates had become embroiled in violence or warfare.

In less-developed countries, people have many children for several reasons. One is because they lack access to birth control, or they may have customs or beliefs that do not accept its use. A second reason is due to ineffective or nonexistent government programs such as Social Security or other transfer payments. A couple in a less-developed country with several children can rely on them for assistance if they reach advanced ages. Education, medical care, and stable governments can help address population growth issues.

> ## *QUICKCHECK*
>
> **Would it be good public policy to ensure that prospective parents pay all of the costs of educating their children?**
>
> **Answer:** The question of good public policy is normative, meaning that economics cannot provide a definitive answer. Policymakers might weigh the often-conflicting goals of efficiency and equity for children. For example, the large majority of people think that it is equitable for all children to have equal access to education, even if that means publicly subsidizing that education. This policy leads to inefficiencies, because it gives parents less incentive to hold down family size.

29.3 PRICES AND PROPERTY RIGHTS

price signals the allocation of resources through the price system; prices guide consumption and investment.

For countries to develop, they need capital. Investments from private sources or government are the source of this capital. Consider private investment. In deciding which projects to fund, banks, private investors, and multinational firms look at market prices and the security of property rights. In other words, the investors follow **price signals** to guide them in the direction of the greatest profits. **Because of the central importance of prices in guiding consumption and investment spending throughout the world, the market economy is often called the price system.** Some LDCs have abundant natural resources, such as oil in the countries of the Middle East. Let's see how the price system responds to dwindling supplies of resources.

THE PRICE SYSTEM—FINDING NEW RESOURCES

Prices respond to scarcity. Other things equal, the scarcer are resources, the higher are their prices. Higher prices make it profitable to find or develop substitutes, which would not be economical at lower prices. Well before any resource is depleted, its increasing scarcity drives its price higher. When the price of a nonrenewable resource rises, the market is motivated to explore for additional supplies and to develop substitutes.

In the 1970s, the high price of oil resulted in major new finds in Mexico, Alaska, the North Sea, and elsewhere. Today, oil rigs can be found in many LDCs, as the search for oil has spread to the far corners of the globe. Substitutes for oil include technology to give motor vehicles more miles per gallon, insulation to reduce the energy costs of homes, and fuel alternatives such as coal and natural gas. However, oil prices have not remained high enough for most substitute fuels to be economical.

As price has risen, technology has responded to prevent shortages. At one time, for example, the world's copper supplies appeared to be running out. This shortage threatened growth because copper was needed for electricity and telephone connections. The rising price of copper spurred new technologies, such as fiber optics, that greatly reduced the world's need for copper. In the realm of food, too, technological advances have helped farmers increase yields per acre to meet the needs of growing populations. The hunger spots in the world today have much less to do with agricultural technology than with political instability that interrupt the production and distribution of food.

In the 1800s, an energy crisis was brought about by a scarcity of whale oil, which at the time was used in reading lamps. The scarcity was prompted by tight supplies and high prices, as whaling ships decimated the population of the world's whales in response to growing demand. The price system dangled the lure of profit to successful innovators who could find new energy sources. This incentive eventually brought about the age of petroleum. We can only speculate about whether the next energy age will be of solar power, new efficiencies in energy usage, or other possibilities that few of us currently envision.

Many developing countries' exports are heavily weighted toward natural resources. For example, countries in the Middle East export crude oil, countries with rainforests export tropical hardwoods, and so forth. The problem for these countries occurs when the prices of *commodities,* including natural resources such as copper, tin, and precious metals, and agricultural products such as rice, bananas, and cocoa, are not high enough to sustain development. The **Prebisch–Singer thesis,** which was advanced in the 1950s, states that developing countries will be trapped in poverty because the price of their exports will be driven down by increasing commodity supplies as the price system responds. This can lead to **immiserizing growth,** where increasing supplies of commodities exported by the LDCs causes prices to drop so far that these countries end up worse off because of trade. Although low commodity and agricultural prices are a problem for the LDCs that export these goods, the Prebisch–Singer thesis is not generally accepted by economists as an explanation for the ills of these countries. Thus, in the next section we turn our attention to the role of property rights in economic development.

> **Prebisch–Singer thesis** states that developing countries will remain in poverty because the prices of their exports of commodities are doomed to decrease.
>
> **immiserizing growth** growth that leaves a country worse off; associated with the Prebisch–Singer thesis.

PROPERTY RIGHTS

A key ingredient of the market economy, one lacking in many less-developed countries, is the ingredient of secure **property rights,** meaning rights of ownership. Investors need to know that they will be able to retain the fruits of their investments, or they will not invest. They must not fear that government action in the future will prevent them from reaping the rewards that they envision when they make their investments in the present.

> **property rights** clear rights of ownership.

For example, prospective investors would be deterred if they fear regulatory *takings,* in which government reduces the value of property by restricting how the investor can use it. In extreme cases, investors might fear government expropriation, such as the expropriation of oil wells that occurred in Colombia and other countries in the 1960s and 1970s. Investors must also be confident that government regulations will be enforced evenhandedly, and not skewed by bribery or favoritism. Civil unrest and terrorism are also problems that can drive investors away.

Table 29-4 presents the average annual growth rates, from 1990 to 2000, of selected high-growth countries, medium- to low-growth countries, and countries with negative growth. Most of the high-growth countries share a significant role for the price system and property rights. LDCs that can sustain a high-growth rate experience rising living standards. In general, the growth rates of the developed countries are 4 percent or less.

WATER WAR IN COCHABAMBA

SNAPSHOT

While people in the developed world may take clean, safe drinking water for granted, over a billion people around the world do not enjoy that resource. In Cochabamba, Bolivia's third-largest city, chronic water problems came to a head in 1999. The government chose to privatize the city's water system, selling it to Bechtel, an American-owned firm. The firm held out the hope that infrastructure investments, in the form of dams, pipelines, and purification facilities, would bring ample supplies of clean water to the populace.

Before investments could be made, the new owner said water rates had to rise. Considering that many Bolivians live on the country's $60-a-month minimum wage, the $20 and $30 monthly water bills that residents of Cochabamba began to receive generated outrage. Civil unrest in early 2000 put water back into the hands of the government. Since then, nothing has been done to solve the water problems, and many residents have water only a few hours a week, if at all. Meanwhile, the loss of property put a chill on foreign investment in Bolivia, leaving no winners from this Bolivian water war. ◄

| TABLE 29-4 | AVERAGE ANNUAL GROWTH RATES IN GDP, SELECTED COUNTRIES |

HIGH-GROWTH COUNTRIES (IN PERCENT)		MEDIUM- TO LOW-GROWTH COUNTRIES		NEGATIVE-GROWTH COUNTRIES	
China	10.0	Guatemala	4.1	Moldova	− 8.4
Ireland	7.7	Hong Kong, China	4.0	Ukraine	− 7.9
Myanmar	7.4	Australia	3.9	Russian Federation	− 3.7
Mozambique	6.7	Panama	3.8		
Malaysia	6.5	Pakistan	3.7		
Lao Peoples' Democratic Republic	6.4	United States	3.4		
Chile	6.3	Philippines	3.3		
India	5.9	Mexico	3.1		
South Korea	5.7	New Zealand	3.1		
Lebanon	5.4	Japan	1.3		

Source: 2003 World Bank Development Indicators database. Growth rates cited are for 1990 to 2001.

WARRING OVER REAL ESTATE

Besides poverty, the LDCs have conflict in common. A study of the seventy-five countries that have USAID missions showed that, between 1996 and 2001, two-thirds of them had major conflicts. There is nothing more destructive to standards of living than warfare. Property ownership is central to many of the world's conflicts. Conflict over property can range from boundary disputes to the control of entire countries. Borders between nations are often ill defined, with centuries of warfare shifting them back and forth. Disputes over property have triggered the wars among the countries of the former Yugoslavia and the many clashes between Palestinians and Israelis. Likewise, the Indians and Pakistanis have fought two wars over the Kashmir Province, where ethnic tensions are still running very high. Disputes sap vital energy that could be used to move countries ahead economically.

29.4 COUNTRIES HELPING COUNTRIES: FOREIGN AID, THE IMF, AND THE WORLD BANK

When one country helps another country, the mechanism is often *foreign aid*. Foreign aid consists of donated money or products. Countries provide foreign aid on their own and through membership in two of the most important organizations that channel resources to the poorer countries: the **World Bank** and the **International Monetary Fund,** commonly referred to by its initials (**IMF**).

World Bank institution that was created to loan money to developing countries.

International Monetary Fund (IMF) institution created in 1944 to promote a sound world financial system.

FOREIGN AID—AN ANSWER TO SCARCITY OF CAPITAL?

Polls show that people in the developed countries support the principle of giving aid to the LDCs. The United States plays a major role in foreign aid. For example, as reported by the White House in 2002, the United States is:

- The top importer of goods from developing countries–eight times more than all Official Development Assistance to developing countries from all donors.
- The top source of private capital to developing countries.
- The world leader in charitable donations to developing countries.
- One of the top two providers of Official Development Assistance, targeting the following key sectors:
  - HIV/AIDS (54 percent)
  - Basic education (50 percent)
  - Trade and investment (38 percent)
  - Agriculture (38 percent)

The United States also shoulders a major burden in fighting the war on terrorism and in maintaining the peace throughout the world.

Figure 29-7 shows the breakdown of USAID's core Developmental Assistance. As you can see, by far the greatest share goes to promote economic growth and agricultural development, since agriculture is especially important in LDCs that have difficulty raising enough food to feed themselves. Such aid might take the form of teaching farmers new technologies and techniques that promise to increase crop yields.

Figure 29-8 tracks the total amount of aid from all countries during the 1990s. The value of foreign aid is expressed in nominal terms, meaning the numbers have not been adjusted for inflation. A striking feature of the figure is the more than $10 billion drop in aid in 2001 when compared to 1991.

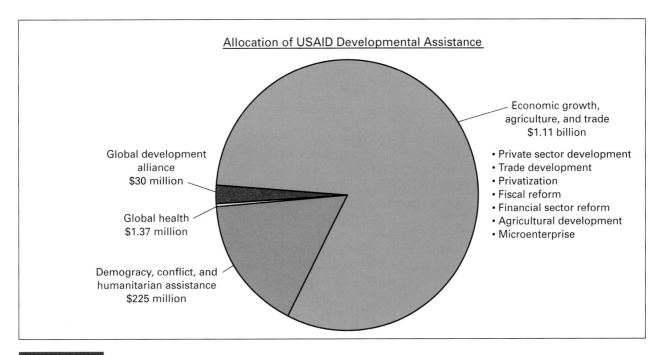

FIGURE 29-7

PURPOSES OF U.S. FOREIGN AID Foreign aid to developing countries by the USAID has a variety of purposes. The four stated pillars of USAID Development Assistance are shown in the pie chart. The largest portion of aid goes toward promoting economic growth and agricultural development. In addition to the spending shown above, USAID manages other spending, such as the huge Food for Peace program, with a budget of nearly $1.2 billion in 2003.

Source: U.S. Agency for International Development, Summary of Fiscal Year 2003 Budget.

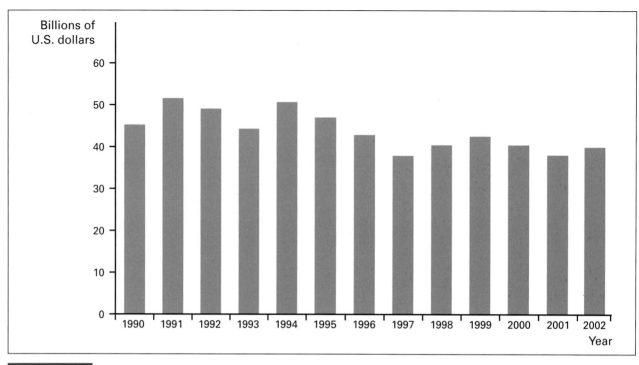

FIGURE 29-8

GOVERNMENT AID TO DEVELOPING COUNTRIES Foreign aid from governments drifted lower since 1990. By 2001 it was $10 billion lower than in 1991. This drop in foreign aid probably reflects the public's lack of support for foreign aid. By 2002, however, governments in the developed world were promising to significantly increase foreign aid, partly because of the war on terrorism.

Source: World Bank, *World Bank Anticipates Global Upturn, Urges Increased Help to Poor Countries,* March 13, 2002. Value for 2002 is author's estimate.

Issues of aid and development received more than the usual media attention in the spring of 2002, when an unlikely pair toured the world's poorest countries. The Irish singer, Bono, of the group U2 was one. The other was Paul O'Neill, U.S. Secretary of the Treasury. Their purpose was to assess opportunities for lifting up poor nations. One of the problems poor nations face is a crushing debt load. Banks in the developed countries have loaned billions of dollars to the governments of LDCs to finance infrastructure. Unfortunately for many LDCs, their economies do not generate enough tax dollars to repay the money owed.

Bono's opinion was that all debt should be forgiven. O'Neill argued for generosity in ongoing aid, but that forgiveness of debt would be inappropriate. Their debate typifies the differences of opinion on the issue of foreign aid. To provide debt relief to impoverished countries, the United States and other countries help to pay for the debt initiative for Heavily Indebted Poor Countries (HIPC). This program was established by the IMF and the World Bank. By late 2003, over $51 billion of debt relief had been granted to participating countries.

THE INTERNATIONAL MONETARY FUND (IMF)

As its name suggests, the IMF is a fund that can be drawn on by member countries needing temporary financing to deal with monetary and financial problems. The IMF was established in 1944 with the goal of ensuring a stable world monetary and financial system. According to its Articles of Agreement, the purposes of the IMF are to:

- Promote international monetary cooperation.
- Facilitate the expansion of international trade.
- Encourage exchange rate stability.
- Further the establishment of a *multilateral* (multicountry) payment system.
- Provide resources to member countries experiencing balance of payments problems.

Money to finance IMF operations comes from membership fees, called quotas, that are proportional to the size and economic strength of its 184 member countries. The United States has the largest quota, amounting to 17.6 percent of IMF funding. All member countries, rich and poor alike, have access to IMF resources.

The main activities of the IMF include:

1. **Surveillance.** This procedure involves a policy discussion between the IMF and a member country. An annual IMF appraisal of each member country's exchange rate policies is part of the process. Surveillance is intended to ensure that a country's economic policies furnish a strong foundation for stable exchange rates, which the IMF believes is a key to world prosperity. For example, the IMF urged Japan in 2000 to promote deregulation and competition in order to stimulate economic growth. Global surveillance is also carried out, such as in 2001 when the IMF pointed out in a *World Economic Outlook* report the need for countries to stimulate aggregate demand in the face of weakening global growth.

2. **Financial assistance.** As of February 2002, the IMF had about $77 billion in credits and loans outstanding to eighty-eight countries. This assistance is provided to countries that have balance of payments problems. The purpose of this assistance is to encourage reforms in the policies of countries receiving the assistance. Some of this assistance is in the form of debt relief provided through the HIPC initiative, mentioned earlier. IMF loans are intended to support reforms aimed at eliminating the root causes of a country's problems. For example, during the Asian financial crisis in 1998, the IMF's $21 billion loan to Korea was targeted toward reforming that country's financial and business sectors. In late 2003, the IMF promised to provide at least $5 billion in financial assistance to aid in rebuilding Iraq.

3. **Technical assistance.** Poor countries are often ill-equipped to develop their own fiscal and monetary policies because the human capital necessary to develop sound policies is not available domestically. Thus, the IMF provides help so that countries can design policies that strengthen their economies. For example, the IMF assisted Russia and other transition economies in setting up central banking and treasury systems. Part of the technical assistance offered is in the area of statistics. For a country to be able to implement and monitor effective policies, there must be statistics on unemployment, inflation, GDP, and other key macro variables. Countries that lack expertise in this area can tap into the IMF's expertise. That expertise was offered to Iraq in late 2003 in the form of training for Iraqi officials in budgeting and taxation.

Through the provision of surveillance, financial assistance, and technical assistance, the IMF aims to tie member countries more closely into the world economy, and advise members on how to deal with problems that arise from their trade and financial interactions with other countries. Sometimes these problems call for IMF financial assistance, which the IMF offers under the condition that the countries undertake economic reforms that are in accord with IMF advice.

The reforms can be painful, which leads some countries to complain about IMF arm-twisting. They might even complain of IMF *imperialism,* saying that the IMF seeks to force the values of Western economies upon countries around the world. The IMF has responded to this criticism by reforms intended to make IMF loan conditions less burdensome.

The IMF is known for the massive loans that it extended to Mexico during the 1994 to 1995 peso crisis, to the countries of Asia during the 1997 to 1998 Asian financial crisis, to Russia in 1998 as that country struggled through multiple economic and social crises, to Turkey in 2000, and to Argentina in 2001. The purpose of these loans was to allow these countries to pay their debts to other countries, while reforming their economic and financial systems. Not surprisingly, when the IMF compiled a ranking of its largest borrowers between the years of 1947 and 2000, Mexico, Korea, and Russia were the top three recipients of IMF loans.

Critics of IMF lending practices term many IMF loans "bailouts" that will lead to more bailouts in the future, because countries' lenders will not be as careful when they realize the IMF will step in with money when the countries get into trouble. Careless lending practices can impede economic development and sound growth because money will go into projects that are unsound and should not be undertaken. The IMF has publicly recognized the *moral hazard* in making unlimited loans—that countries will be prompted to follow unsound policies that will lead to future crises, and that lenders will be encouraged to make unsound loans if they believe that the IMF will see that they are repaid in the event of default by borrowing countries.

THE WORLD BANK

The World Bank does what most people expect banks to do: loan money. **World Bank loans to less-developed member countries are intended to further their economic development.** Since its creation more than fifty years ago, the World Bank has loaned more than $400 billion. The similarities between the World Bank and the IMF include that they are both headquartered in Washington, D.C., they are both owned by the governments of member countries, virtually every country is a member of both institutions, and they were both started in July 1944.

Consider the World Bank's lending practices:

- World Bank loans, which only go to developing countries, must be repaid. Unlike aid programs, the World Bank does not provide grants, which are gifts of money. The money for the Bank's loans comes partly from government grants and partly from borrowings from the private sector and governments.
- Lending is of two types. The first is lending to countries that are able to pay near-market interest on the loans they receive. The second is lending to countries that cannot afford to pay interest. These loans are called *credits* and are provided through a World Bank affiliate, the International Development Association, for terms of thirty-five to forty years. Although interest is not charged, the credits must be repaid. Such credits only go to the very poorest countries and average about $6 billion per year.
- The World Bank can only lend to member governments or under a member government's guarantee.
- To ensure that money is well invested, the Bank evaluates projects and only lends when a project is expected to earn at least a 10-percent rate of economic return.

A top priority of the World Bank is to stimulate development of the private sector, although direct loans to the private sector are prohibited. The Bank seeks to encourage the private sector by promoting stable, honest government economic policies that focus on expanding the significance of markets. Although the Bank cannot make loans to the private sector, an affiliate called the International Finance Corporation exists for that purpose. It also aids governments in privatizing formerly government-owned businesses.

The World Bank's focus on the private sector is a relatively recent development. From its inception through the 1970s, the Bank tended toward policies that emphasized expanding the government sector in developing countries. It was thought that large-scale government projects were the key to bringing about prosperity, including promoting government-owned industries. However, the Bank changed its policies in response to the successes of the U.S. economy and the failure of central planning in the communist countries in the 1980s, along with the successes of market economies in Hong Kong, Malaysia, and elsewhere in the world.

THE BEST-LAID PLANS OF MICE AND GOVERNMENT   *SNAPSHOT*

To see why World Bank policies now emphasize markets, consider the outcome of government planning in Nigeria in the 1970s. To bring the nation up to modern standards required roads, bridges, airports, and other infrastructure. This modernization called for massive quantities of cement, much more than the nation could produce domestically. Thus, Nigeria's government planners ordered the needed cement, which was shipped in the holds of freighters from cement-producing nations around the world.

Oops! One slight oversight threw these best-laid plans into disarray. The Nigerian docks were incapable of handling such quantities of cement. In fact, at one point it would have taken nearly thirty years to unload the cement that lay in the holds of ships anchored offshore. As time passed, the cement commenced to solidify within the ships, thereby providing a concrete example of the dangers inherent in centrally planned development. ◄

Explore & Apply

29.5 RUSSIA—A ROUGH TRANSITION TO THE PRICE SYSTEM

> *"If history could teach us anything, it would be that private property is inextricably linked with civilization."*
>
> —*Ludwig von Mises*

For much of the last century, Russia was part of the former Union of Soviet Socialist Republics (the Soviet Union), with an economy that rejected the price system of the free market. After the overthrow of communism in 1991, Russia embraced its new market economy, but only today is starting to realize its potential. Russia's had a rough transition, as demonstrated in Table 29-5, which shows the country's unemployment rate and output of goods and services (as a percentage of the previous year's output). During the early years of the transition to a market-oriented system, output fell and unemployment increased. Russia had good reason to endure this process.

Unlike capitalist countries, the former communist countries of Eastern Europe and the Soviet Union had no competitive market prices to ensure an efficient allocation of resources. Prices were set to achieve equity and political expediency, not efficiency. Soviet planners tried to match resources to outputs and outputs to needs, but faced a difficult problem. To allocate efficiently, planners must know how much value consumers place on alternative outputs. They also must compute the opportunity costs of inputs. In contrast, free markets reveal this information automatically; it is implicit in market prices.

To acquire the information they need, the Soviet planners estimated *shadow prices,* which are what the market prices would have been if there had been a free market. This undertaking is something like trying to answer the old riddle, "How much wood would a woodchuck chuck, if a woodchuck could chuck wood?" Although the planners resorted to complex mathematical models, the estimated shadow prices were only rough approximations to true market prices. When planners imposed incorrectly estimated prices, people and businesses were led to many wrong decisions about what and how to produce. The result was both surpluses and shortages.

In response, we saw such strange occurrences as children using loaves of bread as footballs, even though the bread did not last long in that usage, and even though the cost of the ingredients to make the loaves far exceeded their value as footballs. The problem was that bread was priced very cheaply for political reasons, and customers bought it in much larger quantities than they would have if bread prices reflected the costs of the ingredients, labor, and other items used in producing that bread. Still, for political reasons, government attempted to turn out as much of this necessity as consumers would choose to buy.

Politically set prices had one interesting positive effect. They forced Soviet authorities to exercise monetary restraint. Too many rubles would just add more purchasing power, which

TABLE 29-5 MACROECONOMIC INDICATORS FOR RUSSIA

YEAR	OUTPUT AS A PERCENTAGE OF THE PREVIOUS YEAR'S OUTPUT	UNEMPLOYMENT RATE
1994	87	7.8%
1995	96	9.0
1996	96.6	10.0
1997	100.9	11.2
1998	95.1	13.3
1999	104.6	12.4
2000	110.2	9.9
2001	105.7	8.7
2002	103.9	8.8
2003	107.3	8.5

Source: The Central Bank of the Russian Federation. Prior to 1999, the output measure used was GDP; in 1999 an index of output replaced GDP. The 1998 unemployment rate is an authors' estimate. All other unemployment rates are from the source indicated. Data for 2003 are current through June.

consumers would spend on underpriced goods. The Soviet Union did not have the where-withal to produce enough of these goods as it was. With the exception of bread and a few other items, shelves were often bare. The only way to prevent even greater shortages was to keep additional money from circulating in the economy. Thus, in the former Soviet Union, price inflation was kept low because government set the prices, and monetary growth was restrained in order to allow the policy of low prices to work. In contrast, when markets are free, the process is reversed. Monetary restraint must be exercised to keep inflation from taking hold in the marketplace.

It was small wonder that the Soviet economy spiraled downward over time. The arms buildup of the 1980s hastened that decline and prompted an overthrow of the central planners. First, there was Mikhail Gorbachev, would-be reformer of the communist system. Then came Boris Yeltsin, a free-market revolutionary who extricated Russia from the splinters of the Soviet Union. Many thought that, with markets freed from the central planners, living standards would quickly rise. The statistics said otherwise, and for good reason.

PROPERTY RIGHTS

Russia embraced capitalist ideas, but at first failed to impose a key ingredient necessary for the success of free markets: certainty over property rights. If individuals and businesses have no confidence that they will be able to keep the fruits of their labors and investments, the profit motive is lost. Few would seek profit in order to turn it over to the government. Unfortunately, in modern Russia, that has been a danger.

After the downfall of the Soviet Union, Russia had too many governments claiming jurisdiction over the same economic activity. For example, while it has been possible to buy land in Russia, it has also at times been nearly impossible to obtain a clear title to it. One government would grant the title, while another government would lie in wait to claim the land in the future. At least one U.S. entrepreneur saw this situation as a profit opportunity, and offered title insurance to remedy it.

Some Russian entrepreneurs have a different strategy. They specialize in having connections with both legitimate and illegitimate authorities. For example, Ben and Jerry's used these entrepreneurs to establish a network of Russian "scoop shops" to sell its ice cream. Even so, Ben and Jerry's ultimately abandoned its efforts to do business in Russia.

With all the governments came a host of taxes. To some extent, all taxes represent an expropriation of private property. Post-Soviet taxes sometimes carried this expropriation to an absurd extreme. Specifically, when taxes from the various jurisdictions were added together, they would often sum to over 100 percent. This means that, for every dollar of profit a business would make, it would owe more than a dollar to the government.

It seems unlikely that any business would voluntarily choose to operate under these conditions. Yet business did go on in Russia. The reason is at least threefold. First, many profits are hidden from the tax collector, either through bribery or techniques of accounting. Second, and related to the first, there has been and continues to be a thriving underground economy that is not reported to authorities. Third, business looked to the future, a future that is already unfolding in the form of greater clarification as to property ownership and taxation. The result of these early problems of transition is that Russia has since seen rapid economic growth.

Much of the underground economy in Russia is ruled by organized crime. Oftentimes, their leaders are former officials of the communist government, officials with connections to networks of "enforcers." In a way, these former officials are entrepreneurs whose skills are in demand. Those skills are the protection of property rights. For a price, the local crime boss will protect your property from other criminals. Through his connections, he can also offer some protection from excessive government regulation and taxation. It is thus not surprising to find that statistics from the Russian government show that the transition to free markets caused the Russian economy to shrink.

When economic activity is not reported, government cannot collect taxes on it directly. There is a way to collect taxes indirectly, however: inflation. Authorities in Russia's central bank printed money freely, allowing government to spend without collecting taxes. Instead, the tax was inflation that eroded purchasing power in the legitimate and underground economies alike.

Russia has undergone a dramatic upheaval, in which the old order of communism was thrown out to make way for the new order of capitalism. However, capitalistic free markets cannot function without the ownership of private property. There has been movement in this direction. For example, Russia now has in place a supply-side tax policy that attempts to secure property rights and avoid prohibitively high tax rates. The underground economy will diminish in importance because of those tax changes. But will the principles of private property that support free-market efficiency ever become firmly entrenched? We need only wait to see the answer, as the story unfolds before the Russian people and the world.

THINKING CRITICALLY

1. Consumers like low prices. Yet the transition from government-set prices to free-market prices leads to higher prices for many goods, such as bread and milk. How can it be in the consumer's interest to accept the transition from command-and-control pricing to free-market pricing? Do you think the typical consumer would recognize your reasoning?

2. Free markets rely on private property rights, but those rights are not absolute. In other words, it would not be in the social interest to allow private property to be put to any use whatsoever, without any restriction. What are some examples that in your opinion are legitimate government restrictions on the use of private property? Should government pay property owners to accept these restrictions?

 Visit www.prenhall.com/ayers for updates and web exercises on this Explore & Apply topic.

SUMMARY AND LEARNING OBJECTIVES

1. **Discuss the problems that are a priority for developing countries.**
   - The poverty and low life expectancy in many less-developed countries provide the motivation for economic development efforts. Extreme poverty is associated with low per capita incomes in less-developed countries (LDCs).
   - Additional problems include lack of infrastructure and high population growth. LDCs need investments in roads, schools, and other infrastructure. They sometimes have trouble feeding their people, a problem compounded by high population growth.

2. **Describe the goals on the United Nations' development agenda.**
   - The eight goals are: (1) Eradicate extreme poverty and hunger. (2) Achieve universal primary education. (3) Promote gender equality and empower women. (4) Reduce child mortality. (5) Improve maternal

health. (6) Combat HIV/AIDS, malaria, and other diseases. (7) Ensure environmental sustainability. (8) Develop a global partnership for development.
   - The UN's objective is to achieve the eight goals by 2015. Attached to each goal are specific targets.
   - Indicators are used to classify countries according to their level of economic development. A common set of fourteen world indicators are used by the UN to assess development. These indicators focus on infrastructure and health.

3. **Point out the incentives for population growth.**
   - Economics is sometimes referred to as "the dismal science" because of the predictions of Thomas Malthus. He forecast a future world in which population growth would outstrip the ability to produce food. To this point, the world has escaped the Malthusian vision because technology has increased productivity in food production.

- Population growth is a problem for many countries, especially the less-developed ones, as these countries must feed and provide jobs for their growing populations. A country's population growth varies according to a number of economic factors, including implicit government subsidies to larger families.

- Government policies can change the price signals facing parents. One way is through subsidizing the expenses associated with raising children. A number of aspects of having and raising children can be subsidized, but the outcome is the same—an increase in the number of births.

4. Explain the connection between economic development and property rights.

- Price signals guide investors in market economies. The price system has proven to be remarkably adept at responding to impending shortages of resources. As resources become more scarce, their prices rise. When resources become sufficiently costly because of scarcity, the price system has responded by offering new substitutes that can replace the older resources.

- A good example of price signals from history is the transition from scarce whale oil to alternative energy sources, where higher whale oil prices increased the demand for substitute energy sources. That increase in demand in turn led to the development of petroleum resources.

- Economic development is impeded by unclear property rights.

- Market economies depend on clear property rights. Many less-developed nations lack this feature, which is a key ingredient in the economic success of nations. Regulatory takings and government expropriation of private property tend to deter investment.

- The desire for territory has motivated many of the world's conflicts. Palestinians and Israelis have fought over the same land. Likewise, the Indians and Pakistanis have faced off over the Kashmir Province. Conflict impedes development.

5. Identify the roles of the International Monetary Fund and the World Bank in economic development.

- The World Bank and the International Monetary Fund (IMF) were created by the industrialized countries to assist the less-developed countries. The World Bank provides loans to finance qualified development projects in poor countries. The mission of the IMF is to maintain a stable financial order that facilitates trade and development.

- The IMF was founded in 1944 with the goal of promoting global prosperity through increased world trade and exchange rate stability. The IMF provides funds to its 184 member countries in the form of temporary loans to countries experiencing balance of payments problems. These funds are provided through fees assessed on member countries. The United States is the largest provider of funds to the IMF. Through surveillance, financial assistance, and technical assistance, the IMF helps countries achieve financial stability.

- The World Bank was founded at the same time as the IMF. Its mission is to make loans to developing countries that finance projects that promise to provide benefits sufficient to earn a 10-percent return. World Bank policies favor the expansion of the market sector in countries receiving loans.

6. Describe how insecure property rights have hindered economic development in Russia.

- Private property is an integral component of a market economy. Unclear ownership of property has hindered Russia's economic development during its transition from central planning to a market economy.

KEY TERMS

TEST YOURSELF

TRUE OR FALSE

1. The United States is an example of a country that lacks infrastructure.

2. The United Nations' development agenda does not address issues relating to the environment.

3. "The dismal science" is a term coined by Adam Smith.

4. When existing resources become more scarce, the price system responds through an increase in the demand for alternative resources.

5. The primary function of the World Bank is to provide grants to deserving poor countries.

MULTIPLE CHOICE

6. Life expectancy in the LDCs is generally
   a. about the same as in developed countries.
   b. higher than in developed countries because the people eat healthier foods.
   c. higher than in developed countries because the people eat less frequently.
   d. lower than in the developed countries.

7. The fourth stage in Rostow's stages model is
   a. traditional society.
   b. takeoff.
   c. drive to maturity.
   d. high mass consumption.

8. Which is not a specific goal of the United Nations' development agenda?
   a. Build mass transit systems.
   b. Universal primary education.
   c. Reduce child mortality.
   d. Combat disease.

9. The price system
   a. hinders economic development.
   b. has no effect on economic development.
   c. promotes economic development by offering people incentives to find and develop new resources.
   d. promotes economic development, but is clearly inferior to central planning in that role.

10. Which would NOT contribute to high population growth?
    a. Reliable retirement benefits to the elderly.
    b. Government subsidies to parents.
    c. Advances in medicine.
    d. Lower death rates.

11. Economics was called "the dismal science" because
    a. students often fell asleep in economics classes.
    b. of Malthus's prediction that immigration would be so great as to destroy a country's unique culture through foreign influences.
    c. of its low level of scientific rigor.
    d. of Malthus's prediction that population growth would outstrip resources, leading to a subsistence standard of living for most people.

12. The downward shift in marginal cost shown in Self-Test Figure 29-1 is most likely caused by
    a. government subsidies to education.
    b. increased opportunities for women in the work force.
    c. Social Security.
    d. higher family income.

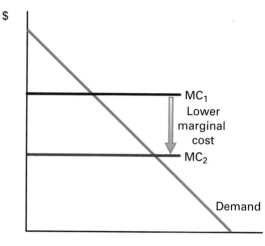

SELF-TEST FIGURE 29-1

13. In recent years annual foreign aid from all countries has totaled about
    a. $10 billion.
    b. $40 billion.
    c. $70 billion.
    d. $100 billion.

14. World Bank loans go only to countries
    a. that have never defaulted on their debts.
    b. that cannot get loans from any other source.
    c. that offer projects with at least a 10-percent expected return.
    d. that have achieved at least Rostow's stage-3 level of development.

15. The World Bank's loans are intended to promote
    a. central planning.
    b. economic development.
    c. policies that reduce world trade.
    d. population growth.

16. The primary role of the International Monetary Fund (IMF) is to
    a. promote central planning of economies.
    b. make sure that countries repay their loans to the World Bank.
    c. show farmers in LDCs how to produce enough food to avoid starvation.
    d. strengthen the world monetary and financial system.

17. Financing for the IMF comes from
    a. only the United States.
    b. only the United States and the countries of Western Europe.
    c. only the United States, Japan, and the countries of Western Europe.
    d. its members through the payment of membership fees that are proportional to the size and economic strength of each country.

18. The moral hazard associated with IMF actions is most closely associated with
    a. the way in which the IMF is financed.
    b. the stated mission of the IMF.
    c. the low life expectancy of citizens in less-developed countries.
    d. the idea that IMF bailouts would encourage countries to follow unsound policies.

19. Less-developed countries have sometimes accused the IMF of imperialism because
    a. the director of the IMF, who must by tradition be selected from the members of Britain's royal family, has often exhibited an imperial manner at public ceremonial events related to the IMF.
    b. the IMF encourages less-developed countries to become imperialists.
    c. of the conditions the IMF attaches to its help.
    d. the IMF offers money to countries but then offers no guidance on the best use of that money.

20. As Russia develops its market economy by reducing taxes and securing property rights, the underground economy in Russia will likely
    a. expand.
    b. diminish.
    c. remain the same.
    d. be legalized by the government.

QUESTIONS AND PROBLEMS

1. *[development indicators]* Why would per capita income be a good indicator of a country's level of development? What other indicators might be used to supplement per capita income in order to assess a country's level of development?

2. *[problems of LDCs]* List four common problems of developing nations. How do these problems affect everyday life in a developing country?

3. *[infrastructure]* Suppose you are a central planner in a less-developed country we shall call Poorlandia. Devise a policy statement that explains the significance of various items of infrastructure in helping Poorlandia grow and increase its standard of living.

4. *[development]* If you were to join the Peace Corps after graduating from college, and you were sent to a less-developed country, what single most important economic principle would you wish to share with the people of that country? Explain that principle in common-sense terms.

5. *[poverty and life expectancy]* Write a short essay that describes how poverty contributes to the short life expectancy of people in many less-developed countries.

6. *[Rostow model]* List Rostow's five stages of economic growth. Briefly describe each stage. Why is this model criticized by economists?

7. *[population]* Ecosystems have carrying capacities for the species within them. Do you think there is a comparable carrying capacity for humans within the world's ecosystem? If so, how far do you think we are from that capacity, and what would be the consequences of overshooting it?

8. *[population]* Explain why farmers in LDCs desire large numbers of children. Why might development slow down population growth?

9. *[population]* What roles do religious beliefs play in either promoting or hindering a solution to the world's population problems? Explain.

10. *[population]* What is your personal desire regarding how many children you would like to have? Explain how the costs and benefits of having children influences your choice.

11. *[price signals]* Explain how the price system responds to scarcity. Use the example in the text of the energy crisis involving whale oil. Is that example from history relevant to any modern energy crisis?

12. *[property rights]* How can clearly defined property rights assist in economic development? How does a country where property rights have been ambiguous go about establishing clearer property rights?

13. *[foreign aid]* Why do some people view foreign aid as a waste of tax dollars? What alternatives to government-provided aid exist? Explain.

14. *[World Bank]* In a series of bullet points, write a one-page policy statement for the World Bank that lists the criteria you would recommend be applied for approving development loans to poorer countries.

15. *[IMF]* In recent years there have been several large protests and demonstrations against the International Monetary Fund (IMF). Discuss the significance of the IMF in the context of economic development. In your discussion, comment on why you think the IMF has generated such hostility among the protestors.

WORKING WITH GRAPHS AND DATA

1. *[price signals]* Use Graph 29-1 to answer questions concerning the lack of market-determined competitive prices.

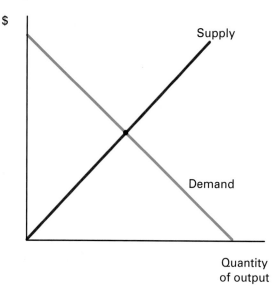

GRAPH 29-1

a. The market shown in Graph 29-1 is operating as a competitive market. Identify the equilibrium price as P_1 and quantity as Q_1.

b. Now assume that, for political reasons, the government takes control and ownership of the firms in this market and sets the legal price at P_1. Shortly after the government takes control of this market there is an increase in demand. Show the increase in demand on Graph 29-1 and label the new demand curve D_2.

c. Show the new quantity demanded as Q_2. What economic problem would occur? Label it on the graph.

d. Suppose that the government ordered the firms to produce the quantity demanded but did not allow them to change the price of the good. Also assume no change in marginal costs, so the supply curve, which reflects marginal costs, does not shift. Show the marginal cost of the last unit produced as MC_1 on the vertical axis. How does it compare to the price?

e. Why would producing enough to satisfy the quantity demanded at P_1 be inefficient in this case?

2. *[property rights and economic development]* Figure 29-2(a) shows the demand for investment and the supply of savings. Figure 29-2(b) shows long-run aggregate supply. Use these graphs to answer the following questions:

(a)

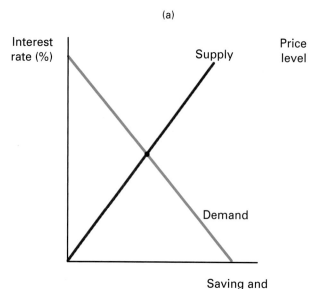

(b)

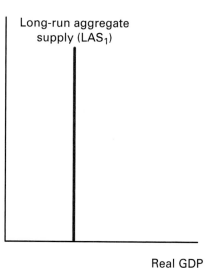

GRAPH 29-2

a. Assume that Figure 29-2(a) shows a country that has unclear property rights. Show the equilibrium quantity of saving and investment as Q_1.

b. Now let the government clearly define and enforce property rights. Show what would happen to the demand for the investment curve and label it D_2. Explain.

c. Show the new equilibrium quantity of saving and investment as Q_2.

d. What would the effect on the long-run supply curve of this economy be? Show the new LAS curve as LAS_2. Why does this happen? (*Hint:* Is there any effect on the amount of capital?)

3. *[population growth]* Use Graph 29-3 to answer the following questions that relate to population growth that shows the demand for children and the marginal cost of raising children.

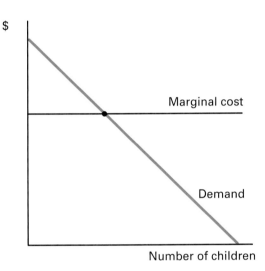

GRAPH 29-3

a. Identify the number of children parents would choose to have and label it Q_1.

b. Suppose that the government decides to subsidize the cost of raising children for equity reasons. Draw

another marginal cost curve that still requires parents to pay part of the cost of raising children. Identify the number of children parents would choose to have in this case and label it Q_2.

c. Show the size of the subsidy and label it "Subsidy."

d. Label the increase in population as "More children."

4. *[population growth]* Use Graph 29-4 to answer the following questions that relate to population growth that shows the demand for children and the marginal cost of raising children.

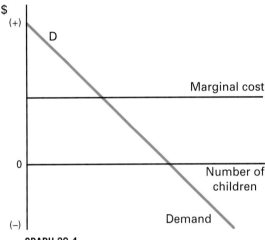

GRAPH 29-4

a. Identify the number of children parents would choose to have if the curves are as currently drawn and label it Q_1.

b. Identify the number of children parents would choose to have if the marginal cost is zero.

c. Suppose the government decides to pay a subsidy so that it covers more than the marginal cost of raising a child. Draw the new marginal cost curve.

d. Show the size of the subsidy and label it "Subsidy."

e. Identify the number of children parents would choose to have if they receive this subsidy.

f. Label the increase in population as "More children."

g. Identify and label the number of unwanted children as "Unwanted children."

Visit www.prenhall.com/ayers for Exploring the Web exercises and additional self-test quizzes.

A

ability-to-pay principle states that those who can afford to pay more taxes than others should be required to do so.

absolute advantage the ability to produce a good with fewer resources than other producers.

action lag time between when the problem is recognized and when policies are enacted.

actual return the value an investment actually had, judged after the fact; expressed as a percentage.

adaptive expectations when we form our expectations about future prices according to our past experiences.

aggregate demand relates how much real GDP consumers, businesses, government, and foreign buyers will purchase at each price level; graphically, aggregate demand slopes downward.

aggregate expenditure function shows the economy's planned spending for each possible level of real GDP.

aggregate expenditures consumption + investment + government + net exports.

aggregate supply the relationship between aggregate output, as measured by real GDP, and the price level.

allocative efficiency involves choosing the most valuable mix of outputs to produce.

antitrust law public policies designed to limit the abuse of market power by monopolies.

appreciation when a currency buys more of other currencies; makes imports cheaper and exports more expensive.

asymmetric information when one person has access to more information than another on a subject of mutual interest.

automatic stabilizers features embedded within existing fiscal policies that act as a stimulant when the economy is sluggish and act as a drag when it is in danger of inflation.

autonomous spending spending that would occur even if people had no incomes.

average cost per-unit cost; total cost divided by the quantity of output; also called average total cost.

average = cost pricing see **rate-of-return regulation**.

average product total quantity of output ÷ total quantity of labor.

average variable cost variable cost per unit; total variable cost divided by the quantity of output.

B

balance of payments accounts measure of a country's economic interactions with other countries.

balance of trade the monetary value of exported goods minus the monetary value of imported goods.

balanced budget occurs when government revenue equals government spending.

balanced-budget multiplier the effect on equilibrium GDP per dollar of additional government spending when that spending is paid for by additional taxation; this multiiplier equals one.

bank reserves vault cash plus deposits held by the Fed.

barriers to entry when investors or entrepreneurs find obstacles to joining a profitable industry.

barter the exchange of goods and services directly for one another, without the use of money.

benefit principle states that a fair tax is one that taxes people in proportion to the benefits they receive when government spends those tax revenues.

bilateral monopoly labor market with a monopsony buyer (employer) and monopoly seller (union) of labor services.

black market market in which goods are bought and sold illegally; associated with price controls.

block grant a sum of money transferred from the federal government to states that is designated for a particular type of spending, but where the exact programs are not specified.

bond a legally binding promise to repay borrowed funds with interest at a specified future date.

breakeven occurs when economic profit is zero.

budget deficit occurs when government collects less revenue than it spends.

budget surplus occurs when government collects more revenue than it spends.

bundled good in the context of voting, occurs when voters must take the whole package, including elements they don't want; candidates represent bundled goods.

business cycle the uneven sequence of trough, expansion, peak, and recession that the economy follows over time.

C

capital anything that is produced in order to increase productivity in the future; includes human capital and physical capital.

capital account records the monetary value of capital inflows from other countries (foreign investment in the United States), and outflows to other countries (U.S. investment abroad).

capital formation the creation of new capital.

capital gains the difference between the current market value of an investment and its purchase price.

capital gains tax a tax on the capital gains from investments that are sold.

cartel occurs when firms collude to eliminate competition among themselves and obtain greater profit.

ceteris paribus holding all else constant.

circular flow a model of the economy that depicts how the flow of money facilitates a counterflow of resources, goods, and services in the input and output markets.

classical a macroeconomic school of thought that emphasizes the long run and reliance upon market forces to achieve full employment.

Coase theorem theory that holds parties to an externality would voluntarily negotiate an efficient outcome without government involvement when property rights are clearly defined.

collective bargaining negotiations between an employer and a labor union.

command and control government decrees that direct economic activity.

common property resource a jointly owned resource, such as groundwater; people have little incentive to conserve common property resources, but rather seek to capture them for their own private use.

comparative advantage the ability to produce a good at a lower opportunity cost (other goods forgone) than others could do.

compensating wage differentials additional pay offered by employers to offset undesirable job characteristics.

complements goods or services that go well with each other, such as cream with coffee.

congestion when adding an additional consumer of a public good detracts from its value to other consumers.

conglomerate merger merger between firms in unrelated businesses.

constant-cost industry when an increase in the industry's output does not affect input prices.

constant returns to scale when increasing all inputs increases output by the same proportion; associated with constant long-run average cost.

consumed-income tax an income tax that does not tax income that is saved.

consumer price index (CPI) measures prices of a market basket of purchases made by consumers living in urban areas.

consumer surplus consumers' total benefit minus cost; graphically, demand minus market price.

consumption function shows planned consumption spending for each possible level of real GDP.

consumption spending purchasing by households; makes up the majority of GDP spending.

consumption tax a tax on spending rather than on income.

contestable markets oligopoly or monopoly market with quick entry and exit; limits market power of firms already in the market.

contractionary fiscal policy (fiscal drag) reduced government spending or increased taxation intended to decrease aggregate demand.

contractionary monetary policy monetary policy intended to slow down the economy; also called a tighter monetary policy.

corporation a type of firm that is a legal entity separate from the people who own, manage, and otherwise direct its affairs.

cost-benefit analysis the process of estimating the costs and benefits of alternative policy choices.

cost–push inflation occurs when an upward shift in short-run aggregate supply causes the economy to move up the aggregate demand curve to a higher price level and less output.

cross elasticity of demand measures how the demand for one good responds to changes in the price of another good; computed as the percentage change in the quantity demanded of one good divided by the percentage change in the price of another.

crowding-out effect when borrowing to finance government spending displaces private-sector spending.

current account account that records the monetary value of imports and exports of goods and services, adjusted for international incomes and transfers.

cyclical unemployment unemployment from a downturn in the business cycle that affects workers simultaneously in many different industries.

cycling when the order of political choices determines the outcome.

D

deadweight loss reduction in social surplus caused by inefficient price; shown graphically as a triangular area.

decreasing-cost industry when an increase in the industry's output causes input prices to fall.

demand relates the quantity of a good that consumers would purchase at each of various possible prices, over some period of time, *ceteris paribus.*

demand deposits checking account deposits at commercial banks.

demand for money quantities of money that people would like to hold at various nominal interest rates, *ceteris paribus;* the demand curve for money shows an inverse relationship between the quantity of money demanded and the interest rate, and thus slopes downward.

demand–pull inflation occurs when a rightward shift in aggregate demand moves the economy up short-run aggregate supply; associated with greater employment and output.

demand-side deflation occurs when aggregate demand shifts to the left. The result is a movement down the long-run aggregate supply curve to a lower price level, but no change in full-employment output.

demand-side inflation occurs when aggregate demand shifts to the right. The result is a movement up the long-run aggregate supply curve to a higher price level, but no change in full-employment output.

deposit multiplier upper bound on the value of the money multiplier; computed as 1 divided by the reserve requirement.

depreciation when a currency buys less of other currencies; makes imports more expensive and exports cheaper.

deregulation the scaling back of government regulation of industry.

derived demand the demand for labor; exists only because there is a demand for the firm's outputs.

developed countries countries such as the United States, Japan, Germany, and the United Kingdom that rely on the free-market system.

development when technology is embodied into capital.

differentiated products products that vary from one producer to another within the same industry.

discount rate interest rate set by the Fed on loans it makes to banks.

discouraged workers people who would like to have a job, but have given up looking; not counted as unemployed because they are not included in the labor force.

discretionary policy public policy adjusted through explicit changes made by lawmakers.

diseconomies of scale when increasing all inputs leads to a less-than-proportional increase in output; associated with increasing long-run average cost; also called decreasing returns to scale.

disutility a negative value for marginal utility; associated with consuming too much of a good.

dominant firm with a competitive fringe when one large firm sets the price to maximize its profit, and the many smaller competitors that are also in the same market sell at that price

dumping selling a good to another country for less than its cost of production.

E

economic development a field of economics that studies the poverty of nations.

economic growth the ability of the economy to produce more or better output; computed as the change in real GDP over time.

economic rent earnings in excess of opportunity cost when an input is unique.

economics studies the allocation of limited resources in response to unlimited wants.

economies of scale when increasing all inputs causes a more-than-proportional increase in output; associated with declining long-run average cost; also called increasing returns to scale.

efficiency means that resources are used in ways that provide the most value; implies that no one can be made better off without someone else becoming worse off.

elastic demand demand has an elasticity that is greater than 1.

elastic supply supply has an elasticity that is greater than 1.

elasticity measures the responsiveness of one thing ("Y") to another ("X"), specifically, the percentage change in Y divided by the percentage change in X.

elasticity of demand measures the responsiveness of quantity demanded to changes in price; computed as the percentage change in quantity demanded divided by the percentage change in price; expressed as an absolute value.

elasticity of supply measures the responsiveness of quantity supplied to price; computed as the percentage change in quantity supplied divided by the percentage change in price.

entrepreneurship personal initiative to combine resources in productive ways; involves risk.

entry when a firm first opens for business; occurs in the long run.

equation of exchange $M \times V = P \times Q$; M represents the quantity of money, V is velocity, P is the price leve, and Q is aggregate output.

equity fairness.

excess profit economic profit; the accounting profit in excess of normal profit.

excess reserves the amount of bank reserves that exceed the amount needed to meet the reserve requirement.

exchange rate price of one currency in terms of another.

exit when a firm goes out of business or changes its line of business; occurs in the long run.

expansionary fiscal policy (fiscal stimulus) increased government spending or reduced taxation intended to stimulate aggregate demand.

expansionary monetary policy monetary policy designed to stimulate the economy; also called a looser monetary policy.

expected return the value of an investment if successful, multiplied by the probability of success; expressed as a percentage.

expenditure approach method of computing GDP that sums consumption, gross investment, government purchases, and net exports.

expenditure equilibrium the level of GDP that the economy tends toward in the short run, at a given price level.

expenditure multiplier the multiple by which equilibrium real GDP grows as a result of an increase (an injection) of new autonomous spending.

explicit costs costs accountants aim to measure.

exports goods and services a country sells to other countries.

external benefit when an externality takes the form of benefits, such as from a neighbor maintaining an attractive yard.

external cost when an externality takes the form of costs, such as from pollution.

externality side effect of production or consumption that affects third parties who have no say in the matter.

F

federal funds rate interest rate on loans that banks make to other banks.

Federal Reserve System U.S. central bank; conducts monetary policy, holds bank deposits, and performs several other functions.

fiat money money not backed by a commodity; money by decree of law.

firm a business that employs inputs to produce output.

fiscal federalism the study of the design of a federal system of government from an economic standpoint.

fiscal illusion when voters focus on visible benefits from projects and ignore the less-obvious costs.

fiscal policy government tax and spending policy designed to shift aggregate demand rightward.

fixed cost a cost that does not vary with changes in output.

fixed exchange rate any exchange rate that the government commits itself to maintaining.

floating exchange rates exchange rates that adjust according to the forces of supply and demand; called managed float or dirty float if the government attempts to influence these forces.

foreign exchange markets markets in which currencies are bought and sold.

four-firm concentration ratio fraction of total market sales by the four largest firms.

franchise monopoly a right to be the exclusive provider of a service.

free markets the collective decisions of individual buyers and sellers that, taken together, determine what outputs are produced, how those outputs are produced, and who receives the outputs; free markets depend on private property and free choice.

free trade international commerce unhindered by policy obstacles.

free-rider problem the incentive to avoid paying for a public good, because no one person's payment will have any appreciable effect on the quantity of the public good.

frictional unemployment unemployment associated with entering the labor market or switching jobs.

full employment 100 percent minus the natural rate of unemployment.

full-employment budget estimate of government revenue and spending were the economy to be at full employment.

full-employment equilibrium the long-run macroeconomic equilibrium that occurs at a full-employment output.

full-employment output (full-employment GDP) the real GDP the economy produces when it fully employs its resources.

fully funded the idea of having enough revenue in the Social Security trust fund to be able to pay off all obligations to current workers without recourse to taxing future workers.

G

game theory analysis of economic strategies in order to predict how firms will behave; uses a decision tree or a payoff matrix to illustrate the outcomes associated with the choices available.

GDP chained price index a price index used to compute real GDP by linking together successive years of data.

GDP implicit price deflator index of prices across the spectrum of GDP; ratio of nominal GDP to real GDP.

General Agreement on Tariffs and Trade (GATT) an agreement signed by most of the major trading countries of the world, which limits the use of protectionist policies; enforced by the World Trade Organization.

general human capital skills such as language and math that are easily transferred from job to job.

government failure the inefficiency of government processes.

Gresham's law bad money drives good money out of circulation.

gross domestic product (GDP) the market value of the final goods and services produced in the economy within some time period, usually one quarter.

gross investment the total amount of investment.

H

Herfindahl-Hirschman index (HHI) an index of market concentration used by the U.S. Justice Department in the merger approval process; computed by squaring and summing the market shares of all firms in a market; ranges in value from 0 (pure competition) to 10,000 (pure monopoly).

homogeneous products products that are identical, no matter which firms in the industry produce the commodities.

horizontal merger merger of competing firms.

housing vouchers government grants that recipients can spend only on housing.

human capital acquired skills and abilities embodied within a person.

I

immiserizing growth growth that leaves a country worse off; associated with the Prebisch-Singer thesis.

imperfect information occurs when we do not fully understand the choices available to us, or the consequences of those choices.

implementation lag time between when policies are enacted and when they take effect.

implicit opportunity costs (implicit costs) the value that the firm's capital and the entrepreneur's time would have in their best alternative uses.

imports goods and services a country buys from other countries.

income approach method of computing GDP that sums various forms of income.

income effect the change in the quantity demanded caused by a price change's effect on real income, which measures a consumer's purchasing power; when the wage rate rises, individuals offer to work fewer hours because their higher incomes increase their demands for normal goods, including leisure.

income elasticity of demand measures how demand responds to income; computed as the percentage change in quantity demanded divided by the percentage change in income.

income–expenditure model shows planned and actual expenditures at each possible real GDP.

increasing-cost industry when an increase in the industry's output causes input prices to rise.

indexing automatically adjusting the terms of an agreement for inflation.

individual retirement accounts (IRAs) tax-free savings accounts earmarked for retirement income.

induced spending spending that depends upon income.

inelastic demand demand has an elasticity that is less than 1.

inelastic supply supply has an elasticity that is less than 1.

infant industries startup industries that might be unable to survive the rigors of competition in their formative years.

inferior goods demand for these goods varies inversely with income.

inflation persistent, widespread increases in the price level.

inflationary expectations predictions about future inflation that people factor into their current behavior.

inflationary gap excess in the aggregate expenditure function above that necessary to achieve a full-employment equilibrium; this gap will be corrected by inflation; when combined with the multiplier effect, the amount by which spending would need to be cut to reduce GDP to full-employment GDP at a constant price level.

inflationary spiral alternately rising and falling output along with a continually rising price level.

inflation rate the annual percentage increase in the price level.

in-kind benefits a government-provided good or service, as opposed to cash.

input market the market where resources are bought and sold.

interest payment made by a borrower to compensate a lender for the use of money.

interest rate price of borrowed money, expressed as a percentage.

interest-rate effect A higher price level increases interest rates, causing households and firms to decrease the quantity of real GDP demanded.

International Monetary Fund (IMF) institution created in 1944 to promote a sound world financial system.

international substitution effect a change in the price level changes the quantity demanded of real GDP through its effects on imports and exports

investment spending now in order to increase output or productivity later; includes spending on capital, new housing, and changes in business inventories.

invisible hand the idea that self-interest and competition promote economic efficiency without any need for action by government.

K

Keynesian a macroeconomic school of thought that emphasizes the short run and the importance of fiscal policy.

kinked demand curve demand curve that is steeper below the current price than above it; predicts that firms will not change price.

L

labor the human capacity to work.

labor force individuals age 16 and over, excluding those in the military, who are either employed or actively looking for work.

labor force participation rate the ratio of the labor force to the population age 16 and over; expressed as a percentage.

labor productivity output per hour worked.

land natural resources in their natural states.

law of demand as price falls, the quantity demanded increases.

law of diminishing marginal utility as consumption of a good increases, marginal utility will eventually decrease.

law of diminishing returns states that when additional units of labor or any other variable input are added in the short run, the marginal product of the variable input must eventually decrease.

law of increasing cost the rise in the marginal opportunity cost of producing a good as more of that good is produced.

law of supply as price rises, the quantity supplied increases.

leading indicators statistics that are expected to change direction before the economy at large does, thereby indicating where the economy is headed.

less-developed countries (LDCs) nations that lag behind the wealthier countries; also known as developing countries.

limit pricing charging the highest price customers will pay, subject to the limit that the price not be so high that potential competitors enter the industry.

line-item veto power that allows a governor to veto parts of appropriations bills, rather than having to accept or reject the bills in their entireties.

liquidity how easily and quickly an item can be turned into a spendable form.

lobbyists agents who promote a special-interest agenda within the political system.

local public good a public good that affects a particular region, such as a city.

logrolling when politicians trade votes in order to obtain projects of direct benefit to constituents in their districts.

long run in macroeconomics, involves underlying economic forces that make themselves felt over time; in microeconomics, the period of time sufficiently long that all inputs are variable.

long-run aggregate supply the idea that, in the long run, the price level does not affect the amount of GDP the economy produces; graphically, long-run aggregate supply is vertical at full-employment GDP.

long-run average cost per-unit cost when all inputs are variable.

long-run supply tells how much will be produced at each of various possible short-run market-equilibrium prices.

loss occurs when economic profit is negative.

M

M1 most liquid measure of money; currency plus demand deposits, traveler's checks, and other checkable deposits.

M2 obtained by adding savings deposits, small time deposits, and money market fund balances to M1.

M3 expands M2 by adding large time deposits and several other near monies.

macroeconomic equilibrium where aggregate demand equals aggregate supply.

macroeconomics analyzes economic aggregates, such as aggregate employment, output, growth, and inflation.

marginal benefit the incremental value of an additional unit of a good.

marginal cost the change in total cost that occurs when there is a one-unit change in output.

marginal cost of labor additional cost of employing an additional unit of labor.

marginal external costs or benefits externalities that cause market outcomes to be inefficient.

marginal product additional output produced by the addition of one more unit of labor; change in output ÷ change in labor.

marginal propensity to consume (mpc) the fraction of additional income that people spend.

marginal propensity to save (mps) the fraction of additional income that people save.

marginal revenue the change in total revenue that occurs when there is a one-unit change in output.

marginal revenue product of labor change in the firm's total revenue resulting from the employment of an additional unit of labor.

marginal tax rate the percentage of incremental income that is taken by the federal income tax.

marginal utility the increments to total utility from changes in consumption.

marginal utility per dollar marginal utility divided by price.

market equilibrium a situation in which there is no tendency for either price or quantity to change.

market failure when markets fail to achieve efficiency, as in the case of public goods, externalities, and common property resources.

market power when individual firms have at least a bit of control over the prices of their outputs; arises from barriers to entry.

market prices serve as signals that guide the allocation of resources.

market structures models of the way markets work.

marketable permits property rights to a specified amount of an activity, such as groundwater pumping or air pollution, where those property rights can be bought and sold; can efficiently achieve quantity targets set by the government.

markets make possible the voluntary exchange of resources, goods, and services; can take physical, electronic, and other forms.

median voter model predicts that, in two-candidate races, the winner will be chosen by the median voter—50 percent of the other voters prefer further to the right and 50 percent prefer further to the left.

medium of exchange the purchasing function of money.

merger when two firms combine into a single firm.

microeconomics analyzes the individual components of the economy, such as the choices made by people, firms, and industries.

minimum wage lowest wage legally allowed to be paid to workers.

mixed economies the mixture of free-market and command-and-control methods of resource allocation that characterize modern economies.

models simplified versions of reality that emphasize features central to answering the questions we ask of them.

monetarism school of thought that emphasizes the importance of the quantity of money in the economy and a rule for monetary policy; associated with economist Milton Friedman.

monetary base sum of currency in circulation plus bank reserves.

money a medium of exchange that removes the need for barter; also a measure of value and a way to store value over time.

money market the market where the determination of the interest rate is by the demand and supply of money.

money multiplier the amount by which a new deposit is multiplied to arrive at the actual increase in the money supply; maximum value is given by the deposit multiplier.

monopolistic competition a market structure with many firms selling differentiated products and relatively easy entry of new firms; associated only with slight market power.

monopoly in the output market, when a single firm sells an output for which there are no close substitutions; in the labor market, when a union is the only seller of labor services.

monopoly by law (legal monopoly) when legal barriers restrict the supply of a good to one firm, and when there are no close substitutes for that good.

monopoly by possession when a single firm owns a resource needed in the production of a good for which there are no close substitutes.

monopsony one buyer of labor services in a labor market.

moral suasion exhortations to do the right thing, as defined by public policymakers.

multi-part pricing a form of price discrimination in which the price depends on the quantity consumed.

multiplier effect occurs when an initial change in spending leads to additional rounds of spending changes; causes aggregate demand to shift further in the same direction as its initial shift; sequence of spending that takes the economy from one equilibrium to another.

mutually interdependent when actions by one firm influence actions taken by other firms in the market.

N

national debt how much money the government owes.

natural monopoly when one firm can supply the entire market at a lower per-unit cost than could two or more separate firms.

natural rate of unemployment the minimum sustainable level of unemployment; associated with zero cyclical unemployment.

net domestic product (NDP) gross domestic product minus depreciation.

net exports exports minus imports.

net investment gross investment minus depreciation.

new growth theory emphasizes the importance of new ideas in generating economic growth, and of intellectual property rights in providing the profit incentive to generate those ideas.

nominal GDP GDP that is stated without adjusting for inflation.

nominal value a value that is not adjusted for inflation.

nontariff barriers any of a variety of actions other than tariffs that make importing more expensive or difficult.

normal goods demand for these goods varies directly with income.

normal profit the portion of accounting profit that equals implicit opportunity costs.

normative having to do with behavioral norms, which are judgments as to what is good or bad.

North American Free Trade Agreement (NAFTA) trading bloc that includes the United States, Canada, and Mexico.

O

occupational segregation the concentration of women workers in a limited number of occupations.

oligopoly a market with more than one seller, where at least one seller can significantly influence price.

open economy an economy with no restrictions on economic interactions with other countries.

open market operations buying and selling of Treasury bonds and Treasury bills by the Fed; tool of monetary policy.

opportunity cost the value of the best alternative opportunity forgone.

output gap the amount by which full-employment GDP exceeds actual GDP.

output market the market where goods and services are bought and sold.

P

pay-as-you-go referring to Social Security, meaning that current workers pay for current retirees.

pegged exchange rate (fixed exchange rate) any exchange rate that the government commits itself to maintaining.

perfect competition special case of pure competition in which all firms are identical, with identical access to resources and information.

perfectly elastic elasticity of infinity; demand would be drawn as a horizontal line.

perfectly inelastic elasticity of zero; demand would be drawn as a vertical line.

perfect price discrimination price discrimination that perfectly matches the demand curve.

Personal Security Accounts retirement accounts individuals own, but that they are forced to contribute to by the government.

Phillips curve a graphical representation of data from the 1960s in the United States that shows a short-run tradeoff between low unemployment and low inflation.

positive having to do with what is, was, or will be.

poverty line a government-set income threshold that varies by household size and composition, set to approximately equal three times the cost of a nutritionally adequate diet.

Prebisch-Singer thesis a thesis that states that developing countries will remain in poverty because the prices of their exports of commodities are doomed to decrease.

precautionary motive holding money to cover unforeseen needs or wants.

price ceiling a maximum price that can legally be charged for a good.

price discrimination charging different prices for different units of output, where the differences do not depend on differences in production costs.

price floor (price support) minimum price guaranteed to producers by the government.

price gouging price increases in response to increased demand related to emergencies.

price leadership when one firm changes its price and others in the industry follow suit.

price level prices of goods and services in the aggregate.

price maker a firm that faces a downward-sloping demand curve.

price rule conducting monetary policy in order to keep price increases in basic commodities within a low range.

price signals the allocation of resources through the price system; prices guide consumption and investment.

price taker a firm that must sell its output at the market price.

principal–agent problem the difficulty of making agents, such as employees or public servants, act in the interests of principals, such as owners or voters.

prisoner's dilemma an oligopoly game that shows the difficulty of enforcing collusion.

private costs or benefits costs or benefits that are borne by the decision maker, such as a buyer or seller.

private goods goods consumed by one person only—excludable and rival; most goods and services are private.

privatization the sale of government industries, or government paying private firms to provide public services.

producer price index (PPI) measures wholesale prices, which are prices paid by firms.

producer surplus producers' revenue minus production cost; graphically, market price minus supply.

production function the relationship between the amounts of inputs and the quantities of output a firm produces.

production possibilities frontier a model that shows the various combinations of two goods the economy is capable of producing.

profit (economic profit) total revenue minus total cost; unlike accounting profit, economic profit defines cost to include implicit opportunity costs.

progressive tax a tax that collects a higher percentage of high incomes than of low incomes.

property rights rights of ownership.

proportional tax a tax that collects the same percentage of high incomes as of low incomes.

public choice the study of economic incentives within government, including those that face voters, politicians, and the administrators of government programs.

public goods goods that are nonexcludable and nonrival, meaning that a person's consumption of the good does not reduce its quantity for others.

purchasing power effect the effect of the price level on consumers' ability to buy goods and services.

purchasing power parity theory that prices would be the same around the world for easily tradeable items.

pure competition a market in which there are numerous firms, all of which are price takers. The product is homogeneous and there are no barriers to entry.

purely competitive labor market labor market with many employers hiring homogeneous labor; employers are wage takers; the equilibrium wage rate is given by the intersection of market supply and demand.

Q

quantity demanded the quantity that consumers would purchase at a given price.

quantity supplied the quantity that will be offered for sale at a given price.

quantity theory of money a theory based upon the equation of exchange; shows that the effect of a change in the money supply is a proportional change in the price level; assumes velocity and aggregate output remain constant.

quota quantity limit on imports.

R

rate-of-return regulation (average-cost pricing) restricts the monopoly from earning more than a normal profit; shown by the intersection of the average-cost curve and demand.

rational expectations when people correctly predict the implications of government policy action and thus cannot be systematically tricked.

rational ignorance when voters make the rational choice to remain uninformed on many public issues.

real business cycle when GDP rises or falls in response to major events that cannot be foreseen.

real GDP the value of GDP after nominal GDP is adjusted for inflation.

real value a value that results from adjusting a nominal value for inflation.

recession a sustained decrease in real GDP.

recessionary gap shortfall in the aggregate expenditure function below that necessary to achieve a full-employment equilibrium; this gap might persist in the short run unless the government takes action; when combined with the multiplier effect, the amount of new spending needed to close the output gap without change to the price level.

recognition lag time before policymakers recognize that a problem exists.

regressive tax a tax that collects a higher percentage of low incomes than of high incomes.

regulation occurs whenever the government acts to influence the specifications of goods and services or the manner in which they are produced.

rent controls a price ceiling applied to the price of rental housing.

rent seeking occurs when lobbyists or others expend resources in an effort to come out a winner in the political process.

required reserves bank reserves held to meet the Fed's reserve requirement; expressed as a percentage of deposits.

research aimed at creating new products or otherwise expanding the frontiers of knowledge and technology.

reservation wage the lowest wage offer an individual will accept.

Rostow's stages of economic development a model that says that countries begin as traditional societies, pass through the preconditions for takeoff, the takeoff, the drive to maturity, and conclude their development with the stage of high mass consumption.

rule of profit maximization produce to the point where marginal revenue equals marginal cost.

rule of utility maximization to maximize utility, a consumer adjusts spending until the marginal utility from the last dollar spent on each good is the same.

S

satiation point quantity for which an additional unit consumed provides zero marginal utility; associated with maximum total utility.

saving putting aside income for later use.

Say's Law supply creates its own demand; the aggregate value of what is produced will provide the income with which to buy it.

scarcity a situation in which there are too few resources to meet all human wants.

search costs the costs of finding something; rent controls increase search costs for rental housing.

seasonal unemployment unemployment that can be predicted to recur periodically, according to the time of year.

shortage the excess of quantity demanded over quantity supplied, which occurs when price is below equilibrium.

short run in macroeconomics, a period of time during which the economy transitions to the long run; in microeconomics, a period of time in which at least one input is fixed.

short-run aggregate supply tells how much output the economy will offer in the short run at each possible price level.

short-run macroeconomic equilibrium where the economy tends in the short run, given by the intersection of aggregate demand and short-run aggregate supply.

shut down when a firm produces no output in order to minimize its loss, which equals total fixed cost; occurs in the short run

signaling the view that education provides information to employers about the characteristics of job applicants.

Smoot-Hawley Act legislation passed by the U.S. Congress in 1930, the Act raised tariffs so high that imports nearly ceased.

social costs or benefits the sum of all costs or all benefits to all members of society; includes both private and external costs and benefits.

Social Security trust fund the buildup of Social Security tax revenues above what is paid out in benefits; kept in the form of government bonds.

social surplus the sum of consumer surplus and producer surplus.

specific human capital human capital that is specific to a particular firm or kind of job.

specificity principle the idea that policies should be targeted as narrowly and directly at a problem as possible.

speculative motive money held because current investment opportunities are unattractive.

sticky prices prices that are slow to adjust, usually in a downward direction.

sticky wages wages that are slow to adjust, usually in a downward direction.

stock shares of ownership in a corporation.

store of value the function of money related to holding wealth.

strategic dumping dumping with the intention of driving the competition out of business.

structural deficit occurs when the economy has a budget deficit, even when at full employment.

structural rigidities impediments within the economy that slow adjustment to a long-run equilibrium.

structural unemployment unemployment caused by a mismatch between a person's human capital and that needed in the workplace.

subsidies payments to promote actions with external benefits or that reduce external costs.

substitutes something that takes the place of something else, such as one brand of cola for another.

substitution effect a lower price of a good causes a person to buy more of that good instead of alternative goods; in the labor market, when the wage rate increases, individuals recognize that the opportunity cost of leisure has risen, choose to substitute labor for leisure, and thus offer to work more hours.

sunk cost an irrecoverable cost; irrelevant to decision making.

supply relates the quantity of a good that will be offered for sale at each of various possible prices, over some period of time, ceteris paribus.

supply shock an unexpected event that is major enough to affect the overall economy; shifts aggregate supply.

supply-side deflation occurs when long-run aggregate supply shifts to the right. The result is a movement down the aggregate demand curve to a lower price level.

supply-side economists (supply siders) economists who emphasize incentives for productivity and economic growth, such as lower marginal tax rates and less regulation.

supply-side inflation occurs when long-run aggregate supply shifts to the left. The result is a movement up the aggregate demand curve to a higher price level and lower full-employment output.

surplus the excess of quantity supplied over quantity demanded, which occurs when price is above equilibrium.

T

tariff tax on imports.

tax base that which is taxed.

tax burden how much the tax costs after taking into account price changes.

tax incidence identifies those who eventually wind up paying a tax.

tax multiplier $-mpc/(1 - mpc)$; when multiplied by a change in taxation, gives the change in equilibrium GDP.

tax shifting when the effects of a tax are transferred from one party to another.

technological efficiency the greatest quantity of output for given inputs; likewise, for any given output, requires the least-cost production technique.

technology possible techniques of production.

technology mandates government rules that instruct producers as to the exact technology to use in a product or its production.

"the dismal science" a name given to economics because of Thomas Robert Malthus's nineteenth-century predictions of mass starvation.

the margin the cutoff point; decision making at the margin refers to deciding on one more or one less of something.

the production effect when a higher price level causes firms to increase output, employing workers who are willing to work extra hours to the extent that they do not correctly anticipate inflation.

total cost the sum of the firm's expenses.

total product the firm's total quantity of output.

total revenue price $\times$ quantity.

total utility the satisfaction a person receives from consuming a specific quantity of a good.

trade creation effect trade that would otherwise not take place; adds to efficiency; caused by lower trade barriers among members of a trading bloc.

trade deficit a negative balance on the merchandise trade account, given when the dollar value of imported goods exceeds the dollar value of exported goods.

trade diversion effect trade among members of a trading bloc that would more efficiently be conducted with other countries outside of the bloc.

trading bloc agreement among a group of countries that provides for lower trade barriers among its members than with the rest of the world.

transaction costs the expense of coordinating market exchanges.

transactions motive holding money to make purchases.

transfer payments the redistribution of income or social surplus from one group to another.

transitional economies countries such as Russia, Hungary, and Poland that are moving away from central planning to the free-market system.

U

underground economy market transactions that go unreported to government.

unemployment equilibrium a short-run equilibrium GDP that is less than full-employment GDP.

unemployment rate the ratio of the number of unemployed persons to the number of persons in the labor force.

unit elastic demand demand has an elasticity that equals 1.

unit elastic supply supply has an elasticity that equals 1.

unit elastic throughout elasticity of 1; demand would be a rectangular hyperbola that never touches either axis.

unit of account a use of money that occurs when the value of one item is compared with the value of another in terms of monetary units.

user fees charges for use of a publicly owned good, service, or resource.

util unit of measurement of utility; used for illustration only.

utility satisfaction received from consumption of a good.

V

value added the difference between revenue and the cost of purchased inputs.

value added tax (VAT) a form of consumption tax that collects the difference between what companies earn in revenues and their previously taxed costs.

variable cost a cost that varies in the same direction as output.

velocity of money the number of times a dollar changes hands in a year.

vertical merger merger between a firm and its supplier, or between the firm and a buyer of its output.

voluntary export restraints an alternative to import quotas in which exporting countries agree to voluntarily limit their exports to the target country; leads to higher price received by exporting countries.

W

Washington Monument strategy when a government agency offers a bare-bones budget that cuts its most popular functions; intended to increase the chances that a more generous budget will be approved.

wealth effect the change in the fraction of current income spent caused by a price-level change affecting the real value of savings.

World Bank institution that was created to loan money to developing countries.

World Trade Organization (WTO) international organization formed to administer the General Agreement on Tariffs and Trade.

ANSWERS TO TEST YOURSELF

CHAPTER 1

1. False
2. False
3. True
4. False
5. True
6. b
7. c
8. a
9. a
10. b
11. d
12. c
13. a
14. b
15. c
16. c
17. b
18. d
19. b
20. d

CHAPTER 2

1. True
2. False
3. True
4. False
5. False
6. b
7. c
8. a
9. d
10. c
11. c
12. a
13. a
14. a
15. a
16. c
17. a
18. c
19. b
20. a

CHAPTER 3

1. False
2. False
3. True

4. False
5. True
6. d
7. d
8. a
9. a
10. d
11. c
12. b
13. c
14. c
15. c
16. b
17. c
18. c
19. c
20. c

CHAPTER 4

1. False
2. False
3. True
4. False
5. False
6. c
7. c
8. a
9. c
10. c
11. b
12. c
13. c
14. c
15. d
16. c
17. b
18. b
19. a
20. b
21. d

CHAPTER 5

1. True
2. False
3. False
4. False
5. False
6. c

7. b
8. a
9. a
10. b
11. d
12. b
13. a
14. c
15. c
16. d
17. d
18. d
19. c
20. d

CHAPTER 6

1. False
2. True
3. False
4. False
5. True
6. a
7. a
8. b
9. b
10. c
11. a
12. c
13. d
14. c
15. c
16. c
17. b
18. b
19. b
20. b

CHAPTER 7

1. False
2. False
3. False
4. False
5. True
6. d
7. b
8. b
9. d
10. d

11. c
12. d
13. c
14. c
15. b
16. b
17. c
18. b
19. a
20. c

CHAPTER 8

1. False
2. True
3. False
4. True
5. False
6. d
7. b
8. a
9. a
10. c
11. d
12. b
13. b
14. b
15. c
16. b
17. c
18. d
19. b
20. c

CHAPTER 9

1. True
2. False
3. True
4. True
5. True
6. d
7. b
8. a
9. d
10. a
11. a
12. b
13. c
14. c

15. b
16. b
17. c
18. a
19. d
20. b

CHAPTER 10

1. False
2. True
3. True
4. False
5. False
6. b
7. a
8. a
9. d
10. b
11. d
12. d
13. b
14. c
15. a
16. d
17. b
18. b
19. b
20. c

CHAPTER 11

1. True
2. False
3. False
4. False
5. False
6. c
7. c
8. d
9. d
10. c
11. d
12. a
13. a
14. d
15. d
16. c
17. c
18. a
19. d
20. b

CHAPTER 12

1. False
2. True
3. False
4. True
5. False
6. a
7. b
8. d
9. d
10. d
11. a
12. d
13. b
14. d
15. c
16. a
17. d
18. d
19. b
20. a

CHAPTER 13

1. False
2. False
3. False
4. True
5. True
6. d
7. b
8. a
9. d
10. d
11. d
12. b
13. c
14. a
15. b
16. c
17. d
18. a
19. c
20. a

CHAPTER 14

1. False
2. False
3. False
4. False
5. False
6. c
7. c
8. d

9. d
10. c
11. c
12. b
13. b
14. b
15. c
16. c
17. c
18. b
19. b
20. d

CHAPTER 15

1. False
2. True
3. True
4. False
5. False
6. c
7. d
8. a
9. b
10. a
11. d
12. d
13. c
14. a
15. a
16. b
17. d
18. a
19. b
20. d

CHAPTER 16

1. False
2. False
3. True
4. True
5. False
6. a
7. c
8. c
9. d
10. a
11. b
12. c
13. c
14. d
15. a
16. c
17. c
18. c

19. c
20. c

CHAPTER 17

1. False
2. False
3. False
4. True
5. False
6. d
7. c
8. d
9. b
10. c
11. d
12. a
13. c
14. c
15. c
16. b
17. b
18. c
19. c
20. c

CHAPTER 18

1. False
2. True
3. True
4. False
5. True
6. b
7. b
8. b
9. b
10. b
11. a
12. c
13. b
14. c
15. a
16. b
17. b
18. d
19. a
20. d

CHAPTER 19

1. False
2. True
3. True
4. True
5. False

6. a
7. d
8. d
9. a
10. d
11. d
12. a
13. c
14. a
15. a
16. a
17. d
18. a
19. b
20. d

CHAPTER 20

1. False
2. True
3. True
4. False
5. False
6. b
7. c
8. c
9. c
10. a
11. d
12. c
13. b
14. b
15. a
16. d
17. d
18. c
19. b
20. b

CHAPTER 21

1. False
2. True
3. False
4. False
5. False
6. a
7. b
8. d
9. c
10. d
11. b
12. a
13. c
14. b
15. a

16. c
17. b
18. c
19. b
20. a

CHAPTER 22

1. True
2. True
3. False
4. False
5. True
6. a
7. b
8. b
9. b
10. c
11. a
12. b
13. c
14. b
15. c
16. c
17. c
18. a
19. d
20. b

CHAPTER 23

1. False
2. False
3. False
4. False
5. True
6. b
7. c
8. d
9. d
10. c
11. d
12. c
13. b
14. c
15. b
16. b
17. d
18. b
19. d
20. c

CHAPTER 24

1. False
2. False

3. False
4. True
5. False
6. c
7. c
8. c
9. d
10. b
11. a
12. b
13. d
14. d
15. b
16. a
17. d
18. a
19. d
20. d

CHAPTER 25

1. False
2. False
3. True
4. False
5. False
6. c
7. c
8. c
9. a
10. d
11. c
12. b
13. c
14. c
15. d
16. a
17. b
18. c
19. c
20. c

CHAPTER 26

1. True
2. False
3. False
4. False
5. True
6. b
7. c
8. a
9. b
10. a
11. c
12. d

13. d
14. a
15. d
16. b
17. d
18. c
19. a
20. b

CHAPTER 27

1. False
2. False
3. True
4. True
5. True
6. b
7. b
8. a
9. c
10. b
11. d
12. a
13. a
14. a
15. a
16. d
17. d
18. b
19. b
20. d

CHAPTER 28

1. False
2. False
3. False
4. False
5. False
6. a
7. a
8. d
9. a
10. d
11. a
12. c
13. c
14. c
15. c
16. d
17. d
18. b
19. a
20. d

CHAPTER 29

1. False
2. False
3. False
4. True
5. False
6. d
7. c
8. a
9. c
10. a
11. d
12. a
13. b
14. c
15. b
16. d
17. d
18. d
19. c
20. b

SOLUTIONS TO EVEN-NUMBERED QUESTIONS AND PROBLEMS

CHAPTER 1

2. Examples of decisions you might have made at the margin in the last twenty-four hours include when to get out of bed, how much cereal to put in the cereal bowl, how much water or juice to drink, how fast to walk to get to class, and how extensively to take notes in class.

4. **a.** Macroeconomics, since it pertains to the whole economy.
   b. Microeconomics, since it pertains to a particular industry.
   c. Macroeconomics, since it pertains to the whole economy.
   d. Macroeconomics, to the extent that it pertains to the whole economy.
   e. Microeconomics, since it pertains to a particular industry.

6. The three types of economic systems are free market economies, command-and-control economies, and mixed economies. All modern economies are mixed, including those of Canada, the United States, and Western Europe. In these countries, the mix tends more toward the free market end of the spectrum than toward command and control. In all mixed economies, free markets play a prominent role, but so too does government.

8. The tax system promotes equity to the extent that it redistributes income from the rich to the poor. This increase in equity comes at the cost of reduced efficiency, however, because it means there is less of an incentive to get the education and to do the hard work required for a high income.

10. Farmers grow food in order to sell it. If some of the farmers decide to quit, the result would be higher prices that would prompt the remaining farmers to produce more output. The food appears in the stores because consumers are willing to pay enough for the stores to more than cover expenses, which leads self-interested store owners to stock the food.

12. Government policy greatly influences what occurs in a mixed economy. Since government policy is strongly influenced by politics, economics is sometimes known as political economy.

14. Saying that movies are too violent is expressing an opinion that is based on normative judgments. How much is too much? The statement about movies would become positive if it was restated as, "Movies are more violent today than they used to be." The statement is positive whether or not it is true. Its accuracy might be determined, however, by defining what kinds of acts involve violence and counting how often those acts of violence occur in a selection of recent movies relative to a selection of older ones of the same general type.

16. **a.** If classes are spread throughout the day and evening, the same number of students could get by with fewer parking places than if classes are bunched together, such as in the morning.

   b. If there is good bus service to and from campus, students have less need to drive and thus less need for parking places. Bunching classes together would make parking more difficult and increase students' willingness to pay for it.

   c. If students have higher incomes, they're more likely to own cars, which would tend to increase students' willingness to pay for parking places.

CHAPTER 2

2. Management skills can overlap with entrepreneurship, but the two are different. Entrepreneurship involves creativity, putting together resources in new and unique ways. While management might include entrepreneurship, it might also be merely carrying out directions from higher levels of management, or organizing activities according to someone else's direction. Those latter aspects are not entrepreneurship.

4. **a.** ten baseball bats.
   b. six baseball bats.

6. The graph you draw should have a horizontal axis labeled with one good and a vertical axis labeled with another good. The production possibilities frontier itself should be increasingly downwardly sloping as you travel along it from the vertical axis to the horizontal axis. To show general growth, draw another production possibilities frontier that is everywhere outside the first one you drew. This means that, wherever the economy started on the first production possibilities frontier, it can increase its production of either good without decreasing the production of the other. In the production possibilities frontier in question 4, general growth would occur if each of the numbers in the list were increased.

8. When used as a medium of exchange, money allows goods and services to be traded for one another. Money's use as a medium of exchange means that barter does not need to take place. The flow of money is an integral part of the circular flow model.

10. **a.** No, consumers in the United States like to make their own choices between California wine and French wine. Those who choose French wine would be worse off if they were not allowed that option. When consumers buy French wine in preference to California wine, they are in effect saying that the opportunity cost of California wine is more than it is worth to them. Therefore, even though Californian winemakers would prefer consumers to buy California wine, the resources producers would need to use to replace the French wine have more value elsewhere in the economy.

   b. Either for variety or because they like it better, some French consumers presumably do drink imported U.S. wine.

12. Absolute advantage means being able to produce a good with fewer resources than it would take someone else to produce it. In reality, people specialize according to their comparative advantages, which means that each individual must compare the opportunity cost of the alternative things that particular person could do and choose those for which they have the lowest opportunity costs. Likewise, a country would also specialize according to comparative advantage. It would produce something, but exactly what it produces would depend on its own alternative opportunities. It would choose to produce goods for which its opportunity costs are relatively low.

14. **a.** A country cannot produce outside its current production possibilities frontier unless it acquires new resources or new technology. That's why the production possibilities frontier is called a "frontier."

   b. The purpose of trade is to expand consumption possibilities beyond the confines of what the country can produce. For this reason, a country that trades with other countries can be expected to consume at a point outside of its production possibilities frontier. The country would consume at a point on its frontier only if it did not trade.

16. **a.** 1*Y.*

   b. 1*X.*

   c. 2*Y.*

   d. 1/2*X.*

   Tryhard will produce good *X*, and Trynot will produce good *Y*, which are the goods in which each country has a comparative advantage.

CHAPTER 3

2. Draw a graph with the horizontal axis labeled "hot dogs" and the vertical axis labeled with "$" or "price." The demand curve that you label "individual's demand" should be a downwardly sloping line. The demand curve that you label "market demand" should start at the same point on the vertical axis as the other demand curve, but should slope downward less steeply, and reach the horizontal axis at the quantity that is twice as much as the quantity at which the first demand curve intersects the horizontal axis.

4. Insurance lowers the cost to you if your house is hit by a hurricane. Because the price is lower, in accordance with the law of demand, you're willing to accept the potential for more hurricanes and are therefore more willing to build a house in hurricane-prone areas. To graph the demand for the new houses in hurricane-prone areas, the horizontal axis would be labeled with "new houses" and the vertical axis would be labeled with "price" or "$". A lower price causes a movement along the demand curve to a greater quantity of new houses demanded.

6. Examples of complementary goods include: pencil and paper, baseball and bat, personal computer and printer, postage stamp and envelope, sugar and cereal, and butter and bread. In each case, if the price of the complement for the good were to increase, the demand for the good itself would decrease. Conversely, if the price of the complement for the good were to decrease, the demand for the good itself would increase.

8. In response to Mr. Johnson's income reduction, his demand for normal goods would decrease and his demand for inferior goods would increase. The following goods are likely to be normal goods for Mr. Johnson: restaurant food, Tommy Hilfiger clothing, fresh vegetables, antique furniture, and tickets to pro football games. The following goods are likely to be inferior goods for Mr. Johnson: generic paper towels, Spam, used cars, and Ramen noodles. Home-brewed coffee would be a normal good for Mr. Johnson if he most prefers the way he makes it himself. Home-brewed coffee would be an inferior good for Mr. Johnson if he prefers coffee from restaurants or coffee shops.

10. There is a difference between a change in demand and change in the quantity demanded. If there is a change in demand, the entire demand curve shifts, showing a new quantity demanded for each possible price. If there is a change in the quantity demanded, the reason might be simply that the price has fallen or risen, which would cause the consumer to move from one point to another along the same demand curve. For movements along demand in response to price changes, the demand curve itself does not shift.

12. For each of the following, you would draw a supply curve with the quantity supplied on the horizontal axis and price or $ on the vertical axis. The supply curve would slope upward to the right. If the supply curve increases, that means that the curve itself is shifted to the right. If the supply curve decreases, the curve is shifted to the left.

   a. Supply increases.

   b. Supply decreases.

   c. Supply decreases.

   d. Supply increases.

14. When the market clears, the quantity demanded just equals the quantity supplied. There is no surplus or shortage. The situation occurs when the market is in equilibrium. If there is a surplus or shortage, the price tends to change until it reaches that equilibrium. For example, if there is a shortage, there are not enough goods to go around to all of the consumers who want them, and sellers would be inclined to raise their prices. If there is a surplus, sellers have more than they can sell at the current price, and so lower their prices in order to sell more. At equilibrium, when quantity demanded equals quantity supplied, the market clears and price has no tendency to change.

16. A shortage results from a price that is below the equilibrium price. At that low price, consumers want to buy more than producers are willing to sell. In response, producers raise their prices.

18. If the market starts at equilibrium and demand increases, the market would experience a shortage if price does not

rise. However, the market forces the price to rise to a new equilibrium.

20. You should have drawn two graphs, labeling the horizontal axis on each as "quantity" and the vertical axis on each as "price" or "$." Also, on each graph, you should have drawn a downward-sloping demand curve and an upward-sloping supply curve. On the first graph, draw another demand curve that has shifted only a little bit to the left and another supply curve that has shifted quite a bit to the right. If you compare the market equilibrium from the second set of supply and demand curves to the first set of curves you drew, you'll find that the equilibrium price has fallen and quantity has increased. The reason is that the change in supply has dominated the change in demand. On the second graph, draw another demand curve that has shifted a large amount to the left and another supply curve that has shifted only a little bit to the right. In this case, you'll find that the equilibrium price and quantity have both fallen because the change in demand has dominated the change in supply.

CHAPTER 4

2. This answer is likely to vary from person to person. For example, it might have been a new car that you are very happy with, or a really great apartment that you rented at a low price. The difference between what you would have been willing to pay in the abstract and the price that you actually did pay would determine the amount of consumer surplus that you receive.

4. Yes, in the absence of market failures which will be discussed later in the book, the market-equilibrium output is efficient. For each unit sold, the value to consumers equals or exceeds the price, which in turn equals or exceeds the cost of producing it. For any output above the market equilibrium, the cost of producing it would exceed its value to consumers, and so consumers would not buy it and firms would not choose to produce it.

6. A country will import a good when the world price of that good is less than the country's price would have been without trade. The result will be a lower price within the country after trade, which causes producers in the country to cut back on their output. The lower price moves them down their supply curve, but normally not so far down that they would produce nothing at all. The country as a whole will gain from trade because the trade increases consumer surplus more than it reduces producer surplus. To show this result graphically, label the horizontal axis with the quantity of some good and the vertical axis with its price, or with a $. Draw a downwardly sloping demand curve and an upwardly sloping supply curve to represent the domestic market. Then add a world price that is lower than what would have been the market-equilibrium price in the absence of imports. The quantity actually consumed will be given by the point on the demand curve at the new lower price. The quantity produced in the domestic market will be given by the point on the supply curve at that

same, lower price. Producer surplus is given by the triangular area below the world price and above the domestic supply curve. Consumer surplus is given by the triangular area above the world price and below the market-demand curve. Note that the sum of these two areas is larger than the sum of the producer and consumer surplus that would occur at the higher price in the absence of trade.

8. For the price ceiling to have an effect, it must be set below the market-equilibrium price. In your first graph, you're instructed to show a ceiling price above the market-equilibrium price and interpret the result. The interpretation is that the ceiling price would be ignored. Anyone who tried to sell at that ceiling price would be undercut by other suppliers willing to sell at a lower price. The price would try to drop to the market equilibrium and there would be nothing to keep it from doing so. Therefore, the market would move to the market-equilibrium price. In your second graph, you're instructed to show a ceiling price that is below the market-equilibrium price and interpret that result. The interpretation is that the ceiling price would prevent price from rising to the market equilibrium, and for that reason would lead to a shortage in which the quantity demanded is greater than the quantity supplied.

10. Ticket scalping is efficient in that it makes sure the tickets go to those who are willing to pay the most for them. However, this may seem inequitable to people who get up early to stand in line for good seats, only to find them already gone because tickets for the best seats were purchased in bulk by the ticket scalpers.

12. Some inefficiencies of rent controls are: some people cannot find apartments who are willing to pay more than those who do find them, people waste time looking for apartments, apartments are not properly maintained, and too few apartments are offered for rent.

14. Price floors decrease consumer surplus because they increase the prices consumers pay and decrease the quantities that they purchase.

16. The minimum wage is a price floor, because it sets a lower bound on what wages employers are allowed to pay.

18. A black market is one that is illegal. When prices are held down, there'll be some consumers unable to buy at the controlled price. It is in the interest of these consumers and producers to break the law and make a deal at a higher price. Such deals are illegal and therefore would be part of the black market. In the case of price supports, however, producers are normally able to sell as much as they want to at the artificially high price, with the government being the buyer of what would otherwise be a surplus. For this reason, producers have no excess production and thus no incentive to undercut the support price by engaging in black market activities.

CHAPTER 5

2. The macro goals are not mentioned explicitly in the Constitution, but the phrase "life, liberty, and the pursuit

of happiness" could be interpreted to include the prosperity implied by the achievement of the goals.

4. Excluding the value of intermediate goods is necessary to avoid counting the value of intermediate goods twice, which would inflate the value of GDP. Their value is included in the value of final goods.

6. Traczania's GDP = $150 + $55 + $75 + $20 − $25 = $275. Neither net investment nor government transfer payments should appear in the calculation of GDP.

8. The difference between GNP and GDP is not large in percentage terms. It revolves around ownership, with GDP including the output of resources located in the United States but owned by foreigners. In contrast, GNP excludes this output but includes U.S.-owned output in foreign countries.

10. The output of the underground economy consists of goods and services that are produced but not reported to government. The usual reason is to avoid taxation or because the activities are illegal. Because the output is not reported, it is not measured in GDP statistics.

12. Per capita GDP refers to GDP per person. It is the total GDP divided by the population. Per capita GDP is in some ways more informative than total GDP because per capita GDP reveals more about the standard of living of an average person. For example, an increase in population could lead to a larger GDP in total, but a lower per capita GDP.

14. Your graph should label the horizontal axis "time" and the vertical axis "real GDP." The curve that shows the business cycle looks like a roller coaster tilted upward. The rising part shows the expansion, the top point shows the peak, the downward-sloping part shows the recession, and the bottom point shows the trough. The upward tilt reflects the upward trend in real GDP.

CHAPTER 6

2. Persons under age 16 are minors, discouraged from working because of the desire of society to have them finish their education. Few of them work, so excluding them from the labor force does not impair the accuracy of the data. Adults over age 65 may or may not be retired, and so many of them will be working. Excluding them from the labor force data would result in inaccuracies.

4. Labor force participation rate = (employed + unemployed)/Adult population; you should poll your classmates about their labor force participation in order to answer the second part of the question.

6. **a.** 9.7 percent in 1982.
   b. 4.0 percent in 2000.
   c. The data show a downward trend in the unemployment rate, interrupted by periodic upward movements, such as during the recession in the early 1990s and in 2001.

8. Worklandia's labor force participation rate equals 73 percent. The unemployment rate is 3 percent.

10. Human capital is a critical factor in employment. For example, to find a job as an airline pilot, a person must know how to fly an airplane. People without human capital or with obsolete human capital will have difficulty in finding and keeping a job.

12. A strong work ethic makes people less willing to stay unemployed. People will be more productive, other things equal. They will begin working earlier in life, and if they become unemployed, they will strive to minimize the period of time between jobs. Countries with weak work ethics are less productive. An argument could be made that too strong a work ethic focuses people too much on work, causing them to ignore other values. For example, some critics of the strong American work ethic maintain that children are harmed by parents spending too much time at work. Other arguments against the work ethic could be made.

14. Full employment occurs when the country achieves the natural rate of unemployment, which is currently thought to be 4 to 5 percent. Thus, an employment rate of 95 or 96 percent represents full employment. As the natural rate of unemployment has changed over time, so has the threshold for full employment. When the natural rate decreases, the full-employment percentage will become larger; when the natural rate increases, the full-employment percentage will become smaller.

CHAPTER 7

2. Inflation rates vary markedly from country to country. There is no reason for other countries' inflation rates to be the same as the inflation rate in the United States. For example, Japan has recently experienced mild deflation, while the United States experienced low inflation, and some other countries experienced high inflation.

4. The overall inflation rate is influenced by food and energy prices, while the core inflation rate excludes those prices. In this case, food and energy prices are rising more than other prices. The core inflation rate is often considered to be a more accurate reflection of inflation because food and energy prices are more volatile than prices in general.

6. Unanticipated inflation catches people by surprise, so they are less able to plan for unanticipated inflation. When inflation is planned for, people can make arrangements to adjust wage agreements, loan agreements, and other contracts for the effects of inflation.

8. The base period is the point of reference to which other time periods are compared. The index is set to 100 during the base period. Any particular value of the CPI can be compared to the base period by noting the difference between that value and the base period value of 100.

10. The value of the price index is 183: $(2 \times 8 + 1 \times 7 + 3 \times 3)/(1 \times 8 + .5 \times 7 + 2 \times 3) \times 100 = 32/17.5 \times 100 = 183$. The index says that prices are 83 percent higher than in the base year.

12. Johnson's nominal income is 25 percent higher than three years ago, computed as $(125 − 100)/100 = 25/100 = 25$ percent. The price index shows that prices have risen 16.7 percent, computed as $(175 − 150)/150 = 25/150 = 16.7$

percent. Since Johnson's nominal income has risen by more than the price index, his real income is higher than three years ago. Alternatively, we can compute Johnson's real income three years ago using the formula that says real income equals nominal income divided by the price index, computed as $100/150 (multiplied by 100) = $66.67. Johnson's current real income equals $125/175 (multiplied by 100) = $71.43.

14. Real GDP = Nominal GDP/Price index × 100: $1,000/125 (multiplied by 100) = $800.

CHAPTER 8

2. Aggregate demand tells how much real GDP consumers, businesses, and others will purchase at each price level. On the graph, the vertical axis should be labeled as the price level and the horizontal axis labeled as real GDP. The aggregate demand curve slopes down in response to the purchasing power effect, the wealth effect, the interest-rate effect, and the international substitution effect.

4. No, the actual GDP could be greater than or less than full-employment GDP. Actual GDP and full-employment GDP are not equal unless the economy is at a full-employment equilibrium.

6. Long-run aggregate supply is a vertical line because full-employment output does not depend on the price level in the long run. So, whatever the price level might be, long-run aggregate supply shows where full-employment output lies, which is given by the horizontal intercept of the long-run aggregate supply curve. Long-run aggregate supply would shift to the right if full-employment output were to increase. That increase could occur in response to an increase in full employment or in the output full employment is able to produce.

8. The upward slope of short-run aggregate supply shows that the price level matters in the short run in the sense that a change in the price level causes a change in the amount of real GDP supplied. A rising price level increases the amount of real GDP supplied, while a decrease in the price level reduces the amount of real GDP supplied.

10. Your graph should show real GDP on the horizontal axis and the price level on the vertical axis. The long-run aggregate supply curve should be vertical at the full-employment GDP. The aggregate demand curve should slope downward and intersect the long-run aggregate supply curve. The long-run macro equilibrium occurs at this point of intersection, which is characterized by no tendency for either price or aggregate output to change.

12. Use the same graph of aggregate demand and aggregate supply that you used in question 10 or question 11. To illustrate overheating, draw another aggregate demand curve that is to the right of the first one. That shift in aggregate demand might be caused by increased government spending, for example. The economy's response would be a higher price level as it moves from one point of macro equilibrium to the next.

14. On each of your graphs, the horizontal axis should be labeled as "real GDP" and the vertical axis labeled as the "price level." On both graphs, start with the long-run macro equilibrium, given by the intersection of aggregate demand and long-run aggregate supply. To show demand-side deflation, draw a second aggregate demand curve that is to the left of the first one and intersects long-run aggregate supply at a lower price level. To show supply-side deflation, draw a second long-run aggregate supply curve that is to the right of the first one and intersects aggregate demand at a lower price level. Demand-side deflation and supply-side deflation might occur together if there is a technological advance and, simultaneously, less spending by consumers in response to concerns over the economy or levels of personal debt.

CHAPTER 9

2. When the economy overheats, fiscal policy would aim to reduce aggregate demand, which could be done through higher taxes or less government spending.

4. Automatic stabilizers can immediately put the brakes on an overheating economy or stimulate one that is falling into recession, without policymakers needing to recognize that the problem exists and enact policy, and without waiting for the new policies to be implemented. For example, as unemployment rises in a recession, the income tax automatically soaks up less purchasing power, because it is based on a percentage of falling income. Likewise, unemployment insurance and other safety-net programs automatically increase government spending, which serves to counteract recessionary tendencies. When problems of unemployment do become visible, however, there is strong pressure on the government to take explicit action, in addition to the automatic stabilizers. Perhaps the reason is that unemployment is so difficult to endure.

6. The full-employment budget has exhibited a tendency toward deficit for decades. The reason largely revolves around politics, where voters like the immediate effects of lower taxes and greater spending.

8. The graph of the short-run aggregate supply curve should have the price level on the vertical axis and real GDP on the horizontal axis. The short-run aggregate supply curve should be upward sloping, preferably with the slope increasing toward vertical a little after the curve crosses the vertical long-run aggregate supply curve, which should be drawn at full-employment GDP. The short-run aggregate supply curve intersects the long-run aggregate supply curve at the expected price level. This expected price level should be marked on the vertical axis directly to the left of the intersection point.

10. The production effect means that workers are fooled by a higher price level into offering more hours of work in response to increases in nominal wages, even when those increases in nominal wages are merely the result of a general inflation. While workers would want to base their supply curves of labor on their real wages, they actually

based their supply curve on nominal wages, with the result that they work more when nominal wages rise. As a consequence, when increasing aggregate demand causes demand-side inflation, it also brings forth more work effort and an increase in real GDP. On the graph, the economy moves up the short-run aggregate supply curve to a higher price level and a larger real GDP.

12. You should draw two separate graphs, each with the price level on the vertical axis and real GDP on the horizontal axis. Both graphs should include a downward-sloping aggregate demand curve and an upward-sloping short-run aggregate supply curve. In the graph showing demand-pull inflation, a second aggregate demand curve should be drawn to the right of the first one, and the change in equilibriums shown as a movement up the short-run aggregate supply curve to a larger output at a higher price level. In the graph showing cost-push inflation, a second aggregate supply curve should be drawn above the first one, and the change in equilibriums shown as a movement up the aggregate demand curve to a higher price level and a smaller output.

14. According to the Phillips curve, inflation and unemployment are inversely related. When you draw the Phillips curve, place "unemployment" on the horizontal axis and "inflation" on the vertical axis. Then draw a downward-sloping line that is inwardly bowed. The Phillips curve fit the data nicely in the 1960s. Since then, however, there has been no obvious Phillips curve.

16. In a nutshell, classical economists advocate consistent government policy and patience until economic problems resolve themselves. Keynesian economists argue that government should actively adjust taxes and spending so as to manage aggregate demand and counter short-run economic difficulties.

CHAPTER 10

2. In the aggregate, national income consists of what is paid for output. The value of aggregate output is thus equal to the value of the aggregate income.

4. Autonomous spending is only the spending that would occur in the absence of any income. The amount of autonomous spending is likely to vary from one family to another, depending on the amounts the families have saved. Actual spending is likely to vary even more, since this will depend on induced spending in addition to autonomous spending. Induced spending is based on income, which for this reason is likely to differ quite a bit from one household to another.

6. Use the income-expenditure graphs to answer this question. Place "real GDP" on a horizontal axis and "expenditure" on the vertical axis. Draw a 45-degree line that exactly splits the difference between the two axes. Starting at a point on the vertical axis, draw an upward-sloping line that crosses over the 45-degree line. Label this line as the aggregate expenditure function and label the point at which it crosses the 45-degree line as the unemployment equilibrium. To

show that this point you have labeled unemployment equilibrium is indeed an unemployment equilibrium, draw a vertical line downward to the horizontal axis. Label the point you reach on the horizontal axis as actual GDP. To the right of actual GDP, mark another point as full-employment GDP. Because full-employment GDP exceeds actual GDP, the point that you marked as the unemployment equilibrium is correctly labeled. To achieve full employment, fiscal policy would need to shift the aggregate expenditure function upward until it crosses the 45-degree line at a point directly above full-employment GDP. The amount of the required upward shift is the recessionary gap. It is the shortfall in aggregate expenditure below that which is necessary to achieve the full-employment GDP.

8. The sum of the marginal propensity to consume and the marginal propensity to save equals one to the extent that all income must either be spent or not spent. Money that is spent represents consumption and money that is not spent represents savings. Your own personal marginal propensity to consume can be found by imagining what you would do if you found some money, such as $100. If you would save $10 of it and spend $90, then your marginal propensity to consume would be 0.9.

10. **a.** The answer is found by multiplying $1 trillion by the expenditure multiplier, which equals $1/(1 - mpc)$. In this example, the expenditure multiplier equals $1/0.6$, or 1.67. The expenditure equilibrium for this economy is thus $1.67 trillion.

   b. To increase the expenditure equilibrium by $1 trillion, the change in autonomous spending multiplied by 1.67 must equal $1 trillion. To find this amount, divide 1.67 into $1 trillion. Doing so reveals the amount of autonomous spending necessary is $599 billion.

12. A decrease in the marginal propensity to save would increase the marginal propensity to consume and thus also increase the expenditure multiplier. Assuming unemployed resources and a constant price level, the higher multiplier would cause a larger equilibrium GDP as autonomous spending is multiplied by this multiplier.

14. The paradox of thrift occurs when people collectively save a larger fraction of their incomes, but see their total savings go down because their incomes fall. The result is less total spending at any given price level, and a shift to the left in aggregate demand. From the perspective of today, if the price level is downwardly sticky and we take a short-run perspective, we might not want to see people increase their marginal propensity to save. However, if we take a long-run perspective or if prices are not downwardly sticky, we do not need to worry about people increasing their propensity to save.

CHAPTER 11

2. Sam's marginal tax rate cannot be determined from the information provided. We would need to know how much taxes would be taken out of an additional dollar of earnings in order to know the marginal tax rate.

4. About 46% of the federal revenue pie consists of personal income tax revenues. About 38% comes from the Social Security tax.

6. What seems fair from one person's point of view might not seem fair from another's. There are many examples, and applying principles of tax equity will depend upon the example chosen. One example would be the personal income tax evaluated from the point of view of horizontal equity. The principle of horizontal equity is to tax people in equal circumstances an equal amount. Yet figuring out what equal circumstances actually are might be quite difficult. The couple with a family to support might think it is equitable to have deductions for the children that the couple must support. However, a childless couple might find it inequitable to be made to pay more in taxes than the couple with a family, merely because the childless couple could not have, or chose not to have, children.

8. A tax on football tickets would seem to satisfy the benefit principle of taxation, since those who go to football games benefit from the student athletics program. By associating the price of the program with the price of tickets, it might also promote efficient choice. Taxing football tickets would only be progressive, however, if college football attendance increased more than in proportion to increases in income. Taxing textbooks or vending machine drinks would not appear to satisfy any principle of tax equity, although such taxes might be relatively efficient in that they would be hard to escape. While taxing textbooks might be the hardest tax for a student to escape, taxing textbooks is also the most likely to be regressive, particularly if the tax is not covered by financial aid.

10. A payroll tax is a tax on paychecks workers receive for the jobs they do. In contrast, an income tax is levied on all income, although there are likely to be deductions allowed.

12. It is difficult to aid the poor without providing disincentives to work, so long as the aid depends upon a person having little or no income. To the extent that aid is reduced as income increases, the aid acts as a drag on that income and reduces the incentive to earn it. In addition, to pay for the many aid programs that make up the social safety net, government must resort to taxation. Taxes reduce the amount of income people get to keep for themselves, and so also reduce work incentives.

14. One possibility for tax reform would be to replace the personal income tax with a consumption tax, such as a sales tax or a value added tax. A consumption tax might be more efficient than the income tax, but would not allow the same possibilities for detailed fine-tuning in order to achieve equity goals.

CHAPTER 12

2. When a recession first hits, firms reduce the production of goods, but are slow to lay off workers. The reason is that there are costs associated with layoffs and with rehiring workers when the economy improves. Many firms would prefer to retain their workers until it becomes clear that it is not economic to do so. As a result, with the reduction in output greater than the reduction in labor, output per worker falls. This effect is reversed when the economy begins to improve. Firms will be slow to increase their use of labor until they are sure that the economic rebound will continue. Output rises more than proportionally to the use of labor, and so labor productivity rises.

4. **a.** When Microsoft was started, the success of the firm would have required capital formation in computers and other office equipment.

   b. When Wal-Mart was started, store buildings, fixtures, and merchandise were examples of the capital formation that occurred.

   c. When Motown Records started, various pieces of recording equipment, billing equipment, and office equipment would have been needed.

6. The supply of savings slopes upward because its slope represents a positive relationship between the quantity saved and the real interest rate. People save more when they get paid more to do so. Likewise, businesses invest more when it costs them less to obtain loans. For this reason, investment demand shows an inverse relationship between the real interest rate and the amount invested. When the quantity of saving supplied just equals the quantity of investment demanded, this market is at an equilibrium.

8. You should label the horizontal axis of your graph as "savings and investment." The vertical axis should be labeled as the "real interest rate." Draw a downward-sloping demand curve and an upward-sloping supply curve. The point of intersection is the initial equilibrium. To show an increase in investment demand, draw a second demand curve that's further out than the first. The new equilibrium will then occur at a higher real interest rate and a greater amount of savings and investment. If the supply of savings were to also shift to the right, it could potentially lower the real interest rate back to what it was originally, or even to below what it was originally.

10. You should label the horizontal axis of your graph as "savings and investment." The vertical axis should be labeled as the "real interest rate." Draw a downward-sloping demand curve and an upward-sloping supply curve. The point of intersection is the initial equilibrium. To show the effect of taxing interest on savings, draw a second supply curve that is above and to the left of the first one. The supply curve has shifted because consumers now require a higher interest rate prior to the tax in order to pay the tax due on that interest. Observe that the equilibrium real interest rate has risen as a result of the tax, causing the equilibrium quantity of savings and investment to fall.

12. During the war, the economy reduced the production of civilian goods in favor of war goods. There were relatively few consumer goods available to purchase. At the same time, employment was high, as were incomes, as war production reduced unemployment. The combination of high incomes and few items to purchase led people to save more. Unless the war on terrorism results in shortages of

consumer goods, an increase in the savings rate is unlikely.

14. Both focus on the causes of economic growth, but with different emphases. New growth theory emphasizes the role of technology in promoting growth, while supply-side economics emphasizes lower tax rates and less government regulation as the keys to growth. New growth theory also recognizes that technological improvements are encouraged when property rights (in the form of monopoly power) are granted to developers of new technologies.

16. The Laffer curve shows the dangers of setting tax rates too high. It might be the case that a tax would bring in more revenue if its rate was lower. For example, some argue that reductions in the capital gains tax rate might increase revenue from that tax. To graph this case, place the capital gains tax rate on the horizontal axis and note that it can go from zero to 100 percent. Place the amount of revenue collected on the vertical axis. Your curve should be hump-shaped, starting at zero on the horizontal axis, then rising to a maximum, before falling back to zero when you reach 100 percent on the horizontal axis. The argument that reducing the capital gains tax rate would lead to more revenue from the tax is equivalent to saying that we are on the downward-sloping portion of that Laffer curve.

CHAPTER 13

2. Once the inefficiencies of barter become apparent we might expect that people will spontaneously decide to adopt some commodity as money. The more people on the island the more likely the limitations of barter will be obvious because there will be more opportunities for exchange that would be facilitated by money. Barter might work for a group that expects to soon be rescued, but if they expect to remain on the island for a long time, money is likely to be adopted sooner. What form the money will take will depend on what is available. For example, if coconuts grow on the island, they might be used as money.

4. The balance sheet you create will depend on your personal circumstances. For example, if you own a car, computer, and television, and have a bank account balance, then these items would appear as assets. If you owe an unpaid balance on the car, that amount would appear as a liability, along with unpaid balances on your credit card, and other debts you owe.

6. Reserves can be kept as cash in the vault or as deposits at a Federal Reserve bank. Because of security concerns, banks must be concerned about keeping too much vault cash. However, vault cash is needed to satisfy customer withdrawals.

8. The Fed's functions and your interactions with the Fed would include:
   a. Banker's bank: Your bank's reserves might be deposited into an account at the Fed.
   b. Lender of last resort: Your bank might have outstanding discount loans from the Fed.
   c. Supervises banks: Your bank would have to be knowledgeable about and comply with Fed regulations.
   d. Issues currency: Your bank would obtain new currency supplies from your district Federal Reserve bank.
   e. Clears checks: Your bank might send checks deposited into the bank to the Fed for payment.

10. It is impossible for the Fed to control the money supply because the money supply depends not only on the Fed's actions, but also the behavior of the public and banks. The public controls how much money it wishes to hold as deposits and how much as currency. Banks control the amount of bank loans. Both of these affect the money multiplier, and hence the money supply.

12. The deposit multiplier assumes that all new deposits in the banking system are loaned out to the maximum extent. The result is that the deposit multiplier is used to compute the maximum expansion in the money supply. The money multiplier allows for banks to hold excess reserves, and the public to hold currency rather than bank deposits. This characteristic of the money multiplier means its value will be less than the value of the deposit multiplier.

14. The federal funds rate is the interest rate on reserves banks borrow from other banks. The discount rate is the interest rate on reserves that banks borrow from the Fed. There is no reason for these interest rates to be equal since the first is determined by the demand and supply of federal funds, while the second is set by the Fed.

CHAPTER 14

2. Bringing down high inflation calls for slowing down the economy, which could lead to a recession. The two recessions in the early 1980s are believed to have occurred in response to Fed efforts to fight the high inflation of the late 1970s. Tradeoffs in monetary policy exist because in order to achieve one goal another goal may have to be sacrificed. For example, to promote high employment, an expansionary monetary policy may risk an increase in inflation.

4. The monetary policy instruments are the money supply and interest rates. The choice of instrument depends on the Fed's assessment of which instrument will most contribute to the achievement of the goals of monetary policy.

6. The interest rate is the opportunity cost of holding money, and is the "price" in that sense. When the interest rate is high, people will reduce their money holdings in order to buy assets that pay interest. When the interest rate is low, the opportunity cost of holding money is reduced, and so people will hold more money and less assets that pay interest.

8. A money market equilibrium occurs when the quantity demanded and the quantity supplied of money are equal. Label the horizontal axis "quantity of money" and the vertical axis "interest rate." Your graph should show a downward-sloping demand curve for money and a vertical money supply curve. The equilibrium occurs at the intersection of the two curves.

10. Both money and bonds are highly liquid assets. The difference is that money pays no interest, while bonds do. When the interest rate is high, people will economize on their holdings of money in order to own bonds.

12. The price level equals $4, found by substituting into the equation of exchange and solving for the price level. If the money supply were $600, then the price level would be $12.

14. Monetarism is a school of thought associated with economist Milton Friedman. Its foundation is the quantity theory of money, which is expressed through the equation of exchange: $M \times V = P \times Q$. A monetary policy that follows monetarism will expand the money supply at a steady rate of about 2 to 3 percent a year. This recommendation follows from the idea that the economy will, over the long run, show an increase in aggregate output of 2 to 3 percent a year, and so the money supply should grow to match the increased output.

16. Keynesians view an increase in the money supply as leading to a lower interest rate, which causes borrowing to increase. When people spend the borrowed money nominal GDP increases.

18. The federal funds rate is the interest rate on reserves that banks borrow from other banks. The Fed targets the federal funds rate primarily by conducting open market operations that affect the federal funds rate. A lower federal funds rate is associated with a looser monetary policy, while a higher rate is associated with a tighter policy.

CHAPTER 15

2. The answer depends upon your estimate of the elasticity. For example, if you estimate an elasticity of one, then increasing your study time by 25 percent would result in a 25 percent increase in your grade. Whether this payoff is worthwhile depends on many considerations, including the opportunity cost of your time.

4. Substituting into the elasticity formula and solving, we have:

$$\left[\frac{5}{(25 + 30) / 2}\right] \div \left[\frac{25}{(200 + 175) / 2}\right] =$$

$$(5/27.5) \div (25/187.5) = 0.18 \div 0.13 = 1.4$$

6. The following examples describe each elasticity category: Elastic: Percentage change in quantity demanded greater than 10 percent, Inelastic: Percentage change in quantity demanded less than 10 percent, Unit elastic: Percentage change in quantity demanded equals 10 percent. A graph of elastic demand will show that quantity demanded is relatively responsive to the price change, while the graph of inelastic demand will show that quantity demanded is relatively unresponsive. The graph for unit elastic demand will show that the percentage change in quantity demanded matches the percentage change in price. Refer to the relevant graphs in the chapter.

8. Since total revenue increased when the price was decreased, demand is elastic.

10. Your examples should have in common that an increase in income decreases demand. Students often mention noodle cups and generic products as examples.

12. The quantity supplied will increase by more than 10 percent.

14. No, because an elastic demand means the demand curve is horizontal. The tax will shift the supply curve by the amount of the tax, but the horizontal demand means that price will not change. Thus, hot dog makers will bear the cost of the tax.

CHAPTER 16

2. Total utility values (including those in the table) are: 6, 11, 15, 18, and 20. The missing values are found by summing the marginal utilities. The missing marginal utility value is equal to 2, which is found by taking the difference between the last two total utility values.

4. No, total utility is maximized when marginal utility equals zero. Consumers maximize total utility, which is the total amount of satisfaction from consumption. Maximizing marginal utility makes no sense, since total utility can be increased so long as marginal utility is a positive value.

6. A negative value for marginal utility indicates the purchase of the good would reduce total utility. Since consumers wish to increase their total utility, the good will not be purchased.

8. Diminishing marginal utility for pizza explains why the utility provided by other foods will at some point exceed that provided by pizza. Once the consumption of pizza reaches a certain amount, so that its marginal utility has decreased to a low enough value, the marginal utility provided by another food that the consumer likes, but not as well as pizza, will be greater than the marginal utility of pizza. At that point, the consumer will stop eating pizza and eat the other food item.

10. Celina will purchase six books, two cartons of ice cream, and no workouts. This combination of goods maximizes her total utility.

12. Let MU_A stand for the marginal utility of good A, MU_B the marginal utility of good B, and MU_C the marginal utility of C. Also let P_A stand for the price of good A, P_B the price of good B, and P_C the price of good C. The equation for the rule of utility maximization is: $MU_A/P_A = MU_B/P_B = MU_C/P_C$. Restated in words, the rule is to spend on each item until the marginal utility of another dollar spent on any item would be the same.

14. Yes, a lower price allows the consumer to increase his or her consumption of the good, thereby increasing total utility.

CHAPTER 17

2. The four methods of finance are: use personal funds, use retained earnings, borrow, and issue shares of stock. Personal funds have no strings attached to their use, but

will generally be limited in amount. Retained earnings also can be used as a firm pleases, but their amount is limited by the profit earned by a firm. Borrowed funds require that a firm find a lender who is satisfied that the firm will be able to repay the funds with interest in the future. Thus, not all firms will be able to borrow. However, borrowed funds can allow a firm to expand beyond its current size. Corporations can obtain funds by issuing stock, but stocks provide only a small fraction of financing for businesses.

4. Internal financing is generated by profits. External financing comes from outside a firm, such as from a bank or the sale of stock. Internal financing is more common.

6. A secondary market is where items are resold after the initial sale. The stock exchanges are secondary markets, meaning that the firms that issued stock originally do not receive monies when the shares are sold on the stock exchanges.

8. Profit equals total revenue minus total cost. Economists usually assume that firms try to maximize profit.

10. Accounting profit = Total revenue − Explicit cost; Economic profit = Total revenue − Explicit cost − Implicit cost. The economic definition of profit recognizes that total revenue must be sufficient to keep resources in their current use.

12. **a.** Opportunity cost associated with depositing the cash in a bank account.
b. Opportunity cost associated with the income the owner could have earned by holding a job for fifteen hours a week.
c. Opportunity cost associated with using the automobile for personal purposes.

14. The principal-agent problem recognizes that agents (managers) may have different objectives than principals (business owners). Managers may seek to further their own interests rather than maximize profit for the owners.

16. The long run and the short run differ according to the variability of inputs. In the long run, all inputs are assumed to be variable. In the short run, at least one input is assumed to be fixed, meaning that it is constant. Capital is usually assumed to be the fixed input. The long run is a longer period of time than the short run, and is sometimes referred to as the planning horizon.

18. Marginal product is the increment to total product when the variable input is increased by one unit. Expressed as an equation, we have: Marginal product = Change in total product ÷ Change in the quantity of input. In contrast, Average product = Total product ÷ Total quantity input. The law of diminishing returns refers to the behavior of marginal product.

20. Your graph should label the horizontal axis as "quantity of input" (labor) and the vertical axis as "quantity of output." Average product rises when marginal product is greater than average product, but falls when marginal product falls below average product. The curves intersect at the maximum point on average product.

CHAPTER 18

2. The cost of the milk is a sunk cost, which is not relevant for making decisions.

4. Refer to Figure 18-1 after you draw your graphs. The graph of total product labels the horizontal axis as "labor" and the vertical axis as "output." Increasing returns is associated with an increase in the slope of total product. Diminishing returns is identified with a positive, but decreasing slope of total product. Negative returns occur when the total product curve turns down. By reversing the axis and drawing the labor requirements curve, you are able to show the amount of labor required to produce any amount of output. The total variable cost curve and the total cost curve have a similar shape as the labor requirements curve.

6. Refer to Figures 18-2 and 18-3 after you draw your graphs. Total cost curves are typically drawn in a graph separate from average and marginal curves since total costs are much larger than average costs.
a. Total fixed cost.
b. Total variable cost.
c. Total cost and total variable cost.
d. Total cost.
e. Marginal cost.
f. Average total cost and average variable cost.
g. Marginal cost, at the minimum point of average total cost.
h. Marginal cost, at the minimum point of average variable cost.

8. **a.** Total revenue equals the price, $1.50, multiplied by the quantity, 1,000, which is $1,500. Total cost equals the sum of total fixed cost, $200, and total variable cost, $150, which is $350. The firm earns a profit of $1,150, the difference between total revenue and total cost.
b. It is impossible to determine whether the firm is maximizing profit, since marginal cost is not given.

10. Marginal cost appears as a J, while average cost appears as a U. Marginal revenue appears as a horizontal line. The profit-maximizing quantity, Q^*, occurs below the intersection of marginal revenue and marginal cost. Refer to Figure 18-7. Too little output and too much output reduce profit below the maximum value because at Q^* on your graph the additional revenue equals the additional cost of that unit of output. When output is less than Q^*, producing more will result in additional revenue that exceeds additional cost, which increases profit. When output is more than Q^*, reducing output will reduce total cost by more than the reduction in total revenue, which again increases profit.

12. A breakeven graph will show the price tangent to the minimum point of the average cost curve. The marginal revenue line is horizontal at the market price. Marginal cost is J-shaped and intersects the minimum point of average cost, which is U-shaped. Because the firm just breaks even, the marginal revenue line is just tangent to the min-

imum point of average cost. The firm produces the quantity for which marginal revenue equals marginal cost, which in this case occurs where marginal revenue is tangent to average cost. The horizontal axis is labeled as the quantity of output and the vertical axis is labeled as "$."

14. The price should be above the minimum point on the average cost curve. Price equals marginal revenue. The profit rectangle will extend from zero to the profit-maximizing quantity, with its height given by the difference between price and average cost. Refer to Figure 18-8.

16. By producing and selling potatoes, Happy Spud earns total revenue equal to $30,000, and has total costs equal to $35,900. The firm's loss equals $5,900. Since price and marginal cost are equal at $3 and the loss is less than the fixed cost of $6,000, the firm is minimizing its loss. Rather than shut down, the firm should continue to produce.

18. In a production context, all inputs are variable in the long run, but in the short run there is at least one fixed input. In a cost context, in the long run all costs are variable, while the firm has both fixed and variable costs in the short run. The law of diminishing returns applies in the short run, while economies of scale are found in the long run.

20. Economies of scale mean lower per unit costs for larger firms. Diseconomies of scale result in per unit costs that are higher than the minimum cost. By downsizing, a firm could reach the minimum cost.

22. Scanners speed up checkout lines, and as a consequence allow a cashier to ring up more customers per hour. This effect saves on labor costs. Not every supermarket must install scanners, though. The reason is that the cost of purchasing scanners must be justified by the cost savings. Busy supermarkets are more likely to be able to justify the cost than are supermarkets with fewer customers. Whether to install scanners is a long-run decision.

CHAPTER 19

2. Market power refers to a firm's ability to influence price. Market power is not found in pure competition, where firms are price takers.

4. Price takers sell at the market price. The first graph will show the market price occurs at the intersection of market demand and supply. The second graph will show the market price as a horizontal line.

6. An industry demand curve will follow the law of demand and be downward sloping.

8. Letting P stand for price and Q for quantity supplied, the supply for Shiny Yellow Gold Mine is: $P = \$100$, $Q = 0$; $P = \$150$, $Q = 0$; $P = \$200$, $Q = 0$ or 5 (firm loses total fixed cost either way); $P = \$250$, $Q = 5$; $P = \$300$, $Q = 6$; $P = \$350$, $Q = 7$; $P = \$400$, $Q = 7$; $P = \$450$, $Q = 8$; $P = \$500$, $Q = 8$; $P = \$550$, $Q = 9$; $P = \$600$, $Q = 9$. As price rises from $100 to $600, the quantity supplied rises from zero to nine, thus confirming that higher prices are associated with a greater quantity supplied.

10. False. Entry is free of barriers to entry, but lack of barriers leads to zero profit.

12. At equilibrium neither entry nor exit will occur. This condition holds when profit is expected to be zero. Graphically, price will be tangent to average cost at its minimum point.

14. The long-run supply curve is horizontal. Cost curves do not shift upward because the expansion of a constant-cost industry has no effect on the demand for resources used by the industry.

16. The long-run supply curve is downward sloping. Cost curves shift downward because of external economies associated with the expansion of the industry.

CHAPTER 20

2. A firm without market power has a demand curve that is a horizontal line. As market power increases, the demand curve slopes down more and more steeply.

4. A natural monopoly occurs in an industry that has economies of scale throughout the relevant range of output, or at least over a large enough portion of that output that dividing it along two or more firms would lead to higher average costs than just having a single firm produce it. A water company or sewage treatment company is likely to have a natural monopoly, because it is cheaper for only one firm to have a set of pipes below the city streets than to have two or more firms competing and each digging up the streets.

6. A monopolist faces a demand curve that is the same as market demand, which slopes downward and to the right.

8. Just because a firm is a monopoly does not guarantee that the firm will earn economic profit. The monopoly firm will be unable to achieve a profit if its average costs of production are everywhere above its demand curve.

10. Label the horizontal axis of your graph as "quantity" and the vertical axis with a "$." Draw a downward-sloping market demand curve, which is also the demand curve facing the monopoly firm. Draw the monopolist's marginal revenue curve so that it starts at the top point on the demand curve, but then slopes down twice as steeply as the demand curve. Draw a J-shaped marginal cost curve. To ensure that the monopolist incurs a loss, draw an average cost curve that is everywhere above the demand curve. This average cost curve should be U-shaped and its minimum point should be intersected by the marginal cost curve. To minimize loss, the monopoly produces the output for which marginal cost equals marginal revenue, or shuts down if it cannot cover all of its variable costs.

12. No, the monopoly firm does not have a supply curve, because there is no unique relationship between price and quantity. Instead, for any given quantity, the price will be higher if demand is less elastic at that quantity.

14. Your graph should show that the monopolist produces at the point where marginal revenue equals marginal cost. This amount will be less than the efficient quantity, which is given by the point where demand equals marginal cost. To achieve the efficient quantity, the price would be given by the demand curve at that point.

16. The goal of rate-of return regulation is to allow the monopolist normal profits, which is zero economic profits. To achieve this result, price should be set according to where the monopolist's average cost curve intersects its demand curve.

CHAPTER 21

2. Answers will depend upon students' personal experiences.
4. By sales, the four largest firms are D, A, B, and F. Adding the sales of these firms, we have $4,200. Total industry sales are the sum of the sales of all seven firms, equal to $5,000. The four largest firms account for 84 percent of industry sales, which means a four-firm concentration ratio of 84.
6. Entry and exit must be quick and easy. Contestability tends to keep market price down because of the threat of entry.
8. **a.** The small number of dealers makes the formation of a cartel possible, but because cartels are illegal, the cartel would have to be kept secret.
   b. City B has more dealers, making cooperation among dealers more difficult, other things equal.
   c. The cartel in City B would be more likely to break up.
   d. Evidence pointing to a cartel would revolve around the effects of reduced competition. For example, if car prices increased in both cities, and there was no other explanation for the price increases, a cartel could be the explanation.
10. Residual demand is the difference between market demand and the quantity supplied by the fringe firms. The dominant firm with competitive fringe is the oligopoly model in which residual demand is a characteristic. For example, when market demand equals thirty units at a particular price, and the firms on the fringe offer twenty-five units for sale, residual demand equals five units.
12. The payoff matrix is an example of the prisoner's dilemma. A will confess because if B confesses and A does not, A will receive the maximum sentence of eighteen years. B reasons similarly, and so both A and B confess and receive sentences of seven years. If both had kept quiet their sentences would have been only four years.
14. Product differentiation is a means to increase the firm's demand and profit. Society obtains a greater variety of goods because firms practice product differentiation.
16. A firm in monopolistic competition has a highly elastic, but not perfectly elastic, demand. Only a price taker has perfectly elastic demand, and monopolistically competitive firms have some measure of control over their prices.
18. The firm's demand curve will be tangent to its average cost curve. Since the demand curve slopes downward, the tangency point will be to the left of the minimum point on the average cost curve.

CHAPTER 22

2. Firms anticipate that demand for their products will pick up when the slowdown in the economy ends. Anticipating that turnaround in product demand, firms hope that laid-off workers will stay available to return to the job they were doing prior to being laid off.
4. Occupation demand for labor refers to the idea that each type of work has its own labor demand to some extent. The same could be said of each city, state, or other geographic area. The industry demand for labor relates to the demand for the different types of labor employed in a particular industry.
6. Using the data in the table along with a price of $5, total revenue equals: $0, $60, $110, $150, $180, $200, and $210. Marginal revenue product equals: not defined, $60, $50, $40, $30, $20, and $10. The highest wage rate consistent with four units of labor employed is $30. For five units of labor to be employed, the wage rate would have to drop to $20.
8. The marginal cost of labor equals the change in total cost divided by the change in labor. The revenue the firm gains from employing another unit of labor must at least equal the marginal cost of labor for that unit of labor.
10. Marginal revenue product = Marginal cost of labor. This rule for employing labor says that the last unit of labor employed will have a value equal to the additional cost to the firm of employing it.
12. A graph of monopsony will show an upward-sloping supply curve of labor. The marginal cost of labor curve will lie above the supply curve. The quantity of labor employed will be below the point where the marginal cost of labor and the demand for labor intersect. By reducing employment below the competitive level the firm is able to decrease the wage rate below the competitive wage.
14. Bilateral monopoly characterizes professional sports, such as baseball, football, and basketball. The wage rate depends on bargaining power. For that reason, it is not possible to predict whether the wage rate will be more or less than the competitive wage.

CHAPTER 23

2. Total labor costs include fringe benefits such as paid vacations and health insurance.
4. Each student will have his or her own reservation wage. Many things can cause a person's reservation wage to change. Examples include education, experience, health, marital status, and access to labor market information.
6. The income effect of a change in the wage rate refers to the change in purchasing power that accompanies a change in the wage rate. An increase in the wage rate will increase purchasing power, which increases the demand for leisure. An increase in the demand for leisure decreases hours of work. Thus, the income effect is associated with the backward-bending part of labor supply. The substitution effect refers to the change in opportunity cost that accompanies a change in

the wage rate. An increase in the wage rate increases the opportunity cost of leisure, and increases the quantity of labor supplied. The substitution effect is associated with the upward-sloping portion of labor supply. So long as the substitution effect is stronger than the income effect, the labor supply curve will slope upward.

8. **a.** Nurses: A compensating differential could be associated with exposure to disease and the stress from the death of patients.

   b. Forest rangers: The danger from fire and the stress from policing large areas of forest could provide a rationale for a compensating differential.

   c. Movie and TV actors: People in these jobs often experience long periods of unemployment. That disadvantage would normally be associated with a compensating differential, but in the case of actors the possibility of fame may offset the need for employers to pay a compensating differential.

   d. There may or may not be a significant compensating differential in the occupation you would like to make your life's work. If the occupation is dangerous or unpleasant, a compensating differential will be included in the pay you receive.

10. Each student's answer will vary. Opinions about unions are often based upon emotion as well as logic. Answers should sort out emotional arguments from fact.

12. Signaling provides an alternative to the human capital view that education increases an individual's productivity. Signals that a college diploma sends to an employer include that a person is intelligent, diligent, and trainable. Other positive traits are also signaled.

14. The answer to this question will depend upon a person's values. One person might be highly productive (and highly paid) because his or her parent could afford the best schools. Another person might be relatively unproductive (and poorly paid) because of poor health.

16. Your graph should label the horizontal axis as the "quantity of a resource," and the vertical axis as "$" or "hourly earnings." The resource is in fixed supply, meaning that the supply curve is vertical. It does not start at the horizontal axis, but rather at the resource's opportunity cost, which is given by what it would earn in an alternative occupation. The price of the resource is determined by the intersection of supply and a downward-sloping demand curve. The economic rent would be the rectangular area that is bounded on the top by price, on the bottom by opportunity cost, on the right by the supply curve, and on the left by the vertical axis.

CHAPTER 24

2. A pure public good is nonexcludable and nonrival, meaning that we can't keep anyone from consuming it and that allowing someone else to consume it doesn't affect our own consumption. If the good is impure, then there might be some degree of rivalry or difficulty in excluding people.

Most public goods are impure. For example, it might be possible to keep people out of parks or off of highways. If so, those public goods are excludable. Those public goods are also rival if they are subject to congestion when too many people use them at once.

4. **a.** Maybell will consume the good because no one can be excluded from consuming a pure public good.

   b. Marshall and Marsha will consume the same amount.

   c. The value of the good is the sum of its value to Marsha, Marshall, and Maybell, which equals $3 + $7 + $1 = $11.

6. Market failures arise when goods are not purely private. A purely private good does not have external effects on others and is not subject to the free-rider problem. In contrast, there are usually market failures associated with public goods because of the free-rider problem, which limits the revenue available to potential producers of the public good.

8. The free-rider problem arises because it makes little or no difference in the quantity of a public good a person consumes whether or not that person pays anything for the good. Since public goods are not excludable, consumers have the incentive to free ride and to pay nothing. In response, producers in the free market tend to produce nothing. There are exceptions, particularly when the public good is tied into a private good. For example, radio commercials attempt to sway consumers to buy private goods and are paid for by private companies. To get potential consumers to listen to the commercials requires that they be given something in exchange, which in this example would be radio programming, a public good.

10. One intangible that was mentioned is noise, such as from airplanes. This might be used in the cost-benefit analysis of alternative forms of airplane equipment, flight patterns, or landing times. The procedure would be to measure the noise at ground level within affected neighborhoods, and then find other neighborhoods with comparable characteristics but without the noise. The cost of the noise could be estimated as the difference in the property values in these two neighborhoods.

12. Debatable arguments that express somebody's opinions about the homeless and that are related to the specificity principle might include: (1) We should visit homeless shelters and allow the homeless to tell us their specific problems so we can address those issues with them; (2) government should subsidize homeless shelters in order to reduce the problem of homelessness; (3) government should subsidize homeless shelters in order to gather the homeless together in one place where they can be given information about their alternatives, such as about jobs; (4) government should not make safety regulations for the homeless shelters so stringent that the homeless shelters cost more than the homeless can afford; and (5) government should not require employers to pay such high wages to the homeless that the employers do not hire the homeless at all.

14. People are willing to take some risks and weigh the value of extra safety from safety measures against the cost of

those measures in terms of money and inconvenience. For this reason, employees might prefer to have higher wages or less hassles rather than have their employers adopt every possible safety precaution. The efficient quantity of safety would have safety devices to protect workers from danger only if their marginal benefit is at least as much as their marginal cost. Many safety devices might fail this test of efficiency.

CHAPTER 25

2. There are many possibilities here, depending upon what you and your family have done. For example, when people admire the outfit that you're wearing, you're bestowing an external benefit on them. If they are admiring your car, that is also conferring an external benefit. Some external benefits are less obvious. For example, taking action to stay disease-free so that you are not contagious to anyone else also provides external benefits. In turn, you might have been the recipient of any of these external benefits from others, or additional ones, such as when you find yourself admiring a nice-looking yard.

4. Perhaps your neighbors play loud music or have a loud dog. If you are disturbed or awakened by their dog or their music, you have been the victim of an external cost. Most times, people just put up with these external costs and hope they go away over time. Sometimes, the cops are called to enforce noise ordinances.

6. That statement is false, with only a few exceptions for especially toxic substances. In most cases, there are benefits that go along with the pollution in terms of output that we wouldn't know how to produce as cheaply or at all without pollution. If firms face no cost of polluting, they'll pollute too much. However, if firms face a cost of polluting equal to the marginal external costs of the pollution, they have the incentive to cut back to an efficient amount of pollution.

8. In general, the efficient quantity of a good is that for which the marginal social cost just equals the marginal social benefit. When all costs and benefits are private, the market produces this efficient quantity. When there are external costs or external benefits, however, those external costs or external benefits must be added to private costs or private benefits to arrive at marginal social cost or marginal social benefit. When marginal social cost is equated to marginal social benefit, as before, the quantity of output is efficient.

10. The Coasian solution to this problem would be to have farmers sue the railroad company for the damages to the farmers' crops. In response, the railroad company would either change its practices or accept the cost of compensating farmers as merely a cost of doing business. Government might enter the picture to regulate the railroad's habits, which would save transaction costs in the legal system. While the Coasian solution sees no need for such government intervention, it does see a role for government in enforcing property rights, which provides the basis for lawsuits when those rights are violated.

12. You might argue that it's hard to police littering at City Park, and the park experience is more pleasant when there is not a heavy-handed police presence. You might also note the police enforcement is expensive. As an alternative, you might suggest appealing to people's consciences so that they are less inclined to strew trash around the park. Maybe your slogan would be "Keep City Park Looking Sharp!"

14. Draw a graph with the horizontal axis labeled as "pollution emissions" and the vertical axis labeled with the "$." Draw a downward-sloping demand curve by firms for emission rights. Draw an upward-sloping curve that is labeled "marginal external costs." If there were no market failure, these marginal external costs would be marginal private costs and represent the industry supply curve. The efficient quantity of pollution emissions is given by the intersection of the marginal external cost curve and the firms' demand curve. Since there is no market to achieve this quantity, government can instead impose a tax in the amount that would have been the market price. The amount of the tax is given by the intersection of the marginal external cost and the firms' demand, and has the same effect as would the efficient market price. In this way, government has replaced the missing market and achieved an efficient quantity of pollution.

16. In question 14, you showed how a tax could achieve the efficient quantity of pollution. Using that same figure, it is easy to show that a pollution permit system could achieve the same result. The supply of permits would be set equal to the efficient quantity of pollution emissions. This would present firms with a vertical supply curve for emission rights—no matter what the price might be, the quantity of emission rights offered to the market would remain constant. The price of an emission right would be determined by the intersection of the supply curve and the firms' demand. This price would be identical to the tax that was used in question 14.

CHAPTER 26

2. A benevolent dictatorship occurs when a government dictator makes all public choices and does so with the best interests of the public in mind. A benevolent dictatorship is more efficient than democracy to the extent that it does not waste resources in competition among candidates or for political favors. However, there is no such thing as a benevolent dictatorship in reality, since it is the process of political competition that chooses leaders who reflect the public interest. Even a well-meaning benevolent dictator could not know what the public truly desires, and the absolute power associated with dictatorship is not generally associated with the most well-meaning of people.

4. The principal-agent problem occurs when elected officials or agency employees do not follow the wishes of the voters. For example, for both selfish and public-spirited reasons, employees of government agencies generally desire

to spend more than the public would like. This leads to budgeting strategies designed to fool oversight committees and the public.

6. When we elect a public official, we are allowing that person to make many choices while in office. A voter might choose a candidate without supporting all of that candidate's views, since one basically must take the good with the bad. In the terminology of economics, candidates are bundled goods. However, with ballot propositions, voters make the decisions themselves instead of leaving those decisions to their elected representatives. While it takes more time to make a decision on your own than to leave it to someone else, you might choose to do so if you don't have confidence that your representatives will act in your interests once they are in office.

8. You should place voters along a spectrum in terms of how strongly they favor tax cuts versus the status quo. Your spectrum should show five voters bunched together favoring tax cuts with another five bunched together favoring the status quo. There will also be one in the middle, who is the median voter.
   a. The median voter is the one for which half of the voters are on one side and half of the voters are on the other side.
   b. The undecided voter is the median voter because that voter has half of the voters on one side and half of the voters on the other.
   c. To achieve a majority of voters, a candidate would need to win over this median voter. In a two-candidate race, the median voter holds the keys to victory.

10. Rational ignorance means the voters do not stay fully informed on the issues or on the activities of their elected representatives. The less watchful are voters, the more freedom representatives have to follow personal agendas and do whatever they want.

12. If you can identify a local transportation project, such as a new expressway or mass transit system, it is likely that federal money is involved. Such money is sometimes termed pork. Elected officials frequently point to the money they have brought into their districts from Washington. Local voters tend to like that direction of money flow, rather than just always seeing tax money flowing out of their paychecks and into the federal coffers.

14. You would be following the Washington Monument strategy, using up your budget first on the least essential projects, so that if a budget crunch were to come along, you could point to the great need for additional money for your agency. One danger of always doing the least important jobs first is that the most important projects might not ever get done.

CHAPTER 27

2. The capital account records the value of investment flows across international borders. In the capital account of the United States, capital inflows represent investment money that comes into the United States, such as to purchase land, factories, stock, or government securities. Capital outflows represent investment money that goes from the United States into other countries, such as to purchase land, factories, or foreign securities. The balance on the capital account is positive, which offsets the negative balance on the current account.

4. For the United States to run a trade deficit means that it imports more goods than it exports, where goods are measured in dollars according to their market values. The trade deficit is more limited than the current account deficit, which includes the value of not only goods, but also of services, incomes, and transfers.

6. If Middle Eastern investors decide to sell their U.S. investments and use the proceeds to buy investments in other countries, they would be acquiring dollars from their sales that they would wish to convert to the currencies of other countries so that they could buy assets in those countries. Supposing these other countries are Middle Eastern countries, then the dollar would depreciate relative to the Middle Eastern currencies. Those Middle Easterners who did not sell their American assets would find that the value of those assets in terms of the Middle Eastern currencies would be less after the depreciation of the dollar.

8. Depreciation of a currency occurs when there is less demand for it by holders of other currencies or when the holders of the currency increase the amount they offer for sale in exchange for other currencies. In terms of a supply and demand graph—measuring the quantity of the currency on the horizontal axis and the price of that currency in terms of other currencies on the vertical axis—depreciation would occur if demand were to shift to the left or supply were to shift to the right. If the currency depreciates, it will buy less in terms of foreign goods and services, which causes the quantity of goods and services imported to decrease. Likewise, goods and services that are priced in the country's currency will seem cheaper to holders of other countries' currencies. For this reason, exports would increase.

10. In considering the location of a new manufacturing plant, a company must consider the relative production costs in various countries, which will depend upon both exchange rates and the transportation costs from production facilities to the products' markets. The market for the luxurious Mercedes-Benz M-class sport utility vehicle includes a large proportion of people with high incomes. The market for the smaller and less expensive Volkswagen Beetle would not be similarly skewed toward those with higher incomes. Since incomes in Mexico are lower than incomes in the United States, it is not surprising that the Beetle has been popular in Mexico, more so than the Mercedes-Benz SUV.

12. a. Specializing according to comparative advantage, country A would produce good Y and country B would produce good X. The reason is that good Y has a lower opportunity cost in country A (opportunity cost of $1X$) than in B (opportunity cost of $2X$). By the same token, good X has a lower opportunity cost in country B

(opportunity cost of $1/2Y$) than in country A (opportunity cost of $1Y$).

b. Whichever country you are trade minister for, you would help your country by recommending trading with the other country. By doing so, your country can consume more than it was previously able to consume.

14. Alphania has a comparative advantage in wine, because it gives up only one yard of cloth for a bottle of wine, which is less than the 2 yards of cloth it would cost in Betalia. Betalia has a comparative advantage in cloth, because it gives up only one-half bottle of wine for a unit of cloth, which is less than the full bottle of wine it would cost in Alphania.

CHAPTER 28

2. The country will export the good. Domestic producers will increase the price within the country to match the world price, which means that domestic consumers will not consume as much as they would without trade. Domestic producers will continue to produce the quantity that domestic consumers demand at this new, higher price. Your graph should show the quantity of the good on the horizontal axis and its price on the vertical axis, with a downward-sloping demand curve by domestic consumers and an upward-sloping supply curve by domestic producers. The world price should be above what would have been the domestic equilibrium price in the absence of trade. At the world price, the quantity demanded by consumers is less than the quantity supplied by producers, with the difference going to exports.

4. An advantage of expanding the membership of NAFTA would be the trade creation effect, and a disadvantage would be the trade diversion effect. Other countries might want to join NAFTA in order to capture the benefits of trade. Because trade can be beneficial for all those involved, the United States and other countries can be expected to gain. However, some individuals and groups within the countries would lose and therefore be expected to oppose the expansion of NAFTA.

6. You're likely to find in your survey that people have very little idea as to the tariff rates that importers face. The reason is most likely that people do not pay tariffs directly, and for this reason do not see them when they make their purchases. Because tariffs are hidden within product prices, consumers tend to be oblivious to their existence.

8. Because either tariffs or quotas can have an equivalent effect, consumers have no particular reason to prefer one to the other.

10. Producers in exporting countries would like to charge as high of a price as possible, which leads them to prefer the voluntary export restraint that is simultaneously agreed to by many different exporting countries. Otherwise, these exporting countries would be in competition with one another and would drive the price of their exports lower.

12. The chapter listed a number of possible reasons to restrict imports, and you could choose any one of these reasons to critique. For example, you might critique using tariffs to punish countries that engage in dumping, because you might argue that those countries are only hurting themselves in that they will never capture the world markets for the products they are dumping. The effect of dumping in that case is just to give consumers in the importing country lower prices at the expense of the other countries' exporters. A counterargument might emphasize the harm to the domestic industry and the people involved in that industry.

14. You're asked to evaluate the national defense argument in several examples of your own choosing. Following are a few possibilities. For reasons of national defense, it's hard to argue against favoring domestic industry in the production of weaponry, the use of a country's own citizens as troops and commanders, and favoring a country's own industries for high-tech research. More questionable is whether a country should restrict the export of its technology that might be used against it someday, since restricting technology exports might encourage new technology to be developed in other countries where no export barriers exist. Some might argue that food, clothing, and all other necessities be produced domestically for reasons of national defense. However, unless it seems likely that an enemy will control all sources of production and that domestic stockpiles cannot be effectively held, the advantages of trade might outweigh any perceived defense needs.

CHAPTER 29

2. Problems include poverty, little infrastructure, poor life expectancy, and high population growth. These and other problems in the LDCs make life a struggle to survive for many people.

4. Answers will vary from one student to another. For example, students might wish to explain how incentives affect population growth, how markets promote economic development, or the role of property rights in development.

6. Rostow's five stages are: traditional society, preconditions for takeoff, takeoff, drive to maturity, and high mass consumption. The first stage is characterized by subsistence agriculture, the second by excess production and the need for transportation, the third by urbanization and investment, the fourth by economic diversification, and the fifth by the dominance of production of consumer goods and services. The model is criticized for not fitting the way that development occurs in some cases, and for not explaining how economies move from one stage to the next.

8. A farmer can raise and harvest more crops with unpaid labor provided by the family's children. Development could slow down population growth as people move to the city where children become viewed as more of an expense and less of a source of labor.

10. Student answers will vary depending on family background, religious beliefs, and other influences on personal preferences regarding family size. Some students will emphasize the benefits from having more children, while others will emphasize the costs.

12. Without clearly defined property rights, the uncertainty about who owns resources will inhibit investment and business formation. Clear property rights must be established through the legal system.

14. There is no one right answer to this question, but policy statements should include items relating to the value of the projects that will be financed by the loans, the ability of the country to repay a loan, and the need for the World Bank to rank loan applications using a consistent set of criteria. Since loan funds are limited in amount, not all projects can receive loans, and thus choices must be made.

INDEX

A

Ability-to-pay principle, 286, 287, 294
Absolute advantage, 43
Accounting profit, 438, 439
Action lag, 233
Actual return, 312
Adaptive expectations, 240
Administrative and compliance costs, 615
Adverse selection, 623
Advertising, role of, 547
Age/earnings profile, 600
Aggregate demand
    demand-side deflation, 213
    demand-side inflation, 212, 213
    expenditure equilibrium, 270
    modeling, 200–201
    shift factors, 200–203
    short-run stickiness, 208–209
    sticky prices, effects of, 208
    sticky wages, effects of, 208
    versus aggregate supply, 194
Aggregate expenditure function, 255, 257
Aggregate expenditures, 254–255
Aggregate supply
    full-employment output, association
        with, 204
    long-run aggregate supply, 204, 211
    production effect, 235
    real business cycle, 212
    shifts, 205–206
    short-run aggregate supply, 204–205,
        234–236, 237–238
    structural rigidities, 234
    supply shock, 212
    supply-side deflation, 214
    supply-side inflation, 212, 214
    versus aggregate demand, 194
Agricultural price supports and subsidies,
    100–101, 471–473, 709
Allocative efficiency, 6, 37
Anticipated inflation, 174
Antitrust issues
    antitrust law, 514
    average-cost pricing, 521
    Cellar-Kefauver Antimerger Act, 516
    Clayton Act, 514, 515, 516
    deregulation, 522
    exclusive dealing, 515, 516
    exclusive territories, 515
    Federal Trade Commission Act, 514, 516
    franchise monopoly, 521–523
    Hart-Scott-Rodino Antitrust Improvement
        Act, 516
    Herfindahl-Hirschman index (HHI), 518–520
    illegal price discrimination, 516
    judicial implications, 516–518
    labor unions, and, 516
    mergers, and, 518–519

    predatory pricing, 515, 516
    price discrimination, 515
    privatization, 523, 525–526
    rate-of-return regulation, 521
    refusals to deal, 515
    regulation, alternatives to, 521–522
    resale price maintenance, 515
    Robinson-Patman Act, 516
    rule of reason, 515
    Sherman Act, 514, 515
    subsidized monopoly, 523–524
    tie-in sales, 515
    vertical foreclosure, 518
Appreciation, 686–689
Assumptions, 13
Asymmetric information, 618, 664
Austrian school of economic thought, 316
Automatic stabilizers, 233
Autonomous expenditure multiplier, 261
Autonomous spending, 255–256, 260
Average cost, 457, 458
Average product, 443, 444
Average profit, 465
Average revenue, 464–465
Average tax rate, 284
Average total cost, 457
Average variable cost, 457, 460
Average-cost pricing, 521

B

Backward tax shifting, 394
Backward-bending supply of labor, 585
Balanced budget, 231
Balanced-budget multiplier, 268, 269
Balance of payments accounts, 676, 681
Balance of trade, 676
Balance sheet, 331
Banking. *See also* Federal Reserve System
    balance sheet, 331
    bank prime lending rate, 332
    bank reserves, 331
    bonds, 332
    Depository Institutions Deregulation and
        Monetary Control Act of 1980, 345
    discount loans, 333
    discount rate, 333
    excess reserves, 332
    failures, 344–346
    Federal Deposit Insurance Corporation
        (FDIC), 332
    federal funds rate, 332
    financial intermediaries, 333
    Glass-Steagall Act of 1933, 331
    interstate banking, 331
    key interest rates, 333, 334
    regulation, 331
    required reserves, 332
    reserve requirements, 332

    role, 335
    securities, 332
    treasury bills, 332
Bank prime lending rate, 332
Bank reserves, 331
Bargaining power, 589
Barriers to entry, 482, 502–503
Barter, 42, 326
Beggar-thy-neighbor protectionist policies, 709
Benefit principle, 286
Benevolent dictatorship, 654
Bilateral monopoly, 569, 572
Black market, 104
Block grants, 662
Bonds, 332, 597
Boycott, 590
Breakeven, 440, 465
Bretton Woods agreement, 689
Broadly based taxes, 294
Budget deficit, 231
Budget surplus, 231
Bundled good, 657
Bureaucracy, role of the, 662–664
Business choices, 2
Business cycle
    coincident indicators, 133
    depression, 130
    expansion stage, 130
    lagging indicators, 133
    leading indicators, 133
    long-run features, 131
    peak, 130
    recession, 130
    seasonal adjustment, 132
    short-run features, 131
    stabilization of, 226
    stages of, 130–131
    trough, 130
Business ethics, 445–447

C

Canada
    government expenditures as percentage of
        GDP, 9
    real GDP, 129
    unemployment rates, 28, 154
Capital, 33, 117
Capital and financial account, 677–678
Capital consumption allowance, 122
Capital formation, role of, 308–309
Capital gains, 313
Capital inflows, 678
Capital intensive, 681
Capital outflows, 678
Capitalism, Socialism, and Democracy, 551
Cartel, 538
Cellar-Kefauver Antimerger Act, 516
Central bank independence reforms, 369–371

PHOTO CREDITS

Chapter 1, page 1, Keren Su/Corbis; page 3, Joel. W. Rogers/Corbis; page 10, © Corbis, page 13, © Bettman/Corbis; page 14, TimePix.

Chapter 2, page 31, Bill Ross/Corbis; page 32, Getty Images, Inc.-Liaison; page 40, AP/Wide World Photos; page 46, AFP/Corbis; page 46, Peter Turnley/Corbis.

Chapter 3, page 57, Eyewire/Getty Images/Eyewire, Inc.; page 61, Angelo Cavalli/Getty Images, Inc./Liaison; page 63, PhotoEdit; page 66, Richard Hamilton Smith/Corbis; page 76, Minnesota Historical Society/Corbis.

Chapter 4, page 87, NASA/Goddard Space Flight Center; page 94, John Kelly/Getty Images, Inc./Liaison; page 99, AP/Wide World Photos; page 104, Robert Maass/Corbis; page 105 AP/Wide World Photos.

Chapter 5, page 113, David Young Wolf/PhotoEdit; page 117, George Hall/Corbis; page 114, Bill Boch/Getty Images, Inc./Taxi; page 125, Christopher Bissell/Getty Images, Inc./Liaison; page 127, Reuters NewMedia Inc./Getty Images Inc./Liaison; page 133, Dennis Cook/AP Wide World Photos.

Chapter 6, page 145, Getty Images, Inc.-Stone; page 148, PhotoEdit; page 156, Annabelle Breakey/Getty Images, Inc./Illustration Works, Inc.; page 159, Index Stock Imagery, Inc; page 159, Keith Brofsky/Getty Images, Inc.

Chapter 7, page 167, TimePix; page 172, Bedford Times-Mail/Scott Brunner/AP/Wide World Photos; page 175, Corbis Digital Stock; page 179, PhotoEdit; page 184, © Todd Gripstein/Corbis.

Chapter 8, page 193, Chris Noble/Getty Images, Inc./Stone; page 199, TimePix; Page 212, PhotoEdit; page 214, Library of Congress; page 215, © Corbis Sygma.

Chapter 9, page 225, Getty Images, Inc./Illustration Works, Inc.; page 231, Getty Images Inc./Illustration Works, Inc.; page 232, The Kobal Collection/Selznick/ MGM/ Picture Desk, Inc./Kobal Collection; page 236, Doug Pizac/AP/Wide World Photos; page 243, PhotoEdit.

Chapter 10, page 253, © Joseph Sohm; ChromoSohm Inc./Corbis; page 259, Melaine Einzig/AP/Wide World Photos; page 264, Greg Miller Photography; page 269, Stanley Fellerman/Corbis Digital Stock; page 271, The Kobal Collection/First National/Charles Chaplin/Picture Desk, Inc./Kobal Collection.

Chapter 11, page 281, Oscar Sosa/AP/Wide World Photos; page 287, © Joseph Sohm; ChromoSohm Inc./Corbis; page 294, Myrleen Ferguson/PhotoEdit; page 295, PhotoEdit; page 296, AP/Wide World Photos.

Chapter 12, page 305, Patagonik Works/PhotoDisc/Getty Images, Inc./PhotoDisc; page 308, © David Young Wolff/PhotoEdit, Inc.; page 315, Getty Images, Inc-Stone; page 318, Eyewire Collection/Getty Images/Eyewire, Inc.; page 319, © Ed Bock/CORBIS.

Chapter 13, page 325, Danny Johnson/AP/Wide World Photos; page 327, Janis Christie/Getty Images, Inc./Photodisc; page 330, Thierry Dosogne/Getty Images, Inc./Liaison; page 333, AP/Wide World Photos; page 344, PhotoEdit.

Chapter 14, page 351, PhotoEdit; page 355, PhotoEdit; page 359, Doug Mills/AP/Wide World Photos; page 367, Paul Sakuma/AP/Wide World Photos; page 369, PhotoEdit.

Chapter 15, page 377, Lynne Sladky/AP/Wide World Photos; page 389, David Young-Wolff/PhotoEdit; page 391, Ken Biggs/Getty Images, Inc.-Liaison; page 395, Bill Ling/Getty Images, Inc.-Liaison; page 396, Corbis Digital Stock.

Chapter 16, page 405, Robert Frerck/Odyssey Productions, Inc.; page 406, Mary Kate Denny/PhotoEdit; page 410, Alissa Crandall/Corbis; page 415 top, Najlah Feanny/SABA Press Photos, Inc.; page 415 bottom, Myrleen Ferguson/PhotoEdit.

Chapter 17, page 433, John Sommers II/Corbis/Sygma; page 436, Bryan F. Peterson/Corbis/Stock Market; page 437, White Castle Management Company; page 442, Liba Taylor/Corbis; page 445, David J. Phillip/AP/Wide World Photos.

Chapter 18, page 453, Wayne Eastep/Getty Images, Inc.-Stone; page 455, Erik Simonsen/Getty Images, Inc.-Liaison; page 464, V.C.L/Getty Images, Inc.- Liasion; page 470 top, Carlos Osorio/AP/Wide World Photos; page 470 bottom, Digital Vision.

Chapter 19, page 481, Tom McCarthy/PhotoEdit; page 484, H. Dratch/The Image Works; page 485, Bernd Kammerer/AP/Wide World Photos; page 488, Tracy Hayes/Bloomberg News Landov LLC; page 492, Michael S. Yamashita/Corbis.

Chapter 20, page 501, PhotoEdit; page 503, Steven Dunwell/Getty Images, Inc.-Liaison; page 520, Joe Marquette/AP/Wide World Photos; page 524 top, Steve Pope/AP/Wide World Photos; page 524 bottom, LWA/Dann Tardif/Corbis.

Chapter 21, page 533, Richard Lord/PhotoEdit; page 534, Kelly-Mooney Photography/Corbis; page 537, Evan Vucci/AP/Wide World Photos; page 549 top, The Coca-Cola Company; page 549 bottom, Mug Shots/Corbis.

Chapter 22, page 559, Jeff Greenberg/PhotoEdit; page 561, Amos Morgan/Getty Images, Inc.; page 563, Frank Siteman/PhotoEdit; page 572, Lennox McLendon/AP/Wide World Photos; page 574, Jose Luis Magana/AP/Wide World Photos.

Chapter 23, page 583, Ryan McVay/Getty Images, Inc.; page 587, Chad Slattery/Getty Images, Inc.-Stone; page 593, Mary Kate Denny/PhotoEdit; page 595, Clay Perry/Corbis; page 598, Andy Sacks/Getty Images, Inc.-Stone.

Chapter 24, page 607, Billy E. Bames/PhotoEdit; page 612, Mike Groll-Buffalo News/Corbis/Sygma; page 617 REUTERS/Mike Blake/Corbis; page 621 top, Richard Chapman/SunTimes/AP/Wide World Photos; page 621 bottom, Mug Shot/Corbis/Stock Market.

Macroeconomic Data

Macroeconomic data can help you get the "big picture" of the U.S. economy. Most of the data goes back to 1929, which marked the start of the Great Depression. You can observe the slump in economic activity in the data. You can also see the increase in production brought about by World War II, the post-war prosperity, and the occasional recessions.

EXPENDITURES APPROACH

		1977	1978	1979	1980	1981	1982	1983	1984	1985	1986	1987
The Sum Of	1. Personal consumption expenditures	1278.4	1430.4	1596.3	1762.9	1944.2	2079.3	2286.4	2498.4	2712.6	2895.2	3105.3
	2. Gross private domestic investment	361.3	436	490.6	477.9	570.8	516.1	564.2	735.5	736.3	747.2	781.5
	3. Government consumption expenditures and gross investment	415.3	455.6	503.5	569.7	631.4	684.4	735.9	800.8	878.3	942.3	997.9
	4. Net exports of goods and services	−23.7	−26.1	−24	−14.9	−15	−20.5	−51.7	−102	−114.2	−131.9	−142.3
Equals	5. Gross domestic product	2031.4	2295.9	2566.4	2795.6	3131.3	3259.2	3534.9	3932.7	4213	4452.9	4742.5
Less	6. Consumption of fixed capital	231.6	261.5	300.4	345.2	394.8	436.5	456.1	482.4	516.5	551.6	586.1
Equals	7. Net domestic product	1799.8	2034.4	2266	2450.3	2736.5	2822.8	3078.8	3450.4	3696.5	3901.3	4156.4

INCOMES APPROACH

		1977	1978	1979	1980	1981	1982	1983	1984	1985	1986	1987
The Sum Of	8. Compensation of employees	1180.4	1336.0	1500.8	1651.7	1825.7	1926.0	2042.7	2255.9	2425.2	2570.7	2755.6
	9. Proprietors' income with inventory valuation and capital consumption adjustments	148.3	170.1	183.7	177.6	186.2	179.9	195.5	247.5	267.0	278.6	303.9
	10. Rental income of persons with capital consumption adjustment	20.4	22.4	24.5	31.3	39.6	39.6	36.9	39.5	39.1	32.2	35.8
	11. Corporate profits with inventory valuation and capital consumption adjustments	190.9	217.2	222.5	198.5	219.0	201.2	254.1	309.8	322.4	300.7	346.6
	12. Net interest	95.7	114.5	144.2	183.9	226.5	256.3	267.2	309.6	326.7	343.6	361.5
Equals	13. National income	1635.8	1860.2	2075.6	2243.0	2497.1	2603.0	2796.5	3162.3	3380.4	3525.8	3803.4
Less	14. Net factor income from rest of world	20.7	22.1	32.9	35.3	34.7	36.5	36.9	35.3	25.3	15.5	13.7
Plus	15. Consumption of fixed capital	231.6	261.5	300.4	345.2	394.8	436.5	456.1	482.4	516.5	551.6	586.1
Plus	16. Indirect business taxes	163.1	175.4	187.6	208.7	246.6	253.8	272.2	304.8	329.7	347	363.4
Plus	17. Statistical discrepancy	21.6	21.0	35.7	33.9	27.5	2.5	47.0	18.6	11.7	43.9	3.3
Equals	18. Gross domestic product	2031.4	2295.9	2566.4	2795.6	3131.3	3259.2	3534.9	3932.7	4213	4452.9	4742.5

OTHER DATA

	1977	1978	1979	1980	1981	1982	1983	1984	1985	1986	1987
19. Real GDP	4511.8	4760.6	4912.1	4900.9	5021.0	4919.3	5132.3	5505.2	5717.1	5912.4	6113.3
20. Percent change in real GDP	4.6	5.5	3.2	−0.2	2.5	−2	4.3	7.3	3.8	3.4	3.4
21. GDP inplicit price deflator (1996 = 100)	45.02	48.23	52.25	57.04	62.37	66.25	68.88	71.44	73.69	75.31	77.58
22. Chain-type price index (1996 = 100)	48.22	52.24	57.05	62.37	66.26	68.87	71.44	73.69	75.32	77.58	80.22
23. Gross saving	398.2	481.6	544.9	555.5	656.5	625.7	608.0	769.4	772.5	735.9	810.4
24. Gross investment	419.8	502.6	580.6	589.5	684.0	628.2	655	787.9	784.2	779.8	813.8
25. Transfer payments to persons	104.9	116.2	131.8	154.2	182.0	204.5	221.7	235.7	253.4	269.2	282.9
26. Real disposable personal income	3360.7	3527.5	3628.6	3658	3741.1	3791.7	3906.9	4207.6	4347.8	4486.6	4582.5
27. Personal saving as a percentage of disposable personal income	8.7	9.0	9.2	10.2	10.8	10.9	8.8	10.6	9.2	8.2	7.3
28. Population (mid-period, millions)	220.3	222.6	225.1	227.7	230.0	232.2	234.3	236.4	238.5	240.7	242.8
29. Current surplus or deficit (2), national income and product accounts	−32	−8.2	1.7	−44.9	−46.2	−134.8	−169.1	−144.2	−154.9	−171.4	−135.7
30. Contributions for social insurance	113.1	131.3	152.7	166.2	195.7	208.9	226	257.5	281.4	303.4	323.1

PERSONAL CONSUMPTION

		1977	1978	1979	1980	1981	1982	1983	1984	1985	1986	1987
The Sum Of	31. Durable goods	181.2	201.7	214.4	214.2	231.3	240.2	281.2	326.9	363.3	401.3	419.7
	32. Nondurable goods	497.2	550.2	624.4	696.1	758.9	787.6	831.2	884.7	928.8	958.5	1015.3
	33. Services	600.0	678.4	757.4	852.7	954.0	1051.5	1174.0	1286.9	1420.6	1535.4	1670.3
	34. Personal consumption expenditures	1278.4	1430.4	1596.3	1762.9	1944.2	2079.3	2286.4	2498.4	2712.6	2895.2	3105.3

MONEY SUPPLY AND INFLATION

	1977	1978	1979	1980	1981	1982	1983	1984	1985	1986	1987
35. Quantity of M1	330.5	356.9	381.4	408.1	436.2	474.3	520.8	551.2	619.1	724.0	749.4
36. Percent increase in M1	8.0	8.0	6.9	7.0	6.9	8.7	9.8	5.8	12.3	16.9	3.5
37. Quantity of M2	1,269.9	1,365.6	1,473.3	1,599.4	1,754.9	1,909.8	2,125.9	2,309.6	2,494.9	2,731.6	2,830.6
38. Percent increase in M2	10.3	7.5	7.9	8.6	9.7	8.8	11.3	8.6	8.0	9.5	3.6
39. Quantity of M3	1,470.1	1,644.2	1,808.3	1,995.1	2,254.0	2,460.2	2,697.0	2,990.5	3,207.5	3,498.7	3,685.8
40. Percent increase in M3	12.2	11.8	10.0	10.3	13.0	9.1	9.6	10.9	7.3	9.1	5.3
41. CPI Inflation rate	6.7	9.0	13.3	12.5	8.9	3.8	3.8	3.9	3.8	1.1	4.4